Julius D. H. Benedict
D. Joseph Mmm

How now, you secret, black, and midnight hags!

Macbeth, Act IV, Sc. 1

PROSE AND POETRY OF ENGLAND

INCLUDING
A HISTORY OF
ENGLISH LITERATURE

EDITED BY
H. WARD McGRAW, A.M.
LATE HEAD OF THE ENGLISH DEPARTMENT
STATE NORMAL SCHOOL, CORTLAND N.Y.

ILLUSTRATED BY
GUY BROWN WISER

THE · L·W · SINGER · COMPANY
SYRACUSE   CHICAGO   DALLAS

Copyright, 1934, 1935, by
THE L. W. SINGER COMPANY

All rights reserved. No part of this book may be reproduced in any form without permission in writing from the publisher.

THE NEW PROSE AND POETRY SERIES

PROSE AND POETRY
FOR ENJOYMENT

PROSE AND POETRY
FOR APPRECIATION

PROSE AND POETRY
OF AMERICA

PROSE AND POETRY
OF ENGLAND

Printed in the United States of America
7752.5

CONTRIBUTING EDITORS

SARAH HEYWORTH BARBER, M.A.
Formerly Supervisor Speech Development
Public Schools, Omaha, Nebraska
Head of the English Department
High School, Peru, New York

HARRIET MARCELIA LUCAS, A.B.
English Department, South High School
Minneapolis, Minnesota

FLORETTE M^{c}NEESE, M.A.
Chairman, Oklahoma State Syllabus Committee on English
Director of English, Classen High School
Oklahoma City, Oklahoma

SARAH E. SIMONS, M.A.
Author, *American Literature through Illustrative Readings*
Head of the English Department, Junior-Senior
High Schools, Washington, D. C.

EMILY EVELETH SNYDER, A.B.
English Department, Little Falls High School
Little Falls, New York

DONALD MacLEAN TOWER, Ph.D.
Author, *Educational Dramatics*
Formerly Director of Curriculum, Public Schools
Binghamton, New York
Superintendent, Rye Neck Public Schools
Mamaroneck, New York

For helpful counsel and suggestions, thanks are extended to Dora V. Smith, Ph.D., University of Minnesota, Minneapolis, Minnesota, specialist in English of the National Survey of Secondary Education

ACKNOWLEDGMENTS

For the courteous permission to use the following selections, grateful acknowledgment and thanks are extended to the following authors and publishers.

D. Appleton-Century Company: Selections from *Disraeli* by André Maurois.

Curtis Brown, Ltd.: "A Study in Dejection" from *Yet Again* by Max Beerbohm.

J. M. Dent & Sons, Ltd.: "The Donkey" by Gilbert K. Chesterton.

Dodd, Mead & Company, Inc.: "On Lying in Bed" from *Tremendous Trifles* by G. K. Chesterton, copyright 1909; "The Soldier" and "The Great Lover" by Rupert Brooke, copyright 1915; "I Meant to Do My Work Today" by Richard Le Gallienne. Used by permission of Dodd, Mead & Company, Inc., publishers.

Doubleday, Doran & Company, Inc.: "Mary's Little Lamb" from *The Book of a Naturalist* by W. H. Hudson, copyright 1919 by Doubleday, Doran & Company, Inc.; "A Daily Miracle" from *How to Live on Twenty-four Hours a Day* by Arnold Bennett, copyright 1910 by Doubleday, Doran & Company, Inc.; "The 'Tremolino'" from *The Mirror of the Sea* by Joseph Conrad, copyright 1906 by Doubleday, Doran & Company, Inc.; "Fuzzy-Wuzzy" and "Gunga Din" from *Departmental Ditties and Barrack Room Ballads* by Rudyard Kipling, copyright 1899, and "Recessional" from *The Five Nations* by Rudyard Kipling, copyright 1903, reprinted by permission from Doubleday, Doran & Company, Inc.

E. P. Dutton & Co., Inc.: Selection from *The Sea and the Jungle* by H. M. Tomlinson; "In Service" from *Songs of Leinster* by Winifred Letts.

Harcourt, Brace and Company, Inc.: "Florence Nightingale" from *Eminent Victorians* by Lytton Strachey. Reprinted by permission of Harcourt, Brace and Company, Inc., publishers.

Harper & Brothers: "The Substitute" from *Ten Tales* by François Coppée.

Henry Holt & Company: "The Listeners" from *The Listeners and Other Poems* and "Silver" from *Peacock Pie* by Walter de la Mare.

Sidney Kiek & Son, Ltd.: "Fish in the Forest" from *Book of Noodles* by W. Clouston.

Alfred A. Knopf, Inc.: "On the Birth of His Son" from *170 Chinese*

ACKNOWLEDGMENTS

Poems by Arthur Waley. By permission of and special arrangement with Alfred A. Knopf, Inc., authorized publishers.

Little, Brown & Company: "The Lost Silk Hat" by Lord Dunsany.

The Macmillan Company: "Weathers" and "The Man He Killed" from *Collected Poems* by Thomas Hardy; "The Lake Isle of Innisfree" and "Song of the Old Mother" from *Collected Poems* by William Butler Yeats; "An Old Woman of the Roads" from *Collected Poems* by Padraic Colum; "The Road" from *Songs from the Clay* by James Stephens; "A Consecration" and "Tewkesbury Road" from *Collected Poems* and "Rounding the Horn" from *Dauber* by John Masefield.

The Paget Literary Agency, Inc.: "A Greeting" from *Foliage* and "The Example" from *Songs of Joy* by W. H. Davies. By permission of Jonathan Cape, Ltd.

Siegfried Sassoon: "The Dreamers."

Charles Scribner's Sons: "Some Platitudes Concerning the Drama" and "Quality" from *The Inn of Tranquillity* by John Galsworthy; "My Brother Henry" by James M. Barrie; "Invictus" and "Margaritae Sorori" by W. E. Henley; "In the Orchard" by Henrik Ibsen.

Frederick A. Stokes Company: "The Barrel Organ" from *Collected Poems,* Volume I, by Alfred Noyes.

The Viking Press, Inc.: "The Sleeper of the Valley" from *The Poets of Modern France* by Ludwig Lewisohn, copyright 1918 by The Viking Press.

A. P. Watt & Son: "Fuzzy-Wuzzy" and "Gunga Din" from *Barrack Room Ballads* and "Recessional" from *The Five Nations* by Rudyard Kipling.

PREFACE

A New Approach to Literature Study

One of the tendencies in the so-called "new education" is a different approach to the study of literature. Traditionally, high school literature courses have emphasized the teaching of the classics, with a method of approach not very different from the translation of foreign masterpieces. The selection, whatever its type, was read slowly and painfully, was completely dissected, and practically paraphrased line by line. The objective evidently was the mastery of the factual material of the piece plus a mastery of analysis of the author's particular technique. More recently the objective seems to be first a genuine love of reading on the part of the pupil, and secondly, the broadening and enriching of his life through the experiences and thoughts of literary characters. The growing emphasis on reading as one of the natural activities for worthy use of leisure has made the change in approach necessary.

The Function of a Key Book

Advocates of both intensive and extensive reading programs have long clashed in their notions of relative values of the two general plans. A middle ground resulting in a less detailed reading of a few typical selections, followed by wide reading of similar pieces of the same type seems to be the preferred procedure. In order to carry out a literature program of this type, well-chosen selections for intensive study, or reading "in common," must be made available in convenient form. Carefully prepared, yet broad lists of suggestions for the follow-up extensive reading activities must also be accessible to the pupil in planning his own reading, and to the teacher in making suggestions.

The New PROSE AND POETRY series offers exactly this plan of organization. Type selections are included in each volume for intensive study. Carefully prepared background material and study suggestions are provided for the purpose of giving direction and assistance in the detailed analyses of the respective selections. Extensive lists of suggestions for outside reading follow each section.

Arrangement by Types

By the time the student has reached the senior high school level, his experience in exploratory reading of wide variety will have revealed to him that literature is divided naturally into types. His use of the library which has been encouraged throughout the earlier years of school, has acquainted him with library classification which is first of all by types. Hence, the type arrangement as followed in the PROSE AND POETRY books is the natural approach to literature study. It further provides a simple, direct organization not possible when all types of literature are intermingled, and an arrangement which lends itself readily to the unit system of teaching.

A further important advantage of type arrangement is that each type of literature receives its due emphasis, and none is neglected or overlooked. Hitherto, it has been the tendency in most anthologies to overemphasize one or two types, notably poetry and Shakespearean drama, and to underemphasize, or completely overlook, other important types. Biography, especially, has received little, if any, treatment in the past, and modern drama and the essay have also been neglected.

But even in the type arrangement it seems unwise to become too detailed in analysis and classification. Introductory work on types of literature is usually most effective if presented from the point of view of assisting students to master difficulties which they encounter in learning to read and enjoy the type in question, rather than from the point of view of literary classification and technique. Such a plan is followed in the PROSE AND POETRY books.

The History of Literature

The literary selections which the pupil will have read by the time he reaches senior high school cover a wide range in both time and type, but the student who has read only detached selections is not likely to have formed any idea of the continuity of literature nor to have seen much relationship between it and the development of the race. It is, therefore, the purpose of the literary history presented in the PROSE AND POETRY books to give the connected facts in the story and to show, as well as space permits, the influences which have been at work in the shaping of our literature.

In the past, the collegiate technique of teaching history of literature by chronological arrangement has been extended downward into the high school. The result has been a high school presentation which has been on the college level. Historical and political events have received more attention than the literature itself and the result has been to make literature study a task rather than a pleasure for the pupil.

The editors of the PROSE AND POETRY books believe that history of literature can be so presented to high school pupils that it becomes a fascinating story which reveals and interprets those influences which have produced great writing. In their presentation of the history of literature they have reduced political facts to a minimum and have given chief attention to showing the spirit and temper of the various

PREFACE

literary periods and to interpreting literature in the light of daily living. The result is a narrative account, written from the point of view of high school students. The biographies of the authors have been written in interesting story form with emphasis on personality rather than on mere historical data.

Again, the arrangement by type is advantageous for it aids in the study of literary history. The history of each type of literature is developed naturally through each of the literary periods and the pupil is not confused by a study of all types within one period. Furthermore, the study of each successive type provides a form of review of the general characteristics of each literary period so that by the time the book has been completed the pupil has a very clear and definite picture of each of the periods and of the influences which have been at work in the shaping of our literature. Only a brief summary and review such as given at the end of the book is necessary to place the whole story of literature in brief, concise form before the pupil.

Study Features

Just as the pupil has learned that literature falls naturally into types and that it reflects biographical incidents of authors, so also has he become aware of the fact that there is such a thing as technical skill. In the PROSE AND POETRY books are to be found carefully prepared study features which will aid the pupil in an appreciation of technical skill and of the reasons why the writers represented have achieved their places in the literary world.

Careful *Introductions* have been prepared to give the setting and background whenever such introductions are necessary for an understanding and appreciation of the selections. *Suggestions for Study* give direction and assistance in the detailed analyses of the respective pieces. Here, emphasis is rather upon questions which lead to appreciation rather than upon mere fact questions. *Creative Work* is provided for by suggestions for précis writing, for outlines, and for original stories, essays, and other compositions. *Vocabulary Study* emphasizes word history, the use of synonyms and antonyms, and pronunciation. Footnotes are used only in the case of difficult words or phrases which cannot be explained by dictionary definitions. All of the study features deliberately avoid the common fault of superfluous details and over-technicality of treatment.

Emphasis on Modern Material

The titles chosen for intensive study have been carefully checked with recent scientific studies of pupil reading interests and with most recent courses of study from many sections of the country. There is a balance of both easy and difficult selections and of early and modern writings. The emphasis, however, has been placed on modern and contemporary literature. In this volume of PROSE AND POETRY 33% of the authors represented are contemporary writers of the twentieth century, and 55% are modern writers—the term "modern" being used here in the generally accepted sense of belonging to the period of the last fifty years.

World Literature

One marked result of the World War was the increased interest in world literature. In attempts to understand the French, the German, the Italian points of view during the War, an interest in European writers was aroused. This interest has continued and authors who had been national have now become international. In the PROSE AND POETRY books, recognition of national, international, and world literatures is kept before the pupils, following the best practices of the best courses of study.

Several selections from world literature have been included in the present volume. They serve to show that literature is by no means confined to England and to America. They reveal the riches of the world's literature and should stimulate a desire to read further in the literature of other nations.

Extensive Reading Program

Extensive lists of suggestions for outside reading follow each section of the book. These lists give a broad scope from which to choose. The selections represent both early and contemporary writers and throw open for study the whole field of literature.

It is obvious that accompanying an extensive reading program there must be generous opportunity for individual reports, class discussions, and the sharing of experiences. A convenient way for the pupil to record his outside reading is by means of card records. A suggested system is for the teacher to have on his desk a file box containing a card for each pupil in the class. As a pupil reads a selection outside of class he makes a record on the card giving the date of the reading, the title, the author, and a brief comment as to his reaction. A complete record of all selections read during the year is thus kept in convenient form and such record can be kept for the entire high school course. As the teacher sees fit, he may require, in addition to the card record, more extensive reports in the form of book reports, outlines, or précis.

Conclusion

It is the hope of the editors that the New PROSE AND POETRY books will meet every need for the new program of teaching literature and will open wide the doors which lead to good reading as a worthy use of leisure.

THE EDITORS

CONTENTS

	PAGE
THE PERIODS OF ENGLISH LITERATURE	1
THE SHORT STORY	15

The Twentieth Century

THE THREE STRANGERS	Thomas Hardy	24
THE "TREMOLINO"	Joseph Conrad	47
MY BROTHER HENRY	James Matthew Barrie	64
MY OWN TRUE GHOST STORY	Rudyard Kipling	68
QUALITY	John Galsworthy	77

In World Literature

THE SUBSTITUTE	François Coppée	85
THE BET	Anton Chekhov	96
FISH IN THE FOREST	A Russian Folk Tale	104

Extensive Reading Program 106

BIOGRAPHY AND AUTOBIOGRAPHY 109

Classicism and the Age of Johnson

JOHNSON AS A CONVERSATIONALIST
(From *The Life of Dr. Samuel
Johnson*) ....James Boswell 112

The Victorian Era

OLIVER GOLDSMITH (From *The English Humorists of the Eighteenth
Century*) ....William Makepeace Thackeray 119

The Twentieth Century

FLORENCE NIGHTINGALE (From *Eminent Victorians*) ....Lytton Strachey 131

In World Literature

DISRAELI IN LONDON (From *Disraeli*) André Maurois 141

Extensive Reading Program 164

CONTENTS

	PAGE
POETRY	169

The Middle English Period

THE KNIGHT (From the *Prologue* to *The Canterbury Tales*)	Geoffrey Chaucer	179

The Age of Elizabeth

UNDER THE GREENWOOD TREE	William Shakespeare	186
HARK, HARK! THE LARK	William Shakespeare	187
WHEN TO THE SESSIONS OF SWEET SILENT THOUGHT	William Shakespeare	188
WHEN IN DISGRACE WITH FORTUNE AND MEN'S EYES	William Shakespeare	189
TO CELIA	Ben Jonson	190
TO THE MEMORY OF MY BELOVED MASTER, WILLIAM SHAKESPEARE	Ben Jonson	191
PSALM 1	The Bible	194
PSALM 23	The Bible	195
PSALM 121	The Bible	196

The Puritan Age and the Restoration

ON HIS BLINDNESS	John Milton	201
L'ALLEGRO	John Milton	202
IL PENSEROSO	John Milton	211

Classicism and the Age of Johnson

From AN ESSAY ON CRITICISM	Alexander Pope	224
ELEGY WRITTEN IN A COUNTRY CHURCHYARD	Thomas Gray	227
THE DESERTED VILLAGE	Oliver Goldsmith	236

The Age of Romanticism

THE TIGER	William Blake	263
JOHN ANDERSON, MY JO	Robert Burns	264
A MAN'S A MAN FOR A' THAT	Robert Burns	265
BANNOCKBURN	Robert Burns	267
SWEET AFTON	Robert Burns	268
MY HEART'S IN THE HIGHLANDS	Robert Burns	270
THE COTTER'S SATURDAY NIGHT	Robert Burns	271
AULD LANG SYNE	Robert Burns	278
TO A MOUSE	Robert Burns	280
MY HEART LEAPS UP	William Wordsworth	282
THE WORLD IS TOO MUCH WITH US	William Wordsworth	283
COMPOSED UPON WESTMINSTER BRIDGE	William Wordsworth	284

CONTENTS

PAGE

It Is a Beauteous Evening, Calm
   and Free ....*William Wordsworth* 285
London, 1802 ....*William Wordsworth* 286
The Daffodils ....*William Wordsworth* 287
The Solitary Reaper ....*William Wordsworth* 288
Jock o' Hazeldean ....*Sir Walter Scott* 289
The Parting of Marmion and
   Douglas (From *Marmion*) ......*Sir Walter Scott* 291
Kubla Khan ....*Samuel Taylor Coleridge*..295
Oft, in the Stilly Night ....*Thomas Moore* 297
The Destruction of Sennacherib..*Lord Byron* 298
She Walks in Beauty ....*Lord Byron* 300
Maid of Athens, Ere We Part....*Lord Byron* 301
The Prisoner of Chillon ....*Lord Byron* 302
The Cloud ....*Percy Bysshe Shelley*.....316
To a Skylark ....*Percy Bysshe Shelley* 319
Ode to the West Wind ....*Percy Bysshe Shelley*....324
Rough Wind, That Moanest Loud.*Percy Bysshe Shelley*.....327
Ozymandias ....*Percy Bysshe Shelley*.....328
Music, When Soft Voices Die....*Percy Bysshe Shelley*.....329
On First Looking Into Chapman's
   Homer ....*John Keats* 330
When I Have Fears That I May
   Cease to Be...................*John Keats* 331
Ode to a Nightingale ....*John Keats* 332
Ode on a Grecian Urn...........*John Keats* 335
The Eve of St. Agnes ....*John Keats* 337

The Victorian Era

The Revenge ....*Alfred, Lord Tennyson* ..355
Ring Out, Wild Bells (From *In
   Memoriam*) ....*Alfred, Lord Tennyson* ...361
Break, Break, Break ....*Alfred, Lord Tennyson* ...362
Ulysses ....*Alfred, Lord Tennyson* ...363
Crossing the Bar ....*Alfred, Lord Tennyson* ...366
The Year's at the Spring ......*Robert Browning* 367
Home Thoughts from Abroad.....*Robert Browning* 368
"De Gustibus—" ....*Robert Browning* 369
My Last Duchess ....*Robert Browning* 371
Prospice ....*Robert Browning* 374
Up at a Villa—Down in the City.*Robert Browning* 376
How Do I Love Thee ....*Elizabeth B. Browning* ...381
Dover Beach ....*Matthew Arnold* 382
Sonnet 86—Lost Days ....*Dante Gabriel Rossetti* ...384
Up-Hill ....*Christina Rossetti* 384

CONTENTS

	PAGE
A Child's Laughter ....Algernon C. Swinburne ..385
Invictus ....William Ernest Henley ..387
Margaritae Sorori ....William Ernest Henley ..388
Requiescat ....Oscar Wilde 389

The Twentieth Century

The Man He Killed ....Thomas Hardy 396
Weathers ....Thomas Hardy 397
Loveliest of Trees ....Alfred Edward Housman 398
Reveille ....Alfred Edward Housman 399
The Lake Isle of Innisfree ......William Butler Yeats 400
The Song of the Old Mother....William Butler Yeats 401
Gunga Din ....Rudyard Kipling 402
Fuzzy-Wuzzy ....Rudyard Kipling 405
Recessional ....Rudyard Kipling 407
I Meant to Do My Work Today...Richard Le Gallienne 409
The Example ....William Henry Davies ...410
A Greeting ....William Henry Davies ...410
Silver ....Walter de la Mare 411
The Listeners ....Walter de la Mare 412
The Donkey ....Gilbert Keith Chesterton 414
Tewkesbury Road ....John Masefield 415
Rounding the Horn ....John Masefield 416
A Consecration ....John Masefield 419
The Barrel Organ ....Alfred Noyes 420
An Old Woman of the Roads.....Padraic Colum 427
The Road ....James Stephens 428
Dreamers ....Siegfried Sassoon 429
In Service ....Winifred M. Letts 430
The Soldier ....Rupert Brooke 431
The Great Lover ....Rupert Brooke 432

In World Literature

The Morning Glory (Chinese)....From the *Shi King* 435
On the Birth of His Son (Chinese) Su Tung-P'o 436
The Ocean (Greek) ....Moschus 437
The Dying Christian to His Soul
  (Latin) ....The Emperor Hadrian ...438
Inscription for a Portrait of
  Dante (Italian) ....Giovanni Boccaccio 439
Wanderer's Night-Songs (German). Johann Wolfgang von
                                Goethe 440
In the Orchard (Norwegian)......Henrik Ibsen 441
The Sleeper of the Valley
  (French) ....Arthur Rimbaud 442

Extensive Reading Program 443

CONTENTS

	PAGE
THE ESSAY AND OTHER PROSE	447

The Age of Elizabeth
| OF STUDIES .... *Francis Bacon* .... 455 |
| OF TRUTH .... *Francis Bacon* .... 458 |

The Puritan Age and the Restoration
IN DEFENSE OF ANGLERS (From *The Compleat Angler*) .... *Izaak Walton* 466
IN THE VALLEY OF HUMILIATION (From *The Pilgrim's Progress*) .... *John Bunyan* 470
FROM A DIARY .... *Samuel Pepys* 475

Classicism and the Age of Johnson
A VOYAGE TO BROBDINGNAG (From *Gulliver's Travels*) .... *Jonathan Swift* 487
SIR ROGER AT CHURCH .... *Addison and Steele* 495
FROZEN WORDS .... *Addison and Steele* 501
THE DISSECTION OF A BEAU'S HEAD .. *Addison and Steele* 506
THE COQUETTE'S HEART .... *Addison and Steele* 509
THE CHARACTER OF THE IDLER (From *The Idler*) .... *Samuel Johnson* 514

The Age of Romanticism
A DISSERTATION UPON ROAST PIG (From *Essays of Elia*) .... *Charles Lamb* 522
OLD CHINA (From *Essays of Elia*) .. *Charles Lamb* 531
ON GOING A JOURNEY .... *William Hazlitt* 540
DREAMS (From *The Confessions of an English Opium Eater*) .... *Thomas de Quincey* 548

The Victorian Era
THE STORMING OF THE BASTILLE (From *The French Revolution*) ... *Thomas Carlyle* 561
LONDON IN 1685 (From *History of England*) .... *Thomas B. Macaulay* 567
THE DEFINITION OF A GENTLEMAN .. *John Henry Newman* 572
OF BOOKS, OF READING, OF NATIONS (From *Sesame and Lilies*) ...... *John Ruskin* 575
A LIBERAL EDUCATION .... *Thomas Henry Huxley* ... 582
THE GREEN DONKEY-DRIVER (From *Travels with a Donkey*) .... *Robert Louis Stevenson* . 587

The Twentieth Century
MARY'S LITTLE LAMB (From *The Book of a Naturalist*) .... *William Henry Hudson* ... 601

    Some Platitudes Concerning Drama (From *The Inn of Tranquillity*) ....John Galsworthy 608
    A Study in Dejection (From *Yet Again*) .... Max Beerbohm 618
    The Daily Miracle (From *How to Live on Twenty-four Hours a Day*) Arnold Bennett 623
    The Sea and the Jungle (A Selection) ....Henry Major Tomlinson ..627
    On Lying in Bed (From *Tremendous Trifles*) ....Gilbert Keith Chesterton 634

In World Literature

    Against Idleness ....Michel de Montaigne 640

    Extensive Reading Program 647

THE DRAMA 649

The Age of Elizabeth

    Macbeth ....William Shakespeare 664

Classicism and the Age of Johnson

    She Stoops to Conquer ....Oliver Goldsmith 782

The Twentieth Century

    The Lost Silk Hat ....Lord Dunsany 861

    Extensive Reading Program 872

THE NOVEL 875

The Victorian Era

    A Tale of Two Cities ....Charles Dickens 883

    Extensive Reading Program 1179

A SUMMARY AND REVIEW 1181

INDEX 1191

PROSE AND POETRY OF ENGLAND

LITERARY PERIODS

THE PERIODS OF ENGLISH LITERATURE

THE ANGLO-SAXON AND MIDDLE ENGLISH PERIODS (BEGINNINGS TO 1550)

THE ANGLO-SAXON PERIOD (BEGINNINGS TO 1066)

The Celts, the Earliest Inhabitants of Britain

The earliest inhabitants of Britain of whom literature takes an account were the Celts. Originally they had made their homes in Central Asia, but had wandered westward and located in what is now northern France. They were a restless people and some of them crossed the English Channel and settled in what is now England, Scotland and Wales. In 55 B.C. they were conquered by the Romans, under whose subjugation they remained for nearly five hundred years.

The Anglo-Saxon Conquest

In the fifth century there swarmed from the continent of Europe those fierce conquering tribes, the Angles, Saxons, and Jutes, whom Tennyson in *The Coming of Arthur* describes as

> a heathen horde,
> Reddening the sun with smoke and earth with blood.

The homeland of these tribes lay along the coast of the North Sea and in southern Denmark in the vicinity now known as Jutland. Their migration was probably part of that great folk-movement which pressed down from the north and east upon the weakening Roman empire; and their conquest, though stubbornly resisted, seems to have been a thorough-going one. The Britons were either killed or driven farther and farther west until the fury of the onslaught had spent itself, and the survivors found refuge in the fastnesses of Wales, in Cornwall, or in Ireland.

At length the conquerors settled upon the lands which they had ravaged, and devoted themselves to husbandry and the arts of peace. From the tribes of Angles the country came to be called Angle-land, or England. From the two tribes, Angles and Saxons, has come the name of the language—Anglo-Saxon.

Anglo-Saxon Literature

The new-comers brought their literature with them, and it is from what has survived that we learn what manner of men they were. Of course, their literature was not what we have in mind when we use that term, for it was still a matter of oral tradition. It consisted largely of tales of heroes and mighty deeds done in battle. The custodians of this literature were the *scops*, who, at the feasts of the warriors, sang or chanted their tales to the accompaniment of the harp. From the surviving fragments of this literature we picture a hardy, warlike, adventuresome people. They were at home upon the water. The sea was their highway and upon it they set out in their sturdy curve-stemmed ships on voyages of plunder and adventure. They were a somewhat serious, dour, if not gloomy race, quite lacking the fanciful imagination of the Briton, or Celt. There is very little in their literature that would indicate a delight in nature. This fact is not astonishing, for the climate of their homeland, lying as it did along the low, misty shores of the North Sea with the dark forests of Germany at its back, was a rigorous one. Winters were cold and long. The struggle for existence was a strenuous one, in which the unkinder aspects of nature were conspicuous, and their imagination peopled the forest, the sea, and the misty moorlands with etens and elves, and monsters and demons.

The Effect of Christianity

In the latter years of the sixth century Christian missionaries from Rome and from Ireland began to find their way among the Anglo-Saxons, in whose temperament there seems to have been a reflective strain which led them at times to musing on the mystery of life. The characteristic is well illustrated by the account of the conversion of King Edwin of Northumbria:

> Another of the king's councilors spoke thus: "King, this earthly life of ours seems to me, when compared with the time of which we are ignorant, as if we were sitting at a feast with your councilors and chieftains in the winter, and the fire were burning and the hall cheerfully heated, while outside it rained, it snowed, and the wind raged; and as if then there came a sparrow and swiftly flew through the hall, coming in through one door and going out at the other. While he is within the hall he is not buffeted by the wintry storm; but in the twinkling of an eye his respite is ended, and from the winter he goes into the winter again. So the life of man appears for a little time; what went before, and what comes after, we know not. If, therefore, this new teaching brings us anything more certain and more valuable, it seems to me that we ought to follow it."

Such was the appeal which the new religion made. Once adopted, Christianity seems to have spread with a fair degree of rapidity. Monasteries were established throughout the realm, especially in Northumbria, in great number. In these learning was cultivated, and the industry of the monks first reduced to writing those remnants of old Anglo-Saxon literature which have come down to us. For two centuries the great bulk of Anglo-Saxon literature continued to be religious in nature, and was the work of either monks or churchmen. It consisted of paraphrases in verse of passages of the Old Testament, religious poems, and collections of sermons.

King Alfred

In the last half of the eighth century England was again well-nigh overwhelmed by another heathen horde. Now came the Danes, who burst upon northern England burning and destroying as they went. The monasteries where literature and learning had flourished were pillaged and the monks killed or dispersed. The Danes pushed southward across the Thames and threatened to overrun all England, but in a great battle at Edington, Alfred, King of the West-Saxons, forced the Danish host to surrender and rolled back the tide of conquest. The Danes, however, were left in possession of nearly all the territory north of the Thames.

Alfred had no sooner forced the Danes to a peace than he turned his attention to the education of his people. He gathered scholars and learned men about him and established a school where "every freeborn youth who possessed the means should abide at his book until he can well understand English writing." He himself undertook various translations of earlier works. "Alfred," says Green, "created English literature. Before him, England had possessed noble poems and a train of ballads and battle songs. Prose she had none. The mighty roll of the books that fill her libraries begins with the translations of Alfred, and above all, with the chronicle of his reign."

The Anglo-Saxon Language

Present day English bears little resemblance to the Anglo-Saxon tongue. Only occasionally do we come across a word which we recognize, as the following three lines from one of the great Anglo-Saxon folk-epics show:

            Hwæt!   We Gar-Dena   in gear-dagum
            Þeod-cyninga   Þrym gefrunon,
            hu ða æÞlingas   ellen fremedon!

The translation of these lines is as follows: "Lo, we have heard of the glory in days of old of the Spear-Danes, of the kings of the people, how the athelings did deeds of valor!"

Here we recognize the words "we" and "in," and perhaps the word "hwæt" (what). Not only was the vocabulary different from that of our tongue, but it was also a far less expressive language than ours. It had fewer words and those for the most part named concrete things such as the sea, night, feast, day, ship, shield, wave, home, etc. In fact, most of the monosyllables in our present day speech come from the Anglo-Saxon. It was lacking in what we call abstract terms, and it was not a language adapted to graceful, fanciful and imaginative writing. It was, moreover, inflected to show conjugation, declension, and comparison. Harsh and somewhat guttural sounds seem to have prevailed. But what it lacked in lightness and grace, it made up for in force and vigor.

THE MIDDLE ENGLISH PERIOD (1066–1550)

The Norman Conquest

In 1066 England again suffered another invasion which was to have a far-reaching effect on English life and literature. In this year came the Normans under the leadership of their great duke, William the Conqueror, who crossed the Channel with an army at his back to enforce his claim to the throne of England. On the battlefield of Hastings, not far from the place where tradition says the Saxons first set foot on English soil, William met and defeated Harold, "the last of the Saxons," and made himself master of England.

There now followed the subjugation of the realm. Most of the great estates passed into the hands of William's followers, and the English bishops were supplanted by Norman churchmen. The whole direction of affairs passed to the newcomers. As their influence extended, Norman manners and customs followed; and Norman-French became the language of all persons of social consequence under whose patronage alone, literature in those days could flourish.

Norman and Saxon

Originally the Normans were what might be called cousins of the Anglo-Saxons, for they were Norsemen. They too had come down out the North in their curve-stemmed ships, coasting the shores and making quick forays inland to ravage and plunder. During the early years of the tenth century they effected a settlement in France about the mouth of the Seine in the region which took from them the name of Normandy. Here the people whom they dispossessed were the Celts, of the same stock as the Britons, but instead of waging a war of extermination upon them, they intermarried with them and adopted their language and their more civilized manners and customs. The result was that in 1066 when the Normans set out on their conquest of England, they were perhaps the most masterful and the most progressive race in Europe.

The Norman and Saxon presented a number of contrasts. The latter was conspicuous for qualities which make for endurance. He was conservative, if not somewhat stolid, and resented innovation. He was matter-of-fact, and heavy-minded rather than romantic or imaginative. He was likewise stubborn and tenacious, and a strong individualist.

The character of Cedric the Saxon in *Ivanhoe* illustrates pretty well the outstanding traits of the race. The Norman, on the other hand, was more progressive and energetic. He was romantic and imaginative, with a more artistic temperament, a keener appreciation of beauty, and a more joyous outlook on life. The Norman conquest was achieved by virtue not of superior bravery but by superior ability. While the Saxon, like Cedric, was content to stand up man to man and fight it out with the brown-bill, the javelin, and the buckler of his fathers, the Norman brought to the field superior weapons and tactics of war; and the subjugation of the realm was as much due to Norman superiority in architecture as to ability in arms, for the Saxons knew no method of attack which would reduce the strong fortresses their conquerors raised on every hilltop throughout the land. And in the business of government, the Normans manifested a vigor, an efficiency, and a degree of executive ability which bewildered the more easy-going Saxons.

The Effect on Literature

As those agencies which fostered the development of literature—the castle hall and the monastery—passed under Norman influence, the change was reflected in the cessation of writing in the Anglo-Saxon, and for nearly a hundred and fifty years after the conquest there was no literature in English worthy the name. When finally it does appear, one of the first things we note is that it is in a language which is much nearer our modern English than the Anglo-Saxon was. As the two races had grown together, they had developed a new tongue. Though it was the English speech which had triumphed, it was a simpler, richer, less cumbersome, and a more expressive language than the Anglo-Saxon, which had lost most of its inflectional endings in the process and been enriched by the addition of many words of Norman-French origin. Two other changes in the literature are also to be noted. First, it is no longer predominantly religious, but reflects new interests. We now find nature poetry, love lyrics, the beginnings of patriotic poetry, a book of travels, some satire, and a great number of romances. And in the second place, we find new literary forms, especially in poetry.

Two great influences of the period upon literature were the Crusades and the establishment of universities. The Crusades were expeditions which were undertaken by the Christians to recover the Holy Land from the Turks. The first Crusade took place in 1096 and the last in 1189. The Crusaders came back from their travels with new ideas, new mannerisms, new clothing, and broader aspects of life.

In the twelfth century, Oxford University was founded and in the thirteenth century, Cambridge. The establishment of these universities meant that education was no longer confined within the walls of the monasteries.

The Fourteenth and Fifteenth Centuries

The fourteenth century was an important one for it produced Geoffrey Chaucer, the first great figure in English literature. It was a period which found Norman and Saxon fighting side by side against a common enemy, and one in which all differences were forgotten and distrust was replaced by friendliness. The popularity of Chaucer's writing was powerful in making his dialect the standard English speech. For the first time we have a single tongue understood by all men. English now became the speech of the court and of parliament as well as of the common people.

The fifteenth century produced no single writer comparable to Chaucer but it did see advances in the field of poetry and a rapid development in the Mystery and Morality plays from which the Shakespearean drama was to develop.

The Renaissance

The term Renaissance is given to that great period of transition during which the Middle Ages passed away and the modern world came into being. Literally translated, the term means "Rebirth" and has been used to describe the revival of classic learning which took place in Europe in the fifteenth and sixteenth centuries. The revival of learning was, however, only one phase of the great change in life which took place during this period. In every department of life the old was being superseded by the new. Feudalism and all the institutions attendant upon it was passing away. A strong sense of nationalism was growing up, a new system of land holding was supplanting feudal tenure, a new form of wealth based upon trade rather than upon land was coming into being, and towns and cities were springing up. It was in this period that the printing press was invented, that America was discovered, and that a religious reformation took place. Everywhere were signs of economic progress and a consequent rise in the standard of living. What the revival of learning did was to open up the rich civilizations of the ancient world, stimulate intellectual curiosity, and spur men on to attempt to reconstruct the culture and civilization of the ancients.

The first step, of course, in the revival of learning in England, was to make the literature of the ancient world available to Englishmen. In the closing years of the fifteenth century the study of Greek was begun at Oxford. Here and soon at other centers of learning assembled scholars whose attention was directed to the study of the classics of antiquity. The study of such books as the *Republic* of Plato, the *Iliad* and the *Odyssey* of Homer, and the Greek philosophers, poets, and dramatists generally, led to a desire on the part of Englishmen to imitate these works. In this way it came about that the ancient classics gave an impulse to English literature.

There was no great literature written during this period. It was, on

PERIODS OF ENGLISH LITERATURE

the whole, a period of experimentation and of preparation for the great productive period which was to follow in the days of Queen Elizabeth.

The Age of Elizabeth (1550–1625)

England Comes of Age

The reign of Elizabeth (1558–1603) may be said to have witnessed England's coming of age. In her day, those changes which had been going on in every department of life, transforming medieval into modern England, reached their culmination. By 1603, the monarchy was firmly established and the authority of the central government made itself felt in every corner of the realm. The religious question, which had so often threatened disruption, had been settled. The great power of Spain had been met and humbled, and England had emerged a world power. Explorers and merchant adventurers were sending their ships to the far corners of the earth, and the foundations of England's great colonial empire were being laid. Commerce and manufacture were receiving promotion and encouragement. Agriculture was being studied and improved. The great middle class was coming into a position of economic and political power. The standard of living generally was rising, and people as a whole were enjoying more of the material comforts of life. The cultivation of learning which had gone on during the sixteenth century was now rewarded by an abundant harvest in letters and learning. In everything there was manifest a new, vigorous, adventuresome, and progressive spirit.

The Elizabethan Spirit

Perhaps the thing which strikes one as most significant when he reads the history of the period is the new spirit. Explaining its origin is a long story. Here it is sufficient to say that in various ways it grew out of the many-sided curiosity and activities of the Renaissance. As the best intelligence and the imagination of the Middle Ages had been preoccupied with the world to come, so now they were directed to the world here and now, with unbounded enthusiasm and vigor born of new delight in living and of a new confidence in the ability of man to master the universe. In countless writings of the age this confidence finds expression. Shakespeare speaks it in *Hamlet*. "What a piece of work is a man! how noble in reason! how infinite in faculty! in form and moving now express and admirable! in action how like an angel! in apprehension how like a god!" Such are the very words. Extravagant hyperbole, perhaps, but valid enough as evidence of the temper of the age.

This was the spirit which was behind the making of the modern world. It animated cold intellectual natures like that of Sir Francis Bacon who declared, "I have taken all knowledge to be my province." It was behind the new science, the new geography, and the new astronomy of the time. It pushed Harvey on to the discovery of the circulation of the blood, as it pushed Hawkins and Drake and Frobisher on to the discovery of new lands beyond the seas. It stirred men like Holinshed to the rediscovery of England's glorious past, and fired others to the celebration of the spacious days of their own time.

Elizabethan Literature

But nowhere is the new spirit better revealed than in the literature of the period. Elizabeth, herself, was a great patron of the arts, and under her interest and encouragement, literature flourished as it had never done before in its history. Although the Elizabethan Age witnessed a remarkable development in prose, it was in the fields of poetry and of drama that the exuberant delight in life found best expression. There was a great outburst of poetry which exhibited a great variety of stanza form and exquisite lyric grace and sweetness. But the supreme literary achievement was in drama. In the days of Elizabeth came the culmination toward which the English drama had been developing for centuries. And here appears the greatest figure in all English literature—that of William Shakespeare. The Age of Elizabeth was truly one of the most productive in all English history.

THE PURITAN AGE AND THE RESTORATION (1625-1700)

Changes Appear in Literature

Although Elizabeth died in 1603, the literary period which bears her name continued until 1625 for her successor, James I, from a literary point of view, belongs in the Elizabethan Age. It was during James' reign that Shakespeare produced some of his greatest plays and that other Elizabethan writers continued to wield great literary influence. The accession of Charles I in 1625, however, marks a new literary period.

Even before the death of Shakespeare in 1616 there were observable signs of a change coming over the face of English literature—a change which became more pronounced in the years following. The spirit of the Renaissance seems to have burned itself out. The delight in life and intense vigor which had characterized the literature of the period gave way to a more sober, less confident mood.

Puritan and Cavalier

Behind this change of spirit was a divided England—Puritan and Cavalier. The two groups were present in English life long before Charles I came to the throne. They date back, indeed, even to the days before Elizabeth—to the days of the Reformation which took place during the Renaissance. Although the Reformation had been attended with new freedom of religious thought, there was a considerable group who were hostile to certain church ceremonies and to the authority of the bishops. This group of extreme Protestants became known as the Puritan party. In spite of Elizabeth's vigorous attempts to unify the church, the Puritans persisted in their belief, but during her reign they did not advance beyond their demands for church reform. It should be noted, however, that the Puritans were not merely a religious sect. They put great stress on the freedom of the individual in politics as well as in religion, and were bitterly opposed to tyrannous government.

Those opposing the Puritans were known as the Cavaliers. They were characterized by loyalty to the king, they delighted in beauty, and they believed in enjoying life. At first the differences between the Puritans and the Cavaliers were not marked by bitterness, but during the reign of James I who believed in the divine right of kings, the chasm between them widened. The Puritans grew stronger and stronger, and under the high-handed rule of Charles I who believed himself responsible to neither parliament nor the people, the differences between the two parties resulted in Civil War. The Puritans, with Oliver Cromwell as their leader, overthrew the supporters of the king, put Charles to death, and in 1649 set up a republican commonwealth in the place of the monarchy.

Puritan Literature

The rise of the Puritans was swift and their power was brief, but in their short reign they exerted an influence that the world still feels. Included in their ranks were some of the foremost names in English politics and literature. As might be expected, literary production was much less than in the Elizabethan Era, but there were, nevertheless, great writings in both poetry and prose. Prose was the chosen form of expression with the Puritan, for it suited his serious purpose. But great as was some of the Puritan prose, equally great was some of the Puritan poetry. Some of the finest poetry in English literature came from the pen of the great Puritan poet, John Milton. In drama, however, there was a notable decline. The Puritans were antagonistic toward all things of the stage, and in 1642 Parliament closed all theaters throughout the kingdom.

The Restoration

In 1660 the Puritan régime came to an end and Charles II ascended the English throne. It was from this reseating of the Stuart dynasty that the period takes its name—the Restoration. For a time there was a natural reaction against what had been the too stern rule of the Puritans. Pleasures and "vanities of the world" ran wild. Theaters were re-opened, music and dancing were encouraged, and there was a wild, extravagant, unrepressed orgy of pleasure. With the return of the King and his Cavaliers from the Continent, whither they had fled during the Puritan régime, came the demand that English writing should follow the style they had known in Paris. Even Shakespeare was considered dull. This was the beginning of the French influence in English literature. The French standard was "correctness and elegance in expression," and the aim in literature became formal correctness, an aim which was to dominate literature for nearly a hundred years. The Puritan influence had not entirely disappeared from all literature, but for the most part, the writings of the Restoration had a low moral tone.

Classicism and the Age of Johnson (1700–1780)

The Early Years of the Century

The first forty years of the eighteenth century saw great activity in England both internally and in foreign affairs. Between the years 1690 and 1750, England fought three wars with France. These wars increased possessions in India, in the Mediterranean, and in America, and laid the foundation for the British Empire. Foreign trade increased and brought with it increased wealth. Luxury and leisure became the order of the day. Internally, however, there were less favorable results. The wars had brought increased taxation, the burden of which fell on the poor. There was great inequality in life and sharp distinctions in social classes. In this period we find the beginnings of city life with its many interests and amusements and its social refinement and sophistication. Social life reflected these changes, and great value came to be placed on grace and ease of bearing. People affected an elaborate society manner. The dress of both men and women was extravagant and elaborate and reflected the artificiality of polite society. General education was at a low ebb and there was little progress in the sciences. Religion, too, was in a low state.

The Literature of the Early Eighteenth Century

All these conditions were reflected in the literature of the period. It was not a period of great enthusiasm; in fact the temper of the age was one that seemed to frown upon enthusiasms and desired most of all an adherence to established forms and customs. This temper is reflected in the absence from literature of the intense interest in life which characterized the literature of the Elizabethan period and the enthusiasm for an ideal which had characterized the best writing of the Puritan period. Literature was predominantly prose and its aim was formal correctness. Classicism dominated all literature.

Classicism

The term classicism as here used has a specialized meaning. It means really a conventional way of writing. Let us study it more closely.

In *form*, classic literature is smooth, regular, polished, elaborate, scholarly, often imitative. It uses long words; long sentences, carefully balanced; ornate figures of speech, and many allusions to Greek and Roman mythology and literature.

In *subject,* classic literature deals with man in his social relationships—his schools, his clubs, his politics, his churches. It is concerned about rank and social position and behavior. It shows more interest in man-made institutions than in man himself, and more interest in art and artificial effects than in nature. A man of classic mind would take more pleasure in smooth lawns and clipped hedges than in the tumbled splendor of the Alps.

In *spirit* or *mood,* classic literature is impersonal and—unless stirred by anger—unemotional. It appeals to the mind rather than to the heart. It is critical, often satiric. At its best, it pleasantly skims the surface of life. It shows the dress and mannerisms of the man but not his heart of hearts. And the classic writer never puts himself into his works save as a spectator or observer.

The Age of Johnson

The second forty years of the eighteenth century are often called "The Age of Johnson." This age takes its name from Dr. Samuel Johnson, literary dictator of the period, and the last of the classicists. During these years wealth continued to increase, but now agriculture made striking advances, important inventions were made, and there was an intellectual awakening on the part of the masses. In religion, too, there was a revival, due mainly to the efforts of John Wesley who went from one end of England to the other, preaching reform from evil ways. Great elaborateness and extravagance in dress continued as did emphasis on elegance of expression, but men were now beginning to pay more attention to ideas than to the way of expressing them. About Dr. Johnson as a center, there grew up a famous group of literary men who were to wield great influence not only on the literature of their own day, but upon the literature of many days to come. Literature was still predominantly prose, and still predominantly classical, but in content it began to savor of new influences which were in the next period to produce a kind of renaissance in literature in general, and in poetry in particular.

THE AGE OF ROMANTICISM (1780–1840)

The Romantic Movement

The changes in literature which have already been detected in the Age of Johnson and which by 1780 were very marked, were the result of several influences. The American Revolution of 1775 and the French Revolution of 1789 resulted in important reforms within England. Suffrage was extended, a national system of schools was established, and slavery was abolished in all the English colonies. In this period there also occurred the Industrial Revolution which brought about a great number of new discoveries and inventions. The use of steam as a source of power revolutionized every kind of manufacture and changed England from an agricultural to a manufacturing country. All of these conditions led to the recognition of the worth of the common man. Now any triumph in the progress of the common man is accompanied by an increased output in literature. The years 1780–1840 were no exception to this rule. England was now on the threshold of one of the greatest poetry periods in its literature, a period in which all literature was prevailingly romantic.

Romanticism

As might be guessed, romantic literature differs from classic literature in every main point of criticism.

In *form,* romantic literature throws aside the restraint of rules and of ancient models. It allows the message to determine the form, and the form is ever subordinate to the thought. There is therefore much variety in romantic expression. It uses simple language; short, direct sentences; and, often, a conversational style. Sometimes a homely dialect is used. Classical references and elaborate figures of speech are abandoned for simple illustrations drawn from nature. The classicist might say, "Madam, there is in Clio the image of Diana." The romanticist says, "There was my mother with her pretty hair and youthful shape, and Peggotty with no shape at all . . . and with cheeks and arms so hard and red that I wondered the birds didn't peck at her in preference to apples."

In *subject,* romantic literature demands originality, freshness of ideas. It is interested in man as an individual, in his experiences, his emotions, and his dreams. It is in sympathy with the poor and oppressed, and finds the common man more interesting than the man of society because he is more natural. Then the romanticist understands and enjoys nature—nature as it really is, with daisies, buttercups, and noisy swallows instead of Philomels (the classic name for the nightingale) and amaranths. And finally the romanticist expresses the ideals and upward-strivings of mankind. He is hopeful, optimistic.

In *spirit* or *mood,* romantic literature is warm and friendly. It is intimate and sympathetic. The romanticist reveals his own joys and sorrows, his hopes and loves and fears. He arouses our emotions at the suffering of others and urges us on to make the world right. He flames, sometimes, with the zeal of the revolutionist. Sometimes he is quietly happy in his communion with nature. His moods take color from his scene and subject, and he himself is a part of the scene.

The romantic spirit found its finest expression in lyric poetry, but prose, too, quickened to the new influence. The period saw the emergence of the familiar essay, the development of the novel, and a revival of the drama.

PERIODS OF ENGLISH LITERATURE

The Victorian Era (1840–1900)

General Characteristics

The Victorian Era takes its name from Queen Victoria whose long reign lasted from 1837 until 1901. These years saw a number of changes in English life, an understanding of which is necessary to an interpretation of the literature which the period produced. There was on the material side, a great growth in wealth following upon the commercial expansion which resulted from the Industrial Revolution. This material prosperity was accompanied by a rapid growth of great industrial towns and brought in its wake a great variety of social and economic problems. An attempt to deal with the economic problems gave rise to the science of economics which produced a number of writers such as Bentham, Mill, and others. On the spiritual side, life was affected by this material prosperity, and also by the activity in natural science which gave to the world the theory of evolution and other theories which upset established opinions based upon Biblical authority. To some men, the materialism of the age was anathema, for it seemed to them that the effect of material prosperity was to make men lose sight of spiritual values; and in other men the new scientific theories which seemed so difficult to reconcile with the old beliefs, gave rise to doubt which unsettled faith. Another characteristic of this age was the growth of political democracy which brought about a reform of Parliament and extension of the franchise—a movement which is also reflected in literature. Democracy had not only its adherents but also its critics who could not see how the right to vote would give men the qualities of mind and soul which it seemed to them that the age was most in need of.

Victorian Literature

The literature of the period was a combination of romanticism and classicism, with classicism—in form, at least—predominating. The age was productive of a great body of poetry but was essentially an age of prose. The novel reached its high-water mark and the short story saw its beginnings. Scientific investigation, social and economic problems, religion, and politics gave rise to a great variety of writing which included essays, criticism, history, and philosophy. A high moral tone characterized all literature.

The Twentieth Century (1900–   )

General Characteristics

The first thing which strikes one about contemporary literature is the great mass of it, and the second thing is that every writer seems to be a law unto himself. Indeed, it appeared for a time that in the desperate desire to achieve something different, artists—writers among them—would make this a "Formless Age." Patterns of all sorts went into the discard. Verseless poetry and sentence-less (and sense-less) prose had their flare. With them came a casting aside of standards and ideals. To be different, to be smart, to be free—these were all that mattered. Classicism and romanticism alike suffered the scorn of the progressive artist. It was and still is, to some extent, an age of *realism*. But the special application of realism seemed to imply that nothing good or beautiful or true was real. Reality meant ugliness and sin and disillusionment.

Now, more than thirty years of this latest century have passed, and one can look back over its works with some sense of perspective. It is rather surprising to note how the books which have lifted themselves above the mass to a position that seems to promise lasting recognition are neither the ultra-smart, nor the formless, nor the sense-less. It begins to dawn on this twentieth century that true realism sees both sides of the picture. Life is sin *and* goodness, ugliness *and* beauty, disillusionment *and* truth. It is just as narrow to pick the bad without the good as it is the other way around. The business of the artist is to select the significant. The ugliness that has a meaning may be—should be—in the picture; but ugliness for the sake of ugliness is worse than beauty for the sake of beauty.

Contemporary Literature

All of which introduction leads to the fact that some exceptionally fine literature has come out of what promised to be an hysterical age. The short story and the novel have seen great development, and the essay has emerged into many different types. The age has witnessed a "new biography" and a revival of the drama. In poetry there is observable a great break with the past in content, form, and treatment. As new aspects of life have developed, new sources of poetic inspiration and material have likewise developed. Except for the tendency to realism, it is quite impossible to classify or group authors with respect to any great movement or tendency of the times. A recent writer says, "Never did the personality of each writer count for more, as compared with the general form of his expression. And never did temperaments more forcibly refuse to comply with a common style, one method, one programme. It has often been noticed that the era of literary doctrines and schools seems to be over."

THE SHORT STORY

THE HISTORY OF THE SHORT STORY IN ENGLAND

ANGLO-SAXON AND MIDDLE ENGLISH PERIODS (BEGINNINGS TO 1550)

Religious Narratives

Although the literary form which we classify as the short story has only recently taken a definite form, narration or story telling is, of course, much older. Many good stories which were undoubtedly told during the Anglo-Saxon and Middle English periods have been lost because they were never recorded. One reason for this was that very few people could read or write. Besides, the making of manuscripts was done almost entirely in the monasteries where interest was naturally focused on religious subjects. Bits of narrative, however, such as wonderful happenings to saints, nuns, and monks, crept into the sermons and histories, and in them is to be found the beginning of the English short story.

Fables

Gradually, stories which were not written about a religious theme were incorporated in the church literature. The purpose of these was to emphasize some point—to serve as an example. By the fourteenth century fables had become numerous. They were included in sermons and treatises for adults because of the morals which could be drawn from them. By giving human characteristics to animals, the fable gained significance over an abstract discussion on human virtues and vices. The purpose of these fables was not to amuse but to teach a lesson and provoke serious thinking in the minds of adults. The idea that fables and fairy tales are suitable only for small children came in recent times.

THE AGE OF ELIZABETH (1550–1625)

Translations from the French and Italian

England was too near the continent geographically, and too much involved in its affairs politically, by the time of Elizabeth, not to be influenced by French and Italian thinking. This influence had first been

ELD

felt during the period of the Renaissance, and it now exerted itself in two directions, in translations and in imitations.

One notable collection of translations was *The Palace of Pleasure* brought out by William Painter, a clerk of her majesty's ordnance in the tower. Painter must have been a reader of both contemporary and ancient writers, for his translations included stories by Boccaccio, Bandello, Margaret of Navarre, Livy, Herodotus, Plutarch, and many others. This was the first time that many of these works had been translated into English and the result was that this book became a source of plots for further stories and especially for dramas. Painter's style was simple in comparison with the elaborate and ornate style of most of the Elizabethan writers.

Imitations of the Novella

The Italian *novella* was a form of short narrative told for amusement. It was popular in translation in England, but when the English mind, given the pattern, attempted to imitate and to write a *novella,* the result was very different from the pattern. Instead of telling the story simply, the writer not only overburdened his writing by the introduction of endless figures of speech, but he felt it necessary to insert lengthy discussions on his philosophy of life and love, morals and manners. No wonder that interest shifted from the story to the drama in the Elizabethan period. Nor is it difficult to see that, when an author felt that he must discuss at length his philosophy of life, the short narrative did not give him room enough and he spread out into the more spacious form which later developed into the novel.

The Puritan Age and the Restoration (1625–1700)

A Decline in the Short Narrative

During the Puritan Age and the Restoration, the little narrative writing that was done was in the form of longer pieces. The shorter narratives in most cases continued to be translations or imitations, now not so much of Italian writings as those from France and Spain. Furthermore, the strictness of the Puritans tended to discourage rather than encourage any kind of fictional writing.

Classicism and the Age of Johnson (1700–1780)

English Influence in the Periodical Essay

The eighteenth century is an important period in the study of English fiction, for in it we have the beginnings of the novel. During this period the short narrative also developed along new lines in the so-called "periodical essay." Although contributions to *The Tatler, The Spectator,* and other periodicals of the day are classified as essays, they are often, more correctly, character sketches, anecdotes, and situations which need only a plot to make them short stories in the modern meaning of the term. The short narrative which until 1700 had drawn so heavily on foreign sources was now getting its sustenance from English soil, for these "periodical essays" dealt with London and the types of people to be found there. They were written not so much for the amusement of the reader as in the attempt "to throw darts, whether blunt or pointed, at the manners, morals, and customs of the times." In these writings we find the characters acting and speaking like Londoners—a new accomplishment for the English writer who had been so long under continental influence.

The Age of Romanticism (1780–1840)

The Development of the Short Story

Although the years 1780 to 1840 are of the greatest importance in the development of the short story in the English language, it was in America rather than in England that the development took place. Washington Irving, Nathaniel Hawthorne, and Edgar Allan Poe gave a new form to the short narrative and thereby furnished a model for other writers. In England, writers were much slower than in America to develop this form. Short narratives were written but the emphasis and proportions differ from those in the short story of today, and during the last part of the eighteenth century the moral was the all-important part of the story. In the first decade of the nineteenth century the romantic, the mysterious, and the pathetic narratives filled the magazines but they lacked the artistry and technique to be found in the narratives of like nature in America.

The Victorian Era (1840–1900)

Novelists Write Short Stories

The names of Charles Dickens, William Makepeace Thackeray, and George Eliot will always be prominent when novelists of the Victorian Era are discussed. Then, as now, writers of novels did not confine themselves wholly to the longer form but wrote short narratives as well. Some of the short narratives of these three authors approximate in form the present short story. Dickens, for example, in 1866, published *The Signal Man* in which, whether intentionally or not, he used the same technique that Poe had used in his stories.

Robert Louis Stevenson (1850–1894)

The English short story as we know it may be said to have begun with Robert Louis Stevenson, when in 1877 he published *A Lodging for the Night*. Stevenson was a born story teller, and that this natural talent might have a proper setting, he developed a most polished style of expression. The method he used is well known—he studied great masters and painstakingly imitated them. He was a close student of Hawthorne in particular, and most of his stories, like Hawthorne's, inquire into the moral nature of man. He added to the moral tone, however, his own originality in the way of romantic atmosphere. He appeals to a variety of readers because of his wide range of interests and his mastery of many forms of expression. He traveled much and turned his travels to literary account in *Travels with a Donkey* and *An Inland Voyage*. He liked adventure and romance and gave them expression in *Treasure Island, Prince Otto,* and *Kidnapped.* In *Dr. Jekyll and Mr. Hyde,* he made a powerful psychological study of the powers of good and evil. *Markheim* is perhaps his best short story.

Later Victorian Writers

A number of short story writers now appear, who, although their work was begun during the Victorian Era, belong more properly to the twentieth century, and will be treated in that period. Thomas Hardy is perhaps the most notable example. Rudyard Kipling is also important, for his *Plain Tales from the Hills,* which was published in 1890, gave the popularity of the short story a great impetus.

The Twentieth Century (1900–   )

General Characteristics

The short story by the beginning of the new century was an established branch of literature, holding its own place, independent of the novel, the essay, or any other form of prose writing. Its growth from the first written narratives has never been direct or continuous. As has been shown, constant influences from one foreign country or another have been at work. Even at the beginning of the twentieth century, the writings of de Maupassant in France and the work of Chekhov in Russia affected contemporary writers. Since literature is no more static now than in the past, the short story, as we know it today—in its compact, incisive form—will be modified to reflect the ideas and temperaments of the writers of the future.

Among the large number of twentieth century short story writers the names of Thomas Hardy, Rudyard Kipling, Joseph Conrad, James M. Barrie, and John Galsworthy stand out as perhaps most important. All of these writers are novelists who have also been interested in the short story form.

Thomas Hardy (1840–1928)

In the very small town of Upper Bockhampton, near Dorchester, Thomas Hardy was born on June 2, 1840. The cottage in which he was born was as simple as those he often describes in his writings. The living room floor was stone flagged and the ceiling was of cross-beams. The large fireplace was built of uncemented bricks.

Hardy was educated in local schools and by private instruction. His writings, particularly his poetry, show that he had a wide knowledge of classical as well as modern literature. When he was sixteen, he was apprenticed to an ecclesiastical architect at Dorchester. Although he must have had considerable ability along this line, he spent his spare time writing poems and essays. In 1862 he went to London as an assistant to Sir Arthur Bloomfield and, while working for him, won the medal of the Royal Institute of British Architects. Since no English writer can excel Hardy in his descriptions of the landscape, it is reasonable to believe that his appreciation of color and proportion was developed by his work as an architect.

In 1865 his first short story was published and from this date he took up writing as a profession. After 1897 Hardy turned from prose to poetry. In this medium he also won for himself a very high place in English literature.

He died on January 12, 1928, and his ashes were placed in Westminster Abbey, but his heart was buried in his parish churchyard. At first thought this strange burial may seem sentimental, yet Hardy was nearer a fatalist than a sentimentalist. But, on second thought, it seems fitting that his heart should have been buried in the churchyard of the community about which he wrote and among just such people as he portrayed in his novels and short stories.

Joseph Conrad (1857–1924)

Joseph Conrad (Teodor Jozef Konrad Korzeniowski) was born on December 3, 1857, in Russian Poland in the Kiev section of Ukraine. His father's family belonged to the landed gentry and were active in attempts to make Poland once more an independent country. When Conrad was four years old, his family moved to Warsaw. There his father became so active in the cause of Poland's independence that the following year he was banished to Vologda. Joseph and his mother went with his father into exile. His mother died a few years after this, and Conrad lived alone with his father, who was a scholar and translator and whose library supplied the young boy with plenty of books in Polish and French.

In 1868, after his father's health had failed, they were given permission to move from Vologda to Cracow, where Joseph entered the Royal and Imperial Gymnasium of St. Anne. Soon after moving to

Cracow, his father died and Joseph was left in the care of his uncle. At fifteen he was so determined to go to sea that he ran away. His tutor, however, followed and brought him back to complete some of his schooling. It is said that the books, *The Toilers of the Sea* by Victor Hugo and *The Pilot* by James Fenimore Cooper, had given him this desire to go to sea. After much discussion with his uncle, that gentleman realized that it was useless to try to make Joseph give up the idea and he did what he could to help him. At eighteen Conrad went to France and sailed for two years on trading vessels. For the next fifteen years Conrad led an adventurous life at sea. He kept no notes but his experiences were later the basis for his stories.

In 1889, while he was taking a vacation in London, he wrote the first seven chapters of *Almayer's Folly*. This manuscript went with him through the African jungle, was nearly lost in a shipwreck on the Congo, and again in a railway station in Germany. Finally it was completed and published in 1895. This was the beginning of Conrad's highly successful literary career.

Although he spoke Polish and French fluently as a child, he did not learn English until he was twenty, and then his textbook was an English newspaper and his teachers fellow seamen.

Sir James Matthew Barrie (1860–1937)

James Matthew Barrie was born at Kirriemuir, in Forfarshire, Scotland. He was educated at Dumfries Academy and Edinburgh University. While in the Academy he wrote up accounts of the cricket matches for the Dumfries' newspapers, and also wrote letters to these papers, using a pen name. The most frequent topic of this correspondence was the desirability of longer school vacations. He continued to write during his university days. In 1883, he became a writer on the Nottingham *Journal*. The following year an article, *An Auld Licht Community*, appeared in a London paper and was well received. Other articles followed this and brought him sufficient success to warrant his moving to London in 1885. *Auld Licht Idylls, When a Man's Single,* and *A Window in Thrums,* all collections of short stories, established his place among contemporary writers. The first and last of these volumes were based on life in his native village, to which he gave the name of "Thrums." A novel, *The Little Minister,* written in 1891, was dramatized and very successfully produced in 1897. The influence of Barrie's mother is noticeable in much of his writing. In 1897, he published a biography of her called *Margaret Ogilvy*. *Peter Pan*, which has endeared Barrie in the hearts of children in England and America, appeared in 1904.

Barrie was knighted in 1913 and in 1922 the Order of Merit was conferred on him. He died in June, 1937, after a long illness.

Rudyard Kipling (1865-1936)

Rudyard Kipling was born in Bombay, India, the son of John Lockwood Kipling, a modeler and designer of pottery, who had gone from England to Bombay to become a teacher in an art school. As is the custom in India, Rudyard's early childhood was largely spent in the charge of native servants. He spoke very little English until he was six years old, but during this time he learned the stories and legends of India in the native tongue. When he was six, he was sent to Portsmouth, England, to be educated. The home in which he lived was as somber and strict as India had been gay and free. Kipling became very familiar with the Bible during this time and this knowledge increased his vocabulary and influenced the rhythm of his poetry. When he was old enough, he entered the United Service College, more familiarly known as "Westward Ho," a school intended for the sons of Englishmen who were in military or government service in the East. *Stalky & Co.* is based on his experiences in this school and Kipling pictures himself as "Beetle" in the story.

At the end of his schooling in the United Service College, Kipling was given his choice of going to a university or returning to India. He was then in his seventeenth year and the memories of his childhood made him choose India. By this time, his father had become Director of the Museum in Lahore in northern India. There Kipling was fortunate enough to be made a sub-editor on the *Civil and Military Gazette*. His style, which is in many ways journalistic, gives evidence of his newspaper experiences. In his spare time he wrote poems that appeared in the paper, often as fillers.  Nevertheless, they pleased the readers so much that letters came from all over India asking that they be published in a book. To this demand Kipling responded by bringing them out in a volume called *Departmental Ditties*.

By 1890 Kipling had gained enough popularity in India to make him want to have his work published in England. He returned to England by way of America, hoping to find a publisher in the United States. Unfortunately, his stories were not accepted by the only publisher to whom he showed them and he continued to London where they were accepted.

In 1892 Kipling married an American girl with whom he returned to this country and for several years made his home in Brattleboro, Vermont. *Captains Courageous,* the two *Jungle Books,* and some of the *Just So Stories* were among the stories he wrote while in Vermont. After a trip to Africa in 1897, Kipling never again made his home in this country, but settled in Sussex, England, where he died in 1936.

For both his poetry and prose Kipling is recognized as an important figure in English literature. His range of subject matter and treatment is very varied and while a reader may not care for everything which Kipling has written, he is almost sure to find something which will appeal to his taste. In 1907 Kipling won the Nobel Prize for Literature, an honor which carries with it the highest international recognition.

John Galsworthy (1867–1933)

John Galsworthy, the son of a lawyer, was born in Surrey, now a suburb of London. He attended Harrow and Oxford. He was prominent in athletics at Oxford where he held the mile record for several years. Although he studied law, he disliked the practice of it and gave up the profession a few years after being called to the bar. For two years he traveled. On one of his sailing voyages he met Joseph Conrad, while the latter was yet a sailor, and a lasting friendship grew up between them. At that time Galsworthy had no intention of trying to write. He did not begin to write until he was twenty-eight. Since he had always been interested in sports, travel, and social affairs, for some years he found it difficult to give up these things and devote himself exclusively to writing. In 1899, his first novel *Jocelyn* was published. In 1901, *Salvation of Forsyte* appeared. This book was the first of a series in which Galsworthy followed the Forsyte family through three generations. These books appeared at intervals for twenty-six years. In between them came the plays *The Silver Box, Joy, Strife,* and *Justice*. Galsworthy believed that humanity could be helped by written propaganda. He frequently presents the conditions which show the injustices of our social system. He does not, however, attempt to formulate a remedy for all these injustices, but his purpose is to make the reader or the playgoer conscious of the inequalities and start him thinking about them. Galsworthy made long visits to this country. *Escape* was written in California, and he spent the winter of 1930 in Arizona. His home in England during the later part of his life was in Sussex. He died in 1933.

Other Short Story Writers of the Twentieth Century

The list of English authors who have developed and practiced the art of short story writing is long. Their names appear with great frequency in the best American magazines. Only a few of them can be listed here.

Arnold Bennett was a versatile writer who is known as an editor, novelist, playwright, essayist, and short story writer. Some of his short stories appear in *Old Wives' Tale* and *The Matador of the Five Towns*.

HISTORY OF THE SHORT STORY

H. G. Wells, better known as a novelist and as a writer in the field of history and the sciences, has also turned his hand to the short story. Here he has made use of his scientific knowledge in the creation of such fantastic tales as *The Time Machine*. Hugh Walpole is also better known as a novelist, but some of his short stories are *Enemy, Silly Old Fool,* and *Chinese Horses*.

E. M. Delafield is the pen name used by Mrs. Arthur Paul Dashwood. Miss Delafield's deep interest in psychology is reflected in her books. *Women Are Like That* is a collection of seventeen of her short stories. V. Sackville-West is an English noblewoman. Knole Castle, where she was born, was a gift to the Sackville family from Queen Elizabeth. The castle has been described by Miss Sackville-West and many other writers in fiction and poetry. *The Heir,* a volume of short stories, was very favorably received by the reading public. Katherine Mansfield, during her short life, showed brilliant talent as a short story writer. *Bliss* is a collection of her short stories.

Gilbert K. Chesterton began his career as an artist but turned to writing after he had been asked to contribute an art criticism to a London magazine. He has written poetry, biography, detective stories, and essays. Among his detective stories is the *Father Brown* series, some of which have been recently published in an American magazine. L. A. G. Strong has won recognition in this country for both his poetry and prose. *The English Captain* is a volume of short stories. J. C. Squire is considered the ablest living parodist in verse. For a number of years he has been editor of the *London Mercury*. He is a contributor to magazines and *Grub Street Nights Entertainments* is a collection of short stories. Sir Arthur Quiller-Couch signed some of his early writings "Q" and since then he has been familiarly known by that initial. He is one of the most important of contemporary English writers. He is well known for his short stories, essays, and poems. W. Somerset Maugham, a dramatist and novelist, is also author of short stories, some of which have been collected in a volume entitled *The Trembling Leaf*. He is a wide traveler and uses foreign backgrounds very effectively. Sir Arthur Conan Doyle, a very versatile writer, is most often thought of as the creator of the Sherlock Holmes stories. P. G. Wodehouse writes humorous stories full of the most amusing complications. Jeeves, the ever-necessary valet, is one of his best known characters. In June, 1929, it was recorded that Wodehouse had published one hundred and fifty-two short stories. William Wymark Jacobs is known especially for his sea stories. His familiarity with the wharves and the people who frequented them gave him material for these stories. E. Phillips Oppenheim has written over a hundred and fifty books in forty-eight years, a large number of which are collections of short stories. His popularity as a writer of international mystery and intrigue stories is as great in America as it is in England.

Short Stories of the Twentieth Century

THE THREE STRANGERS

Thomas Hardy

AMONG the few features of agricultural England which retain an appearance but little modified by the lapse of centuries, may be reckoned the high, grassy and furzy downs,[1] coombs, or ewe-leases, as they are indifferently called, that fill a large area of certain counties in the south and southwest. If any mark of human occupation is met with hereon, it usually takes the form of the solitary cottage of some shepherd.

Fifty years ago such a lonely cottage stood on such a down, and may possibly be standing there now. In spite of its loneliness, however, the spot, by actual measurement, was not more than five miles from a county-town. Yet that affected it little. Five miles of irregular upland, during the long inimical seasons, with their sleets, snows, rains, and mists, afford withdrawing space enough to isolate a Timon[2] or a Nebuchadnezzar;[3] much

---

[1] FURZY DOWNS—Rolling pasture land covered with spiny shrubs.
[2] TIMON—An Athenian who lived a life of almost total seclusion from society.
[3] NEBUCHADNEZZAR—A king of ancient Babylonia.

less, in fair weather, to please that less repellent tribe, the poets, philosophers, artists, and others who "conceive and meditate of pleasant things."

Some old earthen camp or barrow, some clump of trees, at least some starved fragment of ancient hedge is usually taken advantage of in the erection of these forlorn dwellings. But, in the present case, such a kind of shelter had been disregarded. Higher Crowstairs, as the house was called, stood quite detached and undefended. The only reason for its precise situation seemed to be the crossing of two footpaths at right angles hard by, which may have crossed there and thus for a good five hundred years. Hence the house was exposed to the elements on all sides. But, tho the wind up here blew unmistakably when it did blow, and the rain hit hard whenever it fell, the various weathers of the winter season were not quite so formidable on the coomb as they were imagined to be by dwellers on low ground. The raw rimes [4] were not so pernicious as in the hollows, and the frosts were scarcely so severe. When the shepherd and his family who tenanted the house were pitied for their sufferings from the exposure, they said that upon the whole they were less inconvenienced by "wuzzes and flames" (hoarses and phlegms) than when they had lived by the stream of a snug neighboring valley.

The night of March 28, 182–, was precisely one of the nights that were wont to call forth these expressions of commiseration. The level rainstorm smote walls, slopes, and hedges like the clothyard shafts of Senlac and Crécy.[5] Such sheep and outdoor animals as had no shelter stood with their buttocks to the wind; while the tails of little birds trying to roost on some scraggy thorn were blown inside-out like umbrellas. The gable-end of the cottage was stained with wet, and the eavesdroppings flapped against the wall. Yet never was commiseration for the shepherd more misplaced. For that cheerful rustic was entertaining a large party in glorification of the christening of his second girl.

The guests had arrived before the rain began to fall, and they were all now assembled in the chief or living room of the dwell-

---

[4] RIMES—Hoarfrost.
[5] SENLAC AND CRÉCY—The scenes of famous battles in which the long bow was used. "Clothyard shafts" means arrows.

ing. A glance into the apartment at eight o'clock on this eventful evening would have resulted in the opinion that it was as cozy and comfortable a nook as could be wished for in boisterous weather. The calling of its inhabitant was proclaimed by a number of highly-polished sheep-crooks without stems that were hung ornamentally over the fireplace, the curl of each shining crook varying from the antiquated type engraved in the patriarchal pictures of old family Bibles to the most approved fashion of the last local sheep-fair. The room was lighted by half-a-dozen candles, having wicks only a trifle smaller than the grease which enveloped them, in candlesticks that were never used but at high-days, holy-days, and family feasts. The lights were scattered about the room, two of them standing on the chimney-piece. This position of candles was in itself significant. Candles on the chimney-piece always meant a party.

On the hearth, in front of the back-brand to give substance, blazed a fire of thorns, that crackled "like the laughter of the fool."

Nineteen persons were gathered here. Of these, five women, wearing gowns of various bright hues, sat in chairs along the wall; girls shy and not shy filled the window-bench; four men, including Charley Jake the hedge-carpenter, Elijah New the parish-clerk, and John Pitcher, a neighboring dairyman, the shepherd's father-in-law, lolled in the settle; a young man and maid, who were blushing over tentative *pourparlers* [6] on a life-companionship, sat beneath the corner-cupboard; and an elderly engaged man of fifty or upward moved restlessly about from spots where his betrothed was not to the spot where she was. Enjoyment was pretty general, and so much the more prevailed in being unhampered by conventional restrictions. Absolute confidence in each other's good opinion begat perfect ease, while the finishing stroke of manner, amounting to a truly princely serenity, was lent to the majority by the absence of any expression or trait denoting that they wished to get on in the world, enlarge their minds, or do any eclipsing thing whatever— which nowadays so generally nips the bloom and *bonhomie* [7] of all except the two extremes of the social scale.

Shepherd Fennel had married well, his wife being a dairyman's daughter from a vale at a distance, who brought fifty

[6] *Pourparlers*—Conversations.   [7] *Bonhomie*—Good nature.

guineas in her pocket—and kept them there, till they should be required for ministering to the needs of a coming family. This frugal woman had been somewhat exercised as to the character that should be given to the gathering. A sit-still party had its advantages; but an undisturbed position of ease in chairs and settles was apt to lead on the men to such an unconscionable deal of toping that they would sometimes fairly drink the house dry. A dancing party was the alternative; but this, while avoiding the foregoing objection on the score of good drink, had a counterbalancing disadvantage in the matter of good victuals, the ravenous appetites engendered by the exercise causing immense havoc in the buttery. Shepherdess Fennel fell back upon the intermediate plan of mingling short dances with short periods of talk and singing, so as to hinder any ungovernable rage in either. But this scheme was entirely confined to her own gentle mind: the shepherd himself was in the mood to exhibit the most reckless phases of hospitality.

The fiddler was a boy of those parts, about twelve years of age, who had a wonderful dexterity in jigs and reels, tho his fingers were so small and short as to necessitate a constant shifting for the high notes, from which he scrambled back to the first position with sounds not of unmixed purity of tone. At seven the shrill tweedle-dee of this youngster had begun, accompanied by a booming ground-bass from Elijah New, the parish-clerk, who had thoughtfully brought with him his favorite musical instrument, the serpent.[8] Dancing was instantaneous, Mrs. Fennel privately enjoining the players on no account to let the dance exceed the length of a quarter of an hour.

But Elijah and the boy, in the excitement of their position, quite forgot the injunction. Moreover, Oliver Giles, a man of seventeen, one of the dancers, who was enamored of his partner, a fair girl of thirty-three rolling years, had recklessly handed a new crown-piece to the musicians, as a bribe to keep going as long as they had muscle and wind. Mrs. Fennel, seeing the steam begin to generate on the countenances of her guests, crossed over and touched the fiddler's elbow and put her hand on the serpent's mouth. But they took no notice, and fearing she might lose her character of genial hostess if she were to

[8] SERPENT—A bass musical instrument consisting of an eight foot tapered tube of wood, covered with leather and twisted about like a serpent.

interfere too markedly, she retired and sat down helpless. And so the dance whizzed on with cumulative fury, the performers moving in their planet-like courses, direct and retrograde, from apogee to perigee, till the hands of the well-kicked clock at the bottom of the room had travelled over the circumference of an hour.

While these cheerful events were in course of enactment within Fennel's pastoral dwelling, an incident having considerable bearing on the party had occurred in the gloomy night without. Mrs. Fennel's concern about the growing fierceness of the dance corresponded in point of time with the ascent of a human figure to the solitary hill of Higher Crowstairs from the direction of the distant town. This personage strode on through the rain without a pause, following the little worn path which, further on in its course, skirted the shepherd's cottage.

It was nearly the time of full moon, and on this account, tho the sky was lined with a uniform sheet of dripping cloud, ordinary objects out of doors were readily visible. The sad wan light revealed the lonely pedestrian to be a man of supple frame; his gait suggested that he had somewhat passed the period of perfect and instinctive agility, tho not so far as to be otherwise than rapid of motion when occasion required. At a rough guess, he might have been about forty years of age. He appeared tall, but a recruiting sergeant, or other person accustomed to the judging of men's heights by the eye, would have discerned that this was chiefly owing to his gauntness, and that he was not more than five-feet-eight or nine.

Notwithstanding the regularity of his tread, there was caution in it, as in that of one who mentally feels his way; and despite the fact that it was not a black coat nor a dark garment of any sort that he wore, there was something about him which suggested that he naturally belonged to the black-coated tribes of men. His clothes were fustian, and his boots hobnailed, yet in his progress he showed not the mud-accustomed bearing of hobnailed and fustianed peasantry.

By the time that he had arrived abreast of the shepherd's premises the rain came down, or rather came along, with yet more determined violence. The outskirts of the little settlement partially broke the force of wind and rain, and this induced him to stand still. The most salient of the shepherd's domestic erections was an empty sty at the forward corner of his hedgeless garden, for in these latitudes the principle of masking the homelier features of your establishment by a conventional frontage was unknown. The traveller's eye was attracted to this small building by the pallid shine of the wet slates that covered it. He turned aside, and, finding it empty, stood under the pent-roof for shelter.

While he stood, the boom of the serpent within the adjacent house, and the lesser strains of the fiddle, reached the spot as an accompaniment to the surging hiss of the flying rain on the sod, its louder beating on the cabbage-leaves of the garden, on the eight or ten beehives just discernible by the path, and its dripping from the eaves into a row of buckets and pans that had been placed under the walls of the cottage. For at Higher Crowstairs, as at all such elevated domiciles, the grand difficulty of housekeeping was an insufficiency of water; and a casual rainfall was utilized by turning out, as catchers, every utensil that the house contained. Some queer stories might be told of the contrivances for economy in suds and dish-waters that are absolutely necessitated in upland habitations during the droughts of summer. But at this season there were no such exigencies; a mere acceptance of what the skies bestowed was sufficient for an abundant store.

At last the notes of the serpent ceased and the house was silent. This cessation of activity aroused the solitary pedestrian from the reverie into which he had lapsed, and, emerging from the shed, with an apparently new intention, he walked up the path to the house-door. Arrived here, his first act was to kneel down on a large stone beside the row of vessels, and to drink a copious draft from one of them. Having quenched his thirst, he rose and lifted his hand to knock, but paused with his eye upon the panel. Since the dark surface of the wood revealed absolutely nothing, it was evident that he must be mentally looking through the door, as if he wished to measure thereby all the possibilities that a house of this sort might include, and how they might bear upon the question of his entry.

In his indecision he turned and surveyed the scene around. Not a soul was anywhere visible. The garden-path stretched downward from his feet, gleaming like the track of a snail; the roof of the little well (mostly dry), the well-cover, the top rail of the garden-gate, were varnished with the same dull liquid glaze; while, far away in the vale, a faint whiteness of more than usual extent showed that the rivers were high in the meads. Beyond all this winked a few bleared lamplights through the beating drops—lights that denoted the situation of the county-town from which he had appeared to come. The absence of all notes of life in that direction seemed to clinch his intentions, and he knocked at the door.

Within, a desultory chat had taken the place of movement and musical sound. The hedge-carpenter was suggesting a song to the company, which nobody just then was inclined to undertake, so that the knock afforded a not unwelcome diversion.

"Walk in!" said the shepherd promptly.

The latch clicked upward, and out of the night our pedestrian appeared up the door-mat. The shepherd arose, snuffed two of the nearest candles, and turned to look at him.

Their light disclosed that the stranger was dark in complexion and not unprepossessing as to feature. His hat, which for a moment he did not remove, hung low over his eyes, without concealing that they were large, open, and determined, moving with a flash rather than a glance round the room. He seemed pleased with his survey, and, baring his shaggy head, said, in a rich, deep voice, "The rain is so heavy, friends, that I ask leave to come in and rest awhile."

"To be sure, stranger," said the shepherd. "And faith, you've been lucky in choosing your time, for we are having a bit of a fling for a glad cause—tho, to be sure, a man could hardly wish that glad cause to happen more than once a year."

"Nor less," spoke up a woman. "For 'tis best to get your family over and done with, as soon as you can, so as to be all the earlier out of the fag o't."

"And what may be this glad cause?" asked the stranger.

"A birth and christening," said the shepherd.

The stranger hoped his host might not be made unhappy either by too many or too few of such episodes, and being invited by a gesture to a pull at the mug, he readily acquiesced. His manner, which, before entering, had been so dubious, was now altogether that of a careless and candid man.

"Late to be traipsing athwart this coomb-hey?" said the engaged man of fifty.

"Late it is, master, as you say.—I'll take a seat in the chimney-corner if you have nothing to urge against it, ma'am; for I am a little moist on the side that was next the rain."

Mrs. Shepherd Fennel assented, and made room for the self-invited comer, who, having got completely inside the chimney-corner, stretched out his legs and his arms with the expansiveness of a person quite at home.

"Yes, I am rather cracked in the vamp," he said freely, seeing that the eyes of the shepherd's wife fell upon his boots, "and I am not well fitted either. I have had some rough times lately, and have been forced to pick up what I can get in the way of wearing, but I must find a suit better fit for working-days when I reach home."

"One of hereabouts?" she inquired.

"Not quite that—further up the country."

"I thought so. And so be I; and by your tongue you come from my neighborhood."

"But you would hardly have heard of me," he said quickly. "My time would be long before yours, ma'am, you see."

This testimony to the youthfulness of his hostess had the effect of stopping her cross-examination.

"There is only one thing more wanted to make me happy," continued the new-comer. "And that is a little baccy, which I am sorry to say I am out of."

"I'll fill your pipe," said the shepherd.

"I must ask you to lend me a pipe likewise."

"A smoker, and no pipe about 'ee?"

"I have dropped it somewhere on the road."

The shepherd filled and handed him a new clay pipe, saying, as he did so, "Hand me your baccy box—I'll fill that too, now I am about it."

The man went through the movement of searching his pockets.

"Lost that too?" said his entertainer, with some surprise.

"I am afraid so," said the man with some confusion. "Give it to me in a screw of paper." Lighting his pipe at the candle with a suction that drew the whole flame into the bowl, he resettled himself in the corner and bent his looks upon the faint steam from his damp legs, as if he wished to say no more.

Meanwhile the general body of guests had been taking little notice of this visitor by reason of an absorbing discussion in which they were engaged with the band about a tune for the next dance. The matter being settled, they were about to stand up when an interruption came in the shape of another knock at the door.

At sound of the same the man in the chimney-corner took up the poker and began stirring the brands as if doing it thoroughly were the one aim of his existence; and a second time the shepherd said, "Walk in!" In a moment another man stood upon the straw-woven door-mat. He too was a stranger.

This individual was one of a type radically different from the first. There was more of the commonplace in his manner, and a certain jovial cosmopolitanism sat upon his features. He was several years older than the first arrival, his hair being slightly frosted, his eyebrows bristly, and his whiskers cut back from his cheeks. His face was rather full and flabby, and yet it was not altogether a face without power. A few grog-blossoms marked the neighborhood of his nose. He flung back his long drab greatcoat, revealing that beneath it he wore a suit of cinder-gray shade throughout, large heavy seals, of some metal or other that would take a polish, dangling from his fob as his only personal ornament. Shaking the water-drops from his low-crowned glazed hat, he said, "I must ask for a few minutes' shelter, comrades, or I shall be wetted to my skin before I get to Casterbridge."

"Make yourself at home, master," said the shepherd, perhaps a trifle less heartily than on the first occasion. Not that Fennel had the least tinge of niggardliness in his composition; but the room was far from large, spare chairs were not numerous, and damp companions were not altogether desirable at close quarters for the women and girls in their bright-colored gowns.

However, the second comer, after taking off his greatcoat, and hanging his hat on a nail in one of the ceiling-beams as if he had been specially invited to put it there, advanced and sat down at the table. This had been pushed so closely into the chimney-corner, to give all available room to the dancers, that its inner edge grazed the elbow of the man who had ensconced himself by the fire; and thus the two strangers were brought into close companionship. They nodded to each other by way of breaking the ice of unacquaintance, and the first stranger handed his neighbor the family mug—a huge vessel of brown ware, having its upper edge worn away like a threshold by the rub of whole generations of thirsty lips that had gone the way of all flesh, and bearing the following inscription burnt upon its rotund side in yellow letters:

> THERE IS NO FUN
> UNTILL I CUM

The other man, nothing loth, raised the mug to his lips, and drank on, and on, and on—till a curious blueness overspread the countenance of the shepherd's wife, who had regarded with no little surprise the first stranger's free offer to the second of what did not belong to him to dispense.

"I knew it!" said the toper to the shepherd with much satisfaction. "When I walked up your garden before coming in, and saw the hives all of a row, I said to myself, 'Where there's bees there's honey, and where there's honey there's mead.' But mead of such a truly comfortable sort as this I really didn't expect to meet in my older days." He took yet another pull at the mug, till it assumed an ominous elevation.

"Glad you enjoy it!" said the shepherd warmly.

"It is goodish mead," assented Mrs. Fennel, with an absence of enthusiasm which seemed to say that it was possible to buy praise for one's cellar at too heavy a price. "It is trouble enough to make—and really I hardly think we shall make any more. For honey sells well, and we ourselves can make shift with a drop o' small mead and metheglin for common use from the comb-washings."

"O, but you'll never have the heart!" reproachfully cried the stranger in cinder-gray, after taking up the mug a third time and setting it down empty. "I love mead, when 'tis old like this, as I love to go to church o' Sundays, or to relieve the needy any day of the week."

"Ha, ha, ha!" said the man in the chimney-corner, who, in spite of the taciturnity induced by the pipe of tobacco, could not or would not refrain from this slight testimony to his comrade's humor.

Now the old mead of those days, brewed of the purest first-year or maiden honey, four pounds to the gallon—with its due complement of white of eggs, cinnamon, ginger, cloves, mace, rosemary, yeast, and processes of working, bottling, and cellaring—tasted remarkably strong; but it did not taste so strong as it actually was. Hence, presently, the stranger in cinder-gray at the table, moved by its creeping influence, unbuttoned his waistcoat, threw himself back in his chair, spread his legs, and made his presence felt in various ways.

"Well, well, as I say," he resumed, "I am going to Casterbridge, and to Casterbridge I must go. I should have been almost there by this time; but the rain drove me into your dwelling, and I'm not sorry for it."

"You don't live in Casterbridge?" said the shepherd.

"Not as yet; tho I shortly mean to move there."

"Going to set up in trade, perhaps?"

"No, no," said the shepherd's wife. "It is easy to see that the gentleman is rich, and don't want to work at anything."

. The cinder-gray stranger paused, as if to consider whether he would accept that definition of himself. He presently rejected it by answering, "Rich is not quite the word for me, dame. I do work, and I must work. And even if I only get to Casterbridge by midnight I must begin work there at eight tomorrow morning. Yes, het or wet, blow or snow, famine or sword, my day's work tomorrow must be done."

"Poor man! Then, in spite o' seeming, you be worse off than we?" replied the shepherd's wife.

" 'Tis the nature of my trade, men and maidens. 'Tis the nature of my trade more than my property. . . . But really and truly I must up and off, or I shan't get a lodging in the town." However, the speaker did not move, and directly added, "There's time for one more draft of friendship before I go; and I'd perform it at once if the mug were not dry."

"Here's a mug o' small," said Mrs. Fennel. "Small, we call it, tho to be sure 'tis only the first wash o' the combs."

"No," said the stranger disdainfully. "I won't spoil your first kindness by partaking o' your second."

"Certainly not," broke in Fennel. "We don't increase and multiply every day, and I'll fill the mug again." He went away to the dark place under the stairs where the barrel stood. The shepherdess followed him.

"Why should you do this?" she said reproachfully, as soon as they were alone. "He's emptied it once, tho it held enough for ten people; and now he's not contented wi' the small, but must needs call for more o' the strong! And a stranger unbeknown to any of us. For my part, I don't like the look o' the man at all."

"But he's in the house, my honey; and 'tis a wet night, and a christening. Daze it, what's a cup of mead more or less? There'll be plenty more next bee-burning."

"Very well—this time, then," she answered, looking wistfully at the barrel. "But what is the man's calling, and where is he one of, that he should come in and join us like this?"

"I don't know. I'll ask him again."

The catastrophe of having the mug drained dry at one pull by the stranger in cinder-gray was effectually guarded against this time by Mrs. Fennel. She poured out his allowance in a small cup, keeping the large one at a discreet distance from him. When he had tossed off his portion the shepherd renewed his inquiry about the stranger's occupation.

The latter did not immediately reply, and the man in the chimney-corner, with sudden demonstrativeness, said, "Anybody may know my trade—I'm a wheelwright."

"A very good trade for these parts," said the shepherd.

"And anybody may know mine—if they've the sense to find it out," said the stranger in cinder-gray.

"You may generally tell what a man is by his claws," observed the hedge-carpenter, looking at his own hands. "My fingers be as full of thorns as an old pin-cushion is of pins."

The hands of the man in the chimney-corner instinctively sought the shade, and he gazed into the fire as he resumed his pipe. The man at the table took up the hedge-carpenter's remark, and added smartly, "True; but the oddity of my trade is that, instead of setting a mark upon me, it sets a mark upon my customers."

No observation being offered by anybody in elucidation of this enigma, the shepherd's wife once more called for a song. The same obstacles presented themselves as at the former time— one had no voice, another had forgotten the first verse. The stranger at the table, whose soul had now risen to a good working temperature, relieved the difficulty by exclaiming that, to start the company, he would sing himself. Thrusting one thumb into the armhole of his waistcoat, he waved the other hand in the air, and, with an extemporizing gaze at the shining sheep-crooks above the mantelpiece, began:—

> O my trade it is the rarest one,
>   Simple shepherds all—
> My trade is a sight to see;
> For my customers I tie, and take them up on high,
>   And waft 'em to a far countree!

The room was silent when he had finished the verse—with one exception, that of the man in the chimney-corner, who, at the singer's word, "Chorus!" joined him in a deep bass voice of musical relish—

> And waft 'em to a far countree!

Oliver Giles, John Pitcher the dairyman, the parish-clerk, the engaged man of fifty, the row of young women against the wall, seemed lost in thought not of the gayest kind. The shepherd looked meditatively on the ground, the shepherdess gazed keenly at the singer, and with some suspicion; she was doubting whether this stranger were merely singing an old song from recollection, or was composing one there and then for the occasion. All were as perplexed at the obscure revelation as the guests at Belshazzar's Feast,[9] except the man in the chimney-corner, who quietly said, "Second verse, stranger," and smoked on.

The singer thoroughly moistened himself from his lips inwards, and went on with the next stanza as requested:—

> My tools are but common ones,
>   Simple shepherds all—
> My tools are no sight to see:
> A little hempen string, and a post whereon to swing,
>   Are implements enough for me!

Shepherd Fennel glanced round. There was no longer any doubt that the stranger was answering his question rhythmically. The guests one and all started back with suppressed exclamations. The young woman engaged to the man of fifty fainted half-way, and would have proceeded, but finding him wanting in alacrity for catching her she sat down trembling.

"O, he's the—!" whispered the people in the background, mentioning the name of an ominous public officer. "He's come

---

[9] BELSHAZZAR'S FEAST—See *Daniel* v.

to do it! 'Tis to be at Casterbridge jail tomorrow—the man for sheep-stealing—the poor clock-maker we heard of, who used to live away at Shottsford and had no work to do—Timothy Summers, whose family were a-starving, and so he went out of Shottsford by the high-road, and took a sheep in open daylight, defying the farmer and the farmer's wife and the farmer's lad, and every man jack among 'em. He" (and they nodded towards the stranger of the deadly trade) "is come from up the country to do it because there's not enough to do in his own county-town, and he's got the place here now our own county man's dead; he's going to live in the same cottage under the prison wall."

The stranger in cinder-gray took no notice of this whispered string of observations, but again wetted his lips. Seeing that his friend in the chimney-corner was the only one who reciprocated his joviality in any way, he held out his cup towards that appreciative comrade, who also held out his own. They clinked together, the eyes of the rest of the room hanging upon the singer's actions. He parted his lips for the third verse; but at that moment another knock was audible upon the door. This time the knock was faint and hesitating.

The company seemed scared; the shepherd looked with consternation towards the entrance, and it was with some effort that he resisted his alarmed wife's deprecatory glance, and uttered for the third time the welcoming words, "Walk in!"

The door was gently opened, and another man stood upon the mat. He, like those who had preceded him, was a stranger. This time it was a short, small personage, of fair complexion, and dressed in a decent suit of dark clothes.

"Can you tell me the way to—?" he began: when, gazing round the room to observe the nature of the company amongst whom he had fallen, his eyes lighted on the stranger in cinder-gray. It was just at the instant when the latter, who had thrown his mind into his song with such a will that he scarcely heeded the interruption, silenced all whispers and inquiries by bursting into his third verse:—

>   Tomorrow is my working day,
>   Simple shepherds all—
>   Tomorrow is a working day for me:
> For the farmer's sheep is slain, and the lad who did it ta'en,
>   And on his soul may God ha' merc-y!

The stranger in the chimney-corner, waving cups with the singer so heartily that his mead splashed over on the hearth, repeated in his bass voice as before:—

And on his soul may God ha' merc-y!

All this time the third stranger had been standing in the doorway. Finding now that he did not come forward or go on speaking, the guests particularly regarded him. They noticed to their surprise that he stood before them the picture of abject terror—his knees trembling, his hand shaking so violently that the door-latch by which he supported himself rattled audibly: his white lips were parted, and his eyes fixed on the merry officer of justice in the middle of the room. A moment more and he had turned, closed the door, and fled.

"What a man can it be?" said the shepherd.

The rest, between the awfulness of their late discovery and the odd conduct of this third visitor, looked as if they knew not what to think, and said nothing. Instinctively they withdrew further and further from the grim gentleman in their midst, whom some of them seemed to take for the Prince of Darkness himself, till they formed a remote circle, an empty space of floor being left between them and him—

". . . *circulus, cuius centrum diabolus.*" [10]

The room was so silent—tho there were more than twenty people in it—that nothing could be heard but the patter of the rain against the window-shutters, accompanied by the occasional hiss of a stray drop that fell down the chimney into the fire, and the steady puffing of the man in the corner, who had now resumed his pipe of long clay.

The stillness was unexpectedly broken. The distant sound of a gun reverberated through the air—apparently from the direction of the county-town.

"Be jiggered!" cried the stranger who had sung the song, jumping up.

"What does that mean?" asked several.

"A prisoner escaped from the jail—that's what it means."

All listened. The sound was repeated, and none of them

---

[10] *Circulus . . . diabolus*—A circle with the devil in the center.

spoke but the man in the chimney-corner, who said quietly, "I've often been told that in this county they fire a gun at such times; but I never heard it till now."

"I wonder if it is *my* man?" murmured the personage in cinder-gray.

"Surely it is!" said the shepherd involuntarily. "And surely we've zeed him! That little man who looked in at the door by now, and quivered like a leaf when he zeed ye and heard your song!"

"His teeth chattered, and the breath went out of his body," said the dairyman.

"And his heart seemed to sink within him like a stone," said Oliver Giles.

"And he bolted as if he'd been shot at," said the hedge-carpenter.

"True—his teeth chattered, and his heart seemed to sink; and he bolted as if he'd been shot at," slowly summed up the man in the chimney-corner.

"I didn't notice it," remarked the hangman.

"We were all a-wondering what made him run off in such a fright," faltered one of the women against the wall, "and now 'tis explained!"

The firing of the alarm-gun went on at intervals, low and sullenly, and their suspicions became a certainty. The sinister gentleman in cinder-gray roused himself. "Is there a constable here?" he asked, in thick tones. "If so, let him step forward."

The engaged man of fifty stepped quavering out from the wall, his betrothed beginning to sob on the back of the chair.

"You are a sworn constable?"

"I be, sir."

"Then pursue the criminal at once, with assistance, and bring him back here. He can't have gone far."

"I will, sir, I will—when I've got my staff. I'll go home and get it, and come sharp here, and start in a body."

"Staff!—never mind your staff; the man'll be gone!"

"But I can't do nothing without my staff—can I, William, and John, and Charles Jake? No; for there's the king's royal crown a painted on en in yaller and gold, and the lion and the unicorn, so as when I raise en up and hit my prisoner, 'tis made a lawful blow thereby. I wouldn't 'tempt to take up a man without my staff—no, not I. If I hadn't the law to gie me courage, why, instead o' my taking up him he might take up me!"

"Now, I'm a king's man myself, and can give you authority enough for this," said the formidable officer in gray. "Now then, all of ye, be ready. Have ye any lanterns?"

"Yes—have ye an lanterns?—I demand it!" said the constable.

"And the rest of you able-bodied——"

"Able-bodied men—yes—the rest of ye!" said the constable.

"Have you some good stout staves and pitchforks——"

"Staves and pitchforks—in the name o' the law! And taken 'em in yer hands and go in quest, and do as we in authority tell ye!"

Thus aroused, the men prepared to give chase. The evidence was, indeed, tho circumstantial, so convincing, that but little argument was needed to show the shepherd's guests that after what they had seen it would look very much like connivance if they did not instantly pursue the unhappy third stranger, who could not as yet have gone more than a few hundred yards over such uneven country.

A shepherd is always well provided with lanterns; and, lighting these hastily, and with hurdle-staves in their hands, they poured out of the door, taking a direction along the crest of the hill, away from the town, the rain having fortunately a little abated.

Disturbed by the noise, or possibly by unpleasant dreams of her baptism, the child who had been christened began to cry heart-brokenly in the room overhead. These notes of grief came down through the chinks of the floor to the ears of the women below, who jumped up one by one, and seemed glad of the excuse to ascend and comfort the baby, for the incidents of the last half-hour greatly oppressed them. Thus in the space of two or three minutes the room on the ground-floor was deserted quite.

But it was not for long. Hardly had the sound of footsteps died away when a man returned round the corner of the house from the direction the pursuers had taken. Peeping in at the door, and seeing nobody there, he entered leisurely. It was the stranger of the chimney-corner, who had gone out with the rest. The motive of his return was shown by his helping himself to a cut piece of skimmer-cake that lay on a ledge beside where he had sat, and which he had apparently forgotten to take with him. He also poured out half a cup more mead from the quantity that remained, ravenously eating and drinking these as he stood. He had not finished when another figure came in just as quietly—his friend in cinder-gray.

"O—you here?" said the latter, smiling. "I thought you had gone to help in the capture." And this speaker also revealed the object of his return by looking solicitously round for the fascinating mug of old mead.

"And I thought you had gone," said the other, continuing his skimmer-cake with some effort.

"Well, on second thoughts, I felt there were enough without me," said the first confidentially, "and such a night as it is, too. Besides, 'tis the business o' the Government to take care of its criminals—not mine."

"True; so it is. And I felt as you did, that there were enough without me."

"I don't want to break my limbs running over the humps and hollows of this wild country."

"Nor I neither, between you and me."

"These shepherd-people are used to it—simple minded souls, you know, stirred up to anything in a moment. They'll have him ready for me before the morning, and no trouble to me at all."

"They'll have him, and we shall have saved ourselves all labor in the matter."

"True, true. Well, my way is to Casterbridge; and 'tis as much as my legs will do to take me that far. Going the same way?"

"No, I am sorry to say! I have to get home over there" (he nodded indefinitely to the right), "and I feel as you do, that it is quite enough for my legs to do before bedtime."

The other had by this time finished the mead in the mug, after which, shaking hands heartily at the door, and wishing each other well, they went their several ways.

In the meantime the company of pursuers had reached the end of the hog's-back elevation which dominated this part of the down. They had decided on no particular plan of action; and finding that the man of the baleful trade was no longer in their company, they seemed quite unable to form any such plan now. They descended in all directions down the hill, and straightway several of the party fell into the snare set by Nature for all misguided midnight ramblers over this part of the cretaceous formation. The "lanchets," or flint slopes, which belted the escarpment at intervals of a dozen yards, took the less cautious ones unawares, and losing their footing on the rubbly steep they slid sharply downwards, the lanterns rolling from their hands to the bottom, and there lying on their sides till the horn was scorched through.

When they had again gathered themselves together, the shepherd, as the man who knew the country best, took the lead, and guided them round these treacherous inclines. The lanterns, which seemed rather to dazzle their eyes and warn the fugitive than to assist them in the exploration, were extinguished; due silence was observed; and in this more rational order they plunged into the vale. It was a grassy, briery, moist defile, affording some shelter to any person who had sought it; but the party perambulated it in vain, and ascended on the other side. Here they wandered apart, and after an interval closed together again to report progress. At the second time of closing in they found themselves near a lonely ash, the single tree on this part of the coomb, probably sown there by a passing bird some fifty years before. And here, standing a little to one side of the trunk, as motionless as the trunk itself, appeared the man they were in quest of, his outline being well defined against the sky beyond. The band noiselessly drew up and faced him.

"Your money or your life!" said the constable sternly to the still figure.

"No, no," whispered John Pitcher. " 'Tisn't our side ought to say that. That's the doctrine of vagabonds like him, and we be on the side of the law."

"Well, well," replied the constable impatiently, "I must say something, mustn't I? and if you had all the weight o' this undertaking upon your mind, perhaps you'd say the wrong thing too!—Prisoner at the bar, surrender, in the name of the Father —the Crown, I mane!"

The man under the tree seemed now to notice them for the

first time, and, giving them no opportunity whatever for exhibiting their courage, he strolled slowly towards them. He was, indeed, the little man, the third stranger; but his trepidation had in a great measure gone.

"Well, travellers," he said, "did I hear ye speak to me?"

"You did: you've got to come and be our prisoner at once!" said the constable. "We arrest 'ee on the charge of not biding in Casterbridge jail in a decent proper manner to be hung tomorrow morning. Neighbors, do your duty, and seize the culpet!"

On hearing the charge, the man seemed enlightened, and, saying not another word, resigned himself with preternatural civility to the search-party, who, with their staves in their hands, surrounded him on all sides, and marched him back towards the shepherd's cottage.

It was eleven o'clock by the time they arrived. The light shining from the open door, a sound of men's voices within, proclaimed to them as they approached the house that some new events had arisen in their absence. On entering they discovered the shepherd's living room to be invaded by two officers from Casterbridge jail, and a well-known magistrate who lived at the nearest county-seat, intelligence of the escape having become generally circulated.

"Gentlemen," said the constable, "I have brought back your man—not without risk and danger; but every one must do his duty! He is inside this circle of able-bodied persons, who have lent me useful aid, considering their ignorance of Crown work. Men, bring forward your prisoner!" And the third stranger was led to the light.

"Who is this?" said one of the officials.

"The man," said the constable.

"Certainly not," said the turnkey; and the first corroborated his statement.

"But how can it be otherwise?" asked the constable. "Or why was he so terrified at sight o' the singing instrument of the law who sat there?" Here he related the strange behavior of the third stranger on entering the house during the hangman's song.

"Can't understand it," said the officer coolly. "All I know is that it is not the condemned man. He's quite a different character from this one; a gauntish fellow, with dark hair and eyes, rather good-looking, and with a musical bass voice that if you heard it once you'd never mistake as long as you lived."

"Why, souls—'twas the man in the chimney-corner!"

"Hey-what?" said the magistrate, coming forward after inquiring particulars from the shepherd in the background. "Haven't you got the man after all?"

"Well, sir," said the constable, "he's the man we were in search of, that's true; and yet he's not the man we were in search of. For the man we were in search of was not the man we wanted, sir, if you understand my every-day way; for 'twas the man in the chimney-corner!"

"A pretty kettle of fish altogether!" said the magistrate. "You had better start for the other man at once."

The prisoner now spoke for the first time. The mention of the man in the chimney-corner seemed to have moved him as nothing else could do. "Sir," he said, stepping forward to the magistrate, "take no more trouble about me. The time is come when I may as well speak. I have done nothing; my crime is that the condemned man is my brother. Early this afternoon I left home at Shottsford to tramp it all the way to Casterbridge jail to bid him farewell. I was benighted, and called here to rest and ask the way. When I opened the door I saw before me the very man, my brother, that I thought to see in the condemned cell at Casterbridge. He was in this chimney-corner; and jammed close to him, so that he could not have got out if he had tried, was the executioner who'd come to take his life, singing a song about it and not knowing that it was his victim who was close by, joining in to save appearances. My brother looked a glance of agony at me, and I knew he meant, "Don't reveal what you see; my life depends on it!" I was so terror-struck that I could hardly stand, and, not knowing what I did, I turned and hurried away."

The narrator's manner and tone had the stamp of truth, and his story made a great impression on all around. "And do you know where your brother is at the present time?" asked the magistrate.

"I do not. I have never seen him since I closed this door."

"I can testify to that, for we've been between ye ever since," said the constable.

"Where does he think to fly to?—what is his occupation?"

"He's a watch-and-clock-maker, sir."

" 'A said 'a was a wheelwright—a wicked rogue," said the constable.

"The wheels of clocks and watches he meant, no doubt," said Shepherd Fennel. "I thought his hands were palish for's trade."

"Well, it appears to me that nothing can be gained by retaining this poor man in custody," said the magistrate; "your business lies with the other unquestionably."

And so the little man was released off-hand; but he looked nothing the less sad on that account, it being beyond the power of magistrate or constable to raze out the written troubles in his brain, for they concerned another whom he regarded with more solicitude than himself. When this was done, and the man had gone his way, the night was found to be so far advanced that it was deemed useless to renew the search before the next morning.

Next day, accordingly, the quest for the clever sheep-stealer became general and keen, to all appearances at least. But the intended punishment was cruelly disproportioned to the transgression, and the sympathy of a great many country-folk in that district was strongly on the side of the fugitive. Moreover, his marvellous coolness and daring in hob-and-nobbing with the hangman, under the unprecedented circumstances of the shepherd's party, won their admiration. So that it may be questioned if all those who ostensibly made themselves so busy in exploring woods and fields and lanes were quite so thorough when it came to the private examination of their own lofts and outhouses. Stories were afloat of a mysterious figure being occasionally seen in some old overgrown trackway or other, remote from turnpike roads; but when a search was instituted in any of these suspected quarters nobody was found. Thus the days and weeks passed without tidings.

In brief, the bass-voiced man of the chimney-corner was never recaptured. Some said that he went across the sea, others that he did not, but buried himself in the depths of a populous city. At any rate, the gentleman in cinder-gray never did his morning's work at Casterbridge, nor met anywhere at all, for business purposes, the genial comrade with whom he had passed an hour of relaxation in the lonely house on the coomb.

The grass has long been green on the graves of Shepherd Fennel and his frugal wife; the guests who made up the christening party have mainly followed their entertainers to the tomb; the baby in whose honor they all had met is a matron in the sere and yellow leaf. But the arrival of the three strangers at the shepherd's that night, and the details connected therewith, is a story as well known as ever in the country about Higher Crowstairs.

The Type of Hardy's Stories: Very few writers have confined themselves as closely to one locality and to one type of characters as Hardy has done. Although he renames the towns and rivers in his stories, it is easy for a person familiar with England to recognize real towns and places. He has remarkable ability in describing landscapes in which he shows an exceedingly well developed appreciation for color. His descriptions of the sky are always worth noticing. Hardy's characters are most often inhabitants of rural sections. Underlying all of his stories is a pessimism and a feeling of the one-sidedness of man's struggle against natural forces, such as environment and heredity. Somewhat offsetting this is a sprinkling of humor which lessens the oppressiveness of the story.

For Appreciation: How are the setting and characters typical of Hardy's writings? Another characteristic of his work is the great wealth of detail he uses in depicting scenes. The description of the interior of the shepherd's cottage is an example of this. Reread the passage and try to visualize the room as you read. The rise and fall of interest or action is very noticeable in this story. Explain how it is brought about. The first stranger is the only one who is described before he enters the cottage. What is the purpose of this emphasis? Where is the climax of the story? How does Hardy present the character of the "bass-voiced man of the chimney-corner" so that the reader is satisfied when he is not recaptured?

For Further Study: Explain the meaning of each of the following words or expressions: *inimical; repellent; formidable; sheep-crooks; frugal; apogee to perigee; fustian; desultory; mead; ensconced; reciprocated his joviality; king's man; cretaceous; horn was scorched through.*

Select passages to show the attitudes of the shepherd and his wife toward hospitality at the party. Why was the first stranger uneasy when the talk turned to ability to tell occupations by the condition of a person's hands? Do you think the constable was an efficient officer of the law? Explain. What were the reasons why the first stranger and the man in the gray clothes returned to the cottage? Did you think the condemned man's brother was the criminal? Why?

Exercises and Creative Work: Reread the description of the rain storm. Notice all the ways by which Hardy produces the picture of the storm. Write a description of a storm in a town. Try to produce your effect in the same way.

THE "TREMOLINO"

Joseph Conrad

By Way of Introduction: Several people, among whom were the narrator and Dominic Cervoni, belonged to the Royalist party which was supporting Don Carlos, the Pretender to the Spanish throne. The boat *Tremolino* was in the service of these Royalists. The boat was used to carry messages and "various unlawful goods landed secretly from under the *Tremolino's* hatches."

Dominic Cervoni is described as follows: "His thick black moustaches, curled every morning with hot tongs by the barber at the corner of the quay, seemed to hide a perpetual smile. But nobody, I believe, had even seen the true shape of his lips. From the slow, imperturbable gravity of the broad-chested man you would think he had never smiled in his life. In his eyes lurked a look of perfectly remorseless irony, as though he had been provided with an extremely experienced soul; and the slightest distension of his nostrils would give his bronzed face a look of extraordinary boldness. This was the only play of feature of which he seemed capable. . . . He may have been forty years old, and he was a voyager on the inland sea. . . . For want of more exalted adversaries Dominic turned his audacity fertile in impious stratagems against the powers of the earth, as represented by the institution of Custom-houses and every mortal belonging thereto—scribes, officers, and *guardacostas* afloat and ashore. He was the very man for us, this modern and unlawful wanderer with his own legend of loves, dangers and bloodshed. . . . On board the *Tremolino*, wrapped up in the black *caban*, the picturesque cloak of Mediterranean seamen, with those massive moustaches and his remorseless eyes set off by the shadow of the deep hood, he looked piratical and monkish and darkly initiated into the most awful mysteries of the sea."

Anyway, he was perfect, as Doña Rita had declared. The only thing unsatisfactory (and even inexplicable) about our Dominic was his nephew, Cesar. It was startling to see a desolate expression of shame veil the remorseless audacity in the eyes of that man superior to all scruples and terrors.

"I would never have dared to bring him on board your balancelle," he once apologized to me. "But what am I to do? His mother is dead, and my brother has gone into the bush."

In this way I learned that our Dominic had a brother. As to "going into the bush," this only means that a man has done his duty successfully in the pursuit of a hereditary vendetta.[1] The feud which had existed for ages between the families of Cervoni and Brunaschi was so old that it seemed to have smouldered out at last. One evening Pietro Brunaschi, after a laborious day amongst his olive-trees, sat on a chair against the wall of his house with a bowl of broth on his knees and a piece of bread in his hand. Dominic's brother, going home with a gun on his shoulder, found a sudden offence in this picture of content and rest so obviously calculated to awaken the feelings of hatred and revenge. He and Pietro had never had any personal quarrel; but, as Dominic explained, "all our dead cried out to him." He shouted from behind a wall of stones, "O Pietro! Behold what is coming!" And as the other looked up innocently he took aim at the forehead and squared the old vendetta account so neatly, that, according to Dominic, the dead man continued to sit with the bowl of broth on his knees and the piece of bread in his hand.

This is why—because in Corsica your dead will not leave you alone—Dominic's brother had to go into the *maquis*, into the bush on the wild mountain-side, to dodge the gendarmes[2] for the insignificant remainder of his life, and Dominic had charge of his nephew with a mission to make a man of him.

[1] Vendetta—A private feud for revenge by bloodshed.
[2] Gendarmes—Military police.

No more unpromising undertaking could be imagined. The very material for the task seemed wanting. The Cervonis, if not handsome men, were good sturdy flesh and blood. But this extraordinarily lean and livid youth seemed to have no more blood in him than a snail.

"Some cursed witch must have stolen my brother's child from the cradle and put that spawn of a starved devil in its place," Dominic would say to me. "Look at him! Just look at him!"

To look at Cesar was not pleasant. His parchment skin, showing dead white on his cranium through the thin wisps of dirty brown hair, seemed to be glued directly and tightly upon his big bones. Without being in any way deformed, he was the nearest approach which I have ever seen or could imagine to what is commonly understood by the word "monster." That the source of the effect produced was really moral I have no doubt. An utterly, hopelessly depraved nature was expressed in physical terms, that taken each separately had nothing positively startling. You imagined him clammily cold to the touch, like a snake. The slightest reproof, the most mild and justifiable remonstrance, would be met by a resentful glare and an evil shrinking of his thin dry upper lip, a snarl of hate to which he generally even added the agreeable sound of grinding teeth.

It was for this venomous performance rather than for his lies, impudence, and laziness that his uncle used to knock him down. It must not be imagined that it was anything in the nature of a brutal assault. Dominic's brawny arm would be seen describing deliberately an ample horizontal gesture, a dignified sweep, and Cesar would go over suddenly like a ninepin—which was funny to see. But, once down, he would writhe on the deck, gnashing his teeth in impotent rage—which was pretty horrible to behold. And it also happened more than once that he would disappear completely—which was startling to observe. This is the exact truth. Before some of the majestic cuffs Cesar would go down and vanish. He would vanish heels overhead into open hatchways, into scuttles, behind up-ended casks, according to the place where he happened to come into contact with his uncle's mighty arm.

Once—it was in the old harbour, just before the *Tremolino's* last voyage—he vanished thus overboard to my infinite consternation. Dominic and I had been talking business together aft, and Cesar had sneaked up behind us to listen, for, amongst his other perfections, he was a consummate eavesdropper and spy. At the sound of the heavy plop alongside horror held me rooted to the spot; but Dominic stepped quietly to the rail and leaned over waiting for his nephew's miserable head to bob up for the first time.

"Ohé, Cesar!" he yelled, contemptuously, to the spluttering wretch. "Catch hold of that mooring hawser—*charogne!*"[3]

He approached me to resume the interrupted conversation.

"What about Cesar?" I asked, anxiously.

"*Canallia!*"[4] Let him hang there," was his answer. And he went on talking over the business in hand calmly, while I tried vainly to dismiss from my mind the picture of Cesar steeped to the chin in the water of the old harbour, a decoction of centuries of marine refuse. I tried to dismiss it, because the mere notion of that liquid made me feel very sick. Presently Dominic, hailing an idle boatman, directed him to go and fish his nephew out; and by and by Cesar appeared walking on board from the quay, shivering, streaming with filthy water, with bits of rotten straws in his hair and a piece of dirty orange-peel stranded on his shoulder. His teeth chattered; his yellow eyes squinted balefully at us as he passed forward. I thought it my duty to remonstrate.

"Why are you always knocking him about, Dominic?" I asked. Indeed, I felt convinced it was no earthly good—a sheer waste of muscular force.

"I must try to make a man of him," Dominic answered, hopelessly.

I restrained the obvious retort that in this way he ran the risk of making, in the words of the immortal Mr. Mantalini, "a demnition damp, unpleasant corpse of him."

"He wants to be a locksmith!" burst out Cervoni. "To learn how to pick locks, I suppose," he added with sardonic bitterness.

"Why not let him be a locksmith?" I ventured.

"Who would teach him?" he cried. "Where could I leave him?" he asked, with a drop in his voice; and I had my first glimpse of genuine despair. "He steals, you know, alas! *Par*

---

[3] *Charogne*—Carrion.
[4] *Canallia*—Scoundrel.

la Madonne![5] I believe he would put poison in your food and mine—the viper!"

He raised his face and both his clenched fists slowly to heaven. However, Cesar never dropped poison into our cups. One cannot be sure, but I fancy he went to work in another way.

This voyage, of which the details need not be given, we had to range far afield for sufficient reasons. Coming up from the South to end it with the important and really dangerous part of the scheme in hand, we found it necessary to look into Barcelona for certain definite information. This appears like running one's head into the very jaws of the lion, but in reality it was not so. We had one or two high, influential friends there, and many others humble but valuable because bought for good hard cash. We were in no danger of being molested; indeed, the important information reached us promptly by the hands of a Custom-house officer, who came on board full of showy zeal to poke an iron rod into the layer of oranges which made the visible part of our cargo in the hatchway.

I forgot to mention before that the *Tremolino* was officially known as a fruit and cork-wood trader. The zealous officer managed to slip a useful piece of paper into Dominic's hand as he went ashore, and a few hours afterwards, being off duty, he returned on board again athirst for drinks and gratitude. He got both as a matter of course. While he sat sipping his liqueur in the tiny cabin Dominic plied him with questions as to the whereabouts of the guardacostas.[6] The preventive service afloat was really the one for us to reckon with, and it was material for our success and safety to know the exact position of the patrol craft in the neighbourhood. The news could not have been more favourable. The officer mentioned a small place on the coast some twelve miles off, where, unsuspicious and unready, she was lying at anchor, with her sails unbent, painting yards[7] and scraping spars. Then he left us after the usual compliments, smirking reassuringly over his shoulder.

I had kept below pretty close all day from excess of prudence. The stake played on that trip was big.

"We are ready to go at once, but for Cesar, who has been

---

[5] *Par la Madonne*—By the Madonna. [6] GUARDACOSTAS—Coast guards.
[7] YARDS—A slender spar hung crosswise to a mast, used to support a sail.

missing ever since breakfast," announced Dominic to me in his slow, grim way.

Where the fellow had gone, and why, we could not imagine. The usual surmises in the case of a missing seaman did not apply to Cesar's absence. He was too odious for love, friendship, gambling, or even casual intercourse. But once or twice he had wandered away like this before.

Dominic went ashore to look for him, but returned at the end of two hours alone and very angry, as I could see by the token of the invisible smile under his moustache being intensified. We wondered what had become of the wretch, and made a hurried investigation amongst our portable property. He had stolen nothing.

"He will be back before long," I said, confidently.

Ten minutes afterwards one of the men on deck called out loudly:

"I can see him coming."

Cesar had only his shirt and trousers on. He had sold his coat, apparently for pocket-money.

"You knave!" was all Dominic said, with a terrible softness of voice. He restrained his choler [8] for a time. "Where have you been, vagabond?" he asked, menacingly.

Nothing would induce Cesar to answer that question. It was as if he even disdained to lie. He faced us, drawing back his lips and gnashing his teeth, and did not shrink an inch before the sweep of Dominic's arm. He went down as if shot, of course. But this time I noticed that, when picking himself up, he remained longer than usual on all fours, baring his big teeth over his shoulder and glaring upwards at his uncle with a new sort of hate in his round, yellow eyes. That permanent sentiment seemed pointed at that moment by especial malice and curiosity. I became quite interested. If he ever manages to put poison in the dishes, I thought to myself, this is how he will look at us as we sit at our meal. But I did not, of course, believe for a moment that he would ever put poison in our food. He ate the same things himself. Moreover, he had no poison. And I could not imagine a human being so blinded by cupidity as to sell poison to such an atrocious creature.

We slipped out to sea quietly at dusk, and all through the

[8] CHOLER—A'nger.

night everything went well. The breeze was gusty; a southerly blow was making up. It was fair wind for our course. Now and then Dominic slowly and rhythmically struck his hands together a few times, as if applauding the performance of the *Tremolino*. The balancelle [9] hummed and quivered as she flew along, dancing lightly under our feet.

At daybreak I pointed out to Dominic, amongst the several sail in view running before the gathering storm, one particular vessel. The press of canvas she carried made her loom up high, end on, like a grey column standing motionless directly in our wake.

"Look at this fellow, Dominic," I said. "He seems to be in a hurry."

The Padrone [10] made no remark but wrapping his black cloak about him stood up to look. His weather-tanned face, framed in the hood, had an aspect of authority and challenging force, with the deep-set eyes gazing far away fixedly, without a wink, like the intent, merciless, steady eyes of a sea-bird.

"*Chi va piano va sano*," [11] he remarked at last, with a derisive glance over the side, in ironic allusion to our own tremendous speed.

The *Tremolino* was doing her best, and seemed hardly to touch the great bursts of foam over which she darted. I crouched down again to get some shelter from the low bulwark. After more than half an hour of swaying immobility expressing a concentrated, breathless watchfulness, Dominic sank on the deck by my side. Within the monkish cowl his eyes gleamed with a fierce expression which surprised me. All he said was:

"He has come out here to wash the new paint off his yards, I suppose."

"What?" I shouted, getting up on my knees. "Is she the guardacosta?"

The perpetual suggestion of a smile under Dominic's piratical moustaches seemed to become more accentuated—quite real, grim, actually almost visible through the wet and uncurled hair. Judging by that symptom, he must have been in a towering rage. But I could also see that he was puzzled, and that dis-

---

[9] BALANCELLE—Small sailboat.
[10] PADRONE—The master of a small coaster in the Mediterranean.
[11] *Chi va piano va sano*—He who goes slow goes safe.

covery affected me disagreeably. Dominic puzzled! For a long time, leaning against the bulwark, I gazed over the stern at the grey column that seemed to stand swaying slightly in our wake always at the same distance.

Meanwhile Dominic, black and cowled, sat cross-legged on the deck, with his back to the wind, recalling vaguely an Arab chief in his *burnous* [12] sitting on the sand. Above his motionless figure the little cord and tassel on the stiff point of the hood swung about inanely in the gale. At last I gave up facing the wind and rain, and crouched down by his side. I was satisfied that the sail was a patrol craft. Her presence was not a thing to talk about, but soon, between two clouds charged with hail-showers, a gleam of sunshine fell upon her sails, and our men discovered her character for themselves. From that moment I noticed that they seemed to take no heed of each other or of anything else. They could spare no eyes and no thought but for the slight column-shape astern of us. Its swaying had become perceptible. For a moment she remained dazzlingly white, then faded away slowly to nothing in a squall, only to reappear again, nearly black, resembling a post stuck upright against the slaty background of solid cloud. Since first noticed she had not gained on us a foot.

"She will never catch the *Tremolino*," I said, exultingly.

Dominic did not look at me. He remarked absently, but justly, that the heavy weather was in our pursuer's favour. She was three times our size. What we had to do was to keep our distance till dark, which we could manage easily, and then haul off to seaward and consider the situation. But his thought seemed to stumble in the darkness of some non-solved enigma, and soon he fell silent. We ran steadily, wing-and-wing. Cape San Sebastian nearly ahead seemed to recede from us in the squalls of rain, and come out again to meet our rush, every time more distinct between the showers.

For my part I was by no means certain that this *gabelou* (as our men alluded to her opprobriously) was after us at all. There were nautical difficulties in such a view which made me express the sanguine opinion that she was in all innocence simply changing her station. At this Dominic condescended to turn his head.

"I tell you she is in chase," he affirmed, moodily, after one short glance astern.

[12] *Burnous*—Cloak and hood combined, worn by the Moors and Arabs.

I never doubted his opinion. But with all the ardour of a neophyte [13] and the pride of an apt learner I was at that time a great nautical casuist.[14]

"What I can't understand," I insisted, subtly, "is how on earth, with this wind, she has managed to be just where she was when we first made her out. It is clear that she could not and did not gain twelve miles on us during the night. And there are other impossibilities. . . ."

Dominic had been sitting motionless, like an inanimate black cone posed on the stern deck, near the rudder-head, with a small tassel fluttering on its sharp point, and for a time he preserved the immobility of his meditation. Then, bending over with a short laugh, he gave my ear the bitter fruit of it. He understood everything now perfectly. She was where we had seen her first, not because she had caught us up, but because we had passed her during the night while she was already waiting for us, hove-to, most likely, on our very track.

"Do you understand—already?" Dominic muttered in a fierce undertone. "Already! You know we left a good eight hours before we were expected to leave, otherwise she would have been in time to lie in wait for us on the other side of the Cape, and" —he snapped his teeth like a wolf close to my face—"and she would have had us like—that."

I saw it all plainly enough now. They had eyes in their heads and all their wits about them in that craft. We had passed them in the dark as they jogged on easily towards their ambush with the idea that we were yet far behind. At daylight, however, sighting a balancelle ahead under a press of canvas, they had made sail in chase. But if that was so, then——

Dominic seized my arm.

"Yes, yes! She came out on an information—do you see it? —on information. . . . We have been sold—betrayed. Why? How? What for? We always paid them all so well on shore. . . . No! But it is my head that is going to burst."

He seemed to choke, tugged at the throat button of the cloak, jumped up open-mouthed as if to hurl curses and denunciation, but instantly mastered himself, and, wrapping up the cloak closer about him, sat down on the deck as quiet as ever.

---

[13] NEOPHYTE—A novice, a beginner.
[14] CASUIST—One who studies questions of right and wrong conduct.

"Yes, it must be the work of some scoundrel ashore," I observed.

He pulled the edge of the hood well forward over his brow before he muttered:

"A scoundrel . . . Yes. . . . It's evident."

"Well," I said, "they can't get us, that's clear."

"No," he assented, quietly, "they cannot."

We shaved the Cape very close to avoid an adverse current. On the other side, by the effect of the land, the wind failed us so completely for a moment that the *Tremolino's* two great lofty sails hung idle to the masts in the thundering uproar of the seas breaking upon the shore we had left behind. And when the returning gust filled them again, we saw with amazement half of the new mainsail, which we thought fit to drive the boat under before giving way, absolutely fly out of the bolt-ropes. We lowered the yard at once, and saved it all, but it was no longer a sail; it was only a heap of soaked strips of canvas cumbering the deck and weighting the craft. Dominic gave the order to throw the whole lot overboard.

"I would have had the yard thrown overboard, too," he said, leading me aft again, "if it had not been for the trouble. Let no sign escape you," he continued, lowering his voice, "but I am going to tell you something terrible. Listen: I have observed that the roping stitches on that sail have been cut! You hear? Cut with a knife in many places. And yet it stood all that time. Not enough cut. That flap did it at last. What matters it? But look! there's treachery seated on this very deck. By the horns of the devil! seated here at our very backs. Do not turn, signorino."

We were facing aft then.

"What's to be done?" I asked, appalled.

"Nothing. Silence! Be a man, signorino."

"What else?" I said.

To show I could be a man, I resolved to utter no sound as long as Dominic himself had the force to keep his lips closed. Nothing but silence becomes certain situations. Moreover, the experience of treachery seemed to spread a hopeless drowsiness over my thoughts and senses. For an hour or more we watched our pursuer surging out nearer and nearer from amongst the squalls that sometimes hid her altogether. But even when not seen, we felt her there like a knife at our throats. She gained on us frightfully. And the *Tremolino,* in a fierce breeze and in much smoother water, swung on easily under her one sail, with something appallingly careless in the joyous freedom of her motion. Another half-hour went by. I could not stand it any longer.

"They will get the poor barky," I stammered out, suddenly, almost on the verge of tears.

Dominic stirred no more than a carving. A sense of catastrophic loneliness overcame my inexperienced soul. The vision of my companions passed before me. The whole Royalist gang was in Monte Carlo now, I reckoned. And they appeared to me clear-cut and very small, with affected voices and stiff gestures, like a procession of rigid marionettes upon a toy stage. I gave a start. What was this? A mysterious, remorseless whisper came from within the motionless black hood at my side.

"*Il faut la tuer.*"

I heard it very well.

"What do you say, Dominic?" I asked, moving nothing but my lips.

And the whisper within the hood repeated mysteriously. "She must be killed."

My heart began to beat violently.

"That's it," I faltered out. "But how?"

"You love her well?"

"I do."

"Then you must find the heart for that work, too. You must steer her yourself, and I shall see to it that she dies quickly, without leaving as much as a chip behind."

"Can you?" I murmured, fascinated by the black hood turned immovably over the stern, as if in unlawful communion with that old sea of magicians, slave-dealers, exiles, and warriors, the sea of legends and terrors, where the mariners of remote antiquity used to hear the restless shade of an old wanderer weep aloud in the dark.

"I know a rock," whispered the initiated voice within the hood secretly. "But—caution! It must be done before our men perceive what we are about. Whom can we trust now? A knife drawn across the fore halyards would bring the foresail down, and put an end to our liberty in twenty minutes.

And the best of our men may be afraid of drowning. There is our little boat, but in an affair like this no one can be sure of being saved."

The voice ceased. We had started from Barcelona with our dinghy in tow; afterwards it was too risky to try to get her in, so we let her take her chance of the seas at the end of a comfortable scope of rope. Many times she had seemed to us completely overwhelmed, but soon we would see her bob up again on a wave, apparently as buoyant and whole as ever.

"I understand," I said, softly. "Very well, Dominic. When?"

"Not yet. We must get a little more in first," answered the voice from the hood in a ghostly murmur.

It was settled. I had now the courage to turn about. Our men crouched about the decks here and there with anxious, crestfallen faces, all turned one way to watch the chaser. For the first time that morning I perceived Cesar stretched out full length on the deck near the foremast and wondered where he had been skulking till then. But he might in truth have been at my elbow all the time for all I knew. We had been too absorbed in watching our fate to pay attention to each other. Nobody had eaten anything that morning, but the men had been coming constantly to drink at the water-butt.

I ran down to the cabin. I had there, put away in a locker, ten thousand francs in gold, of whose presence on board, so far as I was aware, not a soul except Dominic had the slightest inkling. When I emerged on deck again Dominic had turned about and was peering from under his cowl at the coast. Cape Creux closed the view ahead. To the left a wide bay, its waters torn and swept by fierce squalls, seemed full of smoke. Astern the sky had a menacing look.

Directly he saw me, Dominic, in a placid tone, wanted to know what was the matter. I came close to him and, looking as unconcerned as I could, told him in an undertone that I had found the locker broken open and the money-belt gone. Last evening it was still there.

"What did you want to do with it?" he asked me, trembling violently.

"Put it round my waist, of course," I answered, amazed to hear his teeth chattering.

"Cursed gold!" he muttered. "The weight of the money

might have cost you your life, perhaps." He shuddered. "There is no time to talk about that now."

"I am ready."

"Not yet. I am waiting for that squall to come over," he muttered. And a few leaden minutes passed.

The squall came over at last. Our pursuer, overtaken by a sort of murky whirlwind, disappeared from our sight. The *Tremolino* quivered and bounded forward. The land ahead vanished, too, and we seemed to be left alone in a world of water and wind.

"*Prenez la barre, monsieur,*" Dominic broke the silence suddenly in an austere voice. "Take hold of the tiller." He bent his hood to my ear. "The balancelle is yours. Your own hands must deal the blow. I—I have yet another piece of work to do." He spoke up loudly to the man who steered. "Let the signorino take the tiller, and you with the others stand by to haul the boat alongside quickly at the word."

The man obeyed, surprised, but silent. The others stirred, and pricked up their ears at this. I heard their murmurs: "What now? Are we going to run in somewhere and take to our heels? The Padrone knows what he is doing."

Dominic went forward. He paused to look down at Cesar, who, as I have said before, was lying full length face down by the foremast, then stepped over him, and dived out of my sight under the foresail. I saw nothing ahead. It was impossible for me to see anything except the foresail open and still, like a great shadowy wing. But Dominic had his bearings. His voice came to me from forward, in a just audible cry:

"Now, signorino!"

I bore on the tiller, as instructed before. Again I heard him faintly, and then I had only to hold her straight. No ship ran so joyously to her death before. She rose and fell, as if floating in space, and darted forward, whizzing like an arrow. Dominic, stooping under the foot of the foresail, reappeared, and stood steadying himself against the mast, with a raised forefinger in an attitude of expectant attention. A second before the shock his arm fell down by his side. At that I set my teeth. And then——

Talk of splintered planks and smashed timbers! This shipwreck lies upon my soul with the dread and horror of a homicide, with the unforgettable remorse of having crushed a living, faithful heart at a single blow. At one moment the rush and the soaring swing of speed; the next a crash, and death, stillness—a moment of horrible immobility, with the song of the wind changed to a strident wail, and the heavy waters boiling up menacing and sluggish around the corpse. I saw in a distracting minute the foreyard fly fore and aft with a brutal swing, the men all in a heap, cursing with fear, and hauling frantically at the line of the boat. With a strange welcoming of the familiar I saw also Cesar amongst them, and recognized Dominic's old, well-known, effective gesture, the horizontal sweep of his powerful arm. I recollect distinctly saying to myself, "Cesar must go down, of course," and then, as I was scrambling on all fours, the swinging tiller I had let go caught me a crack under the ear, and knocked me over senseless.

I don't think I was actually unconscious for more than a few minutes, but when I came to myself the dinghy was driving before the wind into a sheltered cove, two men just keeping her straight with their oars. Dominic, with his arm around my shoulders, supported me in the stern sheets.

We landed in a familiar part of the country. Dominic took one of the boat's oars with him. I suppose he was thinking of the stream we would have presently to cross, on which there was a miserable specimen of a punt, often robbed of its pole. But first of all we had to ascend the ridge of land at the back of the Cape. He helped me up. I was dizzy. My head felt very large and heavy. At the top of the ascent I clung to him, and we stopped to rest.

To the right, below us, the wide, smoky bay was empty. Dominic had kept his word. There was not a chip to be seen around the black rock from which the *Tremolino*, with her plucky heart crushed at one blow, had slipped off into deep water to her eternal rest. The vastness of the open sea was smothered in driving mists, and in the centre of the thinning squall, the unconscious guardacosta dashed on, still chasing to the northward. Our men were already descending the reverse slope to look for that punt which we knew from experience was not always to be found easily. I looked after them with dazed, misty eyes. One, two, three, four.

"Dominic, where's Cesar?" I cried.

As if repulsing the very sound of the name, the Padrone made that ample, sweeping, knocking-down gesture. I stepped back a pace and stared at him fearfully. His open shirt uncovered his muscular neck and the thick hair on his chest. He planted the oar upright in the soft soil, and rolling up slowly his right sleeve, extended the bare arm before my face.

"This," he began, with an extreme deliberation, whose superhuman restraint vibrated with the suppressed violence of his feelings, "is the arm which delivered the blow. I am afraid it is your own gold that did the rest. I forgot all about your money." He clasped his hands together in sudden distress. "I forgot, I forgot," he repeated, disconsolately.

"Cesar stole the belt?" I stammered out, bewildered.

"And who else? *Canallia!* He must have been spying on you for days. And he did the whole thing. Absent all day in Barcelona. *Traditore!* Sold his jacket—to hire a horse. Ha! ha! A good affair! I tell you it was he who set him at us. . . ."

Dominic pointed at the sea, where the guardacosta was a mere dark speck. His chin dropped on his breast.

". . . On information," he murmured, in a gloomy voice. "A Cervoni! Oh! my poor brother! . . ."

"And you drowned him," I said, feebly.

"I struck once, and the wretch went down like a stone—with the gold. Yes. But he had time to read in my eyes that nothing could save him while I was alive. And had I not the right—I, Dominic Cervoni, Padrone who brought him aboard your felucca [15]—my nephew, a traitor?"

He pulled the oar out of the ground and helped me carefully down the slope. All the time he never once looked me in the face. He punted us over, then shouldered the oar again and waited till our men were at some distance before he offered me his arm. After we had gone a little way, the fishing hamlet we were making for came into view. Dominic stopped.

"Do you think you can make your way as far as the houses by yourself?" he asked me, quietly.

"Yes, I think so. But why? Where are you going, Dominic?"

"Anywhere. What a question! Signorino, you are but little more than a boy to ask such a question of a man having this tale in his family. Ah! *Traditore!* What made me ever own

[15] FELUCCA—Sailboat.

that spawn of a hungry devil for our own blood! Thief, cheat, coward, liar—other men can deal with that. But I was his uncle, and so . . . I wish he had poisoned me—*charogne!* But this: that I, a confidential man and a Corsican, should have to ask your pardon for bringing on board your vessel, of which I was Padrone, a Cervoni, who has betrayed you—a traitor!—that is too much. It is too much. Well, I beg your pardon; and you may spit in Dominic's face because a traitor of our blood taints us all. A theft may be made good between men, a lie may be set right, a death avenged, but what can one do to atone for a treachery like this? . . . Nothing."

He turned and walked away from me along the bank of the stream, flourishing a vengeful arm and repeating to himself slowly, with savage emphasis: "Ah! *Canaille! Canaille! Canaille!* . . ." He left me there trembling with weakness and mute with awe. Unable to make a sound, I gazed after the strangely desolate figure of that seaman carrying an oar on his shoulder up a barren, rock-strewn ravine under the dreary leaden sky of *Tremolino's* last day. Thus, walking deliberately, with his back to the sea, Dominic vanished from my sight.

With the quality of our desires, thoughts, and wonder proportioned to our infinite littleness we measure even time itself by our own stature. Imprisoned in the house of personal illusions thirty centuries in mankind's history seem less to look back upon than thirty years of our own life. And Dominic Cervoni takes his place in my memory by the side of the legendary wanderer on the sea of marvels and terrors, by the side of the fatal and impious adventurer, to whom the evoked shade of the soothsayer predicted a journey inland with an oar on his shoulder, till he met men who had never set eyes on ships and oars. It seems to me I can see them side by side in the twilight of an arid land, the unfortunate possessors of the secret lore of the sea, bearing the emblem of their hard calling on their shoulders, surrounded by silent and curious men: even as I, too, having turned my back upon the sea, am bearing these few pages in the twilight, with the hope of finding in an inland valley the silent welcome of some patient listener.

The Type of Conrad's Stories: If you were to read a large number of Conrad's stories, you would be able to appreciate the diversity of his experiences, for the backgrounds and often the happenings themselves are based on actual experiences. The sea attracted him at an early age and it is the sea that figures prominently in his writings. It is remarkable that a man who could not speak English until he was twenty should have mastered the language so thoroughly that he has a place in the foremost ranks of English writers. He is an artist in the choice of the particular word or phrase that will convey his meaning. He avoids the common, threadbare expressions and when necessary to attain some shade of meaning he does not hesitate to use another language. His characters are vivid—strong people, sometimes, battling with the sea—broken people, often, struggling against the adversities of life.

For Appreciation: *The "Tremolino"* is built on an actual experience. At the age of nineteen, Conrad bought the *Tremolino* and with three other Royalists attempted to aid the cause of Don Carlos. The boat was deliberately wrecked to avoid its capture by the *guardacosta*. Shortly after this adventure, Conrad joined the crew of a steamer which transported grain. In the complete introduction to this story, Conrad gives a description of the boat which shows his feeling for it. This same feeling is noticeable throughout the story. In many stories told in the first person the narrator is the hero. In this, although the reader is in sympathy with the narrator at all times, Dominic Cervoni is the leading character. Find passages where the narrator's emotions are affected by some look or gesture of Dominic. To tell a story, such as this, in the first person and yet keep the narrator a secondary character requires real artistry. At what point did you think that the conflict would be between Dominic and Cesar? Read again the description of the chase by the *guardacosta*. How does the weather intensify the feeling of the chase? Where is the climax of the story?

For Further Study: Explain the meanings of the following words and expressions: *parchment skin; cranium; venomous; horizontal gesture; impotent rage; non-solved enigma; opprobriously; inanimate; marionettes; remorseless; slightest inkling.*

Why was it necessary for Dominic Cervoni to bring his nephew on board the boat? Has Cesar any redeeming qualities? What is the attitude of the Custom-house officer toward the cargo of the *Tremolino*? What is the significance of Dominic's remark, "He has come out here to wash the new paint off his yards, I suppose"? How did the narrator feel about running the boat on the rocks? How was the theft of the money partly responsible for Cesar's death? Explain Dominic Cervoni's attitude toward the narrator at the end of the story. Explain the meaning of the last paragraph.

Exercises and Creative Work: Imagine that you are a member of the crew of the *guardacosta*. Write a story in which you tell how the information was received about the *Tremolino* and describe the chase which followed.

MY BROTHER HENRY

James Matthew Barrie

STRICTLY speaking I never had a brother Henry, and yet I can not say that Henry was an impostor. He came into existence in a curious way, and I can think of him now without malice as a child of smoke. The first I heard of Henry was at Pettigrew's house, which is in a London suburb, so conveniently situated that I can go there and back in one day. I was testing some new Cabanas, I remember, when Pettigrew remarked that he had been lunching with a man who knew my brother Henry. Not having any brother but Alexander, I felt that Pettigrew had mistaken the name. "Oh, no," Pettigrew said; "he spoke of Alexander too." Even this did not convince me, and I asked my host for his friend's name. Scudamour was the name of the man, and he had met my brothers Alexander and Henry years before in Paris. Then I remembered Scudamour, and I probably frowned, for I myself was my own brother Henry. I distinctly recalled Scudamour meeting Alexander and me in Paris, and calling me Henry, though my name begins with a J. I explained the mistake to Pettigrew, and here, for the time being, the matter rested. However, I had by no means heard the last of Henry.

Several times afterward I heard from various persons that Scudamour wanted to meet me because he knew my brother Henry. At last we did meet, in Jimmy's chambers; and, almost as soon as he saw me, Scudamour asked where Henry was now.

This was precisely what I feared. I am a man who always looks like a boy. There are few persons of my age in London who retain their boyish appearance as long as I have done; indeed, this is the curse of my life. Though I am approaching the age of thirty, I pass for twenty; and I have observed old gentlemen frown at my precocity when I said a good thing or helped myself to a second glass of wine. There was, therefore, nothing surprising in Scudamour's remark, that, when he had the pleasure of meeting Henry, Henry must have been about the age that I had now reached. All would have been well had I explained the real state of affairs to this annoying man; but, unfortunately for myself, I loathe entering upon explanations to anybody about anything. This it is to smoke the Arcadia. When I ring for a time-table and William John brings coals instead, I accept the coals as a substitute.

Much, then, did I dread a discussion with Scudamour, his surprise when he heard that I was Henry, and his comments on my youthful appearance. Besides, I was smoking the best of all mixtures. There was no likelihood of my meeting Scudamour again, so the easiest way to get rid of him seemed to be to humor him. I therefore told him that Henry was in India, married, and doing well. "Remember me to Henry when you write to him," was Scudamour's last remark to me that evening.

A few weeks later some one tapped me on the shoulder in Oxford Street. It was Scudamour. "Heard from Henry?" he asked. I said I had heard by the last mail. "Anything particular in the letter?" I felt it would not do to say that there was nothing particular in a letter which had come all the way from India, so I hinted that Henry was having trouble with his wife. By this I meant that her health was bad; but he took it up in another way, and I did not set him right. "Ah, ah!" he said, shaking his head sagaciously; "I'm sorry to hear that. Poor Henry!" "Poor old boy!" was all I could think of replying. "How about the children?" Scudamour asked. "Oh, the children," I said, with what I thought presence of mind, "are coming to England." "To stay with Alexander?" he asked. My answer was that Alexander was expecting them by the middle of next month; and eventually Scudamour went away muttering, "Poor Henry!" In a month or so we met again. "No word of Henry's getting leave of absence?" asked Scudamour. I replied shortly that Henry had gone to live in Bombay, and would not be home for years. He saw that I was brusk, so what does he do but draw me aside for a quiet explanation. "I suppose," he said, "you are annoyed because I told Pettigrew that Henry's wife had run away from him. The fact is, I did it for your good. You see, I happened to make a remark to Pettigrew about your brother Henry, and he said that there was no such person. Of course I laughed at that, and pointed out not only that I had the pleasure of Henry's acquaintance, but that you and I had talked about the old fellow every time we met. 'Well,' Pettigrew said, 'this is a most remarkable thing; for he,' meaning you, 'said to me in this very room, sitting in that very chair, that Alexander was his only brother.' I saw that Pettigrew resented your concealing the existence of your brother Henry from him, so I thought the most friendly thing I could do was to tell him that your reticence was doubtless due to the unhappy state of poor Henry's private affairs. Naturally in the circumstances you did not want to talk about Henry." I shook Scudamour by the hand, telling him that he had acted judiciously; but if I could have stabbed him in the back at that moment I dare say I would have done it.

I did not see Scudamour again for a long time, for I took care to keep out of his way; but I heard first from him and then of him. One day he wrote to me saying that his nephew was going to Bombay, and would I be so good as to give the youth an introduction to my brother Henry? He also asked me to dine with him and his nephew. I declined the dinner, but I sent the nephew the required note of introduction to Henry. The next I heard of Scudamour was from Pettigrew. "By the way," said Pettigrew, "Scudamour is in Edinburgh at present." I trembled, for Edinburgh is where Alexander lives. "What has taken him there?" I asked, with assumed carelessness. Pettigrew believed it was business; "but," he added, "Scudamour asked me to tell you that he meant to call on Alexander, as he was anxious to see Henry's children." A few days afterward I had a telegram from Alexander, who generally uses this means of communication when he corresponds with me.

"Do you know a man, Scudamour? Reply," was what Alexander said. I thought of answering that we had met a man of that name when we were in Paris; but after consideration, I replied boldly: "Know no one of name of Scudamour."

About two months ago I passed Scudamour in Regent Street, and he scowled at me. This I could have borne if there had been no more of Henry; but I knew that Scudamour was now telling everybody about Henry's wife.

By and by I got a letter from an old friend of Alexander's asking me if there was any truth in a report that Alexander was going to Bombay. Soon afterward Alexander wrote to me saying he had been told by several persons that I was going to Bombay. In short, I saw that the time had come for killing Henry. So I told Pettigrew that Henry had died of fever, deeply regretted; and asked him to be sure to tell Scudamour, who had always been interested in the deceased's welfare. Pettigrew afterward told me that he had communicated the sad intelligence to Scudamour. "How did he take it?" I asked. "Well," Pettigrew said, reluctantly, "he told me that when he was up in Edinburgh he did not get on well with Alexander. But he expressed great curiosity as to Henry's children." "Ah," I said, "the children were both drowned in the Forth; a sad affair—we can't bear to talk of it." I am not likely to see much of Scudamour again, nor is Alexander. Scudamour now goes about saying that Henry was the only one of us he really liked.

The Type of Barrie's Stories: Barrie is best known as a playwright. However, he has written successful novels and short stories. In all of his writings there is both pathos and humor. Added to these, there is a whimsicality which makes it possible for him to introduce fairies and unreal situations with great effectiveness. Barrie uses the Scotch dialect in much of his writing.

For Appreciation: *My Brother Henry* is short and humorous. The story is told in a mild fashion—as one would relate it to a friend. Yet it is written with such skill that the reader senses, without being told in so many words, the annoyance of the narrator. The evasion of an immediate explanation brought about further fabrications. Trace the growth of this "myth" about Henry.

For Further Study: Explain the meanings of the following words: *precocity; brusk; reticence.*

Why did the narrator not explain that Scudamour was mistaken about his brother? Why was it necessary to "kill off" the non-existent brother? Explain the meaning of the last sentence in the story.

Exercises and Creative Work: Read *My Double and How He Undid Me* by Edward Everett Hale and make a short outline of it.

Write a story of a mistaken identity.

MY OWN TRUE GHOST STORY

Rudyard Kipling

As I came through the Desert thus it was—
As I came through the Desert.
—*The City of Dreadful Night.*

Somewhere in the Other World, where there are books and pictures and plays and shop-windows to look at, and thousands of men who spend their lives in building up all four, lives a gentleman who writes real stories about the real insides of people; and his name is Mr. Walter Besant. But he will insist upon treating his ghosts—he has published half a workshopful of them—with levity. He makes his ghost-seers talk familiarly, and, in some cases, flirt outrageously, with the phantoms. You may treat anything, from a Viceroy to a Vernacular Paper with levity; but you must behave reverently toward a ghost, and particularly an Indian one.

There are, in this land, ghosts who take the form of fat, cold, pobby corpses, and hide in trees near the roadside till a traveler passes. Then they drop upon his neck and remain. There are also terrible ghosts who wander along the pathways at dusk, or hide in the crops near a village, and call seductively. But to answer their call is death in this world and the next. There are ghosts of little children who have been thrown into wells. These haunt well-curbs and the fringes of jungles, and wail under the stars, or catch women by the wrist and beg to be taken up and carried. These and the corpse-ghosts, however, are only vernacular articles and do not attack Sahibs.[1] No native ghost has yet been authentically reported to have frightened an Englishman; but many English ghosts have scared the life out of both white and black.

Nearly every other Station owns a ghost. There are said to be two at Simla, not counting the woman who blows the bellows at Syree dâk-bungalow[2] on the Old Road; Mussoorie has a house haunted of a very lively Thing; a White Lady is supposed to be night watchman round a house in Lahore; Dalhousie says that one of her houses "repeats" on autumn evenings all the incidents of a horrible horse-and-precipice accident; Murree has a merry ghost, and, now that she has been swept by cholera, will have room for a sorrowful one; there are Officers' Quarters in Mian Mir whose doors open without reason, and whose furniture is guaranteed to creak, not with the heat of June but with the weight of Invisibles who come to lounge in the chair; Peshawur possesses houses that none will willingly rent; and there is something—not fever—wrong with a big bungalow in Allahabad. The older Provinces simply bristle with haunted houses, and march phantom armies along their main thoroughfares.

Some of the dâk-bungalows on the Grand Trunk Road have handy little cemeteries in their compound—witnesses to the "changes and chances of this mortal life" in the days when men drove from Calcutta to the Northwest. These bungalows are objectionable places to put up in. They are generally very old, always dirty, while the *khansamah*[3] is as ancient as the bungalow. He either chatters senilely, or falls into the long trances of age. In both moods he is useless. If you get angry with him, he refers to some Sahib dead and buried these thirty years, and says that when he was in that Sahib's service not a *khansamah* in the Province could touch him. Then he jabbers

---

[1] SAHIBS—Sahib is a term used in India by the natives when referring to a European gentleman or master.

[2] DÂK-BUNGALOW—The dâk-bungalows are rest-houses constructed by Indian authorities for the convenience of travelers.

[3] *Khansamah*—The person in charge at a dâk-bungalow.

and mows and trembles and fidgets among the dishes, and you repent of your irritation.

In these dâk-bungalows, ghosts are most likely to be found, and when found, they should be made a note of. Not long ago it was my business to live in dâk-bungalows. I never inhabited the same house for three nights running, and grew to be learned in the breed. I lived in Government-built ones with red brick walls and rail ceilings, an inventory of the furniture posted in every room, and an excited snake at the threshold to give welcome. I lived in "converted" ones—old houses officiating as dâk-bungalows—where nothing was in its proper place and there wasn't even a fowl for dinner. I lived in second-hand palaces where the wind blew through open-work marble tracery just as uncomfortably as through a broken pane. I lived in dâk-bungalows where the last entry in the visitors' book was fifteen months old, and where they slashed off the curry-kid's head with a sword. It was my good-luck to meet all sorts of men, from sober traveling missionaries and deserters flying from British Regiments, to drunken loafers who threw whiskey bottles at all who passed. Seeing that a fair proportion of the tragedy of our lives out here acted itself in dâk-bungalows, I wondered that I had met no ghosts. A ghost that would voluntarily hang about a dâk-bungalow would be mad of course; but so many men have died mad in dâk-bungalows that there must be a fair percentage of lunatic ghosts.

In due time I found my ghost, or ghosts rather, for there were two of them. Up till that hour I had sympathized with Mr. Besant's method of handling them, as shown in *The Strange Case of Mr. Lucraft and Other Stories*. I am now in the Opposition.

We will call the bungalow Katmal dâk-bungalow. But *that* was the smallest part of the horror. A man with a sensitive hide has no right to sleep in dâk-bungalows. He should marry. Katmal dâk-bungalow was old and rotten and unrepaired. The floor was of worn brick, the walls were filthy, and the windows were nearly black with grime. It stood on a by-path largely used by native Sub-Deputy Assistants of all kinds, from Finance to Forests; but real Sahibs were rare. The *khansamah*, who was nearly bent double with old age, said so.

When I arrived, there was a fitful, undecided rain on the

face of the land, accompanied by a restless wind, and every gust made a noise like the rattling of dry bones in the stiff toddy-palms outside. The *khansamah* completely lost his head on my arrival. He had served a Sahib once. Did I know that Sahib? He gave me the name of a well-known man who has been buried for more than a quarter of a century, and showed me an ancient daguerreotype of that man in his prehistoric youth. I had seen a steel engraving of him at the head of a double volume of Memoirs a month before, and I felt ancient beyond telling.

The day shut in and the *khansamah* went to get me food. He did not go through the pretence of calling it *"khana"*—man's victuals. He said *"ratub,"* and that means, among other things, "grub"—dog's rations. There was no insult in his choice of the term. He had forgotten the other word, I suppose.

While he was cutting up the dead bodies of animals, I settled myself down, after exploring the dâk-bungalow. There were three rooms, beside my own, which was a corner kennel, each giving into the other through dingy white doors fastened with long iron bars. The bungalow was a very solid one, but the partition-walls of the rooms were almost jerry-built in their flimsiness. Every step or bang of a trunk echoed from my room down the other three, and every footfall came back tremulously from the far walls. For this reason I shut the door. There were no lamps—only candles in long glass shades. An oil wick was set in the bath-room.

For bleak, unadulterated misery that dâk-bungalow was the worst of the many that I had ever set foot in. There was no fireplace, and the windows would not open; so a brazier [4] of charcoal would have been useless. The rain and the wind splashed and gurgled and moaned round the house, and the toddy-palms rattled and roared. Half a dozen jackals went through the compound singing, and a hyena stood afar off and mocked them. A hyena would convince a Sadducee of the Resurrection of the Dead—the worst sort of Dead. Then came the *ratub*—a curious meal, half native and half English in composition—with the old *khansamah* babbling behind my chair about dead and gone English people, and the wind-blown candles playing shadow-bopeep with the bed and the mosquito-curtains. It was just the sort of dinner and evening to make a man think

[4] BRAZIER—An open pan for burning charcoal.

of every single one of his past sins, and of all the others that he intended to commit if he lived.

Sleep, for several hundred reasons, was not easy. The lamp in the bathroom threw the most absurd shadows into the room, and the wind was beginning to talk nonsense.

Just when the reasons were drowsy with blood-sucking I heard the regular—"Let-us-take-and-heave-him-over" grunt of doolie[5]-bearers in the compound. First one doolie came in, then a second, and then a third. I heard the doolies dumped on the ground, and the shutter in front of my door shook. "That's some one trying to come in," I said. But no one spoke, and I persuaded myself that it was the gusty wind. The shutter of the room next to mine was attacked, flung back, and the inner door opened. "That's some Sub-Deputy Assistant," I said, "and he has brought his friends with him. Now they'll talk and spit and smoke for an hour."

But there were no voices and no footsteps. No one was putting his luggage into the next room. The door shut, and I thanked Providence that I was to be left in peace. But I was curious to know where the doolies had gone. I got out of bed and looked into the darkness. There was never a sign of a doolie. Just as I was getting into bed again, I heard, in the next room, the sound that no man in his senses can possibly mistake —the whir of a billiard ball down the length of the slates when the striker is stringing for break. No other sound is like it. A minute afterward there was another whir, and I got into bed. I was not frightened—indeed I was not. I was very curious to know what had become of the doolies. I jumped into bed for that reason.

Next minute I heard the double click of a cannon and my hair sat up. It is a mistake to say that hair stands up. The skin of the head tightens and you can feel a faint, prickly bristling all over the scalp. That is the hair sitting up.

There was a whir and a click, and both sounds could only have been made by one thing—a billiard ball. I argued the matter out at great length with myself; and the more I argued the less probable it seemed that one bed, one table, and two chairs—all the furniture of the room next to mine—could so exactly duplicate the sounds of a game of billiards. After an-

[5] Doolie—A low litter.

other cannon, a three-cushion one to judge by the whir, I argued no more. I had found my ghost and would have given worlds to have escaped from that dâk-bungalow. I listened, and with each listen the game grew clearer. There was whir on whir and click on click. Sometimes there was a double click and a whir and another click. Beyond any sort of doubt, people were playing billiards in the next room. And the next room was not big enough to hold a billiard table!

Between the pauses of the wind I heard the game go forward —stroke after stroke. I tried to believe that I could not hear voices; but that attempt was a failure.

Do you know what fear is? Not ordinary fear of insult, injury or death, but abject, quivering dread of something that you cannot see—fear that dries the inside of the mouth and half of the throat—fear that makes you sweat on the palms of the hands, and gulp in order to keep the uvula at work? This is a fine Fear—a great cowardice, and must be felt to be appreciated. The very improbability of billiards in a dâk-bungalow proved the reality of the thing. No man—drunk or sober—could imagine a game at billiards, or invent the spitting crack of a "screw-cannon."

A severe course of dâk-bungalows has this disadvantage—it breeds infinite credulity. If a man said to a confirmed dâk-bungalow-haunter:—"There is a corpse in the next room, and there's a mad girl in the next but one, and the woman and the man on that camel have just eloped from a place sixty miles away," the hearer would not disbelieve because he would know that nothing is too wild, grotesque, or horrible to happen in a dâk-bungalow.

This credulity, unfortunately, extends to ghosts. A rational person fresh from his own house would have turned on his side and slept. I did not. So surely as I was given up as a bad carcass by the scores of things in the bed because the bulk of my blood was in my heart, so surely did I hear every stroke of a long game at billiards played in the echoing room behind the iron-barred door. My dominant fear was that the players might want a maker. It was an absurd fear; because creatures who could play in the dark would be above such superfluities. I only know that that was my terror; and it was real.

After a long long while, the game stopped, and the door

banged. I slept because I was dead tired. Otherwise I should have preferred to have kept awake. Not for everything in Asia would I have dropped the door-bar and peered into the dark of the next room.

When the morning came, I considered that I had done well and wisely, and inquired for the means of departure.

"By the way, *khansamah*," I said, "what were those three doolies doing in my compound in the night?"

"There were no doolies," said the *khansamah*.

I went into the next room and the daylight streamed through the open door. I was immensely brave. I would, at that hour, have played Black Pool with the owner of the big Black Pool down below.

"Has this place always been a dâk-bungalow?" I asked.

"No," said the *khansamah*. "Ten or twenty years ago, I have forgotten how long, it was a billiard-room."

"A how much?"

"A billiard-room for the Sahibs who built the Railway. I was *khansamah* then in the big house where all the Railway-Sahibs lived, and I used to come across with brandy-*shrab*. These three rooms were all one, and they held a big table on which the Sahibs played every evening. But the Sahibs are all dead now, and the Railway runs, you say, nearly to Kabul."

"Do you remember anything about the Sahibs?"

"It is long ago, but I remember that one Sahib, a fat man and always angry, was playing here one night, and he said to me:—'Mangal Khan, brandy-*pani do*,' and I filled the glass, and he bent over the table to strike, and his head fell lower and lower till it hit the table, and his spectacles came off, and when we—the Sahibs and I myself—ran to lift him he was dead. I helped to carry him out. Aha, he was a strong Sahib! But he is dead and I, old Mangal Khan, am still living, by your favor."

That was more than enough! I had my ghost—a first-hand, authenticated article. I would write to the Society for Psychical Research—I would paralyze the Empire with the news! But I would, first of all, put eight miles of assessed crop-land between myself and that dâk-bungalow before nightfall. The Society might send their regular agent to investigate later on.

I went into my own room and prepared to pack after noting

down the facts of the case. As I smoked I heard the game begin again—with a miss in balk this time, for the whir was a short one.

The door was open and I could see into the room. *Click—click!* That was a cannon. I entered the room without fear, for there was sunlight within and a fresh breeze without. The unseen game was going on at a tremendous rate. And well it might, when a restless little rat was running to and fro inside the dingy ceiling-cloth, and a piece of loose window-sash was making fifty breaks off the window-bolt as it shook in the breeze!

Impossible to mistake the sound of billiard balls! Impossible to mistake the whir of a ball over the slate! But I was to be excused. Even when I shut my enlightened eyes the sound was marvelously like that of a fast game.

Entered angrily the faithful partner of my sorrows, Kadir Baksh.

"This bungalow is very bad and low caste! No wonder the Presence was disturbed and is speckled. Three sets of doolie-bearers came to the bungalow late last night when I was sleeping outside, and said that it was their custom to rest in the rooms set apart for the English people! What honor has *khansamah?* They tried to enter, but I told them to go. No wonder, if these *Oorias* have been here, that the Presence is sorely spotted. It is shame, and the work of a dirty man!"

Kadir Baksh did not say that he had taken from each gang two annas for rent in advance, and then, beyond my earshot, had beaten them with the big green umbrella whose use I could never before divine. But Kadir Baksh has no notions of morality.

There was an interview with the *khansamah*, but as he promptly lost his head, wrath gave place to pity, and pity led to a long conversation, in the course of which he put the fat Engineer-Sahib's tragic death in three separate stations—two of them fifty miles away. The third shift was to Calcutta, and there the Sahib died while driving a dogcart.

If I had encouraged him the *khansamah* would have wandered all through Bengal with his corpse.

I did not go away as soon as I intended. I stayed for the night, while the wind and the rat and the sash and the window-bolt played a ding-dong "hundred and fifty up." Then the wind ran out and the billiards stopped, and I felt that I had ruined my one genuine, hall-marked ghost story.

Had I only stopped at the proper time, I could have made *anything* out of it.

That was the bitterest thought of all!

The Type of Kipling's Stories: Kipling was the first writer to make stories of India popular with the general reading public. He wrote of natives, the British soldiers and government officials, and the animals in the jungles. With the instinct of a journalist he created characters who were interesting and unusual. In a sense, his stories are "local color" stories. Any writing of this kind calls for exactness of expression and Kipling possesses to a very high degree the ability to select or even to coin words which convey the shade of meaning which he desires. His use of Indian words and the dialects of some of his British soldiers make many of his stories a little difficult for an American reader. To many people the name of Kipling is linked only with India. This gives too narrow an impression of his scope, for some of his best writing has other countries for the settings. Canby has written of Kipling, "It is as difficult to review Kipling's stories as it is to characterize East Side New York. They are quite as multifarious."

For Appreciation: *My Own True Ghost Story* appears in the volume entitled *The Phantom 'Rickshaw and Other Stories*. It is of the type known as a "flash-back" or a "story in a frame." In the matter of time, stories are either told with the events happening in chronological order or after the story is started the reader is taken back to something which happened in the past. The latter kind is called the "flash-back." Kipling uses this method of telling a story very frequently. Would you call this story one of "local color"? The narrator sometimes admits he was frightened; sometimes he tries to pretend he was not. Find these passages. Does the story end in the "flash-back"? Can you explain why this story might also be called "a story in a frame"?

For Further Study: Give the meanings of the following words and expressions: *levity; vernacular; prehistoric youth; ancient daguerreotype; jerry-built; uvula; dominant fear.*

What is the purpose of the long introduction to this story? What kinds of dâk-bungalows are described? Can you explain why the native ghosts were not supposed to frighten the white people? Weather plays an important part in many stories. In this story and in *The Three Strangers* much depends on the weather. Explain.

For Creative Work: Write a description of the *khansamah.*

Write an account of something which has frightened you that was later explainable.

QUALITY

John Galsworthy

I knew him from the days of my extreme youth, because he made my father's boots; inhabiting with his elder brother two little shops let into one, in a small by-street—now no more, but then most fashionably placed in the West End.

That tenement had a certain quiet distinction; there was no sign upon its face that he made for any of the Royal Family— merely his own German name of Gessler Brothers; and in the window a few pairs of boots. I remember that it always troubled me to account for those unvarying boots in the window, for he made only what was ordered, reaching nothing down, and it seemed so inconceivable that what he made could ever have failed to fit. Had he bought them to put there? That, too, seemed inconceivable. He would never have tolerated in the house, leather on which he had not worked himself. Besides, they were too beautiful—the pair of pumps, so inexpressibly slim, the patent leathers with cloth tops, making water come into one's mouth, the tall brown riding boots with marvelous sooty glow, as if, though new, they had been worn a hundred years. Those pairs could only have been made by one who saw before him the Soul of Boot—so truly were they prototypes incarnating the very spirit of all footgear. These thoughts, of course, came to me later, though even when I was promoted to him, at the age of perhaps fourteen, some inkling haunted me of the dignity of himself and brother. For to make boots—such boots as he made—seemed to me then, and still seems to me, mysterious and wonderful.

I remember well my shy remark, one day, while stretching out to him my youthful foot:

"Isn't it awfully hard to do, Mr. Gessler?"

And his answer, given with a sudden smile from out of the sardonic redness of his beard: "Id is an Ardt!"

Himself, he was a little as if made from leather, with his yellow crinkly face, and crinkly reddish hair and beard, and neat folds slanting down his cheeks to the corners of his mouth, and his guttural and one-toned voice; for leather is a sardonic substance, and stiff and slow of purpose. And that was the character of his face, save that his eyes, which were gray-blue, had in them the simple gravity of one secretly possessed by the Ideal. His elder brother was so very like him—though watery, paler in every way, with a great industry—that sometimes in early days I was not quite sure of him until the interview was over. Then I knew that it was he, if the words, "I will ask my brudder," had not been spoken; and that, if they had, it was his elder brother.

When one grew old and wild and ran up bills, one somehow never ran them up with Gessler Brothers. It would not have seemed becoming to go in there and stretch out one's foot to that blue iron-spectacled glance, owing him for more than—say—two pairs, just the comfortable reassurance that one was still his client.

For it was not possible to go to him very often—his boots lasted terribly, having something beyond the temporary—some, as it were, essence of boot stitched into them.

One went in, not as into most shops, in the mood of: "Please serve me, and let me go!" but restfully, as one enters a church; and, sitting on the single wooden chair, waited—for there was never anybody there. Soon, over the top edge of that sort of well—rather dark, and smelling soothingly of leather—which formed the shop, there would be seen his face, or that of his elder brother, peering down. A guttural sound, and the tip-tap of bast slippers beating the narrow wooden stairs, and he would stand before one without coat, a little bent, in leather apron, with sleeves turned back, blinking—as if awakened from some dream of boots, or like an owl surprised in daylight and annoyed at this interruption.

And I would say: "How do you do, Mr. Gessler? Could you make me a pair of Russia leather boots?"

Without a word he would leave me, retiring whence he came, or into the other portion of the shop, and I would continue to rest in the wooden chair, inhaling the incense of his trade. Soon he would come back, holding in his thin, veined hand a piece of gold-brown leather. With eyes fixed on it, he would remark: "What a beaudiful biece!" When I, too, had admired it, he would speak again. "When do you wand dem?" And I would answer: "Oh! As soon as you conveniently can." And he would say: "To-morrow fordnighd?" Or if he were his elder brother: "I will ask my brudder!"

Then I would murmur: "Thank you! Good morning, Mr. Gessler." "Goot morning!" he would reply, still looking at the leather in his hand. And as I moved to the door, I would hear the tip-tap of his bast slippers restoring him, up the stairs, to his dream of boots. But if it were some new kind of footgear that he had not yet made me, then indeed he would observe ceremony—divesting me of my boot and holding it long in his hand, looking at it with eyes at once critical and loving, as if recalling the glow with which he had created it, and rebuking the way in which one had disorganized this masterpiece. Then, placing my foot on a piece of paper, he would two or three times tickle the outer edges with a pencil and pass his nervous fingers over my toes, feeling himself into the heart of my requirements.

I cannot forget that day on which I had occasion to say to him: "Mr. Gessler, that last pair of town walking boots creaked, you know."

He looked at me for a time without replying, as if expecting me to withdraw or qualify the statement, then said:

"Id shouldn'd 'ave greaked."

"It did, I'm afraid."

"You goddem wed before dey found demselves?"

"I don't think so."

At that he lowered his eyes, as if hunting for memory of those boots, and I felt sorry I had mentioned this grave thing.

"Zend dem back!" he said; "I will look at dem."

A feeling of compassion for my creaking boots surged up in me, so well could I imagine the sorrowful long curiosity of regard which he would bend on them.

"Zome boods," he said slowly, "are bad from birdt. If I can do noding wid dem, I dake dem off your bill."

Once (once only) I went absent-mindedly into his shop in a pair of boots bought in an emergency at some large firm's. He took my order without showing me any leather, and I could feel his eyes penetrating the inferior integument of my foot. At last he said:

"Dose are nod my boods."

The tone was not one of anger, nor of sorrow, not even of

ELD

contempt, but there was in it something quiet that froze the blood. He put his hand down and pressed a finger on the place where the left boot, endeavoring to be fashionable, was not quite comfortable.

"Id 'urds you dere," he said. "Dose big virms 'ave no self-respect. Drash!" And then, as if something had given way within him, he spoke long and bitterly. It was the only time I ever heard him discuss the conditions and hardships of his trade.

"Dey ged id all," he said, "dey ged id by adverdisement, nod by work. Dey dake id away from us, who lofe our boods. Id gomes to this—bresently I haf no work. Every year id gets less —you will see." And looking at his lined face I saw things I had never noticed before, bitter things and bitter struggle—and what a lot of gray hairs there seemed suddenly in his red beard!

As best I could, I explained the circumstances of the purchase of those ill-omened boots. But his face and voice made so deep an impression that during the next few minutes I ordered many pairs. Nemesis fell! They lasted more terribly than ever. And I was not able conscientiously to go to him for nearly two years.

When at last I went I was surprised to find that outside one of the two little windows of his shop another name was painted, also that of a bootmaker—making, of course, for the Royal Family. The old familiar boots, no longer in dignified isolation, were huddled in the single window. Inside, the now contracted well of the one little shop was more scented and darker than ever. And it was longer than usual, too, before a face peered down, and the tip-tap of the bast slippers began. At last he stood before me, and, gazing through those rusty iron spectacles, said:

"Mr. ——, isn'd it?"

"Ah! Mr. Gessler," I stammered, "but your boots are really *too* good, you know! See, these are quite decent still!" And I stretched out to him my foot. He looked at it.

"Yes," he said, "beople do nod wand good boods, id seems."

To get away from his reproachful eyes and voice I hastily remarked: "What have you done to your shop?"

He answered quietly: "Id was too exbensif. Do you wand some boods?"

I ordered three pairs, though I had only wanted two, and

quickly left. I had, I do not know quite what feeling of being part, in his mind, of a conspiracy against him; or not perhaps so much against him as against his idea of boot. One does not, I suppose, care to feel like that; for it was again many months before my next visit to his shop, paid, I remember, with the feeling: "Oh! well, I can't leave the old boy—so here goes! Perhaps it'll be his elder brother!"

For his elder brother, I knew, had not character enough to reproach me, even dumbly.

And, to my relief, in the shop there did appear to be his elder brother, handling a piece of leather.

"Well, Mr. Gessler," I said, "how are you?"

He came close, and peered at me.

"I am breddy well," he said slowly: "but my elder brudder is dead."

And I saw that it was indeed himself—but how aged and wan! And never before had I heard him mention his brother. Much shocked, I murmured: "Oh! I am sorry!"

"Yes," he answered, "he was a good man, he made a good bood; but he is dead." And he touched the top of his head, where the hair had suddenly gone as thin as it had been on that of his poor brother, to indicate, I suppose, the cause of death. "He could nod ged over losing de oder shop. Do you wand any boods?" And he held up the leather in his hand: "Id's a beautiful biece."

I ordered several pairs. It was very long before they came —but they were better than ever. One simply could not wear them out. And soon after that I went abroad.

It was over a year before I was again in London. And the first shop I went to was my old friend's. I had left a man of sixty, I came back to one of seventy-five, pinched and worn and tremulous, who genuinely, this time, did not at first know me.

"Oh! Mr. Gessler," I said, sick at heart; "how splendid your boots are! See, I've been wearing this pair nearly all the time I've been abroad; and they're not half worn out, are they?"

He looked long at my boots—a pair of Russia leather, and his face seemed to regain steadiness. Putting his hand on my instep, he said:

"Do dey vid you here? I 'ad drouble wid dat bair, I remember."

I assured him that they had fitted beautifully.

"Do you wand any boods?" he said. "I can make dem quickly; id is a slack dime."

I answered: "Please, please! I want boots all round—every kind!"

"I will make a vresh model. Your food must be bigger." And with utter slowness, he traced round my foot, and felt my toes, only once looking up to say:

"Did I dell you my brudder was dead?"

To watch him was painful, so feeble had he grown; I was glad to get away.

I had given those boots up, when one evening they came. Opening the parcel, I set the four pairs out in a row. Then one by one I tried them on. There was no doubt about it. In shape and fit, in finish and quality of leather, they were the best he had ever made me. And in the mouth of one of the town walking boots I found his bill. The amount was the same as usual, but it gave me quite a shock. He had never before sent it in till quarter day. I flew downstairs, and wrote a cheque, and posted it at once with my own hand.

A week later, passing the little street, I thought I would go in and tell him how splendidly the new boots fitted. But when I came to where his shop had been, his name was gone. Still there, in the window, were the slim pumps, the patent leathers with cloth tops, the sooty riding boots.

I went in, very much disturbed. In the two little shops—again made into one—was a young man with an English face.

"Mr. Gessler in?" I said.

He gave me a strange, ingratiating look.

"No, sir," he said, "no. But we can attend to anything with pleasure. We've taken the shop over. You've seen our name, no doubt, next door. We make for some very good people."

"Yes, yes," I said; "but Mr. Gessler?"

"Oh!" he answered; "dead."

"Dead! But I only received these boots from him last Wednesday week."

"Ah!" he said; "a shockin' go. Poor old man starved 'imself."

"Good God!"

"Slow starvation, the doctor called it! You see he went to work in such a way! Would keep the shop on; wouldn't have a soul touch his boots except himself. When he got an order, it took him such a time. People won't wait. He lost everybody. And there he'd sit, goin' on and on—I will say that for him—not a man in London made a better boot! But look at the competition! He never advertised! Would 'ave the best leather, too, and do it all 'imself. Well, there it is. What could you expect with his ideas?"

"But starvation——"

"That may be a bit flowery, as the sayin' is—but I know myself he was sittin' over his boots day and night, to the very last. You see I used to watch him. Never gave 'imself time to eat; never had a penny in the house. All went in rent and leather. How he lived so long I don't know. He regular let his fire go out. He was a character. But he made good boots."

"Yes," I said, "he made good boots."

And I turned and went out quickly, for I did not want that youth to know that I could hardly see.

The Type of Galsworthy's Stories: It has been written of Galsworthy: "He was 'Devonshire,' and proud of being Devonshire and proud that the chief attribute of the Devonshire man is a surface softness under which lies the grimmest of obstinacies—the velvet glove on a hand of marble." Galsworthy's stories are like that. Strong—but written with restraint, they make a lasting impression on the mind of the reader. Galsworthy's plots are slight; his themes, which have to do with the inequality in society and the disappointments of less fortunate individuals, carry his stories along and sustain the interest.

For Appreciation: *Quality* might be considered as a short story in which the theme rather than the plot predominates. There is a conflict in the story, but it occurs "off stage." With the exception of one passage, the reader learns of Mr. Gessler's troubles in an indirect way. The story is significant because the theme has to do with an individual who rather than surrender his ideals as a master craftsman suffers material defeat. Notice how Galsworthy appeals to the senses of smell and touch to produce his effects. The story is told with restraint, yet its emotional value is increased rather than decreased by this means.

For Further Study: Give the meaning of each of the following: *prototypes; sardonic; bast slippers; nemesis; integument; ingratiating.*

Select five passages which show Mr. Gessler's feeling toward his boots. What changes in the shop gave evidence of the decrease in business? Why was the narrator ill at ease when he entered the shop wearing a pair of boots which had not been made by Mr. Gessler?

Exercises and Creative Work: Write a few paragraphs telling why you like or do not like this story.

Discuss the effects of the machine age on the attitude of a person toward the article which he is making.

The Short Story in World Literature

General Characteristics

French and Russian writers have probably developed the short story to a greater degree than the writers of other European nations. The Spanish and the Germans have not taken so kindly to this type of literature, although there are excellent examples of the short story found in their literature. The French, especially, are masters of the short story, having developed a sharp, clear, photographic style, without superfluous words. The effect is all the stronger for the brevity. Here we find finish of plot and style and finely drawn characters and scenes. A French writer and a Russian writer are represented in this volume.

François Coppée (1842–1908)

François Coppée was born in Villers-Cotterets in France. His father was a clerk in the War Department. After a few years of study in the Lycée Saint-Louis, it became necessary for him to leave school in order to help support his family. However, his desire for an education was so great that he spent his evenings in the library. Coppée's first book of poems appeared in 1866. Three years later, a French actress recited one of the poems from this collection. The poem stimulated her interest in the author so much that she asked him to write a play for her. *Le Passant,* a drama in verse, was written in response to this request. Lofty ideals are always expressed in Coppée's dramas.

Coppée was a successful writer of short stories and novels as well as of poetry and drama. In all of his writings he was profoundly French.

Anton Chekhov (1860–1904)

Anton Chekhov, whose name is sometimes spelled Tchekhov, Tchekov, or Chekov, was born in southern Russia near the Sea of Azov on January 17, 1860. His parents were liberated serfs, who, though uneducated themselves, helped their son to receive a good education. He completed the medical course at Moscow University, but practiced little, preferring to devote himself to writing. Chekhov had published a number of humorous stories while he was a student and after experimenting for several years with various types of literature, he turned more and more to a certain psychological type. In these stories he is often concerned chiefly with a mood or state of mind and with great skill he shows how constant, though small, incidents intensify or change this state of mind.

Ill health, after 1897, made it necessary for him to live in Crimea or in other countries where the climate was favorable. He died in 1904 at the age of forty-four. Chekhov's writings have been translated into German, French, and English.

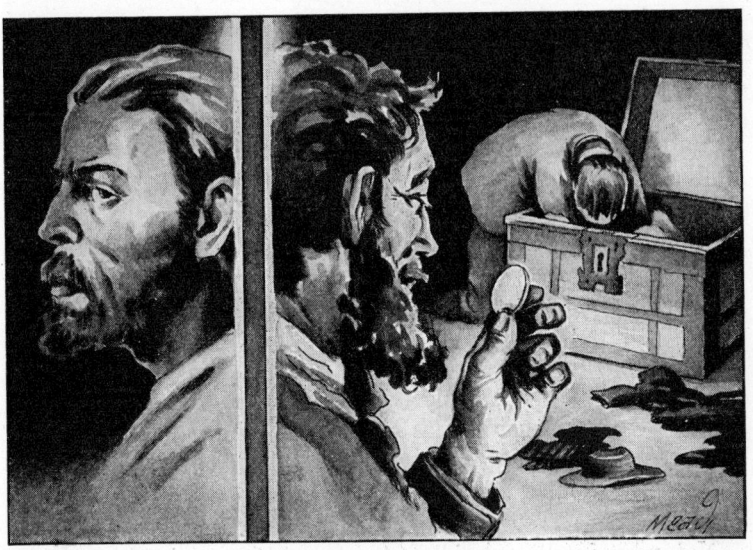

THE SUBSTITUTE

François Coppée

He was scarcely ten years old when he was first arrested as a vagabond.

He spoke thus to the judge:

"I am called Jean François Leturc, and for six months I was with the man who sings and plays upon a cord of catgut[1] between the lanterns at the Place de la Bastille. I sang the refrain with him, and after that I called, 'Here's all the new songs, ten centimes, two sous!' He was always drunk, and used to beat me. That is why the police picked me up the other night. Before that I was with the man who sells brushes. My mother was a laundress, her name was Adèle. She was a good workwoman and liked me. She made money because she had for customers waiters in the cafés, and they use a good deal of linen. On Sundays she used to put me to bed early so that she could go to the ball. On week-days she sent me to Les Frères,[2] where I learned to read. Well, the sergent-de-ville[3]

---

[1] Cord of catgut—A tough cord used on stringed instruments.
[2] Les Frères—A school maintained by priests.
[3] Sergent-de-ville—A policeman.

whose beat was in our street used always to stop before our windows to talk with her—a good-looking chap, with a medal from the Crimea. They were married, and after that everything went wrong. He didn't take to me, and turned mother against me. Every one had a blow for me, and so, to get out of the house, I spent whole days in the Place Clichy, where I knew the mountebanks.[4] My father-in-law lost his place, and my mother her work. She used to go out washing to take care of him; this gave her a cough—the steam . . . She is dead at Lamboisière. She was a good woman. Since that I have lived with the seller of brushes and the catgut scraper. Are you going to send me to prison?"

He said this open, cynically, like a man. He was a little, ragged street-arab, as tall as a boot, his forehead hidden under a queer mop of yellow hair.

Nobody claimed him, and they sent him to the Reform School.

Not very intelligent, idle, clumsy with his hands—the only trade he could learn there was not a good one—that of reseating straw chairs. However, he was obedient, naturally quiet and silent, and he did not seem to be profoundly corrupted by that school of vice. But when, in his seventeenth year, he was thrown out again on the streets of Paris, he unhappily found there his prison comrades, all great scamps, exercising their dirty professions: teaching dogs to catch rats in the sewers, and blacking shoes on ball nights in the passage of the Opera—amateur wrestlers, who permitted themselves to be thrown by the Hercules of the booths—or fishing at noontime from rafts; all of these occupations he followed to some extent, and, some months after he came out of the house of correction, he was arrested again for a petty theft—a pair of old shoes prigged from a shop-window. Result: a year in the prison of Sainte Pélagie, where he served as valet to the political prisoners.

He lived in much surprise among this group of prisoners, all very young, negligent in dress, who talked in loud voices, and carried their heads in a very solemn fashion. They used to meet in the cell of one of the oldest of them, a fellow of some thirty years, already a long time in prison and quite a fixture at Sainte Pélagie—a large cell, the walls covered with colored

[4] MOUNTEBANKS—Boastful and unscrupulous pretenders; sellers of quack medicines or other questionable articles.

caricatures, and from the window of which one could see all Paris—its roofs, its spires, and its domes—and far away the distant line of hills, blue and indistinct upon the sky. There were upon the walls some shelves filled with volumes and all the old paraphernalia of a fencing-room: broken masks, rusty foils, breastplates, and gloves that were losing their tow.[5] It was there that the "politicians" used to dine together, adding to the everlasting "soup and beef," fruit, cheese, and pints of wine which Jean François went out and got by the can—a tumultuous repast interrupted by violent disputes, and where, during the dessert, the *Carmagnole* and *Ça Ira*[6] were sung in full chorus. They assumed, however, an air of great dignity on those days when a newcomer was brought in among them, at first entertaining him gravely as a citizen, but on the morrow using him with affectionate familiarity and calling him by his nickname. Great words were used there: Corporation, Responsibility, and phrases quite unintelligible to Jean François—such as this, for example, which he once heard imperiously put forth by a frightful little hunchback who blotted some writing-paper every night:

"It is done. This is the composition of the Cabinet: Raymond, the Bureau of Public Instruction; Martial, the Interior; and for Foreign Affairs, myself."

His time done, he wandered again around Paris, watched afar by the police, after the fashion of cockchafers,[7] made by cruel children to fly at the end of a string. He became one of those fugitive and timid beings whom the law, with a sort of coquetry, arrests and releases by turn—something like those platonic fishers who, in order that they may not exhaust their fish-pond, throw immediately back into the water the fish which has just come out of the net. Without a suspicion on his part that so much honor had been done to so sorry a subject, he had a special bundle of memoranda in the mysterious portfolios[8] of the Rue de Jérusalem. His name was written in round hand on the gray paper of the cover, and the notes and reports, carefully classified, gave him his successive appellations: "Name, Leturc"; "the prisoner Leturc," and, at last, "the criminal Leturc."

[5] Tow—A kind of stuffing in the gloves.
[6] THE *Carmagnole* AND *Ça Ira*—Revolutionary songs.
[7] COCKCHAFER—A kind of beetle.
[8] MYSTERIOUS PORTFOLIOS—Criminal records.

He was two years out of prison, dining where he could, sleeping in night lodging-houses and sometimes in lime-kilns, and taking part with his fellows in interminable games of pitch-penny on the boulevards near the barriers. He wore a greasy cap on the back of his head, carpet slippers, and a short white blouse. When he had five sous he had his hair curled. He danced at Constant's at Montparnasse; bought for two sous to sell for four at the door of Bobino, the jack of hearts or the ace of clubs serving as a countermark; sometimes opened the door of a carriage; led horses to the horse-market. From the lottery of all sorts of miserable employments he drew a goodly number. Who can say if the atmosphere of honor which one breathes as a soldier, if military discipline might not have saved him? Taken, in a cast of the net, with some young loafers who robbed drunkards sleeping on the streets, he denied very earnestly having taken part in their expeditions. Perhaps he told the truth, but his antecedents were accepted in lieu of proof, and he was sent for three years to Poissy. There he made coarse playthings for children, was tattooed on the chest, learned thieves' slang and the penal code. A new liberation, and a new plunge into the sink of Paris; but very short this time, for at the end of six months at the most he was again compromised in a night robbery, aggravated by climbing and breaking—a serious affair, in which he played an obscure rôle, half dupe and half fence.[9] On the whole his complicity was evident, and he was sent for five years at hard labor. His grief in this adventure was above all in being separated from an old dog which he had found on a scrap-heap, and cured of the mange. The beast loved him.

Toulon, the ball and chain, the work in the harbor, the blows from a stick, wooden shoes on bare feet, soup of black beans dating from Trafalgar,[10] no tobacco money, and the terrible sleep in a camp swarming with convicts; that was what he experienced for five broiling summers and five winters raw with the Mediterranean wind. He came out from there stunned, was sent under surveillance to Vernon, where he worked some time on the river. Then, an incorrigible vagabond, he broke his exile and came again to Paris. He had his savings, fifty-six

---

[9] HALF DUPE AND HALF FENCE—An easily deceived person who would receive stolen goods.

[10] TRAFALGAR—A battle in 1805 when the British fleet defeated the combined fleets of France and Spain.

francs, that is to say, time enough for reflection. During his absence his former wretched companions had dispersed. He was well hidden, and slept in a loft at an old woman's, to whom he represented himself as a sailor, tired of the sea, who had lost his papers in a recent shipwreck, and who wanted to try his hand at something else. His tanned face and his calloused hands, together with some sea phrases which he dropped from time to time, made his tale seem probable enough.

One day when he risked a saunter in the streets, and when chance had led him as far as Montmartre, where he was born, an unexpected memory stopped him before the door of Les Frères, where he had learned to read. As it was very warm the door was open, and by a single glance the passing outcast was able to recognize the peaceable schoolroom. Nothing was changed: neither the bright light shining in at the great windows, nor the crucifix over the desk, nor the rows of benches with the tables furnished with inkstands and pencils, nor the table of weights and measures, nor the map where pins stuck in still indicated the operations of some ancient war. Heedlessly and without thinking, Jean François read on the blackboard the words of the Evangelist which had been set there as a copy:

"Joy shall be in heaven over one sinner that repenteth, more than over ninety and nine just persons, which need no repentance."

It was undoubtedly the hour for recreation, for the Brother Professor had left his chair, and, sitting on the edge of a table, he was telling a story to the boys who surrounded him with eager and attentive eyes. What a bright and innocent face he had, that beardless young man, in his long black gown, and white necktie, and great ugly shoes, and his badly cut brown hair streaming out behind! All the simple figures of the children of the people who were watching him seemed scarcely less childlike than his; above all when, delighted with some of his own simple and priestly pleasantries, he broke out in an open and frank peal of laughter which showed his white and regular teeth, a peal so contagious that all the scholars laughed loudly in their turn. It was such a sweet, simple group in the bright sunlight, which lighted their dear eyes and their blond curls.

Jean François looked at them for some time in silence, and for the first time in that savage nature, all instinct and appetite, there awoke a mysterious, a tender emotion. His heart, that seared and hardened heart, unmoved when the convict's cudgel or the heavy whip of the watchman fell on his shoulders, beat oppressively. In that sight he saw again his infancy; and closing his eyes sadly, the prey to torturing regret, he walked quickly away.

Then the words written on the blackboard came back to his mind.

"If it wasn't too late, after all!" he murmured; "if I could again, like others, eat honestly my brown bread, and sleep my fill without nightmare! The spy must be sharp who recognizes me. My beard, which I shaved off down there, has grown out thick and strong. One can burrow somewhere in the great ant-hill, and work can be found. Whatever is not worked to death in the hell of the galleys comes out agile and robust, and I learned there to climb ropes with loads upon my back. Building is going on everywhere here, and the masons need helpers. Three francs a day! I never earned so much. Let me be forgotten, and that is all I ask."

He followed his courageous resolution; he was faithful to it, and after three months he was another man. The master for whom he worked called him his best workman. After a long day upon the scaffolding, in the hot sun and the dust, constantly bending and raising his back to take the hod from the man at his feet and pass it to the man over his head, he went for his soup to the cook-shop, tired out, his legs aching, his hands burning, his eyelids stuck with plaster, but content with himself, and carrying his well-earned money in a knot in his handkerchief. He went out now without fear, since he could not be recognized in his white mask, and since he had noticed that the suspicious glances of the policeman were seldom turned on the tired workman. He was quiet and sober. He slept the sound sleep of fatigue. He was free!

At last—oh, supreme recompense!—he had a friend!

He was a fellow-workman like himself, named Savinien, a little peasant with red lips who had come to Paris with his stick over his shoulder and a bundle on the end of it, fleeing from the wine-shops and going to mass every Sunday. Jean François loved him for his piety, for his candor, for his honesty, for all that he himself had lost, and so long ago. It was a passion, profound and unrestrained, which transformed him by fatherly cares and attentions. Savinien, himself of a weak and egotistical nature, let things take their course, satisfied only in finding a companion who shared his horror of the wine-shop. The two friends lived together in a fairly comfortable lodging, but their resources were very limited. They were obliged to take into their room a third companion, an old Auvergnat,[11] gloomy and rapacious, who found it possible out of his meager salary to save something with which to buy a place in his own country. Jean François and Savinien were always together. On holidays they together took long walks in the environs of Paris, and dined under an arbor in one of those small country inns where there are a great many mushrooms in the sauces and innocent rebusses on the napkins. There Jean François learned from his friend all lore of which they who are born in the city are ignorant; learned the names of the trees, the flowers, and the plants; the various seasons for harvesting; he heard eagerly the thousand details of a laborious country life—the autumn sowing, the winter chores, the splendid celebrations of harvest and vintage days, the sound of the mills at the water-side, and the flails striking the ground, the tired horses led to water, and the hunting in the morning mist; and, above all, the long evenings around the fire of vineshoots, that were shortened by some marvelous stories. He discovered in himself a source of imagination before unknown, and found a singular delight in the recital of events so placid, so calm, and so monotonous.

One thing troubled him, however: it was the fear lest Savinien might learn something of his past. Sometimes there escaped from him some low word of thieves' slang, a vulgar gesture—vestiges of his former horrible existence—and he felt the pain one feels when old wounds reopen; the more because he fancied that he sometimes saw in Savinien the awakening of an unhealthy curiosity. When the young man, already tempted by the pleasures which Paris offers to the poorest, asked him about the mysteries of the great city, Jean François feigned ignorance and turned the subject; but he felt a vague inquietude for the future of his friend.

His uneasiness was not without foundation. Savinien could not long remain the simple rustic that he was on his arrival in

[11] AUVERGNAT—A man from the province of Auvergne.

Paris. If the gross and noisy pleasures of the wine-shop always repelled him, he was profoundly troubled by other temptations, full of danger for the inexperience of his twenty years. When spring came he began to go off alone, and at first he wandered about the brilliant entrance of some dancing-hall, watching the young girls who went in with their arms around each other's waists, talking in low tones. Then, one evening, when lilacs perfumed the air and the call to quadrilles was most captivating, he crossed the threshold, and from that time Jean François observed a change, little by little, in his manners and his visage. He became more frivolous, more extravagant. He often borrowed from his friend his scanty savings, and he forgot to repay. Jean François, feeling that he was abandoned, jealous and forgiving at the same time, suffered and was silent. He felt that he had no right to reproach him, but with the foresight of affection he indulged in cruel and inevitable presentiments.

One evening, as he was mounting the stairs to his room, absorbed in his thoughts, he heard, as he was about to enter, the sound of angry voices, and he recognized that of the old Auvergnat who lodged with Savinien and himself. An old habit of suspicion made him stop at the landing-place and listen to learn the cause of the trouble.

"Yes," said the Auvergnat, angrily, "I am sure that some one has opened my trunk and stolen from it the three louis that I had hidden in a little box; and he who has done this thing must be one of the two companions who sleep here, if it were not the servant Maria. It concerns you as much as it does me, since you are the master of the house, and I will drag you to the courts if you do not let me at once break open the valises of the two masons. My poor gold! It was here yesterday in its place, and I will tell you just what it is, so that if we find it again nobody can accuse me of having lied. Ah, I know them, my three beautiful gold-pieces, and I can see them as plainly as I see you! One piece was more worn than the others; it was of greenish gold, with a portrait of the great emperor. The other was a great old fellow with a queue and epaulettes; and the third, which had on it a Philippe with whiskers, I had marked with my teeth. They don't trick me. Do you know that I only wanted two more like that to pay for my vineyard? Come, search these fellows' things with me, or I will call the police! Hurry up!"

"All right," said the voice of the landlord; "we will go and search with Maria. So much the worse for you if we find nothing, and the masons get angry. You have forced me to it."

Jean François' soul was full of fright. He remembered the embarrassed circumstances and the small loans of Savinien and how sober he had seemed for some days. And yet he could not believe that he was a thief. He heard the Auvergnat panting in his eager search, and he pressed his closed fists against his breast as if to still the furious beating of his heart.

"Here they are!" suddenly shouted the victorious miser. "Here they are, my louis, my dear treasure; and in the Sunday vest of that little hypocrite of Limousin![12] Look, landlord, they are just as I told you. Here is the Napoleon, the man with a queue, and the Philippe that I have bitten. See the dents! Ah, the little beggar with the sanctified air. I should have much sooner suspected the other. Ah, the wretch! Well, he must go to the convict prison."

At this moment Jean François heard the well-known step of Savinien coming slowly up the stairs.

He is going to his destruction, thought he. Three stories. I have time!

And, pushing open the door, he entered the room, pale as death, where he saw the landlord and servant stupefied in a corner, while the Auvergnat, on his knees, in the disordered heap of clothes, was kissing the pieces of gold.

"Enough of this," he said, in a thick voice; "I took the money, and put it in my comrade's trunk. But that is too bad. I am a thief, but not a Judas. Call the police; I will not try to escape, only I must say a word to Savinien in private. Here he is."

In fact, the little Limousin had just arrived, and seeing his crime discovered, believing himself lost, he stood there, his eyes fixed, his arms hanging.

Jean François seized him forcibly by the neck, as if to embrace him; he put his mouth close to Savinien's ear, and said to him in a low, supplicating voice:

"Keep quiet."

Then turning towards the others:

"Leave me alone with him. I tell you I won't go away. Lock us in if you wish, but leave us alone."

[12] Limousin—Mason.

With a commanding gesture he showed them the door.
They went out.

Savinien, broken by grief, was sitting on the bed, and lowered his eyes without understanding anything.

"Listen," said Jean François, who came and took him by the hands. "I understand! You have stolen three gold-pieces to buy some trifle for a girl. That costs six months in prison. But one only comes out from there to go back again, and you will become a pillar of police courts and tribunals. I understand it. I have been seven years at the Reform School, a year at Sainte Pélagie, three years at Poissy, five years at Toulon. Now, don't be afraid. Everything is arranged. I have taken it on my shoulders."

"It is dreadful," said Savinien; but hope was springing up again in his cowardly heart.

"When the elder brother is under the flag, the younger one does not go," replied Jean François. "I am your substitute, that's all. You care for me a little, do you not? I am paid. Don't be childish—don't refuse. They would have taken me again one of these days, for I am a runaway from exile. And then, do you see, that life will be less hard for me than for you. I know it all, and I shall not complain if I have not done you this service for nothing, and if you swear to me that you will never do it again. Savinien, I have loved you well, and your friendship has made me happy. It is through it that, since I have known you, I have been honest and pure, as I might always have been, perhaps, if I had had, like you, a father to put a tool in my hands, a mother to teach me my prayers. It was my sole regret that I was useless to you, and that I deceived you concerning myself. Today I have unmasked in saving you. It is all right. Do not cry, and embrace me, for already I hear heavy boots on the stairs. They are coming with the *posse*, and we must not seem to know each other so well before those chaps."

He pressed Savinien quickly to his breast, then pushed him from him, when the door was thrown wide open.

It was the landlord and the Auvergnat, who brought the police. Jean François sprang forward to the landing-place, held out his hands for the handcuffs, and said, laughing, "Forward, bad lot!"

Today he is at Cayenne, condemned for life as an incorrigible.

The Type of Coppée's Stories: Fortunately for French literature, Princess Mathilde used her influence to have Coppée appointed an assistant-librarian at the Senate. In this way Coppée was assured of a living and of the necessary leisure for his literary work, because the position was more honorary than arduous. A great deal of his time seems to have been spent loitering—feeding the birds in the squares and gardens, standing in public squares, strolling along the banks of the Seine. But this loitering while it may have seemed unimportant bore fruit in that Coppée by his sympathetic understanding of the people won their hearts in his stories. He was called the "poet of the lowly," beloved by the common people who "felt that he belonged to them by every right of inheritance and environment." On the other hand, he was praised by the critics. It is unusual for a writer to win the esteem of both the common people and the critics.

Coppée's stories are more popular today than his other forms of writing. He portrayed familiar scenes in a simple yet truthful and vivid manner.

For Appreciation: The underlying theme of *The Substitute* is the development of the character of Jean François Leturc. But a careful reader will realize that he has learned of many things besides the changes which took place in Jean François. He feels the attitude of the law toward the criminal in each offense from his first arrest to his life imprisonment. He is made conscious of the atmosphere of Les Frères as Jean François looks into the schoolroom. He has a glimpse of rural France through the association of Jean François and Savinien. All this makes it easy to understand why the common people appreciated Coppée's writings.

What facts about the lives of young criminals are told? What does the reader learn about the types of prisoners with whom Jean is associated? It is interesting to note that in 1897 Coppée published *Le Coupable*, a novel of criminal psychology.

For Further Study: Give the meanings of the following words and phrases: *street-arab; prigged; political prisoners; platonic fishers; surveillance; rapacious; rebusses; inquietude.* Why was Jean François arrested the first time? In what ways was his environment the cause of his arrest? What did the different entries in the police book tell about Jean François? Why was he sad when he was sentenced to five years' hard labor? What was his first steady employment? Why was he not recognized by the police? For what reason was Jean attracted to Savinien? What circumstance made it necessary to share a room with the old Auvergnat? For what was the old man saving his money? Why did Jean François make the great sacrifice that he did?

Exercises and Creative Work: Write another ending for the story.

Write a short story in which Savinien is tempted to do something, but is restrained by his memory of the sacrifice of Jean François.

THE BET

Anton Chekhov

It was a dark autumn night. The old banker was pacing from corner to corner of his study, recalling to his mind the party he gave in the autumn fifteen years before. There were many clever people at the party and much interesting conversation. They talked among other things of capital punishment. The guests, among them not a few scholars and journalists, for the most part disapproved of capital punishment. They found it obsolete as a means of punishment unfitted to a Christian State and immoral. Some of them thought that capital punishment should be replaced universally by life-imprisonment.

"I don't agree with you," said the host. "I myself have experienced neither capital punishment nor life-imprisonment, but if one may judge *a priori*,[1] then in my opinion capital punishment is more moral and more humane than imprisonment. Execution kills instantly, life-imprisonment kills by degrees. Who is the more humane executioner, one who kills you in a

---

[1] *A priori*—Self-evidently or from cause to effect.

few seconds or one who draws the life out of you incessantly, for years?"

"They're both equally immoral," remarked one of the guests, "because their purpose is the same, to take away life. The State is not God. It has no right to take away that which it cannot give back, if it should so desire."

Among the company was a lawyer, a young man of about twenty-five. On being asked his opinion, he said:

"Capital punishment and life-imprisonment are equally immoral; but if I were offered the choice between them, I would certainly choose the second. It's better to live somehow than not to live at all."

There ensued a lively discussion. The banker, who was then younger and more nervous, suddenly lost his temper, banged his fist on the table, and turning to the young lawyer, cried out:

"It's a lie. I bet you two millions you wouldn't stick in a cell even for five years."

"If you mean it seriously," replied the lawyer, "then I bet I'll stay not five but fifteen."

"Fifteen! Done!" cried the banker. "Gentlemen, I stake two millions."

"Agreed. You stake two millions, I my freedom," said the lawyer.

So this wild, ridiculous bet came to pass. The banker, who at that time had too many millions to count, spoiled and capricious, was beside himself with rapture. During supper he said to the lawyer jokingly:

"Come to your senses, young man, before it's too late. Two millions are nothing to me, but you stand to lose three or four of the best years of your life. I say three or four, because you'll never stick it out any longer. Don't forget either, you unhappy man, that voluntary is much heavier than enforced imprisonment. The idea that you have the right to free yourself at any moment will poison the whole of your life in the cell. I pity you."

And now the banker, pacing from corner to corner, recalled all this and asked himself:

"Why did I make this bet? What's the good? The lawyer loses fifteen years of his life and I throw away two millions. Will it convince people that capital punishment is worse or better than imprisonment for life? No, no! all stuff and rubbish. On my part, it was the caprice of a well-fed man; on the lawyer's pure greed of gold."

He recollected further what happened after the evening party. It was decided that the lawyer must undergo his imprisonment under the strictest observation, in a garden wing of the banker's house. It was agreed that during the period he would be deprived of the right to cross the threshold, to see living people, to hear human voices, and to receive letters and newspapers. He was permitted to have a musical instrument, to read books, to write letters, to drink wine and smoke tobacco. By the agreement he could communicate, but only in silence, with the outside world through a little window specially constructed for this purpose. Everything necessary, books, music, wine, he could receive in any quantity by sending a note through the window. The agreement provided for all the minutest details, which made the confinement strictly solitary, and it obliged the lawyer to remain exactly fifteen years from twelve o'clock of November 14th, 1870, to twelve o'clock of November 14th, 1885. The least attempt on his part to violate the conditions, to escape if only for two minutes before the time, freed the banker from the obligation to pay him the two millions.

During the first year of imprisonment, the lawyer, as far as it was possible to judge from his short notes, suffered terribly from loneliness and boredom. From his wing day and night came the sound of the piano. He rejected wine and tobacco. "Wine," he wrote, "excites desires, and desires are the chief foes of a prisoner; besides, nothing is more boring than to drink good wine alone, and tobacco spoils the air in his room." During the first year the lawyer was sent books of a light character; novels with a complicated love interest, stories of crime and fantasy, comedies, and so on.

In the second year the piano was heard no longer and the lawyer asked only for classics. In the fifth year, music was heard again, and the prisoner asked for wine. Those who watched him said that during the whole of that year he was only eating, drinking, and lying on his bed. He yawned often and talked angrily to himself. Books he did not read. Sometimes at nights he would sit down to write. He would write for a long time and tear it all up in the morning. More than once he was heard to weep.

In the second half of the sixth year, the prisoner began zealously to study languages, philosophy, and history. He fell on these subjects so hungrily that the banker hardly had time to get books enough for him. In the space of four years about six hundred volumes were bought at his request. It was while that passion lasted that the banker received the following letter from the prisoner: "My dear gaoler, I am writing these lines in six languages. Show them to experts. Let them read them. If they do not find one single mistake, I beg you to give orders to have a gun fired off in the garden. By the noise I shall know that my efforts have not been in vain. The geniuses of all ages and countries speak in different languages; but in them all burns the same flame. Oh, if you knew my heavenly happiness now that I can understand them!" The prisoner's desire was fulfilled. Two shots were fired in the garden by the banker's order.

Later on, after the tenth year, the lawyer sat immovable before his table and read only the New Testament. The banker found it strange that a man who in four years had mastered six hundred erudite[2] volumes should have spent nearly a year in reading one book, easy to understand and by no means thick. The New Testament was then replaced by the history of religions and theology.

During the last two years of his confinement the prisoner read an extraordinary amount, quite haphazard. Now he would apply himself to the natural sciences, then he would read Byron or Shakespeare. Notes used to come from him in which he asked to be sent at the same time a book on chemistry, a textbook of medicine, a novel, and some treatise on philosophy or theology. He read as though he were swimming in the sea among broken pieces of wreckage, and in his desire to save his life was eagerly grasping one piece after another.

The banker recalled all this, and thought:

"Tomorrow at twelve o'clock he receives his freedom. Under the agreement, I shall have to pay him two millions. If I pay, it's all over with me. I am ruined forever . . ."

Fifteen years before he had too many millions to count, but

[2] ERUDITE—Scholarly.

now he was afraid to ask himself which he had more of, money or debts. Gambling on the Stock-Exchange, risky speculation, and the recklessness of which he could not rid himself even in old age, had gradually brought his business to decay; and the fearless, self-confident, proud man of business had become an ordinary banker, trembling at every rise and fall in the market.

"That cursed bet," murmured the old man clutching his head in despair . . . "Why didn't the man die? He's only forty years old. He will take away my last farthing, marry, enjoy life, gamble on the Exchange, and I will look on like an envious beggar and hear the same words from him every day: 'I'm obliged to you for the happiness of my life. Let me help you.' No, it's too much! The only escape from bankruptcy and disgrace—is that the man should die."

The clock had just struck three. The banker was listening. In the house every one was asleep, and one could hear only the frozen trees whining outside the windows. Trying to make no sound, he took out of his safe the key of the door which had not been opened for fifteen years, put on his overcoat, and went out of the house. The garden was dark and cold. It was raining. A damp, penetrating wind howled in the garden and gave the trees no rest. Though he strained his eyes, the banker could see neither the ground, nor the white statues, nor the garden wing, nor the trees. Approaching the garden wing, he called the watchman twice. There was no answer. Evidently the watchman had taken shelter from the bad weather and was now asleep somewhere in the kitchen or the greenhouse.

"If I have the courage to fulfill my intention," thought the old man, "the suspicion will fall on the watchman first of all."

In the darkness he groped for the steps and the door and entered the hall of the garden-wing, then poked his way into a narrow passage and struck a match. Not a soul was there. Some one's bed, with no bedclothes on it, stood there, and an iron stove loomed dark in the corner. The seals on the door that led into the prisoner's room were unbroken.

When the match went out, the old man, trembling from agitation, peeped into the little window.

In the prisoner's room a candle was burning dimly. The prisoner himself sat by the table. Only his back, the hair on his head and his hands were visible. Open books were strewn about on the table, the two chairs, and on the carpet near the table.

Five minutes passed and the prisoner never once stirred. Fifteen years' confinement had taught him to sit motionless. The banker tapped on the window with his finger, but the prisoner made no movement in reply. Then the banker cautiously tore the seals from the door and put the key into the lock. The rusty lock gave a hoarse groan and the door creaked. The banker expected instantly to hear a cry of surprise and the sound of steps. Three minutes passed and it was as quiet inside as it had been before. He made up his mind to enter.

Before the table sat a man, unlike an ordinary human being. It was a skeleton, with tight-drawn skin, with long curly hair like a woman's, and a shaggy beard. The color of his face was yellow, of an earthy shade; the cheeks were sunken, the back long and narrow, and the hand upon which he leaned his hairy head was so lean and skinny that it was painful to look upon. His hair was already silvering with gray, and no one who glanced at the senile emaciation of the face would have believed that he was only forty years old. On the table, before his bended head, lay a sheet of paper on which something was written in a tiny hand.

"Poor devil," thought the banker, "he's asleep and probably seeing millions in his dreams. I have only to take and throw this half-dead thing on the bed, smother him a moment with the pillow, and the most careful examination will find no trace of unnatural death. But, first, let us read what he has written here."

The banker took the sheet from the table and read:

"Tomorrow at twelve o'clock, midnight, I shall obtain my freedom and the right to mix with people. But before I leave this room and see the sun I think it necessary to say a few words to you. On my own clear conscience and before God who sees me I declare to you that I despise freedom, life, health, and all that your books call the blessings of the world.

"For fifteen years I have diligently studied earthly life. True, I saw neither the earth nor the people, but in your books I drank fragrant wine, sang songs, hunted deer and wild boar in the forests, loved women . . . And beautiful women, like clouds ethereal, created by the magic of your poets' genius, visited me by night and whispered to me wonderful tales, which made my head drunken. In your books I climbed the summits of Elburz and Mont Blanc and saw from there how the sun rose in the morning, and in the evening suffused the sky, the ocean, and the mountain ridges with a purple gold. I saw from there how above me lightnings glimmered cleaving the clouds; I saw green forests, fields, rivers, lakes, cities; I heard the wings of beautiful devils who came flying to me to speak of God. . . . In your books I cast myself into bottomless abysses, worked miracles, burned cities to the ground, preached new religions, conquered whole countries. . . .

"Your books gave me wisdom. All that unwearying human thought created in the centuries is compressed to a little lump in my skull. I know that I am cleverer than you all.

"And I despise your books, despise all worldly blessings and wisdom. Everything is void, frail, visionary and delusive as a mirage. Though you be proud and wise and beautiful, yet will death wipe you from the face of the earth like the mice underground; and your posterity, your history, and the immortality of your men of genius will be as frozen slag, burnt down together with the terrestrial [3] globe.

"You are mad, and gone the wrong way. You take falsehood for truth and ugliness for beauty. You would marvel if suddenly apple and orange trees should bear frogs and lizards instead of fruit, and if roses should begin to breathe the odor of a sweating horse. So do I marvel at you, who have bartered heaven for earth. I do not want to understand you.

"That I may show you in deed my contempt for that by which you live, I waive the two millions of which I once dreamed as of paradise, and which I now despise. That I may deprive myself of my right to them, I shall come out from here five minutes before the stipulated term, and thus shall violate the agreement."

When he had read, the banker put the sheet on the table, kissed the head of the strange man, and began to weep. He went out of the wing. Never at any other time, not even after his terrible losses on the Exchange, had he felt such contempt for himself as now. Coming home, he lay down on his bed, but agitation and tears kept him a long time from sleeping. . . .

[3] TERRESTRIAL—Pertaining to the earth.

The next morning the poor watchmen came running to him and told him that they had seen the man who lived in the wing climb through the window into the garden. He had gone to the gate and disappeared. The banker instantly went with his servants to the wing and established the escape of his prisoner. To avoid unnecessary rumors he took the paper with the renunciation from the table and, on his return, locked it in his safe.

The Type of Chekhov's Stories: Chekhov began to write humorous stories while he was a student in medical school. From 1886 to 1888 he experimented with various other types. Although he died at the age of forty-four, he had written over one hundred and fifty short stories, besides plays and a novel. His popularity in Russia was tremendous and his work has been translated into French, German and English. In England his stories which have a psychological emphasis appreciably influenced contemporary writers. The characters about whom Chekhov writes with the greatest sympathy are not strong, efficient people, but rather those sensitive ones who are capable of intense feeling.

For Appreciation: Chekhov's interest in criminals is reflected in the beginning of *The Bet* when life-imprisonment and capital punishment are under discussion. In 1890, he visited the convict colony of Sakhalin. The book which he wrote on his return brought about some reforms in the treatment of prisoners. *The Bet* is a psychological story in that the interest is carried along not by action but by the reactions of the men's minds to their situations. Read again the part of the story which tells how the lawyer spent his time during his voluntary imprisonment. What he asked for is an index of his mental state. Explain this fully. In the beginning, the lawyer's greed causes him to make the bet. Later the same desire prompts the banker to go to the sealed room. Compare the feelings of the two men toward life and toward each other at the conclusion of the story.

For Further Study: Give the meanings of the following words: *humane; zealously; ethereal; abysses; stipulated; agitation; renunciation.* The last sentence in the third paragraph of page 102 contains an excellent figure of speech. Explain what it means. Which of the two men had the finer character? On what is your opinion based? After the bet is made, the banker and the lawyer have no more conversation with each other. The story takes up first one and then the other. Could any other method have been as effective? Explain.

Exercises and Creative Work: Imagine that a passer-by saw the lawyer as he climbed over the fence. Write a few paragraphs in which the passer-by tells of his experience.

Make a list of ten books you would choose to take with you if you were going into solitary confinement for six months. Be able to give a reason for each selection.

FISH IN THE FOREST
A Russian Folk Tale

In tilling the ground a labourer found a treasure, and carrying it home, said to his wife, "See! Heaven has sent us a fortune. But where can we conceal it?"

She suggested he should bury it under the floor, which he did accordingly. Soon after this the wife went out to fetch water, and the labourer reflected that his wife was a dreadful gossip, and by tomorrow night all the village would know their secret. So he removed the treasure from its hiding-place and buried it in his barn, beneath a heap of corn. When the wife came back from the well, he said to her quite gravely, "Tomorrow we shall go to the forest to seek fish; they say there's plenty there at present."

"What! fish in the forest?" she exclaimed.

"Of course," he rejoined; "and you'll see them there."

Very early next morning he got up, and took some fish, which he had concealed in a basket. He went to the grocer's and bought a quantity of sweet cakes. He also caught a hare and killed it. The fish and cakes he disposed of in different parts of the wood, and the hare he hooked on a fishing-line, and then threw it in the river. After breakfast he took his wife with him into the wood, which they had scarcely entered when she found a pike, then a perch, and then a roach, on the ground. With many exclamations of surprise, she gathered up the fish and put them in her basket. Presently they came to a pear-tree, from the branches of which hung sweet cakes.

"See!" she cried. "Cakes on a pear-tree."

"Quite natural," replied he; "it has rained cakes, and some have remained on this tree; travellers have picked up the rest."

Continuing their way to the village, they passed a stream.

"Wait a little," said the husband; "I set my line early this morning, and I'll look if anything is caught on it."

He then pulled in the line, and behold, there was a hare hooked on to it!

"How extraordinary!" cries the wife; "a hare in the water!"

"Why," says he, "don't you know there are hares in the water as well as rats?"

"No, indeed, I knew it not."

They now returned home, and the wife set about preparing all the nice eatables for supper.

In a day or two the labourer found from the talk of his acquaintances that his finding the treasure was no secret in the village, and in less than a week he was summoned to the castle.

"Is it true," says the lord, "that you have found a treasure?"

"It is not true," was the reply.

"But your wife has told me all."

"My wife does not know what she says—she is mad, my lord."

Hereupon the woman cries, "It is the truth, my lord! He has found a treasure and buried it beneath the floor of our cottage."

"When?"

"On the eve before the day when we went into the forest to look for fish."

"What do you say?"

"Yes; it was on the day that it rained cakes; we gathered a basketful of them, and coming home, my husband fished a fine hare out of the river."

My lord declared the woman to be an idiot; nevertheless he caused his servants to search under the labourer's cottage floor, but nothing was found there, and so the shrewd fellow secured his treasure.

For Appreciation: Before people could read or write they told tales one to another, and from early times have come down to us vast numbers of traditional stories known as folk tales. They were told primarily to amuse, but in their simple directness they express the instinctive feeling of tribes and races in a kind of story-philosophy.

A great many of such folk tales are to be found in Russia. They are told in simple language but deal with dramatic incidents. In *Fish in the Forest*, there is no attempt to tell the thoughts of the man or his wife. The incidents are related in an orderly fashion and the climax of the tale comes when the wife relates the extraordinary things she and her husband found in the woods.

For Further Study: The word "study" is obviously out of place in discussing a narrative of this type. The tale is simple in structure and language, and the philosophy is evident. Yet it serves as an excellent example of an early form of that branch of literature which we know as the short story. In what ways does it differ from the modern short story in style and in theme? What can you say of the humor? Would this early tale indicate to you that the Russian has a genuine talent for the narrative?

EXTENSIVE READING PROGRAM—THE SHORT STORY

The Victorian Era (1840–1900)

Robert Louis Stevenson
Adventure of Prince Florizel and a Detective
Adventure of the Hansom Cab
A Lodging for the Night
Markheim
The Rajah's Diamond
The Sire de Maletroit's Door
Story of a Lie
Story of a Bandbox
Story of the Young Man with the Cream Tarts
Will o' the Mill

The Twentieth Century (1900–)

Thomas Hardy
Fiddler of the Reels
For Conscience' Sake
Superstitious Man's Story
Distracted Preacher
Fellow-Townsmen
Imaginative Woman
Withered Arm

Joseph Conrad
The Informer
The Brute
The Anarchist
The Duel
The Lagoon
A Smile of Fortune
The Secret Sharer
Freya of the Seven Isles

Sir James Matthew Barrie
How Gavin Birse Put It to Mag Lownie
Auld Licht Kirk
Family Honor
Fox Terrier "Frisky"
Cree Queery and Mysy Drolly

H. G. Wells
Beautiful Suit
Catastrophe
The Time Machine
Stolen Bacillus
Empire of Ants
The Flying Man

Rudyard Kipling
The City of Dreadful Night
Courting of Dinah Shadd
The Man Who Was
Mot Guj, Mutineer
The Phantom 'Rickshaw
Wee Willie Winkie
The Brushwood Boy

John Galsworthy
The Lost Dog
Demos
Old Age
The Careful Man
Fear
Fashion
Sport

W. W. Jacobs
The Lady of the Barge
The Monkey's Paw
Cupboard Love
A Change of Treatment
A Love Passage
Taking Pains
Handsome Harry

L. A. G. Strong
Storm
Quartette for Two Voices

Gilbert K. Chesterton
Secret of Father Brown
Mirror of the Magistrates
Man with Two Beards

EXTENSIVE READING PROGRAM

Sheila Kaye-Smith
  Old Gadgett
  Joanna Godden Married
  Mrs. Adis
  Fear of Streets
  The Mock Beggar
  Mr. John Arnold
Arnold Bennett
  The Baby's Bath
  Burglary
  Death of Simon Fuge
  Lion's Share
  A Letter Home
  Mary with the High Hand
  Phantom
V. Sackville-West
  Christmas Party
  Heir
  Parrot
  Patience
A. Conan Doyle
  Captain Sharkey
  How Copley Banks Slew Captain Sharkey
  Case of Lady Sannox
  Heather Funnel
Hugh Walpole
  Little Donkeys with Crimson Saddles
  No Unkindness Intended
  Chinese Horses
  Silly Old Fool
  Enemy
Frank Swinnerton
  Percy and Pansy
Sir Arthur Quiller-Couch
  Old Aeson
  Roll Call of the Reef
  Statement of Gabriel Foot, Highwayman
P. G. Wodehouse
  Heel of Achilles
  Long Hole
  Mixed Threesome
Storm Jameson
  Splendid Days

E. M. Delafield
  "And Never the Twain Shall Meet"
  Gallant Little Lady
  Hotel-Child
  Lost in Transmission
  Time Works Wonders
  Entertainment
  Incidental
  Life Is Like That
  Tortoise
Rebecca West
  Gray Men
  In a City That Is Now Ploughed Fields
  They That Sit in Darkness
Katherine Mansfield
  Prelude
  Bliss
  Pictures
  Man without a Temperature
  Daughters of the Late Colonel
  Life of Ma Parker
  Voyage
  Stranger
  Mary
  Poison
  Something Childish but Very Natural
William McFee
  Deckers on the Coast
Somerset Maugham
  In a Strange Land
  Mackentosh
  The Fall of Edward Barnard
  The Pool
  Honolulu
  Rain
  The Taipan
J. C. Squire
  Cemetery
  Best Seller
  Baxteriana
  Man Who Kept a Diary
E. Philips Oppenheim
  He Laughed at the Gods

THE SHORT STORY IN WORLD LITERATURE

French
  François Coppée
    The Piece of Bread
    The Captain's Vices
  Alphonse Daudet
    The Last Lesson
  Prosper Mérimée
    Mateo Falcone
  Honoré de Balzac
    The Mysterious Mansion
  Alexandre Dumas
    Zodomirsky's Duel
    When Pierrot Was Young
    Countess Bertha's Honey-Feast
  Guy de Maupassant
    The Piece of String
    A Coward
  Théophile Gautier
    The Mummy's Foot
Russian
  Anton Chekhov
    The Schoolmistress
    A Nervous Breakdown
    Misery
    In Exile
  Alexander Pushkin
    The Snowstorm
  Ivan Turgenev
    The District Doctor
  Leo Tolstoy
    The Long Exile
    God Sees the Truth But Waits
  Maxim Gorky
    One Autumn Night
  Leonid Andreyev
    Silence

Spanish
  Vicente Ibáñez
    Sunset
  Miguel Cervantes
    Ninconete and Cortadillo
Hungarian
  Ferenc Molnar
    The Silver Hilt
Yiddish
  David Pinski
    In the Storm
German
  Thomas Mann
    Loulou
  E. T. W. Hoffmann
    A Cremona Violin
Italian
  Grazia Deledda
    Two Men and a Woman
    Two Miracles
  Gabriele d'Annunzio
    Fire
Norwegian
  Björnstjerne Björnson
    The Father
  Johan Bojer
    Skobelef
Swedish
  Selma Lagerlöf
    The Girl from the Marsh Croft
    The Silver Mine
    A Christmas Guest
  H. A. Larsen
    Sweden's Best Stories
Hindustani
  Rabindranath Tagore
    On the Calcutta Road

BIOGRAPHY

THE HISTORY OF BIOGRAPHY IN ENGLAND

ANGLO-SAXON AND MIDDLE ENGLISH PERIODS (BEGINNINGS TO 1550)

General Characteristics

"Society is founded on hero-worship," says Carlyle, and Emerson declares that "there is properly no history, only biography." While the case for biography is somewhat overstated by these two great men, the study of biography has, or should have, a most important place in any scheme of education.

Biography, the story of human life, makes an instant appeal to all of us. We like to learn how great men and women—who are, after all, mere human beings like ourselves—lived and moved, and had their being. We enjoy reading about the intimate details of their daily lives. Their struggles give us courage, their achievements fascinate us, their predicaments make us laugh.

Biography as we know it did not exist in the early days of English literature. The bard chanted songs of daring deeds of the hero in the chase or in war to his fellow tribesmen gathered round the glowing camp fire, and the story of tribal life from age to age lived through its heroic figures. These songs and tales were not recorded, however, and the lives of the early heroes have come down to us only through legend, song, and folklore. It was not until after 1500 that biography in England really begins.

THE AGE OF ELIZABETH (1550–1625)

Biography Makes Its First Appearance

In the impetus which the reign of Elizabeth gave to all literature, we find not only great drama and great poetry, but also the beginnings of prose writing, including biography. The two biographies of the period which are deserving of mention as the ones with which literature in this form may be said to have begun, are William Roper's life of his father-in-law, Sir Thomas More, and George Cavendish's memoir of Cardinal Wolsey. A proposal to write the lives of the poets of the period was unfortunately never carried out, although at this time a need was being felt for preserving records of illustrious authors of the day.

The Puritan Age and the Restoration (1625–1700)

Biography Continues Its Development

The writing of biography which began in the Elizabethan Age was to continue in the Puritan and Restoration Periods. Izaak Walton, better known for his *Compleat Angler,* was also a writer of biography. In fact, his five lives of John Donne, Sir Henry Wotton, Richard Hooker, George Herbert, and Dr. Robert Saunderson, which were later collected under the title of *Walton's Lives,* were the forerunners of a large number of biographies. Here, as in the *Compleat Angler,* Walton's style is simple and charming, and his *Lives* met with great public favor.

Two other biographies of the period are worthy of notice—*Minutes of Lives* by John Aubrey and *Life of Cowley* by Thomas Sprat. The latter was much admired in its day but it was to have a baneful influence on English biography for many years to come. Sprat's idea of a biography was something that should teach a lesson. His emphasis was on conduct and he omitted all picturesque detail and familiar anecdote. The result was a biography that was artificial, solemn, and stilted.

Classicism and the Age of Johnson (1700–1780)

Biography Reaches Its Greatest Heights

The moralizing biography started by Sprat in the Restoration Period was to continue well into the eighteenth century. This type was further encouraged by the tendencies of the day in all literature. Just as poetry and the essay followed the classic mold, so also did biography continue to be a highly artificial and rhetorical thing.

By 1750, however, a change was to be noted in the general style of biographical writing. Theophilus Cibber in his *Lives of the Poets* gave interesting anecdotes with regard to the personal adventures of his subjects, and Mason in his *Life and Letters of Gray* for the first time made use of letters to intimate friends as means of illustrating the real character of the writer.

Boswell's Life of Dr. Samuel Johnson

Excellent as were these newer forms, they fade into insignificance when compared with the biography for which this age will always be remembered—James Boswell's *Life of Dr. Samuel Johnson.* In this biography, Boswell combined with his intimate knowledge of his subject the use of incidents and conversations which up to this time would have been disregarded as insignificant trifles. The result was the most interesting example of biography existing in English, or perhaps in any language. The book is indeed more than a biography—it is "a transcript of life—of men, women, conversation, character, manners, and wisdom, such as no novel ever assembled."

The Age of Romanticism (1780-1840)
Biography Is Patterned after Boswell's Johnson

Biographies in this period—in fact, in all periods succeeding the age of Johnson—were more or less founded on Boswell's work. While the Age of Romanticism was mainly one of poetry, there were, nevertheless, a few important biographies. Robert Southey, better known as a poet, produced a number of prose works among which were his excellent lives of Nelson and of John Wolsey. Another biography of the period which was to become a classic was John Lockhart's *Life of Sir Walter Scott*. This has been called, after Boswell's *Johnson*, the most admirable biography in the English language.

The Victorian Era (1840-1900)
The Critical Biography

Although the Victorian Era was one of prose, there were very few outstanding biographies. Perhaps the most noteworthy ones were Carlyle's lives of Cromwell and Frederick the Great. This period did, however, see the rise of the critical appreciation, or literary biography. This form is both essay and biography and is sometimes called biographical essay and sometimes critical biography. Macaulay's *Samuel Johnson* is an excellent example of this type of writing. This was written for the eighth edition of the *Encyclopedia Britannica*, published in 1856. What Boswell did at length in his famous biography, Macaulay did in miniature in his essay. Other notable critical biographies were Ruskin's *Modern Painters*, Carlyle's *Essay on Burns*, and Thackeray's *English Humorists*, a selection from the last named of which appears in this book.

The Twentieth Century (1900-   )
The New Biography

It remained for the twentieth century to produce the *new* biography, the type of literature which has seen such rapid growth in popularity within the past two decades. The kind of biography which is a mere chronicle of the events in a man's life is out of date. It has been supplanted by a method which is largely interpretative—Gamaliel Bradford calls it "psychography." It presents struggles in the mental and moral life of the subject—struggles with which we are all familiar. Pursuit of ideas until their final fruition in deeds fascinates us. The evolution of thought into deeds interests us. The new biography is vivid, colorful, dramatic, and fascinating to both young and old. The leaders in this new movement which is world wide are Lytton Strachey in England, Emil Ludwig in Germany, André Maurois in France, and Gamaliel Bradford in America. Strachey and Maurois are represented in this volume.

A Biography of the Classic Age

JOHNSON AS A CONVERSATIONALIST

From *The Life of Dr. Samuel Johnson*

JAMES BOSWELL

By Way of Introduction: Samuel Johnson, literary dictator of the London of the eighteenth century, was more noted for his conversational ability than for his writings. He had a dominating and at the same time a winning personality and was virtually ruler of all things literary in England for many years. He was, indeed, czar of the Literary Club which he and Sir Joshua Reynolds founded in 1764. Johnson was the author of the first English *Dictionary*, the *Lives of the Poets, Rasselas,* and many other works, but his lasting fame is based on his talk as recorded in Boswell's *Johnson.* According to Thomas Macaulay, "The influence exercised by his [Johnson's] conversation, directly upon those with whom he lived, and indirectly on the whole literary world, was altogether without a parallel." Kind-hearted, erratic, brilliant, with a prodigious command of language, Johnson was the perfect subject for the greatest of all English biographies.

THE LITERARY CLUB

IN February [1764] was founded that Club which existed long without a name, but at Mr. Garrick's[1] funeral became distinguished by the title of "The Literary Club." Sir Joshua

---

[1] MR. GARRICK—David Garrick, famous actor and theatrical manager. Although not one of the original members of the Club, he was made a member shortly after its organization.

Reynolds had the merit of being the first proposer of it, to which Johnson acceded; and the original members were Sir Joshua Reynolds, Dr. Johnson, Mr. Edmund Burke, Dr. Nugent, Mr. Beauclerk, Mr. Langton, Dr. Goldsmith, Mr. Chamier, and Sir John Hawkins.[2] They met at the Turk's Head, in Gerrard Street, Soho,[3] one evening in every week, at seven, and generally continued their conversation till a pretty late hour. This club has been gradually increased to its present number, thirty-five. After about ten years, instead of supping weekly, it was resolved to dine together once a fortnight during the meeting of Parliament.

Not very long after the institution of [the] club Sir Joshua Reynolds was speaking of it to Garrick. "I like it much," said he; "I think I shall be of you." When Sir Joshua mentioned this to Dr. Johnson, he was much displeased. *"He'll be of us,"* said Johnson; "how does he know we will *permit* him? The first Duke in England has no right to hold such language." However, when Garrick was regularly proposed some time afterwards, Johnson warmly and kindly supported him, and he was accordingly elected, was a most agreeable member, and continued to attend our meetings to the time of his death.

[2] SIR JOSHUA REYNOLDS . . . SIR JOHN HAWKINS—In addition to the name of Dr. Johnson himself, the most familiar names are those of Sir Joshua Reynolds, famous portrait painter; Mr. Edmund Burke, famous orator who is remembered for his *Speech on Conciliation with America;* and Dr. Goldsmith, author of *The Deserted Village* and *The Vicar of Wakefield*.

[3] SOHO—A section of London.

JOHNSON'S REGARD FOR CONVERSATION

ANOTHER evening Dr. Goldsmith and I called on him [Johnson] with the hope of prevailing on him to sup with us at the Mitre.[1]

We found him indisposed and resolved not to go abroad. "Come, then," said Goldsmith, "we will not go to the Mitre tonight, since we cannot have the big man [2] with us." Johnson then called for a bottle of port, of which Goldsmith and I partook, while our friend, now a water drinker, sat by us. GOLDSMITH. "I think, Mr. Johnson, you don't go near the theaters now. You give yourself no more concern about a new play than if

[1] THE MITRE—A popular tavern of the day.
[2] BIG MAN—Johnson was an extremely large man.

you had never had anything to do with the stage." JOHNSON. "Why, sir, our tastes greatly alter. The lad does not care for the child's rattle. As we advance in the journey of life, we drop some of the things which have pleased us; whether it be that we are fatigued and don't choose to carry so many things any farther, or that we find other things which we like better." BOSWELL. "But, sir, why don't you give us something in some other way?" GOLDSMITH. "Aye, sir, we have a claim upon you." JOHNSON. "No, sir, I am not obliged to do any more. No man is obliged to do as much as he can do. A man is to have part of his life to himself. If a soldier has fought a good many campaigns, he is not to be blamed if he retires to ease and tranquillity. A physician who has practiced long in a great city may be excused if he retires to a small town, and takes less practice. Now, sir, the good I can do by my conversation bears the same proportion to the good I can do by my writings that the practice of a physician, retired to a small town, does to his practice in a great city." BOSWELL. "But I wonder, sir, you have not more pleasure in writing than in not writing." JOHNSON. "Sir, you *may* wonder."

JOHNSON CONVERSES WITH HIS FRIENDS

ON Friday, May 7, I breakfasted with him [Johnson] at Mr. Thrale's[1] in the Borough.[2] I dined with him this day at the house of my friends, Messieurs Edward and Charles Dilly, booksellers in the Poultry.[3]

BOSWELL. "I am well assured that the people of Otaheite[4] who have the bread tree, the fruit of which serves them for bread, laughed heartily when they were informed of the tedious process necessary with us to have bread—plowing, sowing, harrowing, reaping, threshing, grinding, baking." JOHNSON. "Why, sir, all ignorant savages will laugh when they are told of the advantages of civilized life. Were you to tell men who live without houses, how we pile brick upon brick, and rafter upon rafter, and that after a house is raised to a certain height, a man

---

[1] MR. THRALE—Henry Thrale, at whose home Johnson spent a great deal of time.
[2] BOROUGH—A section of London.
[3] POULTRY—A section of London.
[4] OTAHEITE—Tahiti, an island in the southern Pacific.

tumbles off a scaffold, and breaks his neck, he would laugh heartily at our folly in building; but it does not follow that men are better without houses. No, sir (holding up a slice of a good loaf), this is better than the bread tree."

He repeated an argument, which is to be found in his *Rambler*,[5] against the notion that the brute creation is endowed with the faculty of reason: "Birds build by instinct; they never improve; they build their first nest as well as any one they ever build." GOLDSMITH. "Yet we see if you take away a bird's nest with the eggs in it, she will make a slighter nest and lay again." JOHNSON. "Sir, that is because at first she has full time and makes her nest deliberately. In the case you mention she is pressed to lay, and must therefore make her nest quickly, and consequently it will be slight."

I introduced the subject of toleration. JOHNSON. "Every society has a right to preserve public peace and order, and therefore has a good right to prohibit the propagation of opinions which have a dangerous tendency." MAYO.[6] "I am of opinion, sir, that every man is entitled to liberty of conscience in religion; and that the magistrate cannot restrain that right." JOHNSON. "Sir, I agree with you. Every man has a right to liberty of conscience, and with that the magistrate cannot interfere. People confound liberty of thinking with liberty of talking; nay, with liberty of preaching. Every man has a physical right to think as he pleases; for it cannot be discovered how he thinks. He has not a moral right, for he ought to inform himself, and think justly. But, sir, no member of a society has a right to *teach* any doctrine contrary to what the society holds to be true. The magistrate may be wrong in what he thinks; but while he thinks himself right, he may and ought to enforce what he thinks." MAYO. "Then, sir, we are to remain always in error, and truth never can prevail; and the magistrate was right in persecuting the first Christians." JOHNSON. "I am afraid there is no other way of ascertaining the truth but by persecution on the one hand and enduring it on the other." GOLDSMITH. "But how is a man to act, sir? Though firmly convinced of the truth of his doctrine, may he not think it wrong to expose himself to persecution? Has he a right to do so? Is it not, as it were, commit-

---

[5] *Rambler*—A series of short essays on morals, manners, and literature.
[6] MAYO—The Reverend Doctor Mayo, a member of the Club.

ting voluntary suicide?" JOHNSON. "Sir, as to voluntary suicide, as you call it, there are twenty thousand men in an army who will go without scruple to be shot at, and mount a breach for five pence a day."

[This conversation lasted a long time.]

During this argument, Goldsmith sat in restless agitation, from a wish to get in and *shine*. Finding himself excluded, he had taken his hat to go away, but remained for some time with it in his hand, like a gamester, who, at the close of a long night, lingers for a little while to see if he can have a favorable opening to finish with success. Once when he was beginning to speak, he found himself overpowered by the loud voice of Johnson, who was at the opposite end of the table and did not perceive Goldsmith's attempt. Thus disappointed of his wish to obtain the attention of the company, Goldsmith in a passion threw down his hat, looking angrily at Johnson, and exclaimed in a bitter tone, *"Take it."* When Toplady [7] was going to speak, Johnson uttered some sound which led Goldsmith to think that he was beginning again and taking the words from Toplady. Upon which, he seized this opportunity of venting his own envy and spleen, under the pretext of supporting another person: "Sir," said he to Johnson, "the gentleman has heard you patiently for an hour; pray allow us now to hear him." JOHNSON (sternly). "Sir, I was not interrupting the gentleman. I was only giving him a signal of my attention. Sir, you are impertinent." Goldsmith made no reply, but continued in the company for some time.

[7] TOPLADY—The Reverend Doctor Toplady, a member of the Club.

JOHNSON AND GOLDSMITH

HE [Johnson] and Mr. Langton and I went together to the Club, where we found Mr. Burke, Mr. Garrick, and some other members, and amongst them our friend Goldsmith, who sat silently brooding over Johnson's reprimand to him after dinner. Johnson perceived this, and said aside to some of us, "I'll make Goldsmith forgive me"; and then called to him in a loud voice, "Dr. Goldsmith—something passed today where you and I dined; I ask your pardon." Goldsmith answered placidly, "It must be much from you, sir, that I take ill." And so at once the difference was over, and they were on as easy terms as ever, and Goldsmith rattled away as usual.

Goldsmith's incessant desire of being conspicuous in company was the occasion of his sometimes appearing to such disadvantage as one should hardly have supposed possible in a man of his genius. One evening, in a circle of wits, he found fault with me for talking of Johnson as entitled to the honor of unquestionable superiority. "Sir," said he, "you are for making a monarchy of what should be a republic." He was still more mortified when, talking in a company with fluent vivacity, a German who sat next to him and perceived Johnson rolling himself as if about to speak, suddenly stopped him, saying, "Stay, stay—Toctor Shonson is going to say something." This was, no doubt, very provoking, especially to one so irritable as Goldsmith, who frequently mentioned it with strong expressions of indignation.

It may also be observed that Goldsmith was sometimes content to be treated with an easy familiarity, but, upon occasions, would be consequential and important. An instance of this occurred in a small particular. Johnson had a way of contracting the names of his friends; as Beauclerk, Beau; Boswell, Bozzy; Langton, Lanky; Murphy,[1] Mur; Sheridan,[2] Sherry. I remember one day, when Tom Davies[3] was telling what Dr. Johnson said, "We are all in labor for a name to Goldy's play," Goldsmith seemed displeased that such a liberty should be taken with his name, and said, "I have often desired him not to call me 'Goldy.'" Tom was remarkably attentive to the most minute circumstance about Johnson. I recollect his telling me once, on my arrival in London, "Sir, our great friend has made an improvement on his appellation of old Mr. Sheridan. He calls him now 'Sherry derry.'"

---

[1] MURPHY—An editor and critic.
[2] SHERIDAN—Richard Brinsley Sheridan, famous playwright of the day, remembered for *The Rivals* and *The School for Scandal*.
[3] TOM DAVIES—Thomas Davies, an actor and bookseller.

The Biographer—James Boswell (1740-1795): James Boswell, a Scotch lawyer, came to London at the age of nineteen. In 1762 he met Johnson, who was thirty years his senior, in a little bookshop and there began a lifelong friendship. He had always sought out celebrities—he had the modern reporter's point of view—but after he met Johnson, his interest narrowed to this one supreme personality and he devoted the rest of his life to him. Boswell, indeed, became one of Johnson's favorites. For twenty years he devoted himself to Johnson, taking down meticulously every word that fell from his lips. He once said to Johnson, "I plan to write your life." To this Johnson replied, "If I thought you were telling the truth, I should take yours." Nevertheless, Boswell *did* write Johnson's life and thus made immortal the man whose literary works would never have brought him such fame. For Boswell created a new kind of biography, an intimate, day-by-day recital of the hero's life. Since then, many biographies of the same character have been written but none has equalled Boswell's life of the learned doctor.

Suggestions for Study: What are Johnson's leading traits as shown in the selections from Boswell? Give instances of leadership, of service, of human sympathy as revealed in these selections. In your opinion, is Johnson one of the great men who, on becoming great, "grows out of proportion to himself"? Prove your statement with definite references. What is Boswell's estimate of Goldsmith? Give illustrations to uphold your statements.

Exercises and Creative Work: Give an account of the founding of the famous Literary Club, its object, its membership, its meetings.

Prepare a collective biography of short lives of each of the original members of the Literary Club.

Dramatize an imaginary meeting of the Club. Select a topic on which the various members are to express themselves, taking care to make Johnson the dominating personality.

Discuss the following quotations from Johnson.

"Before dinner men meet with great inequality of understanding; and those who are conscious of their inferiority, have the modesty not to talk. But when they have drunk wine, every man feels himself happy, and loses that modesty, and grows impudent and vociferous; but he is not improved; he is only not sensible of his defects."

"A man of sense and education should meet a suitable companion in a wife. It is a miserable thing when the conversation can only be such as, whether the mutton should be boiled or roasted, and probably a dispute about that."

"What we read with inclination makes a much stronger impression. If we read without inclination half the mind is employed in fixing the attention; so there is but one half to be employed on what we read."

"If a man does not make new acquaintance as he advances through life, he will soon find himself left alone. A man, Sir, should keep his friendship in constant repair."

"If a man begins to read in the middle of a book and feels an inclination to go on, let him not quit it to go to the beginning. He may perhaps not feel again the inclination."

For Further Reading: It is recommended that as much as possible be read in Boswell's *Johnson*. The following topics are recommended: *The Dictionary; Lord Chesterfield's Patronage and Later Neglect.*

A Biography of the Victorian Era

OLIVER GOLDSMITH

From *The English Humorists of the Eighteenth Century*

WILLIAM MAKEPEACE THACKERAY

By Way of Introduction: In 1851 Thackeray wrote *The English Humorists of the Eighteenth Century* which had been delivered as a series of lectures in the same year. In 1852 and 1853 he re-delivered these lectures in the United States. In the introductory remarks to the first lecture he said: "In treating of the English humorists of the past age, it is of the men and of their lives, rather than of their books, that I ask permission to speak to you; and in doing so, you are aware that I cannot hope to entertain you with a merely humorous or facetious story.... But the men regarding whose lives and stories your kind presence here shows that you have curiosity and sympathy, appeal to a great number of other faculties, besides our mere sense of ridicule. The humorous writer professes to awaken and direct your love, your pity, your kindness—your scorn for untruth, pretension, imposture—your tenderness for the weak, the poor, the oppressed, the unhappy. To the best of his means and ability he comments on all the ordinary actions and passions of life almost. He takes upon himself to be the week-day preacher, so to speak. Accordingly, as he finds, and speaks, and feels the truth best, we regard him, esteem him—sometimes love him. And as his business is to mark other people's lives and peculiarities, we moralize upon *his* life when he is gone—and yesterday's preacher becomes the text for today's sermon." The first lecture of the series was on Jonathan Swift. The last lecture was on Oliver Goldsmith.

BIOGRAPHY

Who, of the millions whom he [Goldsmith] has amused, doesn't love him? To be the most beloved of English writers, what a title that is for a man! A wild youth, wayward, but full of tenderness and affection, quits the country village where his boyhood has been passed in happy musing, in idle shelter, in fond longing to see the great world out-of-doors, and achieve name and fortune; and after years of dire struggle, and neglect and poverty, his heart turning back as fondly to his native place as it has longed eagerly for change when sheltered there, he writes a book and a poem, full of the recollections and feelings of home: he paints the friends and scenes of his youth, and peoples Auburn[1] and Wakefield with remembrances of Lissoy.[2] Wander he must, but he carried away a home-relic with him, and dies with it on his breast. His nature is truant; in repose it longs for change: as on the journey it looks back for friends and quiet. He passes today in building an air-castle for tomorrow, or in writing yesterday's elegy; and he would fly away this hour, but that a cage and necessity keep him. What is the charm of his verse, of his style, and humor? His sweet regrets, his delicate compassion, his soft smile, his tremulous sympathy, the weakness which he owns? Your love for him is half pity. You come hot and tired from the day's battle, and this sweet minstrel sings to you. Who could harm the kind vagrant harper? Whom did he ever hurt? He carries no weapon, save the harp on which he plays to you; and with which he delights great and humble, young and old, the captains in the tents, or the soldiers round the fire, or the women and children in the villages, at whose porches he stops and sings his simple songs of love and beauty. With that sweet story of the *"Vicar of Wakefield"*[3] he has found entry into every castle and every hamlet in Europe. Not one of us, however busy or hard, but once or twice in our lives has passed an evening with him, and undergone the charm of his delightful music.

Goldsmith's father was no doubt the good Doctor Primrose,[4]

---

[1] Auburn—The "sweet Auburn" of Goldsmith's *Deserted Village*.
[2] Lissoy—Goldsmith's boyhood home in Ireland.
[3] *Vicar of Wakefield*—Goldsmith's famous novel by that name.
[4] Doctor Primrose—The Reverend Charles Primrose, vicar of Wakefield, in Goldsmith's novel. He was a clergyman rich in heavenly wisdom, but poor indeed in all worldly knowledge.

whom we all of us know. Swift[5] was yet alive, when the little Oliver was born at Pallas, or Pallasmore, in the county of Longford, in Ireland. In 1730, two years after the child's birth, Charles Goldsmith removed his family to Lissoy, in the county Westmeath, that sweet "Auburn" which every person who hears me has seen in fancy. Here the kind parson brought up his eight children; and loving all the world, as his son says, fancied all the world loved him. He had a crowd of poor dependents besides those hungry children. He kept an open table; round which sat flatterers and poor friends, who laughed at the honest rector's many jokes, and ate the produce of his seventy acres of farm. Those who have seen an Irish house in the present day can fancy that one of Lissoy. The old beggar still has his allotted corner by the kitchen turf; the maimed old soldier still gets his potatoes and buttermilk; the poor cottier still asks his honor's charity, and prays God bless his reverence for the sixpence: the ragged pensioner still takes his place by right and sufferance. There's still a crowd in the kitchen, and a crowd round the parlor-table, profusion, confusion, kindness, poverty. If an Irishman comes to London to make his fortune, he has a half-dozen of Irish dependents who take a percentage of his earnings. The good Charles Goldsmith left but little provision for his hungry race when death summoned him: and one of his daughters being engaged to a Squire of rather superior dignity, Charles Goldsmith impoverished the rest of his family to provide the girl with a dowry.

The smallpox, which scourged all Europe at that time, and ravaged the roses off the cheeks of half the world, fell foul of poor little Oliver's face, when the child was eight years old, and left him scarred and disfigured for his life. An old woman in his father's village taught him his letters, and pronounced him a dunce: Paddy Byrne, the hedge-schoolmaster, took him in hand; and from Paddy Byrne, he was transmitted to a clergyman at Elphin. When a child was sent to school in those days, the classic phrase was that he was placed under Mr. So-and-So's *ferule*. Poor little ancestors! It is hard to think how ruthlessly you were birched; and how much of needless whipping and tears our small forefathers had to undergo! A relative—

---

[5] SWIFT—Jonathan Swift, the subject of Thackeray's first lecture on the English humorists.

kind uncle Contarine, took the main charge of little Noll,[6] who went through his school-days righteously doing as little work as he could: robbing orchards, playing at ball, and making his pocket-money fly about whenever fortune sent it to him. Everybody knows the story of that famous "Mistake of a Night,"[7] when the young schoolboy, provided with a guinea and a nag, rode up to the "best house" in Ardagh, called for the landlord's company over a bottle of wine at supper, and for a hot cake for breakfast in the morning; and found, when he asked for the bill, that the best house was Squire Featherstone's, and not the inn for which he mistook it. Who does not know every story about Goldsmith? That is a delightful and fantastic picture of the child dancing and capering about in the kitchen at home, when the old fiddler gibed at him for his ugliness, and called him Æsop;[8] and little Noll made his repartee of "Heralds proclaim aloud this saying—See Æsop dancing and his monkey playing." One can fancy a queer pitiful look of humor and appeal upon that little scarred face—the funny little dancing figure, the funny little brogue. In his life, and his writings, which are the honest expression of it, he is constantly bewailing that homely face and person; anon, he surveys them in the glass ruefully; and presently assumes the most comical dignity. He likes to deck out his little person in splendor and fine colors. He presented himself to be examined for ordination in a pair of scarlet breeches, and said honestly that he did not like to go into the church, because he was fond of colored clothes. When he tried to practise as a doctor, he got by hook or by crook a black velvet suit, and looked as big and grand as he could, and kept his hat over a patch on the old coat; in better days he bloomed out in plum-color, in blue silk, and in new velvet. For some of those splendors the heirs and assignees of Mr. Filby, the tailor, have never been paid to this day: perhaps the kind tailor and his creditor have met and settled the little account in Hades.

[6] LITTLE NOLL—Goldsmith's nickname as a child was "Nolly." An impromptu epitaph on Goldsmith written by David Garrick reads as follows:
"Here lies Nolly Goldsmith, for shortness called Noll,
Who wrote like an angel, and talk'd like poor Poll."
[7] MISTAKE OF A NIGHT—Goldsmith's play, *She Stoops to Conquer, or The Mistakes of a Night* probably drew its theme from this incident.
[8] ÆSOP—A Greek slave in the sixth century, B.C., who wrote a large number of fables. According to tradition, he was ugly and deformed.

They showed until lately a window at Trinity College, Dublin, on which the name of O. Goldsmith was engraved with a diamond. Whose diamond was it? Not the young sizar's,[9] who made but a poor figure in that place of learning. He was idle, penniless, and fond of pleasure: he learned his way early to the pawnbroker's shop. He wrote ballads, they say, for the street-singers, who paid him a crown for a poem: and his pleasure was to steal out at night and hear his verses sung. He was chastised by his tutor for giving a dance in his rooms, and took the box on the ear so much to heart, that he packed up his all, pawned his books and little property, and disappeared from college and family. He said he intended to go to America, but when his money was spent, the young prodigal came home ruefully, and the good folks there killed their calf—it was but a lean one—and welcomed him back.

After college, he hung about his mother's house, and lived for some years the life of a buckeen[10]—passed a month with this relation and that, a year with one patron, a great deal of time at the public-house. Tired of this life, it was resolved that he should go to London, and study at the Temple;[11] but he got no farther on the road to London and the woolsack[12] than Dublin, where he gambled away the fifty pounds given to him for his outfit, and whence he returned to the indefatigable forgiveness of home. Then he determined to be a doctor, and uncle Contarine helped him to a couple of years at Edinburgh. Then from Edinburgh he felt that he ought to hear the famous professors of Leyden and Paris, and wrote most amusing pompous letters to his uncle about the great Farheim, Du Petit, and Duhamel du Monceau,[13] whose lectures he proposed to follow. If uncle Contarine believed those letters—if Oliver's mother believed that story which the youth related of his going to Cork, with the purpose of embarking for America, of his having paid his passage-money, and having sent his kit on board; of the anonymous cap-

---

[9] SIZAR—A student at Trinity College, Dublin, allowed free commons (board) for performing menial services.

[10] BUCKEEN—A shabby, genteel idler; in Ireland, the younger son of the lower gentry.

[11] TEMPLE—The buildings originally built for the Knights Templars, and later occupied by law students.

[12] WOOLSACK—The seat of the Lord Chancellor in the House of Lords.

[13] FARHEIM, DU PETIT, AND DUHAMEL DU MONCEAU—The first named, a famous Dutch scientist, the last two, noted French chemists.

tain sailing away with Oliver's valuable luggage, in a nameless ship, never to return; if uncle Contarine and the mother at Ballymahon believed his stories, they must have been a very simple pair; as it was a very simple rogue indeed who cheated them. When the lad, after failing in his clerical examination, after failing in his plan for studying the law, took leave of these projects and of his parents, and set out for Edinburgh, he saw mother, and uncle, and lazy Ballymahon, and green native turf, and sparkling river for the last time. He was never to look on old Ireland more, and only in fancy revisit her.[14]

I spoke in a former lecture of that high courage which enabled Fielding,[15] in spite of disease, remorse, and poverty, always to retain a cheerful spirit and to keep his manly benevolence and love of truth intact, as if these treasures had been confided to him for the public benefit, and he was accountable to posterity for their honorable employ; and a constancy equally happy and admirable I think was shown by Goldsmith, whose sweet and friendly nature bloomed kindly always in the midst of life's storm, and rain, and bitter weather. The poor fellow was never so friendless but he could befriend some one; never so pinched and wretched but he could give of his crust, and speak his word of compassion. If he had but his flute[16] left, he could give that, and make the children happy in the dreary London court. He could give the coals in that queer coal-scuttle we read of to his poor neighbor: he could give away his blankets in college to the poor widow, and warm himself as he best might in the feathers: he could pawn his coat to save his landlord from gaol: when he was a school-usher he spent his earnings in treats for the boys, and the good-natured schoolmaster's wife said justly that she ought to keep Mr. Goldsmith's money as well as the young gentlemen's. When he met his pupils in later life, nothing would satisfy the Doctor but he must treat them still. "Have you seen the print of me after Sir Joshua Reynolds?"[17] he asked one of his old pupils. "Not seen it? not bought it? Sure, Jack, if your picture had been published, I'd not have been without it half an hour." His purse and his heart were everybody's, and

[14] IN FANCY REVISIT HER—In *The Deserted Village,* Goldsmith in fancy revisits Ireland and the scenes of his youth.

[15] FIELDING—Henry Fielding, an eighteenth century novelist.

[16] FLUTE—Goldsmith was very musical, and his flute was an inseparable companion.

[17] SIR JOSHUA REYNOLDS—A famous portrait painter of the day.

his friends' as much as his own. When he was at the height of his reputation, and the Earl of Northumberland, going as Lord Lieutenant to Ireland, asked if he could be of any service to Dr. Goldsmith, Goldsmith recommended his brother, and not himself, to the great man. "My patrons,"[18] he gallantly said, "are the booksellers, and I want no others." Hard patrons they were, and hard work he did; but he did not complain much: if in his early writings some bitter words escaped him, some allusions to neglect and poverty, he withdrew these expressions when his works were republished, and better days seemed to open for him; and he did not care to complain that printer or publisher had overlooked his merit, or left him poor. The Court face was turned from honest Oliver, the Court patronized Beattie;[19] the fashion did not shine on him—fashion adored Sterne.[20] Fashion pronounced Kelly[21] to be the great writer of comedy of his day. A little—not ill-humor, but plaintiveness— a little betrayal of wounded pride which he showed render him not the less amiable. The author of the *Vicar of Wakefield* had a right to protest when Newbery[22] kept back the MS. for two years; had a right to be a little peevish with Sterne; a little angry when Colman's[23] actors declined their parts in his delightful comedy, when the manager refused to have a scene painted for it, and pronounced its damnation before hearing. He had not the great public with him; but he had the noble Johnson, and the admirable Reynolds, and the great Gibbon, and the great Burke, and the great Fox[24]—friends and admirers illustrious indeed, as famous as those who fifty years before, sat round Pope's[25] table.

[18] PATRONS—Formerly, a patron was one to whom, in return usually for gifts of money or other favors, an author would dedicate a book.
[19] BEATTIE—A Scottish poet of the eighteenth century.
[20] STERNE—Laurence Sterne, a popular author of Goldsmith's time.
[21] KELLY—Hugh Kelly, an Irish dramatist and poet. His first comedy, *False Delicacy*, was produced in 1768 and had a great vogue in London.
[22] NEWBERY—John Newbery, a bookseller and publisher.
[23] COLMAN—George Colman, a dramatist and producing manager.
[24] JOHNSON, REYNOLDS, GIBBON, BURKE, FOX—Samuel Johnson, Sir Joshua Reynolds, Edward Gibbon, Edmund Burke, and Charles James Fox, leaders in the literary and art world of London of the eighteenth century. Gibbon wrote *The Decline and Fall of the Roman Empire* which made him famous for all time; Burke delivered his great speech, *On Conciliation with America;* Fox was leader of the liberals in Parliament for many years. They were all members of the famous Literary Club.
[25] POPE—Alexander Pope, famous poet of the early part of the century.

Nobody knows, and I dare say Goldsmith's buoyant temper kept no account of all the pains which he endured during the early period of his literary career. Should any man of letters in our day have to bear up against such, heaven grant he may come out of the period of misfortune with such a pure, kind heart as that which Goldsmith obstinately bore in his breast. The insults to which he had to submit are shocking to read of—slander, contumely, vulgar satire, brutal malignity perverting his commonest motives and actions; he had his share of these, and one's anger is roused at reading of them, as it is at seeing a woman insulted or a child assaulted, at the notion that a creature so very gentle and weak, and full of love, should have had to suffer so. And he had worse than insult to undergo—to own to fault and deprecate the anger of ruffians. There is a letter of his extant to one Griffiths, a bookseller, in which poor Goldsmith is forced to confess that certain books sent by Griffiths are in the hands of a friend from whom Goldsmith had been forced to borrow money. "He was wild, sir," Johnson said, speaking of Goldsmith to Boswell, with his great, wise benevolence and noble mercifulness of heart—"Dr. Goldsmith was wild, sir; but he is so no more." Ah! if we pity the good and weak man who suffers undeservedly, let us deal very gently with him from whom misery extorts not only tears, but shame; let us think humbly and charitably of the human nature that suffers so sadly and falls so low. Whose turn may it be tomorrow? What weak heart, confident before trial, may not succumb under temptation invincible? Cover the good man who has been vanquished—cover his face and pass on.

For the last half-dozen years of his life Goldsmith was far removed from the pressure of any ignoble necessity: and in the receipt, indeed, of a pretty large income from the booksellers, his patrons. Had he lived but a few years more, his public fame would have been as great as his private reputation, and he might have enjoyed alive a part of that esteem which his country has ever since paid to the vivid and versatile genius who has touched on almost every subject of literature, and touched nothing that he did not adorn. Except in rare instances, a man is known in our profession, and esteemed as a skilful workman, years before the lucky hit which trebles his usual gains, and stamps him a popular author. In the strength of his age, and the dawn of his reputation, having for backers and friends the most illustrious literary men of his time, fame and prosperity might have been in store for Goldsmith, had fate so willed it; and, at forty-six, had not sudden disease carried him off. I say prosperity rather than competence, for it is probable that no sum could have put order into his affairs or sufficed for his irreclaimable habits of dissipation. It must be remembered that he owed £2,000 when he died. "Was ever poet," Johnson asked, "so trusted before?" As has been the case with many another good fellow of his nation, his life was tracked and his substance wasted by crowds of hungry beggars and lazy dependents. If they came at a lucky time (and be sure they knew his affairs better than he did himself, and watched his pay-day), he gave them of his money: if they begged on empty-purse days he gave them his promissory bills: or he treated them to a tavern where he had credit; or he obliged them with an order upon honest Mr. Filby for coats, for which he paid as long as he could earn, and until the shears of Filby were to cut for him no more. Staggering under a load of debt and labor, tracked by bailiffs and reproachful creditors, running from a hundred poor dependents, whose appealing looks were perhaps the hardest of all pains for him to bear, devising fevered plans for the morrow, new histories, new comedies, all sorts of new literary schemes, flying from all these into seclusion, and out of seclusion into pleasure —at last, at five-and-forty, death seized him and closed his career. I have been many a time in the chambers in the Temple which were his, and passed up the staircase, which Johnson, and Burke,[26] and Reynolds trod to see their friend, their poet, their kind Goldsmith—the stair on which the poor women sat weeping bitterly when they heard that the greatest and most generous of all men was dead within the black oak door. Ah, it was a different lot from that for which the poor fellow sighed, when he wrote with heart yearning for home those most charming of all fond verses, in which he fancies he revisits Auburn—

> Here, as I take my solitary rounds,
> Amidst thy tangling walks and ruined grounds,
> And, many a year elapsed, return to view
> Where once the cottage stood, the hawthorn grew,

[26] JOHNSON AND BURKE—Dr. Samuel Johnson and Mr. Edmund Burke.

> Remembrance wakes, with all her busy train,
> Swells at my breast, and turns the past to pain. . . .

In these verses, I need not say with what melody, with what touching truth, with what exquisite beauty of comparison—as indeed in hundreds more pages of the writings of this honest soul—the whole character of the man is told—his humble confession of faults and weakness; his pleasant little vanity, and desire that his village should admire him; his simple scheme of good in which everybody was to be happy—no beggar was to be refused his dinner—nobody in fact was to work much, and he to be the harmless chief of the Utopia,[27] and the monarch of the Irish Yvetot.[28] He would have told again, and without fear of their failing, those famous jokes which had hung fire in London: he would have talked of his great friends of the Club [29]—of my Lord Clare and my Lord Bishop, my Lord Nugent—sure he knew them intimately, and was hand and glove with some of the best men in town—and he would have spoken of Johnson and of Burke, and of Sir Joshua who had painted him—and he would have told wonderful sly stories of Ranelagh [30] and the Pantheon,[31] and the masquerades at Madame Cornelis'; and he would have toasted, with a sigh, the Jessamy Bride [32]—the lovely Mary Horneck.

The figure of that charming young lady forms one of the prettiest recollections of Goldsmith's life. She and her beautiful sister, who married Bunbury, the graceful and humorous amateur artist of those days, when Gilray had but just begun to try his powers, were among the kindest and dearest of Goldsmith's many friends, cheered and pitied him, travelled abroad with him, made him welcome at their home, and gave him many a pleasant holiday. He bought his finest clothes to figure at their country-house at Barton—he wrote them droll verses. They loved him, laughed at him, played him tricks and made him happy. He

---

[27] UTOPIA—Any place or state of ideal perfection.
[28] YVETOT—A town in France the lords of which had borne the title of king during the fifteenth century. Their petty monarchy was popularized in a song of the day.
[29] CLUB—The famous Literary Club.
[30] RANELAGH—A place of entertainment on the Thames, near London.
[31] PANTHEON—A place of public amusement opened in London in 1772.
[32] JESSAMY BRIDE—*Jessamy Bride*, a novel by F. F. Moore, gives an interesting account of Goldsmith and his friends.

WILLIAM MAKEPEACE THACKERAY

asked for a loan from Garrick, and Garrick kindly supplied him, to enable him to go to Barton: but there were to be no more holidays, and only one brief struggle more for poor Goldsmith. A lock of his hair was taken from the coffin and given to the Jessamy Bride. She lived quite into our time. Hazlitt[33] saw her an old lady, but beautiful still, in Northcote's [34] painting-room, who told the eager critic how proud she always was that Goldsmith had admired her. The younger Colman has left a touching reminiscence of him.

"I was only five years old," he says, "when Goldsmith took me on his knee one evening whilst he was drinking coffee with my father, and began to play with me, which amiable act I returned, with the ingratitude of a peevish brat, by giving him a very smart slap on the face: it must have been a tingler, for it left the marks of my spiteful paw on his cheek. This infantile outrage was followed by summary justice, and I was locked up by my indignant father in an adjoining room to undergo solitary imprisonment in the dark. Here I began to howl and scream most abominably, which was no bad step towards my liberation, since those who were not inclined to pity me might be likely to set me free for the purpose of abating a nuisance.

"At length a generous friend appeared to extricate me from jeopardy, and that generous friend was no other than the man I had so wantonly molested by assault and battery—it was the tender-hearted Doctor himself, with a lighted candle in his hand, and a smile upon his countenance, which was still partially red from the effects of my petulance. I sulked and sobbed as he fondled and soothed, till I began to brighten. Goldsmith seized the propitious moment of returning good-humor, when he put down the candle and began to conjure. He placed three hats, which happened to be in the room, and a shilling under each. The shillings he told me were England, France and Spain. 'Hey Presto cockalorum!' cried the Doctor, and lo, on uncovering the shillings, which had been dispersed each beneath a separate hat, they were all found congregated under one. I was no politician at five years old, and therefore might not have wondered at the sudden revolution which brought England, France, and Spain all under one crown; but, as also I was no conjurer,

---

[33] HAZLITT—William Hazlitt (1778–1830), a famous writer.
[34] NORTHCOTE—James Northcote (1776–1831), a famous portrait painter.

it amazed me beyond measure. . . . From that time, whenever the Doctor came to visit my father, 'I plucked his gown to share the good man's smile;' a game at romps constantly ensued, and we were always cordial friends and merry playfellows."

Think of him reckless, thriftless, vain if you like—but merciful, gentle, generous, full of love and pity. He passes out of our life, and goes to render his account beyond it. Think of the poor pensioners weeping at his grave; think of the noble spirits that admired and deplored him; think of the righteous pen that wrote his epitaph—and of the wonderful and unanimous response of affection with which the world has paid back the love he gave it. His humor delighting us still: his song fresh and beautiful as when first he charmed with it; his words in all our mouths: his very weakness beloved and familiar—his benevolent spirit seems still to smile upon us: to do gentle kindnesses: to succor with sweet charity: to soothe, caress, and forgive: to plead with the fortunate for the unhappy and the poor.

The Biographer—William Makepeace Thackeray (1811–1863). Thackeray ranks with Charles Dickens and George Eliot as one of the three leading Victorian novelists. He was famous also as a lecturer and essayist. His peculiar genius was satire; his subjects the upper classes of society; his art sophisticated yet human; his appeal universal. He was a master of English style.

Suggestions for Study: Describe the hospitality of Goldsmith's father. Read the parallel in *The Vicar of Wakefield* (Dr. Primrose's Open House). Give an account of Goldsmith's early school days. Tell about his college career (Trinity College, Dublin). Give instances of his fondness for fine clothes. Tell about his failures in search of a profession. What was Goldsmith's leading character trait? Give several references to prove your point. In the extract from Boswell's *Life of Johnson* in this book what character trait of Goldsmith is emphasized? Give an account of the attitude of the public and of other authors towards Goldsmith. Give a résumé of the last six years of his life.

Exercises and Creative Work: Write a paragraph on one of the following topics: *"His Purse and His Heart Were Everybody's"; Dr. Johnson's Friendship; Goldsmith, the Lavish Lender; Goldsmith's Friendship with the Jessamy Bride; Colman's Reminiscence; The Character of Goldsmith* (based on Thackeray's biography).

For Further Reading: Goldsmith's poem, *The Deserted Village,* and his play, *She Stoops to Conquer,* appear in this book. In addition to these two selections, you will want to read his novel, *The Vicar of Wakefield.* It is as popular today as it was yesterday because of its human interest. Human nature does not change.

A Biography of the Twentieth Century

FLORENCE NIGHTINGALE

From *Eminent Victorians*

LYTTON STRACHEY

By Way of Introduction: Florence Nightingale, whose name is identified with the Crimean War (1854–56) as the person who exposed the shocking conditions in the English camps in the Crimea and who was responsible for improved sanitary conditions, devoted her long life after her return to England to a campaign for reform of military hospitals by Parliamentary action. It was through her influence and indefatigable efforts, in spite of shattered health, that a Royal Commission was finally appointed and that its report, embodying all of her suggestions, was finally adopted by Parliament in spite of strong political opposition led by Lord Panmure, the Secretary of War.

Her method of indirect attack through her coterie of faithful followers whom she gathered round her, forms an interesting chapter in feminine psychology. She lived to see the triumph of her ideas. She was eighty-eight years old when she died.

I

EVERYONE knows the popular conception of Florence Nightingale. The saintly, self-sacrificing woman, the delicate maiden of high degree who threw aside the pleasures of a life of ease to succour the afflicted, the Lady with the Lamp [1] gliding through

---

[1] LADY WITH THE LAMP—Florence Nightingale became known by this name for she was ever passing about at night visiting the wounded.

the horrors of the hospital at Scutari,[2] and consecrating with the radiance of her goodness the dying soldier's couch—the vision is familiar to all. But the truth was different. The Miss Nightingale of fact was not as facile fancy painted her. She worked in another fashion, and towards another end; she moved under the stress of an impetus which finds no place in the popular imagination. A Demon possessed her. Now demons, whatever else they may be, are full of interest. And so it happens that in the real Miss Nightingale there was more than was interesting than in the legendary one; there was also less that was agreeable.

Her family was extremely well-to-do, and connected by marriage with a spreading circle of other well-to-do families. There was a large country house in Derbyshire; there was another in the New Forest; there were Mayfair[3] rooms for the London season and all its finest parties; there were tours on the Continent with even more than the usual number of Italian operas and of glimpses at the celebrities of Paris. Brought up among such advantages, it was only natural to suppose that Florence would show a proper appreciation of them by doing her duty in that state of life unto which it had pleased God to call her—in other words, by marrying, after a fitting number of dances and dinner-parties, an eligible gentleman, and living happily ever afterwards. Her sister, her cousins, all the young ladies of her acquaintance, were either getting ready to do this or had already done it. It was inconceivable that Florence should dream of anything else; yet dream she did. Ah! To do her duty in that state of life unto which it had pleased God to call her! Assuredly she would not be behindhand in doing her duty; but unto what state of life *had* it pleased God to call her? That was the question. God's calls are many, and they are strange. Unto what state of life had it pleased Him to call Charlotte Corday,[4] or Elizabeth of Hungary?[5] What was that secret voice in her ear, if it was not a call? Why had she felt, from her

---

[2] SCUTARI—A city in the Crimea, a peninsula in southern Russia extending into the Black Sea. Crimea was the scene of the Crimean War (1854–56) in which England, France, and Turkey were allied against Russia.

[3] MAYFAIR—A fashionable district in London, named from the fair which was held there every May.

[4] CHARLOTTE CORDAY—A French patriot who assassinated Marat during the French Revolution. She believed she was serving France.

[5] ELIZABETH OF HUNGARY—Elizabeth devoted herself to religion and works of charity.

earliest years, those mysterious promptings towards ... she hardly knew what but certainly towards something very different from anything around her? Why, as a child in the nursery, when her sister had shown a healthy pleasure in tearing her dolls to pieces, had *she* shown an almost morbid one in sewing them up again? Why was she driven now to minister to the poor in their cottages, to watch by sick-beds, to put her dog's wounded paw into elaborate splints as if it was a human being? Why was her head filled with queer imaginations of the country house at Embley turned, by some enchantment, into a hospital, with herself as matron moving about among the beds? Why was even her vision of heaven itself filled with suffering patients to whom she was being useful? So she dreamed and wondered, and, taking out her diary, she poured into it the agitations of her soul. And then the bell rang, and it was time to go and dress for dinner.

As the years passed, a restlessness began to grow upon her. She was unhappy, and at last she knew it.

The thoughts and feelings that I have now (she wrote) I can remember since I was six years old. A profession, a trade, a necessary occupation, something to fill and employ all my faculties, I have always felt essential to me, I have always longed for. The first thought I can remember, and the last, was nursing work; and in the absence of this, education work, but more the education of the bad than of the young.... Everything has been tried, foreign travel, kind friends, everything. My God! What is to become of me?

A desirable young man? Dust and ashes! What was there desirable in such a thing as that? "In my thirty-first year," she noted in her diary, "I see nothing desirable but death."

Three more years passed, and then at last the pressure of time told; her family seemed to realise that she was old enough and strong enough to have her way; and she became the superintendent of a charitable nursing home in Harley Street. She had gained her independence, though it was in a meagre sphere enough; and her mother was still not quite resigned: surely Florence might at least spend the summer in the country. At times, indeed, among her intimates, Mrs. Nightingale almost wept. "We are ducks," she said with tears in her eyes, "who have hatched a wild swan." But the poor lady was wrong; it was not a swan that they had hatched; it was an eagle.

II

Miss Nightingale had been a year in her nursing home in Harley Street, when Fate knocked at the door. The Crimean War broke out; the battle of the Alma was fought; and the terrible condition of our military hospitals at Scutari began to be known in England. It sometimes happens that the plans of Providence are a little difficult to follow, but on this occasion all was plain; there was a perfect co-ordination of events. For years Miss Nightingale had been getting ready; at last she was prepared—experienced, free, mature, yet still young—she was thirty-four—desirous to serve, accustomed to command: at that precise moment the desperate need of a great nation came, and she was there to satisfy it. If the war had fallen a few years earlier, she would have lacked the knowledge, perhaps even the power, for such a work; a few years later and she would, no doubt, have been fixed in the routine of some absorbing task, and moreover, she would have been growing old. Nor was it only the coincidence of Time that was remarkable. It so fell out that Sidney Herbert [1] was at the War Office and in the Cabinet; and Sidney Herbert was an intimate friend of Miss Nightingale's, convinced, from personal experience in charitable work, of her supreme capacity. After such premises, it seems hardly more than a matter of course that her letter, in which she offered her services for the East, and Sidney Herbert's letter, in which he asked for them, should actually have crossed in the post. Thus it all happened, without a hitch. The appointment was made, and even Mrs. Nightingale, overawed by the magnitude of the venture, could only approve. A pair of faithful friends offered themselves as personal attendants; thirty-eight nurses were collected; and within a week of the crossing of the letters Miss Nightingale, amid a great burst of popular enthusiasm, left for Constantinople.

[1] Sidney Herbert—An English statesman, who at the time of the Crimean War was connected with the War Office. It was through his efforts that Miss Nightingale was sent to Scutari.

III

The name of Florence Nightingale lives in the memory of the world by virtue of the lurid and heroic adventure of the Crimea. Had she died—as she nearly did—upon her return to England, her reputation would hardly have been different; her legend would have come down to us almost as we know it today—that gentle vision of female virtue which first took shape before the adoring eyes of the sick soldiers at Scutari. Yet, as a matter of fact, she lived for more than half a century after the Crimean War; and during the greater part of that long period all the energy and all the devotion of her extraordinary nature were working at their highest pitch. What she accomplished in those years of unknown labour could, indeed, hardly have been more glorious than her Crimean triumphs; but it was certainly more important. The true history was far stranger even than the myth. In Miss Nightingale's own eyes the adventure of the Crimea was a mere incident—scarcely more than a useful stepping-stone in her career. It was the fulcrum. For more than a generation she was to sit in secret, working her lever: and her real life began at the very moment when, in the popular imagination, it had ended.

She arrived in England in a shattered state of health. The hardships and the ceaseless effort of the last two years had undermined her nervous system; her heart was pronounced to be affected; she suffered constantly from fainting fits and terrible attacks of utter physical prostration. The doctors declared that one thing alone would save her—a complete and prolonged rest. But that was also the one thing with which she would have nothing to do. She had never been in the habit of resting; why should she begin now? Now, when her opportunity had come at last; now, when the iron was hot, and it was time to strike? No, she had work to do; and, come what might, she would do it. The doctors protested in vain; in vain her family lamented and entreated, in vain her friends pointed out to her the madness of such a course. . . .

One of her very first steps was to take advantage of the invitation which Queen Victoria had sent her to the Crimea, together with the commemorative brooch.[1] Within a few weeks of

[1] Commemorative brooch—A jeweled brooch which had been designed by the Prince Consort and which bore the inscription, "Blessed are the Merciful."

her return, she visited Balmoral,[2] and had several interviews both with the Queen and the Prince Consort. "She put before us," wrote the Prince in his diary, "all the defects of our present military hospital system and the reforms that are needed." She related the whole story of her experiences in the East; and, in addition, she managed to have some long and confidential talks with His Royal Highness on metaphysics and religion. The impression which she created was excellent. "Sie gefällt uns sehr," noted the Prince, "ist sehr bescheiden."[3] Her Majesty's comment was different—"Such a *head!* I wish we had her at the War Office. . . ."

Of Miss Nightingale's friends, the most important was Sidney Herbert. He was a man upon whom the good fairies seemed to have showered, as he lay in his cradle, all their most enviable gifts. Well born, handsome, rich, the master of Wilton—one of those great country-houses, clothed with the glamour of historic past, which are the peculiar glory of England—he possessed, besides all these advantages, so charming, so lively, so gentle a disposition that no one who had once come near him could ever be his enemy. He was, in fact, a man of whom it was difficult not to say that he was a perfect English gentleman. For his virtues were equal even to his good fortune. He was religious—deeply religious: "I am more and more convinced every day," he wrote, when he had been for some years a Cabinet Minister, "that in politics, as in everything else, nothing can be right which is not in accordance with the spirit of the Gospel." No one was more unselfish; he was charitable and benevolent to a remarkable degree; and he devoted the whole of his life with an unwavering conscientiousness to the public service. With such a character, with such opportunities, what high hopes must have danced before him, what radiant visions of accomplished duties, of ever-increasing usefulness, of beneficent power, of the consciousness of disinterested success! Some of those hopes and visions were, indeed, realized; but, in the end, the career of Sidney Herbert seemed to show that, with all their generosity, there was some gift or other—what was it?—some essential gift —which the good fairies had withheld, and that even the quali-

[2] BALMORAL—Balmoral Castle in Scotland.
[3] SIE GEFÄLLT UNS SEHR, IST SEHR BESCHEIDEN—She pleases us greatly; is very modest.

ties of a perfect English gentleman may be no safeguard against anguish, humiliation, and defeat.

That career would certainly have been very different if he had never known Miss Nightingale. The alliance between them, which had begun with her appointment to Scutari, which had grown closer and closer while the war lasted, developed, after her return, into one of the most extraordinary of friendships. It was the friendship of a man and a woman intimately bound together by their devotion to a public cause; mutual affection, of course, played a part in it, but it was an incidental part; the whole soul of the relationship was a community of work. Perhaps out of England such an intimacy could hardly have existed —an intimacy so utterly untinctured not only by passion itself but by the suspicion of it. For years Sidney Herbert saw Miss Nightingale almost daily, for long hours together, corresponding with her incessantly when they were apart; and the tongue of scandal was silent; and one of the most devoted of her admirers was his wife. But what made the connection still more remarkable was the way in which the parts that were played in it were divided between the two. The man who acts, decides, and achieves; the woman who encourages, applauds, and—from a distance—inspires:—the combination is common enough; but Miss Nightingale was neither an Aspasia [4] nor an Egeria.[5] In her case it is almost true to say that the rôles were reversed; the qualities of pliancy and sympathy fell to the man, those of command and initiative to the woman. There was one thing only which Miss Nightingale lacked in her equipment for public life; she had not—she never could have—the public power and authority which belong to the successful politician. That power and authority Sidney Herbert possessed; the fact was obvious, and the conclusion no less so: it was through the man that the woman must work her will. She took hold of him, taught him, shaped him, absorbed him, dominated him through and through. He did not resist—he did not wish to resist; his natural inclination lay along the same path as hers; only that terrific personality swept him forward at her own fierce pace and with her

---

[4] ASPASIA—An Athenian woman who inspired admiration of many distinguished men of Greece. Her home was the meeting place of learned men.
[5] EGERIA—In Roman mythology, a nymph from whom Numa, a legendary king of Rome, derived religious inspiration.

own relentless stride. Swept him—where to? Ah, Why had he ever known Miss Nightingale? If Lord Panmure [6] was a bison, Sidney Herbert, no doubt, was a stag—a comely, gallant creature springing through the forest; but the forest is a dangerous place. One has the image of wide eyes fascinated suddenly by something feline, something strong; there is a pause; and then the tigress has her claws in the quivering haunches; and then—!

Besides Sir Herbert, she had other friends who, in a more restricted sphere, were hardly less essential to her. If, in her condition of bodily collapse, she were to accomplish what she was determined that she should accomplish, the attentions and the services of others would be absolutely indispensable. Helpers and servers she must have; and accordingly there was soon formed about her a little group of devoted disciples upon whose affections and energies she could implicitly rely. Devoted, indeed, these disciples were, in no ordinary sense of the term; for certainly she was no light task-mistress, and he who set out to be of use to Miss Nightingale was apt to find, before he had gone very far, that he was in truth being made use of in good earnest —to the very limit of his endurance and his capacity. Perhaps, even beyond those limits; why not? Was she asking of others more than she was giving herself? Let them look at her lying there pale and breathless on the couch; could it be said that she spared herself? Why, then, should she spare others? And it was not for her own sake that she made these claims. For her own sake, indeed! No! They all knew it! It was for the sake of the work. And so the little band, bound body and soul in that strange servitude, laboured on ungrudgingly. Among the most faithful was "Aunt Mai," her father's sister, who from the earliest days had stood beside her, who had helped her to escape from the thraldom of family life, who had been with her at Scutari, and who now acted almost the part of a mother to her, watching over her with infinite care in all the movements and uncertainties which her state of health involved. Another constant attendant was her brother-in-law, Sir Harry Verney, whom she found particularly

---

[6] LORD PANMURE—Lord Panmure was War Secretary at the time. He was called the "Bison" because he was a large, phlegmatic Scotchman, who was not to be moved quickly. He was quite ready to agree with Miss Nightingale "in principle" to the need for reform, but he could not be induced to action.

valuable in parliamentary affairs. Arthur Clough,[7] the poet, also a connection by marriage, she used in other ways. Ever since he had lost his faith at the time of the Oxford Movement,[8] Clough had passed his life in a condition of considerable uneasiness, which was increased rather than diminished by the practise of poetry. Unable to decide upon the purpose of an existence whose savour had fled together with his belief in the Resurrection, his spirits lowered still further by ill-health, and his income not all that it should be, he had determined to seek the solution of his difficulties in the United States of America. But, even there, the solution was not forthcoming; and when, a little later, he was offered a post in a government department at home, he accepted it, came to live in London, and immediately fell under the influence of Miss Nightingale. Though the purpose of existence might be still uncertain and its nature still unsavoury, here, at any rate, under the eye of this inspired woman, was something real, something earnest: his only doubt was—could he be of any use? Certainly he could. There was a great number of miscellaneous little jobs which there was nobody handy to do. For instance, when Miss Nightingale was travelling, there were the railway-tickets to be taken; and there were proof-sheets to be corrected; and then there were parcels to be done up in brown paper, and carried to the post. Certainly he could be useful. And so, upon such occupations as these, Arthur Clough was set to work. "This that I see, is not all," he comforted himself by reflecting, "and this that I do is but little; nevertheless it is good, though there is better than it."

As time went on, her "Cabinet," as she called it, grew larger. Officials with whom her work brought her into touch and who sympathised with her objects were pressed into her service; and old friends of the Crimean days gathered round her when they returned to England. Among these the most indefatigable was Dr. Sutherland, a sanitary expert, who for more than thirty years acted as her confidential private secretary, and surrendered to her purposes literally the whole of his life. Thus sustained

---

[7] ARTHUR CLOUGH—A Victorian poet, whose most famous poem is, *Say Not the Struggle Naught Availeth*.

[8] OXFORD MOVEMENT—A movement in the Church of England to bring the church back to greater ritualism. This movement was started in 1833 at Oxford.

and assisted, thus slaved for and adored, she prepared to beard the Bison. . . .

And, if the need came, she meant to be as good as her word. For she had now determined, whatever might be the fate of the Commission, to draw up her own report upon the questions at issue. The labour involved was enormous; her health was almost desperate; but she did not flinch, and after six months of incredible industry she had put together and written with her own hand her "Notes affecting the Health, Efficiency, and Hospital Administration of the British Army." This extraordinary composition, filling more than eight hundred closely printed pages, laying down vast principles of far-reaching reform, discussing the minutest details of a multitude of controversial subjects, containing an enormous mass of information of the most varied kinds—military, statistical, sanitary, architectural—was never given to the public, for the need never came; but it formed the basis of the Report of the Royal Commission; and it remains to this day the leading authority on the medical administration of armies.

The Biographer—Lytton Strachey (1880–1932): Lytton Strachey, eminent biographer, was the founder of the new school of biography, and his recent death was a blow to literary London, as indeed it was to the entire world of letters. When in 1918 Strachey published *Eminent Victorians*, the book from which *Florence Nightingale* is taken, he was almost unknown; when he died, he ranked as the most eminent biographer of England, if not of the world.

Suggestions for Study: Describe the early home life of Florence Nightingale. What were her dreams and her longings? Tell about her dissatisfaction with her life as she grew up, as shown by notes in her diary. Give an account of her first appointment. What was the attitude of her mother toward her work? Show how the Crimean War was her great opportunity. Discuss her career after her return to England—her visits to Balmoral to see Queen Victoria and the Prince Consort; her friendship with Sidney Herbert; her devoted band of followers, Aunt Mai, Sir Harry Verney, and Arthur Clough. Tell how she won her final victory for improvement of military hospitals.

Exercises and Creative Work: Write a short character sketch of Sidney Herbert.

Write a short character sketch of Florence Nightingale.

For Further Reading: You will want to read the other biographies which appear in Strachey's *Eminent Victorians*. You will also be interested in Strachey's *Queen Victoria* and *Elizabeth and Essex*.

Biography in World Literature

General Characteristics

In searching for biographies representing various nations, one is necessarily restricted to the literature of the so-called western nations. The East has little to offer in the way of biography.

Emil Ludwig's *Napoleon*, George Brandes' *Napoleon Bonaparte*, Maurois' *Disraeli*, Dimnet's *The Brontë Sisters*, Harold Lamb's *Genghis Khan* are recent evidences that hero worship has little regard for nationality. In fact, the field of biography has no boundaries. Here, only the man matters. And it is often true that distance and freedom from local or traditional prejudices produces a saner, truer biography than similar nationality or intimacy can give. No form of literature, unless it be the essay, offers so interesting a glimpse of the author. In no way does one so reveal himself as in his estimate and interpretation of another. Hence biography is a reliable source of information concerning the ideals of individuals and nations.

DISRAELI IN LONDON *

From *Disraeli*

ANDRÉ MAUROIS

By Way of Introduction: Disraeli, brilliant Prime Minister of England, adored by the élite of London, admired by his colleagues in Parliament, and great favorite of Queen Victoria, was the grandson of a Venetian Jew who had settled in England. His father was a distinguished man of letters who spent his days and nights at the British Mu-

* From *Disraeli* by André Maurois. Copyright D. Appleton-Century Company. Used by permission of the publishers.

seum, communing with books. The son, Benjamin, inherited his father's literary tastes and was the author of several novels that had a real vogue in their day. The best known today, as yesterday, are *Vivian Grey* and *Coningsby*. A scintillating wit, a rare personality, a gift for constructive statesmanship make his name famous among great Victorians.

At the magic touch of André Maurois, the life story of this unique figure in English public affairs becomes as all absorbing as any romance.

THE CONQUEST OF LONDON

It turned out that I had a very fine leg, which I never knew before.
Letter of Disraeli.

ABSENCE had worked the expected effects. London knew nothing of Disraeli the Younger beyond that he was a writer of talent, a very handsome lad, who dressed with an amazing extravagance, and had returned from the East with a wealth of stories which it was diverting to hear. It required only one invitation to set in gear all those that mattered. It came quite as a matter of course from Edward Bulwer.[1]

Bulwer, no less ambitious than Disraeli and better endowed than he by birth, had advanced considerably ahead of his friend during the past two years. At the time when they had published, one his *Vivian Grey*, the other his *Pelham*,[2] it could only be supposed that they were setting off along much the same lines. But Bulwer had husbanded his youthful fame better than Disraeli. In April 1831 he had had himself nominated a member of Parliament and sat among the advanced Radicals; his books had conquered a public; he was editor of an important review.

This imposing façade concealed grave domestic difficulties. Such fruitful prizes could only have been won by relentless toil, to which all else, and Mrs. Bulwer in particular, had been sacrificed. Poor Poodle came to feel that she had lost her Pups forever. When she saw him alone (which was seldom) she complained. In society, the couple appeared to be as one.

A few weeks after his return, Disraeli received a letter from Bulwer:

[1] EDWARD BULWER—A Victorian novelist, best known, perhaps, for *The Last Days of Pompeii*. He also wrote plays. His *Richelieu* and *The Lady of Lyons* were often given by the great English actor, Sir Henry Irving.

[2] *Vivian Grey, Pelham*—The former was written by Disraeli, the latter by Bulwer.

"My Dear Disraeli,—If I am not among the very first, let me, at least, be not the last, to congratulate you on your safe return. I only heard of it yesterday. . . . 'Mr. Disraeli, sir, is come to town,—young Mr. Disraeli! Won't he give us a nice light article about his travels?'"

A few weeks later Disraeli rented a bachelor's flat in Duke Street. Sarah[3] knew that her brother was wretched the moment he was deprived of flowers, and sent him from Bradenham a few pots of geraniums, which were lovingly tended. Straight away he dined at the Bulwers'. The house and the table were absurdly and magnificently lavish. Mrs. Bulwer, prettier and more elegant than ever, had on her knee a dog "not larger than a bird of paradise, and at least as brilliant." Champagne was poured out in cup shaped glasses; Disraeli had never seen this, and it struck him as a detail of admirable refinement. The company was worthy of the setting: great names, great beauties, great talents. Especially did he eye the ravishing Mrs. Norton, one of Sheridan's[4] granddaughters, and Count Alfred D'Orsay, who had lately arrived in London and won the position, unprecedented for a Frenchman, of grand master of the dandies.

Many of the ladies requested that the author of *Vivian Grey* and *The Young Duke* should be presented to them. A certain Mrs. Wyndham Lewis, wife of a member of Parliament, was very insistent.

"I was introduced 'by particular desire,'" he wrote to his sister, "to Mrs. Wyndham Lewis, a pretty little woman, a flirt, and a rattle; indeed gifted with a volubility I should think unequalled, and of which I can convey no idea. She told me that she liked 'silent, melancholy men.' I answered 'that I had no doubt of it.'"

He reaped an invitation from Mrs. Norton. He had pleased her; he had spoken little, but with brilliance, and she had need of conversationalists. The English at that period had the trick of replacing the essential verb of every sentence with a gesture.

[3] SARAH—Disraeli's sister, of whom he was very fond.
[4] SHERIDAN—Richard Sheridan, author of seven plays which were very popular in their day. Two of them, *The Rivals* and *The School for Scandal* are given occasionally on our modern stage. Sheridan's wife was a very beautiful woman and his grandchildren inherited her beauty.

This young man with his few and perfect periods was cutting into that fashion of inarticulacy.

He went to Caroline Norton's in a coat of black velvet, poppy-coloured trousers broidered with gold, a scarlet waistcoat, sparkling rings worn on top of white kid gloves.[5]

The Nortons occupied a flat in Storey's Gate so small that one large sofa filled the whole of the drawing-room. White muslin curtains were crossed over the windows, before a flower-covered balcony. It was from this same balcony that Caroline Norton used to greet her old friend Lord Melbourne as he passed every morning on his way to Parliament. Norton, said rumour, tolerated this sentimental friendship because he found it profitable.

The tiny drawing-room was filled with a tightly packed crowd of politicians and celebrated men of letters, and positively illuminated by the extraordinary beauty of the Sheridans. In one arm-chair sat the mother, of whom it was said that she remained more beautiful than any woman in the world except her three daughters. These were the mistress of the house (Mrs. Norton), Mrs. Blackwood, and, loveliest of the three, Georgiana (Lady Seymour) beside whom even her sisters paled. Mrs. Norton had black hair, which she coiled in tresses round her head, the features of a Greek beauty, and an adorable way of blushing. If some phrase in the conversation touched her, a pinkish tint would suddenly mingle with her slightly olive hue, linger for an instant—and vanish. Her eyes and lips flashed such colour that she seemed to be made of precious stones: diamonds and rubies and sapphires. Lady Seymour, with her pale and limpid complexion, was quite different, and her softly lit eyes looked like fountains in the light of the moon. When any one commented to Mrs. Norton on the emotion left by such a galaxy of beauty, she would look round her tiny drawing-room and her dazzling family with a complacent smile, and say: "Yes, we are rather good-looking people."

Mrs. Norton's conversation was an enchantment to Disraeli. She had an exquisite way of telling free stories, modestly lowering those eyelids of hers fringed with their long thick lashes. "Yesterday I dined with the Nortons," he wrote to Sarah. "It

---

[5] COAT OF BLACK VELVET . . . WHITE KID GLOVES—Disraeli was romantic by nature and was inclined to elaborate, even dandyish, dress.

was her eldest brother's birthday, who, she says, is 'the only respectable one of the family, and that is because he had a liver complaint.' The only lady beside Mrs. Norton, her sister Mrs. Blackwood, was very handsome and very Sheridanic. She told me she was nothing. 'You see Georgy's the beauty, and Carrie's the wit, and I ought to be the good one, but then I am not.' I must say I liked her exceedingly; besides she knows all my works by heart, and spouts whole pages of *V. G.* and *C. F.* and *Y. D.*" [6]

The three Sheridanic Graces were soon to play a charming rôle in the life of the young author. All three were very free-and-easy; Mrs. Norton, delighted to leave an intolerable husband, liked to have Disraeli as her escort for the theatre or a ball. He found it agreeable to show himself in her company.

London in those days had a Watteau-like charm: [7] dinners, balls, river-parties. Disraeli shared in everything. He was amusing, he brought pretty women, he was fresh from foreign travel. He was sought after: "I make my way easily in the highest set, where there is no envy, malice, &c., and where they like to admire and be amused...." The table of "Dizzy" (as Mayfair [8] had nicknamed him) was strewn with noble invitations, which he accepted with pleasure. In this brilliant, witty, and cordial world, he felt himself more at his ease and more in his proper sphere than amongst the middle-class people of his childhood. The free and fearless grace of these young women and young noblemen cast a spell over him. In their midst he met with the friends of his dreams, the fair-haired youths, lithe and splendid Englishmen, and with Englishwomen of high birth, the loveliest. He relished the luxury of the houses, the beauty of the flowers, the splendour of the women. On the surface at least, his dry pride was dissolved. He took confidence. He lived in a fever of joy. "I wish that your organization," his father wrote to him, "allowed you to write calmer letters." But Ben was quite incapable of writing a calm letter. The beauty of life was intoxicating him.

[6] *V. G., C. F., Y. D.*—*Vivian Grey, Contarini Fleming,* and *The Young Duke*, three books written by Disraeli.
[7] WATTEAU-LIKE CHARM—The paintings of Watteau, a French artist of the eighteenth century, were very much in vogue in England. The style of dress depicted in the paintings became very fashionable.
[8] MAYFAIR—Fashionable London.

His deep interest in history led him to seek out old people. One of his closest women friends was the aged Lady Cork, who still, in spite of her eighty-seven years, entertained guests every evening. She was the prettiest and most diverting of dowagers. The heroes and heroines of her youth, of her maturity, and then of her old age, favourites, soldiers, poets, had all vanished. She had seen revolutions in every country of the world; she remembered Brighton when it was a fishing harbour, and Manchester as a village. But she still remained unaltered, alert and gay, thirsting for amusement and novelty. Finding both wit and curiosity in this young man, she accorded him her protection, a powerful one, in the social world.

"A good story!" he wrote to Sarah. "On Monday, I think, Lady Sykes was at Lady Cork's, and Lord Carrington paid her a visit.

"Lady C. Do you know young Disraeli?

"Lord C. Hem! Why? Eh?

"Lady C. Why, he is your neighbour, isn't he, eh?

"Lord C. His father is.

"Lady C. I know that. His father is one of my dearest friends. I dote on the Disraelis.

"Lord C. The young man is an extraordinary sort of person. The father I like; he is very quiet and respectable.

"Lady C. Why do you think the young man extraordinary? I should not think that *you* could taste him.

"Lord C. He is a great agitator. Not that he troubles us much *now*. He is never amongst us now. I believe he has gone abroad again.

"Lady C. (*literatimo* [9]) You old fool! Why, he sent me this book this morning. You need not look at it; you can't understand it. It is the finest book ever written. Gone abroad, indeed! Why, he is the best *ton* [10] in London! There is not a party that goes down without him. The Duchess of Hamilton says there is nothing like. Lady Lonsdale would give her head and shoulders for him. He would not dine at your house if you were to ask him. He does not care for people because they are lords; he must have fashion, or beauty, or wit, or something:

---

[9] *Literatimo*—Very learnedly.
[10] *Ton*—Style; vogue.

and you are a very good sort of person, but you are nothing more.
"The old Lord took it very good-humouredly, and laughed. Lady Cork has read every line of the new book. I don't doubt the sincerity of her admiration, for she has laid out 17s. in crimson velvet, and her maid is binding it. . . ."

A story for Sarah, no doubt; it would be rash to believe every word of it; when Benjamin's success was in question, the family tolerated a rather garishly coloured picture, and he himself realized that Sarah, as she read it, shared in Ben's imaginative powers.

In the evening the whole of the English aristocracy assembled at Almack's, a kind of private dance-club, under the patronage of the most exclusive of great ladies and governed by the strictest rules. One could enter its precincts only in breeches and silk stockings. Once the Duke of Wellington had tried to enter differently attired, but the doorkeeper had stepped forward and said: "Your Grace cannot be admitted in trousers." Whereupon the Duke, as a disciplined soldier, had gone off with not a word of complaint. Disraeli became a regular attender at Almack's. Many marriages were arranged there, and dazzling alliances were proposed to him: "By the bye, would you like Lady Z. for a sister-in-law, very clever, £25,000 and domestic? As for 'love,' all my friends who have married for love and beauty either beat their wives or live apart from them. This is literally the case. I may commit many follies in life, but I never intend to marry for 'love,' which I am sure is a guarantee of infelicity."

. . . .

Feminine favour brought in its wake, but more slowly, the man. By some he had been invited to political luncheons, and this was his foremost desire. One evening, at Lord Eliot's, he found himself seated beside Sir Robert Peel, the great chief of the Tory party. The whole table seemed to be sorely intimidated. With hungry curiosity Disraeli scrutinized this stern and powerful personage on whom, from his adolescence, destiny had lavished everything which Disraeli, for his part, was coveting.

The son of a great manufacturer, owner of one of the seven largest fortunes in England, Peel had as a child been brought up to become Prime Minister. At five years old, he was hoisted on to tables and made to repeat his speeches. He had come down from Oxford with a "double first" in classics and mathematics, a rare achievement. At twenty-one, his father had bought a seat for him in Parliament. At twenty-three he had been a secretary of state. For some time he had been reproached for his ingratitude towards Canning, whom he had fought sternly to the death after having been his friend, but the political world had forgotten, and now at forty-three he had acquired an unbelievable prestige, even amongst his adversaries. He was the very symbol of English honesty and solidity. It was found good that he was tall in stature and had features of Roman firmness; it was accepted that he should be haughty and chilling. Disraeli caught unawares the nervous movements of a susceptibility which was almost morbid, but only natural in a man accustomed to power, and realized that the Minister must be difficult to live with. But on that evening Peel had decided to make himself agreeable; he treated the young writer with slightly condescending familiarity, and joked with appropriate dignity; he was far from imagining that this insignificant neighbour was taking the measure of a great man.

Sometimes Disraeli would reflect: "But is it really essential to enter Parliament? This life of pleasure, idleness, literary work, is altogether delightful. At bottom, I am indolent, like all men of high imagination . . . I wish to be idle and enjoy myself, muse over the stormy past and smile at the placid present. Alas! I struggle from Pride. Yes! It is Pride that now prompts me, not Ambition. They shall not say I have failed."

One day, on expressing these feelings to Bulwer, his friend turned towards him, took his arm, and said with every sign of sincerity: "It is true, my dear fellow, it is true. We are sacrificing our youth, the time of pleasure, the light season of enjoyment—but we are bound to go on, we are *bound*. How our enemies would triumph were we to retire from the stage!"

Yes, without a doubt, the game must go on. But sometimes, when some evening party had been charming, when London at night gleamed dimly in the fog as he came out from some ball, when a pretty woman had lingered as she pressed his hand in farewell, he would tell himself that ambition was a vain folly, that this frivolity he had feigned so long was his true nature, and was wisdom too, that it would be delightful to live on for ever at the feet of the three Sheridan sisters, a fond and indolent page. . . .

THE MAIDEN SPEECH

At Bradenham it was possible to believe that all England was agog with the entrance of Benjamin Disraeli to Parliament. In London conversation centered rather on the young Queen,[1] her ease of bearing, her intelligence, the affection which she seemed to feel for her Prime Minister, Melbourne. Many people too, coming back from holidays, were talking of their first railway journey; they had experienced a certain sense of danger, but soon put it out of their heads.

Immediately Disraeli found his Wyndham Lewis "colleagues" again. Mrs. Wyndham Lewis, proud of her protégé, took him to the theatre to see Kean,[2] in a well-heated box. He went to receive Lord Lyndhurst's[3] congratulations, and to compliment him in his return, for this sturdy old man had just married a young girl and his sole topic was of having a son. Then Wyndham Lewis showed him the Houses of Parliament.

As the old Palace of Westminster had been partly burnt down, the Lords and Commons were sitting in temporary halls. There they were rather crowded, but Disraeli managed to make sure of a seat for himself just behind his chief, Sir Robert Peel. The latter was cordial and invited the new member to join him at a small dinner-party at the Carlton on the following Thursday. "A House of Commons dinner purely. By that time we shall know something of the temper of the House." That "we" was very acceptable. Wyndham Lewis, when he came home, said to his wife: "Peel took Disraeli by the hand in the most cordial fashion."

From the first divisions it was plain that Lord Melbourne's

---

[1] Young Queen—Victoria who had come to the throne when she was only eighteen years old.
[2] Kean—Edmund Kean, famous tragedian.
[3] Lord Lyndhurst—A member of the Conservative party to whom Disraeli had attached himself.

Whig Ministry with the support of the Irish, was going to retain power. For a fortnight Disraeli remained a silent spectator of the debates. He had a great desire to speak, but was terribly intimidated. He saw himself set about with great men. Opposite him, on the ministerial bench, in front of the official red box, was the Whig leader, Lord John Russell, very small in the black frock-coat of old fashioned cut, his face half hidden beneath a hat with an enormous brim, and with a stricken air, Lord John, the perfect symbol of his party, who advanced the most daring ideas in the most archaic style, and uttered the word "democracy" with an aristocratic drawl. Near him was Lord Palmerston, the Foreign Secretary, with his dyed and carefully brushed side-whiskers, Palmerston of whom Granville said that he looked like some old retired croupier from Baden, and whom the Whigs deemed vulgar, because he had not that ceremonious respect for the Crown which the Whigs had always shown, even when they were dethroning kings. Nearer to him, standing out against the massive table which separated the Ministers from the Opposition, Disraeli could see from behind the imposing figure of Sir Robert Peel, and in profile, the brilliant Lord Stanley, with his fine curved nose, his sensitive mouth, his curled and slightly unruly hair, Stanley the indolent, the disdainful, the intelligent, dressed with a carefully considered negligence that was full of lessons for Dizzy. Over by the entrance, amongst the Radicals, was his friend Bulwer; and in the midst of the Irish band, his formidable foe, Daniel O'Connell.

He was troubled also by the contrast in this assembly between the majesty of its ritual and its carelessness for appearances. Nobody listened; members chattered during the speeches and moved endlessly in and out; but the Speaker was in robes and wig, the ushers brought in and removed the mace, and a fellow member was referred to only by the appellation of "the honourable gentleman." All these small details delighted a neophyte who had so long observed them from without. He was certain that on the day when he would rise to speak, he would commit no blunder, would address himself solely to the Speaker, following the accepted fiction of the place, would call every barrister-member "the honourable and learned gentleman," every officer-member "the honourable and gallant gentleman," Sir Robert Peel, "the right honourable baronet," and Lord John, "the noble Lord opposite." Already in his thoughts, his phrases were cast in the parliamentary mould. If he became a Minister, how grandly he would strike his fist on that scarlet box! At the close of a loudly acclaimed speech, with what an air of negligence would he drop into his seat on the Treasury bench, wiping his lips with handkerchief of fine cambric! But now that he had measured at closer quarters the powerful inertia of this great body, a certain anxiety was mingled with his impatience.

. . . .

In establishing the powers of the House, a discussion had opened on a subscription opened by a Mr. Spottiswoode to furnish Protestant candidates with the funds necessary to fight the Catholics in Ireland. This subscription had been extremely distasteful, not only to the Irish, but also to the Liberals, who held it to be contrary to the liberty of the electors. O'Connell had just spoken on the subject with vehemence when Disraeli rose in his place. It had been arranged that Lord Stanley should reply on behalf of the Conservatives, but Disraeli had gone up and asked for his place as spokesman, and Stanley, surprised but indifferent, had granted it.

Irish and Liberals both looked with curiosity at the new orator who now rose opposite them. Many of them had heard it said that he was a charlatan, an old Radical turned Conservative,[4] a novel-writer, a pompous orator. It was known that he had had a violent quarrel with O'Connell, and a strong detachment of the latter's friends had grouped together as soon as Disraeli rose. On the Conservative benches, the country gentlemen examined with some disquietude this decidedly un-English face. The curls vexed them, and the costume. Disraeli wore a bottle-green coat, a white waistcoat covered with gold chains ("Why so many chains, Dizzy?" Bulwer had said to him. "Are you practising to become Lord Mayor, or what?"), and a great black cravat accentuated the pallor of his complexion. It was a grave moment and he was playing a great part. He had to show to the Liberals what manner of man they had lost in him,

---

[4] RADICAL TURNED CONSERVATIVE—Disraeli, upon first entering politics, had offered himself as a Radical candidate for the House of Commons, but he later changed his party affiliations and turned Tory, or Conservative. O'Connell, mentioned in the next sentence, had supported Disraeli as a Radical, and the latter's change of politics had precipitated a bitter quarrel.

to the Conservatives, that a future leader was in their midst, to O'Connell, that the day of expiation was at hand. He had several reasons for confidence; his speech had been elaborately prepared, and contained several phrases of sure effectiveness; and the tradition of Parliament was such that these beginners' speeches were greeted with kindliness. "The best maiden speech since Pitt's,"[5] was the remark generally passed to the orator. Young Gladstone,[6] for example, whom Disraeli now found again on the benches of the Commons, had delivered his five years before amid general sympathy: "Spoke my first time for fifty minutes," he had noted in his diary. "The House heard me very kindly and my friends were satisfied. Tea afterwards at the Carlton." But Gladstone came from Eton and Oxford; he had a handsome English face, with firm and familiar features, dark-coloured clothes, and a grave manner.

Disraeli's voice was a trifle forced; its effect, one of unpleasing astonishment. Disraeli tried to show that the Irish, and O'Connell in particular, had themselves profited by very similar subscriptions. "This majestic mendicancy . . ." he said. The House had a horror of long words and there was a titter of laughter. "I do not affect to be insensible to the difficulty of my position. (*Renewed laughter.*) I am sure I shall receive the indulgence of honourable gentlemen—(*Laughter and 'Question!'*); but I can assure them that if they do not wish to hear me, I, without a murmur, will sit down. (*Applause and laughter.*)" After a moment of comparative calm, another slightly startling association of words roused the storm. From the Irish group came hisses, scraping of feet, and cat-calls. Disraeli kept calm. "I wish I really could induce the House to give me five minutes more. (*Roars of laughter.*) I stand here tonight, sir, not formally, but in some degree virtually, the representative of a considerable number of members of Parliament. (*Loud and general laughter.*) Now, why smile? (*Continued laughter.*) Why envy me? (*Loud laughter.*) Why should I not have a tale to unfold tonight? (*Roars of laughter.*)"

---

[5] PITT—William Pitt (1708–1778), famous orator, and Prime Minister during the American Revolution.

[6] GLADSTONE—William Gladstone (1809–1898), a brilliant orator, and four times Prime Minister.

From that moment onwards the uproar became such that only a few phrases could be heard.

"About that time, sir, when the bell of our cathedral announced the death of the monarch—(*'Oh, oh!' and much laughter.*) . . . If honourable members think it is fair to interrupt me, I will submit. (*Great laughter.*) I would not act so towards any one, that is all I can say. (*Laughter and cries of 'Go on!'*) But I beg simply to ask—(*'Oh!' and loud laughter.*) Nothing is so easy as to laugh. (*Roars of laughter.*) We remember the amatory eclogue—(*Roars of laughter*)—the old loves and the new loves that took place between the noble Lord, the Tityrus of the Treasury Bench,[7] and the learned Daphne of Liskeard[8]—(*Loud laughter and 'Question!'*) . . . When we remember at the same time that with emancipated Ireland and enslaved England, on the one hand a triumphant nation, on the other a groaning people, and notwithstanding the noble Lord, secure on the pedestal of power, may wield in one hand the keys of St. Peter, and—(*Here the hon. Member was interrupted with such loud and incessant laughter that it was impossible to know whether he closed his sentence or not.*) Now, Mr. Speaker, we see the philosophical prejudices of man. (*Laughter and cheers.*) I respect cheers, even when they come from the lips of political opponents. (*Renewed laughter.*) I think, sir—(*'Hear, hear!' and 'Question, question!'*)—I am not at all surprised, sir, at the reception I have received. (*Continued laughter.*) I have begun several things many times—(*Laughter*)—and I have often succeeded at last—(*Fresh cries of 'Question!'*)—although many had predicted that I must fail, as they had done before me. (*'Question, question!'*)"

And then, in formidable tones, staring indignantly at his interruptors, raising his hands and opening his mouth as wide as he could, he cried out in a voice which was almost terrifying and suddenly dominated the clamour: "Ay, sir, and though I sit down now, the time will come when you will hear me."

He was silent. His adversaries were still laughing; his friends gazed at him, saddened and surprised. During the whole of his ordeal, one man had supported him with great firmness—the

---

[7] TITYRUS OF THE TREASURY BENCH—Young blades of the better class.
[8] DAPHNE OF LISKEARD—A nymph, pursued by Apollo and turned into a laurel tree.

right honourable baronet, Sir Robert Peel. Sir Robert was not in the habit of showing noisy approval of the orators of his party; he listened to them in an almost hostile silence. But on this occasion he turned round several times to the young orator, saying "Hear, hear!" in a loud voice. When he turned towards the Chamber he could not contain a slight smile.

Lord Stanley had risen, and scornfully, without saying one single word on the incredible reception of which one of his colleagues had just been the victim, had resumed the question seriously. He was listened to with respect. Silent and sombre, Disraeli leaned his head on his hand. Once again a defeat,[9] once again hell. Never, since he had followed the debates of the Commons, had he known of so degrading a scene. Was the life of the Cogan school [10] going to begin again for him now in Parliament? Would he still have to fight and hate, when he desired so much to love and be loved? Why was everything more difficult for him than for others? But why, in his first speech, had he challenged O'Connell and his band? It would be hard now to swim against the stream. Would it even be possible at all? He had lost all standing in the eyes of this assembly. He reflected with bitterness on the idea he had conjured up to this début. He had imagined a House overwhelmed by his phrases, charmed by his images, delighted by his sarcasms; prolonged applause; a complete and immediate success. . . . And these insulting guffaws. . . . Defeat. . . . O for the haven of the Bradenham woods!

A division forced him to rise. He had not heard the debate. The excellent Lord Chandos came up to him with congratulations. He replied that there was no cause here for congratulations, and murmured: "It is a reverse. . . ." "No such thing!" said Chandos, "you are quite wrong. I have just seen Peel and I asked him, 'Now tell me exactly what you think of Disraeli.' Peel replied, 'Some of my party were disappointed and talk of failure. I say *just the reverse*. He did all that he could do under the circumstances. I say anything but failure; he must make his way.'"

[9] ONCE AGAIN A DEFEAT—Disraeli had suffered many personal and political defeats before finally becoming a member of the House.
[10] THE COGAN SCHOOL—The school kept by Rev. Eli Cogan which Disraeli had attended in his youth. Disraeli was most unhappy in this school.

In the lobby the Liberal Attorney-General stopped him and asked with cordiality: "Now, Mr. Disraeli, can you tell me how you finished one sentence in your speech, we are anxious to know: 'In one hand the keys of St. Peter and in the other——'?"

" 'In the other the cap of liberty,' Sir John."

The other smiled and said: "A good picture!"

"Yes," replied Disraeli, with a touch of bitterness, "but your friends will not allow me to finish my pictures."

"But I assure you," said the Attorney-General, "there was the liveliest desire to hear you from us. It was a party at the bar, over whom we have no control; but you have nothing to be afraid of."

What was this? On others, then, the impression of an irreparable collapse had not been so unmistakable as on himself? Like many highly-strung men, Disraeli picked up confidence again as quickly as he lost heart. Already the cloud of despair was lifting. Writing to Sarah on the following day, he circumscribed the extent of the disaster: "As I wish to give you an *exact* idea of what occurred, I state at once that my *début* was a *failure*, so far that I could not succeed in gaining an opportunity of saying what I intended; but the failure was not occasioned by my breaking down or any incompetency on my part, but from the physical powers of my adversaries. I can give you no idea how bitter, how factious, how unfair they were. I fought through all with undaunted pluck and unruffled temper, made occasionally good isolated hits when there was silence, and finished with spirit when I found a formal display was ineffectual." He signed it: "Yours, D —— in very good spirits."

On the same day, entering the Athanaeum,[11] Bulwer saw old Sheil, the famous Irish member and O'Connell's lieutenant, surrounded by a group of young Radicals who were rejoicing in the Disraeli incident. Bulwer went over to them and remained silent. Suddenly Sheil threw down his newspaper and said in his shrill voice: "Now, gentlemen, I have heard all you have to say, and, what is more, I heard this same speech of Mr. Disraeli, and I tell you this: if ever the spirit of oratory was in a man, it is in that man. Nothing can prevent him from

---

[11] ATHANAEUM—A literary club.

being one of the first speakers in the House of Commons. Ay! I know something about that place, I think, and I tell you what besides: that if there had not been this interruption, Mr. Disraeli might have been a failure; I don't call this a failure, it is a crash. My *début* was a failure, because I was heard, but my reception was supercilious, his indignant. A *début* should be dull. The House will not allow a man to be a wit and an orator, unless they have the credit of finding it out. There it is."

This little oration, coming from an opponent, left a shock of astonishment. The young men dispersed, rather embarrassed. Bulwer went up to Sheil and said: "Disraeli is dining with me this evening. Would you like to meet him?"

"In spite of my gout," said Sheil, "I long to know him. I long to tell him what I think."

Sheil was charming at dinner. He took Disraeli aside and explained to him that this noisy reception had been a great opportunity for him. "For," said he, "if you had been listened to, what would have been the result? You would have done what I did; you would have made the best speech that you ever would have made: it would have been received frigidly, and you would have despaired of yourself. I did. As it is, you have shown to the House that you have a fine organ, an unlimited command of language, courage, temper, and readiness. Now get rid of your genius for a session. Speak often, for you must not show yourself cowed, but speak shortly. Be very quiet, try to be dull, only argue and reason imperfectly, for if you reason with precision, they will think you are trying to be witty. Astonish by speaking on subjects of detail. Quote figures, dates, calculations. And in a short time the House will sigh for the wit and eloquence which they all know are in you. They will encourage you to pour them forth, and then you will have the ear of the House and be a favourite."

A speech so intelligent, and showing so deep an understanding of the English, flooded the future with light for Disraeli. Nobody was more capable than he of understanding and following such counsel. He liked to fashion himself with his own hands like a work of art. He was always ready to touch up the picture. Once more he had fallen into the mistake wherewith his father had so often reproached him, that of being in a hurry, of wanting to be famous at one stroke. But he would know how to advance slowly.

A week later he rose in the midst of a discussion on authors' rights. Almost every one was inclined to give him a favourable welcome. Tories and Liberals were of one mind, that this man had been unfairly treated. That was distasteful to them. They were sportsmen; they preferred that an orator, like the game, should have his chance. A sense of shame lingered in their minds from that brutal afternoon. They were inclined to support this odd young man if he dared to make another trial. They would even put up with the excessive brilliance of his phrases and with his unheard-of images. But to the general surprise, he uttered nothing but what was common place and obvious, on a subject with which he was thoroughly familiar, and sat down amid general approval. The author of the project replied that he would carefully bear in mind the excellent remarks of the honourable member for Maidstone, himself one of the most remarkable ornaments of modern literature. Sir Robert Peel was strong in his approval, "Hear, hear!" and many members went up and congratulated Disraeli. An old Tory colonel came up to him and said, after some amiable growling: "Well, you have got in your saddle again; now you may ride away." To Sarah he wrote: "Next time I rise in the House, I shall sit down amidst loud cheers."

Far from having been of disservice to him, this sorry beginning had given him the prestige of a victim. Within three weeks he had acquired, in this extremely difficult assembly, a kind of popularity. He was courageous; he spoke well; he seemed to have an exact knowledge of the subjects he dealt with. "Why not?" thought the English gentlemen. . . .

ACTION

On November 15th, 1875,[1] Frederick Greenwood, the editor of the *Pall Mall Gazette,* called upon Lord Derby at the Foreign Office. He had dined on the previous evening with a financier well versed in Egyptian affairs, and had learned that the Khedive,[2] being short of money, was desirous of pledging his 177,000

---

[1] November 15th, 1875—Disraeli was at this time Prime Minister, having been appointed to that office in 1868.

[2] Khedive—Governor of Egypt.

shares in the Suez Canal. There were in all 400,000 Suez shares, the majority in the hands of French capitalists. Greenwood considered that it was in England's interest to acquire the Khedive's holding, as the Canal was the highway to India. Derby showed no great enthusiasm; he had a horror of large projects. But Disraeli's imagination was fired. He telegraphed to the British Agent in Egypt and learned that the Khedive had given an option to a French syndicate for £3,680,000 up to the following Tuesday. The Khedive was glad enough to deal with England, but he required money at once. Parliament was not in session, and four millions was not a sum which could be taken on to the Budget without a vote of credit. "Scarcely breathing time! But the thing must be done," wrote Disraeli to the Queen. The French Government offered no obstacles; on the contrary, the Duc Decazes[3] was very anxious for Disraeli's support against Bismarck,[4] and discouraged the French banks, who renounced their option. But £4,000,000 had to be found. On the day of the Cabinet's deliberation, Montagu Corry was posted in the anteroom. The Chief put his head round the half-opened door, and said one word. "Yes." Ten minutes later Corry was in New Court at Rothschild's,[5] whom he found at table. He told him that Disraeli needed four millions on the following day. Rothschild was eating grapes. He took one, spat out the skin, and said: "What is your security?"

"The British Government."

"You shall have it."

"Mr. Disraeli, with his humble duty to your Majesty:

"It is just settled. You have it, Madam. . . . Four millions sterling! and almost immediately. There was only one firm that could do it—Rothschild's. They behaved admirably; advanced the money at a low rate, and the entire interest of the Khedive is now yours, Madam."

The Queen was overjoyed. Never had Disraeli seen her so smiling; she kept him to dinner, "nothing but smiles and in-

---

[3] Duc Decazes—The French minister of foreign affairs.
[4] Bismarck—Chancellor of Germany.
[5] Rothschild—Nathan Rothschild, London member of the famous international banking house.

finite *agaceries*."[6] What particularly delighted the Faery[7] was the thought of Bismarck's fury, for only shortly before he had insolently declared that England had ceased to be a political force.

Under Gladstone, with England abstaining and France crushed by the war, the German Chancellor had acquired a habit of playing the master of Europe. With Disraeli, England once more had a foreign policy and desires which she meant to have respected. In 1875, when Bismarck menaced Belgium and then threatened France, Disraeli wrote to Lady Chesterfield that Bismarck was really another old Bonaparte, and had to be bridled. He spoke of it to the Queen, who approved and offered to write to the Emperor of Russia. England and Russia acted simultaneously at Berlin, and Bismarck beat a retreat. England's return into European politics had been triumphant, and the Queen was in ecstasies. How strong she felt, Disraeli being Consul!

All of a sudden she demanded the title of Empress of India. There had been some question of this in 1858, at the time when India, after the Mutiny, had been brought under the Crown, and Disraeli had supported it in principle. But in 1875 the moment was unfavourable. Disraeli knew that this rather un-English idea would be attributed to the Prime Minister's taste for Oriental tinsel. He made endless attempts to obtain a few years of patience from Her Majesty. But in vain. She was obstinate, and a Bill had to be brought forward.

The public outcry was great. The English do not like changes. The Queen had always been the Queen: why should she not continue so? "The title of Emperor," said the puritans, "evokes the images of conquest, of persecution, and even of debauchery." Pamphlets were published: "How Little Ben, the innkeeper, changed the Sign of the Queen's Inn to the Empress Hotel Limited and what was the Result," or "Dizzi-ben-dizzi, the Orphan of Bagdad." The embassies found it a comical story. "It is the freak of an artist and a king-maker in Dizzy," wrote the French *chargé d'affaires*. "In the Queen, the freak of an upstart; she

---

[6] *Agaceries*—Allurements, coquetries.

[7] FAERY—Disraeli called the Queen, the "Faery," from Edmund Spenser's famous poem *The Faerie Queene* which had been written in honor of Queen Elizabeth.

imagines that her standing will be raised and that her children find a better place for themselves in life with this Imperial title. It is my impression that it is a grave mistake thus to raise the veil which ought to cover the origins of Crowns; these things ought not to be played with. One is born emperor and king, but it is very dangerous to become one."

Dizzy was to reassure everybody. As regards the evil associations of the name of Emperor, he pointed out that the golden age of humanity had been the era of the Antonines.[8] As for the title of Queen, that would be maintained in England, and in all documents relating to Europe; only in acts concerning India and in the commissions of officers (who might be called upon to serve in India), the title of "Empress of India" would follow that of "Defender of the Faith." The Queen was much grieved by the opposition showed to *her* law, and especially by the personal attacks which her wishes had loosed against her dear Mr. Disraeli, but she was all the more closely drawn to him. When at last she had her title, she wrote him a letter of thanks, signing it, "Victoria, Regina et Imperatrix," with a childlike delight. Then the new Empress gave a dinner, at which she appeared, contrary to all her customs, covered with Oriental jewels presented to her by the Indian princes. At the end of the repast, Disraeli rose, in conscious violation of etiquette, and proposed the health of the Empress of India in a short speech as crowded with imagery as a Persian poem, and the Queen, far from being scandalized, responded with a smiling bow that was almost a curtsey.

. . . .

Thus the political vessel, tossed on the waves of fortune and climate, of the favour of the House and the humour of the Sovereign, rode the seas pretty well. But the skipper was very ill. So poor did his health become that more than once he told the Queen that he wanted to leave political life. This was a prospect which she would not have at any price, and she suggested that it would be easy to elevate the Prime Minister to the House of Lords, "where the fatigue would be *far less* and where he would be able to *direct* everything." This time he accepted. He took the name which he had bestowed on Mary Anne, that of

---

[8] THE ANTONINES—Two Roman emperors of the second century, B.C.

Beaconsfield, but whereas she had been only a Viscountess, he became the Earl of Beaconsfield and Viscount Hughenden of Hughenden. "Earl!" said Gladstone ironically, when he learned of his new avatar of the Evil One, "I cannot forgive him for not having himself made a Duke."

To avoid a farewell scene, affecting but unwelcome to his taste, he spoke for the last time in the Commons on the eve before the decision was announced. The secret had been well kept, and members were far from supposing, that they would never again hear their leader. When the House rose, he walked slowly down the floor, right to the end, at the bar of the House. There he turned, and for a moment or two looked round the long room, at its benches and galleries, at the seat from which he had made his first speech, the Treasury Bench where he had seen the massive figure and the fine features of Peel at the Opposition bench which he himself had occupied for so long a time. Then he came back, passed in front of the Speaker's chair, and, wrapped in his long white overcoat, leaning on the arm of his secretary, went out. A young man who was passing noticed that there were tears in his eyes, but could not tell why.

When members learned the news at the meeting of the House next day, they gathered in groups, deeply moved. Voices were lowered on the benches, as if there were a coffin in the chamber. A supporter, Sir William Hart Dyke, said: "All the real chivalry and delight of party politics seem to have departed; nothing remains but routine." And that was the feeling of the whole House. The interest taken by this old man in the game of life had in the end communicated itself to all those about him. With him one never knew what the morrow might not bring, but one could be certain that at least it would be nothing dull. "He corrected an immense platitude." The presence of this great artist in living had succeeded in making debates into works of art. "He was not only brilliant in himself, but he made others brilliant." Since his conquest of a position of authority, he had used it to impose a universal courtesy and respect for forms. An interruption from one of his own followers would make him turn round and cast a displeased look in his direction. In a discussion on finance he contrived to see a veritable tournament, and he made others see the same. "Your departure," wrote Manners, "terminates for me all personal interest in House of Commons life"; and Sir William Harcourt, an opponent, wrote: "Henceforth the game will be like a chessboard when the queen is gone—a petty struggle of pawns." And he quoted in conclusion the words of Matternich on the death of Napoleon: "You will perhaps think that when I heard of his death I felt a satisfaction at the removal of the great adversary of my country and my policy. It was just the reverse. I experienced only a sense of regret at the thought that I should never again have converse with that great intelligence." "Alas! alas!" wrote another, "we shall never see your like again. The days of the giants are over. Ichabod![9] Ichabod!"

When shortly afterwards the Queen opened the session of Parliament, a strange, motionless figure was seen standing by her side, draped in scarlet and ermine. It was the new Lord Beaconsfield. The fairest peeresses had come to see him take his seat. Derby and Bradford were his sponsors. With perfect composure he came forward and bowed, shook hands, raised his hat, as the ritual demanded, and then, having become Leader of the House of Lords on the very day of his entering it, he had to speak at its very first sitting. At twenty-five he had written in *The Young Duke*: "One thing is quite clear—that a man may speak very well in the House of Commons, and fail very completely in the House of Lords. There are two distinct styles requisite: I intend, in the course of my career, to give a specimen of both. In the Lower House, *Don Juan*[10] may perhaps be our model; in the Upper House, *Paradise Lost*."[11] In both cases he had been mistaken, but even if it had taken him some time in the House of Commons to abjure his Byronic manner, he never in the House of Lords adopted the Miltonic style. A shade of difference there was, but it was subtle, and more indefinable than his youthfulness had foreseen. He noted it with perfect artistry. "I am dead," he said on coming out from his first sitting, "dead, but in the Elysian Fields."[12]

[9] ICHABOD—Ichabod is an old Hebrew name meaning "the glory has departed."
[10] *Don Juan*—Byron's dramatic poem.
[11] *Paradise Lost*—Milton's majestic epic.
[12] ELYSIAN FIELDS—The dwelling place of happy souls after death.

The Biographer—André Maurois (1855–   ): As a student at the lyceé of Rouen, Maurois distinguished himself for his mastery of English.

ANDRÉ MAUROIS

During the World War he was detailed to the British General Headquarters where English-speaking Frenchmen were in demand. Here he began his writing. After the war he published *Ariel: A Life of Shelley* which brought him international fame. He has since written fascinating biographies of Disraeli and Byron, as well as many novels and short stories. His work illustrates the modern method of interpreting the life of a great man. It is brilliant, sympathetic, and compels the attention of the reader. He is one of the four great masters of the new biography, the others being Lytton Strachey, Emil Ludwig, and Gamaliel Bradford.

Suggestions for Study: *The Conquest of London*—Why was Disraeli so much in demand at the salons of the rich and fashionable in London? Discuss the following quotation: "He was not only brilliant in himself, but he made others brilliant."

The Maiden Speech—Why did Disraeli have confidence that his maiden speech in Parliament would be a success? What was the subject of his speech? Describe the reception of the speech by the House. Repeat the closing sentence. Give Peel's estimate of the speech. Give Sheil's estimate. What was his advice? What did Disraeli write his sister about the speech? Show how his apparent failure led to real success.

Action—What was the effect on the House of Commons of Disraeli's leaving for the House of Lords? Give a picture of the new Lord Beaconsfield at the opening of Parliament. Give an account of his first speech in the House of Lords.

Exercises and Creative Work: Give instances to show the sympathetic relationship between Disraeli and his sister Sarah. Tell the story of the bestowal of the title "Empress of India" on Queen Victoria; the purchase of the Suez Canal.

Write a paragraph on one of the following topics: *Disraeli, the Popular Author; Disraeli, the Dandy; Disraeli, the Social Idol.*

Write a paragraph on each of the following topics: *Disraeli's Maiden Speech as a Failure; Disraeli's Maiden Speech as a Prophecy.*

For Further Reading: You will enjoy Maurois' entire book, *Disraeli*. It is lively, dramatic, and holds the interest of the reader throughout.

Maurois' *Ariel: The Life of Shelley* is also fascinating. It is a romantic, poetic, treatment of the life of the poet and it reads like a novel. This book made Maurois famous on two continents.

Other authors have written about Disraeli. L. N. Parker's *Disraeli* is a drama which has proved a stage success.

EXTENSIVE READING PROGRAM—BIOGRAPHY

Reports of Biographies Read

Since the reading of biography is largely a matter of individual interest, most of your reading in this form of literature will be done outside the classroom. You will want to make a report on each biography you read, and the following questions will help you to prepare such reports.

1. Does the book seem long-drawn out or is it firmly organized?
2. Do the characters seem real?
3. Are personal details, habits, mannerisms, made to seem important? Are they over-emphasized?
4. Has the author a sense of humor? Give instances.
5. Is there a sympathetic understanding between the biographer and the subject? Cite cases.
6. Is there such a vivid re-creation of the times that you see, feel, and live in them?
7. Select instances of wit, of humor, of keenness of observation, in any of the biographies you read.
8. Is the author poetic, sarcastic, satirical?
9. Has he a pictorial quality in his work? Is his vocabulary interesting?
10. Does the biographer intrude his own personality in a way that makes or mars the book?
11. Examine the vocabulary used. Is it commonplace? unique? picturesque? Give examples.
12. Have you discovered in your reading that background influences character development? Illustrate.

Literary Prizes

The Nobel Prize was established by the will of Alfred Bernard Nobel (1833–1896), Swedish chemist and originator of dynamite. A sum of $9,200,000 was left for the annual award of five prizes to the persons in the world making the greatest contribution to chemistry, physics, physiology or medicine, literature, and to the cause of world peace.

The Pulitzer Prize was established by Pulitzer, naturalized citizen of the United States, member of Congress, newspaper editor and owner (New York *World*). In 1903 he endowed the School of Journalism, Columbia University, and gave $1,000,000 for the award of annual prizes to Americans distinguishing themselves in the field of letters. From $500 to $1,000 are given annually for each of the following—the best novel, play, poetry, biography, history on the United States, cartoon, editorial, and reporter's story.

What books that you have read have been awarded these prizes? Write two paragraphs on the Nobel prize awards in literature for the last three years. Write two paragraphs on the Pulitzer prize awards in literature for the last five years.

Exercises and Creative Work

Throughout this volume of PROSE AND POETRY are interesting biographies of writers of English literature. Choose the ones which you think should go in a collection entitled *Famous English Writers*. Other collective biographies can be made under such titles as *English Poets, Writers of the Romantic Period, The Writers of English Essays, English Novelists*.

Outstanding Modern Biographies

The following list of biographies and autobiographies includes not only great English biographies, but also outstanding American, French, German, Italian, and Swedish writings. The movement in the new biography is world-wide and we are interested in the productions of all countries.

OUTSTANDING ENGLISH BIOGRAPHIES

James Matthew Barrie　　　　　　　　　　　　*Margaret Ogilvy*
　　Barrie writes the life story of his mother in such a fascinating way as to make it read like a novel. It has the Barrie touch of quaint humor.

Gilbert K. Chesterton　　　　　　　　　　　　*Charles Dickens*
　　Chesterton is one of England's leading writers of today. His style is brilliant, paradoxical, and compels attention. He is a phrase-maker and John Drinkwater says "he writes in flashes of lightning." He has written *A Short History of England* and much literary criticism.

May Sinclair　　　　　　　　　　　　　　*The Brontë Sisters*
　　Miss Sinclair, one of England's leading women novelists of today, here gives us the story of the three Brontë sisters—Charlotte, famous for her novel, *Jane Eyre;* Emily, who deserves a place in the annals of English literature for her weird tale of *Wuthering Heights;* and Anne, who also wrote a novel, *Agnes Grey,* which Mr. Chesterton says "is interesting only as the work of a famous woman's sister."

Lytton Strachey　　　　　　　　　　　　*Elizabeth and Essex*
　　This is a colorful account of the life and times of Elizabeth, the great queen of England.

Lytton Strachey　　　　　　　　　　　　　　*Queen Victoria*
　　Queen Victoria is practically a history of nineteenth century England, told dramatically in Strachey's interesting way.

Virginia Woolf　　　　　　　　　　　　*Flush: A Biography*
　　A unique book, giving the life story of Flush, Elizabeth Barrett Browning's dog, and through the experiences of Flush, the biography of Mrs. Browning. It is short, amusing, and very much worth reading. Virginia Woolf, the author, has a worthwhile literary inheritance. She is the

daughter of Sir Leslie Stephen, eminent critic, and is related to the great literary families in England, Lytton Strachey's among them. She has written many novels, some in the traditional manner, others which break away from established rules and which are, indeed, highly original.

OUTSTANDING BIOGRAPHIES BY WRITERS IN OTHER COUNTRIES

Henry Adams (American) *The Education of Henry Adams*
This autobiography, published after the death of the author in 1918, is a remarkable document. Each generation of the Adams family since John Adams, second President of the United States, has produced one or more great personalities. In addition to two Presidents, there are cabinet officers, statesmen, and historians numbered among their contribution to our country. Henry Adams ranks as perhaps our leading historian of today.

Gamaliel Bradford (American) *The Quick and the Dead*
This is a collection of sketches of famous people written in Bradford's convincing and interesting manner. Bradford is America's leading biographer today. His recent death has robbed us of an outstanding personality in the realm of letters. Read also his *Portraits of American Women* and *Lee, the American.*

R. H. Davis and **A. B. Maurice** (American) *The Caliph of Bagdad*
This book is a biography of O. Henry who called New York City "Old Bagdad of the Subway." The authors give us a dramatic account of O. Henry's dramatic career.

George H. Palmer (American) *Life of Alice Freeman Palmer*
The story of the life and work of a remarkable woman, told in an understanding and sympathetic way by her husband.

George H. Palmer (American) *The Autobiography of a Philosopher*
Mr. Palmer, familiar to high school students through his *Self-Cultivation in English* and his translation of the *Odyssey,* here gives us many of his interesting experiences as a college professor at Harvard. We also get glimpses of his happy, domestic life with his wife, Alice Freeman Palmer.

Edith Wharton (American) *A Glance Backward*
Charmingly written, delightfully intimate, and informing withal. This book is as absorbing as any of Mrs. Wharton's stories. It is full of interesting accounts of interesting events in the life of an interesting woman. She met and knew intimately many celebrities—authors, actors, artists, musicians,—and recounts amusing incidents of her intercourse with them. The book is highly recommended for your book list.

Selma Lagerlöf (Swedish) *Marbacka*
Selma Lagerlöf, the first woman to receive the Nobel prize for literature (1909), writes this delightful account of her early childhood, which incidentally gives us a fine picture of Swedish country life, and also much of the folklore of her native land. She tells her story up to the time she was sent to Stockholm for her health.

Selma Lagerlöf (Swedish) *Memories of My Childhood*
In this book Miss Lagerlöf continues the story of her childhood life at the beautiful manor house, Marbacka.

Emil Ludwig (German) *Napoleon*
In this book, Ludwig, the leading German representative of the new biography, gives the story of Napoleon in a dramatic and picturesque way. You will also be interested in his *Bismarck*.

Vallentin-Luchaire (German) *Stresemann*
This book has been translated by Eric Sutton and contains a foreword by Dr. Albert Einstein. In it, Gustav Stresemann, former President of the German Republic, is shown as the idealist, working for internationalism, each for all, and all for each.

Jacob Wassermann (German) *Bula Matari, Conqueror of a Continent*
This book is a biography of Henry M. Stanley, African explorer. Stanley had a most unhappy childhood with relatives who did not want him. He never saw his father, and he saw his mother only once. Finally he ran away to sea. His ship stopped at New Orleans. Here he left the ship and began his life of strange adventure. He was adopted by a Mr. Stanley; served on the Southern side in the Civil War, was taken prisoner and employed on a Union ship as reporter. His rise in the newspaper world was rapid. His great opportunity came when James Gordon Bennett sent him on the mission to Africa to find David Livingston. The story of his adventures on the search and of his final discovery of Livingston is most dramatically told in this book and holds the reader in breathless suspense. You should read this book if you like adventure stories.

André Maurois (French) *Ariel: A Life of Shelley*
This is the book which made Maurois world-famous. It reads like an all-absorbing novel.

Benito Mussolini (Italian) *My Autobiography*
The introduction of this book is written by Richard Washburn Child, former American minister to Italy, who says, "No man knows Mussolini." If you read this book, see if you think Mussolini reveals himself or still remains a mystery.

OTHER BIOGRAPHIES OF INTEREST

George Arliss
Up the Years from Bloomsbury

Graham Balfour
Life of Robert Louis Stevenson

Mrs. L. S. Boas
A Great Rich Man (Scott)

W. H. Davies
Autobiography of a Super-Tramp

Jeanette Eaton
The Flame (St. Catherine)

R. D. Evans
Sailor's Log

Burton J. Hendrick
Life and Letters of Walter H. Page

W. H. Hudson
Far Away and Long Ago

Washington Irving
Life of Oliver Goldsmith

David Loth
The Brownings

Cyril Maude
Lest I Forget

Raphael Pumpelly
Travels and Adventures

A. D. Sedgwick
A Childhood in Brittany Eighty Years Ago

Charles Turley
Voyages of Captain Scott

Plays Based on Biographies

Maxwell Anderson *Mary of Scotland*
An appealing picture of the Queen of Scots and of her struggle with Elizabeth.

Rudolf Besier *The Barretts of Wimpole Street*
An intimate portrayal of Elizabeth Barrett's life with her father in Wimpole Street, London; of her meeting with Robert Browning; of their flight together to Italy.

Gordon Daviot *Mary, Queen of Scots*
An English playwright gives us another interesting play about Mary of Scotland. The dramatic quality is achieved by the dialogue rather than by the presentation of events. The period covered is from the time of her landing in Scotland until she loses her crown.

John Drinkwater *Abraham Lincoln*
A notable portrayal of Lincoln's life while President.

John Drinkwater *Robert E. Lee*
A sympathetic delineation of Lee, the Southern gentleman, the idol of his people.

Percy Mackaye *Jeanne d'Arc*
A romantic treatment of the ideas and ideals of the Maid of Orleans.

Percy Mackaye *Washington, the Man Who Made Us*
An understanding dramatization of Washington's ideals and achievements.

L. N. Parker *Disraeli*
A splendid dramatic treatment of a most dramatic personality.

George Bernard Shaw *Saint Joan*
A dynamic, convincing, and artistic dramatization of the life of the Maid of Orleans, in Shaw's usual manner—preachings and expositions largely taking the place of action.

Movies Based on Biographies

The following biographical movies are well worth seeing. Though truth is often sacrificed to situation, the pictures of the times given are, in all instances, remarkable. *Cardinal Richelieu; Catherine the Great; Disraeli; The Private Life of Henry the Eighth; The House of Rothschild; Queen Christina; The Scarlet Empress: Elizabeth of Russia; Voltaire; The Barretts of Wimpole Street.*

POETRY FORMS

Poetry may be classified under three main divisions: narrative, lyric, and dramatic.

In *narrative* poetry the poet describes or relates events. In *lyric* poetry he expresses his thoughts and feelings on a subject. In *dramatic* poetry he creates characters who speak and act.

Narrative Poetry

Under the heading of narrative poetry are *epics, metrical romances,* and *ballads.*

Epic poetry deals with stories told in verse form and arranged as a series of related events. Each story is complete in itself, but all are connected in thought. The style is dignified. The stories tell of the heroic deeds performed by great heroes. Homer's *Iliad* and *Odyssey* are examples of two great epics.

The *metrical romance* deals with love, chivalry, and religion, all with a romantic element closely woven throughout the story. Tennyson's *Idylls of the King* and Lowell's *Vision of Sir Launfal* are excellent examples.

Ballads are short narrative poems or story-songs. They were originally sung to the accompaniment of a stringed instrument on festival days and about the fireside. They have been handed down to us by word of mouth from father to son. Among the earliest ballads are those about Robin Hood. Ballads were originally written in one form which consisted of four lines with the second and fourth lines rhyming. The first and third lines contained four accents and the second and fourth contained three. The following is the last stanza of *Bonny Barbara Allen* which illustrates this form:

> O Mother, Mother, make my bed
> O make it soft and narrow.
> Since my love died for me today
> I'll die for him tomorrow.

Lyric Poetry

Lyric poetry consists of *songs, odes, sonnets,* and *elegies.* It deals with the emotions and expresses the author's thoughts and feelings on a subject. The lyric in poetry corresponds to the essay in prose. There are lyrics on love, patriotism, duty, death, joy, sorrow, courage, and many others. The subjects are abstract. The form of the lyric is usually short. Its general characteristics are sincerity, broadness of scope, and unity of thought. It must come from true emotions; must appeal to the general rather than to the specific, and must be direct in its line of thought.

An *ode* is addressed in an exalted manner to some object or person. It was primarily intended to be accompanied by music. Keats' *Ode on a Grecian Urn* and *Ode to a Nightingale* are excellent examples.

Songs express the poet's personal hopes, fears, joys, sorrows, loves, or ideals. They may be religious, national, or personal. Burns' *A Red, Red Rose,* Shakespeare's *Under the Greenwood Tree,* and Johnson's *To Celia* are only a few examples of songs which have lasted through the years.

The *sonnet* is a name used to designate a certain definite verse form. Like the ode, it was originally meant to be sung, and was accompanied by music. The sonnet has fourteen lines and a fixed rhyming scheme. The first eight lines are called an *octave,* with a rhyming scheme of a b b a a b b a, and the last six, or *sestet,* having a rhyming scheme of c d e c d e or c d c d c d. Milton's *Sonnet on His Blindness,* Wordsworth's *The World Is Too Much With Us,* and Mrs. Browning's *How Do I Love Thee* are among the finest sonnets in literature.

The *elegy* has death or mourning as its theme. It is quiet in its mood and contemplative rather than exalted. Gray's *Elegy in a Country Churchyard,* Milton's *Lycidas,* and Shelley's *Adonis* are probably the best known of the elegies.

Dramatic Poetry

Dramatic poetry includes *dramatic monologues* and the *drama.*

The *dramatic monologue* is a one-sided conversation in verse form which gives throughout the underlying ideas and thoughts of the speaker. It reveals the character of the speaker himself. In Browning's *My Last Duchess,* the real traits of the man are clearly shown. He is apparently speaking to someone else, but this the reader knows only by the remarks he makes, for there are no words uttered by any other character. Browning is the poet who makes the most use of the dramatic monologue.

The *drama* presents a story of human life. The characters play their parts before our eyes and unfold the plot to us as it would happen

VERSIFICATION

in real life. The best examples of the drama in poetry are Shakespeare's plays.

VERSIFICATION

The elements which enter into poetry may be divided into four classes: *rhyme, rhythm, foot,* and *meter.*

Rhyme

Rhyme, which is the simplest to understand, means the corresponding of end words as to sound. Stanzas have what is called a "rhyming scheme" and are given various names according to this scheme.

The *couplet* consists of two lines, the end line of each having the same sound, such as:

> Words are like leaves; and where they most abound,
> Much fruit of sense beneath is rarely found.
> ALEXANDER POPE, *Essay on Criticism*

The *quatrain* consists of four lines with a rhyming scheme of two choices. Lines 1 and 3 and 2 and 4 may rhyme, or lines 1 and 4 and 2 and 3 may rhyme. The first rhyming scheme may be represented by a b a b, and the second by a b b a. Following are examples of the two rhyming schemes:

> The curfew tolls the knell of parting day,   a
> The lowing herd winds slowly o'er the lee,   b
> The plowman homeward plods his weary way,   a
> And leaves the world to darkness and to me.   b
> THOMAS GRAY, *Elegy Written in a Country Churchyard*

> I held it truth, with him who sings   a
> To one clear harp in divers tone,   b
> That men may rise on stepping-stones   b
> On their dead selves to higher things.   a
> ALFRED TENNYSON, *In Memoriam*

The *sestet* contains six lines and several rhyming schemes such as a b a b c c, or a b b a c c, or a b c a b c.

The *octave* contains eight lines with a various arrangement of rhyming schemes. The most frequently used is that of a b a b c d c d.

Rhythm

Rhythm is the regular repetition of accented and unaccented syllables in a line of poetry as:

> Ă mán hĕ wás tŏ áll thĕ cóuntrў déar.
> OLIVER GOLDSMITH, *The Deserted Village*

Here the accented syllable follows the unaccented. This regular stress of syllables gives a rhythm to the line.

Foot

A *foot* in poetry means a division of the line into groups of syllables, each group having an accented syllable. There may be one accented and one unaccented syllable, or there may be one accented with two unaccented syllables in the group. The principal feet which we have in poetry are called:

Iambic—Two syllables with the accent on the last syllable.

> The sún thăt brief Decémbĕr dáy
> Rŏse chéerlĕss óvĕr hílls ŏf gráy.
>   JOHN G. WHITTIER, *Snow-Bound*

Trochaic—Two syllables with accent on the first syllable.

> Heárd thĕ whíspĕring óf thĕ píne trĕes,
> Heárd thĕ laúghĭng óf thĕ wátĕrs.
>   HENRY W. LONGFELLOW, *Hiawatha*

Anapestic—Three syllables with accent on the last of the three.

> Thĕ Ăssýrĭăn cămé dówn lĭke ă wólf ŏn thĕ fóld.
>   LORD BYRON, *The Destruction of Sennacherib*

Dactylic—Three syllables with the accent on the first syllable.

> Thís ĭs thĕ fórĕst prĭmévăl, thĕ múrmŭrĭng pínes ănd thĕ hémlŏcks.
>   HENRY W. LONGFELLOW, *Evangeline*

Meter

The *meter* is determined by the number of feet in the line. If there is one foot, the meter is *monometer*. If there are two feet, the meter is *dimeter;* three feet, *trimeter;* four feet, *tetrameter;* five feet, *pentameter;* and six feet, *hexameter*.

The most commonly used kinds of verse are the following:

Iambic Trimeter

> Ĭ né/vĕr sáw/ ă móor
> Ĭ né/vĕr sáw/ thĕ śea.
>   EMILY DICKINSON, *I Never Saw a Moor*

Iambic Tetrameter

> Ŏ Má/rў át/ thy wín/dŏw bé
> Ĭt ís/ thĕ wíshed,/ thĕ trýs/tĕd hóur.
>   ROBERT BURNS, *Mary Morison*

VERSIFICATION

Iambic Pentameter

When I/ consi/der how/ my light/ is spent
Ere half/ my days/ in this/ dark world/ and wide.
JOHN MILTON, *On His Blindness*

Trochaic Trimeter

Hail to/ thee, blithe/ spirit
Bird thou/ never/ wert.
PERCY BYSSHE SHELLEY, *To a Skylark*

Trochaic Tetrameter

Birds are/ singing/ round my/ window
Tunes the/ sweetest/ ever heard.
And I/ hang my/ cage there/ daily
But I/ never/ catch a/ bird.
RICHARD HENRY STODDARD, *Birds*

Anapestic Tetrameter

For the moon/ never beams/ without bring/ing me dreams.
EDGAR ALLAN POE, *Annabel Lee*

Dactylic Dimeter

Honor the/ charge they made
Honor the/ Light Brigade.
ALFRED TENNYSON, *Charge of the Light Brigade*

Dactylic Hexameter

This is the/ forest pri/meval, the/ murmuring/ pines and the/ hemlocks.
HENRY W. LONGFELLOW, *Evangeline*

Other Definitions

Without some change in the rhythm, the poem would become monotonous, so the poet often combines different feet and meters within the poem.

When the line is divided into feet and the accented syllable is stressed, it is called *scanning* the poem.

A *verse* is a line of poetry. A *stanza* is made up of two or more lines of verse.

Blank verse is iambic pentameter without the end words rhyming. Shakespeare makes frequent use of this form of verse.

Free verse is the new type of verse that is free from rhyme, rhythm, regular length of line or regular stanzas. Its chief value lies in its imagery and the expression of sentiment.

THE HISTORY OF POETRY IN ENGLAND

The Anglo-Saxon and Middle English Periods (Beginnings to 1550)

THE ANGLO SAXON PERIOD (BEGINNINGS TO 1066)

General Characteristics

It was the custom of the Anglo-Saxons, after their sea voyages and conquests, to gather in their mead-halls to feast and drink. As the mead cup passed around, the *scops* or gleemen sang or chanted their tales of heroes and mighty deeds done in battle to the accompaniment of the harp. Their greatest hero was Beowulf from whom the most noted poem of the period takes its name.

Beowulf

Beowulf is the greatest piece of Anglo-Saxon literature which has come down to us. It is the story of a warrior, or thane, of Hygelac, king of the Geats, a tribe dwelling in southern Sweden. Hearing that the mead-hall of Hrothgar, a king of the Spear-Danes who had befriended his father, was being ravaged nightly by a great monster, Grendel, Beowulf set out with his chosen band of "shoulder-companions" to slay the hideous "night-prowler." This he did in single-handed combat, and afterward, pursued Grendel's dam to her lair beneath the sea and there slew her. This done, Beowulf returned to his homeland, bearing the rich gifts given him to his king. There now intervenes in the story a period of fifty years. Upon the death of Hygelac, his son being only a boy, Beowulf was offered the throne by the Queen, but he would not take it. He chose rather to uphold the prince, Heardred, with counsel and good will, until the latter was older and able to rule the Geats. Upon the death of Heardred, slain in battle, Beowulf then became king and ruled the people well, defending them from their enemies and dealing justice among them. In his old age, a fire-dragon began to ravish his lands, and Beowulf went forth against him. In this last battle, his companions, save one, the young Wiglaf, deserted him. Though he killed the monster, he himself was slain.

This, in barest outline, is the story. It is a story filled with vivid pictures of the primitive life of the Anglo-Saxons. Written in a rough, vigorous chant, its movement echoes the surge and thunder of the sea. But perhaps its most compelling interest is in the character of Beowulf. In him we see many of those qualities which the race has always valued in a man. He is the embodiment of the heroic idea. His outstanding physical characteristic is strength. His most conspicuous moral quality was courage, but the story makes it plain that he was no bully. Accompanying his strength was prudence of mind and modesty. Upon loyalty he set a high value. In all his actions he displayed a high sense of honor. "Death," he held, "is better to every man than a life of disgrace."

Other Anglo-Saxon Poems

In addition to *Beowulf* there have survived a number of shorter poems and fragments, giving us glimpses of the Anglo-Saxons and their life. Conspicuous among these is a magnificent lyric poem, *The Seafarer,* which breathes a passion for the sea that has run through English literature from then until Masefield's cry, "I must down to the seas again." And somewhat later in the period came two great battle poems, *The Battle of Brunanburh* and *The Battle of Maldon,* the former of which exists in a spirited translation by Tennyson.

The rhythm of all the earliest poetry depends upon alliteration and accent. There is no rhyme, but the accent gives a musical effect.

Cædmon, the Father of English Song

In the latter years of the sixth century, missionaries from Rome introduced Christianity into England. With their coming, monasteries and churches were founded, and schools and libraries came into existence. This had a stimulating effect upon the literature of the world.

The legend of Cædmon, sometimes called "The Father of English Song," symbolizes the influence of Christianity. The story has come down to us in the *Ecclesiastical History of the English People,* a Latin work, written by the "venerable Bede," a monk and scholar who died in 735. Cædmon was a cowherd in the monastery of Abbess Hilda at Whitby. "Being sometimes at feasts, when all agreed for glee's sake to sing in turn, he no sooner saw the harp come towards him than he rose from the board and turned homewards. Once when he had done thus, and had gone from the feast to the stable where he had that night charge of the cattle, there appeared to him in his sleep One who said . . . 'Sing, Cædmon, some song for Me.' 'I cannot sing,' he answered; 'for this cause I left the feast and came hither.' He who talked with him answered, 'However that be, you shall sing for Me.' 'What shall I sing?' rejoined Cædmon. 'The beginning of created things,' replied He." In the morning when Cædmon told his dream to the Abbess, she concluded that "heavenly grace had been conferred on him by the Lord." A passage in the Holy Writ was read to Cædmon and he was bade to put it into poetic form. The next morning he gave it "composed in excellent verse." Cædmon became a monk, and in subsequent years, so the story goes, put the Scriptures into verse. Cædmon's *Hymn,* the first recorded piece of literature created on English soil, is given by Bede:

> Now ought we to praise   the prince of heaven's kingdom
> The Maker's might   and the thought of His mind
> The work of the Father,   since he of all wonders,
> Eternal Lord,   the beginning established.
> First did he shape   for the sons of mankind
> Heaven as a roof,   the holy Creator
> Then the middle-world   did the warden of men,
> The eternal prince,   after prepare
> As a dwelling for men,   the Lord Almighty.

Other Religious Pieces

The great bulk of Anglo-Saxon literature written after the days of Cædmon was religious in nature. It was the work of either monks or churchmen. In addition to paraphrases in verse of *Genesis*, *Exodus*, and *Daniel*, at one time attributed to Cædmon, there are a number of religious poems believed to have been written by Cynewulf, a monk who lived in Mercia or Northumbria. Among the best of those which are attributed to him are *The Swan* and *The Storm Spirit*.

THE MIDDLE ENGLISH PERIOD (1066–1550)

Effect of the Norman Conquest

For nearly a hundred and fifty years after the Norman conquest in 1066 there was little English literature of any kind, and no poetry. When poetry finally does appear, however, a change in its substance is to be noted. We now find nature poetry, love lyrics, and the beginnings of patriotic poetry. There is also a difference in form. Poetry now exhibits rhyme, meter, and a variety of stanza forms. Much of the new poetry is, furthermore, graceful and musical. Most of it is anonymous and this fact has significance. Literature was still composed to be sung or recited. To those who heard it, it was the substance of story which was important, rather than the author.

The Metrical Romances

There grew up in England after the Conquest, a great mass of legend. This legendary material had to do with great folk-heroes, and it is with the wonderful deeds and exploits of King Arthur and his Knights that the outstanding metrical romances in English have to do. By far the best of these is *Sir Gawayne and the Grene Knight*.

Sir Gawayne and the Grene Knight

This story opens with a description of the Christmas festivities at King Arthur's Court. The spirit of romance is reflected in the description of the great hall with its hangings of rich tapestry and in the character of those who are present. All are in their youth, the ladies are of surpassing fairness and beauty and the knights of great renown and valor. At the height of the festivities there comes riding into the hall on his steed a knight clad all in green, bearing a remarkable challenge. He offers to let any knight of King Arthur's Court strike off his head, if the knight accepting the challenge will suffer a blow in return. Sir Gawayne accepts, and strikes off the head of the green knight who calmly takes his head up and rides from the hall. After the festivities of the following Christmas, Sir Gawayne in accordance with the conditions laid down by the Grene Knight sets out in search of the latter. After a number of adventures in the course of which the knighthood

HISTORY OF POETRY

of Sir Gawayne is proved by a series of temptations, he arrives at the Grene Chapel, the appointed rendezvous. Since Sir Gawayne has been true to his vows, the Grene Knight is unable to strike off Sir Gawayne's head. The purpose of the romance is to picture the perfect knight, Sir Gawayne, who has been found faultless in five virtues—purity, compassion, fellowship, courtesy, and frankness. This metrical tale was written about 1370. It reflects in both form and substance the influence of the French and the English.

Nature Poetry

In both *Sir Gawayne* and in other poems of the period is to be seen a delight in nature not found in the older Anglo-Saxon poetry. Perhaps the best example of this nature interest is the short lyric known as the *Cuckoo Song*.

> Sumer is icumen in, lhude sing, cucu;
> Groweþ sed and bloweþ med and springþ þe wude nu;
>   Sing, cucu.
> Awe bleteþ after lomb, lhouþ after calue cu;
> Bulluc sterteþ bucke uerteþ, murie sing cucu.
>   Cucu, cucu.
> Well singes þu, cucu; ne swik þu nauer nu.

> Summer is a-coming in, loudly sing, cuckoo;
> Groweth seed and bloweth mead and springeth the woodland now;
>   Sing cuckoo.
> Ewe bleateth after lamb, lows after calf the cow;
> Bullock starteth, buck darteth, merry sing, cuckoo.
>   Cuckoo, cuckoo,
> Well singest thou, cuckoo; cease thou never now.

Geoffrey Chaucer

The first great figure in English literature is Geoffrey Chaucer, sometimes called "The Father of English Poetry." Chaucer was born in London in 1340. The known facts of his life are few. His father was a wine-merchant. As a boy Chaucer was a page in the household of Elizabeth, the wife of the Duke of Clarence, in whose army he later served in France where he was taken prisoner. Throughout his life he was in the service of the Crown in some capacity. At one time he went on diplomatic business to France and Italy, and he was for a number of years a collector of customs at the port of London. Chaucer's visits to the continent brought him in contact with both French and Italian literature which served to develop his genius. In these literatures he found both material and models, and his first longer poems were written in imitation of pieces he had read in Italian or in French. Chaucer's masterpiece is the *Canterbury Tales,* a selection from which appears in this book.

Chaucer wrote in the midland dialect spoken in the vicinity of London and the popularity of the *Canterbury Tales* was powerful in making Chaucer's dialect the standard English speech. His poetry shows a greater love for nature than that of any of his predecessors. Birds sing, flowers bloom, and a spirit of gladness pervades his poems.

Other Poets of Chaucer's Day

Two other poets of this period deserve mention. One of these is William Langland, author of a poem which in its day seems to have been very popular, *Vision of William Concerning Piers, the Plowman*. The poem is a protest against selfishness, luxury, covetousness, and many of the evils of the period. A second is John Gower, a very learned poet and voluminous writer whose didacticism earned for him the sobriquet conferred upon him by Chaucer of "Moral Gower."

The Ballads

The fifteenth century produced no single writer comparable to Chaucer, but it did see the development of a great number of short, popular, verse tales known as ballads. The origin of these ballads has been a matter of a great deal of speculation and investigation. They are all anonymous. One theory of their origin is that they originated as the musical accompaniments to folk dances, for they all are intended to be sung.

The English ballads deal for the most part with subjects which appeal to the popular imagination. To use a modern expression, their subjects have what we designate by the term "news value"—deeds of violence resulting from jealousy and love triangles, bride stealing, heroic deeds, battles and individual combats, relationships between men and supernatural beings, and occasionally humorous domestic incidents. A great number of these ballads deal with the prowess and exploits of the famous legendary bandit character, Robin Hood, who is represented as the friend of the poor, and as a kind of agent for effecting social justice. Some of the best known of the ballads are *Sir Patrick Spens, The Nut-Browne Mayde, Robin Hood,* and *Bonny Barbara Allen.*

The Poetry of the Renaissance

As Englishmen became more aware of their cultural deficiencies, they began to turn to the continent, especially to Italy, for models of literary excellence. In the early years of the sixteenth century two Englishmen, Sir Thomas Wyatt and Henry Howard, Earl of Surrey, began to write in imitation of Italian verse. They introduced into English literature the sonnet. Surrey also attempted a translation of Vergil's *Æneid* in which he used blank verse for the first time that it is to be found in our literature. The poetry of Wyatt and Surrey had a tremendous influence on others. There followed now a number of men, notably Thomas Sackville and George Gascoigne who, experimenting with new verse forms, were to show what could be done in English.

Poetry of the Middle English Period

THE KNIGHT

From the *Prologue* to *The Canterbury Tales*

Geoffrey Chaucer

Poem Interest: In Chaucer's day, pilgrimages to various shrines were common. One of the journeys most frequently undertaken was that to the shrine of Thomas à Becket, Archbishop of Canterbury, who had been murdered during the reign of Henry II. It was the custom of the pilgrims desiring to visit this shrine to gather at the Tabard Inn across the Thames from London. Here they waited until a sufficient number came to make the journey pleasant and safe. Chaucer represents an imaginary group of these pilgrims in his *Canterbury Tales* and in the *Prologue* gives a description of each of these persons.

As a result of a suggestion made by the landlord of the Tabard Inn, who proposed to ride with the company to Canterbury as its guide, each pilgrim, to furnish entertainment on the journey, was to tell four tales, two during the ride to Canterbury and two during the return. Whoever was judged to be the best story-teller would be given a fine supper by all the rest when they returned.

This plan, of course, was but a device enabling Chaucer to tell a great number of stories. Had he carried out his plans there would have been more than one hundred tales, for there were twenty-nine pilgrims. Only twenty-four were written but they cover a wide range of subjects.

There are legends, love stories, adventures, satires, allegories, fables—all written in verse. Many of the stories are old tales retold. Chaucer did not trouble much about the originality of his subject matter but in his retelling he gave to these stories a new life and vividness which is all his own.

The following selection is from the *Prologue* and it introduces the Knight. Many of the words will at first appear strange to you, but after you have read a line or two you will recognize our own English words with only a slightly different spelling. Those words and phrases which need special interpretation will be found in the footnotes.

<pre>
      A KNYGHT ther was, and that a worthy man,
    That fro the tyme that he first bigan
    To riden out he lovede chivalrye,
    Trouthe and honour, fredom and curteisye.
 5 Ful worthy was he in his lordes werre,
    And therto hadde he riden, no man ferre,
    As wel in cristendom as in hethenesse,
    And ever honoured for his worthinesse.
    At Alsiaundre he was when it was wonne;
10 Ful ofte tyme he hadde the bord bigonne
    Aboven alle naciouns in Pruce.
    In Lettow hadde he reysed and in Ruce;
    No Cristen man so ofte of his degree.
    In Gernade at the seege eek hadde he be
15 Of Algezir, and riden in Belmarye.
    At Leyes was he, and at Satalye,
    Whan they were wonne; and in the Grete See
</pre>

1. WORTHY—Valiant.
3. RIDEN OUT—Ride out seeking adventures.
4. FREDOM—Liberality.
5. LORDES WERRE—Lord's war.
6. FERRE—Farther.
7. HETHENESSE—Heathendom.
9. ALISAUNDRE—Alexandria, taken in 1365.
10. THE BORD BIGONNE—Sat at the head of the table.
11. NACIOUNS—Nations; that is, knights of other nations.
11. PRUCE—Prussia.
12. LETTOW—Lithuania.   12. REYSED—Campaigned.   12. RUCE—Russia.
14. GRENADE—Granada in Spain.   14. SEEGE—Siege.   14. EEK—Also.
15. ALGEZIR—Algeciras, a city in Granada.
15. BELMARYE—Belmaria, in north Africa.
16. LEYES—Layas, in Asia Minor.
16. SATALYE—Adalia, in Asia Minor.
17. GRETE SEE—Great Sea, the Mediterranean.

At many a noble armee hadde he be.
At mortal batailles hadde he been fiftene,
20 And foughten for our feith at Tramyssene
In lystes thryes, and ay slayn his foo,
This ilke worthy knight hadde been also
Somtyme with the lord of Palatye,
Agayn another hethen in Turkye;
25 And evermore he hadde a sovereyn prys.
And though that he were worthy, he was wys,
And of his port as meeke as is a mayde.
He never yet no vileinye ne sayd e
In al his lyf, unto no maner wight.
30 He was a verray, parfit, gentil knyght.
But for to tellen yow of his array,
His hors weren goode, but he was nat gay.
Of fustian he wered a gipoun
Al bismotered with his habergeoun.
35 For he was late y-come from his viage,
And wente fro to doon his pilgrymage.

19. BATAILLES—Battles.
20. FEITH—Faith.   20. TRAMYSSENE—Tramissene, in Asia Minor.
21. LYSTES THRYES—Lists three; that is, three lists or tournaments.
21. AY SLAYN HIS FOO—Always slain his foe.
22. ILKE—Same.
23. PALATYE—Palatia, in Asia Minor.
24. AGAYN—Against.
25. SOVEREYN PRYS—Great renown.
26. WYS—Wise; that is, modest.
27. PORT—Manner, bearing.   27. MAYDE—Maid.
28. VILEINYE—Villainy; that is, discourteous talk.
29. NO MANER WIGHT—Any man.
30. VERRAY, PARFIT, GENTIL—True, perfect, gentle.
31. FOR TO TELLEN YOU—To tell you.
32. HIS HORS WEREN GOODE—His horse was good.
33. FUSTIAN—A coarse cloth.   33. GIPOUN—A doublet or short coat.
34. BISMOTERED—Begrimed.   34. HABERGEOUN—Ring-mail or coat of mail.
35. LATE Y-COME—Lately come.   35. VIAGE—Journey.
36. TO DOON—To do.

Poem Development: The first thing which strikes one about Chaucer is his vivid realism in description. In the *Prologue* he has left us a picture gallery of the Middle Ages. His pilgrims come from different social levels and represent different occupations. In addition to the knight, we meet a forester, a farm laborer, a lawyer, a doctor, a merchant, a shipman, and a prioress, to name only a few of them. Each one is drawn true to life.

The knight, for example, is not the shining knight in armor of the medieval romances, but one such as might have been met on the highways and byways of England in Chaucer's time. He is a veteran of many campaigns. (Lines 5–24.) It will be noted (Lines 31–36) that "his hors was goode"—a strong, serviceable animal, but that "he was not gay," that is, gayly clad as were those battle-steeds which romance delights to picture. The knight himself wears a "gypon," or doublet, not of silk or some rich material but of cotton or "fustain," and his doublet is all begrimed or "bismotered" with rust from his ring-mail, or "habergeoun."

In the delineation of character Chaucer also excels. Each of his pilgrims is an individual; whereas the knights, for example, one meets in the medieval romances are all very much the same. In a few lines (25–30) Chaucer shows us the character of his knight. We have pictured a soldier who has everywhere won great renown (sovereyn prys). He is valiant (worthy, but he is also discreet and modest (wys) and no swaggerer—his manner (port) is as meek as that of any maid. We note here one of those characteristics which distinguished the hero Beowulf and which is still admired in the English ideal of a gentleman. In all his life, Chaucer's knight had never taken advantage of his prowess to pick a quarrel—he never yet "no vileynye (discourteous talk) sayde . . . unto no maner wight (any man)." "He was a verray, parfit, gentil (gentle, as in gentleman) knyght."

A further characteristic of Chaucer is his sly humor which comes out in his description of the weaknesses and failings of some of his characters, but his humor is only gently satirical, rarely if ever biting or sarcastic.

In your own words, first describe the Knight, and then characterize him. Briefly tell about some of his campaigns. Remember that the lines given here are from the *Prologue* and merely introduce the Knight. When the lots were drawn for the first story, it fell to the Knight. In a copy of *The Canterbury Tales,* look up the tale he tells, and give it to the class in your own words. You will be interested in other descriptions given in the *Prologue,* especially those of the squire, the prioress, the monk, the cook, and the wife of Bath, and you will also enjoy some of the tales that they tell.

Significant Expressions: Quote four lines which give an ideal picture of a knight in Chaucer's day. Quote one line which gives the character of the knight.

THE HISTORY OF POETRY IN ENGLAND

The Age of Elizabeth (1550–1625)

General Characteristics

With the marked advance in national and individual prosperity during Elizabeth's reign, together with extended education and religious tolerance, came leisure and opportunity to appreciate beauty. Now the English people changed the type of their homes from the old, heavy, feudal castles to stately villas built upon the Italian plan. Their mode of living changed, too, and in it and in their dress, we note great elaborateness and extravagance. This new interest and joy in living found expression in the literary productions of the period, especially in poetry and in drama. It has been said that everybody wrote poetry during Elizabeth's reign. The whole nation burst into song. The happy, carefree life was reproduced in the poetry of the home, of spring flowers, of birds, of battles on land and sea, of youth, and of love. England was a "Merrie England" and good Queen Bess was a revered and honored sovereign.

Much of the poetry of the period shows an Italian influence for Italy had a higher development of civilization and literature than did England. We have already noted the Italian influence in Chaucer's poetry, and in the blank verse and sonnets of Wyatt and Surrey. In the Elizabethan Age we find further imitations of Italian verse.

Edmund Spenser (1552–1599)

The first great poet of the Elizabethan Age, sometimes called "the poets' poet," is Edmund Spenser. Spenser was a product of the new education, and in him unite the new learning, medieval romance, and English seriousness. His first important poem was *The Shepherd's Calendar*, a pastoral poem dealing with country life. It is divided into twelve parts, one for each month, and in it are recorded the poet's unreturned love for a lady named Rosalind, some little condemnation of church practices, and homage to the Queen.

The Faerie Queene

Spenser's greatest work is his allegorical romance, the *Faerie Queene*, which he never finished. The plan of the *Faerie Queene* is as follows: Spenser pretends that at a feast held by the Queen of Faerie, on each of the twelve successive days a stranger in distress presents himself asking the Queene for a knight to champion his cause. Each book is concerned with one adventure; the first book, for example, deals with the legend of the Red Cross Knight. Spenser completed only six books and a fragment of the seventh. The characters and the incidents throughout carry an allegorical meaning. The Faerie Queene, for example, is Queen Elizabeth, and the Red Cross Knight represents Holiness. Other knights are Temperance, Chastity, Friendship, Justice, and Courtesy. The lady, Una, represents Religion. Throughout the poem Spenser brings in actual happenings of the day, religious discussions, wars of the times, and popular heroes.

In writing the *Faerie Queene,* Spenser devised a new stanza form which takes its name from him—the Spenserian stanza. This stanza has nine lines with the following rhyming scheme: a b a b b c b c c. So well adapted is this stanza to the work that one reads page after page of Spenser's smooth, flowing, liquid verse without any sense of monotony. The following selection from the first book of the *Faerie Queene* will illustrate both the style and the beautiful melody of the poem.

> A Gentle Knight was pricking on the plaine,
> Ycladd in mightie armes and silver shielde,
> Wherein old dints of deepe woundes did remaine,
> The cruell markes of many a bloudy fielde;
> Yet armes till that time did he never wield:
> His angry steede did chide his foaming bitt,
> As much disdayning to the curbe to yield:
> Full jolly knight he seemed, and faire did sitt,
> As one for knightly giusts and fierce encounters fitt.

William Shakespeare (1564-1616)

Of Shakespeare, the greatest figure in English literature, a more complete account will be given in the study of the drama. Although he is best known as a dramatist, it has been said that his poetry alone would have made him famous even if he had never written any drama. In addition to two long narrative poems, *Venus and Adonis* and *The Rape of Lucrece,* he wrote one hundred and fifty-four sonnets, exquisitely beautiful in their expression and deeply thoughtful in their content.

His songs are bits of charming lyrical verse found in many of his dramas. Among the most beautiful lyrics is *When Icicles Hung by the Wall* from *Love's Labor Lost.* From *The Merchant of Venice* we have *Tell Me Where is Fancy Bred,* sung when Bassanio is about to make his choice of the caskets which will result in Portia's hand. *Under the Greenwood Tree* and *Blow, Blow, Thou Winter Wind* are nature lyrics from *As You Like It* and they extol the charm of outdoor life.

All of Shakespeare's poetry reflects his love of nature and his keen observance of human characteristics. Nothing was too trivial to be overlooked by his keen intellect. His poetry reaches a state of perfection in its naturalness of setting that no other writer has ever equalled.

Ben Jonson (1573-1637)

Like Shakespeare, Jonson is better known as a dramatist, but a number of his poems will always live in English literature. He was at his best in lyric poetry, some of his most widely read lyrics being *To the Memory of My Beloved Mother, To the Memory of My Beloved Master,* and *To Celia.* The last named is a song which is as much loved today by those who are fond of music as it was over three hundred years ago when it was written. Jonson was named Poet Laureate on the accession of James I in 1603.

The Authorized Translation of the Bible

No study of the poetry of the Elizabethan period can overlook the authorized version of the Bible which was completed in 1611, for in it are examples of some of the most beautiful poetry in existence. In the *Psalms*, particularly, are to be found simple, eloquent, and beautiful verse which has had tremendous influence on the literary expression of many of our great poets.

Minor Poets of the Elizabethan Age

It is impossible within the brief limits of this story to give anything approximating an adequate account of the great number of poets who produced excellent verse between the years 1550 and 1625. Between the publication in 1557 of Tottel's *Miscellany*, a collection of about three hundred poems, and the end of the period there appeared several collections of songs from dozens of young poets. These songs, many of which are yet well known, exhibit a great variety of stanza form and exquisite lyric grace and sweetness. Among the most important poets of this minor group were Sir Walter Raleigh, Christopher Marlowe, Sir Philip Sidney, and John Lyly.

Sir Walter Raleigh (1552–1618) led a life of adventure. He was a court favorite, but most of his life was spent in organizing expeditions, in explorations, in colonizing new countries, in wars, even in prison. Rarely were his expeditions successful, however, and most of his poetry reflects his moods of despondency. He wrote both sonnets and lyrics, two of his best known poems being *The Nymph's Reply to the Shepherd* and *A Vision upon the Conceit of the Fairy Queen*. His poem entitled *Conclusion* was said to have been written the night before his execution.

Christopher Marlowe (1564–1593), like Raleigh, led an adventurous life. But he was wild and reckless and at twenty-nine was killed in a drunken brawl. In poetry he is best remembered for his development of blank verse which had already been introduced by Surrey. *Hero and Leander* is considered his best poem but he is also noted for *The Passionate Shepherd to His Love* and a number of sonnets.

Sir Philip Sidney (1554–1586) was a soldier who traveled extensively and was a great court favorite. He was at one time betrothed to Lady Penelope Devereux to whom he addressed *Astrophel and Stella*, a collection of songs and sonnets which contain many beautiful passages.

John Lyly (1554–1606) received his education at Magdalen College, Oxford, and was elected to Parliament several times. One of his best songs is *Appelles' Song* taken from his comedy *Alexander and Campaspé*. His *Hymn to Apollo* is another short song with charming rhythm.

Poetry of the Elizabethan Age

UNDER THE GREENWOOD TREE

William Shakespeare

Poem Interest: On a bright sunny day when you are lying under a tree watching the leaves move lazily in the breeze and listening to the singing of the birds, do you not feel sorry for those who have to be working? Perhaps Shakespeare had something of this idea when he wrote the following poem.

<pre>
     Under the greenwood tree
     Who loves to lie with me,
     And turn his merry note
     Unto the sweet bird's throat,
  5 Come hither, come hither, come hither:
        Here shall he see
        No enemy
     But winter and rough weather.

     Who doth ambition shun
 10 And loves to live i' the sun,
     Seeking the food he eats
     And pleased with what he gets,
</pre>

> Come hither, come hither, come hither;
> > Here shall he see
> 15   No enemy
> > But winter and rough weather.

Poem Development: Whom does the poet call "hither" in the first stanza? What were the only enemies those living a free life in the forest would encounter? In the second stanza whom does the poet call to the forest? What is the effect of the short lines of the poem? What are the theme and the central thought?
Interpretations: How is the word "who" used in each stanza? Turn his merry note; ambition; lines 11 and 12.
Significant Expressions: Quote the lines which for you present the pleasantest picture.

HARK, HARK! THE LARK

William Shakespeare

Poem Interest: In England, the lark truly does seem to sing at heaven's gate because it flies straight up and up and up into the sky until it is lost from sight, while its song floats back, fainter and fainter, until it too, is lost in the blue haze. Listen for the note of his song in this musical little poem.

> Hark, hark! the lark at heaven's gate sings;
> > And Phœbus 'gins arise,
> > His steeds to water at those springs
> > On chaliced flowers that lies;
> 5   And winking Mary-buds begin
> > To ope their golden eyes.
> > With every thing that pretty is,
> > > My lady sweet, arise,
> > > > Arise, arise!

2. Phœbus—God of the sun.
5. Mary-buds—Marigold buds.

Poem Development: Perhaps you have sung this song to the beautiful music composed by Franz Schubert. If you have, you can never read the words without also hearing the music. Look up the story of Phœbus, the sun god. What are his steeds? Give a word picture of the poem. What is the theme? What is the central thought?

Interpretations: 'Gins; chaliced. Name some flowers which you think are "chaliced."

Significant Expressions: Quote a line describing a flower. What is the figure of speech in line 6?

WHEN TO THE SESSIONS OF SWEET SILENT THOUGHT

William Shakespeare

Poem Interest: You will find that the appeal of Shakespeare lies in the artistry and accuracy with which he depicts the truisms of human nature. In this sonnet, he has given us a study of the inspiration of today's friendship as it overweighs all sorrow and loss of the past.

When to the sessions of sweet silent thought
I summon up remembrance of things past,
I sigh the lack of many a thing I sought,
And with old woes new wail my dear time's waste;
5 Then can I drown an eye, unused to flow,
For precious friends hid in death's dateless night,
And weep afresh love's long-since-canceled woe,
And moan the expense of many a vanished sight.
Then can I grieve at grievances foregone,
10 And heavily from woe to woe tell o'er
The sad account of fore-bemoanèd moan
Which I new pay as if not paid before;
But if the while I think on thee, dear friend,
All losses are restored, and sorrows end.

Poem Development: What were the things the author remembered first when he thought of the past? What were the things he next remembered? Summarize in your own words the things he grieved about. What causes his sorrow to cease? Give the theme and the central thought.

Interpretations: Sessions; summon up remembrance; sigh the lack; dear time; drown an eye; line 8; fore-bemoanèd moan; losses are restored.

Significant Expressions: What is the figure of speech in line 1? Quote the lines expressing mourning for old friends. Quote a line meaning the end of sorrow.

WHEN IN DISGRACE WITH FORTUNE AND MEN'S EYES

William Shakespeare

Poem Interest: It is said that love alone opens the gates of a human heart to true thankfulness and power. For Shakespeare, just the memory of love made new the world, redressing all the wrong of failure and despair.

    When in disgrace with fortune and men's eyes
    I all alone beweep my outcast state,
    And trouble deaf heaven with my bootless cries,
    And look upon myself, and curse my fate,
5   Wishing me like to one more rich in hope,
    Featured like him, like him with friends possessed,
    Desiring this man's art, and that man's scope,
    With what I most enjoy contented least;
    Yet in these thoughts myself almost despising,
10 Haply I think on thee,—and then my state,
    (Like to the lark at break of day arising
    From sullen earth,) sings hymns at heaven's gate;
    For thy sweet love remembered, such wealth brings
    That then I scorn to change my state with kings.

Poem Development: This sonnet is distinctly human, as all of Shakespeare's writings are. Have you felt "all alone" when you have been particularly discouraged? What is the meaning of line 1? Why does the poet say "deaf heaven" in line 3? Have you ever wished you were in some one else's place? What were the things the poet envied the other men? Can you give an instance from your own experience which will illustrate line 8? Why should the poet despise himself? Whom do you suppose he thought about? Why should this change his attitude? What is the theme? What is the central thought?

Interpretations: Beweep; outcast state; bootless; this man's art; that man's scope; haply I think on thee.

Significant Expressions: Quote a line which tells what the author desired. Quote a line which tells what he thought of himself. Quote a simile. Quote lines telling the poet's final state of happiness, and what changed his thoughts.

TO CELIA

BEN JONSON

Poem Interest: Probably no finer compliment can be paid to a woman than to have a beautiful poem written to her. When the poem can be set to music, the compliment is doubly enhanced. Such a poem is the following—a poem which the world has been singing for over three centuries.

> DRINK to me only with thine eyes,
>   And I will pledge with mine;
> Or leave a kiss but in the cup
>   And I'll not look for wine.
> 5 The thirst that from the soul doth rise
>   Doth ask a drink divine;
> But might I of Jove's nectar sup,
>   I would not change for thine.
>
> I sent thee late a rosy wreath,
> 10   Not so much honoring thee
> As giving it a hope that there
>   It could not withered be;
> But thou thereon didst only breathe
>   And sent'st it back to me;
> 15 Since when it grows, and smells, I swear
>   Not of itself, but thee!

7. JOVE—Father of the gods.
7. NECTAR—A drink prepared for the gods.

Poem Development: In the old days it was customary, whenever the occasion offered, to drink a toast to the fair ladies present. In the opening line the poet substitutes something in the place of the wine. What is it? In line 3 the poet says that if the fair lady will but touch her lips to the cup, it will suffice for him and the wine will be unnecessary. What further compliment is paid Celia in the first stanza? What are the compliments in the second stanza? What is the theme? What is the central thought?

Interpretations: I will pledge with mine; drink divine; lines 10, 11 and 12.

Significant Expressions: Quote a line expressing a compliment. Quote a line showing the poet's depth of feeling for Celia.

TO THE MEMORY OF MY BELOVED MASTER, WILLIAM SHAKESPEARE

BEN JONSON

Poem Interest: There were but ten years between the birth dates of Shakespeare and Jonson. We are told they were great friends. "I loved the man," said Jonson, "and do honor his memory, on this side idolatry." In this light, we can understand the beauty of his poem.

    To DRAW no envy, Shakespeare, on thy name,
    Am I thus ample to thy book and fame;
    While I confess thy writings to be such
    As neither man nor muse can praise too much.
5   'Tis true, and all men's suffrage. But these ways
    Were not the paths I meant unto thy praise;
    For silliest ignorance on these may light,
    Which, when it sounds at best, but echoes right;
    Or blind affection, which doth ne'er advance
10 The truth, but gropes, and urgeth all by chance;
    Or crafty malice might pretend this praise,
    And think to ruin, where it seemed to raise. . . .
    But thou art proof against them, and, indeed,
    Above the ill fortune of them, or the need.
15 I therefore will begin. Soul of the age,
    The applause, delight, the wonder of our stage,
    My Shakespeare, rise! I will not lodge thee by
    Chaucer, or Spenser, or bid Beaumont lie
    A little further, to make thee a room:
20 Thou art a monument without a tomb,
    And art alive still while thy book doth live,
    And we have wits to read and praise to give.
    That I not mix thee so my brain excuses—
    I mean with great, but disproportioned Muses;
25 For if I thought my judgment were of years,

    2. AMPLE—Abundant in praise.
    4. MUSE—The Muses were goddesses of song, poetry and the arts.
    5. SUFFRAGE—Opinion, decision.
    18. CHAUCER, SPENSER, BEAUMONT—Chaucer was an earlier English poet, sometimes called the "father of English literature." Spenser and Beaumont were Shakespeare's contemporaries.
    25. OF YEARS—That is, mature.
    26. COMMIT—Compare.

I should commit thee surely with thy peers,
And tell how far thou didst our Lyly outshine,
Or sporting Kyd, or Marlowe's mighty line.
And though thou hadst small Latin and less Greek,
30 From thence to honor thee, I would not seek
For names, but call forth thundering Æschylus,
Euripides, and Sophocles to us,
Pacuvius, Accius, him of Cordova dead,
To life again, to hear thy buskin tread,
35 And shake a stage; or when thy socks were on,
Leave thee alone for the comparison
Of all that insolent Greece or haughty Rome
Sent forth, or since did from their ashes come.
Triumph, my Britain, thou hast one to show
40 To whom all scenes of Europe homage owe.
He was not of an age, but for all time!
And all the Muses still were in their prime,
When, like Apollo, he came forth to warm
Our ears, or like a Mercury to charm.
45 Nature herself was proud of his designs
And joyed to wear the dressing of his lines,
Which were so richly spun, and woven so fit,
As, since, she will vouchsafe no other wit.
The merry Greek, tart Aristophanes,
50 Neat Terence, witty Plautus, now not please,
But antiquated and deserted lie,
As they were not of Nature's family.
Yet must I not give Nature all; thy art,
My gentle Shakespeare, must enjoy a part;
55 For though the poet's matter nature be,
His art doth give the fashion; and that he

27–28. LYLY, KYD, MARLOWE—Dramatists of Shakespeare's day.
31–32. ÆSCHYLUS, EURIPIDES, SOPHOCLES—Dramatists of ancient Greece.
33. PACUVIUS, ACCIUS—Dramatists of ancient Rome.
33. HIM OF CORDOVA—Seneca, a Roman dramatist.
34. BUSKIN—A very thick-soled high boot worn by actors of tragedy.
35. SOCKS—Thin-soled low slippers worn by actors of comedy.
43. APOLLO—God of the sun.
44. MERCURY—Messenger of the gods.
49. ARISTOPHANES—A writer of ancient Greek comedy.
50. TERENCE, PLAUTUS—Writers of Roman comedy.

Who casts to write a living line must sweat,
(Such as thine are) and strike the second heat
Upon the Muses' anvil, turn the same
60 (And himself with it) that he thinks to frame,
Or, for the laurel, he may gain a scorn;
For a good poet's made, as well as born.
And such wert thou; look how the father's face
Lives in his issue, even so the race
65 Of Shakespeare's mind and manners brightly shines
In his well turnèd and filèd lines,
In each of which he seems to shake a lance,
As brandished at the eyes of ignorance.
Sweet Swan of Avon! what a sight it were
70 To see thee in our waters yet appear,
And make those flights upon the banks of Thames,
That so did take Eliza and our James!
But stay, I see thee in the hemisphere
Advanced, and made a constellation there!
75 Shine forth, thou Star of poets, and with rage
Or influence chide or cheer the drooping stage,
Which, since thy flight from hence, hath mourned like night,
And despairs day, but for thy volume's light.

57. CASTS—Attempts.
61. LAUREL—A symbol of victory or achievement.
72. ELIZA AND OUR JAMES—Queen Elizabeth, and her successor, King James I.

Poem Development: What does Jonson say about the worth of Shakespeare's writings? What does he say of the opinions of other men about Shakespeare's works? Name the things Jonson says Shakespeare's writings are proof against. Name the men whom he thinks Shakespeare surpasses. Do you think the dramatists mentioned in lines 31–44 wrote tragedy or comedy? Why? Describe the art of writing as Jonson sees it. What evidences do you find of the sincerity of Jonson's praise of his friend? What is the theme? the central thought?

Interpretations: But these ways were not the paths I meant unto thy praise (l. 5–6); thou art a monument without a tomb (l. 20); art alive still while thy book doth live (l. 21); line 22; peers (l. 26); thy buskin tread (l. 34); when thy socks were on (l. 35); vouchsafe (l. 48); line 41; sweet Swan of Avon (l. 69).

Significant Expressions: Can you quote at least three famous lines which you recognize as having heard or read before? What is the figure of speech in line 69? Quote a line which tells what Shakespeare's writings do for the stage.

PSALM I

Poem Interest: According to the interpretation given of old, a psalm is a song or a hymn, the singing of which is accompanied by the music of a stringed instrument. Most of the psalms we know are attributed to David, "sweetest singer of Israel." Although the score of their music has long since been lost, the poetry of the psalms remains, lovely in its lyric beauty.

BLESSED is the man that walketh not in the counsel of the
    ungodly,
Nor standeth in the way of sinners,
Nor sitteth in the seat of the scornful.
But his delight is in the law of the Lord;
5 And in His law doth he meditate day and night.
And he shall be like a tree planted by the rivers of water,
    that bringeth forth his fruit in his season;
His leaf also shall not wither;
And whatsoever he doeth shall prosper.
The ungodly are not so;
10 But are like the chaff which the wind driveth away.
Therefore the ungodly shall not stand in the judgment,
Nor sinners in the congregation of the righteous.
For the Lord knoweth the way of the righteous;
But the way of the ungodly shall perish.

1. COUNSEL OF THE UNGODLY—Advice of the wicked.

Poem Development: This psalm is said to have been written as an introduction after the rest of the psalter was completed. It does not abound in imagery as some of the others do, but rather emphasizes the idea of retribution. What are the two parallel ideas? In your own words, give the admonitions to, and the rewards of, the godly; of the ungodly. What is the theme of the poem? Give the central thought.

Interpretations: Walketh not in the counsel of the ungodly; sitteth in the seat of the scornful; congregation.

Significant Expressions: This psalm is so often quoted that it is worth memorizing. What is the figure of speech in line 6? in line 10?

PSALM 23

Poem Interest: Great thankfulness welled up in David's heart as he contemplated the goodness of God's ever-present protection. Living as he did, in a shepherd's country, his thought turned to something familiar to which this care could be likened—the love of a shepherd for his sheep. And so his grateful voice rings out ...

THE Lord is my shepherd;
I shall not want.
He maketh me to lie down in green pastures,
He leadeth me beside the still waters.
5 He restoreth my soul.
He leadeth me in the paths of righteousness for His name's sake.
Yea, though I walk through the valley of the shadow of death,
I will fear no evil,
For Thou art with me.
10 Thy rod and thy staff they comfort me.
Thou preparest a table before me in the presence of mine enemies;
Thou anointest my head with oil;
My cup runneth over.
Surely goodness and mercy shall follow me all the day of my life,
15 And I will dwell in the house of the Lord forever.

Poem Development: Much of the reference in this psalm is to the customs of the shepherd of old in the care of his sheep, and here used symbolically to express the great assurance and comfort that the thought of God brings to David. What are the references in the first 10 lines to customs of the shepherd? What is the thought in lines 11-13? What is the final expression of confidence in God? What is the central thought of this psalm?

Interpretations: Line 12; line 13; dwell in the house of the Lord.

Significant Expressions: If you have not already memorized this psalm, you will want to learn it. Go over the lines, quoting those which express the restoring power of God; those telling the bounty of God's care. Quote a line containing a metaphor; also give the figure of speech in line 14.

PSALM 121

Poem Interest: From what crystal-clear depths of faith springs the white light of these splendidly confident songs of David! With limitless assurance, he lifts his eyes and voice in prayer, up to the eternal hills.

> I WILL lift up mine eyes unto the hills,
> From whence cometh my help.
> My help cometh from the Lord,
> Which made heaven and earth.
> 5 He will not suffer thy foot to be moved;
> He that keepeth thee will not slumber.
> Behold, He that keepeth Israel
> Shall neither slumber nor sleep.
> The Lord is thy keeper;
> 10 The Lord is thy shade upon thy right hand.
> The sun shall not smite thee by day,
> Nor the moon by night.
> The Lord shall preserve thee from all evil;
> He shall preserve thy soul.
> 15 The Lord shall preserve thy going out and thy coming in
> From this time forth, and even for evermore.

Poem Development: It is interesting to note here, as in many of the psalms, that the thought is expressed first in the first person, and is then carried on in the third person. This does not necessarily involve the interpolation of a second party—more often than not it is but the singer's way of reiterating the assurance he has given in the first lines of his own faith. Interpret the first four lines. You will see that this thought is general. The next section, given in third person, is an elaboration of this confident assurance of God's help. What significance do you attach to line 5? Again we find the reiteration of assurance. The psalmist seems so overflowing with thankfulness and faith that he hardly mentions the things that trouble him. For a understanding of lines 10-12, it should be explained that one of the greatest dangers in Jerusalem by day is that of sunstroke, and also that in the language of the mystic, the right hand is considered the position of comforter and protector. Also, in many countries of the East, the rays of the moon are considered dangerous. In the last four lines we again find the deep assurance and the climax—lines embracing all human activity from dawn to dusk, from birth to death, and into eternity. Give in your own words, the fullest meaning of lines 15-16. Briefly summarize the message of this psalm.

Significant Expressions: Quote the lines of assurance that you like the best. What is the figure of speech in line 5?

THE HISTORY OF POETRY IN ENGLAND

The Puritan Age and the Restoration (1625-1700)

The Puritan Age (1625-1660)

In the days of Queen Elizabeth the Puritans had been strong, but Elizabeth had been stronger, and she, not they, had controlled the country. During her reign the people were joyous and carefree and there were unified patriotism and loyalty to the queen. As the Puritans came into power after her death, however, all these things were changed. The Puritans were a stern, unrelenting people, who did not believe in festivities or celebrations. The theaters were closed, maypole dancing was prohibited, and holidays were abolished. The two parties, Puritans and Royalists, were constantly at variance with each other.

These conditions necessarily had their effect on the literature of the times. Not only were poetic productions lessened in number, but their character was changed. We now find that poetry reflects a sad, gloomy mood. Much of it is unnatural and fantastic, and it is often obscure and eccentric. It has little of the romantic element and it reflects the moral earnestness of the Puritans. The name of only one Puritan poet, that of John Milton, stands out as pre-eminently great. There were many minor writers, both Puritan and Royalist, but their importance consists not so much in the productions which they left us, as in the new forms which they used and which influenced the writings of later poets.

John Milton (1608-1674)

Milton was born eight years before the death of Shakespeare, but his poetry was not to be the product of that exuberant delight in life which animated the poets of the Elizabethan age. His inspiration was to be the most austere ideal of life which was the guiding star of Puritanism. He was the child of a Puritan home, and received there a careful, devout, and dutiful training. His father, who had become a Puritan while a student at Oxford and had been disinherited for doing so, was a man of independence of mind and conspicuous integrity. Milton seems to have owed much to him. He was a man of literary tastes and a musician and composer of considerable ability.

Milton's formal education began at the age of eight when his father engaged as his tutor Thomas Young, a young Scotch clergyman whom Milton credits with having infused into him a taste for classic literature and poetry. At the age of twelve he went as a day scholar to the justly famous St. Paul's School where he further developed the love of learning which characterized him to the end of his life. In 1625 he entered Christ College, Cambridge, where he remained for seven years. After leaving Cambridge he retired to his father's country place at Horton in Buckinghamshire, about seventeen miles from London. Here he spent five years in study and in wide reading in the Latin, Greek, French,

Italian and English. In 1638 Milton made a tour of Italy, making the acquaintance of Italian literary men and scholars, visiting places of interest, and collecting books and manuscripts. Upon his return to London he received into his house "the sons of some gentlemen that were his intimate friends" as pupils and interested himself in education.

About 1641, he was attracted into the controversy then raging over church reform. Now began a period of about twenty years during which he left "a calm and pleasing solitariness, fed with cheerful and confident thoughts" to "embark in a troubled sea of noises and hoarse disputes." In 1649 he became Latin Secretary to the Council of State. In addition to the performance of the duties which this office lay upon him, he wrote a number of tracts in defense of the policies of the Commonwealth. His eyesight, which it would seem had never been strong, was severely tasked by these undertakings, yet he felt that it was his duty to continue even in the face of the warning by his physician that blindness would result; and in 1652 he became totally blind.

After the restoration of the Stuarts in 1660, he was obliged for some time to live in concealment. There now followed what from the standpoint of literature was the most important period in his life, during which he wrote the greatest epic in our language, *Paradise Lost,* which was published in 1667. Critics are generally agreed that this work is his masterpiece. The poem deals with the fall of man and the promise of his redemption, and was written for the purpose of justifying the ways of God toward man.

Milton's life bears out the belief which he once expressed in middle age. "I was confirmed," he wrote, "in this opinion, that he who would not be frustrated of his hope to write well hereafter in laudable things ought himself to be a true poem—not presuming to sing high praises of heroic men or famous cities, unless he have in himself the experience and practice of all that is praiseworthy."

The Religious and Metaphysical Poets

The sober, less confident mood, which in the Puritan Age replaced the delight in life and intense vigor which had characterized Elizabethan literature, is particularly observable in the religious and so-called metaphysical poets. While many of the poems of this group were deeply religious, there is often to be found in them a strain of the unreal, the mysterious, the fantastic, and the obscure.

John Donne (1573–1631)

In point of time, John Donne who died in 1631 belongs perhaps with the Elizabethans but his poetry does not have the Elizabethan flavor.

Donne's life is in fact a kind of symbol of the change which was taking place. As a young man Donne seems to have been an Elizabethan gallant but the love poetry which he wrote in his youth is quite different from that of Ben Jonson and those whom we think of as typical Elizabethans. Instead of the blind, intense devotion expressed by other Elizabethan poets, Donne takes a more realistic if not a somewhat cynical view of love. He seems to have felt that life after all could not yield enduring satisfaction. His poetry reflects a melancholy which appears to proceed from a consciousness that life regardless of what it seems to promise is, after all, a fleeting thing. When middle age was upon him, he entered the church. He rose rapidly to be Dean of St. Paul's and became perhaps the most celebrated preacher of his time. His poetry is intellectual, perhaps, rather than emotional and concerns itself with religious and philosophical aspects of life.

Robert Herrick (1591-1674)

Herrick, the most gifted of all the minor poets of this period, was a clergyman. His poetry, while not reflecting an intense delight in life, is, however, not in the vein of the other religious poets. It displays a quiet, bright joy in living, without intensity of feeling. His touch was light and in his poetry there is nothing of the weightiness of the metaphysical poets. His best known poem and one of the most charming lyrics in English is *Corinna's Going A-Maying,* descriptive of the English custom of bringing in the May.

Other Religious Poets

Richard Crashaw, George Herbert, and Henry Vaughan are sometimes referred to as "the school of Donne." Crashaw at times attains great beauty in his poetry, but it is more often heavy with the over-niceties of style and extravagant "conceits" of expression so peculiar to the Metaphysicists. His first collection of poems was published under the title of *Delights of the Muses.* George Herbert, after his graduation from Cambridge, entered the church. He led a saintly life and contributed some very beautiful religious poems which were published in a book entitled *The Temple.* Henry Vaughan was a Welsh doctor and a great disciple of Herrick in sacred writings. He saw "God revealed in the living world of nature." *The Retreat* and *Childhood* are two of his most beautiful poems.

The Cavalier Poets

Under the designation of Cavalier poets are usually included Thomas Carew, Sir John Suckling, and Richard Lovelace. Their poetry is characterized by a carefree, dashing gayety which stands in great contrast to the melancholy of the religious poets. Carew wrote love poetry, the poem *Song* being perhaps his best work. Lovelace was well educated and a social favorite at court. He was devoted to the King and imprisoned for the cause, finally dying in dire poverty. While in prison he wrote the poem which has lived through the years, *To Lucasta on Going to the Wars*. Sir John Suckling was also a brilliant courtier and gallant royalist. His lyrics are characterized by their melody and lightness of verse. His best known poem is *Ballad upon a Wedding*.

Two other poets of the period, Abraham Cowley and Edmund Waller, were very popular in their day. Waller developed what is known as the heroic couplet and Cowley gave us the Pindaric ode. Both of these new forms were later used by the poets of the eighteenth century.

The Restoration

In 1660 the Puritan régime came to an end and Charles II ascended the English throne. His followers returned from the Continent where they had been obliged to flee during the days of the Commonwealth. For a time there was a wild, extravagant, unrepressed orgy of pleasure, but after this natural reaction to the soberness of the Puritan days, all England seems to have been possessed by a desire to get back to normal conditions. From the Cavaliers came the demand that English poetry should follow the style and type they had known in France and in Italy. The aim in literature became formal correctness and we find the beginnings of the classicism which was to dominate the literature of the next century.

John Dryden (1631–1700)

Dryden was the outstanding figure of the Restoration Period and is a link between the seventeenth and eighteenth centuries. He was a most voluminous writer, having to his credit a number of long poems, a narrative account of the year 1666 during which the English achieved a number of naval victories over the Dutch and the great fire of London occurred, a number of satirical poems, several dramas, translations from Homer and the chief Latin poets, and a great many critical essays. In poetry, he is especially remembered for his odes, two of which, *Alexander's Feast* and *A Song for St. Cecilia's Day*, are considered among the best in the English language. He appealed to the people by writing of the topics of the time and he utilized a plainer style of writing than that formerly used. However, while one admires Dryden's literary skill, the keenness of his intellect, and his remarkable versatility, one is not carried away by anything that Dryden wrote. He evidences little sense of the beauty of nature and almost no tenderness in his lines. He is chiefly noted for his satires and for his development of the heroic couplet.

Samuel Butler (1612–1680)

In the early years of the Restoration, the Puritan spirit was active, even though the Royalists were in power, and it was the object of much ridicule. Butler's one work entitled *Hudibras* was a satire upon the Puritans in which he ridiculed their hypocrisy and intolerance.

Poetry of the Puritan Age

ON HIS BLINDNESS

John Milton

Poem Interest: It is difficult for any of us to put ourselves in Milton's place; to realize what exquisite torture the man must have endured when he knew he had become incurably blind. Doubtless his first thought was of his writing—of anguished wondering if he would ever again be able to use his wonderful talent for putting into words the things he felt so keenly and so truly. We can understand something of the great sorrow he experienced through reading this poem.

When I consider how my light is spent,
Ere half my days in this dark world and wide,
And that one talent which is death to hide
Lodged with me useless, though my soul more bent
5 To serve therewith my Maker, and present
My true account, lest He returning chide—
"Doth God exact day-labor, light denied."
I fondly ask.—But patience, to prevent
That murmur, soon replies, "God doth not need
10 Either man's work, or His own gifts; who best
Bear His mild yoke, they serve Him best. His state
Is kingly; thousands at His bidding speed
And post o'er land and ocean without rest;
They also serve who only stand and wait."

1. Light—Sight.
1. Is spent—Is gone, used up.
2. Talent—The power to write.
4. Bent—Desirous or willing.
8. Fondly—Foolishly.

Poem Development: Rewrite the first two lines in your own words. What is the meaning of "lodged with me useless?" What question does the poet ask? What is the answer? Whom does the poet say serve the Lord best? Do you think this is true? What is the meaning of the last line? What is the theme? What is the central thought?

Interpretations: Line 1; true account; light denied; line 7; lines 11 and 12.

Significant Expressions: Find an illustration of personification. There is a line of this sonnet which is very often quoted. Which one is it?

L'ALLEGRO

John Milton

Poem Interest: *L'Allegro* and the following poem, *Il Penseroso*, are companion poems. The titles are usually translated as meaning "the cheerful man" and "the serious, or thoughtful man," and the poems as describing a day in the lives of each. The poems do not, however, describe the day of two distinct individuals; rather they describe the alternating moods of one man, and that man in this case is Milton himself. Nor should it be supposed that all the pleasures which mark the day of the cheerful man, for example, were enjoyed in the one round of twenty-four hours. What Milton is doing is describing a kind of composite day into which he has compressed the pleasures which appealed to him.

Hence, loathèd Melancholy,
   Of Cerberus and blackest Midnight born
In Stygian cave forlorn
   'Mongst horrid shapes, and shrieks, and sights unholy!

1. Hence—Be gone!
2. Cerberus (sŭr' bẽr ŭs)—The huge three-headed dog, with a serpent's tail, which in Greek mythology stood guard at the approach to Hades. The myth that Cerberus and Midnight were the parents of Melancholy is Milton's own invention.
3. Stygian (stĭj' ĭ ăn)—That is, in the region of the Styx, the chief river of Hades.

5   Find out some uncouth cell,
      Where brooding Darkness spreads his jealous wings,
      And the night-raven sings;
      There, under ebon shades and low-browed rocks,
      As ragged as thy locks,
10   In dark Cimmerian desert ever dwell.
      But come, thou Goddess fair and free,
      In heaven yclept Euphrosyne,
      And by men heart-easing Mirth;
      Whom lovely Venus, at a birth,
15   With two sister Graces more,
      To ivy-crownèd Bacchus bore:
      Or whether (as some sager sing)
      The frolic wind that breathes the spring,
      Zephyr, with Aurora playing,
20   As he met her once a-Maying,
      There, on beds of violets blue,
      And fresh-blown roses washed in dew,
      Filled her with thee, a daughter fair,
      So buxom, blithe, and debonair.
25   Haste thee, Nymph, and bring with thee
      Jest, and youthful Jollity,
      Quips and Cranks and wanton Wiles,

5. UNCOUTH—Wild, mysterious.
6. JEALOUS WINGS—Because unwilling to let light enter.
7. NIGHT-RAVEN—The night-owl, night-heron.
10. CIMMERIAN—The land of the Cimmerians in classic mythology was a region of mist and darkness across the stream Oceanus, which surrounded the world of men. Beyond the land of the Cimmerians was Hades.
12. YCLEPT—Called.
12. EUPHROSYNE (ū frŏs′ ĭ nē)—One of the three Graces, lesser deities, who as their designation indicates were the goddesses of gentility and the polite amenities. Euphrosyne means joy or cheerfulness. The other two were Aglaïa (brightness) and Thalïa (bloom). They were generally regarded as daughters of Zeus.   14. VENUS—The goddess of love and beauty.
16. BACCHUS—God of wine and revelry. He was generally represented as wearing a crown of ivy.
17. SOME SAGER—That is, some wiser poets. That Mirth (Euphrosyne) is the child not of Venus and Bacchus but of Zephyr and Aurora is Milton's own invention.   19. ZEPHYR—The West Wind.   19. AURORA—The Dawn.
20. A-MAYING—The allusion is to the old English custom of going out into the fields early on May-day to celebrate the return of spring and bring in the "may" or hawthorn.
24. BUXOM—In Milton's time the word "buxom" meant blithesome.
25. NYMPH—That is, Euphrosyne or Mirth.
27. QUIPS—Flashes of wit.   27. CRANKS—Plays on words.
27. WANTON WILES—Sportive tricks.

Nods and Becks and wreathèd Smiles,
Such as hang on Hebe's cheek,
30   And love to live in dimple sleek;
Sport that wrinkled Care derides,
And Laughter holding both his sides.
Come, and trip it, as you go,
On the light fantastic toe;
35   And in thy right hand lead with thee
The mountain-nymph, sweet Liberty;
And, if I give thee honor due,
Mirth, admit me of thy crew,
To live with her, and live with thee,
40   In unreprovèd pleasures free;
To hear the lark begin his flight,
And, singing, startle the dull night,
From his watch-tower in the skies,
Till the dappled dawn doth rise;
45   Then to come, in spite of sorrow,
And at my window bid good-morrow,
Through the sweet-briar or the vine,
Or the twisted eglantine;
While the cock, with lively din,
50   Scatters the rear of darkness thin;
And to the stack, or the barn-door,
Stoutly struts his dames before:
Oft listening how the hounds and horn
Cheerly rouse the slumbering Morn,

28. BECKS—Bows, beckonings.
29. HEBE (hē' bē)—Goddess of youth, and cupbearer to the gods.
31. CARE—Care is the object of derides.
34. FANTASTIC—The word as Milton uses it here designates movements in the dance made according to the fancy of those dancing.
36. MOUNTAIN-NYMPH, SWEET LIBERTY—Here is another of Milton's inventions. The idea of a mountain-nymph, Liberty, was suggested to Milton, it is safe to say, by the love of freedom and hatred of tyranny which has seemed peculiarly characteristic of mountain dwellers, notably the Swiss.
39. HER—Liberty.
40. UNREPROVÈD—Innocent.
41. TO HEAR, etc.—Here begins the delineation of the "unreprovèd pleasures" which appeal to the cheerful mood.
41. TO HEAR THE LARK—The lark is a small, brownish bird, which nests on the ground. In flight it sings almost continuously, soaring up until it becomes lost to sight and then dropping to its nest.
45. THEN TO COME—The infinitive "to come" is co-ordinate with "to hear." The sense is: To hear the lark . . . [and] Then to come . . .

JOHN MILTON

55 From the side of some hoar hill,
Through the high wood echoing shrill:
Sometime walking, not unseen,
By hedgerow elms, on hillocks green,
Right against the eastern gate
60 Where the great Sun begins his state,
Robed in flames and amber light,
The clouds in thousand liveries dight;
While the ploughman, near at hand,
Whistles o'er the furrowed land,
65 And the milkmaid singeth blithe,
And the mower whets his scythe,
And every shepherd tells his tale
Under the hawthorn in the dale.
Straight mine eye hath caught new pleasures,
70 Whilst the landskip round it measures:
Russet lawns, and fallows gray,
Where the nibbling flocks do stray;
Mountains on whose barren breast
The laboring clouds do often rest;
75 Meadows trim, with daisies pied;
Shallow brooks, and rivers wide;
Towers and battlements it sees
Bosomed high in tufted trees,
Where perhaps some beauty lies,
80 The cynosure of neighboring eyes.
Hard by a cottage chimney smokes
From betwixt two aged oaks,
Where Corydon and Thyrsis met

55. HOAR—White with blossoming trees.
58. HEDGEROW ELMS—The elms which grow along the lines of the hedges. In England fields and lanes are bordered not by fences as in America but generally by dense hedges.
60. SUN—Sun is personified and compared to a great monarch setting out on a procession of "state" richly robed and attended by a great retinue of clouds in livery.
62. DIGHT—Dressed or garbed. 67. TELLS HIS TALE—Counts his sheep.
70. LANDSKIP—Landscape.   74. LABORING—"Teeming, heavy with rain."
75. PIED—Variegated. Pied modifies meadows, and alludes to the color effect which the daisies produce. Have you ever looked down from some hilltop on "meadows trim with daisies pied"?
80. CYNOSURE—The center of attraction.
83. CORYDON AND THYRSIS (Cŏr' ў dŏn, Thĕr' sĭs)—Shepherds in one of Vergil's poems of country life. Used here to indicate two English shepherds or rustics.

>   Are at their savory dinner set
> 85 Of herbs and other country messes,
>   Which the neat-handed Phyllis dresses;
>   And then in haste her bower she leaves,
>   With Thestylis to bind the sheaves;
>   Or, if the earlier season lead,
> 90 To the tanned haycock in the mead.
>   Sometimes, with secure delight,
>   The upland hamlets will invite,
>   When the merry bells ring round,
>   And the jocund rebecks sound
> 95 To many a youth and many a maid
>   Dancing in the chequered shade,
>   And young and old come forth to play
>   On a sunshine holiday,
>   Till the livelong daylight fail:
> 100 Then to the spicy nut-brown ale,
>   With stories told of many a feat,
>   How Faery Mab the junkets eat.
>   She was pinched and pulled, she said;
>   And he, by Friar's lantern led,

    86. PHYLLIS—A shepherdess in one of Vergil's poems. Here used, of course, to designate an English maid.   87. BOWER—Cottage.
    88. THESTYLIS (thĕs' tў lĭs)—A shepherdess in one of Vergil's poems.
    89. IF THE EARLIER SEASON LEAD—That is, if it is in the haying season which is earlier, of course, than the grain harvest.
    92. INVITE—Appeal to the fancy.
    93. RING ROUND—That is, ring one after another from the churches in the "upland hamlets." Milton is here describing a holiday, or holy-day, such as was celebrated in his day in every village.
    94. REBECKS—An old-fashioned fiddle or violin.
    102. FAERY MAB, etc.—The allusion is best explained by quoting from Ben Jonson, a contemporary of Shakespeare and Milton:

>   This is Mab, the mistress fairy,
>   That doth nightly rob the dairy.
>
>   She that pinches country wenches
>   If they rub not clean their benches.

    102. JUNKETS—A dish made of curds mixed with cream.
    102. EAT—This is the past tense of eat (ēt)—the form that Americans spell and pronounce *āte*.
    103. SHE—One of the villagers, a country maid.
    104. HE—Another of the villagers, a country fellow, or rustic.
    104. FRIAR'S—Friar Rush. This was a Christmas game. Milton evidently refers to Will-o'-the-Wisp who led travelers astray.

105   Tells how the drudging goblin sweat
      To earn his cream-bowl duly set,
      When in one night, ere glimpse of morn,
      His shadowy flail hath threshed the corn
      That ten day-laborers could not end;
110   Then lies him down, the lubber fiend,
      And, stretched out all the chimney's length,
      Basks at the fire his hairy strength,
      And crop-full out of doors he flings,
      Ere the first cock his matin rings.
115   Thus done the tales, to bed they creep,
      By whispering winds soon lulled asleep.
      Towered cities please us then,
      And the busy hum of men,
      Where throngs of knights and barons bold,
120   In weeds of peace, high triumphs hold,
      With store of ladies, whose bright eyes
      Rain influence, and judge the prize
      Of wit or arms, while both contend
      To win her grace whom all commend.

105. DRUDGING GOBLIN—Robin Goodfellow, another fairy or brownie, who in return for a bowl of cream set out for him would do no end of work during the night.

110. LUBBER—Drudging. Note the description of Robin. He was a pretty husky fairy.

110. FIEND—Used here simply to designate a supernatural being, a demon, not necessarily evil.

113. CROP-FULL—That is, stomach-full, well fed.

114. ERE THE FIRST COCK HIS MATIN RINGS—Fairies, goblins, etc., had to return to their abodes before sunrise.

115. THEY—The villagers.

119. WHERE THRONGS OF KNIGHTS . . . HIGH TRIUMPHS HOLD—Tournaments, such as the one described in *Ivanhoe*, had long since ceased to be held by Milton's day. There survived, however, a kind of mock tournament, known as a "triumph" or "joust of peace," which was the occasion for brilliant assemblage and courtly ceremony. It is to such a "triumph" that Milton alludes.

120. WEEDS OF PEACE—Garments of peace, there being no actual fighting to the death as in the old tournaments.

123. OF WIT OR ARMS—In the days of Elizabeth, especially, both "wit," that is, speeches of elaborate courtly compliment, and "arms," mimic contests with swords, lances, and pikes, featured these triumphs.

124. HER GRACE—That is, the favor of the Queen of Love and Beauty.

125   There let Hymen oft appear
      In saffron robe, with taper clear,
      And pomp, and feast, and revelry,
      With mask and antique pageantry;
      Such sights as youthful poets dream,
130   On summer eves by haunted stream.
      Then to the well-trod stage anon,
      If Jonson's learnèd sock be on,
      Or sweetest Shakespeare, Fancy's child,
      Warble his native wood-notes wild,
135   And ever, against eating cares,
      Lap me in soft Lydian airs,
      Married to immortal verse,
      Such as the meeting soul may pierce,
      In notes with many a winding bout

   125. THERE—That is, at Court. Court weddings were matters of elaborate ceremony and display.
   125. HYMEN—The god of marriage. Hymen was represented as wearing a yellow robe and bearing in his hand a torch.
   128. MASK—A dramatic entertainment, generally written for some particular occasion. *Comus* by Milton is a good example. The mask, or masque, was a much favored form of entertainment at Court in the days of Milton. One characteristic of its production was elaborate staging.
   128. PAGEANTRY—Pageants were frequent and extravagant in Elizabeth's day.
   131. TO THE WELL-TROD STAGE—That is, to the theater, well-trod, because in Milton's youth London had a number of well-trained companies of professional players.
   132. IF JONSON'S LEARNÈD SOCK BE ON—That is, to see if one of learnèd Ben Jonson's comedies is playing. The "sock" was a term used to designate comedy, and the "buskin" to designate tragedy. The "sock" was a light shoe worn by actors in comedy on the ancient stage, and the "buskin," a laced boot, was worn by tragic actors.
   133. FANCY'S CHILD—Imagination's child. Milton refers here to those lighter, gayer and more fanciful products of Shakespeare's imagination—the comedies such as *As You Like It, Twelfth Night*, and *A Midsummer Night's Dream*.
   134. HIS NATIVE WOOD-NOTES WILD—An oft repeated distinction between Shakespeare and Jonson is that Shakespeare had nature and Jonson had art. The meaning is that the latter taught himself to write drama by studying the dramas of the ancients whose rules he followed, whereas the former was a dramatist "by nature," so to speak, and was guided not by learning but by native ability only.
   135. EATING CARES—That is, cares that eat the heart.   136. LAP—Enfold.
   136. LYDIAN—A term designating one of the ancient Greek "modes" or scales, of which there were three: the Lydian, Dorian, and Phrygian. The Dorian was "soft and effeminate."
   137. MARRIED TO IMMORTAL VERSE—He would have immortal verse set to the Lydian airs.
   138. THE MEETING SOUL—That is, "the soul which lends itself to the music."
   139. BOUT—What in music is called a "phrase."

140   Of linkèd sweetness long drawn out
       With wanton heed and giddy cunning,
       The melting voice through mazes running,
       Untwisting all the chains that tie
       The hidden soul of harmony;
145   That Orpheus' self may heave his head
       From golden slumber on a bed
       Of heaped Elysian flowers, and hear
       Such strains as would have won the ear
       Of Pluto to have quite set free
150   His half-regained Eurydice.
       These delights if thou canst give,
       Mirth, with thee I mean to live.

141. WITH WANTON HEED AND GIDDY CUNNING—"Wanton heed" refers to playing that is frolicsome and sportive yet done with care and accuracy. "Giddy cunning" refers to the rapidity of skill shown by the player. If you have seen a violinist play a light, frolicsome piece which called for almost lightning swift manipulation of his instrument, you will know to what Milton, who was himself an accomplished musician, refers.

142. THE MELTING VOICE THROUGH MAZES RUNNING—That is, while the voice blending with the music accompanies it through its rapid and intricate changes.

143–44. UNTWISTING ALL THE CHAINS THAT TIE THE HIDDEN SOUL OF HARMONY—That is, freeing the soul from the worries and cares of life and restoring harmony to it.

145. ORPHEUS—Son of Apollo and Calliope, the muse of epic poetry.

147. ELYSIAN—(ê lĭzh' ăn)—The allusion is to the Elysian fields, the abode of the blessed or good, in Greek mythology.

149. PLUTO—God of Hades or the underworld.

150. EURYDICE (ū rĭd' ĭ sē)—A nymph, the wife of Orpheus. Orpheus was inconsolable at the death of Eurydice. Taking a lyre, given him by Apollo, he made his way to Hades. His music "drew iron tears down Pluto's cheek" and so moved that god that he granted Orpheus's petition to let Eurydice return to the upper world. One condition was attached to this permission. Orpheus who was to precede Eurydice was forbidden to look back, but as he was about to leave Hades he turned to see if Eurydice followed, whereupon she was carried back and lost to him.

Poem Development: The specific pleasures described in *L'Allegro* are those in which Milton himself delighted—the leisurely walk in the cool of the morning through the English countryside where there were sights and sounds to charm the ear and delight the eye; the upland hamlet, with its quaint customs and folklore, where old and young came forth to play on a sunshine holiday; the colorful pageantry of London and the Court; the comedies of Jonson and Shakespeare, and finally music "married to immortal verse such as the meeting soul may pierce."

The poem opens with the banishment of Melancholy. In Milton's day, Melancholy was a term to which attached a wide signification.

As used here, Milton probably had in mind what we usually understand by melancholy—a gloomy, unwholesome depression—the kind of melancholy which might most appropriately be thought of as born of "Cerberus and blackest Midnight, in Stygian cave forlorn." In direct contrast, it is interesting to note that the invocation to Mirth delineates a "goddess fair and free"—the patroness of "unreprovèd pleasures free," the healthy pleasures which do not enslave the spirit and mind of man. It is an uncloying Mirth, forever to be enjoyed, partaking of the west wind and the brightness of the dawn. Nor are her companion nymphs mere riotous bacchanals who by ceaseless activity and "making whoopee" endeavor to put boredom out of mind; rather are they representative of things which give delight to all those who can recognize that reality is within themselves, that "mind is its own place, and in itself can make a heaven of hell, a hell of heaven."

There are eight natural divisions into which the poem falls—lines 1–10; 11–40; 41–68; 69–90; 91–116; 117–134; 135–150; 151–152. For full appreciation of their poetic quality, study them carefully, keeping in mind the following points. Lyric poetry is the expression of a personal impression of the author, associated always with feeling—the poet is interested not merely in giving us mere items of information, he desires to make us feel as he does about the situation. To achieve this end, he employs the poetic device of imagery—a kind of sense experience which the poet, through the power of language, makes us seem to see, hear, feel, taste, or smell, as the case may be. In this way, he makes real to us his own experience, and to the degree that he causes us truly to sense it, to that degree do we feel as he does about it—for sensation is always accompanied by definite reactions of feeling. Too, the vividness of imagery is often heightened by the movement in the verse—you can note this fine point by scanning the lines for variety of meter.

Question yourself on each division: What is the idea or thought? What is the feeling? Note striking pieces of imagery, and classify each according to its appeal—is it visual or auditory, or of another type? what feeling does it give you? Point out lines which you consider most effective and tell why. Write a précis of one or more of the divisions. What is the theme of the entire poem? Give the central thought.

Interpretations: Horrid (l. 4); line 62; dresses (l. 86); chequered shade (l. 96); matin (l. 114).

Significant Expressions: What is the figure of speech in line 3? in line 44? in line 146? Read line 4 aloud for dramatic effect. Read line 6 in the same way and notice the different effects produced by the use of the consonants in the 4th line and the vowels in the 6th. Quote the lines describing the meadows. Quote the lines giving a picture of the dance. Memorize at least eight lines which you consider significant.

IL PENSEROSO

John Milton

Hence, vain deluding Joys,
  The brood of Folly without father bred!
How little you bested,
  Or fill the fixèd mind with all your toys!
5 Dwell in some idle brain,
  And fancies fond with gaudy shapes possess,
As thick and numberless
  As the gay motes that people the sun-beams,
Or likest hovering dreams,
10 The fickle pensioners of Morpheus' train.
But, hail! thou Goddess sage and holy!
Hail, divinest Melancholy!
Whose saintly visage is too bright
To hit the sense of human sight,

  2. Without father bred—They are wholly the offspring of Folly, and, therefore, quite senseless.
  3. Bested—Profit, avail.
  4. Fixèd—Serious.
  6. Fancies fond with gaudy shapes possess—The object of "possess" is "fancies." The meaning is: Fill foolish imaginations with showy ideas.
  10. Pensioners—Members of a retinue or body-guard.
  10. Morpheus—The god of sleep.
  14. To hit the sense of human sight—To look upon.

15   And therefore to our weaker view
     O'erlaid with black, staid Wisdom's hue;
     Black, but such as in esteem
     Prince Memnon's sister might beseem,
     Or that starred Ethiop queen that strove
20   To set her beauty's praise above
     The Sea-Nymphs, and their powers offended.
     Yet thou art higher far descended:
     Thee bright-haired Vesta long of yore
     To solitary Saturn bore;
25   His daughter she; in Saturn's reign
     Such mixture was not held a stain.
     Oft in glimmering bowers and glades
     He met her, and in secret shades
     Of woody Ida's inmost grove,
30   Whilst yet there was no fear of Jove.
     Come, pensive Nun, devout and pure,
     Sober, steadfast, and demure,
     All in a robe of darkest grain,
     Flowing with majestic train,
35   And sable stole of cypress lawn
     Over thy decent shoulders drawn.

18. PRINCE MEMNON'S SISTER—An Ethiopian prince of great beauty who fought on the side of the Trojans in the war with the Greeks. He was the son of Tithonius and Eos (Aurora). He had a sister Hemera who Milton thinks must have possessed her brother's beauty.

19. STARRED ETHIOP QUEEN, etc.—The allusion is to Cassiopea, a queen of Ethiopia, who boasted that she was more beautiful than the Nereids, or Sea-Nymphs. Offended by her boasting, the sea-nymph prevailed upon Poseidon to send a monster to ravage the coast of Ethiopia, and the queen's daughter, Andromeda, was exposed on a rock to appease the monster. Both Cassiopea and Andromeda were later changed to constellations—which explains "starred Ethiop queen."

23. VESTA—Goddess of the hearth and the divinity of the home. She was the first-born child of Saturn and Rhea.

24. SOLITARY SATURN—Called solitary probably because for a long period preceding the rule of the Olympian gods, Saturn (Cronos) was the sole lord of heaven and earth.

29. WOODY IDA—The woody slopes of Mount Ida on the island of Crete.

30. FEAR OF JOVE—Saturn, or Cronos, was told by his parents that he should be dethroned by his children. It was Jove (Jupiter or Zeus) the sixth child of Saturn who led the revolt against his father, and established the Olympian dynasty. Cronos, to prevent the fulfillment of the prophecy, swallowed the first five of his children as soon as they were born, but his wife, Rhea, caused Jove to be spirited away and concealed on Mount Ida.

33. GRAIN—Color, hue.

35. SABLE STOLE OF CYPRESS LAWN—A black robe of fine lawn or crape.

36. DECENT—Shapely.

JOHN MILTON

    Come; but keep thy wonted state,
    With even step, and musing gait,
    And looks commercing with the skies,
40   Thy rapt soul sitting in thine eyes:
    There, held in holy passion still,
    Forget thyself to marble, till
    With a sad leaden downward cast
    Thou fix them on the earth as fast.
45   And join with thee calm Peace and Quiet,
    Spare Fast, that oft with gods doth diet,
    And hears the Muses in a ring
    Aye round about Jove's altar sing;
    And add to these retirèd Leisure,
50   That in trim gardens takes his pleasure;
    But, first and chiefest, with thee bring
    Him that yon soars on golden wing,
    Guiding the fiery-wheelèd throne,
    The Cherub Contemplation;
55   And the mute Silence hist along,
    'Less Philomel will deign a song,
    In her sweetest, saddest plight,
    Smoothing the rugged brow of Night,

---

37. WONTED STATE—Accustomed dignity of bearing.
39. COMMERCING—Communing, conversing.
42. FORGET THYSELF TO MARBLE—That is, forgetting everything in holy contemplation until you become as motionless as a figure cut from marble.
44. THEM—"Thine eyes."
46. SPARE FAST, THAT OFT WITH GODS DOTH DIET—Among the ancients, fasting was practiced in connection with certain religious observances as a preparation for the sacrificial meal.
47. MUSES—The lesser deities who inspired the artistic powers in mortals. They were nine in number, the daughters of Jove and Mnemosyne (Memory).
48. AYE (ā)—Ever.
49. RETIRÈD—Living in retirement, withdrawn from the haunts of men.
52. HIM THAT YON SOARS ON GOLDEN WING—The allusion is to the vision of Ezekiel, related in Chapter 10: "Then I looked, and, behold, in the firmament that was above the head of the cherubims there appeared over them as it were a sapphire stone, as the appearance of the likeness of a throne. . . . And when I looked, behold the four wheels by the cherubims, one wheel by one cherub, and another wheel by another cherub, etc." These cherubims are nameless in the Scriptures. It is Milton's invention that one was Contemplation.
55. HIST—This is a verb in the imperative. Its object is "Silence." It means to urge along without making noise.
56. PHILOMEL—The nightingale.
57. PLIGHT—Mood, strain.

While Cynthia checks her dragon yoke
60   Gently o'er the accustomed oak.
Sweet bird, that shunn'st the noise of folly,
Most musical, most melancholy!
Thee, chauntress, oft the woods among
I woo, to hear thy even-song;
65   And, missing thee, I walk unseen
On the dry smooth-shaven green,
To behold the wandering moon,
Riding near her highest noon,
Like one that had been led astray
70   Through the heaven's wide pathless way,
And oft, as if her head she bowed,
Stooping through a fleecy cloud.
Oft, on a plat of rising ground,
I hear the far-off curfew sound,
75   Over some wide-watered shore,
Swinging slow with sullen roar;
Or, if the air will not permit,
Some still removèd place will fit,
Where glowing embers through the room
80   Teach light to counterfeit a gloom,
Far from all resort of mirth,
Save the cricket on the hearth,
Or the bellman's drowsy charm
To bless the doors from nightly harm.
85   Or let my lamp, at midnight hour,
Be seen in some high lonely tower,

---

59. CYNTHIA—Diana, goddess of the moon, called Cynthia because she was born on Mount Cynthus in Delos. Her chariot was drawn across the heavens by two white steeds. Milton substitutes dragons.

59. YOKE—Team.

60. THE ACCUSTOMED OAK—The oak over which the moon is accustomed to rise.

67. WANDERING—So called, since the moon, in contrast to the punctual and regular sun, seems to be a wanderer in the heavens, appearing and disappearing at odd times.

68. HIGHEST NOON—The highest point in the sky, the zenith.

73. PLAT—Plot.   77. AIR—Weather.   78. STILL REMOVÈD—Quiet, secluded.

80. TEACH LIGHT TO COUNTERFEIT A GLOOM—That is, the effect of the dim light from the embers is such that the gloom seems to result from the light.

83. BELLMAN'S DROWSY CHARM—The allusion is to the call of the watchman who went about the village streets at night swinging his bell and calling the hours.

JOHN MILTON

>   Where I may oft outwatch the Bear,
>   With thrice great Hermes, or unsphere
>   The spirit of Pluto, to unfold
> 90   What worlds or what vast regions hold
>   The immortal mind that hath forsook
>   Her mansion in this fleshly nook;
>   And of those demons that are found
>   In fire, air, flood, or underground,
> 95   Whose power hath a true consent
>   With planet or with element.
>   Sometime let gorgeous Tragedy
>   In sceptred pall come sweeping by,
>   Presenting Thebes, or Pelops' line,
> 100 Or the tale of Troy divine,

87. OUTWATCH THE BEAR—The allusion is to the constellation of the Bear which never sets in northern latitudes. Hence to outwatch it, means to sit up until dawn.

88. THRICE GREAT HERMES—Hermes, Trismegistus (thrice-great), an ancient philosopher and king. The meaning is to sit up reading a book by Hermes.

88. UNSPHERE THE SPIRIT OF PLATO—That is, call back the spirit of Plato from the "sphere" to which it passed after Plato's death. Plato was a great Greek philosopher. The meaning here is, of course, to read Plato's works, and thus "unsphere" him.

89. TO UNFOLD ... THIS FLESHLY NOOK—That is, to discover what becomes of the soul after death. The question is discussed in the *Phaedo*, one of the works of Plato, which gives an account of the death of Socrates.

93. AND OF THOSE—That is, And to tell of those.

96. FOUND IN FIRE ... OR WITH ELEMENT—There was a belief among the ancients that before man there was created a class of beings—variously referred to as spirits, genii, demons, angels—servants of God, sometimes called "sons of God," who were His servants in the creation and, afterward, in the government of the world. There is reference to these demons in Plato. Medieval philosophers divided them into four classes corresponding to the four elements —earth, air, fire, and water—of which they believed the universe made up. These demons were believed to be "in harmony" with the planets also—to have "a true consent with planet and with element." They were, of course, factors in human destiny since the planet or star under which one was born was thought to exert an influence on the individual and since the body itself was composed of the four elements. The "genius" or "demon" of Plato, however, is rather an attendant spirit or guardian angel who accompanies man through life and leads him afterward to the other world.

98. IN SCEPTRED PALL—That is, in the garb of royalty, bearing a sceptre. This personification of Tragedy indicates that Milton had in mind the great tragedies of the Greek dramatists Æschylus, Sophocles, and Euripides, all of whom wrote plays dealing with the legendary royalty of ancient Greece.

99. THEBES—Sophocles, in particular, dramatized the legend of Œdipus, King of Thebes, a city of Boetia.

99. PELOPS' LINE—The allusion here is to the tragedies of Æschylus and Euripides dealing with the great hero Agamemnon and his children.

100. TALE OF TROY—Sophocles and Euripides both dramatized incidents of the Trojan war.

>   Or what (though rare) of later age
>   Ennobled hath the buskined stage.
>   But, O sad Virgin; that thy power
>   Might raise Musæus from his bower;
> 105   Or bid the soul of Orpheus sing
>   Such notes as, warbled to the string,
>   Drew iron tears down Pluto's cheek,
>   And made Hell grant what love did seek;
>   Or call up him that left half-told
> 110   The story of Cambuscan bold,
>   Of Camball, and of Algarsife,
>   And who had Canace to wife,
>   That owned the virtuous ring and glass,
>   And of the wondrous horse of brass
> 115   On which the Tartar king did ride;
>   And if aught else great bards beside
>   In sage and solemn tunes have sung,
>   Of turneys, and of trophies hung,
>   Of forests, and enchantments drear,
> 120   Where more is meant than meets the ear.

101. OR WHAT (THOUGH RARE) OF LATER AGE—That is, of Milton's own time. Although Milton in *L'Allegro* refers to the comedies of Shakespeare and Jonson, he does not seem to have entertained so high an opinion of their tragedies as he did of those of the Greeks.

103. SAD VIRGIN—That is, Melancholy—the pensive Nun of line 31.

104. MUSÆUS—A legendary Greek poet whose power to move men was similar to that of Orpheus. None of his poems has survived; hence, Milton's desire to raise him from his bower.

105. ORPHEUS—See the note to line 150 of *L'Allegro*.

110. CAMBUSCAN—The allusion here is to *The Squire's Tale*, which was left unfinished by Chaucer. Geoffrey Chaucer, sometimes called the "Father of English Poetry," lived 1340–1400. His greatest work was *The Canterbury Tales*. *The Squire's Tale* is the story of Cambyuskan, a king of Tartary, his sons, Algarsyf and Cambalo, and his daughter, Canace. As Cambyuskan was holding his birthday feast there came riding in at the hall door a knight upon a steed of brass, bearing in his hand a broad mirror of glass and upon his thumb a ring of gold—presents for the King and Canace from his master, "King of Araby and Ind."

112. WHO HAD CANACE TO WIFE—*The Squire's Tale* does not get this far.

113. VIRTUOUS—Magic.

117. TUNES—Verses. 118. TURNEYS—Tournaments.

119. OF FORESTS, AND ENCHANTMENTS—An allusion to Spenser's *Faerie Queene*, a long, allegorical romance "of Knights' and Ladies' gentle deeds," written in the days of Queen Elizabeth. The First Book of the *Faerie Queene* tells the story of the Knight of the Red Crosse and Lady Una who are lost in an enchanted forest.

120. WHERE MORE IS MEANT THAN MEETS THE EAR—The *Faerie Queene* is an allegory, a story which has a secondary meaning.

JOHN MILTON

  Thus, Night, oft see me in thy pale career,
  Till civil-suited Morn appear,
  Not tricked and frounced, as she was wont
  With the Attic boy to hunt,
125 But kerchieft in a comely cloud,
  While rocking winds are piping loud,
  Or ushered with a shower still,
  When the gust hath blown his fill,
  Ending on the rustling leaves,
130 With minute-drops from off the eaves.
  And, when the sun begins to fling
  His flaring beams, me, Goddess, bring
  To archèd walks of twilight groves,
  And shadows brown, that Sylvan loves,
135 Of pine, or monumental oak,
  Where the rude axe with heavèd stroke
  Was never heard the nymphs to daunt,
  Or fright them from their hallowed haunt.
  There, in close covert, by some brook,
140 Where no profaner eye may look,
  Hide me from day's garish eye,
  While the bee with honeyed thigh,
  That at her flowery work doth sing,
  And the waters murmuring,
145 With such consort as they keep,
  Entice the dewy-feathered Sleep.
  And let some strange mysterious dream
  Wave at his wings, in airy stream
  Of lively portraiture displayed,
150 Softly on my eyelids laid;

121. PALE—Dim.
122. CIVIL-SUITED—That is, soberly garbed.
123. TRICKED—Gaily adorned.   123. FROUNCED—With hair curled.
124. ATTIC BOY—The allusion is to Cephalus, the young huntsman, whom Aurora (the Dawn) stole away because of his beauty.
125. KERCHIEFT—Enveloped in a kerchief or head-cover, to cover her "frounced" head.   130. MINUTE-DROPS—Drops falling at minute intervals.
134. SYLVAN—Sylvanus, god of woods and fields.
142. BEE WITH HONEYED THIGH—How do bees carry pollen?
145. WITH SUCH CONSORT AS THEY KEEP—"They" refers to "waters" and "bees." "Consort" means harmony. The allusion is to the harmony of murmuring water and murmuring bees.
148. WAVE AT HIS WINGS—That is, hover at the wings of dewy-feathered sleep.   149. LIVELY PORTRAITURE—Life-like pictures.

And, as I wake, sweet music breathe
Above, about, or underneath,
Sent by some Spirit to mortals good,
Or the unseen Genius of the wood.
155 But let my due feet never fail
To walk the studious cloister's pale,
And love the high embowèd roof,
With antique pillars massy-proof,
And storied windows richly dight,
160 Casting a dim religious light.
There let the pealing organ blow,
To the full-voiced quire below,
In service high and anthems clear,
As may with sweetness, through mine ear,
165 Dissolve me into ecstasies,
And bring all Heaven before mine eyes.
And may at last my weary age
Find out the peaceful hermitage,
The hairy gown and mossy cell,
170 Where I may sit and rightly spell
Of every star that heaven doth shew,
And every herb that sips the dew,
Till old experience do attain
To something like prophetic strain.
175 These pleasures, Melancholy, give;
And I with thee will choose to live.

151. SWEET MUSIC BREATHE—That is, let sweet music breathe.
153. GOOD—That is, by some spirit who is good to mortals.
154. GENIUS—The spirit or deity of the wood.
155. DUE—Duteous.   156. PALE—Enclosure.   157. EMBOWÈD—Arched.
158. MASSY-PROOF—Ponderous, able to support the mass resting on them.
159. STORIED WINDOWS—Windows of stained and leaded glass portraying scenes from Biblical stories.
163. SERVICE HIGH—That is, the high service of the Church. It is probably that in lines 155-166 Milton had in mind King's College Chapel, Cambridge, said to be the "finest college chapel in existence and probably the finest example of its style or architecture in the world, in size, form, and decoration. It contains some of the best glass and wood carving in England." The service at King's College Chapel, moreover, has always enjoyed great renown.
168. HERMITAGE—That is, a cottage or simple dwelling in some retired spot.
169. HAIRY GOWN AND MOSSY CELL—Used figuratively to describe a plain and simple way of life. Milton does not mean that he will don the hairy gown of the religious hermit.
170. SPELL—Study.
174. TO SOMETHING LIKE PROPHETIC STRAIN—That is, to an understanding of the mysteries and secrets of creation.

Poem Development: Like *L'Allegro, Il Penseroso* reflects Milton's own way of life. The particular things which appeal to the serious or thoughtful mood tell us in part how he spent many years of his life—the evening walk and the hours by the hearth given to silent contemplation, the study and pondering of Plato and the classic philosophers, the reading of classic and English poets and dramatists, and the walk through the "studious cloister's pale" to hear "the pealing organ blow."

The introduction to the poem is similar to that of *L'Allegro,* but here Joys are banished. Notice particularly that Milton says "vain, deluding Joys"—"the brood of folly," the inane, fatuous delights which so conveniently serve as substitutes for thinking—not the "goddess fair and free" of *L'Allegro.* Too, the Melancholy of *Il Penseroso* is a creation utterly different from the Melancholy of *L'Allegro.* Here she stands for a mood of calm and quiet favorable to contemplation and high thought, the daughter of bright Vesta, goddess of the hearth. Why does Milton picture her clothed in royal black? Find out the composition of the color we call black. What companions does he call for Melancholy?

Il Penseroso also falls into natural divisions. Find the divisions and study each section as you did with *L'Allegro.* Give the idea or thought of each section, find striking bits of imagery and note their effect on your feelings. Point out lines which appeal to you most.

Write a précis of one or more of the divisions. What is the theme of the poem? Give the central thought.

Interpretations: Lines 7 and 8; likest (l. 9); rapt (l. 40); shunn'st the noise of folly (l. 61); bards (l. 116); archèd walks (l. 133); studious cloister's pale (l. 156). What part of speech is "spare" in line 46?

Significant Expressions: Quote a line telling of the little use of Joys as Milton interprets them in this mood. Quote the lines describing Melancholy. Quote lines which tell of music. What are the figures of speech in lines 58, 76 and 107? Memorize lines in contrast to those you chose from *L'Allegro.*

A Comparison of L'Allegro and Il Penseroso: *L'Allegro* and *Il Penseroso* are poems of the lyric type—which means that they are poems which give expression to personality—to mood and feeling, and aim to stir in the reader the feeling which the writer himself experiences.

The tastes which the poems reveal are those of the man of culture, wide education and refinement, and of the scholar and man of leisure, rather than those of the doer and man of affairs. Compare the things which the serious, thoughtful man liked with those of the cheerful man's liking. Are there likes common to both? Which of the two moods do you think Milton himself preferred, and why? Would you say that in both moods Milton had chosen the most desirable pleasures? Would you subtract any, or add others?

THE HISTORY OF POETRY IN ENGLAND

Classicism and the Age of Johnson (1700-1780)

General Characteristics

Classicism which had seen its beginning in the Restoration Period was to dominate English literature for nearly a hundred years. Its emphasis on formal correctness and conformity to the generally accepted standards had an important effect on poetry. To let one's self go in verse, to burst into raptures about anything was regarded by the classicists as something not done by the best people in literature. Reason and common sense were to be observed. The result is that this period produced little nature poetry and little poetry that breathes delight in life or strong feeling of any kind. Most of it was addressed to the intelligence, and a great deal of the work of the lesser poets is little more than rhymed information—unimaginative and lifeless. The great variety of verse forms which had been developed in the days of Elizabeth fell into disuse, and a kind of standardized form—the heroic couplet came into use. Nowhere is the conventional nature of the poetry of the period better illustrated than in the diction or idiom which it developed—a cottage is a "bower," a peasant is a "rustic" or a "swain," a crowd is a "train" and so on until such common things as pigs and hens had developed high flown stock-designations, and to write poetry one had to forget the language of life and learn the jargon of classicism.

Alexander Pope (1688–1744)

Alexander Pope is the chief representative of classicism in English literature. His outstanding characteristic is formal correctness. He brought the heroic couplet to a high degree of perfection, and his verse is written with precision and exactness.

Pope was a strange mixture of incongruity in nature, for in spite of acknowledged disagreeable traits which he had, he was a leader in literature, a man of tremendous intellect, and probably, next to Shakespeare, the most often quoted of the English poets. His *Essay on Criticism* gives the principles of writing poetry. This was followed by *The Rape of the Lock* which was a mock epic, the story of which, briefly, is as follows. Lord Petre had cut a lock of hair from the curls of Arabella Fermor. The lady resented the liberty and both families were immediately plunged into a quarrel. Pope satirized the event and the result was not particularly complimentary to the manners and customs of the day. His *Dunciad*, a satire as great as any ever written, was the result of his anger at the literary men of the day. His *Essay on Man* is concerned with man's relations to his environment and abounds in apt sayings which the world has quoted ever since they were written. One reason why they are so often quoted is because each couplet as Pope uses it embodies a complete thought stated in a neat and compact form. Good examples are the following well-known quotations:

> Honor and shame from no condition rise:
> Act well your part, there all the honor lies.
>
> Hope springs eternal in the human breast:
> Man never is but always to be blest.
>
> Know then thyself, presume not God to scan:
> The proper study of mankind is man.
>
> A wit's a feather, and a chief a rod;
> An honest man's the noblest work of God.
>
> 'Tis education forms the common mind:
> Just as the twig is bent the tree's inclined.
>
> To err is human, to forgive divine.
>
> For fools rush in where angels fear to tread.

Pope was witty and his verse was melodious. In form, finish, and compactness, he stands alone. His deficiencies are lack of emotional power and force. His appeal is almost wholly to the intellect. The subjects on which he wrote for the most part might as well have been treated in prose.

Other Classic Poets

Following closely the ideas of Pope were three minor writers who deserve mention. Matthew Prior wrote odes and lyrics which, though reflecting Pope's careful precision of thought, are lighter in tone. John Gay is best remembered for *The Beggars' Opera* from which we have two songs which have been very popular. These are *Sweet William's Farewell to Blackey'd Susan* and *'Twas When the Seas Were Roaring*. Thomas Parnell, in his poems *The Hermit* and *A Hymn to Contentment*, shows a deeper feeling than is to be found in the writing of Pope's other followers.

Beginnings of the Romantic Movement

The years from 1740 to 1780 saw the beginnings of a revolt against the formalism of Pope and Dryden which was to culminate in what is known as the Romantic Movement. The poetry in form is still predominantly classical, but in content and feeling it savors of the new influences, as if men were pouring new wine into old bottles. Lyric poetry began to appear and the poets again turned to Nature's vast storehouse of beauty for their themes. Satirical verse was replaced by that showing a sympathy by man for his fellow beings.

The Naturalistic Poets

A revival of a feeling for nature, a feeling conspicuously absent from the poetry of Pope and Dryden, is to be seen in the naturalistic poets, the first of whom was James Thomson, a Scotchman, who completed in 1730 a poem entitled *The Seasons*. This poem was in four parts, *Spring, Summer, Autumn,* and *Winter,* and it exhibits a genuine feeling for nature and a first hand acquaintance with it. A second and perhaps the most important of this group is William Collins, whose poem *Ode to Evening* is a nature poem of the first rank.

Forerunners of Romantic Poetry

Three poets of this age were forerunners of romantic poetry—Thomas Gray, Oliver Goldsmith, and William Cowper. Their poetry in form is still predominantly classical, but in content there are changes to be noted. We find a return to life for subject matter and inspiration, a quickening of emotion—especially a feeling for nature and for the common man, a return of idealism, and an awakening of the imagination.

Thomas Gray (1716–1771)

Thomas Gray was born in London. His father was moderately well-to-do, but was selfish and brutal—a poor husband and a poor father. To the efforts of his "careful, tender mother," who was a milliner, Gray owed his education and it was her earnings which put him through the great school at Eton. He was not a boy who strove for popularity, or cared for attention, but he and three other boys, who found sufficient comradeship in one another's company, formed what was called the "Quadruple Alliance." They were studious and literary, caring little for the amusements of their fellows. One of the members of this group was Horace Walpole, son of the Prime Minister of England.

In 1734 Gray entered Peterhouse College, Cambridge, his mother continuing to pay his expenses. Gray was obliged to live very modestly, and it is not difficult to see where his sympathy with the poor and his appreciation of the worth of their useful toil originated.

It was about 1740 that Gray's first published poem, an ode on the death of a Richard West, who had been a member of the "Quadruple Alliance," appeared. His *Elegy in a Country Churchyard* was finished about 1750. It is said that Gray had worked over it some eight or nine years, revising it until it finally suited him. This is quite characteristic of his manner of writing. He never let himself go to write in the heat of feeling. Indeed, it is difficult to imagine Gray wrought to a white heat. His feelings evidently never ran away with him. His poetry is much what the man was—quiet, somewhat somber, neat, and intellectual rather than impassioned. In these respects he reflects the classicism of the age in which he lived. His output of poetry was small, and all worked over with the same carefulness. For literary fame he seems to have cared little. It is characteristic of him that he was offered the place of Poet Laureate, and that he declined. He is said next to Milton to have been the most learned poet in our literature.

Oliver Goldsmith (1728-1774)

Goldsmith's life was a pathetic one, marked by disappointments, blunders and failures. He went to various schools but never stayed long. He entered Trinity College but because of his escapades was forced to leave. For the next few years he was first an under school teacher and then an apothecary's assistant. Finally he was engaged by a book seller and publisher to contribute to a literary review. This engagement began his literary career. His pay was small and he was often in want, but he still had his jovial, kindly temperament which attracted other literary men of the day to him. Dr. Samuel Johnson became his friend, and he was taken into the famous Literary Club.

As his circumstances improved, his expenditures became greater. He had no money sense, and he was easily imposed upon by every kind of sharper. Unable to withstand an appeal to his sympathy, he gave to the unfortunate when he himself was in want. When he was in funds he spent recklessly. The result was that he was obliged to work always under the pressure of debt, and the strain at last contributed largely to breaking his health and spirit.

Goldsmith's literary activity covered a period of about sixteen years. He displayed an astonishing ability to handle varied literary forms, writing essays, poems, dramas, and a novel. Whereas many a man's reputation, like that of Gray, rests upon one great poem, Goldsmith wrote a series of essays, a poem, a novel, and two dramas, any one of which would have been sufficient to entitle him to an enduring place in literature. In the field of poetry he is best known for his long poem *The Deserted Village*. This is written in heroic couplet and portrays many delightful pictures of country scenes.

William Cowper (1731-1800)

As a child, Cowper was sensitive and dominated by what today would be called fear complexes. His whole life was a struggle against insanity, but he was always optimistic and cheerful. His poems are neither widely read nor greatly discussed today, but when we realize the dearth of nature subjects in his day, and the absolute lack of a touch of human affection, we may get some idea of what an innovation and shock his commonplace subjects of humanity, of nature, and of the emotions must have been to the readers of the day. His poetry is sincere and much of it is humorous. His *John Gilpin's Ride* is well known for its delightful humor, and *The Task,* which was written in blank verse, shows clearly the discarding of the shackles of the classic age, both in form and choice of theme.

Poetry of the Classic Age

From AN ESSAY ON CRITICISM

Alexander Pope

Poem Interest: During the age of classicism, all writing was regulated by rule, and the true test of a poet's work was the amount of imitation of the classics that he was able to put into his poetry. Pope expresses in Part I of the *Essay on Criticism* his ideas of false criticism, and in Part II he tells of what he considers true criticism should consist.

From Part I

'Tis hard to say, if greater want of skill
Appear in writing or in judging ill;
But, of the two, less dangerous is th' offence
To tire our patience, than mislead our sense.
5   Some few in that, but numbers err in this,
Ten censure wrong for one who writes amiss;
A fool might once himself alone expose,
Now one in verse makes many more in prose.
'Tis with our judgments as our watches, none
10 Go just alike, yet each believes his own.
In poets as true genius is but rare,
True taste as seldom is the critic's share;
Both must alike from Heaven derive their light,
These born to judge, as well as those to write.
15 Let such teach others who themselves excel,
And censure freely who have written well.
Authors are partial to their wit, 'tis true,
But are not critics to their judgment too?

---

5. Some few in that—Some few (err) in that.
8. Now one in verse, etc.—For one poor poet there are many foolish critics.
11. In poets, etc.—True genius is rare among poets.
12. True taste, etc.—Critics seldom have true judgment.
17. Partial—Biased, in favor of.
17–18. Authors are partial, etc.—The meaning is that authors have as much right to think their work is good as the critics have to think their criticisms are right.

ALEXANDER POPE

From Part II

True wit is nature to advantage dressed,
What oft was thought, but ne'er so well expressed:
Something, whose truth convinced at sight we find.
That gives us back the image of our mind.
5   As shades more sweetly recommend the light,
So modest plainness sets off sprightly wit.
For works may have more wit than does 'em good,
As bodies perish through excess of blood.
   Others for language all their care express,
10 And value books, as women men, for dress;
Their praise is still—the style is excellent;
The sense they humbly take upon content.
Words are like leaves; where they most abound,
Much fruit of sense beneath is rarely found.
15 False eloquence, like the prismatic glass,
Its gaudy colors spreads on every place.
The face of nature we no more survey;
All glares alike, without distinction gay;
But true expression, like the unchanging sun,
20 Clears and improves whate'er it shines upon;
It gilds all objects, but it alters none.
Expression is the dress of thought, and still
Appears more decent, as more suitable;
A vile conceit in pompous words expressed
25 Is like a clown in regal purple dressed;
For different styles with different subjects sort,
As several garbs with country, town and court.
Some by old words to fame have made pretense,
Ancients in phrase, mere moderns in their sense;
30 Such labored nothings, in so strange a style,
Amaze the unlearned, and make the learnèd smile.
Unlucky, as Fungoso in the play,

  1. Wit—Used in the meaning of writing.
  9. Language—Style.
  12. Content—Trust.
  23. Decent—Attractive.
  24. Vile conceit—An unnatural expression.
  32. Fungoso—A character in Ben Jonson's play, *Every Man Out of His Humour.*

>   These sparks with awkward vanity display
>   What the fine gentleman wore yesterday;
> 35   And but so mimic ancients wits at best,
>   As apes our grandsires, in their doublets dressed.
>   In words, as fashions, the same rule will hold,
>   Alike fantastic, if too new, or old:
>   Be not the first by whom the new is tried,
> 40   Nor yet the last to lay the old aside.
>
>   .   .   .   .
>
>   True ease in writing comes from art, not chance,
>   As those move easiest who have learned to dance.
>   'Tis not enough no harshness gives offense,
>   The sound must seem an echo to the sense.

Poem Development: The ideas which Pope expresses were not only his, but were the accepted theories of the times. The exuberance which had dominated Elizabethan literature, the unnatural religious tone of the Puritan writings, the sensuality of the Restoration Period, all gave way during the classic age to formality. *Part I*—What is Pope's opinion of the literary critics? How does he think the number of poor writers compares with the number of worthless critics? What are the qualifications a critic should have? Is it true that one should be able to write well before becoming a critic? What is the theme of Part I? The central thought? *Part II*—What is Pope's idea of writing? How do the first two lines accord with the rules of the times? Would this allow for any originality? To what period of literature does he refer in line 7? Whom does he mean in line 9? What is Pope's idea of true expression? Give some of the rules Pope wanted to have followed in writing. Give the theme and central thought of Part II.

Interpretations: *Part I*—Judging ill; mislead our sense; writes amiss; true taste; partial to their wit. *Part II*—Advantage dressed; image of our mind; take upon content; fruit of sense; dress of thought; ancients in phrase; echo to the sense.

Significant Expressions: *Part I*—Memorize lines 15 and 16. Quote the line showing Pope's preference for writers rather than for critics. Quote the line giving the qualifications of a critic. *Part II*—Memorize lines 13 and 14, 23 and 24, 32 and 33, 34 and 35. What is the figure of speech in line 14? in line 35? Quote the lines giving Pope's idea of true expression.

ELEGY WRITTEN IN A COUNTRY CHURCHYARD

Thomas Gray

Poem Interest: Most of us have had the experience at one time or another of wandering through an old graveyard—a graveyard whose old marble slabs and markers, with their interesting inscriptions, immediately set us musing and wondering about the people who lie buried there. We gather from the poem that the poet, too, often wandered among the graves of a little English churchyard where he mused over the rude inscriptions on the tombstones, and pondered the lives of those who lay beneath them.

> The curfew tolls the knell of parting day;
>   The lowing herd winds slowly o'er the lea;
> The plowman homeward plods his weary way,
>   And leaves the world to darkness and to me.
>
> 5 Now fades the glimmering landscape on the sight,
>   And all the air a solemn stillness holds,
> Save where the beetle wheels his droning flight,
>   And drowsy tinklings lull the distant folds;

Elegy—An elegy is a lyric poem which voices the poet's feelings, his lament or grief, at the death of another. Usually the elegy is called forth by the death of some one individual, but in this poem the poet gives his reflection on all those who lie buried in the little churchyard.

Save that from yonder ivy-mantled tow'r
10   The moping owl does to the moon complain
Of such as, wandering near her secret bow'r,
    Molest her ancient solitary reign.

Beneath those rugged elms, that yew-tree's shade,
    Where heaves the turf in many a mold'ring heap,
15 Each in his narrow cell forever laid,
    The rude forefathers of the hamlet sleep.

The breezy call of incense-breathing Morn,
    The swallow twitt'ring from the straw-built shed,
The cock's shrill clarion, or the echoing horn,
20   No more shall rouse them from their lowly bed.

For them no more the blazing hearth shall burn,
    Or busy housewife ply her evening care;
No children run to lisp their sire's return,
    Or climb his knees the envied kiss to share.

25 Oft did the harvest to their sickle yield,
    Their furrow oft the stubborn glebe has broke;
How jocund did they drive their team a-field!
    How bowed the woods beneath their sturdy stroke!

Let not Ambition mock their useful toil,
30   Their homely joys and destiny obscure;

10. MOPING—Melancholy, sad—so appearing because of its gloomy call.
12. ANCIENT SOLITARY REIGN—From time immemorial the owl is found not in flocks, but alone.
13. YEW-TREE—A tree conspicuous in the English landscape.
15. CELL—Grave.
16. RUDE—Unpolished, country-bred.
17. Contrast the sensation called up by this line with that by line 6. Here the poet would have us feel the faint, fragrant breeze which comes up with the sun.
18. STRAW-BUILT SHED—In Gray's time, outbuildings were often constructed of straw, the straw being woven into a network of slender saplings and branches to form the side walls, and the room thatched with straw.
19. HORN—The hunter's horn.
23. LISP THEIR SIRE'S RETURN—Greet in childish speech their father on his return from the fields.
26. GLEBE—Turf, sward. The meaning is: Their plows have often broken the glebe into furrows.
29. AMBITION—Those who have made it their purpose in life to achieve power, wealth, social position, world fame, etc.
30. DESTINY—Lot, position in life.

Nor Grandeur hear with a disdainful smile
    The short and simple annals of the poor.

The boast of heraldry, the pomp of pow'r,
    And all that beauty, all that wealth e'er gave,
35 Awaits alike the inevitable hour:
    The paths of glory lead but to the grave.

Nor you, ye proud, impute to these the fault,
    If Memory o'er their tomb no trophies raise,
Where, through the long-drawn aisle and fretted vault,
40   The pealing anthem swells the note of praise.

Can storied urn or animated bust
    Back to its mansion call the fleeting breath?
Can Honor's voice provoke the silent dust,
    Or Flatt'ry soothe the dull, cold ear of Death?

45 Perhaps in this neglected spot is laid
    Some heart once pregnant with celestial fire;
Hands that the rod of empire might have swayed,
    Or waked to ecstasy the living lyre.

31. GRANDEUR—Those of great wealth and social position.
32. ANNALS—Story, history.
33. BOAST OF HERALDRY—Family greatness or fame. Whenever a man did a famous deed, it was the practice to have it symbolized on his coat of arms. Heraldry comprises the body of customs and practices which govern the designing of coats of arms.
33. POMP OF POW'R—The magnificence and display which accompany power.
35. INEVITABLE—Unavoidable, not to be escaped. The "inevitable hour" is death. "Hour" is the subject of "awaits." "The boast of heraldry," etc., are the objects. The sense is that death awaits the boast of heraldry, etc., not that they await death.
39. WHERE—Gray probably had in mind Westminster Abbey where it is the custom to bury England's great dead. "Fretted vault" is the arched ceiling ornamented by fretwork. Find a picture of the interior of Westminster Abbey—"the long-drawn aisle and fretted vault."
41. STORIED URN—The ashes of the dead are sometimes enclosed in urns on the exterior of which is inscribed their great deeds—hence "storied" urn.
41. ANIMATED—Life-like. Find a picture of Poet's Corner in Westminster where may be seen the "busts" of those buried there.
46. PREGNANT WITH CELESTIAL FIRE—Full of poetic inspiration which is often spoken of as celestial, or divine, in origin.
47. HANDS—Men who had ability to govern empires.
48. OR WAKED—Those who might have been great musicians. The "lyre" is an ancient musical instrument; it symbolizes here any instrument.

But Knowledge to their eyes her ample page,
  50   Rich with the spoils of time, did ne'er unroll;
       Chill Penury repressed their noble rage,
          And froze the genial current of their soul.

       Full many a gem of purest ray serene
          The dark unfathomed caves of ocean bear;
  55   Full many a flower is born to blush unseen,
          And waste its sweetness on the desert air.

       Some village-Hampden that with dauntless breast
          The little tyrant of his fields withstood,
       Some mute inglorious Milton, here may rest,
  60   Some Cromwell guiltless of his country's blood.

       Th' applause of list'ning senates to command,
          The threats of pain and ruin to despise,
       To scatter plenty o'er a smiling land,
          And read their hist'ry in a nation's eyes,

51. PENURY REPRESSED THEIR NOBLE RAGE—Poverty held down their genius.
52. FROZE THE GENIAL CURRENT OF THEIR SOUL—Prevented them from following their natural inclinations. "Genial" is here used in the old sense of natural.
57. HAMPDEN—An English squire who refused to pay the "tax of ship money" because he believed it unjust. This refusal was the beginning of the Puritan Revolution, in which Charles I, who had caused the ship tax to be levied, was beheaded.
58. THE LITTLE TYRANT OF HIS FIELDS—His landlord. The men who lay buried in this churchyard were the tenant farmers on great estates, and they were called upon often to resist the petty tyrannies and injustices of their landlords. By "village-Hampden," Gray means some independent and sturdy peasant who resisted an unjust landlord as the great Hampden resisted King Charles.
59. SOME MUTE INGLORIOUS MILTON—Some man who had the poetic power of Milton, but, because he had no opportunity, died "mute," i.e., without writing, and inglorious—without glory.
60. SOME CROMWELL—Some man who had the military genius of Cromwell, commander of the republican army in the Puritan Revolution.
60. GUILTLESS OF HIS COUNTRY'S BLOOD—Unlike Cromwell, never having been the cause of shedding the blood of his countrymen.
61. The infinitives in this stanza: "to command," "to despise," "to scatter" and "(to) read" are the direct objects of "forbade" in the stanza below. "Lot" is the subject of "forbade." The sense is as follows: Their lowly position in life prevented them from becoming great statesmen whose oratory moved listening legislatures (senates) to applaud. It prevented them also from resisting, like Hampden, the unjust King who threatened to ruin and perhaps execute for treason all who opposed him. It forbade them being the authors of legislation which would bring prosperity to the land, and from seeing in the pleased expressions of people the reflection of what they had done—i.e., "their history."

65 Their lot forbade: nor circumscribed alone,
       Their growing virtues, but their crimes confined;
    Forbade to wade through slaughter to a throne,
       And shut the gates of mercy on mankind;

    The struggling pangs of conscious truth to hide,
70   To quench the blushes of ingenuous shame,
    Or heap the shrine of Luxury and Pride
       With incense kindled at the Muse's flame.

    Far from the madding crowd's ignoble strife,
       Their sober wishes never learned to stray;

65. CIRCUMSCRIBED—Set limits to. The sense here is: If their lot prevented them from becoming benefactors of their fellow men, it also prevented them from bringing pain and suffering to them—it "confined their crimes." It forbade the village-Cromwell from making himself master of England through war, as Cromwell did, and it prevented him likewise from being the author of the merciless consequences of war—from "shutting the gates of mercy on mankind." Gray held the opinion, common in his day, that Cromwell was moved by selfish ambition.

69. "To hide" is the object of "forbade" in line 67. To get the sense of this stanza it is necessary to know something of the relationship between patron and author as it was known to Gray. There used to be a very practical purpose in dedicating a book to another. Before the reading public was as numerous as it is to-day, and only a few people bought books, it was customary for an author to dedicate his book often to a great nobleman, called his patron. In the dedication he found it advisable to say as many splendid things of his patron as possible, and oftentimes in the book or poem itself he would pay compliments to his patron. The patron responded by giving the author a present, by securing for him a pension from the government, or by some other reward. In this stanza Gray has reference to this practice. He says in effect that if there lies in this churchyard some poet whose lot forbade him from becoming known, that lot likewise saved him from the pain (pangs) which he must have felt at being obliged to hide the truth about his patron, and it saved him also from being obliged to quench the blushes of admitted (ingenuous) shame which rose to his cheeks as he wrote the flattery which his patron expected. The sense of the last two lines is: Their lot forbade them flattering the rich and the proud with poetry.

71-72—In these last two lines is a good example of what is called symbolism in poetry—i.e., the presentation of a thought imaginatively through a picture. The symbolism here is classical; and before one can see the picture he must know something of the practices and beliefs of antiquity. The ancients believed that poetry was inspired by deities called Muses. To their gods they used to erect shrines or altars before which they offered sacrifices and burned incense. When one wished for poetic inspiration, he sacrificed before the altar of the Muse, and invoked, or called upon her for inspiration. Here Gray pictures the poet as lighting his incense at the flame on the altar of the Muse, and then carrying it to "the shrine of Luxury and Pride" as an offering for which he asks a reward. The "incense kindled at the Muse's flame" is his poetry, and his heaping "the shrine of Luxury and Pride" is his flattery of his patron.

75   Along the cool sequestered vale of life
       They kept the noiseless tenor of their way.

    Yet e'en these bones from insult to protect,
       Some frail memorial still erected nigh,
    With uncouth rhymes and shapeless sculpture decked,
80   Implores the passing tribute of a sigh.

    Their name, their years, spelt by th' unlettered Muse,
       The place of fame and elegy supply;
    And many a holy text around she strews,
       That teach the rustic moralist to die:

85   For who, to dumb Forgetfulness a prey,
       This pleasing, anxious being e'er resigned,
    Left the warm precincts of the cheerful day,
       Nor cast one longing, ling'ring look behind?

    On some fond breast the parting soul relies,
90   Some pious drops the closing eye requires;
    E'en from the tomb the voice of nature cries,
       E'en in our ashes live their wonted fires.

77. INSULT—From being walked upon.

79. UNCOUTH RHYMES—Crudely constructed verses. Best illustrated by finding examples on the tombstones in old cemeteries.

79. SHAPELESS SCULPTURE DECKED—Crudely cut figures and ornaments.

81. UNLETTERED MUSE—Some village poet whose rhymes were crude, and whose English was rough and ready.

83. That is, many a holy text the "unlettered Muse" (she) has cut on the various tombstones.

84. MORALIST—One who tries to guide his life according to right principles.

84. TEACH . . . TO DIE—Give him strength in face of death.

85. The sense of the stanza is: For who among men, however resigned to death, ever left this life with its pleasures and anxieties, without some longing to stay yet a little while with those who loved him?

85. TO DUMB FORGETFULNESS A PREY—Likely to be forgotten in the silence of the grave. "Prey" is in apposition with "who."

89. The first two lines state illustrations of the "one longing, ling'ring look." The dying do not wish to depart abruptly from earthly associations. Death is eased by the very lingering of life when one reposes in the arms of a loved one. And the yearning to remain is in a measure satisfied by the tears of those at the bedside, for these "pious drops" give assurance that the dying will continue to live in memory.

91. The sense of this line is that "the voice of nature," i.e., our words and the echo of our voices, lingers in the ears of those who love us, long after we have gone.

92. The sense here is that our ideas and thoughts and the inspiration and influence we shed while living continue after we are dust.

For thee who, mindful of th' unhonored dead,
    Dost in these lines their artless tale relate,
95 If chance, by lonely Contemplation led,
    Some kindred spirit shall inquire thy fate,

Haply some hoary-headed swain may say,
    "Oft have we seen him at the peep of dawn,
Brushing with hasty steps the dews away,
100   To meet the sun upon the upland lawn.

"There, at the foot of yonder nodding beech
    That wreathes its old fantastic roots so high,
His listless length at noontide would he stretch,
    And pore upon the brook that babbles by.

105 "Hard by yon wood, now smiling as in scorn,
    Mutt'ring his wayward fancies, he would rove;
Now drooping, woful—wan, like one forlorn
    Or crazed with care or crossed in hopeless love.

"One morn I missed him from the customed hill,
110   Along the heath, and near his fav'rite tree.
Another came, nor yet beside the rill,
    Nor up the lawn, nor at the wood was he;

"The next, with dirges due, in sad array,
    Slow through the churchway path we saw him borne:
115 Approach and read (for thou canst read) the lay
    Graved on the stone beneath yon aged thorn.

93. THEE—Gray is here speaking of himself. In this and the following six stanzas, Gray is himself casting "one longing, ling'ring look behind." He is expressing the hope that after he is gone his "voice" and his "wonted fires" will live in the memory of the villagers.
95. CHANCE—Perchance.
96. KINDRED SPIRIT—Person with a contemplative turn of mind similar to Gray's.
97. HAPLY—Perhaps.
102. WREATHES—Refers to the way in which the roots of the beech hump up and sometimes push through the surface of the ground.
105. SMILING AS IN SCORN—Like one who scorned human companionship, wishing to be alone.
106. MUTT'RING HIS WAYWARD FANCIES—Composing his poetry. "Wayward" here means capricious.
115. APPROACH AND READ—These words are directed by the "hoary-headed swain" to the "kindred spirit" who has inquired for Gray. "For thou canst read" seems to imply that the swain could not.

"There scattered oft, the earliest of the year,
  By hands unseen are showers of vi'lets found
The redbreast loves to build and warble there,
120   And little footsteps lightly print the ground."

THE EPITAPH

Here rests his head upon the lap of Earth,
  A youth to Fortune and to Fame unknown:
Fair Science frowned not on his humble birth,
  And Melancholy marked him for her own.

125 *Large was his bounty, and his soul sincere;*
  Heaven did a recompense as largely send:
He gave to Mis'ry (all he had) a tear,
  He gained from Heav'n ('twas all he wished) a friend.

No farther seek his merits to disclose,
130   *Or draw his frailties from their dread abode,*
(There they alike in trembling hope repose),
  The bosom of his Father and his God.

117. THERE—Beneath the "aged thorn."
120. THE EPITAPH—In this epitaph Gray describes himself.
122. TO FORTUNE AND TO FAME UNKNOWN—Who was neither rich nor famous.
123. SCIENCE—Learning. The meaning is that though he was of humble birth, education was not denied to him. His mother, who was a milliner, put him through Eton and Cambridge.
124. MELANCHOLY MARKED HIM FOR HER OWN—He was given all his life to meditation.
126. RECOMPENSE—Heaven was as kind toward him, as he was toward others.
127. He had nothing to give to "Mis'ry" (those who were in need) but sympathy. Heaven did not give him wealth (Gray was a poor man) but it gave him contentment—a friend.
132. THE BOSOM—In the bosom—known only to God.

Poem Development: The poem first appeared in 1752, and it is probably safe to say that when he wrote, Gray had in mind the churchyard of Stoke Poges in Buckinghamshire, although two others near Cambridge each lay claim to being the churchyard of the poem. But this is after all not so important; the significant point is that the *Elegy* gives expression to Gray's reflections on the lives of men who might have been found lying in their narrow cells in the shadow of a hundred village churches throughout England.

Lines 1–16: The poet is alone in the village churchyard as evening falls. These first stanzas give a perfect description of twilight. To what sense do most of the pictures of the first three stanzas appeal?

Lines 17–28: These lines describe what had been the daily life of those who lie buried beneath the yew tree's shade. Name these daily happenings.

Lines 29–44: These are given over to reflection on the leveling power of death. Give the meaning of lines 29–36. These lines are so often quoted that it would be wise to memorize them. What idea is the poet expressing in lines 37–44?

Lines 45–76: Here occurs the reflection that only lack of opportunity, not lack of ability or worth, distinguished these men from the great of the earth. In which line is this idea summed up? To what does the poet refer when he says "gem" and "flower" in lines 53 and 55? Memorize lines 53–56. Does the fact that "many a flower is born to blush unseen, and waste its fragrance on the desert air" reflect to any degree upon its indispensability in the plan of things?

Lines 77–92: These lines tell of the rude tombstones, with the reflection that they are an expression of the desire which we all feel not to be forgotten. Describe the memorials and their inscriptions.

Lines 93–120: Here the poet reflects what one day may be said of him after he himself shall have been buried in the village churchyard. Give in your own words the ideas he expresses.

Lines 121–132: These constitute such an epitaph as Gray would have on his tombstone. Give the meaning of these lines. The meaning of this epitaph, in its deepest sense, refers not to death, but to life. Look at yourself, as Gray does here, and write down what you would desire to have your life express.

Combine your impressions of each section of the poem into a précis. Considering the poem as a whole—the contemplation, the rhythm, the imagery, etc.—what would you like most to remember about it? What is the theme of the poem? Give the central thought.

Interpretations: Lea (l. 2); bow'r (l. 11); molest (l. 12); rugged (l. 13); yew tree (l. 13—find a description of a yew tree); cock's shrill clarion (l. 19); ply her evening care (l. 22); jocund (l. 27); homely joys (l. 30); hear with disdainful smile (l. 31); impute (l. 37); line 38; its mansion (l. 42); lines 43 and 44; rich with the spoils of time (l. 50); full many (l. 53); line 73; sober wishes (l. 74); sequestered (l. 75); noiseless tenor (l. 76); implores (l. 80); resigned (l. 86); pious (l. 90); unhonored dead (l. 93); artless tale (l. 94); inquire thy fate (l. 96); hoary-headed swain (l. 97); pore upon the brook (l. 104); crossed (l. 108); customed hill (l. 109); dirges due (l. 113); bounty (l. 125); his merits to disclose (l. 129); line 130.

Significant Expressions: Quote the stanzas describing twilight. Quote the lines telling of the father's return from the day's work. Quote the famous lines meaning that everything must end in death. What is the figure of speech in line 6? in line 17? in line 29?

THE DESERTED VILLAGE

Oliver Goldsmith

Poem Interest: In early days in England, the tillers of the soil lived not in widely separated farmhouses, each on his own land, but in little villages encompassed by their fields. Nor in those days did every farmer have his separate pasture for his live stock. These he turned out to graze on the "common," the unenclosed open meadows which were regarded as common property. But such village life which Goldsmith knew as a boy was fast disappearing during his lifetime. England was becoming the workshop of the world and changing from an agricultural to an industrial country. This industrial expansion seriously affected village life. In the first place, the growth of towns made necessary better farming that the city populations might be fed, and capital accumulated in trade was now turned to the improvement of agriculture. The new methods also made necessary a change in the system of landholding to which the peasant had long been accustomed. In order that a crop, like wheat for example, might be grown over a large area instead of in scattered patches, the peasants' holdings were thrown together and, by the Enclosure Acts, the commons which had been regarded as public property for generations were fenced in. The government tried to be fair and gave the peasants the equivalent in land or money for whatever was taken, but the peasants were unable to adjust themselves to the new conditions. They soon lost the money they re-

OLIVER GOLDSMITH

ceived; some became farm laborers, or drifted off the land to find work in the growing industrial towns; others emigrated to America. The result was a large number of deserted villages up and down England.

Goldsmith felt great sympathy for the peasant. It meant little to him that these changes were necessary from a practical standpoint. He saw the hardships they caused the peasant, and from his indignation and sympathy came *The Deserted Village*.

    SWEET Auburn, loveliest village of the plain,
      Where health and plenty cheer'd the laboring swain,
      Where smiling spring its earliest visit paid,
      And parting summer's lingering blooms delayed;
5   Dear lovely bowers of innocence and ease,
      Seats of my youth, when every sport could please,
      How often have I loitered o'er thy green,
      Where humble happiness endeared each scene!
      How often have I paused on every charm—
10   The sheltered cot, the cultivated farm,
      The never-failing brook, the busy mill,
      The decent church that topt the neighboring hill,
      The hawthorn bush, with seats beneath the shade,
      For talking age and whisp'ring lovers made.
15   How often have I blest the coming day
      When toil, remitting, lent its turn to play,
      And all the village train, from labor free,
      Led up their sports beneath the spreading tree;
      While many a pastime circled in the shade,
20   The young contending as the old surveyed,
      And many a gambol frolicked o'er the ground,
      And sleights of art and feats of strength went round;
      And still, as each repeated pleasure tired,
      Succeeding sports the mirthful band inspired:

  1. AUBURN—Goldsmith had in mind an idealized picture of Lissoy, his native village in Ireland.
  1. PLAIN—Countryside.
  2. SWAIN—Peasant, tenant farmer.
  5. BOWERS—Shelters.
 10. COT—Cottage.
 12. DECENT—Modest, becoming.
 15. THE COMING DAY—The approaching holiday.
 17. TRAIN—Here, people of the village. A favorite word with Goldsmith.
 22. SLEIGHTS OF ART—Tricks. Compare the expression "sleight of hand."
 22. FEATS OF STRENGTH—Feats, such as throwing the sledge, or hammer, at which Goldsmith himself was a "champion."

25 The dancing pair that simply sought renown
By holding out to tire each other down;
The swain mistrustless of his smutted face,
While secret laughter tittered round the place;
The bashful virgin's side-long looks of love,
30 The matron's glance that would those looks reprove.
These were thy charms, sweet village: sports like these,
With sweet succession, even toil to please;
These round thy bowers their cheerful influence shed,
These were thy charms—but all these charms are fled.

35 Sweet smiling village, loveliest of the lawn,
Thy sports are fled and all thy charms withdrawn;
Amidst thy bowers the tyrant's hand is seen,
And desolation saddens all thy green:
One only master grasps the whole domain,
40 And half a tillage stints thy smiling plain.
No more thy glassy brook reflects the day,
But, choked with sedges, works its weedy way;
Along thy glades, a solitary guest,
The hollow sounding bittern guards its nest;
45 Amidst thy desert walks the lapwing flies,
And tires their echoes with unvaried cries;
Sunk are thy bowers in shapeless ruin all,
And the long grass o'ertops the moldering wall;

25. SIMPLY—In a simple manner.
27. SWAIN—Here used to mean country lad.
27. SMUTTED—The old trick of smearing his face with black, while he was not aware (mistrustless) of what was being done, had been played on him.
32. The meaning of the line is: Sports like these, coming every so often (in sweet succession), were something to look forward to, and made daily toil less wearisome.
33. BOWERS—Used here somewhat in the sense of haunts.
35. LAWN—The countryside.
39. ONE ONLY MASTER—Goldsmith probably had in mind General Robert Napier and his turning a large number of peasant families from their cottages. This happened near Lissoy and was one of the few instances in which peasants were evicted.
40. The meaning of the line is that the fields (plain) about the village are but half tilled.
44. BITTERN—A bird of the heron family. Its cry is best described in Goldsmith's words "the booming of the bittern."
45. LAPWING—European plover. Its call is a shrill, wailing cry repeated over and over, which explains the next line.
47. BOWERS—Here the word means cottages.

And trembling, shrinking from the spoiler's hand,
50 Far, far away thy children leave the land.

Ill fares the land, to hastening ills a prey,
Where wealth accumulates, and men decay:
Princes and lords may flourish, or may fade—
A breath can make them, as a breath has made;
55 But a bold peasantry, their country's pride,
When once destroyed, can never be supplied.

A time there was, ere England's griefs began,
When every rood of ground maintained its man:
For him light labor spread her wholesome store,
60 Just gave what life required but gave no more;
His best companions, innocence and health;
And his best riches, ignorance of wealth.

But times are altered; trade's unfeeling train
Usurp the land, and dispossess the swain;
65 Along the lawn, where scattered hamlets rose,
Unwieldly wealth and cumbrous pomp repose,
And every want to opulence allied,
And every pang that folly pays to pride.
These gentle hours that plenty bade to bloom,
70 Those calm desires that asked but little room,
Those healthful sports that graced the peaceful scene,
Lived in each look and brightened all the green,

54. BREATH—Princes and lords may be created by the word of a king.
58. ROOD—Plot. The rood, a unit of measurement, here used to indicate the land itself.
66. The meaning is that where there were formerly little hamlets one now sees only great manor houses and their numerous outbuildings (cumbrous pomp)—the evidence of wealth so great that men do not know what to do with it, that is, it is "unwieldly."
67. OPULENCE—Wealth. The meaning is that one sees satisfied on these great estates every want that wealth can satisfy.
68. PANG—Pain, misery. The meaning is that in the sufferings of the poor peasants who have been dispossessed to make these great estates, one can see the pain and hardship which the foolishness born of pride can make one man inflict on another.
69. THESE GENTLE HOURS—The pleasant hours of innocent mirth which Goldsmith has described, that were the result of the villagers' having plenty for the ordinary needs of life.
72. LIVED IN EACH LOOK—That were reflected in the happiness on every face.

ELD

>   These, far departing, seek a kinder shore,
>   And rural mirth and manners are no more.
>
> 75   Sweet Auburn, parent of the blissful hour,
>   Thy glades forlorn confess the tyrant's power.
>   Here, as I take my solitary rounds
>   Amidst thy tangling walks and ruined grounds,
>   And, many a year elapsed, return to view
> 80   Where once the cottage stood, the hawthorn grew,
>   Remembrance wakes with all her busy train,
>   Swells at my breast, and turns the past to pain.
>
>   In all my wanderings round this world of care,
>   In all my griefs—and God has given my share,—
> 85   I still had hopes, my latest hours to crown,
>   Amidst these humble bowers to lay me down;
>   To husband out life's taper at the close,
>   And keep the flame from wasting by repose:
>   I still had hopes—for pride attends us still—
> 90   Amidst the swains to show my book-learned skill;
>   Around my fire an evening group to draw,
>   And tell of all I felt, and all I saw;
>   And, as an hare whom hounds and horns pursue
>   Pants to the place from whence at first she flew,
> 95   I still had hopes, my long vexations past,
>   Here to return, and die at home at last.
>
>   O blest retirement, friend to life's decline,
>   Retreats from care, that never must be mine,
>   How happy he who crowns, in shades like these,
> 100 A youth of labor with an age of ease,
>   Who quits a world where strong temptations try,
>   And, since 't is hard to combat, learns to fly.
>   For him no wretches, born to work and weep,
>   Explore the mine, or tempt the dangerous deep;

---

87. HUSBAND OUT—To burn with care, to prolong; literally, to economize.

103. WRETCHES—The use of this word to designate factory hands, and especially the men and women who worked in the coal mines of Wales, before laws protecting labor were enacted, is quite justified.

104. TEMPT THE DANGEROUS DEEP—Man the merchant ships of the rich. Life in these ships was one of great hardship.

105 No surly porter stands in guilty state,
     To spurn imploring famine from the gate;
     But on he moves to meet his latter end,
     Angels around befriending Virtue's friend;
     Bends to the grave with unperceived decay,
110 While resignation gently slopes the way;
     And, all his prospects brightening to the last,
     His heaven commences ere the world be past.

        Sweet was the sound when oft, at evening's close,
     Up yonder hill the village murmur rose;
115 There, as I passed with careless steps and slow,
     The mingling notes came softened from below:
     The swain responsive as the milk-maid sung,
     The sober herd that lowed to meet their young,
     The noisy geese that gabbled o'er the pool,
120 The playful children just let loose from school,
     The watch-dog's voice that bayed the whispering wind,
     And the loud laugh that spoke the vacant mind;
     These all in sweet confusion sought the shade,
     And filled each pause the nightingale had made.
125 But now the sounds of population fail;
     No cheerful murmurs fluctuate in the gale,
     No busy steps the grass-grown footway tread,
     For all the bloomy flush of life is fled—
     All but yon widowed, solitary thing,
130 That feebly bends beside the plashy spring;
     She, wretched matron, forced in age, for bread,
     To strip the brook with mantling cresses spread,
     To pick her wintry fagot from the thorn,
     To seek her nightly shed, and weep till morn;

105. IN GUILTY STATE—Conscious of his shameful occupation in turning the hungry (famine) who come begging (imploring) bread.
107. HE—Refers to "he who crowns," etc., in line 99.
107. MOVES TO MEET HIS LATTER END—Sees the end of his life approach.
113. EVENING—Used here to mean afternoon.
122. VACANT—Care-free.
123. THESE—These sounds.
123. SOUGHT THE SHADE—Came to Goldsmith listening in the shade.
129. WIDOWED THING—Said to refer to Catherine Geharty whose cottage near Lissoy, and the creek where she gathered water cress, were often shown to travelers.
132. MANTLING—Refers to the way in which water cress overgrows the surface of a brook.

135   She only left of all the harmless train,
     The sad historian of the pensive plain.

       Near yonder copse, where once the garden smiled,
     And still where many a garden flower grows wild,
     There, where a few torn shrubs the place disclose,
140   The village preacher's modest mansion rose.
     A man he was to all the country dear,
     And passing rich with forty pounds a year.
     Remote from towns he ran his godly race,
     Nor e'er had changed, nor wished to change his place;
145   Unpractised he to fawn, or seek for power,
     By doctrines fashioned to the varying hour;
     Far other aims his heart had learned to prize,
     More skilled to raise the wretched than to rise.
     His house was known to all the vagrant train;
150   He chid their wanderings but relieved their pain:
     The long-remembered beggar was his guest,
     Whose beard, descending, swept his aged breast;
     The ruined spendthrift, now no longer proud,
     Claimed kindred there, and had his claims allowed;
155   The broken soldier, kindly bade to stay,
     Sat by his fire and talked the night away,
     Wept o'er his wounds, or, tales of sorrow done,
     Shouldered his crutch and shewed how fields were won.
     Pleased with his guests, the good man learned to glow,
160   And quite forgot their vices in their woe;
     Careless their merits or their faults to scan,
     His pity gave ere charity began.

       Thus to relieve the wretched was his pride,
     And e'en his failings leaned to Virtue's side;
165   But in his duty prompt at every call,
     He watched and wept, he prayed and felt for all:

  142. PASSING—Surpassing.
  142. FORTY POUNDS—About $200.
  145. UNPRACTICED HE TO FAWN—He was so honest and simple that he did not know how to curry favor with his superiors by preaching whatever happened to be the favorite doctrine of those above him.
  151. LONG-REMEMBERED BEGGAR—One which Goldsmith remembers from long ago in his boyhood.
  162. GAVE ERE CHARITY BEGAN—He gave from a sense of sympathy rather than because he felt it his duty. (charity).

    And, as a bird each fond endearment tries
    To tempt its new-fledged offspring to the skies,
    He tried each art, reproved each dull delay,
170 Allured to brighter worlds, and led the way.

    Beside the bed where parting life was laid,
    And sorrow, guilt, and pain by turns dismayed,
    The reverend champion stood: at his control
    Despair and anguish fled the struggling soul;
175 Comfort came down the trembling wretch to raise,
    And his last faltering accents whispered praise.

    At church, with meek and unaffected grace,
    His looks adorned the venerable place;
    Truth from his lips prevailed with double sway,
180 And fools who came to scoff remained to pray.
    The service past, around the pious man,
    With steady zeal, each honest rustic ran;
    Even children followed, with endearing wile,
    And plucked his gown to share the good man's smile.
185 His ready smile a parent's warmth exprest;
    Their welfare pleased him, and their cares distrest;
    To them his heart, his love, his griefs were given,
    But all his serious thoughts had rest in heaven:
    As some tall cliff, that lifts its awful form,
190 Swells from the vale, and midway leaves the storm,
    Tho' round its breast the rolling clouds are spread,
    Eternal sunshine settles on its head.

    Beside yon straggling fence that skirts the way,
    With blossom'd furze unprofitably gay,
195 There, in his noisy mansion, skill'd to rule,
    The village master taught his little school.
    A man severe he was, and stern to view;
    I knew him well, and every truant knew:

172. DISMAYED—Dismayed the dying.
179. DOUBLE SWAY—Because he himself practiced what he preached.
184. GOWN—The gown he wore in the pulpit.
189. AWFUL—Majestic, inspiring awe.
194. Furze has a bright yellow flower. "Unprofitably gay" means that although it is of no practical use it is pleasant to look at.

Well had the boding tremblers learned to trace
200　The day's disasters in his morning face;
Full well they laughed with counterfeited glee
At all his jokes, for many a joke had he;
Full well the busy whisper, circling round,
Conveyed the dismal tidings when he frowned.
205　Yet he was kind; or if severe in aught,
The love he bore to learning was in fault.
The village all declared how much he knew:
'Twas certain he could write, and cypher too;
Lands he could measure, terms and tides presage;
210　And even the story ran that he could gauge.
In arguing, too, the parson owned his skill,
For, even though vanquished he could argue still,
While words of learned length and thundering sound
Amazed the gazing rustics ranged around;
215　And still they gazed, and still the wonder grew
That one small head could carry all he knew.

But past is all his fame; the very spot
Where many a time he triumphed is forgot:
Near yonder thorn, that lifts its head on high,
220　Where once the sign-post caught the passing eye,
Low lies that house where nut-brown draughts inspired,
Where grey-beard Mirth and smiling Toil retired,
Where village statesmen talked with looks profound,
And news much older than their ale went round.
225　Imagination fondly stoops to trace
The parlor splendors of that festive place:

209. PRESAGE—Foretell. "Terms" has reference to term days, on which terms, or sessions of the law courts, opened. "Tides" is used here in the old sense of times or seasons as it is still used in Whitsuntide and Yuletide. What the schoolmaster could do was tell by a simple arithmetical reckoning the date on which these days and seasons would fall. The line rather implies that this ability was one which entitled its possessor to be looked up to by the simple folk of the village.

210. GAUGE—Measure the capacity of such things as barrels and similar containers.

211. OWNED—Admitted.

221. DRAUGHTS—Of nut-brown ale.

221. INSPIRED—Caused mirth and talk such as are mentioned in the lines below.

222. GREY-BEARD MIRTH AND SMILING TOIL—There the old men gathered (retired) to spin yarns, and those still vigorous sat about after the day's work to listen and laugh.

*And still they gazed, and still
the wonder grew
That one small head could carry
all he knew.*

The white-washed wall; the nicely sanded floor;
The varnished clock that clicked behind the door;
The chest contrived a double debt to pay—
230 A bed by night, a chest of drawers by day;
The pictures placed for ornament and use;
The twelve good rules; the royal game of goose;
The hearth, except when winter chilled the day,
With aspen boughs and flowers and fennel gay;
235 While broken tea-cups, wisely kept for show,
Ranged o'er the chimney, glistened in a row.

Vain, transitory splendors! could not all
Reprieve the tottering mansion from its fall?
Obscure it sinks, nor shall it more impart
240 An hour's importance to the poor man's heart.
Thither no more the peasant shall repair
To sweet oblivion of his daily care;
No more the farmer's news, the barber's tale,
No more the wood-man's ballad shall prevail;
245 No more the smith his dusky brow shall clear,
Relax his ponderous strength, and lean to hear;
The host himself no longer shall be found
Careful to see the mantling bliss go round,
Nor the coy maid, half willing to be prest,
250 Shall kiss the cup to pass it to the rest.

227. SANDED FLOOR—It was customary to cover the stone floors with fine, clean sand.

231. USE—That is, to cover spots on the walls.

232. TWELVE GOOD RULES—Twelve rules for conduct often hung up in taverns. These rules, said to have been originated by Charles I, were: 1. Urge no healths. 2. Profane no divine ordinances. 3. Touch no state matters. 4. Reveal no secrets. 5. Pick no quarrels. 6. Make no comparisons. 7. Maintain no ill opinions. 8. Keep no bad company. 9. Encourage no vice. 10. Make no long meals. 11. Repeat no grievances. 12. Lay no wagers.

232. GAME OF GOOSE—A game somewhat like checkers, so called because a goose was painted on certain squares of the board.

234. WITH ASPEN BOUGHS—In summer it was customary to fill the fireplace with flowers or green branches.

238. REPRIEVE—Delay.

244. WOOD-MAN—Hunter.

248. BLISS—The nut-brown ale, called "mantling" because there formed on the top of it a mantle, or covering, of creamy froth.

249. MAID—The bar-maid.

Yes, let the rich deride, the proud disdain,
These simple blessings of the lowly train;
To me more dear, congenial to my heart,
One native charm, than all the gloss of art.
255 Spontaneous joys, where nature has its play,
The soul adopts, and owns their first-born sway;
Lightly they frolic o'er the vacant mind,
Unenvied, unmolested, unconfined.
But the long pomp, the midnight masquerade,
260 With all the freaks of wanton wealth arrayed,
In these, ere triflers half their wish obtain,
The toiling pleasure sickens into pain;
And, even while Fashion's brightest arts decoy,
The heart, distrusting, asks if this be joy.

265 Ye friends to truth, ye statesmen who survey
The rich man's joys increase, the poor's decay,
'Tis yours to judge, how wide the limits stand
Between a splendid and an happy land.
Proud swells the tide with loads of freighted ore,
270 And shouting Folly hails them from her shore;
Hoards e'en beyond the miser's wish abound,
And rich men flock from all the world around,
Yet count our grains; this wealth is but a name,
That leaves our useful products still the same.
275 Not so the loss: the man of wealth and pride
Takes up a space that many poor supplied—

254. GLOSS—Elaborate entertainment. Goldsmith means that he much prefers the simple pleasures which are to be found among peasants who act naturally to the elaborate entertainments of the rich.
256. The meaning is that man naturally responds to these simpler spontaneous pleasures, and that they are harmless—"They lightly frolic o'er" the care-free mind.
260. FREAKS—The meaning is: The masquerade in which the dancers are garbed (arrayed) in every fantastic costume (freaks) which imagination can devise and unlimited (wanton) wealth provide.
267. That is: It is your business, as those who have the welfare of the country to look out for, to note that there is a vast difference between a country which shines with the splendor of great wealth in the hands of a few, and a country in which the great mass of people are happy, and contented with enough to live on.
269. ORE—"Ore" here stands for rich cargoes of merchandise. The line describes England's great merchant trade on the seas.
270. It was Goldsmith's opinion that the creation of wealth by trade in which he saw the cause for such distress as he describes in the poem was unwise (folly). 276. SUPPLIED—Maintained in comfort.

            Space for his lake, his park's extended bounds,
            Space for his horses, equipage, and hounds;
            The robe that wraps his limbs in silken sloth
280   Has robbed the neighboring fields of half their growth;
            His seat, where solitary sports are seen,
            Indignant spurns the cottage from the green;
            Around the world each needful product flies,
            For all the luxuries, the world supplies;
285   While thus the land, adorned for pleasure all,
            In barren splendor feebly waits the fall.

                As some fair female, unadorned and plain,
            Secure to please while youth confirms her reign,
            Slights every borrowed charm that dress supplies,
290   Nor shares with art the triumph of her eyes;
            But when those charms are past—for charms are frail,—
            When time advances, and when lovers fail,
            She then shines forth, solicitous to bless,
            In all the glaring impotence of dress:
295   Thus fares the land, by luxury betrayed,
            In Nature's simplest charms at first arrayed;
            But, verging to decline, its splendors rise,
            Its vistas strike, its palaces surprise,
            While, scourged by famine from the smiling land,
300   The mournful peasant leads his humble band;
            And while he sinks, without one arm to save,
            The country blooms—a garden and a grave.

280. ROBBED THE NEIGHBORING FIELDS—Half the produce of the fields has been sent abroad in exchange for the silk.
281. SOLITARY SPORTS—He rides alone perhaps on horseback where formerly the whole population of the village used to gather for sports such as those described at the opening of the poem.
281. HIS SEAT . . . INDIGNANT SPURNS THE COTTAGE FROM THE GREEN—The meaning is that the rich, who had made their money in trade, bought up the land to create great estates and arrogantly (indignant) turned off the cotters, or peasants.
283. Goldsmith implies here that products which were needed at home are now sent abroad in exchange for unneeded luxuries, to gratify the desires of the wealthy.   288. That is, sure to be attractive because of her youth.
289. Makes no use of dress or artificial beauty to render herself attractive.
294. IMPOTENCE—Inability, lack of power. That is, she now tries to win favor by her dress, which Goldsmith says is conspicuously (glaring) unable to do what the unadorned charm of youth once did.
302. GARDEN AND A GRAVE—A pleasure garden for those who have created great estates which are really private parks; a grave, because these parks are made where formerly were villages and farms, now deserted, or dead.

       Where, then, ah where shall poverty reside,
       To scape the pressure of contiguous pride?
305 If to some common's fenceless limits strayed,
       He drives his flock to pick the scanty blade,
       Those fenceless fields the sons of wealth divide,
       And even the bare-worn common is denied.

       If to the city sped, what waits him there?
310 To see profusion that he must not share;
       To see ten thousand baneful arts combined
       To pamper luxury and thin mankind;
       To see those joys the sons of pleasure know,
       Extorted from his fellow-creature's woe.
315 Here while the courtier glitters in brocade,
       There the pale artist plies the sickly trade;
       Here while the proud their long-drawn pomps display,
       There the black gibbet glooms beside the way.
       The dome where Pleasure holds her midnight reign,
320 Here, richly deckt, admits the gorgeous train;
       Tumultuous grandeur crowds the blazing square,
       The rattling chariots clash, the torches glare:
       Sure, scenes like these no troubles e'er annoy;
       Sure, these denote one universal joy!
325 Are these thy serious thoughts? Ah, turn thine eyes
       Where the poor houseless shivering female lies:
       She once, perhaps, in village plenty blest,
       Has wept at tales of innocence distrest;
       Her modest looks the cottage might adorn,
330 . Sweet as the primrose peeps beneath the thorn;
       Nor lost to all—her friends, her virtue, fled—
       Near her betrayer's door she lays her head,

    304. CONTIGUOUS PRIDE—Where can the poor find land which some adjoining (contiguous) great landowner will not be demanding?
    315. HERE . . . THERE—While in one place . . . in the other.
    316. ARTIST—Workman—probably the maker of the brocade which the courtier wears, or possibly the tailor.
    318. GIBBET—Gallows. Even in Goldsmith's time executions were public. The gallows was often erected on a hilltop or by the road in a conspicuous place, and the executed person left hanging as a warning to passers-by against crime.
    319. DOME—The ballroom, so called because often on the upper floor of great houses, beneath the cupola or dome.
    320. RICHLY DECKT—Elaborately decorated—refers to "dome."
    332. HER BETRAYER—The aristocrat and usurper of the land.

And, pinch'd with cold, and shrinking from the shower,
With heavy heart deplores that luckless hour
When idly, first, ambitious of the town,
She left her wheel and robes of country brown.

Do thine, sweet Auburn, thine, the loveliest train,
Do thy fair tribes participate her pain?
Even now, perhaps, by cold and hunger led,
At proud men's doors they ask a little bread.

Ah, no! To distant climes, a dreary scene,
Where half the convex world intrudes between,
Through torrid tracts with fainting steps they go,
Where wild Altama murmurs to their woe.
Far different there from all that charm'd before
The various terrors of that horrid shore:
Those blazing suns that dart a downward ray,
And fiercely shed intolerable day;
Those matted woods, where birds forget to sing,
But silent bats in drowsy clusters cling;
Those poisonous fields with rank luxuriance crowned,
Where the dark scorpion gathers death around,
Where at each step the stranger fears to wake
The rattling terrors of the vengeful snake,
Where crouching tigers wait their hapless prey,
And savage men more murderous still than they;

336. WHEEL—Spinning wheel.
338. PARTICIPATE HER PAIN—Have thy young women come to a like end?
344. ALTAMA—The Altamaha River in Georgia. Georgia was first settled by a group of families out of debtors' prisons in England. It was hoped that here in the New World, those who had lost out in the Old would get a new start. James Oglethorpe, the philanthropist, who conceived the idea of sending England's unfortunates to Georgia was a friend of Goldsmith. The attempt to colonize Georgia with debtors and other delinquents fell through. Perhaps the things which made for successful farming in the Old World were unsuited to it in Georgia. At any rate, the first colonists lacked the ability to make the necessary adjustments to the conditions of climate and soil they found in the New World. Goldsmith evidently thought the failure of the colony due to climate and local circumstances rather than to any weakness of the colonists. The picture he draws of Georgia makes it a most unattractive place; perhaps it appeared thus to people accustomed to the English countryside.
346. Read: "Are" the various terrors, etc.
355. TIGERS—Possibly wildcats or panthers, certainly not tigers.
356. SAVAGE MEN—Indians.

While oft in whirls the mad tornado flies,
Mingling the ravaged landscape with the skies.
Far different these from every former scene—
360 The cooling brook, the grassy-vested green,
The breezy covert of the warbling grove,
That only sheltered thefts of harmless love.

    Good Heaven! what sorrows gloom'd that parting day
That called them from their native walks away,
365 When the poor exiles, every pleasure past,
Hung round the bowers, and fondly looked their last,
And took a long farewell, and wished in vain
For seats like these beyond the western main,
And, shuddering still to face the distant deep,
370 Returned and wept, and still returned to weep.
The good old sire the first prepared to go
To new-found worlds, and wept for others' woe;
But for himself, in conscious virtue brave,
He only wished for worlds beyond the grave.
375 His lovely daughter, lovelier in her tears,
The fond companion of his helpless years,
Silent went next, neglectful of her charms,
And left a lover's for a father's arms.
With louder plaints the mother spoke her woes,
380 And blest the cot where every pleasure rose,
And kist her thoughtless babes with many a tear,
And claspt them close, in sorrow doubly dear,
Whilst her fond husband strove to lend relief
In all the silent manliness of grief.

385   O Luxury! thou curst by Heaven's decree,
How ill exchanged are things like these for thee!
How do thy potions, with insidious joy,
Diffuse their pleasure only to destroy!
Kingdoms by thee, to sickly greatness grown,

---

362. THEFTS OF HARMLESS LOVE—Stolen kisses.
368. WESTERN MAIN—The Atlantic.
373. CONSCIOUS VIRTUE BRAVE—Unafraid to meet death because he knew his conscience clear.
387. POTIONS—The pleasure-giving things which come with luxury. A potion is a drink concocted for some particular purpose, such as a sleeping potion. Goldsmith compares the pleasure-giving things of luxury to a potion which, though producing joy for the time, poisons the drinker in the end.

390　Boast of a florid vigor not their own:
　　　At every draught more large and large they grow,
　　　A bloated mass of rank unwieldly woe;
　　　Till, sapped their strength, and every part unsound,
　　　Down, down they sink, and spread a ruin round.

395　　Even now the devastation is begun,
　　　And half the business of destruction done;
　　　Even now, methinks, as pondering here I stand,
　　　I see the rural Virtues leave the land.
　　　Down where yon anchoring vessel spreads the sail
400　That idly waiting, flaps with every gale,
　　　Downward they move, a melancholy band,
　　　Pass from the shore, and darken all the strand:
　　　Contented Toil, and hospitable Care,
　　　And kind connubial Tenderness are there,
405　And Piety with wishes placed above,
　　　And steady Loyalty, and faithful Love.
　　　And thou, sweet Poetry, thou loveliest maid,
　　　Still first to fly where sensual joys invade,
　　　Unfit in these degenerate times of shame
410　To catch the heart, or strike for honest fame;
　　　Dear, charming nymph, neglected and decried,
　　　My shame in crowds, my solitary pride,
　　　Thou source of all my bliss, and all my woe,
　　　That found'st me poor at first, and keep'st me so,
415　Thou guide by which the nobler arts excel,
　　　Thou nurse of every virtue, fare thee well!
　　　Farewell, and oh, where'er thy voice be tried,
　　　On Torno's cliffs, or Pambamarca's side,
　　　Whether where equinoctial fervors glow,
420　Or winter wraps the polar world in snow,

390. FLORID—Blooming, highly colored. The term is often applied to the high color which often characterizes the faces of excessive drinkers.
411. NYMPH—Poetry.
412. MY SOLITARY PRIDE—The thing which gives me the most pride in myself, regardless of the attitude of the crowd toward poetry.
415. NOBLER ARTS—Music, sculpture, painting. The meaning seems to be that poetry furnishes the inspiration for these sister arts.
418. TORNO'S CLIFFS—Thought to refer to the cliffs on Lake Tornea in northern Sweden.
418. PAMBAMARCA'S SIDE—A height of the Andes in Ecuador.
419. WHERE EQUINOCTIAL FERVORS—In the torrid regions.

Still let thy voice, prevailing over time,
Redress the rigors of the inclement clime;
Aid slighted truth with thy persuasive strain;
Teach erring man to spurn the rage of gain:
425 Teach him that states of native strength possest,
Though very poor, may still be very blest;
That trade's proud empire hastes to swift decay,
As ocean sweeps the labored mole away,
While self-dependent power can time defy,
430 As rocks resist the billows and the sky.

428. MOLE—A breakwater. "Labored" means belabored by the sea.
429. SELF-DEPENDENT—Power resulting from strength of character (self) rather than from money (things).

Poem Development: *The Deserted Village* is what is known as an idyll, that is, a poem which presents a series of pictures, especially of rustic life. It does not give us a history, but rather a kind of composite picture into which Goldsmith worked the idyllic aspects of village life in general. These aspects he saw disappearing, and in their stead he saw poverty and misery for the many, and wealth and luxury for the few. It seemed to him that the changes which the development of trade had brought about were all for the worse. Throughout the poem, the old is contrasted with the new and the whole is shot through and through with indignation at "trade's unfeeling train" and with sympathy for the bewildered peasant; while over the poem broods a melancholy tenderness born of his own longing for the days that were gone.

Lines 1–34 give a picture of the simple, happy life of a peasant village as Goldsmith idealized it. Give the description in your own words. What were the pleasures enjoyed in the evenings? Describe the village after it became deserted (lines 34–50).

Lines 51–56 express Goldsmith's belief in the worth of the common man. The poem reflects the age in which it was written, for it voices the same sentiment which five years later, in 1775, found expression in the American Declaration of Independence. The philosophy that "all men are created free and equal" was in the air.

Lines 57–112 describe some of the "griefs," contrast the new with the old, and picture the old age which he dreamed of bringing to a close among the scenes of his childhood. Describe some of the unjust social conditions which existed at this time. Do you agree with the philosophy in lines 99–102?

Lines 113–136 contrast the evening scenes in the village before and after the Enclosure Acts. What is the picture that makes the latter description the more effective?

Lines 137–192 describe the village preacher. This passage is well worth memorizing. Goldsmith's father, his brother Henry, and his uncle Contarine were all village curates in Ireland. They were one and all distinguished for their simplicity of manner, their kindliness, and their goodness of heart, rather than for any ability to get on in the world. The picture of the village preacher is probably a composite of all three. Give a description of him. Describe the schoolmaster.

Lines 217–302 contrast the simple pleasures of the village with the elaborate entertainments of the rich, and the expression of the belief that wealth has brought only evil in its train. Give a description of the tavern. What were the sights that Goldsmith says would no more be seen? What reasons does the poet give for preferring the simple pleasures of the poor to those of the wealthy?

Lines 303–308 refer to the enclosure of the commons. Lines 309–340 describe the condition of the great mass of workers in the cities, and contrast their condition with the luxury of the rich. The state of the poor in the towns was wretched in the extreme. Describe some of the conditions and customs of the time.

Is the picture of Georgia (lines 341–362) true? What can you say about the reference to a tornado in line 357?

Lines 363–430 picture the parting from the old homes, and the poem closes with an indignant outburst of feeling against luxury and its attendant evils, and a portrayal of the rural virtues. In lines 407–430 Goldsmith sees the disappearance of poetry with the life which made poetry possible. It is true, of course, that with the disappearance of the village life Goldsmith knew, poetry springing from that life could no longer be possible. Here is a good illustration of the fact that to fully appreciate any poem one must first re-create the picture of the conditions which gave it birth; and one must also understand that poetry never dies; it simply changes as life changes.

Combine the paramount thoughts you have gained from the independent study of each section into a smoothly running summary or précis of the poem as a whole. What would you say is the chief poetic appeal of this poem? What is the theme? The central thought?

Interpretations: Seats of my youth (l. 6); line 19; line 20; lines 53 and 54; England's griefs (l. 56); line 64; calm desires (l. 70); far departing (l. 73); my latest hours to crown (l. 85); unperceived decay (l. 109); resignation (l. 110); fluctuate in the gale (l. 126); chid their wanderings (l. 150); line 160; line 164; lines 169 and 170; line 185; lines 205 and 206; vain, transitory splendors (l. 237); by luxury betrayed (l. 295); ambitious of the town (l. 335); ravaged landscape (l. 358); lines 421–422.

Significant Expressions: What is the figure of speech in line 3? in line 119? in line 222? in line 270? in line 403? Select three passages that appeal to you most and memorize one of them. Give reasons for your choice (poetic quality, feeling, etc.).

THE HISTORY OF POETRY IN ENGLAND

THE AGE OF ROMANTICISM (1780-1840)

General Characteristics

Any triumph in the progress of the common man is always reflected in the literature of the period. All of the poetry of the Romantic Age shows a broader sympathy with humanity which was an outgrowth of the American and French revolutions for liberty and of the reforms which swept England. As the rights of the individual increased, the poets found new themes for the expression of their thoughts—the rights of man, the worth of the individual. They found new interests, too, in the old legends of the country and these formed the subject of many of their poems. But by far the most important characteristic of the poetry of this period was the revival of a feeling for nature. The great poetry of the period reveals writers who were tremendously sensitive to the outward charms and aspects of the natural world. Subjects which to Dryden or Pope would hardly have been sufficiently dignified to justify a heroic couplet are now the themes of the romantic poetry.

No such age of poetic production had been known since the age of Elizabeth. It was characterized by an abandonment of old ideas and by the acceptance of new standards in regard to society and the rank of the common man. The new spirit of liberty was reflected in a great production of lyrics, ballads, and odes, and these were written in the language of common every-day use with a complete avoidance of the old flowery, artificial language of the classicists. It was an age of simplicity and genuineness.

William Blake (1757-1827)

The first of the poets of the Romantic Age was William Blake. He was the son of a well-to-do hosier in London who sent him to school when he was ten years old. He soon began to write verses and to copy prints. He was a strange boy who seemed to live in a dream world, but who worked patiently, diligently, and cheerfully all through his life. Blake had little education for he became an engraver's apprentice at fourteen, but he read constantly and he was a great lover of nature.

He wrote lyrics dealing with nature subjects, all simple in expression and often containing a spiritual and mystical element. He wrote, too, of childhood and of animals, subjects rarely before expressed in verse. Some of his nursery songs are very musical. He is probably best known for *The Tiger*, but *Introduction to Songs of Innocence* and *To the Evening Star* are also exquisitely beautiful.

Robert Burns (1759-1796)

Burns is the best embodiment of all those tendencies exhibited by the Romantic movement. In the choice of subject matter he stands in marked contrast to the classicists. In addition to this individuality in choice of material, he exhibits strong feeling, especially for nature and for his fellow man, and he wrote his poetry not in the form approved by the classicists, but in Scotch dialect.

Burns was born in Alloway, Scotland. His parents were poor, honest Scotch peasants, who worked early and late to make a meager living. Burns received little education, for he had to do a man's work on the farm, but he was extremely interested in the old folk songs and legends of Scotland and spent considerable time familiarizing himself with them. It is said of him that he sang as he plowed, and made his verses to suit the melody. He loved nature intensely. It is easy to picture him stopping to listen to the song of a bird, or the wind in the trees, or the whisper of the grass, as he worked about the farm.

At seventeen, Burns left his home to study surveying. It was then that he became associated with a rough class of men and began drinking. Drink was to be his worst enemy the rest of his life.

When he was about twenty-seven years old, he decided to go to America, and he published his first book of poems in order to raise money to pay for his passage. The book proved so popular that he gave up the intended trip. He spent a winter in Edinburgh where he was lionized and where he became a popular hero, but his dissipation soon offended his entertainers and he went back to farm life. He married Jean Armour in 1788 and had he been able to abstain from drinking, he would have had a very happy life. As it was, his last years were filled with poverty and trouble.

He nevertheless gave us some of the most inspiring and beautiful songs and lyrics ever written. Burns saw beauty in every flower, rock, bird, shrub, or animal that came into his vision. He wrote of them in such a simple, unaffected way that they seemed to come straight from his heart. All lyric themes were to him inspirations, and he moves the reader to tears or smiles at will. Besides this love for nature, Burns had a strong feeling for the equality of man. He lived during the time of the American and French Revolutions, and these struggles no doubt left their impression on him. Burns was a man who was sincere, big-hearted, cheerful, and tender.

William Wordsworth (1770–1850)

Wordsworth was born in a small village in Cumberland and grew up as a boy in the beautiful Lake District of England. Both of his parents died before he was fourteen years old, but they left to him an inheritance of love and sympathy for all things connected with country life, for they were of families who had for generations been landowners in the country. Wordsworth's boyhood life spent as it was close to nature, no doubt, too, exerted a strong tendency toward making him one of the greatest of nature poets.

He attended Cambridge University and after his graduation spent two years in continental travel. In France he came into contact with the ideas which produced the French Revolution, and as a young man his sympathies were wholly with the revolutionists. The excesses of the Revolution resulted in disillusionment and he returned to England somewhat despondent.

After three years of rather unhappy, unsettled life, he received a small legacy which enabled him to take a cottage in the country and here he established himself with his sister Dorothy and devoted himself to writing poetry. The rest of his life was simple and an example of "plain living and high thinking." In the preface to a book, *Lyrical Ballads*, produced in collaboration with Coleridge, Wordsworth took his stand against the classicists, declaring that poetry is "the spontaneous overflow of powerful feelings" and is not to be encased in hard and fast rules. Recognition of Wordsworth's ability as a poet was slow but in 1843 he was appointed Poet Laureate.

Wordsworth is primarily an interpreter of nature—nature in a calm, majestic mood. He found beauty in the most commonplace object and so re-created its image that we live over beautiful scenes that we ourselves have known. He awakens memories and stirs the imagination, always in a calm, quiet, deeply sincere manner. Wordsworth is also one of the great masters of the sonnet and his odes have been called the greatest in the English language. Perhaps his greatest poem is the *Ode on the Intimations of Immortality* in which he voices his belief in the immortality of the soul. Wordsworth's poetry is characterized by sincerity of feeling, simplicity, and accuracy of description in the portrayal of nature. In diction, he was particularly careful to avoid the stilted idiom of the classicists and to use only the language of common speech.

Sir Walter Scott (1771–1832)

Not very long after his birth in 1771, Walter Scott became lame as a result of illness. He was sent to his grandmother's farm at Sandy-knowe on the Scottish border, and there he learned many tales and legends of border life. A few years of life in the open brought a big improvement in the sickly child, and he was able after a time to return to his home in Edinburgh. While in school he was fond of stories of ancient battles, of brave knights, and of adventure. He enjoyed riding through the country in search of old legends and in a few years knew every battle-field around Edinburgh, and the tales of witches and goblins that were a part of the magic country near his home.

While at the University of Edinburgh, he became more and more interested in reading from the old masters, and even after he began to practice law his greatest interest was in the romantic tales of old Scotland. Often he left his office to travel to the Highlands and to the Border Country in search of ballads, myths, and history. In 1799, he married Miss Charlotte Carpenter. Shortly after, he was appointed Sheriff of Selkirkshire with a salary which permitted him to devote much of his time to literature. Between the ages of thirty and forty he wrote his best poems. At forty-three he began writing novels, and he wrote twenty-nine before his death.

Meanwhile he had built a castle on the banks of the Tweed not far from where the last of the great battles between the clans had been fought in 1526. But now occurred an unfortunate business failure. An Edinburgh publishing firm with which he was connected failed and left a debt of £117,000. Scott might have taken advantage of the bankruptcy law, but he did not. The remainder of his life was a heroic struggle to die with honor by paying up all of the debt.

Scott's poetry is noted for the absorbing interest which it creates in the reader's mind, for its vivid descriptions and stirring action. He wrote several long narrative poems of which *The Lay of the Last Minstrel, Marmion,* and *The Lady of the Lake* are perhaps the best known. All of these show Scott's great love for Scotland and its customs. From *Minstrelsy of the Scottish Border* we have many ballads, oftentimes with a charming lyrical touch to them. Scott reveled in a world of romance, with its knights and ladies and chivalry of old, but he described them to us with a realness that re-creates the scenes so vividly we can picture ourselves a part of them.

Samuel Taylor Coleridge (1772–1834)

Coleridge was born at Ottery St. Mary in southwest England. His father was a school teacher and vicar of the parish church. He was educated at Christ's Hospital and later attended Cambridge University, but he did not graduate for he had a somewhat adventurous spirit and was not inclined to settle down to work. Coleridge was a bright child and could read before he was four years old. As he grew older he delighted in the *Arabian Nights* and in reading the classics. As he advanced in years, he became more and more a dreamer and more and more weak in character, never seeming to have any fixed purpose or to keep steadily at any one line of work. He studied a while in Germany and in Italy, started a paper, and lectured on poetry. He married but was unable to support his wife and family.

Coleridge and Robert Southey were great friends for they had married sisters, and Southey often supplied the necessary funds for the Coleridge family. After wandering about, Coleridge finally returned to England in 1800 and settled near the home of Wordsworth. Here he began taking an opiate to alleviate the pain which he suffered from neuralgia, and for fifteen years he was unable to conquer the opiate habit.

All through his life, Coleridge was a nature lover. But while his friend Wordsworth wrote of nature in a high, lofty, exalted manner, Coleridge expressed a tenderness of thought which endears him to his readers. His contributions to poetry are few in number, but they are wonderful in their beauty and in their musical lines. In *The Ancient Mariner* he shows his love for God's created things. The entire poem is one of musical tone with one vivid, colorful picture following another. In it there is also expressed a moral truth. *Kubla Khan* gives the same reality to the supernatural that is found in *The Ancient Mariner,* and an atmosphere of  dreamlike uncertainty is carried out by the arrangement of accented syllables. It is full of melody and imaginative pictures. Coleridge's gentle nature made verses which cause the reader to love him in spite of his weaknesses.

Thomas Moore (1779-1852)

Moore was born in Dublin, Ireland. He attended Trinity College where he was extremely popular because he could sing and play. This ability made him welcome in London also, where he went to study law. Moore and Byron became friends, and this friendship resulted in his becoming Byron's official biographer. Moore wrote many lyrics and it is for those songs dealing with love and Ireland that we know him best. These songs are gay with an occasional touch of sadness, and they are appealing both in their musical tone and in their sentiment. Moore often wrote the music to accompany his songs. *Oft in the Stilly Night* and *The Harp That Once Through Tara's Halls* are two favorites which have been sung for many years.

George Gordon, Lord Byron (1788-1824)

Byron, an only child, was born in London in 1788. Shortly thereafter his parents separated. His father, an unprincipled spendthrift, had gone through his wife's fortune in two years, and fled to France to escape his creditors. The mother took her boy to Aberdeen where she lived in a shabby Scotch flat on a slender income. In 1798 there came a change in the family circumstances. On the death of his great-uncle, Byron succeeded to his title and estates, and became the sixth Lord Byron. Mrs. Byron now took up her residence at Newstead Abbey, and Byron was put to school first at Dulwich, and then at the great school of Harrow, where he remained four years, going from there to Trinity College, Cambridge.

Many of the outstanding characteristics of Byron the man are to be seen in him as a boy. Among the good housewives of Aberdeen upon whom he played his pranks he was known as "Mrs. Byron's crockit deevil." Although he is spoken of as having been lively, warm-hearted,  and companionable, he was capable of a deep vindictive anger against those who crossed his path. He was proud and self-centered. Silent rages, moody sullenness and revenge are by one biographer called his general characteristics as a boy. From the standpoint of heredity he came honestly enough by his make-up, for on both sides of his house were to be found men of violent temper and dark imaginings, and his up-bringing was such as to confirm his faults rather than to remove them. His mother was a woman of most uneven disposition and she mismanaged the boy from the outset.

Among other characteristics of Byron as a boy are to be noted a love of attention and a desire to excel. He had been born with a deformed foot, and to this blemish he became morbidly sensitive. It seems to have embittered him, and to have engendered in him a sense of inferiority which but stimulated his natural ambition to outstrip other boys. Because of it he threw himself with the more vigor into athletic exercises, and possibly because of it he developed the rather contentious, quarrelsome spirit which he sometimes manifested in his school days. He became a "record" swimmer, and enough of a "cricketer" to play for his school.

He was never distinguished for scholarship, yet he was a devourer of books, especially of such as fed the imagination. His first published poems, a thin volume entitled *Hours of Idleness,* were done while he was yet at Trinity College. The *Edinburgh Review* made them the target for sarcastic and brutal criticism. His pride stung to the quick, Byron retorted in a poem—*English Bards and Scotch Reviewers*—which demonstrated his own power in satire, and his ability to write poetry as well.

In 1809 he began a tour of the Mediterranean world, visiting Greece, Albania, and Syria. The effect of the Orient upon his development as a poet can hardly be overestimated. Romantic landscape seems always to have moved him as it did Scott, and the colorful and picturesque East

HISTORY OF POETRY

fired his imagination. He recorded his impressions in a long poem entitled *Childe Harold's Pilgrimage,* part of which was published after his return to England in 1812. The poem made him famous "over night." In 1813 he was at the height of his popularity. His poetry was on everyone's lips, he was sought after socially, and his manner and style were aped by the dandies of the time.

In 1815 Byron married. Hardly a year had elapsed before his wife left him, alleging that his conduct had been harsh, violent, and eccentrical. London took her side in the controversy, and public opinion drove Byron from society. In April, 1816, he left England, never to return. He finally settled in Italy, living at Venice, Ravenna, and Genoa. During these years he continued to write, producing some of his best known poems. He interested himself first in the movement for Italian liberty, and then in the struggle which the Greeks were making to throw off the rule of Turkey. It was while in command of a Greek force that death overtook him. He died of a rheumatic fever at Missolonghi, April 19, 1824.

Percy Bysshe Shelley (1792–1822)

Shelley was born in Field Place, Sussex. He was descended from old families who had been famous in the history of England. He was sent to a public school where he was most unhappy for those were the days of floggings and harsh treatment as a means of educating the young. Shelley was a sensitive, nervous child of unusual beauty, but he was never a coward. On the contrary he always stood out against oppression and was called "mad Shelley" by his schoolmates because he resented the flogging system and the persecution put upon him by the bigger boys at the school. At Eton and later at Oxford, he was constantly in trouble with the masters for he continued to express his revolutionary ideas. Finally
he was expelled from college, and married Harriet Westbrook, who also imagined that she was an object of persecution. The marriage was an unhappy one and resulted in a separation. Later he married Mary Godwin, who proved loyal and faithful to him until he died.

Shelley's field of poetry is the lyric. No greater lyric poet has ever lived. True it is that one must have a soul to appreciate flights of fancy into infinite spaces to really appreciate Shelley, but his lyrics contain some of the sweetest and most liquid harmonies ever written. His notes are as clear as a flute, now high, now low, but always in a minor key. Shelley is at his best in *To a Skylark, The Cloud,* and *Ode to the West Wind.* In *Prometheus Unbound,* a lyric drama, Shelley shows his rebellion against all oppressions of the world. He believed in the brotherhood of man, and a world of beauty and love, but he was an idealist who could not adjust himself to the arrangements of a practical world. Byron said of him, "he was the best and least selfish man I ever knew, I never met one who was not a beast in comparison."

Shelley was drowned in the Gulf of Lerici off the Italian coast when he was only thirty years old.

John Keats (1795–1821)

Keats was born in London. His father was a stable keeper and no more unpoetic environment could be imagined than that which surrounded the poet's early days. His parents died before he was fifteen, but he had already had a little schooling. He was apprenticed to a surgeon with whom he remained for five years. It was during this time that someone presented him with a copy of Spenser's *Faerie Queene*, and this so inspired him that he immediately began writing poetry. There were brutal attacks made upon his verse by the critics, but Shelley and Lamb both encouraged him, and he kept on with his work. About this time Keats' beloved brother died with consumption and Keats felt that the dread disease was fastening itself upon him. He had fallen in love with a charming girl, Fannie Brawne, and knowing that he could not marry her because of his poverty and illness, the despondency to which he was naturally disposed, increased. Worry and dejection of mind undermined his health and he went to Italy, but it was too late. He died at the age of twenty-six.

Keats was a lover of beauty and no poet ever kept more steadfastly to his ideal. His finest poetry was lyric, and some of the best of his poems are *Ode on a Grecian Urn, Ode to a Nightingale,* and *To Autumn. The Eve of St. Agnes* is a delightful story of medieval days. Had Keats lived he would probably have become the greatest poet of his generation. While he did not represent quite so strongly the characteristic of the Romantic Age in wishing to influence society, he is nevertheless typical of that age for he writes of beauty in nature, in man, in everything. With him, beauty and truth were one—"Beauty is truth, truth beauty—that is all ye know on earth, and all ye need to know."

Minor Poets of the Romantic Age

The chief minor poets of the period are Robert Southey, Poet Laureate after Wordsworth, and the author of a number of romantic narrative poems among which *The Battle of Blenheim* is perhaps best known, and Thomas Campbell, remembered for his spirited battle ballads, *Ye Mariners of England, Hohenlinden,* and *The Battle of the Baltic.*

Poetry of the Romantic Age

THE TIGER

William Blake

Poem Interest: More than anything we meet in life, the contrasts of nature cause us to pause in wonder. On one hand, we see the uplifting freshness of trees and flowers; on the other the destructive fury of the storm. Blake's poem captures this mood of wonder in a simple, perfect way.

Tiger, Tiger, burning bright
In the forests of the night,
What immortal hand or eye
Could frame thy fearful symmetry?

5   In what distant deeps or skies
Burnt the fire of thine eyes?
On what wings dare he aspire?
What the hand dare seize the fire?

And what shoulder, and what art,
10   Could twist the sinews of thy heart?
When thy heart began to beat,
What dread hand forged thy dread feet?

What the hammer? What the chain?
In what furnace was thy brain?

15   What the anvil? What dread grasp
     Dared its deadly terrors clasp?

     When the stars threw down their spears,
     And watered heaven with their tears,
     Did He smile His work to see?
20   Did He who made the Lamb make thee?

     Tiger, Tiger, burning bright
     In the forests of the night,
     What immortal hand or eye
     Dare frame thy fearful symmetry?

Poem Development: This has been called Blake's best poem. Back of its apparent simplicity there is a deeper meaning. Briefly give your thoughts on the message of the poem. Is the poem one of masterful imagery? Give examples. What is the effect of the series of questions in the poem? What emotion is aroused by reading the poem?

Significant Expressions: Quote the line giving the most vivid picture. Quote the line conveying an expression of fear.

JOHN ANDERSON, MY JO

Robert Burns

Poem Interest: Many are the poems dedicated to young love—to the beauty and strength of men and women young in years. Therefore, it is quite unusual, and delightful too, to find a "love lyric" written to one whose "brow is beld," whose "locks are like the snaw." We feel in its lines the sincere contentment and fulfillment of a love which is also a fine friendship.

     John Anderson, my jo, John,
        When we were first acquent,
     Your locks were like the raven,
        Your bonie brow was brent;
5   But now your brow is beld, John,
        Your locks are like the snaw;
     But blessings on your frosty pow,
        John Anderson, my jo.

1. Jo—Sweetheart.   2. Acquent—Acquainted.
4. Brent—Unwrinkled.   5. Beld—Bald.
7. Frosty pow—White head.

>   John Anderson, my jo, John,
> 10   We clamb the hill thegither;
>   And mony a canty day, John,
>   We've had wi' ane anither;
>   Now we maun totter down, John,
>   But hand in hand we'll go,
> 15 And sleep thegither at the foot,
>   John Anderson, my jo.

11. CANTY—Merry, cheerful.   13. MAUN—Must.

Poem Development: Describe the youthful sweetheart. Describe him in old age. What do you think the poet means by "hill" in line 10? Can you find in the lines of the poem a secret of the old couple's happiness together? Give the theme and central thought of the poem.

Significant Expressions: Quote the line in the first stanza which is the most vividly descriptive.

A MAN'S A MAN FOR A' THAT

ROBERT BURNS

Poem Interest: Burns lived during the time of the American and French Revolutions, and he was profoundly affected by the doctrine of democracy which was the impetus for both these great conflicts. From this movement he drew inspiration, and in turn, his simple, faithfully presented pictures exalt the individual and champion the worth of man.

>   Is THERE for honest Poverty
>   That hings his head, an' a' that;
>   The coward slave—we pass him by,
>   We dare be poor for a' that!
> 5   For a' that, an' a' that,
>   Our toils obscure an' a' that,
>   The rank is but the guinea's stamp,
>   The Man's the gowd for a' that.
>
>   What though on hamely fare we dine,
> 10   Wear hoddin greay, an' a' that;
>   Gie fools their silks, and knaves their wine,
>   A Man's a Man for a' that:

2. HINGS—Hangs.
7. GUINEA—An English gold coin worth about $5.11.
8. GOWD—Gold. Burns meant that it is the gold, not the mark, or stamp, which makes the coin valuable.
9. HAMELY—Common; coarse.   10. HODDIN GREAY—Coarse grey woolen.

> For a' that, and a' that,
>   Their tinsel show, an' a' that;
> 15 The honest man, tho' e'er sae poor,
>   Is king o' men for a' that.
>
> Ye see yon birkie ca'd a lord,
>   Wha struts, an' stares, an' a' that;
> Tho' hundreds worship at his word,
> 20 He's but a coof for a' that:
>
> For a' that, an' a' that,
>   His ribband, star, an' a' that:
> The man o' independent mind
>   He looks an' laughs at a' that.
>
> 25 A prince can mak a belted knight,
>   A marquis, duke, an' a' that;
> But an honest man's aboon his might,
>   Gude faith, he maunna fa' that!
> For a' that, an' a' that,
> 30 Their dignities an' a' that;
> The pith o' sense, an' pride o' worth,
>   Are higher rank than a' that.
>
> Then let us pray that come it may,
>   (As come it will for a' that,)
> 35 That Sense and Worth, o'er a' the earth,
>   Shall bear the gree, an' a' that.
> For a' that, an' a' that,
>   It's coming yet for a' that,
> That Man to Man, the world o'er,
> 40 Shall brothers be for a' that.

17. BIRKIE—Conceited fellow.
20. COOF—Dull fellow; dolt; ninny.
22. RIBBAND, STAR—Symbols of orders of nobility.
27. ABOON—Above.
28. MAUNNA FA'—Must not claim that.
36. BEAR THE GREE—Have the first place.

Poem Development: In what other poems have you noticed the theme of democracy and the worth of man? Give specific quotations. What is meant by "rank" in line 7? To whom does "their" refer in line 14? Give in your own words the picture of the poor which the poet portrays in the second stanza. Contrast this with that which he says of the rich. Why is the honest man king of men? Describe the lord as the poet sees him. What qualities can place the poor man above prince, knight, or duke? What are the theme and central thought?

Interpretations: The rank is but the guinea's stamp; line 19; line 31; lines 35 and 36.

Significant Expressions: Quote the lines giving praise to the true but poor man. Quote the line showing the triumph of real worth.

BANNOCKBURN

Robert Bruce's Address to His Army

ROBERT BURNS

Poem Interest: In his *Essay on Burns,* Thomas Carlyle writes: "[*Bannockburn*] was composed on horseback; in riding in the middle of tempests, over the wildest Galloway moor. . . . Doubtless this stern hymn was singing itself, as he formed it, through the soul of Burns: but to the external ear, it should be sung with the throat of the whirlwind. So long as there is warm blood in the heart of Scotchman or man, it will move in fierce thrills under this war-ode; the best, we believe, that was ever written by any pen."

The battle of Bannockburn (so called because its field was traversed by the brook, or burn, of Bannock) was fought on June 24, 1314, and proved an overwhelming victory for the Scots under the leadership of Robert Bruce. The battle was so decisive that it freed Scotland, and established her independence. Before Bannockburn, Bruce had told his Scottish pikemen, and told them truly, that they fought "not for glory, truth or honour, but for that liberty which no virtuous man will survive." It is that spirit, still white-hot after over four hundred years, that Burns has poured into the enduring mold of this battle hymn of independence.

SCOTS, wha hae wi' Wallace bled,
Scots, wham Bruce has aften led,
Welcome to your gory bed,
    Or to Victorie!

5   Now's the day, and now's the hour;
See the front o' battle lour;
See approach proud Edward's power—
    Chains and Slaverie!

1. WALLACE—Sir William Wallace who had raised the standard of Scottish independence in 1296, and had rallied the commons against the English invader. He was defeated, captured, and executed in London in August, 1305.
7. EDWARD—Edward II, king of England.

Wha will be a traitor knave?
10 Wha can fill a coward's grave?
Wha sae base as be a Slave?
    Let him turn and flee!

Wha, for Scotland's King and Law,
Freedom's sword will strongly draw,
15 Free-man stand, or Free-man fa',
    Let him on wi' me!

By Oppression's woes and pains!
By your Sons in servile chains!
We will drain our dearest veins,
20   But they shall be free!

Lay the proud Usurpers low!
Tyrants fall in every foe!
Liberty's in every blow!—
    Let us Do or Die!

Poem Development: Why is reference made to Wallace? To whom does "him" refer in line 12? Which stanza do you consider the strongest? What is the theme of the poem? What is the central thought?

Interpretations: Gory bed; servile chains; line 19.

Significant Expressions: Quote the lines which you like best.

SWEET AFTON

Robert Burns

Poem Interest: The tender sentiment, the appropriate background of natural beauty, and a melodiousness which is readily appreciated even without its beautiful musical setting make this poem deservedly one of the most popular of Burns' songs. You will particularly like the perfect union of sound and sense in many of the lines, and the smooth flowing rhythm of the stanzas.

Flow gently, sweet Afton! among thy green braes,
Flow gently, I'll sing thee a song in thy praise;
My Mary's asleep by thy murmuring stream,
Flow gently, sweet Afton, disturb not her dream.

1. Braes—Small hills.

5   Thou stock dove whose echo resounds thro' the glen,
    Ye wild whistling blackbirds, in yon thorny den,
    Thou green crested lapwing thy screaming forbear,
    I charge you, disturb not my slumbering Fair.

    How lofty, sweet Afton, thy neighbouring hills,
10 Far mark'd with the courses of clear, winding rills;
    There daily I wander as noon rises high,
    My flocks and my Mary's sweet cot in my eye.

    How pleasant thy banks and green valleys below,
    Where, wild in the woodlands, the primroses blow;
15 There oft, as mild Ev'ning weeps over the lea,
    The sweet-scented birk shades my Mary and me.

    Thy crystal stream, Afton, how lovely it glides,
    And winds by the cot where my Mary resides;
    How wanton thy waters her snowy feet lave,
20 As, gathering sweet flowerets, she stems thy clear wave.

    Flow gently, sweet Afton, among thy green braes,
    Flow gently, sweet river, the theme of my lays;
    My Mary's asleep by thy murmuring stream,
    Flow gently, sweet Afton, disturb not her dream.

  5. STOCK DOVE—European wild pigeon.
  7. LAPWING—Plover; noted for its shrill, wailing cry.
12. COT—Cottage; humble home.
15. LEA—Grass or pasture land; untilled land.
16. BIRK—Birch.
19. LAVE—Wash; flow against.
22. LAYS—Songs.

Poem Development: If you have studied physical geography you will be interested in classifying the Afton River as an old age river, for the old age rivers flow slowly and gently. It is thought that Burns used the idea of the sleeping Mary merely to make the poem more effective, and that there was no real Mary meant. Notice the long sounds of the vowels which are continually used and which give to the sound of the stanzas a smoothness almost like the sound of the gently flowing river. What are the sounds the poet asks to cease? What does he see at noon? What is the picture he paints of the evening? Is the poem made more effective by the repetition at the end of the poem of the third and fourth lines? Give the theme and central thought of the poem.

Interpretations: Line 12; line 15; theme of my lays.

Significant Expressions: What is the figure of speech in line 3? in line 6? Quote the lines which appeal most to you, and tell what qualities they possess from a poetic standpoint.

MY HEART'S IN THE HIGHLANDS

Robert Burns

Poem Interest: It is said that Burns continually sang as he worked and this probably accounts for the singing quality of so many of his poems. And a pleasant, galloping little song is this. You can almost see it wave a gay farewell to "green valleys below" and chase off to the highlands to "follow the roe."

> Farewell to the Highlands, farewell to the North,
> The birth-place of valour, the country of worth;
> Wherever I wander, wherever I rove,
> The hills of the Highlands for ever I love.
>
> 5 My heart's in the Highlands, my heart is not here;
> My heart's in the Highlands, a-chasing the deer;
> A-chasing the wild deer, and following the roe,
> My heart's in the Highlands wherever I go.
>
> Farewell to the mountains, high-cover'd with snow;
> 10 Farewell to the straths and green valleys below;
> Farewell to the forests and wild-hanging woods,
> Farewell to the torrents and loud-pouring floods.
>
> My heart's in the Highlands, my heart is not here;
> My heart's in the Highlands, a-chasing the deer;
> 15 A-chasing the wild deer, and following the roe,
> My heart's in the Highlands wherever I go.

Poem Development: Many of Burns' lyrics were based upon old folk songs and we are told that he "repeatedly hummed over an old air" and then fitted his words to it. What made the Highlands attractive to the poet? Describe the Highlands as the poet pictures them. What is the theme? What is the central thought?

Interpretations: Roe; straths.

Significant Expressions: What is the figure of speech in line 1? Quote the lines which you think the most descriptive of the Highlands.

THE COTTER'S SATURDAY NIGHT
Robert Burns

Poem Interest: There is an old, old truth (all truth is old, but our finding makes it new) which says true living and true happiness depend not on our worldly wealth, but on our love of life itself and on the thankfulness with which we meet the gifts and blessings of each day. The cotter in this story, and his family, lived in this spirit, drawing riches from essential things, although they dwelt in what we would call poverty.

Inscribed to Robert Aiken, Esq.

Let not Ambition mock their useful toil,
Their homely joys, and destiny obscure;
Nor Grandeur hear, with a disdainful smile,
The short and simple annals of the poor.

My loved, my honoured, much respected friend!
  No mercenary bard his homage pays;
With honest pride, I scorn each selfish end,
  My dearest meed a friend's esteem and praise:

Title—A cotter is a cottager.
Inscription—Robert Aiken was a lawyer of Ayr who had often helped Burns and who was a life-long friend. He is the "friend" referred to in the first line of the poem.

5   To you I sing, in simple Scottish lays,
        The lowly train in life's sequester'd scene;
          The native feelings strong, the guileless ways,
        What Aiken in a cottage would have been;
        Ah, tho' his worth unknown, far happier there, I ween!

10   November chill blaws loud wi' angry sugh;
          The short'ning winter-day is near a close;
        The miry beasts retreating frae the pleugh;
          The black'ning trains o' craws to their repose.
          The toil-worn cotter frae his labour goes—
15   This night his weekly moil is at an end,—
          Collects his spades, his mattocks, and his hoes,
        Hoping the morn in ease and rest to spend,
        And weary, o'er the moor, his course does hameward bend.

        At length his lonely cot appears in view,
20   Beneath the shelter of an aged tree;
        Th' expectant wee-things, toddlin, stacher through
          To meet their dad, wi' flichterin' noise and glee.
          His wee bit ingle, blinkin bonilie,
        His clean hearth-stane, his thrifty wifie's smile,
25   The lisping infant, prattling on his knee,
        Does a' his weary kiaugh and care beguile,
        And makes him quite forget his labour and his toil.

        Belyve the elder bairns come drapping in,
          At service out, amang the farmers roun';
30   Some ca' the pleugh, some herd, some tentie rin
          A cannie errand to a neebor town.
          Their eldest hope, their Jenny, woman-grown,
        In youthfu' bloom, love sparkling in her e'e,
          Comes hame, perhaps to shew a braw new gown,
35   Or deposite her sair-won penny-fee,
        To help her parents dear if they in hardship be.

---

10. Sugh—Sough, or rushing sound.   12. Frae the pleugh—From the plough.   13. Craws—Crows.   15. Moil—Toil or labor.   16. Mattocks—Implements for digging.   21. Stacher—Toddle or stagger.   22. Flichterin'—Fluttering.   23. Ingle—Fireplace or fire.   26. Kiaugh—Trouble, anxiety.   28. Belyve—By and by.   30. Ca'—Drive.   30. Tentie rin—Heedfully run.   31. Cannie—Carefully.   34. Braw—Handsome.   35. Sair-won—Hard earned.

With joy unfeigned, brothers and sisters meet,
    And each for other's weelfare kindly spiers;
The social hours, swift-winged, unnoticed fleet;
    Each tells the uncos that he sees or hears.
The parents, partial, eye their hopeful years;
Anticipation forward points the view.
The mother, wi' her needle and her sheers,
Gars auld claes look amaist as weel's the new;
    The father mixes a' wi' admonition due:

Their master's and their mistress's command
    The yonkers a' are warnèd to obey,
And mind their labours wi' an eydent hand,
    And ne'er, tho' out o' sight, to jauk or play:
"And O be sure to fear the Lord alway,
And mind your duty duly, morn and night;
    Lest in temptation's path ye gang astray,
Implore His counsel and assisting might:
They never sought in vain that sought the Lord aright."

But hark! a rap comes gently to the door.
    Jenny, wha kens the meaning o' the same,
Tells how a neebor lad came o'er the moor,
    To do some errands and convoy her hame.
The wily mother sees the conscious flame
Sparkle in Jenny's e'e, and flush her cheek;
    With heart-struck anxious care enquires his name,
While Jenny hafflins is afraid to speak;
Weel-pleased the mother hears it's nae wild, worthless rake.

With kindly welcome Jenny brings him ben:
    A strappin' youth, he takes the mother's eye;
Blythe Jenny sees the visit's no ill-taen;
    The father cracks of horses, pleughs, and kye.
The youngster's artless heart o'erflows wi' joy,
But blate and laithfu', scarce can weel behave;

---

38. SPIERS—Inquires.   40. UNCOS—Strange happenings.   44. GARS AULD CLAES—Makes old clothes.   48. EYDENT—Diligent.   49. JAUK—Trifle.   62. HAFFLINS—Halfway, partly.   64. BEN—Into the parlor.   67. CRACKS—Talks.   67. KYE—Cattle.   69. BLATE AND LAITHFU'—Shy and bashful.

70 The mother, wi' a woman's wiles, can spy
What makes the youth sae bashfu' and sae grave,
Weel-pleased to think her bairn's respected like the lave.

Oh happy love, where love like this is found!
  Oh heart-felt raptures! bliss beyond compare!
75 I've pacèd much this weary, mortal round,
  And sage experience bids me this declare:
  "If Heaven a draught of heavenly pleasure spare,
One cordial in this melancholy vale,
  'T is when a youthful, loving, modest pair
80 In other's arms breathe out the tender tale,
Beneath the milk-white thorn that scents the evening gale."

Is there, in human form, that bears a heart,
  A wretch! a villain! lost to love and truth!
That can, with studied, sly, ensnaring art,
85   Betray sweet Jenny's unsuspecting youth?
  Curse on his perjured arts! dissembling, smooth!
Are honour, virtue, conscience, all exiled?
  Is there no pity, no relenting ruth,
Points to the parents fondling o'er their child?
90 Then paints the ruined maid, and their distraction wild?

But now the supper crowns their simple board:
  The halesome parritch, chief o' Scotia's food:
The sowpe their only hawkie does afford,
  That 'yont the hallan snugly chows her cood.
95   The dame brings forth, in complimental mood,
To grace the lad, her weel-hained kebbuck, fell,
  And aft he's prest and aft he ca's it guid;
The frugal wifie, garrulous, will tell
How 't was a towmond auld sin' lint was i' the bell.

72. LAVE—Others, the rest.
92. HALESOME PARRITCH—Wholesome porridge.
93. SOWPE—Sup of milk.   93. HAWKIE—Cow.
94. 'YONT THE HALLAN—Beyond the partition.
96. WEEL-HAINED KEBBUCK, FELL—Well-saved strong cheese.
99. TOWMOND AULD, etc.—Twelve-month old since flax was in the flower.

100 The cheerfu' supper done, wi' serious face
        They round the ingle form a circle wide;
    The sire turns o'er, wi' patriarchal grace,
        The big ha'-Bible, ance his father's pride;
    His bonnet rev'rently is laid aside,
105 His lyart haffets wearing thin and bare;
    Those strains that once did sweet in Zion glide,
    He wales a portion with judicious care,
    And "Let us worship God!" he says, with solemn air.

    They chant their artless notes in simple guise;
110   They tune their hearts, by far the noblest aim:
    Perhaps "Dundee's" wild-warbling measures rise,
        Or plaintive "Martyrs," worthy of the name;
    Or noble "Elgin" beets the heavenward flame,
    The sweetest far of Scotia's holy lays.
115   Compared with these, Italian trills are tame;
    The tickled ears no heart-felt raptures raise;
    Nae unison hae they with our Creator's praise.

    The priest-like father reads the sacred page:
        How Abram was the friend of God on high;
120 Or Moses bade eternal warfare wage
        With Amalek's ungracious progeny;
    Or how the royal bard did groaning lie
    Beneath the stroke of Heaven's avenging ire;
    Or Job's pathetic plaint and wailing cry;
125   Or rapt Isaiah's wild, seraphic fire;
    Or other holy seers that tune the sacred lyre.

    Perhaps the Christian volume is the theme:
        How guiltless blood for guilty man was shed;
    How He Who bore in Heaven the second name

103. HA'-BIBLE—Hall Bible, that is the Bible belonging in the hall, or living room.
105. LYART HAFFETS—Grey locks.   107. WALES—Chooses.
111. DUNDEE'S, MARTYRS, ELGIN—Names of hymns.
113. BEETS—Fans.
119. ABRAM—See *Genesis* xv.   120. MOSES—See *Exodus* xvii.
121. AMALEK'S UNGRACIOUS PROGENY—The descendants of Amalek, a heathen tribe that attacked the Israelites in the desert.
122. ROYAL BARD—King David.
127. CHRISTIAN VOLUME—The New Testament.

130   Had not on earth whereon to lay His head;
      How His first followers and servants sped;
    The precepts sage they wrote to many a land;
      How he, who lone in Patmos banishèd,
    Saw in the sun a mighty angel stand,
135   And heard great Bab'lon's doom pronounced by Heaven's command.

    Then kneeling down to heaven's Eternal King,
      The saint, the father, and the husband prays;
    Hope "springs exulting on triumphant wing,"
      And thus they all shall meet in future days,
140   There ever bask in uncreated rays,
    No more to sigh or shed the bitter tear,
      Together hymning their Creator's praise,
    In such society, yet still more dear,
    While circling Time moves round in an eternal sphere.

145   Compared with this, how poor Religion's pride,
      In all the pomp of method and of art,
    When men display to congregations wide
      Devotion's ev'ry grace except the heart!
    The Power, incensed, the pageant will desert,
150   The pompous strain, the sacerdotal stole;
      But haply, in some cottage far apart,
    May hear, well pleased, the language of the soul,
    And in His Book of Life the inmates poor enroll.

    Then homeward all take off their sev'ral way;
155   The youngling cottagers retire to rest;
    The parent-pair their secret homage pay,
      And proffer up to Heaven the warm request
      That He Who stills the raven's clam'rous nest,
    And decks the lily fair in flow'ry pride,
160   Would, in the way His wisdom sees the best,
    For them and for their little ones provide,
    But chiefly in their hearts with grace divine preside.

---

133. HE—Saint John, who was imprisoned on the island of Patmos in the Ægean Sea. He wrote the Book of Revelations referred to in the next lines.
150. SACERDOTAL STOLE—Priestly garment.

From scenes like these old Scotia's grandeur springs,
   That makes her loved at home, revered abroad:
165 Princes and lords are but the breath of kings,
   "An honest man's the noblest work of God."
   And certes in fair virtue's heavenly road,
   The cottage leaves the palace far behind:
   What is a lordling's pomp? a cumbrous load,
170 Disguising oft the wretch of human kind,
   Studied in arts of hell, in wickedness refined!

   O Scotia! my dear, my native soil!
   For whom my warmest wish to Heaven is sent!
   Long may thy hardy sons of rustic toil
175 Be blest with health and peace and sweet content!
   And O may Heaven their simple lives prevent
   From luxury's contagion, weak and vile!
   Then, howe'er crowns and coronets be rent,
   A virtuous populace may rise the while,
180 And stand a wall of fire around their much-loved isle.

   O Thou, Who poured the patriotic tide
   That streamed thro' Wallace's undaunted heart,
   Who dared to nobly stem tyrannic pride,
   Or nobly die, the second glorious part!
185   (The patriot's God peculiarly Thou art,
   His friend, inspirer, guardian, and reward!)
   Oh never, never Scotia's realm desert,
   But still the patriot and the patriot-bard
   In bright succession raise, her ornament and guard!

165. Find a similar thought in Goldsmith's *Deserted Village*.
166. A quotation from Alexander Pope.
167. CERTES—Certainly.
182. WALLACE—A Scottish leader of the thirteenth century. See Burns' poem *Bannockburn*.

Poem Development: Of this poem, Gilbert Burns, Robert's brother, writes: "Robert had frequently remarked to me that he thought there was something peculiarly venerable in the phrase, 'Let us worship God,' used by a decent, sober head of a family, introducing family worship. To this sentiment of the author, the world is indebted for *The Cotter's Saturday Night*." The description of the cotter is supposed to be almost exactly that of Burns' father.

Why is the stanza from Gray's *Elegy Written in a Country Churchyard* an appropriate introduction to this poem? Do you find any similarity between the poems? In the first stanza the poet tells what the poem will be about. Give this thought in your own words. Describe the return of the peasant from his work on Saturday night. Who welcomes him as he reaches the cottage? Who later comes in to greet him? Describe the evening. What admonitions does the father give? Tell the story of Jenny's lover. Describe the supper. Tell the story of the worship hour after the supper was finished. What does Burns say is left out of the worship of the rich? Compare the life in the cottage with the life in the palace. What is the poet's fervent wish for the hardy sons of Scotia? It has been written of the poem that it is a "perfect picture of noble poverty." Explain. What is the theme of the poem? the central thought?

Interpretations: Mercenary bard (l. 2); life's sequester'd scene (l. 6); lines 28 and 29; line 42; see the visit's no ill-taen (l. 66); Scotia (l. 92); line 97; luxury's contagion (l. 177).

Significant Expressions: Quote the line addressed to Burns's friend. Quote the line describing November. Quote the line showing the friendly spirit of the brothers and sisters. Quote the lines of admonition. What is the figure of speech in line 165? Quote the line describing an honest man.

AULD LANG SYNE

Robert Burns

Poem Interest: You are of course familiar with this poem, for it is one of the most widely sung of all songs among English-speaking peoples. But as you read it now, weigh the words as if you had never before heard them. You will be delighted to find in them a new poem, instinct with life, possessed of real power to move because of connection with real experiences—*Auld Lang Syne* is a universal song of friendship, the property of all mankind.

> Should auld acquaintance be forgot,
>   And never brought to mind?
> Should auld acquaintance be forgot,
>   And auld lang syne!
>
> *Chorus*
> 5   *For auld lang syne, my dear,*
>   *For auld lang syne,*

Title—The title means, literally, "long, long since." It is, however, practically untranslatable, as it suggests a wealth of memories clustering about a friendship of many years' growth and standing.

*We'll tak a cup o' kindness yet,
For auld lang syne.*

    And surely ye'll be your pint stowp
10   And surely I'll be mine!
    And we'll tak a cup o' kindness yet,
        For auld lang syne.

    We twa hae run about the braes,
        And pou'd the gowans fine;
15   But we've wander'd mony a weary fit,
        Sin' auld lang syne.

    We twa hae paidl'd in the burn,
        Frae morning sun till dine;
    But seas between us braid hae roar'd
20   Sin' auld lang syne.

    And there's a hand, my trusty fere!
        And gie's a hand o' thine!
    And we'll tak a right gude-willie waught,
        For auld lang syne.

    9. PINT STOWP—A kind of jug with a handle, holding from half a pint to two quarts. The meaning is that each of the old acquaintances will take a loving cup.
    13. TWA—Two.   14. GOWANS—Wild daisies.   15. FIT—Foot.
    17. PAIDL'D—Paddled; waded.   17. BURN—Brook; rivulet.
    18. DINE—Dinner.   19. BRAID—Broad.   21. FERE—Comrade.
    22. GIE'S—Give us.   23. RIGHT GUDE-WILLIE WAUGHT—Hearty good-will draught.

    Poem Development: Burns is said to have taken the air for *Auld Lang Syne* from a tune he had heard an old man sing. One likes to think that perhaps he wrote it after meeting an old acquaintance whom he had not seen in years. What is meant by "cup o' kindness"? What makes you think these two were childhood friends? What gives you the idea that both men are now rather old? What is the theme of the poem? Give the central thought.
    Interpretations: Line 15; line 19.
    Significant Expressions: Perhaps you already have the poem memorized. If not, choose at least three verses and the chorus and commit them to memory.

TO A MOUSE

*On Turning Her Up in Her Nest with the Plough,
November, 1785*

Robert Burns

Poem Interest: Only from a heart full of tenderness for the weak and defenceless could have come the following poem. In *To a Mouse*, unconventional as the topic may seem to us, we cannot but perceive the fine, true sensitivity which always shows the mark of God in man.

<blockquote>
Wee, sleekit, cowrin, tim'rous beastie,
O, what a panic's in thy breastie!
Thou need na start awa sae hasty,
    Wi' bickering brattle!
5 I wad be laith to rin an' chase thee,
    Wi' murd'ring pattle!
</blockquote>

1. Sleekit—Sleek.
4. Bickering brattle—Hurrying scamper.
5. Laith—Loath.
6. Pattle—Plough staff.

I'm truly sorry man's dominion,
Has broken nature's social union,
An' justifies that ill opinion,
    Which makes thee startle
At me, thy poor, earth-born companion,
    An' fellow-mortal!

I doubt na, whiles, but thou may thieve;
What then? poor beastie, thou maun live!
A daimen icker in a thrave
    'S a sma' request;
I'll get a blessin wi' the lave,
    An' never miss't!

Thy wee bit housie, too, in ruin!
It's silly wa's the win's are strewin!
An' naething, now, to big a new ane,
    O' foggage green!
An' bleak December's winds ensuin,
    Baith snell an' keen!

Thou saw the fields laid bare an' waste,
An' weary winter comin fast,
An' cozie here, beneath the blast,
    Thou thought to dwell—
Till crash! the cruel coulter past
    Out thro' thy cell.

That wee bit heap o' leaves an' stibble,
Has cost thee mony a weary nibble!
Now thou's turn'd out, for a' thy trouble,
    But house or hald,
To thole the winter's sleety dribble,
    An' cranreuch cauld!

---

15. DAIMEN ICKER—Occasional ear of corn.
15. THRAVE—Twenty-four sheaves of corn.
17. LAVE—Remainder.   20. WA'S—Walls.   21. BIG—Build.
22. FOGGAGE—Coarse.   24. SNELL—Bitter.   29. COULTER—Plough share.
31. STIBBLE—Stubble.   34. HALD—Abiding place.   34. BUT—Without.
35. THOLE—Endure.   35. DRIBBLE—Drizzle.   36. CRANREUCH—Hoar frost.

> But Mousie, thou art no thy lane,
> In proving foresight may be vain;
> The best-laid schemes o' mice an' men
>   Gang aft agley,
> An' lea'e us nought but grief an' pain,
>   For promis'd joy!
>
> Still thou art blest, compar'd wi' me
> The present only toucheth thee:
> But och! I backward cast my e'e,
>   On prospects drear!
> An' forward, tho' I canna see,
>   I guess an' fear!

37. THY LANE—Alone.
40. GANG AFT AGLEY—Go oft askew.

Poem Development: Burns seems always to have been at one with every manifestation of nature which is the basis of true poetic expression, and, incidentally, of truer living. Paint a word picture of the mouse as he makes you see it. What is meant by "nature's social union" in line 8? Why was there nothing from which the mouse could build a new home? What is the comparison to Man which Burns draws? Why did he think the mouse more blessed than he? Do you agree with him? What is the theme of the poem? the central thought?

    Interpretations: Lines 7–10; win's are strewin; lines 37–38.

    Significant Expressions: Memorize lines 39–42. This oft-quoted moral is a charming and appropriate part of the whole poem. Of its kind it is perfect.

MY HEART LEAPS UP

WILLIAM WORDSWORTH

    Poem Interest: Every thinking person has his own vision of the great Intelligence which guides the universe. To some, God dwells only in a far-distant heaven; to others, He is revealed in the essential mechanics of things; and to still others, as with Wordsworth, the whole glorious panorama of nature reveals Him in all His splendour. With this knowledge of Wordsworth's philosophy, we can understand his reverent exultation at seeing the rainbow in the sky, and echo his hope that he will always perceive beauty in this way.

> My heart leaps up when I behold
>   A rainbow in the sky;

So was it when my life began,
So is it now I am a man,
So be it when I shall grow old
 Or let me die!
The child is father of the man;
And I could wish my days to be
Bound each to each by natural piety.

Poem Development: Give the thought in the first two lines. What conclusion would you draw from the next four lines? Would you say that the quality expressed in these first six lines is indispensable to the production of true poetry? What do you understand by line 7? Interpret "natural piety." Now give the central thought of the poem as a whole. What is the theme?

Interpretations: My heart leaps up; line 7.

Significant Expressions: Quote lines which you would like to remember as a guiding point to better living. Give the figure of speech in line 1.

THE WORLD IS TOO MUCH WITH US

William Wordsworth

Poem Interest: A famous physician had the habit—an exceedingly annoying one, to many of his patients, by the way—of suddenly packing up and leaving for a day in the open whenever the impulse came. Upon being asked the reason for these sudden excursions, he smiled and quoted the first four lines of the following poem . . .

 The world is too much with us; late and soon,
 Getting and spending, we lay waste our powers;
 Little we see in Nature that is ours;
 We have given our hearts away, a sordid boon!
5 The sea that bares her bosom to the moon;
 The winds that will be howling at all hours,
 And are upgathered now like sleeping flowers;
 For this, for everything, we are out of tune;
 It moves us not.—Great God! I'd rather be
10 A Pagan suckled in a creed outworn;
 So might I, standing on this pleasant lea,
 Have glimpses that would make me less forlorn;

10. Pagan—An irreligious person; meaning here a worshipper of nature and its deities.

Have sight of Proteus rising from the sea;
Or hear old Triton blow his wreathèd horn.

13. PROTEUS—A sea god who could assume different shapes.
14. TRITON—A sea god who is pictured as blowing a conch-shell trumpet to raise or calm the waves. The names of Proteus and Triton as here used are symbolic of the great love for nature which the pagan Greeks and Romans had.

Poem Development: In what way do we "lay waste our powers"? What does the poet suggest as a way to increase our efficiency in living? How would the physician's day in the open have added to his success with his patients? Interpret lines 3 and 4. How would a pagan faith bring one nearer to nature? Do you gain from the poem a thought that would help you in your own life? Give the theme of the poem.

Interpretations: Lay waste; a sordid boon; out of tune; creed outworn; wreathèd horn.

Significant Expressions: Quote the line which tells of our failure to appreciate nature. Which line shows the strongest emotion? What are the figures of speech in lines 6 and 7?

COMPOSED UPON WESTMINSTER BRIDGE

WILLIAM WORDSWORTH

Poem Interest: There is something about the silence of an unawakened city in the early morning hours that is awe-inspiring. From Westminster Bridge, Wordsworth watched London, born anew with the dawn, and saw the city almost as if it were some great nature object.

EARTH has not anything to show more fair:
Dull would he be of soul who could pass by
A sight so touching in its majesty:
This City now doth, like a garment, wear
5   The beauty of the morning; silent, bare,
Ships, towers, domes, theatres and temples lie
Open unto the fields, and to the sky;
All bright and glittering in the smokeless air.
Never did sun more beautifully steep
10   In his first splendour, valley, rock, or hill;
Ne'er saw I, never felt, a calm so deep!
The river glideth at his own sweet will:
Dear God! the very houses seem asleep;
And all that mighty heart is lying still!

WILLIAM WORDSWORTH

Poem Development: What structures did the poet see from the bridge? What is the river referred to in line 12? What feeling is created by the poem? Upon what central thought is this poem constructed?

Interpretations: Dull would he be of soul; steep; all that mighty heart.

Significant Expressions: Quote the lines which for you make the most vivid impression. Give the figure of speech in line 4.

IT IS A BEAUTEOUS EVENING, CALM AND FREE

William Wordsworth

Poem Interest: There are few sights in nature lovelier than that of a sunset on the broad expanse of ocean. The long breakers roll ceaselessly in to the shore; the sun sinks quietly below the horizon and the whole world seems at peace. A delicate perception of the loveliness of such scenes is always to be found in Wordsworth, a true reflection of his passionate love of nature, combined with a deeper thought of reverence.

> It is a beauteous evening, calm and free,
> The holy time is quiet as a Nun
> Breathless with adoration; the broad sun
> Is sinking down in its tranquillity;
> 5 The gentleness of heaven broods o'er the Sea:
> Listen! the mighty Being is awake,
> And doth with his eternal motion make
> A sound like thunder—everlastingly.
> Dear Child! dear Girl! that walkest with me here,
> 10 If thou appear untouched by solemn thought,
> Thy nature is not therefore less divine:
> Thou liest in Abraham's bosom all the year;
> And worship'st at the Temple's inner shrine,
> God being with thee when we know it not.

12. THOU LIEST IN ABRAHAM'S BOSOM ALL THE YEAR—Thou art near God always.

Poem Development: Describe the scene, noting the touches of reverence. List the words and phrases which give a feeling of calm and peace. How does the sea sound? It is thought that Wordsworth meant his sister, Dorothy, when he wrote "Dear Child." This allusion, however is to all Youth. What interpretation would you give the last five lines, in the light of this symbology? Find the theme and the central thought of the poem.

Interpretations: Broad sun; eternal motion; line 13.

Significant Expressions: Quote the line or lines which for you make the most vivid sense perception. Give the figure of speech in line 2; line 8.

LONDON, 1802

William Wordsworth

Poem Interest: The history of all countries moves somewhat like a graph, striking highs of true living and rich idealism, then sinking to lows of artificiality and corruption. In the latter periods do the hopes of thinking men hark back and invoke the free, bold spirits of better days to lend their aid in present crises. Thus does Wordsworth, in his desire to arouse England to a realization of what he believed to be national stagnation, call out to Milton.

> Milton! thou shouldst be living at this hour;
> England hath need of thee: she is a fen
> Of stagnant waters; altar, sword, and pen,
> Fireside, the heroic wealth of hall and bower,
> 5   Have forfeited their ancient English dower
> Of inward happiness. We are selfish men:
> O raise us up, return to us again;
> And give us manners, virtue, freedom, power.
> Thy soul was like a star, and dwelt apart;
> 10 Thou hadst a voice whose sound was like the sea;
> Pure as the naked heavens, majestic, free,
> So didst thou travel on life's common way,
> In cheerful godliness, and yet thy heart
> The lowliest duties on herself did lay.

Poem Development: The title of this poem is taken from the place and time of its writing and has nothing to do with the theme. Why did the poet wish Milton were alive again? Describe the conditions in England as Wordsworth sees them. What did the poet desire England to regain? What does he say of Milton? What is the theme? What is the central thought?

Interpretations: Fen of stagnant waters; altar, sword and pen; fireside.

Significant Expressions: Quote the line most descriptive of Milton's greatness. Give the figures of speech in lines 2–3; line 9; line 10.

WILLIAM WORDSWORTH

THE DAFFODILS
William Wordsworth

Poem Interest: It is said that the brain of man acts much like the film of a camera—it takes pictures. More than that, it has the unique faculty of developing them, and storing them away on carefully labeled shelves. Year after year they remain, undiminished in color and form. *The Daffodils* was one of Wordsworth's choice bits of photography, which he brought forth in words for all to enjoy.

> I WANDERED lonely as a cloud
> That floats on high o'er vales and hills,
> When all at once I saw a crowd,
> A host of golden daffodils,
> 5 Beside the lake, beneath the trees,
> Fluttering and dancing in the breeze.
>
> Continuous as the stars that shine
> And twinkle on the milky way,
> They stretched in never-ending line
> 10 Along the margin of a bay;
> Ten thousand saw I at a glance
> Tossing their heads in sprightly dance.
>
> The waves beside them danced, but they
> Outdid the sparkling waves in glee—
> 15 A poet could not but be gay
> In such a jocund company!
> I gazed—and gazed—but little thought
> What wealth the show to me had brought;
>
> For oft, when on my couch I lie
> 20 In vacant or in pensive mood,
> They flash upon that inward eye
> Which is the bliss of solitude;
> And then my heart with pleasure fills,
> And dances with the daffodils.

Poem Development: Can you see the poet meandering along "lonely as a cloud that floats on high o'er vales and hills"? From this point on, notice the careful attention he gave to the picture he was taking—

he got color, motion, and setting. Describe the scene as you see it through his eyes. What made the daffodils seem to dance? What is the meaning of the last stanza? This poem has been set to music. Can you suggest why? What is the thought that you get from the poem as a whole?

Interpretations: Host; milky way; jocund; pensive; inward eye.

Significant Expressions: Find two similes. Which lines give an idea of the number of the daffodils?

THE SOLITARY REAPER

William Wordsworth

Poem Interest: In 1803, Wordsworth went on a walking tour through Scotland. Doubtless the new scenes were many and varied, yet of them all the simple sweetness of this picture of a peasant girl singing in her native tongue of Gaelic as she worked, fired Wordsworth's poetic fancy to such a degree that *The Solitary Reaper* has come down to us through the years.

BEHOLD her, single in the field,
Yon solitary highland lass!
Reaping and singing by herself;
Stop here, or gently pass!
5   Alone she cuts and binds the grain,
And sings a melancholy strain;
O listen! for the vale profound
Is overflowing with the sound.

No nightingale did ever chaunt
10   More welcome notes to weary bands
Of travelers in some shady haunt,
Among Arabian sands;
A voice so thrilling ne'er was heard
In springtime from the cuckoo-bird,
15   Breaking the silence of the seas
Among the farthest Hebrides.

Will no one tell me what she sings?
Perhaps the plaintiff numbers flow
For old, unhappy, far-off things,
20   And battles long ago;

16. HEBRIDES—A group of islands off the Coast of Scotland.

> Or is it some more humble lay,
> Familiar matter of today?
> Some natural sorrow, loss, or pain,
> That has been, and may be again!
>
> 25 Whate'er the theme, the maiden sang
> As if her song could have no ending;
> I saw her singing at her work,
> And o'er the sickle bending—
> I listened, motionless and still;
> 30 And, as I mounted up the hill,
> The music in my heart I bore
> Long after it was heard no more.

Poem Development: Paint a word picture of the highland lassie as Wordsworth saw her. Describe her song. Why does the poet say, "Will no one tell me what she sings?" What did he think the song might be about? What was the most vivid impression of the reaper which the poet carried away with him? Give the theme and central thought of the poem.

Interpretations: Melancholy strain; vale profound; chaunt; plaintive numbers; humble lay.

Significant Expressions: Quote the lines which for you produce the most vivid sense image.

JOCK O' HAZELDEAN

Sir Walter Scott

Poem Interest: We do not know who Jock was, nor where he was, but this we do know, that he was much beloved by the "ladie." The "ladie" had been urged to marry Frank, the chief of Errington and laird of Langley-Dale, and on the wedding morn, the priest and bridegroom and wedding guests were gathered in the gayly decked church. At this point—but read, and learn for yourself.

> "Why weep ye by the tide, ladie?
> Why weep ye by the tide?
> I'll wed ye to my youngest son,
> And ye sall be his bride;
> 5 And ye sall be his bride, ladie,
> Sae comely to be seen"—
> But aye she loot the tears down fa'
> For Jock o' Hazeldean.

1. Ladie—Lady. Do not confuse with "laddie."   7. Loot—Let.

"Now let this wilfu' grief be done,
    And dry that cheek so pale;
Young Frank is chief of Errington,
    And lord of Langley-Dale;
His step is first in peaceful ha',
    His sword in battle keen"—
But aye she loot the tears down fa'
    For Jock o' Hazeldean.

"A Chain of gold ye sall not lack,
    Nor braid to bind your hair;
Nor mettled hound, nor managed hawk,
    Nor palfrey fresh and fair;
And you, the foremost o' them a',
    Shall ride our forest queen"—
But aye she loot the tears down fa'
    For Jock o' Hazeldean.

The kirk was decked at morning tide,
    The tapers glimmered fair;
The priest and bridegroom wait the bride,
    And dame and knight are there.
They sought her baith by bower and ha'
    The ladie was not seen!
She's o'er the Border, and awa'
    Wi' Jock o' Hazeldean.

13. Ha'—Hall.
19. Mettled hound nor managed hawk—Spirited hunting dog nor trained hawk.
20. Palfrey—Riding horse.
25. Kirk—Church.   29. Baith—Both.

Poem Development: Sir Walter Scott also wrote another poem about an elopement. If you are familiar with it, give the story. How does the "ladie" feel in the first stanza? How would the reading of the last two lines of the stanza differ from the preceding lines? How did Frank's father try to win the "ladie's" affections for his son? Describe the wedding scene. Notice how Scott holds your interest by withholding the climax until the very end. Give the theme of the poem. What is the central thought?

Interpretations: Tide; sae comely; aye she loot the tears down fa'; lines 13 and 14; bower; Border.

Significant Expressions: Quote the lines which give you the complete story of the poem.

THE PARTING OF MARMION AND DOUGLAS

From *Marmion*

Sir Walter Scott

Poem Interest: The scene of *Marmion* is laid in Scotland. In 1513, James IV of Scotland had ordered his chiefs to assemble and arm their men preparatory to an invasion of England. To quell the uprising, English forces were sent into Scotland under the command of the Earl of Surrey. Before they went, however, the English king sent Marmion as messenger to the court of Scotland to ask the meaning of the gathering clans. Marmion was protected by the seal of the king and traveled unharmed to Holyrood Castle, one of the palaces of James IV. He not only traveled unharmed but the hospitality of the times was so great and exercised so freely that he was entertained at first one castle and then another on his way. At Tantallon, at the king's request, he spent some little time. This was the home of Douglas, the Earl of Angus, who failed in nothing as a host, though he was only coolly courteous to the English noble. The scene given here is the one in which Marmion takes leave of his host. Picture the two men—the one young, fair, eager to be gone, yet lingering to make friendly advances—the other old, white-haired, a courteous host, but unwilling to be more.

>   Not far advanced was morning day,
>   When Marmion did his troops array
>   To Surrey's camp to ride;

He had safe-conduct for his band,
5 Beneath the royal seal and hand,
   And Douglas gave a guide;
The ancient Earl, with stately grace,
Would Clara on her palfrey place,
And whispered in an undertone,
10 "Let the hawk stoop, his prey is flown."
The train from out the castle drew,
But Marmion stopped to bid adieu:—
"Though something I might plain," he said,
"Of cold respect to stranger guest,
15 Sent hither by your king's behest,
While in Tantallon's towers I stayed,
Part we in friendship from your land,
And, noble Earl, receive my hand."—
But Douglas round him drew his cloak,
20 Folded his arms and thus he spoke:—
"My manors, halls, and bowers shall still
Be open, at my sovereign's will,
To each one whom he lists, howe'er
Unmeet to be the owner's peer.
25 My castles are my king's alone,
From turret to foundation stone,—
The hand of Douglas is his own;
And never shall in friendly grasp
The hand of such as Marmion clasp."—

30 Burned Marmion's swarthy cheek like fire,
And shook his very frame for ire,
   And—"This to me!" he said,—
"An't were not for thy hoary beard,
Such hand as Marmion's had not spared
35   To cleave the Douglas' head!
And, first, I tell thee, haughty Peer,
He who does England's message bear,
Although the meanest in her state,
May well, proud Angus, be thy mate:

8. CLARA—The girl with whom Marmion fell in love; she, however, loved Ralph De Wilton, a brave knight.
13. PLAIN—Complain, *i.e.*, I might complain somewhat.

40 And, Douglas, more I tell thee here,
     Even in thy pitch of pride,
   Here in thy hold, thy vassals near
   (Nay never look upon your lord,
   And lay your hands upon your sword),
45   I tell thee, thou'rt defied!
   And if thou said'st I am not peer
   To any lord in Scotland here,
   Lowland or Highland, far or near,
     Lord Angus, thou hast lied!"—
50 On the Earl's cheek the flush of rage
   O'ercame the ashen hue of age:
   Fierce he broke forth,—"And dar'st thou then
   To beard the lion in his den,
     The Douglas in his hall?
55 And hop'st thou hence unscathed to go?
   No, by Saint Bride of Bothwell, no!
   Up drawbridge, grooms,—what, Warder, ho!
     Let the portcullis fall."—
   Lord Marmion turned,—well was his need!—
60 And dashed the rowels in his steed;
   Like arrow through the archway sprung;
   The ponderous grate behind him rung;
   To pass there was such scanty room,
   The bars descending razed his plume.
65 The steed along the drawbridge flies,
   Just as it trembled on the rise;
   Not lighter does the swallow skim
   Along the smooth lake's level brim;
   And when Lord Marmion reached his band,
70 He halts, and turns with clenched hand,
   And shout of loud defiance pours,
   And shook his gauntlet at the towers.
   "Horse! horse!" the Douglas cried, "and chase!"

43–44. These two lines were addressed to the vassals.
56. SAINT BRIDE OF BOTHWELL—A patron saint.
57. DRAWBRIDGE—Around the old castles were ditches or moats filled with water for protection; over the ditches were bridges which were raised and lowered by chains.
58. PORTCULLIS—A heavy grating made to slide up and down; when let down it barred the entrance to the castle.
60. ROWELS—Spurs.

ROMANTIC POETRY

<blockquote>

But soon he reined his fury's pace:
75 "A royal messenger he came,
Though most unworthy of the name.—
A letter forged! Saint Jude to speed!
Did ever knight so foul a deed?
At first in heart it liked me ill
80 When the king praised his clerkly skill.
Thanks to Saint Bothan, son of mine,
Save Gawain, ne'er could pen a line;
So swore I, and I swear it still,
Let my boy bishop fret his fill.—
85 Saint Mary, mend my fiery mood!—
Old age ne'er cools the Douglas blood
I thought to slay him where he stood
'Tis pity of him, too," he cried;
"Bold can he speak, and fairly ride:
90 I warrant him a warrior tried."
With this his mandate he recalls
And slowly seeks his castle halls.

</blockquote>

77. A LETTER FORGED—Douglas thinks that Marmion might have forged the king's name to the letter.
81. SAINT BOTHAN—A monk who lived at Iona.
82. GAWAIN—One of Douglas' sons.
81–84. Saint Bothan's advice, no son of Douglas', except Gawain, could write; this pleased Douglas because he knew then his sons could not forge any written letters.

Poem Development: Besides entertaining Marmion and his men, what other courtesy did Douglas extend? With whom was Clara in love? Evidently Marmion would have liked to capture Clara's love. Why didn't he? What complaint did Marmion make? Was Marmion friendly? How did he show this? Paint a word picture of Douglas and give his answer to Marmion. Describe the manner in which Marmion left. Why did Douglas recall the order to follow Marmion? What can you say of the spirit of the poem as a whole? What was the cause of the antipathy which sprang up between these two? Under similar conditions how would men of today react?

Interpretations: Marmion did his troops array; safe-conduct; cold respect; each one whom he lists; unmeet; pitch of pride; in thy hold; thou'rt defied; ashen hue of age; line 74; it liked me ill; mend my fiery mood.

Significant Expressions: Quote Douglas' first answer to Marmion. Quote Marmion's reply. Quote Douglas' command to the Warder. What is the figure of speech in line 30? in line 68?

KUBLA KHAN

Samuel Taylor Coleridge

Poem Interest: In the summer of 1797 Coleridge, who was in ill health, went to a farm house near Porlock, England, hoping the rest would cure him. One morning as he sat reading *Purchas's Pilgrimage* he fell asleep in his chair. The last words he read were: "In Xanadu did Cublai Can build a stately Palace, encompassing sixteene miles of plaine ground with a wall, wherein are fertile Medowes, pleasant Springs, delightfull Streames, and all sorts of beasts of chase and game, and in the middest thereof a sumptuous house of pleasure." He said upon awakening that he had composed during his sleep about three hundred lines telling of magnificent scenes of oriental splendor. He immediately began writing them down and had completed fifty-four lines when he was interrupted by a visitor who stayed an hour. Coleridge was never able to remember any more of the dream.

> In Xanadu did Kubla Khan
> A stately pleasure-dome decree,
> Where Alph, the sacred river, ran
> Through caverns measureless to man
> 5   Down to a sunless sea.
> So twice five miles of fertile ground
> With walls and towers were girdled round;
> And here were gardens bright with sinuous rills,
> Where blossomed many an incense-bearing tree;

Title—Khan is equivalent to king or emperor. It is sometimes spelled "cham."
1. Xanadu—A region of Tartary.

10 And here were forests ancient as the hills,
　　Enfolding sunny spots of greenery.

　　But O that deep romantic chasm which slanted
　　Down the green hill athwart a cedarn cover!
　　A savage place! as holy and enchanted
15 As e'er beneath a waning moon was haunted
　　By woman wailing for her demon-lover!
　　And from this chasm, with ceaseless turmoil seething,
　　As if this earth in fast thick pants were breathing,
　　A mighty fountain momently was forced;
20 Amid whose swift half-intermitted burst,
　　Huge fragments vaulted like rebounding hail,
　　Or chaffy grain beneath the thresher's flail;
　　And 'mid these dancing rocks at once and ever
　　It flung up momently the sacred river.
25 Five miles meandering with a mazy motion,
　　Through wood and dale the sacred river ran,
　　Then reached the caverns measureless to man,
　　And sank in tumult to a lifeless ocean;
　　And 'mid this tumult Kubla heard from far
30 Ancestral voices prophesying war!

　　　　The shadow of the dome of pleasure
　　　　Floated midway on the waves;
　　　　Where was heard the mingled measure
　　　　From the fountain and the caves.
35 It was a miracle of rare device,
　　A sunny pleasure-dome with caves of ice!
　　　　A damsel with a dulcimer
　　　　In a vision once I saw;
　　　　It was an Abyssinian maid,
40 　　And on her dulcimer she played,
　　　　Singing of Mount Abora.
　　　　Could I revive within me
　　　　Her symphony and song,
　　　　To such a deep delight 't would win me

41. MOUNT ABORA—Probably a mountain in Abyssinia.

45　　That with music loud and long
　　　　I would build that dome in air,
　　　　That sunny dome! those caves of ice!
　　　　And all who heard should see them there,
　　　　And all should cry, "Beware! beware!
50　　His flashing eyes, his floating hair!
　　　　　　Weave a circle round him thrice,
　　　　　　And close your eyes with holy dread,
　　　　　　For he on honey-dew hath fed,
　　　　　　And drunk the milk of Paradise.

Poem Development: Even though we have these comparatively few lines of an uncompleted poem, the poet has given us wonderfully vivid images, and he has made the unreal real for us. The beauty of the poem is like that of far-away mysterious music of haunting loveliness. What is the image the poet creates of the river? Paint a word picture of the walls and gardens. Re-create in prose the image of the chasm and fountain. What is the image in lines 31–36? Coleridge then saw in the dream a maiden. What sense image does she create? Are you more doubtful of the images in this latter part of the poem? What is the theme? What is the central thought?

Interpretations: Sunless sea; sinuous rills; incense-bearing tree; momently; meandering; holy dread.

Significant Expressions: Which line best describes the chasm? Quote the line telling how the poet would build the dome.

OFT, IN THE STILLY NIGHT

Thomas Moore

Poem Interest: How quickly in the stillness of the night do memories flood in upon one! The poet has well expressed this dreaming attitude in the following musical lines . . .

　　　　Oft, in the stilly night,
　　　　　　Ere Slumber's chain has bound me,
　　　　From Memory brings the light
　　　　　　Of other days around me:
5　　　　　　The smiles, the tears,
　　　　　　Of boyhood's years,
　　　　The words of love then spoken;
　　　　　　The eyes that shone,
　　　　　　Now dimmed and gone,
10　　　　The cheerful hearts now broken!

Thus in the stilly night,
   Ere Slumber's chain has bound me,
Sad Memory brings the light
   Of other days around me.

15 When I remember all
      The friends, so linked together,
   I've seen around me fall,
      Like leaves in wintry weather,
         I feel like one
20   Who treads alone
   Some banquet-hall deserted,
      Whose lights are fled,
      Whose garlands dead,
   And all but he departed.
25 Thus in the stilly night,
      Ere Slumber's chain has bound me,
   Sad Memory brings the light
      Of other days around me.

Poem Development: What are the things the poet thinks about? How old would you think the author might be? Are most of his friends dead? How does he feel? Should he feel sad, or should there also be pleasant memories for him? How does the form of the poem add to its singing quality? Give the theme and central thought.

Interpretations: Line 2; 'whose garlands dead.

Significant Expressions: Quote the line meaning the time. Quote lines which express the poet's feelings. What is the figure of speech in line 18?

THE DESTRUCTION OF SENNACHERIB

George Gordon, Lord Byron

Poem Interest: About seven hundred years before the coming of Christ, there lived in Asia Minor many tribes of people, among whom were the Jews and the Assyrians. Hezekiah was ruler of the Jews, and Sennacherib was king of the Assyrians. Desirous of increasing his power, Sennacherib invaded the land of Judea, capturing forty-six cities and taking two hundred thousand people into captivity. Upon reaching Jerusalem, the capital city, he demanded its surrender, whereupon Hezekiah went into the temple and prayed for the deliverance of the city. Read the poem for the rest of the story.

GEORGE GORDON, LORD BYRON

The Assyrian came down like a wolf on the fold,
And his cohorts were gleaming in purple and gold;
And the sheen of their spears was like stars on the sea,
When the blue wave rolls nightly on deep Galilee.

5 Like the leaves of the forest when Summer is green,
That host with their banners at sunset were seen:
Like the leaves of the forest when Autumn hath blown,
That host on the morrow lay withered and strewn.

For the Angel of Death spread his wings on the blast,
10 And breathed in the face of the foe as he passed;
And the eyes of the sleepers waxed deadly and chill,
And their hearts but once heaved, and forever grew still!

And there lay the steed with his nostril all wide,
But through it there rolled not the breath of his pride;
15 And the foam of his gasping lay white on the turf,
And cold as the spray of the rock-beating surf.

And there lay the rider distorted and pale,
With the dew on his brow and the rust on his mail:
And the tents were all silent, the banners alone,
20 The lances unlifted, the trumpet unblown.

And the widows of Ashur are loud in their wail,
And the idols are broke in the temple of Baal;
And the might of the Gentile, unsmote by the sword,
Hath melted like snow in the glance of the Lord!

1. Assyrian—Sennacherib.
4. Galilee—A sea near Jerusalem.   21. Ashur—Assyria.
22. Baal—A heathen god which the Assyrians worshipped.
23. Gentile—One not of the Jewish faith. Here, Sennacherib.

Poem Development: This story is told in *II Kings* 19:35-37. Describe the advance of the Assyrians. Paint a word picture of the army. What sense is appealed to in lines 2, 3 and 4? What idea of the size of Sennacherib's army is given? What is the comparison used when the hosts of men are alive? What is the comparison when they are dead? How did the Lord answer Hezekiah's prayer? What is the theme of the poem? the central thought?

Significant Expressions: Find five similes. Find two phrases which are often quoted. Quote lines which illustrate the poetic quality of the poem.

SHE WALKS IN BEAUTY

George Gordon, Lord Byron

Poem Interest: It is a beautiful and charming woman whom Byron pictures here. She partakes of all the finest things of earth and yet is wound about with a soft, ethereal light that constitutes "the nameless grace which waves in every raven tress, or softly lightens o'er her face."

She walks in beauty, like the night
  Of cloudless climes and starry skies;
And all that's best of dark and bright
  Meet in her aspect and her eyes:
5 Thus mellowed to that tender light
  Which heaven to gaudy day denies.

One shade the more, one ray the less,
  Had half impaired the nameless grace
Which waves in every raven tress,
10   Or softly lightens o'er her face;
Where thoughts serenely sweet express
  How pure, how dear, their dwelling-place.

And on that cheek, and o'er that brow,
  So soft, so calm, yet eloquent,
15 The smiles that win, the tints that glow,
  But tell of days in goodness spent,
A mind at peace with all below,
  A heart whose love is innocent!

Poem Development: The inspiration of this poem is said to have been Mrs. Wilmot, the poet's cousin by marriage, who appeared at a ball in a black gown covered with spangles. What would lead you to think she wore this kind of a dress? In what terms does the poet describe this woman? In what sense does he use the term "beauty" throughout the poem? Give a description of the woman as she appears to you. Is she your ideal of a truly lovely woman? Give the theme and central thought of the poem.

Significant Expressions: Choose phrases or lines which most appeal to you, giving the reasons for your choice. What is the figure of speech in line 1? in line 2? in line 11?

MAID OF ATHENS, ERE WE PART
GEORGE GORDON, LORD BYRON

Poem Interest: The sorrow of parting has often been inspiration for great verse. Among Byron's beautiful lyrics, this farewell song to an Athenian maiden charms us with its lovely music.

    MAID of Athens, ere we part,
      Give, oh, give me back my heart!
    Or, since that has left my breast,
    Keep it now, and take the rest!
5 Hear my vow before I go,
      My life, I love you.

    By those tresses unconfined,
    Wooed by each Ægean wind;
    By those lids whose jetty fringe
10 Kiss thy soft cheeks' blooming tinge;
    By those wild eyes like the roe,
      My life, I love you.

    By that lip I long to taste;
    By that zone-encircled waist;
15 By all the token-flowers that tell
    What words can never speak so well;
    By love's alternate joy and woe,
      My life, I love you.

    Maid of Athens! I am gone:
20 Think of me, sweet! when alone.
    Though I fly to Istambol,
    Athens holds my heart and soul;
    Can I cease to love thee? No!
      My life, I love you.

8. ÆGEAN WIND—Winds from the Ægean Sea.
14. ZONE—Sash.   21. ISTAMBOL—Constantinople.

Poem Development: Byron was evidently about to leave Athens when he wrote this poem. How does he address the girl? Which line do you like best in the first stanza? Why? Describe the girl as the poet saw her. How does he assure her of his continued love? Summarize the meaning of each stanza into an explanation of the poem as a whole. Give the theme and central thought.

Significant Expressions: Which lines gives the effect of song? What are the figures of speech in lines 2; 9 and 10; 11; 22?

THE PRISONER OF CHILLON

George Gordon, Lord Byron

Poem Interest: Although the poem is only remotely founded upon historical fact, in the background are the struggles for political liberty and the complicated religious controversies which raged in and about Geneva, Switzerland, in the fifteenth and sixteenth centuries. The historic prisoner of Chillon was François de Bonnivard, a churchman who in the early years of the sixteenth century was Prior of St. Victor's, a small religious house near Geneva. However, the offense for which he was imprisoned was not religious as suggested by the poem, but rather political. In the struggles for liberation which the republican city of Geneva waged against the feudal claims of the Duke of Savoy, Bonnivard took the side of the city, thus offending the Duke, who seized him by treachery and shut him up in the castle of Chillon from 1530 to 1536. Four of these years he spent in a dungeon below the level of Lake Leman, or Lake Geneva.

In 1816 Lord Byron and the poet Shelley made a yachting tour about Lake Geneva. They visited the castle of Chillon and heard the story of its prisoner. Being detained for two days by unseasonable weather at the little village of Ouchy, Byron made use of the time to write *The Prisoner of Chillon.* Although Byron was an aristocrat, and had little love for the masses, he was always sympathetic toward any struggle for political liberty—an attitude which grew out of his own hatred of restraint. In Bonnivard, the prisoner, he saw a fellow rebel against things as they are, and his sympathy went out toward him.

MY HAIR is gray, but not with years,
    Nor grew it white
    In a single night,
As men's have grown from sudden fears.
5 My limbs are bowed, though not with toil,
    But rusted with a vile repose.
For they have been a dungeon's spoil,
    And mine has been the fate of those
To whom the goodly earth and air
10 Are banned and barred—forbidden fare.
But this was for my father's faith
I suffered chains and courted death:
That father perished at the stake
For tenets he would not forsake;
15 And for the same his lineal race
In darkness found a dwelling place.
We were seven—who now are one;
    Six in youth and one in age
Finished as they had begun,
20   Proud of Persecution's rage:
One in fire and two in field,
Their belief with blood have sealed,
Dying as their father died,
For the God their foes denied;
25 Three were in a dungeon cast,
Of whom this wreck is left the last.

There are seven pillars of Gothic mold
In Chillon's dungeons deep and old;
There are seven columns massy and gray,
30 Dim with a dull imprisoned ray,
A sunbeam which hath lost its way,
And through the crevice and the cleft
Of the thick wall is fallen and left,

15. LINEAL RACE—Descendants; here his six sons.
20. PERSECUTION'S RAGE—Proud in the face of persecution.

ELD

Creeping o'er the floor so damp,
35 Like a marsh's meteor lamp:
And in each pillar there is a ring,
    And in each ring there is a chain;
That iron is a cankering thing,
    For in these limbs its teeth remain,
40 With marks that will not wear away
Till I have done with this new day,
Which now is painful to these eyes,
Which have not seen the sun so rise
For years—I cannot count them o'er,
45 I lost their long and heavy score
When my last brother drooped and died,
And I lay living by his side.

They chained us each to a column stone,
And we were three—yet each alone;
50 We could not move a single pace,
We could not see each other's face,
But with that pale and livid light
That made us strangers in our sight.
And thus together, yet apart,
55 Fettered in hand but joined in heart,
'Twas still some solace, in the dearth
Of the pure elements of earth,
To hearken to each other's speech,
And each turn comforter to each
60 With some new hope, or legend old,
Or song heroically bold:
But even these at length grew cold;
Our voices took a dreary tone,
An echo of the dungeon stone,
65   A grating sound—not full and free
  As they of yore were wont to be;
  It might be fancy, but to me
They never sounded like our own.

---

35. MARSH'S METEOR LAMP—Will-o'-the-wisp, a phosphorescent light which appears at night over marshy grounds.
57. PURE ELEMENTS—Light and fresh air.

GEORGE GORDON, LORD BYRON

        I was the eldest of the three,
70   And to uphold and cheer the rest
        I ought to do—and did—my best;
      And each did well in his degree.
      The youngest, whom my father loved
      Because our mother's brow was given
75   To him, with eyes as blue as heaven,
        For him my soul was sorely moved:
      And truly might it be distressed
      To see such bird in such a nest;
      For he was beautiful as day—
80   (When day was beautiful to me
        As to young eagles, being free)—
      A polar day, which will not see
      A sunset till its summer's gone,
        Its sleepless summer of long light,
85   The snow-clad offspring of the sun;
        And thus he was as pure and bright,
      And in his natural spirit gay,
      With tears for naught but others' ills,
      And then they flowed like mountain rills,
90   Unless he could assuage the woe
      Which he abhorred to view below.

      The other was as pure of mind,
      But formed to combat with his kind;
      Strong in his frame, and of a mood
95   Which 'gainst the world in war had stood,
      And perished in the foremost rank
       With joy—but not in chains to pine:
      His spirit withered with their clank;
        I saw it silently decline—
100   And so perchance in sooth did mine;
      But yet I forced it on to cheer
      Those relics of a home so dear.

  82. A POLAR DAY—A long, bright day. The six-months' day at the poles corresponds to the summer season.
  85. The line is in apposition with light. The light is the more bright from being reflected by the polar snows; hence it is "the snow-clad offspring of the sun."   91. BELOW—Among men.
  95. HAD STOOD—Could have stood, was made to stand.
  102. RELICS—His two brothers who were all that was left of the home.

He was a hunter of the hills,
    Had followed there the deer and wolf;
105   To him this dungeon was a gulf,
And fettered feet the worst of ills.

Lake Leman lies by Chillon's walls:
A thousand feet in depth below
Its massy waters meet and flow;
110   Thus much the fathom-line was sent
From Chillon's snow-white battlement,
    Which round about the wave inthrals;
A double dungeon wall and wave
Have made—and like a living grave
115   Below the surface of the lake
The dark vault lies wherein we lay:
We heard it ripple night and day;
    Sounding o'er our heads it knocked;
And I have felt the winter's spray
120   Wash through the bars when winds were high
And wanton in the happy sky;
    And then the very rock hath rocked,
    And I have felt it shake, unshocked,
Because I could have smiled to see
125   The death that would have set me free.

I said my nearer brother pined,
I said his mighty heart declined;
He loathed and put away his food:
It was not that 't was coarse and rude,
130   For we were used to hunter's fare,
And for the like had little care.
The milk drawn from the mountain goat
Was changed for water from the moat;
Our bread was such as captives' tears
135   Have moistened many a thousand years,
Since man first pent his fellow men

---

110. FATHOM-LINE—The line used to measure the depth of the water.

111. SNOW-WHITE BATTLEMENT—The castle was built of white limestone. Battlement here is used for castle.

112. INTHRALS—Encompasses, shuts in. "Wave" is the subject of "inthrals," and "battlement" is the object.

126. NEARER—In age.

> Like brutes within an iron den.
> But what were these to us or him?
> These wasted not his heart or limb:
> 140 My brother's soul was of that mold
> Which in a palace had grown cold,
> Had his free breathing been denied
> The range of the steep mountain's side.
> But why delay the truth?—he died.
> 145 I saw, and could not hold his head,
> Nor reach his dying hand—nor dead,—
> Though hard I strove, but strove in vain,
> To rend and gnash my bonds in twain.
> He died—and they unlocked his chain,
> 150 And scooped for him a shallow grave
> Even from the cold earth of our cave.
> I begged them, as a boon, to lay
> His corse in dust whereon the day
> Might shine—it was a foolish thought,
> 155 But then within my brain it wrought,
> That even in death his freeborn breast
> In such a dungeon could not rest.
> I might have spared my idle prayer—
> They coldly laughed, and laid him there:
> 160 The flat and turfless earth above
> The being we so much did love;
> His empty chain above it leant,
> Such murder's fitting monument!
>
> But he, the favorite and the flower,
> 165 Most cherished since his natal hour,
> His mother's image in fair face,
> The infant love of all his race,
> His martyred father's dearest thought,
> My latest care, for whom I sought
> 170 To hoard my life, that his might be
> Less wretched now, and one day free;
> He, too, who yet had held untired
> A spirit natural or inspired,

138. THESE—Water and bread.   155. IT WROUGHT—The thought appeared.
170. HOARD—To prolong, for the purpose of comforting him.

He, too, was struck, and day by day
175 Was withered on the stalk away.
Oh, God! it is a fearful thing
To see the human soul take wing
In any shape, in any mood:
I've seen it rushing forth in blood,
180 I've seen it on the breaking ocean
Strive with a swoln convulsive motion,
I've seen the sick and ghastly bed
Of Sin delirious with its dread;
But these were horrors—this was woe
185 Unmixed with such—but sure and slow.
He faded, and so calm and meek,
So softly worn, so sweetly weak,
So tearless, yet so tender—kind,
And grieved for those he left behind;
190 Withal the while a cheek whose bloom
Was as a mockery of the tomb,
Whose tints as gently sunk away
As a departing rainbow's ray;
An eye of most transparent light
195 That almost made the dungeon bright;
And not a word of murmur—not
A groan o'er his untimely lot;
A little talk of better days,
A little hope my own to raise,
200 For I was sunk in silence—lost
In this last loss, of all the most;
And then the sighs he would suppress
Of fainting nature's feebleness,
More slowly drawn, grew less and less:
205 I listened, but I could not hear—
I called, for I was wild with fear;
I knew 't was hopeless, but my dread

181. That is, battle frantically against drowning.
183. DREAD—Of death.
184. THESE—The forms of death described above.
184. THIS—The slow death of the younger brother.
185. The other deaths filled him with horror, but this with woe, that is grief and sorrow. There was no horror in it—it was "unmixed" with horror.
190. WITHAL THE WHILE—And with it all the time.

>   Would not be thus admonishèd;
>   I called, and thought I heard a sound—
> 210   I burst my chain with one strong bound,
>   And rushed to him:—I found him not;
>   *I* only stirred in this black spot,
>   *I* only lived—*I* only drew
>   The accursed breath of dungeon-dew;
> 215   The last—the sole—the dearest link
>   Between me and the eternal brink,
>   Which bound me to my failing race,
>   Was broken in this fatal place.
>   One on the earth, and one beneath—
> 220   My brothers—both had ceased to breathe:
>   I took that hand which lay so still,
>   Alas! my own was full as chill;
>   I had not strength to stir or strive,
>   But felt that I was still alive—
> 225   A frantic feeling, when we know
>   That what we love shall ne'er be so.
>   I know not why
>   I could not die;
>   I had no earthly hope—but faith,
> 230   And that forbade a selfish death.
>
>   What next befell me then and there
>   I know not well—I never knew.
>   First came the loss of light and air,
>   And then of darkness too:
> 235   I had no thought, no feeling—none;
>   Among the stones I stood a stone,
>   And was, scarce conscious what I wist,
>   As shrubless crags within the mist;
>   For all was blank, and bleak, and gray;

208. BE THUS ADMONISHÈD—His very dread of the possibility of his brother's death would not let him believe that it could actually have happened. In other words, he hoped against hope.
212. *I* ONLY—Only *I* stirred—only *I* lived.
230. A SELFISH DEATH—His faith forbade his killing himself to end his own misery.
237. WIST—Knew, used here more in the sense of "felt."

240 It was night—it was not day;
It was not even the dungeon-light,
So hateful to my heavy sight,
But vacancy absorbing space,
And fixedness—without a place;
245 There were no stars—no earth—no time—
No check—no change—no good—no crime—
But silence, and a stirless breath
Which neither was of life nor death;
A sea of stagnant idleness,
250 Blind, boundless, mute, and motionless!

A light broke in upon my brain—
It was the carol of a bird;
It ceased, and then it came again,
The sweetest song ear ever heard;
255. And mine was thankful till my eyes
Ran over with the glad surprise,
And they that moment could not see
I was the mate of misery.
But then by dull degrees came back
260 My senses to their wonted track:
I saw the dungeon walls and floor
Close slowly round me as before;
I saw the glimmer of the sun
Creeping as it before had done,
265 But through the crevice where it came
That bird was perched, as fond and tame,
And tamer than upon the tree;
A lovely bird, with azure wings,
And song that said a thousand things,
270 And seemed to say them all for me!
I never saw its like before,
I ne'er shall see its likeness more:
It seemed like me to want a mate,
But was not half so desolate;
275 And it was come to love me when
None lived to love me so again,
And cheering from my dungeon's brink,
Had brought me back to feel and think.

GEORGE GORDON, LORD BYRON

   I know not if it late were free,
280 Or broke its cage to perch on mine;
   But knowing well captivity,
    Sweet bird, I could not wish for thine!
   Or if it were, in wingèd guise,
   A visitant from Paradise;
285 For—Heaven forgive that thought, the while
   Which made me both to weep and smile—
   I sometimes deemed that it might be
   My brother's soul come down to me;
   But then at last away it flew,
290 And then 't was mortal, well I knew,
   For he would never thus have flown,
   And left me twice so doubly lone,—
   Lone—as the corse within its shroud,
   Lone—as a solitary cloud,
295   A single cloud on a sunny day
   While all the rest of heaven is clear,
   A frown upon the atmosphere,
   That hath no business to appear
    When skies are blue and earth is gay.

300 A kind of change came in my fate,
   My keepers grew compassionate;
   I know not what had made them so,
   They were inured to sights of woe,
   But so it was:—my broken chain
305 With links unfastened did remain,
   And it was liberty to stride
   Along my cell from side to side,
   And up and down, and then athwart,
   And tread it over every part,
310 And round the pillars one by one,
   Returning where my walk begun,
   Avoiding only, as I trod,
   My brothers' graves without a sod;

---

 283. OR IF IT WERE—These two lines are the object of "I know not." The two lines above are parenthetical.
 308. ATHWART—From one corner to the opposite corner.

*And it was liberty to stride
Along my cell from side to side,
And round the pillars one by one,
Returning where my walk begun.*

GEORGE GORDON, LORD BYRON

  For if I thought with heedless tread
315 My step profaned their lowly bed,
  My breath came gaspingly and thick,
  And my crushed heart fell blind and sick.

  I made a footing in the wall:
   It was not therefrom to escape,
320 For I had buried one and all
   Who loved me in a human shape,
  And the whole earth would henceforth be
  A wider prison unto me;
  No child—no sire—no kin had I,
325 No partner in my misery;
  I thought of this, and I was glad,
  For thought of them had made me mad;—
  But I was curious to ascend
  To my barred windows, and to bend
330 Once more, upon the mountains high,
  The quiet of a loving eye.

  I saw them—and they were the same,
  They were not changed like me in frame;
  I saw their thousand years of snow
335 On high—their wide long lake below,
  And the blue Rhone in fullest flow;
  I heard the torrents leap and gush
  O'er channell'd rock and broken bush;
  I saw the white-walled distant town,
340 And whiter sails go skimming down:
  And then there was a little isle,
  Which in my very face did smile,
   The only one in view;
  A small green isle, it seemed no more,
345 Scarce broader than my dungeon floor,
  But in it there were three tall trees,
  And o'er it blew the mountain breeze,
  And by it there were waters flowing,
  And on it there were young flowers growing,

327. HAD MADE ME MAD—Would have made me mad—insane.
336. RHONE—The river rises in Lake Leman.

350   Of gentle breath and hue.
   The fish swam by the castle wall,
   And they seemed joyous each and all;
   The eagle rode the rising blast,
   Methought he never flew so fast
355 As then to me he seemed to fly;
   And then new tears came in my eye,
   And I felt troubled—and would fain
   I had not left my recent chain;
   And when I did descend again,
360 The darkness of my dim abode
   Fell on me as a heavy load;
   It was as is a new-dug grave,
   Closing o'er one we sought to save,—
   And yet my glance, too much oppressed,
365 Had almost need of such a rest.

   It might be months, or years, or days—
     I kept no count, I took no note;
   I had no hope my eyes to raise,
     And clear them of their dreary mote:
370 At last men came to set me free:
     I asked not why, and recked not where;
   It was at length the same to me,
   Fettered or fetterless to be;
   I learned to love despair.
375 And thus when they appeared at last,
   And all my bonds aside were cast,
   These heavy walls to me had grown
   A hermitage—and all my own!
   And half I felt as they were come
380 To tear me from a second home:
   With spiders I had friendship made,
   And watched them in their sullen trade;
   Had seen the mice by moonlight play,

364. TOO MUCH OPPRESSED—Too long prevented from looking at the light of day. His eyes had become so adjusted to the dim light of his dungeon, that, after looking out of his window, they needed rest.

369. CLEAR THEM OF THEIR DREARY MOTE—Mote is an obstruction of the vision. To clear them of their dreary mote would be to accustom them to a brighter light than the dreary half-light of the dungeon.

And why should I feel less than they?
385 We were all inmates of one place,
And I, the monarch of each race,
Had power to kill—yet, strange to tell!
In quiet we had learned to dwell;
My very chains and I grew friends,
390 So much a long communion tends
To make us what we are:—even I
Regained my freedom with a sigh.

384. FEEL LESS—Feel less attached to this place, feel less than they that the dungeon was home.

Poem Development: *The Prisoner of Chillon* is not intended to be history. Byron's conception of Bonnivard as a victim of religious persecution can hardly be justified, although it is true that the political rebellion of Geneva had also its religious side. Upon the capture of Chillon by the Genevans, Bonnivard was released, made a member of the city council, and granted a pension. He lived well beyond his allotted three score years and ten, and died a natural death some thirty-five years after his release from prison. It is possible that the original incident had been modified by legend and that Byron tells the story as he heard it from a "citizen of Geneva"; but it is more likely that the story as it stands in his poem is in a large measure the product of the poet's dramatic imagination. But while it is true that Byron takes liberty with the facts of history, it is equally true that he succeeds in making us feel the strength of mind, the fearlessness, and the tenacity of purpose which made the reformers of the Middle Ages face imprisonment, torture, and death for their beliefs. Some one has said that history tells us what men have done, while literature tells us why they did it. This poem is another illustration of the fact that it is not the office of literature to give facts, but to give rather the meaning or soul of fact.

Lines 1–26: How did the father perish? How many brothers were there? Three of the brothers were dead at the opening of this story. How had they met death?

Lines 27–68: Describe the dungeon. How does the poet gain the effect of the tinyness of the sunbeam? Describe the manner in which the prisoners were confined. How did they cheer one another?

Lines 69–125: Which brother is telling the story? Describe the youngest brother. Describe the second brother. Why was the dungeon called a "double dungeon"?

Lines 126–250: What was the most pitiful thing about the first brother's death? Where was he buried? What happened to the elder brother when his second brother died?

Lines 251–317: After the period of forgetfulness what brought the prisoner back to a sense of realization? What kind of a bird was it? What did the prisoner think the bird might symbolize? Why do you think the keepers became more compassionate?

Lines 318–392: What desire did the prisoner have? What did he see when he climbed up to look through the window? How did he feel when he descended into the dungeon again? How did the walls of the dungeon at last seem to him? What friendships did he make? Did he wish for his freedom when it was at last granted him?

In your study of the poem, consider not only the story but also expressions which you think illustrate the state of mind of a man in prison. Write a précis of the poem. What is the theme of the poem? Give the central thought.

Interpretations: Vile repose (l. 6); perished at the stake (l. 13); tenets (l. 14); this wreck (l. 26); Gothic (l. 27); cankering thing (l. 38); livid light (l. 52); joined in heart (l. 55); dearth (l. 56); in his degree (l. 72); to pine (l. 97); in sooth (l. 100); unshocked (l. 123); nearer brother (l. 126); lines 134–135; pent (l. 136); boon (l. 152); corse (l. 153); lines 162–163; line 166; lines 190–191; I found him not (l. 211); line 234; ran over (l. 256); their wonted track (l. 260); line 284; line 292; lines 330–331; sullen trade (l. 382).

Significant Expressions: What is the figure of speech in line 35? in line 81? Quote some vivid lines of description; some lines expressing despair; terror; hopefulness.

THE CLOUD

Percy Bysshe Shelley

Poem Interest: Imagine yourself lying on the grassy bank of a winding river. The day is warm and sunny. White foamy clouds float lazily across the blue sky. You feel yourself slowly transported to the cloud itself and as you float dreamily along with it, the cloud begins to speak . . .

    I BRING fresh showers for the thirsting flowers,
        From the seas and the streams;
    I bear light shade for the leaves when laid
        In their noonday dreams.
5   From my wings are shaken the dews that waken
        The sweet buds every one,
    When rocked to rest on their mother's breast,
        As she dances about the sun.
    I wield the flail of the lashing hail,
10   And whiten the green plains under,

And then again I dissolve it in rain,
   And laugh as I pass in thunder.

I sift the snow on the mountains below,
   And their great pines groan aghast;
And all the night 'tis my pillow white,
   While I sleep in the arms of the blast.
Sublime on the towers of my skyey bowers,
   Lightning my pilot sits;
In a cavern under is fettered the thunder,
   It struggles and howls at fits;
Over earth and ocean, with gentle motion,
   This pilot is guiding me,
Lured by the love of the genii that move
   In the depths of the purple sea;
Over the rills, and the crags, and the hills,
   Over the lakes and the plains,
Wherever he dream, under mountain or stream,
   The Spirit he loves remains;
And I all the while bask in heaven's blue smile.
   Whilst he is dissolving in rains.

The sanguine Sunrise, with his meteor eyes,
   And his burning plumes outspread,
Leaps on the back of my sailing rack,
   When the morning star shines dead,
As on the jag of a mountain crag,
   Which an earthquake rocks and swings,
An eagle alit one moment may sit
   In the light of its golden wings.
And when sunset may breathe, from the lit sea beneath,
   Its ardors of rest and of love,
And the crimson pall of eve may fall
   From the depth of heaven above,
With wings folded I rest, on mine airy nest,
   As still as a brooding dove.

That orbèd maiden with white fire laden,
   Whom mortals call the Moon,

---

31. SANGUINE—Red, like blood.   33. RACK—Thin, floating, broken clouds.

Glides glimmering o'er my fleece-like floor,
    By the midnight breezes strewn;
And wherever the beat of her unseen feet,
50   Which only the angels hear,
May have broken the woof of my tent's thin roof,
    The stars peep behind her and peer;
And I laugh to see them whirl and flee,
    Like a swarm of golden bees,
55 When I widen the rent in my wind-built tent,
    Till the calm rivers, lakes, and seas,
Like strips of the sky fallen through me on high,
    Are each paved with the moon and these.

I bind the Sun's throne with a burning zone,
60   And the Moon's with a girdle of pearl;
The volcanoes are dim, and the stars reel and swim,
    When the whirlwinds my banner unfurl.
From cape to cape, with a bridge-like shape,
    Over a torrent sea,
65 Sunbeam-proof, I hang like a roof—
    The mountains its columns be.
The triumphal arch through which I march
    With hurricane, fire, and snow,
When the Powers of the air are chained to my chair,
70   Is the million-colored bow;
The sphere-fire above its soft colors wove,
    While the moist earth was laughing below.

I am the daughter of Earth and Water,
    And the nursling of the Sky;
75 I pass through the pores of the ocean and shores;
    I change, but I cannot die.
For after the rain when with never a stain
    The pavilion of heaven is bare,
And the winds and sunbeams with their convex gleams,
80   Build up the blue dome of air,

59. ZONE—Girdle; belt.
67. TRIUMPHAL ARCH—The rainbow.

> I silently laugh at my own cenotaph,
>   And out of the caverns of rain,
> Like a child from the womb, like a ghost from
>   the tomb,
>   I arise and unbuild it again.

81. CENOTAPH—Empty tomb.

Poem Development: A changing, rhythmic panorama of the varying moods of cloud life—the tender calm, the laughing thunder, the weeping storm—sweeps across our vision. Apparently the cloud in this poem, like all other clouds, is going places and doing things, and has not time to stop to classify the experiences it meets. It swings gaily along from plain to mountain top, shouting and still by turns, through hail, rain, snow; into the sunrise, on to the sunset, and then garlands the moon with a "girdle of pearls." Choose a word picture from one of the stanzas and carefully reproduce it in your own words—lines 31-38; 49-58; 61-67 are suggested. Comment on the central thought of the sixth stanza. Would you say that the cloud's laughter is an expression of joy in realizing the essential immortality of its life, though it may change in form? Read the poem again, and write a brief summary of its content. Give also the theme of the poem, and its central thought.

Interpretations: Wield the flail (l. 9); skyey bowers (l. 17); genii (l. 23); burning plumes (l. 32); shines dead (l. 34); crimson pall of eve (l. 41); white fire laden (l. 45); woof (l. 51); rent (l. 55); burning zone (l. 59); line 66; convex gleams (l. 79).

Significant Expressions: In the first stanza, choose the line which paints the most vivid picture. Quote the line describing thunder. Quote lines expressing color; quietness; mirth. Give the figures of speech in the following lines: 4; 14; 18; 19; 29; 38; 44; 47; 54; 57; 63; 65; 78.

TO A SKYLARK

PERCY BYSSHE SHELLEY

Poem Interest: Shelley and his wife were wandering one day along an English lane, when suddenly the varied, pulsating sound of a skylark's song flowed down upon them in a golden cascade of melody. The delicate perception of the poet caught every tone, and the divine flood of rapture awakened in him comes to us in the following poem which is probably one of the most beautiful lyrics in existence.

Hail to thee, blithe spirit!
　　Bird thou never wert,
That from heaven, or near it,
　　Pourest thy full heart
In profuse strains of unpremeditated art.

　　Higher still and higher
　　　From the earth thou springest
　　Like a cloud of fire;
　　　The blue deep thou wingest,
And singing still dost soar, and soaring ever singest.

　　In the golden lightning
　　　Of the sunken sun,
　　O'er which clouds are brightening,
　　　Thou dost float and run,
Like an unbodied joy whose race is just begun.

　　The pale purple even
　　　Melts around thy flight;
　　Like a star of heaven,
　　　In the broad daylight
Thou art unseen, but yet I hear thy shrill delight,

　　Keen as are the arrows
　　　Of that silver sphere,
　　Whose intense lamp narrows
　　　In the white dawn clear,
Until we hardly see, we feel that it is there.

　　All the earth and air
　　　With thy voice is loud,
　　As, when night is bare,
　　　From one lonely cloud
The moon rains out her beams, and heaven is overflowed.

　　What thou art we know not;
　　　What is most like thee?

From rainbow clouds there flow not
  Drops so bright to see
35 As from thy presence showers a rain of melody.

  Like a poet hidden
    In the light of thought,
  Singing hymns unbidden,
    Till the world is wrought
40 To sympathy with hopes and fears it heeded not;

  Like a high-born maiden
    In a palace tower,
  Soothing her love-laden
    Soul in secret hour
45 With music sweet as love, which overflows her
    bower;

  Like a glowworm golden
    In a dell of dew,
  Scattering unbeholden
    Its aërial hue
50 Among the flowers and grass, which screen it
    from the view;

  Like a rose embowered
    In its own green leaves,
  By warm winds deflowered,
    Till the scent it gives
55 Makes faint with too much sweet those heavy-
    winged thieves.

  Sound of vernal showers
    On the twinkling grass,
  Rain-awakened flowers,
    All that ever was
60 Joyous, and clear, and fresh, thy music doth
    surpass.

Teach us, sprite or bird,
  What sweet thoughts are thine;
I have never heard
  Praise of love or wine
65 That panted forth a flood of rapture so divine.

Chorus Hymeneal
  Or triumphal chaunt
Matched with thine, would be all
  But an empty vaunt—
70 A thing wherein we feel there is some hidden want.

What objects are the fountains
  Of thy happy strain?
What fields, or waves, or mountains?
  What shapes of sky or plain?
75 What love of thine own kind? what ignorance of pain?

With thy clear keen joyance
  Languor cannot be;
Shadow of annoyance
  Never came near thee;
80 Thou lovest—but ne'er knew love's sad satiety.

Waking or asleep
  Thou of death must deem
Things more true and deep
  Than we mortals dream,
85 Or how could thy notes flow in such a crystal stream?

We look before and after,
  And pine for what is not;
Our sincerest laughter
  With some pain is fraught;
90 Our sweetest songs are those that tell of saddest thought.

66. CHORUS HYMENEAL—Wedding music; from Hymen, the god of marriage.

        Yet if we could scorn
           Hate, and pride, and fear;
        If we were things born
           Not to shed a tear,
95   I know not how thy joy we ever should come near.

        Better than all measures
           Of delightful sound,
        Better than all treasures
           That in books are found,
100   Thy skill to poet were, thou scorner of the ground!

        Teach me half the gladness
           That thy brain must know,
        Such harmonious madness
           From my lips would flow,
105   The world should listen then, as I am listening now.

Poem Development: This poem is an ode, an ode being a lyric which is exalted in tone and deals with a single dignified theme. It is really one long figure of speech. Tell what figure of speech this is. Why does the poet say "from heaven or near it" in line 3? Look up the English skylark in an encyclopedia. Have we any bird in America similar to it? How does the verse form help suggest the motion of the bird? Lines 1–30 tell about the song. Give these thoughts in your own words. Lines 31–60 compare the song with other beauties of nature and with people. Name the comparisons. Lines 61–85 show a contrast between the bird's divine music and various human emotions. What are these contrasting ideas? Lines 85–105 express the wish of the poet to bring forth beauty in words as the bird does in song. Give the meaning of these four stanzas in your own words. What are the theme and central thought of the poem?

Interpretations: Unpremeditated art (l. 5); unbodied joy (l. 15); silver sphere (l. 22); aërial hue (l. 49); deflowered (l. 53); heavy-winged thieves (l. 55); vernal (l. 56); fountains (l. 71); satiety (l. 80); scorner of the ground (l. 100).

Significant Expressions: Quote the lines descriptive of the bird's flight. Quote the line which best describes the skylark. Quote the stanza which tells of human disappointment. Quote and learn the four last stanzas, relative to the poet's wish. Find five similes. Find two metaphors. Find three illustrations of alliteration.

ODE TO THE WEST WIND

Percy Bysshe Shelley

Poem Interest: We love that thing whose power we love—that thing most like ourselves, through which we see ourselves, in whole or in part, as we are or as we desire to be. Shelley, "tameless, swift, and proud," creature of moods, loved the west wind, and in this ode pours forth praise of all its beauty, strength and power. According to Shelley's notes, "This poem was conceived and chiefly written in a wood that skirts the Arno, near Florence [Italy], and on a day when that tempestuous wind, whose temperature is at once mild and animating, was collecting the vapours which pour down the autumnal rains. [The rains] began, as I foresaw, at sunset with a violent tempest of hail and rain, attended by that magnificent thunder and lightning peculiar to the Cisalpine regions."

I

O wild West Wind, thou breath of Autumn's being,
Thou, from whose unseen presence the leaves dead
Are driven, like ghosts from an enchanter fleeing,

Yellow, and black, and pale, and hectic red,
5 Pestilence-stricken multitudes; O thou,
Who chariotest to their dark wintry bed

The wingèd seeds, where they lie cold and low,
Each like a corpse within its grave, until
Thine azure sister of the spring shall blow

10 Her clarion o'er the dreaming earth, and fill
(Driving sweet buds like flocks to feed in air)
With living hues and odors plain and hill;

Wild Spirit, which art moving everywhere;
Destroyer and preserver; hear, O hear!

II

15 Thou on whose stream, 'mid the steep sky's commotion,
Loose clouds like earth's decaying leaves are shed,
Shook from the tangled boughs of heaven and ocean,

---

9. AZURE SISTER—The mild west wind of spring as contrasted to the wild west wind of autumn.

     Angels of rain and lightning; there are spread
     On the blue surface of thine airy surge,
20 Like the bright hair uplifted from the head

     Of some fierce Mænad, even from the dim verge
     Of the horizon to the zenith's height,
     The locks of the approaching storm. Thou dirge

     Of the dying year, to which the closing night
25 Will be the dome of a vast sepulcher,
     Vaulted with all thy congregated might

     Of vapors, from whose solid atmosphere
     Black rain, and fire, and hail will burst; O hear!

III

     Thou who didst waken from his summer dreams
30 The blue Mediterranean, where he lay,
     Lulled by the coil of his crystalline streams,

     Beside a pumice isle in Baiae's bay,
     And saw in sleep old palaces and towers
     Quivering within the wave's intenser day,

35 All overgrown with azure moss and flowers
     So sweet, the sense faints picturing them! thou
     For whose path the Atlantic's level powers

     Cleave themselves into chasms, while far below
     The sea-blooms and the oozy woods which wear
40 The sapless foliage of the ocean, know

     Thy voice, and suddenly grow gray with fear,
     And tremble and despoil themselves; O hear!

21. MÆNAD—A frenzied priestess of Bacchus, the god of wine.
32. BAIAE—A site of many ruins of ancient luxury near Naples. The region is volcanic, hence "pumice" or volcanic isle.
39–42. The explanation of these lines is to be found in Shelley's notes as follows: "The phenomenon alluded to at the conclusion of the third stanza is well known to naturalists. The vegetation at the bottom of the sea, of rivers, and of lakes, sympathizes with that of the land in the change of seasons, and is consequently influenced by the winds which announce it."

IV

If I were a dead leaf thou mightest bear;
If I were a swift cloud to fly with thee;
A wave to pant beneath thy power, and share

The impulse of thy strength, only less free
Than thou, O uncontrollable! If even
I were as in my boyhood, and could be

The comrade of thy wanderings over heaven,
As then, when to outstrip thy skyey speed
Scarce seemed a vision, I would ne'er have striven

As thus with thee in prayer in my sore need.
O lift me as a wave, a leaf, a cloud!
I fall upon the thorns of life! I bleed!

A heavy weight of hours has chained and bowed
One too like thee—tameless, and swift, and proud.

V

Make me thy lyre, even as the forest is;
What if my leaves are falling like its own!
The tumult of thy mighty harmonies

Will take from both a deep, autumnal tone,
Sweet though in sadness. Be thou, spirit fierce,
My spirit! Be thou me, impetuous one!

Drive my dead thoughts over the universe
Like withered leaves to quicken a new birth!
And, by the incantation of this verse,

Scatter, as from an unextinguished hearth
Ashes and sparks, my words among mankind!
Be through my lips to unawakened earth

The trumpet of a prophecy! O Wind,
If winter comes, can spring be far behind?

Poem Development: This poem is a very complete picture, and each stanza has a distinct, contributing thought. Study each of the stanzas carefully—notice that in turn they deal with the wind and earth; the wind and sky; the wind and sea; to the fourth stanza which sweeps quickly through the allusions in the first, second and third, and applies them to the wind and Shelley; then on to the fifth stanza which is the climax and the end. Tell the effect of the west wind on the earth; on the sky; on the sea. Explain the relationship Shelley would have with the wind. Give the meaning of the last two lines. What is the mood of the poem? Is there any change in mood in the fifth stanza? What is the theme of the poem? Give the central thought.

Interpretations: Pestilence-stricken multitudes (l. 5); wingèd seeds (l. 7); destroyer and preserver (l. 14); zenith's height (l. 22); dirge of the dying year (l. 23); saw in sleep (l. 33); cleave themselves into chasms (l. 38); skyey speed (l. 50); lyre (l. 57); incantation (l. 65).

Significant Expressions: Quote the line painting the most vivid picture of the flying leaves; of the clouds; of the waves. Quote the poet's prayer. Memorize the last two lines. What figure of speech is this entire poem? Make a list of similes and metaphors.

ROUGH WIND, THAT MOANEST LOUD

Percy Bysshe Shelley

Poem Interest: Shelley had the delightful habit of personifying the natural sounds and sights which appealed to him. Here again we find him tuning in to the voice of the wind—

> Rough wind, that moanest loud
>   Grief too sad for song;
> Wild wind, when sullen cloud
>   Knells all the night long;
>
> Sad storm, whose tears are vain,
> Bare woods, whose branches strain,
> Deep caves and dreary main,
>   Wail, for the world's wrong!

Poem Development: What thought has the poet expressed through the medium of the wind's wailing? This poem was written sometime during the last two years of Shelley's life. From your study of the circumstances of his life, can you explain why he heard the sound of the wind as he did? What does the rush of the rough wind and storm symbolize to you? What is the theme of the poem? Give the central thought.

Interpretations: Sullen cloud; knells; vain; main.

Significant Expressions: Quote the line giving a feeling of intense sadness. Quote lines which describe the wind.

OZYMANDIAS

Percy Bysshe Shelley

Poem Interest: There is an eastern fascination to this story of Ozymandias, an ancient Egyptian king. It flings a challenge to us to ferret out the veiled truth hidden in its passages.

> I met a traveler from an antique land
> Who said: "Two vast and trunkless legs of stone
> Stand in the desert . . . Near them, on the sand,
> Half sunk, a shattered visage lies, whose frown,
> 5 And wrinkled lip, and sneer of cold command,
> Tell that its sculptor well those passions read
> Which yet survive, stamped on these lifeless things,
> The hand that mocked them, and the heart that fed;

1. Antique land—Egypt.
8. "Hand" and "heart" are the objects of "survive." The meaning is that the passions of the king as shown by the sculptor's art have survived both the sculptor and the king. "Mocked" has the meaning of "imaged."

And on the pedestal these words appear;
10 'My name is Ozymandias, king of kings;
Look on my works, ye Mighty, and despair!'
Nothing beside remains. Round the decay
Of that colossal wreck, boundless and bare
The lone and level sands stretch far away."

Poem Development: Describe the general scene that the traveler saw. Now tell in detail the characteristic of the face of the statue. Picture the King Ozymandias as he might have been during life. Tell the story, as you see it, of how he achieved his "mighty works," and why they did not survive. Summarize the lesson, using your own interpretation or a combination of lines from the poem.

Interpretations: Shattered visage; cold command; boundless.

Significant Expressions: Quote the lines which you consider most significant in contributing to the meaning of the poem as a whole.

MUSIC, WHEN SOFT VOICES DIE

Percy Bysshe Shelley

Poem Interest: Each experience of beauty leaves with us its own particular loveliness—a sound, a fragrance, an emotion. For Shelley, too, memories were precious possessions.

> Music, when soft voices die,
> Vibrates in the memory—
> Odors when sweet violets sicken,
> Live within the sense they quicken.
>
> Rose leaves, when the rose is dead,
> Are heap'd for the beloved's bed;
> And so thy thoughts, when thou art gone,
> Love itself shall slumber on.

7. Thy thoughts—Thoughts of thee.

Poem Development: Explain lines 2, 4, 6 and 8. To what senses do the first four lines appeal? What is the theme of the poem? Give the central thought.

Interpretations: Soft voices die; sicken.

Significant Expressions: Quote the two lines which you like best.

ON FIRST LOOKING INTO CHAPMAN'S HOMER

John Keats

Poem Interest: Keats himself was not able to read Greek. A friend, however, brought him a copy of George Chapman's translation of Homer, and the two stayed up all night reading the book, "Keats shouting with delight as some passage of special energy struck his imagination." Fired by the splendors of the Greek culture thus opened to him, Keats composed the following sonnet after his friend had left, and presented it to him the next morning. It is considered one of the best sonnets in English literature.

    Much have I traveled in the realms of gold
    And many goodly states and kingdoms seen;
    Round many western islands have I been
    Which bards in fealty to Apollo hold.
5 Oft of one wide expanse had I been told
    That deep-browed Homer ruled as his demesne;
    Yet did I never breathe its pure serene
    Till I heard Chapman speak out loud and bold.
    Then felt I like some watcher of the skies
10 When a new planet swims into his ken;
    Or like stout Cortez, when with eagle eyes
    He stared at the Pacific—and all his men
    Looked at each other with a wild surmise—
    Silent, upon a peak in Darien.

  1. Realms of gold—Great literature.
  3–4. That is, I have read much poetry by English writers. "Western islands" refers to the British Isles. "Bards in fealty to Apollo" means "poets who have kept faith with Apollo, the god of song and music."
  6. Demesne—Domain.
  8. Chapman—George Chapman (1559–1634), whose translation of Homer gives him a high place in English literature.
  11. Cortez—Balboa, not Cortez, was discoverer of the Pacific Ocean.
  14. Darien—The Isthmus of Panama.

Poem Development: Give the meaning of the first four lines; also lines 5–8. Have you ever experienced a feeling akin to that described in lines 9–14? Express these lines in your own words. Summarize the poem, giving its theme and central thought.

Interpretations: Fealty; deep-browed Homer; its pure serene; ken; wild surmise.

Significant Expressions: Quote lines most significant of the meaning of the poem as a whole. What is the figure of speech in line 9? line 11?

WHEN I HAVE FEARS THAT I MAY CEASE TO BE

John Keats

Poem Interest: Early in his life, Keats found himself face to face with approaching death. Possessed of an extraordinary ability for poetic expression, and ardently in love with a beautiful girl, he saw life as he would have it just within his grasp. But knowing that a dread disease had already fastened upon him, he was forced to stand helplessly by and watch his dreams crumble into dust and sweep away into the darkness of the unknown . . .

> When I have fears that I may cease to be
> Before my pen has gleaned my teeming brain,
> Before high-pilèd books, in charact'ry,
> Hold like rich garners the full-ripened grain;
> 5 When I behold, upon the night's starred face,
> Huge cloudy symbols of a high romance,
> And think that I may never live to trace
> Their shadows, with the magic hand of chance;
> And when I feel, fair creature of an hour,
> 10 That I shall never look upon thee more,
> Never have relish in the faery power
> Of unreflecting love; then on the shore
> Of the wide world I stand alone, and think
> Till love and fame to nothingness do sink.

Poem Development: What is the first fear that the poet expresses? The second fear? Give the meaning of lines 5–8 in your own words. Give the theme and central thought.

Although the influencing factors in each case differ to some extent, Keats' situation as pictured here is not unlike the stark nothingness with which Milton was faced when he first realized the permanency of his blindness. Both Keats and Milton felt themselves flooded with the desire to write on and on, the one slowly dying from an incurable malady; the other already dead, as he then believed, to any hope of using his one great talent. Reread Milton's *On His Blindness* and compare the thoughts of one who clung to his faith and his God in spite of the crushing weight of his blindness, with the thoughts of the other who wandered off alone in bleak and utter discouragement. Comment on these two reactions.

Interpretations: Line 2; the full-ripened grain; magic hand of chance; never have relish.

Significant Expressions: Quote the lines which give the feeling of utter discouragement. Give the figure of speech in line 4.

ODE TO A NIGHTINGALE

John Keats

Poem Interest: On a fragrant summer eve, shortly after the sad death of his dearly loved brother, Keats sought the solitude of a garden spot where he might be quiet and alone. Suddenly, a nightingale in a nearby tree burst into song, and the music accompanied and inspired his thought. This poem is a delicately sad blending of the anguished musing of the poet, and the pure notes of the bird's melody.

    My heart aches, and a drowsy numbness pains
        My sense, as though of hemlock I had drunk,
    Or emptied some dull opiate to the drains
        One minute past, and Lethe-wards had sunk;
5   'Tis not through envy of thy happy lot,
        But being too happy in thine happiness—
          That thou, light-wingèd Dryad of the trees,
            In some melodious plot
    Of beechen green, and shadows numberless,
10   Singest of summer in full-throated ease.

    O, for a draught of vintage! that hath been
        Cooled a long age in the deep-delvèd earth,
    Tasting of Flora and the country green,
        Dance, and Provençal song, and sun-burnt mirth!
15   O for a beaker full of the warm South,
        Full of the true, the blushful Hippocrene,
          With beaded bubbles winking at the brim,
            And purple-stainèd mouth;
    That I might drink, and leave the world unseen,
20   And with thee fade away into the forest dim;
    Fade far away, dissolve, and quite forget
        What thou among the leaves hast never known,

    2. Hemlock—A drug made from hemlock, a poisonous herb.
    4. Lethe-wards—Lethe is a river in Hades, whose water when drunk would cause one to forget the past. "Lethe-wards" of course means "toward" or "in the direction of Lethe."
    7. Dryads—Wood nymphs.
    13. Flora—Goddess of flowers and the spring.
    14. Provençal song—Songs of the troubadours of Provençal in southern France.
    16. Hippocrene—A spring sacred to the goddesses who presided over poetry, art and sciences (the Muses).

The weariness, the fever, and the fret
　　Here, where men sit and hear each other groan;
25 Where palsy shakes a few, sad, last gray hairs;
　　　Where youth grows pale, and specter-thin and dies;
　　　　Where but to think is to be full of sorrow
　　　　　And leaden-eyed despairs;
　　Where Beauty cannot keep her lustrous eyes
30 　　　Or new Love pine at them beyond tomorrow.

Away! away! for I will fly to thee,
　　Not charioted by Bacchus and his pards,
But on the viewless wings of Poesy,
　　Though the dull brain perplexes and retards
35 Already with thee! tender is the night,
　　And haply the Queen-Moon is on her throne,
　　　Clustered around by all her starry Fays;
　　　　But here there is no light,
　　Save what from heaven is with the breezes blown
40 　　　Through verdurous glooms and winding mossy ways.

I cannot see what flowers are at my feet,
　　Nor what soft incense hangs upon the boughs,
But, in embalmèd darkness, guess each sweet
　　Wherewith the seasonable month endows
45 The grass, the thicket, and the fruit-tree wild;
　　White hawthorne, and the pastoral eglantine;
　　　Fast fading violets covered up in leaves;
　　　　And mid-May's eldest child,
　　The coming musk-rose, full of dewy wine,
50 　　　The murmurous haunt of flies on summer eves.

Darkling I listen; and, for many a time
　　I have been half in love with easeful Death,
Called him soft names in many a musèd rhyme,
　　To take into the air my quiet breath;
55 Now more than ever seems it rich to die,
　　To cease upon the midnight with no pain,
　　　While thou are pouring forth thy soul abroad
　　　　In such an ecstasy!

　32. BACCHUS—God of wine. His chariot is often represented as being drawn by two leopards (pards).　　37. FAYS—Fairies.

> Still wouldst thou sing, and I have ears in vain—
> 60   To thy high requiem become a sod.
>
> Thou wast not born for death, immortal Bird!
>   No hungry generations tread thee down;
> The voice I hear this passing night was heard
>   In ancient days by emperor and clown;
> 65 Perhaps the self-same song that found a path
>   Through the sad heart of Ruth, when, sick for home,
>   She stood in tears amid the alien corn;
>   The same that oft-times hath
>   Charmed magic casements, opening on the foam
> 70   Of perilous seas, in faëry lands forlorn.
>
> Forlorn! the very word is like a bell
>   To toll me back from thee to my sole self!
> Adieu! the fancy cannot cheat so well
>   As she is famed to do, deceiving elf.
> 75 Adieu! adieu! thy plaintive anthem fades
>   Past the near meadows, over the still stream,
>   Up the hill-side; and now 'tis buried deep
>   In the next valley-glades.
>   Was it a vision, or a waking dream?
> 80   Fled is that music:—Do I wake or sleep?

60. REQUIEM—Hymn for the dead.
64. CLOWN—Peasant.
66. RUTH—See *Ruth* in the Bible. With her mother-in-law Naomi, Ruth left her home and went to Bethlehem.

Poem Development: Why does the poet's heart ache? What is the wish expressed in the second stanza? The third stanza refers to what sorrow that Keats had recently experienced? In what way could the poet join the bird? What sense is appealed to in the fifth stanza? How could the song of the nightingale make death easier? Who have been charmed by the bird in years gone by? How does the poet feel when the song dies away? Write a précis of the poem as a whole, giving the theme and central thought.

Interpretations: Pains my sense (l. 1); line 3; draught of vintage (l. 11); beaker (l. 15); youth grows pale (l. 26); verdurous gloom (l. 40); enbalmèd darkness (l. 43); pastoral eglantine (l. 46); coming musk-rose (l. 49); line 60; alien corn (l. 67).

Significant Expressions: Quote the most significant lines in each stanza and give your reason for choosing them. Give the figure of speech in line 17. Memorize stanza 7.

JOHN KEATS

ODE ON A GRECIAN URN

John Keats

Poem Interest: Our appreciation of any work of art is measured by our sensitivity to beauty. To Keats, a passionate lover of all beauty, the sight of a Grecian urn with its beautifully carved figures and scenes was inspiration for the following ode . . .

Thou still unravished bride of quietness,
 Thou foster-child of silence and slow time,
Sylvan historian, who canst thus express
 A flowery tale more sweetly than our rhyme:
5 What leaf-fringed legend haunts about thy shape
 Of deities or mortals, or of both,
  In Tempe or the dales of Arcady?
What men or gods are these? What maidens loth?
What mad pursuit? What struggle to escape?
10 What pipes and timbrels? What wild ecstasy?

Heard melodies are sweet, but those unheard
 Are sweeter; therefore, ye soft pipes, play on;
Not to the sensual ear, but, more endeared,
 Pipe to the spirit ditties of no tone.
15 Fair youth, beneath the trees, thou canst not leave
 Thy song, nor ever can those trees be bare;
  Bold Lover, never, never canst thou kiss,
Though winning near the goal—yet, do not grieve;
 She cannot fade, though thou hast not thy bliss,
20 Forever wilt thou love, and she be fair!

Ah, happy, happy boughs! that cannot shed
 Your leaves, nor ever bid the Spring adieu;
And, happy melodist, unwearièd,
 Forever piping songs forever new;

1. Because undisturbed and unmolested, the urn has retained its original beauty and purity.
2. So-called because it has been preserved by silence and time.
3. Sylvan historian—Historian of rural scenes.
7. Tempe—A valley in Greece, famed for its beauty and sacred to Apollo the sun god.
7. Arcady—A district of Greece inhabited by simple, contented people. It has become a symbol of peace and happiness.

ELP

25   More happy love! more happy, happy love!
      Forever warm and still to be enjoyed,
        Forever panting, and forever young;
   All breathing human passion far above,
      That leaves a heart high-sorrowful and cloyed,
30   A burning forehead, and a parching tongue.

   Who are these coming to the sacrifice?
      To what green altar, O mysterious priest,
   Lead'st thou that heifer lowing at the skies,
      And all her silken flanks with garlands dressed?
35   What little town by river or sea shore,
      Or mountain-built with peaceful citadel,
        Is emptied of this folk, this pious morn?
   And, little town, thy streets for evermore
      Will silent be; and not a soul to tell
40   Why thou art desolate, can e'er return.

   O Attic shape! Fair attitude! with brede
      Of marble men and maidens overwrought,
   With forest branches and the trodden weed;
      Thou, silent form, dost tease us out of thought
45   As doth eternity. Cold Pastoral!
      When old age shall this generation waste,
        Thou shalt remain, in midst of other woe
   Than ours, a friend to man, to whom thou say'st,
      "Beauty is truth, truth beauty,"—that is all
50   Ye know on earth, and all ye need to know.

   41. ATTIC SHAPE—The urn. "Attic" means "Athenian." Attic sculpture is marked by its simplicity and purity.   41. BREDE—Decoration.
   45. PASTORAL—That which pictures rural life and scenes.

   Poem Development: Try to find a picture of a Grecian urn which will show how the figures and scenes are depicted. The wonderful poetic imagination of Keats made the figures come to life. The first four lines are a salutation to the urn. Why is the urn called "sylvan historian"? Lines 5–10 give the pictures as the poet saw them at first glance. What were they? Now give in detail the specific pictures that the poet saw (stanzas 2, 3 and 4). The last stanza is addressed to the urn. What is the thought expressed in it? Give the theme of the poem as a whole. What is the central thought?
   Interpretations: Flowery tale; pipes and timbrels; lines 11 and 12; line 14; cloyed; fair attitude; teas; cold Pastoral.

THE EVE OF ST. AGNES

John Keats

Poem Interest: January 21st is supposedly the date of the death of Saint Agnes, a Roman maiden who died a martyr. The evening of January 20th is therefore kept in memory as St. Agnes' Eve, and is attended with celebration and festivity. There is an old superstition, too, connected with this night which promises each maiden who follows certain rites a vision of her future husband in a dream. Madeline, a beautiful maiden of medieval times meticulously obeyed all the rules. The poem will tell you how the charm worked.

> St. Agnes' Eve—ah, bitter chill it was!
> The owl, for all his feathers, was a-cold;
> The hare limped trembling through the frozen grass,
> And silent was the flock in woolly fold;
> 5   Numb were the beadsman's fingers, while he told
> His rosary, and while his frosted breath,
> Like pious incense from a censer old,
> Seemed taking flight for heaven, without a death,
> Past the sweet Virgin's picture, while his prayer he saith.

5. Beadsman—One who "tells his beads" or prays for his benefactor.
7. Censer—A vessel in which incense is burned.

10 　　His prayer he saith, this patient, holy man;
　　　　Then takes his lamp, and riseth from his knees,
　　　　And back returneth, meagre, barefoot, wan,
　　　　Along the chapel aisle by slow degrees.
　　　　The sculptured dead, on each side, seem to freeze,
15 　　Emprisoned in black, purgatorial rails:
　　　　Knights, ladies, praying in dumb orat'ries,
　　　　He passeth by; and his weak spirit fails,
　　To think how they may ache in icy hoods and mails.

　　　　Northward he turneth through a little door,
20 　　And scarce three steps ere Music's golden tongue
　　　　Flattered to tears this aged man and poor;
　　　　But no—already had his death-bell rung;
　　　　The joys of all his life were said and sung;
　　　　His was harsh penance on St. Agnes' Eve:
25 　　Another way he went, and soon among
　　　　Rough ashes sat he for his soul's reprieve,
　　And all night kept awake, for sinners' sake to grieve.

　　　　That ancient beadsman heard the prelude soft;
　　　　And so it chanced, for many a door was wide,
30 　　From hurry to and fro. Soon, up aloft,
　　　　The silver, snarling trumpets 'gan to chide;
　　　　The level chambers, ready with their pride,
　　　　Were glowing to receive a thousand guests;
　　　　The carvèd angels, ever eager-eyed,
35 　　Stared, where upon their heads the cornice rests,
　　With hair blown back, and wings put cross-wise on their breasts.

　　　　At length burst in the argent revelry,
　　　　With plume, tiara, and all rich array,
　　　　Numerous as shadows haunting faerily
40 　　The brain, new stuffed, in youth, with triumphs gay
　　　　Of old romance. These let us wish away,

15. PURGATORIAL—Atoning, cleansing.
16. ORAT'RIES—Oratories; places of prayer.
37. ARGENT—Silvery; shining like silver.
38. TIARA—An ornament worn on the head; a crown.

And turn, sole-thoughted, to one lady there,
Whose heart had brooded, all that wintry day,
On love, and winged St. Agnes' saintly care,
45 As she had heard old dames full many times declare.

They told her how, upon St. Agnes' Eve,
Young virgins might have visions of delight,
And soft adorings from their loves receive
Upon the honeyed middle of the night,
50 If ceremonies due they did aright:
As, supperless to bed they must retire,
And couch supine their beauties, lily-white;
Nor look behind, nor sideways, but require
Of Heaven with upward eyes for all that they desire.

55 Full of this whim was thoughtful Madeline:
The music, yearning like a god in pain,
She scarcely heard; her maiden eyes divine,
Fixed on the floor, saw many a sweeping train
Pass by—she heeded not at all; in vain
60 Came many a tip-toe, amorous cavalier,
And back retired, not cooled by high disdain,
But she saw not—her heart was otherwhere:
She sighed for Agnes' dreams, the sweetest of the year.

She danced along with vague, regardless eyes,
65 Anxious her lips, her breathing quick and short:
The hallowed hour was near at hand; she sighs
Amid the timbrels, and the thronged resort
Of whisperers in anger or in sport;
'Mid looks of love, defiance, hate, and scorn,
70 Hoodwinked with faery fancy, all amort
Save to St. Agnes and her lambs unshorn,
And all the bliss to be before to-morrow morn.

52. COUCH SUPINE THEIR BEAUTIES—Lay down their bodies.
67. TIMBRELS—Hand-drums; tambourines.
70. AMORT—Deadened; oblivious.
71. LAMBS UNSHORN—A few days after her death, Saint Agnes was seen by her parents, in a vision, surrounded by angels and with a lamb close beside her. Thereafter the lamb was symbolic of her purity, and on the day sacred to her, two unshorn lambs were dedicated to her.

So, purposing each moment to retire,
She lingered still. Meantime, across the moors,
75 Had come young Porphyro, with heart of fire
For Madeline. Beside the portal doors,
Buttressed from moonlight, stands he, and implores
All saints to give him sight of Madeline,
But for one moment in the tedious hours,
80 That he might gaze and worship all unseen;
Perchance speak, kneel, touch, kiss—in sooth such things have been.

He ventures in: let no buzzed whisper tell;
All eyes be muffled, or a hundred swords
Will storm his heart, Love's fev'rous citadel:
85 For him, those chambers held barbarian hordes,
Hyena foemen, and hot-blooded lords,
Whose very dogs would execrations howl
Against his lineage; not one breast affords
Him any mercy, in that mansion foul,
90 Save one old beldame, weak in body and in soul.

Ah, happy chance! the aged creature came,
Shuffling along with ivory-headed wand,
To where he stood, hid from the torch's flame,
Behind a broad hall-pillar, far beyond
95 The sound of merriment and chorus bland:
He startled her; but soon she knew his face,
And grasped his fingers in her palsied hand,
Saying, "Mercy, Porphyro! hie thee from this place;
They are all here to-night, the whole blood-thirsty race!

100 "Get hence! get hence! there's dwarfish Hildebrand;
He had a fever late, and in the fit
He cursèd thee and thine, both house and land.
Then there's that old Lord Maurice, not a whit
More tame for his gray hairs.—Alas me! flit!
105 Flit like a ghost away."—"Ah, gossip dear,

85. BARBARIAN HORDES—Porphyro came from a bordering country at war with the inmates of the castle.
88. AGAINST HIS LINEAGE—Against his family or ancestors.
90. BELDAME—An old woman.
105. GOSSIP—Godmother; grandmother.

We're safe enough; here in this arm-chair sit,
And tell me how"—"Good saints! not here, not here!
Follow me, child, or else these stones will be thy bier."

He followed through a lowly archèd way,
110 Brushing the cobwebs with his lofty plume;
And as she muttered "Well-a—well-a-day!"
He found him in a little moonlight room,
Pale, latticed, chill, and silent as a tomb.
"Now tell me where is Madeline," said he,
115 "O tell me, Angela, by the holy loom
Which none but secret sisterhood may see,
When they St. Agnes' wool are weaving piously."

"St. Agnes! ah, it is St. Agnes' Eve—
Yet men will murder upon holy days:
120 Thou must hold water in a witch's sieve,
And be liege-lord of all the elves and fays,
To venture so; it fills me with amaze
To see thee, Porphyro!—St. Agnes' Eve!
God's help! my lady fair the conjuror plays
125 This very night: good angels her deceive!
But let me laugh awhile, I've mickle time to grieve."

Feebly she laugheth in the languid moon,
While Porphyro upon her face doth look,
Like puzzled urchin on an aged crone
130 Who keepeth closed a wondrous riddle-book,
As spectacled she sits in chimney nook.
But soon his eyes grew brilliant, when she told
His lady's purpose; and he scarce could brook
Tears, at the thought of those enchantments cold,
135 And Madeline asleep in lap of legends old.

Sudden a thought came like a full-blown rose,
Flushing his brow, and in his painèd heart

115–118 On St. Agnes' day, her sheep are shorn and the wool spun and woven into garments for the poor by chosen sisters or nuns.
120. HOLD WATER IN A WITCH'S SIEVE—That is, lead a charmed life.
124. CONJUROR PLAYS—Plays up to the superstition.
126. MICKLE—Much.

       Made purple riot; then doth he propose
       A stratagem, that makes the beldame start:
140   "A cruel man and impious thou art!
       Sweet lady, let her pray, and sleep, and dream
       Alone with her good angels, far apart
       From wicked men like thee. Go, go! I deem
  Thou canst not surely be the same that thou didst seem."

145   "I will not harm her, by all saints I swear,"
       Quoth Porphyro. "O may I ne'er find grace
       When my weak voice shall whisper its last prayer,
       If one of her soft ringlets I displace,
       Or look with ruffian passion in her face!
150   Good Angela, believe me by these tears;
       Or I will, even in a moment's space,
       Awake, with horrid shout, my foemen's ears,
  And beard them, though they be more fanged than wolves and bears."

       "Ah, why wilt thou affright a feeble soul?
155   A poor, weak, palsy-stricken, churchyard thing,
       Whose passing-bell may ere the midnight toll;
       Whose prayers for thee, each morn and evening,
       Were never missed." Thus plaining, doth she bring
       A gentler speech from burning Porphyro;
160   So woeful, and of such deep sorrowing,
       That Angela gives promise she will do
  Whatever he shall wish, betide her weal or woe.

       Which was, to lead him, in close secrecy,
       Even to Madeline's chamber, and there hide
165   Him in a closet, of such privacy
       That he might see her beauty unespied,
       And win perhaps that night a peerless bride,
       While legioned faeries paced the coverlet,
       And pale enchantment held her sleepy-eyed.
170   Never on such a night have lovers met,
  Since Merlin paid his demon all the monstrous debt.

171. Merlin, the son of a demon, was a wizard or magician, who became a victim of his own magic.

"It shall be as thou wishest," said the dame:
"All cates and dainties shall be storèd there
Quickly on this feast-night; by the tambour frame
Her own lute thou wilt see: no time to spare,
For I am slow and feeble, and scarce dare
On such a catering trust my dizzy head.
Wait here, my child, with patience; kneel in prayer
The while. Ah, thou must needs the lady wed,
Or may I never leave my grave among the dead."

So saying, she hobbled off with busy fear.
The lover's endless minutes slowly passed.
The dame returned, and whispered in his ear
To follow her, with aged eyes aghast
From fright of dim espial. Safe at last,
Through many a dusky gallery, they gain
The maiden's chamber, silken, hushed, and chaste,
Where Porphyro took covert, pleased amain.
His poor guide hurried back, with agues in her brain.

Her faltering hand upon the balustrade,
Old Angela was feeling for the stair,
When Madeline, St. Agnes' charmèd maid,
Rose, like a missioned spirit, unaware.
With silver taper's light, and pious care,
She turned, and down the aged gossip led
To a safe level matting. Now prepare,
Young Porphyro, for gazing on that bed:
She comes, she comes again, like ring-dove frayed and fled.

Out went the taper as he hurried in;
Its little smoke, in pallid moonshine, died:
She closed the door, she panted, all akin
To spirits of the air and visions wide:
No uttered syllable, or woe betide!

173. CATES—Delicacies.
174. TAMBOUR FRAME—A frame for embroidery shaped like a tambour or drum.
188. PLEASED AMAIN—Greatly pleased.
193. MISSIONED SPIRIT—Spirit with a mission.
203. NO UTTERED SYLLABLE—One of the rites was to speak to no one upon retiring.

But to her heart, her heart was voluble,
205 Paining with eloquence her balmy side,
As though a tongueless nightingale should swell
Her throat in vain, and die, heart-stifled, in her dell.

A casement high and triple-arched there was,
All garlanded with carven imageries
210 Of fruits and flowers and bunches of knot-grass,
And diamonded with panes of quaint device,
Innumerable of stains and splendid dyes
As are the tiger-moth's deep damasked wings;
And in the midst, 'mong thousand heraldries,
215 And twilight saints, and dim emblazonings,
A shielded scutcheon blushed with blood of queens and kings.

Full on this casement shone the wintry moon,
And threw warm gules on Madeline's fair breast,
As down she knelt for Heaven's grace and boon;
220 Rose-bloom fell on her hands, together prest,
And on her silver cross soft amethyst,
And on her hair a glory, like a saint:
She seemed a splendid angel, newly drest,
Save wings, for heaven. Porphyro grew faint,
225 She knelt so pure a thing, so free from mortal taint.

Anon his heart revives: her vespers done,
Of all its wreathèd pearls her hair she frees:
Unclasps her warmèd jewels one by one;
Loosens her fragrant bodice; by degrees
230 Her rich attire creeps rustling to her knees;
Half-hidden, like a mermaid in sea-weed,
Pensive awhile she dreams awake, and sees,
In fancy, fair St. Agnes in her bed,
But dares not look behind or all the charm is fled.

235 Soon, trembling in her soft and chilly nest,
In sort of wakeful swoon, perplexed she lay,

206. TONGUELESS NIGHTINGALE—Look up the legend of Philomel.
216. SCUTCHEON—Escutcheon; a surface, usually in the form of a shield upon which armorial bearings are depicted and displayed.
218. GULES—Red color.
234. DARES NOT LOOK BEHIND—Another requirement of the charm.

Until the poppied warmth of sleep oppressed
Her soothed limbs, and soul fatigued away;
Flown, like a thought, until the morrow-day;
240 Blissfully havened both from joy and pain;
Clasped like a missal where swart Paynims pray;
Blinded alike from sunshine and from rain,
As though a rose should shut, and be a bud again.

Stolen to this paradise, and so entranced,
245 Porphyro gazed upon her empty dress,
And listened to her breathing, if it chanced
To wake into a slumberous tenderness;
Which when he heard, that minute did he bless,
And breathed himself; then from the closet crept,
250 Noiseless as fear in a wide wilderness,
And over the hushed carpet, silent, stept,
And 'tween the curtains peeped, where, lo! how fast she slept.

Then by the bedside, where the faded moon
Made a dim, silver twilight, soft he set
255 A table, and, half-anguished, threw thereon
A cloth of woven crimson, gold, and jet—
O for some drowsy Morphean amulet!
The boisterous, midnight, festive clarion,
The kettle-drum, and far-heard clarionet
260 Affray his ears, though but in dying tone;
The hall door shuts again, and all the noise is gone.

And still she slept an azure-lidded sleep,
In blanchèd linen, smooth and lavendered,
While he from forth the closet brought a heap
265 Of candied apple, quince, and plum, and gourd;
With jellies soother than the creamy curd,
And lucent syrops, tinct with cinnamon;

241. MISSAL—Prayer book. The meaning is that her eyes are as tightly closed in sleep as a prayer book would be in the land of pagans (Paynims).
252. CURTAINS—Curtains of the bed.
257. MORPHEAN AMULET—A charm of Morpheus to produce sleep. Morpheus was the god of dreams.
265. GOURD—A hard-shelled fruit.   266. SOOTHER—Smoother.

>   Manna and dates, in argosy transferred
>   From Fez; and spiced dainties, every one
> 270   From silken Samarcand to cedared Lebanon.
>
>   These delicates he heaped with glowing hand
>   On golden dishes and in baskets bright
>   Of wreathed silver; sumptuous they stand
>   In the retired quiet of the night,
> 275   Filling the chilly room with perfume light.
>   "And now, my love, my seraph fair, awake!
>   Thou art my heaven, and I thine eremite;
>   Open thine eyes, for meek St. Agnes' sake,
>   Or I shall drowse beside thee, so my soul doth ache."
>
> 280 Thus whispering, his warm, unnervèd arm
>   Sank in her pillow. Shaded was her dream
>   By the dusk curtains—'t was a midnight charm
>   Impossible to melt as icèd stream;
>   The lustrous salvers in the moonlight gleam;
> 285   Broad golden fringe upon the carpet lies.
>   It seemed he never, never could redeem
>   From such a stedfast spell his lady's eyes;
>   So mused awhile, entoiled in woofèd phantasies.
>
>   Awakening up, he took her hollow lute—
> 290   Tumultuous,—and in chords that tenderest be,
>   He played an ancient ditty, long since mute,
>   In Provence called "La belle dame sans mercy,"
>   Close to her ear touching the melody;
>   Wherewith disturbed, she uttered a soft moan;
> 295 He ceased—she panted quick—and suddenly
>   Her blue affrayed eyes wide open shone;
>   Upon his knees he sank, pale as smooth-sculptured stone.
>
>   Her eyes were open, but she still beheld,
>   Now wide awake, the vision of her sleep:

268–269. IN ARGOSY TRANSFERRED FROM FEZ—Transferred by ship from Fez in northern Africa.
  270. SAMARCAND—A city in Turkestan noted for its fine silks.
  270. LEBANON—A mountain range in Syria from which the "cedars of Lebanon" came.   277. EREMITE—A hermit or holy man.
  284. SALVERS—Trays.   288. WOOFÈD PHANTASIES—Confused fancies.
  292. LA BELLE DAME SANS MERCY—The beautiful lady without pity.

300 There was a painful change that nigh expelled
     The blisses of her dream so pure and deep;
     At which fair Madeline began to weep,
     And moan forth witless words with many a sigh,
     While still her gaze on Porphyro would keep,
305 Who knelt, with joined hands and piteous eye,
   Fearing to move or speak, she looked so dreamingly.

     "Ah, Porphyro!" said she, "but even now
     Thy voice was at sweet tremble in mine ear,
     Made tuneable with every sweetest vow;
310 And those sad eyes were spiritual and clear:
     How changed thou art! how pallid, chill, and drear!
     Give me that voice again, my Porphyro,
     Those looks immortal, those complainings dear!
     Oh leave me not in this eternal woe,
315 For if thou diest, my love, I know not where to go."

     Beyond a mortal man impassioned far
     At these voluptuous accents, he arose,
     Ethereal, flushed, and like a throbbing star
     Seen 'mid the sapphire heaven's deep repose;
320 Into her dream he melted, as the rose
     Blendeth its odour with the violet—
     Solution sweet: meantime the frost-wind blows
     Like Love's alarum pattering the sharp sleet
   Against the window-panes; St. Agnes' moon hath set.

325 'T is dark; quick pattereth the flaw-blown sleet.
     "This is no dream, my bride, my Madeline!"
     'T is dark; the icèd gusts still rave and beat.
     "No dream, alas! alas! and woe is mine!
     Porphyro will leave me here to fade and pine—
330 Cruel! what traitor could thee hither bring?
     I curse not, for my heart is lost in thine,
     Though thou forsakest a deceivèd thing,
   A dove forlorn and lost, with sick unprunèd wing."

     "My Madeline! sweet dreamer! lovely bride!
335 Say, may I be for aye thy vassal blest?

Thy beauty's shield, heart-shaped and vermeil-dyed?
Ah, silver shrine, here will I take my rest
After so many hours of toil and quest,
A famished pilgrim—saved by miracle.
340 Though I have found, I will not rob thy nest,
Saving of thy sweet self; if thou think'st well
To trust, fair Madeline, to no rude infidel.

"Hark! 't is an elfin-storm from faery land,
Of haggard seeming but a boon indeed:
345 Arise—arise! the morning is at hand;
The bloated wassailers will never heed.
Let us away, my love, with happy speed;
There are no ears to hear, or eyes to see,—
Drowned all in Rhenish and the sleepy mead.
350 Awake! arise! my love, and fearless be,
For o'er the southern moors I have a home for thee."

She hurried at his words, beset with fears,
For there were sleeping dragons all around,
At glaring watch, perhaps, with ready spears—
355 Down the wide stairs a darkling way they found:—
In all the house was heard no human sound;
A chain-dropped lamp was flickering by each door;
The arras, rich with horseman, hawk, and hound,
Fluttered in the besieging wind's uproar;
360 And the long carpets rose along the gusty floor.

They glide, like phantoms, into the wide hall;
Like phantoms to the iron porch they glide,
Where lay the porter in uneasy sprawl,
With a huge empty flaggon by his side.
365 The wakeful bloodhound rose, and shook his hide,
But his sagacious eye an inmate owns.
By one, and one, the bolts full easy slide;—
The chains lie silent on the footworn stones;—
The key turns, and the door upon its hinges groans.

336. VERMEIL-DYED—Dyed red, or vermilion.
346. WASSAILERS—Revelers.
349. RHENISH—Rhenish wine; that is, from the region of the Rhine River.
349. MEAD—A drink made from honey. Why "sleepy"?
358. ARRAS—Tapestries.

370   And they are gone; aye, ages long ago
      These lovers fled away into the storm.
      That night the Baron dreamt of many a woe;
      And all his warrior-guests, with shade and form
      Of witch, and demon, and large coffin-worm,
375   Were long be-nightmared. Angela the old
      Died palsy-twitched, with meagre face deform.
      The beadsman, after thousand aves told,
      For aye unsought-for slept among his ashes cold.

377. AVES—Prayers (Ave Marias).

Poem Development: Lines 1–36: What is the sense most appealed to in the first stanza? How were medieval castles heated? Describe the old beadsman. Why did he not join the revelers? What sense is appealed to in the fourth stanza? How many guests were expected?

Lines 36–72: Describe the costumes at the feast. Of what was Madeline thinking? How did she receive the cavaliers who came for her?

Lines 73–189: Why was Porphyro not welcome at the castle? Who was the friend from whom he might expect help? Why was Angela worried? What was Porphyro's plan?

Lines 190–288: What sense is appealed to in lines 208–225? 257–261? 262–270? What are the chief impressions you gain from this section? What is the chief appeal of Keats' style of writing as illustrated in this section?

Lines 289–378: How did Porphyro awaken Madeline? Had she already seen him in her dreams? Describe their departure. What happened to old Angela and the beadsman? Is the last stanza a fitting one?

Write a précis of the poem. Give the theme and the central thought of the poem.

Interpretations: Lines 8 and 9; sculptured dead (l. 14); icy hoods and mails (l. 18); upon their heads the cornice rests (l. 35); amorous cavaliers (l. 60); buttressed from moonlight (l. 77); hyena foeman (l. 86); had a fever late (l. 101); line 103; fays (l. 121); stratagem (l. 139); line 144; lines 152 and 153; line 156; plaining (l. 158); weal or woe (l. 162); lines 176 and 177; dim espial (l. 185); agues in her brain (l. 189); poppied warmth (l. 237); noiseless as fear (l. 250); line 260; line 267; line 277; unnervèd arm (l. 280); lines 298 and 299; flaw-blown (l. 325); lines 343 and 344; sleeping dragons (l. 353).

Significant Expressions: Give the figure of speech in each of the following lines: 7, 20, 31, 39, 84, 113, 136, 361. List the words in the first stanza that give the feeling of cold. Lines 1–9, 208–225, and 262–270 are famous passages which are often quoted. Give reasons why you think these passages are so famous. Memorize the passage which you like best.

THE HISTORY OF POETRY IN ENGLAND

The Victorian Era (1840-1900)

General Characteristics

Victorian poetry, although flavored strongly with romanticism, reflects new tendencies in science and religion, and also the great growth of the country itself. The age was one of development of inventions and scientific discoveries, but even out of these unromantic fields, inspiration was found for poetry. There is a reflection, too, of the religious unrest caused by scientific writings, for the poetry of the period is distinctly of a thoughtful type and is characterized by a high moral tone. The Victorian era has been called an age of prose, but it gave us the names of two outstanding poets, Tennyson and Browning, and of many minor poets. A large number of new verse forms were introduced, and a new literary form, the dramatic monologue, came into existence.

Alfred, Lord Tennyson (1809-1892)

Tennyson was born in Lincolnshire. He was one of twelve children, nearly every one of whom wrote poetry. His father was a preacher. At an early age, he was sent to school, but like Shelley, he hated it because of the brutality of the teachers. His father finally tutored him

and prepared him for college. It was while in college that he contracted a friendship with Arthur Hallam which was to last until the latter's death and which was to have a great influence upon the poet's life.

Tennyson seems to have had the writing of poetry always dominant in his mind, for early in his college days he began publishing poems. Because of the death of his father in 1830 he left college without taking a degree. He had already published his first volume of poems, *Poems Chiefly Lyrical*, and two years later he published another volume called *Poems*. The latter was published when he was only twenty-three, and among the poems are to be found the familiar *Lady of Shalott*.

Although the death of Hallam plunged Tennyson into despair, he continued to write, even though he published nothing for ten years. Finally, in 1842, he published *Poems by Alfred Tennyson*. These were immediately received with favor. They contained *Ulysses*, *Morte d'Arthur*, and the appealing lyric, *Break, Break, Break*, written on the death of Hallam. Tennyson continued to write with success and in 1850 was made Poet Laureate.

Of the Victorian poets, Tennyson is probably the one who most truly reflects the spirit of the times. His poetry is thoughtful and at times reflective of the new discoveries in science. Some of his verse is deeply religious and concerned with the reforms of the day. He wrote both narrative and lyric poetry. His narratives include *Idylls of the King, Enoch Arden,* and the *Princess.* Of his lyrics, several which are widely known are *Sweet and Low, Bugle Song, Tears, Idle Tears,* and *Flower in the Crannied Wall.* There seems almost no end to his lyrical themes. He writes of faith, of love, of war, of national loyalty and pride, and of death, all in a musical rhythm which is exquisite in its form and skill. Two of his famous elegies are *Break, Break, Break* and *Crossing the Bar.* He died in 1892 at the age of eighty-three.

Robert Browning (1812–1889)

Robert Browning was born in a suburb of London. His father, who held a position in the Bank of England, was a man of some means; moreover, he sympathized with his son's love of poetry. Browning's education was most unusual. He owed little of it to schools. His early training came from his father who read him the tales of Troy, sang him to sleep with lyrics from the Greek, or taught him Latin grammar by twisting it into grotesque rhymes. From his mother, a woman of gentle nature, and simple, earnest religious faith, Browning inherited a love for drawing and music and a faith that remained steadfast in an age of doubt.

As he grew older he educated himself from his father's rich store of books. He attended a school in the neighborhood for four years; had a French tutor from the age of fourteen to sixteen, and in his eighteenth year attended some Greek lectures at London University. This was the extent of his schooling, yet he was one of the best educated men of his day.

Browning began writing poetry early. By the time he was twelve he had composed a number of poems, somewhat after the style of Byron, and tried to find a publisher who would bring them out. In 1833, when he was twenty-one, his first published poem, *Pauline,* appeared. He paid the printer with a hundred and fifty pounds given him by his aunt. Not a single copy of the poem was sold. It was indeed fortunate for Browning that he did not have to depend upon poetry for a living. Recognition from the general public was slow in coming. *Paracelsus,* published in 1835, met with little better success than *Pauline,* but it did win recognition in literary circles, where its author was looked upon as a man of genius of whom great things might be expected.

In 1846 Browning married Elizabeth Barrett, and the fifteen years of their married life were spent in Italy. The marriage is said to have been one of the happiest ever known. Browning's love for his wife finds expression in a number of his poems, particularly in *One Word More*. The years spent in Italy saw the maturing of Browning's genius. Italy itself was an inspiration to him, and here he wrote most of the poems published in the volume, *Men and Women*.

After his wife's death in 1861, Browning returned to England. He never visited Florence again. He took up his residence in London, spending his winters either in Switzerland or in Brittany. The fame and recognition which had been denied him in his earlier years came with interest in his later days. He was honored by Oxford, Cambridge, and Edinburgh. In 1861 there was formed the Browning Society for the study of his works. Poets dead and gone have frequently been the objects of such societies, but Browning alone in the history of our literature seems to have been so honored in his lifetime.

Elizabeth Barrett Browning (1806-1861)

Elizabeth Barrett began early to write and publish poetry. In 1840 a beloved brother died and she was prostrated with grief. Illness and the shock of her brother's death resulted in her becoming an invalid and for years she hardly left her room. She was intensely interested in the social problems of the day, as illustrated in the poem *Cry of the Children*. In 1846 she married Robert Browning and this marriage was an ideally happy one. Her *Sonnets from the Portuguese* are written of her love for her husband. They are exquisite lyrics. Mrs. Browning shows a great sympathy for humanity and a tenderness and sweetness of spirit that is unexcelled. She ranks among the greatest of women poets.

Matthew Arnold (1822-1888)

Arnold's father was headmaster at Rugby, and the boy received his education at Rugby and Oxford. In college Arnold won prizes for writing poetry. After his graduation he was inspector of schools for thirty-five years. For ten years he was professor of poetry at Oxford. Twice he visited the United States to study educational methods. Arnold had a happy home life, and was a cheerful, sincere man with a profound belief in culture as a means of advancement of civilization. He wrote narratives of which *Sohrab and Rustum* is considered the finest, and elegies, among which *Thyrsis* and *Rugby Chapel* are the best known. The first named elegy was written on the death of his friend, Arthur Clough, and the latter on the death of his father.

Dante Gabriel Rossetti (1828-1882)

Rossetti was born in London. His father had left Italy to escape political persecution, and was professor of Italian at King's College, University of London. At fourteen Rossetti began to study painting and at the same time to write verses. With a group of young painters and sculptors he organized the "Pre-Raphaelite Society." The members of this society believed that the purest form of pictorial art could be found among the painters who worked before the time of the great Italian artist, Raphael. Their slogan was naturalness and simplicity and they drew their inspiration from the painters preceding Raphael. Many of them wrote as well as painted, and Rossetti "often expressed the same or similar conceptions in both color and verse." Pictures were painted which were suggested by verse, and poetry was written which was suggested by pictures. Rossetti was known both as a painter and as a poet. One of his best poems, *The Blessed Damozel*, was written when he was only twenty. All of his poems contain careful detail which carried out the principles of the group which he represented. Their aim was to create beauty in a too formal and artificial world.

Christina Georgina Rossetti (1830-1894)

Christina Rossetti, the sister of Dante Rossetti, was born in London. In her early life she had an unhappy love affair because of a difference in religion and this cast a shadow of sadness over her whole life. She turned to religion for solace. She was often used as a model by her brothers because of the saint-like beauty of her face. She wrote religious lyrics and it has been said that she attained a purity of verse almost equal to that of Browning. She has been called the greatest poetess in the English language. In all of her poetry there is the simplicity of the Pre-Raphaelite group—it glows with an almost spiritual light. Her touch is delicate, as she combines nature and art in her verse. One of her best known lyrics is *Up Hill*.

Algernon Charles Swinburne (1837-1909)

Swinburne was born in London of aristocratic parents. His father was an admiral in the British Navy and his mother was the daughter of an Earl. He received his education at Eton and Balliol College, Oxford. He was thoroughly trained in French and Italian by his parents, and at college obtained exhaustive knowledge of Latin and Greek. Before settling in London, he travelled extensively. We have in Swinburne a thoroughly cultured, travelled, and aristocratic man. It would naturally follow that his productions would have as their themes, incidents from the classics. In London, he identified himself with the Pre-Raphaelite group. Swinburne, however, was something of a non-conformist, and Victorian England was a bit shocked by some of his verses. He was erratic and lived the life of a Bohemian. He felt that the Victorians took themselves too seriously, and that there was much pleasure to be gotten out of the world. His writing is remarkable for its perfection of technique and for its amazing fluency of vocabulary. Had Swinburne been a bit more conservative and not scorned conventionalities, he would undoubtedly have been made Poet Laureate, for he was called the greatest poet living at the time of Tennyson's death. He wrote a great number of poems dealing with nature, with child life, and of incidents based upon classic themes. His poetry is wonderfully melodious and contains vivid images. In *Songs before Sunrise* we see the Italian struggle for independence. Arthurian romance is depicted in *Tristram of Lyonesse*. One of his most beautiful lyrics is *A Child's Laughter*.

Oscar Wilde (1856–1900)

Wilde was born in Dublin. He finished his education at Oxford University, and it was while at Oxford that he was influenced by the Pre-Raphaelites. He is sometimes called "the apostle of beauty." He was among the last of the Victorians, and while he posed as an exponent of new ideas, he was really of an old school of thought. People were beginning to tire of a world of dreams and turn to everyday facts. Wilde was for a time regarded in the light of a social hero, but he did not remain long in London. He went to France and spent the rest of his life in Paris. Wilde wrote poetry in a witty vein but he is at times somewhat insincere. His best poem is *The Ballad of Reading Gaol*, written during a brief period of imprisonment.

William Ernest Henley (1849–1903)

Henley was born in Gloucester. All his life he suffered from a tubercular disease, and at one time he was forced to spend a period of twenty months in a hospital. During this time he became acquainted with Robert Louis Stevenson, and the friendship lasted many years. Stevenson and Henley wrote several plays together. Probably because of his affliction, Henley's poetry is imbued with a courage and vigor which he so desired to have himself and lacked. Some of it is redolent with the atmosphere of a sick room but all of it is musical and very beautiful. His nature lyrics are full of vivid images and beautiful melody of verse. He was an experimenter with free verse, but is best known for his short poem, *Invictus*.

Other Victorian Poets

One of the most interesting characters of the later Victorian days was William Morris, the author of a great deal of excellent, vivid, narrative poetry, inspired by his interest in the Middle Ages and in the old Norse legends. He was particularly successful in creating the atmosphere of the time of which he writes.

During the 90's come a number of poets whom it is difficult to classify. In many of them are evidences of some of the tendencies observable in contemporary poetry. Many of them lived on into the first decade of the twentieth century but in the case of all of them, their work was practically done by 1900. Among these are John Davidson, a realist, author of *Fleet Street Ecologues* and *Testaments*, a genuine poet but somewhat of a skeptic; Francis Thompson, a religious mystic, author of one great poem, *The Hound of Heaven;* Stephen Phillips, writer of dramas and lyrics; and Alfred Austin, Poet Laureate from 1896 to 1913.

Poetry of the Victorian Era

THE REVENGE

A BALLAD OF THE FLEET

Alfred, Lord Tennyson

Poem Interest: In the fall of 1591, at a time when England and Spain were at war, six English ships under the command of Lord Thomas Howard lay at anchor near Flores, one of the islands of the Azores. Many of the crews were on shore, and some of the men of every ship were sick and utterly unserviceable. Upon information of the approach of the Spanish fleet, the English ships took to flight, with the exception of the *Revenge*, commanded by Sir Richard Grenville. ... Tennyson tells the rest of the story ...

> At Flores in the Azores Sir Richard Grenville lay,
> And a pinnace, like a flutter'd bird, came flying from far away;
> "Spanish ships of war at sea! we have sighted fifty-three!"

1. Flores—One of the islands of the Azores group which lie in the mid-Atlantic, west of Portugal.
2. Pinnace—A light sailing vessel used as a tender.

355

Then sware Lord Thomas Howard: " 'Fore God I am no coward;
5 But I cannot meet them here, for my ships are out of gear,
And the half my men are sick. I must fly, but follow quick,
We are six ships of the line: can we fight with fifty-three?"

Then spake Sir Richard Grenville: "I know you are no coward;
You fly them for a moment to fight with them again,
10 But I've ninety men and more that are lying sick ashore;
I should count myself the coward if I left them, my Lord Howard,
To these Inquisition dogs and the devildoms of Spain."

So Lord Howard passed away with five ships of war that day,
Till he melted like a cloud in the silent summer heaven;
15 But Sir Richard bore in hand all his sick men from the land
Very carefully and slow,
Men of Bideford in Devon,
And we laid them on the ballast down below;
For we brought them all aboard,
20 And they blest him in their pain, that they were not left to Spain,
To the thumbscrew and the stake, for the glory of the Lord.
He had only a hundred seamen to work the ship and to fight,
And he sailed away from Flores till the Spaniard came in sight,
With his huge sea castles heaving upon the weather bow.

7. OF THE LINE—Equipped to fight.
12. INQUISITION DOGS—These were the days of the Spanish Inquisition. The *inquisitors,* or those charged with finding out heretics, sometimes tortured suspects to make them reveal their beliefs. The English were regarded as heretics by the Spaniards.   17. BIDEFORD—A seaport town in England.
17. DEVON—A section of England from which came many sea heroes.
24. SEA CASTLES—The Spanish galleons had three or four decks built up at the stern and bow giving the appearance of a castle.

25   "Shall we fight or shall we fly?
Good Sir Richard, tell us now,
For to fight is but to die!
There'll be little of us left, by the time this sun be set."
And Sir Richard said again: "We be all good Englishmen;
30 Let us bang these dogs of Seville, the children of the devil,
For I never turned my back upon Don or Devil yet."

Sir Richard spoke and he laugh'd and we roar'd a hurrah, and so
The little *Revenge* ran on, sheer into the heart of the foe,
With her hundred fighters on deck and her ninety sick below;
35 For half of their fleet to the right and half to the left were seen,
And the little *Revenge* ran on, thro' the long sea lane between.

Thousands of their soldiers looked down from their decks and laugh'd,
Thousands of their seamen made mock at the mad little craft
Running on and on, till delay'd
40 By their mountain-like *San Philip,* that, of fifteen hundred tons,
And up-shadowing high above us with her yawning tiers of guns,
Took the breath from our sails and we stay'd,
And while now the great *San Philip* hung above us like a cloud
Whence the thunderbolt will fall
45 Long and loud,
Four galleons drew away
From the Spanish fleet that day,
And two upon the larboard and two upon the starboard lay,
And the battle thunder broke from them all.

30. SEVILLE—A seaport town of Spain.
31. DON—A term given to Spanish noblemen or gentlemen.
42. AND WE STAY'D—Were becalmed and could not move.

50 And the sun went down, and the stars came out, far over the summer sea,
But never a moment ceased the fight of the one and the fifty-three.
Ship after ship, the whole night long, their high-built galleons came,
Ship after ship, the whole night long, with her battle thunder and flame;
Ship after ship, the whole night long, drew back with her dead and her shame,
55 For some were sunk, and many were shatter'd, and so could fight us no more—
God of battles, was ever a battle like this in the world before?

For he said: "Fight on! fight on!"
Tho' his vessel was all but a wreck;
And it chanced that, when half of the short summer night was gone,
60 With a grisly wound to be dressed, he had left the deck,
But a bullet struck him that was dressing it suddenly dead,
And himself he was wounded again, in the side of the head,
And he said: "Fight on! fight on!"
And the night went down, and the sun smiled far out over the summer sea,
65 And the Spanish fleet, with broken sides, lay round us, all in a ring;
But they dared not touch us again, for they feared that we still could sting,
So they watched what the end would be.
And we had not fought them in vain,
But in perilous plight were we,
70 Seeing forty of our poor hundred were slain,
And half of the rest of us were maim'd for life
In the crash of the cannonades and the desperate strife.

And the sick men down in the hold were most of them stark and cold,
And the pikes were all broken or bent, and the powder was all of it spent;
75 And the masts and the rigging were lying over the side;
But Sir Richard cried in his English pride;
"We have fought such a fight for a day and a night
As may never be fought again!
We have won great glory, my men!
80 And a day less or more
At sea or ashore,
We die—does it matter when?
Sink the ship, Master Gunner—sink her, split her in twain!
Fall into the hands of God, not into the hands of Spain!"
85 And the gunner said: "Ay, ay," but the seamen made reply:
"We have children, we have wives,
And the Lord hath spared our lives.
We will make the Spaniard promise, if we yield, to let us go;
We shall live to fight again, and to strike another blow."
90 And the lion there lay dying, and they yielded to the foe.

And the stately Spanish men to their flagship bore him then,
Where they laid him by the mast, old Sir Richard caught at last,
And they praised him to his face with their courtly foreign grace;
But he rose upon their decks, and he cried:
95 "I have fought for Queen and Faith, like a valiant man and true;
I have only done my duty, as a man is bound to do;
With a joyful spirit, I, Sir Richard Grenville, die!"
And he fell upon their decks, and he died.

74. PIKES—Weapons; long wooden shafts with steel points.

And they stared at the dead that had been so valiant and true,
100 And had holden the power and glory of Spain so cheap
That he dared her with one little ship and his English few;
Was he devil or man? He was devil for aught they knew,
But they sank his body with honor down into the deep,
And they mann'd the *Revenge* with a swarthier alien crew,
105 And away she sail'd with her loss, and long'd for her own;
When a wind from the lands they had ruin'd awoke from sleep,
And the water began to heave, and the weather to moan,
And or ever that evening ended a great gale blew,
And a wave like the wave that is raised by an earthquake grew,
110 Till it smote on their hulls and their sails and their masts and their flags,
And the whole sea plunged and fell on the shot-shatter'd navy of Spain,
And the little *Revenge* herself went down by the island crags,
To be lost evermore in the main.

108. OR EVER—Before.

Poem Development: The first written account of this great sea-fight was the work of Sir Walter Raleigh, a cousin of Sir Richard Grenville. Raleigh's account is fully as stirring as Tennyson's poem, which is in fact, based upon the story as Raleigh gives it. If you are interested to read Raleigh's account you will find it in Hakluyt's *Voyages,* or in *Sir Walter Raleigh, The Shepherd of the Ocean.* Characterize Lord Thomas Howard and Sir Richard Grenville. Look up accounts of the Spanish Inquisition and determine why the English especially feared capture by Spaniards. Describe the fight. Why was the *Revenge* becalmed? Even the Spaniards admired Sir Richard's bravery. Show how they evidenced their admiration. Do you like the ending of the poem? This fight has been called "a defeat exceeding a victory." Explain. Give the theme and central thought of the poem.

Interpretations: Out of gear (l. 5); ballast (l. 18); thumbscrew and the stake (l. 21); larboard, starboard (l. 48); sting (l. 67).

Significant Expressions: Quote lines which show Sir Richard's bravery. Give the figures of speech in lines 14 and 33.

RING OUT, WILD BELLS

From *In Memoriam*

ALFRED, LORD TENNYSON

Poem Interest: During the seventeen years immediately following Arthur Hallam's death, Tennyson wrote many short poems in his memory. In 1850 these were arranged and published as stanzas of one long poem entitled *In Memoriam*. Some of the stanzas of this poem are personal in nature, and others, like *Ring Out, Wild Bells* treat of universal problems. There is a reflection in many of them of the changes which were taking place in religious and scientific thought of the day. *Ring Out, Wild Bells* is complete in itself and has become a favorite hymn to the New Year for the whole world. Let the bells ring out their message to you . . .

RING out, wild bells, to the wild sky,
    The flying cloud, the frosty light;
    The year is dying in the night;
Ring out, wild bells, and let him die.

5 Ring out the old, ring in the new,
    Ring, happy bells, across the snow;
    The year is going, let him go;
Ring out the false, ring in the true.

Ring out the grief that saps the mind,
10   For those that here we see no more;
    Ring out the feud of rich and poor,
Ring in redress to all mankind.

Ring out a slowly dying cause,
    And ancient forms of party strife;
15   Ring in the nobler modes of life,
With sweeter manners, purer laws.

Ring out the want, the care, the sin,
    The faithless coldness of the times;
    Ring out, ring out my mournful rhymes,
20 But ring the fuller minstrel in.

Ring out false pride in place and blood,
    The civic slander and the spite;
    Ring in the love of truth and right,
Ring in the common love of good.

<pre>
25   Ring out old shapes of foul disease;
          Ring out the narrowing lust of gold;
          Ring out the thousand wars of old,
        Ring in the thousand years of peace.

        Ring in the valiant man and free,
30   The larger heart, the kindlier hand;
          Ring out the darkness of the land,
        Ring in the Christ that is to be.
</pre>

Poem Development: What in the poem structure gives you the feeling of ringing bells? List the things which the poet wishes rung out. Make a contrasting list of the things he wishes to be rung in. From your knowledge of this period in English history can you suggest how this poem reflects the changing thought of the times? Which lines make reference to a personal sorrow? Give the theme of the poem. What is the central thought?

Interpretations: Saps the mind; redress; fuller minstrel.

Significant Expressions: Memorize the stanza which has the greatest appeal for you.

BREAK, BREAK, BREAK

Alfred, Lord Tennyson

Poem Interest: When Tennyson was in Trinity College, Cambridge, he formed a deep and sincere friendship with a fellow student, Arthur Hallam. During college and in later years the men were constantly together, and Hallam's sudden death in 1833 left Tennyson heartbroken. *Break, Break, Break* was Tennyson's first cry of sadness at the loss of his friend.

<pre>
        Break, break, break,
          On thy cold gray stones, O Sea!
        And I would that my tongue could utter
          The thoughts that arise in me.

5   O, well for the fisherman's boy,
          That he shouts with his sister at play!
        O, well for the sailor lad,
          That he sings in his boat on the bay!

        And the stately ships go on
10   To their haven under the hill;
</pre>

But O for the touch of a vanish'd hand,
  And the sound of a voice that is still!

Break, break, break,
  At the foot of thy crags, O Sea!
15 But the tender grace of a day that is dead
  Will never come back to me.

Poem Development: In the first stanza what gives the feeling of great loneliness? To what sense does this stanza most appeal? What effect did the sight of the fisherman's boy and his sister have on Tennyson? Lines 11 and 12 are frequently quoted. Can you suggest why? What is the thought in the last two lines? What is the theme of the poem? Give the central thought.
Interpretations: Haven under the hill.
Significant Expressions: Quote the lines which express the hopelessness of the poet's grief.

ULYSSES

ALFRED, LORD TENNYSON

Poem Interest: Homer tells the story of Ulysses in both the *Iliad* and the *Odyssey*. In the *Iliad* he tells of Ulysses' part in the ten-years' siege of Troy, and in the *Odyssey* of Ulysses' wanderings from Troy to Ithaca, his island home in Greece. According to Homer, Ulysses, upon his return, spent the rest of his life contentedly at home. Tennyson, however, visions a different future for the sturdy wanderer . . .

It little profits that an idle king,
By this still hearth, among these barren crags,
Matched with an aged wife, I mete and dole
Unequal laws unto a savage race,
That hoard, and sleep, and feed, and know not me.
I cannot rest from travel; I will drink
Life to the lees. All times I have enjoyed
Greatly, have suffered greatly, both with those
That loved me, and alone; on shore, and when
Through scudding drifts the rainy Hyades
Vext the dim sea. I am become a name;
For always roaming with a hungry heart,
Much have I seen and known; cities of men
And manners, climates, councils, governments,
Myself not least, but honored of them all;
And drunk delight of battle with my peers,
Far on the ringing plains of windy Troy.
I am a part of all that I have met;
Yet all experience is an arch wherethrough
Gleams that untraveled world whose margin fades
Forever and forever when I move.
How dull it is to pause, to make an end,
To rust unburnished, not to shine in use!
As though to breathe were life! Life piled on life
Were all too little, and of one to me
Little remains; but every hour is saved
From that eternal silence, something more,
A bringer of new things; and vile it were
For some three suns to store and hoard myself,
And this gray spirit yearning in desire
To follow knowledge like a sinking star,
Beyond the utmost bound of human thought.

This is my son, my own Telemachus,
To whom I leave the scepter and the isle—
Well-loved of me, discerning to fulfill
This labor, by slow prudence to make mild
A rugged people, and through soft degrees
Subdue them to the useful and the good.

10. HYADES—Rain nymphs, placed by Zeus in the sky.

Most blameless is he, centered in the sphere
40 Of common duties, decent not to fail
In offices of tenderness, and pay
Meet adoration to my household gods,
When I am gone. He works his work, I mine.

There lies the port; the vessel puffs her sail;
45 There gloom the dark, broad seas. My mariners,
Souls that have toiled, and wrought, and thought with me—
That ever with a frolic welcome took
The thunder and the sunshine, and opposed
Free hearts, free foreheads—you and I are old;
50 Old age hath yet his honor and his toil.
Death closes all; but something ere the end,
Some work of noble note, may yet be done,
Not unbecoming men that strove with Gods.
The lights begin to twinkle from the rocks;
55 The long day wanes; the slow moon climbs; the deep
Moans round with many voices. Come, my friends,
'Tis not too late to seek a newer world.
Push off, and sitting well in order smite
The sounding furrows; for my purpose holds
60 To sail beyond the sunset, and the baths
Of all the western stars, until I die.
It may be that the gulfs will wash us down;
It may be we shall touch the Happy Isles,
And see the great Achilles, whom we knew.
65 Though much is taken, much abides; and though
We are not now that strength which in old days
Moved earth and heaven, that which we are, we are—
One equal temper of heroic hearts,
Made weak by time and fate, but strong in will
70 To strive, to seek, to find, and not to yield.

42. MEET—Fit, due.
63. HAPPY ISLES—The Islands of the Blest; the home of heroes after death.
64. ACHILLES—A celebrated Greek hero with whom Ulysses fought in the Trojan War.

Poem Development: Relate some of the incidents in Ulysses' life before his return to Ithaca. Can you suggest why Tennyson chose Ulysses rather than some other hero to carry out the theme of his poem? How does Ulysses feel about the quiet life he is now leading? Why does the serenity of his life so pall on him? Lines 22 and 23 are frequently quoted. What do they mean? To whom does Ulysses give control of his property? What is meant by "He works his work, I mine"? Do you think father and son were alike? What does Ulysses purpose to do? Relate some of the incidents to which reference is made in line 53. What fine attribute of power is left to Ulysses even though he is growing old? This poem was written shortly after the death of Arthur Hallam. Select lines which voice the way in which Tennyson is trying to face this tragedy. Can you suggest what the entire poem might symbolize? What is the theme of the poem? Give the central thought.

Interpretations: Mete and dole (l. 3); I will drink life to the lees (l. 6, 7); I am become a name (l. 11); as though to breathe were life (l. 24); soft degrees (l. 37); line 42; line 53; line 65.

Significant Expressions: Characterize Ulysses by quoting lines from the poem. Quote lines which you think best express the theme of the poem.

CROSSING THE BAR

Alfred, Lord Tennyson

Poem Interest: In his eighty-first year, Tennyson wrote this most beautiful of all his poems. Its words picture for us the serene old man of unwavering faith, looking out across the sea and watching the end of his life draw near.

   Sunset and evening star,
    And one clear call for me!
   And may there be no moaning of the bar,
    When I put out to sea,

5   But such a tide as moving seems asleep,
    Too full for sound and foam,
   When that which drew from out the boundless deep
    Turns again home.

   Twilight and evening bell,
10   And after that the dark!
   And may there be no sadness of farewell,
    When I embark;

3. Moaning of the bar—In some seacoast regions it is believed that the outgoing tide moans when a death has occurred.

> For though from out our bourne of time
>   and place
>   The flood may bear me far,
> 15 I hope to see my Pilot face to face
>   When I have crossed the bar.

13. BOURNE—Boundary or limit, referring here to earthly existence.

Poem Development: "Mind," said Tennyson to his son, "you put *Crossing the Bar* at the end of all my poems." Why do you think he made this request? The sunset, twilight, evening bell and evening star so simply and yet so beautifully symbolize the close of day and for Tennyson the close of life, that we marvel at such perfect poetic expression. What is the thought in the first stanza? In the second stanza there is given us the manner in which Tennyson would like to have death come to him. Tennyson makes death seem almost beautiful in this poem—makes it something to be anticipated rather than dreaded. In the third stanza we have the effect of death on those who remain behind. What is the poet's thought here? The fourth stanza radiates anticipation. Give the meaning in your own words. What are the theme and central thought of the poem?

Interpretations: Line 6; lines 7 and 8; embark; flood; Pilot.

Significant Expressions: Quote the lines which appeal to you most as an attitude toward approaching death. What is the figure of speech in line 3?

THE YEAR'S AT THE SPRING

ROBERT BROWNING

Poem Interest: Among a number of dramas which Browning published, probably the best known is *Pippa Passes*. Pippa, the heroine, is a little girl from an Italian silk factory who sings happily as she enjoys her one holiday of the year. During the course of the day, her path crosses that of each of four people who are facing great crises in their lives, and they are influenced toward good by her song. Entirely unconscious of the good she has wrought, Pippa happily returns home from her holiday. Here is her morning song:

> THE year's at the spring,
> And day's at the morn;
> Morning's at seven;
> The hillside's dew-pearled;
> The lark's on the wing;
> The snail's on the thorn;

> God's in His heaven—
> All's right with the world.

Poem Development: What mood does the song express? Notice the way in which the lines rhyme. Now read the poem again. What effect does this method of rhyming have? This poem has been set to music. If possible, have it sung in class. Give the theme and central thought of the poem.

Interpretations: Dew-pearled; on the wing.

Significant Expressions: The poem is so significant and so often quoted that it would be worth while to memorize it.

HOME THOUGHTS FROM ABROAD

Robert Browning

Poem Interest: Homesickness is truly a malady, and one which seems at its worst in the spring of the year when the sweetest beauty bursts forth in the beloved home land. Browning, though he loved Italy with a poet's passion for its loveliness, found himself possessed in April of a yearning for his first love, an English spring.

> Oh, to be in England
> Now that April's there,
> And whoever wakes in England
> Sees, some morning, unaware,
> 5 That the lowest boughs and the brushwood sheaf
> Round the elm tree bole are in tiny leaf,
> While the chaffinch sings on the orchard bough
> In England—now!
>
> And after April, when May follows,
> 10 And the whitethroat builds, and all the swallows!
> Hark, where my blossomed pear tree in the hedge
> Leans to the field and scatters on the clover
> Blossoms and dewdrops—at the bent spray's edge—
> That's the wise thrush; he sings each song twice over,
> 15 Lest you should think he never could recapture
> The first fine careless rapture!
> And though the fields look rough with hoary dew,

7. CHAFFINCH—A European song bird.
10. WHITETHROAT—A common name for the whitethroat warbler.

All will be gay when noontide wakes anew
The buttercups, the little children's dower
20 —Far brighter than this gaudy melon flower!

Poem Development: As you would guess, this poem was written during one of the many years Browning lived in Italy. What senses are appealed to in the poem? How do April and May in England differ from these months in Italy? What sights and sounds appeal to you in the spring of the year? What is the theme of the poem? Give the central thought.

Interpretations: Brushwood sheaf; at the bent spray's edge; hoary dew; little children's dower; gaudy melon flower.

Significant Expressions: Quote phrases indicating the poet's love for birds.

"DE GUSTIBUS—"

Robert Browning

Poem Interest: Dear to Browning's heart were both his native England and his adopted Italy. In a beautifully drawn comparison of the two countries he expresses his final preference for Italian scenes.

Your ghost will walk, you lover of trees,
  (If our loves remain)
  In an English lane,
By a cornfield side a-flutter with poppies.
5 Hark, those two in the hazel coppice—
A boy and a girl, if the good fates please,
  Making love, say—
  The happier they!
Draw yourself up from the light of the moon,
10 And let them pass, as they will too soon,
  With the bean flowers' boon,
  And the blackbird's tune,
  And May, and June!

"*De Gustibus*"—The title means "concerning tastes." The words come from a familiar quotation: *de gustibus non est disputandum*—there is no disputing about tastes.
  4. CORNFIELD—A field of grain.
  4. POPPIES—In Europe poppies grow wild amid the grain.
  9. DRAW YOURSELF UP . . . MOON—Step into the shadow.

What I love best in all the world
15 Is a castle, precipice-encurled,
In a gash of the wind-grieved Apennine.
Or look for me, old fellow of mine,
(If I get my head from out the mouth
O' the grave, and loose my spirit's bands,
20 And come again to the land of lands)—
In a seaside house to the farther South,
Where the baked cicala dies of drouth,
And one sharp tree—'tis a cypress—stands
By the many hundred years red-rusted,
25 Rough iron-spiked, ripe fruit o'ercrusted,
My sentinel to guard the sands
To the water's edge. For, what expands
Before the house, but the great opaque
Blue breadth of sea without a break?
30 While, in the house, forever crumbles
Some fragment of the frescoed walls,
From blisters where a scorpion sprawls.
A girl barefooted brings, and tumbles
Down on the pavement, green-flesh melons,
35 And says there's news to-day—the king
Was shot at, touched in the liver wing,
Goes with his Bourbon arm in a sling:
—She hopes they have not caught the felons.
Italy, my Italy!
40 Queen Mary's saying serves for me—
(When fortune's malice
Lost her, Calais)

16. APENNINE—The mountains of central Italy. Florence, in which Browning lived a number of years, is in the foothills of the Apennines.
21. FARTHER SOUTH—In the vicinity of Naples.
22. CICALA (sĭ-kä′là)—The cicada, locust.
31. FRESCOED—A kind of ornamental painting done on plaster. Italian houses are frequently frescoed both inside and out.
36. LIVER WING—The right arm.
37. BOURBON—The kings of Naples before the unification of Italy were of the Bourbon line.
40. QUEEN MARY—Mary I of England (1516–58).
42. CALAIS—The last of the English possessions on the continent. Mary's foreign policy lost Calais to France.

> Open my heart and you will see
> Graved inside of it, "Italy."
> 45 Such lovers old are I and she:
> So it always was, so shall ever be!

43. The loss of Calais, which she called "the chief jewel of my realm," grieved Mary I greatly, and hastened her death. She is reported to have said that if her heart were opened there would be found written there the word "Calais."

Poem Development: Describe the two scenes as Browning pictures them. Which do you prefer? Does Browning always prefer Italian scenes to English ones? Give a reason for your answer. From a study of Browning's life can you suggest a possible reason why he springs to defense of the Italian scene in this poem? In line 38, why does the girl express the hope that the felons will not be caught? Do you think Browning sympathized with this feeling? Browning died in Italy and on the wall of the house in which he died the Venetians placed an inscription from *"De Gustibus."* Can you suggest which two lines were used? Give the theme and central thought of the poem.

Interpretations: Hazel coppice; precipice-encurled; blisters; green-flesh melons; felons.

Significant Expressions: Quote lines which give the effect of music. Quote lines which present a vivid picture. What is the figure of speech in line 29?

MY LAST DUCHESS

(FERRARA)

ROBERT BROWNING

Poem Interest: This poem is a dramatic monologue.

SPEAKER: The Duke of Ferrara.
SETTING: The ducal palace.
TIME: During the Italian Renaissance,
      in the fifteenth century.

The Duke of Ferrara has just finished his business with an ambassador who has come to negotiate a marriage between the Duke and the daughter of some neighboring Count. With the ambassador, he is about to descend the stairs, but pauses to draw aside the curtain which hangs before the portrait of his first wife, the last Duchess of Ferrara. The Duke speaks:

THAT's my last Duchess painted on the wall,
Looking as if she were alive. I call
That piece a wonder, now: Frà Pandolf's hands
Worked busily a day, and there she stands.
5 Will 't please you sit and look at her? I said
"Frà Pandolf" by design, for never read
Strangers like you that pictured countenance,
The depth and passion of its earnest glance,
But to myself they turned (since none puts by
10 The curtain I have drawn for you, but I)
And seemed as they would ask me, if they durst,
How such a glance came there; so, not the first
Are you to turn and ask thus. Sir, 'twas not
Her husband's presence only, called that spot
15 Of joy into the Duchess' cheek: perhaps
Frà Pandolf chanced to say, "Her mantle laps
Over my lady's wrist too much," or "Paint
Must never hope to reproduce the faint
Half flush that dies along her throat:" such stuff
20 Was courtesy, she thought, and cause enough
For calling up that spot of joy. She had
A heart—how shall I say?—too soon made glad,
Too easily impressed: she liked whate'er
She looked on, and her looks went everywhere.
25 Sir, 'twas all one! My favor at her breast,
The dropping of the daylight in the west,
The bough of cherries some officious fool
Broke in the orchard for her, the white mule

---

3. FRÀ—Italian for brother. Many of the Italian painters of the Renaissance were monks.

5. The Duke offers the ambassador a chair.

6. BY DESIGN—That is for the purpose of concealing the name of the real painter. Frà Pandolf is evidently a fictitious name.

16–19. The Duke throws out as an explanation for the "spot of joy" the tactful compliments to the Duchess' beauty in the remarks of the painter. He implies his contempt for a woman in the Duchess' position who would be affected by the compliments of such an ordinary person as a portrait painter. See lines 19–20.

23–31. The Duke describes an eager soul that delighted in life.

27. OFFICIOUS—Impertinent, one who should have minded his own business.

She rode with round the terrace—all and each
30 Would draw from her alike the approving speech,
Or blush, at least. She thanked men—good! but thanked
Somehow—I know not how—as if she ranked
My gift of a nine-hundred-years-old name
With anybody's gift. Who'd stoop to blame
35 This sort of trifling? Even had you skill
In speech—(which I have not)—to make your will
Quite clear to such an one, and say, "Just this
Or that in you disgusts me; here you miss,
Or there exceed the mark"—and if she let
40 Herself be lessoned so, nor plainly set
Her wits to yours, forsooth, and made excuse
—E'en then would be some stooping; and I choose
Never to stoop. Oh, sir, she smiled, no doubt,
Whene'er I passed her; but who passed without
45 Much the same smile? This grew; I gave commands;
Then all smiles stopped together. There she stands
As if alive. Will 't please you rise? We'll meet
The company below, then. I repeat,
The Count your master's known munificence
50 Is ample warrant that no just pretence
Of mine for dowry will be disallowed;
Though his fair daughter's self, as I avowed
At starting, is my object. Nay, we'll go

34. WHO'D ... TRIFLING—That is, who would lower himself to explain to such a person that her conduct was vulgar?
41. SET HER WITS—That is, argued.
45. I GAVE COMMANDS—Hiram Corson once asked Browning if he meant that the Duke gave commands that the Duchess be put to death. "Yes," Browning said, "I meant that the commands were that she should be put to death," and then he added after a pause, "or he might have had her shut up in a convent."
47. The Duke intimates that the ambassador has looked at the picture long enough.
48–51. The Duke says that knowing the Count's reputation for doing things in a magnificent way, he has no fear that the latter will refuse the dowry which he, the Duke, wishes, and then he adds that it is, of course, not the wedding gift which he wants but the Count's fair daughter. Do you believe him?
53. The ambassador has stepped back to let the Duke precede him, but the latter condescends to treat him as an equal.

Together down, sir. Notice Neptune, though,
55 Taming a sea horse, thought a rarity,
Which Claus of Innsbruck cast in bronze for me!

54. NEPTUNE—That is, a statue of Neptune, the ancient god of the sea.
56. CLAUS OF INNSBRUCK—An imaginary artist.

Poem Development: The dramatic monologue was a favorite with Browning, and one well suited to his genius. This form of poetry gives the speech of one person. It differs from the soliloquy in that the latter is simply a kind of thinking aloud, whereas in the dramatic monologue the speech is always addressed to some person or persons. Browning made it the means of revealing character, and *My Last Duchess* is one of the best examples of his success in handling this form. No description of the Duke is given us, yet in his speech his character is completely revealed. The Duke admires the picture and treasures it for its qualities as a consummate work of art, yet he shows no whit of feeling for the woman who was his wife.

During the Renaissance, the Italian nobility were especially noted for their interest in art. What gives an impression of the beauty of the portrait? Characterize the Duchess. What characteristics of the Duke are suggested in lines 32–34? In line 36, the Duke claims to lack skill in speech. Do you think he evidences such a lack? What characteristic is indicated in the line "I choose never to stoop"? What does the Duke's nonchalance in turning so quickly from the Duchess' portrait show as to his character? Can you account for the Duke's blindness to the beauties of the Duchess' character? The section of Italy known as Ferrara produces a famous marble. Can you now attach any significance to the word "Ferrara" used in connection with the title of the poem? Were the Duke's characteristics common to noblemen in the fifteenth century? Read the poem aloud for its dramatic effect. What is the theme of the poem? the central thought?

Interpretations: Lines 6–12; spot of joy; too soon made glad; 'twas all one; let herself be lessoned so; thought a rarity.

Significant Expressions: Quote lines which give characteristics of the Duchess. Choose lines which most accurately characterize the Duke.

PROSPICE

ROBERT BROWNING

Poem Interest: One of the happiest marriages of which we have any knowledge was that of Robert Browning and his wife Elizabeth Barrett. They were completely devoted to each other, and Mrs. Browning's death left her husband heartbroken. This poem was written shortly after her death. The title means "Look forward."

ROBERT BROWNING

Fear death?—to feel the fog in my throat,
    The mist in my face,
When the snows begin, and the blasts denote
    I am nearing the place,
5 The power of the night, the press of the storm,
    The post of the foe;
Where he stands, the Arch Fear in a visible form,
    Yet the strong man must go:
For the journey is done and the summit attained,
10   And the barriers fall,
Though a battle's to fight ere the guerdon be gained,
    The reward of it all.
I was ever a fighter, so—one fight more,
    The best and the last!
15 I would hate that death bandaged my eyes, and forbore,
    And bade me creep past.
No! let me taste the whole of it, fare like my peers
    The heroes of old,
Bear the brunt, in a minute pay glad life's arrears
20   Of pain, darkness and cold.
For sudden, the worst turns the best to the brave,
    The black minute's at end,
And the elements' rage, the fiend-voices that rave,
    Shall dwindle, shall blend,
25 Shall change, shall become first a peace out of pain,
    Then a light, then thy breast,
O thou soul of my soul! I shall clasp thee again,
    And with God be the rest!

Poem Development: With what does the poet compare death? What wish does he express in lines 15 and 16? Beginning with line 21 the mood changes somewhat. What is this change? What is the effect of the lessening storm? Which lines show Browning's love for his wife? What kind of man does this poem show Browning to have been? Give the theme of the poem. What is the central thought?

Interpretations: The place; guerdon; peers; life's arrears; fiend-voices.

Significant Expressions: Quote lines which might be termed a war cry. Quote lines which are beautiful bits of imagery.

UP AT A VILLA—DOWN IN THE CITY

(As Distinguished by an Italian Person of Quality)

Robert Browning

Poem Interest: Given the privilege of choice, which would you choose—the country or the city—as the place in which to live? The speaker of the poem has a very definite preference. As the complete title of the poem indicates, he is an Italian person of quality—an impoverished nobleman, perhaps. Whether or not you agree with him, you will enjoy his enthusiastic sighs for the place of his choice.

> Had I but plenty of money, money enough and to spare,
> The house for me, no doubt, were a house in the city square;
> Ah, such a life, such a life, as one leads at the window there!
>
> Something to see, by Bacchus, something to hear, at least!
> 5   There, the whole day long, one's life is a perfect feast;
> While up at a villa one lives, I maintain it, no more than a beast.

2. City square—Browning lived from 1848–61 in an old house, the Casa Guidi (kä′sà gwē′dê), which looked out upon the Piazza S. Felice, a city square in Florence, Italy.
4. By Bacchus—In Roman mythology Bacchus was the god of wine. The expression here is a mild oath.

Well now, look at our villa! stuck like the horn of a bull
Just on a mountain edge as bare as the creature's skull,
Save a mere shag of a bush with hardly a leaf to pull!
10 —I scratch my own, sometimes, to see if the hair's turned wool.

But the city, oh the city—the square with the houses! Why?
They are stonefaced, white as a curd, there's something to take the eye!
Houses in four straight lines, not a single front awry;
You watch who crosses and gossips, who saunters, who hurries by;
15 Green blinds, as a matter of course, to draw when the sun gets high;
And the shops with fanciful signs which are painted properly.

What of a villa? Though winter be over in March by rights,
'Tis May perhaps ere the snow shall have withered well off the heights:
You've the brown ploughed land before, where the oxen steam and wheeze,
20 And the hills oversmoked behind by the faint gray olive trees.
Is it better in May, I ask you? You've summer all at once;
In a day he leaps complete with a few strong April suns.
'Mid the sharp short emerald wheat, scarce risen three fingers well,
The wild tulip, at end of its tube, blows out its great red bell
25 Like a thin clear bubble of blood, for the children to pick and sell.

12. WHITE AS A CURD—Because built of white stone, which looks the whiter in the Italian sunlight.
20. OVERSMOKED—The faint gray olive trees, which cover the hills about Florence, look like "a smoke upon the hills."

Is it ever hot in the square? There's a fountain to spout and splash!
In the shade it sings and springs; in the shine such foam-bows flash
On the horses with curling fish tails, that prance and paddle and pash
Round the lady atop in her conch—fifty gazers do not abash,
30 Though all that she wears is some weeds round her waist in a sort of sash.

All the year long at the villa, nothing to see though you linger,
Except yon cypress that points like death's lean lifted forefinger.
Some think fireflies pretty, when they mix i' the corn and mingle,
Or thrid the stinking hemp till the stalks of it seem a-tingle.
35 Late August or early September, the stunning cicala is shrill,
And the bees keep their tiresome whine round the resinous firs on the hill.
Enough of the seasons—I spare you the months of the fever and chill.

Ere you open your eyes in the city, the blessed church bells begin:
No sooner the bells leave off than the diligence rattles in:
40 You get the pick of the news, and it costs you never a pin.

27. FOAMBOWS—The miniature rainbows in the spray from the fountain.
28–29. The horses with curling fishtails are sea horses, fabulous animals with the body of the horse and the tail of a fish. The lady atop her conch is Venus. The fountain depicts Venus being drawn ashore in a great shell, or conch, by sea horses. According to one Greek myth Venus sprang from the sea foam and was drawn to the island of Cyprus in the manner here depicted. During the Renaissance subjects from classical mythology were frequently employed by the painters and sculptors of Florence.
34. THRID—Thread the stalks.
34. STINKING HEMP—After being cut, hemp is spread on the ground so that the gums which hold the fibers together may rot.
35. CICALA—Locust.
37. I SPARE YOU THE MONTHS OF THE FEVER AND CHILL—That is, I won't tell you about the cold months.
39. DILIGENCE—Stage coach. This poem was published first in 1855.

By and by there's the traveling doctor gives pills, lets
   blood, draws teeth;
Or the Pulcinello trumpet breaks up the market beneath.
At the post office such a scene picture—the new play,
   piping hot!
And a notice how, only this morning, three liberal thieves
   were shot.
45 Above it, behold the Archbishop's most fatherly of rebukes,
And beneath, with his crown and his lion, some little new
   law of the Duke's!
Or a sonnet with flowery marge, to the Reverend Don So-
   and-so,
Who is Dante, Boccaccio, Petrarca, Saint Jerome, and
   Cicero,
"And moreover" (the sonnet goes rhyming,) "the skirts of
   Saint Paul has reached,
50 Having preached us those six Lent lectures more unctuous
   than ever he preached."

41. LETS BLOOD—Letting blood was formerly a common remedy for many ailments.

42. PULCINELLO TRUMPET—Pulcinello, (pōōl'chē-nĕl-lô), a fat, short, humpbacked character in Italian puppet shows, corresponding to Punch in a Punch and Judy show. The trumpet is that blown to announce the play.

42. BREAKS UP THE MARKET BENEATH—That is the people in the market place below leave their buying and selling to see the scene play.

43. AT THE POST OFFICE—The play was given in the square before the post office.

44–50. In these lines the speaker voices the thrill which he gets from the "news" on the official bulletin board. Here one might see the announcement of the execution of three men whose crime was trying to bring about popular government—"liberal thieves" the speaker calls them, for he is no sympathizer with democracy. Above it is a letter from the Archbishop reprimanding perhaps those who have liberal sympathies. And below the announcement is the proclamation, bearing the coat of arms of the Duke, declaring some new law. Or it may be that there is to be found posted here a poem (sonnet), the margin of the manuscript decorated with a flowery drawing, dedicated to some clergyman whom the writer thinks is as great as Dante, Boccaccio, Petrarch, Saint Jerome, and Cicero, all rolled into one.

47. DON—A title of respect.

48. DANTE, BOCCACCIO, AND PETRARCA—Famous names in Italian literature. Saint Jerome was one of the early Church Fathers and a famous preacher. Cicero was a great orator of ancient Rome.

48–50. These two lines are quoted from the sonnet. Line 49 says that the Reverend Don So-and-so even has a touch of Saint Paul about him. In line 50 we learn that the occasion of the sonnet in his praise is a series of six Lent lectures.

Noon strikes—here sweeps the procession! our Lady borne smiling and smart
With a pink gauze gown all spangles, and seven swords stuck in her heart!
Bang-whang-whang goes the drum, *tootle-te-tootle* the fife;
No keeping one's haunches still: it's the greatest pleasure in life.

55 But bless you, it's dear—it's dear! fowls, wine, at double the rate.
They have clapped a new tax upon salt, and what oil pays passing the gate
It's a horror to think of. And so, the villa for me, not the city!
Beggars can scarcely be choosers: but still—ah, the pity, the pity!
Look, two and two go the priests, then the monks with cowls and sandals,
60 And the penitents dressed in white shirts, a-holding the yellow candles;
One, he carries a flag up straight, and another a cross with handles,
And the Duke's guard brings up the rear, for the better prevention of scandals:
Bang-whang-whang goes the drum, *tootle-te-tootle* the fife.
Oh, a day in the city square, there is no such pleasure in life!

51. PROCESSION—A religious procession in which the image of the Virgin was borne through the streets.
52. SEVEN SWORDS—Emblematical of the seven sorrows of the Virgin.
55–58. These four lines constitute a digression on the high cost of living in the city. In line 59 the speaker returns again to his description of the holy procession.
56. TAX UPON SALT—The line refers to the practice of levying an import duty upon salt and oil brought into the city.
62. FOR THE BETTER PREVENTION OF SCANDALS—That is, to guard against ribaldry and mischief on the part of the spectators.

Poem Development: Like *My Last Duchess*, this poem is a dramatic monologue, and the speaker another Renaissance Italian. In giving voice to his preference for the city, the nobleman gives us so many attractive glimpses of life in a country villa that we rather envy him. With what aspect of city life does he first express a preference? Describe the villa. Why do the city houses seem beautiful to the nobleman? How does he compare the seasons in the country and the city? Do you think he appreciates the beauties of nature? What do you think he likes best about life in the city? Give reasons for your opinion. Religious processions are common in Italian towns and are occasionally to be seen in movie news pictorials. Describe such a procession. Why must the nobleman live in the villa? Why was Browning able to picture Italian life so vividly? Read the poem aloud to get its dramatic effect as a monologue. To what degree does the monologue reveal the character of the Italian? What is the theme of the poem? Give the central thought.

Interpretations: Villa (Title); to see if the hair's turned wool (l. 10); emerald wheat (l. 23); pash (l. 28); corn (l. 33); unctuous (l. 50).

Significant Expressions: Make a list of words and phrases which are descriptive of the country. Make a contrasting list of phrases which are descriptive of the city. Quote a line appealing to the sense of hearing. Give the figures of speech in lines 7; 12; 23; 25.

HOW DO I LOVE THEE

Elizabeth Barrett Browning

Poem Interest: When we remember that the Brownings' life together was one of the most perfectly happy marriages of which we know, and that, although Mrs. Browning was in very poor health, she lived many years because of her happiness with her husband, we can understand the deep sincerity of her tribute to their love.

    How do I love thee? Let me count the ways.
    I love thee to the depth and breadth and height
    My soul can reach, when feeling out of sight
    For the ends of Being and ideal Grace.
5   I love thee to the level of every day's
    Most quiet need, by sun and candle-light.
    I love thee freely, as men strive for Right;
    I love thee purely, as they turn from Praise.
    I love thee with the passion put to use
10 In my old griefs, and with my childhood's faith.
    I love thee with a love I seemed to lose
    With my lost saints—I love thee with the breath,
    Smiles, tears, of all my life! and, if God choose,
    I shall but love thee better after death.

Poem Development: This poem appeals to the emotional sense. After you have read it, read Shakespeare's sonnet on love beginning: "Let me not to the marriage of true minds admit impediment." Shakespeare's sonnet has a "reasoning appeal." Note which you prefer.

Can the poet's love be measured? How does she express the freedom and purity of her love? Grief is a destructive emotion, requiring the negative expenditure of a great deal of energy which might be used to better advantage. Now can you explain, "I love thee with the passion put to use in my old griefs"? Most people can remember the adoration felt in youth for certain people, which amounted almost to worship. These were probably the "lost saints" of early life referred to in the poem. What is the climax of the poem? Give the theme and the central thought.

Interpretations: To the depth and breadth and height my soul can reach; to the level of every day's most quiet need.

Significant Expressions: Quote the line you think the most expressive. Quote the line expressive of the lasting quality of the poet's love for her husband.

DOVER BEACH

Matthew Arnold

Poem Interest: It is a calm and lovely night on the seashore. The ceaseless wash of the waves can be heard and the moon throws a radiance over all. But to the poet, the beauty of the scene is clouded by the confused struggle and lack of faith which he sees in the world, and he turns for solace to his loved one.

> The sea is calm tonight.
> The tide is full, the moon lies fair
> Upon the straits; on the French coast the light
> Gleams and is gone; the cliffs of England stand,
> 5 Glimmering and vast, out in the tranquil bay.
> Come to the window, sweet is the night-air!
> Only, from the long line of spray
> Where the sea meets the moon-blanched land,
> Listen! you hear the grating roar
> 10 Of pebbles which the waves draw back, and fling,
> At their return, up the high strand,
> Begin, and cease, and then again begin,
> With tremulous cadence slow, and bring
> The eternal note of sadness in.

Dover Beach—On the southeast coast of England on the English Channel.

15   Sophocles long ago
     Heard it on the Ægean, and it brought
     Into his mind the turbid ebb and flow
     Of human misery; we
     Find also in the sound a thought,
20   Hearing it by this distant northern sea.

     The sea of faith
     Was once, too, at the full, and round earth's shore
     Lay like the folds of a bright girdle furled.
     But now I only hear
25   Its melancholy, long, withdrawing roar,
     Retreating, to the breath
     Of the night-wind, down the vast edges drear
     And naked shingles of the world.

     Ah, love, let us be true
30   To one another! for the world which seems
     To lie before us like a land of dreams,
     So various, so beautiful, so new,
     Hath really neither joy, nor love, nor light,
     Nor certitude, nor peace, nor help for pain;
35   And we are here as on a darkling plain
     Swept with confused alarms of struggle and flight,
     Where ignorant armies clash by night.

15. SOPHOCLES—One of the great tragic poets of Greece.
16. ÆGEAN—The sea lying between Greece and Asia Minor.
28. SHINGLES—Pebbles.

Poem Development: Arnold has painted some beautiful pictures in this poem but they are touched with sadness. The sea seems to typify an endless struggle with no attainment. What is the poet's mood in the first 14 lines? His next thought is also sad. What is it? Give lines 20–28 in your own words. What does he think will make up for the lack of faith in the world? What is the theme of the poem? Give the central thought.

Interpretations: The straits; moon-blanched land; turbid; darkling plain.

Significant Expressions: Quote a line of description that seems very effective to you. Which line best describes the sound of the sea? What is the figure of speech in line 9? in line 23?

SONNET 86—LOST DAYS

Dante Gabriel Rossetti

Poem Interest: Time is a table of measurement by which we gauge the glory of life really lived, or by which we are judged before the grim accusation of life lived in vain. Our poet faces the specters of lost days as they spring up suddenly before him . . .

    The lost days of my life until today,
      What were they, could I see them on the street
      Lie as they fell? Would they be ears of wheat
    Sown once for food but trodden into clay?
5   Or golden coins squandered and still to pay?
      Or drops of blood dabbling the guilty feet?
      Or such spilt water as in dreams must cheat
    The undying throats of Hell, athirst alway?
    I do not see them here: but after death
10 God knows I know the faces I shall see,
      Each one a murdered self, with low last breath.
    "I am thyself,—what hast thou done to me?"
    "And I—and I—thyself" (lo! each one saith),
    "And thou thyself to all eternity!"

Poem Development: This poem makes the wasting of time seem like a very serious offense, and one that each of us may be called upon to answer for sometime in another world. What does the poet imagine the lost days might be here on earth? What might the days like the ears of wheat be? Do you think he meant the days spent in foolish spending of money by line 5? Line 6 could have several interpretations. What would be your interpretation of it? One interpretation for lines 7 and 8 might be the days spent in worthless pursuits when so many people need help. Have you another interpretation for these lines? What will the faces the poet sees in eternity represent? What will they say to him? What is the theme of the poem? What is the central thought?

Significant Expressions: Quote lines representing three lost days. Quote a line which contains a reproach.

UP-HILL

Christina Rossetti

Poem Interest: In this poem we listen first to the eager question and then to the steady, confident reply; to the one who is just starting; and to the one who has found the way.

Does the road wind up-hill all the way?
   Yes, to the very end.
Will the day's journey take the whole long day?
   From morn to night, my friend.

5 But is there for the night a resting-place?
   A roof for when the slow dark hours begin.
May not the darkness hide it from my face?
   You cannot miss that inn.

Shall I meet other wayfarers at night?
10   Those who have gone before.
Then must I knock, or call when just in sight?
   They will not keep you standing at that door.

Shall I find comfort, travel-sore and weak?
   Of labour you shall find the sum.
15 Will there be beds for me and all who seek?
   Yea, beds for all who come.

Poem Development: What interpretation do you give to "up-hill"? Does the answer in line 2 carry out this interpretation? Is the second question a repetition of the first, or is there a new idea? Does line 10 make you feel assured that the poet means this long journey is the journey of life with death at the end? Why? Is line 14 comforting or somewhat appalling? Give the theme and central thought of the poem.

Interpretations: Morn to night; slow dark hours; line 10; line 14.

Significant Expressions: Quote the line containing what you consider the most helpful thought. Tell why you chose it.

A CHILD'S LAUGHTER

Algernon Charles Swinburne

Poem Interest: Only one intensely fond of children could create such an exquisite sound image of a child's laughter . . .

    All the bells of heaven may ring,
    All the birds of heaven may sing,
    All the wells on earth may spring,
    All the winds on earth may bring

3. Wells . . . may spring—That is, wells may become springs and bubble forth.

5   All sweet sounds together;
Sweeter far than all things heard,
Hand of harper, tone of bird,
Sound of woods at sundawn stirred,
Welling water's winsome work,
10   Wind in warm, wan weather—

One thing yet there is, that none
Hearing ere its chime be done
Knows not well the sweetest one
Heard of man beneath the sun,
15   Hoped in heaven hereafter;
Soft and strong and loud and light—
Very sound of very light
Heard from morning's rosiest height—
When the soul of all delight
20   Fills a child's clear laughter.
Golden bells of welcome rolled
Never forth such notes, nor told
Hours so blithe in tones so bold,
As the radiant mouth of gold

25   Here that rings forth heaven.
If the golden crested wren
Were a nightingale—why then
Something seen and heard of men
Might be half as sweet as when
30   Laughs a child of seven.

Poem Development: What are the sound images of the first ten lines? Describe the sounds of the child's laughter. What does her laughter tell? Give the poet's last comparison. What is the theme of the poem? Give the central thought.

Interpretations: Hand of harper; line 9; mouth of gold.

Significant Expressions: Quote the line giving the clearest sound image. Quote the line best describing the child's laughter. What is the figure of speech in line 21?

WILLIAM ERNEST HENLEY

INVICTUS

William Ernest Henley

Poem Interest: Some poems appeal to us because they create images of beauty; some because they stir the emotions; some because they carry us on thrilling journeys of adventure; but there is still another type of poem which encourages and gives a message of faith and bravery which spurs us to "carry on" in spite of obstacles.

> Out of the night that covers me,
>   Black as the Pit from pole to pole,
> I thank whatever gods may be
>   For my unconquerable soul.
>
> 5 In the fell clutch of circumstance
>   I have not winced nor cried aloud.
> Under the bludgeonings of chance
>   My head is bloody, but unbowed.
>
> Beyond this place of wrath and tears
> 10   Looms but the Horror of the shade,
> And yet the menace of the years
>   Finds, and shall find, me unafraid.
>
> It matters not how strait the gate,
>   How charged with punishments the scroll,
> 15 I am the master of my fate;
>   I am the captain of my soul.

Poem Development: Henley and Stevenson were great friends and this poem is said to have been "the portrait of Stevenson." What does the poet mean by "the night that covers me"? In the first stanza he gives an idea of a general thankfulness for having been able to meet the struggles of life unconquered. In the second stanza he becomes a little more specific. Give the meaning of this second stanza. The third stanza goes from life to death. Even though uncertain of life after death, is the poet's courage lessened? Give the meaning of the last stanza in your own words. What is the theme? What is the central thought?

Interpretations: Fell clutch of circumstances; bludgeonings of chance; menace of the years; charged with punishments the scroll.

Significant Expressions: Quote the lines telling for what the poet is thankful. Memorize the last two lines.

MARGARITAE SORORI

William Ernest Henley

Poem Interest: Death and the quiet beauty of the night—both are the benediction of the sunset hour. Our souls serenely follow the last sunset rays, a late lark softly sings his notes of eventide, the dusky, star-lit shadows fall—and all is finished, day is done.

> The late lark twitters from the quiet skies
> And from the west,
> Where the sun, his day's work ended,
> Lingers as in content,
> 5   There falls on the old, gray city
> An influence luminous and serene,
> A shining peace.
>
> The smoke ascends
> In a rosy-and-golden haze. The spires
> 10 Shine, and are changed. In the valley
> Shadows rise. The lark sings on. The sun,
> Closing his benediction,
> Sinks, and the darkening air
> Thrills with a sense of the triumphing night—
> 15 Night with her train of stars
> And her great gift of sleep.
>
> So be my passing!
> My task accomplished and the long day done,
> My wages taken, and in my heart
> 20 Some late lark singing,
> Let me be gathered to the quiet west,
> The sundown splendid and serene,
> Death.

Poem Development: What is the mood of the first stanza? What is the sound image? List the words that help convey the mood of peace. Name the words that enhance the feeling of quietness. What are the images in the second stanza? With what does the poet compare this serene twilight scene? What is the theme? Give the central thought.

Significant Expressions: Quote the lines giving sound impressions. Quote the lines describing night. What is the figure of speech in line 9? in line 22?

REQUIESCAT

Oscar Wilde

Poem Interest: *Requiescat* was written after the death of Wilde's younger sister. The poet speaks, as with him you stand by the grave of his loved one.

       Tread lightly, she is near
          Under the snow,
      Speak gently, she can hear
          The daisies grow.

5   All her bright golden hair
          Tarnished with rust,
      She that was young and fair
          Fallen to dust.

      Lily-like, white as snow,
10   She hardly knew
      She was a woman, so
          Sweetly she grew.

      Coffin-board, heavy stone,
          Lie on her breast;
15   I vex my heart alone,
          She is at rest.

      Peace, peace; she cannot hear
          Lyre or sonnet;
      All my life's buried here,
20   Heap earth upon it.

Requiescat—May she rest in peace.

Poem Development: The delicate touches of this poem make it very appealing. Give the most descriptive line about the dead girl. Which stanza seems to express the poet's heaviness of heart? Which line shows his greatest grief? What is the theme of the poem? Give the central thought.

Interpretations: Tarnished with rust; vex my heart alone; all my life's buried here.

Significant Expressions: Quote a line giving a color image; one giving a sound image.

THE HISTORY OF POETRY IN ENGLAND

The Twentieth Century (1900–   )

General Characteristics

With the advancement of learning, increased travel, and contact with the world of the first decades of the twentieth century, came a revolt against Victorian poetry. Victorian poets had written of legends and a dream sort of world, and all of their writings were strongly flavored with romanticism. This kind of poetry now seemed unreal and trivial and tinsel-like. The knights and ladies, and all the exactness of verse forms annoyed the new writers. These writers had traveled and seen the splendors of the Orient, had experienced adventures of their own, had met with danger, and had faced the realities of life. Therefore, only the real and genuine had any appeal to them. They objected to the use of poetry to teach a moral and they also discarded the romantic tendency.

Out of this revolt have grown several changes worthy of note. The new poetry is realistic; it is written of adventure with the attractiveness of actuality; it deals with a bolder range of subjects; it has a franker mode of expression; and it is genuine in that it deals with ordinary happenings of ordinary people. The subjects are varied. Many poems have been written of the sea, of adventures, of the poor, of the old, and of nature. Out of the World War came a great number of war poems, some of them depicting the ghastliness of the war and all its horrors, and others seeming to be great cries of men who wished for peace and home. All poetic forms are used, with perhaps the exception of free verse. This, the English have not adopted as have the American writers. Another result of the revolt against romanticism has been the Celtic revival. The Irish poets have gone back to their own legends, folk-lore and Irish history for their inspirations, and the movement has produced a number of lyric poets of distinction.

It is impossible to write of a period which is so near to us with any accuracy. The names of some contemporary writers will probably live forever in English literature. There is a great mass of poetry to choose from, dealing with subjects of all kinds, and written in all forms of verse. We can say this of the modern poetry: It is sincere and strong and it is exalted in its tone.

Thomas Hardy (1840–1928)

Hardy was born at Upper Brockhampton near Dorchester. He stayed in school until he was sixteen and was then apprenticed to an architect, with whom he remained for six years. He then went to London. During all of this time he read all that he could, both during and outside of working hours. He was also fond of music and he studied French at evening classes at Kings' College. Hardy was a master of the novel, but after 1898 he devoted his time to the writing of poetry. It is said that Hardy's lyric ability will be recognized more and more as time goes on. England mourned his death in 1928, and thousands waited in the pouring rain at the door of Westminster Abbey to attend the memorial service. Among the pall-bearers were Kipling, Housman, Galsworthy, Barrie, and Prime Minister Baldwin.

Alfred Edward Housman (1859-1936)

Housman was born in Shropshire. He received his education in a preparatory school and then attended St. John's College, Oxford. Here he devoted himself to a study of the classics. After his graduation he became professor of Latin at University College, London, and finally professor of Latin at Cambridge University. He died in 1936.

Housman is best known for *A Shropshire Lad,* a volume of poems which he published in 1896. These poems are lyrics which are light and delicate and have a touch of haunting melody in their tone. In 1922 he published another volume called *Last Poems.*

William Butler Yeats (1865-   )

Yeats was born in Dublin, Ireland. His father was an artist. Yeats attended school in Hammersmith and later the Erasmus Smith School in London. His father wanted him to study painting and he spent three years in its study, but he always preferred to seek out the old Irish legends and folk-lore, and it was his delight to listen to the tales of old Ireland as told by the Irish peasants. He identified himself with the Celtic movement and became deeply interested in the development of Irish literature. Yeats has made several trips to America.

The idea of mysticism hovers over his poems. He is an exponent of the doctrine of simple expression in verse and has had a great influence on many other poets. We know Yeats best for his lyrics which are simple in style and frank in utterance. *The Wild Swans at Coole* is one of his best poems.

Rudyard Kipling (1865-1936)

Kipling was born in Bombay, India, but received his education in England. He returned to India when he was seventeen to take a position on the *Civil and Military Gazette.* He remained there until he was about twenty-five when he returned to England. Kipling married an American girl, Caroline Balestier of Brattleboro, Vermont. They lived in Brattleboro for several years and two children were born to them there. Many of Kipling's best poems were published while he lived in America. After a trip to Africa in 1897, the Kipling family made their home in England. Kipling lost his only son in the World War.

His place in literature is probably assured to him by his short stories rather than by his verse. However, he is well-known for several volumes of verse, among which is *Barrack Room Ballads* published in 1892. Poems such as the *Recessional, The Sons of Martha,* and *The Return,* show him at his best. He was the outstanding exponent in verse of British imperialism and the father of "drum and trumpet" poetry. His verse and his thought were always forceful and vigorous and in this respect he stood in marked contrast to many of his contemporaries. He was a popular poet, which is no doubt in a great measure due to the fact that he was the master of powerful and striking rhythms.

Walter de la Mare (1873-)

De la Mare was born in Charlestown, England. He is related to Browning. He was educated in St. Paul's Cathedral Choir School. With no further education he became a bookkeeper and is now a book reviewer. It has been said of him that he has the trick of revealing the ordinary in whimsical colors, and a second gift is his sense of the supernatural. His is a delicate touch and his poems have a mysterious, haunting beauty. He has written lyrics and dramatic poems, and in them we see nature in all its beauty and the homely scenes of life made lovely by a master touch.

Richard Le Gallienne (1866-)

Le Gallienne was born in Liverpool. He was educated at Liverpool College and then went into business. He continued in business for about seven years but then turned to literary pursuits. In 1887 he wrote a book of poetry entitled *My Ladies' Sonnets* which led to his becoming critic for the London *Star*. He is called a "sane and kindly critic." Le Gallienne was connected with several papers. In 1898 he visited America, and finally settled in New York. He is father of the actress, Eva Le Gallienne, who founded the New York Civic Repertory Theatre. His poetry is graceful and contains considerable melody. His images are clear and delicate and his perceptions are true and sincere.

William Henry Davies (1870-)

Davies was born at Newport, Wales. His schooling was mediocre, most of it having been gained by experience. He was apprenticed to a picture frame maker and as soon as his apprenticeship was over, he came to America. For six years he led the life of a vagabond, sometimes working a bit, often "riding the rails," and begging from door to door for food. He tripped, as he was about to board a train and his foot was cut off. After this accident he returned to England and peddled notions from door to door for a living. All this time he was reading and writing whenever opportunity permitted him. He sent a collection of his poems to Bernard Shaw who recognized his talent and helped him. He became popular as a poet, and life grew easier for him. His poems reflect the hardships of his early years and the contacts with life in its hardest forms.

Gilbert K. Chesterton (1874-1936)

Chesterton was born at Campden Hill, Kensington. He attended St. Paul's School where he studied art and spent much of his time writing poetry. Chesterton was a prolific writer and contributed biography, essays, fiction, plays, and poetry to the field of literature. He was an enthusiast and a master of rhythm and sound in his verse.

John Masefield (1874-   )

Masefield, the present Poet Laureate, is probably entitled to be called the greatest living English poet. Masefield was born in 1874. At the age of fourteen he went to sea and spent a number of years before the mast, winding up in New York in 1896 where he worked for a time as a kind of porter in Luke O'Connor's saloon and in a Yonkers carpet factory. Although as a boy he had made a few juvenile attempts at poetry, he had not felt the urge to write until one Sunday afternoon in a Yonkers rooming house he read Chaucer's *Canterbury Tales.* It was Chaucer, so to speak, who unlocked his genius and became his model. His long narrative poems *The Everlasting Mercy, The Widow in the Bye Street,* and *Dauber* come directly from his experiences and contacts with life and show how deep is his sympathy for all those who are "hemmed in  by the spears" of life. They are written in verse resembling the rime royal of Chaucer. These poems illustrate his realism. *The Everlasting Mercy* tells the story of Saul Kane, a drunken poacher, of his fist fight with another of his kind, of the stirrings within him of compunction, of his drunken debauch, and of his regeneration and reaching out to the "everlasting mercy." The story is told in Saul Kane's own language—coarse and at times blasphemous—but it is the authentic record of the struggle of a soul against evil and of its yearning for peace. It is not Saul Kane's fault that he does not talk the dignified language of philosophy. *The Widow in the Bye Street,* whose son must die on the gallows, has deep pathos. *Dauber* is in some respects the best of these three as poetry. Of all contemporary poets, Masefield is preëminently the poet of the sea. *Sea Fever* is the work of a sailor—no landsman could write it.

Alfred Noyes (1880-   )

Noyes has produced a great body of poetry written in conventional meters and having a popular appeal. His verse is full of color and alive with action, and people enjoy reading him. He inclines to a rather romantic treatment. He is rather lacking in intensity of feeling and thought, and is quite lacking in the conviction and realism that one imagines Masefield would give to the same subjects. He is best known for a few short poems such as *Kilmeny, The Barrel Organ,* and *The Highwayman.*

Siegfried Sassoon (1886-   )

Sassoon was born in England and was educated at Marlborough and Clare College. His father was of Persian Jew descent and his mother was English. From earliest youth he was fond of poetry and, although he was an outdoor boy, he always found time to read and study. He received much inspiration from Masefield and greatly admired both Keats and Shelley. Sassoon enlisted in the army in 1914 and went into the war filled with the enthusiasm of youth fighting in a valiant cause. He served four years and a half and received the Military Cross for valor in rescue work. Until he entered the war his poetry had been of a lovely, lyrical nature. The war turned his poetry into bitter exposure of the horrors of war, and violent and passionate protest against the "glorification of war." His volumes of poems, which are three in number, give us the most vivid and truthful records of the war that exist.

Padraic Colum (1881-   )

Colum was born in Longford, Ireland. As a child he was intensely interested in the folk-lore of the Irish people and he missed no opportunity to delve into old Irish melodies and songs. He came to America in 1914 and has lived here since. Colum began writing when he was very young. He helped to found the *Irish Review* and edited it in 1911. It is a delight to hear him talk of Ireland or give a reading of his own poems and tales. His poetry is full of whimsical humor and melody that hold the reader's interest to the last word. Colum is also a writer of books for children and of two books on Hawaiian folk-lore.

James Stephens (1882-   )

Stephens was born in Ireland. His boyhood was spent in poverty and what education he had was self-taught. He learned stenography and obtained a position in a lawyer's office. Here he came in contact with

George Russell, an Irish poet, who immediately helped him to get his writings before the public and who drew him into the group who were interested in the Irish literary revival. He has written prose as well as poetry. He delights in putting the legends of early Ireland into verse, and his poetry is filled with a quaint, whimsical beauty through which runs a thread of profound thought. He delights as well as teaches.

Winifred M. Letts (1887-   )

Miss Letts was born in Ireland. She was educated at Alexandra College in Dublin and makes her home there. She has written novels and children's stories. During the World War she served as a nurse in the base hospitals. Her *Spires of Oxford* reflects a mood of contrast between the peace of the surroundings of Oxford College and the terrible war scenes through which so many of the Oxford boys went. Miss Letts gives us clear, mental pictures and there is a charming lilt to her verse. There is a thought element underlying her lines which causes a bit of reflection on the reader's part.

Rupert Brooke (1887-1915)

Brooke was born at Rugby where his father was an assistant master in the Rugby School. He participated in all forms of athletics and was highly proficient as an athlete. When he was nineteen he entered Kings' College. While there one of his poems was published in the college magazine. He was early interested in poetry and published his first volume of poems in 1911 when he was only twenty-four years old. At the outbreak of the World War, he enlisted. He was in a training camp for a winter and was then sent to take part in the Dardanelles campaign. He died on board ship of blood poison. Had Brooke lived he would un-  doubtedly have given a large amount of valuable poetry to the world. His poems are colorful and filled with the joy of just being alive. *The Soldier* was written a few months before his death. Both this and *The Dead* give us an idea of the bravery and unselfishness of the young men who fought in the Great War of 1914.

Other Twentieth Century Poets

New anthologies of contemporary poetry come daily from the press. They contain literally hundreds of names each represented by one or more creditable poems. Poets like Coventry Patmore, Alice Meynell, Sir Henry Newboldt, W. W. Gibson, Ralph Hodgson, John Drinkwater, Robert Grave, Harold Monro, Robert Bridges, George William Russell, have all produced poems which will make their names long remembered.

Poetry of the Twentieth Century

THE MAN HE KILLED *

Thomas Hardy

Poem Interest: How can man *en masse* commit brutal, bloody acts which as an individual he would consider unthinkable? This is a question which has been asked since the beginning of time.

"Had he and I but met
   By some old ancient inn,
We should have sat us down to wet
   Right many a nipperkin!

5 "But ranged as infantry,
   And staring face to face,
I shot at him as he at me,
   And killed him in his place.

"I shot him dead because—
10   Because he was my foe,
Just so: my foe of course he was;
   That's clear enough; although

"He thought he'd 'list, perhaps,
   Off-hand like—just as I—

---

* From *Collected Poems* by Thomas Hardy. Reprinted by permission of The Macmillan Company, publishers.
4. Nipperkin—A small drink.   13. 'List—Enlist.

15   Was out of work—had sold his traps—
       No other reason why.

     "Yes; quaint and curious war is!
       You shoot a fellow down
       You'd treat, if met where any bar is,
20   Or help to half-a-crown."

Poem Development: If the two men of the poem had met during times of peace, what would have happened? What did actually take place? What are the poet's thoughts about this? Do you think he was trying to figure out the problem of war or justifying his own act? Give the theme of the poem. What is the central thought?

Interpretations: Ranged as infantry; traps; help to half-a-crown.

WEATHERS *

Thomas Hardy

Poem Interest: *Weathers* is more than an expression of preference; it is a charming peep into the English countryside.

     This is the weather the cuckoo likes,
     And so do I;
     When showers betumble the chestnut spikes,
     And nestlings fly:
5   And the little brown nightingale bills his best,
     And they sit outside at "The Travellers' Rest,"
     And maids come forth sprig-muslin drest,
     And citizens dream of the south and west,
     And so do I.

10   This is the weather the shepherd shuns,
     And so do I;
     When beeches drip in browns and duns,
     And thresh, and ply;
     And hill-hid tides throb, throe on throe,
15   And meadow rivulets overflow,
     And drops on gate-bars hang in a row,
     And rooks in families homeward go,
     And so do I.

* From *Collected Poems* by Thomas Hardy. Reprinted by permission of The Macmillan Company, publishers.

Poem Development: Who, besides the poet, likes sunny weather? Paint a word picture of the inn scene. Who shuns the rainy weather? How do the trees look? Give another picture to be seen in rainy weather. Do you always prefer a sunny day? What color effects are produced in the poem? What is your reaction to the last line of each stanza? What pictures in the poem are distinctly English? Give the theme and central thought of the poem.

Interpretations: Showers betumble; bills his best; thresh and ply; hill-hid tides; throe on throe.

Significant Expressions: Quote the line most descriptive of the sunny day; of the rainy day.

LOVELIEST OF TREES

Alfred Edward Housman

Poem Interest: It is good to drink deeply of today's beauty for its loveliness too quickly vanishes from sight. Whatever time is left to us, it is all too short to let a fragrance pass unclaimed, a blossom fade unseen.

> Loveliest of trees, the cherry now
> Is hung with bloom along the bough,
> And stands about the woodland ride,
> Wearing white for Eastertide.
>
> 5 Now, of my threescore years and ten,
> Twenty will not come again,
> And take from seventy springs a score,
> It only leaves me fifty more.
> And since to look at things in bloom
> 10 Fifty springs are little room,
> About the woodlands I will go
> To see the cherry hung with snow.

Poem Development: Many poems have been written about trees. Most of them have been of trees in summer. Which tree does the poet think is the loveliest? Paint a word picture of the tree in bloom. How old is the lad? Why does he regret the passing of youth? What is the theme of the poem? Give the central thought.

Interpretations: Woodland ride; threescore years and ten; score; hung with snow.

Significant Expressions: Quote the line which you think best describes the cherry tree.

REVEILLE

Alfred Edward Housman

Poem Interest: In army terms, "reveille" is the bugle call to awaken soldiers at the appointed morning hour. Our poem *Reveille* is the poet's call to awaken sleepers to the beauties of nature. Its verses are an invitation to satisfying things to do, to interesting things to see . . .

    Wake: the silver dusk returning
        Up the beach of darkness brims,
    And the ship of sunrise burning
        Strands upon the eastern rims.

5   Wake: the vaulted shadow shatters,
        Trampled to the floor it spanned,
    And the tent of night in tatters
        Straws the sky-pavilioned land.

    Up, lad, up, 'tis late for lying:
10   Hear the drums of morning play;
    Hark, the empty highways crying
        "Who'll beyond the hills away?"

    Towns and countries woo together,
        Forelands beacon, belfries call;
15   Never lad that trod on leather
        Lived to feast his heart with all.

    Up, lad: thews that lie and cumber
        Sunlit pallets never thrive;
    Morns abed and daylight slumber
20   Were not meant for man alive.

    Clay lies still, but blood's a rover;
        Breath's a ware that will not keep.
    Up, lad: when the journey's over
        There'll be time enough to sleep.

1. Silver dusk—Moonlight.   8. Straws—Strews.
17. Thews—Muscles.   18. Pallets—Beds.

ELD

Poem Development: There is beautiful imagery in this poem. With what is the sunrise compared? Paint a word picture of the dawn as the poet sees it. What are some of the morning sounds? As in *Loveliest of Trees,* the poet expresses regret at the passing of youth. Which lines express this feeling? Does the rhythm of the poem suggest a bugle call? What is the theme of the poem? Give the central thought.

Interpretations: Strands; vaulted shadow; spanned; sky-pavilioned; forelands beacon; trod on leather; clay lies still; breath's a ware.

Significant Expressions: Quote two lines which for you present the most vivid image. What is the figure of speech in line 1? in line 3?

THE LAKE ISLE OF INNISFREE *

William Butler Yeats

Poem Interest: The poet himself tells us how he came to write this poem: "I had still the ambition, formed . . . in my teens, of living in imitation of Thoreau on Innisfree, a little island in Lough Gill, and when walking through Fleet Street, very homesick, I heard a little tinkle of water and saw a fountain in a shop window which balanced a little ball upon its jet, and began to remember lake water. From the sudden remembrance came my poem 'Innisfree.'"

I will arise and go now, and go to Innisfree,
And a small cabin build there, of clay and wattles made;
Nine bean rows will I have there, a hive for the honey bee,
And live alone in the bee-loud glade.

5   And I shall have some peace there, for peace comes dropping slow,
Dropping from the veils of the morning to where the cricket sings;
There midnight's all a-glimmer, and noon a purple glow,
And evening full of the linnet's wings.

I will arise and go now, for always night and day
10 I hear lake water lapping with low sounds by the shore;
While I stand on the roadway, or on the pavements gray,
I hear it in the deep heart's core.

* From *Collected Poems* by William Butler Yeats. Reprinted by permission of The Macmillan Company, publishers.
   2. Wattles—Interwoven twigs.

Poem Development: In the explanation of how the poem came to be written, who is Thoreau to whom reference is made? Innisfree is evidently a definite place which the poet has in mind, but do you think the poem could be merely expressive of a desire for peace and a wish to be alone and undisturbed? What sound image has the poet kept in his mind all the years he has been away? What effect does it have in the poem? How is peace symbolized in the second stanza? Give the theme and central thought of the poem.

Interpretations: Bee-loud glade; linnet's wings.

Significant Expressions: Quote the line which gives the sound of the water. What is the figure of speech in line 5?

THE SONG OF THE OLD MOTHER *

William Butler Yeats

Poem Interest: There is an interesting comparison to be drawn between the discontented old mother of this poem, and the forlorn old woman of whom Padraic Colum later tells in *An Old Woman of the Roads*. Both poems are the productions of Irish poets, dealing with representatives of aged womankind in the same country.

    I RISE in the dawn, and I kneel and blow
    Till the seed of the fire flicker and glow.
    And then I must scrub, and bake, and sweep,
    Till stars are beginning to blink and peep;
5   But the young lie long and dream in their bed
    Of the matching of ribbons, the blue and the red,
    And their day goes over in idleness,
    And they sigh if the wind but lift up a tress.
    While I must work, because I am old
10 And the seed of the fire gets feeble and cold.

* From *Collected Poems* by William Butler Yeats. Reprinted by permission of The Macmillan Company, publishers.

Poem Development: Paint a word picture of the old mother as you see her. What is the contrast in this poem? Explain the last line. What is the mood of the poem? What are the theme and central thought of this poem?

Interpretations: Seed of the fire (l. 2 and also line 10); lift up a tress.

Significant Expressions: Quote lines which express a feeling of discouragement.

GUNGA DIN

Rudyard Kipling

Poem Interest: A number of British soldiers lie sprawled about their quarters, smoking and exchanging yarns. One of their number who has seen service in India now speaks . . .

You may talk o' gin and beer
When you're quartered safe out 'ere,
An' you're sent to penny-fights an' Aldershot it;
But when it comes to slaughter
5 You will do your work on water,
An' you'll lick the bloomin' boots of 'im that's got it.
Now in Injia's sunny clime,
Where I used to spend my time
A-servin' of 'Er Majesty the Queen,
10 Of all them blackfaced crew
The finest man I knew
Was our regimental *bhisti*, Gunga Din.
   He was "Din! Din! Din!
   You limping lump o' brick-dust, Gunga Din!
15 Hi! *slippy hitherao!*
   Water! get it! *Panee lao!*
   You squidgy-nosed old idol, Gunga Din."

The uniform 'e wore
Was nothin' much before,
20 An' rather less than 'arf o' that be'ind,
For a piece o' twisty rag
An' a goatskin water-bag
Was all the field-equipment 'e could find.
When the sweatin' troop-train lay
25 In a sidin' through the day,

2. QUARTERED SAFE OUT 'ERE—Quartered at Aldershot, near London.
3. PENNY-FIGHTS—Sham battles.
6. IT—Water. That is, you will do anything, no matter how servile, for a drink of water.
12. *Bhisti*—Water-carrier.
15. *Slippy hitherao*—Slide here quickly.
16. *Panee lao*—Bring water swiftly.

Where the 'eat would make your bloomin' eyebrows
    crawl,
We shouted *"Harry By!"*
Till our throats were brick-dry,
Then wopped 'im cause 'e couldn't serve us all.
30   It was "Din! Din! Din!
You 'eathen, where the mischief 'ave you been?
You put some *juldee* in it
Or I'll *marrow* you this minute
If you don't fill up my helmet, Gunga Din!"

35 'E would dot an' carry one
Till the longest day was done;
An' 'e didn't seem to know the use o' fear.
If we charged or broke or cut,
You could bet your bloomin' nut,
40 'E'd be waitin' fifty paces right flank rear.
With 'is *mussick* on 'is back
'E would skip with our attack,
An' watch us till the bugles made "Retire,"
An' for all 'is dirty 'ide
45 'E was white, clear white, inside
When 'e went to tend the wounded under fire!
    It was "Din! Din! Din!"
With the bullets kickin' dust-spots on the green,
When the cartridges ran out,
50   You could hear the front-files shout,
"Hi! ammunition-mules an' Gunga Din!"

I shan't forgit the night
When I dropped be'ind the fight
With a bullet where my belt-plate should 'a' been.
55 I was chokin', mad with thirst,
An' the man that spied me first
Was our good old grinnin', gruntin' Gunga Din.
'E lifted up my 'ead,
An' he plugged me where I bled,
60 An' 'e guv me 'arf-a-pint o' water—green;

27. *Harry By*—O, brother.   32. *Juldee*—Speed.   33. *Marrow*—Hit.
41. *Mussick*—Water bag made of skin.

>   It was crawlin' and it stunk,
>   But of all the drinks I've drunk,
>   I'm gratefullest to one from Gunga Din.
>   It was "Din! Din! Din!
> 65   'Ere's a beggar with a bullet through 'is spleen,
>   'E's chawin' up the ground,
>   An' 'e's kickin' all around:
>   For Gawd's sake git the water, Gunga Din!"
>
>   'E carried me away
> 70   To where a *dooli* lay,
>   An' a bullet come an' drilled the beggar clean.
>   'E put me safe inside,
>   An' just before 'e died:
>   "I hope you liked your drink," sez Gunga Din.
> 75   So I'll meet 'im later on
>   At the place where 'e is gone—
>   Where it's always double drill and no canteen;
>
>   'E'll be squattin' on the coals,
>   Givin' drink to poor damned souls,
> 80   An' I'll get a swig in hell from Gunga Din!
>   Yes, Din! Din! Din!
>   You Lazarushian-leather Gunga Din!
>   Though I've belted you and flayed you,
>   By the livin' Gawd that made you,
> 85   You're a better man than I am, Gunga Din!

70. *Dooli*—A litter for the wounded.
82. LAZARUSHIAN—From Lazarus, a kindly beggar.

Poem Development: Give in your own words the meaning of the first six lines. Where had the speaker seen active fighting? Who was the finest man he knew? Would an Indian water-carrier be appreciated by the men of the regiment? What were some of the outstanding qualities of Gunga Din? Relate the incident when he gave the British soldier water. Why was the soldier so grateful for this service? What happened to Gunga Din? What is the highest compliment that the soldier pays Gunga Din? Give the theme of the poem. What is the central thought?

Interpretations: Quartered (l. 2); do your work on water (l. 5); troop-train (l. 24); wopped 'im (l. 29); 'e was white (l. 45).

Significant Expressions: Quote lines which express appreciation of Gunga Din.

FUZZY-WUZZY

Rudyard Kipling

Poem Interest: Here's a tribute from one fighting man to another! With traditional pride in the power of his own country's troops, the British soldier has nothing but admiration for the spirit of the native "Fuzzy-Wuzzy."

We've fought with many men acrost the seas,
   An' some of 'em was brave an' some was not:
The Paythan an' the Zulu an' Burmese;
   But the Fuzzy was the finest o' the lot.
5 We never got a ha'porth's change of 'im:
   'E squatted in the scrub an' 'ocked our 'orses,
'E cut our sentries up at *Suakim,*
   An' 'e played the cat an' banjo with our forces.
     So 'ere's *to* you, Fuzzy-Wuzzy, at your 'ome in the Soudan;
10   You're a pore benighted 'eathen but a first-class fightin' man;
     We gives you your certifikit, an' if you want it signed
     We'll come an' 'ave a romp with you whenever you're inclined.

Fuzzy-Wuzzy—The native soldier of the Sudan in Africa, so named, probably for his huge head of fuzzy hair.
5. Ha'porth's—Half-penny's worth.
7. *Suakim*—Suakin, in the African Sudan.

    We took our chanst among the Kyber 'ills,
        The Boers knocked us silly at a mile,
15   The Burman give us Irriwaddy chills,
        An' a Zulu *impi* dished us up in style:
    But all we ever got from such as they
        Was pop to what the Fuzzy made us swaller;
    We 'eld our bloomin' own, the papers say,
20   But man for man the Fuzzy knocked us 'oller.
        Then 'ere's *to* you, Fuzzy-Wuzzy, an' the missis and the kid;
          Our orders was to break you, an' of course we went and did.
          We sloshed you with Martinis, an' it wasn't 'ardly fair;
          But for all the odds agin you, Fuzzy-Wuz, you broke the square.

25 'E 'asn't got no papers of 'is own,
       'E 'asn't got no medals nor rewards,
    So we must certify the skill 'e's shown
       In usin' of 'is long two-'anded swords:
    When 'e's 'oppin' in an' out among the bush
30   With 'is coffin-'eaded shield an' shovel-spear,
    A 'appy day with Fuzzy on the rush
       Will last a 'ealthy Tommy for a year.
        So 'ere's *to* you, Fuzzy-Wuzzy, an' your friends which are no more,
          If we 'adn't lost some messmates we would 'elp you to deplore;
35   But give an' take's the gospel, an' we'll call the bargain fair,
          For if you 'ave lost more than us, you crumpled up the square!

    'E rushes at the smoke when we let drive,
       An', before we know, 'e's 'ackin' at our 'ead;
    'E's all 'ot sand an' ginger when alive,
40   An' 'e's generally shammin' when 'e's dead.

13. KYBER—Khyber Pass, in India.
15. IRRIWADDY—The Irrawaddy River in Burma.
16. ZULU *impi*—A South African warrior.
23. MARTINIS—Probably a kind of gun.
32. TOMMY—A British soldier.

'E's a daisy, 'e's a ducky, 'e's a lamb!
'E's a injia-rubber idiot on the spree,
'E's the only thing that doesn't give a damn
For a Regiment o' British Infantree!
45   So 'ere's *to* you, Fuzzy-Wuzzy, at your 'ome in the Soudan;
You're a pore benighted 'eathen but a first-class fightin' man;
An' 'ere's *to* you, Fuzzy-Wuzzy, with your 'ayrick 'ead of 'air—
You big black boundin' beggar—for you broke a British square!

Poem Development: The British soldier mentions some of the people whom he has fought against. How do they compare with Fuzzy-Wuzzy? What can you say of Fuzzy's skill with his sword and spear? What is the meaning of line 40? What are the soldier's words of highest praise? What is the theme of the poem? What is the central thought?

Interpretations: 'Ocked our 'orses (l. 6); all the odds agin you (l. 24); coffin-'eaded shield and shovel-spear (l. 30); 'ayrick 'ead of 'air (l. 47).

Significant Expressions: Quote lines which express admiration for the fighting spirit of Fuzzy-Wuzzy.

RECESSIONAL

Rudyard Kipling

Poem Interest: The Diamond Jubilee which marked Queen Victoria's sixty years of sovereignty was held in England in 1897. As the appointed hours of June 22nd drew nigh, kings, princes, and potentates began to gather in London. There were British troops, and troops from every colony—there were white people, yellow people, black people, brown people. The streets were ablaze with color as this cavalcade of assorted peoples started the two weeks' festivities with a procession six miles long from Buckingham Palace to St. Paul's. The power of England, her extensive possessions, her wealth were all subjects of song and story. As the Jubilee was being brought to a close, it remained for Kipling in his *Recessional* to sound a plea for balance; to utter a prayer for humbleness.

God of our fathers, known of old,
Lord of our far-flung battle-line,

Beneath whose awful hand we hold
  Dominion over palm and pine—
5 Lord God of Hosts, be with us yet,
  Lest we forget—lest we forget!

The tumult and the shouting dies;
  The Captains and the Kings depart
Still stands Thine ancient sacrifice,
10   An humble and a contrite heart.
Lord God of Hosts, be with us yet,
  Lest we forget—lest we forget!

Far-called our navies melt away;
  On dune and headland sinks the fire;
15 Lo, all our pomp of yesterday
  Is one with Nineveh and Tyre!
Judge of the nations, spare us yet,
  Lest we forget—lest we forget!

If, drunk with sight of power, we loose
20   Wild tongues that have not Thee in awe,
Such boasting as the gentiles use
  Or lesser breeds without the Law—
Lord God of Hosts, be with us yet,
  Lest we forget—lest we forget!

25 For heathen heart that puts her trust
  In reeking tube and iron shard,
All valiant dust that builds on dust,
  And guarding calls not Thee to guard,
For frantic boast and foolish word—
30   Thy mercy on Thy people, Lord!

4. PALM AND PINE—Representative of the extent of the British colonies.
16. NINEVEH AND TYRE—The Assyrian empire, after existing as a great power for more than twelve centuries, came to an end with the fall of Nineveh. Tyre was a splendid Phoenician city which was captured by Alexander the Great in 332 B.C. and never recovered its greatness. The cities are representative of great glory and pomp which have long since disappeared.
21. GENTILES—Kipling thinks of the English as being God's chosen people of modern times—the Israelites. Hence, the gentiles would be other nations, outside or "without" God's law.
26. TUBE AND IRON SHARD—Cannon and bombshell.

Poem Development: The first stanza begins the prayer. How extensive is England's domain as Kipling represents it? As the potentates and rulers depart for their own countries, what does the poet say is left in England? What is meant by the reference to Nineveh and Tyre? How does Kipling address God in the third stanza? Is excess of power likely to make nations and people forget God? Give the plea of the last stanza in your own words? What is the meaning of the most repeated line? Tell the story of the Golden Jubilee and of Kipling's reaction as given in the poem. What is the theme of the poem? Give the central thought.

Interpretations: Far-flung battle-line; awful hand; our navies melt away; dune and headland; pomp of yesterday; drunk with sight of power; loose wild tongues; line 27.

Significant Expressions: Quote lines which to you are especially imaginative and striking. Quote lines descriptive of the end of the celebration.

I MEANT TO DO MY WORK TODAY

Richard Le Gallienne

Poem Interest: Have the flowers in your garden ever called you to come and pick them? Have the birds ever enticed you to follow them into the woods? Have you ever answered an oriole's call and had him call back to you? If so you will understand how the poet feels.

> I meant to do my work today
>   But a brown bird sang in the apple-tree,
> And a butterfly flitted across the field,
>   And all the leaves were calling me.
>
> And the wind went sighing over the land,
>   Tossing the grasses to and fro,
> And a rainbow held out its shining hand—
>   So what could I do but laugh and go?

Poem Development: What were the reasons the work was left undone? Did the poet come back better able to work, do you think? What is the theme? Give the central thought.

Significant Expressions: Quote the line containing the most vivid call. Quote a line containing a sound image.

THE EXAMPLE

William Henry Davies

Poem Interest: It is not what life holds for us, it is what we hold for life that makes for happiness. We may gain all the world can offer of luxuries, but if we know not the happy heart which can transform simple things into beauty, our lot is sad indeed.

> Here's an example from
>   A Butterfly;
> That on a rough, hard rock
>   Happy can lie;
> 5 Friendless and all alone
>   On this unsweetened stone.
>
> Now let my bed be hard,
>   No care take I;
> I'll make my joy like this
> 10 Small Butterfly;
> Whose happy heart has power
>   To make a stone a flower.

Poem Development: What is the significance of the title? What is the example? Where did the butterfly lie? How did it make a stone a flower? Express the thought of the poem in your own words.

Interpretations: Unsweetened stone.

Significant Expressions: Quote a line giving a feeling image; one giving a visual image. What is the figure of speech in lines 9 and 10?

A GREETING

William Henry Davies

Poem Interest: There is a charming woman, who, no matter what the weather, greets the day by saying, "It's a beautiful day to be glad in." Here is another greeting, this time in poem form . . .

> Good morning, Life—and all
> Things glad and beautiful.
> My pockets nothing hold,
> But he that owns the gold,

5   The Sun, is my great friend—
    His spending has no end.

    Hail to the morning sky,
    Which bright clouds measure high;
    Hail to you birds whose throats
10 Would number leaves by notes;
    Hail to you shady bowers,
    And you green fields of flowers.

    Hail to you women fair,
    That make a show so rare
15 In cloth as white as milk—
    Be't calico or silk:
    Good morning, Life—and all
    Things glad and beautiful.

Poem Development: What is the opening greeting? Who owns the gold? Name the other greetings. What perfect whole do they all make? What special thoughts would come with your own "Good morning, Life"? What is the theme of the poem? What is the central thought?

Interpretations: His spending has no end; would number leaves by notes; be't calico or silk.

Significant Expressions: Quote lines which express the poet's love of life.

SILVER *

WALTER DE LA MARE

Poem Interest: Create in your mind a picture which is in just one color. Try first a rainy day and make this picture all in gray. Then picture a sunset all in reds. The Grand Canyon in some lights can be seen in shades of purple. Now read the following poem for still another color picture.

SLOWLY, silently, now the moon
Walks the night in her silvery shoon;
This way, and that, she peers, and sees
Silver fruit upon silver trees;

---

* From *Peacock Pie* by Walter de la Mare. Reprinted by permission of Henry Holt and Company, publishers.

5   One by one the casements catch
    Her beams beneath the silvery thatch;
    Couched in his kennel, like a log,
    With paws of silver sleeps the dog;
    From their shadowy cote the white breasts peep
10 Of doves in a silver-feathered sleep;
    A harvest mouse goes scampering by,
    With silver claws and a silver eye;
    And moveless fish in the water gleam,
    By silver reeds in a silver stream.

Poem Development: The whole poem is a study in silver. Notice the constant recurrence of the letter *s*. Could an artist paint this picture? Notice how the rhythm adds smoothness and quietness to the picture. Can you see the dog with only his paws showing in the kennel opening? Which do you think is the most vivid image? the most beautiful? What is the theme of the poem? Give the central thought.

Interpretations: Walks the night; casements; cote.

Significant Expressions: Quote words or lines which you think make a pleasant sound. Give the figure of speech in lines: 2, 4, 7.

THE LISTENERS *

Walter de la Mare

Poem Interest: Have you ever let your voice ring out in an old, deserted house? How weirdly it echoes back to you through the bare and empty rooms! In the uncanny silence you can almost feel the presence of former dwellers who listen to your voice, but cannot answer.

    "Is there anybody there?" said the traveler,
        Knocking on the moonlit door;
    And his horse in the silence champed the grasses
        Of the forest's ferny floor;
5   And a bird flew up out of the turret,
        Above the traveler's head;
    And he smote upon the door again a second time;
        "Is there anybody there?" he said.
    But no one descended to the traveler;
10   No head from the leaf-fringed sill

* From *The Listeners and Other Poems* by Walter de la Mare. Reprinted by permission of Henry Holt and Company, publishers.

Leaned over and looked into his gray eyes,
   Where he stood perplexed and still.

But only a host of phantom listeners
   That dwelt in the lone house then
15 Stood listening in the quiet of the moonlight
   To that voice from the world of men;
Stood thronging the faint moonbeams on the dark stair
   That goes down to the empty hall,
Hearkening in an air stirred and shaken
20   By the lonely traveler's call.
And he felt in his heart their strangeness,
   Their stillness answering his cry,
While his horse moved, cropping the dark turf,
   'Neath the starred and leafy sky;

25 For he suddenly smote on the door, even
   Louder, and lifted his head—
"Tell them I came, and no one answered,
   That I kept my word," he said.
Never the least stir made the listeners,
30   Though every word he spake
Fell echoing through the shadowiness of the still house
   From the one man left awake;
Ay, they heard his foot upon the stirrup,
   And the sound of iron on stone,
35 And how the silence surged softly backward,
   When the plunging hoofs were gone.

Poem Development: De la Mare is an adept at creating a mysterious and supernatural atmosphere in his poetry. *The Listeners* does not so much tell a story as it creates a mood. Select some words or lines which you think add to the mysterious atmosphere. Who listened to the traveler's knock? What is the effect of the last two lines? Give the theme of the poem. What is the central thought?

Interpretations: Champed; ferny floor; leaf-fringed sill; leafy sky; the one man left awake.

Significant Expressions: Quote the line giving the first sound image; the second sound image. Quote lines which add to the uncanny atmosphere.

THE DONKEY

Gilbert Keith Chesterton

Poem Interest: In the life of even the most humble of creatures there comes a supreme moment. Chesterton chooses to tell of that which came to the donkey.

> When fishes flew and forests walked
>   And figs grew upon thorn,
> Some moment when the moon was blood,
>   Then surely I was born;
>
> 5 With monstrous head and sickening cry
>   And ears like errant wings,
> The devil's walking parody
>   On all four-footed things.
>
> The tattered outlaw of the earth,
> 10   Of ancient crooked will;
> Starve, scourge, deride me: I am dumb,
>   I keep my secret still.
>
> Fools! For I also had my hour;
>   One far fierce hour and sweet:
> 15 There was a shout about my ears,
>   And palms before my feet.

13. My hour—A reference to the time when Christ rode into Jerusalem upon a donkey.

Poem Development: Someone has said that Chesterton has the ability to present an unexpected subject in a way that nobody ever happened to think of before. Would the above poem make you think this to be true? Do fishes ever fly or forests walk? What is the thought conveyed by these paradoxes? With what thought does the donkey console himself for all the things he lacks? Why does he say "Fools"? What is the theme of the poem? Give the central thought.

Interpretations: Sickening cry; errant wings; walking parody; palms before my feet.

Significant Expressions: Give two illustrations of alliteration; one of simile; one of metaphor. Quote a line showing dejection; one showing exultation.

TEWKESBURY ROAD *

John Masefield

Poem Interest: What a delightful contrast to the crowded pushing of a city street is an aimless tramp down "Tewkesbury Road" . . .

It is good to be out on the road, and going one knows not where,
    Going through meadow and village, one knows not whither nor why;
Through the grey light drift of the dust, in the keen cool rush of the air,
    Under the flying white clouds, and the broad blue lift of the sky.

5 And to halt at the chattering brook, in the tall green fern at the brink
    Where the harebell grows, and the gorse, and the foxgloves purple and white;
Where the shy-eyed delicate deer troop down to the pools to drink,
    When the stars are mellow and large at the coming on of the night.

O! to feel the warmth of the rain, and the homely smell of the earth,
10   Is a tune for the blood to jig to, a joy past power of words;
And the blessed green comely meadows seem all a-ripple with mirth
    At the lilt of the shifting feet, and the dear wild cry of the birds.

* From *Collected Poems* by John Masefield. Reprinted by permission of The Macmillan Company, publishers.

Poem Development: The poet's first picture is that of motion. Through what places does he pass? What senses does he appeal to in the first stanza? The second stanza is predominately quiet. Where does the poet stop? What points does he touch upon in his description of the scene? What human emotions does the last stanza arouse? Write a précis of the poem, giving the theme and central thought.

Significant Expressions: Quote lines which produce color effects. Quote the line giving the most vivid picture.

ROUNDING THE HORN *

John Masefield

Poem Interest: During his early days as cabin boy on a sailing vessel, John Masefield learned much of the ways of the sea. *Rounding the Horn*, with its wild, shocking blows of the storm at the Cape, the mad, shrill sea noises, and the tormented agony of the Dauber, reveals his intimate knowledge of the cruelty and capriciousness of that mightiest of monarchs, old King Neptune.

>   Then came the cry of "Call all hands on deck!"
>   The Dauber knew its meaning; it was come:
>   Cape Horn, that tramples beauty into wreck,
>   And crumples steel and smites the strong man dumb.
> 5 Down clattered flying kites and staysails; some
>   Sang out in quick, high calls: the fair-leads skirled,
>   And from the south-west came the end of the world . . .
>
>   "Lay out!" the Bosun yelled. The Dauber laid
>   Out on the yard, gripping the yard, and feeling
> 10 Sick at the mighty space of air displayed
>   Below his feet, where mewing birds were wheeling.
>   A giddy fear was on him; he was reeling.

* From *Dauber* by John Masefield. Reprinted by permission of The Macmillan Company, publishers.
  5. Kites—Light, lofty sails for use in light breezes.
  6. Fair-leads—Blocks or rings which serve as guides for running rigging.
  9. Yard—A long spar which supports the sail.

He bit his lip half through, clutching the jack.
A cold sweat glued the shirt upon his back.

15 The yard was shaking, for a brace was loose.
He felt that he would fall; he clutched, he bent,
Clammy with natural terror to the shoes
While idiotic promptings came and went.
Snow fluttered on a wind-flaw and was spent;
20 He saw the water darken. Someone yelled,
"Frap it; don't stay to furl! Hold on!" He held.

Darkness came down—half darkness—in a whirl;
The sky went out, the waters disappeared.
He felt a shocking pressure of blowing hurl
25 The ship upon her side. The darkness speared
At her with wind; she staggered, she careered;
Then down she lay. The Dauber felt her go,
He saw her yard tilt downwards. Then the snow

Whirled all about—dense, multitudinous, cold—
30 Mixed with the wind's one devilish thrust and shriek,
Which whiffled out men's tears, defeated, took hold,
Flattening the flying drift against the cheek.
The yards buckled and bent, man could not speak.
The ship lay on her broadside; the wind's sound
35 Had devilish malice at having got her downed.

How long the gale had blown he could not tell,
Only the world had changed, his life had died.
A moment now was everlasting hell.
Nature an onslaught from the weather side,
40 A withering rush of death, a frost that cried,
Shrieked, till he withered at the heart; a hail
Plastered his oilskins with an icy mail. . . .

"Up!" yelled the Bosun; "up and clear the wreck!"
The Dauber followed where he led; below
45 He caught one giddy glimpsing of the deck

21. FRAP IT—Bind it tightly together.

Filled with white water, as though heaped with snow.
He saw the streamers of the rigging blow
Straight out like pennons from the splintered mast,
Then, all sense dimmed, all was an icy blast.

50 Roaring from nether hell and filled with ice,
Roaring and crashing on the jerking stage,
An utter bridle given to utter vice,
Limitless power mad with endless rage
Withering the soul; a minute seemed an age.
55 He clutched and hacked at ropes, at rags of sail,
Thinking that comfort was a fairy tale,

Told long ago—long, long ago—long since
Heard of in other lives—imagined, dreamed—
There where the basest beggar was a prince.
60 To him in torment where the tempest screamed,
Comfort and warmth and ease no longer seemed
Things that a man could know; soul, body, brain,
Knew nothing but the wind, the cold, the pain.

52. AN UTTER BRIDLE GIVEN TO UTTER VICE—That is, there was no restraint whatever on the wind.

Poem Development: This selection is taken from a longer poem entitled *Dauber*. The Dauber was a poor artist who had shipped on a sailing vessel in the hope of learning sea colors, ship's lines, sunsets to enable him "to paint great ships at sea." Instead, he was "done to death" by the heartless seamen who could not understand him nor appreciate his love of beauty and art. You will want to read the whole poem to get the complete story of this tragic sailor-painter.

Can you picture a storm coming with such force that it seems to bring the end of the world? Paint a word picture of the Dauber out on the yard arm. What happened to the ship? Can you feel the wind and the cold? Can you picture the onslaught of the hail? Describe the deck after the storm. What were the Dauber's thoughts about warmth and comfort? What is the theme of the poem? Give the central thought.

Interpretations: Crumples steel; furl; the sky went out; icy mail; Bosun; pennons.

Significant Expressions: Quote the lines describing Cape Horn. Quote the lines best describing the Dauber's fear and discomfort. Quote lines which describe the wind and the cold. Find examples of similes, metaphors, onomatopoeia, and alliteration.

JOHN MASEFIELD

A CONSECRATION *

John Masefield

Poem Interest: Behind the scenes of every accomplishment are to be found the tireless efforts of unheralded workers who keep the wheels of life going round. Masefield has thought of these men who carry the burdens of life . . .

    Not of the princes and prelates with periwigged charioteers
    Riding triumphantly laurelled to lap the fat of the years,—
    Rather the scorned—the. rejected—the men hemmed in with the spears;

    The men of the tattered battalion which fights till it dies,
5 Dazed with the dust of the battle, the din and the cries.
    The men with the broken heads and the blood running into their eyes.

    Not the be-medalled Commander, beloved of the throne,
    Riding cock-horse to parade when the bugles are blown,
    But the lads who carried the koppie and cannot be known.

10 Not the ruler for me, but the ranker, the tramp of the road,
    The slave with the sack on his shoulders pricked on with the goad,
    The man with too weighty a burden, too weary a load.

    The sailor, the stoker of steamers, the man with the clout,
    The chantyman bent at the halliards putting a tune to the shout,
15 The drowsy man at the wheel and the tired look-out.

    Others may sing of the wine and the wealth and the mirth,
    The portly presence of potentates goodly in girth;—
    Mine be the dirt and the dross, the dust and scum of the earth!

    * From *Collected Poems* by John Masefield. Reprinted by permission of The Macmillan Company, publishers.
    9. Koppie—A word used in South Africa to mean kop, or small hill. The reference is to the Boer War.
    13. Clout—Cloth or rag.
    14. Chantyman—The sailor who leads in the singing as the men work at the halliards (sails).

Theirs be the music, the colour, the glory, the gold;
20 Mine be a handful of ashes, a mouthful of mold.
  Of the maimed, of the halt and the blind in the rain and the
      cold—
  Of these shall my songs be fashioned, my tales be told.

Poem Development: From your knowledge of Masefield's own life why do you think he would choose to sing of the toiling and suffering types of humanity? The poem is a series of comparisons between the powerful and the weak, the successful and the scorned, the rich and the poor. What is the comparison in the first stanza? What picture do you see? In your own words describe the picture in the second stanza; in the third stanza. Why would Masefield think of the men mentioned in the fifth stanza? What is the meaning of line 20? What is the theme of the poem? Give the central thought.

Interpretations: Prelates; periwigged charioteers; laurelled; lap the fat of the years; riding cock-horse; carried the koppie; ranker; pricked on with the goad; the man with the clout; look-out; potentates.

Significant Expressions: Quote the stanza which you think presents the most vivid picture. Quote the lines which best express the poet's sympathy for the workers of the world. What is the figure of speech in line 1? in line 2? in line 20?

THE BARREL ORGAN *

Alfred Noyes

Poem Interest: Music, perhaps more than any other art, has power to recall images of the past and to awaken memories long forgotten. The sound of a hurdy-gurdy on a London street sends the thoughts of each hurrying passer-by back to the sweetness and sorrow of memories of days gone by . . .

  There's a barrel organ caroling across a golden street
    In the City as the sun sinks low;
  And the music's not immortal; but the world has made it
      sweet
    And fulfilled it with the sunset glow;
5 And it pulses through the pleasures of the City and the pain
    That surround the singing organ like a large eternal light;

* Reprinted by permission from *Collected Poems,* Volume I, by Alfred Noyes. Copyright, 1906, by Frederick A. Stokes Company.

And they've given it a glory and a part to play again
　　In the symphony that rules the day and night.

And now it's marching onward through the realms of old romance,
10　And trolling out a fond familiar tune,
And now it's roaring cannon down to fight the King of France,
　　And now it's prattling softly to the moon,

And all around the organ there's a sea without a shore
　　Of human joys and wonders and regrets;
15 To remember and to recompense the music evermore
　　For what the cold machinery forgets. . . .

　　　Yes; as the music changes,
　　　　Like a prismatic glass,
　　　It takes the light and ranges
20　　　Through all the moods that pass;
　　　Dissects the common carnival
　　　　Of passions and regrets,
　　　And gives the world a glimpse of all
　　　　The colors it forgets.

25　　And there *La Traviata* sighs
　　　　Another sadder song;
　　　And there *Il Trovatore* cries
　　　　A tale of deeper wrong;
　　　And bolder knights to battle go
30　　　With sword and shield and lance,
　　　Than ever here on earth below
　　　　Have whirled into—*a dance!*—

Go down to Kew in lilac time, in lilac time, in lilac time;
Go down to Kew in lilac time (it isn't far from London!)
35 And you shall wander hand in hand with love in summer's wonderland;
Go down to Kew in lilac time (it isn't far from London!)

25. *La Traviata*—An opera by Verdi, an Italian composer.
27. *Il Trovatore*—Another opera by Verdi.
33. Kew—A village and park near London, the popular resort of tired people from London in the spring and summer.

The cherry trees are seas of bloom and soft perfume and
    sweet perfume,
  The cherry trees are seas of bloom (and oh, so near to
    London!)
And there they say, when dawn is high and all the world's
    a blaze of sky
40 The cuckoo, though he's very shy, will sing a song for
    London.

The Dorian nightingale is rare, and yet they say you'll hear
    him there
  At Kew, at Kew in lilac time (and oh, so near to London!)
The linnet and the throstle, too, and after dark the long
    halloo
  And golden-eyed *tu-whit, to-whoo* of owls that ogle
    London.

45 For Noah hardly knew a bird of any kind that isn't heard
    At Kew, at Kew in lilac time (and oh, so near to London!)
And when the rose begins to pout, and all the chestnut
    spires are out,
  You'll hear the rest without a doubt, all chorusing for
    London—

Come down to Kew in lilac time, in lilac time, in lilac time;
50 *Come down to Kew in lilac time (it isn't far from*
    London!)
And you shall wander hand in hand with love in summer's
    wonderland;
  Come down to Kew in lilac time (it isn't far from
    London!)

And then the troubadour begins to thrill the golden street,
  In the City as the sun sinks low;
55 And in all the gaudy busses there are scores of weary feet
Marking time, sweet time, with a dull mechanic beat,
And a thousand hearts are plunging to a love they'll never
    meet,

41. DORIAN—Simple, natural.

Through the meadows of the sunset, through the poppies and the wheat,
    In the land where the dead dreams go.

60 Verdi, Verdi, when you wrote *Il Trovatore* did you dream
    Of the City when the sun sinks low,
Of the organ and the monkey and the many-colored stream
On the Piccadilly pavement, of the myriad eyes that seem
To be litten for a moment with a wild Italian gleam
65 As *Ah che la morte* parodies the world's eternal theme
    And pulses with the sunset glow?

There's a thief, perhaps, that listens with a face of frozen stone
    In the City as the sun sinks low,
There's a portly man of business with a balance of his own,
70 There's a clerk and there's a butcher of a soft reposeful tone,
And they're all of them returning to the heavens they have known;
They are crammed and jammed in busses and—they're each of them alone
    In the land where the dead dreams go.

There's a very modish woman, and her smile is very bland
75   In the City as the sun sinks low;
And her hansom jingles onward, but her little jeweled hand
Is clenched a little tighter and she cannot understand
What she wants or why she wanders to that undiscovered land,
For the parties there are not at all the sort of thing she planned,
80   In the land where the dead dreams go.

There's a rowing man that listens and his heart is crying out
    In the City as the sun sinks low,
For the barge, the eight, the Isis, and the coach's whoop and shout,

---

  63. PICCADILLY—A famous London street.
  65. *Ah che la morte*—The first words of *Il Trovatore*.
  83. THE EIGHT—The crew of eight.
  83. ISIS—The upper part of the Thames where the Cambridge-Oxford races are held.

For the minute gun, the counting and the long disheveled
       rout,
85 For the howl along the towpath and a fate that's still in
       doubt,
  For a roughened oar to handle and a race to think about
    In a land where the dead dreams go.

  There's a laborer that listens to the voices of the dead
    In the City as the sun sinks low;
90 And his hand begins to tremble and face to smolder red
  As he sees a loafer watching him and—there he turns his
       head
  And stares into the sunset where his April love is fled,
  For he hears her softly singing and his lonely soul is led
    Through the land where the dead dreams go.

95 There's an old and haggard demi-rep, it's ringing in her
       ears,
    In the City as the sun sinks low;
  With the wild and empty sorrow of the love that blights
       and sears,
  Oh, and if she hurries onward, then be sure, be sure she
       hears,
  Hears and bears the bitter burden of the unforgotten years,
100 And her laugh's a little harsher and her eyes are brimmed
       with tears
    For the land where the dead dreams go.

  There's a barrel organ caroling across a golden street
    In the City as the sun sinks low;
  Though the music's only Verdi there's a world to make it
       sweet,
105 Just as yonder yellow sunset where the earth and heaven
       meet
  Mellows all the sooty City! Hark, a hundred thousand feet
  Are marching on to glory through the poppies and the wheat
    In the land where the dead dreams go.

         So it's Jeremiah, Jeremiah,
110   What have you to say

When you meet the garland girls
Tripping on their way?

All around my gala hat
I wear a wreath of roses
(A long and lonely year it is
I've waited for the May!)
If any one should ask you,

The reason why I wear it is—
My own love, my true love
Is coming home today.

And it's buy a bunch of violets for the lady
(*It's lilac time in London; it's lilac time in London!*)
Buy a bunch of violets for the lady
While the sky burns blue above;
On the other side the street you'll find it shady
(*It's lilac time in London; it's lilac time in London!*)
But buy a bunch of violets for the lady,
And tell her she's your own true love.

There's a barrel organ caroling across a golden street
In the City as the sun sinks glittering and slow;
And the music's not immortal; but the world has made it sweet
And enriched it with the harmonies that make a song complete
In the deeper heavens of music where the night and morning meet,
As it dies into the sunset glow;
And it pulses through the pleasures of the City and the pain
That surround the singing organ like a large eternal light,
And they've given it a glory and a part to play again
In the symphony that rules the day and night.

And there, as the music changes,
The song runs round again.
Once more it turns and ranges
Through all its joy and pain,
Dissects the common carnival

<pre>
                    Of passions and regrets;
145   And the wheeling world remembers all
                The wheeling song forgets.
            Once more *La Traviata* sighs
                Another sadder song;
            Once more *Il Trovatore* cries
150   A tale of deeper wrong;
            Once more the knights to battle go
                With sword and shield and lance
            Till once, once more, the shattered foe
                Has whirled into—*a dance!*
</pre>

155 *Come down to Kew in lilac time, in lilac time, in lilac time;*
    Come down to Kew in lilac time (it isn't far from London!)
And you shall wander hand in hand with love in summer's wonderland;
    Come down to Kew in lilac time (it isn't far from London!)

Poem Development: There are few hurdy-gurdies to be heard on American streets today. Extra quarters and dimes go for other pleasures, and none are left for the organ-grinder and his monkey. What kind of music does the barrel-organ play? How does the poet suggest a change in the music? Name the rhythm and meter used in the first two stanzas; in the third and fourth; in the five stanzas of the dance. What is the next selection played? Name the people who are listening. Why are they "alone"? What effect does the music have on the society woman? What does the old varsity man long for? What does the music make the laborer think of? How does it affect the woman of the streets? Tell about the music in your own words. Note the change in the rhythm and meter in the next five stanzas. What type of music do these suggest? Why does the poet repeat the lines which began the poem? What human emotions are touched upon in the poem? What is the theme of the poem? Give the central thought.

Interpretations: Golden street (l. 1); the music's not immortal (l. 3); trolling (l. 10); prismatic glass (l. 18); lines 21 and 22; troubadour (l. 53); litten (l. 64); parodies the world's eternal theme (l. 65).

Significant Expressions: Quote as many lines as you can find which appeal to the auditory sense. Quote a line appealing to the sense of smell. Quote a line having the rhythm of a dance. Quote a line showing great grief. Find four examples of metonomy; two examples of simile; two examples of metaphor.

AN OLD WOMAN OF THE ROADS *

Padraic Colum

Poem Interest: In Ireland, the woman beggar is a familiar figure. She is frequently seen wandering forlornly along the public roads—a human derelict without home or place to lay her head. It is therefore not to be wondered at that she cherishes a hope such as that expressed in the poem . . .

O, to have a little house!
To own the hearth and stool and all!
The heaped-up sods upon the fire,
The pile of turf against the wall!

5 To have a clock with weights and chains
And pendulum swinging up and down!
A dresser filled with shining delph,
Speckled and white and blue and brown!

I could be busy all the day
10 Clearing and sweeping hearth and floor,
And fixing on their shelf again
My white and blue and speckled store!

I could be quiet there at night
Beside the fire and by myself,

* From *Collected Poems* by Padraic Colum. Reprinted by permission of The Macmillan Company, publishers.

15 Sure of a bed and loath to leave
    The ticking clock and the shining delph!

    Och! but I'm weary of mist and dark,
    And roads where there's never a house nor bush,
    And tired I am of bog and road,
20 And the crying wind and the lonesome hush!

    And I am praying to God on high,
    And I am praying Him night and day,
    For a little house—a house of my own—
    Out of the wind's and the rain's way.

Poem Development: Compare the old woman of this poem with the discontented mother in Yeats' poem, *The Song of the Old Mother*. Which of the two women do you think is the more satisfied? What is the old woman's wish? Paint a word picture of her little house as she would like it. How would she busy herself? Why would the old woman be contented alone? Of what is she tired? What is her prayer? Do you like this poem? What is the theme of the poem? What is the central thought?

Significant Expressions: Quote the line which seems most descriptive to you of the house. Quote the line which seems to you to contain the most vivid image. Quote the line most expressive of weariness.

THE ROAD *

James Stephens

Poem Interest: To be our finest and our best at all times is to step up out of secrecy and darkness to openness and sunlight. James Stephens suggests the way . . .

> Because our lives are cowardly and sly,
> Because we do not dare to take or give,
> Because we scowl and pass each other by,
> We do not live; we do not dare to live.
>
> 5 We dive, each man, into his secret house,
>   And bolt the door, and listen in affright,
>   Each timid man beside a timid spouse,
>   With timid children huddles out of sight.

* From *Songs from the Clay* by James Stephens. Reprinted by permission of The Macmillan Company, publishers.

SIEGFRIED SASSOON

       Kissing in secret, fighting secretly!
10   We crawl and hide like vermin in a hole,
       Under the bravery of sun and sky,
       We flash our meannesses of face and soul.

       Let us go out and walk upon the road,
       And quit for evermore the brick-built den,
15   And lock and key, the hidden, shy abode
       That separates us from our fellow-men.

       And by contagion of the sun we may,
       Catch at a spark from that primeval fire,
       And learn that we are better than our clay,
20   And equal to the peaks of our desire.

Poem Development: Stephens says we do not live. What are the reasons he gives? Do you agree with him? Is the second stanza true? What does the poet want us to do? If we consider the "brick-built den" to be symbolic of our fear and lack of love of fellow-men, and the "road" symbolic of the path of knowledge and the full realization of the divine nature of each individual, how does the poet think we can throw off our cowardice and really live? Give the theme and central thought of the poem.

Interpretations: We do not dare to take or give; contagion of the sun; primeval fire; we are better than our clay.

DREAMERS

Siegfried Sassoon

Poem Interest: Sassoon bitterly protested against the glorification and false glamour of war. He was a soldier and knew the anguish and misery which are far removed from the romantic patriotism of flying flags and beating drums. *Dreamers* is a vivid picture of what he felt.

       Soldiers are citizens of death's grey land,
       Drawing no dividend from time's tomorrows.
       In the great hour of destiny they stand,
       Each with his feuds, and jealousies, and sorrows.
5   Soldiers are sworn to action; they must win
       Some flaming, fatal climax with their lives.
       Soldiers are dreamers; when the guns begin
       They think of firelit homes, clean beds, and wives.

I see them in foul dug-outs, gnawed by rats,
And in the ruined trenches, lashed with rain,
Dreaming of things they did with balls and bats,
And mocked by hopeless longing to regain
Bank-holidays, and picture shows, and spats,
And going to the office in the train.

Poem Development: Note the hopelessness of the first line. Does the poet think the soldier is ever repaid? Do you agree with him? In the words of the poet, what must soldiers win? Of what do they think when the gun-fire begins? Paint a word picture of the men as Sassoon saw them. What did the soldiers dream of? Give the theme and central thought.

Interpretations: Death's grey land; line 2; hour of destiny.

Significant Expressions: Quote the lines descriptive of the soldier's lot. Quote the lines telling what they must give for the winning of war. Quote lines which voice Sassoon's bitterness against war.

IN SERVICE

Winifred M. Letts

Poem Interest: Here is a picture of homesick little Nellie who suddenly meets an old friend . . .

Little Nellie Cassidy has got a place in town,
    She wears a fine white apron,
    She wears a new black gown,
An' the quarest little cap at all with straymers hanging down.

I met her one fine evening stravagin' down the street,
    A feathered hat upon her head,
    And boots upon her feet.
"Och, Mick," says she, "may God be praised that you and I should meet.

"It's lonesome in the city with such a crowd," says she;
    "I'm lost without the bog-land,
    I'm lost without the sea,
An' the harbor an' the fishing-boats that sail out fine and free.

5. Stravagin'—Walking, strolling.

"I'd give a golden guinea to stand upon the shore,
　　To see the big waves lepping,
15　　　To hear them splash and roar,
　To smell the tar and the drying nets, I'd not be asking
　　　　more.

"To see the small white houses, their faces to the sea,
　　The childher in the dooway,
　　　Or round my mother's knee;
20　For I'm strange and lonesome missing them, God keep
　　　them all," says she.

Little Nellie Cassidy earns fourteen pounds and more,
　　Waiting on the quality,
　　　And answering the door—
But her heart is some place far away upon the Wexford
　　　shore.

Poem Development: Describe Nellie as she is "in service." How does she look on the street? What feeling is expressed in her words of greeting to Mike? What did she miss? What and whom did she want to see? How was Nellie employed and how much did she earn? What are the theme and central thought of the poem?
Interpretations: A place in town; bog-land; golden guinea; waiting on the quality.
Significant Expressions: Quote the lines best describing Nellie. Quote the line expressing the most intense homesickness.

THE SOLDIER

RUPERT BROOKE

Poem Interest: The love of country is an outstanding characteristic of Englishmen. It is a part of them. Listen to these words, straight from the English heart of this soldier-poet . . .

IF I should die, think only this of me;
　　That there's some corner of a foreign field
　That is for ever England. There shall be
　　In that rich earth a richer dust concealed;

ELD

5   A dust whom England bore, shaped, made aware,
      Gave, once, her flowers to love, her ways to roam,
   A body of England's, breathing English air,
      Washed by the rivers, blest by suns of home.

   And think, this heart, all evil shed away,
10   A pulse in the eternal mind, no less
      Gives somewhere back the thoughts by England given;
   Her sights and sounds; dreams happy as her day;
     And laughter, learnt of friends; and gentleness,
      In hearts at peace, under an English heaven.

Poem Development: What is the meaning of the first three lines? What would indicate the soldier's love for England? What does he give back to England though his life is sacrificed? What is the theme of the poem? What is the central thought?

Interpretations: Richer dust; made aware; pulse in the eternal mind.

Significant Expressions: Quote the lines which best describe what England meant to the poet.

THE GREAT LOVER

Rupert Brooke

Poem Interest: It is a lover of life who speaks to us in this poem —a lover of the little familiar details which make up everyday living.

   I have been so great a lover: filled my days
   So proudly with the splendour of Love's praise,
   The pain, the calm, the astonishment,
   Desire illimitable, and still content,
5   And all dear names men use, to cheat despair,
   For the perplexed and viewless streams that bear
   Our hearts at random down the dark of life.
   Now, ere the unthinking silence on that strife
   Steals down, I would cheat drowsy Death so far,
10 My night shall be remembered for a star
   That outshone all the suns of all men's days.
   Shall I not crown them with immortal praise
   Whom I have loved, who have given me, dared with me
   High secrets, and in darkness knelt to see

15　　The inenarrable godhead of delight?
　　　Love is a flame;—we have beaconed the world's night.
　　　A city:—and we have built it, these and I.
　　　An emperor:—we have taught the world to die.
　　　So, for their sakes I loved, ere I go hence,
20　　And the high cause of Love's magnificance,
　　　And to keep loyalties young, I'll write those names
　　　Golden for ever, eagles, crying flames,
　　　And set them as a banner, that men may know,
　　　To dare the generations, burn, and blow
25　　Out on the wind of Time, shining and streaming. . . .
　　　These I have loved:
　　　　　　　　　　　White plates and cups, clean-gleaming,
　　　Ringed with blue lines; and feathery, faëry dust;
　　　Wet roofs, beneath the lamp-light; the strong crust
　　　Of friendly bread; and many-tasting food;
30　　Rainbows; and the blue bitter smoke of wood;
　　　And radiant raindrops couching in cool flowers;
　　　And flowers themselves, that sway through sunny hours,
　　　Dreaming of moths that drink them under the moon;
　　　Then, the cool kindliness of sheets, that soon
35　　Smooth away trouble; and the rough male kiss
　　　Of blankets; grainy wood; live hair that is
　　　Shining and free; blue-massing clouds; the keen
　　　Unpassioned beauty of a great machine;
　　　The benison of hot water; furs to touch;
40　　The good smell of old clothes; and other such—
　　　The comfortable smell of friendly fingers,
　　　Hair's fragrance, and the musty reek that lingers
　　　About dead leaves and last year's ferns. . . .
　　　　　　　　　　　　　　　　　　Dear names,
　　　And thousand others throng to me! Royal flames;
45　　Sweet water's dimpling laugh from tap or spring;
　　　Holes in the ground; and voices that do sing:
　　　Voices in laughter, too; and body's pain,
　　　Soon turned to peace; and the deep-panting train;
　　　Firm sands; the little dulling edge of foam
50　　That browns and dwindles as the wave goes home;
　　　And washen stones, gay for an hour; the cold
　　　Graveness of iron; moist black earthen mould;

Sleep; and high places; footprints in the dew;
And oaks; and brown horse-chestnuts, glossy-new;
55 And new-peeled sticks; and shining pools on grass;—
All these have been my loves. And these shall pass.
Whatever passes not, in the great hour,
Nor all my passion, all my prayers, have power
To hold them with me through the gate of Death.
60 They'll play deserter, turn with the traitor breath,
Break the high bond we made, and sell Love's trust
And sacramented covenant to the dust.
—Oh, never a doubt but, somewhere, I shall wake,
And give what's left of love again, and make
65 New friends, now strangers. . . .
      But the best I've known,
Stays here, and changes, breaks, grows old, is blown
About the winds of the world, and fades from brains
Of living men, and dies.
     Nothing remains.

O dear my loves, O faithless, once again
70 This one last gift I give: that after men
Shall know, and later lovers, far-removed
Praise you, "All these were lovely"; say, "He loved."

Poem Development: With what has the poet filled his days? Before he dies he wishes to cheat death by leaving something for the world to remember him by. What is it? What are the things he has loved which most appeal to you? Would you like to know well a person who could find such unending joy in the commonplace objects and events of life? What American poet had an abounding joy in the commonplace? What are the three reasons the poet gives for telling the names of the things he has loved? Does he regret being unable to take these loved things with him to another world? What thought comforts him? What is his last gift? What is the theme? What is the central thought?

Interpretations: Desire illimitable (l. 4); perplexed and viewless streams (l. 6); at random (l. 7); drowsy Death (l. 9); we have beaconed the world's night (l. 16); benison (l. 39); they'll play deserter (l. 60).

Significant Expressions: Choose lines throughout the poem which tell you the manner of man who wrote it. Quote the lines which express his thought of continued life and love. Find five metaphors.

Poetry in World Literature

General Characteristics

Poetry is the universal language. The souls of men change little. Nature was as beautiful and as full of meaning to the Chinese poet in 500 B.C. as it is today. Italian poets felt and expressed the same emotions years ago as they do today—the same emotions that are felt by the Russian, the German, the Scandinavian, the Frenchman, the Englishman, the American. But every poet says what he has to say in his own way, and every nation has had its feelings voiced through the words of poets whom it honors. Nothing gives such a realization of the brotherhood of man as reading the poetry of other lands. In the novel, the drama, the short story, the customs of each country are given such a prominent place that one is conscious of the differences. But in reading the poetry, one loses the differences in the oneness of emotional experience.

The following poems are illustrative of some of the world's greatest poetry. Since many of the poems have been translated by great English authors, they are of added interest. They reveal the riches of the world's poetry thus far gathered into readable English, and present a delightful display of beautiful verse written throughout the ages by poets of all the western and eastern worlds.

Chinese

THE MORNING GLORY

From the *Shi King*, or *Book of Odes* 500 B. C.

Poem Interest: Confucius, a celebrated Chinese philosopher, descendant of an illustrious but impoverished family, was born about the year 550 B. C. When he was twenty-two years old, he became a teacher. A government position was given him when he was fifty-two years old, but he resigned after seven years. Following a period of travel, Confucius returned to China, and spent the rest of his life in writing and teaching. The *Shi King* was compiled by Confucius from earlier collections which had long been in existence. It was through the poems in this book that the great Eastern teacher led his people to an understanding and respect for the feelings and wisdom of the men of old.

> THE morning glory climbs above my head,
>   Pale flowers of white and purple, blue and red.
>   I am disquieted.

Down in the withered grasses something stirred;
5   I thought it was his footfall that I heard.
Then a grasshopper chirred.

I climbed the hill just as the new moon showed,
I saw him coming on the southern road.
My heart lays down its load.

Poem Development: How does this poem illustrate the statement that poetry is ageless? If the date had not been given you, would you have known that it had been written 3,000 years ago, instead of yesterday? What are the theme and the central thought of this poem?

ON THE BIRTH OF HIS SON

Su Tung-p'o (1036–1101)

(*Translated by* Arthur Waley)

Poem Interest: Su Tung-p'o is the elaborated version of the name of Su Shih, a brilliant Chinese essayist and poet. So worthy were his writings that it is said his examiner found it difficult to believe that the compositions he submitted to win his final college degree were not the work of another man. Su Shih rose to be a statesman, but because he had the unfortunate faculty of making more enemies than friends, he was constantly struggling against the machinations of unscrupulous opponents. He is still read with delight by the Chinese.

FAMILIES, when a child is born
Want it to be intelligent.
I, through intelligence,
Having wrecked my whole life,
5   Only hope the baby will prove
Ignorant and stupid.
Then he will crown a tranquil life
By becoming a Cabinet Minister.

Poem Development: How does the thought of the poem reflect the experiences of the poet's own life? Do you think fashions in politics, and natures of politicians, have changed much in the last 1000 years? Give the theme and central thought.

Greek

THE OCEAN

MOSCHUS (THIRD CENTURY B. C.)

(*Translated by* PERCY BYSSHE SHELLEY)

Poem Interest: Moschus was a Greek poet, born at Syracuse, who flourished about the time 150 B.C. He wrote some interesting short epic poetry—a few pieces of which have been preserved. His poems are nearly all in hexameters.

WHEN winds that move not its calm surface sweep
The azure sea, I love the land no more;
The smiles of the serene and tranquil deep
Tempt my unquiet mind.—But when the roar
5   Of Ocean's gray abyss resounds, and foam
Gathers upon the sea, and vast waves burst,
I turn from the drear aspect to the home
Of earth and its deep woods, where intersperst,
When winds blow loud, pines make sweet melody.
10 Whose house is some lone bark, whose toil the sea,
Whose prey the wondering fish, an evil lot
Has chosen.—But I my languid limbs will fling
Beneath the plane, where the brook's murmuring
Moves the calm spirit, but disturbs it not.

Poem Development: What is the mood of this poem? How would a modern poet say the same thing? What is the meaning of "plane"?

Give in your own words, the comparison between the land and sea. Give the theme and central thought.

Latin

THE DYING CHRISTIAN TO HIS SOUL

The Emperor Hadrian (76–138)

(Translated by Alexander Pope*)*

Poem Interest: Hadrian was emperor of Rome through the years 117-138. It was he who renounced the policy of conquest, and established the eastern boundary of the empire at the Euphrates. You will be interested to note from his poem that he who reigned in peace, and built, as a protection against invasion from the north, the great wall which bears his name, also thought constructively upon relatively deeper problems.

    Vital spark of heavenly flame!
    Quit, oh quit this mortal frame:
      Trembling, hoping, lingering, flying,
     Oh the pain, the bliss of dying!
5   Cease, fond Nature, cease thy strife,
    And let me languish into life.

    Hark! they whisper; Angels say,
    Sister Spirit, come away.
      What is this absorbs me quite?
10   Steals my senses, shuts my sight,
    Drowns my spirits, draws my breath?
    Tell me, my Soul, can this be Death?

    The world recedes: it disappears!
    Heaven opens on my eyes! my ears
15   With sounds seraphic ring:
    Lend, lend your wings! I mount! I fly!
    O Grave! where is thy Victory?
    O Death! where is thy Sting.

Poem Development: This poetic version of the soul's passing is undeniably triumphant. In what way does it reflect the accepted Christian philosophy of death, which still prevails today?

GIOVANNI BOCCACCIO

Italian

INSCRIPTION FOR A PORTRAIT OF DANTE

Giovanni Boccaccio (1313–1375)

(Translated by Dante Gabriel Rossetti*)*

Poem Interest: Dante Alighieri was born in Florence in 1265. He became passionately absorbed in the love of his country, fought in her behalf, was entrusted with several foreign missions, and finally elected one of the Priors of Florence. Later, however, his home was destroyed and he was temporarily banished, as the result of a class struggle. His idealism crushed by this failure and humiliation, Dante gave up all connections with the established government and social order, and passed the remainder of his life in wandering from place to place. It was during this time that he wrote his finest piece of poetry, *The Divine Comedy*. In 1320, he retired to Ravenna, and there died in 1321.

It is appropriate that the celebrated Italian novelist and poet, Boccaccio, should be inspired to pen a tribute to the immortal Dante, the master who preceded him. The portrait referred to in the following poem probably is the portrait of Dante as a young man which hangs in Florence. Though injured by time and vandalism, it has been restored and is now among the present treasured masterpieces of the world.

> Dante Alighieri, a dark oracle,
> Of wisdom and of art, I am; whose mind
> Has to my country such great gifts assign'd
> That men account my powers a miracle.
> 5 My lofty fancy passed as low as Hell,
> As high as Heaven, secure and unconfin'd;
> And in my noble book doth every kind
> Of earthly lore and heavenly doctrine dwell.
> Renownéd Florence was my mother,—nay,
> 10 Stepmother unto me her piteous son,
> Through sin of cursed slander's tongue and tooth.
> Ravenna sheltered me so cast away;
> My body is with her,—my soul with One
> For whom no envy can make dim the truth.

Poem Development: Who is speaking, in the poem? What has he to say to those who pass by? Tell the meaning of "stepmother." Also explain what is meant by the last two lines. Comment upon the substance of the poem as a whole.

German

WANDERER'S NIGHT-SONGS

JOHANN WOLFGANG VON GOETHE (1749–1832)

(*Translated by* HENRY WADSWORTH LONGFELLOW)

Poem Interest: The name of Goethe, poet, dramatist, and prose writer, is the greatest in German literature. He first studied law and afterwards held important government posts. In 1782, he was ennobled. After the year 1794, Goethe devoted himself entirely to literature. Of his works, *Faust,* the tragedy, is probably the best known.

I

THOU that from the heavens art,
Every pain and sorrow stillest,
And the doubly wretched heart
Doubly with refreshment fillest,

5   I am weary with contending!
Why this rapture and unrest?
Peace descending
Come, ah, come into my breast!

II

O'er all the hill-tops
Is quiet now,
In all the tree-tops
Hearest thou
5   Hardly a breath;
The birds are asleep in the trees:
Wait; soon like these
Thou too shalt rest.

Poem Development: What is the poet seeking in the first song? It is interesting to note that in most cases the translators choose world poetry expressive of their own deepest experiences. Longfellow, upon the death of his wife, wrote an appealing poem of his own, called *Hymn to the Night,* telling much the same story as this one of Goethe's. Thus we again see the kinship between the poets and poetry of our own and other lands.

Norwegian

IN THE ORCHARD

Henrik Ibsen (1828–1906)

Poem Interest: Ibsen, noted Norwegian dramatic poet, started his career with the study of medicine, but soon abandoned it for literature. Along with his literary pursuits, he also served for some time as director of the Norwegian theater in Christiania. His most widely known dramatic poem is *Peer Gynt*.

In the sunny orchard closes,
    While the warblers sing and swing,
Care not whether blustering Autumn
    Break the promises of Spring!
5 Rose and white, the apple blossom
    Hides you from the sultry sky—
Let it flutter, blown and scatter'd,
    On the meadows by-and-by!

Will you ask about the fruitage
10   In the season of the flowers?
Will you murmur, will you question,
    Count the run of weary hours?
Will you let the scarecrow clapping
    Drown all happy sounds and words?
15 Brothers! there is better music
    In the singing of the birds.

From your heavy-laden garden
    Will you hunt the mellow thrush;
He will play you for protection
20   With his crown-song's liquid rush.
O but you will win the bargain,
    Though your fruit be spare and late,
For remember Time is flying
    And will shut the garden gate.

25 With my living, with my singing,
    I will tear the hedges down.
Sweep the grass and heap the blossom!
    Let it shrivel, pale and brown!

Swing the wicket! Sheep and cattle,
30   Let them graze among the best!
I broke off the flowers; what matter
Who may revel with the rest?

Poem Development: Yesterday is past; tomorrow is not yet born; only today is ours! Show how the poem expresses this oft-repeated advice for daily living.

French

THE SLEEPER OF THE VALLEY

Arthur Rimbaud (1854–1891)

Poem Interest: At the early age of ten, Jean Arthur Rimbaud began to write poetry, showing forth rich intellectual ability. But he also possessed a sullen, violent temperament, and at nineteen, suddenly abandoned his writing. Thus the poetry of this French adventurer all belongs to his early youth.

There's a green hollow where a river sings
Silvering the torn grass in its glittering flight,
And where the sun from the proud mountain flings
Fire—and the little valley brims with light.

5   A soldier young, with open mouth, bare head,
Sleeps with his neck in dewy water cress,
Under the sky and on the grass his bed,
Pale in the deep green and the light's excess.

He sleeps amid the iris and his smile
10   Is like a sick child's slumbering for a while.
Nature, in thy warm lap his chilled limbs hide!

The perfume does not thrill him from his rest.
He sleeps in sunshine, hand upon his breast,
Tranquil—with two red holes in his right side.

Poem Development: Paint your own word picture of the scene of this poem, building it around the line which contains the most vivid image. What does the theme reveal of the poet's nature? Might these verses find acceptance in the experience of any nation?

EXTENSIVE READING PROGRAM

Anglo-Saxon and Middle English Periods (Beginnings to 1550)

Unknown Author
  Sir Gawayne and the Grene Knight
William Langland
  Piers the Plowman

Sir Thomas Wyatt
  A Renouncing of Love
Henry Howard, Earl of Surrey
  Description of Spring
  Translation of Æneid

The Age of Elizabeth (1550–1625)

William Shakespeare
  Venus and Adonis
  Sonnets 12, 29, 30, 116
  Who Is Silvia?
  When Icicles Hang By the Wall
  Take, O Take Those Lips Away
  Over Hill, Over Dale
  Blow, Blow, Thou Winter Wind
  Tell Me Where Is Fancy Bred
Ben Jonson
  The Triumph of Charis
  On My First Son
  Inviting a Friend to Supper
  Epitaph on Elizabeth

Edmund Spenser
  The Faerie Queene
Christopher Marlowe
  Hero and Leander
  The Herdman's Happy Life
Sir Walter Raleigh
  The Nymph's Reply to the Shepherd
  The Lie
Sir Philip Sidney
  Astrophel and Stella
  The Nightingale
John Lyly
  Spring's Welcome

The Puritan Age and the Restoration (1625–1700)

John Milton
  The Hymn
  Lycidas
  Comus
  Paradise Lost
John Donne
  The Computation
  A Hymn to God the Father
  Good Morrow
Thomas Carew
  Ask Me No More Where Jove Bestows
  Persuasions of Joy
  The True Beauty
Richard Crashaw
  In the Holy Nativity of Our Lord God
  The Flaming Heart

George Herbert
  The Temple
  Virtue
  The Pilgrimage
  Love
Henry Vaughn
  The Timber
  The Retreat
Robert Herrick
  Corinna's Maying
  Delight in Disorder
  The Argument of His Book
  Gather Ye Rosebuds While Ye May
  To Daffodils
Sir John Suckling
  The Constant Lover
  Ballad upon a Wedding

Richard Lovelace
  To Lucasta on Going to the Wars
  To Althea from Prison
Abraham Cowley
  The Swallow
  The Wish
Edmund Waller
  Go, Lovely Rose
  To Phyllis

John Dryden
  A Song for St. Cecilia's Day
  Stanzas on Oliver Cromwell
  On Chaucer
  Alexander's Feast
Samuel Butler
  Hudibras
  God in Nature
  The Spacious Firmament on High

Classicism and the Age of Johnson (1700–1780)

Alexander Pope
  Essay on Criticism
  Essay on Man
  The Rape of the Lock
  The Universal Prayer
Matthew Prior
  The Hind and the Panther
  A Smile
John Gay
  The Hare with Many Friends
  Black-Eyed Susan
Thomas Parnell
  The Hermit
  A Hymn of Contentment
James Thomson
  A Snow Scene
  The Coming of the Rain
  Storm in Harvest

William Collins
  Ode to Evening
  An Ode to Music
  How Sleep the Brave
  Ode Written in 1746
Thomas Gray
  On the Spring
  Hymn to Adversity
  The Progress of Poesy
Oliver Goldsmith
  Elegy on Madam Blaize
  Song
  The Traveller
William Cowper
  John Gilpin's Ride
  Conversation
  Light Shining Out of Darkness
  The Rose

The Age of Romanticism (1780–1840)

William Blake
  Laughing Song
  Love's Secret
  Songs of Innocence
  The Chimney Sweeper
Robert Burns
  To a Louse
  To a Mountain Daisy
  Tam O'Shanter
  Highland Mary
  Mary Morison
  The Banks O' Doon

William Wordsworth
  We Are Seven
  Ode on Intimations of Immortality
  Tintern Abbey
  Lucy Gray
  She Was a Phantom of Delight
Sir Walter Scott
  The Lay of the Last Minstrel
  Lady of the Lake
  Marmion
  Lochinvar

Percy Bysshe Shelley
 When the Lamp Is Shattered
 Lament
 Dirge
 The Indian Serenade
 To Night
 Prometheus Unbound
John Keats
 Lines on the Mermaid Tavern
 La Belle Dame Sans Merci
 Endymion
 The Grasshopper and the Cricket
George Gordon, Lord Byron
 Childe Harold's Pilgrimage
 To Thomas Moore
 Night before Waterloo
 The Coliseum

Samuel Taylor Coleridge
 Frost at Midnight
 Work without Hope
 Hymn before Sunrise
 Rime of the Ancient Mariner
Thomas Moore
 'Tis the Last Rose of Summer
 The Harp That Once through Tara's Halls
 Believe Me, If All Those Endearing Young Charms
Robert Southey
 Inchcape Rock
 The Battle of Blenheim
Thomas Campbell
 Ye Mariners of England
 Battle of the Baltic

The Victorian Era (1840-1900)

Alfred, Lord Tennyson
 The Lady of Shalott
 Idylls of the King
 Flower in the Crannied Wall
 Sir Galahad
 In Memoriam
 The Bugle Song
 Tears, Idle Tears
Robert Browning
 Cavalier Tunes
 Home Thoughts from the Sea
 Rabbi Ben Ezra
 Incident of the French Camp
 The Pied Piper of Hamelin
 How They Brought the Good News
Elizabeth Barrett Browning
 The Sleep
 Sonnets from the Portuguese
 The Cry of the Children
William Ernest Henley
 In Hospital
 The Ways of Death
 What Is to Come We Know Not
 England, My England

Dante Gabriel Rossetti
 The Blessed Damozel
 Jenny
 Chimes
 Silent Noon
Christina Georgina Rossetti
 A Birthday
 Remember
Algernon Charles Swinburne
 The Salt of the Earth
 After Sunset
 The Garden of Proserpine
Oscar Wilde
 Ravenna
 The Ballad of Reading Gaol
Matthew Arnold
 The Forsaken Merman
 Rugby Chapel
 To Marguerite
William Morris
 Summer Dawn
 June
Francis Thompson
 The Hound of Heaven
 Daisy

The Twentieth Century (1900–   )

Thomas Hardy
Afterwards
In Time of "The Breaking of Nations"

Alfred Edward Housman
Westward on the High-Hilled Plains
With Rue My Heart Is Laden
The Carpenter's Son

William Butler Yeats
The Stolen Child
When You Are Old
Wild Swans at Coole

Rudyard Kipling
Road to Mandalay
The White Man's Burden
L'Envoi
Ballad of East and West

Richard Le Gallienne
An Echo from Horace
May Is Back
A Ballade-Catalogue of Lovely Things

James Stephens
The Poppy Field
The Shell

Winifred M. Letts
The Spires of Oxford

Walter de la Mare
Nod
Old Susan
All That's Past
Children

Gilbert K. Chesterton
The Wild Knight
Lepanto

John Masefield
The Story of the Round House
On Growing Old
The West Wind
Sea-Fever
Cargoes

Alfred Noyes
The Highwayman
Song of Sherwood
Forty Singing Seamen

Padraic Colum
The Fair Hills of Erie
A Cradle Song

William Henry Davies
Days Too Short
The Moon
Nature's Friend

Rupert Brooke
The Dead
Nineteen-fourteen

THE ESSAY AND OTHER PROSE

THE HISTORY OF PROSE LITERATURE IN ENGLAND

ANGLO-SAXON AND MIDDLE ENGLISH PERIODS (BEGINNINGS TO 1550)

Early English Prose

Although it is customary to begin any discussion of early English literature with the fifth century, the history of English prose literature does not go back so far for two reasons. The first is the fact that in England as in other countries the earliest prose was written for use, not pleasure, and hence is not truly literature. The second reason is that early learning was centered in the Church and the literary language was Latin. Any important work like a history of the country or a record of early miracles was written in the classic tongue. The language of the people was looked upon as a sort of jargon, hardly fit for polite use.

King Alfred

It was thus not until the end of the ninth century that there appeared any English prose literature. In 871 Alfred became king of the West-Saxons. After he had forced the neighboring Danish invaders to a peace, he turned to the education of his people. He knew that if there was to be a strong nation in "Englelond" (he used the name which the Angles had given Britain), it must be a united nation. There must be a national language which the people would respect and use for writing as well as talking. He therefore hired scholars to come to his capital at Winchester and establish a school where "every freeborn youth who possessed the means 'should abide at his book until he can well understand English writing.'" Alfred set himself the task of learning Latin so that he might translate from it the most helpful books for his people. Three books which he chose to work on were Bede's *Ecclesiastical History of England,* Boethius' *On the Consolation of Philosophy,* and Orosius' *Universal History.* In his translating he did some careful editing and made additions which often show more judgment and vision than the originals. He may rightly be called "the Father of English Prose."

The Anglo-Saxon Chronicle

One interesting, original work was developed during Alfred's reign. About one hundred years earlier there had been started in one of the monasteries a sort of year-book in which were recorded—miraculously, not in Latin—the names and dates of national and religious events. In the days of Alfred it was expanded into an interesting historical journal. Important battles were carefully described and there seemed to be a conscious attempt to make it good reading. Probably most of these later entries were written by Alfred himself. This *Anglo-Saxon Chronicle*, which continued for many generations, is not only our first authoritative English history, but also our first native prose literature.

The Norman Conquest

Unfortunately there was no one after the death of Alfred in 901 to carry on the work which he had started, and the annals of English prose record a long stretch of years in which little was written that may be called literature. There came in 1066 the Norman Conquest and English again fell into disrepute. Latin was the language of the Church, of the law-courts, and of the schools; French was the language of society and of polite letters. The Saxons clung stubbornly to their native speech and though eventually there came a merging of the Anglo-Saxon speech with the Norman-French to produce the basis of our modern English, it was generations before this combination language was used for serious literature.

Religious Writings

It made its first appearance, as might be expected, in religious writings. About the year 1225, there appeared a quaint document called the Ancren Riwle (Rule of the Anchoresses) written for three pious ladies who went into seclusion in Dorsetshire. It gives detailed directions for their mode of living, together with much spiritual advice.

One hundred and fifty years later came John Wyclif and his followers to translate the Bible (the Latin Vulgate) into English, and to preach and scatter abroad passages from the translations. So widespread was Wyclif's influence that his Bible did much to set a new standard of written English.

Sir John Mandeville

About this time there appeared in England a book known as *The Voyage and Travaile of Sir John Mandeville*. It was evidently a translation from the Latin or French of an earlier collection from tales of famous travelers. There are hearsay accounts of prodigious wonders, but the unknown English translator (Mandeville was apparently a pen-name) only vouches for the truth of the accounts about places he has seen himself. These descriptions are sober enough, and he further proves his wisdom by advancing a very good argument that the earth is round—this, in 1356. The book is important because its popularity helped to further establish the Midland dialect as the literary language of England, and because its marvelous tales have made Sir John Mandeville the father of all tellers of tall tales.

HISTORY OF PROSE LITERATURE

Geoffrey Chaucer (1340-1400)

Wyclif and the translator of the *Travailes* belonged to the fourteenth century, a period made famous by one of England's greatest poets, Geoffrey Chaucer. If Chaucer had not written a line of poetry, histories of English literature would be full of praise for his prose, for it is far superior to other prose of the times. One of the choicest touches of humor in the *Canterbury Tales* is given when it is Chaucer's turn to tell a story. He begins in a short-lined verse, but before he has gone far, he is stopped by the host because of the wretchedness of his rime—"nothing better than doggerel." Chaucer gravely says that he doesn't know any better verse but that he can tell a story without rime. Thus he is one of the two characters to tell his tale in prose! The poor parson is the other.

Especially charming is a piece of writing that Chaucer composed for his little son Louis. The child, who was in school at Oxford wanted an astrolabe (an astronomical instrument then much used) and Chaucer got him one. Then he sat down and carefully wrote out directions for its use. These he sent with the instrument to the boy. The first paragraphs are a personal note to "Litell Lowis, my sone." They show Chaucer's rare judgment, his logical mind, and a touching affection for his son. He says that he is giving only the most important general principles because some of the rules "are too hard for thy tender age of ten years to conceive." The treatise follows, logical and clear. The student of Chaucer should read the introduction, either done over into modern English, or in the original. It brings this fourteenth-century writer very close to us.

The Renaissance

From the death of Chaucer in 1400 to the ascension of Elizabeth in 1558, there was little original literature in England. The century and a half was a period of preparation. The Renaissance had reached England. It was a period of scholarship, of invention, of rediscovery of old treasures in literature and art. There were researches and translations, but men were too busy reading the writings of others—particularly of the ancient Greeks—to do much writing themselves. The "Humanists" believed that the culture derived from classic training would satisfy all man's intellectual needs. Leaders of the Reformation were exposing the abuses and questioning the authority of the Church. Caxton had set up his printing press and the price of a book had suddenly dropped from about a dollar and a half a page to a dollar and a half a volume. There was some use now in a man's knowing how to read. Books had become available.

Writings of the Early Renaissance Period

The writings of the period are characteristic. In 1470, Sir Thomas Malory's *Morte d'Arthur* appeared, a valuable compilation of the legends of the Round Table. In 1477, Caxton printed the first book in England. To his books he added very interesting, though lengthy prefaces. In 1516, Sir Thomas More's *Utopia* was published, an important social treatise in the guise of a romance, but written in Latin. In 1525, William Tyndale's translation of the New Testament from the original Greek was completed; and in 1539 the Great Bible appeared in England.

Translations of the Bible

Most important of these works in influence, were the translations of the Bible. In 1500 it was against the law for an English version of the Bible to appear in England, and Tyndale had to flee to the Continent to finish his work. His New Testament was published at Worms in Germany. He then began translating the Old Testament from the original Hebrew, but he was ambushed, imprisoned, and put to death by religious enemies in 1536. His work was completed by a follower named Miles Coverdale, and the Great Bible was a version of his translation. It was the first English Bible *printed in England,* and because of Henry VIII's changing religions it was not only permitted but ordered into all the churches of England. Its effect upon English speech and style can never be measured. It was this Bible which served as the basis for the King James Version, and for generations it was the most widely owned and read book in the English tongue.

By the middle of the sixteenth century the preparatory period of English literature had ended. All was in readiness for the burst of creative genius which was to come.

The Age of Elizabeth (1550–1625)

General Characteristics

In the exuberance of Elizabethan activity, every kind of writing was quickened. Interests were centered in poetry and the drama, but prose had its share in the awakening of more expressive power. More and more, English was being used for scholarly works in history and religion.

Travel and History

The Elizabethan zeal for discovery found expression in the works of two clergymen, Richard Hakluyt and Samuel Purchas. After a careful study of original sources, Hakluyt published his *Principal Navigations, Voyages and Discoveries of the English Nation,* in three volumes (1589, 1598–1600). At his death, Purchas continued the undertaking, producing two books, *Purchas, His Pilgrimage* in 1613 and *Hakluytus Posthumous, or Purchas, His Pilgrims* in 1625. Not so reliable was Raleigh's *Discovery of Guiana.* Gallant Sir Walter believed in giving folks what they wanted so he filled his pages with misleading tales of wonders in the New World. His ambitious *History of the World,* written while

HISTORY OF PROSE LITERATURE

he was in prison, is equally untrustworthy. It is made notable chiefly by its closing lines—a moving apostrophe to Death.

History had, however, begun to assume real significance. Holingshed's *Chronicles of England, Ireland, and Scotland* (1578) is important because Shakespeare drew heavily from it for his historical and traditional plays. Camden's *Britannica* is important in itself. It is a piece of careful research—an attempt to present the facts of English history in an orderly chronicle. In 1563 John Foxe published the English version of his *Acts and Monuments*, better known as the *Book of Martyrs*. Though gruesome and somber, it was much esteemed by our Puritan forefathers. Then there was John Knox's *The History of the Reformation in Scotland*, inspired in parts, but biased in viewpoint.

Other Elizabethan Prose

From the pen of John Lyly came a book called *Euphues* from the chief character in the book, a young Athenian who visits England. In Euphues' comment on English life and manners, Lyly voices his own criticism of the rather unpolished contemporary Englishman, intending thereby to stimulate an interest in and attention to polite amenities. The book was written in a somewhat high-flown, affected style which seems to have been much affected in speech by the courtiers of the day. The word "euphuism" which we use to describe an artificially elegant mode of literary expression is a derivation of Euphues.

The most dignified and polished prose of the period appeared in the work of Richard Hooker, who wrote *The Laws of Ecclesiastical Polity* to explain the laws and practice of the English Church.

Great Translations

The translation of foreign and classic books which had begun in the days of the early Renaissance continued in the days of Elizabeth. Translations came from Latin and Greek, from French, Italian, and Spanish, and included not only works of classic literature, but a number of historical works, the most famous of which was perhaps North's *Plutarch*.

The Authorized Version of 1611

An outstanding literary monument of the age was the authorized translation of the Bible, completed in 1611, made by forty-seven scholars assembled by James I. This version was not a translation anew, but rather a revision which represented the best work of scholars and translators from the days of Wyclif. The text was chiefly that of the Tyndale-Coverdale translation.

All these studies in their various fields show a working toward a convenient prose style. They are, as a rule, free from the long, complicated, over-ornamented sentences of the prose romances which are noticeable in the development of fiction.

The Emergence of the Essay

The creative genius of the age reached its greatest heights, in prose, in a hitherto unknown form—the literary essay. The Frenchman, Montaigne, who died in 1592, had used the term *Essais* as the title for his collection of little papers commenting on men and affairs. "To essay" means to attempt or try, and "Attempts" would probably be the closest modern synonym for Montaigne's title. It implies some modesty on the part of the author. Among admiring English readers of the *Essais* were William Shakespeare and Francis Bacon; and when the latter in 1597 published his first ten short prose reflections, he adopted Montaigne's term and called them *Essays*. Bacon had apparently not rated his papers very highly, and he was surprised at their success. In two later editions (1612 and 1625) he increased their number to thirty-eight and then to fifty-eight.

The essay—that versatile, flexible form of self-expression—was certain to have emerged in English literature; but fortunate it was that its christening was so auspicious. The brilliance of Bacon's style and the arresting power of his thought made the essay at once a most important type of English literature.

Sir Francis Bacon (1561–1625)

Were one to read the works of Francis Bacon without knowing anything of his life and personality, one might well question, "What manner of man is this?" Brilliant, certainly, one should guess, for his

scientific treatises disclose a modern point of view startling in its contrast to the sixteenth century English in which it is expressed. He is witty, too, and clear and crisp in manner of speech. An essay like *Of Truth* shows an appreciation of virtue and a true discrimination betwixt right and wrong. *Of Studies* shows good judgment and genuine common-sense. But through the lines in *Of Love* and *Of Marriage and the Single Life* glints cold calculation, unsoftened by any hint of sentiment. He writes *Of Friendship*, merely to tell of the uses to which one may put a friend. He lists a number of things which a man cannot do for himself but which he can have some friend do for him. Therefore, reasons Bacon, a man should cultivate friends. Nowhere is there any mention of the loyalty and devotion which one should return to his friend, nor of the love between friends which may pass all understanding.

The mirror of his works, then, reflects this portrait—a man brilliant, keen, clear-headed, cold, unaffectionate, hard.

Nor is the picture far from the truth when checked by the details of his life. Francis Bacon was indeed clever. More than that he was intelligent and studious. Born the son of the Lord Keeper of the Seal, he found the finest educational facilities of the age open to him. There was private instruction under tutors, followed by college work at Cambridge, and travel with study abroad. We find him in his early teens disgusted with Cambridge, not because he disliked his books but because he found his instructors stupid and their methods antiquated. Generations later the world was to acknowledge the correctness of the boy's insistence that knowledge is drawn not from the works of dead philosophers but from observation and experimentation.

Bacon was also ambitious. He had the disadvantage of being a youngest son and at the death of his father, the eighteen-year-old Francis found himself without income. He turned to the practice of law for his living and his rise was rapid. Within ten years he was Counsel-extraordinary to Queen Elizabeth. His success was due partly to his own great ability and partly to his knowledge of how to use a friend. Robert Devereux, the second Earl of Essex, then a favorite at the Court, gave his patronage to the young lawyer.

And Bacon was heartless. In 1601 came the downfall of Lord Essex. With the usefulness of his friend destroyed, Bacon now became active in securing the conviction and beheading of Essex on the charge of high treason.

After the death of Elizabeth in 1603, Bacon's rise was even more rapid. He was at once knighted by James I. In succeeding years he rose from post to post, until in 1621 he became Lord High Chancellor of England. In the meantime he had married a rich London heiress. In the days of Elizabeth he had been a member of Parliament; in 1618 he took his place in the House of Lords. An eloquent speaker, he drew throngs of listeners whenever he made an address. In 1621 then, Sir Francis Bacon, Baron Verulan, Viscount St. Albans (for these were his titles) appeared one of the wealthiest and most influential men in England. His ascent had been gradual; his fall was disastrously swift.

That very year he was accused of having accepted bribes. Bacon made a complete confession exonerating his associates—some of them of higher rank than himself. Punishment was severe but left him his life. He was fined nearly $200,000; he was barred from ever again holding public office; he was denied admittance to Court and to Parliament; he was committed to imprisonment in the Tower. The intervention of the king made his prison term a short one and part of his fine was restored to him; but Bacon never again entered public life.

From his nineteenth year Bacon had been writing more or less steadily—chiefly scientific, political, and economic discussions in Latin and English. Now he gave himself over to scientific studies. It is a matter of common knowledge that he contracted the bronchitis which caused his death while he was trying an initial experiment in the modern principle of cold storage. He wanted to see whether packing a chicken with snow would preserve it.

His works have impressive titles, many of them in Latin. *The Advancement of Learning* and the *Novum Organum* are particularly interesting to the student of philosophy and science; but the general reader knows only his essays. And these are well worth knowing. His changing views on life show up sharply in the subjects and treatments of his essays. The most admired essay of all, *Of Studies,* appeared in the first edition of his papers. It best illustrates his wit, his eloquence, his intellectual interests. The essays added to the second edition, which appeared during his rapid rise to power, contain more worldly wisdom and seem on the whole more cold and calculating. The last twenty, written in retirement, have a sober, moral tone. It is in this group, for instance, that *Of Truth* appears. Aside from their remarkable style, the essays in themselves reflect almost completely the man whom Pope characterized as "the wisest, brightest, meanest of all time."

Ben Jonson (1573–1637)

It is not generally known that another writer of the age added to the store of English essays. We are well acquainted with Ben Jonson the poet and Jonson the dramatist; but Jonson the essayist is less familiar. In the last years of his life, this lusty writer pondered much on men, on books, on learning; and from time to time he jotted down his meditations. Some, like the reminiscence on Bacon, are very short; some are much longer. He grouped them under the name *Timbers,* but they were not published until 1641, four years after his death. Most interesting are his comments on the famous men he has known, such as the following one on Shakespeare in which he criticizes the dramatist for writing too much; but in which he also pays a splendid tribute to the man and his work.

> . . . For I loved the man, and do honor his memory on this side idolatry as much as any. He was, indeed, honest, and of an open and free nature; had an excellent phantasy, brave notions, and gentle expressions, wherein he flowed with that facility that sometimes it was necessary he should be stopped. *"Sufflaminandus erat"* (He should have been checked), as Augustus said of Haterius. His wit was in his own power; would the rule of it had been so, too! . . .

Following is his tribute to Francis Bacon:

> . . . No man ever spake more neatly, more pressly, more weightily, or suffered less emptiness, less idleness in what he uttered. No member of his speech but consisted of his own graces. His hearers could not cough, or look aside from him, without loss. He commanded where he spoke, and had his judges angry and pleased at his devotion. No man had their affections more in his power. The fear of every man that heard him was lest he should make an end.

Essays of the Elizabethan Age

OF STUDIES

Francis Bacon

By Way of Introduction: Every once in a while the average American boy feels somewhat "fed up" on school and grumbles, "Why do I have to study?" What would he say if he were told in reply, "For profit, for appearances, and for fun"? The first point he might be ready to admit; on the second, he might be convinced after some talking; for the third—well, he might just laugh in derision. Yet Bacon considered the pleasure derived from studies so important that he puts it first of these three benefits. And isn't he right? Just suppose, for instance, that a man has reached the age of thirty with no education at all. He cannot even read and write. Think of the pleasures you enjoy which are denied to such a one! Every new field in which one acquires knowledge offers a new field of pleasure. Oh, yes, Bacon was right when he said, "Studies serve for delight." He is right in almost everything else that he says about studies. See if you don't agree with him.

STUDIES serve for delight, for ornament, and for ability. Their chief use for delight is in privateness and retiring; for ornament, is in discourse; and for ability, is in the judgment and disposition of business. For expert men [1] can execute and perhaps judge of particulars, one by one; but the general counsels, and the plots and marshaling of affairs, come best from those

---

[1] EXPERT MEN—Specialists who lack general information or culture.

that are learned. To spend too much time in studies is sloth; to use them too much for ornament is affectation; to make judgment wholly by their rules is the humor [2] of a scholar. They perfect nature, and are perfected by experience; for natural abilities are like natural plants, that need proyning [3] by study; and studies themselves do give forth directions too much at large, except they be bounded in by experience. Crafty men [4] contemn studies; simple men admire them; and wise men use them: for they teach not their own use; but that [5] is a wisdom without them and above them, won by observation. Read not to contradict and confute; nor to believe and take for granted; nor to find talk and discourse; but to weigh and consider. Some books are to be tasted, others to be swallowed, and some few to be chewed and digested: that is, some books are to be read only in parts; others to be read, but not curiously; [6] and some few to be read wholly, and with diligence and attention. Some books also may be read by deputy,[7] and extracts made of them by others; but that would be only in the less important arguments, and the meaner sort of books; else distilled books are like common distilled waters, flashy [8] things. Reading maketh a full man; conference a ready man; [9] and writing an exact man. And therefore, if a man write little, he had need have a great memory; if he confer [10] little, he had need have a present wit; and if he read little, he had need have much cunning, to seem to know that he doth not. Histories make men wise; poets witty; the mathematics subtile; natural philosophy deep; moral grave; logic and rhetoric able to contend. *Abeunt studia in mores.*[11] Nay, there is no stond or impediment in the wit, but may be wrought out by fit studies: [12] like as diseases of the body may have appropriate exercises. Bowling is good for the stone and reins; [13]

[2] Humor—Peculiarity or tendency.
[3] Proyning—Pruning.
[4] Crafty men—Laborers; workmen of various crafts or guilds.
[5] That—The knowledge of how to use one's learning.
[6] Curiously—With close attention.
[7] Read by deputy—"Read" through reviews or reports by others.
[8] Flashy—Flat, tasteless.
[9] Conference a ready man—Conversation (or repartee) makes a man quick-witted.
[10] Confer—Converse.
[11] *Abeunt studia in mores*—Studies pass into (or grow into) manners.
[12] No stond . . . wrought out by fit studies—No lack of mental ability but may be remedied by.
[13] Stone and reins—Gall-stones and similar affections.

shooting for the lungs and breast; gentle walking for the stomach; riding for the head; and the like. So if a man's wit be wandering, let him study the mathematics; for in demonstrations, if his wit be called away never so little, he must begin again: if his wit be not apt to distinguish or find differences, let him study the Schoolmen; [14] for they are *cymini sectores:* [15] if he be not apt to beat over matters, and to call one thing to prove and illustrate another, let him study the lawyers' case: so every defect of the mind may have a special receipt.

[14] SCHOOLMEN—Theologians or philosophers.
[15] *Cymini sectores*—Hair-splitters or quibblers.

Vocabulary Study: Bacon must be read thoughtfully. He sometimes packs a world of meaning into a single sentence. Be sure that you understand the sense in which he used the following words: *sloth; affectation; contemn; confute; discourse* (note pronunciation); *distilled; subtile; contend.*

Distinguish between the synonyms: *taste, flavor, tang.*

By Way of Appreciation: The first half of Bacon's *Of Studies* (through the sentence, "Reading maketh a full man; conference a ready man; and writing an exact one") is such a remarkable discussion of the use and place of learning in man's life that it is worth memorizing. There are several single clauses which might serve as texts for addresses on education or on reading. The author's terse, pithy sentences, written in a day when most prose was tediously eloquent and over-ornamented, have an almost modern echo. The theory which Bacon advances in the last half of the essay—that the different faculties of the mind may be developed by various mental exercises—has long been debated and is now generally rejected by psychologists.

Suggestions for Study: Ponder the opening sentence of the essay. Be prepared to participate in a class discussion on how the various subjects offered in your school serve one or more of these uses of education. Courses in music, for example, may serve all three: they often prepare a pupil to earn his living; they certainly help him to "shine" in society; and they afford a real source of pleasure for his leisure time.

To *paraphrase* means to reword a passage without changing its meaning. As a test of your understanding of the essay, try paraphrasing any three of sentences 2 to 10. Give some definite illustrations of the truth of the statement that the chief use of studies "for delight is in privateness and retiring." Why, for instance, would our uneducated man be more at a loss for amusement when he was alone than when he was with others?

Bacon says that we should read "to weigh and consider." Apply this precept to the last part of the essay. That is, do you agree that a man lacking a logical mind can develop one by studying geometry? Or that a slow-witted person may become a clever conversationalist through much practice? There might be an informal class debate on the question.

Exercises and Creative Work: Choose any sentence (or part of a sentence) which seems to you to express a particularly important truth, and using it as a topic sentence expand into a paragraph of at least one hundred words.

Write a précis of the essay.

The following topics are suggested as subjects for themes: *Studies That Serve for Delight; Books to Be Tasted; Books to Be Swallowed; Books to Be Chewed and Digested.*

OF TRUTH

Francis Bacon

By Way of Introduction: *If,* in the words of Shakespeare, *to do were as easy as to know what were well to do*—Francis Bacon would have died a happier man. This second essay shows how well he knew the worth of truth. There is something almost touching in his statement that it is "heaven upon earth to have a man's mind move in charity . . . and turn upon the poles of truth." The essay takes on special interest when we realize that it was written in the closing years when Bacon was living in retirement. Bitterly had he learned that "there is no vice that doth so cover a man with shame as to be found false and perfidious."

WHAT is *truth?* said jesting Pilate,[1] and would not stay for an answer. Certainly there be that [2] delight in giddiness, and count it a bondage to fix a belief; affecting free-will in thinking, as well as in acting. And though the sects of philosophers of that kind be gone, yet there remain certain discoursing wits [3] which are of the same veins, though there be not so much blood in them as was in those of the ancients. But it is not only the difficulty and labor which men take in finding out of truth, nor again that when it is found it imposeth upon men's thoughts, that doth bring lies in favor; but a natural though corrupt love of the lie itself. One of the later schools of the Grecians

---

[1] PILATE—The Roman official to whom Jesus was brought for examination. See *John* 18:37, 38.

[2] THERE BE THAT—There be those that.

[3] CERTAIN DISCOURSING WITS—Certain talkative gallants.

examineth the matter, and is at a stand to think what should be in it, that men should love lies; where neither they make for pleasure, as with poets; nor for advantage, as with the merchant; but for the lie's sake. But I cannot tell: this same truth is a naked and open daylight, that doth not show the masques and mummeries and triumphs of the world, half so stately and daintily as candlelights. Truth may perhaps come to the price of a pearl, that sheweth best by day; but it will not rise to the price of a diamond or carbuncle, that sheweth best in varied lights. A mixture of a lie doth ever add pleasure. Doth any man doubt, that if there were taken out of men's minds vain opinions, flattering hopes, false valuations, imaginations as one would, and the like, but it would leave the minds of a number of men poor shrunken things, full of melancholy and indisposition, and unpleasing to themselves? One of the fathers,[4] in great severity, called poesy *vinum dæmonum*,[5] because it filleth the imagination, and yet it is but with the shadow of a lie. But it is not the lie that passeth through the mind, but the lie that sinketh in and settleth in it, that doth the hurt such as we spake of before. But however these things are thus in men's depraved judgments and affections, yet truth, which only doth judge itself, teacheth that the inquiry of truth, which is the love-making or wooing of it, the knowledge of truth, which is the presence of it, and the belief of truth, which is the enjoying of it, is the sovereign good of human nature. The first creature [6] of God, in the works of the days, was the light of the sense; the last was the light of reason; and his sabbath work, ever since, is the illumination of his Spirit. First he breathed light upon the face of the matter or chaos; then he breathed light into the face of man; and still he breatheth and inspireth light into the face of his chosen. The poet [7] that beautified the sect [8] that was otherwise inferior to the rest, saith yet excellently well: *It is a pleasure to stand upon the shore, and to see ships tossed upon the sea: a pleasure to stand in*

---

[4] ONE OF THE FATHERS—St. Augustine (345–430), bishop of Hippo, Africa. The early teachers of Christianity were called "Fathers of the Church."
[5] *Vinum dæmonum*—Wine of demons, or deviis' wine.
[6] CREATURE—Creation.
[7] THE POET—Lucretius (95–51 B.C.), a Roman poet and philosopher.
[8] THE SECT—Epicureans, adherents of the teachings of the Greek philosopher, Epicurus (341–270 B.C.), that pleasure is the chief good in life.

the window of a castle, and to see a battle and the adventures thereof below: but no pleasure is comparable to the standing upon the vantage ground of truth (a hill not to be commanded, and where the air is always clear and serene), *and to see the errors, and wanderings, and mists, and tempests, in the vale below:* so always that [9] this prospect be with pity, and not with swelling or pride. Certainly, it is heaven upon earth, to have a man's mind move in charity, rest in providence, and turn upon the poles of truth.

To pass from theological and philosophical truth, to the truth of civil business: it will be acknowledged, even by those that practice it not, that clear and round dealing is the honor of man's nature; and that mixture of falsehood is like alloy in coin of gold and silver; which may make the metal work the better, but it embaseth it. For these winding and crooked courses are the goings of the serpent; which goeth basely upon the belly, and not upon the feet. There is no vice that doth so cover a man with shame as to be found false and perfidious. And therefore Montaigne [10] saith prettily, when he inquired the reason, why the word of the lie should be such a disgrace and such an odious charge; saith he, *If it be well weighed, to say that a man lieth is as much to say as that he is brave towards God and a coward towards men.* For a lie faces God, and shrinks from man. Surely the wickedness of falsehood and breach of faith cannot possibly be so highly expressed, as in that it shall be the last peal to call the judgments of God upon the generations of men; it being foretold that, when Christ cometh, *he shall not find faith upon the earth.*[11]

[9] So ALWAYS THAT—Providing that; if only; so long as.
[10] MONTAIGNE—Michel Eyquem de Montaigne (1533–1592), French philosopher and essayist.
[11] *He shall not find faith upon the earth*—Luke 18:8. "Nevertheless, when the Son of man cometh, shall he find faith on the earth?"

Vocabulary Study: *Affecting; sects; masques; mummeries; carbuncle; indisposition; poesy; depraved; sovereign good; vantage-ground; prospect; providence; civil business; odious.*

Find three synonyms for the word *dainty*, and give an antonym for at least one of them.

By Way of Appreciation: When Bacon wrote about studies, he showed how wisdom is drawn from the proper mixture of experience with learning. When he wrote about truth, he showed that he had acquired that sort of wisdom. Some of his thoughts reflect the philosophies that he studied as a boy; some of them have grown out of life itself. In many ways, *Of Truth* seems the most mellow of his essays. It is not so brittle, nor so cold. There is a touch of spirituality rather surprising in this man of the world. His expression, as always, is rhythmic—almost poetic. He loves the balanced sentence. Clauses in twos and threes parallel each other with measured precision. As a prose writer, he is worthy of honor in an age that produced Shakespeare, and the King James Version of the Bible.

Suggestions for Study: The following outline lists the points which Bacon covers in his discussion of truth:

I   The avoidance by some men of any fixed belief
II The apparent preference of some men for falsehood
    1. The pleasant glamour of the lie
       (*a*) Spoken to others (flattery)
       (*b*) Believed of oneself (self-deception)
    2. The mental pleasure of romancing (poesy)
    3. The danger of the lie accepted as truth
III The real value of truth—"the sovereign good of human nature"
IV The evils of falsehood

For each topic determine the exact sentences in which Bacon develops the thought. For example, the first point is expressed in the first three sentences.

Choose for memory work three sentences which you judge really worthy of being remembered. Discuss the statement, "The mixture of a lie doth ever add pleasure." Is it true? Can you give an illustration of what Bacon had in mind? Is it genuine pleasure? Discuss the type of person described in the ninth sentence. Can you think of any such characters in fiction? In life? Our great-grandmothers discouraged the reading of novels for the reason expressed in the tenth sentence. Does the objection still hold for some of our modern fiction? For some of our movies? What is your reaction to Lucretius' description of three sources of pleasure?

The most debatable point in the essay is Bacon's comparison of falsehood to an alloy in gold or silver. What do you think—does the addition of falsehood "make the metal work the better"? Explain the statement, "For a lie faces God and shrinks from man." What are the indications in this essay that Bacon was a well-educated man?

Exercises and Creative Work: Summarize briefly the thoughts in the essay which appeal to you.

It will be interesting for you to develop an essay of your own on *Truth*. Or you may wish to choose one of the following titles: *Dishonesty; White Lies; An Honest Man; Caught in a Lie.*

THE HISTORY OF PROSE LITERATURE IN ENGLAND

THE PURITAN AGE AND THE RESTORATION (1625–1700)

General Characteristics

The impetus which the reign of Elizabeth had given literature carried it on through the reign of King James, but by 1625 new forces were at work and there was a definitely different tone in English prose. The years between the death of James I and the end of the century might well be called "The Age of Conflict." At no other time in England were party lines so sharply and so bitterly drawn, nor were there ever before or after such dramatic reversals of power in government. Behind the upheavals was a divided England—Puritan and Cavalier. The rise of the Puritan was impressively swift; his power was brief. But in his short reign he exerted an influence that the world still feels. He sent his Pilgrims to America, and they upset the political and economic balance of the nations. He wrote his poems and allegories, and they have flowed into and directed the spiritual forces of mankind. A review of the writings of the period will indicate why, after all, it is proper to call this age of conflict the Puritan Period; books by Cavalier and Puritan alike caught the sobering spirit of the times, and the religious fervor outlasted the Restoration.

Puritan Writings

As might be expected, prose was the chosen form of expression with the Puritan. It suited his serious purpose. In the middle of the century he was as much concerned with politics and government as with religion. Milton, the great Puritan poet, lost his eyesight writing state papers for Cromwell's Protectorate. His *Tenure of Kings and Magistrates* and his *Areopagitica: A Speech for the Liberty of Unlicensed Printing* are examples of his sonorous, dignified pleas for liberty. Though Milton called prose his "left hand," these works show much the same rhythmic solemnity as his poetry.

Many religious and secular works of the period were not controversial in nature. Among them one notes Jeremy Taylor's *Holy Living* and *Holy Dying*, two noble and gentle books that found their way into pious homes of Cavalier and Puritan alike; and Richard Baxter's *Saints' Everlasting Rest*, written with simple, evangelical fervor. Thomas Fuller was a royalist clergyman with an overflowing sense of humor, and even when he writes of churchly things, there is a sparkle of wit on nearly every page. His best known book was *A History of the Worthies of England*. Even today it is not dull reading. Another man whose books found large circles of readers was Sir Thomas Browne, an honest physician with widely diversified interests. His *Religion of a Physician* under the Latin title, *Religio Medici*, was considered dangerously liberal, but modern readers find him tolerant, reverent, and rather sweet. Even more enduringly popular were the works of Izaak Walton, tradesman and gentleman of sports, and John Bunyan, the greatest prose genius of the century.

Cavalier Writings

There are two works which round out the Cavalier side of the picture. They are the diaries of John Evelyn and Samuel Pepys. John Evelyn was a prosperous, conservative royalist, nearly thirteen years older than Pepys and outliving him by three years. Most of his life he kept a diary. Unlike Pepys he made his entries carefully and methodically. Though he probably had no idea that the world would read his journal, he made no efforts to keep it secret and seemed conscious always of the historical significance of the times in which he lived (1620–1706). He not only recorded events, but commented on them. He was fair-minded and honest, loyal to his kings even while deploring their faults. His diary is not such a human document as Pepys', but the two complement each other beautifully and give the world an almost perfect picture of England immediately after the Restoration.

The two Puritan writers, Izaak Walton and John Bunyan, and the Cavalier writer, Samuel Pepys are deserving of special mention.

Izaak Walton (1593–1683)

The life of Izaak Walton spans ninety of the most unsettled years of English history. Born in the reign of good Queen Bess, he was ten years old when she died. Then came the unhappy reigns of James I and Charles I, the Civil War, the Protectorate, the Restoration, and the disappointingly unwise rule of Charles II. Through these years, Izaak Walton kept faith with the monarchs of England and lived himself a quiet, blameless life.

Most of his first fifty years were spent in London where he became a merchant, evidently a prosperous one, for at fifty he was able to shut up shop and retire to the country. The civil war had already started and perhaps Walton—a peace-loving man—preferred the hedgerows of the countryside to the uneasy stir of London with its militant Puritans growing daily stronger. At any rate in 1643 Walton closed his shop and moved into the country.

There he began a quiet career of writing. He first published the *Lives*, careful biographies of contemporary writers like Hooker and Herbert and Donne. They are the first significant English biographies. Ten years later appeared *The Compleat Angler,* a little book that has lived through two hundred and fifty years and almost as many editions. It has none of the controversial spirit of the age but reflects, rather, the personality of its author—gentle, lovable, grateful for English sunshine and shower and for the little pools where the trout lie hidden. Walton died in Winchester in 1683.

ELD

John Bunyan (1628-1688)

In the troublous days of King Charles I there was born, in the home of a poor tinker, a boy who was christened John and who, as he grew older, was given the training common to the sons of English tradesmen. That is, he received a smattering of schooling, enough to teach him to read and write; he was sent to church on Sundays; and he helped in his father's shop in between times. From these commonplace beginnings developed one of the world's greatest preachers and the author of one of the world's greatest books.

Trivial as the above facts seem, at least two of them are significant. If John Bunyan had not learned to read and write, *The Pilgrim's Progress* would have died unborn in Bedford Jail. If he had not listened to white-hot sermons on hell-fire and the wrath of God, his sensitive nature would never have been stirred to preach the message of salvation.

Now for the boy himself! He seems to have been a curious combination of the robust and the sensitive. He entered into the teeming life around him: he worked and sweated and swore before his father's anvils; he played ball, sometimes on the Sabbath; he joined in all sorts of roistering pranks. Then at night he turned and tossed, unable to sleep, tormented by the thoughts of his sins. These spiritual battles are vividly described in his autobiography *Grace Abounding to the Chief of Sinners*.

An early marriage intensified Bunyan's religious zeal. His wife was a pious woman. Bunyan began to listen to the call to preach. From the first he displayed a real gift for the work. His language was simple and vigorous, and he illustrated his sermons with understandable incidents from the life around him. He became rapidly popular.

In the meantime the government was changing. The growing Puritan power of the days of his youth had culminated in the overthrow of Charles I and the establishment of the Protectorate. During these years Bunyan got his start as an independent preacher. Then came the Restoration of 1660 with the re-establishment of the State Church. Laws were passed prohibiting unlicensed preachers from holding public services. Bunyan's conscience acknowledged a higher law than that of the state, and he continued to hold services. He was arrested and sent to Bedford Jail where he remained a prisoner for nearly twelve years. It was there that he saw the vision of the Christian pilgrim working his hazardous way through the world, and it was there undoubtedly that the great allegory was written.

The Pilgrim's Progress was not published until 1678, but it became instantly popular. The ten remaining years of Bunyan's life were years of great activity,—of traveling and preaching and writing. His fame was as great in London as in his native Bedford. And it was not only the ignorant who crowded to hear him. Scholars and dignified clergymen who came out of curiosity, soberly acknowledged his power and charm. He impressed one with his great sincerity and his sweetness. Withal, he seemed inspired.

Bunyan, despite his meagre learning, produced nearly sixty works besides countless sermons and tracts. His *Holy War* is a prose account of the fall of the angels and of man. *The Life and Death of Mr. Bad Man* is another allegory. But if he had written nothing besides *The Pilgrim's Progress*, he would forever be counted great.

Samuel Pepys (1633–1703)

Granted that a man desires an undying name, what must he do to secure it? Well, human nature being most complex and perverse, he may make himself a hero, or a rascal, or an artist, and *perhaps* the histories will carry a line about him. The very perversity of fate appears in the case of a man—no better than most of his contemporaries, and not much worse; ambitious; moderately successful, but in no sense heroic—who has survived to be paraphrased and quoted almost daily, three hundred years after his birth, and all because he kept a diary that he wanted no one else to read.

Samuel Pepys (pēps or pĕp'ĭs), loyal subject of the Crown, has enjoyed this ironic fate. He might be styled a self-made man, for he began life humbly as clerk in a government office in London and advanced until he became Secretary to the Admiralty. He was alert and politic; he knew what friends to make and how to keep them. He also managed to have a busy, entertaining time. For nine years he kept a diary, and as he wished it to be private, he wrote it in a special shorthand with a code of his own. He wrote freely all the gossipy details of his life and the life about him. He used real names and exact figures, for he supposed that no one else would ever read it. Nor did any one during his life-time.

More than a hundred years after his death, the books were discovered. The code was deciphered and the entries transcribed. The result was a unique record of a section of one man's life and personal glimpses of hundreds of others. There is also a truthful, though somewhat prejudiced account of public events from 1660 to 1669. The style is careless, but so distinctive and amusing that it has been the inspiration of half the newspaper columnists of America; and one oft-recurring line from the diary has become the title of a recent popular song.

Samuel Pepys perhaps congratulated himself on amassing a considerable fortune, on being elected president of the Royal Society, and on having a speaking acquaintance at Court; but if his Diary had proved undecipherable, the twentieth century would never have heard of him.

Prose of the Puritan and Restoration Periods
IN DEFENSE OF ANGLERS

From *The Compleat Angler*

Izaak Walton

By Way of Introduction: On a "fine, fresh May morning" two men on their way up Tottenham Hill toward the town of Ware are overtaken by a third—a pleasant, talkative body, who proceeds to get acquainted with the travellers. One man, it develops, is a falconer who is on his way to see about a hawk which a friend is keeping for him. The second is an ardent hunter who is going out shooting otter with a friend who has a pack of otter-dogs. With this program the third is in hearty accord, for he confesses himself a fisherman and therefore a foe of the fish-eating otter.

The huntsman and the falconer show some surprise at the sport of their companion, one remarking, "I have heard many Huntsmen make sport and scoff at Anglers" and the other declaring, "I have heard many grave and serious men pity them,—it is such a heavy, contemptible, dull recreation."

With an indulgent smile, the fisherman sets them straight. Angling is the most noble of all sports and anglers the most peaceable of all men. But let us hear his defense first hand.

Piscator.[1] You know, Gentlemen, it is an easy thing to scoff at any art or recreation; a little wit mixed with ill nature, confidence, and malice, will do it; but though they often venture boldly, yet they are often caught, even in their own trap, according to that of Lucian,[2] the father of the family of Scoffers:

> Lucian, well skilled in scoffing, this hath writ,
> Friend, that's your folly, which you think your wit:
> This you vent oft, void both of wit and fear,
> Meaning another, when yourself you jeer.

If to this you add what Solomon[3] says of Scoffers, that they are an abomination to mankind, let him that thinks fit scoff on, and be a Scoffer still; but I account them enemies to me and all that love Virtue and Angling.

And for you that have heard many grave, serious men pity Anglers; let me tell you, Sir, there be many men that are by others taken to be serious and grave men, whom we[4] contemn and pity. Men that are taken to be grave, because nature hath made them of a sour complexion;[5] money-getting men, men that spend all their time, first in getting, and next, in anxious care to keep it; men that are condemned to be rich, and then always busy or discontented: for these poor rich-men, we Anglers pity them perfectly, and stand in no need to borrow their thoughts to think ourselves so happy. No, no, Sir, we enjoy a contentedness above the reach of such dispositions, and as the learned and ingenuous Montaigne says, like himself, freely, "When my Cat and I entertain each other with mutual apish tricks, as playing with a garter, who knows that I make my Cat more sport than she makes me? Shall I conclude[6] her to be simple, that has her time to begin or refuse, to play as freely as I myself have? Nay, who knows but that it is a defect of my not understanding her language, for doubtless Cats talk and reason with one another, that we agree no better: and who knows but that she pities me for being no wiser than to play with her, and laughs and censures my folly, for making sport for her, when we two play together?"

---

[1] *Piscator*—Fisherman, from the Latin.
[2] Lucian—A Greek writer and satirist (125?–210?).
[3] Solomon—See *Proverbs* 24:9, "The thought of foolishness is sin and the scorner is an abomination to men."   [4] We—Anglers.
[5] Sour complexion—Solemn faced.   [6] Conclude—Suppose.

Thus freely speaks Montaigne concerning Cats; and I hope I may take as great a liberty to blame any man, and laugh at him too, let him be never so grave, that hath not heard what Anglers can say in the justification of their Art and Recreation; which I may again tell you, is so full of pleasure, that we need not borrow their thoughts, to think ourselves happy.

Venator.[7] Sir, you have almost amazed me; for though I am no Scoffer, yet I have, I pray let me speak it without offense, always looked upon Anglers, as more patient, and more simple men, than I fear I shall find you to be.

Piscator. Sir, I hope you will not judge my earnestness to be impatience: and for my simplicity, if by that you mean a harmlessness, or that simplicity which was usually found in the primitive Christians, who were, as most Anglers are, quiet men, and followers of peace; men that were so simply wise, as not to sell their consciences to buy riches, and with them [8] vexation and a fear to die; if you mean such simple men as lived in those times when there were fewer lawyers; when men might have had a lordship safely conveyed to them in a piece of parchment no bigger than your hand, though several sheets will not do it safely in this wiser age; I say, Sir, if you take us Anglers to be such simple men as I have spoke of, then myself and those of my profession will be glad to be so understood: But if by simplicity you meant to express a general defect in those that profess and practice the excellent Art of Angling, I hope in time to disabuse you, and make the contrary appear so evidently, that if you will but have patience to hear me, I shall remove all the anticipations that discourse, or time, or prejudice, have possessed you with against that laudable and ancient Art; for I know it is worthy the knowledge and practice of a wise man.

O, Sir, doubt not but that Angling is an art; is it not an art to deceive a Trout with an artificial Fly? A Trout! That is more sharp-sighted than any Hawk you have named, and more watchful and timorous than your high-mettled Merlin [9] is bold? And yet, I doubt not to catch a brace or two to-morrow, for a friend's breakfast: doubt not therefore, Sir, but that angling is an art, and an art worth your learning. The question is rather, whether you be capable of learning it? For angling is

---

[7] *Venator*—Hunter.
[8] WITH THEM—With riches.
[9] MERLIN—A kind of falcon.

somewhat like poetry, men are to be born so: I mean, with inclinations to it, though both may be heightened by discourse and practice: but he that hopes to be a good angler, must not only bring an inquiring, searching, observing wit, but he must bring a large measure of hope and patience, and a love and propensity to the art itself; but having once got and practiced it, then doubt not but angling will prove to be so pleasant, that it will prove to be, like virtue, a reward to itself.

Vocabulary Study: Though *The Compleat Angler* is about three hundred years old, it is very easy reading. Walton's vocabulary is simple and his style straightforward. These words you probably know; however, they are worth studying. Some have interesting histories. *Angler* (note derivation); *vent* (verb); *void; ingenuous* (note pronunciation and distinguish from *ingenious*); *censures; conveyed; disabuse; anticipations; laudable; timorous; mettled; brace; propensity.*

Distinguish between the synonyms: *despise, contemn, scorn, disdain.*

By Way of Appreciation: The seventeenth century in England was a turbulent, revolutionary age, and many writers arose to comment on its panorama of change. Some were physicians; some were statesmen; many were clergymen. They expounded and declaimed, then died and were forgotten. Few of us know their scholarly works save by hearsay. But one quiet little tradesman, disturbed by changing governments, retired from business and moved to the country. There he took his leisure, writing a bit and fishing between chapters. From his pen appeared some interesting biographies of writers of his day and one little volume—*The Compleat Angler*—about his chosen sport.

Curiously, this unpretentious book has outlived many weightier works. Fishermen still turn its pages with an appreciative smile. And it has no sensational features. It tells no "fish-stories." The reader rambles along an English road, meets a shepherd, hears a milk-maid singing in a farmyard, casts a fly, catches a trout or two, and speculates upon the world and all the pleasant things within it. Of course more than one philosopher has affirmed that catching the fish is the least of the pleasures of fishing. The charm of the sport lies in the fact that it gives one a chance to "loaf and invite his soul." To all such day-dreaming anglers Izaak Walton gives a happy hour now and then. It is usually as men grow older and the size and number of the catch matter less, that the book with its meditations becomes a real acquaintance. If you have an angling grandfather, see if he isn't a friend of Izaak Walton.

Suggestions for Study: What is Izaak Walton's recipe for scoffing? In what sense is it true that the scornful one really jeers at, or humiliates, himself? For what reasons does the angler pity rich men? Find two places where the angler refers to the troubles that accompany riches. Do you agree that most anglers are "quiet men and followers of peace"? Illustrate by references to some well-known men who have found fishing a favorite pastime. Why is trout-fishing a test of the angler's skill? (Only those who have fished for trout, especially brook-trout, should answer the question.) Comment on the statement, "Angling is like poetry; men are born to be so." Do you agree? Point out some similarities between the vocabularies of Bacon and Walton. Who was Montaigne? What other writer has mentioned him?

Exercises and Creative Work: Make a booklet entitled *In Praise of Izaak Walton*. In it include poetry on fish or fishing, titles of stories or other prose about fish, pictures, etc.

Make a report on the Izaak Walton League.

Write an essay on fishing which may be based on a personal experience or may be imaginary; it may be humorous or serious. Choose your own title for this essay.

IN THE VALLEY OF HUMILIATION

From *The Pilgrim's Progress*

JOHN BUNYAN

By Way of Introduction: "As I walked through the wilderness of this world, I lighted on certain place where there was a Den, and I laid me down in that place to sleep: and as I slept, I dreamed a dream."

The writer was John Bunyan; the den was Bedford jail; and the dream grew into *The Pilgrim's Progress*, his great religious allegory. The book represents the life of any Christian as a pilgrim's journey toward the Celestial City. "Christian" flees from his home, with a burden of sins upon his back. He tumbles into the Slough of Despond, but is helped out by Evangelist. He picks up fellow travellers who weaken and turn back. He is misled by Mr. Worldly Wiseman, but Evangelist sets him right. He passes the roaring lions and finally reaches the House Beautiful where he is refreshed and rested and where he enjoys the friendship of the Christian virtues. Pleasant as the House Beautiful is, it is not his destination and he must push on. His friends provide him with armour and weapons. Again he sets out. Since he had been on the crest of the hill, he must now descend into the Valley of Humiliation.

But let us go a ways with Christian and participate in one of his adventures.

THEN he began to go forward; but Discretion, Piety, Charity, and Prudence would accompany him down to the foot of the hill. So they went on together, reiterating their former discourses, till they came to go down the hill. Then said Christian, As it was difficult coming up, so (so far as I can see) it is dangerous going down. Yes, said Prudence, so it is, for it is a hard matter for a man to go down into the Valley of Humiliation, as thou art now, and to catch no slip by the way; therefore, said they, are we come out to accompany thee down the hill. So he began to go down, but very warily; yet he caught a slip or two.

Then I saw in my dream that these good companions, when Christian was gone to the bottom of the hill, gave him a loaf of bread, a bottle of wine, and a cluster of raisins; and then he went on his way.

But now, in this Valley of Humiliation, poor Christian was hard put to it; for he had gone but a little way, before he espied a foul fiend coming over the field to meet him; his name is Apollyon.[1] Then did Christian begin to be afraid, and to cast in his mind whether to go back or to stand his ground. But he considered again that he had no armour for his back; and therefore thought that to turn the back to him might give him the greater advantage with ease to pierce him with his darts. Therefore he resolved to venture and stand his ground; for, thought he, had I no more in mine eye [2] than the saving of my life, it would be the best way to stand.

So he went on, and Apollyon met him. Now the monster

[1] APOLLYON—A spirit of evil, the Destroyer. See *Revelation* 9:11.
[2] HAD I NO MORE IN MINE EYE—Were I considering nothing more.

was hideous to behold; he was clothed with scales, like a fish (and they are his pride); he had wings like a dragon, feet like a bear, and out of his belly came fire and smoke, and his mouth was as the mouth of a lion. When he was come up to Christian, he beheld him with a disdainful countenance, and thus began to question with him.

Apollyon. Whence come you? and whither are you bound?

Christian. I am come from the City of Destruction,[3] which is the place of all evil, and am going to the City of Zion.[4]

Apollyon. By this I perceive thou art one of my subjects, for all that country is mine, and I am the prince and god of it. How is it, then, that thou hast run away from thy king? Were it not that I hope thou mayest do me more service, I would strike thee now, at one blow, to the ground.

Christian. I was born, indeed, in your dominions, but your service was hard, and your wages such as a man could not live on, "for the wages of sin *is* death";[5] therefore, when I was come to years, I did as other considerate persons do, look out, if, perhaps, I might mend myself.[6]

Apollyon. There is no prince that will thus lightly lose his subjects, neither will I as yet lose thee; but since thou complainest of thy service and wages, be content to go back: what our country will afford, I do here promise to give thee.

Christian. But I have let myself to another, even to the King of princes, and how can I, with fairness, go back with thee?

Then Apollyon broke out into a grievous rage, saying, I am an enemy to this Prince; I hate his person, his laws, and people; I am come out on purpose to withstand thee.

Christian. Apollyon, beware what you do; for I am in the king's highway, the way of holiness; therefore take heed to yourself.

Then Apollyon straddled quite over the whole breadth of the way, and said, I am void of fear in this matter: prepare thyself to die; for I swear by my infernal den, that thou shalt go no farther; here will I spill thy soul.

And with that he threw a flaming dart at his breast; but

---

[3] CITY OF DESTRUCTION—Worldly living.
[4] CITY OF ZION—The Celestial City, Heaven.
[5] FOR THE WAGES OF SIN IS DEATH—See *Romans* 6:23.
[6] MEND MYSELF—Improve my condition.

Christian had a shield in his hand,[7] with which he caught it, and so prevented the danger of that.

Then did Christian draw, for he saw it was time to bestir him: and Apollyon as fast made at him, throwing darts as thick as hail; by the which, notwithstanding all that Christian could do to avoid it, Apollyon wounded him in his head, his hand, and foot. This made Christian give a little back; Apollyon therefore followed his work amain, and Christian again took courage, and resisted as manfully as he could. This sore combat lasted for above half a day, even till Christian was almost quite spent; for you must know that Christian, by reason of his wounds, must needs grow weaker and weaker.

Then Apollyon, espying his opportunity, began to gather up close to Christian, and wrestling with him, gave him a dreadful fall; and with that Christian's sword flew out of his hand. Then said Apollyon, I am sure of thee now. And with that he had almost pressed him to death, so that Christian began to despair of life: but as God would have it, while Apollyon was fetching of his last blow, thereby to make a full end of this good man, Christian nimbly stretched out his hand for his sword, and caught it, saying, "Rejoice not against me, O mine enemy: when J fall I shall arise";[8] and with that gave him a deadly thrust, which made him give back, as one that had received his mortal wound. Christian perceiving that, made at him again, saying, "Nay, in all these things we are more than conquerors through him that loved us."[9] And with that Apollyon spread forth his dragon's wings, and sped him away, that Christian for a season saw him no more.

[7] A SHIELD IN HIS HAND—Christian had been armed in the House Beautiful with the "breast plate of righteousness," the "shield of faith," the "helmet of salvation," and the "sword of the Spirit, which is the Word of God." See *Ephesians* 6:12-18.
[8] REJOICE NOT AGAINST ME . . . I SHALL ARISE—See *Micah* 7:8.
[9] NAY, IN ALL THESE THINGS . . . THAT LOVED US—See *Romans* 8:37, 39 and *James* 4:7.

Vocabulary Study: Notice the distinctly Biblical flavor of Bunyan's style and vocabulary. Notice also that most of his words are of Anglo-Saxon rather than Latin origin. Do you know the exact meaning of the following? *Warily* (see *wary*); *infernal; amain; spent; fetching.*

Determine the difference between *considerate* and *thoughtful.* Also look up the meanings for the synonyms of *wages.*

By Way of Appreciation: The high school boy or girl who is meeting Bunyan's masterpiece for the first time is often disappointed. He has heard so many references to the book as one of the world's immortals, that the simple allegory falls short of his expectations. What is there about it that is great? Why should people differing so greatly in years and personality as Cotton Mather, the Alcott sisters, and Theodore Roosevelt II be alike in naming it the most vividly remembered, the most deeply influential reading of their youth? There are probably many varying reasons, but two seem generally apparent.

In the first place, folks of an earlier day—a day which was not flooded with easy fiction and tabloids—were delighted with the story element of the book. When libraries were small and mainly religious, stories were rare. To the Puritan child who had spent a weary three hours at morning service and who saw stretching ahead a weary afternoon to be devoted to a study of the Catechism or a reading of Jonathan Edward's sermons—to such a child, Christian and his adventures would be an exciting diversion. The book which won an easy race for popularity with Foxe's *Book of Martyrs* or Baxter's *Saints' Everlasting Rest* is facing a different sort of competition in the neighborhood movie and the Sunday "funnies."

But more important is the fact that years ago readers made the acquaintance of Christian early in their youth. Much as the grown boy or girl despises fairy tales, his small brother adores them. The child lives in a visual world. He pictures vividly, if not always accurately, the pirates, giants, princesses, lions, dragons of his stories. He dramatizes the events in his playing. The meaning of an allegory is a matter of no concern to him, but the characters and action become a part of him. Then as he grows older and the experiences of life crowd in upon him, he clothes them with the images of his boyhood. Thus the allegory grows up with him and becomes rich and real. Fortunate is the boy or girl, who, like young Theodore Roosevelt, first hears *Pilgrim's Progress* from the lips of his mother!

But what if one has missed that childhood acquaintance? How can the high school senior, for instance, who has had *Pilgrim's Progress* assigned to him as a book report, get a thrill out of the reading? Probably best through the medium of a child. Let him hunt up a six-year-old for an audience—a younger brother or a neighborhood pal. Now let him read or retell the story and watch the youngster drink it up. The child's wide-eyed concern as Christian passes the lions, only to find them chained, will be infectious. The reader catches the pleasure of the listener.

Too, the reader will catch something of Bunyan's grace in writing. The scriptural richness and simplicity of his language, the earnestness of his purpose, the directness of his message—these challenge one's appreciation. The reader begins to sense the truth that despite its naïveté, *Pilgrim's Progress* is a great book.

Suggestions for Study: Why is the Valley of Humiliation an appropriate place for Christian to meet Apollyon? Can you parallel the events in this selection from the allegory with typical real-life experiences? For example, if the House Beautiful represents the Church in its broadest sense, what sort of incident might be represented by the descent into Humiliation? Or by the fight with Apollyon? Notice how Christian employs the Word of God as his sword.

Bunyan had only the most meager education. How do you account for the excellence of his style? Can you name any other men with slight educational advantages who drew a similarly noble manner of speaking and writing from a similar source? How do you explain the small percentage of words of Latin and French origin in Bunyan's works? What indications are there that Bunyan would be a powerful, convincing speaker?

Exercises and Creative Work: Can you fit real-life experiences to one of the following titles: *My Slough of Despond; My Valley of Humiliation; Mr. Worldly Wiseman?* If so, write a short essay developing the topic.

FROM A DIARY

SAMUEL PEPYS

By Way of Introduction: Have you ever wondered about ordinary folks in the days that now are history—about what they ate, how they dressed, what sorts of amusement they had? You need have no unsatisfied curiosities about such homely details in the days of Charles II. Thanks to the diaries of John Evelyn and Samuel Pepys we know as much about the folks in London then as we do about those in our own home town. Pepys' diary is especially revealing; for you remember he wrote it in secret code, and then besides, he was a gossipy soul. He was as interested in clothes and food as any woman ever was, and he was always surrounded by people. He is very frank in confessing his own misdemeanors—the crafty acceptance of a small bribe, or a little flirtation with the maid. He scolds his wife for being untidy, and then is sorry about it—all in all, a very human sort of chap.

But here is the diary—a small portion of it—and you may see for yourself what manner of man was Samuel. The style has been imitated enough so that you should find it familiar.

Jan. 1st, 1660. (Lord's Day.) This morning (we living lately in the garret,[1]) I rose, put on my suit with great skirts,[2] having not lately worn any other clothes but them. Went to

---

[1] GARRET—In 1660, Pepys was just getting started financially. As he was a Royalist, he was eagerly hoping for a restoration of the monarchy.

[2] GREAT SKIRTS—A coat very full from waist to knees.

Mr. Gunning's chapel at Exeter House, where he made a very good sermon. Dined at home in the garret, where my wife dressed the remains of a turkey, and in the doing of it she burned her hand. I staid at home all the afternoon, looking over my accounts; then went with my wife to my father's, and in going observed the great posts which the City have set up at the Conduit in Fleet-street.

Mar. 5th, 1660. To Westminster by water, only seeing Mr. Pinkney at his own house, where he showed me how he had alway kept the Lion and the Unicorn, in the back of his chimney, bright, in expectation of the King's coming again. At home I found Mr. Hunt, who told me how the Parliament had voted that the Covenant be printed and hung in churches again. Great hopes of the King's coming again. To bed.

Mar. 6th, 1660. (Shrove Tuesday.) To the Bell, where were Mr. Eglin, Veezy, Vincent a butcher, one more, and Mr. Tanner, with whom I played upon a viall, and he a viallin, after dinner, and were very merry, with a special good dinner, a leg of veal and bacon, two capons and sausages and fritters, with abundance of wine. After that I went home, where I found Kate Sterpin who hath not been here a great while before. She gone I went to see Mrs. Jem, at whose chamber door I found a couple of ladies, but she not being there, we hunted her out, and found that she and another had hid themselves behind a door. Well, they all went down into the diningroom, where it was full of tag, rag, and bobtail, dancing, singing, and drinking, of which I was ashamed, and after I had staid a dance or two I went away. This day I hear that the Lords do intend to sit, and great store of them are now in town, and I see in the Hall today. My Lord told me, that there was great endeavours to bring in the Protector[3] again; but he told me, too, that he did believe it would not last long if we were brought in; no, nor the King neither (though he seems to think that he will come in), unless he carry himself very soberly and well. Every body now drinks the King's health without any fear, whereas before it was very private that a man dare do it.

Oct. 13th, 1660. To my Lord's in the morning, where I met with Captain Cuttance, but my Lord not being up I went out

---

[3] PROTECTOR—Richard Cromwell, the son of Oliver, who had succeeded his father but had resigned in May, 1659.

to Charing Cross,[4] to see Major-General Harrison [5] hanged, drawn, and quartered; which was done there, he looking as cheerful as any man could do in that condition. He was presently cut down, and his head and heart shown to the people, at which there was great shouts of joy. It is said that he said that he was sure to come shortly at the right hand of Christ to judge them that now had judged him; and that his wife do expect his coming again. Thus it was my chance to see the King beheaded at White Hall,[6] and to see the first blood shed in revenge for the blood of the King at Charing Cross. From thence to my Lord's, and took Captain Cuttance and Mr. Shepley to the Sun Tavern, and did give them some oysters. After that I went by water home, where I was angry with my wife for her things lying about, and in my passion kicked the little fine basket, which I bought her in Holland, and broke it, which troubled me after I had done it. Within all the afternoon setting up shelves in my study. At night to bed.

Nov. 22d, 1660. This morning came the carpenters to make me a door at the other side of my house, going into the entry, which I was much pleased with. At noon my wife and I walked to the Old Exchange, and there she bought her a white whisk and put it on, and I a pair of gloves, and so we took coach for Whitehall to Mr. Fox's, where we found Mrs. Fox within, and an alderman of London paying £1,000 or £1,400 in gold upon the table for the King, which was the most gold that ever I saw together in my life. Mr. Fox came in presently and did receive us with a great deal of respect; and then did take my wife and I to the Queen's presence-chamber, where he got my wife placed behind the Queen's chair, and I got into the crowd, and by and by the Queen and the two Princesses [7] came to dinner. The Queen a very little plain old woman, and nothing more in her presence in any respect nor garb than any ordinary woman. The Princess of Orange I had often seen before. The Princess Henrietta is very pretty, but much below my expecta-

---

[4] CHARING CROSS—A busy section of London.
[5] MAJOR-GENERAL HARRISON—One of the judges that had sentenced Charles I to be beheaded. Charles II had promised that there would be no reprisals for his father's death. Of course he did not keep the promise.
[6] WHITE HALL—At that time the palace of the English kings.
[7] QUEEN AND THE TWO PRINCESSES—The mother of Charles, and his two sisters. The King was not married until 1662.

tion; and her dressing of herself with her hair frizzed short up to her ears, did make her seem so much the less to me. But my wife standing near with two or three black patches [8] on, and well dressed, did seem to me much handsomer than she. Dinner being done, we went to Mr. Fox's again, where many gentlemen dined with us, and most princely dinner, all provided for me and my friends, but I bringing none but myself and wife, he did call the company to help to eat up so much good victuals. At the end of dinner, my Lord Sandwich's health was drunk in the gilt tankard that I did give to Mrs. Fox the other day. After dinner I took coach for my wife and me homewards, and I light at the Maypole in the Strand, and sent my wife home. I to the new playhouse and saw part of the "Traitor," a very good Tragedy; Mr. Moon did act the Traitor very well. I went home on foot, it being very late and dirty, and so weary to bed.

Feb. 27th, 1661. At the office all the morning, that done I walked in the garden with little Captain Murford, where he and I had some discourse concerning the Light-House again, and I think I shall appear in the business, he promising me that if I can bring it about, it will be worth £100 per annum. Then I called for a dish of fish, which we had for dinner, this being the first day of Lent; and I do intend to try whether I can keep it or no.

Feb. 28th, 1661. Early to wait on my Lord, and after a little talk with him I took boat at Whitehall for Redriffe, but in my way overtook Captain Cuttance and Teddiman in a boat and so ashore with them at Queenhithe, and so to a tavern with them to a barrel of oysters, and so away. Capt. Cuttance and I walked from Redriffe to Deptford, where I found both Sir William and Sir G. Carteret at Mr. Uthwayt's, and there we dined, and notwithstanding my resolution, yet for want of other victualls, I did eat flesh this Lent, but am resolved to eat as little as I can. This month ends with two great secrets under dispute but yet known to very few: first, Who the King will marry; and What the meaning of this fleet is which we are now sheathing to set out for the southward.

Apr. 4th, 1661. To my workmen, then to my Lord's, and there dined with Mr. Shepley. After dinner I went in to my

---

[8] BLACK PATCHES—Beauty-spots, much the fashion.

Lord and there we had a great deal of musique, and then came my cozen Tom Pepys and there did accept of the security which we gave him for his £1,000 that we borrowed of him, and so the money to be paid next week. Then to the Privy Seal, and so with Mr. Moore to my father's, where some friends did sup there and we with them and late went home, leaving my wife still there. So to bed.

Apr. 4th, 1663. Up betimes and to my office. I returned home to dinner, whither by and by comes Roger Pepys, Mrs. Turner, her daughter, Joyce Norton, and a young lady, a daughter of Coll. Cockes, my uncle Wight, his wife and Mrs. Anne Wight. Very merry, at, before, and after dinner, and the more for that my dinner was great, and most neatly dressed by our only maid. We had a fricasee of rabbits and chickens, a leg of mutton boiled, three carps in a dish, a great dish of a side of lamb, a dish of roasted pigeons, a dish of four lobsters, three tarts, a lamprey pie (a most rare pie), a dish of anchovies, good wine of several sorts, and all things mighty noble and to my great content.

Apr. 5th, 1663. (Lord's day.) Up and spent the morning, till the Barber came, in reading in my chamber part of Osborne's Advice to his Son (which I shall not never enough admire for sense and language), and being by and by trimmed, to Church, myself, wife, Ashwell,[9] &c. Home to dinner, it raining, while that was prepared to my office to read over my vows with great affection and to very good purpose. So to dinner, and very well pleased with it. Then to church again, where a simple bawling young Scot preached. So home to my office alone till dark, reading some papers of my old navy precedents, and so home to supper, and, after some pleasant talk, my wife, Ashwell, and I to bed.

Apr. 19th, 1663. (Easter day.) Up and this day put on my close-kneed coloured suit, which, with new stockings of the colour, with belt, and new gilt-handled sword, is very handsome. To church alone, and so to dinner, where my father and brother Tom dined with us, and after dinner to church again, my father sitting below in the chancel. After church done, where the young Scotchman preaching I slept all the while, my father and

---

[9] Ashwell—Mary Ashwell, maid to Mrs. Pepys, addressed without a title because she was a servant. Notice how the Pepyses have prospered.

Then came my cozen Tom Pepys and there did accept of the security which we gave him.

I to see my uncle and aunt Wight, and after a stay of an hour there my father to my brother's and I home to supper, and after supper fell in discourse of dancing, and I find that Ashwell hath a very fine carriage,[10] which makes my wife almost ashamed of herself to see herself so outdone, but to-morrow she begins to learn to dance [11] for a month or two. So to prayers and to bed.

[10] FINE CARRIAGE—That is, carries herself well.
[11] LEARN TO DANCE—To improve her carriage.

Vocabulary Study: Pepys' vocabulary is surprisingly easy. You see he favors words of Anglo-Saxon birth, the stand-bys of our language. Most of the words that you will need to look up are special names for foods or fashions: *whisk; capon; fricasee; lamprey; anchovies; precedents; chancel.*
What is an antonym for *precedents?*

By Way of Appreciation: Fads and fashions may change from year to year. Human nature never changes. There will always be readers for the writer who can catch the ever-living features of men and women. Therein lies the charm of Pepys. True, his style is quaint, and his facts are interesting; but it is the people that his pages make live again who fascinate us. There is Pepys himself, his pretty wife, the boy he loves but must chastise, the crude young preacher, the friendly patron (my lord), her charming Ladyship—and oh, a host of others, all very real, the good mixed with the bad and even the badness somehow engaging. The *Diary* is not a text in English; it is a text in human nature.

Suggestions for Study: The *Diary* furnishes glimpses of the manners and customs of the age. What did you learn about the fashions in clothes during the Restoration period? What are the most striking differences between their dinner menus and ours? Is there any evidence that Pepys was an educated man? How many accomplishments did he have? What evidence did you find that Pepys was in sympathy with the King rather than with the Puritans? What details from these selections do you think would have been omitted if the *Diary* had not been written in shorthand? What proves that Pepys was not guilty of self-deception, that he never "kidded himself"? From these selections, what do you gather about the author's attitude toward religion? What admirable traits of character did the writer possess?

Exercises and Creative Work: Write an objective description of Samuel Pepys, covering his personal appearance as well as character.
Keep a diary for a week, recording any little detail of dress or manners that interests you. Have you noticed that Pepys makes little mention of the weather?

THE HISTORY OF PROSE LITERATURE IN ENGLAND

CLASSICISM AND THE AGE OF JOHNSON (1700-1780)

General Characteristics

Literature in England during the first part of the eighteenth century was prevailing classic—it was scholarly, critical, often satiric. The emphasis which classicism placed upon formal correctness and literary finish was fatal to great poetry, but it was what English prose stood in need of. The age was consequently a great prose period. The first, and perhaps the chief representative of classicism in English prose literature was Jonathan Swift, whose writings serve as excellent illustration of classic satire.

Jonathan Swift (1667-1745)

The tragedy of Swift's life was largely the result of the times in which he lived. It was a period of hot political strife, with the Whigs pitted against the Tories. It was a period of bitter prejudices and general snobbishness. Intelligence and learning were respected, but poverty was a personal disgrace. Swift came from a good Irish family and was

given a college education at Trinity in Dublin and later at Oxford. But he was poor, and his first position was that of an undersecretary to Sir William Temple, a distant relative, who snubbed and humiliated the youth.

Swift had been trained for the church, and when he was twenty-eight he was ordained. There followed several small "livings" in Ireland. He became vicar of Larasor in 1700. The next fourteen years he divided between his Irish parish and London where he became active in literary and political warfare. It was an age of pamphlets, and Swift was a powerful pamphleteer. His keen mind, cutting wit, and lively imagination made his satiric articles against opposing religions and parties feared and respected. First the Whigs and later the Tories employed his pen. Swift rejoiced in his power and was probably more nearly happy from 1701 to 1713 than at any other time in his life. He had hopes of being appointed to a high position in Church or State, and Queen Anne did make him Dean of St. Patrick's Cathedral (episcopal) in Dublin. But the fact that the appointment was to Ireland robbed it of joy for Swift. He had hoped to be in London, in the center of affairs. From that moment Swift was an embittered man, as he had always been a proud one. His later satires emphasize his belief that influence and flattery were more certain of reward than honest merit.

He wrote prodigiously, issuing most of his works—as was the fashion—anonymously or under an assumed name. His three best known satires are *A Tale of a Tub* (on religion), *The Battle of the Books* (on education), and *Gulliver's Travels*.

The happiest of his works, the *Journal to Stella*, was not written for publication. It is a series of letters written from 1710 to 1713 to Esther Johnson in Ireland. They contain simple, unaffected accounts of his activities in London, and show a tenderness that convinces the reader of his love for "Stella." That affection lasted until her death in 1728, but Swift never married. His last years were clouded by insanity of which he was at times conscious and which finally became violent. At his death in 1745, he was buried in St. Patrick's Cathedral.

Swift was a strange, unhappy man—loyal to his parish and sympathetic with suffering Ireland even while he chafed at the injustice which held him there. The world had hurt him, and his impulse was ever to hit back. The pen was his weapon.

The Literary Magazine

The most happy development within the age was the literary magazine and the light essay. Periodical literature increased enormously in the eighteenth century. In 1622 the first weekly newspaper had appeared, but it was not until 1702 that there was a regular daily paper. In the early years of the century Daniel Defoe was busy with journalism. To him is given the credit of writing the first "interview" and of making the "leading editorial" a feature of the newspaper. Then Sir Richard Steele, with his background of newspaper work, produced the *Tatler*, and a new type of periodical had been discovered. It was so often imitated through the rest of the century that, as Johnson says, it was difficult to find new names for succeeding publications.

The Light Essay

The feature of every issue of these magazines was a light essay. We have seen how Bacon introduced the essay to England; but here were essays of a different sort. Instead of being instructive or mentally stimulating, they were amusing. Sometimes they lightly ridiculed fashions of the day—fans, snuff-boxes, wigs. Sometimes they were half-humorous studies of character. Sometimes they were comments on the latest fashionable poet. Often the essay told a story. Any diverting subject might furnish the author with his essay for the day. But no matter what the subject, the essays of the period illustrate the aloof, impersonal tone of classic literature.

Nearly every writer tried his hand at the light essay but Joseph Addison, Richard Steele, and Samuel Johnson were its leading exponents.

Joseph Addison (1672–1719)

Joseph Addison is the fine gentleman of a polite age. He was tactful, courteous, and always correct. Of the same age as Steele, the friendship which he formed with the Irish lad lasted until the year of Addison's death, when a political quarrel came between them.

Addison knew how to write the proper thing at the proper time, and at the age of twenty-five he received a 300-pound pension from the Government as the result of a Latin poem on *The Peace of Ryswick.* Another poem, *The Campaign,* celebrating the Duke of Marlborough and his part in the Battle of Blenheim, was a stepping-stone in his political rise. Beginning as an under-secretary of the Government, he progressed until in April, 1717, he became Secretary of State.

Through these years he wrote many types of literature—poems, a tragic drama, an opera—but he is remembered chiefly as co-author of the *Spectator* papers. Addison and Steele had one ideal in common, the desire to hold up for public approval not vice but virtue. They wished to make goodness fashionable. They shunned the personal satire of their contemporaries and used a sort of general satire as a weapon against the follies of society. Until the appearance of the *Tatler,* the essay had been a formal thing; in the hands of Addison and Steele it became delightfully entertaining.

Addison was only forty-seven when he died in 1719. Steele lived ten years longer. In literature their names are seldom divided. Together they produced the most finished and most readable prose of the early eighteenth century.

Sir Richard Steele (1672–1729)

Dick Steele was a rollicking Irishman who became an English writer. Whatever his failings, and he had many, two achievements stand to his credit—the production of the first popular magazine and the creation of Sir Roger de Coverley.

Steele was a student in the Charterhouse charity school, where he first met Addison, and later in Queen's College, Oxford. After leaving school he drifted from one job to another, taking a turn at journalism, at soldiering, and at politics. Always he managed to write—sketches, articles, pamphlets, comedies—whatever the public wanted.

In 1709 there appeared a little four-page paper called the *Tatler.* It was issued two or three times a week and purported to be written by one Isaac Bickerstaff. It differed from the newspapers which had been appearing in that it had no news stories but, rather, chatty comments on news, a little society gossip, and an essay of some sort for each number. It was designed for pleasant entertainment and so may rightly be termed the first English magazine. It became exceedingly popular and many speculations were made as to the author. Joseph Addison was the first to guess that it was Steele. After that he became a contributor to the periodical, which continued to appear until 1711 when it was replaced by the *Spectator*. The second magazine was the work of Addison and Steele jointly, though Addison is given credit for most of the essays.

The second paper in the new series, written by Steele, contained a description of Sir Roger de Coverley who became the chief feature of the series. Addison collaborated in the succeeding sketches about the famous squire. Of their work, William J. Long says—"Steele is the original genius of Sir Roger and of many other characters and essays for which Addison usually receives the whole credit. It is often impossible in the *Tatler* essays to separate the works of the two men; but the majority of critics hold that the more original parts, the characters, the overflowing kindliness are largely Steele's creation; while to Addison fell the work of polishing and perfecting the essays and of adding that touch of humor which made them the most welcome literary visitors that England had ever received."

The *Spectator* was discontinued after two years, but the bound essays had a tremendous sale. They continue to hold an important place in the library of English literature. And Sir Richard Steele's share in them was his finest contribution to the world.

Samuel Johnson (1709–1784)

This age partly takes its designation from Dr. Samuel Johnson, the man who dominated English literature for forty years. In the literary memory, Johnson survives as the greatest paradox of his age. It was a fastidious age. Dress, manners, and art were elaborate and formal. The artificial was admired and cultivated; the simple and natural despised. Yet through this gilded finery stalks a man who stoops to no artifices, who is natural to the point of barbarism. Miraculously, without distinction of birth, without money, without patronage or "pull," he becomes a leader—almost a dictator in the world of fashion and letters. He is accepted everywhere; his opinions are listened to with respect. He counts among his friends the most gifted of his contemporaries.

He was born in 1709 in Lichfield, where his father was a bookseller. "In the child, the physical, intellectual, and moral peculiarities which afterwards distinguished the man were plainly discernible: great muscular strength accompanied by much awkwardness and many infirmities; great quickness of parts, with a morbid propensity to sloth and procrastination; a kind and generous heart, with a gloomy and irritable temper. . . . Indolent as he was, he acquired knowledge with such ease and rapidity that at every school to which he was sent he was soon the best scholar."

He entered Oxford, but had to leave at the end of three years because he was at the end of his resources. His life during the next thirty years was one hard struggle with poverty. He supported himself by tutoring and by work for magazines. Finally he conceived the idea of the *Dictionary* by which he was to become famous. Although Johnson is also remembered for *Rasselas* and *The Life of Savage,* some of his best writings appear in two series of short essays called the *Idler* and the *Rambler.*

Johnson's writings reflect little of the society in which he moved or of the influence he wielded. In fact, they reflect little of his own greatness, for they are written in the elaborate formality of the period. It remained for others to preserve this strange, incongruous personality. Boswell did it at length in his famous biography, a selection from which appears elsewhere in this book. Macaulay was to do it in miniature in his essay, *Samuel Johnson.*

The Literary Club

In 1764, Johnson and a group of his friends formed themselves into a club which gradually became a formidable power in the commonwealth of letters. It is deserving of mention here because in addition to Dr. Johnson himself, at least three of the original members were outstanding figures in the prose literature of the period. They are Oliver Goldsmith, Edmund Burke, and Edward Gibbon.

Oliver Goldsmith (1728–1774)

Oliver Goldsmith, better known as a poet, also tried his hand at the light essay, and issued an interesting series which he called *The Citizen of the World.* The papers are presumably written by a cultured Chinaman visiting in London. His companion, "The Man in Black," is Goldsmith. The device gave the author an opportunity to comment on life in London as it might appear to a courteous but puzzled foreigner.

Edmund Burke (1729–1797)

Though Americans know Burke chiefly through his *Speech on Conciliation with America,* his collected works fill fourteen volumes. He was a member of Samuel Johnson's famous Literary Club and his writings often show the influence of Johnson's style. He had a logical mind, a sense of fairness, and a remarkable command of language. With his magnetic personality he takes his place as one of England's great literary orators.

Edward Gibbon (1737–1794)

Edward Gibbon gave to English literature the first history that combined authoritative fact with a conscious literary style. His subject, suggested to him while he was visiting in Rome, was *The Decline and Fall of the Roman Empire.* It is in six volumes and covers the history of Rome from the reign of Trajan in 98 A.D. to the fall of the Byzantine Empire in 1453. It is a masterly piece of work. Its almost flawless expression reserves to it the privilege of being listed as the last of the classic works of the eighteenth century.

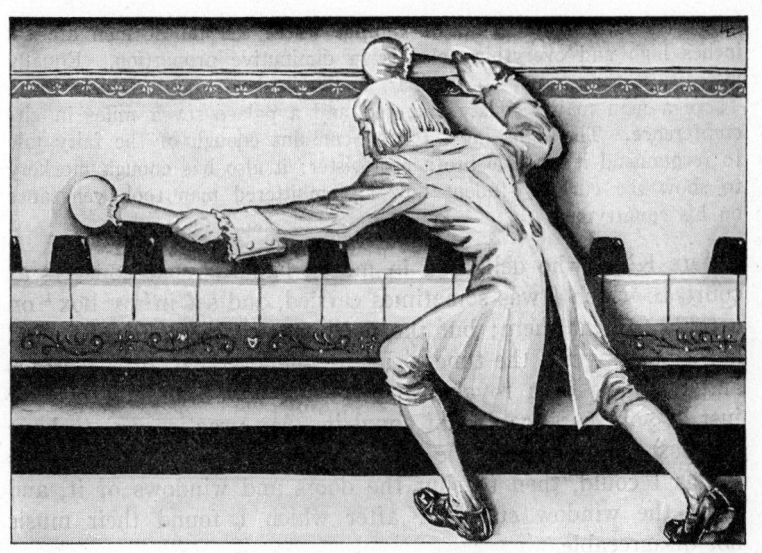

Prose and Essays of the Classic Age

A VOYAGE TO BROBDINGNAG

From *Gulliver's Travels*

Jonathan Swift

By Way of Introduction: Sometimes books written for children prove interesting to grown-ups, but the reverse is seldom true; children rarely enjoy a grown man's reading, particularly if it expresses views on politics, finance, customs or morals. There is one notable exception. *Gulliver's Travels* was written to show the politicians and statesmen of England how much the writer despised them and their country. It amused or enraged a current generation and then, according to precedent, it should have found a place with sister satires in the musty chambers of forgotten books.

It should have, but it didn't. The children discovered it. Now for over one hundred and fifty years it has proved fascinating reading for six- to ten-year olds wherever English is read. The satire, you see, is masqueraded under the guise of fairy-tale adventures in four amazing countries.

Brobdingnag—The general name of the country. Swift locates the land on an undiscovered continent between California and Japan. Its capital was called "Lorbrulgrud" which Gulliver translates as "Pride of the Universe."

Best known is the land of Lilliput where the tallest men are six inches high and everything else is in diminutive proportion. Equally interesting, though not so familiar, is the land of giants, Brobdingnag. There a man may be sixty feet tall and a palace seven miles in circumference. The following selection contains enough of the fairy tale to recommend it to little brother or sister; it also has enough mockery to show the curious student how an embittered man took vengeance on his countrymen.

The King, who delighted in music, had frequent concerts at court, to which I was sometimes carried, and set in my box [1] on a table to hear them; but the noise was so great, that I could hardly distinguish the tunes. I am confident that all the drums and trumpets of a royal army, beating and sounding together just at your ears, could not equal it. My practice was to have my box removed from the places where the performers sat, as far as I could, then to shut the doors and windows of it, and draw the window curtains; after which I found their music not disagreeable.

I had learned in my youth to play a little upon the spinet. Glumdalclitch [2] kept one in her chamber, and a master attended twice a week to teach her: I call it a spinet, because it somewhat resembled that instrument, and was played upon in the same manner. A fancy came into my head that I would entertain the King and Queen with an English tune upon this instrument. But this appeared extremely difficult; for the spinet was near sixty foot long, each key being almost a foot wide, so that, with my arms extended, I could not reach to above five keys, and to press them down required a good smart stroke with my fist, which would be too great a labour, and to no purpose. The method I contrived was this. I prepared two round sticks about the bigness of common cudgels; they were thicker at one end than the other, and I covered the thicker ends with a piece of a mouse's skin,[3] that by rapping on them I might neither damage the tops of the keys, nor interrupt the sound. Before the spinet

---

[1] Box—Gulliver was kept in a box about twelve feet square and ten feet deep. It was lined with cloth and furnished with doll bed, etc. When Gulliver accompanied the king and queen on a progress through the realm, the box was strapped about the waist of "some grave or trusty servant."

[2] Glumdalclitch—"Little Nurse," the name which Gulliver gave to the nine-year-old girl who became his care-taker. He describes her as "very good-natured, and not above forty feet high, being little for her age."

[3] Mouse's skin—The mice were the size of large English dogs.

a bench was placed, about four foot below the keys, and I was put upon the bench. I ran sideling upon it that way and this, as fast as I could, banging the proper keys with my two sticks, and made a shift to play a jig, to the great satisfaction of both their Majesties: but it was the most violent exercise I ever underwent, and yet I could not strike above sixteen keys, nor, consequently, play the bass and treble together, as other artists do; which was a great disadvantage to my performance.

The King, who, as I before observed, was a prince of excellent understanding, would frequently order that I should be brought in my box, and set upon the table in his closet. He would then command me to bring one of my chairs out of the box, and sit down within three yards' distance upon the top of the cabinet, which brought me almost to a level with his face. In this manner I had several conversations with him. I one day took the freedom to tell his Majesty, that the contempt he discovered towards Europe, and the rest of the world, did not seem answerable to those excellent qualities of mind he was master of. That, as inconsiderable as he took me to be, I hoped I might live to do his Majesty some signal service. The King heard me with attention, and began to conceive a much better opinion of me than he had ever before. He desired I would give him as exact an account of the government of England as I possibly could; because, as fond as princes commonly are of their own customs, he should be glad to hear of any thing that might deserve imitation.

Imagine with thyself, courteous reader, how often I then wished for the tongue of Demosthenes [4] or Cicero,[5] that might have enabled me to celebrate the praise of my own dear native country in a style equal to its merits and felicity.

I began my discourse by informing his Majesty that our dominions consisted of two islands, which composed three mighty kingdoms under one sovereign, besides our plantations in America. I dwelt long upon the fertility of our soil, and the temperature of our climate. I then spoke at large upon the constitution of an English Parliament, partly made up of an illustrious body called the House of Peers, persons of the noblest blood, and of the most ancient and ample patrimonies. I de-

---

[4] DEMOSTHENES—An Athenian orator and patriot (384–322 B.C.)
[5] CICERO—A Roman orator and patriot (106–43 B.C.)

scribed that extraordinary care always taken of their education in arts and arms, to qualify them for being counsellors born to the king and kingdom, to have a share in the legislature, to be members of the highest Court of Judicature, from whence there could be no appeal, and to be champions always ready for the defence of their prince and country, by their valour, conduct, and fidelity. That these were the ornament and bulwark of the kingdom, worthy followers of their most renowned ancestors, whose honour had been the reward of their virtue, from which their posterity were never once known to degenerate. To these were joined several holy persons, as part of that assembly, under the title of Bishops, whose peculiar business it is to take care of religion, and of those who instruct the people therein. These were searched and sought out through the whole nation, by the prince and his wisest counsellors, among such of the priesthood as were most deservedly distinguished by the sanctity of their lives, and the depth of their erudition; who were indeed the spiritual fathers of the clergy and the people.

That the other part of the Parliament consisted of an assembly called the House of Commons, who were all principal gentlemen, freely picked and culled out by the people themselves, for their great abilities and love of their country, to represent the wisdom of the whole nation. And these two bodies make up the most august assembly in Europe, to whom, in conjunction with the prince, the whole legislature [6] is committed.

I then descended to the Courts of Justice, over which the Judges, those venerable sages and interpreters of the law, presided, for determining the disputed rights and properties of men, as well as for the punishment of vice, and protection of innocence. I mentioned the prudent management of our treasury; the valour and achievements of our forces by sea and land. I computed the number of our people, by reckoning how many millions there might be of each religious sect, or political party among us. I did not omit even our sports and pastimes, or any other particular which I thought might redound to the honour of my country. And I finished all with a brief historical account of affairs and events in England for about an hundred years past.

[6] THE WHOLE LEGISLATURE—All legislation.

This conversation was not ended under five audiences, each of several hours, and the King heard the whole with great attention, frequently taking notes of what I spoke, as well as memorandums of several questions he intended to ask me.

When I had put an end to these long discourses, his Majesty, in a sixth audience, consulting his notes, proposed many doubts, queries, and objections, upon every article. He asked what methods were used to cultivate the minds and bodies of our young nobility, and in what kind of business they commonly spent the first and teachable part of their lives. What course was taken to supply that assembly when any noble family became extinct. What qualifications were necessary in those who were to be created new lords. Whether the humour of the prince, a sum of money to a court lady, or a prime minister, or a design of strengthening a party opposite to the public interest, ever happened to be motives in those advancements. What share of knowledge these lords had in the laws of their country, and how they came by it, so as to enable them to decide the properties of their fellow-subjects in the last resort. Whether they were always so free from avarice, partialities, or want, that a bribe, or some other sinister view, could have no place among them. Whether those holy lords I spoke of were always promoted to that rank upon account of their knowledge in religious matters, and the sanctity of their lives, had never been compliers with the times while they were common priests, or slavish prostitute chaplains to some nobleman, whose opinions they continued servilely to follow after they were admitted into that assembly.

He then desired to know what arts were practised in electing those whom I called commoners: whether a stranger with a strong purse might not influence the vulgar voters to choose him before their own landlord, or the most considerable gentleman in the neighborhood. How it came to pass, that people were so violently bent upon getting into this assembly, which I allowed to be a great trouble and expense, often to the ruin of their families, without any salary or pension: because this appeared such an exalted strain of virtue and public spirit, that his Majesty seemed to doubt it might possibly not be always sincere: and he desired to know whether such zealous gentlemen could have any views of refunding themselves for the charges and trouble they were at, by sacrificing the public good to the designs of a weak and vicious prince in conjunction with a corrupted ministry. He multiplied his questions, and sifted me thoroughly upon every part of this head, proposing numberless enquiries and objections, which I think it not prudent or convenient to repeat.

Upon what I said in relation to our Courts of Justice, his Majesty desired to be satisfied in several points: and this I was the better able to do, having been formerly almost ruined by a long suit in chancery, which was decreed for me with costs. He asked, what time was usually spent in determining between right and wrong, and what degree of expense. Whether advocates and orators had liberty to plead in causes manifestly known to be unjust, vexatious, or oppressive. Whether party in religion or politics were observed to be of any weight in the scale of justice. Whether those pleading orators [7] were persons educated in the general knowledge of equity, or only in provincial, national, and other local customs. Whether they or their judges had any part in penning those laws which they assumed the liberty of interpreting and glossing upon at their pleasure. Whether they had ever at different times pleaded for and against the same cause, and cited precedents to prove contrary opinions. Whether they were a rich or a poor corporation. Whether they receive any pecuniary reward for pleading, whether they were ever admitted as members in the lower senate.

He fell next upon the management of our treasury; and said he thought my memory had failed me, because I computed our taxes at above five or six millions a year, and when I came to mention the issues,[8] he found they sometimes amounted to more than double; for the notes he had taken were very particular in this point, because he hoped, as he told me, that the knowledge of our conduct might be useful to him, and he could not be deceived in his calculations. But, if what I told him were true, he was still at a loss how a kingdom could run out of its estate [9] like a private person. He asked me, who were our creditors; and where we should find money to pay them. He won-

---

[7] THOSE PLEADING ORATORS—Lawyers.
[8] ISSUES—Bonds of indebtedness for expenditures.
[9] RUN OUT OF ITS ESTATE—Live beyond its income.

dered to hear me talk of such chargeable and extensive wars; that certainly we must be a quarrelsome people, or live among very bad neighbours, and that our generals must needs be richer than our kings. He asked what business we had out of our own islands, unless upon the score of trade or treaty, or to defend the coasts with our fleet. Above all, he was amazed to hear me talk of a mercenary standing army in the midst of peace, and among a free people. He said, if we were governed by our own consent in the persons of our representatives, he could not imagine of whom we were afraid, or against whom we were to fight; and would hear my opinion, whether a private man's house might not better be defended by himself, his children, and family, than by half a dozen rascals picked up at a venture in the streets, for small wages, who might get an hundred times more by cutting their throats.

He was perfectly astonished with the historical account I gave him of our affairs during the last century, protesting it was only an heap of conspiracies, rebellions, murders, massacres, revolutions, banishments, the very worst effects that avarice, faction, hypocrisy, perfidiousness, cruelty, rage, madness, hatred, envy, lust, malice, or ambition could produce.

His Majesty in another audience was at the pains to recapitulate the sum of all I had spoken, compared the questions he made with the answers I had given, then taking me into his hands, and stroking me gently, delivered himself in these words, which I shall never forget nor the manner he spoke them in: My little friend Grildrig,[10] you have made a most admirable panegyric upon your country; you have clearly proved that ignorance, idleness, and vice, may be sometimes the only ingredients for qualifying a legislator; that laws are best explained, interpreted, and applied by those whose interest and abilities lie in perverting, confounding, and eluding them. I observe among you some lines of an institution, which in its original might have been tolerable, but these half erased, and the rest wholly blurred and blotted by corruptions. It doth not appear from all you have said, how any one virtue is required towards the procurement of any one station among you; much less that men are ennobled on account of their virtue,

---

[10] GRILDRIG—The Brobdingnagians' name for Gulliver, signifying "mannikin," or "little man."

that priests are advanced for their piety or learning, soldiers for their conduct or valour, judges for their integrity, senators for the love of their country, or counsellors for their wisdom. As for yourself (continued the King) who have spent the greatest part of your life in travelling, I am well disposed to hope you may hitherto have escaped many vices of your country. But by what I have gathered from your own relation, and the answers I have with much pains wringed and extorted from you, I cannot but conclude the bulk of your natives to be the most pernicious race of little odious vermin that nature ever suffered to crawl upon the surface of the earth.

Vocabulary Study: You will find a number of very common words in the list below, included because in the present selection they are used in uncommon ways. The dictionary, however, gives definitions to fit each case. Be sure to find the right ones. *Spinet; discovered; answerable; felicity; patrimonies; judicature; fidelity; bulwark; posterity; erudition; article; servilely; vulgar; chancery; equity; glossing; pecuniary; creditors; mercenary; venture; avarice; faction; perfidiousness; recapitulate; panegyric; perverting; eluding; procurement; integrity; pernicious; odious; vermin.*

What are synonyms of the verb *describe?* of the noun *imagine?*

By Way of Appreciation: *Gulliver's Travels* like *The Pilgrim's Progress* should first be read when one is very young. Then its stories are enchanting. Swift employs one device which children adore in stories—he furnishes an abundance of elaborate detail. And his details are very carefully worked out. In the descriptions of the kingdoms of Lilliput and Brobdingnag every item is sized precisely to scale. Even the older reader is interested in noting how nicely proportions are maintained.

Again like *The Pilgrim's Progress, Gulliver's Travels* should be reread in later years, though for a different reason. The student of history and literature finds the work a clever, though biased, commentary on institutions and individuals of eighteenth century England. Today we need footnotes to point out the personal jibes. We must be told, for instance, that Flimnap, the somersaulting treasurer of Lilliput, represented Walpole. The general satire, however, is obvious; the most careless reader can hardly miss it.

Two points of contact between Swift and Bunyan have been noted. There the likeness ends. *The Pilgrim's Progress,* written in sober sincerity, remains a book of "sweetness and light." *Gulliver's Travels,* written in disappointment and spite, leaves a bitter taste upon the tongue and one hastens to more pleasant fare.

Suggestions for Study: To appreciate Gulliver's achievement in playing the spinet, try to imagine yourself playing a piano whose keys are a foot wide and whose keyboard is sixty feet long. Can you devise any more satisfactory method of playing it than Gulliver used? What is the effect gained by having Gulliver praise the institutions of his country and having the condemnation of them come from the king of Brobdingnag? How has Swift prepared the reader to respect the opinion of the king? Point out the irony in Gulliver's experience with the Courts of Justice. How many public abuses which the king pointed out still exist? Name them.

Make a list of the important events in English history from the death of Elizabeth in 1603 to the ascension of Anne in 1702. Was the king justified in his condemnation of the century as one of rebellion and bloodshed? Why was Swift especially bitter about the methods of advancement in politics and in the church? Is the closing sentence of the selection in keeping with the character of the king? How do you explain it?

Exercises and Creative Work: Read Gulliver's contrasting voyage to Lilliput where everything is on a tiny scale, and make a class report on it. In your reading, see if you can discover the satire involved.

SIR ROGER AT CHURCH

JOSEPH ADDISON, WITH RICHARD STEELE

By Way of Introduction: One of the most lovable figures moving through the pages of English literature is the country gentleman. Whether we meet him as the white-bearded franklin jogging along the Canterbury road or as the hearty squire of a dozen English novels, he is always delightful, and somehow very typically British. But at no time is he more lovable than in the person of Sir Roger de Coverley—an eccentric, good-hearted country landlord in the days of Queen Anne.

Steele introduced him in the second number of the *Spectator*, and he quickly became the feature of the paper. His ardent, if timorous, devotion to the widow was followed with as much eager suspense as are the modern comic-strip love-adventures of Uncle Bim. When the co-authors suffered him to die, readers of the *Spectator* protested their loss and were not at all consoled by the magnificence of his funeral.

But here is the good squire alive, and very much himself!

SIR ROGER HIMSELF

THE first of our society is a gentleman of Worcestershire, of ancient descent, a baronet, his name Sir Roger de Coverley. His great grandfather was inventor of that famous country-dance which is called after him. All who know that shire, are very well acquainted with the parts and merits of Sir Roger. He is a gentleman that is very singular in his behaviour, but his singularities proceed from his good sense, and are contradictions to the manners of the world, only as he thinks the world is in the wrong. However, this humour creates him no enemies, for he does nothing with sourness or obstinacy; and his being unconfined to modes and forms, makes him but the readier and more capable to please and oblige all who know him. When he is in town, he lives in Soho-square.[1] It is said, he keeps himself a bachelor by reason he was crossed in love by a perverse beautiful widow of the next county to him. Before this disappointment, Sir Roger was what you call a fine gentleman, had often supped with Lord Rochester and Sir George Etherege, fought a duel upon his first coming to town, and kicked Bully Dawson [2] in a public coffee-house for calling him youngster. But being ill used by the above mentioned widow, he was very serious for a year and a half; and though, his temper being naturally jovial, he at last got over it, he grew careless of himself, and never dressed [3] afterwards. He continues to wear a coat and doublet of the same cut that were in fashion at the time of his repulse, which, in his merry humours, he tells us, has been in and out [4] twelve times since he first wore it. He is now in his fifty-sixth year, cheerful, gay, and hearty; keeps a good house both in town and country; a great lover of mankind; but there is such a mirthful cast in his behaviour, that he is rather beloved than esteemed; his tenants grow rich, his servants look satisfied; all the young women profess love to him, and the young men are glad of his company: when he comes into a house, he calls the servants by their names, and talks all the way up stairs to a visit. I must not omit, that Sir Roger is a justice of the quorum;[5] that he fills the chair at a quarter-session [6] with

[1] Soho-square—A square in London.
[2] Lord Rochester, Sir George Etherege, Bully Dawson—The first, John Wilmot, an English poet and courtier of Charles II; the second, an English dramatist; the third, a notorious London sharper. These three are typical of the dissolute gentlemen prominent in London society in the closing years of the reign of Charles II.
[3] Dressed—Dressed up.
[4] In and out—In and out of fashion.
[5] Justice of the quorum—Justice of the peace.
[6] Quarter-session—A court held four times a year, trying many petty offences and exercising a minor civil jurisdiction.

great abilities, and three months ago gained universal applause by explaining a passage in the game act.

SIR ROGER AT CHURCH

I AM always very well pleased with a country Sunday, and think, if keeping holy the seventh day were only a human institution, it would be the best method that could have been thought of for the polishing and civilizing of mankind. It is certain the country people would soon degenerate into a kind of savages and barbarians, were there not such frequent returns of a stated time, in which the whole village meet together with their best faces, and in their cleanliest habits,[1] to converse with one another upon indifferent subjects, hear their duties explained to them, and join together in adoration of the Supreme Being. Sunday clears away the rust of the whole week, not only as it refreshes in their minds the notions of religion, but as it puts both the sexes upon appearing in their most agreeable forms, and exerting all such qualities as are apt to give them a figure in the eye of the village. A country fellow distinguishes himself as much in the churchyard, as a citizen does upon the 'Change, the whole parish-politics being generally discussed in that place either after sermon or before the bell rings.

My friend Sir Roger, being a good churchman, has beautified the inside of his church with several texts of his own choosing. He has likewise given a handsome pulpit-cloth, and railed in the communion-table at his own expense. He has often told me, that at his coming to his estate he found his parishioners very irregular; and that in order to make them kneel and join in the responses, he gave every one of them a hassock and a common prayer-book; and at the same time employed an itinerant singing-master, who goes about the country for that purpose, to instruct them rightly in the tunes of the psalms:[2] upon which they now very much value themselves, and indeed outdo most of the country churches that I have ever heard.

As Sir Roger is landlord to the whole congregation, he keeps them in very good order, and will suffer nobody to sleep in it besides himself; for if by chance he has been surprised into a

---
[1] HABITS—Clothes.
[2] PSALMS—All the earliest church hymns were paraphrases of the Psalms set to music.

short nap at sermon, upon recovering out of it he stands up and looks about him, and if he sees anybody else nodding, either wakes them himself, or sends his servant to them. Several other

of the old knight's peculiarities break out upon these occasions. Sometimes he will be lengthening out a verse in the singing psalms, half a minute after the rest of the congregation have done with it; sometimes when he is pleased with the matter of his devotion, he pronounces Amen three or four times to the same prayer: and sometimes stands up when everybody else is upon their knees, to count the congregation, or see if any of his tenants are missing.

I was yesterday very much surprised to hear my old friend in the midst of the service calling out to one John Matthews to mind what he was about, and not disturb the congregation. This John Matthews it seems is remarkable for being an idle fellow, and at that time was kicking his heels for his diversion. This authority of the knight, though exerted in that odd manner which accompanies him in all circumstances of life, has a very good effect upon the parish, who are not polite [3] enough to see anything ridiculous in his behaviour; besides that the general good sense and worthiness of his character make his friends observe these little singularities as foils that rather set off than blemish his good qualities.

As soon as the sermon is finished, nobody presumes to stir till Sir Roger is gone out of the church. The knight walks down from his seat in the chancel between a double row of his tenants, that stand bowing to him on each side: and every now and then inquires how such an one's wife, or mother, or son, or father

[3] POLITE—Here, sophisticated.

do, whom he does not see at church; which is understood as a secret reprimand to the person that is absent.

The chaplain [4] has often told me, that upon a catechising day, when Sir Roger has been pleased with a boy that answers well, he has ordered a Bible to be given him next day for his encouragement; and sometimes accompanies it with a flitch of bacon to his mother. Sir Roger has likewise added five pounds a year to the clerk's place; and, that he may encourage the young fellows to make themselves perfect in the church service, has promised upon the death of the present incumbent, who is very old, to bestow it according to merit.

The fair understanding between Sir Roger and his chaplain, and their mutual concurrence in doing good, is the more remarkable, because the very next village is famous for the differences and contentions that rise between the parson and the squire, who live in a perpetual state of war. The parson is always preaching at the squire; and the squire, to be revenged on the parson, never comes to church. The squire has made all his tenants atheists and tithe-stealers; while the parson instructs them every Sunday in the dignity of his order, and insinuates to them almost in every sermon that he is a better man than his patron. In short, matters are come to such an extremity, that the squire has not said his prayers either in public or private this half year; and that the parson threatens him, if he does not mend his manners, to pray for him in the face of the whole congregation.

Feuds of this nature, though too frequent in the country, are very fatal to the ordinary people; who are so used to be dazzled with riches, that they pay as much deference to the understanding of a man of an estate, as of a man of learning; and are very hardly brought to regard any truth, how important soever it may be that is preached to them, when they know there are several men of five hundred a year [5] who do not believe it.

[4] CHAPLAIN—Here, the resident clergyman, one of Sir Roger's household.
[5] FIVE HUNDRED A YEAR—Five hundred pounds a year, about $2,500.

Vocabulary Study: Although written during the classic period of English literature, the *Spectator* essays are not difficult reading. These words you will want to be sure to know in order to enjoy the essay: *hassock; itinerant; foils; chancel; flitch; incumbent; mutual; concurrence; tithe-stealers* (see *tithe*); *insinuates; extremity.*

By Way of Appreciation: The essays of Bacon were formal and precise. They were the work of a scholar and were read by the cultured few. With the coming of the newspapers and the gossipy periodical, the essay became popular. The *Tatler* and *Spectator* papers, written by two men-about-town and read to the accompaniment of clattering coffee cups and snapping snuff-box lids, have a lively, friendly tone. The essay has grown familiar.

There is great variety and charm in the essays of Addison and Steele—the more so since they preserve the sparkle of the age without its sharpness. There is wit, of course, and satire; but it is different from that of Pope and Swift. The satire that offends is the satire that is maliciously personal. Addison and Steele were never malicious, and their satire was never personal. Fashions and types of the day they delicately play with. But all is in the kindliest, happiest manner. Sir Roger is not any certain squire. He is enough different so that no country gentleman of the day could see himself in the picture; at the same time, he is typical enough of the breed to give many a man a chuckle at the expense of some neighbor. And if Sir Roger has some of the peculiarities of the country-bred gentleman, he has also all his virtues. He is honest and hospitable and kind-hearted. The professed aim of Addison and Steele was to make virtue popular. Their success is measured by the extent to which Sir Roger, the epitome of simplicity in manner and character, won the hearts of a sophisticated age. And the proof of the real genius of this team of writers is the fact that Sir Roger has held his charm through a good two hundred years and that we of a different age and civilization still read him with delight and understanding.

Suggestions for Study: Do you know of anyone who, like Sir Roger, is "rather beloved than esteemed"? Is it possible for one to be both beloved and esteemed? Explain the last sentence in the first paragraph of *Sir Roger at Church*. So far as you can judge, is the statement still true? Sir Roger being a conservative is, of course, "Church of England" or Episcopalian. What comment might be made upon the Squire's methods of encouraging devotion among his parishioners? Satire ridicules the follies and vices of individuals or of society—(*a*) what passages are a mild satire on Sir Roger? (*b*) what passages are a satire upon society or upon any special class of people? Compare Sir Roger with any other English country gentlemen that you have read about; such as, for instance Squire Cass from *Silas Marner*.

Exercises and Creative Work: Many a writer has helped himself develop style by imitating (for practice) essays from the *Spectator*. Here are two exercises in writing which you might try:

If you are acquainted with an eccentric personality, try writing a pleasantly whimsical characterization of this sort.

Try reproducing Sir Roger (or better, one of his descendants) in a modern setting. What would he be today? A farmer? A rancher?

FROZEN WORDS

Joseph Addison with Richard Steele

By Way of Introduction: Our grandfathers called it spinning yarns. We call it telling tall stories. But no matter what the name, the fun of extravagant tale-telling remains. Often the teller refuses responsibility for his story and gives the credit to some Baron von Münchausen.[1] Before the days of the Baron, most fabulous stories were laid to Sir John Mandeville. And indeed that famous traveler hardly surpassed the heights of imagination reached by Addison and Steele in working up the idea of word-congealing cold.

THERE are no books which I more delight in than in travels, especially those that describe remote countries, and give the writer an opportunity of showing his parts without incurring any danger of being examined or contradicted. Among all the authors of this kind, our renowned countryman Sir John Mandeville[2] has distinguished himself, by the copiousness of his inven-

---

[1] BARON VON MÜNCHAUSEN—Have you wondered why a popular radio comedian (Jack Pearl) calls himself Baron Münchausen? Look up the name in an encyclopedia for the answer.
[2] SIR JOHN MANDEVILLE—See Anglo-Saxon Period in the *History of Prose Literature*.

tion,[3] and the greatness of his genius. The second to Sir John I take to have been, Ferdinand Mendez Pinto,[4] a person of infinite adventure, and unbounded imagination. One reads the voyages of these two great wits, with as much astonishment as the travels of Ulysses in Homer, or of the Red-Cross Knight in Spenser. All is enchanted ground, and fairyland.

I have got into my hands, by great chance, several manuscripts of these two eminent authors, which are filled with greater wonders than any of those they have communicated to the public; and indeed, were they not so well attested, they would appear altogether improbable. I am apt to think the ingenious authors did not publish them with the rest of their works, lest they should pass for fictions and fables: a caution not unnecessary, when the reputation of their veracity was not yet established in the world. But as this reason has now no farther weight, I shall make the public a present of these curious pieces, at such times as I shall find myself unprovided with other subjects.

The present paper I intend to fill with an extract from St. John's Journal, in which that learned and worthy knight gives an account of the freezing and thawing of several short speeches, which he made in the territories of Nova Zembla.[5] I need not inform my reader, that the author of *Hudibras*[6] alludes to this strange quality in that cold climate, when, speaking of abstracted notions[7] clothed in a visible shape, he adds that apt simile,

>Like words congealed in northern air.

Not to keep my reader any longer in suspense, the relation[8] put into modern language, is as follows:

"We were separated by a storm in the latitude of seventy-three, insomuch, that only the ship which I was in, with a Dutch and French vessel, got safe into a creek of Nova Zembla. We landed, in order to refit our vessels, and store ourselves with provisions. The crew of each vessel made themselves a cabin

---

[3] INVENTION—Imagination.
[4] FERDINAND MENDEZ PINTO—Portuguese adventurer and traveler (1509–1583) in China and Japan. *Peregrinaçao* is a record of his adventures.
[5] NOVA ZEMBLA—Russian islands in the Arctic Ocean.
[6] *Hudibras*—A poem by Samuel Butler (1612–1680), a satire on the Puritans.
[7] ABSTRACTED NOTIONS—Abstract, or intangible, ideas.
[8] RELATION—Narrative.

of turf and wood, at some distance from each other, to fence themselves against the inclemencies of the weather, which was severe beyond imagination. We soon observed, that in talking to one another we lost several of our words, and could not hear one another at above two yards distance, and that too when we sat very near the fire. After much perplexity, I found that our words froze in the air, before they could reach the ears of the persons to whom they were spoken. I was soon confirmed in this conjecture, when, upon the increase of the cold, the whole company grew dumb, or rather deaf; for every man was sensible, as we afterwards found, that he spoke as well as ever; but the sounds no sooner took air than they were condensed and lost. It was now a miserable spectacle to see us nodding and gaping at one another, every man talking, and no man heard. One might observe a seaman that could hail a ship at a league's distance, beckoning with his hand, straining his lungs, and tearing his throat; but all in vain:

Nec vox nec verba sequuntur [9]

"We continued here three weeks in this dismal plight. At length, upon a turn of wind, the air about us began to thaw. Our cabin was immediately filled with a dry clattering sound, which I afterwards found to be the crackling of consonants that broke above our heads, and were often mixed with a gentle hissing, which I imputed to the letter *s,* that occurs so frequently in the English tongue. I soon after felt a breeze of whispers rushing by my ear; for those, being of soft and gentle substance, immediately liquefied in the warm wind that blew across our cabin. These were soon followed by syllables and short words, and at length by entire sentences, that melted sooner or later, as they were more or less congealed; so that we now heard everything that had been *spoken* during the whole three weeks that we had been *silent,* if I may use that expression. It was now very early in the morning, and yet, to my surprise, I heard somebody say, 'Sir John, it is midnight, and time for the ship's crew to go to bed.' This I knew to be the pilot's voice; and, upon recollecting myself, I concluded that he had spoken these words to me some days before, though I could not hear them until the present thaw. My reader will easily imagine how the whole crew was amazed to hear every man

---

[9] *Nec vox nec verba sequuntur*—Neither voice nor words followed.

talking, and see no man opening his mouth. In the midst of this great surprise we were all in, we heard a volley of oaths and curses, lasting for a long while, and uttered in a very hoarse voice, which I knew belonged to the boatswain, who was a very choleric fellow, and had taken his opportunity of cursing and swearing at me, when he thought I could not hear him; for I had several times given him the strappado on that account, as I did not fail to repeat it for these his pious soliloquies, when I got him on shipboard.

"I must not omit the names of several beauties in Wapping,[10] which were heard every now and then, in the midst of a long sigh that accompanied them; as, 'Dear Kate!' 'Pretty Mrs. Peggy!' 'When shall I see my Sue again!' This betrayed several amours, which had been concealed until that time, and furnished us with a great deal of mirth in our return to England.

"When this confusion of voices was pretty well over, though I was afraid to offer at speaking, as fearing I should not be heard, I proposed a visit to the Dutch cabin, which lay about a mile farther up in the country. My crew were extremely rejoiced to find they had again recovered their hearing; though every man uttered his voice with the same apprehensions that I had done,

Et timide verba intermissa retentat [11]

"At about a half-a-mile's distance from our cabin we heard the groanings of a bear, which at first startled us; but, upon enquiry, we were informed by some of our company, that he was dead, and now lay in salt, having been killed upon that very spot about a fortnight before, in the time of the frost. Not far from the same place, we were likewise entertained with some posthumous snarls, and barkings of a fox.

"We at length arrived at the little Dutch settlement; and, upon entering the room, found it filled with sighs that smelt of brandy, and several other unsavoury sounds, that were altogether inarticulate.[12] My valet, who was an Irishman, fell into so great a rage at what he heard, that he drew his sword; but not knowing where to lay the blame, he put it up again. We were stunned with these confused noises, but did not hear a single

[10] WAPPING—A part of London, along the Thames.
[11] *Et timide . . . retentat*—And timidly held back the halting words.
[12] INARTICULATE—Unintelligible, not clearly sounded.

word until about half-an-hour after; which I ascribed to the harsh and obdurate sounds of that language, which wanted more time than ours to melt, and become audible.

"After having here met with a very hearty welcome, we went to the cabin of the French, who, to make amends for their three weeks' silence, were talking and disputing with greater rapidity and confusion than I ever heard in an assembly, even of that nation. Their language, as I found, upon the first giving of the weather, fell asunder and dissolved. I was here convinced of an error, into which I had before fallen; for I fancied, that for the freezing of the sound, it was necessary for it to be wrapped up, and, as it were, preserved in breath: but I found my mistake when I heard the sound of a kit [13] playing a minuet over our heads. I asked the occasion of it; upon which one of the company told me that it would play there above a week longer; 'for,' says he, 'finding ourselves bereft of speech, we prevailed upon one of the company, who had his musical instrument about him, to play to us from morning to night; all which time was employed in dancing in order to dissipate our chagrin, and *tuer le temps*." [14]

Here Sir John gives very good philosophical reasons, why the kit could not be heard during the frost; but, as they are something prolix I pass them over in silence, and shall only observe, that the honourable author seems, by his quotations, to have been well versed in the ancient poets, which perhaps raised his fancy above the ordinary pitch of historians, and very much contributed to the embellishment of his writings.

[13] KIT—A small violin with three strings.
[14] *Tuer le temps*—To kill time.

Vocabulary Study: *Copiousness; attested; ingenious; veracity; league; choleric; strappado; amours; posthumous; unsavoury; obdurate; dissipate; chagrin; prolix; embellishment.*

Give synonyms for *copious;* also state the exact meaning of two of its antonyms, *sparse* and *scanty*.

By Way of Appreciation: In the *Tatler* essays, Steele assumed the personality of "Isaac Bickerstaff," an imaginary London club-man. The name had been used first by Jonathan Swift in one of his practical jokes. When Addison began to work with Steele, Mr. Bickerstaff was retained as the narrator of the essays. *Frozen Words,* which appeared in one of the later numbers of the *Tatler* and which is generally attributed to Addison, is one of the most entertaining of the essays.

There is no underlying meaning. It was written as a lark and should be read for fun.

Suggestions for Study: What sentence in the second paragraph is ironic? Explain the words "pious soliloquies." What are the two most humorous situations in the essay? Explain some of the phonetic differences between the English and the Dutch and the French languages. Show how, as a result of these differences, the thawing sounds in the three camps varied. Do you notice a discrepancy on the part of the author in the last two paragraphs?

Exercises and Creative Work: If you wish to try an imitative theme for practice, think of other settings in which a similar idea might be worked out; a schoolroom, for instance, or an office. Make the theme short but entertaining.

THE DISSECTION OF A BEAU'S HEAD
AND
THE COQUETTE'S HEART

JOSEPH ADDISON WITH RICHARD STEELE

By Way of Introduction: Every age has its belles and beaux; few, however, could rival the days of Queen Anne in extravagant vanity. It was a period of satins, laces, frills, and ribboned wigs for men; of "puffs, powders, patches, Bibles, *billet-doux*" (with the stress *not* on the Bibles) for women. Coiffures were tremendous—eighteen and twenty inches high and elaborated with birds, feathers, fruits, ships' models and the like. The frivolities of the court were immortalized in Alexander Pope's burlesque poem, *The Rape of the Lock,* and in the clever dissections of a beau's head and a flirt's heart by Addison and Steele. The beau of the essay was just such a fop as Pope's

> Sir Plume, of amber snuff-box justly vain
> And the nice conduct of clouded cane.

The coquette might have been one of the bevy that fluttered about the Queen—

> With varying vanities from every part,
> They shift the moving toyshop of their heart;
> Where wigs with wigs, with sword-knots sword-knots strive,
> Beaux banish beaux, and coaches coaches drive.

THE DISSECTION OF A BEAU'S HEAD

I WAS yesterday engaged in an assembly of virtuosos, where one of them produced many curious observations which he had lately made in the anatomy of an human body. Another of the company communicated to us several wonderful discoveries, which he had also made on the same subject by the help of very fine glasses. This gave birth to a great variety of uncommon remarks, and furnished discourse for the remaining part of the day.

The different opinions which were started on this occasion, presented to my imagination so many new ideals, that by mixing with those which were already there, they employed my fancy all the last night, and composed a very wild extravagant dream.

I was invited, methought, to the dissection of a beau's head and of a coquette's heart, which were both of them laid on a table before us. An imaginary operator opened the first with a great deal of nicety, which upon a cursory and superficial view, appeared like the head of another man;[1] but upon applying our glasses to it, we made a very odd discovery, namely, that what we looked upon as brains, were not such in reality, but an heap of strange materials wound up in that shape and texture, and packed together with wonderful art in the several cavities of the skull. For as Homer tells us that the blood of the gods is not real blood but only something like it, so we found that the brain of a beau is not real brain but only something like it.

The pineal gland, which many of our modern philosophers[2] suppose to be the seat of the soul, smelt very strong of essence[3] and orange-flower water, and was encompassed with a kind of horny substance cut into a thousand little faces or mirrors, which were imperceptible to the naked eye; insomuch that the soul, if there had been any here, must have been always taken up in contemplating her[4] own beauties.

We observed a large *antrum* or cavity in the *sinciput*, that was filled with ribbons, lace, and embroidery, wrought together in a most curious piece of network, the parts of which were likewise imperceptible to the naked eye. Another of these *antrums* or cavities was stuffed with invisible *billet-doux*, love-

---

[1] OF ANOTHER MAN—Of any other man.
[2] PHILOSOPHERS—Until the nineteenth century the term *philosopher* included, in fact was often considered synonymous with, *scientist*.
[3] ESSENCE—Perfume.
[4] HER—The antecedent is "soul." Psyche, the Greek personification of the soul, was a lovely woman.

letters, pricked dances, and other trumpery of the same nature. In another we found a kind of powder, which set the whole company a sneezing, and by the scent discovered itself to be right Spanish. The several other cells were stored with commodities of the same kind, of which it would be tedious to give the reader an exact inventory.

There was a large cavity on each side of the head, which I must not omit. That on the right side was filled with fictions, flatteries, and falsehoods, vows, promises, and protestations; that on the left with oaths and imprecations. There issued out a duct from each of these cells, which ran into the root of the tongue, where both joined together and passed forward in one common duct to the tip of it. We discovered several little roads or canals running from the ear into the brain, and took particular care to trace them out through their several passages. One of them extended itself to a bundle of sonnets and little musical instruments. Others ended in several bladders, which were filled with wind or froth. But the large canal entered into a great cavity of the skull, from whence there went another canal into the tongue. This great cavity was filled with a kind of spongy substance, which the French anatomists call *galimatias*,[5] and the English, nonsense.

The skins of the forehead were extremely tough and thick, and, what very much surprised us, had not in them any single blood vessel that we were able to discover, either with or without our glasses; from whence we concluded, that the party, when alive, must have been entirely deprived of the faculty of blushing.

The *os cribriforme* was exceedingly stuffed, and in some places damaged with snuff. We could not but take notice in particular of that small muscle, which is not often discovered in dissections, and draws the nose upwards, when it expresses the contempt which the owner of it has, upon seeing anything he does not like, or hearing anything he does not understand. I need not tell my learned reader, that is that muscle which performs the motion so often mentioned by the Latin poets, when they talk of a man's cocking his nose, or playing the rhinoceros.

We did not find anything very remarkable in the eye, saving

[5] *Galimatias*—According to a French dictionary, "balderdash," "bosh."

only that the *musculi amatorii*,⁶ or, as we may translate it into English, the ogling muscles, were very much worn and decayed with use; whereas, on the contrary, the *elevator,* or the muscle which turns the eye towards heaven, did not appear to have been used at all.

I have only mentioned in this dissection such new discoveries as we were able to make, and have not taken any notice of those parts which are to be met with in common heads. As for the skull, the face, and indeed the whole outward shape and figure of the head, we could not discover any difference from what we observe in the heads of other men. We were informed that the person to whom this head belonged has passed for a man above five-and-thirty years; during which time he ate and drank like other people, dressed well, talked loud, laughed frequently, and on particular occasions had acquitted himself tolerably at a ball or an assembly; to which one of the company added, that a certain knot of ladies took him for a wit. He was cut off in the flower of his age by the blow of a paring-shovel, having been surprised by an eminent citizen as he was tending some civilities to his wife.

When we had thoroughly examined this head with all its apartments and its several kinds of furniture, we put up the brain, such as it was, into its proper place, and laid it aside under a broad piece of scarlet cloth, in order to be prepared and kept in a great repository of dissections, our operator telling us that the preparation would not be so difficult as that of another brain, for that he had observed several of the little pipes and tubes which ran through the brain were already filled with a kind of mercurial substance, which he looked upon to be true quicksilver.

He applied himself in the next place to the coquette's heart, which he likewise laid open with great dexterity. There occurred to us many particularities in this dissection; but being unwilling to burden my reader's memory too much, I shall reserve this subject for the speculation of another day.

THE COQUETTE'S HEART

HAVING already given an account of the dissection of a beau's head, with the several discoveries made on that occasion, I shall

⁶ *Musculi amatorii*—Literally, muscles of love-making.

here, according to my promise, enter upon the dissection of a coquette's heart, and communicate to the public such particularities as we observed in that curious piece of anatomy.

I should perhaps have waived this undertaking, had not I been put in mind of my promise by several of my unknown correspondents, who are very importunate with me to make an example of the coquette, as I have already done of the beau. It is therefore in compliance with the request of friends, that I have looked over the minutes of my former dream, in order to give the public an exact relation of it, which I shall enter upon without farther preface.

Our operator, before he engaged in this visionary dissection, told us that there was nothing in his art more difficult than to lay open the heart of a coquette, by reason of the many labyrinths and recesses which are to be found in it, and which do not appear in the heart of any other animal.

He desired us first of all to observe the pericardium, or outward case of the heart, which we did very attentively; and by the help of our glasses discerned in it millions of little scars, which seemed to have been occasioned by the points of innumerable darts and arrows, that from time to time had glanced upon the outward coat; though we could not discover the smallest orifice by which any of them had entered and pierced the inward substance.

Every smatterer in anatomy knows that this pericardium, or case of the heart, contains in it a thin reddish liquor, supposed to be bred from the vapors which exhale out of the heart, and being stopped here, are condensed into this watery substance. Upon examining this liquor, we found that it had in it all the qualities of that spirit which is made use of in the thermometer to show the change of weather.

Nor must I here omit an experiment one of the company assured us he himself had made with this liquor, which he found in great quantity about the heart of a coquette whom he had formerly dissected. He affirmed to us, that he had actually inclosed it in a small tube made after the manner of a weather-glass; but that, instead of acquainting him with the variations of the atmosphere, it showed him the qualities of those persons who entered the room where it stood. He affirmed also, that it rose at the approach of a plume of feathers, an embroidered coat, or a pair of fringed gloves; and that it fell as soon as an ill-shaped periwig, a clumsy pair of shoes, or an unfashionable coat came into his house. Nay, he proceeded so far as to assure us, that upon his laughing aloud when he stood by it, the liquor mounted very sensibly, and immediately sunk again upon his looking serious. In short, he told us that he knew very well by this invention, whenever he had a man of sense or a coxcomb in his room.

Having cleared away the pericardium, or the case, and liquor above-mentioned, we came to the heart itself. The outward surface of it was extremely slippery, and the mucro, or point, so very cold withal, that upon endeavoring to take hold of it, it glided through the fingers like a smooth piece of ice.

The fibers were turned and twisted in a more intricate and perplexed manner than they are usually found in other hearts; insomuch that the whole heart was wound up together like a Gordian knot,[1] and must have had very irregular and unequal motions, while it was employed in its vital function.

One thing we thought very observable, namely, that upon examining all the vessels which came into it, or issued out of it, we could not discover any communication that it had with the tongue.

We could not but take notice likewise that several of those little nerves in the heart which are affected by the sentiments of love, hatred, and other passions, did not descend to this before us from the brain, but from the muscles which lie about the eye.

Upon weighing the heart in my hand, I found it to be extremely light, and consequently very hollow, which I did not wonder at, when, upon looking into the inside of it, I saw multitudes of cells and cavities running one within another, as our historians describe the apartments of Rosamond's bower.[2] Several of these little hollows were stuffed with innumerable sorts of trifles, which I shall forbear giving any particular account of, and shall, therefore, only take notice of what lay first and uppermost, which, upon our unfolding it, and applying our microscopes to it, appeared to be a flame-colored hood.

[1] GORDIAN KNOT—A difficult knot tied by Gordius, a king of ancient Phrygia. For the whole story, see a dictionary or encyclopedia.
[2] ROSAMOND'S BOWER—An underground labyrinth in Blenheim Park, said to have been built by Henry II for his favorite, Rosamond Clifford.

We are informed that the lady of this heart, when living, received the addresses of several who made love to her, and did not only give each of them encouragement, but made every one she conversed with believe that she regarded him with an eye of kindness; for which reason we expected to have seen the impression of multitudes of faces among the several plaits and foldings of the heart; but to our great surprise not a single print of this nature discovered itself till we came into the very core and center of it. We there observed a little figure, which, upon applying our glasses to it, appeared dressed in a very fantastic manner. The more I looked upon it, the more I thought I had seen the face before, but could not possibly recollect either the place or time; when at length one of the company, who had examined this figure more nicely than the rest, showed us plainly by the make of its face, and the several turns of its features, that the little idol which was thus lodged in the middle of the heart was the deceased beau, whose head I gave some account of in my last Tuesday's paper.

As soon as we had finished our dissection, we resolved to make an experiment of the heart, not being able to determine among ourselves the nature of its substance, which differed in so many particulars from that in the heart of other females. Accordingly, we laid it into a pan of burning coals, when we observed in it a certain salamandrine quality, that made it capable of living in the midst of fire and flame, without being consumed or so much as singed.

As we were admiring this strange phenomenon, and standing round the heart in a circle, it gave a most prodigious sigh, or rather crack, and dispersed all at once in smoke and vapor. This imaginary noise, which methought was louder than the burst of a cannon, produced such a violent shake in my brain, that it dissipated the fumes of sleep, and left me in an instant broad awake.

Vocabulary Study: To give the proper scientific tone, the authors made use of certain anatomical terms. Most of them can be found in the ordinary desk-size dictionary. Still, there would be added interest in the essays if a member of the class who has had biology would explain the following terms, perhaps with the aid of blackboard drawings or charts: THE HEAD—*pineal gland; antrum; sinciput; duct; os cribriforme.* THE HEART—*pericardium; mucro.*

Other words which may require special study are the following: From THE BEAU'S HEAD—*beau* (look it up, even though you have a general idea of its meaning); *virtuosos; cursory; superficial; soul; encompassed; billet-doux; trumpery; protestations; imprecations; repository.* From THE COQUETTE'S HEART—*coquette; waived; importunate; orifice; periwig; coxcomb; plaits; deceased; salamandrine; dissipated; fumes.*

By Way of Appreciation: These companion essays are classic English prose at its best. They deal with polite society; they reflect the artificiality of the age; they are lightly satiric; they are delicately impersonal; they are gracefully polished in expression. Addison, the perfect gentleman of a sophisticated age, and Steele, the Irish wit, play with satire and even the beaux and ladies laugh.

The introduction to the essays points out a likeness between them and Pope's mock epic. There is, however, an important difference. The essays were pleasant reading because their satire was impersonal. As in the de Coverley papers, it is a type, a fashion that is being ridiculed —not some certain man and woman. With *The Rape of the Lock,* it is different. We know the incident that inspired the poem. We know the real name of Sir Plume of the "round, unthinking face." We know the name and history of the fair but frivolous Belinda. And Pope wrote the poem for spite.

After all, the mark of the gentleman is kindness; and with all their wit, Addison and Steele never stepped beyond the bounds of courtesy.

Suggestions for Study: Each discovery in the beau's head symbolizes some characteristic of the dandy of the day. Make a list of these characteristics in the order in which they are presented. Similarly, each peculiarity of the coquette's heart represents a characteristic of the coquette. List her qualities in the order of their presentation. (The girls of the class might take the former question and the boys the latter.)

What modern word is most nearly synonymous with *beau?* with *coquette?* If one were to do a modern "dissection" in this manner, what differences would there be in the contents of head and heart? What similarities? How do the lists of qualities for the first two questions correspond with the qualities of a shallow boy or girl of the present?

Exercises and Creative Work: Ever since these essays made their appearance, imitations of them have flourished. As an exercise in writing, it is good fun to dissect a quarter-back's brain, or a teacher's heart (if any), or a golfer's head. Try one, if you like. Be as clever as you can, but keep your satire impersonal. Of course, your paper may be in the nature of a tribute and thus be entirely free from satire. And remember to give credit for the idea to Addison and Steele.

THE CHARACTER OF THE IDLER

From *The Idler*

SAMUEL JOHNSON

By Way of Introduction: "Every man is, or hopes to be, an Idler." Yet Johnson, physically disposed as he was to laziness, was not idle, as a long list of literary labors shows. He could not afford, even in his most comfortable days, to live at ease. Yet the desire is there. It is like the pot of gold at the rainbow's end—the more to be dreamed of because it is unattainable.

Naturally inclined toward thunderous Latin phrases, Johnson is in a surprisingly easy mood as he pens the *Idler* papers and assumes neatly the character which he describes in the first number. The *Idler* papers, by the way, were essays which appeared in a feature column of a Saturday newspaper, the *Universal Chronical*. According to Boswell, "they at once became the chief attraction" of the weekly.

THOSE who attempt periodical essays seem to be often stopped in the beginning by the difficulty of finding a proper title. Two writers, since the time of the *Spectator,* have assumed his name, without any pretensions to lawful inheritance; an effort was once made to revive the *Tatler;* and the strange appellations by which other papers have been called, show that the authors were distressed, like the natives of America, who come to the Europeans to beg a name.[1]

It will be easily believed of the Idler, that if his title had required any search, he never would have found it. Every mode of life has its conveniences. The Idler who habituates himself to be satisfied with what he can most easily obtain, not only escapes labours which are often fruitless, but sometimes succeeds better than those who despise all that is within their reach, and think every thing more valuable as it is harder to be acquired.

If similitude of manners be a motive to kindness, the Idler may flatter himself with universal patronage. There is no single character under which such numbers are comprised. Every man is, or hopes to be, an Idler. Even those who seem to differ most from us are hastening to increase our fraternity; as peace is the end of war, so to be idle is the ultimate purpose of the busy.

There is perhaps, no appellation by which a writer can better denote his kindred to the human species. It has been found hard to describe man by an adequate definition. Some philosophers have called him a reasonable animal; but others have considered reason as a quality of which many creatures partake. He has been termed, likewise, a laughing animal; but it is said that some men have never laughed. Perhaps man may be more properly distinguished as an idle animal; for there is no man who is not sometimes idle. It is at least a definition from which none that shall find it in this paper can be excepted; for who can be more idle than the reader of the *Idler?*

That the definition may be complete, idleness must be not only general, but the peculiar characteristic of man; and, perhaps, man is the only being that can be properly called idle, that does by others what he might do himself, or sacrifices duty or pleasure to the love of ease.

Scarcely any name can be imagined from which less envy or competition is to be dreaded. The Idler has no rivals or enemies. The man of business forgets him; the man of enterprise despises him; and though such as tread the same track of life fall commonly into jealousy and discord, Idlers are always found to associate in peace; and he who is most famed for doing nothing, is glad to meet another as idle as himself.

[1] LIKE THE NATIVES OF AMERICA . . . TO BEG A NAME—A reference to the American tendency to name places in the New World after those in the Old.

What is to be expected from this paper, whether it will be uniform or various, learned or familiar, serious or gay, political or moral, continued or interrupted, it is hoped that no reader will inquire. That the Idler has some scheme cannot be doubted; for to form schemes is the Idler's privilege. But though he has many projects in his head, he is now grown sparing of communication, having observed, that his hearers are apt to remember what he forgets himself; that his tardiness of execution exposes him to the encroachments of those who catch a hint and fall to work; and that very specious plans, after long contrivance and pompous displays, have subsided in weariness without a trial, and without miscarriage have been blasted by derision.

Something the Idler's character may be supposed to promise. Those that are curious after diminutive history, who watch the revolutions of families, and the rise and fall of characters either male or female, will hope to be gratified by this paper; for the Idler is always inquisitive and seldom retentive. He that delights in obloquy and satire, and wishes to see clouds gathering over any reputation that dazzles him with its brightness, will snatch up the *Idler's* essays with a beating heart. The Idler is naturally censorious; those who attempt nothing themselves, think every thing easily performed, and consider the unsuccessful always as criminal.

I think it necessary to give notice, that I make no contract nor incur any obligation. If those who depend on the Idler for intelligence and entertainment, should suffer the disappointment which commonly follows ill-placed expectations, they are to lay the blame only on themselves.

Yet hope is not wholly to be cast away. The Idler, though sluggish, is yet alive and may sometimes be stimulated to vigour and activity. He may descend into profoundness, or tower into sublimity; for the diligence of an Idler is rapid and impetuous, as ponderous bodies forced into velocity move with violence proportionate to their weight.

But these vehement exertions of intellect cannot be frequent, and he will therefore gladly receive help from any correspondent, who shall enable him to please without his own labour. He excludes no style, he prohibits no subject; only let him that writes to the Idler remember, that his letters must not be long: no words are to be squandered in declaration of esteem, or confessions of inability; conscious dullness has little right to be prolix, and praise is not so welcome to the Idler as quiet.

Vocabulary Study: Are you sure of the meanings of the following words? If not, look them up in a dictionary. Remember that many of the definitions and illustrations in our modern dictionaries have come down to us through Samuel Johnson. *Idler* (what is its history?); *appellations; similitude; comprised; fraternity* (note derivation); *ultimate; kindred; execution; specious* (how many syllables?); *contrivance; diminutive; obloquy; censorious, intelligence; velocity; prolix.*

By Way of Appreciation: It seems at first strange that books of English literature usually contain more literature about Samuel Johnson than by him. But most of Johnson's works are too ponderous to be represented in the ordinary anthology. The man who, in his *Dictionary*, defined "network" as "anything reticulated or decussated at equal distances with interstices between the intersections," did not—one may guess—produce much light reading. However, as Johnson grew older and spent more time in conversation than in composition, his style gradually lightened. His essays in the *Rambler* had been so involved in construction and vocabulary that it was jokingly said they were made hard to help sell the *Dictionary*. A sentence of 180 words is not unusual. The curious reader may find some even longer. The *Idler* papers, which appeared eight years later, are much lighter and pleasanter reading. The modern reader will do well to make his first acquaintance with Johnson's genius by curious examination of some pages from the *Dictionary*, by reading occasional essays from the *Idler*, and indirectly, by listening to the famous conversations recorded by Boswell.

Suggestions for Study: Explain the first main clause of the second sentence of the essay. Explain—"to be idle is the ultimate purpose of the busy." What objections, if any, do you raise to the definition of man as an idle animal? What are some of the things that man "does by others that he might do himself"? Can you supply a concrete illustration of the statement that "he who is most famed for doing nothing is glad to meet another as idle as himself"? What do you think is meant by "diminutive history"? What, if any, evidence of humor do you find in the essay? Select at least two quotations from the essay (other than those quoted above) which show Johnson's understanding of human nature.

Exercises and Creative Work: Write a character sketch of an idler. Keep it objective.

Conduct an informal debate on the subject: *Congenial Work Is the Most Desirable Asset Man Can Possess.*

Suggestive topics for essays are: *An Apology for Idlers; In Defense of Idleness; Against Idleness.*

THE HISTORY OF PROSE LITERATURE IN ENGLAND

The Age of Romanticism (1780–1840)

General Characteristics

As the literature of the eighteenth century was prevailingly classic, so that of the early nineteenth century was prevailingly romantic. The romantic spirit found its finest expression in lyric poetry, but prose, too, quickened to the new influence. The familiar essay reflects most clearly the change in mood and subject. The essayist is no longer afraid to talk about himself. He confesses his likes and dislikes, his little whims and fancies. He talks freely about his mistakes and failings, about his plans for the future. He takes us into his home and shows us his books and his china. He takes us a-journeying and invites us in to supper. He talks about the friends he knows and the interesting things they do. The essays, in this volume, by Lamb and Hazlitt and de Quincey are illustrations of the familiar essay. These writers have not freed themselves entirely from classic traditions in style. Their educations had been classic, and their vocabularies are still stocked with resounding Latinisms. De Quincey, particularly, used the sonorous balanced sentence of the eighteenth century. In Lamb, however, in spite of the learned diction, there is a distinctly conversational tone.

Charles Lamb (1775–1834)

It does not take a large man to make a hero; it does take courage. Charles Lamb was a small man, shabby and insignificant looking. He did nothing sensational, but he was heroic just the name. He had the courage to accept the support of himself, his sister, his father, and—at times—other dependents. Though he loved deeply, he was strong enough not to consider a marriage that would have been selfish and perhaps unwise. And he was brave enough to care for his insane sister Mary in the periods of temporary relief and to walk with her to the asylum when a fit of violence was coming on. Here was the most cruel tragedy of his life. One day in his early twenties he had come home to learn that Mary had killed their mother. The girl was put into an institution, her brother paying the fees out of his slender earnings. When her mind cleared, Lamb took her home to keep her busy and amused until the next spell should come on. For the rest of his life the care of Mary was his chief concern.

There was heroism, too, in Lamb's smiling acceptance of everyday hardships. The family had always been poor. Lamb's father was servant to a lawyer, and the boy spent his early years in the curious old Temple Court which was headquarters for most of the London barristers. Then for seven years Charles was a charity student in the Blue-coat School of Christ's Hospital. His ability to find the good in every trying situation is illustrated here. Most English boys found

HISTORY OF PROSE LITERATURE

little but suffering in the charity schools. Lamb absorbed an excellent education and made one good friend, Samuel Coleridge. When he was fourteen, his school days came to an end, and he went out to earn his living. He was a clerk first in the South Sea House; and then two years later he entered the India House where he worked for the next thirty-three years. Some would have found the long hours over a clerk's desk tiring and monotonous; but Lamb liked people and he enjoyed the bustle and stir of business. In his last years of leisure, he was almost homesick for the office.

Lamb showed an early interest in writing, but his first works were poems and plays, now little remembered. He had always been interested in Elizabethan drama, and his first successful works grew out of this field. In 1807 he and Mary published their *Tales from Shakespeare*—short, easily read synopses of the important plays of the poet. It was a successful venture, and so was the critical study of *English Dramatic Poets* which Charles had published a year later. However, his genius was to flower in a different sort of writing. Lamb was about forty-five when he began contributing to the *London Magazine* little sketches which he signed "Elia." Thus began the famous *Essays of Elia*. The first volume is a collection of twenty-five of these sketches. Later there was a second series. They are delightful. Addison and Steele a century before had made the essay entertaining; Lamb made it personal. The *Essays of Elia* are as self-revealing as an autobiography. In *Christ's Hospital Five and Thirty Years Ago* and in *Recollections of the South Sea House,* there are glimpses of his youth. So one might go on. All the little details of his life are there. And in between the lines shines his happy, courageous spirit. There is no sham about it; Lamb did really find happiness in what seems to us unhappy circumstances. He had a sense of fun, an appreciation of books and people, and a brave heart. Out of these he fashioned a pleasant and a noble life.

William Hazlitt (1778–1830)

William Hazlitt heads a line of literary scholars, for his son and grandson—both Williams—have also been successful writers. It was probably the influence of Coleridge that started the first Hazlitt writing. He had been trained for the ministry; but discovering in himself no serious liking for the work, he turned for a time to art. He had long been an admirer of Coleridge and when an acquaintance with the older poet grew into friendship, Hazlitt felt drawn to writing. Through Coleridge he met Wordsworth and Lamb and de Quincey, forming acquaintances that intensified his interests in literature. He was twenty-seven when his first work, *Principles of Human Action,* was published. Its success settled his choice of a career.

Most of Hazlitt's works were critical rather than imaginative. There are for instance, his *Lectures on the Literature of the Elizabethan Age* and *Lectures on the English Poets*—both subjects on which he was well prepared to speak. To his own careful study there was added the advantage of an interchange of ideas with the greatest writers and scholars of his own day. He wrote, too, a very successful *Life of Napoleon* in four volumes. Of lighter nature are his essays; yet even they are scarcely easy reading. His pages are filled with references to writers, living or dead, famous or almost unknown. The essays that are most widely read are in the volume *Table Talk.*

It was Hazlitt's misfortune to allow his love for an argument to develop into a quarrelsome disposition. Before his death in 1830, he was estranged from most of his former friends.

Thomas de Quincey (1785–1859)

Picture for a moment a tiny man with gentle manners, a man with a delicate womanly face illumined by brilliant eyes, a man somehow marked with mystery—and you have a notion of Thomas de Quincey. Carlyle once said that he looked like a beautiful little child but that there was an expression in his face that said, "Behold, this child has been in Hell." De Quincey himself has explained the look in his *Confessions of an English Opium Eater.* At different periods in his life he was a slave of the drug, at one time using enormous quantities of it. Before he died he had broken the habit, but the marks of his suffering were never erased.

The *Confessions* are in truth an account of his early life. His father, who was wealthy, died when Thomas was seven, leaving the lad to the guardianship of relatives. They were conscientious but not understanding. De Quincey particularly hated the first school in which he was placed. He was a brilliant boy, a great reader, and proficient beyond his years—and his teachers—in Latin and Greek. At fourteen he ran away. For weeks he tramped through Wales and then nearly starved in London. He was finally found and persuaded to enter Oxford. He remained for the four years; but terrified at the thought of the examinations, he again fled, never to return to school. It was while he was in Oxford that he began taking drugs. In his late twenties, he was most completely in their grip; but by the time of his marriage in 1816, he had broken the habit.

A great admirer of Wordsworth and Coleridge, he moved as a young man to the Lake district, into the very Dove Cottage where Wordsworth had lived. He dabbled a bit in literature because it pleased him but did no regular writing until an unwise investment cost him his fortune. Then he began to contribute steadily to various literary magazines. There was a constant market for his articles, which were unusual in

HISTORY OF PROSE LITERATURE

learning and in style. The *Confessions* appeared serially in the *London Magazine*. Their popularity was sensational.

His later years were restless ones, spent chiefly in Edinburgh. He would rent a room, live in it alone for weeks (letting no one know where he was), fill it with books and papers until he could no longer work in the litter, then lock the door and go off to find another room. At his death, it is said, six such rooms were discovered.

All sorts of subjects he treated with distinction: history, recent and ancient, literature, manners, customs, morals, personalities. His vocabulary was prodigious; he was never at loss for words. The reader brings these judgments against him: his sentences are often too elaborate to be easily understood; he often is led away from his subject; and he is not averse to gossiping about his neighbors. He is most reliable when he talks about himself, and nowhere is he more interesting than in his *Confessions*.

Magazines of Literary Criticism

The years from 1800 to 1820 saw the establishment of the famous magazines of literary criticism: The *Edinburgh Review,* the *Quarterly Review, Blackwoods,* the *Examiner,* and the *London Magazine.* With the exception of the last two, these were very conservative periodicals and were distinctly unfriendly to romantic writers. The first works of Wordsworth, Coleridge, Keats, and Byron were all ridiculed by the *Edinburgh Review* and the *Quarterly;* and it was the adverse criticism of the two magazines that called forth Byron's satiric retaliation, *English Bards and Scotch Reviewers.*

Literary Critics and Other Essayists

It was Leigh Hunt, himself a poet, who began the *Examiner,* and he proved a loyal friend to the younger poets. Time has revealed that he was the best critic of them all. The writers to whom he opened his pages are the ones that the world calls great.

Two other poets should be mentioned for their work in literary criticism—Samuel Coleridge and Robert Southey. Coleridge was an inspired lecturer, but he was unable to hold himself to a task long enough adequately to release his brilliant mind. Two prose works deserve mention—his *Sketches of My Literary Life and Opinions* and the collected *Essays on Shakespeare.* Robert Southey was Coleridge's friend. He too wrote critical essays, but his best prose is in his biographies, *The Life of Nelson* and *Lives of the British Admirals.*

A prose writer of the period who reached some prominence was Walter Savage Landor. He was a stormy fellow, but his prose is surprisingly placid. He is best known for his *Imaginary Conversations,* a work that is classic both in subject and in manner. It is based upon his great reading in history and literature, and is of value chiefly because of the way in which it has caught the spirit of ages long ago.

Essays of the Romantic Age

A DISSERTATION UPON ROAST PIG

From *Essays of Elia*

Charles Lamb

By Way of Introduction: Before the American Indian introduced wild turkey to the white man, the Englishman's favorite holiday dish was roast pig. Not roast pork, mind you, but young pig—from three to six weeks old—roasted whole with appropriate stuffing and served with a festive apple in his mouth! One who has enjoyed the tender sweetness of a crisply browned loin of pork can easily imagine the delicacy of its baby brother. 'Tis small wonder that Lamb was inspired to rhapsodize in its praise.

In the opening paragraphs, Lamb qualifies as a member of the "tall-story club." We can see the twinkle in his eye as he gravely recounts the wasteful method by which man learned to cook his food. There's an idea to speculate upon! How *did* man first get the idea of cooking his meat? There may be logical flaws in Lamb's explanation, but it makes a right good tale.

Mankind, says a Chinese manuscript, which my friend M—[1] was obliging enough to read and explain to me, for the first seventy thousand ages ate their meat raw, clawing or biting it from the living animal, just as they do in Abyssinia to this day.

---

[1] M—Thomas Manning. The Chinese manuscript is, of course, purely imaginative.

This period is not obscurely hinted at by their great Confucius[2] in the second chapter of his *Mundane Mutations*, where he designates a kind of golden age by the term *Cho-fang*, literally the Cook's holiday. The manuscript goes on to say that the art of roasting, or rather broiling (which I take to be the elder brother), was accidentally discovered in the manner following. The swineherd, Ho-ti, having gone out into the woods one morning, as his manner was, to collect mast for his hogs, left his cottage in the care of his eldest son, Bo-bo, a great lubberly boy, who being fond of playing with fire, as younkers of his age commonly are, let some sparks escape into a bundle of straw which, kindling quickly, spread the conflagration over every part of their poor mansion, till it was reduced to ashes. Together with the cottage (a sorry antediluvian makeshift of a building, you may think it), what was of much more importance a fine litter of new-farrowed pigs, no less than nine in number, perished. China pigs have been esteemed a luxury all over the East from the remotest periods that we read of. Bo-bo was in utmost consternation, as you may think, not so much for the sake of the tenement,[3] which his father and he could easily build up again with a few dry branches, and the labor of an hour or two, at any time, as for the loss of the pigs. While he was thinking what he should say to his father, and wringing his hands over the smoking remnants of one of these untimely sufferers, an odor assailed his nostrils, unlike any scent which he had before experienced. What could it proceed from?—not from the burnt cottage—he had smelt that smell before—indeed this was by no means the first accident of the kind which had occurred through the negligence of this unlucky young firebrand. Much less did it resemble that of any known herb, weed, or flower. A premonitory moistening at the same time overflowed his nether lip. He knew not what to think. He next stooped down to feel the pig, if there were any signs of life in it. He burnt his fingers, and to cool them he applied them in his booby fashion to his mouth. Some of the crumbs of the scorched skin had come away with his fingers, and for the first time in his life (in the world's life indeed, for before him no man had

---

[2] CONFUCIUS—Famous Chinese philosopher and teacher (551–478 B.C.) The allusion is used to give an air of authenticity to the tale.
[3] TENEMENT—Here, merely "dwelling."

known it) he tasted—*crackling!* Again he felt and fumbled at the pig. It did not burn him so much now, still he licked his fingers from a sort of habit. The truth at length broke into his slow understanding, that it was the pig that smelt so, and the pig that tasted so delicious; and, surrendering himself up to the newborn pleasure, he fell to tearing up whole handfuls of the scorched skin with the flesh next to it, and was cramming it down his throat in his beastly fashion, when his sire entered amid the smoking rafters, armed with retributory cudgel, and finding how affairs stood, began to rain blows upon the young rogue's shoulders, as thick as hailstones, which Bo-bo heeded not any more than if they had been flies. The tickling pleasure, which he experienced in his lower regions, had rendered him quite callous to any inconveniences he might feel in those remote quarters. His father might lay on, but he could not beat him from his pig, till he had fairly made an end of it, when, becoming a little more sensible of his situation, something like the following dialogue ensued.

"You graceless whelp, what have you got there devouring? Is it not enough that you have burnt me down three houses with your dog's tricks, and be hanged to you, but you must be eating fire, and I know not what—what have you got there, I say?"

"O, father, the pig, the pig, do come and taste how nice the burnt pig eats."

The ears of Ho-ti tingled with horror. He cursed his son, and he cursed himself that ever he should beget a son that should eat burnt pig.

Bo-bo, whose scent was wonderfully sharpened since morning, soon raked out another pig, and fairly rending it asunder, thrust the lesser half by main force into the fists of Ho-ti, still shouting out, "Eat, eat, eat the burnt pig, father, only taste—O Lord,"—with such-like barbarous ejaculations, cramming all the while as if he would choke.

Ho-ti trembled in every joint while he grasped the abominable thing, wavering whether he should not put his son to death for an unnatural young monster, when the crackling scorching his fingers, as it had done his son's, and applying the same remedy to them, he in his turn tasted some of its flavor, which, make what sour mouths he would for a pretense, proved not altogether displeasing to him. In conclusion (for the manuscript here is a little tedious) both father and son fairly sat down to the mess, and never left till they had despatched all that remained of the litter.

Bo-bo was strictly enjoined not to let the secret escape, for the neighbors would certainly have stoned them for a couple of abominable wretches, who could think of improving upon the good meat which God had sent them. It was observed that Ho-ti's cottage was burnt down now more frequently than ever. Nothing but fires from this time forward. Some would break out in broad day, others in the nighttime. As often as the sow farrowed, so sure was the house of Ho-ti to be in a blaze; and Ho-ti himself, which was the more remarkable, instead of chastising his son, seemed to grow more indulgent to him than ever. At length they were watched, the terrible mystery discovered, and father and son summoned to take their trial at Pekin,[4] then an inconsiderable assize town. Evidence was given, the obnoxious food itself produced in court, and verdict about to be pronounced, when the foreman of the jury begged that some of the burnt pig, of which the culprits stood accused, might be handed into the box. He handled it, and they all handled it, and burning their fingers, as Bo-bo and his father had done before them, and Nature prompting to each of them the same remedy, against the face of all the facts, and the clearest charge which judge had ever given,—to the surprise of the whole court, townsfolk, strangers, reporters, and all present—without leaving the box, or any manner of consultation, whatever, they brought in a simultaneous verdict of Not Guilty.

The judge, who was a shrewd fellow, winked at the manifest iniquity of the decision; and, when the court was dismissed, went privily, and bought up all the pigs that could be had for love or money. In a few days his Lordship's town house was observed to be on fire. The thing took wing, and now there was nothing to be seen but fires in every direction. Fuel and pigs grew enormously dear all over the district. The insurance offices one and all shut up shop. People built slighter and slighter every day, until it was feared that the very science of architecture would in no long time be lost to the world. Thus this custom of firing houses continued, till in process of time,

---

[4] PEKIN—Now "Peiping," a principal city of northern China.

says my manuscript, a sage arose, like our Locke,[5] who made a discovery, that the flesh of swine, or indeed of any other animal, might be cooked (*burnt,* as they called it) without the necessity of consuming a whole house to dress it. Then first began the rude form of a gridiron. Roasting by the string, or spit, came in a century or two later, I forget in whose dynasty. By such slow degrees, concludes the manuscript, do the most useful, and seemingly the most obvious arts, make their way among mankind.

Without placing too implicit faith in the account above given, it must be agreed that if a worthy pretext for so dangerous an experiment as setting houses on fire (especially in these days) could be assigned in favor of any culinary object, that pretext and excuse might be found in Roast Pig.

Of all the delicacies in the whole *mundus edibilis,*[6] I will maintain it to be the most delicate—*princeps obsoniorum.*[7]

I speak not of your grown porkers—things between pig and pork—those hobbydehoys—but a young and tender suckling—under a moon old—guiltless as yet of the sty—with no original speck of the *amor immunditiæ*[8] the hereditary failing of the first parent, yet manifest—his voice as yet not broken, but something between a childish treble, and a grumble—the mild forerunner or *præludium,* of a grunt.

He must be roasted. I am not ignorant that our ancestors ate them seethed, or boiled but what a sacrifice of the exterior tegument!

There is no flavor comparable, I will contend, to that of the crisp, tawny, well-watched, not over-roasted, *crackling,* as it is well called—the very teeth are invited to their share of the pleasure at this banquet in overcoming the coy, brittle resistance —with the adhesive oleaginous—O call it not fat—but an indefinable sweetness growing up to it—the tender blossoming of fat—fat cropped in the bud—taken in the shoot—in the first innocence—the cream and quintessence of the child-pig's yet pure food—the lean, no lean, but a kind of animal manna—or, rather, fat and lean (if it must be so), so blended and running

---

[5] LOCKE—John Locke (1632–1704), an English philosopher.
[6] *Mundus edibilis*—World of food, eatables.
[7] *Princeps obsoniorum*—Chief of dainties.
[8] *Amor immunditiæ*—Love of dirt.

into each other, that both together make but one ambrosian result, or common substance.

Behold him, while he is doing—it seemed rather a refreshing warmth, than a scorching heat, that he is so passive to. How equably he twirleth round the string!—Now he is just done. To see the extreme sensibility of that tender age, he hath wept out his pretty eyes—radiant jellies—shooting stars——

See him in the dish, his second cradle, how meek he lieth!—wouldst thou have had this innocent grow up to the grossness and indocility which too often accompany maturer swinehood? Ten to one he would have proved a glutton, a sloven, an obstinate, disagreeable animal—wallowing in all manner of filthy conversation—from these sins he is happily snatched away—

> Ere sin could blight, or sorrow fade,
> Death came with timely care— [9]

his memory is odoriferous—no clown curseth, while his stomach half rejecteth, the rank bacon—no coal-heaver bolteth him in reeking sausages—he hath a fair sepulchre in the grateful stomach of the judicious epicure—and for such a tomb might be content to die.

He is the best of sapors. Pineapple [10] is great. She is indeed almost too transcendent—a delight, if not sinful, yet so like to sinning, that really a tender-conscienced person would do well to pause—too ravishing for mortal taste, she woundeth and excoriateth the lips that approach her—like lovers' kisses, she biteth—she is a pleasure bordering on pain from the fierceness and insanity of her relish—but she stoppeth at the palate [11]—she meddleth not with the appetite—and the coarsest hunger might barter her consistently for a mutton chop.

Pig—let me speak his praise—is no less provocative of the appetite, than he is satisfactory to the criticalness of the censorious palate. The strong man may batten on him, and weakling refuseth not his mind juices.

Unlike to mankind's mixed characters, a bundle of virtues and vices, inexplicably intertwisted, and not to be unraveled without hazard, he is good throughout. No part of him is bet-

---

[9] These lines are from Coleridge's *Epitaph on an Infant*.
[10] PINEAPPLE—A rare delicacy in eighteenth-century England.
[11] SHE STOPPETH AT THE PALATE—Pleases the taste without satisfying one's hunger.

ter or worse than another. He helpeth, as far as his little means extend, all around. He is the least envious of banquets. He is all neighbors' fare.

I am one of those who freely and ungrudgingly impart a share of the good things of this life which fall to their lot (few as mine are in this kind) to a friend. I protest I take as great an interest in my friend's pleasures, his relishes, and proper satisfactions, as in mine own. "Presents," I often say, "endear Absents." Hares, pheasants, partridges, snipes, barndoor chickens (those "tame villatic fowl" [12]), capons, plovers, brawn, barrels of oysters, I dispense as freely as I receive them. I love to taste them, as it were, upon the tongue of my friend. But a stop must be put somewhere. One would not, like Lear,[13] "give everything." I make stand upon pig. Methinks it is an ingratitude to the Giver of all good flavors, to extra-domiciliate,[14] or send out of the house, slightly (under pretext of friendship, of I know not what), a blessing so particularly adapted, predestined, I may say, to my individual palate—it argues an insensibility.

I remember a touch of conscience in this kind at school. My good old aunt, who never parted from me at the end of a holiday without stuffing a sweetmeat, or some nice thing, into my pocket, had dismissed me one evening with a smoking plum-cake, fresh from the oven. In my way to school (it was over London Bridge) a gray-headed old beggar saluted me (I have no doubt at this time of day that he was a counterfeit). I had no pence to console him with, and in the vanity of self-denial, and the very coxcombry of charity, schoolboy like, I made him a present of—the whole cake. I walked on a little, buoyed up, as one is on such occasions, with a sweet soothing of self-satisfaction; but before I had got to the end of the bridge, my better feelings returned, and I burst into tears, thinking how ungrateful I had been to my good aunt, to go and give her good gift away to a stranger, that I had never seen before, and who might be a bad man for aught I knew; and then I thought of the pleasure my aunt would be taking in thinking that I—I myself, and not

[12] "Tame villatic fowl—From John Milton's *Samson Agonistes*.
[13] Lear—The tragic hero of Shakespeare's *King Lear,* who gave up his kingdom to his children before his death.
[14] Extra-domiciliate—Lamb uses an Anglicized expression in its literal Latin meaning, translating it for the reader in the following words.

another—would eat her nice cake—and what should I say to her the next time I saw her—how naughty I was to part with her pretty present—and the pleasure and the curiosity I had taken in seeing her make it, and her joy when she sent it to the oven, and how disappointed she would feel that I had never had a bit of it in my mouth at last—and I blamed my impertinent spirit of alms-giving, and out-of-place hypocrisy of goodness, and above all I wished never to see the face again of that insidious good-for-nothing, old gray impostor.

Our ancestors were nice in their method of sacrificing these tender victims. We read of pigs whipped to death with something of a shock, as we hear of any other obsolete custom. The age of discipline is gone by, or it would be curious to inquire (in a philosophical light merely) what effect this process might have towards intenerating and dulcifying a substance, naturally so mild and dulcet as the flesh of young pigs. It looks like refining a violet. Yet we should be cautious, while we condemn the inhumanity, how we censure the wisdom of the practice. It might impart a gusto——

I remember an hypothesis, argued upon by the young students, when I was at St. Omer's,[15] and maintained with much learning and pleasantry on both sides, "Whether, supposing that the flavor of a pig who obtained his death by whipping (*per flagellationem extremam*) superadded a pleasure upon the palate of a man more intense than any possible suffering we can conceive in the animal, is man justified in using that method of putting the animal to death?" I forget the decision.

His sauce [16] should be considered. Decidedly, a few bread crumbs, done up with his liver and brains, and a dash of mild sage. But banish, dear Mrs. Cook, I beseech you, the whole onion tribe. Barbecue your whole hogs to your palate, steep them in shalots, stuff them out with plantations of the rank and guilty garlic; you cannot poison them, or make them stronger than they are—but consider, he is a weakling—a flower.

[15] St. Omer's—An imaginative touch. Lamb attended a charity school not, by the way, "over London Bridge."
[16] His sauce—Dressing.

Vocabulary Study: If one had doubts as to the thoroughness with which a boy might be educated in one of the English charity schools, those doubts would vanish after reading Lamb or Coleridge. Besides these writers' Latin fluency, there is an amazing English vocabulary at their command. Note, for instance, the interesting words from *A Dissertation upon Roast Pig*, and the precision with which they are used: *dissertation; mundane; mutations; mast; younkers* (note derivation); *antediluvian* (note derivation); *farrowed; premonitory; nether; crackling; retributory* (note pronunciation); *abominable; chastising; assize; obnoxious; simultaneous; manifest; iniquity; privily; obvious; implicit; pretext; culinary.*

Hobbydehoy (see *hobbledehoy*); *præludium* (see *prelude*); *seethed; tegument* (see *integument*); *adhesive; oleaginous; quintessence; manna; ambrosian; equably; indocility* (see *docility*); *odoriferous; clown* (not a funny-man); *epicure* (a common noun); *sapors; transcendent; excoriateth; provocative; batten; inexplicable* (see *explicate,* and note pronunciation); *villatic; capons; plovers; brawn; predestined; insensibility* (see *sensibility*); *coxcombry; impertinent; insidious; impostor; nice; obsolete; intenerating; dulcifying; dulcet; gusto; hypothesis.*

Explain the difference between the synonyms *radiant* and *beaming*. Also list all the meanings you can find for the word *nice*.

By Way of Appreciation: A sense of humor is a saving grace. Lamb's ability to see the fun in life must have spared him many a heartsick hour. The big things in life were tragic, but he knew how to find pleasure in the little things. Most of his essays have a whimsical touch; *A Dissertation upon Roast Pig* is humorous throughout. Everyone enjoys the ridiculous story with which the essay begins; not everyone, however, appreciates the humor of the dissertation itself. There are two ways of achieving the burlesque. The first is to treat a serious theme frivolously. The second is to treat a slight theme with mock solemnity. The latter is the method which Lamb here employs. True, roast pig is delicious and Lamb was fond of it. Yet it hardly merits the extravagant praise he lavishes upon it. No, the essay is burlesque of high order. The learned manner, the Latin phrases, the poetic—and sometimes scriptural—style are all a part of the fun.

Suggestions for Study: What touches of human nature make the story of Bo-bo and his father entertaining? Look up, if necessary, the meaning of "anachronism." What anachronistic touches lend humor to the tale? Aside from the intentional absurdities of the story, there is a point which makes it seem most improbable that man discovered the art of cooking by the accidental route of "burnt pig." Do you find the flaw? How was meat roasted in Lamb's day? Why must the pig be "well-watched" to insure the proper delicacy? Why is roast young pig a greater luxury today than it was in the eighteenth century? Why is pineapple no longer a luxury?

Explain Lamb's pun, "Presents endear Absents." Explain the sentence, "I love to taste them [delicacies] upon the tongue of my friends." What do you think was the real cause of the schoolboy's tears after his generosity to the beggar? What is the thought that links the incident of the plum cake with roast pig? Why is the vocabulary more elaborate in the latter part of the essay than in the first part? Contrast the style of Bacon's *Of Truth* with the style of this essay as to length, sentence structure, general plan, vocabulary, and the like. What differences in the personalities of the two writers are reflected in their works? Is *A Dissertation upon Roast Pig* comic or humorous?

Exercises and Creative Work: Make a topical outline of the essay, and then develop one of the topics into a paragraph of about one hundred words.

Write a dissertation upon some other accidental discovery. You may choose something as prosaic as rice pudding, or as sublime as one of the chance scientific discoveries which have benefited mankind. The essay may be imaginative or true.

OLD CHINA

From *Essays of Elia*

Charles Lamb

By Way of Introduction: *Old China* is an essay with a setting. The stage directions should read about like this: "The scene is the living-room of a poorer middle-class English home of the early nineteenth century. The room is simply furnished, with everything in quiet good taste. There is a fireplace center-back, before which stands a table set for tea with china of blue and white in a Japanese pattern. At one side of the table sits a small, mild-mannered man of about sixty. Facing him is a woman, somewhat older, and rather nervous."

The characters—as you have guessed—are Charles Lamb and his sister Mary (Bridget). Except for the first eight paragraphs, which serve as a sort of prologue, the essay is the tea-table conversation in which Mary does most of the talking.

I HAVE an almost feminine partiality for old china. When I go to see any great house, I inquire for the china closet, and next for the picture-gallery. I cannot defend the order of preference, but by saying that we have all some taste or other, of too ancient a date to admit of our remembering distinctly that it was an acquired one. I can call to mind the first play, and the first exhibition, that I was taken to; but I am not conscious of a time when china jars and saucers were introduced into my imagination.

I had no repugnance then—why should I now have?—to those little, lawless, azure-tinctured grotesques, that, under the notion of men and women, float about, uncircumscribed by any element, in that world before perspective—a china tea-cup.

I like to see my old friends—whom distance cannot diminish—figuring up in the air (so they appear to our optics [1]), yet on *terra firma* [2] still—for so we must in courtesy interpret that speck of deeper blue, which the decorous artist, to prevent absurdity, has made to spring up beneath their sandals.

I love the men with women's faces, and the women, if possible, with still more womanish expressions.

Here is a young and courtly Mandarin handing tea to a lady from a salver—two miles off. See how distance seems to set off respect! And here the same lady, or another—for likeness is identity on tea-cups—is stepping into a little fairy boat, moored on the hither side of this calm garden river, with a dainty mincing foot, which in a right angle of incidence [3] (as angles go in our world) must infallibly land her in the midst of a flowery mead—a furlong off on the other side of the same strange stream!

Farther on—if far or near can be predicated of their world—see horses, trees, pagodas, dancing the hays.[4]

---

[1] OPTICS—Here, eyes.
[2] *Terra firma*—Solid ground.
[3] A RIGHT ANGLE OF INCIDENCE—A technical expression used for effect.
[4] THE HAYS—An English country dance. "Dancing the hays" here probably means "helter skelter," or "all jumbled together."

Here—a cow and rabbit couchant and coextensive—so objects show, seen through the lucid atmosphere of fine Cathay.

I was pointing out to my cousin [5] last evening, over our Hyson (which we are old-fashioned enough to drink unmixed still of an afternoon) some of these *speciosa miracula* [6] upon a set of extraordinary old blue china (a recent purchase) which we were now for the first time using; and could not help remarking, how favourable circumstances had been to us of late years, that we could afford to please the eye sometimes with trifles of this sort—when a passing sentiment seemed to overshade the brows of my companion. I am quick at detecting these summer clouds in Bridget.

"I wish the good old times would come again," she said, "when we were not quite so rich. I do not mean that I want to be poor; but there was a middle state"—so she was pleased to ramble on—"in which I am sure we were a great deal happier. A purchase is but a purchase, now that you have money enough to spare. Formerly it used to be a triumph. When we coveted a cheap luxury (and O! how much ado I had to get you to consent in those times!) we were used to have a debate two or three days before, and to weigh the *for* and *against,* and think what we might spare it out of, and what saving we could hit upon, that should be an equivalent. A thing was worth buying then when we felt the money that we paid for it.

"Do you remember the brown suit, which you made to hang upon you, till all your friends cried shame upon you, it grew so threadbare—and all because of that folio Beaumont and Fletcher [7] which you dragged home late at night from Barker's in Covent Garden? [8] Do you remember how we eyed it for weeks before we could make up our minds to the purchase, and

---

[5] COUSIN—In these essays, which Lamb wrote under the pseudonym of James Elia, he refers to his sister Mary as his cousin, "Bridget Elia."

[6] *Speciosa miracula*—Literally, "fair miracles"; more freely, "pretty absurdities."

[7] BEAUMONT AND FLETCHER—Francis Beaumont (1584–1616) and John Fletcher (1579–1625), Elizabethan dramatists who worked together. Lamb was especially interested in the works of Shakespeare and his contemporaries.

[8] COVENT GARDEN—A space in London between the Strand and Longacre, which at one time had been a convent garden belonging to the monks of St. Peter. Later it was filled with markets, book-stalls, taverns, coffee-houses, and the like. It was a favorite lounging place for authors, actors, and men-about-town.

how not come to a determination till it was near ten o'clock of the Saturday night, when you set off from Islington [9] fearing you should be too late—and when the old bookseller with some grumbling opened his shop, and by the twinkling taper (for he was setting bedwards) lighted out the relic from his dusty treasures—and when you lugged it home, wishing it were twice as cumbersome—and when you presented it to me—and when we were exploring the perfectness of it (*collating,* you called it) —and while I was repairing some of the loose leaves with paste, which your impatience would not suffer to be left till day-break —was there no pleasure in being a poor man? or can those neat black clothes which you wear now, and are so careful to keep brushed, since we have become rich and finical, give you half the honest vanity with which you flaunted it about in that overworn suit—your old corbeau [10]—for four or five weeks longer than you should have done, to pacify your conscience for the mighty sum of fifteen—or sixteen shillings [11] was it?—a great affair we thought it then—which you had lavished on the old folio. Now you can afford to buy any book that pleases you, but I do not see that you ever bring me home any nice old purchases now.

"When you came home with twenty apologies for laying out a less number of shillings upon that print after Lionardo [12] which we christened the 'Lady Blanche'; when you looked at the purchase, and thought of the money—and thought of the money, and looked again at the picture—was there no pleasure in being a poor man? Now, you have nothing to do but walk into Colnaghi's, and buy a wilderness of Lionardos. Yet do you?

"Then, do you remember our pleasant walks to Enfield,[13] and Potter's Bar, and Waltham,[14] when we had a holiday—holidays and all other fun are gone, now we are rich—and the little handbasket in which I used to deposit our day's fare of savory cold lamb and salad—and how you could pry about at noontide for

[9] ISLINGTON—One of the boroughs of London.
[10] CORBEAU—A coat of dark green goods.
[11] FIFTEEN—OR SIXTEEN SHILLINGS—About $4.00.
[12] LIONARDO—Leonardo da Vinci (1452–1519), a famous Italian artist.
[13] ENFIELD—A town within the metropolitan district of London, visited because of its picturesque ruins.
[14] WALTHAM—A town in Essex, about twelve miles from London, containing an interesting old abbey.

some decent house, where we might go in, and produce our store —only paying for the ale that you must call for—and speculate upon the looks of the landlady, and whether she was likely to allow us a table-cloth—and wish for such another honest hostess, as Izaak Walton has described many a one on the pleasant banks of the Lea, when he went a-fishing—and sometimes they would prove obliging enough, and sometimes they would look grudgingly upon us—but we had cheerful looks still for one another, and would eat our plain food savorily, scarcely grudging Piscator his Trout Hall? Now, when we go out a day's pleasuring, which is seldom moreover, we *ride* part of the way—and go into a fine inn, and order the best of dinners, never debating the expense—which, after all, never has half the relish of those chance country snaps,[15] when we were at the mercy of uncertain usage, and a precarious welcome.

"You are too proud to see a play anywhere now but in the pit. Do you remember where it was we used to sit when we saw *The Battle of Hexam* and *The Surrender of Calais,* and Bannister and Mrs. Bland in *The Children in the Wood*—when we squeezed out our shilling a-piece to sit three or four times in a season in the one-shilling gallery—where you felt all the time that you ought not to have brought me—and more strongly I felt obligation to you for having brought me—and the pleasure was the better for a little shame—and when the curtain drew up, what cared we for our place in the house or what mattered it where we were sitting, when our thoughts were with Rosalind in Arden, or with Viola at the court of Illyria? You used to say, that the gallery was the best place of all for enjoying a play socially—that the relish of such exhibitions must be in proportion to the infrequency of going—that the company we met there, not being in general readers of plays, were obliged to attend the more, and did attend, to what was going on, on the stage—because a word lost would have been a chasm, which it was impossible for them to fill up. With such reflections we consoled our pride then—and I appeal to you, whether, as a woman, I met generally with less attention and accommodation than I have done since in more expensive situations in the house? The getting in indeed, and the crowding up those incon-

---

[15] SNAPS—A hasty meal, a snack.

venient staircases, was bad enough,—but there was still a law of civility to women recognized to quite as great an extent as we ever found in the other passages—and how a little difficulty overcome heightened the snug seat and the play afterwards! Now we can only pay our money, and walk in. You cannot see, you say, in the galleries now. I am sure we saw, and heard too, well enough then—but sight, and all, I think is gone with our poverty.

"There was pleasure in eating strawberries, before they became quite common—in the first dish of peas, while they were yet dear—to have them for a nice supper, a treat. What treat can we have now? If we were to treat ourselves now—that is, to have dainties a little above our means, it would be selfish and wicked. It is the very little more that we allow ourselves beyond what the actual poor can get at, that makes what I call a treat—when two people, living together as we have done, now and then indulge themselves in a cheap luxury which both like; while each apologizes, and is willing to take both halves of the blame to his single share. I see no harm in people making much of themselves, in that sense of the word. It may give them a hint how to make much of others. But now—what I mean by the word—we never do make much of ourselves. None but the poor can do it. I do not mean the veriest poor of all, but persons as we were, just above poverty.[16]

"I know what you were going to say, that it is mighty pleasant at the end of the year to make all meet—and much ado we used to have every thirty-first night of December to account for our exceedings—many a long face did you make over your puzzled accounts, and in contriving to make it out how we had spent so much—or that we had not spent so much—or that it was impossible we should spend so much next year—and still we found our slender capital decreasing—but then, betwixt ways, and projects, and compromises of one sort or another, and talk of curtailing this charge, and doing without that for the future—and the hope that youth brings, and laughing spirits (in which you were never poor till now), we pocketed up our loss, and in conclusion, with 'lusty brimmers' (as you used to quote it out of

---

[16] PERSONS . . . JUST ABOVE POVERTY—At one time Lamb's income was just £100 (about $500) a year.

hearty cheerful Mr. Cotton,[17] as you called him), we used to welcome in the 'coming guest.'[18] Now we have no reckoning at all at the end of the old year—no flattering promises about the new year doing better for us."

Bridget is so sparing of her speech on most occasions, that when she gets into a rhetorical vein, I am careful how I interrupt it. I could not help, however, smiling at the phantom of wealth which her dear imagination had conjured up out of a clear income of poor — hundred pounds [19] a year. "It is true we were happier when we were poorer, but we were also younger, my cousin. I am afraid we must put up with the excess, for if we were to shake the superflux [20] into the sea, we should not much mend ourselves. That we had much to struggle with, as we grew up together, we have reason to be most thankful. It strengthened, and knit our compact closer. We could never have been what we have been to each other, if we had always had the sufficiency which you now complain of. The resisting power—those natural dilations of the youthful spirit, which circumstances cannot straiten—with us are long since passed away. Competence to age is supplementary youth; a sorry supplement indeed, but I fear the best that is to be had. We must ride, where we formerly walked; live better, and lie softer—and shall be wise to do so—than we had means to do in those good old days you speak of. Yet could those days return—could you and I once more walk our thirty miles a-day, could Bannister and Mrs. Bland again be young, and you and I be young to see them—could the good old one-shilling gallery days return—they are dreams, my cousin, now—but could you and I at this moment, instead of this quiet argument, by our well-carpeted fireside, sitting on this luxurious sofa—be once more struggling up those inconvenient staircases, pushed about, and squeezed, and elbowed by the poorest rabble of poor gallery scramblers—could I once more hear those anxious shrieks of yours—and the delicious *Thank God, we are safe*, which always followed when the topmost stair, conquered, let in the first light of the whole cheerful theatre down beneath us—I know not the fathom line

---

[17] MR. COTTON—Probably Charles Cotton (1630–1687), an English poet and translator with a humorous or satiric turn.
[18] COMING GUEST—The new year.
[19] POOR — HUNDRED POUNDS A YEAR—Four hundred pounds a year.
[20] SUPERFLUX—Superfluity.

that ever touched a descent so deep as I would be willing to bury more wealth in than Crœsus had, or the great Jew R—, is supposed to have, to purchase it.

"And now do just look at that merry little Chinese waiter holding an umbrella, big enough for a bed-tester, over the head of that pretty insipid half-Madonna-ish chit of a lady in that very blue summer-house."

Vocabulary Study: Lamb's essays are conversational in expression; but since there are differences between the conversational vocabularies of a well-read, nineteenth-century Englishman and of a present-day American, there are some words that we need to get acquainted with. The dictionary will help you with the following: *repugnance; azure-tinctured* (look up both parts of the compound); *grotesques; decorous; Mandarin; incidence; furlong; predicated; couchant; lucid; Cathay; Hyson; folio; collating; finical; precarious; dilations; straiten* (see *strait*, a verb); *competence.*

Look up the word history of each of the following: *tea; pagoda; salver*. It is interesting to note that English is not all-English, but a blending of the influences of many languages. Find synonyms for *insipid;* also an antonym.

By Way of Appreciation: *Old China* is a significant essay for several reasons. In the first place, it exemplifies the easy conversational style which was Lamb's special contribution to the development of the English essay. The author writes just as folks talk, without too nice a regard for the right word or the proper sentence construction. He rambles a bit, for people seldom talk in a straight line when they talk informally. One idea may lead to another so entertaining that the first is forgotten. But the talk is always friendly and cheerful.

Then, the essay is especially interesting because it is in the truest sense autobiographical. The thin disguise of names does not mislead us. Such a conversation may really have passed between Charles and Mary. Certainly the glimpses of their early poverty and their later ease are true. Each illustration came from their lives; and each idea, right from the heart. Thus it accurately reflects the tastes and interests of brother and sister.

And finally, *Old China* is an engaging essay because it presents a question for the reader to ponder: Does increase of income bring a corresponding increase in happiness? Do you agree with Bridget, or can you find some valid answers to her argument? Here is a question of universal interest presented in a concrete way.

Suggestions for Study: Lamb's manner of expression is pleasingly picturesque. Explain the meaning of the following selections: Paragraph

2: "Those little, lawless, azure-tinctured grotesques"; Paragraph 2: "That world before perspective—a china tea-cup"; Paragraph 5: "Likeness is identity on tea-cups" (If you have any china of Japanese design, study the figures and landscape with eye to proportion and perspective.); Paragraph next to the last: "Competence to age is supplementary youth." Can you select at least five other effective word-combinations from the essay? They need not be whole sentences.

How does the punctuation reveal the conversational style? Which mark is used with notable frequency? Do you find any expressions which verge upon slang of the English variety (words purposely inaccurately used)? What are they? Point out any sentence so broken or involved that it is difficult to follow its meaning. Why did Lamb allow it to stand? Why did Lamb return to the tea-cup in the last paragraph?

Jot down five or six sentences in the essay which prove that Lamb was a well-educated man. You will recall that Lamb entered a charity school at the age of seven and left it to work at the age of fourteen. How does his general educational and cultural background compare with that of an American of our day who has had to leave school after finishing the eighth grade? (Think of the things you knew or didn't know when you were fourteen.) How does it compare with that of the average high school senior? How do you account for the differences noted above? From the contents of the essay, justify the statement in the introduction that the Lamb living-room was furnished in quiet good taste. Can you specify any of the details in the furnishings?

Exercises and Creative Work: Make an outline of the essay. Then show how Lamb leads from one idea to another.

Following are some suggested topics for original essays: *A China Tea-Cup; Tea-Leaves; Money versus True Happiness.*

Following are some questions for written work or informal debate:
1. Do you believe with Bridget that people who just escape actual poverty are happier than those who have money enough to supply every reasonable desire?
    (a) If you do not, how do you answer her points
       (1) That the fewer purchases one can make, the greater the pleasure in those purchases?
       (2) That people in the gallery seem to have more fun at a play than those who sit downstairs? (Have you ever "rushed the gallery"? Did you enjoy it?)
    (b) If you do agree with Bridget, how do you explain the fact that most people, if given a choice between wealth and bare sufficiency, would choose wealth?
2. Does Lamb effectually answer Bridget's question? Are there other points that you would like to add?
3. What do you think is the true ratio between happiness and money?

ON GOING A JOURNEY

William Hazlitt

By Way of Introduction: Travel has always been one of the most interesting of human experiences. People who could not get away themselves have been eager to listen to or read about the journeys of others. And as we do not all travel for the same reasons in the same way, it is interesting to hear another person's philosophy on the subject. There is a good deal of personal philosophy in Hazlitt's essay, *On Going a Journey*. You will notice that travel in nineteenth-century England was quite different from travel in twentieth-century America, but Hazlitt's comments are still engaging.

One of the pleasantest things in the world is going a journey; but I like to go by myself. I can enjoy society in a room; but out of doors, nature is company enough for me. I am then never less alone than when alone.

> The fields his study, nature was his book.[1]

I cannot see the wit of walking and talking at the same time. When I am in the country, I wish to vegetate like the country.

---

[1] The fields, etc.—From *The Farmer's Boy* by Robert Bloomfield.

I am not for criticising hedge-rows and black cattle. I go out of town in order to forget the town and all that is in it. There are those who for this purpose go to watering-places, and carry the metropolis with them. I like more elbow-room, and fewer incumberances. I like solitude, when I give myself up to it, for the sake of solitude; nor do I ask for

> a friend in my retreat
> Whom I may whisper solitude is sweet.[2]

The soul of a journey is liberty, perfect liberty, to think, feel, do just as one pleases. We go on a journey chiefly to be free of all impediments and of inconveniences; to leave ourselves behind, much more to get rid of others. It is because I want a little breathing space to muse on indifferent matters, where Contemplation

> May plume her feathers and let grow her wings,
> That in the various bustle of resort
> Were all too-ruffled, and sometimes impair'd,[3]

that I absent myself from the town for a while, without feeling at a loss the moment I am left by myself. Instead of a friend in a post-chaise or in a tilbury, to exchange good things with, and vary the same stale topics over again, for once let me have a truce with impertinence. Give me the clear blue sky over my head, and the green turf beneath my feet, and a three hours' march to dinner—and then to thinking. It is hard if I cannot start some game on these lone heaths. I laugh, I run, I leap, I sing for joy. From the point of yonder rolling cloud, I plunge into my past being, and revel there, as the sun-burnt Indian[4] plunges headlong into the wave that wafts him to his native shore. Then long-forgotten things like "sunken wrack and sumless treasuries" burst upon my eager sight, and I begin to feel, think, and be myself again.

To give way to our feelings before company seems extravagance or affectation; and on the other hand, to have to unravel this mystery of our being at every turn, and to make others take an equal interest in it (otherwise the end is not answered) is a task to which few are competent. We must "give it an

---

[2] A FRIEND IN MY RETREAT, etc.—From *Retirement* by William Cowper.
[3] MAY PLUME HER FEATHERS, etc.—From *Comus* by John Milton.
[4] SUN-BURNT INDIAN—Here, probably any dark-skinned, tropic islander.

understanding, but no tongue." My old Friend C——,[5] however, could do both. He could go on in the most delightful explanatory way over hill and dale, a summer's day, and convert a landscape into a didactic poem or a Pindaric ode.[6] "He talked far above singing." If I could so clothe my ideas in sounding and flowing words, I might perhaps wish to have some one with me to admire the swelling theme; or I could be more content, were it possible for me still to hear his echoing voice in the woods of All-Foxden. They had "that fine madness in them which our first poets had"; and if they could have been caught by some rare instrument, would have breathed such strains as the following:

> Here be woods as green
> As any, air likewise as fresh and sweet
> As when smooth Zephyrus plays on the fleet
> Face of the curled stream, with flow'rs as many
> As the young spring gives, and as choice as any;
> Here be all new delights, cool streams and wells,
> Arbours o'ergrown with woodbine, caves and dells;
> Choose where thou wilt, while I sit by and sing,
> Or gather rushes to make many a ring
> For thy long fingers; tell thee tales of love,
> How the pale Phoebe, hunting in a grove,
> First saw the boy Endymion, from whose eyes
> She took eternal fire that never dies;
> How she convey'd him softly in a sleep,
> His temples bound with poppy, to the steep
> Head of old Latmos, where she stoops each night,
> Gilding the mountain with her brother's light,
> To kiss her sweetest.
>
> *Faithful Shepherdess* [7]

Had I words and images at command like these, I would attempt to wake the thoughts that lie slumbering on golden ridges in the evening clouds: but at the sight of nature my fancy, poor as it is, droops and closes up its leaves, like flowers at sunset. I can make nothing out on the spot:—I must have time to collect myself.

---

[5] My old Friend C———Samuel Taylor Coleridge.
[6] Pindaric ode—Pindar was a lyric poet of ancient Greece. Any ode written in a constantly changing meter is called Pindaric. Coleridge wrote several such odes.
[7] *Faithful Shepherdess*—A play by John Fletcher.

In general, a good thing spoils out-of-door prospects: it should be reserved for Table-talk. L——[8] is for this reason, I take it, the worst company in the world out of doors; because he is the best within. I grant, there is one subject on which it is pleasant to talk on a journey; and that is, what one shall have for supper when we get to our inn at night. The open air improves this sort of conversation or friendly altercation, by setting a keener edge on appetite. Every mile of the road heightens the flavour of the viands we expect at the end of it. How fine it is to enter some old town, walled and turreted, just at the approach of night-fall, or to come to some straggling village, with the lights streaming through the surrounding gloom; and then after inquiring for the best entertainment that the place affords, to "take one's ease at one's inn."[9] What a delicate speculation it is, after drinking whole goblets of tea,—

The cups that cheer, but not inebriate,—[10]

and letting the fumes ascend into the brain, to sit considering what we shall have for supper—eggs and a rasher, a rabbit smothered in onions, or an excellent veal-cutlet! These hours are sacred to silence and to musing, to be treasured up in the memory, and to feed the source of smiling thoughts hereafter. I would not waste them in idle talk; or if I must have the integrity of fancy broken in upon, I would rather it were by a stranger than by a friend. A stranger takes the hue and character from the time and place; he is a part of the furniture and costume of an inn. If he is a Quaker, or from the West Riding of Yorkshire so much the better. I do not even try to sympathize with him, and he breaks no squares.[11] I associate nothing with my travelling companion but present objects and passing events. In his ignorance of me and my affairs, I in a manner forget myself.

I have certainly spent some enviable hours at inns—sometimes when I have been left entirely to myself, and have tried to solve some metaphysical problem, as once at Witham-

---

[8] L—— —Charles Lamb.
[9] TAKE ONE'S EASE AT ONE'S INN—From Shakespeare's *Henry IV*.
[10] THE CUPS THAT CHEER, etc.—From *The Task* by William Cowper.
[11] BREAKS NO SQUARES—Perhaps a reference to "the integrity of fancy" mentioned above.

common, where I found out the proof that likeness is not a case of the association of ideas—at other times, when there have been pictures in the room, as at St. Neot's (I think it was), where I first met with Gribelin's engravings of the Cartoons,[12] into which I entered at once, and at a little inn on the borders of Wales, where there happened to be hanging some of Westall's drawings, which I compared triumphantly with the figure of a girl who had ferried me over the Severn,[13] standing up in the boat between me and the twilight—at other times I might mention luxuriating in books, with a peculiar interest in this way, as I remember sitting up half the night to read *Paul and Virginia*,[14] which I picked up at an inn in Bridgewater, after being drenched in the rain all day; and at the same place I got through two volumes of Madame D'Arblay's *Camilla*.[15]

There is hardly any thing that shows the shortsightedness or capriciousness of the imagination more than travelling does. With change of place we change our ideas; nay, our opinions and feelings. We can by an effort indeed transport ourselves to old and long-forgotten scenes, and then the picture of the mind revives again; but we forget those that we have just left. It seems that we can think of but one place at a time. The canvas of the fancy is but of a certain extent, and if we paint one set of objects upon it, they immediately efface every other. We cannot enlarge our conceptions, we only shift our point of view. The landscape bares its bosom [16] to the enraptured eye, we take our fill of it, and seem as if we could form no other image of beauty or grandeur. We pass on, and think no more of it: the horizon that shuts it from our sight, also blots it from our memory like a dream. In travelling through a wild barren country, I can form no idea of a woody and cultivated one. It appears to me that all the world must be barren, like

---

[12] GRIBELIN'S ENGRAVINGS OF THE CARTOONS—The Cartoons of Raphael were seven Biblical subjects designed to be reproduced in tapestry. Gribelin, an engraver, had recently reproduced the drawings. Be sure to look up *cartoon* in the dictionary.

[13] SEVERN—A river in western England.

[14] *Paul and Virginia*—An English translation of a French novel by de Saint-Pierre, published in 1788.

[15] MADAME D'ARBLAY'S *Camilla*—Madame D'Arblay's (Fanny Burney) popular novel, *Camilla*, was published in 1796.

[16] LANDSCAPE BARES ITS BOSOM—Reminiscent of a line in Wordsworth's sonnet, *The World Is Too Much With Us*.

what I see of it. In the country we forget the town, and in town we despise the country. "Beyond Hyde Park,"[17] says Sir Fopling Flutter, "all is a desert." All that part of the map that we do not see before us is a blank. The world in our conceit of it is not much bigger than a nutshell. It is not one prospect expanded into another, county joined to county, kingdom to kingdom, lands to seas, making an image voluminous and vast; —the mind can form no larger idea of space than the eye can take in at a single glance. The rest is a name written in a map, a calculation of arithmetic. For instance, what is the true signification of that immense mass of territory and population known by the name of China to us? An inch of paste-board on a wooden globe, or no more account than a China orange! Things near us are seen of the size of life: things at a distance are diminished to the size of the understanding. We measure the universe by ourselves, and even comprehend the texture of our own being only piecemeal. To return to the question I have quitted above.

I have no objection to go to see ruins, aqueducts, pictures, in company with a friend or party, but rather the contrary, for the former reason reversed. They are intelligible matters, and will bear talking about. The sentiment here is not tacit, but communicable and overt. Salisbury Plain is barren of criticism, but Stonehenge[18] will bear a discussion antiquarian, picturesque, and philosophical. In setting out on a party of pleasure, the first consideration always is where shall we go to: in taking a solitary ramble, the question is what shall we meet with by the way. "The mind is its own place";[19] nor are we anxious to arrive at the end of our journey. I can myself do the honours indifferently well to works of art and curiosity. I once took a party[20] to Oxford with no mean *éclat*—shewed them that seat of the Muses[21] at a distance,—

"With glistering spires and pinnacles adorn'd"—[22]

[17] HYDE PARK—In Westminster. It is one of the largest of London's parks.
[18] STONEHENGE—A ruined structure of giant stones on Salisbury Plain, England; perhaps the ruins of a Druid temple.
[19] THE MIND IS ITS OWN PLACE—From *Paradise Lost,* by John Milton.
[20] PARTY—Charles Lamb and his sister.
[21] MUSES—The nine Greek goddesses who presided over poetry, the arts, and science; here used merely in the sense of learning or culture.
[22] WITH GLISTERING SPIRES, etc.—From *Paradise Lost.*

descanted on the learned air that breathes from the grassy quadrangles and stone walls of halls and colleges. As another exception to the above reasoning, I should not feel confident in venturing on a journey in a foreign country without a companion. I should want at intervals to hear the sound of my own language. There is an involuntary antipathy in the mind of an Englishman to foreign manners and notions that requires the assistance of social sympathy to carry it off. As the distance from home increases, this relief, which was at first a luxury, becomes a passion and an appetite. A person would almost feel stifled to find himself in the deserts of Arabia without friends and countrymen: there must be allowed to be something in the view of Athens or old Rome that claims the utterance of speech; and I own that the Pyramids are too mighty for any single contemplation. In such situations, so opposite to all one's ordinary train of ideas, one seems a species by one's self, a limb torn off from society, unless one can meet with instant fellowship and support.

There is undoubtedly a sensation in travelling into foreign parts that is to be had nowhere else: but it is more pleasing at the time than lasting. It is too remote from our habitual associations to be a common topic of discourse or reference, and, like a dream or another state of existence, does not piece into our daily modes of life. Dr. Johnson remarked how little foreign travel added to the facilities of conversation in those who had been abroad. In fact, the time we have spent there is both delightful and in one sense instructive; but it appears to be cut out of our substantial, downright existence, and never to join kindly on to it. We are not the same, but another, and perhaps more enviable individual, all the time we are out of our own country. We are lost to ourselves, as well as our friends. So the poet somewhat quaintly sings,—

> Out of my country and myself I go.

Those who wish to forget painful thought, do well to absent themselves for a while from the ties and objects that recall them: but we can be said only to fulfill our destiny in the place that gave us birth. I should on this account like well enough to spend the whole of my life in travelling abroad, if I could anywhere borrow another life to spend afterwards at home!

Vocabulary Study: These words, which you should know in order to appreciate Hazlitt's essay, may be found in the ordinary dictionary: *metropolis; impediments; contemplation; impaired; post-chaise* (note pronunciation); *tilbury; truce; impertinence; wrack; didactic; altercation; viands; inebriate* (verb); *metaphysical; ferried; capriciousness; efface; descanted; quadrangle; aqueducts; intelligible; tacit; communicable; overt; éclat* (note pronunciation); *involuntary; antipathy; mariner; arbitrary; facilities.*

Find two synonyms in good use for *viands,* for *tacit,* for *overt.* Find an antonym for *truce; impertinence; overt.* Notice the derivation of *wrack.* What common modern word comes from the same root?

By Way of Appreciation: Even a glance at *On Going a Journey* tells one that its author was a scholar, a lover of books and the arts. A closer study of the liberal sprinkling of allusions from Milton, from Shakespeare, and from lesser writers old and new, suggests that William Hazlitt had the wells of English literature in his heart to draw from. The interest of his allusions to writers of the day is increased by our realization that he knew these writers well. It was an early friendship with Coleridge that influenced Hazlitt to become a writer. Lamb, de Quincey, and Hunt were other friends who shared Hazlitt's critical and creative interests in literature.

The essay reveals, too, something of Hazlitt's independent nature. He could be satisfied with his own company; in fact, he often preferred it. For one thing he had such an argumentative turn of mind that solitude was more restful than companionship. But the chief reason for his pleasure in solitude was the great store of interests he carried with him. He is an excellent illustration of the way in which "studies serve for delight."

Suggestions for Study: Can you list four reasons which Hazlitt gives for going on a journey? Which, if any, of these reasons for traveling do you share? What other reasons are there for traveling? Which do you think Hazlitt enjoyed more, traveling in England or traveling abroad? Why? The author says, "With change of place, we change our ideas, our opinions and feelings." Can you give an illustration from experience or observation? Explain his statement that to most of us China is an inch of pasteboard on a wooden globe. Discuss the remark of Dr. Johnson that foreign travel adds little to the conversational facilities of the traveler.

Exercises and Creative Work: Make a topical outline of the essay. Then using your outline, but not referring again to the essay, develop one of the main topics into a paragraph of about one hundred words.

Write your answer to the following question in the form of a discussional essay: If you had the opportunity to go abroad, would you choose (*a*) to go alone, (*b*) to go with a tour-party, (*c*) to go with a companion who had never been abroad, (*d*) to go with a companion or companions who had been abroad before?

DREAMS

From *The Confessions of an English Opium Eater*

THOMAS DE QUINCEY

By Way of Introduction: People are always interested in dreams. If the conversation lags at any gathering, let some one mention an unusual dream and instantly the ball of talk starts rolling again. No doubt this common interest is one reason for the continued popularity of Thomas de Quincey's *Confessions of an English Opium Eater,* for much of that work is given over to a discussion of his opium dreams. Strange as are the dreams of health, they are pallid in comparison with the dreams that accompany fever, artificial sleep induced by anesthetics or drugs, or, in fact, any abnormal physical condition.

Contrary to general belief, the dreams that follow drugs are not pleasant, but horrifying and depressing. This fact is well attested by writers who have been the unfortunate victims of drugs—such writers as Samuel Taylor Coleridge, Edgar Allan Poe, and Thomas de Quincey. In his *Confessions,* de Quincey makes reference to the "pains" of opium. In this selection, note that almost immediately he speaks of his "acutest suffering." He shares with Poe and Coleridge the faculty of describing these weird, unreal experiences with convincingly vivid detail.

I NOW pass to what is the main subject of these latter confessions, to the history and journal of what took place in my dreams; for these were the immediate and proximate cause of my acutest suffering.

The first notice I had of any important change going on in this part of my physical economy was from the re-awakening of a state of eye generally incident to childhood, or exalted states of irritability. I know not whether my reader is aware that many children, perhaps most, have a power of painting, as it were, upon the darkness, all sorts of phantoms; in some, that power is simply a mechanic affection of the eye; others have a voluntary, or a semi-voluntary power to dismiss or to summon them; or, as a child once said to me when I questioned him on this matter, "I can tell them to go, and they go; but sometimes they come, when I don't tell them to come." Whereupon I told him that he had almost as unlimited a command over apparitions as a Roman centurion over his soldiers.—In the middle of 1817, I think it was, that this faculty became positively distressing to me: at night, when I lay awake in bed, vast processions passed along in mournful pomp; friezes of never-ending stories, that to my feelings were as sad and solemn as if they were stories drawn from times before Œdipus[1] or Priam[2]—before Tyre[3]—before Memphis.[4] And, at the same time a corresponding change took place in my dreams; a theatre seemed suddenly opened and lighted up within my brain, which presented nightly spectacles of more than earthly splendour. And the four following facts may be mentioned, as noticeable at this time:

1. That, as the creative state of the eye increased, a sympathy seemed to arise between the waking and the dreaming states of the brain in one point—that whatsoever I happened to call up and to trace by a voluntary act upon the darkness was very apt to transfer itself to my dreams; so that I feared to exercise this faculty; for, as Midas[5] turned all things to gold, that yet baffled his hopes and defrauded his human desires, so whatsoever things capable of being visually represented I did but think of in the darkness, immediately shaped themselves into phantoms of the eye; and, by a process apparently no less inevitable, when thus once traced in faint and visionary colours, like writings in sympathetic ink, they were drawn out by the fierce chemistry of my dreams, into insufferable splendour that fretted my heart.

2. For this, and all other changes in my dreams, were accompanied by deep-seated anxiety and gloomy melancholy, such as are wholly incommunicable by words. I seemed every night to descend, not metaphorically, but literally to descend, into chasms and sunless abysses, depths below depths, from which it seemed hopeless that I could ever re-ascend. Nor did I, by waking, feel that I *had* re-ascended. This I do not dwell upon; because the state of gloom which attended these gorgeous spectacles, amounting at last to utter darkness, as of some suicidal despondency, cannot be approached by words.

3. The sense of space, and in the end, the sense of time, were

---

[1] ŒDIPUS—King of Thebes, whose story is told in Greek mythology.
[2] PRIAM—King of ancient Troy, father of Hector and Paris.
[3] TYRE—An ancient city in Phoenicia.
[4] MEMPHIS—An ancient city in Egypt.
[5] MIDAS—King of Phrygia, who was granted the power of turning everything he touched into gold.

both powerfully affected. Buildings, landscapes, &c. were exhibited in proportions so vast as the bodily eye is not fitted to receive. Space swelled, and was amplified to an extent of unutterable infinity. This, however, did not disturb me so much as the vast expansion of time; I sometimes seemed to have lived 70 or 100 years in one night; nay, sometimes had feelings representative of a millennium passed in that time, or, however, of a duration far beyond the limits of any human experience.

4. The minutest incidents of childhood, or forgotten scenes of later years, were often revived: I could not be said to recollect them; for if I had been told of them when waking, I should not have been able to acknowledge them as parts of my past experience. But placed as they were before me, in dreams like intuitions, and clothed in all their evanescent circumstances and accompanying feelings, I *recognised* them instantaneously. I was once told by a near relative of mine, that having in her childhood fallen into a river, and being on the very verge of death but for the critical assistance which reached her, she saw in a moment her whole life, in its minutest incidents, arrayed before her simultaneously as in a mirror; and she had a faculty developed as suddenly for comprehending the whole and every part. This, from some opium experiences of mine, I can believe; I have, indeed, seen the same thing asserted twice in modern books, and accompanied by a remark which I am convinced is true; viz. that the dread book of account, which the Scriptures speak of is, in fact, the mind itself of each individual. Of this at least, I feel assured, that there is no such thing as *forgetting* possible to the mind; a thousand accidents may, and will interpose a veil between our present consciousness and the secret inscriptions on the mind; accidents of the same sort will also rend away this veil; but alike, whether veiled or unveiled, the inscription remains for ever; just as the stars seem to withdraw before the common light of day, whereas, in fact, we all know that it is the light which is drawn over them as a veil—and that they are waiting to be revealed when the obscuring daylight shall have withdrawn.

Having noticed these four facts as memorably distinguishing my dreams from those of health, I shall now cite a case illustrative of the first fact; and shall then cite any others that I remember, either in their chronological order, or any other that may give them more effect as pictures to the reader.

I had been in youth, and even since, for occasional amusement, a great reader of Livy,[6] whom, I confess, that I prefer, both for style and matter, to any other of the Roman historians: and I had often felt as most solemn and appalling sounds, and most emphatically representative of the majesty of the Roman people, the two words so often occurring in Livy—*Consul Romanus;*[7] especially when the consul is introduced in his military character. I mean to say that the words king—sultan—regent, &c. or any other titles of those who embody in their own persons the collective majesty of a great people, had less power over my reverential feelings. I had also, though no great reader of history, made myself minutely and critically familiar with one period of English history, viz. the period of the Parliamentary War,[8] having been attracted by the moral grandeur of some who figured in that day, and by the many interesting memoirs which survive those unquiet times. Both these parts of my lighter reading,[9] having furnished me often with matter of reflection, now furnished me with matter for my dreams. Often I used to see, after painting upon the blank darkness a sort of rehearsal whilst waking, a crowd of ladies, and perhaps a festival, and dances. And I heard it said, or I said to myself, "These are English ladies from the unhappy times of Charles I. These are the wives and the daughters of those who met in peace, and sate at the same table, and were allied by marriage or by blood; and yet, after a certain day in August 1642, never smiled upon each other again, nor met but in the field of battle; and at Marston Moor, at Newbury, or at Naseby[10] cut asunder all ties of love by the cruel sabre, and washed away in blood the memory of ancient friendship."—The ladies danced, and looked as lovely as the court of George IV. Yet I knew, even in my dream, that they had been in the grave for nearly two centuries.—This pageant would suddenly dissolve: and, at a clapping of hands would be heard the heart-quaking sound of *Consul Romanus:* and immediately came

[6] LIVY—A Roman historian (59 B.C.–17 A.D.).

[7] *Consul Romanus*—The title given to the chief magistrate of ancient Rome.

[8] PARLIAMENTARY WAR—The civil war which deposed Charles I and made Cromwell Protector of England. It began in August, 1642.

[9] LIGHTER READING—An interesting sidelight on the author's wide reading. Livy is considered heavy reading in college today.

[10] MARSTON MOOR, NEWBURY, NASEBY—Battles in the Parliamentary War.

"sweeping by," in gorgeous paludaments,[11] Paulus or Marius,[12] girt round by a company of centurions, with the crimson tunic hoisted on a spear, and followed by the *alalagmos*[13] of the Roman legions.

Many years ago, when I was looking over Piranesi's Antiquities of Rome, Mr. Coleridge, who was standing by, described to me a set of plates by that artist, called his *Dreams*, and which record the scenery of his own visions during the delirium of a fever: Some of them (I describe only from memory of Mr. Coleridge's account) represented vast Gothic halls: on the floor of which stood all sorts of engines and machinery, wheels, cables, pulleys, levers, catapults, &c. &c. expressive of enormous power put forth, and resistance overcome. Creeping along the sides of the walls, you perceive a staircase; and upon it, groping his way upwards, was Piranesi himself: follow the stairs a little further, and you perceive it come to a sudden and abrupt termination, without any balustrade, and allowing no step onwards to him who had reached the extremity, except into the depths below. Whatever is to become of poor Piranesi, you suppose, at least, that his labours must in some way terminate here. But raise your eyes, and behold a second flight of stairs still higher: on which again Piranesi is perceived, but this time standing on the very brink of the abyss. Again elevate your eye, and a still more aerial flight of stairs is beheld: and again is poor Piranesi busy on his aspiring labours: and so on, until the unfinished stairs and Piranesi both are lost in the upper gloom of the hall.—With the same power of endless growth and self reproduction did my architecture proceed in dreams. In the early stage of my malady, the splendours of my dreams were indeed chiefly architectural: and I beheld such pomp of cities and palaces as was never yet beheld by the waking eye, unless in the clouds.

And now came a tremendous change, which, unfolding itself slowly like a scroll, through many months, promised an abiding torment; and, in fact, it never left me until the winding up of my case.[14] Hitherto the human face had mixed often in my

[11] PALUDAMENTS—Military cloaks.
[12] PAULUS, MARIUS—The former a Roman consul (died 216 B.C.); the latter a Roman consul and general (155–86 B.C.).
[13] *Alalagmos*—A word coined from the war cry of the Romans.
[14] WINDING UP OF MY CASE—By phenomenal will-power, de Quincey broke himself of the habit of taking drugs.

dreams, but not despotically nor with any special power of tormenting. But now that which I have called the tyranny of the human face began to unfold itself. Perhaps some part of my London life might be answerable for this. Be that as it may, now it was that upon the rocking waters of the ocean the human face began to appear; the sea appeared paved with innumerable faces, upturned to the heavens: faces, imploring, wrathful, despairing, surged upward by thousands, by myriads, by generations, by centuries:—my agitation was infinite,—my mind tossed—and surged with the ocean.

Vocabulary Study: De Quincey furnishes good exercise for anyone's vocabulary. Following are listed some of the most interesting words from the present essay: *economy* (my physical economy); *incident* (*incident* to childhood); *voluntary; apparitions; centurion; pomp; friezes; sympathy* (note derivation); *inevitable* (see *evitable*); *metaphorically; literally* (note that this word is the opposite of *metaphorically*); *chasms* (note pronunciation); *abysses* (note pronunciation); *infinity; millennium; evanescent; critical; simultaneously; appalling; memoirs; sabre; legions; catapults; terminate; malady; despotically.*

Distinguish between *finite* and *infinite*. Give synonyms of *infinite*.

By Way of Appreciation: Aside from the peculiar interest of de Quincey's subject, there is much in his manner of writing to please the reader. His wording is scholarly, but picturesque. His remarkable fund of literary and historical knowledge provided strangely colorful figures and backgrounds for his word-paintings. A sensitiveness to rhythm guided his phrases into happy cadences. It is pleasant to read de Quincey aloud or to listen while another reads. His critical and historical studies will well repay the attention of the scholar; but *The Confessions*, because they are most personal, are most interesting to the general reader.

Suggestions for Study: Coleridge began one of his poems, "My eyes make pictures when they are shut." If you share with him and de Quincey this power to paint pictures in the dark, how do your experiences correspond with those described in the first part of the second paragraph of this essay? Explain the allusion to Midas in the first numbered paragraph. Do you think that it is a common experience to have one's dreams grow out of one's last waking thoughts? Can you furnish any illustrations? Jot down at least three ways in which de Quincey's dream experiences differed from the dreams of a person in normal health. What is de Quincey's theory about *forgetting?* Do you agree with him? What two periods of history often furnished him with material for his dreams? Which of all the dream experiences described do you think would be the most disturbing?

Exercises and Creative Work: Write a précis of the essay, and add a final paragraph giving your reactions to the essay.

THE HISTORY OF PROSE LITERATURE IN ENGLAND

THE VICTORIAN ERA (1840-1900)

General Characteristics

The Age of Romanticism was a revolutionary age; it was followed by a period of great conservatism. The literature of the later nineteenth century was a combination of romanticism and classicism, with classicism —in form, at least—predominating. Prose shows both influences. Its general tone was sober, but it displays an interest in many new subjects. Discoveries in science, the development of new theories, general industrial expansion—these brought a wealth of new ideas to be discussed. A glance at the fields of activity represented by the greatest essayists of the age will indicate the great diversity of subject. Carlyle was a philosopher; Macaulay, a Member of Parliament; Newman, a churchman and theologian; Ruskin, a critic of art, and a social reformer; Huxley, a scientist; Stevenson, a writer. It is interesting to note, however, that except for the work of Stevenson, there is nothing that approaches the light essay from their pens.

Thomas Carlyle (1795-1881)

Not unlike the dour, rugged country from which he came was Thomas Carlyle. He had the rather common Scotch combination of a crusty exterior and a sweet, sound core.

There are four important settings in the drama of Carlyle's life. The first is a farmer's cottage at Ecclefechan, near Dumfries in Scotland. Thomas himself is a peasant lad—sturdy, ruddy-cheeked, accustomed to hard work. He is the oldest child and his parents have decided that he is to be a Presbyterian minister. At fourteen, therefore, he sets off on foot for the University of Edinburgh, eighty miles away.

The second scene is a poor student's lodgings at college. Carlyle is friendless and miserable. The indigestion which tormented him the rest of his days has begun—undoubtedly the result of privation. But he has found an enthusiasm in German literature and philosophy—an enthusiasm which inspired his own first writings and which was the one happy association of his college years.

Half a century later Carlyle returned to this scene, one of the most famous men in Britain and newly elected Lord Rector of the University. His election to the office was the greatest honor that came to him.

The third scene is not a parsonage but a farmhouse. Carlyle was convinced that he was not to be a minister. After some luckless experimenting with jobs, he settled down to write. In 1826 he had married Jane Welsh, a beautiful girl who had also some genius as a writer. Though her father was a physician, Jane owned a farm at Craigenputtock; here the couple decided to live while Thomas was getting established. It was a lonely place, and life was hard—especially for Jane, who baked bread, scrubbed floors, washed clothes, and wheedled her husband. Carlyle responded by writing *The Life of Burns* and *Sartor Resartus* (reflective of his interest in German philosophy). It was at Craigenputtock that Carlyle first entertained Emerson and made a lifelong friend. At the end of seven years he was finding a regular market for his writings and decided to leave the farm.

For the next forty-seven years a house in Cheyne Row, Chelsea, in London is the setting. It was here that fame came to Thomas; it was here that he and Jane entertained the wise and great of England. Carlyle's books had always commanded readers, but it took *The French Revolution* with its unusual style and vigor to make him famous. The book was published in 1837. When the last line was written, Carlyle gave his wife the manuscript, with the words, "This I could tell the world, 'You have not had for a hundred years any book that comes more directly and flamingly from the heart of a living man.'" And Mrs. Carlyle, after reading it through, replied, "A work of genius, dear!"

From the appearance of *The French Revolution* until the death of Mrs. Carlyle in 1865, the author was busy lecturing and writing. His house became a Mecca for everyone interested in books and philosophy. But when Jane Carlyle died, Thomas was a broken man. His last fifteen years were sadly lonely.

Many anecdotes are told of the Scotchman's flaming temper and general ill humor and of his amazing meekness in moments of great stress. He confessed that during the years he was working on *Frederick the Great* he "devastated homelife and happiness,"—but then, he was ever given to exaggeration. And when the manuscript for the first volume of *The French Revolution*, which he had lent to John Stuart Mill, was destroyed through the carelessness of a servant, Carlyle's only concern was to keep Mill from knowing how disastrous the loss was! The whole thing had to be rewritten, and not a note had been saved.

When the curtain falls on Thomas Carlyle he is being carried back for burial to the little town where he had been born eighty-five years before.

Thomas Babington Macaulay (1800–1859)

"If I had to choose a lot from all that there are in human life, I am not sure that I should prefer any to that which has fallen to me. I am sincerely and thoroughly contented."

This remarkable statement comes from a letter written by Thomas Macaulay when he was at the height of his career. He would probably have counted it the final blessing that he died very suddenly at the comparatively early age of fifty-nine, while he was still happily active.

What were the circumstances of this contented life? In the first place, Macaulay had a rare combination of natural gifts. His mind was phenomenally quick and retentive. He could read at three, was studying serious books at five, talked like an encyclopedia at six, had written a *Compendium of Universal History* at ten; and instead of being a self-conscious little prig, was a pretty child whom everyone adored. In maturity he could read like lightning and he seemed to remember, literally, everything that he had ever read. He could recite at will from *Paradise Lost,* from novels or histories or newspapers.

He had, besides, a tall, fine figure, excellent health, and a happy disposition. Everyone liked him. More, everyone respected him. He was thoroughly honest and conscientious in his business and political life. In Parliament, besides being its most eloquent speaker, he was

a trustworthy leader. He accepted some high offices—such as a cabinet position—and refused others. At no time did he sacrifice his honor to success. Once he was not re-elected to Parliament because of his loyalty to an unpopular cause. A later election, however, returned him to his seat. Two years before his death he was made Baron Macaulay of Rothley.

With money he was also fortunate. His father had been wealthy but lost his money when Macaulay was a young man. Thomas then set vigorously to work to make a living for himself and his brothers and sisters. He eventually built up a fortune of his own. He never married but made his home with a sister and her sons.

The success that he enjoyed in other things came to him also as a writer. In fact the sale of his works contributed largely to his fortune. When he was twenty-five, his *Essay on Milton* appeared in the *Edinburgh Review.* It was a sensational success. For the next twenty years he contributed to magazines, essays on literary and historical themes—essays like those on Bunyan, Addison, and Goldsmith; on Lord Clive, Warren Hastings, and William Pitt. Then he began the *History of England* on which he worked until his death. He finished five volumes. Scholars have estimated that the work completed on the scale that he had started would have filled fifty volumes.

Macaulay made history and literature popular. He wrote, not for scholars, but for everyone. His style was direct, easy to read. He chose details with an eye to human interest and did not hesitate to overdraw the curious or appealing. In fact he said, "We are not certain that the best histories are not those in which a little of the exaggeration of fictitious narrative is judiciously employed. Something is lost in accuracy, but much is gained in effect." Unfortunately, most historians do not agree with him; and his work is recommended more as an introduction to the subject than for intensive study. Macaulay followed the same principles in writing literary criticisms, with a similar result. His books are always read with pleasure. No student finds them dull; but they must be read with the proverbial grain of salt. The heroes were probably not quite so good nor the villains quite so bad as he drew them. Historical facts, though, are easy to find; it is not so easy to make them come alive, and a certain liveliness of subject was Macaulay's greatest contribution to the art of writing.

John Henry Newman (1801–1890)

Much of the prose of the nineteenth century was of practical nature and its writers were active in other callings. John Henry Newman, for example, was a churchman, and the greatest part of his thirty-six volumes are of first interest to the theologian. The student of literature chooses from among them his two excellent novels, *Loss and Gain* and *Callista;* his autobiography, *Apologia Pro Vita Sua* with its sub-title *A History of His Religious Opinions;* the five-hundred-page collection of his Dublin addresses and essays, *The Idea of a University;* his long poem, *The Dream of Gerontius;* and his famous hymn, *Lead, Kindly Light.*

The student is interested in Newman's clear, precise style—the result of careful labor. "I have been obliged," he said, "to take great pains with everything I have ever written, and I often write chapters over and over again, besides innumerable corrections and interlinear additions."

Like Macaulay, Newman began writing as a child. Two magazine articles were printed when he was only fourteen. He was graduated from Oxford at nineteen, took orders in the Episcopal Church and became Vicar of St. Mary's at Oxford. In middle life serious convictions led him to become a Roman Catholic. The storm of protests over England were silenced by his *Apologia*—it was so evidently sincere. For four years he was rector of the Catholic University in Dublin; then he retired to Edgbaston near Birmingham, spending his remaining years in an Oratory there. In 1879 he was made a Cardinal.

Through changing religious experiences he remained a gentle, noble soul.

John Ruskin (1819–1900)

It is refreshing to read of a reformer sincere enough to try putting his theories into practice and sensible enough to have practical ideas. That is the kind of man Ruskin was. Of course, he was sometimes prejudiced and unreasonable; but many of his undertakings were successful and his influence was wholly good. His own wealth had not blinded him to the injustices of the day, and he worked and put his money to work to correct them. He became interested in social conditions in a roundabout way, the chain beginning in his childhood.

Ruskin's father was a wine-merchant, wealthy and interested in art; his mother was very religious. The father hoped that his boy would be a poet; the mother wanted him to be a minister. Both parents were very strict. They did not believe in toys save simple hand-made ones, and the tiny fellow amused himself for hours by tracing the pattern in the carpet or counting the bricks in nearby walls. He did, of course, have books as soon as he could read. As he grew older, he shared his father's interest in art, planning at first to become a painter. He therefore followed his Oxford courses with two years of study in Italy.

When he was twenty-four his first work was published—the introductory volume of *Modern Painters* in which he warmly defended nineteenth century art, especially the work of the landscape painter, Joseph William Turner. Some of his ideas were very different from those of the established critics, so the volume was much discussed. Other volumes followed; and before long young Ruskin was the most influential art critic in England. Besides *Modern Painters,* he had written *The Seven Lamps of Architecture; Pre-Raphaelitism* (a defense of one of the newer movements in art and poetry); and *The Stones of Venice*—all before he was forty-one.

It was at this time that his love for art led him to realize the need for changes in living-and-working conditions in England. He did not think of art as a pleasure to be reserved for a wealthy few. He thought of it as something to enrich and beautify the lives of everyone. What use was there in writing about the glories of Gothic architecture in Venice when a million Londoners were living in tenement slums? Ruskin set to work to get rid of the slums. He did not, to be sure, wipe them out, but he did much to improve the conditions of the working-man and to put within his reach things that were lovely and inspiring. Ruskin's father had left him about three-quarters of a million dollars, and most of this fortune Ruskin used in works of public welfare.

His writings from 1860 on, all reveal this new interest. Many of them were delivered as lectures to schools or clubs for working-men. Among them are *Sesame and Lilies, Crown of Wild Olives,* and *Fors Clavigera* (letters to the working-men of England). Ruskin's titles are usually allegories that need interpretation, but his style became more and more simple and forceful. From 1870 to 1879 Ruskin was also connected with Oxford as professor of fine arts. The students found his lectures profoundly moving—as one of them said, "far above the religious height of the most solemn service I have ever heard."

Ruskin was wise and good, but there had been disappointments and sorrows in his life. He had married a girl of his mother's choosing, and the venture was not happy. His wife obtained a divorce and remarried. A girl whom he later loved died, leaving him grief-stricken. At sixty-five his health was failing him, and he went to spend his closing years in his home at Coniston in the lovely Lake District of England.

Thomas Henry Huxley (1825-1895)

As Macaulay, in the nineteenth century, popularized history, Huxley popularized science. He did it in something the same way—that is, by using easy English and by supplying illustrations for every vague or difficult point. Huxley, however, was always scientifically exact. He was interested in many fields of activity. He was an expert student of biology and anatomy; he served for a while as a ship's surgeon, as a professor of natural history, as a lecturer, as president of the Royal Society. For three years he was Lord Rector of Aberdeen University. His technical writings are many and authoritative. In literature he is remembered chiefly for these works: *Lay Sermons*, containing the famous essay *On a Piece of Chalk*; *Science and Culture*; and his *Autobiography*, which reveals his gracious personality. He was fond of children, saying once of his four-year-old grandson, "I like that chap. I like the way he looks you straight in the face and disobeys you." There was later a delightful interchange of letters between Julian and his "Grandpater."

Robert Louis Stevenson (1850-1894)

Robert Louis Stevenson wrote brave books, but braver than all his books was his life. And brave, you remember means *gay* as well as *courageous*. He did not let ill health keep him from living fully and richly. His father and grandfather were famous lighthouse engineers, but Louis had no inclination to follow their profession. As a schoolboy he began teaching himself to write by carefully imitating the styles of his favorite authors. In *Memories and Portraits* there are delightful essays reminiscent of his youth, his father, and scenes of his boyhood. In *A College Magazine* from that collection he tells of his self-training in the art of writing. When his accounts of two short trips in Europe were

successful, he was encouraged to give up law, which he hated, for literature. It was *An Inland Voyage* and *Travels with a Donkey* that thus decided his career.

While Stevenson was on his "inland voyage" he fell in love with an American woman, Mrs. Osbourne, whom he later married. Most of the fourteen years remaining to him were filled with his writings and with his pilgrimages in search of a healthful climate. At last the ideal location was found in Samoa. There with his wife and his step-children, of whom he was very fond, six happy years were spent. The Stevenson home Vailima was built on the mountain side, three miles back of Apia. Devoted natives built the "Road of the Loving Heart" up to Stevenson's door and at his death, cleared a way to the mountaintop where he was buried. Over the grave are the lines of his noble "Requiem."

ELD

There is an amazing variety of style and form in the things that Stevenson wrote. Though he was tender-hearted as a woman, his novels are mostly blood-and-thunder adventure tales. His stories deal often with crime and criminals. His lyric poems are delightfully simple and childlike. His books of travel are lightly whimsical. His essays are scholarly and often sober. Besides *Memories and Portraits,* his essay groups include *Virginibus Puerisque (For Boys and Girls), Studies of Men and Books,* and *Essays in the Art of Writing.* These essays are not all easy reading for the author adopted in them a complex style and they are filled with references to his own broad background of reading. However there is in them much real wisdom colored by his charming personality.

Matthew Arnold (1822–1888)

A writer who gained great distinction in the field of literary criticism was Matthew Arnold, the schoolman. His father was headmaster at Rugby, and Matthew was connected with the public schools of England as Inspector for most of his mature life. Writing was his avocation. He produced both poetry and prose, both showing a decided classic tendency. That is, he was a scholarly man; he was especially fond of ancient classic literature; he labored to achieve perfection of style; and he had rather the aloof manner of the professor before a class. He believed in education for culture rather than for use, and his essays make their greatest appeal to the man of learning. He has even a delicate satire with which to jibe the unbeliever—of his doctrine. His best essays are in four main groups: *Essays in Criticism, Culture and Anarchy, Friendship's Garland,* and *Discourses in America. Sweetness and Light* from *Culture and Anarchy* is an excellent illustration of Arnold's favorite subject and his style. Schoolboys like best of all his narrative poem *Sohrab and Rustum.*

Other Essayists of the Victorian Era

Many writers who are best known for work in other literary fields wrote occasional essays. There was, for instance, William Morris—a designer, an artist, a cabinet-maker, a printer, and a poet—who wrote a very charming series of essays. There is Walter Pater, whose best known work is a kind of idealized novel in classic vein, *Marius the Epicurean.* Pater wrote essays expressive of his philosophy that man should search for and cherish moments of ideal pleasure. And finally there is William Makepeace Thackeray, author of *Vanity Fair* and a half dozen other novels. But Thackeray produced a number of volumes of sketches illustrated by his funny, disproportionate drawings. These sketches are very short light essays. Characteristic of the man, they are chiefly satires on society. *Christmas Sketches* is such a collection. Then there are the *Roundabout Papers* which Thackeray contributed to the *Cornhill Magazine* when he was its editor.

Prose and Essays of the Victorian Era

THE STORMING OF THE BASTILLE

From *The French Revolution*

THOMAS CARLYLE

By Way of Introduction: It has remained for a twentieth-century invention to furnish a satisfactory simile for Carlyle pouring forth his almost incoherent account of the French Revolution. He was a glorified radio announcer, standing, as it were, at the ringside of the battle of the century—the tumultous eighteenth century. Though the battle was fought and won six years before Carlyle was born, it comes to us hot from his pages as if, instead, he were being borne by the crowd through the streets of Paris, microphone to his lips, shouting to the world the moment-by-moment blows that are felling the Bastille.

"And now, friends, we switch you over to our announcer, Mr. Thomas Carlyle, who will pick up the story. Here we are—"

THE Bastille[1] is besieged!

On, then, all Frenchmen that have hearts in your bodies! Roar with all your throats of cartilage and metal, ye sons of liberty; stir spasmodically whatsover of utmost faculty is in you,

---

[1] BASTILLE—The former state-prison of France, begun in 1370, one of the strongest fortresses and most dreaded prisons of Europe. On July 14, 1789, the mobs of Paris stormed the fortress and demanded its surrender. The governor of the prison pretended to comply, then had his soldiers fire into the mob and the fight was on.

561

soul, body, or spirit, for it is the hour! Smite thou, Louis Tournay, cartwright of the Marais, old soldier of the Regiment Dauphine;[2] smite at that outer drawbridge chain, though the fiery hail whistles around thee! Never, over nave or felloe, did thy axe strike such a stroke. Down with it, man; down with it to Orcus;[3] let the whole accursed edifice sink thither, and tyranny be swallowed up forever! Mounted, some say, on the roof of the guard-room, some "on bayonets stuck into joints of the wall," Louis Tournay smites, brave Aubin Bonnemère (also an old soldier) seconding him. The chain yields, breaks; the huge drawbridge slams down, thundering. Glorious! and yet, alas! it is still but the outworks. The eight grim towers with their invalide musketry,[4] their paving-stone and cannon-mouths still soar aloft intact; ditch yawning impassable, stone-faced; the inner drawbridge with its back toward us; the Bastille is still to take!

To describe this siege of the Bastille (thought to be one of the most important in history) perhaps transcends the talent of mortals. . . . Paris, wholly,[5] has got to the acme of its frenzy, whirled all ways by panic madness. At every street-barricade there whirls, simmering a minor whirlpool, strengthening the barricade, since God knows what is coming; and all minor whirlpools play distractedly into that grand fire-maelstrom which is lashing round the Bastille.

And so it lashes and roars. Cholat, the wine-merchant, has become an impromptu cannoneer. See Georget, of the marine service, fresh from Brest,[6] play the King of Siam's cannon. Singular (if we were not used to the like). Georget lay last night taking his ease at his inn; the King of Siam's cannon also lay, knowing nothing of *him* for a hundred years; yet now, at the right instant, they have got together, and discourse eloquent music; for, hearing what was toward, Georget sprang from the Brest diligence, and ran. Gardes Francaises,[7] also, will be here with real artillery. Were not the walls so thick! Upward from

[2] REGIMENT DAUPHINE—Regiment of the prince.
[3] ORCUS—In Roman mythology, the underworld, the abode of the dead.
[4] INVALIDE MUSKETRY—The handful of soldiers defending the Bastille; *invalide* meaning originally a wounded soldier, later, any veteran.
[5] PARIS, WHOLLY—A mob of about 12,000 citizens, armed with whatever they could lay hands on.
[6] BREST—A French seaport.
[7] GARDES FRANCAISES—French guards.

the esplanade, horizontally from all neighboring roofs and windows, flashes one irregular deluge of musketry, without effect. The invalides lie flat, firing comparatively at their ease from behind stone; hardly through port-holes show the tip of a nose. We fall, shot, and make no impression!

Let conflagration rage of whatsoever is combustible! Guard rooms are burnt, invalides mess-rooms. A distracted "perukemaker with two fiery torches" is burning "the saltpeters of the arsenal," had not a woman run screaming, had not a patriot, with some tincture of natural philosophy, instantly struck the wind out of him (butt of musket on pit of stomach), overturned barrels, and stayed the devouring element. A young, beautiful lady seized, escaping, in these outer courts, and thought, falsely, to be de Launay's [8] daughter, shall be burnt in de Launay's sight; she lies, swooned, on a paillasse; [9] but, again, a patriot—it is brave Aubin Bonnemère, the old soldier—dashes in, and rescues her. Straw is burnt; three cartloads of it, hauled hither, go up in white smoke, almost to the choking of patriotism itself; so that Elie had, with singed brows, to drag back one cart, and Réole, the "gigantic haberdasher," another. Smoke as of Tophet,[10] confusion as of Babel,[11] noise as of the crack of doom!

Blood flows, the aliment of new madness. The wounded are carried into houses of the Rue Cerisaie,[12] the dying leave their last mandate not to yield till the accursed stronghold fall. And yet, alas! how fall? The walls are so thick! Deputations, three in number, arrive from the Hôtel-de-Ville.[13] . . . These wave their town flag in the arched gateway, and stand, rolling their drum, but to no purpose. In such crack of doom de Launay cannot hear them, dare not believe them; they return, with justified rage, the whew of lead still singing in their ears. What to do? The firemen are here, squirting with their fire-pumps on the invalides cannon to wet the touch-holes; they unfortunately cannot squirt so high, but produce only clouds of

---

[8] DE LAUNAY—The governor of the prison. He was killed by the mob.
[9] PAILLASSE—Bed of straw.
[10] TOPHET—Tō'phet, part of a valley near Jerusalem, used for burning refuse; hence, hell.
[11] BABEL—Bā'bel, the tower described in *Genesis* xi:9; hence, confusion of sound, tumult.
[12] RUE CERISAIE—A neighboring street.
[13] HÔTEL-DE-VILLE—Town-house, guild-hall.

spray. Individuals of classical knowledge propose *catapults*. Santerre, the sonorous brewer of the suburb Saint-Antoine, advises rather that the place be fired by "a mixture of phosphorous and oil of turpentine spouted up through forcing-pumps." O Spinola-Santerre,[14] hast thou the mixture *ready?* Every man his own engineer! And still the fire-deluge abates not; even women are firing, and Turks—at least one woman (with her sweetheart) and one Turk. Gardes Francaises have come; real cannon, real cannoneers. Usher Maillard is busy; half-pay Elie, half-pay Hulin, rage in the midst of thousands.

How the great Bastille clock ticks (inaudible) to its inner court, there, at its ease, hour after hour; as if nothing special, for it or the world, were passing! It tolled one when the firing began, and is now pointing toward five, and still the firing slakes not. Far down in their vaults, the seven prisoners hear muffled din as of earthquakes; their turnkeys answer vaguely.

Woe to thee, de Launay, with thy poor hundred invalides! . . .

What shall de Launay do? One thing only de Launay could have done—what he said he would do. Fancy him sitting, from the first, with lighted taper, within arm's-length of the powder-magazine; motionless, like an old Roman senator, or bronze lamp-holder; coldly apprising Thuriot,[15] and all men, by a slight motion of his eye, what his resolution was. Harmless he sat there, while unharmed; but the king's fortress, meanwhile, could, might, would, or should in nowise be surrendered, save to the king's messenger; one old man's life is worthless, so it be lost with honor; but think, ye brawling *canaille*, how will it be when a whole Bastille springs skyward? In such statuesque, taper-holding attitude, one fancies de Launay might have left Thuriot, the red clerks of the Basoche,[16] cure of St. Stephen, and all the tagrag and bobtail of the world, to work their will.

And yet, withal, he could not do it. Hast thou considered how each man's heart is so tremulously responsive to the hearts

---

[14] SPINOLA-SANTERRE—Santerre was a leader of the mob; Spinola was an Italian general who fought valiantly with the Spanish against the Netherlands in the early seventeenth century.

[15] THURIOT—A revolutionary leader.

[16] RED CLERKS OF BASOCHE, etc.—The revolutionists.

of all men? Hast thou noted how omnipotent is the very sound of many men? How their shriek of indignation palsies the strong soul? Their howl of contumely withers with unfelt pangs? . . . Great is the combined voice of men, the utterance of their *instincts,* which are truer than their *thoughts;* it is the greatest a man encounters, among the sounds and shadows which make up this world of time. He who can resist that, has his footing somewhere *beyond* time. Distracted he hovers between two—hopes in the middle of despair; surrenders not his fortress; declares that he will blow it up, seizes torches to blow it up, and does not blow it. Unhappy old de Launay, it is the death agony of the Bastille and thee! Jail, jailoring, and jailor, all three, such as they may have been, must finish.

For four hours now has the world-bedlam roared; call it the world-chimera, blowing fire! The poor invalides have sunk under their battlements, or rise only with reversed muskets; they have made a white flag of napkins, go beating the chamade, or seeming to beat, for one can hear nothing. The very Swiss[17] at the portcullis look weary of firing, disheartened in the firedeluge; a port-hole at the drawbridge is opened, as by one that would speak. See Huissier Maillard, the shifty man! On his plank, swinging over the abyss of that stoned ditch, plank resting on parapet, balanced by weight of patriots, he hovers perilous—such a dove toward such an ark! Deftly, thou shifty ushers; one man already fell and lies smashed, far down there against the masonry! Usher Maillard falls not; deftly, unerringly, he walks, with outspread palm. The Swiss holds a paper through the port-hole; the shifty usher snatches it and returns. Terms of surrender: Pardon, immunity to all! Are they accepted? *"Foi d'officer* (on the word of an officer)," answers half-pay Hulin, or half-pay Elie—for men do not agree on it—"they are!" Sinks the drawbridge, Usher Maillard bolting it when down; rushes in the living deluge; the Bastille is fallen!

Victorie! La Bastille est prise![18]

[17] Swiss—Swiss mercenaries.
[18] *Victorie! La Bastille est prise*—Victory! The Bastille is taken.

Vocabulary Study: If there are pupils in the class who have studied French, it would be helpful for them to list on the blackboard all French names and words occurring in the essay, indicating the correct pronunciation for each and, if translatable, the meaning. In the case of doubtful words, one of the teachers should be consulted. Be sure you know the meaning of: *cartilage; nave; felloe; maelstrom; diligence; esplanade; peruke; saltpeter; arsenal; haberdasher; aliment; deputations; catapults; slakes; turnkey; canaille; bedlam; chimera; chamade; portcullis; usher; immunity.*

Give the word-history of *maelstrom;* of *bedlam;* of *chimera.* What are synonyms for *slakes;* for *immunity?* How many different languages are represented in the root-words for the above list?

By Way of Appreciation: The *French Revolution* was Carlyle's masterpiece. It remains his most readable work, perhaps chiefly because here was a subject admirably suited to the Scotchman's explosive style. Glance at a page of any of Carlyle's works and you will find it peppered with dashes, exclamation points, and question marks. There are many incomplete sentences. Yet Carlyle ranks as one of the great Victorians. Why?

Well, in the first place, he was a personality as distinctive as his writings—strong, brusque, honest, fiery. Then, he was a student of letters and of men. He was especially interested in German literature and philosophy. His opinions are the result of careful reflection and he utters them with conviction.

Carlyle's curious style is undoubtedly a handicap to the general reader. In his more deeply philosophical works such as *Sartor Resartus (The Tailor Retailored),* besides the sometimes chaotic sentences, there is a complicated allegory—an allegory within an allegory—to perplex the reader. As a result, Carlyle, a leading figure in literary London little over fifty years ago, has today fewer readers than his more smooth-spoken contemporaries—Ruskin, for instance, or Newman or Macaulay.

Suggestions for Study: Instead of leaving us with the general notion that men of all trades helped storm the Bastille, Carlyle mentions ten different occupations represented in the mob. Can you find them all? Note the scarcity of adjectives and adverbs. Why? List ten vivid nouns and ten expressive verbs from the essay. Read the description of mob action in Ruskin's *Of Nations.* Can you illustrate Ruskin's points by passages from *The Fall of the Bastille?* Where do Carlyle's sympathies lie—with the mob or with the defenders of the prison? How do you know? Should de Launay have blown up the Bastille?

Exercises and Creative Work: Retell *The Fall of the Bastille* in condensed form, using the past tense, but keeping the account lively and specific. How will this account differ from a précis of the essay?

Prepare a short history of the Bastille to give before the class.

Dozens of novels have been set in the background of the French Revolution; notably, Dickens' *Tale of Two Cities,* D'Orczy's *Scarlet Pimpernel,* Davis' *The Whirlwind,* and Sabatini's *Scaramouche.* An interesting critical essay might be written on the subject, *Living through the Revolution in Fiction.*

LONDON IN 1685

From *History of England*, Vol. 1, Chap. 3

THOMAS BABINGTON MACAULAY

By Way of Introduction: Defining *history*, Macaulay once said, "It should invest with the reality of human flesh and blood, beings whom we are all too much inclined to consider as personified qualities in an allegory; call up our ancestors before us with all their peculiarities of language, manners, and garb; show us over their houses, seat us at their tables, rummage their old-fashioned wardrobes, explain the uses of their ponderous furniture."

It was his conscientious efforts to meet that definition which stretched his discussion of sixteen years of English history into five full-length volumes and which at the same time made those volumes the best-sellers of the day. The work ran through ten thousand copies in a few weeks. Said Macaulay (and he was a modest man), "I remember no success so complete, and I remember all Byron's poems and all Scott's novels."

A short selection from the *History* is enough to convince one that it is still entertaining and valuable reading.

THE position of London, relatively to the other towns of the empire, was, in the time of Charles the Second far higher than at present. For at present the population of London is little more than six times the population of Manchester or of Liverpool. In the days of Charles the Second the population of London was more than seventeen times the population of Bristol or of Norwich. It may be doubted whether any other instance can be mentioned of a great kingdom in which the first city was more than seventeen times as large as the second. There is reason to believe that, in 1685, London had been, during about half a century, the most populous capital in Europe. The inhabitants, who are now[1] at least nineteen hundred thousand, were then probably a little more than half a million. London had in the world only one commercial rival, now long outstripped, the mighty and opulent Amsterdam.

Of the metropolis, the City, properly so called, was the most important division. At the time of the Restoration it had been built, for the most part, of wood and plaster;[2] the few bricks that were used were ill baked; the booths where goods were exposed to sale projected far into the streets, and were overhung by the upper stories. A few specimens of this architecture may still be seen in those districts which were not reached by the great fire.[3] That fire had, in a few days, covered a space of little less than a square mile with the ruins of eighty-nine churches and of thirteen thousand houses. But the city had risen again with a celerity which had excited the admiration of neighboring countries. Unfortunately, the old lines of the streets had been to a great extent preserved; and those lines, originally traced in an age when even princesses performed their journeys on horseback, were often too narrow to allow wheeled carriages to pass each other with ease, and were therefore ill adapted for the residence of wealthy persons in an age when a coach and six was a fashionable luxury. The style of building was, however, far superior to that of the city which had perished. The ordinary material was brick, of much better quality than had formerly been used.

[1] Now—The first volume of the *History,* from which this selection is taken, was published in 1848. The estimated population in 1933 was 4,396,421 for London proper and 8,202,818 for London and its suburbs.
[2] BUILT OF WOOD AND PLASTER—For this reason the houses and buildings were infested with rats, spreaders of disease. It is interesting to note that after the great fire the city was never again the victim of a great plague such as that which raged in 1665.
[3] GREAT FIRE—The great fire of London in 1666.

We should greatly err if we were to suppose that any of the streets and squares then bore the same aspect as at present. The great majority of the houses, indeed, have, since that time, been wholly or in great part rebuilt. If the most fashionable parts of the capital could be placed before us, such as they then were, we should be disgusted by their squalid appearance and poisoned by their noisome atmosphere. In Covent Garden a filthy and noisy market was held close to the dwellings of the great. Fruit women screamed, carters fought, cabbage stalks and rotten apples accumulated in heaps at the thresholds of the Countess of Berkshire and of the Bishop of Durham. The center of Lincoln's Inn Fields [4] was an open space where the rabble congregated every evening, within a few yards of Cardigan House and Winchester [5] House, to hear mountebanks harangue, to see bears dance, and to set dogs at oxen.

The houses were not numbered. There would indeed have been little advantage in numbering them; for of the coachmen, chairmen, porters, and errand boys of London, a very small portion could read. It was necessary to use marks which the most ignorant could understand. The shops were therefore distinguished by painted signs, which gave a gay and grotesque aspect to the streets. The walk from Charing Cross to Whitechapel [6] lay through an endless succession of Saracen's Heads, Royal Oaks, Blue Bears, and Golden Lambs, which disappeared when they were no longer required for the direction of the common people.

When the evening closed in, the difficulty and danger of walking about London became serious indeed. The garret windows were opened, and pails were emptied, with little regard to those who were passing below. Falls, bruises, and broken bones were of constant occurrence. For, till the last year of the reign of Charles the Second, most of the streets were left in profound darkness. Thieves and robbers plied their trade with impunity; yet they were hardly so terrible to peaceable citizens as another class of ruffians. It was a favorite amusement of dissolute young gentlemen to swagger by night about the town, breaking windows, upsetting sedans, beating quiet men, and offering rude

[4] LINCOLN'S INN FIELDS—The largest square in London, named from its proximity to Lincoln's Inn.
[5] CARDIGAN . . . WINCHESTER—Great residences.
[6] CHARING CROSS TO WHITECHAPEL—Across London.

caresses to pretty women. The machinery for keeping the peace was utterly contemptible. There was an act of Common Council which provided that more than a thousand watchmen should be constantly on the alert in the city, from sunset to sunrise, and that every inhabitant should take his turn of duty. But the act was negligently executed. Few of those who were summoned left their homes; and those few generally found it more agreeable to tipple in alehouses than to pace the streets.

It ought to be noticed that, in the last year of the reign of Charles the Second, began a great change in the police of London,—a change which has perhaps added as much to the happiness of the great body of the people as revolutions of much greater fame. An ingenious projector, named Edward Heming, obtained letters patent conveying to him, for a term of years, the exclusive right of lighting up London. He undertook, for a moderate consideration, to place a light before every tenth door, on moonless nights, from Michaelmas to Lady Day,[7] and from six to twelve of the clock. Those who now see the capital all the year round, from dusk to dawn, blazing with a splendor compared with which the illuminations for La Hogue[8] and Blenheim[9] would have looked pale, may perhaps smile to think of Heming's lanterns, which glimmered feebly before one house in ten during a small part of one night in three. But such was not the feeling of his contemporaries. His scheme was enthusiastically applauded and furiously attacked. The friends of improvement extolled him as the greatest of all the benefactors of his city. What, they asked, were the boasted inventions of Archimedes[10] when compared with the achievement of the man who had turned the nocturnal shades into noonday? In spite of these eloquent eulogies, the cause of darkness was not left undefended. There were fools in that age who opposed the introduction of what was called the new light as strenuously as fools in our age have opposed the introduction of vaccination and

[7] MICHAELMAS TO LADY DAY—September 29 to the day of the Feast of the Annunciation, March 25.
[8] LA HOGUE—The English victory of La Hogue. This naval battle was fought between the English and the French in the war which Louis XIV brought against England in an attempt to put King James II back on the throne after the English had expelled him.
[9] BLENHEIM—The battle in which Marlborough defeated the French in 1704.
[10] ARCHIMEDES—An ancient Greek scientist.

railroads, as strenuously as the fools of an age anterior to the dawn of history doubtless opposed the introduction of the plough and of alphabetical writing. Many years after the date of Heming's patent, there were extensive districts in which no lamp was seen.

Vocabulary Study: *Celerity; squalid* (note pronunciation); *rabble; mountebanks; harangue; impunity; sedan; police; eulogies; anterior.*
Note the histories of *squalid* and *rabble.*
Give two synonyms each for *eulogy* and *anterior.*

By Way of Appreciation: When the *History of England* first issued from the press, while Macaulay was still in doubt about its success, he wrote in his diary, "At all events, I have aimed high; I have tried to do something that may be remembered; I have had the year 2000, or even 3000, often in my mind; I have sacrificed nothing to temporary fashions of thought and style; and if I fail, my failure will be honorable."

But he did not fail. Nearly ninety years have passed since the words were written, and the *History* has an assured place among the world's great books. It was written with an honest purpose. Years of labor were spent in gathering the material. It sparkles with the brilliance of an extraordinary genius. It carries its message in an easy, direct style. For these reasons, it is not only history but art, and therefore enduring.

Suggestions for Study: Find, if possible, a map of the city of London and locate upon it the limits of the City proper. Locate also the parts of the city which you have read about in this and other selections—such places as Westminster, Covent Garden, Fleet Street, Lincoln's Inn Fields, etc.

Why are the streets of old London narrow and crooked? How were shops and inns designated in 1685? Why? In an essay entitled *On the Naming of Streets,* Max Beerbohm protests against the modern rebuilding of some sections of London, with streets being widened, straightened, and renamed. Do you think that in such a case progress should be sacrificed to sentiment? or sentiment to progress? Which period (so far as you can judge) has produced the greater changes—the 165 years between the death of Charles II and Macaulay's *History,* or the 85 years between 1850 and the present? Illustrate by specific examples. Select at least five examples of Macaulay's use of specific detail as a means to vivid impressiveness.

Exercises and Creative Work: Many interesting topics for long themes may be found in the city of London and its history. Two interesting ones are the Great Plague and the Great Fire.

The following are suggestive topics for short themes: *The Fascination of Facts* (for an essay of appreciation on history); *This Modern Age—a Study in Relativity.*

THE DEFINITION OF A GENTLEMAN

From *The Idea of a University*

JOHN HENRY NEWMAN

By Way of Introduction: Someone has said, "Politeness is kindness"—an easy definition, but like many another, easier to learn than to apply. The kindness of the gentleman shows itself in so many ways that a superficial acceptance of the word is not enough. In the following essay, Cardinal Newman—who was himself a gentleman loved and honored over all Europe—shows the many ways in which one may manifest his kindness.

IT IS almost a definition of a gentleman to say he is one who never inflicts pain. This description is both refined and, as far as it goes, accurate. He is mainly occupied in merely removing the obstacles which hinder the free and unembarrassed action of those about him, and he concurs with their movements rather than takes the initiative himself. His benefits may be considered as parallel to what are called comforts or conveniences in arrangements of a personal nature; like an easy chair or a good fire, which do their part in dispelling cold and fatigue, though nature provides both means of rest and animal heat without them. The true gentleman in like manner carefully avoids whatever may cause a jar or a jolt in the minds of those with whom he is cast—all clashing of opinion, or collision of feeling, all restraint, or suspicion, or gloom, or resentment; his great concern being to make every one at their ease and at home. He has his eyes on all his company; he is tender towards the bashful, gentle towards the distant, and merciful towards the absurd; he can recollect to whom he is speaking; he guards against unreasonable allusions, or topics which may irritate; he is seldom prominent in conversation, and never wearisome. He makes light of favors while he does them, and seems to be receiving when he is conferring. He never speaks of himself except when compelled, never defends himself by a mere retort, he has no ears for slander or gossip, is scrupulous in imputing motives to those who interfere with him, and interprets everything for the best. He is never mean or little in his disputes, never takes unfair advantage, never mistakes personalities or sharp sayings for arguments, or insinuates evil which he dare not say out. From a long sighted prudence, he observes the maxim of the ancient sage, that we should ever conduct ourselves towards our enemy as if he were one day to be our friend. He has too much good sense to be affronted at insults, he is too well employed to remember injuries, and too indolent to bear malice. He is patient, forbearing, and resigned, on philosophical principles; he submits to pain because it is inevitable, to bereavement because it is irreparable, and to death because it is his destiny. If he engages in controversy of any kind, his disciplined intellect preserves him from the blundering discourtesy of better, perhaps, but less educated minds, who, like blunt weapons, tear and hack, instead of cutting clean, who mistake the point in argument, waste their strength on trifles, misconceive their adversary, and leave the question more involved than they find it. He may be right or wrong in his opinion, but he is too clear-headed to be unjust; he is as simple as he is forcible, and as brief as he is decisive. Nowhere shall we find greater candor, consideration, indulgence; he throws himself into the minds of his opponents, he accounts for their mistakes. He knows the weakness of human reason as well as its strength, its province and its limits. If he be an unbeliever, he will be too profound and large-minded to ridicule religion or to act against it; he is too wise to be a dogmatist or fanatic in his infidelity. He respects piety and devotion; he even supports institutions as venerable, beautiful, or useful, to which he does not assent; he honors the ministers of religion, and it contents him to decline its mysteries without assailing or denouncing them. He is a friend of religious toleration, and that not only because his philosophy has taught him to look on all forms of faith with an impartial eye, but also from the gentleness and effeminacy of feeling which is the attendant on civilization.

Vocabulary Study: The following words are probably not strangers to you; but unless you know them well, they will repay study. Note the context of each, and try to find the exact shade of meaning in each case. Notice how many have been formed by joining a common Latin prefix to a common Latin stem. *Concur; parallel; dispel; allusion; confer; scrupulous; impute; insinuate; prudence; maxim; sage; affronted; indolent; philosophical; irreparable* (note pronunciation); *controversy* (note pronunciation); *misconceive; adversary; candor; indulgence; dogmatist; fanatic; infidelity; venerable; effeminacy.*

Distinguish between the synonyms, *indolent, lazy, slothful.* Distinguish between *dogmatist* and *fanatic.* Find synonyms for *scrupulous, insinuate, misconceive,* and *candor.* Find antonyms for *adversary, infidelity,* and *effeminate.*

By Way of Appreciation: Literature has been called "the art that expresses life in words." Sometimes it expresses broadly the life of a nation or a period. Sometimes it expresses the life of an individual—the writer himself—and then we like it best, for it then seems warm and real.

Cardinal Newman's writings have this personal significance. We feel that what he wrote he believed and practiced. He was a teacher and a preacher of singular sweetness of character. Writing was only one of many ways in which he gave himself to the world. In middle life he renounced the Episcopal church for the Catholic. As rector of the University of Dublin, he gave before the faculties a series of addresses on *The Idea of a University.* It is from one of those lectures that *The Definition of a Gentleman* is taken. Even such a short selection discloses Newman's wide learning, his clear expression, and his gentle nature.

Suggestions for Study: In what sense is the word *refined* used in the second sentence? Explain also the uses of *indolent, indulgence* and *effeminacy* in their respective sentences. How many of the distinctions of the gentleman are fundamental in his character? How many are habits or manners that may be acquired? What are the discourtesies of conversation that a gentleman avoids? How does he conduct himself in any controversy? Do you accept all of Newman's qualifications as essential to the gentleman? If there are any which you question, make note of them for class discussion. Do you think of any qualifications which might be added? Can you think of any person—man or woman—who meets most of these requirements? If so, what is the effect of his company on you and on others? Which of these characteristics have you most need of cultivating? Which of them seem already inherent in your character?

Exercises and Creative Work: Write a précis of the essay.

You may find an idea for a thoughtful essay in one of the following subjects: *Group Courtesy* (Do Americans show it? Can schools develop it? Should they?); *Behavior and the Movies; Wanted: a Gentle Nation* (See Ruskin's *Of Nations*); *Ladies, Yesterday and Today.*

Another lecture delivered by Cardinal Newman begins, "A university is not a birthplace of poets or of immortal authors, of founders of schools, leaders of colonies, or conquerors of nations." Thus we learn what a university is *not.* Read the rest of the lecture and be prepared to tell the class what a university *is.*

OF BOOKS, OF READING, OF NATIONS

From *Sesame and Lilies*

JOHN RUSKIN

By Way of Introduction: *Sesame*[1] *and Lilies* is the composite title given to two lectures which Ruskin delivered in 1864 before a group of working men at Manchester. The first lecture, which is about books, has the special title "Of Kings' Treasuries." The address closed with a plea to have more good books made easily available to the people of England, for these books would be the "Sesame which opens doors— doors not of robbers', but of kings' treasuries." The second lecture, "Of Queens' Gardens," presents Ruskin's view on education for women and on woman's place in the world. The three selections which follow are from the first lecture. The "King's Treasuries"—as you have guessed —are the riches to be found in books.

OF BOOKS

ALL books are divisible into two classes,—the books of the hour, and the books of all time. Mark this distinction; it is not one of quality only. It is not merely the bad book that does not last, and the good one that does; it is a distinction of species. There are good books for the hour, and good ones for all time; bad books for the hour, and bad ones for all time. I must define the two kinds before I go farther.

The good book of the hour, then,—I do not speak of the bad ones,—is simply the useful or pleasant talk of some person whom you cannot otherwise converse with, printed for you. Very useful often, telling you what you need to know; very pleasant often, as a sensible friend's present talk would be. These bright accounts of travel; good-humored and witty discussions of question; lively or pathetic story-telling in the form of novel; firm fact-telling, by the real agents concerned in the events of passing history,—all these books of the hour, multiplying among us as education becomes more general, are a peculiar possession of the present age. We ought to be entirely thankful for them, and entirely ashamed of ourselves if we make no good use of them. But we make the worst possible use if we allow them to usurp the place of true books; for strictly speaking, they are not

---

[1] *Sesame*—In the story of *Ali Baba and the Forty Thieves* from *The Arabian Nights*, "Open Sesame (Sĕs′à-mē)" was the magic phrase which would open the entrance to the robbers' cave.

575

books at all, but merely letters or newspapers in good print. Our friend's letter may be delightful or necessary today,—whether worth keeping or not, is to be considered. The newspaper may be entirely proper at breakfast-time, but assuredly it is not reading for all day; so, though bound up in a volume, the long letter which gives you so pleasant an account of the inns and roads and weather last year at such a place, or which tells you that amusing story, or gives you the real circumstances of such and such events, however valuable for occasional reference, may not be in the real sense of the word, a "book" at all, nor, in the real sense, to be "read." A book is essentially not a talked thing, but a written thing, and written not with a view of mere communication, but of permanence. The book of talk is printed only because its author cannot speak to thousands of people at once; if he could he would,—the volume is mere *multiplication* of his voice. You cannot talk to your friend in India; if you could, you would. You write instead; that is mere *conveyance* of voice. But a book is written, not to multiply the voice merely, not to carry it merely, but to perpetuate it. The author has something to say which he perceives to be true and useful, or helpfully beautiful. So far as he knows, no one has yet said it; so far as he knows, no one else can say it. He is bound to say it clearly and melodiously if he may; clearly, at all events. In the sum of his life he finds this to be the thing or group of things manifest to him,—this, the piece of true knowledge or sight which his share of sunshine and earth has permitted him to seize. He would fain set it down forever, engrave it on rock if he could, saying, "This is the best of me; for the rest, I ate and drank and slept, loved and hated, like another. My life was as the vapor, and is not; but this I saw and knew,—this, if anything of mine, is worth your memory." This is his "writing"; it is in his small human way, and with whatever degree of true inspiration is in him, his inscription or scripture. That is a "Book."

OF READING

VERY ready we are to say of a book, "How good this is,—that's exactly what I think!" But the right feeling is, "How strange that is! I never thought of that before, and yet I see it is true; or if I do not now, I hope I shall some day." But whether thus submissively or not, at least be sure that you go to the author to get at *his* meaning, not to find yours. Judge it afterward if you think yourself qualified to do so; but ascertain it first. And be sure also, if the author is worth anything, that you will not get at his meaning all at once—nay, that at his whole meaning you will not for a long time arrive in any wise. Not that he does not say what he means, and in strong words too; but he cannot say it all, and what is more strange, *will* not, but in a hidden way and in parable, in order that he may be sure you want it. I cannot quite see the reason of this, nor analyze that cruel reticence in the breasts of wise men which makes them always hide their deeper thought. They do not give it you by way of help, but of reward, and will make themselves sure that you deserve it before they allow you to reach it. But it is the same with the physical type of wisdom, gold. There seems, to you and me, no reason why the electric forces of the earth should not carry whatever there is of gold within it at once to the mountain-tops; so that kings and people might know that all the gold they could get was there, and without any trouble of digging, or anxiety, or chance, or waste of time, cut it away, and coin as much as they needed. But Nature does not manage it so. She puts it in little fissures in the earth, nobody knows where; you may dig long and find none; you must dig painfully to find any.

And it is just the same with men's best wisdom. When you come to a good book, you must ask yourself, "Am I inclined to work as an Australian miner would? Are my pickaxes and shovels in good order, and am I in good trim, myself, my sleeves well up to the elbow, and my breath good, and my temper?" And keeping the figure a little longer, even at a cost of tiresomeness, for it is a thoroughly useful one, the metal you are in search of being the author's mind or meaning, his words are as the rock which you have to crush and smelt in order to get at it. And your pickaxes are your own care, wit, and learning; your smelting furnace is your own thoughtful soul. Do not hope to get any good author's meaning without those tools and that fire; often you will need sharpest, finest chiselling and patientest fusing, before you can gather one grain of the metal.

And, therefore, first of all, I tell you earnestly and authoritatively (I *know* I am right in this), you must get into the habit of looking intensely at words, and assuring yourself of their meaning, syllable by syllable—nay, letter by letter. For though it is only by reason of the opposition of letters in the function of signs, to sounds in the function of signs, that the study of books is called "literature," and that a man versed in it is called, by the consent of nations, a man of letters instead of a man of books or of words, you may yet connect with that accidental nomenclature this real fact,—that you might read all the books in the British Museum (if you could live long enough) and remain an utterly "illiterate," uneducated person; but that if you read ten pages of a good book, letter by letter,—that is to say, with real accuracy,—you are forevermore in some measure an educated person. The entire difference between education and non-education (as regards the merely intellectual part of it) consists in this accuracy. A well-educated gentleman may not know many languages, may not be able to speak any but his own, may have read very few books. But whatever language he knows, he knows precisely; whatever word he pronounces, he pronounces rightly. Above all, he is learned in the *peerage* of words, knows the words of true descent and ancient blood, at a glance, from the words of modern *canaille*, remembers all their ancestry, their intermarriages, distant relationships, and the extent to which they were admitted, and offices they held, among the national *noblesse* of words at any time and in any country. But an uneducated person may know, by memory, many languages, and talk them all, and yet truly know not a word of any,—not a word even of his own.

OF NATIONS

As IN nothing is a gentleman better to be discerned from a vulgar person, so in nothing is a gentle nation (such nations have been) better to be discerned from a mob, than in this,—that their feelings are constant and just, results of due contemplation, and of equal thought. You can talk a mob into anything; its feelings may be—usually are—on the whole, generous and right; but it has no foundation for them, no hold of them; you may tease or tickle it into any, at your pleasure; it thinks by infection, for the most part, catching an opinion like a cold, and there is nothing so little that it will not roar itself wild about, when the fit is on;—nothing so great but it will forget in an hour, when the fit is past. But a gentleman's, or a gentle nation's, passions are just, measured, and continuous. A great nation, for instance, does not spend its entire national wits[1] for a couple of months in weighing evidence of a single ruffian's having done a single murder; and for a couple of years see its own children murder each other by their thousands or tens of thousands a day, considering only what the effect is likely to be on the price of cotton,[2] and caring nowise to determine which side of battle is in the wrong. Neither does a great nation send its poor little boys to jail for stealing six walnuts; and allow its bankrupts to steal their hundreds of thousands with a bow, and its bankers, rich with poor men's savings, to close their doors "under circumstances over which they have no control," with a "by your leave"; and large landed estates to be bought by men who have made their money by going with armed steamers up and down the China Seas, selling opium at the cannon's mouth,[3] and altering, for the benefit of the foreign nation, the common highwayman's demand of "your money *or* your life," into that of "your money *and* your life." Neither does a great nation allow the lives of its innocent poor to be parched out of them by fog fever, and rotted out of them by dunghill plague, for the sake of sixpence a life extra per week to its landlords; and then debate, with drivelling tears, and diabolical sympathies, whether it ought not piously to save, and nursingly cherish, the lives of its murderers. Also, a great nation having made up its mind that hanging is quite the wholesomest process for its homicides in general, can yet with mercy distinguish between the degrees of guilt in homicides, and does not yelp like a pack of frost-pinched wolf-cubs on the blood track of an unhappy crazed boy, or gray-haired clodpate Othello,[4] "perplexed i' the extreme," at the very moment that it

[1] DOES NOT SPEND ITS ENTIRE NATIONAL WITS, etc.—This and the following illustrations Ruskin took from abuses current in England in 1864.

[2] EFFECT . . . ON THE PRICE OF COTTON—In spite of recent reform legislation, shocking conditions still existed in factories which continued to employ child labor.

[3] SELLING OPIUM AT THE CANNON'S MOUTH—One of Great Britain's blackest sins was her enforcing trade in opium when the Chinese government wished to prohibit traffic in the drug.

[4] CRAZED BOY, OR . . . CLODPATE OTHELLO—A reference to two sensational murders of the time, the "Othello" being a man who had killed his wife in a frenzy of jealousy. "Perplexed i' the extreme" is a quotation from Shakespeare's *Othello*.

is sending Minister of the Crown to make polite speeches to a man who is bayoneting young girls in their fathers' sight, and killing noble youths in cool blood, faster than a country butcher kills lambs in spring. And, lastly, a great nation does not mock Heaven and its Powers, by pretending belief in a revelation which asserts the love of money to be the root of *all* evil, and declaring, at the same time, that it is actuated, and intends to be actuated, in all chief national deeds and measures, by no other love.

No nation can last, which has made a mob of itself, however generous at heart. It must discipline its passions, and direct them, or they will discipline *it*, one day, with scorpion-whips. Above all, a nation cannot last as a money-making job: it cannot with impunity,—it cannot with existence,—go on despising literature, despising science, despising art, despising nature, despising compassion, and concentrating its soul on Pence.

Vocabulary Study: Ruskin was a precise scholar; and his words, while not uncommon or difficult, are used with accuracy and care. Study these words, as the author advises, syllable by syllable, absorbing their meanings and descent as well as mastering their pronunciation: OF BOOKS—*Species; agent; usurp; communication; permanence; conveyance; perpetuate; manifest; fain; inscription; scripture.* OF READING—*Submissively; ascertain; parable; reticence; physical; fissures; fusing* (see *fuse*); *function; literature; letters; literate; illiterate; nomenclature; peerage; canaille; noblesse.* OF NATIONS—*Constant; just; contemplation; infection; drivelling; homicides; clodpate; actuated; despising; pence.*

By Way of Appreciation: "The child is father of the man," said Wordsworth. When we find, then, a great and noble man, it is wise to learn something of the childhood that fathered him. In *Praeterita* Ruskin has given us some revealing glimpses of his early years. In part, he says—

"I had Walter Scott's novels and the *Iliad* (Pope's translation) for my only reading when I was a child, on week days; on Sunday their effect was tempered by *Robinson Crusoe* and *The Pilgrim's Progress,* my mother having it deeply in her heart to make an evangelical clergyman of me.

"I had, however, still better teaching, and that compulsorily and every day of the week. My mother forced me, by steady daily toil, to learn long chapters of the Bible by heart, as well as to read it every syllable through, aloud, hard names and all, from Genesis to the *Apocalypse* [*Revelation*] about once a year; and to that discipline—patient, accurate, and resolute—I owe not only a knowledge of the book which

I find occasionally serviceable, but much of my general power of taking pains, and the best part of my taste in literature. Once knowing the 32d of *Deuteronomy*, or the 119th *Psalm*, the 15th of 1st *Corinthians*, The Sermon on the Mount, and most of the *Apocalypse*, every syllable by heart, and having always a way of thinking with myself what words meant, it was not possible for me, even in the foolishest times of my youth to write entirely superficial or formal English."

It is not strange that from such a childhood grew a man sober, sincere, painstaking. Books were to him something almost sacred, but only when they too were sincere and painstaking. Reading was a challenge, more exciting than the most intricate puzzle. Words, like bits of jigsaw, must be labored over before they yielded the full picture of the author's thought. With this honesty in reading and study, it is not surprising that Ruskin was distressed by insincerity and greed in life, especially in national life. He saw things straight. Why should it not be possible to conceive a nation which would think straight and act soberly? The idea is not impossible of achievement. Ruskin was an idealist, but he also had a good measure of common sense. He believed that the means to national reform lay in national education.

Have these selections made you feel that you should like to read all of *Sesame and Lilies?* It will not be easy reading; you will need your pickaxes and shovels. But you will find rich veins of ore, truths to be smelted in the furnace of "your own thoughtful soul." And if you read at least ten pages of it, "letter by letter, with real accuracy," you will be "forever in some measure an educated person." That is the kind of education that can save civilization.

Suggestions for Study: *Of Books:* Which prose selections in this volume of English literature are from books which Ruskin would designate as "good books of the hour"? Which are from "books of all time"? Which of the ten best-sellers of last year do you think will survive as books for all time? What kinds of printed matter today serve as mere *multiplication* or *conveyance* of voice?

Of Reading—Do you think Ruskin would advise the student of English to study Latin? French? German? Other languages? Why, or why not? What is meant by the *peerage* of words? Their ancestry? Their intermarriages? In the lists of words given above under *Vocabulary Study*, which are related to each other? Do you find any that have "intermarried"? What do you think would be Ruskin's attitude toward such expressions as *enthuse, contact* (as a verb), *yeah?* Why?

Of Nations—Which, if any, of the accusations that Ruskin brings against nineteenth-century England would be pertinent to twentieth-century America? The young aldermen, representatives, mayors of today were in high school twenty years ago. In a score of years, the government will be in *your* hands. What will you do to prepare yourselves for the responsibility?

Exercises and Creative Work: Write a précis of the one of these three essays which has the greatest appeal to you.

Write the life history of some word which you have discovered to have had an interesting development.

As a special assignment, make an outline of "Of Kings' Treasuries" or "Of Queens' Gardens"; then using your outline as a guide, give an oral summary of the essay to the class.

A LIBERAL EDUCATION

Thomas Henry Huxley

By Way of Introduction: The pupil who has read thoughtfully the prose selections up to this point must have observed certain great differences between the older systems of education and modern American systems. He must have noticed the classical complexion of English learning. Children barely able to talk were set at work upon the Greek alphabet and the rules of Latin grammar. A good scholar, ten or twelve years old, could turn out original verses in Latin—in fact, was expected to. De Quincey tells us that one of his diversions in his early teens was to translate the daily newspapers into Greek. All of which brings us to a second observation, that the older English system was very rigid and very thorough. There was little variation in the subjects taught or the classics read in the different schools; and the amount of reading—in English, Latin, and Greek literature and philosophy—expected of the young scholar seems to us staggering. For five hundred years the same traditions governed the classrooms of England. It was education for culture rather than for use. With these facts in mind, you will appreciate the revolutionary nature of Huxley's address on the subject *A Liberal Education* from which the following essay has been taken. Try to reconstruct the mental attitude of the British audience who first listened to these words.

Suppose it were perfectly certain that the life and fortune of every one of us would, one day or other, depend upon his winning or losing a game of chess. Don't you think that we should all consider it to be a primary duty to learn at least the names and the moves of the pieces; to have a notion of gambit, and a keen eye for all the means of giving and getting out of check? Do you not think that we should look with a disapprobation amounting to scorn, upon the father who allowed his son, or the state which allowed its members, to grow up without knowing a pawn from a knight?

Yet it is a very plain and elementary truth, that the life,

the fortune, and the happiness of every one of us, and, more or less, of those who are connected with us, do depend upon our knowing something of the rules of a game infinitely more difficult and complicated than chess. It is a game which has been played for untold ages, every man and woman of us being one of the two players in a game of his or her own. The chessboard is the world, the pieces are the phenomena of the universe, the rules of the game are what we call the laws of Nature. The player on the other side is hidden from us. We know that his play is always fair, just, and patient. But also we know, to our cost, that he never overlooks a mistake, or makes the smallest allowance for ignorance. To the man who plays well, the highest stakes are paid, with that sort of overflowing generosity with which the strong shows delight in strength. And one who plays ill is checkmated—without haste, but without remorse.

My metaphor will remind some of you of the famous picture in which Retzsch[1] has depicted Satan playing at chess with man for his soul. Substitute for the mocking fiend in that picture, a calm, strong angel who is playing for love, as we say, and would rather lose than win—and I should accept it as an image of human life.

Well, what I mean by Education is learning the rules of this mighty game. In other words, education is the instruction of the intellect in the laws of Nature, under which name I include not merely things and their forces but men and their ways; and the fashioning of the affections and of the will into an earnest and loving desire to move in harmony with those laws. For me education means neither more nor less than this. Anything which professes to call itself education must be tried by this standard, and if it fails to stand the test, I will not call it education, whatever may be the force of authority, or of numbers, upon the other side.

It is important to remember that, in strictness, there is no such thing as an uneducated man. Take an extreme case. Suppose that an adult man, in the full vigor of his faculties, could be suddenly placed in the world, as Adam is said to have been, and then left to do as he best might. How long would he be left uneducated? Not five minutes. Nature would begin to teach him, through the eye, the ear, the touch, the properties

[1] RETZSCH—Moritz Retzsch (1779–1857), a German painter and etcher.

of objects. Pain and pleasure would be at his elbow telling him to do this and avoid that; and by slow degrees the man would receive an education, which, if narrow, would be thorough, real, and adequate to his circumstances, though there would be no extras and very few accomplishments.

And if to this solitary man entered a second Adam, or better still, an Eve, a new and greater world, that of social and moral phenomena, would be revealed. Joys and woes, compared with which all others might seem but faint shadows, would spring from the new relations. Happiness and sorrow would take the place of the coarser monitors, pleasure and pain; but conduct would still be shaped by the observation of the natural consequences of action; or, in other words, by the laws of the nature of man.

To every one of us the world was once as fresh and new as to Adam. And then, long before we were susceptible of any other mode of instruction, Nature took us in hand, and every minute of waking life brought its educational influence, shaping our actions into rough accordance with Nature's laws, so that we might not be ended untimely by too gross disobedience. Nor should I speak of this process of education as past for any one, be he as old as he may. For every man the world is as fresh as it was at the first day, and as full of untold novelties for him who has the eyes to see them. And Nature is still continuing her patient education of us in that great university, the universe, of which we are all members—Nature having no Test-Acts.[2]

Those who take honors in Nature's university, who learn the laws which govern men and things and obey them, are the really great and successful men in this world. The great mass of mankind are the "Poll,"[3] who pick up just enough to get through without much discredit. Those who won't learn at all are plucked;[4] and then you can't come up again. Nature's pluck means extermination.

Thus the question of compulsory education is settled so far

---

[2] TEST-ACTS—Until 1871 there was enforced in all English universities a Test-Act, requiring every student to subscribe to the articles of belief of the Church of England before he could come up for a degree.

[3] POLL—An English college term for one who receives an ordinary degree without honors or distinction.

[4] PLUCKED—English slang for failed; like "flunked."

as Nature is concerned. Her bill on that question was framed and passed long ago. But, like all compulsory legislation, that of Nature is harsh and wasteful in its operation. Ignorance is visited as sharply as willful disobedience—incapacity meets with the same punishment as crime. Nature's discipline is not even a word and a blow, and the blow first; but the blow without the word. It is left to you to find out why your ears are boxed.

The object of what we commonly call education—that education in which man intervenes and which I shall distinguish as artificial education—is to make good these defects in Nature's methods; to prepare the child to receive Nature's education, neither incapably nor ignorantly, nor with willful disobedience; and to understand the preliminary symptoms of her displeasure, without waiting for the box on the ear. In short, all artificial education ought to be an anticipation of natural education. And a liberal education is an artificial education, which has not only prepared a man to escape the great evils of disobedience to natural laws, but has trained him to appreciate and to seize upon the rewards, which Nature scatters with as free a hand as her penalties.

That man, I think, has had a liberal education, who has been so trained in youth that his body is the ready servant of his will, and does with ease and pleasure all the work that, as a mechanism, it is capable of; whose intellect is a clear, cold, logic engine, with all its parts of equal strength, and in smooth working order; ready, like a steam engine, to be turned to any kind of work, and spin the gossamers as well as forge the anchors of the mind; whose mind is stored with a knowledge of the great and fundamental truths of Nature and of the laws of her operations; one who, no stunted ascetic, is full of life and fire, but whose passions are trained to come to heel by a vigorous will, the servant of a tender conscience; who has learned to love all beauty, whether of Nature or of art, to hate all vileness, and to respect others as himself.

Such an one and no other, I conceive, has had a liberal education; for he is, as completely as a man can be, in harmony with Nature. He will make the best of her, and she of him. They will get on together rarely; she as his ever beneficent mother; he as her mouthpiece, her conscious self, her minister and interpreter.

Vocabulary Study: In a dictionary or encyclopedia find an explanation of the game of *chess* and the terms used in it; such terms as *gambit, check, checkmate, pawn* and *knight*.

Like the words used by Newman and Ruskin, those in the following list are neither hard nor strange, but they will repay study. It is well to note how precisely Huxley has used them. *Phenomenon; adequate; social; moral; monitor; susceptible; extermination; compulsory; incapacity; intervenes; anticipation; liberal; mechanism; gossamers; ascetic; beneficent* (note the spelling and pronunciation); *minister.*

Look up the word history of *education,* and give the exact meaning of the word, as its derivation implies. Also indicate synonyms, and illustrate their various shades of meaning. You will be interested also to find antonyms for each synonym. Write a paragraph or so, giving your ideas about education, using these words.

By Way of Appreciation: Thomas Henry Huxley is remembered as one of the most important scientists of Victorian England. He was actively interested in the rapid developments being made in physics, chemistry, and biology; and he was influential in making science generally popular. However, his interests were not restricted to this one field. His educational background was the traditional classic one. Nor did he despise it. He was conservative in his literary tastes and recommended to every English child a careful study of the Bible, Chaucer, and Shakespeare as a means to literary culture of the highest kind.

He did believe that practical and cultural education should unite in showing men how to live wisely and happily. He was liberal and tolerant and, like Ruskin, was uncommonly blessed with a good portion of "common" sense. Living in a controversial age, he himself avoided controversies. He wanted learning to be accurate and useful; and he proved that, granted these two qualities, it may also be beautiful. Notice how clearly and reasonably he has developed his ideas in the present selection, and what a pleasantly conversational tone he has maintained.

Suggestions for Study: Put Huxley's definition of education into your own words. Distinguish between *pleasure* and *happiness,* and between *pain* and *sorrow.* Explain the sentence, "Nature's pluck means extermination." Can you name any persons who may be said to have "taken honors in Nature's university"? Give an illustration of Nature's method of teaching, "the blow without the word." Would you be satisfied with this statement of the objective of education—"to learn to love all beauty, whether of nature or of art, to hate all vileness, and to respect others as oneself"? If not, how would you change it? Was Huxley an atheist? Prove the correctness of your answer by reference to the essay. How do you think Huxley would judge the education offered by the American high school? By the American college?

Exercises and Creative Work: Make an outline of what seems to you to be an ideal course of study for a senior high school.

THE GREEN DONKEY-DRIVER

From *Travels with a Donkey*
ROBERT LOUIS STEVENSON

By Way of Introduction: Hitch-hiking is one way of getting there —somewhere. But in out-of-the-way spots with roads that are only by-paths, one still must depend upon the hike without the hitch. Then it is well to have some nimble-footed, though balky, creature to carry the pack. In southern France one still travels with a donkey if out for adventure rather than speed; and the adventures one finds differ little from those of Stevenson with that most capricious of donkeys—Modestine—way back in the 1870's.

THE bell of Monastier [1] was just striking nine as I got quit of these preliminary troubles and descended the hill through the common. As long as I was within sight of the windows, a secret shame and the fear of some laughable defeat withheld me from tampering with Modestine. She tripped along upon

[1] MONASTIER—In southern France. Stevenson's route was to take him about sixty miles through the Cévennes mountains, working southward from Monastier to Alais. The Cévennes divide the basins of the Loire and Garonne on the north from the Rhône and the Saône on the south.

her four small hoofs with a sober daintiness of gait; from time to time she shook her ears or her tail; and she looked so small under the bundle that my mind misgave me. We got across the ford without difficulty—there was no doubt about the matter, she was docility itself—and once on the other bank, where the road begins to mount through pine-woods, I took in my right hand the unhallowed staff, and with a quaking spirit applied it to the donkey. Modestine brisked up her pace for perhaps three steps, and then relapsed into her former minuet. Another application had the same effect, and so with the third. I am worthy the name of an Englishman, and it goes against my conscience to lay my hand rudely on a female. I desisted, and looked her all over from head to foot; the poor brute's knees were trembling and her breathing was distressed; it was plain that she could go no faster on a hill. God forbid, thought I, that I should brutalize this innocent creature; let her go at her own pace, and let me patiently follow.

What that pace was, there is no word mean enough to describe; it was something as much slower than a walk as a walk is slower than a run; it kept me hanging on each foot for an incredible length of time; in five minutes it exhausted the spirit and set up a fever in all the muscles of the leg. And yet I had to keep close at hand and measure my advance exactly upon hers; for if I dropped a few yards into the rear, or went on a few yards ahead, Modestine came instantly to a halt and began to browse. The thought that this was to last from here to Alais nearly broke my heart. Of all conceivable journeys, this promised to be the most tedious. I tried to tell myself it was a lovely day; I tried to charm my foreboding spirit with tobacco; but I had a vision ever present to me of the long, long roads, up hill and down dale, and a pair of figures ever infinitesimally moving, foot by foot, a yard to the minute, and, like things enchanted in a nightmare, approaching no nearer to the goal.

In the meantime there came up behind us a tall peasant, perhaps forty years of age, of an ironical snuffy countenance, and arrayed in the green tail-coat of the country. He overtook us hand over hand, and stopped to consider our pitiful advance.

"Your donkey," says he, "is very old?"

I told him, I believed not.

Then, he supposed, we had come far.

I told him, we had but newly left Monastier.

"*Et vous marchez comme ça!*"[2] cried he; and, throwing back his head, he laughed long and heartily. I watched him, half prepared to feel offended, until he had satisfied his mirth; and then, "You must have no pity on these animals," said he; and, plucking a switch out of a thicket, he began to lace Modestine about the sternworks, uttering a cry. The rogue pricked up her ears and broke into a good round pace, which she kept up without flagging, and without exhibiting the least symptom of distress, as long as the peasant kept beside us. Her former panting and shaking had been, I regret to say, a piece of comedy.

My *deus ex machina*,[3] before he left me, supplied some excellent, if inhumane, advice; presented me with the switch, which he declared she would feel more tenderly than my cane; and finally taught me the true cry or masonic[4] word of donkey-drivers, "Proot!" All the time, he regarded me with a comical incredulous air, which was embarrassing to confront; and smiled over my donkey-driving, as I might have smiled over his orthography, or his green tail-coat. But it was not my turn for the moment.

I was proud of my new lore, and thought I had learned the art to perfection. And certainly Modestine did wonders for the rest of the afternoon, and I had a breathing space to look about me. It was Sabbath; the mountain-fields were all vacant in the sunshine; and as we came down through St. Martin de Frugères, the church was crowded to the door, there were people kneeling without upon the steps, and the sound of the priest's chanting came forth out of the dim interior. It gave me a home feeling on the spot; for I am a countryman of the Sabbath, so to speak, and all Sabbath observances, like a Scotch accent, strike in me mixed feelings, grateful and the reverse. It is only a traveller, hurrying by like a person from another planet, who can rightly enjoy the peace and beauty of the great

---

[2] *Et vous marchez comme ça*—And you walk like that!

[3] *Deus ex machina*—The god of the machine. In Greek literature, the action of the characters was predetermined by the gods of destiny. Later the term was used of any providential interference in the action of the story by which the author rescued the characters from their dilemmas.

[4] MASONIC—Brotherhood. "Proot" was the term used by all donkey-drivers.

ascetic feast. The sight of the resting country does his spirit good. There is something better than music in the wide unusual silence; and it disposes him to amiable thoughts, like the sound of a little river or the warmth of sunlight.

In this pleasant humor I came down the hill to where Goudet [5] stands in the green end of a valley, with Château Beaufort opposite upon a rocky steep, and the stream, as clear as crystal, lying in a deep pool between them. Above and below, you may hear it wimpling over the stones, an amiable stripling of a river, which it seems absurd to call the Loire.[6] On all sides, Goudet is shut in by mountains; rocky foot-paths, practicable at best for donkeys, join it to the outer world of France; and the men and women drink and swear, in their green corner, or look up at the snow-clad peaks in winter from the threshold of their homes, in an isolation, you would think, like that of Homer's Cyclops.[7] But it is not so; the postman reaches Goudet with the letter-bag; the aspiring youth of Goudet are within a day's walk of the railway at Le Puy; and here in the inn you may find an engraved portrait of the host's nephew, Régis Senac, "Professor of Fencing and Champion of the two Americas," a distinction gained by him, along with the sum of five hundred dollars, at Tammany Hall, New York, on the 10th April, 1876.[8]

I hurried over my midday meal, and was early forth again. But, alas, as we climbed the interminable hill upon the other side, "Proot!" seemed to have lost its virtue. I prooted like a lion, I prooted mellifluously like a sucking-dove;[9] but Modestine would be neither softened nor intimidated. She held doggedly to her pace; nothing but a blow would move her, and that only for a second. I must follow at her heels, incessantly belaboring. A moment's pause in this ignoble toil, and she relapsed into her own private gait. I think I never heard of any one in as mean a situation. I must reach the lake of Bouchet,[10] where I meant to camp, before sundown, and, to have even a

[5] GOUDET—About five miles from Monastier.
[6] LOIRE—The Loire has its source in these mountains.
[7] CYCLOPS—The one-eyed giants that Ulysses discovered on an island, perhaps Sicily. See the *Odyssey*, Book IX.
[8] RÉGIS SENAC . . . 1876—Senac actually did win the title at the time and place mentioned. He defeated one Colonel T. H. Monstery.
[9] LIKE A SUCKING-DOVE—An allusion to Shakespeare's *Midsummer Night's Dream*, Act I, Sc. 2.   [10] BOUCHET—About ten miles from his starting point.

hope of this, I must instantly maltreat this uncomplaining animal. The sound of my own blows sickened me. Once, when I looked at her, she had a faint resemblance to a lady of my acquaintance who formerly loaded me with kindness; and this increased my horror of my cruelty.

To make matters worse, we encountered another donkey, ranging at will upon the roadside; and this other donkey chanced to be a gentleman. He and Modestine met nickering for joy, and I had to separate the pair and beat down their young romance with a renewed and feverish bastinado. If the other donkey had had the heart of a male under his hide, he would have fallen upon me tooth and hoof; and this was a kind of consolation—he was plainly unworthy of Modestine's affection. But the incident saddened me, as did everything that spoke of my donkey's sex.

It was blazing hot up the valley, windless, with vehement sun upon my shoulders; and I had to labor so consistently with my stick that the sweat ran into my eyes. Every five minutes, too, the pack,[11] the basket, and the pilot-coat would take an ugly slew to one side or the other; and I had to stop Modestine, just when I had got her to a tolerable pace of about two miles an hour, to tug, push, shoulder, and readjust the load. And at last, in the village of Ussel, saddle and all, the whole hypothec[12] turned round and grovelled in the dust below the donkey's belly. She, none better pleased, incontinently drew up and seemed to smile; and a party of one man, two women, and two children came up, and, standing round me in a half-circle, encouraged her by their example.

I had the devil's own trouble to get the thing righted; and the instant I had done so, without hesitation, it toppled and fell down upon the other side. Judge if I was hot! And yet not a hand was offered to assist me. The man, indeed, told me I ought to have a package of a different shape. I suggested, if he knew nothing better to the point in my predicament, he

[11] THE PACK—In writing about this journey, Mrs. Stevenson said: "The management of Modestine's pack must have been a source of perplexity and exasperation to her master, for my husband was, like his father before him, what the Scotch call a 'handless man.' Neither of them could tie a knot that would hold."

[12] HYPOTHEC—A Scotch term for a lien given upon property to secure payment of a debt. Modestine here is the creditor and the pack the hypothec.

might hold his tongue. And the good-natured dog agreed with me smilingly. It was the most despicable fix. I must plainly content myself with the pack for Modestine, and take the following items for my own share of the portage: a cane, a quart flask, a pilot-jacket heavily weighted in the pockets, two pounds of black bread, and an open basket full of meats and bottles. I believe I may say I am not devoid of greatness of soul; for I did not recoil from this infamous burthen. I disposed it, Heaven knows how, so as to be mildly portable, and then proceeded to steer Modestine through the village. She tried, as was indeed her invariable habit, to enter every house and every courtyard in the whole length; and, encumbered as I was, without a hand to help myself, no words can render an idea of my difficulties. A priest, with six or seven others, was examining a church in process of repair, and he and his acolytes laughed loudly as they saw my plight. I remembered having laughed myself when I had seen good men struggling with adversity in the person of a jackass, and the recollection filled me with penitence. That was in my old light days, before this trouble came upon me. God knows at least that I shall never laugh again, thought I. But O, what a cruel thing is a farce to those engaged in it!

A little out of the village, Modestine, filled with the demon, set her heart upon a by-road, and positively refused to leave it. I dropped all my bundles, and, I am ashamed to say, struck the poor sinner twice across the face. It was pitiful to see her lift up her head with shut eyes, as if waiting for another blow. I came very near crying; but I did a wiser thing than that, and sat squarely down by the roadside to consider my situation under the cheerful influence of tobacco and a nip of brandy. Modestine, in the meanwhile, munched some black bread with a contrite hypocritical air. It was plain that I must make a sacrifice to the gods of shipwreck. I threw away the empty bottle destined to carry milk; I threw away my own white bread, and, disdaining to act by general average, kept the black bread for Modestine; lastly, I threw away the cold leg of mutton and the egg-whisk, although this last was dear to my heart. Thus I found room for everything in the basket, and even stowed the boating-coat on the top. By means of an end of cord I slung it under one arm; and although the cord cut my shoulder, and the jacket hung almost to the ground, it was with a heart greatly lightened that I set forth again.

I had now an arm free to thrash Modestine, and cruelly I chastised her. If I were to reach the lakeside before dark, she must bestir her little shanks to some tune. Already the sun had gone down into a windy-looking mist; and although there were still a few streaks of gold far off to the east on the hills and the black fir-woods, all was cold and gray about our onward path. An infinity of little country by-roads led hither and thither among the fields. It was the most pointless labyrinth. I could see my destination overhead, or rather the peak that dominates it; but choose as I pleased, the roads always ended by turning away from it, and sneaking back towards the valley, or northward along the margin of the hills. The failing light, the waning color, the naked, unhomely, stony country through which I was travelling, threw me into some despondency. I promise you, the stick was not idle; I think every decent step that Modestine took must have cost me at least two emphatic blows. There was not another sound in the neighborhood but that of my unwearying bastinado.

Suddenly, in the midst of my toils, the load once more bit the dust, and, as by enchantment, all the cords were simultaneously loosened, and the road scattered with my dear possessions. The packing was to begin again from the beginning; and as I had to invent a new and better system, I do not doubt but I lost half an hour. It began to be dusk in earnest as I reached a wilderness of turf and stones. It had the air of being a road which should lead everywhere at the same time; and I was falling into something not unlike despair when I saw two figures stalking towards me over the stones. They walked one behind the other like tramps, but their pace was remarkable. The son led the way, a tall, ill-made, sombre, Scotch-looking man; the mother followed, all in her Sunday's best, with an elegantly-embroidered ribbon to her cap, and a new felt hat atop, and proffering, as she strode along with kilted petticoats, a string of obscene and blasphemous oaths.[13]

I hailed the son and asked him my direction. He pointed

---

[13] BLASPHEMOUS OATHS—The common talk of most European countries is sprinkled thick with oaths which would sound blasphemous if they were translated literally but which are not so intended.

loosely west and north-west, muttered an inaudible comment, and, without slacking his pace for an instant, stalked on, as he was going, right athwart my path. The mother followed without so much as raising her head. I shouted and shouted after them, but they continued to scale the hillside, and turned a deaf ear to my outcries. At last, leaving Modestine by herself, I was constrained to run after them, hailing the while. They stopped as I drew near, the mother still cursing; and I could see she was a handsome, motherly, respectable-looking woman. The son once more answered me roughly and inaudibly, and was for setting out again. But this time I simply collared the mother, who was nearest me, and, apologizing for my violence, declared that I could not let them go until they had put me on my road. They were neither of them offended—rather mollified than otherwise; told me I had only to follow them; and then the mother asked me what I wanted by the lake at such an hour. I replied, in the Scotch manner, by inquiring if she had far to go herself. She told me, with another oath, that she had an hour and a half's road before her. And then, without salutation, the pair strode forward again up the hillside in the gathering dusk.

I returned for Modestine, pushed her briskly forward, and, after a sharp ascent of twenty minutes, reached the edge of a plateau. The view, looking back on my day's journey, was both wild and sad. Mount Mézenc [14] and the peaks beyond St. Julien stood out in trenchant gloom against a cold glitter in the east; and the intervening field of hills had fallen together into one broad wash of shadow, except here and there the outline of a wooded sugar-loaf in black, here and there a white irregular patch to represent a cultivated farm, and here and there a blot where the Loire, the Gazeille, or the Lausonne wandered in a gorge.

Soon we were on a highroad, and surprise seized on my mind as I beheld a village of some magnitude close at hand; for I had been told that the neighborhood of the lake was uninhabited except by trout. The road smoked in the twilight with children driving home cattle from the fields; and a pair of mounted stride-legged women, hat and cap and all, dashed past me at a hammering trot from the canton where they had been to church

---

[14] MOUNT MÉZENC—The highest peak in the Cévennes, 5,750 feet high.

and market. I asked one of the children where I was. At Bouchet St. Nicolas, he told me. Thither, about a mile south of my destination, and on the other side of a respectable summit, had these confused roads and treacherous peasantry conducted me. My shoulder was cut, so that it hurt sharply; my arm ached like toothache from perpetual beating; I gave up the lake and my design to camp, and asked for the *auberge*.[15]

[15] *Auberge*—Inn.

Vocabulary Study: *Common* (a noun); *docility; infinitesimally; incredulous; orthography; amiable; mellifluously; interminable; intimidated; bastinado; vehement* (note pronunciation); *incontinently; despicable* (note pronunciation); *portage; infamous* (note pronunciation); *acolytes; contrite; hypocritical; labyrinth; dominates; kilted; blasphemous; athwart; mollify; trenchant; canton.*

Give the derivation of *mellifluously*. Distinguish between *docility, obedience,* and *gentleness.* Name two synonyms for *contrite.*

By Way of Appreciation: *Travels with a Donkey* is one of the earliest and one of the pleasantest of Stevenson's books. It was published when the author was twenty-eight. Because of his frail health, he had had to find a softer climate than that of his native Scotland, and his first journeyings took him to Belgium and France. With a companion, he took a canoe trip through the waterways of Belgium; and his first published book, *An Inland Voyage,* tells of the delightful ventures of the two canoes, the *Cigarette* and the *Arethusa.* Later, when he tramped through the Cévennes, he went alone—that is, alone except for Modestine; and his second book followed. The success of these two little volumes gave Stevenson the courage to take up writing as his profession. Each chapter is a refreshing narrative, graced with the quaintness of the French countryside and enlivened with bits of humor.

Suggestions for Study: The essay is full of Stevenson's happy phrasings, such as Modestine's "sober daintiness of gait." Make a list of ten picturesque word-groups. Can you find five good similes in the essay? Why does Stevenson call Sabbath church-going an "ascetic feast"? Explain: "What a cruel thing is a farce to those engaged in it!" Explain: "I must make a sacrifice to the gods of shipwreck."—(See the story of Jonah in the Bible.) Why did Stevenson spend the night in the inn instead of camping out as he had planned? What picture do you get of French peasantry from the essay? What picture do you get of French country? What makes this simple sketch entertaining?

Exercises and Creative Work: Experiences which are uncomfortable at the time often furnish material for interesting sketches, especially if they are told with a whimsical air. Can you build such an essay around one of the following topics? *I Rode the Horse!; Four Boys and a Flivver; Mud; The First Hundred Miles.*

THE HISTORY OF PROSE LITERATURE IN ENGLAND

The Twentieth Century (1900–   )

General Characteristics

Victorian prose was chiefly serious, and according to the law of action and reaction, some changes were to be expected of the new century. In the desire to achieve something different, classicism and romanticism alike were discarded and realism became the note of the day. It was at first a one-sided sort of realism that emphasized the sordid and ugly. Nevertheless, out of what promised to be an hysterical age, has come some exceptionally fine literature. In the field of prose, there are many, many good essays; there are essays of all types—of careful criticism, of playful lightness, of science, of travel, of religion, of history, of art—in fact, of every phase of modern life. To acquaint you with the pleasing diversity of the modern English essay, the present volume has chosen papers by six representative English essayists—William Henry Hudson, Arnold Bennett, John Galsworthy, Max Beerbohm, H. M. Tomlinson, and Gilbert K. Chesterton.

William Henry Hudson (1841–1922)

Straightforward and open as are the writings of W. H. Hudson, there was mystery and romance in his life. South America seems always a fascinating land, and that is where Mr. Hudson was born and grew up. One may read about his happy life on the pampas in *Far Away and Long Ago,* a charming tale of his childhood; and all of his most pleasing books—*Green Mansions,* for example—go back to South America for their setting.

When Mr. Hudson was twenty-nine, he left the Argentines. Why? He never told. One sensed that he left youth and joy behind him. It was to London that he came, and his first years there were difficult ones. He was poor and friendless. He married a woman considerably older than himself, only scantily educated, but very devoted to her husband. Together they struggled to make a living while he, from time to time, sent his books and articles out into the world. Though he wrote, in all, twenty-four volumes, popularity came late. He was past sixty when the publication of *Green Mansions* made him famous.

He was really a naturalist, studying the ways of animals, small and large, in their native environments. *The Book of a Naturalist* is an example of the subjects that engaged his interests and of the simplicity of his style. He wrote, besides, entertaining short stories and some novels.

He was an unusual looking man—a sort of Lincoln-like form, tall and gaunt. He had rough, shaggy hair and beard, and very sharp eyes. He rebelled against old age and kept himself active almost to the time of his death just before his eighty-first birthday.

Arnold Bennett (1867–1931)

In *The Truth about an Author* Mr. Bennett has himself told us a good deal about Arnold Bennett and his rise from obscure clerkships in "The Five Towns" and in London to a commanding position in the literary world of to-day. As in others of his books, he has been entirely candid and veracious—or at least, he gives us the impression of having been so.

"The Five Towns," which Mr. Bennett was later to place on the literary map, are great pottery manufacturing communities in the north of England. Enoch Arnold Bennett, their future historian, was born near Hanley (the "Hanbridge" of the novels) in 1867. He received a somewhat limited education at the neighboring "middle school" of Newcastle. He then entered the University of London, and adopted the law as his profession. He read law at first in his father's office, and then went to London as a solicitor's (lawyer's) clerk. In that capacity he earned a modest livelihood by (as he says) "a natural gift for the preparation of bills for taxation." Meanwhile he made some slight beginnings in journalism, won a prize competition, and entered newspaper work with the Staffordshire *Sentinel*.

Later he became sub-editor of *Woman* and contributor to the *Academy*, both British periodicals. His book reviews, dramatic criticisms, and incidental writings had drawn attention to him; and his first novel, *A Man from the North*, had been published both in England and America. With respect to the novel, he tells us that with the excess of profits over the cost of typewriting he bought a new hat. But, although he could look back upon his rise during the past ten years and see how far he had come, he was not satisfied. He resigned his editorial position with its assured income, and retired, first to the country, and then to Fontainebleau, on the outskirts of Paris, to devote himself seriously to literature.

In the autumn of 1903 he was accustomed to dine frequently at a certain Paris restaurant. One day there came in a fat old woman who aroused universal merriment by her eccentric behavior. The novelist reflected: "This woman was once young, slim, perhaps beautiful; certainly free from those ridiculous mannerisms. Very probably she is unconscious of her singularities. Her case is a tragedy. One ought to be able to make a heart-rending novel out of a woman such as she." The incident was the origin of *The Old Wives' Tale*, published in 1908, and recognized both in England and America as a work of genius. Since that time Mr. Bennett has given us other equally faithful accounts of life in provincial towns. He has also written books of essays in which he has given us a private view of the workings of his active and inquiring mind.

John Galsworthy (1867–1933)

The Galsworthys have been in Devonshire, England, "since the flood—of Saxons, at all events," as the writer once put it. John was born at Coombe, in Surrey in 1867, and his works are typical of good English birth and breeding.

After his schooling at Harrow and Oxford, he made an attempt at the practice of law, his father's profession. But it proved uncongenial.

"I read," he said, "in various chambers, practiced almost not at all, and disliked my profession thoroughly." His father's wealth and generosity enabled the young man to close his office and go vagabonding. He traveled for two years, visiting most of the out-of-the-way places of the world. On one of his voyages he made the acquaintance of Joseph Conrad, then still a sailor. John Galsworthy encouraged Conrad to begin writing, but apparently thought nothing of becoming a writer himself.

It was the girl he was later to marry that encouraged him to write. Though one had little different to offer the world, he said, one might try writing "to please her of whom one was fond." In the next two years he wrote nine tales, all of which he later characterized as "very bad." But the start had been made. From that time there was a steady succession of novels, essays, and plays.

The most notable work is the history of three generations of the Forsyte family, the nucleus of which has been gathered into one thick volume, *The Forsyte Saga*. However, later volumes carried on the history until in *Swan Song* the centralizing character, Soames Forsyte, died. It is a most unusual cycle of fiction, for the settings of the books are cotemporaneous with John Galsworthy's life, from the mid-Victorian days of his youth until well into the post-war period. The chief characters are from the social class that he knew best—the upper middle class.

In 1906, Mr. Galsworthy became very much interested in the stage, and for the next twelve years wrote chiefly plays. About two thirds of his work are novels and dramas, the rest including short stories, sketches, essays, and a few poems.

Max Beerbohm (1872–   )

Max Beerbohm is something of a cosmopolite. He was born in London, married an American girl from Memphis, Tennessee, and has lived in Italy ever since. In the year of their marriage, 1910, the

Beerbohms took a villa in that sunny land and it is there that they spend most of their time. Mr. Beerbohm is a cartoonist as well as a writer, indeed some critics call his drawings more clever than his books. Though now past sixty Mr. Beerbohm keeps the manner and mind of youth. His essays are always refreshing reading; his novels are rather bewildering fantasies of this modern age.

One writer has described Mr. Beerbohm as having a small round head, a huge forehead, an encircling fringe of soft white hair, and a countenance altogether "cherubic." He is slight, quick, and dapper.

With mock solemnity he called his first collection of essays *The Works of Max Beerbohm.* Succeeding volumes have been designated *More, Yet Again,* and *And Even Now.* His current essays find eager acceptance in a score of English and American periodicals. *Observations* is a book of caricatures.

Gilbert K. Chesterton (1874–1936)

Gilbert Keith Chesterton, often known by his initials, G. K. C., was an impressive personality. His frame was huge, and he enjoyed a rough unkempt appearance. He started out to be an artist, but some early art criticisms were so well liked and he had such a good time doing them, that he decided to make his living as a journalist and writer. He became an established essayist, poet, journalist, critic, and lecturer. He was one of those Englishmen that must come over once in a while to tell what is wrong with America. And how Americans love it! He had a fund of wit and was as clever with his tongue as with his pen.

Chesterton died suddenly of a heart attack in June 1936.

One of his most popular works is the collection of detective stories entitled, *The Innocence of Father Brown.* There are a number of volumes of light essays to his credit: *Heretics, Tremendous Trifles, Generally Speaking,* and *Come to Think of It.* His serious criticisms appear in studies of Dickens and Browning in the *English Men of Letters* series, and in *The Victorian Age in Literature.*

H. M. Tomlinson (1873–   )

Propinquity to ships does not always make a sailor. Henry Major Tomlinson was born near the docks of London, and had his first job in a shipping office on the wharves; but it was not until he was a newspaper man that he went on his first voyage. Since that first trip up the Amazon, which he described in *The Sea and the Jungle,* he has visited other far-away places.

In "Some Hints for Those about to Travel" Mr. Tomlinson says, "I do not know how one plans a long voyage, and maintains the excellent plan scientifically through all its difficulties. I have never done any planning. A ship seems to have drifted my way at last, by chance, and then, if I did not hesitate too long, I went in her, though always for a reason very inadequate."

It was in 1904 that, tiring of the routine of his shipping-office job, he exchanged it for a position on *The Morning Leader*, a newspaper to which he had been contributing articles. When that paper merged with *The Daily News*, Tomlinson continued with the second daily. The paper sent him on his voyage up the Amazon, and in 1914 sent him as war correspondent to France and Belgium. From 1915 to 1917 he was Official Staff Correspondent, attached to Headquarters of the British Armies in France. Tomlinson said that war "was no inspiration, only horror"; however, out of his experiences have grown two books, *Waiting for Daylight* and the novel, *All Our Yesterdays*. A second book of travel is *Tidemarks,* in which he has recorded a trip through the Malay Archipelago. A group of essays he has called *Gifts of Fortune*.

From boyhood Mr. Tomlinson has been a great reader, catching much inspiration from the works of others. Ralph Waldo Emerson and Herman Melville are his favorite American writers.

Other Essayists of the Twentieth Century

It is impossible in a short space to give a complete list of the writers of excellent contemporary essays. However, there are a few names which deserve special mention.

There is George Bernard Shaw who is startling enough and individual enough to be typical "twentieth-century"; and his critical views in *Dramatic Opinions and Essays* are worth reading. Whether one always agrees with Mr. Shaw or not, his writings start one thinking, and thought-stimulation is one of the functions of literature.

In this older school of writers there are also James M. Barrie and Rudyard Kipling, who, though usually engaged in writing of another sort, have given some very fine addresses and lectures. *Courage* by Barrie and *Independence* by Kipling are thoughtful essays, first delivered as addresses, that will well repay the careful reader.

Sir Philip Gibbs in *Now It Can be Told* and *Since Then* voices the mind of the soldier after the War. In lighter vein is the work of the Anglicized Frenchman, Hilaire Belloc (Hilary Bel-lock'), poet, essayist, and novelist. *On Nothing and Kindred Subjects* are light, very light, essays; and *The Path to Rome* is an account of a walking tour. A. A. Milne is delightful in whatever he writes, his essays in *Not That It Matters* proving no exception to the rule.

One of the most finished of the English essayists is Edward Verrall Lucas, and there are many volumes for one to read with pleasure, *Old Lamps for New,* for instance, or *Adventures and Enthusiasms*. Then his "Wanderer" series is a fine list of travel books. The titles run *A Wanderer in Florence,* and the like.

Essays of the Twentieth Century

MARY'S LITTLE LAMB

From *The Book of a Naturalist*

WILLIAM HENRY HUDSON

By Way of Introduction: William Henry Hudson was the same sort of naturalist as the American John Burroughs—that is, he was a patient observer and recorder of natural life. He was no laboratory scientist. He liked to work under the sky, sitting two hours, perhaps, beside a little stream to watch the slow progress of a turtle to the water. Many of his observations were made in England, but the most fascinating accounts are the reminiscences of his youth in the Argentine. *Mary's Little Lamb* takes us back with the author to the pampas.

THIS is the history of a pet lamb that differed mentally from other lambs I have known. One does not look for anything approaching to marked individuality in that animal, yet sheep do show it on occasions though not in the same degree as cats and dogs. Goats exhibit more character than sheep, probably because we do not compel them to live in a crowd. Indeed, when we consider how our poor domesticated sheep is kept we can see that they have little chance of developing individuality of mind. A sheep cannot "follow his own genius," so to speak, without infringing the laws we have made for his kind. His condition in this respect is similar to that of human beings under a purely socialistic form of government: for example, like that of the ancient civilised Peruvians. In that state every man did as he was told: worked and rested, got up and sat down, ate, drank, and slept, married, grew old and died in the precise way prescribed. And I daresay if he tried to be original or to do something out of the common he was knocked on the head. So with our sheep. The shepherd, assisted by his dog, maps out his whole life for him, from birth to death, and he is not permitted to stray from the path in which he is made to walk. But if a lamb be taken from the flock and reared at a farm and given the same liberty that cats and dogs and even many goats enjoy, he will in almost every case develop a character of his own.

I remember a tame sheep we once had at my home on the pampas [1] who in thieving could give points to many thievish dogs, not excepting the pointer himself, the most accomplished thief in the entire canine gang. Tobacco and books were the objects this mischievous beast was perpetually foraging for when she could get into the house. Tobacco was hard to come at even when she had a good long time to look for it before some one came on the scene to send her about her business with a good whack or a kick. But books were often left lying about on tables and chairs and were easily got at. She knew very well that it was wrong and that if detected she would have to suffer, but she was exceedingly cunning, and from a good distance would keep an eye on the house, and when she saw or cunningly guessed that no person was in the sitting- or dining-room or any other room with the door standing open, she would steal quietly in and finding a book would catch it hastily up and make off with it. Carrying it off to the plantation she would set it down, put her hoof on it, and start tearing out the leaves and devouring them as expeditiously as possible. Once she had got hold of a book she would not give it up—not all the shouting and chasing after her would make her drop it. Away she would rush until fifty yards or more ahead of her hunters; then she would stop, set it down and begin hurriedly tearing out the leaves; then when the hunt drew near with loud

---

[1] PAMPAS—Hudson, you remember, was born in the Argentine and lived on the pampas for nearly thirty years.

hallo she would snatch it up and rush on with it flapping about her face, and leave us all far behind. Eventually, when her depredations could no longer be tolerated, she was sent away to the flock.

An English settler in Patagonia[2] I used to stay with when visiting that part kept a tame guanaco[3] at his estancia,[4] which had a habit resembling that of our book-stealing sheep. This animal had been captured when small by some guanaco-hunters, and my friend reared and made a pet of it. When grown up it associated with the sheep and other domestic animals and was friendly with the dogs, but spent much of its time roaming by itself over the plains. He had the run of the house as well, but at length had to be excluded on account of his passion for devouring any white linen or cotton which he could get hold of. But the guanaco, like our sheep, was cunning and would approach the house from the back and make his way into a bedroom to snatch up and make off with a towel, night-shirt, handkerchief, or anything he could find of linen or cotton, so long as it was white. One day my host came in to get himself ready to attend a meeting and dinner at a neighbouring estancia, and after putting out his linen on his bed he went into an adjoining room for a hot bath. Coming back to his bedroom he was just in time to see his pet guanaco pick up his beautifully-got-up snow-white shirt from the bed and make a dash for the open door. He uttered a wild yell, which had no effect, but he was determined not to lose his shirt, for at that moment he remembered that it was the only clean one he possessed; he rushed out just as he was with nothing but a towel round him, and jumping on his horse, which stood saddled at the gate, started in pursuit. Away he went, shouting to the dogs to come and help him recover his shirt. His yell and shouts brought all the men about the place on the scene, and running out they too mounted their horses in hot haste and started after him. And away far ahead of them went the guanaco at a pace no horse could equal, the shirt held firmly in his teeth waving and flapping like a white banner in the

[2] PATAGONIA—A region at the southern tip of South America, divided by Chile and the Argentine Republic, inhabited by wild tribes.
[3] GUANACO (gwä-nä′kō)—A South American grazing animal, belonging to the camel family. It is light brown in color, shading into white below.
[4] ESTANCIA—A country estate or ranch.

wind. But from time to time he made a stop, and bringing the shirt down to the ground would hurriedly tear a piece out of it, then picking it up would rush on again. The dogs overtook him only to dance round him, barking joyfully to encourage him to run on and keep the fun going. He was their friend and playmate, and it was to them nothing but a jolly sham hunt got up by their sport-loving master for their amusement. The chase led up the valley of the river, a great flat plain, and continued for about four to five miles; by that time the precious shirt had dwindled to something quite small—nothing in fact was left but the hard starched front, which the guanaco found it difficult to masticate and swallow. Then at long last the hunt was given up and my poor shirtless friend in his towel rode mournfully home in the midst of laughing companions, attended, too, by a lot of dogs, lolling their tongues out and over-flowingly happy at having had such an exciting run.

Let me now come to the subject I sat down to write about—namely, Mary's little lamb. It was little to begin with, when my youngest sister, who was not then very big herself, and was always befriending forlorn creatures, came in one day from the shepherd's ranch with a young lamb which had unhappily lost its mother. Oddly enough this little sister's name was Mary—one seldom hears it in these Doris, Doreen days, but in that distant Mary-Jane-Elizabeth period it was quite common. And the motherless lamb she had brought in grew to be her pet lamb, with fleece as white as snow; nor was the whiteness strange seeing that it was washed every day with scented soap, its beauteous neck beribboned and often decorated with garlands of scarlet verbenas which looked exceedingly brilliant against the snowy fleece. A pretty, sweet-tempered and gentle creature it proved and never developed any naughty proclivities like the tobacco- and book-plundering sheep of an earlier date. They were very fond of each other, those two simple beings, and just as in the old familiar rhyme wherever Mary went her little lamb would go. But there was a little rift within the lute [5] which by and by would widen till it made the music mute. The lamb was excessively playful and frisky, but its mistress had her little lessons and duties to attend to, and the

---

[5] LUTE—A reference to an old moralizing rime.

lamb couldn't understand it, and often after frisking and jumping about to challenge the other to a fresh race in vain it would run away to get up a race or game of some sort with the youngest of the dogs. The dogs were responsive, so that they were quite happy together.

We kept eight dogs at that time; two were pointers, all the others just the common dog of the country, a smooth-haired animal about the size of a collie. Like all dogs allowed to exist in their own way, they formed a pack, the most powerful one being their leader and master. They spent most of their time lying stretched dog-fashion in the sun in some open place near the house, fast asleep. They had little to do except bark at strangers approaching the house and to hunt off the cattle that tried to force their way through the fences into the plantation. They would also go off on hunting expeditions of their own. Strange playmates and companions for Libby, as she was named, the pretty pet lamb with fleece as white as snow; yet so congenial did she find the dogs' society that by and by she passed her whole time with them, day and night. When they came to the door to bark and whine and wag their tails to call attention to their wants or to be noticed, the lamb would be with them but would not cross the threshold since the dogs were not permitted in the rooms. Nor would she come to her mistress when called, and having discovered that grass was her proper food she wanted nothing that human beings could give her. Not even a lump of sugar! She was no longer a pet lamb; she was one of the dogs. The dogs on their part, although much given to quarrels and fights among themselves, never growled or snapped at Libby; she never tried to snatch a bone from them, and she made them a comfortable pillow when they slept and slumbered for hours at a stretch. And Libby, just to be always with them and to do exactly as they did, would sleep too. Or rather she would lie stretched out on the ground pretending to sleep, always with the head of one of the dogs pillowed on her neck. Two or three or four of the other dogs who had failed to secure the pillow would lie round her with their heads pressed against her fleece. They would form a curiously amusing group. Then if a shrill whistle was emitted by some one, or the cry of "Up and at 'em," the lamb would spring like lightning to her feet, throwing the drowsy dog off, and away she would dash down the avenue to get outside the plantation and find out what the trouble was. Then the dogs, shaking off their sleep, would start off and perhaps overtake her a couple of hundred yards away.

Most amusing of all the lamb's acting was when the dogs had their periodical hunting fits, when they would vanish for half a day's vizcacha-hunting on the plain, just as fox-terriers and other dogs in which the hunting instinct still survives steal out of the village to chase or dig out rabbits on their own account.

The vizcacha is a big rodent and lives in communities, in warrens or villages composed of a group of huge burrows, and the native dogs are fond of assaulting these strongholds but seldom succeed in getting at their quarry. A dog no bigger than a fox-terrier can make his way in till he comes to grips with the vizcacha, usually with the result that he gets well punished for his audacity. Our dogs would simply labour to enlarge the burrows by scratching and biting away the earth and furiously barking at the animal inside who would emit curious noises and cries, which the dogs appeared to regard as insults and would only cause them to redouble their efforts.

On several occasions, when riding on the plain a mile or two from home, I would come on our dogs—the entire pack and the lamb with them, engaged in the siege and assault of a vizcacha village or earth. A funny sight! The dogs would jump up barking and wagging their tails as if to say, "Here we are, you see, just in the middle of our fight with no time to spare for friendly conversation." And back they would fly to their burrows. The lamb too would dance up to give me a welcome and then back to her duties. Her part was to go frisking about from burrow to burrow, now taking a flying leap over the pit-like mouth, then diving down to see how things were progressing inside, where the dog was tearing at the earth and trying to force himself in and keeping up a running dialogue of threats and insults with the beast inside.

But though Libby, in these her dog days, was a continual joy to us, we thought it best for her own sake to put an end to them. For in spite of her activities she was in very good condition, and any poor gaucho who came upon her, hunting with our dogs a few miles from home, would be justified in saying: "Here is a good fat animal without an ear-mark, consequently without an owner; and though I find it in the company of Neighbour So-and-So's dogs, it can't be his since he has put no mark on it, and as I've found it I have a right to it, and I'm quite sure from its appearance that its flesh when roasted will prove tender and savoury."

Accordingly we took Libby away from her companions and put her with the flock, where in due time she would learn that a sheep is a sheep and not a dog.

Vocabulary Study: Adequate explanations of the following words you will find in an ordinary dictionary: *infringe; pampas; pointer* (a dog); *forage; expeditiously; depredations; verbena; proclivities; rift; lute; congenial; rodent; warrens; burrows; audacity; gaucho.*

Distinguish between the synonyms *expeditiously, hastily, rapidly.* What are common synonyms for *depredations, rift, audacity?* What are the histories of *infringe, gaucho?*

By Way of Appreciation: The chapters in *The Book of a Naturalist* read like a running brook, clear and limpid. Mr. Hudson does not mystify the reader with strange terms or complicated sentences. He tells his story simply. There are pleasant little sketches about animals, wild and tame, which he met in England or in the Argentine. He was bitter against hunters and fishermen, for he did not believe in needless killing of wild life. He was especially interested in birds, and in addition to several books, he wrote many pamphlets for the Society for Protection of Birds. As a fitting memorial to Mr. Hudson, a bird sanctuary was erected to his memory in Hyde Park, London, in 1925.

Suggestions for Study: Why do sheep have little personality? What sort of picture have you formed of the Hudson estancia? Hudson spent his last fifty years in England, mostly in London, but he once said that his life ended when he left the pampas. Does this essay help you to understand the statement?

Exercises and Creative Work: Write a précis of the essay.

If you have enjoyed *Mary's Little Lamb,* you will want to read other selections from *The Book of a Naturalist.* Be prepared to make a class report on one of these selections.

If you are interested in birds, you will especially enjoy some of the bird adventures which Mr. Hudson relates in his autobiography, *Far Away and Long Ago.* Make a class report on some of these adventures, making special note of birds which are different from those with which you are familiar.

Pets furnish unending opportunities for sketches and stories. Here are a few suggestive titles: *Personalities in Pets; The Dog I Couldn't Train; Her Highness, The Cat; Cats—No, Thank You!*

SOME PLATITUDES CONCERNING DRAMA

From *The Inn of Tranquillity*

John Galsworthy

By Way of Introduction: There is over-much modesty in Mr. Galsworthy's title for his essay on the drama. The dictionary tells us that a *platitude* is a "flat, dull, commonplace statement." The essay does challenge our intelligence; but if we have a normal I. Q., we find its statements neither flat nor dull. Galsworthy was a truly modest man; and because he saw certain dramatic principles so clearly, felt them so surely, he perhaps guessed that many another saw and felt them too and that therefore they might appear commonplace in print. Yet even the experienced dramatic critic admits that Galsworthy has here given a fresh vitality to the principles of stage-craft.

In a sense, this is the most thought-provoking essay that has been offered you. It will have an especial message for those who are interested in drama—in reading plays, or seeing plays, or writing plays, or even acting in plays. If you have such an interest, here is something for you to "set your teeth to." There is real meaning in it. Make it yours.

If your knowledge of plays and the theater is slight, read it carefully, once, as a piece of excellent critical writing by a master of English prose; then tuck away in your memory the names of essay and author for future reference if ever you turn your mind to the drama.

A Drama must be shaped so as to have a spire of meaning. Every grouping of life and character has its inherent moral; and the business of the dramatist is so to pose the group as to bring that moral poignantly to the light of day. Such is the moral that exhales from plays like *Lear, Hamlet,* and *Macbeth*. But such is not the moral to be found in the great bulk of contemporary Drama. The moral of the average play is now, and probably has always been, the triumph at all costs of a supposed immediate ethical good over a supposed immediate ethical evil.

The vice of drawing these distorted morals has permeated the Drama to its spine; discoloured its art, humanity, and significance; infected its creators, actors, audience, critics; too often turned it from a picture into a caricature. A Drama which lives under the shadow of the distorted moral forgets how to be free, fair, and fine—forgets so completely that it often prides itself on having forgotten.

Now, in writing plays, there are, in this matter of the moral, three courses open to the serious dramatist. The first is: To definitely set before the public that which it wishes to have set before it, the views and codes of life by which the public lives and in which it believes. This way is the most common, successful, and popular. It makes the dramatist's position sure, and not too obviously authoritative.

The second course is: To definitely set before the public those views and codes of life by which the dramatist himself lives, those theories in which he himself believes, the more effectively if they are the opposite of what the public wishes to have placed before it, presenting them so that the audience may swallow them like powder in a spoonful of jam.

There is a third course: To set before the public no cut-and-dried codes, but the phenomena of life and character, selected and combined, *but not distorted,* by the dramatist's outlook, set down without fear, favour, or prejudice, leaving the public to draw such poor moral as nature may afford. This third method requires a certain detachment; it requires a sympathy with, a love of, and a curiosity as to, things for their own sake; it requires a far view, together with patient industry, for no immediately practical result.

It was once said of Shakespeare that he had never done any good to any one, and never would. This, unfortunately, could not, in the sense of which the word "good" was then meant, be said of most modern dramatists. In truth, the good that Shakespeare did to humanity was of a remote, and, shall we say, eternal nature; something of the good that men get from having the sky and the sea to look at. And this partly because he was, in his greater plays at all events, free from the habit of drawing a distorted moral. Now, the playwright who supplies to the public the facts of life distorted by the moral which it expects, does so that he may do the public what he considers an immediate good, by fortifying its prejudices; and the dramatist who supplies to the public facts distorted by his own advanced morality, does so because he considers that he will at once benefit the public by substituting for its worn-out ethics, his own. In both cases the advantage the dramatist hopes to confer on the public is immediate and practical.

But matters change, and morals change; men remain—and to set men, and the facts about them, down faithfully, so that they draw for us the moral of their natural actions, may also possibly be of benefit to the community. It is, at all events, harder than to set men and facts down, as they ought, or ought not to be. This, however, is not to say that a dramatist should, or indeed can, keep himself and his temperamental philosophy out of his work. As a man lives and thinks, so will he write. But it is certain, that to the making of good drama, as to the practice of every other art, there must be brought an almost passionate love of discipline, a white-heat of self-respect, a desire to make the truest, fairest, best thing in one's power; and that to these must be added an eye that does not flinch. Such qualities alone will bring to a drama the selfless character which soaks it with inevitability.

The word "pessimist" is frequently applied to the few dramatists who have been content to work in this way. It has been applied, among others, to Euripides,[1] to Shakespeare, to Ibsen;[2] it will be applied to many in the future. Nothing, however, is more dubious than the way in which these two words "pessimist" and "optimist" are used; for the optimist appears to be he who cannot bear the world as it is, and is forced by his nature to picture it as it ought to be, and the pessimist one who cannot only bear the world as it is, but loves it well enough to draw it faithfully. The true lover of the human race is surely he who can put up with it in all its forms, in vice as well as in virtue, in defeat no less than in victory; the true seer he who sees not only joy but sorrow, the true painter of human life one who blinks nothing. It may be that he is also, incidentally, its true benefactor.

In the whole range of the social fabric there are only two impartial persons, the scientist and the artist, and under the latter heading such dramatists as desire to write not only for today, but for tomorrow, must strive to come.

But dramatists being as they are made—past remedy—it is perhaps more profitable to examine the various points at which their qualities and defects are shown.

[1] EURIPIDES—A Greek tragic poet and dramatist (480–406 B.C.).
[2] IBSEN—A Norwegian poet and dramatist whose works are chiefly tragic.

The plot! A good plot is that sure edifice which slowly rises out of the interplay of circumstance on temperament, and temperament on circumstance, within the enclosing atmosphere of an idea. A human being is the best plot there is; it may be impossible to see why he is a good plot, because the idea within which he was brought forth cannot be fully grasped; but it is plain that *he is a good plot*. He is organic. And so it must be with a good play. Reason alone produces no good plots; they come by original sin, sure conception, and instinctive after-power of selecting what benefits the germ. A bad plot, on the other hand, is simply a row of stakes, with a character impaled on each—characters who would have liked to live, but came to untimely grief; who started bravely, but fell on these stakes, placed beforehand in a row, and were transfixed one by one, while their ghosts stride on, squeaking and gibbering, through the play. Whether these stakes are made of facts or of ideas, according to the nature of the dramatist who planted them, their effect on the unfortunate characters is the same; the creatures were begotten to be staked, and staked they are! The demand for a good plot, not unfrequently heard, commonly signifies: "Tickle my sensations by stuffing the play with arbitrary adventures, so that I need not be troubled to take the characters seriously. Set the persons of the play to action, regardless of time, sequence, atmosphere, and probability!"

Now, true dramatic action is what characters do, at once contrary, as it were, to expectation, and yet because they have already done other things. No dramatist should let his audience know what is coming; but neither should he suffer his characters to act without making his audience feel that those actions are in harmony with temperament, and arise from previous known actions, together with the temperaments and previous known actions of the other characters in the play. The dramatist who hangs his characters to his plot, instead of hanging his plot to his characters, is guilty of cardinal sin.

The dialogue! Good dialogue again is character, marshalled so as continually to stimulate interest or excitement. The reason good dialogue is seldom found in plays is merely that it is hard to write, for it requires not only a knowledge of what interests or excites, but such a feeling for character as brings misery to the dramatist's heart when his creations speak as they should not speak—ashes to his mouth when they say things for the sake of saying them—disgust when they are "smart."

The art of writing true dramatic dialogue is an austere art, denying itself all license, grudging every sentence devoted to the mere machinery of the play, suppressing all jokes and epigrams severed from character, relying for fun and pathos on the fun and tears of life. From start to finish good dialogue is hand-made, like good lace; clear, of fine texture, furthering with each thread the harmony and strength of a design to which all must be subordinated.

But good dialogue is also spiritual action. In so far as the dramatist divorces his dialogue from spiritual action—that is to say, from progress of events, or toward events which are significant of character—he is stultifying τὸ δρᾶμα [3] the thing done; he may make pleasing disquisitions, he is not making drama. And in so far as he twists character to suit his moral or his plot, he is neglecting, a first principle, that truth to Nature which alone invests art with hand-made quality.

The dramatist's license, in fact, ends with his design. In conception alone he is free. He may take what character or group of characters he chooses, see them with what eyes, knit them with what idea, within the limits of his temperament; but once taken, seen, and knitted, he is bound to treat them like a gentleman, with the tenderest consideration of their mainsprings. Take care of character; action and dialogue will take care of themselves! The true dramatist gives full rein to his temperament in the scope and nature of his subject; having once selected subject and characters, he is just, gentle, restrained, neither gratifying his lust for praise at the expense of his offspring, nor using them as puppets to flout his audience. Being himself the nature that brought them forth, he guides them in the course predestined at their conception. So only have they a chance of defying Time, which is always lying in wait to destroy the false, topical, or fashionable, all—in a word—that is not based on the permanent elements of human nature.

---

[3] Τὸ δρᾶμα—From *to* meaning "the," and *drama* meaning "drama." *Drama* in Greek is the past participle of the verb meaning "to do" or "to perform"; hence, *to drama* means literally "the thing done" as well as "the drama."

The perfect dramatist rounds up his characters and facts within the ring-fence of a dominant idea which fulfils the craving of his spirit; having got them there, he suffers them to live their own lives.

Plot, action, character, dialogue! But there is yet another subject for a platitude. Flavour! An impalpable quality, less easily captured than the scent of a flower, the peculiar and most essential attribute of any work of art! It is the thin, poignant spirit which hovers up out of a play, and is as much its differentiating essence as is caffeine of coffee. Flavour, in fine, is the spirit of the dramatist projected into his work in a state of volatility, so that no one can exactly lay hands on it, here, there, or anywhere. This distinctive essence of a play, marking its brand, is the one thing at which the dramatist cannot work, for it is outside his consciousness. A man may have many moods, he has but one spirit; and this spirit he communicates in some subtle, unconscious way to all his work. It waxes and wanes with the currents of his vitality, but no more alters than a chestnut changes into an oak.

For, in truth, dramas are very like unto trees, springing from seedlings, shaping themselves inevitably in accordance with the laws fast hidden within themselves, drinking sustenance from the earth and air, and in conflict with the natural forces round them. So they slowly come to full growth, until warped, stunted, or risen to fair and gracious height, they stand open to all the winds. And the trees that spring from each dramatist are of different race; he is the spirit of his own sacred grove, into which no stray tree can by any chance enter.

One more platitude. It is not unfashionable to pit one form of drama against another—holding up the naturalistic to the disadvantage of the epic; the epic to the belittlement of the fantastic; the fantastic to the detriment of the naturalistic. Little purpose is thus served. The essential meaning, truth, beauty, and irony of things may be revealed under all these forms. Vision over life and human nature can be as keen and just, the revelation as true, inspiring, delight-giving and thought-provoking, whatever fashion be employed—it is simply a question of doing it well enough to uncover the kernel of the nut. Whether the violet come from Russia, from Parma, or from England, matters little. Close by the Greek temples at Pæstum there are violets that seem redder, and sweeter, than any ever seen—as though they have sprung up out of the footprints of some old pagan goddess; but under the April sun, in a Devonshire lane, the little blue scentless violets capture every bit as much of the spring. And so it is with drama—no matter what its form—it need only be the "real thing," need only have caught some of the precious fluids, revelation, or delight, and imprisoned them within a chalice to which we may put our lips and continually drink.

And yet, starting from this last platitude, one may perhaps be suffered to speculate as to the particular forms that our renascent drama is likely to assume. For our drama is renascent, and nothing will stop its growth. It is not renascent because this or that man is writing, but because of a new spirit. A spirit that is no doubt in part the gradual outcome of the impact on our home-grown art, of Russian, French, and Scandinavian influences, but which in the main rises from an awakened humanity in the conscience of our time.

What, then, are to be the main channels down which the renascent English drama will float in the coming years? It is more than possible that these main channels will come to be two in number and situate far apart.

The one will be the broad and clear-cut channel of naturalism, down which will course a drama poignantly shaped, and inspired with high intention, but faithful to the seething and multiple life around us, drama such as some are inclined to term photographic, deceived by a seeming simplicity into forgetfulness of the old proverb, *"Ars est celare artem,"*[4] and oblivious of the fact that, to be vital, to grip, such drama is in every respect as dependent on imagination, construction, selection, and elimination—the main laws of artistry—as ever was the romantic or rhapsodic play. The question of naturalistic technique will bear, indeed, much more study than has yet been given to it. The aim of the dramatist employing it is obviously to create such an illusion of actual life passing on the stage as to compel the spectator to pass through an experience of his own, to think, and talk, and move with the people he sees thinking, talking, and moving in front of him. A false phrase, a single word out

---

[4] *Ars est celare artem*—It is art to conceal the art.

of tune or time, will destroy that illusion and spoil the surface as surely as a stone heaved into a still pool shatters the image seen there. But this is only the beginning of the reason why the naturalistic is the most exacting and difficult of all techniques. It is easy enough to *reproduce* the exact conversation and movements of persons in a room; it is desperately hard to *produce* the perfectly natural conversation and movements of those persons, when each natural phrase spoken and each natural movement made has not only to contribute toward the growth and perfection of a drama's soul, but also to be a revelation, phrase by phrase, movement by movement, of essential traits of character. To put it another way, naturalistic art, when alive, indeed to be alive at all, is simply the art of manipulating a procession of some delicate symbols. Its service is the swaying and focussing of men's feelings and thoughts in the various departments of human life. It will be like a steady lamp, held up from time to time, in whose light things will be seen for a space clearly and in due proportion, freed from the mists of prejudice and partisanship.

And the other of these two main channels will, I think, be a twisting and delicious stream, which will bear on its breast new barques of poetry, shaped, it may be, like prose, but a prose incarnating through its fantasy and symbolism all the deeper aspirations, yearning, doubts, and mysterious stirrings of the human spirit; a poetic prose-drama, emotionalising us by its diversity and purity of form and invention, and whose province will be to disclose the elemental soul of man and the forces of Nature, not perhaps as the old tragedies disclosed them, not necessarily in the epic mood, but always with beauty and in the spirit of discovery.

Such will, I think, be the two vital forms of our drama in the coming generation. And between these two forms there must be no crude unions; they are too far apart, the cross is too violent. For, where there is a seeming blend of lyricism and naturalism, it will on examination be found, I think, to exist only in plays whose subjects or settings—as in Synge's *Playboy of the Western World*,[5] or in Mr. Masefield's *Nan* [6]—are so re-

[5] *Playboy of the Western World*—An extravagant peasant fantasy by the Irish poet and dramatist, John Millington Synge.
[6] *Nan*—A tragedy by John Masefield.

moved from our ken that we cannot really tell, and therefore do not care, whether an absolute illusion is maintained. The poetry which may and should exist in naturalistic drama, can only be that of perfect rightness of proportion, rhythm, shape—the poetry, in fact, that lies in all vital things. It is the illmating of forms that has killed a thousand plays. We want no more bastard drama; no more attempts to dress out the simple dignity of everyday life in the peacock's feathers of false lyricism; no more straw-stuffed heroes or heroines; no more rabbits and goldfish from the conjurer's pockets, nor any limelight. Let us have starlight, moonlight, sunlight, and the light of our own self-respects.

Vocabulary Study: To understand Mr. Galsworthy's essay you will want to be sure of his vocabulary. The list is long, but it will repay study. *Inherent; poignantly; distorted; permeate; temperamental; pessimist; optimist; edifice; organic; cardinal; austere; license; epigram; pathos; stultifying; disquisitions; conception; scope; impalpable; poignant; essence; caffeine; inevitably; sustenance; epic; detriment; chalice; renascent; situate; rhapsodic; manipulating; ken; lyricism.*

What two words in the list are antonyms? What are the different shades of meaning expressed by *permeate, pierce, pervade?* Give common synonyms for *stultify; disquisition; chalice.*

By Way of Appreciation: "Why do I *have* to read Shakespeare?"

There are, every year, high school students who are putting the question in secret or open disgruntlement. Usually the grumblers are pupils who cannot see beyond the difficulties of sixteenth-century wording or the perplexing mechanics of a page of drama. Some are honestly seeking an answer. Why *is* Shakespeare conceded the world's greatest literary genius?

Some Platitudes Concerning Drama in part answers the question. It tells why Shakespeare is a great *dramatist*, and why his characters are "not of an age, but for all time." It tells us, too, how any writer—but more especially the dramatist—may produce literature with this same time-less quality. Examine the great works of art that have survived the centuries—Homer's *Iliad*, for instance, or Chaucer's *Canterbury Tales*—and you will see that they have lived because they reproduce "the permanent elements of human nature." Galsworthy tells very explicitly how the playwright may build these permanent elements into his plays (perhaps it is more accurate to say, let them grow into his plays).

His rules are the more meaningful because he has himself successfully followed them. He is best known as a novelist, especially through his Forsyte stories. In the Forsytes the author has created a family that is as real as humanity itself. They illustrate how well these same principles of character and action apply in the novel. But Mr. Galsworthy has also written successful plays. In fact, for twelve years he concerned himself principally with the stage. It was during this period that the present essay was written. Most of his dramas are tragedies—*The Silver Box, Strife, Justice, The Eldest Son*—but two—*Joy*, and *The Little Dream*—are in lighter mood. It would be interesting for the student to read one or two of the plays and then judge them by Mr. Galsworthy's own standards as they are set forth in his essay.

Suggestions for Study: Explain the expression, "a spire of meaning," in the first sentence. What part of speech is *situate* in the expression, "two in number and situate far apart"? Comment on the definitions for *optimist* and *pessimist*. What is the difference between *limelight* and the *lights* named in the last sentence?

Express in your own words the three courses in play-writing open to the serious dramatist. Can you name a play (or movie) illustrative of each method? To which course does Galsworthy give his approval? Explain and illustrate what you understand by "drawing a distorted moral." Explain: "The good that Shakespeare did to humanity was of a remote and eternal nature." Ben Jonson, who of all Shakespeare's contemporaries praised him most highly, himself wrote not for all time but for an age—his age. It is interesting to contrast one of his plays (even in synopsis) with Shakespeare's in the light of "drawing a distorted moral" and characterization.

Can you explain why "a human being is a good plot"? Draw an illustration from either a novel or a play. Can you name a play that you have seen that had "flavor"? Now that some moving pictures are being given serious artistic production, perhaps you can name a screen play which had that "thin, poignant spirit" which Mr. Galsworthy calls flavor. What, if any, play have you seen that met all of Mr. Galsworthy's requirements of plot, action, character, dialogue, and flavor? In your own words explain the two types of drama likely to appear in the future. Twenty years have passed since Mr. Galsworthy made this prediction, and plays of both types have appeared. Can you name an example of each?

Exercises and Creative Work: As an aid to your understanding of the essay, make an outline of it, either topical or sentence *but do not combine the two types*. Without referring again to the essay, develop one of the main topics into a paragraph of about one hundred words.

Write a thoughtful review of the best play or movie that you have ever seen (not the most entertaining necessarily).

Write a thoughtful review of the worst play you have even seen. Be sure to tell why it was a poor play, not just why you didn't like it.

A STUDY IN DEJECTION

From *Yet Again*

Max Beerbohm

By Way of Introduction: The light essay is sometimes a mood transferred to paper. Some ordinary object has stirred a sensitive mind until the commonplace features have vanished. It is no longer an object but a symbol which the essayist proceeds to interpret for us—though not in any literal way. It is a free translation with its aim to lift our mood to his. But some thoughts are more easily illustrated than explained. Mr. Beerbohm's *A Study in Dejection* will exemplify better than words can describe the essay which is the crystallization of a mood.

Riderless the horse was, and with none to hold his bridle. But he waited patiently, submissively, there where I saw him, at the shabby corner of a certain shabby little street in Chelsea.[1] "My beautiful, my beautiful, thou standest meekly by," as Mrs. Norton sang of the Arab steed, "with thy proudly-arched and glossy neck, thy dark and fiery eye." Catching the eye of this other horse, I saw that such fire as might once have blazed there had long smouldered away. Chestnut though he was, he had no mettle. His chestnut coat was all dull and rough, unkempt as that of an inferior cab-horse. Of his once luxuriant

[1] Chelsea—A borough of southwest London.

mane there were but a few poor tufts now. His saddle was torn and weather-stained. The one stirrup that dangled therefrom was red with rust.

I never saw in any creature a look of such unutterable dejection. Dejection, in the most literal sense of the word, indeed was his. He had been cast down. He had fallen from higher and happier things. With his "arched neck," and with other points which no neglect nor ill-usage could rob of their old grace, he had kept something of his fallen day about him. In the window of the little shop outside which he stood were things that seemed to match him—things appealing to the sense that he appealed to. A tarnished French mirror, a strip of faded carpet, some rows of battered, tattered books, a few cups and saucers that had erst been riveted [2] and erst been dusted—all these, in a gallimaufry of other languid odds and ends, seen through this mud-splashed window, silently echoed the silent misery of the horse. They were remembering Zion.[3] They had been beautiful once, and expensive, and well cared for, and admired, and coveted. And now . . .

They had, at least, the consolation of being indoors. Public-laughing-stock though they were, they had a barrier of glass between themselves and the irreverent world. To be warm and dry, too, was something. Piteous, they could yet afford to pity the horse. He was more ludicrously, more painfully, misplaced than they. A real blood-horse that has done his work is rightly left in the open air—turned out into some sweet meadow or paddock. It would be cruel to make him spend his declining years inside a house, where no grass is. Is it less cruel that a fine old rocking-horse should be thrust from the nursery out into the open air, upon the pavement?

Perhaps some child had just given the horse a contemptuous shove in passing. For he was rocking gently when I chanced to see him. Nor did he cease to rock, with a slight creak upon the pavement, so long as I watched him. A particularly black and bitter north wind was blowing round the corner of the

---

[2] RIVETED—Very good wares of china may be mended by riveting the broken pieces.
[3] ZION—The site of King David's palace in Jerusalem. *Psalms* 137:1, "We wept when we remembered Zion," written of the Jews held in captivity in Babylon.

street. Perhaps it was this that kept the horse in motion. Boreas[4] himself, invisible to my mortal eyes, may have been astride the saddle, lashing the tired old horse to this futile activity. But no, I think rather that the poor thing was rocking of his own accord, rocking to attract my attention. He saw in me a possible purchaser. He wanted to show me that he was still sound in wind and limb. Had I a small son at home? If so, here was the very mount for him. None of your frisky, showy, first-hand young brutes, on which no fond parent ought to risk his offspring's bones; but a steady-going, sound, well-mannered old hack with never a spark of vice in him! Such was the message that I read in the glassy eye fixed on me. The nostril of faded scarlet seemed for a moment to dilate and quiver. At last, at last, was some one going to inquire his price?

Once upon a time, in a far-off fashionable toy-shop, his price had been prohibitive; and he, the central attraction behind the gleaming shop-window, had plumed himself on his expensiveness. He had been in no hurry to be bought. It had seemed to him a good thing to stand there motionless, majestic, day after day, far beyond the reach of average purses, and having in his mien something of the frigid nobility of the horses on the Parthenon frieze,[5] with nothing at all of their unreality. A coat of real chestnut hair, glossy, glorious! From end to end of the Parthenon frieze not one of the horses had that. From end to end of the toy-shop that exhibited him not one of the horses was thus graced. Their flanks were mere wood, painted white, with arbitrary blotches of grey here and there. Miserable creatures! It was difficult to believe that they had souls. No wonder they were cheap, and "went off," as the shopman said, so quickly, whilst *he* stayed grandly on, cynosure of eyes that dared not hope for him. Into bondage they went off, those others, and would be worked to death, doubtless, by brutal little boys.

When, one fine day, a lady was actually not shocked by the price demanded for him, his pride was hurt. And when, that evening, he was packed in brown paper and hoisted to the roof

---

[4] Boreas—The north wind, symbol of winter, cold, and hardship.
[5] Parthenon frieze—The Parthenon was the temple of Athena on the Acropolis at Athens. The frieze is the broad band of sculpture which adorns the temple. It was designed by Phidias.

of a four-wheeler,[6] he faced the future fiercely. Who was this lady that her child should dare bestride him? With a biblical "ha, ha," he vowed that the child should not stay long in the saddle: he must be thrown—badly—even though it *was* his seventh birthday. But this wicked intention vanished while the child danced around him in joy and wonder. Never yet had so many compliments been showered on him. Here surely, was more the manner of a slave than of a master. And how lightly the child rode him, with never a tug or a kick! And oh, how splendid it was to be flying thus through the air! Horses were made to be ridden; and he had never before savoured the true joy of life, for he had never known his own strength and fleetness. Forward! Backward! Faster, faster! To floor! To ceiling! Regiments of leaden soldiers watched his wild career. Noah's quiet, sedentary beasts gaped up at him in wonderment —as tiny to him as the gaping cows in the fields are to you when you pass by in an express train. This was life indeed! He remembered Katafalto—remembered Eclipse[7] and the rest nowhere. Aye, thought he, and even thus must Black Bess[8] have rejoiced along the road to York. And Bucephalus,[9] skimming under Alexander the plains of Asia, must have had just this glorious sense of freedom. Only less so! Not Pegasus himself can have flown more swiftly. Pegasus, at last, became a constellation in the sky. "Some day," reflected the rocking-horse, when the ride was over, "I, too, shall die: and five stars will appear on the nursery ceiling."

Alas for the vanity of equine ambition! I wonder by what stages this poor beast came down in the world. Did the little boy's father go bankrupt, leaving it to be sold in a "lot" with the other toys? Or was it merely given away, when the little boy grew up, to a poor but procreative relation,[10] who anon became poorer? I should like to think that it had been mourned. But I fear that whatever mourning there may have been for it must have been long ago discarded. The creature did not look

---

[6] FOUR-WHEELER—Truck, or delivery wagon.
[7] ECLIPSE—A famous race-horse.
[8] BLACK BESS—The mare belonging to Dick Turpin, notorious highwayman, whose life she once saved by racing with him to York.
[9] BUCEPHALUS—War horse of Alexander the Great.
[10] PROCREATIVE RELATION—Relative with many children.

as if it had been ridden in any recent decade. It looked as if it had almost abandoned the hope of ever being ridden again. It was but hoping against hope now, as it stood rocking there in the bleak twilight. Bright warm nurseries were for younger, happier horses. Still it went on rocking, to show me that it *could* rock.

The more sentimental a man is, the less is he helpful; the more loth is he to cancel the cause of his emotion. I did not buy the horse.

A few days later, passing that way, I wished to renew my emotion; but lo! the horse was gone. Had some finer person than I bought it?—towed it to the haven where it would be? Likelier, it had but been relegated to some murky recess of the shop . . . I hope it has room to rock there.

Vocabulary Study: Give particular attention to the following words: *chestnut* (the color); *mettle; dejection; erst; gallimaufry; languid; ludicrously; paddock; futile; mien; frigid; arbitrary; cynosure; sedentary; constellation; equine; procreative; loth* (also *loath*); *relegate*.

Give the histories of *dejection; ludicrous; sedentary*. What are common synonyms for *erst; languid; mien?* What is an antonym for *frigid?*

By Way of Appreciation: "I love best in literature, delicate and elaborate ingenuities in form and style," confesses Max Beerbohm, one of England's most engaging essayists. He is speaking, of course, of the works of others; but it is natural that his own writings show this same ingenious delicacy. *A Study in Dejection* is a good illustration. Sympathetic imagination that does not quite run into sentimentality has turned a battered toy into a poetic fancy. The rocking-horse becomes the symbol of vanished splendors. Appealing as Mr. Beerbohm's moods may be, they are usually lightened by glints of humor. He is an excellent caricaturist as well as a writer. He shows the skill of the artist in making visual his subjects. In his later essays there is more than a touch of cynicism, but he is always entertaining and often surprisingly stimulating. He is certainly one of the most artistic of the modern essayists.

Suggestions for Study: Before what kind of shop is the horse standing? In what way are the odds and ends in the window in keeping with the horse? Were you surprised to learn that it was a rocking-horse? How did Mr. Beerbohm manage the surprise? Trace briefly the flight of Beerbohm's imaginings inspired by the horse. Many of the author's phrases have a poetic appeal—such as the "frigid nobility" of the Parthenon horses. Why does the same phrase aptly describe the youthful rocking-horse? Find four or five other pleasing phrases. What are the words that make the horse vivid in our minds? Explain the next-to-the-last paragraph. Do you think of any other illustration of the same idea? Or do you disagree? Would a really sentimental person have bought the horse? Discuss.

Exercises and Creative Work: Follow the plan of the essay by listing in order the topics discussed in each paragraph—one topic to a paragraph. Notice how well defined this thought-development is.

There is no telling what subject may strike a spark in the imagination of another; however the following titles all have possibilities. If one of them appeals to you, try developing it into an imaginative essay. You might jot down a topical plan before you begin to write. *Great-grandmother's Fan; Patchwork; Out of the Rag-bag; At the Rummage Sale; On Seeing an Impoverished Woman Enter a Second-hand Shop; Pathos at the Rummage Sale; The Human Side of the Auction.*

THE DAILY MIRACLE

From *How to Live on Twenty-four Hours a Day*

ARNOLD BENNETT

By Way of Introduction: "I have never," said Arnold Bennett, "seen an essay, 'How to Live on Twenty-four Hours a Day.'" So he proceeded to write one—or rather, a bookful of them. In that book *The Daily Miracle* serves as the introduction. As you may guess, the succeeding chapters present some ideas on how one may get the most for his time; and there are some splendid suggestions. Perhaps this introductory essay will make you want to get acquainted with the book.

"YES, he's one of those men that don't know how to manage. Good situation. Regular income. Quite enough for luxuries as well as needs. Not really extravagant. And yet the fellow's always in difficulties. Somehow he gets nothing out of his money. Excellent flat—half empty! Always looks as if he'd had the brokers[1] in. New suit—old hat! Magnificent necktie—baggy trousers! Asks you to dinner: cut glass—bad mutton, or Turkish coffee—cracked cup! He can't understand it. Explanation simply is that he fritters his income away. Wish I had the half of it! I'd show him——"

So we have most of us criticised, at one time or another, in our superior way.

[1] BROKERS—Here, buyers of furniture.

ELD

We are nearly all chancellors of the exchequer:[2] it is the pride of the moment. Newspapers are full of articles explaining how to live on such-and-such a sum, and these articles provoke a correspondence whose violence proves the interest they excite. Recently, in a daily organ, a battle raged round the question whether a woman can exist nicely in the country on £85 a year.[3] I have seen an essay, "How to live on eight shillings a week." But I have never seen an essay, "How to live on twenty-four hours a day." Yet it has been said that time is money. That proverb understates the case. Time is a great deal more than money. If you have time you can obtain money—usually. But though you have the wealth of a cloak-room attendant at the Carlton Hotel,[4] you cannot buy yourself a minute more time than I have, or the cat by the fire has.

Philosophers have explained space. They have not explained time. It is the inexplicable raw material of everything. With it, all is possible; without it, nothing. The supply of time is truly a daily miracle, an affair genuinely astonishing when one examines it. You wake up in the morning, and lo! your purse is magically filled with twenty-four hours of the unmanufactured tissue of the universe of your life! It is yours. It is the most precious of possessions. A highly singular commodity, showered upon you in a manner as singular as the commodity itself!

For remark! No one can take it from you. It is unstealable. And no one receives either more or less than you receive.

Talk about an ideal democracy! In the realm of time there is no aristocracy of wealth, and no aristocracy of intellect. Genius is never rewarded by even an extra hour a day. And there is no punishment. Waste your infinitely precious commodity as much as you will, and the supply will never be withheld from you. No mysterious power will say:—"This man is a fool, if not a knave. He does not deserve time; he shall be cut off at the meter." It is more certain than consols,[5] and

[2] CHANCELLORS OF THE EXCHEQUER—Ministers of finance.
[3] £85 A YEAR—A pound is worth, at par values, $4.86; a shilling, 24⅓ cents; a guinea, $5.11.
[4] CLOAK-ROOM ATTENDANT AT THE CARLTON HOTEL—A reference to exorbitant tipping.
[5] CONSOLS—A British government security.

payment of income is not affected by Sundays. Moreover, you cannot draw on the future. Impossible to get into debt! You can only waste the passing moment. You cannot waste tomorrow; it is kept for you. You cannot waste the next hour; it is kept for you.

I said the affair was a miracle. Is it not?

You have to live on this twenty-four hours of daily time. Out of it you have to spin health, pleasure, money, content, respect, and the evolution of your immortal soul. Its right use, its most effective use, is a matter of the highest urgency and of the most thrilling actuality. All depends on that. Your happiness—the elusive prize that you are all clutching for, my friends!—depends on that. Strange that the newspapers, so enterprising and up-to-date as they are, are not full of "How to live on a given income of time," instead of "How to live on a given income of money"! Money is far commoner than time. When one reflects, one perceives that money is just about the commonest thing there is. It encumbers the earth in gross heaps.

If one can't contrive to live on a certain income of money, one earns a little more—or steals it, or advertises for it. One doesn't necessarily muddle one's life because one can't quite manage on a thousand pounds a year; one braces the muscles and makes it guineas, and balances the budget. But if one cannot arrange that an income of twenty-four hours a day shall exactly cover all proper items of expenditure, one does muddle one's life definitely. The supply of time, though gloriously regular, is cruelly restricted.

Which of us lives on twenty-four hours a day? And when I say "lives," I do not mean exists, or "muddles through." Which of us is free from that uneasy feeling that the "great spending departments" of his daily life are not managed as they ought to be? Which of us is quite sure that his fine suit is not surmounted by a shameful hat, or that in attending to the crockery, he has forgotten the quality of the food? Which of us is not saying to himself—which of us has not been saying to himself all his life: "I shall alter that when I have a little more time?"

We never shall have any more time. We have, and we have always had, all the time there is. It is the realisation of this profound and neglected truth (which, by the way, I have not discovered) that has led me to the minute practical examination of daily time-expenditure.

Vocabulary Study: *Provoke; organ (daily organ); inexplicable* (note pronunciation); *evolution.*

Note the derivations of the above words. Make a list of the Englishisms in the essay.

By Way of Appreciation: The chapters in *How to Live on Twenty-four Hours a Day* are illustrative of an especially pleasing type of light essay—the essay that has a serious idea to present but does so in a lively, intimate way. It is like a friendly conversation which has drifted into a discussion of the real issues of life but which keeps its light, inconsequential tone. You will notice that Mr. Bennett's manner is gay, but that at the same time he appeals to our sense. Notice, too, Mr. Bennett's crisp modern style—the result of using short, direct sentences and familiar words.

Suggestions for Study: What type of person is being described in the first paragraph? If he were American instead of English what changes in details would be made? Explain: "We are nearly all chancellors of the exchequer." Have you ever thought that you could manage the income of one of your acquaintances better than he does? Have you ever thought that you could make better use of time than any of your friends? Which is the more common thought?

What are the points of contrast between time and money? There is one sense in which a man's time may be said to be "cut off at the meter." What is it? Which of all Mr. Bennett's statements do you consider most strikingly true? Which, if any, would you call in question? Can you guess what will be some of the suggestions for using time in succeeding essays?

Exercises and Creative Work: Write a précis of the paragraphs in which Mr. Bennett develops his idea of *The Miracle of Time.*

Other chapters in *How to Live on Twenty-four Hours a Day* present some interesting ideas on how one may get the most for his time. Read one of the essays and be prepared to make a class report on it.

Mr. Bennett seems to have a tremendous gusto for life—not as it should be, but as it is here and now—and this is perhaps the origin of his books of essays. Read a selection from one of the following books, and then write a précis of it to be read and discussed in class: *Literary Taste and How to Form It, Things That Have Interested Me, How to Make the Best of Life.*

Make a topical outline for a theme on the subject, *My Daily Budget* (in terms of time, not money). If the plan appeals to you, write the theme.

THE SEA AND THE JUNGLE

A Selection

Henry Major Tomlinson

By Way of Introduction: The best possible introduction to *The Sea and the Jungle* would be a reading of Mr. Tomlinson's essay *Hints for Those About to Travel*. In it the author tells how he happened to sail up the Amazon. Briefly, it was something like this:

On a bitterly cold Easter Mr. Tomlinson was reading Bates' *A Naturalist on the River Amazons*. The book with its palms and tropic air fired his imagination. And then one night a sailor told him that on its next voyage his ship was actually going up the Amazon.

"Nonsense," said Mr. Tomlinson, "it cannot be done."

"I've seen the charter," the sailor replied. "We're going, and I wish we weren't. A ship has no right inside a continent. But look here, we have an empty cabin. Come along."

The next day Tomlinson wrote an account of the tramp steamer's proposed voyage for a morning daily. Later in the day he met the editor of the paper on the office stairs.

"That was an amusing lie of yours this morning," said the editor. Tomlinson assured him that it was no lie. "Well," replied the newspaper-man, "you shall go along and prove it."

"Somehow," comments Tomlinson, "as that editor descended the stairs, the attractive old naturalist of the Amazon with his palms at Para [1] was less alluring. This meant packing up; and for what? Even the master of the steamer could not tell me that."

But *The Sea and the Jungle* tells us what he found.

"5 JAN. We seem to have got to a dead end of the trade winds. The heat of the forenoon was oppressively humid and dinner was nearly lost through it. The cook, a fair and plump Dutchman, broke down in the midst of his pans, and was carried out to find his breath again. This poor chef is up at four o'clock every morning coffee making; is working in the galley, which is badly ventilated, all day, getting two hours' rest in the early afternoon. Then he goes on till the saloon tea is over; when he begins to bake bread. He fills in his leisure in peeling potatoes.

"All round the horizon motionless and permanent storm clouds are banked. Their forms do not alter, but their colours change with the hours. They seem to encompass us in a circular lake, a range of precipitous and intricately piled Alps, high and massive. Cleaving those steeps of calamitous rocks—for so they looked, and not in the least like vapour—are chasms full of night, and the upper slopes and summits are lucent in amber and pearl. In the south and east the ranges are indigo, dark and threatening, and the water between us and that closed country is opaque and heavy as molten lead. Across the peaks of the mountains rest horizontal strata of mist. Some petrels were about today. The evening is cool, with a slight head breeze."

.   .   .   .   .   .

After weeks at sea, imprisoned within the walls of the sky, walls which have not opened once to admit another vessel to give the assurance of communion, you begin to doubt your direction and destination, and the possibility of change. Only the clouds change. The ship is no nearer breaking that rigid circle. She cannot escape from her place under the centre of the dome. The most cheering assurance I had was the pulse of the steamer, felt whenever I rested against her warm body. Purposeful life was there, at least. Though the day may have

---

[1] PARA—An estuary of the Amazon, also a state in Brazil.

been brazen, and without a hint of progress, and the sea the same empty wilderness, yet when most disheartened in the blind and the melancholy night I felt under me the beatings, energetic and insistent, of her lively heart, some of that vitality was communicated, and I got sleep as a child would in the arms of a strong and wakeful guardian.

Poised between two profundities—though nearer the clouds, cirrus and lofty though they are, than the land straight beneath the keel—and with morning and night the only variety in the round, the days flicker by white and black like a magic lantern working without a story. Tired of watching for the fruits of our enterprise I went to sleep. Old Captain Morgan must have lived a dull life, monotonous with adventure. What is the use of travel, I asked myself. The stars are as near to London as they are to the Spanish Main.[2] In their planetary journey through the void the passengers at Peckham[3] see as much as their fellows who peer through the windows in Macassar.[4] The sun rises in the east, and the moon is horned; but some of the passengers on the mudball,[5] strangely enough, take their tea without milk. Yet what of that?

In the chart room some days ago I learned we had 3,000 fathoms under us. Well; these waves of the tropics, curling over such abysmal deeps, look much the same as the waves off Land's End.[6] I began to see what I had done. I had changed the murk of winter in London for the discomforts of the dog days. I had come thousands of miles to see the thermometer rise. Where are the Spanish Main, the Guianas, and the Brazils? At last I had discovered them. I found their true bearings. They are in Raleigh's *Golden City of Manoa,* in Burney's *Buccaneers of America,* with Drake,[7] Humboldt,[8] Bates,[9] and Wallace;[10] and I had left them all at home. We borrow the light

---

[2] SPANISH MAIN—The part of the Caribbean close to the northeast coast of South America. It was crossed by the old Spanish merchant ships.

[3] PECKHAM—In England.

[4] MACASSAR—A district of the Celebes, an island of the Malay peninsula.

[5] MUDBALL—The earth.

[6] LAND'S END—A cape in Cornwall, the most westerly point of England.

[7] DRAKE—Sir Francis Drake, English explorer and adventurer on the Spanish Main.

[8] HUMBOLDT—Baron von Humboldt, German scientist, explorer, and author.   [9] BATES—See *Introduction.*

[10] WALLACE—Alfred Russell Wallace, English naturalist and explorer; author of *Palm Trees of the Amazon* and other books.

of an observant and imaginative traveller, and see the foreign land bright with his aura; and we think it is the country which shines.

. . . . .

At eight this morning we crossed the equator. Soon after that, idling under the poop awning, I picked up the Doctor's [11] book from his vacant chair. I took the essays of Emerson carelessly and read at once—the sage plainly had laid a trap for me—"Why covet a knowledge of new facts? Day and night, a house and garden, a few books, a few actions, serve as well as all trades and spectacles." So——. At this moment the first mate crossed my light, and presently I heard the sounding machine whirring, and then stop. There was a pause, and then the mate's unimportant voice, "Twenty-five fathoms, sir, grey sand!"

Emerson went sprawling. I stood up. Twenty-five fathoms! Then that grey sand stuck to the tallow of the weight was the first of the Brazils. The circle of waters was still complete about us, but over the bows, at a great distance, were thunder clouds and wild lights. The oceanic swell had decreased to a languid and glassy beat, and the water had become jade green in colour, shot with turquoise gleams. The Skipper, himself interested and almost jolly, announced a pound of tobacco to the first man who spied the coast. We were nearing it at last. Those far clouds canopied the forests of the Amazon. We stood in at slow speed.

I know those forests. I mean I have often navigated their obscure waterways, rafting through the wilds on a map, in my slippers, at night. Now those forests soon were to loom on a veritable skyline. I should see them where they stood, their roots in the unfrequented floods. I should see Santa Maria de Belem,[12] its aerial foliage over its shipping and squalor. It was quite near now. I should see Santarem and Obydos, and Ita-coatiara; [13] and then, turning from the King of Rivers to his tributary, the Madeira, follow the Madeira to the San Antonio falls in the heart of the South American continent. We drew

---

[11] DOCTOR'S—The ship's doctor.
[12] SANTA MARIA DE BELEM—A seaport town at the mouth of the Amazon, mentioned by Bates.
[13] SANTAREM, OBYDOS, ITA-COATIARA—Towns along the Amazon.

over 23 feet, with this "Capella." [14] We were going to try what had never been attempted before by an ocean steamer. This, too, was pioneering. I also was on an adventure, going two thousand miles under those clouds of the equatorial rains, to live for a while in the forests of the Orellana.[15] And our vessel's rigging, so they tell me, sometimes shall drag the foliage in showers on our decks, and where we anchor at night the creatures of the jungle will call.

Our nearness to land stirs up some old dreads in our minds also. We discuss those dreads again, though with more concern than we did at Swansea.[16] Over the bows is now the prelude. We have heard many unsettling legends of yellow fever, malaria, blackwater fever, dysentery, and beri-beri. The mates, looking for land, swear they were fools to come a voyage like this. They ought to have known better. The Doctor, who does not always smile when he is amused, advises us not to buy a white sun umbrella at Para, but a black one; then it will do for the funerals.

"Land O!" That was the Skipper's own perfunctory cry. He had saved his pound of tobacco.

It was two in the afternoon. There was America. I rediscovered it with some difficulty. All I could see was a mere local thickening of the horizon, as though the pen which drew the faint line dividing the world ahead into an upper and a nether opalescence had run a little freely at one point. That thickening of the horizon was the island of Monjui. Soon, though, there was a palpable something athwart our course. The skyline heightened into a bluish barrier, which, as we approached still nearer, broke into sections. The chart showed that a series of low wooded islands skirted the mainland. Yet it was hard to believe we were approaching land again. What showed as land was of too unsubstantial a quality, too thin and broken a rind on that vast area of water to be of any use as a foothold. Where luminous sky was behind an island, groups of diminutive palms showed, as tiny and distinct as the forms of mildew under a magnifying glass, delicate black pen-

[14] CAPELLA—The steamer.
[15] ORELLANA—Francesco Orellana (1500–1545), Spanish explorer, discovered the course of the Amazons. His name is still sometimes given to the Amazon River.
[16] SWANSEA—A seaport of South Wales.

cillings along the foot of the sky-wall. Often that hair-like tracery seemed to rest upon the sea. The "Capella" continued to stand in, till America was more than a frail and tinted illusion which sometimes faded the more the eye sought it. Presently it cast reflections. The islands grew into cobalt layers, with vistas of silver water between them, giving them body. The course was changed to west, and we cruised along for Atalaia point, towards the pilot station. Over the thin and futile rind of land which topped the sea—it might have undulated on the low swell—ponderous thunder clouds towered, continents of night in the sky, with translucent areas dividing them which were strangely illuminated from the hither side. Curtains as black as bitumen draped to the waters from great heights. Two of these appalling curtains, trailing over America, were a little withdrawn. We could look beyond them to a diminishing array of glowing cloud summits, as if we saw there an accidental revelation of a secret and wonderful region with a sun of its own. And all, gigantic clouds, the sea, the far and frail coast, were serene and still. The air had ceased to breathe. I thought this new lucent world we had found might prove but a lucky dream after all, to be seen but not to be entered, and that some noise would presently shatter it and wake me. But we came alongside the white pilot schooner, and the pilot put off in a boat manned by such a crowd of grinning, ragged, and cinnamon skinned pirates as would have broken the fragile wonder of any spell. Ours, though, did not break, and I was able to believe we had arrived. At sunset the great clouds were full of explosions of electric fire, and there were momentary revelations above us of huge impending shapes. We went slowly over a lower world obscurely lighted by phosphorescent waves.

Vocabulary Study: *Humid; galley; calamitous; lucent; amber; opaque; stratum; petrels; communion; profundities; cirrus; fathom; abysmal; aura; veritable; prelude; perfunctory; nether; opalescence; illusion; cobalt; undulated; translucent; hither; bitumen.*

Note and explain the plural of *stratum*; note also the English pronunciation. Give the derivation of *communion, profundity, lucent.* Give a synonym and an antonym for *nether,* for *prelude.*

By Way of Appreciation: Not all songs of the sea have been written in verse. Mr. Tomlinson writes his in prose. His voyage may have been tedious, hot, empty of comforts; but it is the strange colorful beauty of it that he carries in memory and that he passes on to others in melodious words.

We are reminded of the vivid sea-and-sky pictures of Coleridge's *Rime of the Ancient Mariner;* only with Mr. Tomlinson the clouds hold the center of the stage. Then too the pictures of the later writer hold the conviction of reality. What an inspiration for a painter! Mr. Tomlinson knows, besides, how to catch the changing moods of the sailor —the sense of futility born of long monotony, a what's-the-useness of it all. Then land—and the thrill of quickened life and purpose and discovery! One should like to go on with him over his world of phosphorescent waves into the fresh mystery of the jungle.

Suggestions for Study: It is worth while to make a careful study of Mr. Tomlinson's manner of expression. Much of the effectiveness of his writing is due to his use of sense-appealing words. Here are some examples: Expressive of feeling: *humid, pulse, undulated;* expressive of sound: *whirring, explosions* (Why are they so few?); expressive of color: *lucent, amber, pearl;* expressive of form: *chasms, slopes, summits.* Make a list of ten other *color* words from the essay. Make a list of ten other *form* words from the essay. Choose ten especially effective word-combinations and mark those that are similes or metaphors; thus—

> Vistas of silver water
> Steeps of calamitous rock (metaphor)
> Curtains black as bitumen (simile)

Why would reading Emerson fit Mr. Tomlinson's mood of listless musing on the uselessness of travel? What changes the mood? Explain the sentence which closes the second section of the essay, "We borrow the light, etc." Is this reflection the result of his mood, or is it a general truth? What details throughout the essay keep it "down to earth"? Select a favorite passage for reading aloud to an appreciative audience.

Exercises and Creative Work: Write a précis of one of the sections of the essay. See if, even in condensation, you can preserve something of the tone of the original.

A large expanse of water, mountain ranges, prairie skies—all give opportunities for study of light and shade and color, of clouds and stars, and the like. Even in the city, lights at night, the skyline in early morning, or a little park have picture possibilities. An hour of careful observation should furnish you with the materials for a word-painting of your own. You may even want to write it in verse. The following titles may be suggestive: *Harbor Lights; Sunset over the City; Lights and Shades of the Prairies; The Greens of Summer Landscape; My Cloud-hung Mountaintop.*

If you have studied art, try making an original illustration for the essay—in color.

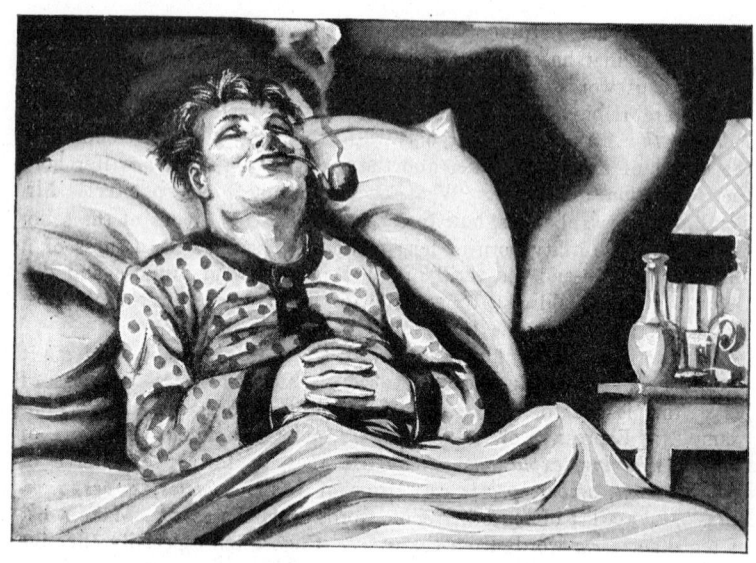

ON LYING IN BED

From *Tremendous Trifles*

GILBERT KEITH CHESTERTON

By Way of Introduction: The light essay often illustrates the manner in which an author uses a title merely as a springboard from which, with many graceful and humorous turns, he dives into a sea of ideas and retrieves something which has been lying unnoticed on the bottom. Mr. Chesterton is a master at this sport. His air of surprised discovery is comparable only to that of the magician who pulls a struggling rabbit from a seemingly empty hat. Incidentally, it pays to watch him closely; the ideas that he displays with such artlessness sometimes trail along with them a pet bit of philosophy. Not that Mr. Chesterton would have us take him seriously on "Lying in bed"!

LYING in bed would be an altogether perfect and supreme experience if only one had a colored pencil long enough to draw on the ceiling. This, however, is not generally a part of the domestic apparatus on the premises. I think myself that the thing might be managed with several pails of Aspinall and a broom. Only if one worked in a really sweeping and masterly way, and laid on the color in great washes, it might drip down again on one's face in floods of rich and mingled color like some strange fairy rain; and that would have its disadvantages. I am afraid it would be necessary to stick to black and white in this form of artistic composition. To that purpose, indeed, the white ceiling would be of the greatest possible use; in fact it is the only use I think of a white ceiling being put to.

But for the beautiful experiment of lying in bed I might never have discovered it. For years I have been looking for some blank spaces in a modern house to draw on. Paper is much too small for any really allegorical design; as Cyrano de Bergerac[1] says: *"Il me faut des géants."*[2] But when I tried to find these fine clear spaces in the modern rooms such as we all live in I was continually disappointed. I found an endless pattern and complication of small objects hung like a curtain of fine links between me and my desire. I examined the walls; I found them to my surprise to be already covered with wall paper, and I found the wall paper to be already covered with very uninteresting images, all bearing a ridiculous resemblance to each other. I could not understand why one arbitrary symbol (a symbol apparently entirely devoid of any religious or philosophical significance) should thus be sprinkled all over my nice walls like a sort of smallpox. The Bible must be referring to wall papers, I think, when it says, "Use not vain repetitions, as the Gentiles do." I found the Turkey carpet a mass of unmeaning colors, rather like the Turkish Empire, or like the sweetmeat called Turkish delight. I do not exactly know what Turkish delight really is; but I suppose it is Macedonian Massacres.[3] Everywhere that I went forlornly, with my pencil or my paint brush, I found that others had unaccountably been before me, spoiling the walls, the curtains, and the furniture with their childish and barbaric designs.

Nowhere did I find a really clear place for sketching until this occasion when I prolonged beyond the proper limit the process of lying on my back in bed. Then the light of that white heaven broke upon my vision, that breadth of mere white

[1] CYRANO DE BERGERAC—Celebrated duelist, wit, poet, and soldier in Rostand's drama of the same name.
[2] *Il me faut des géants*—"Bring me giants" (to fight with).
[3] MACEDONIAN MASSACRES—There has been frequent warfare between Turkey and Macedonia.

which is indeed almost the definition of Paradise, since it means purity and also means freedom. But alas! like all heavens, now that it is seen it is found to be unattainable; it looks more austere and more distant than the blue sky outside the window. For my proposal to paint on it with the bristly end of a broom has been discouraged—never mind by whom; by a person debarred from all political rights—and even my minor proposal to put the other end of the broom into the kitchen fire and turn it into charcoal has not been conceded. Yet I am certain that it was from persons in my position that all the original inspiration came for covering the ceilings of palaces and cathedrals with a riot of fallen angels or victorious gods. I am sure that it was only because Michelangelo [4] was engaged in the ancient and honorable occupation of lying in bed that he ever realized how the roof of the Sistine Chapel [5] might be made into an awful imitation of a divine drama that could be enacted in the heavens.

The tone now commonly taken toward the practice of lying in bed is hypocritical and unhealthy. Of all the marks of modernity that seem to mean a kind of decadence, there is none more menacing and dangerous than the exaltation of very small and secondary matters of conduct at the expense of very great and primary ones, at the expense of eternal public and tragic human morality. If there is one thing worse than the modern weakening of major morals it is the modern strengthening of minor morals. Thus it is considered more withering to accuse a man of bad taste than of bad ethics. Cleanliness is not next to godliness nowadays, for cleanliness is made an essential and godliness is regarded as an offense. A playwright can attack the institution of marriage so long as he does not misrepresent the manners of society, and I have met Ibsenite [6] pessimists who thought it wrong to take beer but right to take prussic acid. Especially this is so in matters of hygiene; notably such matters as lying in bed. Instead of being regarded, as it ought to be, as a matter of personal convenience and adjustment, it has come to be regarded by many as if it were a part of essential morals to get up early in the morning. It is upon the whole part of practi-

---

[4] MICHELANGELO—Italian painter, sculptor, and architect (1475–1564).

[5] SISTINE CHAPEL—The Pope's private chapel in the Vatican.

[6] IBSENITE—Follower of the Norwegian dramatist whose plays are often somber and tragic.

cal wisdom; but there is nothing good about it or bad about its opposite.

Misers get up early in the morning; and burglars, I am informed, get up the night before. It is the great peril of our society that all its mechanism may grow more fixed while its spirit grows more fickle. A man's minor actions and arrangements ought to be free, flexible, creative; the things that should be unchangeable are his principles, his ideals. But with us the reverse is true; our views change constantly; but our lunch does not change. Now, I should like men to have strong and rooted conceptions, but as for their lunch, let them have it sometimes in the garden, sometimes in bed, sometimes on the roof, sometimes in the top of a tree. Let them argue from the same first principles, but let them do it in a bed, or a boat, or a balloon. This alarming growth of good habits really means a too great emphasis on those virtues which mere custom can misuse, it means too little emphasis on those virtues which custom can never quite ensure, sudden and splendid virtues of inspired pity or of inspired candor. If ever that abrupt appeal is made to us we may fail. A man can get used to getting up at five o'clock in the morning. A man cannot very well get used to being burned for his opinions; the first experiment is commonly fatal. Let us pay a little more attention to these possibilities of the heroic and the unexpected. I daresay that when I get out of this bed I shall do some deed of an almost terrible virtue.

For those who study the great art of lying in bed there is one emphatic caution to be added. Even for those who can do their work in bed (like journalists), still more for those whose work cannot be done in bed (as, for example, the professional harpooner of whales), it is obvious that the indulgence must be very occasional. But that is not the caution I mean. The caution is this: if you do lie in bed, be sure you do it without any reason or justification at all. I do not speak, of course, of the seriously sick. But if a healthy man lies in bed, let him do it without a rag of excuse; then he will get up a healthy man. If he does it for some secondary hygienic reason, if he has some scientific explanation, he may get up a hypochondriac.

Vocabulary Study: The following list of words is short; you can afford to study it carefully: *allegorical; arbitrary; austere; awful; decadence; ethics; conception; principle; candor; hypochondriac.*

If you have never mastered the difference between *principal* and *principle,* do so now. You will be glad ever afterward. Find two synonyms for *austere,* for *awful.* Find an antonym for *decadence,* for *candor.*

By Way of Appreciation: Mr. Chesterton's power as a writer and critic is perhaps best shown in his studies of Browning and Dickens. However, he is better known for his light verse, his stories of Father Brown—the delightful clerical detective—his magazine articles, and his essays—the lightness of which is indicated by the title of one collection, *Tremendous Trifles.* There is none of the broom-sweeping strokes that one might expect from so huge a man. He toys with words and ideas daintily, fastidiously. The English essay has learned how to play.

Suggestions for Study: To put yourself in the mood for this essay, recall some time when you have lain in bed—perhaps after an illness—and carefully traced the pattern of the wall paper. What fancies occurred to you then? Note how, in this essay, one idea leads to another. Did the author have a plan for it? Is it merely a ramble? Was it deliberately planned to seem planless? Who do you think the unfeeling person is who prohibited the decorating of the ceiling? Why "debarred from all political rights"? What two significant comments does Mr. Chesterton make on modern morals? Are there any other essays in this collection written on a somewhat similar theme? If so, make a comparison of mood, manner, and general thought.

Exercises and Creative Work: Almost any experience or observation may set up an imaginative train of thought which, if transferred to paper, would be a light essay. Perhaps one of the following subjects will hold a suggestion for you: *Paint; Wall Papers I Have Despised; The Lure of Blank, White Spaces; A Day Off; Dessert First, Why Not?*

The Essay in World Literature

General Characteristics

The Frenchman, Michel de Montaigne, created the essay in the sixteenth century. But there were no more essays in the land of Montaigne until the middle of the nineteenth century when Sainte Beauve again brought it into prominence. Since then the essay has flourished in France as well as in England, the most important French essayists being Gautier, Anatole France, and Jules Lemaitre.

In the other European countries, the writers of histories of literature give little importance to the essay as a separate literary type. Especially is this true in Spain, where the essay seems to be of the formal rather than the personal type, when it is used at all. However, many writers are doing work which we would call essays, as the influence of English, French, and American literature creeps in.

Michel de Montaigne (1533-1592)

The man to whom goes the credit for the discovery of the essay as a type of literature lived an entirely interesting and praiseworthy life. He was born in the château of his father near Bordeaux, France. When he was six, he was put into the College of Guienne at Bordeaux, and by the time he was thirteen he had completed its courses and was ready to take up the study of law. So swiftly did education progress in the sixteenth century! By the time he was twenty-one, he was a practicing lawyer. Montaigne early mingled with the people of prominence in France, and was well and pleasantly known at Court. Like the other young men of France, he served his years with the army, winning distinction for his military service. Until his thirty-eighth year he was active in public life. Then having built up for himself an adequate fortune, he retired to his château to spend the rest of his life in study and writing. He did some translating and some editing but spent most of his time in reading and meditation, jotting down from time to time his reflections on various subjects. Nine years later the world received the results of his study in a small volume called *Essais*. The book was much admired and was speedily translated into other languages. It found its way to England to further inspire the writers of the Age of Elizabeth.

Montaigne was already beginning to suffer from a painful and well-nigh incurable illness. However he practiced the virtues that he preached, keeping busy until his death. He made two revisions of his essays, adding to them at both times. He served for two terms as mayor of Bordeaux. Then followed three years of retirement and literary labor. In September of 1592, when he was fifty-nine years old, he was seized with an attack of quinsy and died very suddenly. His life exemplifies the finest circumstances of the high-born, high-minded Frenchman of the time of Shakespeare.

AGAINST IDLENESS

Michel de Montaigne

By Way of Introduction: "Reader, thou hast here an honest book; it doth at the outset forewarn thee that, in contriving the same, I have proposed to myself no other than a domestic and private end; I have had no consideration at all either to thy service or to my glory. My powers are not capable of any such design. I have dedicated it to the particular use of my kinsfolk and friends, so that, having lost me (which they must do shortly), they may therein recover some traits of my condition and humors, and by that means preserve the more whole and lifelike, the knowledge they had of me. I desire therein to be viewed as I appear in mine own genuine, simple, and ordinary manner, without study and artifice: for it is myself I portray."

These words from Montaigne's preface to the first edition of his *Essays*, which appeared in 1580 while the author was ill and suffering, still serve as the best possible introduction of himself to his reader. A glance at the titles in the volume informs one that it is Montaigne's mind and spirit that is thus being portrayed. He writes *Of Sorrow, Of Fear, Of Constancy, Of Quick or Slow Speech, Of Pedantry, Of the Education of Children,* expressing simply but freely his opinions on these and kindred subjects. He discusses the philosophies of life and death. And though he quotes profusely the sages of his own and older days, the conclusions he draws are the ones he has arrived at through careful meditation.

Yet Montaigne, like many another writer of modest purpose, quite over-shot his mark. His essays have brought him the fame he disregarded, and have been of service to writers ever since. Every writer who has attempted the personal essay is reminded of Montaigne's simple words, "It is myself I portray." If he is a great writer, he will—like Montaigne—show something of the essential truths of life besides.

Against Idleness is merely a sample of the work of this first essayist. It illustrates how, in portraying himself, Montaigne also unconsciously portrayed the age in which he lived.

The Emperor Vespasian,[1] being sick of the disease whereof he died, did not for all that neglect to enquire after the state of the empire; and even in bed continually despatched very many affairs of great consequence; for which, being reproved by his physician, as a thing prejudicial to his health, "An emperor," said he, "must die standing." A fine saying, in my opinion, and worthy a great prince. The Emperor Adrian[2]

---

[1] Vespasian—Emperor of Rome from 70–79 A.D.

[2] Adrian—Also "Hadrian," the nephew of Trajan; Emperor of Rome from 117–138 A.D.

since made use of the same words and kings should be often put in mind of them, to make them know that the great office conferred upon them of the command of so many men, is not an employment of ease; and that there is nothing can so justly disgust a subject, and make him unwilling to expose himself to labour and danger for the service of his prince, than to see him, in the mean time, devoted to his ease and frivolous amusement: and to be solicitous of his preservation who so much neglects that of his people.

Whoever will take upon him to maintain that 'tis better for a prince to carry on his wars by others, than in his own person, fortune will furnish him with examples enough of those whose lieutenants have brought great enterprises to a happy issue, and of those also whose presence has done more hurt than good: but no virtuous and valiant prince can with patience endure so dishonourable councils. Under colour of saving his head, like the statute of a saint, for the happiness of his kingdom, they degrade him from and declare him incapable of his office, which is military throughout. I know one who had rather be beaten, than to sleep while another fights for him; and who never without jealousy heard of any brave thing done even by his own officers in his absence. And Soliman I[3] said, with very good reason, in my opinion, that victories obtained without the master were never complete. Much more would he have said that that master ought to blush for shame to pretend to any share in the honour, having contributed nothing to the work, but his voice and thought; nor even so much of those, considering that in such work as that the direction and command that deserve honour are only such as are given upon the spot, and in the heat of the business. No pilot performs his office by standing still. The princes of the Ottoman family,[4] the chiefest in the world in military fortune, have warmly embraced this opinion, and Bajazet II,[5] with his son who swerved from it, spending their time in science and other retired employments,

---

[3] SOLIMAN I—Also "Solyman," the Magnificent, Sultan of Turkey from 1520–1566. He raised the Turkish Empire to its highest point.
[4] OTTOMAN FAMILY—The branch of Turks which founded and rule the Turkish Empire.
[5] BAJAZET II—Turkish Sultan from 1481–1512. He engaged in almost uninterrupted warfare, was deposed by his son Selim, and died by poison.

gave great blows to their empire; and Amurath III,[6] now reigning, following their example, begins to find the same. Was it not Edward III[7] king of England, who said this of our Charles V: "There never was a king who so seldom put on his armour, and yet never king who cut me out so much work." He had reason to think it strange, as an effect of chance more than of reason. And let those seek out some other to join with them than me, who will reckon the kings of Castile[8] and Portugal among the warlike and magnanimous conquerors, because at the distance of twelve hundred leagues from their lazy abode by the conduct of their captains they made themselves masters of both the Indies; of which it has to be known if they would have had even the courage to go and in person enjoy them.

The Emperor Julian[9] said yet further, that a philosopher and a brave man ought not so much as to breathe; that is to say, not to allow any more to bodily necessities than what we cannot refuse; keeping the soul and body still intent and busy about honourable, great, and virtuous things. He was ashamed if any one in public saw him spit, or sweat (which is said by some, also, of the Lacedæmonian[10] young men, and which Xenephon[11] says of the Persian), forasmuch as he conceived that exercise, continual labour, and sobriety ought to have dried up all those superfluities. What Seneca[12] says will not be unfit for this place; which is, that the ancient Romans kept their youth always standing, and taught them nothing that they were to learn sitting.

'Tis a generous desire to wish to die usefully and like a man, but the effect lies not so much in our resolution as in our good fortune; a thousand have proposed to themselves in battle,

---

[6] AMURATH III—Also "Murad," Sultan of Turkey from 1574–1595, a grandson of Bajazet II.

[7] EDWARD III—King of England, 1327–1377. In his reign began the hundred years' war with France. Edward claimed certain French territories through his mother who had been a French princess. He was at first victorious; but in the war with Charles V he lost all that he had gained except Bordeaux, Calais, and Bayonne. Yet Charles V was a scholar and patron of learning. He founded the Royal Library of Paris.

[8] CASTILE—Spain; a reference especially to conquests in the West Indies and the Americas by Spanish explorers.

[9] EMPEROR JULIAN—Emperor of Rome, 361–363.

[10] LACEDÆMONIAN—Spartan.

[11] XENEPHON—Usually spelled "Xenophon." A Greek historian and writer (430–357 B.C.), a disciple of Socrates. He fought with the Spartans.

[12] SENECA—A Roman Stoic philosopher (4 B.C.–64 A.D.).

either to overcome or to die, who have failed both in the one and the other, wounds and imprisonment crossing their design and compelling them to live against their will. There are diseases that overthrow even our desires and our knowledge. Fortune ought not to second the vanity of the Roman legions, who bound themselves by oath either to overcome or die:—"I will return, Marcus Fabius,[13] a conqueror, from the fight; and if I fail, I wish the indignation of Jove, Mars,[14] and the other offended gods may light upon me." The Portuguese say that in a certain place of their conquest of the Indies, they met with soldiers, who had condemned themselves, with horrible execrations, to enter into no other composition but either to cause themselves to be slain, or to remain victorious; and had their heads and beards shaved in token of this vow. 'Tis to much purpose for us to hazard ourselves and to be obstinate; it seems as if blows avoided those who present themselves too briskly to them, and do not willingly fall upon those who too willingly seek them, and so defeat them of their design. Such there have been, who, after having tried all ways, not having been able with all their endeavour to obtain the favour of dying by the hand of the enemy, have been constrained, to make good their resolution of bringing home the honour of victory or of losing their lives, to kill themselves even in the heat of battle. Of which there are other examples, but this is one; Philistus, general of the naval army of Dionysius[15] the younger against the Syracusans, presented them battle, which was sharply disputed, their forces being equal; in this engagement he had the better at the first, through his own valour; but the Syracusans drawing about his galley to environ him, after having done great things in his own person to disengage himself and hoping for no relief, with his own hand he took away the life he had so liberally and in vain exposed to the enemy.

Muley Moloch, king of Fez,[16] who lately won against Sebas-

[13] MARCUS FABIUS—Designating the Consul or General, administering the oath.
[14] JOVE, MARS—In Roman mythology, Jove was the ruler of the gods, and Mars the god of war.
[15] DIONYSIUS—The Tyrant of Syracuse, 395–343 B.C. He was expelled in 356, restored in 346, and finally expelled in 343. He thus was actively engaged in fighting his countrymen.
[16] FEZ—A Sultanate in the northern part of Morocco (in northwestern Africa), annexed to Morocco in the middle of the sixteenth century, during Montaigne's life.

tian, king of Portugal, the battle so famous for the death of three kings, and for the transmission of that great kingdom to the crown of Castile, was extremely sick when the Portuguese entered in a hostile manner into his dominions; and from that day forward grew worse and worse, still drawing nearer to and foreseeing his end: yet never did man better employ his own sufficiency more vigorously and bravely than he did upon this occasion. He found himself too weak to undergo the pomp and ceremony of entering into his camp, which after their manner is very magnificent, and therefore resigned that honour to his brother; but this was all of the office of a general that he resigned; all the rest of greatest utility and necessity he most exactly and gloriously performed in his own person; his body lying upon a couch, but his judgment and courage upright and firm to his last gasp, and in some sort beyond it. He might have wasted his enemy, indiscreetly advanced into his dominions, without striking a blow; and it was a very unhappy occurrence, that for want of a little life or somebody to substitute in the conduct of this war and the affairs of a troubled state, he was compelled to seek a doubtful and bloody victory, having another by a better and surer way already in his hands. Notwithstanding, he wonderfully managed the continuance of his sickness in consuming the enemy, and in drawing them far from the assistance of their navy and the ports they had on the coast of Africa, even till the last day of his life, which he designedly reserved for this great battle. He arranged his battallia in a circular form, environing the Portuguese army on every side, which round circle coming to close in and to draw up close together, not only hindered them in the conflict (which was very sharp through the valour of the young invading king) considering that they had every way to present a front, but prevented their flight after the defeat, so that, finding all passages possessed and shut up by the enemy, they were constrained to close up together again, "piled up not only in slaughter but in flight," and there they were slain in heaps upon one another, leaving to the conqueror a very bloody and entire victory. Dying, he caused himself to be carried and hurried from place to place where most need was, and passing along the files, encouraged the captains and soldiers one after another; but a corner of his main battallia being broken, he was not to be held from mounting on horseback with his sword in his hand; he did his utmost to break from those about him, and to rush into the thickest of the battle, they all the while withholding him, some by the bridle, some by his robe, and others by his stirrups. This last effort totally overwhelmed the little life he had left; they again laid him upon his bed; but coming to himself, and starting as it were out of his swoon, all other faculties failing, to give his people notice that they were to conceal his death (the most necessary command he had then to give, that his soldiers might not be discouraged with the news), he expired with his finger upon his mouth, the ordinary sign of keeping silence. Who ever lived so long and so far into death? Who ever died so erect, or more like a man?

The most extreme degree of courageously treating death, and the most natural, is to look upon it not only without astonishment but without care, continuing the wonted course of life even into it, as Cato [17] did, who entertained himself in study, and went to sleep, having a violent and bloody death in his heart, and the weapon in his hand with which he was resolved to despatch himself.

[17] CATO—Marcus Porcius Cato (95–46 B.C.). He fought with Pompey against Cæsar and committed suicide at Utica when he learned that Cæsar had been victorious.

Vocabulary Study: Montaigne's essays were translated into English almost at once, and most English texts retain the vocabularies of the sixteenth century translators as most appropriate. You will accordingly find words used in the sense and fashion of Shakespeare's day. Some of the words are common enough, but used in an unfamiliar way. A conference with the dictionary will usually supply you with the proper meaning. *Despatched; prejudicial; solicitous; lieutenants; statute; degrade; embraced; magnanimous; sobriety; second* (a verb); *execrations; hazard* (a verb); *environ* (a verb); *utility.*

What are the word-histories of *prejudicial; lieutenant; magnanimous; execration?* Distinguish between *statue, statute,* and *stature.*

By Way of Appreciation: The statement, often found in books about literature, that art—especially the art of writing—preserves the ideals of former generations is best appreciated after studying an instance of its application. An opportunity for such a study is presented in the essays of Montaigne. Let us see how the principle applies to the present essay.

Imagine, for the sake of comparison, a serious essay against idleness written by a man of our generation—a man prominent in public affairs, well educated, and widely traveled. In how many ways would it differ from Montaigne's essay? Undoubtedly the modern writer would draw his examples from the world of business, for this is an age of industry and materialism. It is with something of amazement that we discover all of Montaigne's illustrations to be drawn from a world of wars and warriors, and we rightly assume that the sixteenth century was an age of militarism. Notice the author's remark that the office of a ruler "is military throughout." And this comes from a scholar! The same war-traced background appears in all his essays. War was taken for granted. It was necessary and praiseworthy. Wars we still have, but notice how public opinion is changing. Ideals must change before the conditions which grow out of them can change. It is significant that no present-day writer would dream of applying his thoughts against idleness to soldiers or generals for common illustration.

If you carry the comparison further, you will see other points on which public opinion has turned right-about-face since 1580—on suicide, for instance; on the right way of meeting defeat; on the proper qualifications of a ruler; on the value of human life; on the most effective kind of education. The reading of Montaigne becomes increasingly interesting as one sees how truly he pictures not only himself, but sixteenth-century France.

Suggestions for Study: After reading Montaigne's essay *Against Idleness*, write down a list of adjectives which you think properly describe his character. The author makes four separate references to men or events of his own lifetime. Can you find all four? The dates supplied in the notes may help you.

Montaigne wrote an account of his childhood in which he said that his first tutor, employed when Michel was hardly more than an infant, addressed him only in Latin and taught him Latin and Greek before French. What effects of that training do you discover in the essay?

What was Montaigne's attitude toward Spanish conquests in Mexico and Peru? What was Montaigne's conception of the duties of a commander or a ruler? Under what circumstances did he consider suicide justifiable, even honorable? Cite one instance in the essay illustrative of the slight value placed upon human life. Do you think that the present belief in the philosophy of being a "good loser" can be carried out in warfare? Discuss. Was the theory of the Roman legionnaire that he should return victorious or die in battle sound? How does this essay compare in style with the essays by Bacon? How do the personalities of the two writers, as revealed by their essays, compare?

Exercises and Creative Work: Write a précis of this essay.

Choose one of the following subjects to develop into an original essay which will reflect twentieth-century ideals as you see them: *Of Peace; Of Self-Defense; Of Money; Against Idleness; Of Governments.*

EXTENSIVE READING PROGRAM—THE ESSAY AND OTHER PROSE *

Anglo-Saxon and Middle English Periods (Beginnings to 1550)

Geoffrey Chaucer
A Treatise on the Astrolabe
Sir Thomas Malory
Morte d'Arthur *

Sir John Mandeville
Of the Star that is Clept Antarctic (From *The Travels of Sir John Mandeville*)

The Age of Elizabeth (1550–1625)

Sir Francis Bacon
Of Friendship
Of Riches
Roger Ascham
The First Books for the Youth

Ben Jonson
De Shakespeare, Nostrati (Of Shakespeare, Our Countryman)
Dominus Verulamius (Baron Verulam, Francis Bacon)

The Puritan Age and the Restoration (1625–1700)

Izaak Walton
The Compleat Angler *
John Bunyan
The Pilgrim's Progress *
Samuel Pepys
Diary *

John Evelyn
His Diary * (Extracts from 1665, the Great Plague; 1666, the Great Fire; 1685, the death of Charles II)

Classicism and the Age of Johnson (1700–1780)

Jonathan Swift
Gulliver's Travels *
Joseph Addison and Richard Steele
Fan Drill
Leonora's Library
The Vision of Mirza
Days with Sir Roger *
Edmund Burke
Speech on Conciliation with America

Oliver Goldsmith
Letters from a Citizen of the World to His Friends in the East * (Chapters XXI, The Chinese Goes to See a Play; XXVI, The Character of the Man in Black; XXVII, The History of the Man in Black)
Samuel Johnson
Letter to Lord Chesterfield
Dictionary * (Random Pages)

The Age of Romanticism (1780–1840)

Charles Lamb
The Superannuated Man
Dream Children
A Chapter on Ears
Essays of Elia *

Leigh Hunt
On Getting Up on Cold Mornings
Thomas de Quincey
Joan of Arc

* If the title is that of a book or collection, instead of a single essay, it has been indicated by the asterisk.

THE ESSAY AND OTHER PROSE

THE VICTORIAN ERA (1840–1900)

Thomas Carlyle
Essay on Burns
Thomas Babington Macaulay
History of England * (Chapter III, England in 1688)
Cardinal John H. Newman
The Idea of a University *
John Ruskin
Sesame and Lilies *
A Crown of Wild Olives *

Matthew Arnold
Sweetness and Light
Thomas Huxley
On a Piece of Chalk
The Method of Scientific Investigation
Robert Louis Stevenson
Virginibus Puerisque *
An Inland Voyage *
Travels with a Donkey *

THE TWENTIETH CENTURY (1900–   )

James M. Barrie
Courage
Max Beerbohm
More *
Going Out for a Walk
Hilaire Belloc
On Nothing and Kindred Subjects *
On Anything *
Arnold Bennett
How to Live on Twenty-four Hours a Day *
Your United States *
The Human Machine *
Arthur C. Benson
From a College Window *
The Joyous Gard *
Sir Philip Gibbs
Now It Can Be Told *
Since Then *
Stephen Graham
The Gentle Art of Tramping *
Tramping with a Poet *
W. H. Hudson
Idle Days in Patagonia *
Sir James Hopwood Jeans
The Universe Around Us *
The Mysterious Universe *
Rudyard Kipling
Letters of Travel *
From Sea to Sea *
Independence

Hugh Black
Friendship *
Gilbert K. Chesterton
Alarms and Discursions *
All Things Considered *
The Uses of Diversity *
On Historical Novels
On Detective Novels
A. A. Milne
If I May *
Not That It Matters *
John Galsworthy
Quality
The Reverie of a Sportsman
Kenneth Graham
Pagan Papers *
Dream Days *
The Romance of the Road
Edward Lucas
The Perfect Guest
The Five Varieties
Wanderings and Diversions *
Joseph Conrad
Overdue and Missing
Some Reflections on the Loss of the Titanic
H. M. Tomlinson
Tide Marks *
Some Hints for Those About to Travel
George Bernard Shaw
Dramatic Opinions and Essays *

THE DRAMA

THE HISTORY OF THE DRAMA IN ENGLAND

ANGLO-SAXON AND MIDDLE ENGLISH PERIODS (BEGINNINGS TO 1550)

The Beginnings of the Drama

English drama had its origin in the various religious rites and ceremonies of the early church. The English church, similar to the Roman, and forerunner of the present Church of England, used much liturgy in the services and gradually came to insert added dramatic scenes for the purpose of simple instruction of the people. The Easter season especially featured the dramatic scenes of Holy Week and Easter, resulting eventually in the Passion Plays, known to us today through the Oberammergau and several American versions. Found to be effective at this season, other dramatic bits were added.

By gradual transition, the strictly biblical subject matter was supplemented by stories from the lives of the great saints and martyrs of the church. In fact, the earliest play of which there is any record in England is called *The Play of St. Catharine* which was represented at Dunstable early in the twelfth century. About 1250, however, many bishops were inclined to prohibit the clergy from taking part in these plays and to forbid the use of the church for their presentation. While the clergy seem to have continued to assist in the writing of the plays, this action of the bishops resulted in the transfer of dramatic activities from the church to groups of people outside. Groups of tradesmen, known as "guilds," became responsible for play acting, different guilds often acting single scenes, which taken together formed a unified story in crude dramatic form. After the plays were put out of the church, they seem to have been given on a platform or rough stage at the church door and later to have been moved into the adjoining fields.

Mystery and Miracle Plays

The general term by which these plays have come to be known in English literature is Mystery or Miracle Plays. While the French seem to have made some distinction between these two, the terms appear to have been used interchangeably among the English. By the year

1400 in most of the leading English towns such as York, Chester, and Coventry, the guilds had taken over these plays. In York, for example, there was developed a series of forty-eight plays, constituting what is called a Cycle. In this Cycle an attempt was made to dramatize the biblical story from the creation of the world to the Resurrection of Christ and the Harrowing of Hell. The various plays, or scenes, were divided up among the different guilds with a naïve appropriateness. In the York Cycle, for example, the creation of the earth was presented by the plasterers' guild, the building of the Ark by the shipwrights, the turning of the water into wine at Cana by the vintners, the Last Supper by the bakers, and at Chester the Harrowing of Hell was presented by the cooks and innkeepers. The plays were performed on holy days, each play on a movable stage or pageant. On Corpus Christi Day, for example, one stood on a street corner and here saw in succession as pageant succeeded pageant the whole series of plays. These pageants were oftentimes elaborately constructed. A sixteenth century churchman describes one as follows: "A high scaffold with two rooms, a higher and a lower, upon four wheels. In the lower they appareled themselves and in the higher room they played." A conspicuous stage property was Hell-Mouth in the form of the head of a great monster with gaping jaws generally supposed to represent Leviathan, or the whale. From Hell-Mouth issued smoke and flame, and into it demons bristling with horse hair and wearing ugly beasts' heads dragged condemned souls. Lists of properties and costumes which have survived show the elaborate preparations which were made in the production of these plays. In one of them the devil is represented as a shaggy beast, horned, clawed, with forked tail, and with pipes of burning gunpowder in his ears and nostrils.

Morality Plays—Everyman

In the fifteenth century there developed another type of play known as the Morality. The Morality Play differed from the Mystery Play in that it was not based upon a Biblical story. A favorite theme of the Morality Plays was the life of man, which it endeavored to present allegorically. Perhaps the best known of these Moralities and the one which serves to illustrate the characteristics of this type of play is *Everyman* in which the chief character Everyman starts out in life accompanied by a number of friends including Beauty, Strength, Discretion, Five Wits, Friendship, Kindred, and Riches. In the course of life he meets other characters such as Good Works, Repentance, and Mercy. Finally he is summoned by the character Death. His companions such as Kindred, Riches, and Strength now leave him, and Good Deeds alone is willing to go with him on the journey to which Death beckons. In these plays the characters were invariably abstractions, and the purpose of the play was of course to give instruction on the conduct of life.

Interludes

Toward the close of the fifteenth century there developed another type of play, much shorter than the Morality Plays, called the Interlude. These Interludes were oftentimes given between the courses of a banquet or on occasions where a short entertainment was desired. They were based frequently upon some life situation. The best known of these Interludes is that known as the *Four P's* in which a Palmer, a Pardoner, a Potycary, and a Pedler vie with one another to see which can tell the greatest lie. The climax comes when the Palmer declares that he has never seen a woman out of patience. The play also embodies some humorous satire for each of the four characters makes himself out to be a rascal.

Contributions of the Early Forms

A brief review of these remote ancestors, so to speak, of the Shakespearean drama will serve to show that the perfected drama like every other literary form did not spring into being all at once. The Elizabethan drama which was to flower at the end of the sixteenth century owes much to these early forms. Katherine Lee Bates distinguishes eight respects in which the Miracle and Mystery Plays contributed to Elizabethan drama, notably intense vitality, truth to human life, dramatic sense, a blending of comedy with tragedy, and reality in characterization. The chief contribution of the Morality Play was that it gave the dramatist a free hand in constructing a plot, whereas the playwright in the Mystery Play was bound more or less to the story as he found it in the Bible. In the Interludes we find the playwright going to life itself for his material.

Effect of the Renaissance

During the first fifty years of the sixteenth century, a mighty revival of learning was in progress and much that was hitherto unknown in the field of literature came for the first time to be available in England. The wonder of the early Greek and Roman dramas served as an inspiration to British writers. The whole realm of ancient dramatic technique was opened to those interested in drama. Copying Greek and Roman style resulted in a rapid dramatic development during the latter part of the century, marked by complete divorce between drama and the church.

Pre-Elizabethan Drama

True British drama, forerunner of present-day drama, is often said to have been born in 1550 when a schoolmaster wrote a crude comedy entitled *Ralph Roister Doister*. This play shows classic influence in the construction of the plot although the subject matter is wholly native. In 1561 appeared what is called the first English tragedy,

Gorboduc, modeled after the Roman dramatist, Seneca, and written in blank verse; and in 1566 came another farcical comedy, *Gammer Gurton's Needle,* written by a bishop.

THE AGE OF ELIZABETH (1550–1625)

Elizabethan Drama

The culmination toward which the English drama had been developing for centuries came in the days of Elizabeth. Until this time the drama had been the product largely of amateur writers. Elizabeth was known as a great patron of the arts, including literature. She was particularly interested in the development of the theater in England, and of a native drama. Because of her patronage, dramatic writing now became a profession. The first men who took it up as a means of livelihood were the so-called University Wits, so named since they were all University men, who, instead of going into the church or teaching, turned to writing to earn their living.

Christopher Marlowe (1564–1593)

The most conspicuous of these University Wits was Christopher Marlowe. Marlowe produced before his death, at twenty-nine, four remarkable dramas, *Tamburlaine, Doctor Faustus, Edward II,* and *The Jew of Malta.* These plays were all written to be performed on the professional stage. The very titles will show how far the drama had traveled since the days of *Everyman.* In these, the characters are concrete personages, one of them an English king. Instead of dealing with simply the conduct of life as *Everyman* did, they deal with great human passions, that of *The Jew of Malta,* for example, with the passion of revenge. Marlowe's principal contributions to the drama were energy, and the "mighty line"—the unrhymed iambic pentameter. Although Marlowe was not the first to use English blank verse, he succeeded in showing that it could be the vehicle of great poetry.

William Shakespeare (1564–1616)

Three centuries after his death, William Shakespeare still ranks as the greatest of England's literary men of all time. He was born in Stratford-on-Avon of excellent parentage. His mother was Mary Arden, daughter of a wealthy landowner of Wilmecote, a neighboring village. His father, John Shakespeare, was an honored citizen and officer of the village.

For its bearing on Shakespeare's education, too much has probably been made of the remark by Ben Jonson that he had "small Latine and less Greek." It is a relative statement, and must be considered in light of the wide acquaintance with the ancient classics which passed for learning in those days. Shakespeare was no university man, it is true; but he certainly had far more schooling than Abraham Lincoln. He must have attended the King's New Grammar School at Stratford, which was a good school, until he was fourteen or fifteen. The course of study was in those days, even in what we call the grades, well ballasted with Latin authors, such as Virgil, Ovid, and Cicero; and the "making of latines" was begun early. For all Jonson's remark, Shakespeare had a better acquaintance with Latin than the average high-school or college graduate of our day, and there is evidence that he read many Latin authors, especially Ovid, with enjoyment.

Moreover, school in those days was heroic business. It usually opened at six o'clock in the morning and held until five in the afternoon. It was believed too "that the best Scholemaster . . . was the greatest beater." It is small wonder that Shakespeare's references to schools are generally uncomplimentary, and that he describes "the whining schoolboy, with his satchel and shining morning face" as "creeping like a snail unwillingly to school." But it was not book learning which made Shakespeare great; it was rather his ability accurately to portray men from his own first-hand experience.

In 1582 Shakespeare married Anne Hathaway, and three children were born to them, Susannah, Hamnet, and Judith. From boyhood Shakespeare had been interested in amateur dramatics and in working with traveling troupes of players that came to Stratford. About 1588 or 1589 he went to London to try his luck at playing. Meager records indicate that he acted in various capacities from stagehand to callboy and eventually as an actor "and did acte exceeding well." Plays which would fill the house were in great demand by the ever-increasing companies of professional actors, just as scenarios which will draw the crowd are in demand in our day. Here again Shakespeare was evidently quick to sense opportunity, and he set himself to supplying the need. The first company of players with whom he became associated was the Earl of Pembroke's Men, and for this company he wrote his earlier plays, most of which are revisions or adaptions of older plays which had long been favorites with the public.

In 1592 and 1593 outbreaks of the plague caused the closing of the theaters in London. Pembroke's Men went on a tour in the country, but meeting with no success, they returned to the city, sold their stock of plays and disbanded. From the time the company went on tour until 1594, Shakespeare was apparently connected with no theater or troupe. During this period he turned to writing poetry with the purpose possibly of establishing a reputation as a literary man. It should be remembered that in his time plays were not published for the reading public, nor were they regarded as worthy the name of literature. He now wrote the poems *Venus and Adonis,* and *Lucrece,* and began the *Sonnets.* These poems were well received and raised their author to a place of eminence in the literary world.

In 1594, the famous company of players, The Lord Chamberlain's Men, later known as The King's Men, was organized. It numbered among its members the most able and popular actors of the day, and it is significant of Shakespeare's reputation that he was taken in as full sharer apparently from the outset. With this company Shakespeare was actively associated as actor and as playwright for nearly twenty years. For it he wrote thirty-two of the thirty-seven plays which have come down to us in the *Folio of 1623,* and he had without doubt a hand in the writing and revision of many more.

Of Shakespeare's career as an actor next to nothing is known. There is a tradition that he played Adam in *As You Like It* and the ghost in *Hamlet,* and he is known to have played in one of Jonson's plays. A man who knew him speaks of his having "played some kingly part in sport," and another contemporary pronounced him "excelent in the quality [profession] he professes." Possibly his fame as a playwright quite eclipsed his reputation as an actor, and for that reason, we hear little of his appearance on the boards.

Of Shakespeare's engaging personality and of his uprightness of character there is the testimony of many who knew him. Jonson said, "I lov'd the man and doe honour his memory, on this side Idolatry, as much as any. He was, indeed, honest, and of an open and free nature." He was evidently a most companionable man, open and gracious, without any touch of affectation. Men spoke of him as "good Will." Aubrey wrote, "He was a handsome, well shap't man: very good company, and a very ready and pleasant smooth wit." And Bishop Fuller, who had in mind no doubt many a tale of the Mermaid Tavern where the wits of the day used to foregather, set down in his book of *Worthies* that Shakespeare's "Genius generally was jocular, and inclining him to festivity."

Shakespeare's death occurred in April, 1616. He was buried simply in the church at Stratford. Although he deserved a place in Westminster Abbey with England's great, his body was never removed there. Tradition has it that local superstition accounts for this, for the inscription on his tombstone, said to have been written "by himselfe a little before his death," reads as follows:

> GOOD FREND FOR IESVS SAKE FORBEARE,
> TO DIGG THE DVST ENCLOASED HEARE:
> BLESE BE Yᴱ MAN Yᵀ SPARES THES STONES,
> AND CVRST BE HE Yᵀ MOVES MY BONES.

HISTORY OF THE DRAMA

Shakespeare's Plays

Between thirty and forty plays were written by Shakespeare. Best known among them are *Richard III, Comedy of Errors, Taming of the Shrew, Two Gentlemen of Verona, Love's Labour's Lost, Romeo and Juliet, Midsummer Night's Dream, Merchant of Venice, Much Ado About Nothing, Julius Cæsar, Merry Wives of Windsor, As You Like It, Twelfth Night, Hamlet, All's Well That Ends Well, Othello, Macbeth, King Lear, Antony and Cleopatra, The Tempest,* and *Henry VIII*. One of the general favorites, as well as one of the most skillfully constructed is *Macbeth* which appears in this book.

The first collected edition of Shakespeare's plays was published in 1623. This is known as the *First Folio,* or the *Folio of 1623.* This first collection of plays was under the editorship of John Heminges and Henri Condell, actors long associated with Shakespeare, and men for whom he evidently entertained an affection.

There is much controversy over the actual dates of production of Shakespeare's plays, but general agreement seems to exist concerning the four major periods of his work: 1590-1594—historical plays and comedies; 1595-1600—comedies; 1601-1609—tragedies; 1610-1612—three comedies.

Shakespeare's Relation to His Age

The spirit of the Elizabethan age is reflected in Shakespeare's plays. We see it in the exuberant delight in life revealed in his comedies, in the renaissance of English history exhibited in his chronicle plays, and in the revelation of human character made in his greater tragedies. It is, however, with Shakespeare as a reflector of the manifestations of the new spirit in the daily life of his time that we are here most concerned. He was in this particular, too, a child of his age. He was not the mouthpiece of the most advanced thought of his time in medicine, in astronomy, and in science generally; it is rather the echoes of these matters, as imperfectly understood by the public, which we hear from the mouths of his characters, in whom, as ever among people at large, old beliefs, ideas, and superstitions linger beside the new. And as among people at large every fundamental change in life is first and most conspicuously reflected in superficial things—in manners, customs, dress, and deportment—so it was in Elizabethan England, and nowhere are these superficial aspects of life better reflected than in the dramas of Shakespeare. It makes little difference when or where a play is laid; it is saturated with Shakespeare's England. We are told that Shakespeare "did gather humors of men dayly where ever" he came. This scrap of tradition illustrates his method. He took the story for *Much Ado About Nothing* from older writers, but he took the characters from his own observation of life. Dogberry, the constable in *Much Ado,* is an officious, self-important, small-town peace-officer, whom the poet "happened to take at Grendon in Bucks" where he lay over night on the road from London to Stratford. It was, however, the teeming, colorful life of the city of London which furnished him his broadest field of observation of those customs, manners, and vagaries of his age which are reflected in the plays.

In nothing does Shakespeare more reveal the fact that he is an Elizabethan than in his numerous allusions to the sports, games, and amusements of his age. He goes again and again to hunting, to hawking, and to riding for figures of speech, and allusions to coursing with the hounds, to fowling, to angling, to tennis, to bowling, to quoits, to leaping and other gymnastic exercises are common. Dancing, which is often mentioned, was popular in his day. Football also comes in for mention in Shakespeare. In *King Lear* one character calls another "you Base foot-ball player," which as used here seems to have something of the meaning of our term "rough-neck."

Like every period of transition, the Elizabethan Age presented many striking contrasts. Old ideas were still strong, especially in what we call the realm of science. The general run of people believed in witches, goblins, and fairies. Astrology still had many followers. Comets and eclipses were regarded as omens. Knowledge of animals, other than those seen in domesticity, was in the main what it had been throughout the Middle Ages. Such fabulous creatures as unicorn and phoenix still lived in popular imagination. In such matters, the allusions in Shakespeare, on the whole, reflect the popular ideas.

However, in making note of the striking and amusing superficial aspects of the time, it should not be forgotten or overlooked that even though Shakespeare reflects the superficialities of his age, he embodies in his characters those great qualities of mind, spirit, and soul which are represented in his time in such men as Sir Philip Sidney and Sir Walter Raleigh.

Ben Jonson (1573-1637)

The next greatest dramatist after Shakespeare, and perhaps the only Englishman ever to approach him in literary greatness, was Ben Jonson. Unlike Marlowe and Shakespeare, Jonson was a learned man and a student of the classics. For his subject matter he went to contemporary life, producing what is known as the comedy of manners. He was a prolific writer, a producer, and occasionally acted in his own plays as well as in those of his contemporaries. Tradition has it that Shakespeare once acted in one of Jonson's plays. Critics disagree concerning the relative importance of Jonson's comedies and tragedies, but in general the tragedies seem to rank higher. Among the better known titles are *Every Man in His Humour, Every Man Out of His Humour, The Cast Is Altered, The Alchemist, The Tale of a Tub,* and an exquisite pastoral, *The Sad Shepherd.*

One very popular type of drama was the *masque,* a diversion in dramatic form usually written in honor or commemoration of a royal wedding or other event. Jonson excelled in this type of dramaturgy and some of his masques are considered among the finest in English literature. Two outstanding ones are *The Faery Prince* and *Masque of Queens*.

Jonson not only enriched English literature through his own contributions, but through his sponsorship and encouragement of a group of younger contemporaries affectionately called by him, "my sons." A few of the more noteworthy of the group deserve mention here.

Other Elizabethan Dramatists

Of all Jonson's "sons," Francis Beaumont and John Fletcher are the most illustrious. The friendship between these two men is one of the most interesting in literary history. In about two decades of continuous collaboration they wrote more than fifty plays, chief among which are, *Philaster, The Maid's Tragedy, The Scornful Lady,* and *Cupid's Revenge*.

Thomas Dekker is best known for his plays *Old Fortunatus* and *The Shoemaker's Holiday*. The outstanding works of Thomas Heywood include *A Woman Kilde with Kindnesse, The Royall Kings,* and *The English Traveller*. Samuel Daniel is noted for three plays, the last named a superior masque, *A Vision of the Twelve Goddesses, The Queen's Arcadia,* and *Hymen's Triumph*. Among the best plays of Thomas Middleton are *The Old Law, The Witch,* and *The Changeling*. Other minor dramatists of the Elizabethan era include James Shirley, author of thirty-odd plays; John Webster, whose claim to greatness lies in three plays; and Thomas Randolph, author of *The Jovial Philosopher* and *The Looking Glass*.

THE ELIZABETHAN THEATER

Plays Given in Innyards

Although the first English playhouse was not erected until 1576, the public had long been familiar with the drama as an amusement. From the beginning of the sixteenth century mention of "Common Players" and "Strolling Players" of one kind or another became increasingly frequent in the documents of the time. Wherever it was possible, such players set up their temporary stage, or scaffold as it was called, in the yard of an inn. These yards were well adapted to dramatic performances. They were open courts, usually quadrangular in shape, in the midst of the inn. As contemporary prints of the yard of the Four Swans in Bishopgate show, there were usually galleries, or porches, looking down upon the yard. The stage was set up at one end of the inclosure, where a near-by room might serve as a "tiring" or dressing room. The spectators, especially the common folk, stood in the yard, while the better class—the gentry, the burghers and the dignitaries of the town—occupied the galleries.

The Theater of 1576

Nowhere, of course, was the popularity of the play more to be marked than in London, where it early attracted the displeasure of the Puritans who were strong enough in 1574 to secure the enactment of an Order of the Common Council in Restraint of Dramatic Exhibitions which read: "from henceforth no Inkeper, Tavern Keper, nor other person whatsover within the liberties of this Cittie shall openlye shewe, or playe, nor cause or suffer to be openlye shewed or played with in the hous yarde or anie other place . . . anie play, interlude, comodye, tragidie, matter or shewe which shall not be firste perused, and allowed." This order led to the building of the first playhouse, called *The Theater*, which was erected by James Burbage in 1576 on a site just north of the city limits where the Order did not apply.

Burbage had formerly been a joiner, who "reaping but a small living by the same, gave it over and became a common player." He now applied his knowledge of building to designing this new structure. For models he seems to have taken the innyard and the Bear Garden—a building south of the Thames where the popular sport of baiting bears was housed. Contemporary prints picture the Bear Garden as an eight-sided tower-like structure enclosing a circular pit in which the bear was baited by the dogs. The picture of the *Globe* theater erected in 1598 from the materials of *The Theater* is on the exterior almost indistinguishable from that of the Bear Garden. It seems probable that the interior of *The Theater* was circular. In this open space, which was called the *pit* or *yard,* on the hard-packed earth stood the "groundlings." About the inside walls on the three sides parallel and opposite to the stage were galleries, probably three tiers, after the fashion of the innyards. There was, likewise, as the picture of the *Fortune* shows, a gallery over the rear stage. This was the "Lords roome."

The Stage

The stage was a raised platform projecting out into the pit. In the *Fortune* theater the contract specified that it should be "in length forty and three foot . . . and in breadth to extend to the middle of the yard of the said house." It was "paled in below with good, strong, and sufficient new oaken boards." Over the "stage forward" was a "shadow or cover" supported by posts, "square and wrought pilaster-wise, with carved proportions called satyrs . . . placed and set on top of every" post. At the rear and under the Lords roome was a kind of recess—"the place behind the stage"—which might be cut off from the stage forward by a curtain or arras. Rising above the gallery was a tower which was used for three purposes. Here was flown a flag giving the name of the theater, as *The Swan, The Fortune,* or *The Globe.* On days when plays were to be given a second flag announcing the fact was also hung out. From this tower also the trumpeter sounded the three blasts which announced that the play was about to begin. On each side of the middle stage were doors opening in to the tiring or dressing rooms.

Interior of the Fortune Theater, London, built in 1599

Scenery and Properties

There was no scenery such as we know on the Elizabethan stage. It is possible that the curtain or arras at the rear sometimes bore a crude painted picture. A character in one of Jonson's plays speaks of "a peece of perspective of some silke curtain . . . to hang the stage." It is probable, however, that the setting was generally indicated by no more than a placard or piece of cloth bearing the legend *Macbeth's Castle* or *A heath*. In Kyd's *The Spanish Tragedy* one of the characters exclaims: "Hang up the title: Our scene is Rhodes."

It has been pointed out that it was this lack of scenery which caused Shakespeare "to make up for the deficiency . . . by his wonderful descriptions of landscapes, castles, and wild moors. All that poetry would have been lost had he had painted scenery at his disposal."

Although there was little or no scenery, considerable use was certainly made of *properties*. A picture of the *Swan* shows a bench or settle on the stage, and other articles of furniture no doubt were used when required. A document of the time mentions "engines, weapons and powder used in plays," and it is known that the *Globe* theater was fired by the wadding of a cannon set off on the stage in the play *Henry VIII.* The diary or expense book of Philip Henslowe, a theater owner and producer of the time, mentions a number of things including a dragon, one rock and one tomb, and gives evidence that such things as a gallows and other "engines" were built as occasion required.

Costumes and Display

Elizabethan actors made little or no attempt to dress according to the time and setting of the play. "Costume," says one writer, "was a means of indicating rank and office more than time or place; it was meant to reveal the characters rather than the setting of the story." The Elizabethan age delighted in extravagant display, especially in clothes. Edward Alleyn, a famous player of the time, paid on one occasion over £20, which in Shakespeare's time was the equivalent of about one thousand dollars in our money, for "one blacke velvet cloake with sleves ymbrodered with silver and gold"; and when *Henry VIII* was first presented at the *Globe* there appeared in the play "Knights of the Order with their Georges and Garter, the guards with their embroidered coats, and the like, sufficient in truth within awhile to make greatness very familiar."

Music, Songs, and Noise

In the mere reading of the plays of Shakespeare, we are likely to overlook one of the chief attractions which appealed to an Elizabethan audience, and that is the appeal which was constantly being made to the ear throughout the play.

To begin with, Elizabethans were fond of music and song. Training in music was part of the education of every person of rank. Henry VIII, father of Queen Elizabeth, was even somewhat of a composer. The actors of the time were also accomplished in music, and there must have been in Shakespeare's company more than one excellent voice. In the *Swan* there was at the left of the stage a place for the musicians—*orchestra*. In Shakespeare's comedies, songs with musical accompaniment were frequently inserted.

But both groundlings and gallants also loved "sound and fury" for its own sake. They liked hurly-burly and commotion. The reader should note the frequency of trumpet calls and fanfares, and other appeals to the ear indicated in the stage directions by *Sennet, Flourish, Cry within, Thunder and lightning, Drum, Flourish and shout,* etc. The frequency of *Alarums* in battle scenes no doubt served both to keep the audience on the alert and to stimulate its imagination. Shakespeare's audience found also in the noise and commotion of mob scenes the movement and excitement in which it delighted.

The Elizabethan Audience

Plays were as popular in the days of Elizabeth as the movies are in our own. Everyone went to the theater except the Puritans, and some of them seem to have had first-hand knowledge of the playhouse.

The bulk of the audience was made up of groundlings—apprentices, serving men, soldiers, water men, carmen, colliers, tinkers, and the like—who stood to see the play on the hard-packed earth of the pit, admission to which might be had by paying a penny to the *gatherer* at the door. The Mayor complained that the theater was the "ordinary meet-

The Globe Theater

ing place of all vagrant persons and masterless men that hang about the city, thieves, horse stealers" and others of ill-repute, and that the plays attracted "great multitudes of the basest sort of people," and were the cause for keeping the Queen's subjects from divine worship on Sundays and holy days at which time such plays were chiefly given; that they separated the poor from their money and were the occasion for robberies by the picking and cutting of purses; and that they corrupted the youth and were the cause of general disorder, frays, and quarrels.

The best seats were in the galleries. In the *Fortune* the galleries had "four convenient divisions for gentlemen's rooms, and other sufficient and convenient division for two-penny rooms," with necessary seats in these rooms and "throughout all the rest of the galleries." Here sat the "gallery-commoner"—the merchants and gentry. In the Lords roome, or "twelve-penny room next the stage," sat the more aristocratic patrons of the play, both men and women, the latter carefully masked. On the very edge of the stage itself sat the swaggering gallants of the day. Here "our fethered Estridge [ostrich]," as Dekker called the gallant, resplendent in satin doublet, white ruff and plumed hat might "have a good stoole for sixpence" and gain "a conspicuous Eminence . . . by which meanes, the best and most essenciall parts of a Gallant (good cloathes, a proportionable legge, white hand, the Persian lock, and a tollerable beard) are perfectly revealed."

At best the audience was a turbulent and unruly one. Expressions of approval and disapproval were common through applause, noisy laughter, hisses, loud spitting, and a whole series of rude guffaws and curses. If the nobles were bored by the play, they interrupted or mimicked the actors or even jumped to the stage and engaged in combat with them.

Actors

Shakespeare's career as a playwright was closely bound up with two famous companies of actors—The Lord Chamberlain's Company, which after the accession of James I, became The King's Men. The plays were written with definite actors in mind, and in some of them it is known for a certainty by whom the different parts were taken.

It can be safely said that Shakespeare's associates included some of the greatest actors who ever lived. The outstanding member of the group was Richard Burbage, son of the builder of *The Theater*. To two famous actors long associated with Shakespeare the world owes a great debt. These are John Heminges and Henri Condell, who "to keep the memory of so worthy a friend and fellow alive as was our Shakespeare" collected and published the plays in the first complete edition, known as the *First Folio of 1623*. Had it not been for these devoted actor friends of Shakespeare, we should probably not now have the complete plays, for the plays were written to be acted rather than read and when they had run their course on the stage there was little further interest in them. In Shakespeare's day plays were not regarded as literature of any merit; furthermore the companies who owned them did not encourage their publication lest they fall into the hands of rival actors.

One peculiarity of the Elizabethan stage was the absence of actresses. Women's parts were taken by boys—the "children"—especially trained. This accounts for the fact that Shakespeare frequently has his women characters impersonate men and for the further fact that in all the plays men predominate.

The leading actors of Shakespeare's day were anything but vagabonds and roisterers. The men of The Lord Chamberlain's Company, like Shakespeare, made for the most part comfortable fortunes from their acting and their shares in the playhouse, and were not only men of substance but men of integrity and good citizens as well. Edward

Alleyn was not only a great actor but an excellent business man as well. He must have made not far from a million dollars, most of which went to the founding of the College of God's Gift at Dulwich, which still exists; and he spent his declining years managing the affairs of the institution.

The actor's life was a strenuous one. Professor Adams in his *A Life of William Shakespeare* writes: "Elizabethan troupes ... not only performed as a rule every week day, and often on Sundays, but also changed their plays from day to day in a most astonishing fashion. The following list from Henslowe's record of performances at the *Rose* in 1594 will illustrate how taxing this must have been on the memory of the actors [the list shows eleven different plays given on eleven consecutive days]. To care for such an elaborate repertoire, the forenoons of the actors were commonly spent in rehearsals, absence or even tardiness being heavily fined. The afternoons, of course, were occupied with performances before the public, lasting from two or three o'clock until five or six. As to the evenings, not a small share of the time surely had to be devoted to learning new, or refreshing the memory on old, plays."

New Plays for Old

After the opening of *The Theater* in 1576, other playhouses followed in quick succession. At the time of Shakespeare's death in 1616 there were in London at least seven well-established theaters in which plays were regularly given, not to mention certain great inns, such as the Boar's Head, where plays evidently continued.

So great was the demand for plays that not only professional literary men, but scholars and courtiers as well, tried their hand at playmaking. In their search for material, they ransacked the past. History, classic myth, legend, medieval romance, and folk tale were all grist to the mill. The situation much resembled that of our own day in which to meet the insatiable demand for movies the literature of the past has been freely used. Originality of subject matter was the last thing sought for. The play was the thing, and the dramatist thought no more of working well-known stories into his play than the scenario writer of our day does of adapting *Silas Marner* or *A Tale of Two Cities* to the screen. In fact, many of the old stories were popular, and people went to see them on the stage for the same reason that we go to see our favorite novel done in the movies.

Shakespeare invariably made use of old material. In fact, he began his distinguished career as a re-vamper of old plays. His originality consisted in the treatment of his borrowed material, and before we criticize the dramatist we should remember Lowell's comment on Chaucer that if a man discover a process for converting a lump of lead into gold, we should not complain, when he hands us the gold, that he stole the lead.

An Elizabethan Drama

MACBETH

William Shakespeare

The Background of Macbeth: For the facts of his story, Shakespeare went to the *Chronicles of England, Ireland, and Scotland,* compiled by Raphael Holinshed. According to the *Chronicles,* there was about the year 1050 a Scottish king, Macbeth, who with the aid of his wife did murder a king. However, the facts which Shakespeare took from Holinshed he rearranged to suit his purpose, treating them not as a historian but as a dramatist. He did not use everything he found in Holinshed nor did he take over Holinshed's conception of Macbeth and Lady Macbeth. These characters as they stand in the play are Shakespeare's own creations.

Macbeth is thought to have been written and first staged shortly after the coming of James I to the throne of England, and the association of the play with the King has interesting aspects. For the material which went into the play, Shakespeare went to the history of Scotland, and James was a Scot. He was the son of Mary, Queen of Scots, and Henry Stuart, Lord Darnley; and at the time of the death of Elizabeth he was James VI of Scotland. Elizabeth was the last of the Tudors, and upon her death James acceded to the throne of England. He was thus the first of the Stuarts to wear the English crown.

In Shakespeare's day the person of the monarch was a matter of great interest among Englishmen; and there must have been a great deal of curiosity about James and about the country from which he came. Shakespeare, who was a practical playwright and, as such, not blind to the necessity of attracting people to the *Globe*, must have recognized what we should call the advertising value of a play dealing with Scottish affairs. And in this connection it should be remembered that in Shakespeare's time the drama was not only a source of entertainment but also one of the chief means through which the mass of people were made aware of the history of the realm. In our day the natural curiosity as to Scotland which the accession of James no doubt aroused would be satisfied by articles in our magazines and newspapers, but these things did not then exist, and furthermore the great mass was probably unable either to read or to write.

But the association of *Macbeth* with James I has what might be called even more intimate aspects. The company of actors to which Shakespeare belonged was, upon the accession of James, taken under the patronage of the monarch and was thereafter known as the King's Men. There is reason to believe that *Macbeth* was played at Court in 1606 on the occasion of the visit to England of the King of Denmark whose sister was Queen Anne. In any event, there are in the play a number of indubitable allusions to James himself—allusions which must have been highly gratifying to that monarch, whose colossal vanity has become a legend of later times. These definite allusions as they appear in the play are explained in the footnotes.

There is yet another aspect in which *Macbeth* must have been gratifying to James and interesting to the public. Both James and the public, for the most part, believed in the existence of witches. In fact, at the time *Macbeth* was being played, London seems to have been agog over witchcraft. An Englishman named Scot had written a book aimed at exposing the trickeries and absurdities of witchcraft and allied superstitions. Shakespeare seems to have been familiar with the book, and in fact he made use of some of the popular beliefs which Scot had set out to expose. The modern reader is perhaps amused by the witch scenes in *Macbeth* or he strives to read into them some symbolic meaning. Shakespeare's audience, on the other hand, was without doubt somewhat awed by the witches and it certainly took them literally enough. To an Elizabethan, a witch was not a supernatural being; she was simply an ugly old hag who had certain supernatural powers. And this is all Shakespeare intended his witches to be.

James was thoroughly convinced of the existence of witches, and it is therefore not difficult to understand how the witch scenes in *Macbeth* might have struck him as among the most remarkable things in the play. There is a tradition that James "was pleased, with his own hand, to write an amicable letter to Mr. Shakespeare," and one wonders if it was *Macbeth* which put James into this "amicable" state of mind.

DRAMATIS PERSONÆ

Duncan, *King of Scotland*
Malcolm \} *his sons*
Donalbain /
Macbeth \} *generals of the*
Banquo / *King's army*
Macduff \}
Lennox |
Ross | *noblemen of*
Menteith| *Scotland*
Angus |
Caithness/
Fleance, *son to* Banquo
Siward, *Earl of Northumberland, general of the English forces*
Young Siward, *his son*
Seyton, *an officer attending on* Macbeth

Boy, *son to* Macduff
An English Doctor
A Scotch Doctor
A Sergeant
A Porter
An Old Man

Lady Macbeth
Lady Macduff
Gentlewoman *attending on* Lady Macbeth

Hecate
Three Witches
Apparitions

Lords, Gentlemen, Officers, Soldiers, Murderers, Attendants, and Messengers

Scene: *Scotland; England*

ACT I

Scene 1. *A desert place.*

Thunder and lightning. Enter three Witches.

1 Witch. When shall we three meet again
In thunder, lightning, or in rain?
2 Witch. When the hurlyburly's done,
When the battle's lost and won.
5 *3 Witch.* That will be ere the set of sun.
1 Witch. Where the place?
2 Witch.   Upon the heath.

Witches—The general run of people in Shakespeare's day believed in the existence of witches. *Macbeth* was probably first staged in 1606. The student should remember that as late as 1692, twenty persons were executed in Salem Village, Massachusetts, for "witchcraft."
  3. Hurlyburly—Tumult. The tumult of the battle.
  4. Battle—The battle being fought under the leadership of Macbeth and Banquo against the enemies of Duncan. See Scene 2.

3 Witch. There to meet with Macbeth.
1 Witch. I come, Graymalkin!
2 Witch. Paddock calls:—Anon!
10 *All.* Fair is foul, and foul is fair;
Hover through the fog and filthy air.

[*Exeunt.*

8. GRAYMALKIN—Gray cat, old cat.
9. PADDOCK—Toad. It was believed that the "familiar spirits" who controlled witches or gave them their power often accompanied them in the form of cats and toads. The implication is that the witches are obeying their familiar spirits who now summon them away.
9. ANON—Immediately. This is the answer of the witch to the call.
11. HOVER—Probably the meaning is, "Let us be off through the fog and filthy air." What does the word "hover" suggest as to the manner in which the witches made their departure?

SCENE 2. *A camp near Forres.*

Alarum within. Enter DUNCAN, MALCOLM, DONALBAIN, LENNOX, *with* Attendants, *meeting a bleeding* Sergeant.

Duncan. What bloody man is that? He can report,
As seemeth by his plight, of the revolt
The newest state.
Malcolm.   This is the sergeant
Who like a good and hardy soldier fought
5 'Gainst my captivity. Hail, brave friend!
Say to the king the knowledge of the broil
As thou didst leave it.
Sergeant.   Doubtful it stood,
As two spent swimmers that do cling together
And choke their art. The merciless Macdonwald—
10 Worthy to be a rebel, for to that
The multiplying villainies of nature
Do swarm upon him—from the western isles
Of kerns and gallowglasses is supplied;

3. NEWEST STATE—Latest news.
9. CHOKE THEIR ART—Prevent each other from swimming.
10. WORTHY TO BE A REBEL—Fit only to be a rebel.
10. FOR TO THAT—For to that end, because.
11. MULTIPLYING VILLAINIES OF NATURE DO SWARM UPON HIM—The reference is to the fact that Macdonwald had uttered "manie slanderous words" and "railing taunts" against Duncan.
12. WESTERN ISLES—Ireland and the islands west of Scotland.
13. KERNS AND GALLOWGLASSES—Light-armed and heavy-armed footsoldiers.

And fortune, on his damned quarrel smiling,
15 Show'd like a rebel's whore: but all's too weak;
For brave Macbeth—well he deserves that name—
Disdaining fortune, with his brandish'd steel,
Which smok'd with bloody execution,
Like valour's minion carv'd out his passage
20 Till he fac'd the slave;
Which ne'er shook hands, nor bade farewell to him,
Till he unseam'd him from the nave to th' chaps,
And fix'd his head upon our battlements.
    Duncan. O valiant cousin! worthy gentleman!
25   *Sergeant.* As whence the sun 'gins his reflection
Shipwrecking storms and direful thunders break,
So from that spring whence comfort seem'd to come
Discomfort swells. Mark, king of Scotland, mark:
No sooner justice had, with valour arm'd,
30 Compell'd these skipping kerns to trust their heels,
But the Norweyan lord, surveying vantage,
With furbish'd arms and new supplies of men,
Began a fresh assault.
    Duncan.   Dismay'd not this
Our captains, Macbeth and Banquo?
    Sergeant.   Yes;
35 As sparrows eagles, or the hare the lion.
If I say sooth, I must report they were
As cannons overcharg'd with double cracks;
So they doubly redoubled strokes upon the foe:
Except they meant to bathe in reeking wounds,

---

14. DAMNED—Doomed.   19. MINION—Darling, favorite.
21. WHICH—Who. Refers to Macbeth.
22. FROM THE NAVE TO TH' CHAPS—From the navel to the jaws.
24. COUSIN—Macbeth and Duncan were first cousins.
25. 'GINS HIS REFLECTION—Begins his return. The allusion is to the return of the sun at the spring equinox, a time of storms. Note the pun on the word "spring" in the third line below. The meaning is that, as the spring is a source not only of gladness but of storms as well, so the course of the battle is a cause for joy—the joy at Macbeth's victory, and a cause also for alarm—alarm at the fresh assault begun by the Norweyan lord.
31. NORWEYAN—Norwegian.
31. SURVEYING VANTAGE—Seeing his opportunity.
32. FURBISH'D—Bright, untarnished, shining.
35. AS SPARROWS EAGLES—That is, as much as sparrows might dismay eagles.
36. SAY SOOTH—Speak truth.   37. CRACKS—Charges of powder.

40 Or memorize another Golgotha,
I cannot tell—
But I am faint, my gashes cry for help.
    Duncan. So well thy words become thee as thy wounds;
They smack of honour both. Go get him surgeons.
                              [*Exit* Sergeant, *attended.*

                    Enter Ross.

45 Who comes here?
    Malcolm.   The worthy thane of Ross.
    Lennox. What a haste looks through his eyes! So should he look
That seems to speak things strange.
    Ross.   God save the king!
    Duncan. Whence cam'st thou, worthy thane?
    Ross.   From Fife, great king;
Where the Norweyan banners flout the sky
50 And fan our people cold.
Norway himself, with terrible numbers,
Assisted by that most disloyal traitor,
The thane of Cawdor, began a dismal conflict;
Till that Bellona's bridegroom, lapp'd in proof,
55 Confronted him with self-comparisons,
Point against point, rebellious arm 'gainst arm,
Curbing his lavish spirit; and, to conclude,
The victory fell on us.
    Duncan.   Great happiness!
    Ross.   That now

    39–41. EXCEPT THEY MEANT . . . I CANNOT TELL—The Sergeant's meaning is: So fierce was their attack that I cannot tell what they meant unless it was to "bathe" in blood or make the place as memorable as another Golgotha. Golgotha is "the place of the skull," the scene of the crucifixion of Christ. See *Matthew* 27:33 and *Mark* 15:22.
    45. THANE—A nobleman.
    49. FLOUT—Mock.
    50. COLD—Cold with terror.
    51. NORWAY HIMSELF—The king of Norway: Sueno or Sweno.
    54. BELLONA—The old Roman goddess of war. Bellona's bridegroom is, of course, Macbeth.
    54. LAPP'D IN PROOF—Clad in impenetrable armor.
    55. CONFRONTED HIM WITH SELF-COMPARISONS—Matched himself against him.
    57. CURBING HIS LAVISH SPIRIT—Checking his unrestrained daring.
    58. THAT NOW—So that now. Note that Duncan's speech "Great happiness!" is an exclamation of pleasure and interrupts the speech of Ross. Ross says: The victory fell on us so that now Sweno . . . craves composition.

Sweno, the Norway's king, craves composition;
60 Nor would we deign him burial of his men
Till he disbursed, at Saint Colme's inch,
Ten thousand dollars to our general use.
 Duncan. No more that thane of Cawdor shall deceive
Our bosom interest. Go pronounce his present death,
65 And with his former title greet Macbeth.
 Ross. I'll see it done.
 Duncan. What he hath lost, noble Macbeth hath won.

[*Exeunt.*

59. COMPOSITION—Terms of peace.
61. SAINT COLME'S INCH—The island of Inchcolm in the Firth of Forth. On this island was the monastery of St. Columba. "Inch" means island, so that "Saint Colme's inch" means St. Columba's Island.
62. DOLLARS—This word, of course, is not used in a modern sense. It was applied in Shakespeare's time to both the German *thaler* and the Spanish *piece of eight*.
64. DECEIVE OUR BOSOM INTEREST—Enjoy our confidence in order to betray it.
64. PRONOUNCE HIS PRESENT DEATH—Sentence him to instant death.

SCENE 3: *A heath near Forres.*

Thunder. Enter the three Witches.

1 Witch. Where hast thou been, sister?
2 Witch. Killing swine.
3 Witch. Sister, where thou?
1 Witch. A sailor's wife had chestnuts in her lap,
5 And munch'd, and munch'd, and munch'd. "Give me," quoth I:
"Aroint thee, witch!" the rump-fed ronyon cries.
Her husband's to Aleppo gone, master o' the Tiger:
But in a sieve I'll thither sail,

2. KILLING SWINE—In Shakespeare's day an animal dying from no apparent cause was popularly believed to have been bewitched.
6. AROINT THEE—Away with you! An expression which was supposed to be especially effective against witches, spirits, and the like.
6. RUMP-FED—Fat.
6. RONYON—An abusive term for a woman.
7. ALEPPO—An ancient city of Syria. In Shakespeare's day it was a great commercial center.
7. TIGER—In a popular book of the day there was a long and interesting account of a trip in the Orient made by a merchant who sailed out in a ship called the *Tyger*. Shakespeare no doubt had read this account and took the name of his ship from it.
8. SIEVE—Witches were believed to go to sea in sieves.

And, like a rat without a tail,
I'll do, I'll do, and I'll do.
   2 Witch. I'll give thee a wind.
   1 Witch. Thou 'rt kind.
   3 Witch. And I another.
   1 Witch. I myself have all the other;
And the very ports they blow,
All the quarters that they know
I' the shipman's card.
I'll drain him dry as hay.
Sleep shall neither night nor day
Hang upon his pent-house lid;
He shall live a man forbid:
Weary se'nnights nine times nine
Shall he dwindle, peak, and pine:
Though his bark cannot be lost,
Yet it shall be tempest-tost.
Look what I have.
   2 Witch. Show me, show me.
   1 Witch. Here I have a pilot's thumb,
Wreck'd as homeward he did come   *[Drum within.*
   3 Witch. A drum, a drum!
Macbeth doth come.
   All. The weird sisters, hand in hand,
Posters of the sea and land,
Thus do go about, about:

  9. WITHOUT A TAIL—Whenever a witch assumed the form of an animal, one might know it by the fact that there would be some defect about the latter—as the "rat without a tail."
  10. I'LL DO—That is, the witch in form of a rat will work the ship some ill, possibly gnawing a hole in the ship's bottom so that it will leak.
  11. GIVE THEE A WIND—Witches were believed to sell winds to sailors. Here the 2nd and 3rd Witches each offer to give the 1st Witch a wind to keep her in her nefarious business.
  17. SHIPMAN'S CARD—The mariner's chart or compass.
  20. PENT-HOUSE LID—Eyelid. The resemblance of the eyebrow to a pent-house is the reason for this figure.
  21. FORBID—Under a curse or ban.
  22. SE'NNIGHTS NINE TIMES NINE—81 weeks.
  23. DWINDLE, PEAK, AND PINE—Grow thin and waste away. Wasting or consumptive diseases were generally believed to be the work of witches.
  33. POSTERS—Swift travellers. Compare with our expression "post-haste."
  34. THUS DO GO ABOUT—That is, join hands and dance about in a ring. The witches go about three times for each "to make up nine." Numbers, especially odd numbers, and in particular three and nine, were formerly believed to have magical properties.

35　Thrice to thine, and thrice to mine,
　　And thrice again, to make up nine.
　　Peace! the charm's wound up.

Enter MACBETH *and* BANQUO

　　Macbeth.　So foul and fair a day I have not seen.
　　Banquo.　How far is 't call'd to Forres? What are these
40　So wither'd, and so wild in their attire,
　　That look not like th' inhabitants o' the earth,
　　And yet are on 't? Live you? or are you aught
　　That man may question? You seem to understand me,
　　By each at once her choppy finger laying
45　Upon her skinny lips: you should be women,
　　And yet your beards forbid me to interpret
　　That you are so.
　　　　Macbeth.　　Speak, if you can: what are you?
　　　1 Witch.　All hail, Macbeth! hail to thee, thane of Glamis!
　　　2 Witch.　All hail, Macbeth! hail to thee, thane of Cawdor!
50　　*3 Witch.*　All hail, Macbeth, that shall be king hereafter!
　　Banquo.　Good sir, why do you start, and seem to fear
　　Things that do sound so fair?—I' the name of truth,
　　Are ye fantastical, or that indeed
　　Which outwardly ye show? My noble partner
55　You greet with present grace and great prediction
　　Of noble having and of royal hope,
　　That he seems rapt withal; to me you speak not.
　　If you can look into the seeds of time,
　　And say which grain will grow and which will not,

　　　38. FOUL AND FAIR—Where have the words appeared before?
　　　44. CHOPPY—Chapped.
　　　52. I' THE NAME OF TRUTH—Banquo is now addressing the witches.
　　　53. FANTASTICAL—Creatures of the fancy or imagination.
　　　55. PRESENT GRACE—This goes with "noble having" in the line below, and "great prediction" goes with "royal hope," so that the meaning is "present grace of noble having" and "great prediction of royal hope." The first expression refers to the greeting of the first two witches who greet Macbeth by the noble titles he at present has. The second expression refers to the greeting of the third witch who hails Macbeth with the prophecy, or prediction, that he shall be king.
　　　57. RAPT WITHAL—As if in a trance with it (your greeting).
　　　58. LOOK INTO THE SEEDS OF TIME—Foretell the future.

*What are these
So wither'd, and so wild?*

60 Speak, then, to me, who neither beg nor fear
Your favours nor your hate.
   1 Witch. Hail!
   2 Witch. Hail!
   3 Witch. Hail!
65   *1 Witch.* Lesser than Macbeth, and greater.
   2 Witch. Not so happy, yet much happier.
   3 Witch. Thou shalt get kings, though thou be none:
So all hail, Macbeth and Banquo!
   1 Witch. Banquo and Macbeth, all hail!
70   *Macbeth.* Stay, you imperfect speakers, tell me more:
By Sinel's death I know I am thane of Glamis;
But how of Cawdor? the thane of Cawdor lives,
A prosperous gentleman, and to be king
Stands not within the prospect of belief
75 No more than to be Cawdor. Say from whence
You owe this strange intelligence? or why
Upon this blasted heath you stop our way
With such prophetic greeting? Speak, I charge you.
                                  [*Witches vanish.*
   Banquo. The earth hath bubbles as the water has,
80 And these are of them. Whither are they vanish'd?
   Macbeth. Into the air; and what seem'd corporal melted
As breath into the wind. Would they had stay'd!
   Banquo. Were such things here as we do speak about?
Or have we eaten on the insane root
85 That takes the reason prisoner?
   Macbeth. Your children shall be kings.
   Banquo.   You shall be king.
   Macbeth. And thane of Cawdor too: went it not so?
   Banquo. To th' selfsame tune and words. Who's here?

    67. GET—Beget.
    70. IMPERFECT—Unfinished. That is, who have not told all.
    71. SINEL—Macbeth's father.
    74. STANDS NOT WITHIN THE PROSPECT OF BELIEF—That is, seems an unbelievable thing.
    79. THE EARTH HATH BUBBLES—To Banquo the witches are of no significance. He neither fears them nor attaches any importance to their words—they are as bubbles.
    81. CORPORAL—Corporeal, having a body, having substance.
    84. INSANE ROOT—It was the belief of the time that there were certain herbs and roots which, when eaten, produced madness.

Enter Ross *and* Angus.

Ross. The king hath happily receiv'd, Macbeth,
90 The news of thy success; and, when he reads
Thy personal venture in the rebels' fight,
His wonders and his praises do contend
Which should be thine or his; silenc'd with that,
In viewing o'er the rest o' the selfsame day,
95 He finds thee in the stout Norweyan ranks,
Nothing afeard of what thyself didst make,
Strange images of death. As thick as hail
Came post with post; and every one did bear
Thy praises in his kingdom's great defence,
100 And pour'd them down before him.
 Angus.   We are sent
To give thee from our royal master thanks;
Only to herald thee into his sight,
Not pay thee.
 Ross. And, for an earnest of a greater honour,
105 He bade me, from him, call thee thane of Cawdor;
In which addition, hail, most worthy thane!
For it is thine.
 Banquo. [*Aside.*] What, can the devil speak true?
 Macbeth. The thane of Cawdor lives; why do you dress me
In borrow'd robes?
 Angus.   Who was the thane lives yet;
110 But under heavy judgment bears that life
Which he deserves to lose. Whether he was combin'd
With those of Norway, or did line the rebel
With hidden help and vantage, or that with both

  91. PERSONAL VENTURE—That is, the risk Macbeth took in person in seeking out and fighting Macdonwald.
  92. HIS WONDERS AND HIS PRAISES DO CONTEND WHICH SHOULD BE THINE OR HIS—"Thine" goes with "praises," and "his" with "wonders." The meaning is: He is struck speechless (silenced with that) between trying to express his own wonder and your praises at the same time.
  97. STRANGE IMAGES OF DEATH—Death as represented, or imaged, in those slain by Macbeth. The meaning is that Macbeth himself did not fear the fate which he saw overtake others at his hand.
  98. POST WITH POST—Messenger after messenger.
  104. EARNEST—Promise.
  106. ADDITION—That is, title added to your name.
  112. LINE—Strengthen, reinforce.

He labour'd in his country's wreck, I know not;
But treasons capital, confess'd and prov'd,
Have overthrown him.
    Macbeth. [*Aside.*] Glamis, and thane of Cawdor!
The greatest is behind. [*To* Ross *and* Angus.] Thanks for
    your pains.
    [*To* Banquo.] Do you not hope your children shall be kings,
When those that gave the thane of Cawdor to me
Promis'd no less to them?
    Banquo.   That trusted home
Might yet enkindle you unto the crown,
Besides the thane of Cawdor. But 'tis strange;
And oftentimes, to win us to our harm,
The instruments of darkness tell us truths,
Win us with honest trifles, to betray 's
In deepest consequence.
Cousins, a word, I pray you.
    Macbeth.   [*Aside.*] Two truths are told,
As happy prologues to the swelling act
Of the imperial theme.—I thank you, gentlemen.—
[*Aside.*] This supernatural soliciting
Cannot be ill; cannot be good. If ill,
Why hath it given me earnest of success,

    114. Labour'd in his country's wreck—Strove to bring about his country's downfall.
    115. Treasons capital—Acts of treason punishable by death.
    117. The greatest is behind—The greatest honor is yet to come.
    120. That trusted home—The prophecy of the witches taken too seriously.
    121. Enkindle you unto the crown—Incite you to obtain the crown.
    122–126. But 'tis strange; and oftentimes . . . deepest consequence—Banquo's meaning is that when men enter upon evil doing they are often so deceived by their initial good fortune that they cannot be convinced that they will come to grief in the end.
    127. Cousins—A form of address applied to a distant relative, or sometimes by one nobleman to another. Banquo here speaks apart to Ross and Angus, leaving Macbeth free to speak his long *Aside*.
    128. Happy prologues . . . imperial theme—This figure is taken from the stage. A prologue is a part delivered before a play by way of introduction or preface to the play. By the "two truths" Macbeth has reference to the fact that the greetings of the first two witches, who hailed him as "thane of Glamis" and "thane of Cawdor," have come true. "Happy" means favorable or propitious. "Swelling" means glorious. "Imperial" means kingly. Macbeth's imagination has caught fire. He conceives of what has happened as a promising prologue to a glorious drama which is about to begin.
    130. Soliciting—Prompting, incitement. 132. Earnest—Promise.

Commencing in a truth? I am thane of Cawdor:
If good, why do I yield to that suggestion
Whose horrid image doth unfix my hair
And make my seated heart knock at my ribs,
Against the use of nature? Present fears
Are less than horrible imaginings.
My thought, whose murder yet is but fantastical,
Shakes so my single state of man that function
Is smother'd in surmise, and nothing is
But what is not.
    Banquo.   Look, how our partner's rapt.
    Macbeth. [*Aside.*] If chance will have me king, why,
        chance may crown me,
Without my stir.
    Banquo.   New honours come upon him,
Like our strange garments, cleave not to their mould
But with the aid of use.
    Macbeth. [*Aside.*] Come what come may,
Time and the hour runs through the roughest day.
    Banquo. Worthy Macbeth, we stay upon your leisure.
    Macbeth. Give me your favour. My dull brain was wrought
With things forgotten. Kind gentlemen, your pains
Are register'd where every day I turn
The leaf to read them. Let us toward the king.
    [*To* BANQUO.] Think upon what hath chanc'd; and, at more
        time,

    134. SUGGESTION—That is, the thought of murdering Duncan.
    135. IMAGE—Macbeth has a vivid imagination. He can see the deed as done.
    135. UNFIX MY HAIR—Make it stand on end.
    139. WHOSE MURDER YET IS BUT FANTASTICAL—In which the murder is now only an imagined deed.
    140. MY SINGLE STATE OF MAN—My whole being.
    141. FUNCTION IS SMOTHER'D IN SURMISE—Power to do the deed is paralyzed by the horror which thinking about it arouses.
    141. NOTHING IS BUT WHAT IS NOT—That is, the only realities to Macbeth are the devisings of his heated imagination.
    147. TIME AND THE HOUR—The meaning is that by biding one's time and seizing favorable opportunity, one can overcome the greatest of difficulties.
    149. GIVE ME YOUR FAVOUR—Pardon me.
    149. WROUGHT—Moved. Macbeth pretends that he has been lost in thought, trying to recall some forgotten matter.
    151. WHERE EVERY DAY . . . TO READ THEM—That is, in his memory.
    152. LET US TOWARD THE KING—This part of the speech is addressed to Banquo.
    153. CHANC'D—Happened. Macbeth here has reference to the meeting with the witches.

The interim having weigh'd it, let us speak
155 Our free hearts each to other.
   Banquo.   Very gladly.
   Macbeth. Till then, enough. Come, friends.   [*Exeunt.*

    154. THE INTERIM HAVING WEIGH'D IT—In the meanwhile having thought it over.

SCENE 4. *Forres. The palace.*

Flourish. Enter DUNCAN, MALCOLM, DONALBAIN, LENNOX, *and* Attendants.

   Duncan. Is execution done on Cawdor? Are not
Those in commission yet return'd?
   Malcolm.   My liege,
They are not yet come back. But I have spoke
With one that saw him die; who did report
5 That very frankly he confess'd his treasons,
Implor'd your highness' pardon, and set forth
A deep repentance. Nothing in his life
Became him like the leaving it; he died
As one that had been studied in his death
10 To throw away the dearest thing he ow'd,
As 'twere a careless trifle.
   Duncan.   There's no art
To find the mind's construction in the face;
He was a gentleman on whom I built
An absolute trust.

Enter MACBETH, BANQUO, ROSS, *and* ANGUS.

                    O worthiest cousin!
15 The sin of my ingratitude even now
Was heavy on me. Thou art so far before,
That swiftest wing of recompense is slow

    2. THOSE IN COMMISSION—Those commissioned, or charged to see the execution done on Cawdor.
    9. AS ONE THAT HAD BEEN STUDIED—As an actor who had studied it as a "part" until he had become perfect in it.
    10. OW'D—Owned.
    11. CARELESS—Uncared for.
    11–12. THERE'S NO ART ... IN THE FACE—There is no way to read a man's character in his face.
    14. WORTHIEST COUSIN—Macbeth.

To overtake thee. Would thou hadst less deserv'd,
That the proportion both of thanks and payment
Might have been mine! Only I have left to say,
More is thy due than more than all can pay.
   Macbeth. The service and the loyalty I owe,
In doing it, pays itself. Your highness' part
Is to receive our duties; and our duties
Are to your throne and state children and servants;
Which do but what they should, by doing everything
Safe toward your love and honour.
   Duncan.   Welcome hither:
I have begun to plant thee, and will labour
To make thee full of growing. Noble Banquo,
That hast no less deserv'd, nor must be known
No less to have done so, let me infold thee
And hold thee to my heart.
   Banquo.   There if I grow,
The harvest is your own.
   Duncan.   My plenteous joys,
Wanton in fulness, seek to hide themselves
In drops of sorrow. Sons, kinsmen, thanes,
And you whose places are the nearest, know,
We will establish our estate upon
Our eldest, Malcolm, whom we name hereafter
The Prince of Cumberland; which honour must

   19-20. THAT THE PROPORTION . . . MIGHT HAVE BEEN MINE—That is, that I might have been able to reward you both in honors and gratitude in proportion to your deserts.
   27. SAFE TOWARD YOUR LOVE AND HONOUR—That is, which will make you loved and honored.   34. WANTON—Unrestrained.
   35. DROPS OF SORROW—Tears. The meaning is: My joys are so great that they bring tears to my eyes.
   39. PRINCE OF CUMBERLAND—The crown of Scotland was elective rather than hereditary, which means that the king's eldest son did not succeed to the throne by right of birth. The final choice of their king lay with the thanes, and they might set aside an immediate heir in favor of one whom they thought more competent. Both Duncan and Macbeth were sons of two daughters of the old King Malcolm, so that Macbeth had some claim to the throne.
   39-42. WHICH HONOUR . . . ON ALL DESERVERS—Duncan's meaning is that Malcolm shall not be the only one to enjoy honor, but that all who have deserved it (especially Banquo and Macbeth) shall be held in high esteem according to their merits. This speech must have irritated Macbeth, for to Malcolm goes the very substantial honor of being named Duncan's successor, while Macbeth who feels himself better fitted to be king must be content with nothing more substantial than high esteem.

40 Not unaccompanied invest him only,
But signs of nobleness, like stars, shall shine
On all deservers. From hence to Inverness,
And bind us further to you.
    Macbeth. The rest is labour, which is not us'd for you.
45 I'll be myself the harbinger, and make joyful
The hearing of my wife with your approach;
So humbly take my leave.
    Duncan.   My worthy Cawdor!
    Macbeth. [*Aside.*] The Prince of Cumberland! that is a step
On which I must fall down, or else o'erleap,
50 For in my way it lies. Stars, hide your fires;
Let not light see my black and deep desires;
The eye wink at the hand; yet let that be
Which the eye fears, when it is done, to see.   [*Exit.*
    Duncan. True, worthy Banquo; he is full so valiant,
55 And in his commendations I am fed;
It is a banquet to me. Let's after him,
Whose care is gone before to bid us welcome.
It is a peerless kinsman.   [*Flourish. Exeunt.*

    42. INVERNESS—Macbeth's castle.
    44. THE REST IS LABOUR, WHICH IS NOT US'D FOR YOU—Macbeth's meaning is that the rest which is not spent in Duncan's service is labor. Is he sincere?
    45. HARBINGER—Forerunner. An officer whose duty it was to go ahead and make provision for the king and his retinue. The connection between this and the preceding line lies in Macbeth's implication that he will employ his "rest" in Duncan's service and carry the news to Inverness.
    52. WINK AT—Pretend not to see.
    54. TRUE, WORTHY BANQUO; HE IS FULL SO VALIANT—The "he" in this speech refers to Macbeth. While Macbeth has been speaking his *Aside* Banquo has been speaking in praise of Macbeth to Duncan. Duncan is confirming some remark of Banquo's with the words: "(That is) true, worthy Banquo."
    58. IT—Refers to Macbeth, who was Duncan's kinsman.

    SCENE 5. *Inverness.* MACBETH'S *castle.*

    Enter LADY MACBETH, *alone, with a letter.*

    Lady Macbeth. [*Reads.*] They met me in the day of success; and I have learn'd by the perfect'st report, they have more in

    1. THEY—The witches.
    2. BY THE PERFECT'ST REPORT—From the most reliable source. Macbeth may be making reference here to the fact that one of the prophecies has actually come true, or it may be that he has been making some inquiry into the power of the witches and is convinced that they actually have more than mortal knowledge.

them than mortal knowledge. When I burn'd in desire to question them further, they made themselves air, into which they vanish'd. Whiles I stood rapt in the wonder of it, came missives from the King, who all-hail'd me "Thane of Cawdor"; by which title, before, these weird sisters saluted me, and referr'd me to the coming on of time, with "Hail, king that shalt be!" This have I thought good to deliver thee, my dearest partner of greatness, that thou mightst not lose the dues of rejoicing, by being ignorant of what greatness is promis'd thee. Lay it to thy heart, and farewell.

Glamis thou art, and Cawdor, and shalt be
What thou art promis'd. Yet do I fear thy nature;
It is too full o' the milk of human kindness
To catch the nearest way. Thou wouldst be great;
Art not without ambition, but without
The illness should attend it. What thou wouldst highly,
That wouldst thou holily; wouldst not play false,
And yet wouldst wrongly win. Thou 'ldst have, great Glamis,
That which cries, "Thus thou must do," if thou have it;
And that which rather thou dost fear to do
Than wishest should be undone. Hie thee hither,
That I may pour my spirits in thine ear,
And chastise with the valour of my tongue
All that impedes thee from the golden round
Which fate and metaphysical aid doth seem
To have thee crown'd withal.

9. DELIVER THEE—Communicate to you.
10. LOSE THE DUES OF REJOICING—That is, that you might not lose any of the rejoicing which is your due.
15. NEAREST WAY—The murder of Duncan.
17. ILLNESS—Wickedness, unscrupulousness.
17–18. WHAT THOU WOULDST HIGHLY, THAT WOULDST THOU HOLILY—Whatever great honors you wish, you prefer to come by them legitimately.
18–19. WOULDST NOT PLAY FALSE, AND YET WOULDST WRONGLY WIN—You will not play false, yet you covet a thing which can be won only by dishonest means. There is perhaps the further meaning here: Although you will not play false yourself, you have no scruples about accepting a result brought about dishonestly, like one who will not steal yet will not hesitate to keep a sum of money which he has found even though he knows the loser.
21. AND THAT—The full sense is: And you would also have that, etc.
21. THAT WHICH—That is, the crown. The meaning is: You would have the crown, which cries, "Thus (murder Duncan) thou must do, if you have me."
25. GOLDEN ROUND—The crown.
26. METAPHYSICAL—Supernatural.

Enter a Messenger.

                                      What is your tidings?
Messenger. The king comes here to-night.
Lady Macbeth.   Thou 'rt mad to say it!
Is not thy master with him? who, were 't so,
30 Would have inform'd for preparation.
   Messenger. So please you, it is true; our thane is coming.
One of my fellows had the speed of him,
Who, almost dead for breath, had scarcely more
Than would make up his message.
   Lady Macbeth.   Give him tending;
35 He brings great news.   [*Exit* Messenger.
                       The raven himself is hoarse
That croaks the fatal entrance of Duncan
Under my battlements. Come, you spirits
That tend on mortal thoughts, unsex me here;
And fill me from the crown to the toe top-full
40 Of direst cruelty! make thick my blood;
Stop up th' access and passage to remorse,
That no compunctious visitings of nature
Shake my fell purpose, nor keep peace between
The effect and it! Come to my woman's breasts,
45 And take my milk for gall, you murd'ring ministers,
Wherever in your sightless substances
You wait on nature's mischief! Come, thick night,
And pall thee in the dunnest smoke of hell,

    32. HAD THE SPEED OF HIM—Outdistanced him.
    35–37. THE RAVEN HIMSELF . . . UNDER MY BATTLEMENTS—The raven formerly enjoyed the reputation of being a bird of ill omen. Lady Macbeth means that the raven that croaks at the entrance of Duncan into Macbeth's castle must croak himself hoarse if his croaking is to be proportionate to the evil which will befall Duncan.
    38. MORTAL—Deadly, murderous.
    38. UNSEX—Divest me of the tender and merciful nature which is woman's.
    40. MAKE THICK MY BLOOD—According to the physiology of Shakespeare's day, "spirits" passed along the blood. Lady Macbeth asks that her blood may become thick to stop the passage of remorse (the "spirit" of pity) so that it may not find access (entrance) into her heart.
    42. COMPUNCTIOUS VISITINGS OF NATURE—Natural feelings of compunction.
    43. FELL—Fierce, cruel.
    43–44. NOR KEEP PEACE BETWEEN THE EFFECT AND IT—Come as a peacemaker between the purpose and the effect, or execution.
    45. TAKE MY MILK FOR GALL—Turn my milk into gall.
    46. SIGHTLESS—Invisible.
    48. PALL—Wrap.

That my keen knife see not the wound it makes,
Nor heaven peep through the blanket of the dark.
To cry, "Hold, hold!"

Enter MACBETH.

                    Great Glamis! worthy Cawdor!
Greater than both, by the all-hail hereafter!
Thy letters have transported me beyond
This ignorant present, and I feel now
The future in the instant.
   Macbeth.   My dearest love,
Duncan comes here to-night.
   Lady Macbeth.   And when goes hence?
   Macbeth. To-morrow, as he purposes.
   Lady Macbeth.   O, never
Shall sun that morrow see!
Your face, my thane, is as a book where men
May read strange matters. To beguile the time,
Look like the time; bear welcome in your eye,
Your hand, your tongue; look like the innocent flower
But be the serpent under 't. He that's coming
Must be provided for; and you shall put
This night's great business into my dispatch,
Which shall to all our nights and days to come
Give solely sovereign sway and masterdom.
   Macbeth. We will speak further.
   Lady Macbeth.   Only look up clear;
To alter favour ever is to fear.
Leave all the rest to me.   [*Exeunt.*

   52. THE ALL-HAIL HEREAFTER—The reference is to the greeting of the third witch: "All hail, Macbeth, that shalt be king hereafter."
   60. TO BEGUILE THE TIME, LOOK LIKE THE TIME—"Time" here means the occasion, which is one for display of hospitality. The lines following make Lady Macbeth's meaning clear—to deceive those present at the "time," behave in the manner the "time" requires.
   65. DISPATCH—Management.
   66. WHICH—Modifies "great business."
   66–67. SHALL TO ALL OUR NIGHTS AND DAYS ... SWAY AND MASTERDOM—That is, shall give us the kingdom and make us masters of the situation henceforth.
   68–69. ONLY LOOK UP CLEAR; TO ALTER FAVOUR EVER IS TO FEAR—That is, do not let your face betray us, to change countenance (alter favour) is to show signs of fear.

Scene 6. *Before* Macbeth's *castle.*

Hautboys and torches. Enter Duncan, Malcolm, Donalbain, Banquo, Lennox, Macduff, Ross, Angus, *and* Attendants.

    Duncan. This castle hath a pleasant seat; the air
Nimbly and sweetly recommends itself
Unto our gentle senses.
    Banquo.   This guest of summer,
The temple-haunting martlet, does approve,
5 By his lov'd mansionry, that the heaven's breath
Smells wooingly here; no jutty, frieze,
Buttress, nor coign of vantage, but this bird
Hath made his pendent bed and procreant cradle.
Where they most breed and haunt, I have observ'd
10 The air is delicate.

Enter Lady Macbeth.

    Duncan.   See, see, our honour'd hostess!
The love that follows us sometime is our trouble,
Which still we thank as love. Herein I teach you
How you shall bid God 'ild us for your pains,
And thank us for your trouble.
    Lady Macbeth.   All our service
15 In every point twice done and then done double
Were poor and single business to contend

    Hautboys (hō'boi)—High-pitched musical instruments, sounded to announce the entrance of important persons, usually royalty.
    1. Seat—Site, situation.
    4. Temple-haunting martlet—An allusion possibly to the martin, which nests in church towers.
    4. Approve—Prove.
    5. Mansionry—Building, nest.
    6. Jutty—Projection.
    7. Coign of vantage—Convenient corner or nook.
    8. Pendent—An allusion possibly to the way in which the nest built on some slight "jutty" projected out or over-hung the edge.
    8. Procreant cradle—Cradle for bringing forth young.
    11–12. The love that follows us . . . we thank as love—Duncan means that the love which others have for us (follows us) sometimes puts us to trouble, yet we are grateful for it.
    12–14. Herein . . . your trouble—The meaning is: Since, therefore, it is our love which puts you to your pains and trouble now, you may ask God to reward us for causing you the trouble of entertaining us.
    16. Single business to contend—That is, a weak repayment for those honors, etc.

Against those honours deep and broad wherewith
Your majesty loads our house: for those of old,
And the late dignities heap'd up to them,
We rest your hermits.
 Duncan.   Where's the thane of Cawdor?
We cours'd him at the heels, and had a purpose
To be his purveyor: but he rides well,
And his great love, sharp as his spur, hath holp him
To his home before us. Fair and noble hostess,
We are your guest to-night.

 Lady Macbeth. Your servants ever
Have theirs, themselves, and what is theirs, in compt,
To make their audit at your highness' pleasure,
Still to return your own.
 Duncan.   Give me your hand;
Conduct me to mine host. We love him highly,
And shall continue our graces towards him.
By your leave, hostess.   [*Exeunt.*

 20. WE REST YOUR HERMITS—We remain, so to speak, your beadsmen. The meaning is made clear by the definition of beadsman—one who having received alms from another is bound to pray for his benefactor.
 21. COURS'D—Pursued, followed closely.
 22. PURVEYOR—Forerunner.
 23. HOLP—Helped.
 26–27. IN COMPT, TO MAKE THEIR AUDIT—The meaning of these lines is that all your subjects have, they hold but in compt, that is, subject to account, against the day it shall please you to make their audit (call them to account).
 31. BY YOUR LEAVE—Duncan, with these words, gives his hand to Lady Macbeth and leads her into the castle.

Scene 7. Macbeth's *castle*.

Hautboys and torches. Enter a Sewer, *and divers* Servants *with dishes and service, over the stage. Then enter* Macbeth.

Macbeth. If it were done when 'tis done, then 'twere well
It were done quickly. If th' assassination
Could trammel up the consequence, and catch
With his surcease success; that but this blow
5 Might be the be-all and the end-all here,
But here, upon this bank and shoal of time,
We'd jump the life to come. But in these cases
We still have judgment here, that we but teach
Bloody instructions, which, being taught, return
10 To plague th' inventor. This even-handed justice
Commends th' ingredients of our poison'd chalice
To our own lips. He's here in double trust:
First, as I am his kinsman and his subject,
Strong both against the deed; then, as his host,
15 Who should against his murderer shut the door,
Not bear the knife myself. Besides, this Duncan
Hath borne his faculties so meek, hath been

Sewer—A servant, or officer of the household, who carried in and arranged dishes for a banquet. These servants pass over the stage to the banquet hall. Macbeth has left the table, much perturbed by the fears and imaginings which he voices in his soliloquy.

1. If it were done when 'tis done—That is, if the deed when done only ended the matter, and there were no consequences.

3. Trammel up—Prevent. To trammel up means literally to catch as in a net—to tangle up, and thus prevent the consequences from following.

4. And catch with his (its) surcease success—That is, bring success with its cessation. Macbeth uses the term surcease, or cessation, to describe such a deed as he has described above—that is over when it is done, and has no consequences—a "be-all and end-all."

4. That but—If only.

6. But here—Only here.

6. Upon this bank and shoal of time—Upon this earth.

7. Jump the life to come—Risk or chance what will happen in the life to come.

8. Have judgment here—Meet retribution here.

8. That—So that; and that judgment is that.

8-10. We but teach bloody instructions . . . plague th' inventor—That is, all we do is to teach others by example what they shall do to us.

11. Commends—Delivers.

11. Chalice—Cup. Pricks of conscience caused Macbeth ever to fear, lest he should be served of the same cup, as he had ministered to his predecessor.

17. Borne his faculties so meek—Exercised his powers in so mild a manner.

So clear in his great office, that his virtues
Will plead like angels, trumpet-tongu'd, against
20 The deep damnation of his taking-off;
And pity, like a naked new-born babe
Striding the blast, or heaven's cherubim hors'd
Upon the sightless couriers of the air,
Shall blow the horrid deed in every eye,
25 That tears shall drown the wind. I have no spur
To prick the sides of my intent, but only
Vaulting ambition, which o'erleaps itself
And falls on th' other.

                Enter LADY MACBETH.

                How now! what news?
  Lady Macbeth. He has almost supp'd. Why have you
    left the chamber?
30 *Macbeth.* Hath he ask'd for me?
  Lady Macbeth.   Know you not he has?
  Macbeth. We will proceed no further in this business:
He hath honour'd me of late; and I have bought
Golden opinions from all sorts of people,
Which would be worn now in their newest gloss
35 Not cast aside so soon.
  Lady Macbeth.   Was the hope drunk
Wherein you dress'd yourself? hath it slept since?
And wakes it now, to look so green and pale
At what it did so freely? From this time

18. SO CLEAR IN HIS GREAT OFFICE—So free from fault as a king.
21–22. LIKE A NAKED NEW-BORN BABE—See *Psalm* 18:10. "And he rode upon a cherub, and did fly: yea, he did fly upon the wings of the wind."
23. SIGHTLESS COURIERS OF THE AIR—The invisible winds.
27–28. VAULTING AMBITION, WHICH O'ERLEAPS ITSELF AND FALLS ON TH' OTHER —The image is that of a horseman who has put his horse over (vaulted) an obstacle only to fall on the other side.
32–35. I HAVE BOUGHT . . . NOT CAST ASIDE SO SOON—The meaning is that Macbeth's deeds have earned him the great esteem of all classes and that he feels he should enjoy that esteem rather than lose it by murdering Duncan.
35–38. WAS THE HOPE DRUNK . . . AT WHAT IT DID SO FREELY—The meaning is: Was the hope (that is, the hope of being able to murder Duncan) like that of a drunken man, who while he is drunk plans and dares great things, but who when he wakes green and pale from his debauch finds himself without the daring which drink gave him?
39. FROM THIS TIME SUCH I ACCOUNT THY LOVE—Lady Macbeth means that henceforth she will regard his love for her as nothing more than the maudlin protestation of a drunken man.

ELD

Such I account thy love. Art thou afeard
40 To be the same in thine own act and valour
As thou art in desire? Wouldst thou have that
Which thou esteem'st the ornament of life,
And live a coward in thine own esteem,
Letting "I dare not" wait upon "I would,"
45 Like the poor cat i' the adage?
    Macbeth.   Prithee, peace:
I dare do all that may become a man;
Who dares do more is none.
    Lady Macbeth.   What beast was 't, then,
That made you break this enterprise to me?
When you durst do it, then you were a man;
50 And, to be more than what you were, you would
Be so much more the man. Nor time nor place
Did then adhere, and yet you would make both:
They have made themselves, and that their fitness now
Does unmake you. I have given suck, and know
55 How tender 'tis to love the babe that milks me;
I would, while it was smiling in my face,
Have pluck'd my nipple from his boneless gums,
And dash'd the brains out, had I so sworn as you
Have done to this.
    Macbeth.   If we should fail?
    Lady Macbeth.   We fail.
60 But screw your courage to the sticking-place,

    42. ORNAMENT—Crown.
    45. THE ADAGE—The proverb alluded to is: "The cat would eat fish, but she will not wet her feet."
    47. BEAST—Lady Macbeth uses this term in contrast with "man" used by Macbeth in the speech above.
    48. BREAK THIS ENTERPRISE—Propose the murder of Duncan. This line indicates to some students of the play that the "enterprise" originated with Macbeth. Others think that the enterprise really originated with her under the inspiration of Macbeth's letter, and that she can believe, or say at least, that she has only followed him.
    52. ADHERE—Agree, that is, present themselves opportunely together. The meaning of the passage is: When you first proposed to murder Duncan, you were held back only by want of a good opportunity. You were so hot to do it then that you were all for creating such an opportunity. Now that opportunity (time and place) has presented itself you are unnerved by it.
    60. SCREW YOUR COURAGE TO THE STICKING-PLACE—The allusion is to screwing up the strings of a musical instrument to their proper degree of tension, "when the peg remains fast in its 'sticking place.'"

And we'll not fail. When Duncan is asleep—
Whereto the rather shall his day's hard journey
Soundly invite him—his two chamberlains
Will I with wine and wassail so convince,
65 That memory, the warder of the brain,
Shall be a fume, and the receipt of reason
A limbeck only. When in swinish sleep
Their drenched natures lie as in a death,
What cannot you and I perform upon
70 Th' unguarded Duncan? what not put upon
His spongy officers, who shall bear the guilt
Of our great quell?
    Macbeth.   Bring forth men-children only,
For thy undaunted mettle should compose
Nothing but males. Will it not be receiv'd,
75 When we have mark'd with blood those sleepy two
Of his own chamber and us'd their very daggers,
That they have done 't?
    Lady Macbeth.   Who dares receive it other,
As we shall make our griefs and clamour roar
Upon his death?
    Macbeth.   I am settled, and bend up
80 Each corporal agent to this terrible feat.
Away, and mock the time with fairest show;
False face must hide what the false heart doth know.
                                                             [*Exeunt.*

    62. THE RATHER—The more quickly.
    64. WASSAIL—Revelry.
    64. CONVINCE—Overcome.
    65–67. THE WARDER OF THE BRAIN . . . A LIMBECK ONLY—According to the anatomy of Shakespeare's day, the brain was believed to be divided into three ventricles, or cavities. The memory was thought to be situated in the one at the base of the brain where the spinal cord enters. In this position the memory served, like the warder or sentinel of a castle, to warn the reason against attack. "When the memory is converted by intoxication into a mere fume, then it fills the brain itself, the receipt or receptacle of reason, which thus becomes like an alembic"—a vessel used in distilling into which the vapor, or fume, rises.
    71. SPONGY—Drunken.
    72. QUELL—Murder, slaying.
    74. RECEIV'D—Thought.
    77. OTHER—Otherwise.
    79–80. BEND UP EACH CORPORAL AGENT—Bring to bear each physical power.

ACT II

Scene 1. *Inverness. Court of* Macbeth's *castle.*

Enter Banquo, *and* Fleance *with a torch before him.*

Banquo. How goes the night, boy?
Fleance. The moon is down; I have not heard the clock.
Banquo. And she goes down at twelve.
Fleance.   I take 't, 'tis later, sir.
Banquo. Hold, take my sword. There's husbandry in heaven;
5 Their candles are all out. Take thee that too.
A heavy summons lies like lead upon me,
And yet I would not sleep. Merciful powers,
Restrain in me the cursèd thoughts that nature
Gives way to in repose!

Enter Macbeth, *and a* Servant *with a torch.*

                          Give me my sword.
10 Who's there?
    Macbeth. A friend.
    Banquo. What, sir, not yet at rest? The king's a-bed:
He hath been in unusual pleasure, and
Sent forth great largess to your offices:
15 This diamond he greets your wife withal,
By the name of most kind hostess; and shut up
In measureless content.
    Macbeth.   Being unprepar'd,
Our will became the servant to defect;

    4. Husbandry—Economy, thrift.
    5. Candles—The stars.
    5. Take thee that too—Banquo hands Fleance some weapon.
    8. The cursed thoughts that nature gives way to in repose—The dreams of the weird sisters which Banquo mentions in a speech below.
    9. Give me my sword—Hearing footsteps approaching, Banquo calls for his sword.
    14. Largess to your offices—Gifts for your household officers or servants.
    16–17. Shut up in measureless content—Probably means "as one whose satisfaction is complete."
    17–19. Being unprepar'd . . . have wrought—The meaning is: Not being prepared for the king's coming, our natural desire (will) to receive him with the ceremony and hospitality due him has been thwarted by our not having had sufficient time to make adequate preparation.

Which else should free have wrought.
  Banquo.   All's well.
20 I dreamt last night of the three weird sisters:
To you they have show'd some truth.
  Macbeth.   I think not of them;
Yet, when we can entreat an hour to serve,
We would spend it in some words upon that business,
If you would grant the time.
  Banquo.   At your kind'st leisure.
25   *Macbeth.* If you shall cleave to my consent, when 't is,
It shall make honour for you.
  Banquo.   So I lose none
In seeking to augment it, but still keep
My bosom franchis'd, and allegiance clear,
I shall be counsell'd.
  Macbeth.   Good repose the while!
30   *Banquo.* Thanks, sir: the like to you!
           [*Exeunt* BANQUO *and* FLEANCE
  Macbeth. Go bid thy mistress, when my drink is ready,
She strike upon the bell. Get thee to bed. [*Exit* Servant.
Is this a dagger which I see before me,
The handle toward my hand? Come, let me clutch thee.
35 I have thee not, and yet I see thee still.
Art thou not, fatal vision, sensible
To feeling as to sight? or art thou but
A dagger of the mind, a false creation,
Proceeding from the heat-oppressed brain?
40 I see thee yet, in form as palpable
As this which now I draw.
Thou marshall'st me the way that I was going;

  22. ENTREAT AN HOUR TO SERVE—That is, find an hour convenient to the purpose.
  25–26. CLEAVE TO MY CONSENT . . . HONOUR FOR YOU—The meaning is: If you shall consent to my plan, when I unfold it to you, it will bring you honor.
  26. SO—Provided that.
  26. NONE—That is, no honor.
  28. BOSOM FRANCHIS'D—That is, free from dishonor.
  28. ALLEGIANCE CLEAR—Loyalty to the king untarnished.
  29. COUNSELL'D—I shall listen to your plan.
  32. *Exit* SERVANT—Macbeth is now left alone in the darkness.
  36–37. SENSIBLE TO FEELING—Perceptible to feeling or to the touch.
  40. PALPABLE—Capable of being touched.
  42. MARSHALL'ST ME—The dagger seems to move farther from him, leading him on.

And such an instrument I was to use.
Mine eyes are made the fools o' the other senses,
45 Or else worth all the rest; I see thee still;
And on thy blade and dudgeon gouts of blood,
Which was not so before. There's no such thing:
It is the bloody business which informs
Thus to mine eyes. Now o'er the one half-world
50 Nature seems dead, and wicked dreams abuse
The curtain'd sleep; witchcraft celebrates
Pale Hecate's offerings; and wither'd murder,
Alarum'd by his sentinel, the wolf,
Whose howl 's his watch, thus with his stealthy pace,
55 With Tarquin's ravishing strides, towards his design
Moves like a ghost. Thou sure and firm-set earth,
Hear not my steps, which way they walk, for fear
Thy very stones prate of my whereabout,
And take the present horror from the time,
60 Which now suits with it. Whiles I threat, he lives:
Words to the heat of deeds too cold breath gives.

[*A bell rings.*

44–45. THE FOOLS O' THE OTHER SENSES, OR ELSE WORTH ALL THE REST—Either his eyes are made the fools of his imagination, since he sees what is not, or else they are worth more, since they can see what he cannot clutch with his hand.

46. DUDGEON—Haft or hilt.

46. GOUTS—Drops, smears.

48. INFORMS—Takes form.

51. CURTAIN'D SLEEP—The Elizabethan bed was hung about with curtains.

51–52. WITCHCRAFT CELEBRATES PALE HECATE'S OFFERINGS—Performs the rites dedicated or offered to Hecate. In Greek mythology Hecate was queen of Hades, or the underworld. The modern pronunciation is hĕk′a-tē. Shakespeare employs it as if it were a word of two syllables, possibly hĕk′āte.

54. WHOSE HOWL 'S HIS WATCH—The "his" refers to murder, that is, the murderer. The allusion is to the watch who used to go about the city and cry out the hour, as, "Twelve o'clock and all's well." The wolf is thought of here as the murder's watch, whose howl means: "Now is the time for your deed and all's well."

55. WITH TARQUIN'S RAVISHING STRIDES—The murderer is pictured as approaching his victim with the stealthy strides of Tarquin. Tarquin was a Roman king whose assault on Lucrece, a Roman matron, so aroused the people that as a result the kingdom was destroyed and a republic established.

58. PRATE—Cry out.

59–60. AND TAKE THE PRESENT HORROR . . . SUITS WITH IT—That is, And break the silence that adds such horror to the night and makes it the more suitable for the murder.

61. WORDS TO THE HEAT OF DEEDS TOO COLD BREATH GIVES—That is, when the time requires action, talking about what one is going to do accomplishes nothing.

I go, and it is done; the bell invites me.
Hear it not, Duncan; for it is a knell
That summons thee to heaven or to hell.   [*Exit.*

<small>62. THE BELL—The bell which Lady Macbeth was to ring when Macbeth's drink was ready. It probably was intended also to signify that Duncan and his grooms were asleep and that the daggers were laid ready for the murder.</small>

SCENE 2. *The same.*

Enter LADY MACBETH.

Lady Macbeth. That which hath made them drunk hath
    made me bold;
What hath quench'd them hath given me fire. Hark! Peace!
It was the owl that shriek'd, the fatal bellman,
Which gives the stern'st good-night. He is about it.
5 The doors are open; and the surfeited grooms
Do mock their charge with snores. I have drugg'd their possets,
That death and nature do contend about them,
Whether they live or die.
    Macbeth. [*Within.*]   Who's there? what, ho!
    Lady Macbeth. Alack, I am afraid they have awak'd,
10 And 'tis not done. Th' attempt and not the deed
Confounds us. Hark! I laid their daggers ready;
He could not miss 'em. Had he not resembled
My father as he slept, I had done 't.

Enter MACBETH.

                                               My husband!
    Macbeth. I have done the deed. Didst thou not hear a noise?

<small>2. QUENCH'D THEM—Put them to sleep. Lady Macbeth refers to the grooms whose drinks she has drugged.
3. OWL—Commonly supposed to be a bird of ill omen.
3. FATAL BELLMAN—It was the custom to have a bellman, or crier, warn the prisoners in Newgate Prison who were to be executed on the day following.
4. HE—Macbeth.
5. SURFEITED—Glutted with food and drink.
6. MOCK THEIR CHARGE—Set at naught their responsibility.
6. POSSETS—A drink made of "hot milk poured on ale or sack, having sugar, grated bisket, and eggs, with other ingredients boiled in it, which all goes to curd." It seems to have been drunk before retiring to induce sleep.
7. THAT—So that.
11. CONFOUNDS—Ruins. That is, to make an unsuccessful attempt will bring ruin.
12. HAD HE NOT RESEMBLED—"He" refers to Duncan.</small>

15   *Lady Macbeth.* I heard the owl scream and the crickets
  Did not you speak?
      Macbeth.   When?
      Lady Macbeth.   Now.
      Macbeth.   As I descended?
      Lady Macbeth. Ay.
      Macbeth. Hark!
  Who lies i' the second chamber?
      Lady Macbeth.   Donalbain.
20   *Macbeth.* This is a sorry sight.   [*Looking on his hands.*

  Lady Macbeth. A foolish thought, to say a sorry sight.
  Macbeth. There's one did laugh in 's sleep, and one cried
      "Murder!"
  That they did wake each other: I stood and heard them;
  But they did say their prayers, and address'd them
25 Again to sleep.
      Lady Macbeth. There are two lodg'd together.
      Macbeth. One cried "God bless us!" and "Amen" the
          other,

   20. SORRY—Woeful, wretched.
   22. THERE'S ONE—One of those in the second chamber.
   25. THERE ARE TWO LODG'D TOGETHER—Two in the second chamber—probably
Malcolm and Donalbain.

As they had seen me with these hangman's hands:
Listening their fear, I could not say "Amen,"
When they did say "God bless us!"
　　Lady Macbeth.　Consider it not so deeply.
　　Macbeth.　But wherefore could not I pronounce "Amen"?
I had most need of blessing, and "Amen"
Stuck in my throat.
　　Lady Macbeth.　These deeds must not be thought
After these ways: so, it will make us mad.
　　Macbeth.　Methought I heard a voice cry "Sleep no more!
Macbeth does murder sleep,"—the innocent sleep,
Sleep that knits up the ravell'd sleave of care,
The death of each day's life, sore labour's bath,
Balm of hurt minds, great nature's second course,
Chief nourisher in life's feast,—
　　Lady Macbeth.　　　　　　What do you mean?
　　Macbeth.　Still it cried "Sleep no more!" to all the house:
"Glamis hath murder'd sleep, and therefore Cawdor
Shall sleep no more; Macbeth shall sleep no more!"
　　Lady Macbeth.　Who was it that thus cried? Why, worthy thane,
You do unbend your noble strength, to think
So brainsickly of things. Go get some water,
And wash this filthy witness from your hand.
Why did you bring these daggers from the place?
They must lie there; go carry them, and smear
The sleepy grooms with blood.
　　Macbeth.　　　　　　I'll go no more:
I am afraid to think what I have done;
Look on 't again I dare not.
　　Lady Macbeth.　　　　　Infirm of purpose!
Give me the daggers: the sleeping and the dead
Are but as pictures; 'tis the eye of childhood
That fears a painted devil. If he do bleed,

27. As—As if.
27. Hangman's—Executioner's.
37. Ravell'd sleave—Floss silk, sometimes called sleave-silk. A "ravell'd sleave" means a tangled skein of silk.
39. Second course—The meat course, or chief course at a banquet.
45. Unbend—Relax, that is, lose your self-control or constancy.
55. Painted devil—The picture of a devil. Lady Macbeth implies that there is nothing to fear from the sight of the murdered Duncan.

I'll gild the faces of the grooms withal;
For it must seem their guilt.   [*Exit. Knocking within.*
    Macbeth.   Whence is that knocking?
How is 't with me, when every noise appals me?
What hands are here? Ha! they pluck out mine eyes!
Will all great Neptune's ocean wash this blood
Clean from my hand? No; this my hand will rather
The multitudinous seas incarnadine,
Making the green one red.

Re-enter LADY MACBETH.

   Lady Macbeth. My hands are of your colour, but I shame
To wear a heart so white. [*Knocking within.*] I hear a knocking
At the south entry: retire we to our chamber.
A little water clears us of this deed.
How easy is it, then! Your constancy
Hath left you unattended. [*Knocking within.*] Hark! more knocking.
Get on your night-gown, lest occasion call us,
And show us to be watchers. Be not lost
So poorly in your thoughts.
    Macbeth. To know my deed, 'twere best not know myself.
                                    [*Knocking within.*
Wake Duncan with thy knocking! I would thou couldst!
                                    [*Exeunt.*

   56. GILD—Make red.
   57. GUILT—Note the pun or "gild" and "guilt"—a rather ghastly play on words.
   59. WHAT HANDS ARE HERE?—Macbeth speaks as if he now saw the blood on his hands for the first time.
   60. NEPTUNE—Roman god of the sea.
   62. MULTITUDINOUS—Is this an effective word to image forth the vastness of the sea?
   62. INCARNADINE—Make red.
   68. YOUR CONSTANCY HATH LEFT YOU UNATTENDED—Your firmness has deserted you.
   70. NIGHT-GOWN—Dressing-gown.
   70–71. LEST OCCASION CALL US, AND SHOW US TO BE WATCHERS—Lady Macbeth admonishes Macbeth to put on his dressing gown so that if the occasion (the knocking) demands them, it will not appear that they have been up.
   73. TO KNOW MY DEED, 'TWERE BEST NOT KNOW MYSELF—Lady Macbeth has urged Macbeth that he cease being "lost so poorly" in his thoughts—in other words, that he be his natural self. His reply means: If to be myself means to realize what I have done, it were best that I should never come back to myself.

Scene 3. *The Same.*

Enter a Porter. *Knocking within.*

Porter. Here's a knocking indeed! If a man were porter of hell-gate, he should have old turning the key. [*Knocking.*] Knock, knock, knock! Who's there, i' the name of Beelzebub? Here's a farmer, that hang'd himself on the expectation of plenty. Come in time; have napkins enough about you; here you'll sweat for 't. [*Knocking.*] Knock, knock! Who's there, in the other devil's name? Faith, here's an equivocator that could swear in both the scales against either scale; who committed treason enough for God's sake, yet could not equivocate to heaven. O, come in, equivocator. [*Knocking.*] Knock, knock, knock! Who's there? Faith, here's an English tailor come hither for stealing out of a French hose. Come in, tailor; here you may roast your goose. [*Knocking.*] Knock, knock; never at quiet! What are you? But this place is too cold for hell. I'll devil-porter it no further: I had thought to have let in some of all professions, that go the primrose way to the everlasting bonfire. [*Knocking.*] Anon, anon! I pray you, remember the porter.
[*Opens the gate.*

Enter Macduff *and* Lennox.

Macduff. Was it so late, friend, ere you went to bed,
That you do lie so late?

Porter—The Porter, who has had his share of the night's wassail is drunk. He imagines that he is porter at hell-gate, and that the knocking is that of damned souls seeking entrance. He fumbles at the lock, as the knocking is repeated.
2. Have old—Grow old; have one's fill of turning the key.
3. Beelzebub—Prince of devils.
4–5. On the expectation of plenty—The farmer had expected a good yield, or a good price for his crop, and being disappointed had hanged himself.
5. Napkins—Handkerchiefs to wipe away the sweat.
7. Equivocator—One who swore falsely. There is an allusion here to a matter familiar to Shakespeare's audience.
9. Equivocate to heaven—Get himself into heaven through equivocation.
12. Stealing out of a French hose—An allusion to the practice commonly charged in those days against tailors, that they stole part of the cloth brought to them to be made up. As used here, "hose" means trousers, or breeches.
13. Goose—A tailor's goose is a heavy pressing iron. It got its name from the fact that the handle somewhat resembled the neck of a goose. A pun on "goose" is intended. 16. Primrose way—Easy way.
17. Anon, anon—The customary reply of porters or waiters to their patrons. It means immediately or at once.
17. Remember the porter—Remember to tip him.

20 *Porter.* Faith, sir, we were carousing till the second cock.
Macduff. I believe drink gave thee the lie last night.
Porter. That it did, sir, i' the very throat on me: but I requited him for his lie; and, I think, being too strong for him, though he took up my legs sometime, yet I made a shift to cast
25 him.
Macduff. Is thy master stirring?

Enter MACBETH.

Our knocking has awak'd him; here he comes.
Lennox. Good morrow, noble sir.
Macbeth.   Good morrow, both.
Macduff. Is the king stirring, worthy thane?
Macbeth.   Not yet.
30 *Macduff.* He did command me to call timely on him.
I have almost slipp'd the hour.
Macbeth.   I'll bring you to him.
Macduff. I know this is a joyful trouble to you;
But yet 'tis one.
Macbeth. The labour we delight in physics pain.
35 This is the door.
Macduff.   I'll make so bold to call,
For 'tis my limited service.   [*Exit.*
Lennox. Goes the king hence to-day?
Macbeth.   He does;—he did appoint so.
Lennox. The night has been unruly: where we lay,
Our chimneys were blown down; and, as they say,
40 Lamentings heard i' the air, strange screams of death,
And, prophesying with accents terrible
Of dire combustion and confus'd events

   20. SECOND COCK—About 3 A.M.
   21. LIE—Note the puns on "lie."
   24. CAST—To throw as in wrestling. The Porter speaks as if he had been wrestling with drink which as he says "took up my legs sometime." There is a pun intended here, "cast" being used also in the sense of to cast up or vomit.
   30. TIMELY—Early.
   34. PHYSICS—Heals, or cures.
   36. MY LIMITED SERVICE—Appointed service.
   38. THE NIGHT HAS BEEN UNRULY—It was formerly a general belief that a great calamity in human affairs was foreshadowed by unusual disturbance in the world of nature.
   42. COMBUSTION—Conflagration, fire. Probably used figuratively for tumult or disturbance.

New hatch'd to th' woeful time, the obscure bird
Clamour'd the livelong night: some say, the earth
45 Was feverous and did shake.
  Macbeth.   'T was a rough night.
  Lennox. My young remembrance cannot parallel
A fellow to it.

Re-enter MACDUFF.

  Macduff. O horror, horror, horror! tongue nor heart
Cannot conceive nor name thee!
  Macbeth. ⎫
  Lennox. ⎬ What's the matter?
50 *Macduff.* Confusion now hath made his masterpiece!
Most sacrilegious murder hath broke ope
The Lord's anointed temple, and stole thence
The life o' the building.
  Macbeth.   What is 't you say? the life?
  Lennox. Mean you his majesty?
55 *Macduff.* Approach the chamber, and destroy your sight
With a new Gorgon. Do not bid me speak;
See, and then speak yourselves.
         [*Exeunt* MACBETH *and* LENNOX.
         Awake, awake!
Ring the alarum-bell. Murder and treason!
Banquo and Donalbain! Malcolm! awake!
60 Shake off this downy sleep, death's counterfeit,
And look on death itself! Up, up, and see
The great doom's image! Malcolm! Banquo!

  43. EVENTS NEW HATCH'D TO TH' WOEFUL TIME—Events born to, that is, in keeping with the woeful time.
  43. OBSCURE—Lovin the darkness. The allusion is to the owl, which was regarded as a bird of ill omen.
  46-47. CANNOT PARALLEL A FELLOW—Cannot call up its equal.
  50. CONFUSION—Destruction.
  51. SACRILEGIOUS—Note the pronunciation of this word: săk rĭ lē′jŭs. Do not confuse the last three syllables with "religious."
  52. ANOINTED TEMPLE—See *I Samuel*, 24:10 where the king is referred to as "the Lord's anointed," and *II Corinthians*, 6:16 where the Christian is called "the temple of the living God."
  56. GORGON—The reference is to Medusa, a character in Greek mythology whose appearance was so terrible that whoever looked at her was turned to stone.
  62. GREAT DOOM'S IMAGE—A sight as terrible as the Last Judgment.

As from your graves rise up, and walk like sprites,
To countenance this horror. Ring the bell. *[Bell rings.*

Enter LADY MACBETH.

65 *Lady Macbeth.* What's the business,
That such a hideous trumpet calls to parley
The sleepers of the house? Speak, speak!
    Macduff.   O gentle lady,
'Tis not for you to hear what I can speak:
The repetition, in a woman's ear,
70 Would murder as it fell.

Enter BANQUO.

                    O Banquo, Banquo,
Our royal master's murder'd!
    Lady Macbeth.   Woe, alas!
What, in our house?
    Banquo.   Too cruel anywhere.
Dear Duff, I prithee, contradict thyself,
And say it is not so.

Re-enter MACBETH *and* LENNOX, *with* ROSS.

75 *Macbeth.* Had I but died an hour before this chance,
I had liv'd a blessed time; for, from this instant,
There's nothing serious in mortality.
All is but toys; renown and grace is dead;
The wine of life is drawn, and the mere lees
80 Is left this vault to brag of.

Enter MALCOLM *and* DONALBAIN.

    Donalbain. What is amiss?
    Macbeth.   You are, and do not know 't:
The spring, the head, the fountain of your blood

---

63. SPRITES—Spirits. The figure of the Judgment Day is continued.
64. COUNTENANCE—Be in keeping with.
66. PARLEY—Conference.
75. CHANCE—Unfortunate event.
77. MORTALITY—Life. There is nothing worthwhile in life.
78. GRACE—Good opinion, esteem.
79. LEES—Dregs.
80. VAULT—Macbeth has in mind a vault or storage place for wine. By "this vault" he means, of course, himself.

Is stopp'd; the very source of it is stopp'd.
    Macduff. Your royal father's murder'd.
    Malcolm.   O! by whom?
85   *Lennox.* Those of his chamber, as it seem'd, had done 't:
Their hands and faces were all badg'd with blood;
So were their daggers, which unwip'd we found
Upon their pillows:
They star'd, and were distracted; no man's life
90 Was to be trusted with them.
    Macbeth. O, yet I do repent me of my fury,
That I did kill them.
    Macduff.   Wherefore did you so?
    Macbeth. Who can be wise, amaz'd, temperate and furious,
The expedition of my violent love
95 Loyal and neutral, in a moment? No man.
Outrun the pauser, reason. Here lay Duncan,
His silver skin lac'd with his golden blood;
And his gash'd stabs look'd like a breach in nature
For ruin's wasteful entrance; there, the murderers,
100 Steep'd in the colours of their trade, their daggers
Unmannerly breech'd with gore. Who could refrain,
That had a heart to love, and in that heart
Courage to make 's love known?
    Lady Macbeth.   Help me hence, ho!
    Macduff. Look to the lady.
    Malcolm. [*Aside to* DONALBAIN.] Why do we hold our tongues,
105 That most may claim this argument for ours?
    Donalbain. [Aside to MALCOLM.] What should be spoken here, where our fate,
Hid in an auger-hole, may rush, and seize us?
Let's away.
Our tears are not yet brew'd.

    86. BADG'D—Marked, smeared.
    94. EXPEDITION—Haste.
    96. PAUSER, REASON—Reason which makes one stop (pause) to think before he acts.
    101. BREECH'D—Covered.
    103. MAKE 'S—Make his.
    105. ARGUMENT—Matter in hand, that is, the murder of Duncan, their father.
    107. HID IN AN AUGER-HOLE—Where no place is so small, not even an auger-hole, but that our fate may lurk therein.

  Malcolm. [*Aside to* DONALBAIN.] Nor our strong sorrow
110 Upon the foot of motion.
  Banquo.   Look to the lady;
         [LADY MACBETH *is carried out.*
And when we have our naked frailties hid,
That suffer in exposure, let us meet
And question this most bloody piece of work,
To know it further. Fears and scruples shake us:
115 In the great hand of God I stand, and thence
Against the undivulg'd pretence I fight
Of treasonous malice.
  Macduff.   And so do I.
  All.   So all.
  Macbeth. Let's briefly put on manly readiness,
And meet i' the hall together.
  All.   Well contented.
     [*Exeunt all but* MALCOLM *and* DONALBAIN.
120 *Malcolm.* What will you do? Let's not consort with them:
To show an unfelt sorrow is an office
Which the false man does easy. I'll to England.
  Donalbain. To Ireland I; our separated fortune
Shall keep us both the safer. Where we are,
125 There's daggers in men's smiles; the near in blood,
The nearer bloody.
  Malcolm.   This murderous shaft that's shot

  109–110. NOR OUR STRONG SORROW UPON THE FOOT OF MOTION—Donalbain has just said "Our tears are not yet brew'd" and Malcolm continues with a remark which means: And our great grief has not yet been given expression. The emotion of fear, for the time, supplants that of grief.
  111. NAKED FRAILTIES—Banquo and the others have rushed forth half-dressed.
  116. UNDIVULG'D PRETENCE—The not-yet-known design or purpose. Banquo means that he stands ready to fight against whatever treasonable purpose is to be found behind the murder.
  118. BRIEFLY—Quickly.
  118. MANLY READINESS—Armor. The implication is that being armed they will feel more ready to act like men.
  119. WELL CONTENTED—Agreed.
  121. OFFICE—Action, "duty."
  125–126. THE NEAR IN BLOOD, THE NEARER BLOODY—The meaning is that being sons of Duncan, the nearer in blood or relationship, the nearer they are to death.
  126–128. THE MURDEROUS SHAFT ... AVOID THE AIM—Whoever killed our father is not yet done, for we stand yet between the murderer and the throne. We must away to avoid being struck by the same arrow.

Hath not yet lighted; and our safest way
Is to avoid the aim. Therefore, to horse;
And let us not be dainty of leave-taking,
But shift away. There's warrant in that theft
Which steals itself, when there's no mercy left. [*Exeunt.*

130. SHIFT AWAY—Steal away.
130. WARRANT—Justification. The meaning is that there can be no blame or discourtesy in stealing away without taking leave from a place where they can expect no mercy.

SCENE 4. *Outside* MACBETH'S *castle.*

Enter Ross *and an* Old Man.

Old Man. Threescore-and-ten I can remember well;
Within the volume of which time I have seen
Hours dreadful and things strange; but this sore night
Hath trifl'd former knowings.
   Ross.   Ah, good father,
Thou see'st the heavens, as troubl'd with man's act,
Threatens his bloody stage; by th' clock 'tis day,
And yet dark night strangles the travelling lamp.
Is 't night's predominance, or the day's shame
That darkness does the face of earth entomb,
When living light should kiss it?
   Old Man.   'Tis unnatural,
Even like the deed that's done. On Tuesday last,
A falcon, tow'ring in her pride of place,
Was by a mousing owl hawk'd at and kill'd.
   Ross. And Duncan's horses—a thing most strange and certain—
Beauteous and swift, the minions of their race,
Turn'd wild in nature, broke their stalls, flung out,

4. HATH TRIFL'D FORMER KNOWINGS—Had made former experiences seem trifling.
4. GOOD FATHER—An expression commonly used in addressing old men.
6. BLOODY STAGE—The earth. The figure is from the theatre, the meaning being: The heavens displeased at man's act threatens to destroy the bloody stage altogether.
7. TRAVELLING LAMP—Sun.
10. UNNATURAL—Monstrous, abnormal, not according to nature.
12. TOW'RING—Soaring. The term was used to designate the soaring of the falcon to the "place" from which it swooped down upon its prey.
13. MOUSING—An owl which was accustomed to attack nothing more vicious than mere mice.
15. MINIONS—Most favored, best cared for.

Contending 'gainst obedience, as they would make
War with mankind.
    Old Man.   'Tis said they eat each other.
    Ross. They did so, to th' amazement of mine eyes,
20 That look'd upon 't.

                      Enter MACDUFF.

                  Here comes the good Macduff.
How goes the world, sir, now?
    Macduff.   Why, see you not?
    Ross. Is 't known who did this more than bloody deed?
    Macduff. Those that Macbeth hath slain.
    Ross.   Alas, the day!
What good could they pretend?
    Macduff.   They were suborn'd.
25 Malcolm and Donalbain, the King's two sons,
Are stol'n away and fled; which puts upon them
Suspicion of the deed.
    Ross.   'Gainst nature still!
Thriftless ambition, that will ravin up
Thine own life's means! Then 'tis most like
30 The sovereignty will fall upon Macbeth.
    Macduff. He is already nam'd; and gone to Scone
To be invested.
    Ross.   Where is Duncan's body?
    Macduff. Carried to Colmekill,
The sacred storehouse of his predecessors,
35 And guardian of their bones.
    Ross.   Will you to Scone?
    Macduff. No, cousin, I'll to Fife.
    Ross.   Well, I will thither.

    18. EAT—The past tense of eat, commonly pronounced ĕt in British usage, where we should say āte.
    24. PRETEND—Expect to derive from the deed.
    24. SUBORN'D—Bribed.
    27. STILL—This word is used frequently in the play and each time means "always."
    28. RAVIN UP—Devour utterly.
    31. SCONE (skoon)—The ancient royal city of Scotland and place of coronation of the Scottish kings.
    33. COLMEKILL—St. Colum's or St. Columba's cell. The island of Iona, where the tombs of the ancient kings may still be seen.
    36. FIFE—Macduff's home. Macduff was Thane of Fife.
    36. THITHER—To Scone.

Macduff. Well, may you see things well done there,—adieu!—
Lest our old robes sit easier than our new!
Ross. Farewell, father.
Old Man. God's benison go with you; and with those
That would make good of bad, and friends of foes! [*Exeunt.*

38. LEST OUR OLD ROBES SIT EASIER THAN OUR NEW—Lest the new order of things be worse than the old.
40. BENISON—Blessing.

ACT III

SCENE 1. *Forres. The palace.*

Enter BANQUO.

Banquo. Thou hast it now: king, Cawdor, Glamis, all,
As the weird women promis'd, and, I fear,
Thou play'dst most foully for 't; yet it was said
It should not stand in thy posterity,
5 But that myself should be the root and father
Of many kings. If there come truth from them,
As upon thee, Macbeth, their speeches shine,
Why, by the verities on thee made good,
May they not be my oracles as well,
10 And set me up in hope? But hush! no more.

Sennet sounded. Enter MACBETH, *as king;* LADY MACBETH, *as queen;* LENNOX, Ross, Lords, Ladies, *and* Attendants.

Macbeth. Here's our chief guest.
Lady Macbeth.   If he had been forgotten,
It had been as a gap in our great feast,
And all-thing unbecoming.
Macbeth. To-night we hold a solemn supper, sir,
15 And I'll request your presence.
Banquo.   Let your highness
Command upon me; to the which my duties

4. IT SHOULD NOT STAND IN THY POSTERITY—See the prophecy of the third witch, Act I, Scene 3.
9. MY ORACLES—Prophets of the truth.
Sennet—A sound of trumpets.
13. ALL-THING—Altogether.
14. SOLEMN—Formal.

Are with a most indissoluble tie
For ever knit.
 Macbeth. Ride you this afternoon?
 Banquo.   Ay, my good lord.
20 *Macbeth.* We should have else desir'd your good advice,
Which still hath been both grave and prosperous,
In this day's council; but we'll take to-morrow.
Is 't far you ride?
 Banquo. As far, my lord, as will fill up the time
25 'Twixt this and supper. Go not my horse the better,
I must become a borrower of the night
For a dark hour or twain.
 Macbeth.   Fail not our feast.
 Banquo. My lord, I will not.
 Macbeth. We hear, our bloody cousins are bestow'd
30 In England and in Ireland, not confessing
Their cruel parricide, filling their hearers
With strange invention: but of that to-morrow,
When therewithal we shall have cause of state
Craving us jointly. Hie you to horse; adieu,
35 Till you return at night. Goes Fleance with you?
 Banquo. Ay, my good lord: our time does call upon 's.
 Macbeth. I wish your horses swift and sure of foot;
And so I do commend you to their backs.
Farewell.   [*Exit* BANQUO.
40 Let every man be master of his time
Till seven at night; to make society
The sweeter welcome, we will keep ourself
Till supper-time alone: while then, God be with you!
      [*Exeunt all but* MACBETH, *and an* Attendant.

 21. GRAVE AND PROSPEROUS—Worth paying attention to and invariably turning out well.
 22. WE'LL TAKE TO-MORROW—We'll let the matter go until to-morrow.
 29. BLOODY COUSINS—Donalbain and Malcolm. 29. BESTOW'D—Lodged.
 31. PARRICIDE—Murder of a parent.
 32. INVENTION—Falsehood.
 33. THEREWITHAL—In addition to the matter of what shall be done about Donalbain and Malcolm.
 33–34. CAUSE OF STATE CRAVING US JOINTLY—Affairs of state which demand our joint attention.
 36. UPON 'S—Upon us. That is, it is already the time we agreed upon to ride out.
 40. BE MASTER OF HIS TIME—Do as he wishes.
 43. WHILE—Until.

Sirrah, a word with you: attend those men
Our pleasure?
    Attendant. They are, my lord, without the palace-gate.
    Macbeth. Bring them before us.   [*Exit* Attendant.
To be thus is nothing,
But to be safely thus. Our fears in Banquo
Stick deep; and in his royalty of nature
Reigns that which would be fear'd. 'Tis much he dares;
And, to that dauntless temper of his mind,
He hath a wisdom that doth guide his valour
To act in safety. There is none but he
Whose being I do fear; and, under him,
My Genius is rebuk'd, as, it is said,
Mark Antony's was by Cæsar. He chid the sisters,
When first they put the name of king upon me,
And bade them speak to him; then prophet-like
They hail'd him father to a line of kings.
Upon my head they plac'd a fruitless crown,
And put a barren sceptre in my gripe,
Thence to be wrench'd with an unlineal hand,
No son of mine succeeding. If 't be so,
For Banquo's issue have I fil'd my mind;
For them the gracious Duncan have I murder'd;
Put rancours in the vessel of my peace
Only for them; and mine eternal jewel
Given to the common enemy of man,
To make them kings, the seed of Banquo, kings!
Rather than so, come, fate, into the list,
And champion me to th' utterance!—Who's there?

    44. SIRRAH—A form commonly used in addressing a servant or an inferior.
    44. ATTEND—Wait.
    44. THOSE MEN—The murderers who soon come upon the scene.
    47. TO BE THUS—To be king.
    51. TO—In addition to.
    55-56. MY GENIUS . . . BY CÆSAR—Genius here means guarding spirit. The allusion is to a passage in North's *Plutarch* in *The Life of Marcus Antonius*. It is related that Antonius was once told by a soothsayer that his fortune was inferior to Octavius Cæsar's.
    62. UNLINEAL HAND—By one not descended from me. The following line makes the meaning clear.   64. FIL'D—Defiled.
    66. RANCOURS IN THE VESSEL—Bitterness in the cup.
    67. MINE ETERNAL JEWEL—My immortal soul.
    68. COMMON ENEMY—Satan.
    71. CHAMPION ME TO TH' UTTERANCE—Fight with me to the death.

Re-enter Attendant, *with two* Murderers.

Now go to th' door, and stay there till we call.—

[*Exit* Attendant.

Was it not yesterday we spoke together?
  1 Murderer. It was, so please your highness.
  Macbeth.   Well then, now.
75 Have you consider'd of my speeches? Know
That it was he, in the times past, which held you
So under fortune; which you thought had been
Our innocent self. This I made good to you
In our last conference, pass'd in probation with you,
80 How you were borne in hand, how cross'd, the instruments,
Who wrought with them, and all things else that might
To half a soul and to a notion craz'd
Say, "Thus did Banquo."
  1 Murderer.   You made it known to us.
  Macbeth. I did so, and went further, which is now
85 Our point of second meeting. Do you find
Your patience so predominant in your nature
That you can let this go? Are you so gospell'd,
To pray for this good man and for his issue,
Whose heavy hand hath bow'd you to the grave
90 And beggar'd yours for ever?
  1 Murderer.   We are men, my liege.
  Macbeth. Ay, in the catalogue ye go for men;
As hounds and greyhounds, mongrels, spaniels, curs,
Shoughs, water-rugs, and demi-wolves, are clept
All by the name of dogs; the valued file
95 Distinguishes the swift, the slow, the subtle,

76–77. HELD YOU SO UNDER FORTUNE—Kept you from being rewarded according to your merits. Macbeth has chosen to do the murder two disgruntled soldiers whom he incites against Banquo by telling them that their misfortunes are the result of Banquo's injustice.

79. PASS'D IN PROBATION WITH YOU—Went over point by point with you, giving you proof in each instance.

80. BORNE IN HAND—Deluded with false hopes or promises.

82. NOTION—Mind, understanding.

87. GOSPELL'D—So filled with the lesson of the gospel which says, "Pray for them which despitefully use you, and persecute you." See *Matthew* 5:44.

93. SHOUGHS, WATER-RUGS, DEMI-WOLVES—Breeds of dogs.

93. CLEPT—Called.

94. VALUED FILE—The list which sets down the values of each dog. This expression is used in contrast to "catalogue" in the first line of the speech.

Ay, in the catalogue ye go for men.

The housekeeper, the hunter, every one
According to the gift which bounteous nature
Hath in him clos'd; whereby he does receive
Particular addition, from the bill
100 That writes them all alike; and so of men.
Now, if you have a station in the file,
Not i' the worst rank of manhood, say 't;
And I will put that business in your bosoms,
Whose execution takes your enemy off,
105 Grapples you to the heart and love of us,
Who wear our health but sickly in his life,
Which in his death were perfect.
   2 Murderer.   I am one, my liege,
Whom the vile blows and buffets of the world
Hath so incens'd, that I am reckless what
110 I do to spite the world.
   1 Murderer.   And I another
So weary with disasters, tugg'd with fortune,
That I would set my life on any chance,
To mend it, or be rid on 't.
   Macbeth.   Both of you
Know Banquo was your enemy.
   Both Murderers.   True, my lord.
115   *Macbeth.* So is he mine; and in such bloody distance,
That every minute of his being thrusts
Against my near'st of life; and though I could
With barefac'd power sweep him from my sight
And bid my will avouch it, yet I must not,

   96. HOUSEKEEPER—Watchdog.
   99. PARTICULAR ADDITION—His own distinctive attribute; his rank.
   99. BILL—The catalogue or general list.
   101. STATION IN THE FILE—If you have that which distinguishes you from the common run of men.
   105. GRAPPLES YOU—Fastens you.
   106. WEAR OUR HEALTH BUT SICKLY IN HIS LIFE—Find our well-being impaired or in danger while he is alive.
   111. TUGG'D WITH FORTUNE—Buffeted about by fortune.
   115. BLOODY DISTANCE—The figure is from duelling. Macbeth speaks of Banquo as one who stands within duelling distance—that is, so close that he (Banquo) can with a single thrust at any minute pierce Macbeth's "near'st of life" (vitals).
   119. AVOUCH IT—Give no explanation to the kingdom other than that it is my will or desire.

For certain friends that are both his and mine,
Whose loves I may not drop, but wail his fall
Who I myself struck down; and thence it is,
That I to your assistance do make love,
Masking the business from the common eye
For sundry weighty reasons.
   2 Murderer.   We shall, my lord,
Perform what you command us.
   1 Murderer.   Though our lives—
   Macbeth. Your spirits shine through you. Within this hour at most
I will advise you where to plant yourselves;
Acquaint you with the perfect spy o' the time,
The moment on 't; for 't must be done to-night,
And something from the palace; always thought
That I require a clearness; and with him—
To leave no rubs nor botches in the work—
Fleance his son, that keeps him company,
Whose absence is no less material to me
Than is his father's, must embrace the fate
Of that dark hour. Resolve yourselves apart;
I'll come to you anon.
   Both Murderers.   We are resolv'd, my lord.
   Macbeth. I'll call upon you straight: abide within.
                            [*Exeunt* Murderers.
It is concluded. Banquo, thy soul's flight,
If it find heaven, must find it out to-night.   [*Exit.*

---

   121. BUT WAIL—Instead of sweeping Banquo from my sight myself, I must bewail (publicly) his murder.
   126. THOUGH OUR LIVES—Though our lives answer for it.
   129. ACQUAINT YOU WITH THE PERFECT SPY O' THE TIME—This probably means: Let you know by means of a perfect spy (the third murderer) when to strike.
   131. SOMETHING—At some distance.
   131. ALWAYS THOUGHT—It being always remembered that I must be kept clear of suspicion.
   133. TO LEAVE NO RUBS NOR BOTCHES—To leave no rough spots, or flaws, and botches such as betray poor workmanship. The expression is parenthetical.
   137. RESOLVE YOURSELVES—Make up your minds.

Scene 2. *The palace.*

Enter Lady Macbeth *and a* Servant.

Lady Macbeth. Is Banquo gone from court?
Servant. Ay, madam, but returns again to-night.
Lady Macbeth. Say to the king, I would attend his leisure
For a few words.
Servant. Madam, I will.
Lady Macbeth. Nought's had, all's spent,
5 Where our desire is got without content.
'Tis safer to be that which we destroy
Than by destruction dwell in doubtful joy.

Enter Macbeth.

How now, my lord! why do you keep alone,
Of sorriest fancies your companions making;
10 Using those thoughts which should indeed have died
With them they think on? Things without all remedy
Should be without regard; what's done is done.
Macbeth. We have scotch'd the snake, not kill'd it:
She'll close and be herself, whilst our poor malice
15 Remains in danger of her former tooth.
But let the frame of things disjoint, both the worlds suffer,
Ere we will eat our meal in fear, and sleep
In the affliction of these terrible dreams
That shake us nightly. Better be with the dead,
20 Whom we, to gain our peace, have sent to peace,
Than on the torture of the mind to lie
In restless ecstasy. Duncan is in his grave;
After life's fitful fever he sleeps well;
Treason has done his worst: nor steel, nor poison,

5. Content—Happiness, peace of mind.
10. Using—Cherishing, constantly thinking.
11. Things without all remedy should be without regard—What cannot be remedied should be ignored.
13. Scotch'd—Cut, slashed.
14. She'll close and be herself—Grow together again and be as formerly.
16. The frame of things—The universe. The meaning of the lines is: Let the universe fall apart and heaven and earth perish before we will eat our meal in fear, etc.
21. On the torture of the mind to lie—The figure alludes to the rack, an instrument of torture employed in the Middle Ages.
22. Ecstasy—Frenzy.

Malice domestic, foreign levy, nothing,
Can touch him further.
 Lady Macbeth. Come on;
Gentle my lord, sleek o'er your rugged looks;
Be bright and jovial among your guests to-night.
 Macbeth. So shall I, love; and so, I pray, be you.
Let your remembrance apply to Banquo;
Present him eminence, both with eye and tongue:
Unsafe the while, that we
Must lave our honours in these flattering streams,
And make our faces vizards to our hearts,
Disguising what they are.
 Lady Macbeth. You must leave this.
 Macbeth. O, full of scorpions is my mind, dear wife!
Thou know'st that Banquo and his Fleance lives.
 Lady Macbeth. But in them nature's copy 's not eterne.
 Macbeth. There's comfort yet; they are assailable;
Then be thou jocund; ere the bat hath flown
His cloister'd flight; ere to black Hecate's summons
The shard-borne beetle with his drowsy hums
Hath rung night's yawning peal, there shall be done
A deed of dreadful note.
 Lady Macbeth. What's to be done?

 25. MALICE DOMESTIC—Rebellion, such as that raised by Macdonwald. See Act I, Scene 2.
 25. FOREIGN LEVY—War from without, such as the attack of Norway. See Act I, Scene 2.
 27. GENTLE MY LORD—My gentle lord.
 30. REMEMBRANCE APPLY TO—Remember to be gracious to him.
 31. PRESENT HIM EMINENCE—Treat him as eminent, make much of him.
 33. LAVE OUR HONOURS IN THESE FLATTERING STREAMS—Wash, for the purpose of keeping unsoiled, our honors in these streams of flattery. The meaning is: We are not safe so long as we are dependent upon the support which can be gained only through flattery.
 34. VIZARDS—Masks.
 38. NATURE'S COPY 'S NOT ETERNE—They will not live forever. The allusion in the figure is to a form of land tenure known as "copyhold." Copyhold did not give perpetual title to the holder.
 39. ASSAILABLE—They may be destroyed. Macbeth interprets Lady Macbeth's remark in a way she probably did not intend it—that Banquo and Fleance can be murdered if necessary.
 40–41. HATH FLOWN HIS CLOISTER'D FLIGHT—Has left the cloisters where perhaps he has hung all day; *i.e.* before nightfall.
 42. SHARD-BORNE—Borne through the air on its hard, scaly wings which are like broken pieces, or shards, of pottery.
 43. YAWNING PEAL—Summons to sleep. The entire clause means before bedtime.

45 *Macbeth.* Be innocent of the knowledge, dearest chuck,
Till thou applaud the deed. Come, seeling night,
Scarf up the tender eye of pitiful day,
And with thy bloody and invisible hand
Cancel and tear to pieces that great bond
50 Which keeps me pale! Light thickens, and the crow
Makes wing to th' rooky wood:
Good things of day begin to droop and drowse,
Whiles night's black agents to their preys do rouse.
Thou marvell'st at my words, but hold thee still;
55 Things bad begun make strong themselves by ill.
So, prithee, go with me. [*Exeunt.*

45. CHUCK—Also chick, a term of endearment.
46. SEELING NIGHT—A technical term from falconry, designating a method of closing the eyes of a hawk. Here "seeling night" means night which closes the eyes.
47. SCARF UP—Blindfold.
49. THAT GREAT BOND—The prophecy of the third witch. The allusion is probably to the "bond of destiny" which guarantees to Banquo's heirs succession to the throne.
51. ROOKY—Rook-haunted, black, dismal.

SCENE 3. *A park near the palace.*

Enter three Murderers.

1 Murderer. But who did bid thee join with us?
3 Murderer. Macbeth.
2 Murderer. He needs not our mistrust; since he delivers
Our offices, and what we have to do
To the direction just.
1 Murderer. Then stand with us.
5 The west yet glimmers with some streaks of day:
Now spurs the lated traveller apace
To gain the timely inn; and near approaches
The subject of our watch.
3 Murderer. Hark! I hear horses.
Banquo. [*Within.*] Give us a light there, ho!

2. HE—The Third Murderer.
2. NEEDS NOT OUR MISTRUST—We need not mistrust him.
2–4. DELIVERS OUR OFFICES . . . DIRECTION JUST—Tells us exactly what we are to do even as we heard it from Macbeth.
6. LATED—Belated.
7. TO GAIN THE TIMELY INN—To reach the inn in good time, that is, before dark.

2 Murderer.   Then 'tis he: the rest
That are within the note of expectation
Already are i' the court.
  1 Murderer.   His horses go about.
  3 Murderer. Almost a mile; but he does usually,
So all men do, from hence to th' palace gate
Make it their walk.

Enter BANQUO, *and* FLEANCE *with a torch.*

  2 Murderer.   A light, a light!
  3 Murderer.   'Tis he.
  1 Murderer. Stand to 't.
  Banquo. It will be rain to-night.
  1 Murderer.   Let it come down.
                           [*They set upon* BANQUO.
  Banquo. O, treachery! Fly, good Fleance, fly, fly, fly!
Thou mayst revenge. O slave!   [*Dies.* FLEANCE *escapes.*
  3 Murderer. Who did strike out the light?
  1 Murderer.   Was 't not the way?
  3 Murderer. There's but one down; the son is fled.
  2 Murderer.   We have lost
Best half of our affair.
  1 Murderer. Well, let's away, and say how much is done.
                                                [*Exeunt.*

9-11. THEN 'TIS HE: THE REST . . . ARE I' THE COURT—It is Banquo, since all others who are expected are already within the court of the castle.

11. HIS HORSES GO ABOUT—Banquo's servants lead the horses along the road which evidently approaches the castle by a circuitous path. Banquo and Fleance dismount and approach the castle by a footpath.

15. STAND TO 'T—Get ready. The remark is directed to the other murderers. It was the part of the First Murderer to strike down Banquo's light, and his remark means: Make ready, I am going to strike down the light.

16. LET IT COME DOWN—The blow. Here is a play on words.

SCENE 4. *Hall in the palace.*

A banquet prepared. Enter MACBETH, LADY MACBETH, ROSS,
LENNOX, LORDS, *and* Attendants.

  Macbeth. You know your own degrees; sit down: at first
And last the hearty welcome.

1. DEGREES—Degrees of rank. It being a state, or formal, banquet, the guests would sit according to rank.

Lords. Thanks to your majesty.
Macbeth. Ourself will mingle with society,
And play the humble host.
5 Our hostess keeps her state, but in best time
We will require her welcome.
Lady Macbeth. Pronounce it for me, sir, to all our friends,
For my heart speaks they are welcome.

First Murderer *appears at the door.*

Macbeth. See, they encounter thee with their hearts' thanks.
10 Both sides are even: here I'll sit i' the midst.
Be large in mirth; anon we'll drink a measure
The table round.—[*Goes to the door.*] There's blood upon thy face.
Murderer. 'Tis Banquo's then.
Macbeth. 'Tis better thee without than he within.
15 Is he dispatch'd?
Murderer. My lord, his throat is cut; that I did for him.
Macbeth. Thou are the best o' the cut-throats; yet he's good
That did the like for Fleance: if thou didst it,
Thou art the nonpareil.
Murderer. Most royal sir,
20 Fleance is scap'd.
Macbeth. Then comes my fit again: I had else been perfect,
Whole as the marble, founded as the rock;
As broad and general as the casing air;
But now I am cabin'd, cribb'd, confin'd, bound in

5. HOSTESS KEEPS HER STATE—Lady Macbeth sits in her chair of state on a dais at the upper end of the hall, while Macbeth "mingles with" his guests—that is, sits at table with them. He has not yet sat down, but lingers near the door, expecting the Murderer.
6. REQUIRE HER WELCOME—Ask her to give you welcome.
9. SEE, THEY ENCOUNTER THEE WITH THEIR HEARTS' THANKS—This is addressed to Lady Macbeth, and refers to the manifestations of thanks returned by the guests.
10. THE MIDST—The chair which Macbeth chooses was evidently at mid-table.
11. LARGE—Unrestrained.   11. ANON—Soon.
14. 'TIS BETTER THEE WITHOUT THAN HE WITHIN—It is better on your face than in his veins.
19. NONPAREIL—One without an equal.
23. AS BROAD AND GENERAL AS THE CASING AIR—As unrestrained and unconfined as the air which envelops the earth but is itself boundless.
24. CABIN'D, CRIBB'D—Shut up, hampered.

To saucy doubts and fears. But Banquo's safe?
　　Murderer. Ay, my good lord; safe in a ditch he bides,
With twenty trenchèd gashes on his head,
The least a death to nature.
　　Macbeth. 　　　　　Thanks for that.
There the grown serpent lies; the worm that's fled
Hath nature that in time will venom breed,
No teeth for th' present. Get thee gone; to-morrow
We'll hear ourselves again. 　　　　　[*Exit* Murderer.
　　Lady Macbeth. 　　　My royal lord,
You do not give the cheer: the feast is sold
That is not often vouch'd, while 'tis a-making,
'Tis given with welcome. To feed were best at home;
From thence the sauce to meat is ceremony;
Meeting were bare without it.

　　Enter the Ghost *of* Banquo, *and sits in* Macbeth's *place.*

　　Macbeth. 　　　　Sweet remembrancer!
Now, good digestion wait on appetite,
And health on both!
　　Lennox. 　　May 't please your highness sit.
　　Macbeth. Here had we now our country's honour roof'd,
Were the grac'd person of our Banquo present;
Who may I rather challenge for unkindness
Than pity for mischance.
　　Ross. 　　　　His absence, sir,

25. To saucy doubts—By insolent doubts.
27. Trenchèd—Deep-cut. 　　　29. Worm—The young serpent—Fleance.
32. Hear ourselves—Hear one another.
33–35. The feast is sold . . . best at home—The meaning is: The feast which is not often vouched (proclaimed by the host as a thing he does out of pleasure) is like a meal which one buys, where there is no sentiment connected with the eating at all. While the feast is on (a-making), the host must make it clear that his guests are welcome. If the purpose of a banquet is merely to eat, then according to Lady Macbeth, it were best to eat at home.
36–37. From thence . . . without it—That which makes eating away from home enjoyable is the ceremony, or attention paid to one. Mere meeting and eating together without the ceremony is no delight.
37. Remembrancer—One who reminds another. He is addressing Lady Macbeth. He has not yet seen the ghost.
40. Our country's honour roof'd—All the worthy men of our country under one roof. The meaning of the lines is: Here we should have our country's honor roof'd if only the gracious person of our Banquo were present.
42. Who may . . . for mischance—Whose absence is due, I hope, to unkindness rather than to mischance or accident.

Lays blame upon his promise. Please 't your highness
45 To grace us with your royal company.
  Macbeth. The table's full!
  Lennox. Here is a place reserv'd, sir.
  Macbeth. Where?
  Lennox. Here, my good lord. What is 't that moves your highness?
  Macbeth. Which of you have done this?
  Lords. What, my good lord?
50 *Macbeth.* Thou canst not say I did it: never shake
Thy gory locks at me.
  Ross. Gentlemen, rise; his highness is not well.
  Lady Macbeth. Sit, worthy friends: my lord is often thus,
And hath been from his youth: pray you, keep seat;
55 The fit is momentary; upon a thought
He will again be well. If much you note him,
You will offend him, and extend his passion.
Feed, and regard him not. [*Aside to* MACBETH.] Are you a man?
  Macbeth. Ay, and a bold one, that dare look on that
60 Which might appal the devil.
  Lady Macbeth. [*Aside to* MACBFTH.] O proper stuff!
This is the very painting of your fear;
This is the air-drawn dagger which, you said,
Led you to Duncan. O, these flaws and starts,
Impostors to true fear, would well become
65 A woman's story at a winter's fire,
Authoriz'd by her grandam. Shame itself!
Why do you make such faces? When all's done,
You look but on a stool.
  Macbeth. Prithee, see there! Behold! look! lo! how say you?

  44. LAYS BLAME UPON HIS PROMISE—Makes him guilty of an unkindness, since he promised to be present.
  50. THOU—This speech is addressed to the ghost of Banquo.
  55. UPON A THOUGHT—In a moment.
  58. *Aside to* MACBETH—Lady Macbeth has left her seat and come down to Macbeth.
  60. O PROPER STUFF!—Nonsense!
  63. FLAWS—A sudden squall of wind, hence in this case, an outburst of feeling or "nerves."
  63. STARTS—Alarms. Compare with our word "startle."
  64. IMPOSTORS TO—Mere allusions when compared to.

Why, what care I? If thou canst nod, speak too.
If charnel-houses and our graves must send
Those that we bury back, our monuments
Shall be the maws of kites. [Ghost *vanishes.*
    Lady Macbeth. [*Aside to* MACBETH.] What, quite un-
      mann'd in folly?
    Macbeth. If I stand here, I saw him!
    Lady Macbeth. [*Aside to* MACBETH.] Fie, for shame!
    Macbeth. Blood hath been shed ere now, i' the olden time,
Ere humane statute purg'd the gentle weal;
Ay, and since too, murders have been perform'd
Too terrible for the ear. The time has been,
That, when the brains were out, the man would die,
And there an end; but now they rise again,
With twenty mortal murders on their crowns,
And push us from our stools: this is more strange
Than such a murder is.
    Lady Macbeth.   My worthy lord,
Your noble friends do lack you.
    Macbeth.   I do forget.
Do not muse at me, my most worthy friends;
I have a strange infirmity, which is nothing
To those that know me. Come, love and health to all;
Then I'll sit down. Give me some wine, fill full.

Re-enter the Ghost.

I drink to th' general joy o' the whole table,
And to our dear friend Banquo, whom we miss;

    70. WHY, WHAT CARE I?—This and the following three lines are addressed to the ghost.
    71. CHARNEL-HOUSES—Sepulchers.
    72. MONUMENTS—Tombs.
    73. MAWS—Stomachs. The meaning is: If the dead may return from ordinary graves, it were better to be left unburied to be devoured by the kites (a kind of hawk).
    76. ERE HUMANE STATUTE PURG'D THE GENTLE WEAL—Before humane laws protecting human life made the commonwealth gentle. Macbeth refers to days before stable government protected life.
    81. WITH TWENTY MORTAL MURDERS—The allusion is to Banquo whom the murderer described as "safe in a ditch . . . with twenty trenched gashes in his head, the least a death to nature."
    84. LACK—Miss, or perceive your absence.
    85. MUSE—Wonder.

ELD

Would he were here! to all and him we thirst,
And all to all.
    Lords.   Our duties, and the pledge.
    Macbeth. Avaunt! and quit my sight! let the earth hide thee!
Thy bones are marrowless, thy blood is cold;
95 Thou hast no speculation in those eyes
Which thou dost glare with!

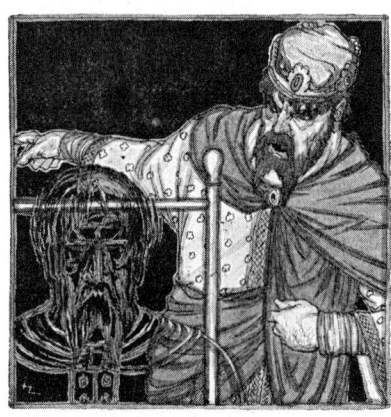

    Lady Macbeth.   Think of this, good peers,
But as a thing of custom: 'tis no other;
Only it spoils the pleasure of the time.
    Macbeth. What man dare, I dare:
100 Approach thou like the rugged Russian bear,
The arm'd rhinoceros, or the Hyrcan tiger;
Take any shape but that, and my firm nerves
Shall never tremble: or be alive again,
And dare me to the desert with thy sword;
105 If trembling I inhabit then, protest me
The baby of a girl. Hence, horrible shadow!
Unreal mockery, hence!   [Ghost *vanishes.*
    Why, so: being gone,

  93. AVAUNT!—Macbeth now sees the ghost.
  95. SPECULATION—Power of sight.
  101. HYRCAN—Hyrcanian. Hyrcania, a region south of the Caspian Sea, mentioned in books of the time as the home of the tiger.
    105. IF TREMBLING I INHABIT THEN—If trembling with fear I then stay in my castle.   105. PROTEST—Declare, call.

I am a man again. Pray you, sit still.
    Lady Macbeth. You have displac'd the mirth, broke the good meeting,
10 With most admir'd disorder.
    Macbeth.   Can such things be,
And overcome us like a summer's cloud,
Without our special wonder? You make me strange
Even to the disposition that I owe,
When now I think you can behold such sights,
15 And keep the natural ruby of your cheeks,
When mine is blanch'd with fear.
    Ross.   What sights, my lord?
    Lady Macbeth. I pray you, speak not; he grows worse and worse;
Question enrages him. At once, good-night.
Stand not upon the order of your going,
20 But go at once.
    Lennox.   Good-night; and better health
Attend his majesty!
    Lady Macbeth. A kind good-night to all!
                      [*Exeunt all but* MACBETH *and* LADY MACBETH.
    Macbeth. It will have blood; they say blood will have blood.
Stones have been known to move and trees to speak;

108. SIT STILL—What were Macbeth's guests doing?
110. ADMIR'D—Strange.
111. AND OVERCOME . . . WITHOUT OUR SPECIAL WONDER—Pass over us like a summer's cloud to which we pay no attention.
112. YOU MAKE ME . . . THAT I OWE—Macbeth has always possessed (owed) a brave and undaunted spirit (disposition). He says in effect to Lady Macbeth who shows no signs of fear, not having seen the ghost, "Your fearlessness makes me hardly know myself, so that I wonder if I am he who has never been afraid of anything."
119. STAND NOT UPON THE ORDER OF YOUR GOING—This being a formal, or state, banquet, the guests were seated according to rank. Lady Macbeth, wishing to have the guests depart as quickly as possible before Macbeth says that which will betray him, calls out to them to depart without regard to rank or precedence.
122. IT WILL HAVE BLOOD—"It" refers to the murder rather than to the ghost. The sense is that the deed cries for vengeance.
122–123. THEY SAY . . . TO SPEAK—The saying that "murder will out" is a very old one. Old wives' tales of astonishing and supernatural means by which murders came to light, when the murderer thought himself safe, were common enough in Shakespeare's day. The allusions here are no doubt to stories of this kind—the one to the story that stones refused to stay over the body of a murdered man, and the other possibly to trees said to have informed on a murderer.

Augures and understood relations have
125 By magot-pies and choughs and rooks brought forth
The secret'st man of blood. What is the night?
   Lady Macbeth. Almost at odds with morning, which is which.
   Macbeth. How say'st thou, that Macduff denies his person
At our great bidding?
   Lady Macbeth.   Did you send to him, sir?
130   *Macbeth.* I hear it by the way, but I will send.
There's not a one of them but in his house
I keep a servant fee'd. I will to-morrow,
And betimes I will, to the weird sisters:
More shall they speak; for now I am bent to know,
135 By the worst means, the worst. For mine own good
All causes shall give way: I am in blood
Stepp'd in so far that, should I wade no more,
Returning were as tedious as go o'er:
Strange things I have in head that will to hand,
140 Which must be acted ere they may be scann'd.
   Lady Macbeth. You lack the season of all natures, sleep.
   Macbeth. Come, we'll to sleep. My strange and self-abuse
Is the initiate fear that wants hard use:
We are yet but young in deed.   [*Exeunt.*

   124. AUGURES—Divinations.
   124. UNDERSTOOD RELATIONS—Relationships revealed by those who understand how to trace them.
   125. MAGOT-PIES AND CHOUGHS—Magpies and jackdaws.
   126. THE SECRET'ST MAN OF BLOOD—The murderer who supposed his secret unknown to any but himself. The sense of the whole passage is that the most carefully covered murders have been disclosed by divinations made upon magpies, etc., by those who have understood how to trace the relationship between the bird examined and the murder.
   128. DENIES HIS PERSON—Macduff refused to attend the banquet.
   130. I HEAR IT BY THE WAY—I hear it indirectly.
   132. I KEEP A SERVANT FEE'D—Macbeth pays a servant in each of the houses of his great subjects to report to him what may be said there about him. He had not received any refusal from Macduff; he had heard through a spy in Macduff's castle what the attitude of the latter was toward him.
   136. ALL CAUSES—Every other consideration.
   139. WILL TO HAND—Press to be done.
   140. SCANN'D—Examined carefully. The implication is that the things Macbeth had in mind doing are of such dreadful nature that it were best to do them first, for thinking about them too much would cause him to refrain.
   141. SEASON—Preservation—that which keeps things fresh and wholesome.
   142-143. MY STRANGE . . . HARD USE—The sense is as follows: Macbeth says that his self-delusion is but the result of the fear which the beginner (initiate fear) naturally has, and that it will disappear with hard use—that is, when he has become hardened and accustomed to killing.

Scene 5. *A heath.*

Thunder. Enter the three Witches, *meeting* Hecate.

1 Witch. Why, how now, Hecate! you look angerly.
   Hecate. Have I not reason, beldams as you are,
Saucy and overbold? How did you dare
To trade and traffic with Macbeth
5 In riddles and affairs of death;
And I, the mistress of your charms,
The close contriver of all harms,
Was never call'd to bear my part,
Or show the glory of our art?
10 And, which is worse, all you have done
Hath been but for a wayward son,
Spiteful and wrathful; who, as others do,
Loves for his own ends, not for you.
But make amends now: get you gone,
15 And at the pit of Acheron
Meet me i' the morning; thither he
Will come to know his destiny.
Your vessels and your spells provide,
Your charms, and every thing beside.
20 I am for th' air; this night I'll spend
Unto a dismal and a fatal end:
Great business must be wrought ere noon:
Upon the corner of the moon
There hangs a vaporous drop profound;
25 I'll catch it ere it come to ground:
And that distill'd by magic sleights
Shall raise such artificial sprites
As by the strength of their illusion

   1. Hecate—See note lines 51–52, Act II, Sc. 1.
   2. Beldams—Hags.
   5. Riddles—In prophecies which have a double or equivocal meaning.
   7. Close—Secret.
   15. Acheron—Acheron was the name of a river in Hades. Here "the pit of Acheron" is used to designate the entrance to the infernal regions, or "hell-mouth."
   24. Vaporous drop—There was a belief among the ancients in "a foam which the moon was supposed to shed on particular herbs or other objects, when strongly solicited by enchantment."
   24. Profound—Full of magic qualities.
   27. Sprites—Spirits.

Shall draw him on to his confusion.
30 He shall spurn fate, scorn death, and bear
His hopes 'bove wisdom, grace, and fear;
And you all know security
Is mortals' chiefest enemy.   [*Music, and a Song.*
Hark! I am call'd; my little spirit, see,
35 Sits in a foggy cloud, and stays for me.   [*Exit.*
              [*Sing within:* "Come away, come away," etc.]
   1 Witch. Come, let's make haste; she'll soon be back
      again.   [*Exeunt.*

32. SECURITY—Over-confidence.

SCENE 6. *Forres. The palace.*

Enter LENNOX *and another* LORD.

Lennox. My former speeches have but hit your thoughts,
Which can interpret farther: only, I say
Things have been strangely borne. The gracious Duncan
Was pitied of Macbeth: marry, he was dead:
5 And the right-valiant Banquo walk'd too late;
Whom, you may say, if 't please you, Fleance kill'd,
For Fleance fled: men must not walk too late.
Who cannot want the thought, how monstrous
It was for Malcolm and for Donalbain
10 To kill their gracious father? damned fact!
How it did grieve Macbeth! did he not straight,
In pious rage, the two delinquents tear,
That were the slaves of drink and thralls of sleep?
Was not that nobly done? Ay, and wisely too;
15 For 't would have anger'd any heart alive
To hear the men deny 't. So that, I say,
He has borne all things well; and I do think

1. FORMER SPEECHES—Lennox and the Lord to whom he is now speaking have talked about the happenings at Macbeth's castle on some former occasion. Lennox makes no direct accusations. He has probably spoken on the former occasion much as he does now—simply stating facts and leaving it to the other to "interpret farther," or in other words, to draw his own conclusions.
   3. BORNE—Managed, carried on. 4. MARRY—A mild oath or expletive.
   8. WHO CANNOT WANT THE THOUGHT—Who can fail to think.
   10. FACT—Deed, especially an evil deed.
   12. TWO DELINQUENTS—Duncan's two grooms.

That, had he Duncan's sons under his key—
As, an 't please heaven, he shall not—they should find
20 What 'twere to kill a father; so should Fleance.
But, peace! for from broad words, and 'cause he fail'd
His presence at the tyrant's feast, I hear,
Macduff lives in disgrace. Sir, can you tell
Where he bestows himself?
    Lord.   The son of Duncan,
25 From whom this tyrant holds the due of birth,
Lives in the English court; and is receiv'd
Of the most pious Edward with such grace
That the malevolence of fortune nothing
Takes from his high respect. Thither Macduff
30 Is gone to pray the holy king, upon his aid
To wake Northumberland and warlike Siward;
That by the help of these, with Him above
To ratify the work, we may again
Give to our tables meat, sleep to our nights;
35 Free from our feasts and banquets bloody knives,
Do faithful homage and receive free honours;
All which we pine for now; and this report
Hath so exasperate the king, that he
Prepares for some attempt of war.
    Lennox.   Sent he to Macduff?
40   *Lord.* He did: and with an absolute "Sir, not I,"
The cloudy messenger turns me his back,
And hums, as who should say, "You'll rue the time
That clogs me with this answer."

    19. AN 'T—If it.
    21. FROM BROAD WORDS—On account of plain speaking.
    24. BESTOWS—Keeps himself, lodges.
    24–25. THE SON OF DUNCAN . . . DUE OF BIRTH—Malcolm. "Holds" means withholds. "Due of birth" means the crown.
    27. MOST PIOUS EDWARD—Edward the confessor, king of England 1042–1066.
    28–29. THAT THE MALEVOLENCE . . . HIGH RESPECT—That his misfortune has not made him the less respected.
    31. NORTHUMBERLAND AND WARLIKE SIWARD—Holinshed says, "Malcolme purchased such favour at King Edward's hands that old Siward earle of Northumberland was appointed with ten thousand men to go with him into Scotland."
    40. WITH AN ABSOLUTE "SIR, NOT I"—This was Macduff's reply to the messenger who brought Macbeth's command.
    41. CLOUDY—Sullen, frowning.
    41. TURNS ME HIS BACK—Turns his back (on Macduff).

Lennox.   And that well might
Advise him to a caution, to hold what distance
45 His wisdom can provide. Some holy angel
Fly to the court of England and unfold
His message ere he come; that a swift blessing
May soon return to this our suffering country
Under a hand accurs'd!
    Lord.   I'll send my prayers with him.
                                                                       [Exeunt.

43. CLOGS—Burdens. The messenger hates to bear the answer to Macbeth so goes with heavy feet.
44. ADVISE HIM TO A CAUTION—Advise Macduff to be cautious.
44. TO HOLD WHAT DISTANCE—To keep what distance from Macbeth.
47. HIS—Macduff's.

ACT IV

SCENE 1. *A cavern. In the middle, a boiling cauldron.*

Thunder. Enter the three Witches.

1 Witch. Thrice the brinded cat hath mew'd.
2 Witch. Thrice, and once the hedge-pig whin'd.
3 Witch. Harpier cries; 'tis time, 'tis time.
1 Witch. Round about the cauldron go;
5 In the poison'd entrails throw.
Toad, that under cold stone
Days and nights has thirty-one
Swelter'd venom sleeping got,
Boil thou first i' the charmed pot.
10   *All.* Double, double toil and trouble;

1. BRINDED CAT—Brindled or streaked cat. This is the graymalkin of Act I, Scene 1, the "familiar" of the first Witch.
2. THRICE, AND ONCE—Odd numbers were thought to possess magical properties. The "thrice" is a repetition of the "thrice" in the first line. The "once" applies to the hedge-pig, which is the familiar of the second Witch.
3. HARPIER—The familiar of the third Witch.
3. 'TIS TIME—That is, to begin the preparations ordered by Hecate. See Act III, Scene 5.
5. POISON'D ENTRAILS—Probably the entrails of some person who has been murdered by poison. Note that the ingredients of this "hell-broth" are chosen for their hideous and diabolical significance. Most of them reflect some dark superstition of Shakespeare's day.
6–8. TOAD . . . SLEEPING GOT—It was the common belief that toads were poisonous. "Swelter'd venom" means poison sweated out.

Fire burn and cauldron bubble.
　2 Witch. Fillet of a fenny snake,
In the cauldron boil and bake;
Eye of newt and toe of frog,
5 Wool of bat and tongue of dog,
Adder's fork and blind-worm's sting,
Lizard's leg and howlet's wing,
For a charm of powerful trouble,
Like a hell-broth boil and bubble.
10 　*All.* Double, double toil and trouble;
Fire burn and cauldron bubble.
　3 Witch. Scale of dragon, tooth of wolf,
Witches' mummy, maw and gulf
Of the ravin'd salt-sea shark;
15 Root of hemlock digg'd i' the dark,
Liver of blaspheming Jew,
Gall of goat, and slips of yew
Sliver'd in the moon's eclipse,
Nose of Turk and Tartar's lips,
20 Finger of birth-strangled babe
Ditch-deliver'd by a drab,
Make the gruel thick and slab:
Add thereto a tiger's chaudron,

　　12. FILLET OF A FENNY SNAKE—Slice of a marsh snake.
　　14. NEWT—Salamander. It was believed that the salamander possessed magic properties, and that it could live in fire.
　　16. FORK—Forked tongue.
　　16. BLIND-WORM—The slow-worm, formerly believed to be venomous.
　　17. HOWLET—Owlet. The owl was regarded as a bird of ill omen.
　　23. MUMMY—In Shakespeare's day a balm for cuts and bruises was made from Egyptian mummies. It was the curious belief that in a mummy might be found the "balsam" by which the body heals a cut or bruise. A witch's mummy might be supposed to retain the evil power which the witch in life possessed.
　　23. MAW AND GULF—Stomach and gullet.
　　24. RAVIN'D—Glutted with food, presumably human flesh, for the shark has an old reputation for being a man-eater.
　　25. HEMLOCK—The poisonous herb of this name.
　　26. BLASPHEMING—So called, because not Christian.
　　27. GOAT—In the Bible the goat represents the wicked, as in the expression to "separate the sheep from the goats."
　　27. YEW—Cuttings from the yew tree, formerly believed to be poisonous.
　　28. MOON'S ECLIPSE—Generally held to be a time of ill omen.
　　29. TURK AND TARTAR—Non-Christian and infidels.
　　30. BIRTH-STRANGLED—Hence unchristened.
　　32. SLAB—Slimy.
　　33. CHAUDRON—Entrails.

For th' ingredients of our cauldron.
35   *All.*   Double, double toil and trouble;
Fire burn and cauldron bubble.
   2 Witch.   Cool it with a baboon's blood,
Then the charm is firm and good.

Enter HECATE *to the other three* Witches.

   Hecate.   O, well done! I command your pains;
40 And every one shall share i' th' gains:
And now about the cauldron sing,
Like elves and fairies in a ring,
Enchanting all that you put in.
              [*Music, and a Song,* "Black spirits," etc.
                                [*Exit* HECATE.
   2 Witch.   By the pricking of my thumbs,
45 Something wicked this way comes:
Open, locks,
Whoever knocks!

Enter MACBETH.

   Macbeth.   How now, you secret, black, and midnight hags!
What is 't you do?
   All.   A deed without a name.
50   *Macbeth.*   I conjure you, by that which you profess,
Howe'er you come to know it, answer me:
Though you untie the winds and let them fight
Against the churches; though the yesty waves
Confound and swallow navigation up;
55 Though bladed corn be lodg'd, and trees blown down;
Though castles topple on their warders' heads;
Though palaces and pyramids do slope
Their heads to their foundations; though the treasure
Of nature's germens tumble all together,

    44. PRICKING—Prickling. The witch interprets the prickling sensation in her thumb as a sign.
    53. YESTY—Foamy, frothy.
    55. BLADED—In the blade. Corn, of course, means grain, not corn in the sense in which Americans think of the word.
    55. LODG'D—Laid flat by the wind.
    59. GERMENS—Seeds.

Even till destruction sicken; answer me
To what I ask you.
 1 Witch.   Speak.
 2 Witch.   Demand.
 3 Witch.   We'll answer.
 1 Witch. Say, if thou 'dst rather hear it from our mouths,
Or from our masters?
 Macbeth.   Call 'em, let me see 'em.
 1 Witch. Pour in sow's blood, that hath eaten
Her nine farrow; grease that's sweaten
From the murderer's gibbet throw
Into the flame.
 All.   Come, high or low;
Thyself and office deftly show!

   Thunder. First Apparition, *an armed Head.*

 Macbeth. Tell me, thou unknown power,—
 1 Witch.   He knows thy thought:
Hear his speech, but say thou nought.
 1 Apparition. Macbeth! Macbeth! Macbeth! beware Macduff;
Beware the thane of Fife.—Dismiss me: enough. [*Descends.*
 Macbeth. Whate'er thou art, for thy good caution, thanks;
Thou hast harp'd my fear aright: but one word more,—
 1 Witch. He will not be commanded: here's another,
More potent than the first.

   Thunder. Second Apparition, *a bloody Child.*

 2 Apparition. Macbeth! Macbeth! Macbeth!
 Macbeth. Had I three ears, I'd hear thee.

 65. NINE FARROW—Litter of nine pigs.
 65. SWEATEN—Sweated.
 66. GIBBET—Gallows.
 67. COME, HIGH OR LOW—The witches with these words summon or call up the apparitions which are to give answer to Macbeth.
 68. OFFICE—Function. The meaning is: Give your message.
 An Armed Head—This is a representation of Macbeth's own head. Macbeth addressing it as "unknown power" fails to recognize what it really is.
 74. HARP'D MY FEAR ARIGHT—Struck the note of my fear.
 A bloody Child—This represents Macduff as a child.
 78. HAD I THREE EARS, I'D HEAR THEE—Had I three ears, I should listen with them all. Three is probably used because the apparition had called his name three times.

  2 Apparition. Be bloody, bold, and resolute; laugh to
   scorn
80 The power of man, for none of woman born
Shall harm Macbeth.   [*Descends.*
  Macbeth. Then live, Macduff: what need I fear of thee?
But yet I'll make assurance double sure,
And take a bond of fate: thou shalt not live;
85 That I may tell pale-hearted fear it lies,
And sleep in spite of thunder.

   Thunder. Third Apparition, *a Child crowned, with a tree
        in his hand.*

         What is this,
That rises like the issue of a king,
And wears upon his baby brow the round
And top of sovereignty?
  All.   Listen, but speak not to 't.
90 *3 Apparition.* Be lion-mettl'd, proud; and take no care
Who chafes, who frets, or where conspirers are:
Macbeth shall never vanquish'd be until
Great Birnam wood to high Dunsinane hill
Shall come against him.   [*Descends.*
  Macbeth.   That will never be:
95 Who can impress the forest; bid the tree
Unfix his earth-bound root? Sweet bodements! good!
Rebellion's head, rise never till the wood
Of Birnam rise, and our high-plac'd Macbeth
Shall live the lease of nature, pay his breath
100 To time and mortal custom. Yet my heart

   83. MAKE ASSURANCE DOUBLE SURE—Macbeth trusts the prophecy implicitly, yet he intends to make doubly sure by killing Macduff.
   84. TAKE A BOND OF FATE—Macbeth means that he will, in effect, by killing Macduff make fate give a guarantee or bond that he need fear no man.
   A Child crowned, with a tree in his hand—This represents Malcolm, the rightful king. 88. ROUND—The crown.
   89. TOP OF SOVEREIGNTY—The symbol of kingly power.
   93. UNTIL GREAT BIRNAM WOOD . . . AGAINST HIM—Until Birnam wood shall move to Dunsinane hill—a seeming impossibility.
   95. IMPRESS—To press, to force to serve as soldiers.
   96. SWEET BODEMENTS—Fair prophecies.
   99. LIVE THE LEASE OF NATURE—Live until he dies a natural death.
   99. PAY HIS BREATH TO TIME AND MORTAL CUSTOM—Live a normal length of life and die a natural death.

Throbs to know one thing: tell me, if your art
Can tell so much: shall Banquo's issue ever
Reign in this kingdom?
    All.   Seek to know no more.
    Macbeth. I will be satisfied: deny me this,
05 And an eternal curse fall on you! Let me know:
Why sinks that cauldron? and what noise is this?
                                          [*Hautboys.*

    1 Witch. Show!
    2 Witch. Show!
    3 Witch. Show!
10   *All.* Show his eyes, and grieve his heart;
Come like shadows, so depart!

A show of eight Kings, *the last with a glass in his hand;*
            BANQUO's Ghost *following.*

    Macbeth. Thou art too like the spirit of Banquo; down!
Thy crown does sear mine eyeballs. And thy hair,
Thou other gold-bound brow, is like the first:
15 A third is like the former. Filthy hags!
Why do you show me this? A fourth! Start, eyes!
What, will the line stretch out to th' crack of doom?
Another yet! A seventh! I'll see no more:
And yet the eighth appears, who bears a glass
20 Which shows me many more; and some I see
That twofold balls and treble sceptres carry:

    A show—A parade or pompous line.
    Eight KINGS—These are the eight Stuart kings of Scotland, Robert II, Robert III, and the six Jameses, the last of whom, James VI, was also James I of England and was on the throne when this play was given. James saw this play and this direct reference to him must have pleased his colossal vanity. The Stuart kings were believed to have been Banquo's descendants.
    There was a legend that Fleance fled into Wales, that he married a daughter of the Prince of Wales, and that his son became Lord High Steward of Scotland. From this office he took the name Walter Stewart (stuart), founding the House of Stuart from which came the Stuart kings.
    112. SPIRIT OF BANQUO—The ghost of Banquo. That is, the first king resembles Banquo. Macbeth remarks each king in turn.
    119. GLASS—A mirror. A mirror or looking-glass was used in Shakespeare's day in making divinations and foretelling future events.
    121. THAT TWOFOLD BALLS AND TREBLE SCEPTRES CARRY—Another reference to James I of England. The "twofold balls" refer probably to the two crowns united by James—those of England and Scotland; the "treble sceptres" to the kingdoms of England, Scotland, and Ireland.

Horrible sight! Now I see 'tis true;
For the bloodbolter'd Banquo smiles upon me,
And points at them for him. [*Apparitions vanish.*] What, is
   this so?
125 *1 Witch.* Ay, sir, all this is so; but why
Stands Macbeth thus amazedly?
Come, sisters, cheer we up his sprites,
And show the best of our delights:
I'll charm the air to give a sound,
130 While you perform your antic round;
That this great king may kindly say
Our duties did his welcome pay.
   [*Music. The* Witches *dance, and vanish with* HECATE.
   Macbeth. Where are they? Gone? Let this pernicious three
      hour
Stand aye accursed in the calendar!
135 Come in, without there!

Enter LENNOX.

Lennox.   What's your grace's will?
Macbeth. Saw you the weird sisters?
Lennox.   No, my lord.
Macbeth. Came they not by you?
Lennox.   No, indeed, my lord.
Macbeth. Infected be the air whereon they ride,
And damn'd all those that trust them! I did hear
140 The galloping of horse: who was 't came by?
   Lennox. 'Tis two or three, my lord, that bring you word
Macduff is fled to England.
   Macbeth.   Fled to England!
   Lennox. Ay, my good lord.
   Macbeth. [*Aside.*] Time, thou anticipat'st my dread exploits:
145 The flighty purpose never is o'ertook
Unless the deed go with it: from this moment

   123. BLOODBOLTER'D—His hair matted with blood.
   127. SPRITES—Spirits.
   130. ANTIC ROUND—Grotesque dance.
   134. AYE—Forever.
   135. WITHOUT THERE—That is, without the "pit of Acheron" or cave where
Macbeth met the witches.
   144. ANTICIPAT'ST—Dost prevent. 145. FLIGHTY—Fleeting, swift.

The very firstlings of my heart shall be
The firstlings of my hand. And even now,
To crown my thoughts with acts, be it thought and done:
50 The castle of Macduff I will surprise;
Seize upon Fife; give to the edge o' the sword
His wife, his babes, and all unfortunate souls
That trace him in his line. No boasting like a fool;
This deed I'll do before this purpose cool:
55 But no more sights. Where are these gentlemen?
Come, bring me where they are. [*Exeunt.*

148. THE VERY FIRSTLINGS . . . OF MY HAND—I shall no sooner think of a thing than I shall do it.

SCENE 2. *Fife.* MACDUFF'S *castle.*

Enter LADY MACDUFF, *her* SON, *and* ROSS.

Lady Macduff. What had he done, to make him fly the land?
Ross. You must have patience, madam.
Lady Macduff. He had none;
His flight was madness: when our actions do not,
Our fears do make us traitors.
Ross. You know not
5 Whether it was his wisdom or his fear.
Lady Macduff. Wisdom! to leave his wife, to leave his babes,
His mansion, and his titles, in a place
From whence himself does fly! He loves us not;
He wants the natural touch: for the poor wren,
10 The most diminutive of birds, will fight,
Her young ones in her nest, against the owl.
All is the fear and nothing is the love;
As little is the wisdom, where the flight
So runs against all reason.
Ross. My dearest coz,

1. WHAT HAD HE DONE—Lady Macduff thinks that Macduff must have committed some act of treason or rebellion. She cannot understand why else one should be obliged to take flight.
7. TITLES—Property, possessions.
9. WANTS THE NATURAL TOUCH—Lacks the natural feeling or instinct which makes the wren protect its young.
11. HER YOUNG ONES IN HER NEST—Her young ones being in the nest.
12. ALL IS THE FEAR—Do you think Shakespeare intends this impression that Macduff fled for fear of his life? Can you justify his leaving his family behind? 14. Coz—Cousin.

15 I pray you, school yourself; but, for your husband,
He is noble, wise, judicious, and best knows
The fits o' the season. I dare not speak much further:
But cruel are the times when we are traitors
And do not know ourselves; when we hold rumour

20 From what we fear, yet know not what we fear,
But float upon a wild and violent sea
Each way and move. I take my leave of you;
Shall not be long but I'll be here again.
Things at the worst will cease, or else climb upward
25 To what they were before. My pretty cousin,
Blessing upon you!
    Lady Macduff. Father'd he is, and yet he's fatherless.
    Ross. I am so much a fool, should I stay longer,
It would be my disgrace and your discomfort.
30 I take my leave at once.   [*Exit*.
    Lady Macduff.   Sirrah, your father's dead:

    17. FITS O' THE SEASON—The turn which things are taking.
    19. DO NOT KNOW OURSELVES—Do not know that we are traitors.
    19–22. WHEN WE HOLD RUMOUR . . . EACH WAY AND MOVE—The meaning is: When having done nothing wrong, yet we fear, because we hear rumors that we are held as having done wrong. In such a case we "float . . . each way and move," that is, like a storm-tossed ship we can take no sure course for we know not what is the right thing to do or what is the wrong.
    25. MY PRETTY COUSIN—This is addressed to Macduff's boy. What acting accompanies the remark?
    29. MY DISGRACE AND YOUR DISCOMFORT—Disgrace myself by weeping and distress you.
    30. SIRRAH—This term was also used in addressing children.

And what will you do now? How will you live?
   Son. As birds do, mother.
   Lady Macduff. What, with worms and flies?
   Son. With what I get, I mean; and so do they.
   Lady Macduff. Poor bird! thou'dst never fear the net nor lime,
35 The pitfall nor the gin.
   Son. Why should I, mother? Poor birds they are not set for. My father is not dead, for all your saying.
   Lady Macduff. Yes, he is dead: how wilt thou do for a father?
   Son. Nay, how will you do for a husband?
40 *Lady Macduff.* Why, I can buy me twenty at any market.
   Son. Then you'll buy 'em to sell again.
   Lady Macduff. Thou speak'st with all thy wit; and yet i' faith,
With wit enough for thee.
   Son. Was my father a traitor, mother?
45 *Lady Macduff.* Ay, that he was.
   Son. What is a traitor?
   Lady Macduff. Why, one that swears and lies.
   Son. And be all traitors that do so?
   Lady Macduff. Every one that does so is a traitor, and must be hang'd.
50 *Son.* And must they all be hang'd that swear and lie?
   Lady Macduff. Every one.
   Son. Who must hang them?
   Lady Macduff. Why, the honest men.
   Son. Then the liars and swearers are fools; for there are liars
55 and swearers enow to beat the honest men and hang up them.
   Lady Macduff. Now, God help thee, poor monkey! But how wilt thou do for a father?

---

34. LIME—Bird-lime, a sticky substance smeared on twigs to catch birds.
35. PITFALL NOR THE GIN—Trap nor snare. All these were common devices for catching small birds, which in Shakespeare's time were still used in pies and other dishes.
42. WIT—Understanding.
47. SWEARS AND LIES—Swears allegiance falsely.
50. THAT SWEAR AND LIE—The boy takes the expression literally.

Son. If he were dead, you'd weep for him; if you would not, it were a good sign that I should quickly have a new father.
60 *Lady Macduff.* Poor prattler, how thou talk'st!

Enter a Messenger.

Messenger. Bless you, fair dame! I am not to you known,
Though in your state of honour I am perfect.
I doubt some danger does approach you nearly:
If you will take a homely man's advice,
65 Be not found here; hence, with your little ones.
To fright you thus, methinks I am too savage;
To do worse to you were fell cruelty,
Which is too nigh your person. Heaven preserve you!
I dare abide no longer. [*Exit*
Lady Macduff. Whither should I fly?
70 I have done no harm. But I remember now
I am in this earthly world; where to do harm
Is often laudable, to do good sometime
Accounted dangerous folly: why then, alas,
Do I put up that womanly defence,
75 To say I have done no harm?

Enter Murderers.

What are these faces?
1 Murderer. Where is your husband?
Lady Macduff. I hope, in no place so unsanctified
Where such as thou mayst find him.
1 Murderer. He's a traitor.
Son. Thou liest, thou shag-ear'd villain!
1 Murderer. [*Stabbing him.*] What, you egg!
80 Young fry of treachery!
Son. He has kill'd me, mother:
Run away, I pray you! [*Dies.*
[*Exit* Lady Macduff, *crying "Murder!"*
[*Exeunt* Murderers, *following her.*

62. IN YOUR STATE OF HONOUR I AM PERFECT—Perfectly acquainted with your rank.
63. DOUBT—Fear.
67. FELL CRUELTY—Direct cruelty.
79. SHAG-EAR'D—Shaggy eared or shaggy haired.
80. YOUNG FRY OF TREACHERY!—Son of a traitor.

Scene 3. *England. Before the King's palace.*

Enter Malcolm *and* Macduff.

Malcolm. Let us seek out some desolate shade, and there
Weep our sad bosoms empty.
    Macduff.   Let us rather
Hold fast the mortal sword, and, like good men,
Bestride our down-fall'n birthdom. Each new morn
5 New widows howl, new orphans cry, new sorrows
Strike heaven on the face, that it resounds
As if it felt with Scotland, and yell'd out
Like syllable of dolour.
    Malcolm.   What I believe, I'll wail;
What know, believe; and what I can redress,
10 As I shall find the time to friend, I will.
What you have spoke, it may be so perchance.
This tyrant, whose sole name blisters our tongues,
Was once thought honest: you have lov'd him well;
He hath not touch'd you yet. I am young; but something
15 You may deserve of him through me, and wisdom
To offer up a weak, poor, innocent lamb
T' appease an angry god.
    Macduff. I am not treacherous.
    Malcolm.   But Macbeth is.
A good and virtuous nature may recoil

    1. Let us seek out some desolate shade—What Malcolm proposes is, in effect, that instead of trying to redress their wrongs, they lose themselves in some wild distant land and try to forget them. This makes Malcolm seem to be a kind of spiritless fellow. It should be remembered that he does not trust Macduff at first, and that throughout most of the scene he puts himself in an unfavorable light in order to try Macduff's sincerity.
    3. Mortal—Deadly.
    4. Bestride our down-fall'n birthdom—Stand astride our fallen native land as a knight does the body of a comrade who has fallen in battle.
    6. It—Heaven.
    8. Like syllable of dolour—A similar cry of pain or grief.
    10. Time to friend—A friendly or favorable time.
    10. I will—Note the reserved nature of Malcolm's entire speech. He implies that as bad as things are, Macduff's account is overdrawn. "I will bewail," he says, "what I believe, and I'll believe only what I know." He professes to be unimpressed by Macduff.
    14–17. But something ... an angry god—Malcolm suggests that it might be worth Macduff's while to betray him (Malcolm) to Macbeth.
    19–20. A good and virtuous nature may recoil in an imperial charge—Macduff's reply to Malcolm's suggestion is to assert that he is not treacherous. To this Malcolm retorts, "No, but Macbeth is. And although you may not

20 In an imperial charge. But I shall crave your pardon;
That which you are, my thoughts cannot transpose
Angels are bright still, though the brightest fell:
Though all things foul would wear the brows of grace,
Yet grace must still look so.
    Macduff.   I have lost my hopes.
25   *Malcolm.* Perchance even there where I did find my doubts.
Why in that rawness left you wife and child,
Those precious motives, those strong knots of love,
Without leave-taking? I pray you,
Let not my jealousies be your dishonours,
30 But mine own safeties: you may be rightly just,
Whatever I shall think.
    Macduff.   Bleed, bleed, poor country!
Great tyranny, lay thou thy basis sure,
For goodness dare not check thee; wear thou thy wrongs;
The title is affeer'd! Fare thee well, lord:
35 I would not be the villain that thou think'st
For the whole space that's in the tyrant's grasp,
And the rich East to boot.
    Malcolm.   Be not offended:

be, yet a good and virtuous man acts contrary (recoil) to his nature when the king lays him under command (imperial charge)."

20–21. BUT I SHALL CRAVE YOUR PARDON . . . CANNOT TRANSPOSE—Malcolm's apology is none at all. What he says is, "I beg your pardon for insinuating that you are treacherous, but whatever the truth is, whether you are treacherous or not my thinking you one thing or the other will not make you what I think you to be." Malcolm, in assuming this attitude, is perhaps more irritating to Macduff than he would be if he accused Macduff outright of treachery, for he seems to be quite disinterested in Macduff's and his country's cause.

22–24. ANGELS ARE BRIGHT STILL . . . YET GRACE MUST STILL LOOK SO—Malcolm says in effect, "I really have no right to accuse you (although I have my own opinion), for some angels are still bright even though the brightest (Lucifer) did fall, and virtue must continue to wear its own looks although vice frequently assumes the outward appearance of virtue."

24. I HAVE LOST MY HOPES—Macduff is discouraged and disappointed. How different have been both Malcolm and his reception from what he must have expected!

25. PERCHANCE EVEN THERE WHERE I DID FIND MY DOUBTS—Malcolm interprets "hopes" in a different sense from that in which Macduff uses it. He says in effect, "Your leaving your wife and child behind is the circumstance which has caused me to doubt your sincerity and to suspect that you came with 'hopes' of enticing me back to Scotland to betray me."

26. RAWNESS—Hastiness, without making adequate provision for their care.

29. JEALOUSIES—Suspicions. The sense is: "Do not interpret my suspicions as insults to you but rather as precautions for myself."

34. AFFEER'D—Confirmed, i.e., "great tyranny's" title.

I speak not as in absolute fear of you.
I think our country sinks beneath the yoke;
40 It weeps, it bleeds; and each new day a gash
Is added to her wounds: I think withal
There would be hands uplifted in my right;
And here from gracious England have I offer
Of goodly thousands: but, for all this,
45 When I shall tread upon the tyrant's head,
Or wear it on my sword, yet my poor country
Shall have more vices than it had before;
More suffer, and more sundry ways than ever,
By him that shall succeed.
    Macduff.   What should he be?
50   *Malcolm.* It is myself I mean; in whom I know
All the particulars of vice so grafted,
That, when they shall be open'd, black Macbeth
Will seem as pure as snow; and the poor state
Esteem him as a lamb, being compar'd
55 With my confineless harms.
    Macduff.   Not in the legions
Of horrid hell can come a devil more damn'd
In evils to top Macbeth.
    Malcolm.   I grant him bloody,
Luxurious, avaricious, false, deceitful,
Sudden, malicious, smacking of every sin
60 That has a name: but there's no bottom, none,
In my voluptuousness; your wives, your daughters,
Your matrons, and your maids, could not fill up
The cistern of my lust, and my desire
All continent impediments would o'erbear,
65 That did oppose my will. Better Macbeth
Than such an one to reign.
    Macduff.   Boundless intemperance
In nature is a tyranny; it hath been

    43. ENGLAND—The king of England.
    48. AND MORE SUNDRY WAYS—And in more sundry ways.
    52. OPEN'D—Disclosed.
    55. CONFINELESS HARMS—Unlimited vices.
    58. LUXURIOUS—Licentious.
    59. SUDDEN—Violent, quick to anger.
    64. CONTINENT IMPEDIMENTS—Restraining motives.

Th' untimely emptying of the happy throne,
And fall of many kings. But fear not yet
70 To take upon you what is yours: you may
Convey your pleasures in a spacious plenty,
And yet seem cold, the time you may so hoodwink.
We have willing dames enough; there cannot be
That vulture in you, to devour so many
75 As will to greatness dedicate themselves,
Finding it so inclined.
    Malcolm.   With this there grows,
In my most ill-compos'd affection such
A stanchless avarice that, were I king,
I should cut off the nobles for their lands,
80 Desire his jewels and this other's house:
And my more-having would be as a sauce
To make me hunger more, that I should forge
Quarrels unjust against the good and loyal,
Destroying them for wealth.
    Macduff.   This avarice
85 Sticks deeper, grows with more pernicious root
Than summer-seeming lust, and it hath been
The sword of our slain kings: yet do not fear;
Scotland hath foisons to fill up your will
Of your mere own: all these are portable,
90 With other graces weigh'd.
    Malcolm. But I have none: the king-becoming graces,
As justice, verity, temperance, stableness,
Bounty, perseverance, mercy, lowliness,
Devotion, patience, courage, fortitude,
95 I have no relish of them; but abound

    71. CONVEY—Pursue in secret.
    72. THE TIME YOU MAY SO HOODWINK—You may so deceive the world.
    76. WITH THIS—In addition to this.
    77. ILL-COMPOS'D AFFECTION—Nature made up of vices.
    78. STANCHLESS—Insatiable.
    80. HIS—This one's.
    86. SUMMER-SEEMING—Like the summer, quickly passing, youthful.
    87. THE SWORD OF OUR SLAIN KINGS—That which has slain our kings.
    88. FOISONS—Abundance.
    89. YOUR MERE OWN—That which is absolutely your own.
    89. PORTABLE—Endurable. The sense is that all these vices are endurable if counterbalanced by other virtues.
    95. RELISH—Savor, smack.

In the division of each several crime,
Acting it many ways. Nay, had I power, I should
Pour the sweet milk of concord into hell,
Uproar the universal peace, confound
100 All unity on earth.
    Macduff.   O Scotland, Scotland!
    Malcolm. If such a one be fit to govern, speak:
I am as I have spoken.
    Macduff.   Fit to govern!
No, not to live. O nation miserable,
With an untitled tyrant bloody-scepter'd,
105 When shalt thou see thy wholesome days again,
Since that the truest issue of thy throne
By his own interdiction stands accurs'd,
And does blaspheme his breed? Thy royal father
Was a most sainted king: the queen that bore thee,
110 Oftener upon her knees than on her feet,
Died every day she liv'd. Fare thee well!
These evils thou repeat'st upon thyself
Hath banish'd me from Scotland. O my breast,
Thy hope ends here!
    Malcolm.   Macduff, this noble passion,
115 Child of integrity, hath from my soul
Wip'd the black scruples, reconcil'd my thoughts
To thy good truth and honour. Devilish Macbeth
By many of these trains hath sought to win me
Into his power; and modest wisdom plucks me
120 From over-credulous haste; but God above
Deal between thee and me! for even now
I put myself to thy direction, and
Unspeak mine own detraction; here abjure
The taints and blames I laid upon myself,
125 For strangers to my nature. I am yet
Unknown to woman, never was forsworn,
Scarcely have coveted what was mine own,

    96. IN THE DIVISION—Variation.
    107. INTERDICTION—Pronouncement.
    108. BLASPHEME HIS BREED—Slander his parentage.
    111. DIED EVERY DAY SHE LIV'D—Each day of her life was a preparation for death.
    118. TRAINS—Lures, devices.
    123. HERE ABJURE—I here disavow.

At no time broke my faith, would not betray
The devil to his fellow, and delight
130 No less in truth than life: my first false speaking
Was this upon myself. What I am truly,
Is thine and my poor country's to command;
Whither, indeed, before thy here-approach,
Old Siward, with ten thousand warlike men,
135 Already at a point, was setting forth:
Now we'll together; and the chance of goodness
Be like our warranted quarrel! Why are you silent?
    Macduff. Such welcome and unwelcome things at once
'Tis hard to reconcile.

Enter a Doctor.

140   *Malcolm.* Well; more anon.—Comes the king forth, I pray you?
    Doctor. Ay, sir; there are a crew of wretched souls
That stay his cure: their malady convinces
The great assay of art; but at his touch,
Such sanctity hath heaven given his hand,
145 They presently amend.
    Malcolm.   I thank you, doctor.   [*Exit* Doctor.
    Macduff. What's the disease he means?
    Malcolm.   'Tis call'd the evil:
A most miraculous work in this good king;
Which often, since my here-remain in England,
I have seen him do. How he solicits heaven,
150 Himself best knows: but strangely-visited people,
All swoln and ulcerous, pitiful to the eye,

    135. AT A POINT—Prepared, armed at point.
    136–137. THE CHANCE OF GOODNESS BE LIKE OUR WARRANTED QUARREL—May the chances of success be as good as the outcome of our quarrel.
    142. STAY HIS CURE—Wait his healing touch. Edward the Confessor was said to have had the gift of healing scrofula, a blood and skin disease, by "touching," and to have passed this gift to his successors. All the kings of England from Edward down are said to have "touched" to cure this disease. This episode has nothing to do with the play, but is generally believed to have been introduced as a compliment to King James who witnessed the play, and who himself "touched" many.
    142–143. THEIR MALADY CONVINCES THE GREAT ASSAY OF ART—Their disease overcomes the best effort of professional skill.
    149. SOLICITS—Invokes and obtains the aid of.
    150. STRANGELY-VISITED—Strangely-afflicted.

The mere despair of surgery, he cures,
Hanging a golden stamp about their necks,
Put on with holy prayers: and 'tis spoken,
To the succeeding royalty he leaves
The healing benediction. With this strange virtue,
He hath a heavenly gift of prophecy,
And sundry blessings hang about his throne,
That speak him full of grace.

Enter Ross.

Macduff. See, who comes here?
Malcolm. My countryman; but yet I know him not.
Macduff. My ever-gentle cousin, welcome hither.
Malcolm. I know him now. Good God, betimes remove
The means that makes us strangers!
Ross. Sir, amen.
Macduff. Stands Scotland where it did?
Ross. Alas, poor country,
Almost afraid to know itself! It cannot
Be call'd our mother, but our grave: where nothing,
But who knows nothing, is once seen to smile;
Where sighs and groans and shrieks that rend the air,
Are made, not mark'd; where violent sorrow seems
A modern ecstasy: the dead man's knell
Is there scarce ask'd for who; and good men's lives
Expire before the flowers in their caps,
Dying or ere they sicken.
Macduff. O, relation
Too nice, and yet too true!
Malcolm. What's the newest grief?

152. MERE—Utter, complete.
153. GOLDEN STAMP—A coin of gold.
160. BUT YET I KNOW HIM NOT—Malcolm recognizes him as a countryman by his dress, but is suspicious of him.
162. BETIMES—Forthwith, soon.
163. MEANS—Cause.
167. WHO KNOWS NOTHING—Such as the idiot and the fool.
169. NOT MARK'D—They are so common as no longer to excite notice.
170. A MODERN ECSTASY—A state of feeling which has become commonplace.
173–174. RELATION TOO NICE—Account or story too accurate.

175   *Ross.* That of an hour's age doth hiss the speaker,
Each minute teems a new one.
    Macduff.   How does my wife?
    Ross. Why, well.
    Macduff.   And all my children?
    Ross.   Well too.
    Macduff. The tyrant has not batter'd at their peace?
    Ross. No; they were well at peace when I did leave 'em.
180   *Macduff.* Be not a niggard of your speech: how goes 't?
    Ross. When I came hither to transport the tidings
Which I have heavily borne, there ran a rumour
Of many worthy fellows that were out;
Which was to my belief witness'd the rather,
185 For that I saw the tyrant's power a-foot:
Now is the time of help; your eye in Scotland
Would create soldiers, make our women fight,
To doff their dire distresses.
    Malcolm.   Be 't their comfort
We are coming thither: gracious England hath
190 Lent us good Siward and ten thousand men;
An older and a better soldier none
That Christendom gives out.
    Ross.   Would I could answer
This comfort with the like! But I have words
That would be howl'd out in the desert air,
195 Where hearing should not latch them.
    Macduff.   What concern they?
The general cause? or is it a fee-grief
Due to some single breast?
    Ross.   No mind that's honest
But in it shares some woe; though the main part
Pertains to you alone.
    Macduff.   If it be mine,

175. DOTH HISS THE SPEAKER—Whoever tells of an atrocity which is only an hour old is regarded much as the player who is hissed for presenting "old stuff."
176. TEEMS—Brings forth.
179. WELL AT PEACE—These are grisly puns.
183. OUT—Up in arms, in rebellion.   188. DOFF—Put off, get rid of.
194. WOULD BE—Ought to be, should only be.
195. LATCH—Catch.
196-197. FEE-GRIEF DUE TO SOME SINGLE BREAST—Private grief which concerns one man only.

Keep it not from me, quickly let me have it.
  Ross.   Let not your ears despise my tongue for ever,
Which shall possess them with the heaviest sound
That ever yet they heard.
  Macduff.   Hum! I guess at it.
  Ross.   Your castle is surpris'd; your wife and babes
Savagely slaughter'd: to relate the manner,
Were, on the quarry of these murder'd deer,
To add the death of you.
  Malcolm.   Merciful heaven!
What, man! ne'er pull your hat upon your brows;
Give sorrow words: the grief that does not speak
Whispers the o'er-fraught heart and bids it break.
  Macduff.   My children too?
  Ross.   Wife, children, servants, all
That could be found.
  Macduff.   And I must be from thence!
My wife kill'd too?
  Ross.   I have said.
  Malcolm.   Be comforted:
Let's make us medicines of our great revenge,
To cure this deadly grief.
  Macduff.   He has no children.—All my pretty ones?
Did you say all? O hell-kite! All?
What, all my pretty chickens and their dam
At one fell swoop?
  Malcolm.   Dispute it like a man.
  Macduff.   I shall do so;
But I must also feel it as a man:
I cannot but remember such things were,
That were most precious to me. Did heaven look on,
And would not take their part? Sinful Macduff,
They were all struck for thee! naught that I am,

  206. QUARRY—Heap, used to designate the game killed.
  207. TO ADD THE DEATH OF YOU—Would be to cause your death.
  210. WHISPERS—As we say "bespeaks." 210. O'ER-FRAUGHT—Over-laden.
  216. HE—Malcolm. Macduff means that it is easy to see that Malcolm has no children. He talks of revenge. Revenge will not bring back those whom Macbeth has slain. Macduff is overcome by his grief; he thinks rather of those whom he will see no more than of revenge. This comes later.
  220. DISPUTE IT—Resist it.
  225. NAUGHT—Worthless.

Not for their own demerits, but for mine,
Fell slaughter on their souls. Heaven rest them now!
   Malcolm. Be this the whetstone of your sword: let grief
Convert to anger; blunt not the heart, enrage it.
230   *Macduff.* O, I could play the woman with mine eyes,
And braggart with my tongue! But, gentle heavens,
Cut short all intermission; front to front
Bring thou this fiend of Scotland and myself;
Within my sword's length set him; if he scape,
235 Heaven forgive him too!
   Malcolm.   This tune goes manly.
Come, go we to the king; our power is ready;
Our lack is nothing but our leave. Macbeth
Is ripe for shaking, and the powers above
Put on their instruments. Receive what cheer you may:
240 The night is long that never finds the day.   [*Exeunt.*

    235. FORGIVE HIM TOO—If for any reason I let him escape, why, then let Heaven let him escape too.
    237. OUR LACK IS NOTHING BUT OUR LEAVE—We lack nothing but taking leave of the king.
    239. PUT ON THEIR INSTRUMENTS—Set their agents at work to shake Macbeth.

ACT V

SCENE I. *Dunsinane. Ante-room in the Castle.*

Enter a Doctor *of Physic and a* Waiting-Gentlewoman.

   Doctor. I have two nights watch'd with you, but can perceive no truth in your report. When was it she last walk'd?
   Gentlewoman. Since his majesty went into the field, I have seen her rise from her bed, throw her night-gown upon her,
5 unlock her closet, take forth paper, fold it, write upon 't, read it, afterwards seal it, and again return to bed; yet all this while in a most fast sleep.
   Doctor. A great perturbation in nature, to receive at once the benefit of sleep, and do the effects of watching! In this

    3. WENT INTO THE FIELD—To put down the "many worthy fellows that were out." See Act IV, Scene 3.
    4. NIGHT-GOWN—Dressing robe.
    8. PERTURBATION—Disturbance.
    9. DO THE EFFECTS OF WATCHING—Do things as if she were awake.

slumbery agitation, besides her walking and other actual performances, what, at any time, have you heard her say?

Gentlewoman. That, sir, which I will not report after her.

Doctor. You may to me; and 'tis most meet you should.

Gentlewoman. Neither to you nor any one; having no witness to confirm my speech.

Enter LADY MACBETH, *with a taper.*

Lo, you, here she comes! This is her very guise; and, upon my life, fast asleep. Observe her; stand close.

Doctor. How came she by that light?

Gentlewoman. Why, it stood by her: she has light by her continually; 'tis her command.

Doctor. You see, her eyes are open.

Gentlewoman. Ay, but their sense are shut.

Doctor. What is it she does now? Look, how she rubs her hands.

Gentlewoman. It is an accustom'd action with her, to seem thus washing her hands; I have known her continue in this a quarter of an hour.

Lady Macbeth. Yet here's a spot.

Doctor. Hark! she speaks: I will set down what comes from her, to satisfy my remembrance the more strongly.

Lady Macbeth. Out, damned spot! out, I say!—One, two; why, then 'tis time to do 't.—Hell is murky!—Fie, my lord, fie! a soldier, and afeard? What need we fear who knows it, when none can call our power to account?—Yet who would

12. WILL NOT REPORT—Will not repeat. What she has heard is of such a damaging nature that she fears getting herself into trouble if she repeats it; she implies in her next speech that what she has heard is something which she dare not report without a confirming witness. What did she hear Lady Macbeth say?

18. STAND CLOSE—Keep out of sight.

34. ONE, TWO—Lady Macbeth seems to hear the bell which she struck to signal Macbeth that his drink was ready and that it was "time to do 't." The student should note that Lady Macbeth's disordered mind recalls disconnected scraps of what had passed between her and her husband, mixed with horrid reminiscences of the crime itself.

have thought the old man to have had so much blood in him?
  Doctor. Do you mark that?
  Lady Macbeth. The thane of Fife had a wife; where is she now?—What, will these hands ne'er be clean?—No more o' that, my lord, no more o' that: you mar all with this starting.
  Doctor. Go to, go to; you have known what you should not.
  Gentlewoman. She has spoke what she should not, I am sure of that: heaven knows what she has known.
  Lady Macbeth. Here's the smell of the blood still: all the perfumes of Arabia will not sweeten this little hand. Oh, oh, oh!
  Doctor. What a sigh is there! The heart is sorely charg'd.
  Gentlewoman. I would not have such a heart in my bosom for the dignity of the whole body.
  Doctor. Well, well, well,—
  Gentlewoman. Pray God it be, sir.
  Doctor. This disease is beyond my practice: yet I have known those which have walk'd in their sleep who have died holily in their beds.
  Lady Macbeth. Wash your hands; put on your nightgown; look not so pale. I tell you yet again, Banquo's buried; he cannot come out on 's grave.
  Doctor. Even so?
  Lady Macbeth. To bed, to bed; there's knocking at the gate: come, come, come, come, give me your hand: what's done cannot be undone: to bed, to bed, to bed. [*Exit.*
  Doctor. Will she go now to bed?
  Gentlewoman. Directly.
  Doctor. Foul whisperings are abroad: unnatural deeds.
Do breed unnatural troubles: infected minds
To their deaf pillows will discharge their secrets:
More needs she the divine than the physician.
God, God forgive us all! Look after her;
Remove from her the means of all annoyance,
And still keep eyes upon her. So, good night:
My mind she has mated, and amaz'd my sight:
I think, but dare not speak.
  Gentlewoman. Good night, good doctor. [*Exeunt.*

48. Sorely charg'd—Heavy, heavily laden.   68. Divine—Priest.
70. Means of all annoyance—Things with which she might harm herself.
71. Still—Always.   71. Keep eyes upon her—Why?
72. Mated—Confounded, bewildered.

Scene 2. *The country near Dunsinane.*

Drum and colours. Enter Menteith, Caithness, Angus, Lennox, *and* Soldiers.

Menteith. The English power is near, led on by Malcolm,
His uncle Siward, and the good Macduff:
Revenges burn in them; for their dear causes
Would to the bleeding and the grim alarm
5 Excite the mortified man.
   Angus.   Near Birnam wood
Shall we well meet them; that way are they coming.
   Caithness. Who knows if Donalbain be with his brother?
   Lennox. For certain, sir, he is not: I have a file
Of all the gentry: there is Siward's son,
10 And many unrough youths, that even now
Protest their first of manhood.
   Menteith.   What does the tyrant?
   Caithness. Great Dunsinane he strongly fortifies:
Some say he's mad; others, that lesser hate him,
Do call it valiant fury: but, for certain,
15 He cannot buckle his distemper'd cause
Within the belt of rule.
   Angus.   Now does he feel
His secret murders sticking on his hands;
Now minutely revolts upbraid his faith-breach;
Those he commands move only in command,
20 Nothing in love: now does he feel his title
Hang loose about him, like a giant's robe
Upon a dwarfish thief.
   Menteith.   Who then shall blame

  3. Dear causes—Grievous complaints.
  4. Bleeding—Bloody deeds.
  4. Alarm—Call to arms.
  5. Excite the mortified man—Rouse the holy or religious man.
  8. File—List.
 10. Unrough—Smooth-faced, beardless.
 11. Protest their first of manhood—Declare themselves no longer mere boys but men, making this the first act of their manhood.
 15. Distemper'd cause—Diseased cause. Macbeth's cause is compared to a body swollen with dropsy which cannot be buckled in. The sense of the lines is: He cannot control his rebellious subjects nor make his plans go right.
 18. Minutely revolts—Revolts breaking out every minute.
 18. Upbraid his faith-breach—Rebuke his breach of allegiance to Duncan.

His pester'd senses to recoil and start,
When all that is within him does condemn
25 Itself for being there?
    Caithness.   Well, march we on,
To give obedience where 'tis truly ow'd:
Meet we the medicine of the sickly weal;
And with him pour we in our country's purge
Each drop of us.
    Lennox.   Or so much as it needs
30 To dew the sovereign flower and drown the weeds.
Make we our march towards Birnam.   [*Exeunt, marching.*

    23. PESTER'D—Perplexed, irritated.
    23. TO RECOIL AND START—For recoiling and starting, that is, for acting, as we say, by fits and starts. We have here a good description of Macbeth alternating between fits of dark depression and starts of "valiant fury."
    24–25. WHEN ALL THAT IS WITHIN HIM DOES CONDEMN ITSELF FOR BEING THERE—When Macbeth turns his thoughts inward, he finds nothing but what should be condemned. It is then he "recoils" to feverish activity.
    27. MEDICINE OF THE SICKLY WEAL—*i.e.* Malcolm who can restore the commonwealth to health.
    28. PURGE—The figure of "medicine" for a "sickly weal" is continued. The sense is: Each of us devote ourselves to restoring our country to health—to purging it.
    30. DEW THE SOVEREIGN FLOWER—Revive or nourish the true king (Malcolm.)

    SCENE 3. *Dunsinane. A room in the castle.*

    Enter MACBETH, *the* Doctor, *and* Attendants.

    Macbeth. Bring me no more reports; let them fly all:
Till Birnam wood remove to Dunsinane
I cannot taint with fear. What's the boy Malcolm?
Was he not born of woman? The spirits that know
5 All mortal consequences have pronounc'd me thus:
"Fear not, Macbeth; no man that's born of woman
Shall e'er have power upon thee." Then fly, false thanes,
And mingle with the English epicures:
The mind I sway by and the heart I bear
10 Shall never sag with doubt nor shake with fear.

    1. THEM—His thanes and their soldiers. He has been receiving reports of their desertions.
    3. TAINT—Become infected.
    8. ENGLISH EPICURES—Holinshed records that the Scotch (whose barren country had accustomed them to plain living and few comforts) looked upon the English not without contempt as gormandizers.
    9. SWAY BY—By which I am ruled.

Act V, Sc. 3   WILLIAM SHAKESPEARE

Enter a Servant.

The devil damn thee black, thou cream-fac'd loon!
Where got'st thou that goose look?
  Servant. There is ten thousand—
  Macbeth.   Geese, villain?
  Servant.   Soldiers, sir.
  Macbeth. Go prick thy face, and over-red thy fear,
Thou lily-liver'd boy. What soldiers, patch?
Death of thy soul! those linen cheeks of thine
Are counsellors to fear. What soldiers, whey-face?
  Servant. The English force, so please you.
  Macbeth. Take thy face hence.   [*Exit* Servant.
                              Seyton! I am sick at heart,
When I behold—Seyton, I say!—This push
Will chair me ever, or disseat me now.
I have liv'd long enough: my way of life
Is fall'n into the sear, the yellow leaf;
And that which should accompany old age,
As honour, love, obedience, troops of friends,
I must not look to have; but, in their stead,
Curses, not loud but deep, mouth-honour, breath,
Which the poor heart would fain deny, and dare not.
Seyton!

Enter Seyton.

  Seyton. What's your gracious pleasure?
  Macbeth.   What news more?
  Seyton. All is confirm'd, my lord, which was reported.

    11. Loon—Stupid fellow. Despite his boast, Macbeth starts at the pallid face of the servant, and tried to bolster his own confidence by his own "valiant fury."
    14. Over-red—Smear your blood over your pallid face; that is, take courage.
    15. Lily-liver'd—Cowardly. The liver was believed to be the seat of courage, much as the heart is still spoken of as the seat of pity.
    15. Patch—Fool.
    16. Linen cheeks—Colorless cheeks.
    17. Are counsellors to fear—Cause all who see them to fear.
    17. Whey-face—What is the color of whey?
    19. Seyton!—Macbeth calls the officer who attends him. Between calls, he gives way to one of his black fits which alternate with moods of fury.
    20. Push—Attack.
    21. Chair me ever, or disseat me now—Will make my seat secure if I win, or disseat me if I lose in the coming attack.

ELD

Macbeth. I'll fight, till from my bones my flesh be hack'd.
Give me my armour.
    Seyton.   'Tis not needed yet.
    Macbeth. I'll put it on.
35 Send out moe horses, skirr the country round;
Hang those that talk of fear. Give me mine armour.
How does your patient, doctor?
    Doctor.   Not so sick, my lord,
As she is troubled with thick-coming fancies,
That keep her from her rest.
    Macbeth.   Cure her of that.
40 Canst thou not minister to a mind diseas'd,
Pluck from the memory a rooted sorrow,
Raze out the written troubles of the brain,
And with some sweet oblivious antidote
Cleanse the stuff'd bosom of that perilous stuff
45 Which weighs upon the heart?
    Doctor.   Therein the patient
Must minister to himself.
    Macbeth. Throw physic to the dogs, I'll none of it.
Come, put mine armour on; give me my staff.
Seyton, send out. Doctor, the thanes fly from me.
50 Come, sir, dispatch. If thou couldst, doctor, cast
The water of my land, find her disease,
And purge it to a sound and pristine health,
I would applaud thee to the very echo,
That should applaud again. Pull 't off, I say.
55 What rhubarb, senna, or what purgative drug,

    35. MOE—More.
    35. SKIRR—Scour.
    42. RAZE OUT—Erase, blot out.
    43. OBLIVIOUS—Causing forgetfulness.
    47. PHYSIC—The whole practice of medicine.
    48. COME, PUT MINE ARMOUR ON; GIVE ME MY STAFF—Note the signs of Macbeth's great perturbation. He orders his armor put on, then pulled off, and finally brought after him. He must talk and he must be doing something. "Come, put mine armour on; give me my staff" is addressed to one (the armorer) whose duty it was to put the armor on.
    49. SEYTON, SEND OUT—To Seyton he turns with the direction to send out for further news; next he addresses the Doctor, and in the same breath orders the armorer to be quick about his business.
    50. CAST—Inspect, examine.
    52. PURGE IT—Restore my land.
    52. PRISTINE—Original, former.
    54. PULL 'T OFF—Macbeth here directs his armorer to pull his armor off.

Would scour these English hence? Hear'st thou of them?
   Doctor.   Ay, my good lord; your royal preparation
Makes us hear something.
   Macbeth.   Bring it after me.
I will not be afraid of death and bane,
60 Till Birnam forest come to Dunsinane.
   Doctor. [*Aside.*] Were I from Dunsinane away and clear,
Profit again should hardly draw me here.   [*Exeunt.*

    58. BRING IT AFTER ME—This probably refers to the armor which had been pulled off.
    59. BANE—Ruin, destruction.

SCENE 4. *Country near Birnam wood.*

Drum and colours. Enter MALCOLM, *old* SIWARD *and his* Son, MACDUFF, MENTEITH, CAITHNESS, ANGUS, LENNOX, ROSS, *and* Soldiers, *marching.*

   Malcolm. Cousins, I hope the days are near at hand
That chambers will be safe.
   Menteith.   We doubt it nothing.
   Siward. What wood is this before us?
   Menteith.   The wood of Birnam.
   Malcolm. Let every soldier hew him down a bough,
5 And bear 't before him: thereby shall we shadow
The numbers of our host, and make discovery
Err in report of us.
   Soldiers.   It shall be done.
   Siward. We learn no other but the confident tyrant
Keeps still in Dunsinane, and will endure
10 Our sitting down before 't.
   Malcolm.   'Tis his main hope:
For, where there is advantage to be given,
Both more and less have given him the revolt,

    2. CHAMBERS WILL BE SAFE—The allusion is probably to the chamber in which Duncan was murdered.
    5. SHADOW—Conceal.
    6-7. MAKE DISCOVERY ERR IN REPORT OF US—Make watchers or scouts (discovery) unable to report accurately of our number.
    10. SITTING DOWN BEFORE 'T—Besieging it.
    11. ADVANTAGE TO BE GIVEN—The sense is: Whenever there has been favorable opportunity.
    12. MORE AND LESS—Great and small.

And none serve with him but constrained things,
Whose hearts are absent too.
   Macduff.   Let our just censures
15 Attend the true event, and put we on
Industrious soldiership.
   Siward.   The time approaches
That will with due decision make us know
What we shall say we have and what we owe.
Thoughts speculative their unsure hopes relate,
20 But certain issue strokes must arbitrate;
Towards which, advance the war.   [*Exeunt, marching.*

   13. CONSTRAINED THINGS—Creatures who are forced to.
   14–15. LET OUR JUST CENSURES ATTEND THE TRUE EVENT—Let our final judgment await the actual outcome.
   18. WHAT WE SHALL SAY WE HAVE AND WHAT WE OWE—Time will show us how our account stands.
   19–20. THOUGHTS SPECULATIVE . . . MUST ARBITRATE—Speculating about the outcome of an issue is only to give expression to hopes—which are not decisive. Fighting alone will yield a decisive result.

SCENE 5. *Dunsinane. Within the castle.*

Enter MACBETH, SEYTON, *and* Soldiers, *with drum and colours.*

   Macbeth. Hang out our banners on the outward walls;
The cry is still, "They come." Our castle's strength
Will laugh a siege to scorn; here let them lie
Till famine and the ague eat them up.
5 Were they not forc'd with those that should be ours,
We might have met them dareful, beard to beard,
And beat them backward home.   [*A cry of women within.*
                             What is that noise?
   Seyton. It is the cry of women, my good lord.   [*Exit.*
   Macbeth. I have almost forgot the taste of fears:
10 The time has been, my senses would have cool'd
To hear a night-shriek, and my fell of hair
Would at a dismal treatise rouse and stir
As life were in 't: I have supp'd full with horrors;
Direness, familiar to my slaughterous thoughts,
15 Cannot once start me.

   5. FORC'D—Reënforced.
   11. FELL OF HAIR—"Fell" means skin of an animal. Hence, "fell of hair" here means scalp.
   12. TREATISE—Story.

Re-enter SEYTON.

Wherefore was that cry?
   Seyton. The queen, my lord, is dead.
   Macbeth. She should have died hereafter;
There would have been a time for such a word.
To-morrow, and to-morrow, and to-morrow,
20 Creeps in this petty pace from day to day,
To the last syllable of recorded time;
And all our yesterdays have lighted fools
The way to dusty death. Out, out, brief candle!
Life's but a walking shadow; a poor player
25 That struts and frets his hour upon the stage
And then is heard no more. It is a tale
Told by an idiot, full of sound and fury,
Signifying nothing.

Enter a Messenger.

Thou com'st to use thy tongue; thy story quickly.
30   *Messenger.* Gracious my lord,
I should report that which I say I saw,
But know not how to do 't.
   Macbeth.   Well, say, sir.
   Messenger. As I did stand my watch upon the hill,
I look'd toward Birnam, and anon, methought,
35 The wood began to move.
   Macbeth.   Liar and slave!
   Messenger. Let me endure your wrath, if 't be not so:
Within this three mile may you see it coming;
I say, a moving grove.
   Macbeth.   If thou speak'st false,
Upon the next tree shalt thou hang alive,
40 Till famine cling thee: if thy speech be sooth,
I care not if thou dost for me as much.

    17. SHE SHOULD HAVE DIED HEREAFTER—Had she not died now, she would have died hereafter.
    18. THERE WOULD HAVE BEEN A TIME FOR SUCH A WORD—And there would have come a time when I should have had to hear of it. Why not now?
    40. CLING—Wither. 40. BE SOOTH—Be the truth.

I pull in resolution, and begin
To doubt th' equivocation of the fiend
That lies like truth: "Fear not, till Birnam wood
45 Do come to Dunsinane"; and now a wood
Comes toward Dunsinane. Arm, arm, and out!
If this which he avouches does appear,
There is nor flying hence nor tarrying here.
I 'gin to be a-weary of the sun,
50 And wish th' estate o' the world were now undone.
Ring the alarum-bell! Blow, wind! come, wrack!
At least we'll die with harness on our back. [*Exeunt.*

42. I PULL IN RESOLUTION—I am no longer so certain of the outcome.
43. EQUIVOCATION—Deceit through double meaning.
47. HE AVOUCHES—The messenger assures me of.
50. TH' ESTATE O' THE WORLD WERE NOW UNDONE—The whole world might fall into destruction.
51. WRACK—Ruin.
52. HARNESS—Armor.

SCENE 6. *Dunsinane. Before the castle.*

Drum and colours. Enter MALCOLM, *old* SIWARD, MACDUFF, *and their* Army, *with boughs.*

Malcolm. Now near enough; your leavy screens throw down,
And show like those you are. You, worthy uncle,
Shall, with my cousin, your right noble son,
Lead our first battle: worthy Macduff and we
5 Shall take upon 's what else remains to do,
According to our order.
   Siward.   Fare you well.
Do we but find the tyrant's power to-night,
Let us be beaten, if we cannot fight.
   Macduff. Make all our trumpets speak; give them all breath,
10 Those clamorous harbingers of blood and death. [*Exeunt.*
[*Alarums continued.*

2. SHOW LIKE THOSE YOU ARE—Appear in your own likenesses without your camouflage.
4. FIRST BATTLE—Vanguard, division of an army.
6. OUR ORDER—The order of battle decided upon beforehand.
10. HARBINGERS—Forerunners, because blown to give the signal to begin the battle.

Scene 7. *Another part of the field.*

Enter Macbeth.

Macbeth. They have tied me to a stake; I cannot fly,
But, bear-like, I must fight the course. What's he
That was not born of woman? Such a one
Am I to fear, or none.

Enter young Siward.

5 *Young Siward.* What is thy name?
Macbeth. Thou 'lt be afraid to hear it.
Young Siward. No; though thou call'st thyself a hotter name
Than any is in hell.
Macbeth. My name's Macbeth.
Young Siward. The devil himself could not pronounce a title
More hateful to mine ear.
Macbeth. No, nor more fearful.
10 *Young Siward.* Thou liest, abhorred tyrant; with my sword
I'll prove the lie thou speak'st.
[They fight, and young Siward *is slain.*
Macbeth. Thou wast born of woman.
But swords I smile at, weapons laugh to scorn,
Brandish'd by man that's of a woman born. *[Exit.*

Alarums. Enter Macduff.

Macduff. That way the noise is. Tyrant, show thy face!
15 If thou be'st slain, and with no stroke of mine,
My wife and children's ghosts will haunt me still.
I cannot strike at wretched kerns, whose arms
Are hir'd to bear their staves: either thou, Macbeth,
Or else my sword, with an unbatter'd edge,
20 I sheathe again undeeded. There thou shouldst be;

1. Tied me to a stake—Macbeth compares himself to the bear in the popular Elizabethan sport of bear-baiting. The bear was tethered to a stake at the end of a rope about fifteen feet long. Relays of dogs were set on him. The "sport" consisted in watching the ensuing battle.
9. Fearful—To be feared.
17. Kerns—Light-armed foot soldiers.
20. Undeeded—Unused.
20. There—Where the noise is—the noise Macduff notes in the first line of his speech.

By this great clatter, one of greatest note
Seems bruited. Let me find him, fortune!
And more I beg not. [*Exit. Alarums.*

Enter MALCOLM *and old* SIWARD.

Siward. This way, my lord. The castle's gently render'd.
25 The tyrant's people on both sides do fight;
The noble thanes do bravely in the war;
The day almost itself professes yours,
And little is to do.
Malcolm. We have met with foes
That strike beside us.
Siward. Enter, sir, the castle. [*Exeunt. Alarums.*

22. SEEMS BRUITED—Seems to be indicated.
24. GENTLY RENDER'D—Surrendered without much resistance.
25. ON BOTH SIDES—Many have come over to Malcolm.
29. STRIKE BESIDE—Strike aside, that is, do not try to hit us. The sense is: They do not oppose us.

SCENE 8. *Another part of the field.*

Enter MACBETH.

Macbeth. Why should I play the Roman fool, and die
On mine own sword? whiles I see lives, the gashes
Do better upon them.

Enter MACDUFF.

Macduff. Turn, hell-hound, turn!
Macbeth. Of all men else I have avoided thee:
5 But get thee back; my soul is too much charg'd
With blood of thine already.
Macduff. I have no words,
My voice is in my sword; thou bloodier villain
Than terms can give thee out! [*They fight.*
Macbeth. Thou losest labour:
As easy mayst thou the intrenchant air

1. PLAY THE ROMAN FOOL—Kill myself, as Brutus and Cassius do in Shakespeare's *Julius Cæsar*.
2. LIVES—Living foes.
8. THAN TERMS CAN GIVE THEE OUT—Than can be described in words.
8. THOU LOSEST LABOUR—Your efforts to kill me will be useless.
9. INTRENCHANT—The "un-cuttable," that is, in the sense that it cannot be cut apart as a material thing can.

10 With thy keen sword impress as make me bleed:
Let fall thy blade on vulnerable crests;
I bear a charmed life, which must not yield
To one of woman born.
  Macduff.   Despair thy charm;
And let the angel whom thou still hast serv'd
15 Tell thee, Macduff was from his mother's womb
Untimely ripp'd.
  Macbeth. Accursed be that tongue that tells me so,
For it hath cow'd my better part of man!
And by these juggling fiends no more believ'd,
20 That palter with us in a double sense;
That keep the word of promise to our ear,
And break it to our hope. I'll not fight with thee.
  Macduff. Then yield thee, coward,
And live to be the show and gaze o' the time:
25 We'll have thee, as our rarer monsters are,
Painted upon a pole, and underwrit,
"Here may you see the tyrant."
  Macbeth.   I will not yield,
To kiss the ground before young Malcolm's feet,
And to be baited with the rabble's curse.
30 Though Birnam wood be come to Dunsinane,
And thou oppos'd, being of no woman born,
Yet I will try the last: before my body
I throw my warlike shield: lay on, Macduff;
And damn'd be him that first cries, "Hold, enough!"
         [*Exeunt fighting. Alarums.*

  12. MUST NOT YIELD—Does not have to yield.
  13. DESPAIR—Put no trust or hope of safety in.
  14. ANGEL—Demon, spirit.
  15–16. MACDUFF ... RIPP'D—That is, Macduff was not "born" in the ordinary sense of a natural birth. Such an exception had never occurred to Macbeth who had interpreted the witches' prophecy to mean that he need fear no man whatever.
  18. COW'D MY BETTER PART OF MAN—Filled my whole being with fear.
  19. JUGGLING—Deceiving.
  20. PALTER—Equivocate.
  21–22. THAT KEEP ... OUR HOPE—That tell us what sounds all right but does not turn out as they lead us to hope.
  26. PAINTED UPON A POLE—Macduff says: "Yield and be put on exhibition in a cage over which suspended from a pole will be a painted cloth bearing 'Here you may see the tyrant.'"
  32. TRY THE LAST—Try the last resort.

*I will not yield,
To kiss the ground before young
Malcolm's feet.*

Act V, Sc. 8

Retreat. Flourish. Enter with drum and colours, MALCOLM,
old SIWARD, ROSS, *the other* Thanes, *and* Soldiers.

35 *Malcolm.* I would the friends we miss were safe arriv'd.
Siward. Some must go off; and yet, by these I see,
So great a day as this is cheaply bought.
Malcolm. Macduff is missing, and your noble son.
Ross. Your son, my lord, has paid a soldier's debt:
40 He only liv'd but till he was a man;
The which no sooner had his prowess confirm'd
In the unshrinking station where he fought,
But like a man he died.
Siward. Then he is dead?
Ross. Ay, and brought off the field: your cause of sorrow
45 Must not be measur'd by his worth, for then
It hath no end.
Siward. Had he his hurts before?
Ross. Ay, on the front.
Siward. Why then, God's soldier be he!
Had I as many sons as I have hairs,
I would not wish them to a fairer death:
50 And so his knell is knoll'd.
Malcolm. He's worth more sorrow,
And that I'll spend for him.
Siward. He's worth no more:
They say he parted well, and paid his score;
And so God be with him! Here comes newer comfort.

Re-enter MACDUFF, *with* MACBETH'S *head.*

Macduff. Hail, king! for so thou art: behold, where
stands

36. GO OFF—Die.
36. BY THESE I SEE—Those killed, who were evidently few.
41. HIS PROWESS CONFIRM'D—His prowess confirmed the fact that he had reached manhood.
42. IN THE UNSHRINKING STATION—Without shrinking from the place where he fought.
46. BEFORE—On the front.
52. PARTED—Departed.
With MACBETH'S *head*—According to Holinshed, Macduff after "cutting his head from his shoulders, he set it upon a pole."
54. STANDS—The head is on the end of a pike or shaft.

55 Th' usurper's cursed head. The time is free.
I see thee compass'd with thy kingdom's pearl,
That speaks my salutation in their minds;
Whose voices I desire aloud with mine:
Hail, King of Scotland!
    All.   Hail, King of Scotland!   [*Flourish.*
60   *Malcolm.* We shall not spend a large expense of time
Before we reckon with your several loves,
And make us even with you. My thanes and kinsmen,
Henceforth be earls, the first that ever Scotland
In such an honour nam'd. What's more to do,
65 Which would be planted newly with the time,
As calling home our exil'd friends abroad
That fled the snares of watchful tyranny;
Producing forth the cruel ministers
Of this dead butcher and his fiend-like queen,
70 Who, as 'tis thought, by self and violent hands
Took off her life; this, and what needful else
That calls upon us, by the grace of Grace,
We will perform in measure, time, and place:
So, thanks to all at once and to each one,
75 Whom we invite to see us crown'd at Scone.
                                        [*Flourish. Exeunt.*

    55. TIME—Age, the world.
    56. COMPASS'D WITH THY KINGDOM'S PEARL—Surrounded by thy kingdom's pearls, that is, the thanes, who encircle him as the pearls in a crown encircle the head of a king.
    57. THAT SPEAK MY SALUTATION IN THEIR MINDS—Who already regard you, as I shall salute you, that is, as king of Scotland.
    61. RECKON WITH YOUR SEVERAL LOVES—Cast up the account of each of you who has been a friend (in order to see what will make us even with you).
    64–65. WHAT'S MORE TO DO, WHICH WOULD BE PLANTED NEWLY WITH THE TIME—The other things that remain to be done under the new order.
    68. PRODUCING FORTH THE CRUEL MINISTERS—Bringing to justice the agents employed by Macbeth to do his murders.

WILLIAM SHAKESPEARE

ON THE READING AND STUDY OF *MACBETH*

Macbeth Is a Tragedy

A tragedy, in the Shakespearean sense at least, is a play in which the chief character, or hero, is defeated in the thing which he wishes to accomplish or gain, and is killed. In outward aspect there is nothing in this definition to distinguish the true tragedy from the mere *tragedy of blood*, or from the *melodrama*, yet there is a sure distinction between them. First, in the tragedy of blood, in the melodrama, and in the mere "thriller" the interest of the audience is held by events, sensational in themselves, which thrill, startle, or excite. Everyone knows movies of this type, filled with exciting and spectacular train-wrecks, airplane crashes, and hair-raising situations. In the tragedy proper our interest is not so much in the happenings as such, however startling they may be, as in the significance of the events in the lives of the persons concerned. We find ourselves absorbed in the characters of the persons of the drama—watching the effects of their deeds upon their fortunes and upon their souls. Second, in the "thriller" or the "blood and thunder" drama, events occur without much relation to probability and with only the loosest relation to character. In the tragedy events are not made to happen just for their own sake. In the true tragedy events are inextricably bound up with character. They issue out of character, with the impression that, given a certain character, the thing which the person does is inevitable. As a result, we find ourselves interested not so much in the act itself as in the reason for the act and in its consequences.

Melodramatic Elements in *Macbeth*

There are, however, a number of incidents in *Macbeth* which were probably intended to provide thrills. The murder of Banquo and of Macduff's son, and the killing of young Siward takes place on the stage. The murder of Duncan, although not done before the audience, is handled in such a way as to make its horror even more pronounced than it would be had the deed been done in the open. Macbeth himself is killed off the stage, but his bleeding head is borne in on a pole by Macduff. There are, moreover, a number of scenes of sound and fury, not to mention the appearance of the Witches and the Apparitions—sights which must have moved Shakespeare's audience more powerfully than they can us who no longer believe in such things. Yet these things do not make *Macbeth* a mere melodrama. They served their purpose no doubt in providing thrills for the groundlings of the *pit* who delighted in such spectacles, but they are not the things which make the play live, and the best proof of the point is to be drawn from the first murder scene itself. Here, it is not the killing itself which interests us; it is the behavior of Macbeth and Lady Macbeth—it is the murder of Duncan as seen through the souls of Macbeth and Lady Macbeth which the dramatist lays bare before us. This is what holds us spellbound, while pity and terror contend within us, and we reflect upon the awful irreparableness of the deed.

The Characters of Macbeth and Lady Macbeth

Macbeth and Lady Macbeth tend to monopolize the reader's interest. Certainly, no other persons of the drama are so well developed or so insistent in their demands upon our attention. Duncan and his sons, Banquo, and Macduff seem to be in the play only because the action demands other characters. But Macbeth and Lady Macbeth rise above the action, and at times it is possible to become so interested in watching the results of events in them that we almost forget the cause.

At the outset it is necessary that the reader get if possible the conception of Macbeth and Lady Macbeth which Shakespeare had when he conceived the play. In the first place, we may note that all of Shakespeare's great characters are persons of unusual qualities. They are invariably great personages and they have great and remarkable personalities. Macbeth and Lady Macbeth are no exceptions. They are not the "deep-dyed" villains of a blood-and-thunder melodrama, nor petty cutthroats such as the police gather in for vile and miserable killings. There is nothing vulgar or ordinary about either of them, and whatever the emotions with which we witness their great crimes, we are not disgusted with them, nor can we view them with contempt.

Macbeth Written to Be Acted

The student should remember that *Macbeth* was written to be acted. Drama is more than dialogue. It includes the acting demanded by the character interpretation and by the situation, the stage setting and scenery, the lighting effects, and everything that is included under the head of *stage business*—the roll of thunder, alarums, the tramp of approaching soldiers, the commotion of battle scenes, and the like. All of these things are synthesized, or united, to produce the effect which we feel when we witness the production of any scene. A play need not be a great piece of literature, but where it is, as in the case of *Macbeth,* the effect of the language is to heighten and make more vivid the effect produced by these other elements. To get the most, therefore, from reading a play, it is necessary to visualize the performance and to hear it in imagination as well.

Dramatic Construction

The student needs also to have in mind as he reads some knowledge of dramatic construction.

The most important of the constitutive elements according to Aristotle is the *plot,* that is, the organization of the incidents of the story. Often the divisions of the plot are designated as follows:

The *Introduction*—The part which gives the situation out of which the conflict rises, and furnishes the reader or beholder with whatever information he needs in order to understand the play.

The *Rising Action*—The part in which the conflict is developed and increases in intensity and interest. The fortunes of the chief character are in the ascendant. The rising action continues in *Macbeth* even beyond the *crisis,* which is reached with the success of the chief character in the murder of Duncan, to the *turning point* of the play which comes with the announcement that Fleance has escaped.

The *Falling Action*—The part in which the tide of circumstance flows against the chief character, and it is apparent that his fortunes are on the decline.

The *Catastrophe*—The definite defeat of the chief character. In *Macbeth* the catastrophe comes with the death of the chief character, Macbeth. This ends the conflict.

The *Conclusion*—There is in *Macbeth* a brief conclusion after the catastrophe, which brings the play to a close without abruptness.

In the organization and management of the incidents of the play, the dramatist endeavors to keep the interest of his audience by so placing incidents that he creates *suspense* and *climax.* A good illustration of suspense is to be seen in the assassination scene (Act II, Scene 2) where the audience is suddenly aroused by Macbeth's "Who's there? What, ho!" to the possibility that "they have awak'd" (Duncan and the grooms). This is followed very quickly by a climax—the appearance of Macbeth, his hands covered with the blood of Duncan, whose shaken voice announces, "I have done the deed," and then the scene goes on to another point of suspense created by the knocking at the gate. The climax in any situation, scene, or act is the point of greatest intensity. It will be noted that within a scene as in this one, there may seem to be a series or concatenation of climaxes. The so-called climax of the play itself is similarly the point of greatest intensity. It may, but it does not always, coincide with the crisis, or with the turning point.

The *conflict* in a drama, to which allusion has been made, is the struggle between the chief character and the forces opposing him in the achievement of his desires. It is sometimes called the soul of the drama, for it is on this contention that interest centers. There is always an outward, visible conflict between characters or groups of characters, and there is in great drama, as in *Macbeth,* an inward struggle between contending forces in the chief character himself.

In the representation of the conflict, Shakespeare employs a number of methods to produce and to heighten the emotional effect of incidents and scenes. He makes frequent use of *contrast,* alternating exciting incidents and scenes with those which are mild and unexciting. The effect of a mild scene following a tense one is to furnish *relief,* or to let down the tension, and by contrast to make the tense scene more effective. The student will find a number of instances of this in *Macbeth.* Occasionally relief is accompanied by a humorous touch, as in the incident of the drunken Porter, who imagines himself devil-porter at the gate of hell; and no sooner do we set ourselves to laugh than the grim truth of the situation strikes us, making the relief itself reinforce the effect of the preceding scene.

After the crisis and, more especially after the turning point, when interest is likely to lag, will be found scenes and incidents which stir emotions not touched in the first part of the play, as the scene between Lady Macduff and her son, or again there may be, as in Act V, a succession of battle scenes, with their alarms and commotion—scenes which, to judge from the frequency in Shakespeare's plays, must have had a strong appeal for his audience.

The Play as Literature

Whatever the effects produced by the management of scenes and incidents, or by acting and stage business, it should be remembered that *Macbeth* is a great piece of literature. This is the reason why a mere reading of the play can move one so powerfully. Although seeing the play or reading it with a knowledge of the theatre, increases one's appreciation of it, it is nevertheless true that the great appeal of *Macbeth* is in a large measure independent of these things. Scenes like the witch scenes or even the drunken porter scene perhaps require to be seen, for it is difficult for the average reader to feel the effect of them, but the great scenes of the play, such as Scenes 5 and 6 of Act I, which portray the intensity of Lady Macbeth's passion, her fierce energy and her all-compelling will, or Scenes 1 and 2 of Act II, which show Macbeth quite unmanned by terrors of the mind, may be said to *compel* the imagination of the reader and to communicate to him the emotion of the speaker, causing him to identify himself imaginatively with the character and to enter imaginatively into the situation. It is here that the great creative imagination of Shakespeare as a literary artist is manifest.

MACBETH BY ACTS AND SCENES

Act I

Scene 1

In producing this scene how would you set the stage to create a "desert place"? What effects do the stage directions *Thunder and lightning* call for? Should the stage be well lighted? Should the witches be distinctly seen by the audience? How would you have them attired? How should they speak? What action would you suggest to accompany their dialogue? What general effect would you aim to produce in this scene?

What information does the scene convey? What is the mood of the scene? What kind of play does it lead you to expect? Does it arouse curiosity? About what? Do you believe that the scene was more effective in Shakespeare's day than it can possibly be today?

Scene 2

The Gentleman's Magazine for March, 1889, gives the following description of the stage setting used by Charles J. Kean at the Princess Theatre, London: "The scene was discovered in night and silence, a couple of semi-savage armed kerns were on guard, prowling to and fro with stealthy steps. A distant trumpet call was heard, another in reply, another, and yet another; a roll of the drum—an alarum. In an instant the whole camp was alive with kerns and gallowglasses, who circled around the old king and the princes. . . . The Bleeding Sergeant was carried in upon a litter, and the scene was illuminated with the ruddy glare of burning pine-knots." Do you call this a good setting?

What information does the scene convey? What do you learn from it as to Malcolm's ability as a soldier? What does Duncan's closing speech tell you? Does the scene increase interest in any character?

Characterization—Macbeth: What inferences as to the character of Macbeth can you draw from this scene? Find instances of direct characterization. Is Macbeth a better soldier than Malcolm? Is there any evidence that Macbeth is a more able man than Duncan?

Scene 3

What stage setting would you suggest for this scene? What do the stage directions call for? To what does Macbeth refer in his opening remark: "So foul . . . a day I have not seen"? What action on the part of the witches is called for before the entrance of Macbeth? Find lines which tell. What does the scene tell you of the appearance of the witches? How would you have Macbeth differ from Banquo in manner and bearing? Find lines which indicate how the part of Macbeth should be acted, especially after the meeting with the witches.

What information does the scene give? What do the witches promise Macbeth? Banquo? What curiosity does the scene arouse? Are you more interested in the events or in the characters? How would you describe the effect created by this scene?

Characterization—Macbeth: What is the effect of the prophecy upon Macbeth? Is he afraid of the witches? What is his manner toward them? In what tone does he speak to them? Whose questions, those of Banquo or Macbeth, seem the more like the disinterested inquiries prompted by mere natural curiosity? Which seems the more interested in the prophecies? What is the effect upon Macbeth of the announcement that he has been made thane of Cawdor? Does it make him tend to trust the witches? Find lines which indicate that he does. Does the announcement excite him? Does it excite Banquo? What is Banquo's comment? Does he feel that the witches are to be trusted? Find lines which tell. Does Banquo feel that whatever truth the witches speak they are evil? Does Macbeth feel, as Banquo does, that the witches are evil? Does he feel that they are good? Find lines which tell. Which man seems to have the stronger moral character? What evidence is there that Macbeth has an active imagination? What is the "horrid image" that "doth unfix my hair"? What is the effect of this "horrid image" upon him? Why doesn't the same "horrid image" trouble Banquo? Can Macbeth put evil aside? What does he mean by saying: "Come what come may, time and the hour runs through the roughest day"? Does Macbeth practice any deception in this scene? Do you think Macbeth has been turning over in his mind possible means whereby he might attain the throne before the meeting with the witches? Why? Do you think the witches originate evil ambition in Macbeth or is it there when he meets them?

Characterization—Banquo: What characteristics does Banquo have in common with Macbeth? How does he differ from Macbeth? Which do you like the better, Macbeth or Banquo? Can you tell why? Which seems to have the warmer human sympathy and the more fellow-feeling?

Scene 4

Suggest a setting for this scene. What persons other than those mentioned would be on the stage? What is a *Flourish?* What "stage business" would you suggest for the scene? Is Duncan seated or standing? What action accompanies Duncan's speech to Banquo? Compare Macbeth's bearing and manner with Banquo's. What distinction would you make between them? Which is the more natural? Which is the more reserved and formal? How would you have Macbeth act at hearing Duncan announce that he intended Malcolm to succeed him?

What information does this scene give? Is it a dramatic scene? Does it give opportunity for display? Is it more important for what happens or what it shows with respect to developments in the mind of Macbeth? Does the scene keep your curiosity aroused? How? What is the effect of the contrast between Duncan's opinion (find this) and your own opinion of Macbeth?

Characterization—Macbeth, Duncan, Banquo: Of the three, Macbeth, Duncan, and Banquo, which seems the more able man and the one best fitted to be king? Why? Compare Duncan's estimate of Macbeth with your own. Do you find any differences? Is Duncan a good judge of men? Why? Which man, Banquo or Macbeth, seems to possess the more likable personality? Why doesn't Duncan embrace Macbeth as he does Banquo? Read the speeches of Macbeth to Duncan. Do they seem sincere? Are they over-drawn? How do you explain Macbeth's eagerness to bear word of Duncan's coming to Lady Macbeth? Does Macbeth wish the death of Duncan? Has he fully resolved to kill him? If not, what holds him back? Is it conscience or "horrible imaginings"? Or lack of favorable opportunity? Do you think Macbeth will go through with it if Lady Macbeth should say *No?* What is Macbeth's great weakness?

Scene 5

The scene is laid in Macbeth's castle—possibly in the great hall whose walls of heavy masonry are hung with thick tapestries or adorned with trophies of the hunt and of battle. It is a somewhat somber and rather cheerless place. In the foreground there is perhaps a massive table to which Lady Macbeth comes as she reads the letter. But our interest is not so much in the setting as in the characters. This is a famous scene. It has called forth the best efforts of some of the greatest Shakespearean actresses. The scene is a good illustration of the fact that the average person probably gets more from seeing the play well acted than from reading it. The part of Lady Macbeth is difficult to do, and probably easy to over-do. To get the most from the scene one must try to see the characters and hear them as they speak.

Lady Macbeth enters reading the letter. Her face, her manner and her voice betray the excitement which the letter has stirred in her. Her words are charged with emotion. What is her facial expression? the expression in her eyes? What emotions play over her face? In what tone of voice does she speak? How does her voice change as she goes on in her speech? Note particularly her reply to the messenger: "Thou art mad to say it." Is this a usual reply? How is the line spoken? What is Lady Macbeth's manner in her next speech? What state of mind does it indicate? Contrast the manner of Macbeth with that of Lady Macbeth. Which is the more intense? What is Macbeth's manner and tone in the speech: "To-morrow, as he purposes"? What is his manner when he speaks: "We will speak further"? Does he act eager? in full accord with his wife?

What is most interesting in this scene? What is the effect of the scene? Do you infer from this scene that Macbeth and Lady Macbeth have talked of Macbeth's ambition to be king? Do you think that they have ever spoken of the murder of Duncan?

Characterization—Lady Macbeth: Read carefully Lady Macbeth's characterization of her husband. Does she thoroughly understand him? Is it the "milk of human kindness" which holds him back from catching "the nearest way"? Is he without the "illness," or unscrupulousness, which should attend ambition? Is it true that he "wouldst wrongly win"? Does her characterization of him seem but partly accurate? How do you account for Macbeth's reserve in this scene? Has he fully resolved to murder Duncan? If not, what holds him back? What is your opinion of Lady Macbeth? Is she merely a "fiend-like" woman? Do you think she has a conscience? Has she more or less conscience than Macbeth? Read the following comment on Lady Macbeth by Stopford Brooke (*On Ten Plays of Shakespeare*). She "was not by nature a bad woman, but a woman who became bad by long cherishing an ambition for the crown. This desire was made much stronger by that which was good in her—by her love for her husband. From the time she receives Macbeth's letter, she is the victim of one of those unbridled impulses whose outburst is the result of inward thoughts and passions directed to one end, increasing during years of silence, and at last reaching the highest point of expansion. . . . Such an impulse arises quickly into action, and is quickly exhausted. It came on Lady Macbeth in a moment—on the reception of Macbeth's letter. That voiced the possibility of the hopes being realized over which she had brooded so long, and the wild image of the reality seized on her brain. Then comes the news that Duncan is coming to spend the night, and the fury of her impulse falls upon her. She sees, hears, feels nothing but the death of the king. When Macbeth enters, the impulse is doubled by her love for him, by her consciousness that in his thought he is at one with her."

What is your opinion of this estimate of Lady Macbeth? Does it seem to you consistent with the facts of the scene? Would this "impulse" be strong enough to overcome conscience? Is it true that where a person has for a long time cherished the desire for something that a sudden and unexpected opportunity to obtain the thing may lead to immediate action and cause other considerations to be forgotten for the time? Is such action in accord with the "laws of human nature"? Is Lady Macbeth acting contrary to what you would expect in a woman? Is she forcing herself to act thus? Why? Would you call force of will an outstanding characteristic in her? What characteristics do Macbeth and Lady Macbeth have in common? Where do they differ?

Scene 6

Where does this scene take place? What time of day is it? What do the stage directions call for? What "stage business" would you suggest for the scene? How does the manner of Lady Macbeth here differ from her manner in the last scene? What action does Duncan's closing speech call for? What is the atmosphere or mood of the scene? Is it less intense than the preceding scene? Does it let down, or furnish "relief" to the intensity of the last scene? How does it increase pity for Duncan? Does it increase feeling against Macbeth and Lady Macbeth? What contrasts does the scene present?

Characterization: Why do you think that Macbeth keeps within? Does Lady Macbeth act her part well? Can she "look like the innocent flower, but be the serpent under 't"? Do you think Macbeth would have acted the part as well? Why? What words of Duncan and Banquo indicate that each has an eye for beauty? Have you ever noticed this characteristic in Macbeth? Do you think of Macbeth as a man who has a well-developed sense of the beautiful? What would you think his interests might be?

Scene 7

This is another great scene. Macbeth has left the banquet table. Now that the meek and gentle Duncan sits at his board, he is unsettled by the prospect of the assassination. He leaves his guests; he must be alone to think, to turn the matter over in his mind. He cannot let the idea of killing Duncan alone, yet he cannot bring himself to it. He has almost decided against it when Lady Macbeth enters. What does Macbeth do while he is thinking aloud in the opening soliloquy? What is Lady Macbeth's manner when she enters? How does Macbeth voice his objections? Is his manner firm and determined? Which shows the greater intensity, Macbeth or Lady Macbeth? How does Lady Macbeth speak the words "We fail"? How does Macbeth's manner change in the closing speeches?

In what are you most interested in this scene? What is there dramatic in it? What elements of contrast heighten its effect? What feelings does Lady Macbeth play upon in her speeches to Macbeth?

Characterization: Read the speeches of Macbeth carefully. What reasons does he find against the killing of Duncan? Does he anywhere say that it is morally wrong to do so? What does he seem to fear most? Does he speak like a man who has a strong moral sense, or strong conscience? Do you get the impression, nevertheless, that at bottom it is the moral aspect of the assassination which troubles him? What inference as to Macbeth's character do you draw from his ready acquiescence after Lady Macbeth points out that the guilt may be put upon Duncan's chamberlains? Is Lady Macbeth her natural self in this scene? Does it prove her a cold-blooded fiend? Is she without conscience? How do you account for her action in this scene? In what state of mind is she? What is the effect of Macbeth's lukewarmness on her? Is Lady Macbeth essentially feminine or not? Read again Lady Macbeth's characterization of Macbeth at the opening of Scene 5. To what extent does Macbeth's manner here bear out her estimate of him? What evidences does the scene give of Lady Macbeth's force of will? Is there any evidence that Macbeth has a high admiration of Lady Macbeth's spirit? What difference in attitude toward the murder of Duncan do you note in Macbeth and Lady Macbeth?

Act II

Scene 1

Capell's idea of the setting intended it as follows: "A large court, surrounded all or in part by an open gallery; chambers opening into that gallery; the gallery ascended into by stairs, open likewise; with addition of a college-like gateway, into which opens a porter's lodge, appears to have been the Poet's idea of the place of this great action." What lighting effects are called for? What part in this scene calls for great acting?

What effect is created by the moonless, starless night? By Banquo's uneasiness? by his suddenly asking for his sword? by the reference to Duncan's measureless content? by the mention of the weird sisters? by the reference to the signal bell? by the air-drawn dagger smeared with "gouts of blood"? by Macbeth's description of the night? by the ringing of the bell? by the closing lines of Macbeth's speech? How does the scene prepare for the following scene?

Characterization: What contrast between Banquo and Macbeth does the scene present? Do you think that the prophecy of the witches has begun to "work" on Banquo? What instance is there in this scene of Macbeth's imagination? Do you get the impression that Macbeth is forcing himself to do the murder? or is he eager to get Duncan out of the way? Why does Macbeth's imagination trouble him?

Scene 2

Read the setting for Scene 1. Where is Lady Macbeth? In what attitude is she? Where is Macbeth? Can any noise be heard from the chambers? What lighting effect is called for? Where is Macbeth when he calls "Who's there? What, ho!"? In what tone of voice does he call? Why does Lady Macbeth exclaim, "My husband!"? In what tones do they speak?

Should the murder be done in sight of the audience, or is it more effective as Shakespeare has had it done? What is the effect of Lady Macbeth's listening? Of the noises which she hears? Of Macbeth's call: "Who's there? What, ho!"? Of Macbeth's hallucinations? Of Macbeth's repeated reference to his hands? Do you pity Macbeth? Why? What is the effect of the knocking? What is the most terrible moment in this scene? Is it the murder or the effect of it upon Macbeth and Lady Macbeth which makes this scene intense?

Characterization: What contrasts do Macbeth and Lady Macbeth present in this scene? Which has the firmer self-control? the more active imagination? Is there any evidence that it is the moral hideousness of the deed which troubles Macbeth? What is Lady Macbeth's attitude toward the murder? Is Lady Macbeth without conscience, or has she suppressed her scruples by sheer force of will? Why cannot Macbeth take the same attitude toward the crime that Lady Macbeth does? What evidence is there in this scene that Lady Macbeth's love for her husband and her desire to see him have his ambition are at the bottom of her action? Is there anything in the scene to indicate that Lady Macbeth is not without tenderness in her nature? Is Macbeth a coward? Is he "infirm of purpose"?

Scene 3

This scene presents a sudden and somewhat startling contrast. While the agonized cry of Macbeth, "Wake Duncan with thy knocking! I wouldst thou couldst!" yet lingers in our ears, the drunken porter stumbles from his lodge and goes with wavering gait to answer the knocking. As he fumbles at the chains and bolts, he pretends in his befuddled humor to be porter at the gate of hell!

Is there any humor in the episode? What irony is there in the porter's pretending? Does the episode relieve the intensity or not?

Does the porter incident create an illusion of the passage of time? What is the effect of the disturbance in nature recounted by Lennox? What is the effect of Macbeth's announcement that he has killed the grooms? Does it surprise you? Why? What is the effect of Macbeth's extravagant language? Does he talk too much? What is the effect of Lady Macbeth's swoon?

Characterization: Speaking of Lady Macbeth and Macbeth after the murder, Stopford Brooke says, "The next day their ideas are entirely changed. Macbeth, having exhausted all his objections, all his fears, and having irreparably committed his murder is absolutely changed from the trembling, reasoning, white-hearted personage of the murder scene. He is cool, determined, quick in action, ruthless. He sticks at nothing—the murder of the grooms. . . . As great a change comes upon Lady Macbeth. The storm of impulse is over. She has slept it away, or it has died in the silent sleeplessness of that dreadful dawn which brought her down to face the terror-stricken crowd and to faint away. She has awakened to the horror of what she has done; and she returns to her natural self—as she was, before the temptation she had cherished rose into fierce action, and transported her beyond herself." Do you agree with this comment? Does it seem to be borne out by the facts of the scene? Is Lady Macbeth's swoon real or pretended? If it is real, how do you account for it? How does Macbeth's manner here contrast with his manner in the preceding scene? What term does Macduff apply to Lady Macbeth in this scene? What example of imagination does the scene give? Read carefully the speech of Macbeth beginning, "Had I but died an hour before this chance." Is this speech such a one as you would expect from Macbeth? Does it excite your sympathy for him? Is it sincere? Why does Macbeth feel thus?

Scene 4

Where is this scene evidently laid? Is the setting important? What "stage business" would you suggest? What information does the scene give? Does it give the impression of the passage of time? Does it convey the impression that Macbeth will succeed in the long run? In what character are you most interested?

Act III

Scene 1

Suggest a setting and "stage business" for this scene. How does the scene arouse your interest anew?

Characterization: What contrast is there in the action of Macbeth before the murder of Duncan and his action here as he questions Banquo to find out the latter's plans? Does Macbeth see any "air-drawn" dagger here? Does he seem self-possessed? What conclusion do you draw from his matter-of-factness here? What troubles Macbeth now that he is king? Find lines which tell. How does Macbeth's reasoning with the murderers affect your attitude toward him?

What characteristics of Banquo does Macbeth enumerate? Contrast the attitude of Banquo toward Macbeth with that of Macduff toward Macbeth? Does Banquo ever think of the prophecy? Do you think he is being affected by it? How? Do you think Macbeth has any special reason to fear Banquo? Do you think that Banquo is thinking more and more of what the weird sisters promised him?

Scene 2

Where is this scene laid? What is the effect of it upon your interest?

Characterization: Why do you think Lady Macbeth inquires about Banquo? Why does she wish to speak with Macbeth? Is there any evidence that she dislikes being alone? What does the scene tell you of the relationship between the two? Does Macbeth need her longer? Does she seem to possess the energy and vigor which she did in Act I? What has happened to her? Does she seem remorseful? repentant? What does Macbeth mean by saying: "Full of scorpions in my mind"? What troubles Macbeth's peace? How has he changed since you last saw the two together? Does Macbeth show any sign of repentance? Is he hesitating and indecisive now? Why? What evidence is there in the scene of womanly qualities in Lady Macbeth?

Scene 3

Where is the scene laid? What lighting effect does it call for? What effect should the setting aim to produce? Where is Banquo when he first speaks? How has Macbeth's plan failed? Where in this scene would you place the turning point of the play? It has been suggested that Macbeth is the Third Murderer. What arguments can you find for and against this contention?

Scene 4

Describe a setting for the scene. What in the scene would make it spectacular? Where is Lady Macbeth seated? Why does Macbeth "mingle with society"? What is his manner? Does he act as though he had something on his mind? Describe his movements. What action accompanies Macbeth's words: "See, they encounter thee with their hearts' thanks"? Can the audience see the Murderer? Does the audience see any ghost in this scene? What great acting is called for in this scene? What is there dramatic in this scene? Where is the turning point of the play? What information with respect to Macduff does the scene give?

Characterization: Does the sight of Banquo's blood affect Macbeth as did the sight of Duncan's? Why not? Do you feel any pity for Macbeth here? What causes Macbeth's "fit" to come on him again? What does he mean by "my fit"? How does his language to the murderer beginning "Then comes my fit again" differ from his previous speeches? Is it more or less imaginative? Can you explain? What change evidently comes over Macbeth's mood? Contrast the action of Macbeth and Lady Macbeth. Does Lady Macbeth act as you would expect her to? Of what other occasions does this remind you? Is Macbeth a coward? How has he changed from the Macbeth of Act I? Is he repentant?

Scene 5

Is this scene necessary? Would the play lose anything if it were left out? What information does it give? Does it increase your interest? Do you think that it had an appeal to Shakespeare's audience which it does not have for a present day audience?

Scene 6

What kind of humor is found in the speech of Lennox? What information does the scene give? Is it necessary to the plot? Does it increase your interest? Are the characters of interest? In what character does the scene revive your interest? How does it affect your attitude toward Macbeth? What impression does it give as to the ultimate success of the play?

Act IV

Scene 1

Macready, a famous actor, suggested the following opening: "Let the witches be placed in different parts of the cavern. Suppose one at the mouth, intently on the watch; another near the cauldron, cowering over the livid flame . . . the third witch on the side opposite the entrance, seated perhaps on a fragment of stone, her arms folded, and rocking to and fro upon the rock, as it were, in impatience. Let not a word be spoken, till the audience have time to study the picture. 'Tis to the point, and they are sure to feel it, if you will allow them. The familiars —the brinded cat, the hedge-pig, and the Harpier—are supposed to be stationed outside the cavern to give notice of the approach of Hecate. The First Witch hears her familiar: 'Thrice the brinded cat hath mew'd.' The eyes of the other Witches are instantly turned towards her; a pause ensues during which they all remain motionless. The Witch near the cauldron hears her familiar; she starts from her cowering attitude: 'Thrice, and once the hedge-pig whined.' Another pause here. Now at length the Third Witch springs upon her feet: 'Harpier cries'; and then addressing her sisters: ' 'Tis time, 'tis time.' "

What action on the part of the witches follows this opening? Do you call the suggested opening an effective one? What mood or impression does the opening create? What is the effect on your feelings of the ingredients of the charmed pot? What is Macbeth's manner as he enters the cavern? Is he timid or imperious in bearing and speech? With what facial expression do you imagine the witches watched Macbeth? From where did the apparitions rise? How does this scene contribute to the plot? Does it give any new information? What dramatic incidents does it present? How does it keep up your interest in Macbeth's affairs? What is the effect of the announcement that Macduff has fled to England?

Characterization: Do you call Macbeth a coward? Of what is he afraid? What does he most desire? Compare Macbeth's attitude toward murder now with his attitude before the murder of Duncan. Is the killing of Macduff's wife and children worse than the killing of Duncan? Is it necessary? What does their murder indicate as to the effect Macbeth's course is having on his character? Is Macbeth lacking in decision? What new trait is coming to the front in Macbeth under the assurance of the witches? Is his "security" breeding overconfidence and recklessness?

Scene 2

Describe a setting and "stage business" for this scene. Is this scene necessary to the plot? Could it be omitted? What is the effect of it? Does it furnish relief after the preceding scene or does it keep interest keyed up? How does it affect your attitude toward Macbeth? What is the effect on the attention of the warnings by Ross and the Messenger? Would the scene be more effective if Lady Macduff were killed on the stage? Is there any pathos in the scene? any humor?

Characterization: What direct characterization of Macduff occurs in this scene? Do you think him wise in leaving his wife and children? Does Macbeth seem more base than you had supposed him? Is Macduff's son a well-developed character? What characteristics does he exhibit? Do you like him?

Scene 3

Is the setting important in this scene? Does it contribute anything by way of effect? Is this scene essential to the plot? In what way? What effect does the length of the scene have? Does it create an impression of the passage of time? Is this an intense or a mild scene? What effect does it have on your interest? Does it hold you in suspense from seeing what you wish to see? Does it make you more eager to see what happens to Macbeth? What is there pathetic in the scene? What is the effect of Macduff's remark: "He has no children"?

Characterization: When did Malcolm last appear in the play? Do you have a very definite idea of him? How does he compare in force of character, soldierly ability, general competence to govern, with Macbeth? with Macduff? Does he impress you as a forceful character? Do you think he would be a match for Macbeth in battle? in personal combat? What direct characterization of Macbeth is given in this scene? Do any of the sins of which he is said to be guilty surprise you? What evidently has been the effect of Macbeth's crimes upon his character? What impression of Macduff does the scene give you? Do you believe that fear for his own life led him to flee from Scotland, leaving his wife and children? Why does Malcolm talk of revenge when he hears of the murder of Macduff's wife and children? Why doesn't Macduff talk as Malcolm does? Are Macduff's actions true to life?

Act V
Scene 1
How should the setting be made to contribute to the effect of this scene? What lighting effect is called for? What is the manner of the Doctor and the Gentlewoman? In what tones do they talk? What is Lady Macbeth's manner? What actions accompany her various speeches? What change has taken place in her. face? Does Lady Macbeth speak in the same confident, forceful manner which characterized her speeches in Acts I and II? What feeling does the scene create in you? How does it affect your feeling toward Lady Macbeth? What is the most horrible moment in the scene?

Characterization: Speaking of the changes which take place in Macbeth and Lady Macbeth after the murder of Duncan, Stopford Brooke says, "As great a change comes upon Lady Macbeth. The storm of impulse is over. She has slept it away, or it has died in the silent sleeplessness of that dreadful dawn which brought her down to face the terror-stricken crowd, and to faint away. She has awakened to the horror of what she has done; and she returns to her natural self—as she was before the temptation she had cherished rose into fierce action, and transported her beyond herself. . . . Her conscience awakes— 'What's done cannot be undone.' It is only the awakened conscience which dwells in the irreparable past. Macbeth does not. He seeks only to secure the future. She lives in the ghastliness of the past." Does this strike you as an accurate explanation of what has gone on in Lady Macbeth?

Scene 2
Describe a setting and "stage business" for this scene. Note the stage directions. What information does the scene give you? What does it tell you of Macbeth's actions? What contrast is there between this and the preceding scene? Do you wonder what Macbeth will do? What is the effect of the brevity of the scene? (Note that the remaining scenes are short and generally full of action. What is the effect?) Are you getting desirous to see the play end? Why? What do you want to happen?

Characterization—Macbeth: What does the scene tell you of Macbeth's state of mind?

Scene 3
What is Macbeth's manner? Does it show agitation or is he calm and self-possessed? How does the pale face of the servant affect him? How does this scene advance the plot? Does it increase your interest? Is there anything pathetic in it? Does it stir your pity for Lady Macbeth?

Characterization: When did you last see Macbeth and Lady Macbeth together? Do you gather that he has left her much alone since the murder of Duncan? Why has he done so? Has his neglect been intentional? What is his attitude toward her present state? What is it that now animates Macbeth? In what mood or state of mind is he? Why does he put on his armor before it is needed? Has he lost any of his physical courage? of his vigor and energy? Why must he keep doing something? Have you any pity for him? Has your attitude toward either Macbeth or Lady Macbeth changed since the first Act? What are the "thick-coming fancies" which trouble Lady Macbeth? Does Macbeth act as if he were confident in the prophecies?

Scene 4

What setting and "stage business" would you suggest for this scene? Would you have the soldiers hew down the boughs on the stage or not? How would you handle this incident? What incident in the scene rouses your interest? Are you interested in the character Malcolm? What moves you to read on?

Scene 5

Where is this scene laid? What activity is suggested? What is Macbeth's manner? What is the cry? What is the manner of Macbeth as he comments on the death of Lady Macbeth? What is the manner of the messenger? of Macbeth's reply? In which case does Macbeth show the more feeling?

Characterization—Macbeth: Why is it that the cry of the women does not cool Macbeth's senses? When was the time that his "senses would have cool'd to hear a night-shriek"? What effect has his course had on his feelings? What is his attitude toward the death of Lady Macbeth? Is his description of life a true description of life in general or only of his life? Why does he call the messenger "Liar and slave"? What is the effect of the announcement on him? Does his mind tell him that his cause is lost? Why does he not commit suicide? or attempt to make his escape? How does he endeavor to keep his spirits up? Does his physical courage remain with him?

Scene 6

What is the effect of the brevity of this scene? What is there exciting in the scene? Do you want to see a general battle or do you wish to see Macduff meet Macbeth?

Scene 7

What information with respect to Macbeth's fortunes does the scene give? What is there dramatic in the scene? How does Macbeth's victory in this scene raise your interest? Does it make you more desirous to see him meet Macduff?

Scene 8

Why does Macbeth say to Macduff, "my soul is too much charg'd with blood of thine already"? Does it indicate that the murder of Lady Macduff and her children has troubled him? Does he really wish to spare Macduff? Does he refuse to fight Macduff because of cowardice? Has his bravery left him at the last, or is there another explanation? Why does he fight in the end? How is suspense created as to the outcome of the fight? How do you suppose the return of Macduff with Macbeth's head affected Shakespeare's audience?

THE HISTORY OF THE DRAMA IN ENGLAND

The Puritan Age and the Restoration (1625-1700)

Drama during the Puritan Period

After the death of Shakespeare there was a notable decline in dramatic writings. This was due in a large measure to the antagonistic attitude of the Puritans who were becoming stronger and whose influence even in the days of Elizabeth had been exerted against playhouses and stage plays. In their zeal to "purify" conditions in England, the Puritans made concentrated attacks on the theater, and the culmination of their program came in 1642, when by order of the king, all theaters were closed. Rigid enforcement of the edict was provided, including such penalties as property confiscation and public whipping.

The Restoration

With the accession of Charles II in 1660, the theaters were reopened and the drama became again a popular form of amusement. With few exceptions, the new dramas were not of particularly high quality. Two significant changes in theatrical technique were developed, however, which had far-reaching effect on the dramas of later periods. In the discussion of the Elizabethan theater it was noted that feminine characters in plays were always interpreted by boys or men and that scenery was clumsy in character and limited in quantity. During the Restoration, movable scenery came quite generally into use and women were allowed to act feminine rôles for the first time in English history.

John Dryden (1631-1700)

The outstanding figure of the Restoration was John Dryden. His work shows strong influence of his classical training, having in form much that smacks of Latin. He is considered the originator of the use of the heroic couplet for dramatic style. The couplet means merely a group of two lines which rhyme, substituted for the common practice of alternating line rhymes. He also used rhymed poetry more commonly than blank verse, the form employed by so many of his predecessors. Among Dryden's works, the most prominent are, *The Wild Gallant, The Rival Ladies, The Rehearsal, All for Love,* and *Love Triumphant.* It is probably fair to state that in most of his plays, Dryden's technique and literary style were superior to his content.

Other Restoration Dramatists

Dryden's contemporaries were few in number and their work so mediocre that little is known of it. It was largely experimental in adaptation from the foreign, chiefly the French, and in the development of heroic tragedies and comedies. Emphasis seemed to be on improvement of style rather than on originality of plot and characterization. Such names as Thomas Otway, William Wycherley, and William Congreve deserved mere notation here. The last named was especially skillful in characterization and dialogue. His *Way of the World* is judged one of the finest plays of the period.

CLASSICISM AND THE AGE OF JOHNSON (1700-1780)

Sentimental Comedy

The moral tone of many of the plays of the Restoration had been distinctly low. Frequently plays were closed officially or suppressed. Even Dryden with his Puritan background and classical style is reported to have written occasional objectionable plays. As might be expected, reaction was strong, and fear was felt that a second closing edict might result. A certain group of dramatists determined to purify the drama from within and began to write overly sentimental and moralizing plays. This movement gave rise to what is known as "sentimental comedy." Three playwrights are distinctly representative of this movement, Colley Cibber, Sir Richard Steele, and Mrs. Susanna Centlivre. Cibber is best known for *The Careless Husband,* Steele for *The Funeral,* and Mrs. Centlivre for *The Busy-Body.*

Moralizing Plays

Moving on from mere purification of the drama, plays now came to take a definite moralizing attitude. Comedy and tragedy alike tried to bring home to readers and audiences the fundamental laws of life and the sure punishment of evil doing. Farce, a type of comedy depending on mimicry, play on words, mechanical devices, and other not strictly dramatic techniques, came into being during the century. While the moral tone was distinctly improved, dramaturgy cannot, in general, be said to have progressed as an art. Perhaps one of the most redeeming features of the period was the recurring tendency to borrow from the classics—either content or style. This, however, tended to halt the progress of a truly *English* drama.

Samuel Johnson (1709-1784)

The outstanding literary figure of the eighteenth century was Samuel Johnson. So far as is known, he wrote only one play that ever merited public performance, a tragedy called *Irene*. Johnson's real contribution to drama came from his influence on the large group of literary men surrounding him, many of whom were dramatists and actors of the day. The stimulus of the group meetings which he dominated and the criticism and encouragement he gave to his followers account in no small part for the excellence of some of the plays of the latter part of the century.

Oliver Goldsmith (1728-1774) and Richard Sheridan (1751-1816)

The two names most noteworthy in the dramatic literature of the period are those of Oliver Goldsmith and Richard Brinsley Sheridan. Goldsmith, well-known for his poem, *The Deserted Village,* and his novel, *The Vicar of Wakefield,* was an Irishman with a rare literary gift. He was educated in medicine but early showed a preference for writing. He was "discovered" by Johnson and became one of his finest pupils. One of his plays, *The Good Natured Man,* showed the author's marked ability, but his real claim to fame lies in the perennial favorite, *She Stoops to Conquer.* This play achieved instant popularity and is still a favorite with amateurs as well as in professional revivals. It is included in this book for special study.

Sheridan was also born in Ireland and was a strong literary rival of Goldsmith. Three plays, *St. Patrick's Day, The Duenna,* and *The Critic,* showed mild literary ability, but it remained for *The Rivals* and *The School for Scandal,* to demonstrate his genius. These two plays, like *She Stoops to Conquer,* are still great stage and reading favorites.

David Garrick (1717-1779)

Although belonging to the group of minor dramatists insofar as his plays are concerned, David Garrick is so important in the development of the art of producing and acting that he deserves special treatment. With the low ebb of drama had come a low ebb of acting and stage production. Garrick, however, proved to be one of those geniuses found within the most unproductive eras. He was a pupil and close follower of Samuel Johnson during his earlier years, but later an avowed enemy of the master. Appearing in an unimportant rôle in an obscure play, and later in several Shakespearean rôles, he commanded instant acclaim as an actor. Turning to producing, he met equal success. His best works as a dramatist are *Lethe, The Guardian,* and *Irish Widow.*

Minor Dramatists of the Period

Many of the dramatic writers of Johnson's time wrote only one or two plays of genuine literary merit and are treated without detail here. Special mention should be made of John Hughes, author of *The Siege of Damascus;* Edward Young, best known for three plays, *Busiris, Revenge,* and *The Brothers;* George Lillo, five of whose plays were fairly successful stage pieces; Henry Fielding, author of *Tom Thumb* and *Author's Farce;* Edward Moore, author of a single success, *The Gamester;* Samuel Foote, author of several puppet shows; and John Home, author of *Douglas,* one of the best plays of the age.

A Drama of the Classic Age

SHE STOOPS TO CONQUER

OLIVER GOLDSMITH

The Background of the Play: The subject of *She Stoops to Conquer* is vastly different from that of *Macbeth*. It is not historical in nature nor so heavy in style. The play is a light comedy based on the foibles of human nature and the amusing weaknesses of so-called "society." Its purpose is entertainment.

DRAMATIS PERSONÆ

SIR CHARLES MARLOW
YOUNG MARLOW, *his son*
HARDCASTLE
HASTINGS
TONY LUMPKIN
DIGGORY
MRS. HARDCASTLE
MISS HARDCASTLE
MISS NEVILLE
MAID
Landlord, Servants, etc

ACT I

SCENE 1. *A chamber in an old-fashioned house.*

Enter MRS. HARDCASTLE *and* MR. HARDCASTLE.

Mrs. Hardcastle. I vow, Mr. Hardcastle, you're very particular. Is there a creature in the whole country but ourselves that does not take a trip to town now and then, to rub off the rust a little? There's the two Miss Hoggs, and our neighbor Mrs. Grigsby, go to take a month's polishing every winter.

Hardcastle. Ay, and bring back vanity and affectation to last them the whole year. I wonder why London cannot keep its own fools at home. In my time, the follies of the town crept slowly among us, but now they travel faster than a stage-coach. Its fopperies come down not only as inside passengers, but in the very basket.[1]

Mrs. Hardcastle. Ay, your times were fine times indeed; you have been telling us of them for many a long year. Here we live in an old rumbling[2] mansion, that looks for all the world like an inn, but that[3] we never see company. Our best visitors are old Mrs. Oddfish, the curate's wife, and little Cripplegate, the lame dancing-master; and all our entertainment your old stories of Prince Eugene and the Duke of Marlborough.[4] I hate such old-fashioned trumpery.

Hardcastle. And I love it. I love everything that's old: old friends, old times, old manners, old books, old wine; and, I believe, Dorothy, [*Taking her hand.*] you'll own I have been pretty fond of an old wife.

Mrs. Hardcastle. Lord, Mr. Hardcastle, you're forever at your Dorothys and your old wives. You may be a Darby, but I'll be no Joan,[5] I promise you. I'm not so old as you'd make me by more than one good year. Add twenty to twenty and make money of that.

---

[1] BASKET—A basket or receptacle for baggage which was fastened at the rear of the stage-coach.

[2] RUMBLING—Rambling.

[3] BUT THAT—Except that.

[4] PRINCE EUGENE AND THE DUKE OF MARLBOROUGH—Prince Eugene was an Austrian general who served in the Turkish campaigns of 1716–17 and the Duke of Marlborough was an English general who fought with Prince Eugene.

[5] DARBY . . . JOAN—Darby and Joan were characters in a popular ballad. They are representative of any happy old couple, devoted to each other.

ELD

Hardcastle. Let me see; twenty added to twenty—makes just fifty and seven!

Mrs. Hardcastle. It's false, Mr. Hardcastle; I was but twenty when I was brought to bed of Tony, that I had by Mr. Lumpkin, my first husband; and he's not come to years of discretion [6] yet.

Hardcastle. Nor ever will, I dare answer for him. Ay, you have taught him finely!

Mrs. Hardcastle. No matter. Tony Lumpkin has a good fortune. My son is not to live by his learning. I don't think a boy wants much learning to spend fifteen hundred [7] a year.

Hardcastle. Learning, quotha! [8] a mere composition of tricks and mischief!

Mrs. Hardcastle. Humor, my dear; nothing but humor. Come, Mr. Hardcastle, you must allow the boy a little humor.

Hardcastle. I'd sooner allow him a horse-pond! If burning the footmen's shoes, frighting the maids, and worrying the kittens, be humor, he has it. It was but yesterday he fastened my wig to the back of my chair, and when I went to make a bow, I popped my bald head in Mrs. Frizzle's face.

Mrs. Hardcastle. And I am to blame? The poor boy was always too sickly to do any good. A school would be his death. When he comes to be a little stronger, who knows what a year or two's Latin may do for him?

Hardcastle. Latin for him! A cat and fiddle! No, no; the alehouse and the stable are the only schools he'll ever go to.

Mrs. Hardcastle. Well, we must not snub the poor boy now, for I believe we shan't have him long among us. Anybody that looks in his face may see he's consumptive.

Hardcastle. Ay, if growing too fat be one of the symptoms.

Mrs. Hardcastle. He coughs sometimes.

Hardcastle. Yes, when his liquor goes the wrong way.

Mrs. Hardcastle. I'm actually afraid of his lungs.

Hardcastle. And truly, so am I; for he sometimes whoops like a speaking-trumpet— [TONY *hallooing behind the scenes.*] —Oh, there he goes—a very consumptive figure, truly!

---

[6] YEARS OF DISCRETION—An age when one is able to judge between what is right and what is wrong.

[7] FIFTEEN HUNDRED—Fifteen hundred pounds.

[8] QUOTHA—Indeed.

Enter Tony, *crossing the stage.*

Mrs. Hardcastle. Tony, where are you going, my charmer? Won't you give papa and I a little of your company, lovey?

Tony. I'm in haste, mother; I cannot stay.

Mrs. Hardcastle. You shan't venture out this raw evening, my dear; you look most shockingly.

Tony. I can't stay, I tell you. *The Three Pigeons* expects me down every moment. There's some fun going forward.

Hardcastle. Ay, the alehouse, the old place; I thought so.

Mrs. Hardcastle. A low, paltry set of fellows.

Tony. Not so low, neither. There's Dick Muggins, the exciseman; Jack Slang, the horse-doctor; little Aminadab, that grinds the music-box; and Tom Twist, that spins the pewter platter.

Mrs. Hardcastle. Pray, my dear, disappoint them for one night at least.

Tony. As for disappointing them, I should not so much mind; but I can't abide to disappoint myself.

Mrs. Hardcastle. [*Detaining him.*] You shan't go.

Tony. I will, I tell you.

Mrs. Hardcastle. I say you shan't.

Tony. We'll see which is the strongest, you or I.

[*Exit, hauling her out.*

Hardcastle. [*Alone.*] Ay, there goes a pair that only spoil each other. But is not the whole age in a combination to drive sense and discretion out of doors? There's my pretty darling, Kate; the fashions of the times have almost infected her too. By living a year or two in town, she is as fond of gauze and French frippery as the best of them.

Enter Miss Hardcastle.

Blessings on my pretty innocence! Dressed out as usual, my Kate. Goodness! what a quantity of superfluous silk hast thou got about thee, girl! I could never teach the fools of this age that the indigent world could be clothed out of the trimmings of the vain.

Miss Hardcastle. You know our agreement, sir. You allow me the morning to receive and pay visits, and to dress in my own manner; and in the evening I put on my housewife's dress to please you.

Hardcastle. Well, remember, I insist on the terms of our agreement; and, by the bye, I believe I shall have occasion to try your obedience this very evening.

Miss Hardcastle. I protest, sir, I don't comprehend your meaning.

Hardcastle. Then, to be plain with you, Kate, I expect the young gentleman I have chosen to be your husband from town this very day. I have his father's letter, in which he informs me his son is set out, and that he intends to follow himself shortly after.

Miss Hardcastle. Indeed! I wish I had known something of this before. Bless me, how shall I behave? It's a thousand to one I shan't like him; our meeting will be so formal, and so like a thing of business, that I shall find no room for friendship or esteem.

Hardcastle. Depend upon it, child, I'll never control your choice; but Mr. Marlow, whom I have pitched upon, is the son of my old friend, Sir Charles Marlow, of whom you have heard me talk so often. The young gentleman has been bred a scholar, and is designed for an employment in the service of his country. I am told he's a man of an excellent understanding.

Miss Hardcastle. Is he?

Hardcastle. Very generous.

Miss Hardcastle. I believe I shall like him.

Hardcastle. Young and brave.

Miss Hardcastle. I'm sure I shall like him.

Hardcastle. And very handsome.

Miss Hardcastle. My dear papa, say no more, [*Kissing his hand.*] he's mine, I'll have him!

Hardcastle. And, to crown all, Kate, he's one of the most bashful and reserved young fellows in all the world.

Miss Hardcastle. Eh! you have frozen me to death again. That word *reserved* has undone all the rest of his accomplishments. A reserved lover, it is said, always makes a suspicious husband.

Hardcastle. On the contrary, modesty seldom resides in a breast that is not enriched with nobler virtues. It was the very feature in his character that first struck me.

Miss Hardcastle. He must have more striking features to catch me, I promise you. However, if he be so young, so handsome, and so everything as you mention, I believe he'll do still; I think I'll have him.

Hardcastle. Ay, Kate, but there is still an obstacle. It's more than an even wager he may not have you.

Miss Hardcastle. My dear papa, why will you mortify one so? Well, if he refuses, instead of breaking my heart at his indifference, I'll only break my glass [9] for its flattery, set my cap to some newer fashion, and look out for some less difficult admirer.

Hardcastle. Bravely resolved! In the mean time, I'll go prepare the servants for his reception; as we seldom see company, they want as much training as a company of recruits the first day's muster. [*Exit.*

Miss Hardcastle. [*Alone.*] Lud, this news of papa's puts me all in a flutter. Young, handsome; these he put last, but I put them foremost. Sensible, good-natured; I like all that. But then, reserved and sheepish; that's much against him. Yet, can't he be cured of his timidity by being taught to be proud of his wife? Yes; and can't I—but I vow I'm disposing of the husband, before I have secured the lover.

Enter Miss Neville.

Miss Hardcastle. I'm glad you're come, Neville, my dear. Tell me, Constance, how do I look this evening? Is there anything whimsical [10] about me? Is it one of my well-looking days, child? Am I in face [11] to-day?

Miss Neville. Perfectly, my dear. Yet, now I look again—bless me!—surely no accident has happened among the canary birds or the gold-fishes? Has your brother or the cat been meddling? Or has the last novel been too moving?

Miss Hardcastle. No; nothing of all this. I have been threatened—I can scarce get it out—I have been threatened with a lover.

Miss Neville. And his name—
Miss Hardcastle. Is Marlow.

---

[9] GLASS—Mirror.
[10] WHIMSICAL—Queer, freakish.
[11] IN FACE—Looking my best.

Miss Neville. Indeed!

Miss Hardcastle. The son of Sir Charles Marlow.

Miss Neville. As I live, the most intimate friend of Mr. Hastings, my admirer. They are never asunder. I believe you must have seen him when we lived in town.

Miss Hardcastle. Never.

Miss Neville. He's a very singular character, I assure you. Among women of reputation and virtue, he is the modestest man alive; but his acquaintance give [12] him a very different character among creatures of another stamp: you understand me.

Miss Hardcastle. An odd character, indeed! I shall never be able to manage him. What shall I do? Pshaw, think no more of him, but trust to occurrences for success. But how goes on your own affair, my dear? Has my mother been courting you for my brother Tony, as usual?

Miss Neville. I have just come from one of our agreeable *tête-à-têtes*. She has been saying a hundred tender things, and setting off her pretty monster as the very pink of perfection.

Miss Hardcastle. And her partiality is such that she actually thinks him so. A fortune like yours is no small temptation. Besides, as she has the sole management of it, I'm not surprised to see her unwilling to let it go out of the family.

Miss Neville. A fortune like mine, which chiefly consists in jewels, is no such mighty temptation. But at any rate, if my dear Hastings be but constant, I make no doubt [13] to be too hard for her at last. However, I let her suppose that I am in love with her son; and she never once dreams that my affections are fixed upon another.

Miss Hardcastle. My good brother holds out stoutly. I could almost love him for hating you so.

Miss Neville. It [14] is a good-natured creature at bottom, and I'm sure would wish to see me married to anybody but himself. But my aunt's bell rings for our afternoon's walk round the improvements. *Allons.*[15] Courage is necessary, as our affairs are critical.

Miss Hardcastle. Would it were bed-time, and all were well.

[*Exeunt.*

---

[12] ACQUAINTANCE GIVE—We should say "acquaintances give."
[13] I MAKE NO DOUBT—I will undoubtedly.
[14] IT—He.
[15] *Allons*—Let's go.

Scene 2. *An alehouse room.*

Several shabby fellows with punch and tobacco; Tony *at the head of the table, a little higher than the rest; a mallet in his hand.*

Omnes.[1] Hurrea, hurrea, hurrea, bravo!
First Fellow. Now, gentlemen, silence for a song. The Squire is going to knock himself down[2] for a song.
Omnes. Ay, a song, a song!
Tony. Then I'll sing you, gentleman, a song I made upon this alehouse, *The Three Pigeons.*

SONG

Let schoolmasters puzzle their brain,
  With grammar, and nonsense, and learning;
Good liquor, I stoutly maintain,
  Gives *genus*[3] a better discerning.
Let them brag of their heathenish gods,
  Their Lethes, their Styxes, and Stygians,[4]
Their quis, and their quæs, and their quods,[5]
  They're all but a parcel of pigeons.[6]
      Toroddle, toroddle, toroll!

[1] *Omnes*—All.
[2] Knock himself down—A term from auctioneering. Tony has a mallet in his hand.   [3] *Genus*—Man.
[4] Lethes, Styxes and Stygians—Rivers of Hades. Here used to ridicule the classics and classical references.
[5] Quis . . . Quæs . . . Quods—A ridicule of Latin.
[6] Pigeons—Dupes; easily deceived.

When Methodist preachers [7] come down,
  A-preaching that drinking is sinful,
I'll wager the rascals a crown,
  They always preach best with a skinful.
But when you come down with your pence,
  For a slice of their scurvy religion,
I'll leave it to all men of sense,
  That you, my good friend, are the pigeon.
              Toroddle, toroddle, toroll!

Then come, put the jorum about,[8]
  And let us be merry and clever,
Our hearts and our liquors are stout,
  Here's the Three Jolly Pigeons for ever.
Let some cry up woodcock or hare,
  Your bustards, your ducks, and your widgeons; [9]
But of all the birds in the air,
  Here's a health to the Three Jolly Pigeons.
              Toroddle, toroddle, toroll!

Omnes. Bravo, bravo!
First Fellow. The Squire has got some spunk in him.
Second Fellow. I loves to hear him sing, bekeays he never gives us nothing that's low.
Third Fellow. Oh, hang anything that's low, I cannot bear it!
Fourth Fellow. The genteel thing is the genteel thing any time; if so be that a gentleman bees in a concatenation accordingly.[10]
Third Fellow. I like the maxum [11] of it, Master Muggins. What though I am obligated to dance a bear, a man may be a gentleman for all that. May this be my poison, if my bear ever dances but to the very genteelest of tunes: *Water Parted,* or *The minuet in Ariadne.*[12]
Second Fellow. What a pity it is the Squire is not come to his own.[13] It would be well for all the publicans within ten miles round of him.

---

[7] METHODIST PREACHERS—In Goldsmith's time the Methodists, a new religious sect, were ridiculed by the adherents of the Established Church.

[8] PUT THE JORUM ABOUT—Pass the drinking bowl.

[9] BUSTARDS; WIDGEONS—Game birds.

[10] IF SO BE . . . ACCORDINGLY—There is no meaning to these words—this fellow is talking nonsense.

[11] MAXUM—Maxim.

[12] *Water Parted* or *The minuet in Ariadne*—Songs in operas of the day.

[13] COME TO HIS OWN—Of age; come into his property.

Tony. Ecod, and so it would, Master Slang. I'd then show what it was to keep choice of company.

Second Fellow. Oh, he takes after his own father for that. To be sure, old Squire Lumpkin was the finest gentleman I ever set my eyes on. For winding the straight horn,[14] or beating a thicket for a hare, he never had his fellow. It was a saying in the place, that he kept the best horses and dogs in the whole county.

Tony. Come, my boys, drink about and be merry, for you pay no reckoning. Well, Stingo, what's the matter?

Enter Landlord.

Landlord. There be two gentlemen in a post-chaise at the door. They have lost their way upo' the forest; and they are talking something about Mr. Hardcastle.

Tony. As sure as can be, one of them must be the gentleman that's coming down to court my sister. Do they seem to be Londoners?

Landlord. I believe they may. They look woundily[15] like Frenchmen.

Tony. Then desire them to step this way, and I'll set them right in a twinkling. [*Exit* Landlord.] Gentlemen, as they may n't be good enough company for you, step down for a moment, and I'll be with you in the squeezing of a lemon.

[*Exeunt mob.*

Tony. [*Alone.*] Father-in-law[16] has been calling me whelp and hound this half year. Now, if I pleased, I could be so revenged upon the old grumbletonian. But then I'm afraid,— afraid of what? I shall soon be worth fifteen hundred a year, and let him frighten me out of *that* if he can.

Enter Landlord, *conducting* MARLOW *and* HASTINGS.

Marlow. What a tedious, uncomfortable day have we had of it! We were told it was but forty miles across the country, and we have come above threescore!

Hastings. And all, Marlow, from that unaccountable reserve

[14] WINDING THE STRAIGHT HORN—Blowing the coaching horn.
[15] WOUNDILY—Very much; exceedingly.
[16] FATHER-IN-LAW—Step-father.

of yours, that would not let us inquire more frequently on the way.

Marlow. I own, Hastings, I am unwilling to lay myself under an obligation to every one I meet, and often stand the chance of an unmannerly answer.

Hastings. At present, however, we are not likely to receive any answer.

Tony. No offence, gentlemen. But I'm told you have been inquiring for one Mr. Hardcastle, in these parts. Do you know what part of the country you are in?

Hastings. Not in the least, sir, but should thank you for information.

Tony. Nor the way you came?

Hastings. No, sir; but if you can inform us—

Tony. Why, gentlemen, if you know neither the road you are going, nor where you are, nor the road you came, the first thing I have to inform you is, that—you have lost your way.

Marlow. We wanted no ghost to tell us that.

Tony. Pray, gentlemen, may I be so bold as to ask the place from whence you came?

Marlow. That's not necessary towards directing us where we are to go.

Tony. No offence; but question for question is all fair, you know.—Pray, gentlemen, is not this same Hardcastle a cross-grained, old-fashioned, whimsical fellow, with an ugly face, a daughter, and a pretty son?

Hastings. We have not seen the gentleman, but he has the family you mention.

Tony. The daughter, a tall, trapesing, trolloping, talkative maypole; the son, a pretty, well-bred, agreeable youth, that everybody is fond of?

Marlow. Our information differs in this. The daughter is said to be well-bred, and beautiful; the son an awkward booby, reared up and spoiled at his mother's apron-string.

Tony. He-he-hem!—Then, gentlemen, all I have to tell you is, that you won't reach Mr. Hardcastle's house this night, I believe.

Hastings. Unfortunate!

Tony. It's a long, dark, boggy, dirty, dangerous way. Stingo, tell the gentlemen the way to Mr. Hardcastle's; [*Winking upon the* Landlord.] Mr. Hardcastle's of Quagmire Marsh, you understand me.

Landlord. Master Hardcastle's! Lack-a-daisy, my masters, you're come a deadly deal wrong! When you came to the bottom of the hill, you should have crossed down Squash-lane.

Marlow. Cross down Squash-lane?

Landlord. Then you were to keep straight forward, till you came to four roads.

Marlow. Come to where four roads meet?

Tony. Ay; but you must be sure to take only one of them.

Marlow. Oh sir, you're facetious.

Tony. Then, keeping to the right, you are to go sideways till you come upon Crack-skull Common: there you must look sharp for the track of the wheel, and go forward till you come to farmer Murrain's barn. Coming to the farmer's barn, you are to turn to the right, and then to the left, and then to the right about again, till you find out the old mill—

Marlow. Zounds, man! we could as soon find out the longitude! [17]

Hastings. What's to be done, Marlow?

Marlow. This house promises but a poor reception; though perhaps the landlord can accommodate us.

Landlord. Alack, master, we have but one spare bed in the whole house.

Tony. And to my knowledge, that's taken up by three lodgers already. [*After a pause in which the rest seem disconcerted.*] I have hit it. Don't you think, Stingo, our landlady could accommodate the gentlemen by the fireside, with—three chairs and a bolster? [18]

Hastings. I hate sleeping by the fireside.

Marlow. And I detest your three chairs and a bolster.

Tony. You do, do you?—then, let me see—what if you go on a mile further, to the Buck's Head; the old Buck's Head on the hill, one of the best inns in the whole country?

Hastings. O ho! so we have escaped an adventure for this night, however.

---

[17] LONGITUDE—In Goldsmith's day, determining the longitude was a difficult matter.

[18] BOLSTER—Cushion.

Landlord. [*Apart to* Tony.] Sure, you be n't sending them to your father's as an inn, be you?

Tony. Mum, you fool you. Let *them* find that out. [*To them.*] You have only to keep on straight forward, till you come to a large old house by the road side. You'll see a pair of large horns over the door. That's the sign. Drive up the yard, and call stoutly about you.

Hastings. Sir, we are obliged to you. The servants can't miss the way?

Tony. No, no; but I tell you, though, the landlord is rich, and going to leave off business; so he wants to be thought a gentleman, saving your presence, he! he! he! He'll be for giving you his company; and, ecod, if you mind him, he'll persuade you that his mother was an alderman and his aunt a justice of peace.

Landlord. A troublesome old blade, to be sure; but a keeps as good wines and beds as any in the whole country.

Marlow. Well, if he supplies us with these, we shall want no further connection. We are to turn to the right, did you say?

Tony. No, no; straight forward. I'll just step myself, and show you a piece of the way. [*To the* Landlord.] Mum!

Landlord. Ah, bless your heart, for a sweet, pleasant, mischievous son. [*Exeunt.*

ACT II

Scene 1. *An old-fashioned house.*

Enter Hardcastle, *followed by three or four awkward* Servants.

Hardcastle. Well, I hope you are perfect in the table exercise I have been teaching you these three days. You all know your posts and your places, and can show that you have been used to good company, without ever stirring from home.

Omnes. Ay, ay.

Hardcastle. When company comes, you are not to pop out and stare, and then run in again, like frighted rabbits in a warren.[1]

Omnes. No, no.

Hardcastle. You, Diggory, whom I have taken from the barn, are to make a show[2] at the side-table; and you, Roger,

---

[1] Warren—A place for keeping such animals as rabbits.
[2] Make a show—Appear.

whom I have advanced from the plough, are to place yourself behind my chair. But you're not to stand so, with your hands in your pockets. Take your hands from your pockets, Roger; and from your head, you blockhead, you. See how Diggory carries his hands. They're a little too stiff, indeed, but that's no great matter.

Diggory. Ay, mind how I hold them. I learned to hold my hands this way, when I was upon drill for the militia. And so being upon drill—

Hardcastle. You must not be so talkative, Diggory. You must be all attention to the guests. You must hear us talk, and not think of talking; you must see us drink, and not think of drinking; you must see us eat, and not think of eating.

Diggory. By the laws, your worship, that's parfectly unpossible. Whenever Diggory sees yeating[3] going forward, ecod, he's always wishing for a mouthful himself.

Hardcastle. Blockhead! Is not a bellyful in the kitchen as good as a bellyful in the parlor? Stay your stomach with that reflection.

Diggory. Ecod, I thank your worship, I'll make a shift[4] to stay my stomach with a slice of cold beef in the pantry.

Hardcastle. Diggory, you are too talkative.—Then, if I happen to say a good thing, or tell a good story at table, you must not all burst out a-laughing, as if you made part of the company.

Diggory. Then, ecod, your worship must not tell the story of the Ould Grouse in the gun-room; I can't help laughing at that—he! he! he!—for the soul of me. We have laughed at that these twenty years—ha! ha! ha!

Hardcastle. Ha! ha! ha! The story is a good one. Well, honest Diggory, you may laugh at that; but still remember to be attentive. Suppose one of the company should call for a glass of wine, how will you behave? A glass of wine, sir, if you please [*To* DIGGORY.] —Eh, why, don't you move?

Diggory. Ecod, your worship, I never have courage till I see the eatables and drinkables brought upo' the table, and then I'm as bauld[5] as a lion.

Hardcastle. What, will nobody move?

---

[3] YEATING—Eating.
[4] MAKE A SHIFT—Contrive with difficulty.
[5] BAULD—Bold.

First Servant. I'm not to leave this pleace.
Second Servant. I'm sure it's no pleace of mine.
Third Servant. Nor mine, for sartain.
Diggory. Wauns,[6] and I'm sure it canna be mine.
Hardcastle. You numskulls! and so while, like your betters, you are quarrelling for places, the guests must be starved. Oh you dunces! I find I must begin all over again—But don't I hear a coach drive into the yard? To your posts, you blockheads! I'll go in the meantime, and give my old friend's son a hearty reception at the gate. [*Exit* HARDCASTLE.
Diggory. By the elevens, my pleace is quite gone out my head!
Roger. I know that my pleace is to be everywhere!
First Servant. Where the devil is mine?
Second Servant. My pleace is to be nowhere at all; and so I'ze go about my business!

[*Exeunt* Servants, *running about as if frighted, different ways. Enter* Servant *with candles, showing in* MARLOW *and* HASTINGS.

Servant. Welcome, gentlemen, very welcome! This way.
Hastings. After the disappointments of the day, welcome once more, Charles, to the comforts of a clean room and a good fire. Upon my word, a very well-looking house; antique but creditable.
Marlow. The usual fate of a large mansion. Having first ruined the master by good house-keeping,[7] it at last comes to levy contributions as an inn.
Hastings. As you say, we passengers are to be taxed to pay all these fineries. I have often seen a good sideboard, or a marble chimney-piece, though not actually put in the bill, inflame a reckoning[8] confoundedly.
Marlow. Travellers, George, must pay in all places. The only difference is that in good inns you pay dearly for luxuries; in bad inns you are fleeced and starved.
Hastings. You have lived pretty much among them. In truth, I have been often surprised, that you who have seen so much of the world, with your natural good sense, and your many opportunities, could never yet acquire a requisite share of assurance.

---

[6] WAUNS—Zounds.
[7] GOOD HOUSE-KEEPING—Probably the meaning is, high cost of upkeep.
[8] INFLAME A RECKONING—Increase a bill.

Marlow. The Englishman's malady. But tell me, George, where could I have learned that assurance you talk of? My life has been chiefly spent in a college or an inn, in seclusion from that lovely part of the creation that chiefly teach men confidence. I don't know that I was ever familiarly acquainted with a single modest woman, except my mother. But among females of another class, you know—

Hastings. Ay, among them you are impudent enough, of all conscience.

Marlow. They are of *us,* you know.

Hastings. But in the company of women of reputation I never saw such an idiot, such a trembler; you look for all the world as if you wanted an opportunity of stealing out of the room.

Marlow. Why, man, that's because I *do* want to steal out of the room. Faith, I have often formed a resolution to break the ice, and rattle away at any rate. But I don't know how, a single glance from a pair of fine eyes has totally overset my resolution. An impudent fellow may counterfeit modesty, but I'll be hanged if a modest man can ever counterfeit impudence.

Hastings. If you could but say half the fine things to them, that I have heard you lavish upon the barmaid of an inn, or even a college bed-maker—

Marlow. Why, George, I can't say fine things to them. They freeze, they petrify me. They may talk of a comet, or a burning mountain, or some such bagatelle; but to me a modest woman, dressed out in all her finery, is the most tremendous object of the whole creation.

Hastings. Ha! ha! ha! At this rate, man, how can you ever expect to marry?

Marlow. Never; unless, as among kings and princes, my bride were to be courted by proxy. If, indeed, like an Eastern bridegroom, one were to be introduced to a wife he never saw before, it might be endured. But to go through all the terrors of a formal courtship, together with the episode of aunts, grandmothers, and cousins, and at last to blurt out the broad staring question of "Madam, will you marry me?" No, no, that's a strain much above me, I assure you.

Hastings. I pity you. But how do you intend behaving to

the lady you are come down to visit at the request of your father?

Marlow. As I behave to all other ladies. Bow very low; answer "Yes" or "No" to all her demands. But for the rest, I don't think I shall venture to look in her face till I see my father's again.

Hastings. I'm surprised that one who is so warm a friend can be so cool a lover.

Marlow. To be explicit, my dear Hastings, my chief inducement down was to be instrumental in forwarding your happiness, not my own. Miss Neville loves you, the family don't know you; as my friend, you are sure of a reception, and let honor do the rest.

Hastings. My dear Marlow! But I'll suppress the emotion. Were I a wretch, meanly seeking to carry off a fortune, you should be the last man in the world I would apply to for assistance. But Miss Neville's person is all I ask, and that is mine, both from her deceased father's consent, and her own inclination.

Marlow. Happy man! you have talents and art to captivate any woman. I'm doomed to adore the sex, and yet to converse with the only part of it I despise. This stammer in my address, and this awkward unprepossessing visage of mine, can never permit me to soar above the reach of a milliner's 'prentice, or one of the Duchesses of Drury Lane.[9] Pshaw! this fellow here to interrupt us.

Enter HARDCASTLE.

Hardcastle. Gentlemen, once more you are heartily welcome. Which is Mr. Marlow? Sir, you are heartily welcome. It's not my way, you see, to receive my friends with my back to the fire. I like to give them a hearty reception, in the old style, at my gate. I like to see their horses and trunks taken care of.

Marlow. [*Aside.*] He has got our names from the servants already. [*To him.*] We approve your caution and hospitality, sir. [*To* HASTINGS.] I have been thinking, George, of changing

---

[9] DUCHESSES OF DRURY LANE—Drury Lane was the theatrical section of London. This expression means the women who frequent the vicinity of the theaters.

our travelling dresses in the morning. I am grown confoundedly ashamed of mine.

Hardcastle. I beg, Mr. Marlow, you'll use no ceremony in this house.

Hastings. I fancy, Charles, you're right; the first blow is half the battle. I intend opening the campaign with the white and gold.

Hardcastle. Mr. Marlow—Mr. Hastings—gentlemen, pray be under no restraint in this house. This is Liberty-hall, gentlemen. You may do just as you please here.

Marlow. Yet, George, if we open the campaign too fiercely at first, we may want ammunition before it is over. I think to reserve the embroidery to secure a retreat.

Hardcastle. Your talking of a retreat, Mr. Marlow, puts me in mind of the Duke of Marlborough, when we went to besiege Denain.[10] He first summoned the garrison—

Marlow. Don't you think the *ventre d'or*[11] waistcoat will do with the plain brown?

Hardcastle. He first summoned the garrison, which might consist of about five thousand men—

Hastings. I think not: brown and yellow mix but very poorly.

Hardcastle. I say, gentlemen, as I was telling you, he summoned the garrison, which might consist of about five thousand men—

Marlow. The girls like finery.

Hardcastle. Which might consist of about five thousand men, well appointed with stores, ammunition, and other implements of war. "Now," says the Duke of Marlborough to George Brooks, that stood next to him—you must have heard of George Brooks—"I'll pawn my dukedom," says he, "but I take that garrison without spilling a drop of blood." So—

Marlow. What, my good friend, if you gave us a glass of punch in the meantime; it would help us to carry on the siege with vigor.

Hardcastle. Punch, sir! [*Aside.*] This is the most unaccountable kind of modesty I ever met with!

Marlow. Yes, sir, punch! A glass of warm punch, after our

---

[10] BESIEGE DENAIN—One of the "old stories of Prince Eugene and the Duke of Marlborough" which Hardcastle so liked to tell.
[11] *Ventre d'or*—Gold-front.

journey, will be comfortable. This is Liberty-hall, you know.

Hardcastle. Here's cup,[12] sir.

Marlow. [*Aside.*] So this fellow, in his Liberty-hall, will only let us have just what he pleases.

Hardcastle. [*Taking the cup.*] I hope you'll find it to your mind. I have prepared it with my own hands, and I believe you'll own the ingredients are tolerable. Will you be so good as to pledge me, sir? Here, Mr. Marlow, here is to our better acquaintance. [*Drinks.*]

Marlow. [*Aside.*] A very impudent fellow this! But he's a character, and I'll humor him a little. Sir, my service to you. [*Drinks.*]

Hastings. [*Aside.*] I see this fellow wants to give us his company, and forgets that he's an innkeeper before he has learned to be a gentleman.

Marlow. From the excellence of your cup, my old friend, I suppose you have a good deal of business in this part of the country. Warm work, now and then, at elections, I suppose.

Hardcastle. No, sir, I have long given that work over. Since our betters have hit upon the expedient of electing each other, there is no business "for us that sell ale."

Hastings. So, then, you have no turn for politics, I find.

Hardcastle. Not in the least. There was a time, indeed, I fretted myself about the mistakes of government, like other people; but, finding myself every day grow more angry, and the government growing no better, I left it to mend itself. Since that, I no more trouble my head about Hyder Ally, or Ally Cawn,[13] than about Ally Croaker.[14] Sir, my service to you.

Hastings. So that with eating above stairs, and drinking below, with receiving your friends within, and amusing them without, you lead a good, pleasant, bustling life of it.

Hardcastle. I do stir about a great deal, that's certain. Half the differences of the parish are adjusted in this very parlor.

Marlow. [*After drinking.*] And you have an argument in

---

[12] HERE'S CUP—A cup is a beverage made from sweetened and flavored liquor. Hardcastle had prepared the drink but it was evidently not the punch which Marlow had asked for. Hence, Marlow's next speech.

[13] HYDER ALLY, OR ALLY CAWN—Probably a reference to Hyder Ali Khan, a regent of India who fought against the British.

[14] ALLY CROAKER—An Irish song, popular at the time. There is a humorous play on the word Ally intended.

your cup, old gentleman, better than any in Westminster-hall.[15]

Hardcastle. Ay, young gentleman, that, and a little philosophy.

Marlow. [*Aside.*] Well, this is the first time I ever heard of an innkeeper's philosophy.

Hastings. So, then, like an experienced general, you attack them on every quarter. If you find their reason manageable, you attack it with your philosophy; if you find they have no reason, you attack them with this. Here's your health, my philosopher. [*Drinks.*]

Hardcastle. Good, very good, thank you; ha! ha! ha! Your generalship puts me in mind of Prince Eugene, when he fought the Turks at the battle of Belgrade.[16] You shall hear—

Marlow. Instead of the battle of Belgrade, I believe it's almost time to talk about supper. What has your philosophy got in the house for supper?

Hardcastle. For supper, sir! [*Aside.*] Was ever such a request to a man in his own house!

Marlow. Yes, sir, supper, sir; I begin to feel an appetite. I shall make devilish work to-night in the larder, I promise you.

Hardcastle. [*Aside.*] Such a brazen dog sure never my eyes beheld. [*To him.*] Why, really, sir, as for supper, I can't well tell. My Dorothy and the cook-maid settle these things between them. I leave these kind of things entirely to them.

Marlow. You do, do you?

Hardcastle. Entirely. By the bye, I believe they are in actual consultation upon what's for supper this moment in the kitchen.

Marlow. Then I beg they'll admit *me* as one of their privy council.[17] It's a way I have got. When I travel I always choose to regulate my own supper. Let the cook be called. No offence, I hope, sir.

Hardcastle. Oh, no, sir, none in the least; yet I don't know how; our Bridget, the cook-maid, is not very communicative upon these occasions. Should we send for her, she might scold us all out of the house.

Hastings. Let's see your list of the larder,[18] then. I ask it

---

[15] WESTMINSTER-HALL—A famous hall in London, for centuries the scene of law trials.
[16] BELGRADE—The scene of one of Prince Eugene's victories.
[17] PRIVY-COUNCIL—Secret council.
[18] LIST OF THE LARDER—Bill-of-fare, menu.

as a favor. I always match my appetite to my bill of fare.

Marlow. [*To* Hardcastle, *who looks at them with surprise.*] Sir, he's very right, and it's my way, too.

Hardcastle. Sir, you have a right to command here. Here, Roger, bring us the bill of fare for to-night's supper; I believe it's drawn out. Your manner, Mr. Hastings, puts me in mind of my uncle, Colonel Wallop. It was a saying of his, that no man was sure of his supper till he had eaten it.

Hastings. [*Aside.*] All upon the high ropes! His uncle a colonel! We shall soon hear of his mother being a justice of peace. But let's hear the bill of fare.

Marlow. [*Perusing.*] What's here? For the first course; for the second course; for the dessert. Zounds, sir, do you think we have brought down the whole Joiners' Company, or the Corporation of Bedford,[19] to eat up such a supper? Two or three little things, clean and comfortable, will do.

Hastings. But let's hear it.

Marlow. [*Reading.*] "For the first course, at the top,[20] a pig, and prune sauce."

Hastings. Away with your pig, I say!

Marlow. And away with your prune sauce, say I!

Hardcastle. And yet, gentlemen, to men that are hungry, pig with prune sauce is very good eating.

Marlow. "At the bottom,[21] a calf's tongue and brains."

Hastings. Let your brains be knocked out, my good sir; I don't like them.

Marlow. Or you may clap them on a plate by themselves. I do.

Hardcastle. [*Aside.*] Their impudence confounds me. [*To them.*] Gentlemen, you are my guests; make what alterations you please. Is there anything else you wish to retrench, or alter, gentlemen?

Marlow. "Item: a pork pie, a boiled rabbit and sausages, a Florentine,[22] a shaking pudding,[23] and a dish of tiff—taff—taffety cream!"[24]

---

[19] Joiners' Company ... Corporation of Bedford—Town officials were supposed to have enormous appetites.
[20] At the top—At the head of the table.
[21] At the bottom—At the foot of the table.
[22] Florentine—A large apple pie drenched with ale.
[23] Shaking pudding—A jelly.
[24] Taffety cream—Probably a smooth, creamy pudding.

Hastings. Confound your made [25] dishes! I shall be as much at a loss in this house as at a green and yellow dinner [26] at the French Ambassador's table. I'm for plain eating.

Hardcastle. I'm sorry, gentleman, that I have nothing you like; but if there be anything you have a particular fancy to—

Marlow. Why, really, sir, your bill of fare is so exquisite, that any one part of it is full as good as another. Send us what you please. So much for supper. And now to see that our beds are aired, and properly taken care of.

Hardcastle. I entreat you'll leave all that to me. You shall not stir a step.

Marlow. Leave that to you! I protest, sir, you must excuse me; I always look to these things myself.

Hardcastle. I must insist, sir, you'll make yourself easy on that head.

Marlow. You see I am resolved on it. [*Aside.*] A very troublesome fellow this, as ever I met with.

Hardcastle. Well, sir, I'm resolved at least to attend you. [*Aside.*] This may be modern modesty, but I never saw anything look so like old-fashioned impudence.

[*Exeunt* Marlow *and* Hardcastle.

Hastings. [*Alone.*] So I find this fellow's civilities begin to grow troublesome. But who can be angry at those assiduities which are meant to please him? Ha! what do I see? Miss Neville, by all that's happy!

Enter Miss Neville.

Miss Neville. My dear Hastings! To what unexpected good fortune, to what accident, am I to ascribe this happy meeting?

Hastings. Rather let me ask the same question, as I could never have hoped to meet my dearest Constance at an inn.

Miss Neville. An inn! sure you mistake! My aunt, my guardian, lives here. What could induce you to think this house an inn?

Hastings. My friend, Mr. Marlow, with whom I came down, and I, have been sent here as to an inn, I assure you. A young

---

[25] Made—Fancy.
[26] Green and yellow—A dinner carrying out a green and yellow color scheme. The meaning here is a fancy, elaborate meal.

I never saw anything look so like old-fashioned impudence.

fellow, whom we accidentally met at a house hard by, directed us hither.

Miss Neville. Certainly it must be one of my hopeful cousin's tricks, of whom you have heard me talk so often; ha! ha! ha!

Hastings. He whom your aunt intends for you? he of whom I have such just apprehensions?

Miss Neville. You have nothing to fear from him, I assure you. You'd adore him if you knew how heartily he despises me. My aunt knows it too, and has undertaken to court me for him, and actually begins to think she has made a conquest.

Hastings. Thou dear dissembler! You must know, my Constance, I have just seized this happy opportunity of my friend's visit here to get admittance into the family. The horses that carried us down are now fatigued with their journey, but they'll soon be refreshed; and then, if my dearest girl will trust in her faithful Hastings, we shall soon be landed in France, where even among slaves the laws of marriage are respected.[27]

Miss Neville. I have often told you that, though ready to obey you, I yet should leave my little fortune behind with reluctance. The greatest part of it was left me by my uncle, the India director, and chiefly consists in jewels. I have been for some time persuading my aunt to let me wear them. I fancy I'm very near succeeding. The instant they are put into my possession, you shall find me ready to make them and myself yours.

Hastings. Perish the baubles! Your person is all I desire. In the meantime, my friend Marlow must not be let into [28] his mistake. I know the strange reserve of his temper is such that, if abruptly informed of it, he would instantly quit the house before our plan was ripe for execution.

Miss Neville. But how shall we keep him in the deception? Miss Hardcastle is just returned from walking; what if we still continue to deceive him?—This, this way— [*They confer.*]

---

[27] LAWS OF MARRIAGE—At this time the English marriage laws were very strict, requiring marriage according to the forms of the Established Church preceded by publication of banns. The laws also demand the assent of parents or guardians to the marriage of minors, so many couples went to Scotland (at that time not affected by the law) and to France to be married.

[28] LET INTO—Informed of.

Enter MARLOW.

Marlow. The assiduities of these good people tease me beyond bearing. My host seems to think it ill manners to leave me alone, and so he claps not only himself but his old-fashioned wife on my back.[29] They talk of coming to sup with us too; and then, I suppose, we are to run the gauntlet through all the rest of the family.—What have we got here?

Hastings. My dear Charles! Let me congratulate you! The most fortunate accident! Who do you think is just alighted?

Marlow. Cannot guess.

Hastings. Our mistresses, boy, Miss Hardcastle and Miss Neville. Give me leave to introduce Miss Constance Neville to your acquaintance. Happening to dine in the neighborhood, they called on their return to take fresh horses here. Miss Hardcastle has just stepped into the next room, and will be back in an instant. Wasn't it lucky? eh!

Marlow. [*Aside.*] I have just been mortified enough of all conscience, and here comes something to complete my embarrassment.

Hastings. Well, but wasn't it the most fortunate thing in the world?

Marlow. Oh, yes. Very fortunate—a most joyful encounter—But our dresses, George, you know, are in disorder—What if we should postpone the happiness till to-morrow?—to-morrow at her own house—It will be every bit as convenient—and rather more respectful—To-morrow let it be.   [*Offering to go.*

Hastings. By no means, sir. Your ceremony will displease her. The disorder of your dress will show the ardor of your impatience. Besides, she knows you are in the house, and will permit you to see her.

Marlow. How shall I support it?[30] Hem! hem! Hastings, you must not go. You are to assist me, you know. I shall be confoundedly ridiculous. Yet, hang it, I'll take courage! Hem!

Hastings. Pshaw, man! it's but the first plunge, and all's over! She's but a woman, you know.

Marlow. And of all women, she that I dread most to encounter!

[29] HE CLAPS . . . ON MY BACK—He thrusts not only himself but his old-fashioned wife on me.
[30] SUPPORT IT—Carry it through.

Enter MISS HARDCASTLE, *as returned from walking, a bonnet, etc.*

Hastings. [*Introducing them.*] Miss Hardcastle, Mr. Marlow; I'm proud of bringing two persons of such merit together, that only want to know, to esteem each other.

Miss Hardcastle. [*Aside.*] Now for meeting my modest gentleman with a demure face, and quite in his own manner. [*After a pause, in which he appears very uneasy and disconcerted.*] I'm glad of your safe arrival, sir. I'm told you had some accidents by the way.

Marlow. Only a few, madam. Yes, we had some. Yes, madam, a good many accidents, but should be sorry—madam— or rather glad of any accidents—that are so agreeably concluded. Hem!

Hastings. [*To him.*] You never spoke better in your whole life. Keep it up, and I'll insure you the victory.

Miss Hardcastle. I'm afraid you flatter, sir. You that have seen so much of the finest company, can find little entertainment in an obscure corner of the country.

Marlow. [*Gathering courage.*] I have lived, indeed, in the world, madam; but I have kept very little company. I have been but an observer upon life, madam, while others were enjoying it.

Miss Neville. But that, I am told, is the way to enjoy it at last.

Hastings. [*To him.*] Cicero never spoke better. Once more, and you are confirmed in assurance for ever.

Marlow. [*To him.*] Hem! stand by me then, and when I'm down, throw in a word or two to set me up again.

Miss Hardcastle. An observer, like you, upon life, were, I fear, disagreeably employed, since you must have had much more to censure than to approve.

Marlow. Pardon me, madam. I was always willing to be amused. The folly of most people is rather an object of mirth than uneasiness.

Hastings. [*To him.*] Bravo, bravo. Never spoke so well in your whole life. Well, Miss Hardcastle, I see that you and Mr. Marlow are going to be very good company. I believe our being here will but embarrass the interview.

Marlow. Not in the least, Mr. Hastings. We like your company of all things. [*To him.*] Zounds, George, sure you won't go? How can you leave us?

Hastings. Our presence will but spoil conversation, so we'll retire to the next room. [*To him.*] You don't consider, man, that we are to manage a little *tête-à-tête* of our own.

[*Exeunt* HASTINGS *with* MISS NEVILLE.

Miss Hardcastle. [*After a pause.*] But you have not been wholly an observer, I presume, sir. The ladies, I should hope, have employed some part of your addresses.

Marlow. [*Relapsing into timidity.*] Pardon me, madam, I—I—I—as yet have studied—only—to—deserve them.

Miss Hardcastle. And that, some say, is the very worst way to obtain them.

Marlow. Perhaps so, madam. But I love to converse only with the more grave and sensible part of the sex.—But I'm afraid I grow tiresome.

Miss Hardcastle. Not at all, sir; there is nothing I like so much as grave conversation myself; I could hear it for ever. Indeed I have often been surprised how a man of sentiment [31] could ever admire those light, airy pleasures, where nothing reaches the heart.

Marlow. It's—a disease—of the mind, madam. In the variety of tastes there must be some who, wanting a relish—for—um—a—um—

Miss Hardcastle. I understand you, sir. There must be some who, wanting a relish for refined pleasures, pretend to despise what they are incapable of tasting.

Marlow. My meaning, madam, but infinitely better expressed. And I can't help observing—a—

Miss Hardcastle. [*Aside.*] Who could ever suppose this fellow impudent upon some occasions! [*To him.*] You were going to observe, sir,—

Marlow. I was observing, madam—I protest, madam, I forget what I was going to observe.

Miss Hardcastle. [*Aside.*] I vow and so do I. [*To him.*] You were observing, sir, that in this age of hypocrisy,—something about hypocrisy, sir.

Marlow. Yes, madam. In this age of hypocrisy there are few who, upon strict inquiry, do not—a—a—

---

[31] SENTIMENT—Judgment, proper feelings.

Miss Hardcastle. I understand you perfectly, sir.

Marlow. [*Aside.*] Egad! and that's more than I do myself!

Miss Hardcastle. You mean that in this hypocritical age there are few who do not condemn in public what they practice in private; and think they pay every debt to virtue when they praise it.

Marlow. True, madam; those who have most virtue in their mouths have least of it in their bosoms. But I'm sure I tire you, madam.

Miss Hardcastle. Not in the least, sir; there's something so agreeable and spirited in your manner, such life and force,—pray, sir, go on.

Marlow. Yes, madam, I was saying—that there are some occasions—when a total want of courage, madam, destroys all the —and puts us—upon—a—a—a—

Miss Hardcastle. I agree with you entirely; a want of courage upon some occasions, assumes the appearance of ignorance, and betrays us when we most want to excel. I beg you'll proceed.

Marlow. Yes, madam. Morally speaking, madam—But I see Miss Neville expecting [32] us in the next room. I would not intrude for the world.

Miss Hardcastle. I protest, sir, I never was more agreeably entertained in all my life. Pray go on.

Marlow. Yes, madam, I was—But she beckons us to join her. Madam, shall I do myself the honor to attend you?

Miss Hardcastle. Well, then, I'll follow.

Marlow. [*Aside.*] This pretty, smooth dialogue has done for me. [*Exit.*

Miss Hardcastle. [*Alone.*] Ha! ha! ha! Was there ever

[32] EXPECTING—Awaiting.

such a sober, sentimental [33] interview? I'm certain he scarce looked in my face the whole time. Yet the fellow, but for his unaccountable bashfulness, is pretty well, too. He has good sense, but then so buried in his fears, that it fatigues one more than ignorance. If I could teach him a little confidence, it would be doing somebody that I know of a piece of service. But who is that somebody? That, faith, is a question I can scarce answer. [*Exit.*

Enter TONY *and* MISS NEVILLE, *followed by* MRS. HARDCASTLE *and* HASTINGS.

Tony. What do you follow me for, cousin Con? I wonder you're not ashamed to be so very engaging.

Miss Neville. I hope, cousin, one may speak to one's own relations, and not be to blame.

Tony. Ay, but I know what sort of a relation you want to make me, though; but it won't do. I tell you, cousin Con, it won't do; so I beg you'll keep your distance. I want no nearer relationship. [*She follows, coquetting him to the back scene.*

Mrs. Hardcastle. Well, I vow, Mr. Hastings, you are very entertaining. There's nothing in the world I love to talk of so much as London, and the fashions, though I was never there myself.

Hastings. Never there! You amaze me! From your air and manner, I concluded you had been bred all your life either at Ranelagh, St. James's, or Tower Wharf.[34]

Mrs. Hardcastle. Oh, sir, you're only pleased to say so. We country persons can have no manner at all. I'm in love with the town, and that serves to raise me above some of our neighboring rustics; but who can have a manner, that has never seen the Pantheon, the Grotto Gardens, the Borough,[35] and such places, where the nobility chiefly resort? All I can do is to enjoy London at second-hand. I take care to know every *tête-à-tête* from

---

[33] SENTIMENTAL INTERVIEW—One of proper sentiments, sensible.

[34] RANELAGH, ST. JAMES'S, OR TOWER WHARF—Ranelagh and St. James were fashionable places in London, but Tower Wharf was a wretched section of the city. Since Mrs. Hardcastle is ignorant of the places mentioned, Hastings is amusing himself by mentioning Tower Wharf.

[35] PANTHEON, THE GROTTO GARDENS, THE BOROUGH—Mrs. Hardcastle unconsciously matches Hastings' wit, for although the Pantheon and Grotto Gardens were fashionable resorts, the Borough was far from fashionable.

the *Scandalous Magazine*,[36] and have all the fashions, as they come out, in a letter from the two Miss Rickets of Crooked-lane. Pray, how do you like this head,[37] Mr. Hastings?

Hastings. Extremely elegant and *degagée*,[38] upon my word, madam. Your friseur [39] is a Frenchman, I suppose?

Mrs. Hardcastle. I protest, I dressed it myself from a print in the *Ladies' Memorandum-book* [40] for the last year.

Hastings. Indeed! Such a head in a side-box, at the playhouse, would draw as many gazers as my Lady Mayoress at a city ball.

Mrs. Hardcastle. I vow, since inoculation began,[41] there is no such thing to be seen as a plain woman; so one must dress a little particular, or one may escape in the crowd.

Hastings. But that can never be your case, madam, in any dress. [*Bowing.*]

Mrs. Hardcastle. Yet what signifies my dressing, when I have such a piece of antiquity by my side as Mr. Hardcastle? All I can say will never argue down a single button from his clothes.[42] I have often wanted him to throw off his great flaxen wig, and where he was bald to plaster it over, like my Lord Pately, with powder.

Hastings. You are right, madam; for, as among the ladies there are none ugly, so among the men there are none old.

Mrs. Hardcastle. But what do you think his answer was? Why, with his usual Gothic [43] vivacity, he said I only wanted him to throw off his wig to convert it into a *tête* [44] for my own wearing.

Hastings. Intolerable! At your age you may wear what you please, and it must become you.

[36] *Scandalous Magazine*—Many of the magazines of the day gave daring bits of scandal and gossip about well-known men and women.
[37] HEAD—Headdress, style of hairdressing.
[38] *Degagée*—Graceful.
[39] FRISEUR—Hairdresser.
[40] *Ladies' Memorandum-book*—A well-known diary or almanac, published once a year.
[41] SINCE INOCULATION BEGAN—Inoculation, or vaccination for smallpox, was introduced in 1721. The meaning of the sentence is probably "since inoculation began there are no scarred faces (plain women).
[42] ARGUE DOWN A SINGLE BUTTON FROM HIS CLOTHES—Probably the meaning is "change his style of clothes."
[43] GOTHIC—Rude, uncouth.
[44] *Tête*—Head. Here, headdress.

Mrs. Hardcastle. Pray, Mr. Hastings, what do you take to be the most fashionable age about town?

Hastings. Some time ago forty was all the mode; but I'm told the ladies intend to bring up fifty for the ensuing winter.

Mrs. Hardcastle. Seriously? Then I shall be too young for the fashion.

Hastings. No lady begins now to put on jewels till she's past forty. For instance, Miss there, in a polite circle, would be considered as a child, as a mere maker of samplers.

Mrs. Hardcastle. And yet, Mistress Niece thinks herself as much a woman, and is as fond of jewels, as the oldest of us all.

Hastings. Your niece, is she? And that young gentleman,—a brother of yours, I should presume?

Mrs. Hardcastle. My son, sir. They are contracted to each other. Observe their little sports. They fall in and out ten times a day, as if they were man and wife already. [*To them.*] Well, Tony, child, what soft things are you saying to your cousin Constance this evening?

Tony. I have been saying no soft things; but that it's very hard to be followed about so. Ecod! I've not a place in the house now that's left to myself, but the stable.

Mrs. Hardcastle. Never mind him, Con, my dear. He's in another story behind your back.

Miss Neville. There's something generous in my cousin's manner. He falls out before faces, to be forgiven in private.

Tony. That's a confounded crack.

Mrs. Hardcastle. Ah, he's a sly one! Don't you think they're like each other about the mouth, Mr. Hastings? The Blenkinsop mouth to a T. They're of a size, too. Back to back, my pretties, that Mr. Hastings may see you. Come, Tony.

Tony. You had as good not make me, I tell you. [*Measuring.*]

Miss Neville. Oh, lud! he has almost cracked my head.

Mrs. Hardcastle. Oh, the monster! For shame, Tony. You a man, and behave so!

Tony. If I'm a man, let me have my fortin. Ecod, I'll not be made a fool of no longer.

Mrs. Hardcastle. Is this, ungrateful boy, all that I'm to get for the pains I have taken in your education? I that have rocked you in your cradle, and fed that pretty mouth with a spoon! Did not I work that waistcoat to make you genteel?

Did not I prescribe for you every day, and weep while the receipt was operating?

Tony. Ecod! you had reason to weep, for you have been dosing me ever since I was born. I have gone through every receipt in the Complete Huswife [45] ten times over; and you have thoughts of coursing me through Quincy [46] next spring. But, Ecod! I tell you, I'll not be made a fool of no longer.

Mrs. Hardcastle. Wasn't it all for your good, viper? Wasn't it all for your good?

Tony. I wish you'd let me and my good alone, then. Snubbing this way when I'm in spirits! If I'm to have any good, let it come of itself; not to keep dinging it, dinging it into one so.

Mrs. Hardcastle. That's false; I never see you when you're in spirits. No, Tony, you then go to the alehouse or kennel. I'm never to be delighted with your agreeable wild notes, unfeeling monster!

Tony. Ecod! mamma, your own notes are the wildest of the two.

Mrs. Hardcastle. Was ever the like? But I see he wants to break my heart; I see he does.

Hastings. Dear madam, permit me to lecture the young gentleman a little. I'm certain I can persuade him to his duty.

Mrs. Hardcastle. Well, I must retire. Come, Constance, my love. You see, Mr. Hastings, the wretchedness of my situation. Was ever poor woman so plagued with a dear, sweet, pretty, provoking, undutiful boy?

[*Exeunt* Mrs. Hardcastle *and* Miss Neville.

Tony. [*Singing.*] "There was a young man riding by, and fain would have his will. Rang do didlo dee."—Don't mind her. Let her cry. It's the comfort of her heart. I have seen her and sister cry over a book for an hour together; and they said they liked the book the better the more it made them cry.

Hastings. Then you're no friend to the ladies, I find, my pretty young gentleman?

Tony. That's as I find 'um.

Hastings. Not to her of your mother's choosing, I dare answer? And she appears to me a pretty, well-tempered girl.

Tony. That's because you don't know her as well as I. Ecod!

---

[45] The Complete Huswife—A ladies' magazine of the period.
[46] Quincy—The author of a home medical book.

I know every inch about her; and there's not a more bitter, cantanckerous toad in all Christendom.

Hastings. [*Aside.*] Pretty encouragement, this, for a lover.

Tony. I have seen her since the height of that. She has as many tricks as a hare in a thicket, or a colt the first day's breaking.

Hastings. To me she appears sensible and silent.

Tony. Ay, before company. But when she's with her playmates, she's as loud as a hog in a gate.

Hastings. But there is a meek modesty about her that charms me.

Tony. Yes, but curb her never so little, she kicks up, and you're flung in a ditch.

Hastings. Well, but you must allow her a little beauty.—Yes, you must allow her some beauty.

Tony. Bandbox! She's all a made-up thing, mun. Ah! could you but see Bet Bouncer of these parts, you might then talk of beauty. Ecod! she has two eyes as black as sloes, and cheeks as broad and red as a pulpit cushion. She'd make two of she.

Hastings. Well, what say you to a friend that would take this bitter bargain off your hands?

Tony. Anan! [47]

Hastings. Would you thank him that would take Miss Neville, and leave you to happiness and your dear Betsy?

Tony. Ay; but where is there such a friend, for who would take *her?*

Hastings. I am he. If you but assist me, I'll engage to whip her off to France, and you shall never hear more of her.

Tony. Assist you! Ecod I will, to the last drop of my blood. I'll clap a pair of horses to your chaise that shall trundle you off in a twinkling, and maybe get you a part of her fortin besides, in jewels, that you little dream of.

Hastings. My dear Squire, this looks like a lad of spirit.

Tony. Come along then, and you shall see more of my spirit before you have done with me. [*Singing.*]

> We are the boys
> That fears no noise
> Where the thundering cannons roar.

[*Exeunt.*

[47] ANAN!—Anon! Here the meaning is probably "Capital!", "Fine!"

ACT III

Scene 1. *The house.*

Enter Hardcastle.

Hardcastle. What could my old friend Sir Charles mean by recommending his son as the modestest young man in town? To me he appears the most impudent piece of brass that ever spoke with a tongue. He has taken possession of the easy chair by the fire-side already. He took off his boots in the parlor, and desired me to see them taken care of. I'm desirous to know how his impudence affects my daughter. She will certainly be shocked at it.

Enter Miss Hardcastle, *plainly dressed.*

Hardcastle. Well, my Kate, I see you have changed your dress, as I bid you; and yet, I believe, there was no great occasion.

Miss Hardcastle. I find such a pleasure, sir, in obeying your commands, that I take care to observe them without ever debating their propriety.

Hardcastle. And yet, Kate, I sometimes give you some cause, particularly when I recommended my *modest* gentleman to you as a lover to-day.

Miss Hardcastle. You taught me to expect something extraordinary, and I find the original exceeds the description.

Hardcastle. I was never so surprised in my life! He has quite confounded all my faculties.

Miss Hardcastle. I never saw anything like it; and a man of the world, too!

Hardcastle. Ay, he learned it all abroad; what a fool was I, to think a young man could learn modesty by travelling. He might as soon learn wit at a masquerade.

Miss Hardcastle. It seems all natural to him.

Hardcastle. A good deal assisted by bad company and a French dancing-master.

Miss Hardcastle. Sure, you mistake, papa. A French dancing-master could never have taught him that timid look—that awkward address—that bashful manner.

ELD

Hardcastle. Whose look, whose manner, child?

Miss Hardcastle. Mr. Marlow's: his *mauvaise honte*,[1] his timidity, struck me at the first sight.

Hardcastle. Then your first sight deceived you; for I think him one of the most brazen first sights that ever astonished my senses.

Miss Hardcastle. Sure, sir, you rally![2] I never saw any one so modest.

Hardcastle. And can you be serious! I never saw such a bouncing, swaggering puppy since I was born. Bully Dawson[3] was but a fool to him.

Miss Hardcastle. Surprising! He met me with a respectful bow, a stammering voice, and a look fixed on the ground.

Hardcastle. He met me with a loud voice, a lordly air, and a familiarity that made my blood freeze again.

Miss Hardcastle. He treated me with diffidence and respect; censured the manners of the age; admired the prudence of girls that never laughed; tired me with apologies for being tiresome; then left the room with a bow, and "Madam, I would not for the world detain you."

Hardcastle. He spoke to me as if he knew me all his life before; asked twenty questions, and never waited for an answer; interrupted my best remarks with some silly pun; and when I was in my best story of the Duke of Marlborough and Prince Eugene, he asked if I had not a good hand at making punch. Yes, Kate, he asked your father if he was a maker of punch!

Miss Hardcastle. One of us must certainly be mistaken.

Hardcastle. If he be what he has shown himself, I'm determined he shall never have my consent.

Miss Hardcastle. And if he be the sullen thing I take him, he shall never have mine.

Hardcastle. In one thing then we are agreed—to reject him.

Miss Hardcastle. Yes—but upon conditions. For if you should find him less impudent, and I more presuming; if you find him more respectful, and I more importunate—I don't know—the fellow is well enough for a man—Certainly we don't meet many such at a horse-race in the country.

---

[1] *Mauvaise honte*—Shyness, bashfulness.
[2] RALLY—Banter, ridicule.
[3] BULLY DAWSON—A notorious braggart or swashbuckler of the time.

Hardcastle. If we should find him so—But that's impossible. The first appearance has done my business. I'm seldom deceived in that.

Miss Hardcastle. And yet there may be many good qualities under that first appearance.

Hardcastle. Ay, when a girl finds a fellow's outside to her taste, she then sets about guessing the rest of his furniture. With her a smooth face stands for good sense, and a genteel figure for every virtue.

Miss Hardcastle. I hope, sir, a conversation begun with a compliment to my good sense, won't end with a sneer at my understanding!

Hardcastle. Pardon me, Kate. But if young Mr. Brazen can find the art of reconciling contradictions, he may please us both, perhaps.

Miss Hardcastle. And as one of us must be mistaken, what if we go to make farther discoveries?

Hardcastle. Agreed. But depend on 't, I'm in the right.

Miss Hardcastle. And, depend on 't, I'm not much in the wrong. [*Exeunt.*

Enter TONY, *running in with a casket.*[4]

Tony. Ecod! I have got them. Here they are. My cousin Con's necklaces, bobs[5] and all. My mother shan't cheat the poor souls out of their fortin neither. Oh! my genus, is that you?

Enter HASTINGS.

Hastings. My dear friend, how have you managed with your mother? I hope you have amused her with pretending love for your cousin, and that you are willing to be reconciled at last? Our horses will be refreshed in a short time, and we shall soon be ready to set off.

Tony. And here's something to bear your charges by the way [*giving the casket*];—your sweetheart's jewels. Keep them; and hang those, I say, that would rob you of one of them!

Hastings. But how have you procured them from your mother?

[4] CASKET—A small case or chest for jewels.
[5] BOBS—Pendants.

Tony. Ask me no questions, and I'll tell you no fibs. I procured them by the rule of thumb.[6] If I had not a key to every drawer in my mother's bureau, how could I go to the alehouse so often as I do? An honest man may rob himself of his own at any time.

Hastings. Thousands do it every day. But, to be plain with you, Miss Neville is endeavoring to procure them from her aunt this very instant. If she succeeds, it will be the most delicate way, at least, of obtaining them.

Tony. Well, keep them, till you know how it will be. But I know how it will be well enough; she'd as soon part with the only sound tooth in her head.

Hastings. But I dread the effects of her resentment when she finds she has lost them.

Tony. Never you mind her resentment; leave *me* to manage that. I don't value her resentment the bounce of a cracker. Zounds! here they are! Morrice![7] Prance!   [*Exit* HASTINGS.

Enter MRS. HARDCASTLE *and* MISS NEVILLE

Mrs. Hardcastle. Indeed, Constance, you amaze me. Such a girl as you want jewels? It will be time enough for jewels, my dear, twenty years hence, when your beauty begins to want repairs.

Miss Neville. But what will repair beauty at forty, will certainly improve it at twenty, madam.

Mrs. Hardcastle. Yours, my dear, can admit of none. That natural blush is beyond a thousand ornaments. Besides, child, jewels are quite out at present. Don't you see half the ladies of our acquaintance, my Lady Kill-day-light, and Mrs. Crump, and the rest of them, carry their jewels to town, and bring nothing but paste and marcasites[8] back?

Miss Neville. But who knows, madam, but somebody that shall be nameless would like me best with all my little finery about me?

Mrs. Hardcastle. Consult your glass, my dear, and then see if, with such a pair of eyes, you want any better sparklers.

---

[6] RULE OF THUMB—Rough and ready manner.
[7] MORRICE—Away with you! Be off!
[8] PASTE AND MARCASITES—Imitation jewelry.

What do you think, Tony, my dear? Does your cousin Con want any jewels, in your eyes, to set off her beauty?

Tony. That's as hereafter may be.

Miss Neville. My dear aunt, if you knew how it would oblige me.

Mrs. Hardcastle. A parcel of old-fashioned rose and table-cut[9] things. They would make you look like the court of King Solomon at a puppet-show.[10] Besides, I believe I can't readily come at them. They may be missing, for aught I know to the contrary.

Tony. [*Apart to* Mrs. Hardcastle.] Then why don't you tell her so at once, as she's so longing for them? Tell her they're lost. It's the only way to quiet her. Say they're lost, and call me to bear witness.

Mrs. Hardcastle. [*Apart to* Tony.] You know, my dear, I'm only keeping them for you. So if I say they're gone, you'll bear me witness, will you? He! he! he!

Tony. Never fear me. Ecod! I'll say I saw them taken out with my own eyes.

Miss Neville. I desire them but for a day, madam, just to be permitted to show them as relics, and then they may be locked up again.

Mrs. Hardcastle. To be plain with you, my dear Constance, if I could find them you should have them. They're missing, I assure you. Lost, for aught I know; but we must have patience, wherever they are.

Miss Neville. I'll not believe it; this is but a shallow pretence to deny me. I know they are too valuable to be so slightly kept,[11] and as you are to answer for the loss—

Mrs. Hardcastle. Don't be alarmed, Constance. If they be lost, I must restore an equivalent. But my son knows they are missing, and not to be found.

Tony. That I can bear witness to. They are missing, and not to be found; I'll take my oath on 't.

Mrs. Hardcastle. You must learn resignation, my dear; for though we lose our fortune, yet we should not lose our patience. See me, how calm I am.

---

[9] Rose and table-cut—Styles of jewel-cutting.

[10] Look like ... puppet-show—i.e., you would be entirely overdressed and out of place.

[11] Slightly kept—Carelessly kept.

I'll say I saw them taken out with my own eyes.

Miss Neville. Ay, people are generally calm at the misfortunes of others.

Mrs. Hardcastle. Now, I wonder a girl of your good sense should waste a thought upon such trumpery. We shall soon find them; and in the meantime you shall make use of my garnets till your jewels be found.

Miss Neville. I detest garnets!

Mrs. Hardcastle. The most becoming things in the world to set off a clear complexion. You have often seen how well they look upon me. You *shall* have them. [*Exit.*

Miss Neville. I dislike them of all things.—You shan't stir. Was ever anything so provoking,—to mislay my own jewels, and force me to wear her trumpery?

Tony. Don't be a fool. If she gives you the garnets take what you can get. The jewels are your own already. I have stolen them out of her bureau, and she does not know it. Fly to your spark; he'll tell you more of the matter. Leave me to manage *her.*

Miss Neville. My dear cousin!

Tony. Vanish. She's here, and has missed them already. [*Exit* Miss Neville.] Zounds! how she fidgets and spits about like a Catherine wheel.[12]

Enter Mrs. Hardcastle.

Mrs. Hardcastle. Confusion! thieves! robbers! we are cheated, plundered, broke open, undone!

Tony. What's the matter, what's the matter, mamma? I hope nothing has happened to any of the good family?

Mrs. Hardcastle. We are robbed. My bureau has been broke open, the jewels taken out, and I'm undone!

Tony. Oh! is that all! Ha! ha! ha! By the laws, I never saw it better acted in my life. Ecod, I thought you was ruined in earnest, ha, ha, ha!

Mrs. Hardcastle. Why, boy, I *am* ruined in earnest. My bureau has been broke open, and all taken away.

Tony. Stick to that; ha, ha, ha! stick to that. I'll bear witness, you know! call me to bear witness.

Mrs. Hardcastle. I tell you, Tony, by all that's precious, the jewels are gone, and I shall be ruined forever.

[12] CATHERINE WHEEL—A pin wheel such as used in fireworks.

Tony. Sure I know they are gone, and I am to say so.

Mrs. Hardcastle. My dearest Tony, but hear me. They're gone, I say.

Tony. By the laws, mamma, you make me for to laugh, ha! ha! I know who took them well enough, ha! ha! ha!

Mrs. Hardcastle. Was there ever such a blockhead, that can't tell the difference between jest and earnest? I can tell you I'm not in jest, booby.

Tony. That's right, that's right! You must be in a bitter passion, and then nobody will suspect either of us. I'll bear witness that they are gone.

Mrs. Hardcastle. Was there ever such a cross-grained brute, that won't hear me? Can you bear witness that you're no better than a fool? Was ever poor woman so beset with fools on one hand, and thieves on the other?

Tony. I can bear witness to that.

Mrs. Hardcastle. Bear witness again, you blockhead, you, and I'll turn you out of the room directly. My poor niece, what will become of *her*? Do you laugh, you unfeeling brute, as if you enjoyed my distress?

Tony. I can bear witness to that.

Mrs. Hardcastle. Do you insult me, monster. I'll teach you to vex your mother, I will!

Tony. I can bear witness to that. [*He runs off; she follows him.*]

Enter Miss Hardcastle *and* Maid.

Miss Hardcastle. What an unaccountable creature is that brother of mine, to send them to the house as an inn; ha! ha! I don't wonder at his impudence.

Maid. But what is more, madam, the young gentleman, as you passed by in your present dress, asked me if you were the bar-maid. He mistook you for the bar-maid, madam!

Miss Hardcastle. Did he? Then, as I live, I'm resolved to keep up the delusion. Tell me, Pimple, how do you like my present dress? Don't you think I look something like Cherry in the *Beaux' Stratagem?* [13]

---

[13] Cherry in the *Beaux' Stratagem*—Cherry was the daughter of the innkeeper in the comedy, the *Beaux' Stratagem.*

Maid. It's the dress, madam, that every lady wears in the country, but when she visits or receives company.

Miss Hardcastle. And are you sure he does not remember my face or person?

Maid. Certain of it.

Miss Hardcastle. I vow I thought so; for though we spoke for some time together, yet his fears were such that he never once looked up during the interview. Indeed, if he had, my bonnet [14] would have kept him from seeing me.

Maid. But what do you hope from keeping him in his mistake?

Miss Hardcastle. In the first place, I shall be *seen,* and that is no small advantage to a girl who brings her face to market. Then I shall perhaps make an acquaintance, and that's no small victory gained over one who never addresses any but the wildest of her sex. But my chief aim is to take my gentleman off his guard, and, like an invisible champion of romance, examine the giant's force before I offer to combat.

Maid. But are you sure you can act your part, and disguise your voice so that he may mistake that, as he has already mistaken your person?

Miss Hardcastle. Never fear me. I think I have got the true bar cant [15]—Did your honor call?—Attend the Lion there. —Pipes and tobacco for the Angel.—The Lamb has been outrageous this half hour!

Maid. It will do, madam. But he's here.   [*Exit* Maid.

Enter MARLOW.

Marlow. What a bawling in every part of the house; I have scarce a moment's repose. If I go to the best room, there I find my host and his story; if I fly to the gallery,[16] there we have my hostess with her curtsey down to the ground. I have at last got a moment to myself, and now for recollection. [*Walks and muses.*]

Miss Hardcastle. Did you call sir? Did your honor call?

Marlow. [*Musing.*] As for Miss Hardcastle, she's too grave and sentimental [17] for me.

[14] BONNET—Deep bonnets were the fashion.
[15] CANT—Mode of speaking.
[16] GALLERY—Hallway, passageway.
[17] SENTIMENTAL—Note the use of this word again and its meaning.

Miss Hardcastle. Did your honor call? [*She still places herself before him, he turning away.*]

Marlow. No, child. [*Musing.*] Besides, from the glimpse I had of her, I think she squints.

Miss Hardcastle. I'm sure, sir, I heard the bell ring.

Marlow. No, no. [*Musing.*] I have pleased my father, however, by coming down, and I'll to-morrow please myself by returning. [*Taking out his tablets and perusing.*]

Miss Hardcastle. Perhaps the other gentleman called, sir?

Marlow. I tell you no.

Miss Hardcastle. I should be glad to know, sir. We have such a parcel of servants.

Marlow. No, no, I tell you. [*Looks full in her face.*] Yes, child, I think I did call. I wanted—I wanted—I vow, child, you are vastly handsome.

Miss Hardcastle. Oh, la, sir, you'll make one ashamed.

Marlow. Never saw a more sprightly, malicious eye. Yes, yes, my dear, I did call. Have you got any of your—a—what d' ye call it, in the house?

Miss Hardcastle. No, sir, we have been out of that these ten days.

Marlow. One may call in this house, I find, to very little purpose. Suppose I should call for a taste, just by way of trial, of the nectar of your lips; perhaps I might be disappointed in that too.

Miss Hardcastle. Nectar? nectar? That's a liquor there's no call for in these parts. French, I suppose. We keep no French wines here, sir.

Marlow. Of true English growth, I assure you.

Miss Hardcastle. Then it's odd I should not know it. We brew all sorts of wines in this house, and I have lived here these eighteen years.

Marlow. Eighteen years! Why, one would think, child, you kept the bar before you were born. How old are you?

Miss Hardcastle. Oh, sir, I must not tell my age. They say women and music should never be dated.

Marlow. To guess at this distance, you can't be much above forty. [*Approaching.*] Yet nearer, I don't think so much. [*Approaching.*] By coming close to some women, they look younger still; but when we come very close indeed— [*Attempting to kiss her.*]

Miss Hardcastle. Pray, sir, keep your distance. One would think you wanted to know one's age as they do horses, by mark of mouth.

Marlow. I protest, child, you use me extremely ill. If you keep me at this distance, how is it possible you and I can be ever acquainted?

Miss Hardcastle. And who wants to be acquainted with you? I want no such acquaintance, not I. I'm sure you did not treat Miss Hardcastle, that was here a while ago, in this obstropalous [18] manner. I'll warrant me, before her you looked dashed, and kept bowing to the ground, and talked, for all the world, as if you was before a justice of peace.

Marlow. [*Aside.*] Egad, she has hit it, sure enough! [*To her.*] In awe of her, child? Ha! ha! ha! A mere awkward, squinting thing! No, no. I find you don't know me. I laughed and rallied her a little; but I was unwilling to be too severe. No, I could not be too severe, curse me!

Miss Hardcastle. Oh, then, sir, you are a favorite, I find, among the ladies!

Marlow. Yes, my dear, a great favorite. And yet, hang me, I don't see what they find in me to follow. At the Ladies' Club in town I'm called their agreeable Rattle. Rattle, child, is not my real name, but one I'm known by. My name is Solomons; Mr. Solomons, my dear, at your service. [*Offering to salute her.*]

Miss Hardcastle. Hold, sir, you are introducing me to your club, not to yourself. And you're so great a favorite there, you say?

Marlow. Yes, my dear. There's Mrs. Mantrap, Lady Betty Blackleg, the Countess of Sligo, Mrs. Langhorns, old Miss Biddy Buckskin, and your humble servant, keep up the spirit of the place.

Miss Hardcastle. Then it's a very merry place, I suppose?

Marlow. Yes, as merry as cards, suppers, wine, and old women can make us.

Miss Hardcastle. And their agreeable Rattle, ha! ha! ha!

Marlow. [*Aside.*] Egad! I don't quite like this chit. She looks knowing, methinks. You laugh, child?

---

[18] OBSTROPALOUS—Obstreperous.

Miss Hardcastle. I can't but laugh to think what time they all have for minding their work, or their family.

Marlow. [*Aside.*] All's well; she don't laugh at me. [*To her.*] Do *you* ever work, child?

Miss Hardcastle. Ay, sure. There's not a screen or a quilt in the whole house but what can bear witness to that.

Marlow. Odso! then you must show me your embroidery. I embroider and draw patterns myself a little. If you want a judge of your work, you must apply to me. [*Seizing her hand.*]

Enter Hardcastle, *who stands in surprise.*

Miss Hardcastle. Ay, but the colors don't look well by candle-light. You shall see it all in the morning. [*Struggling.*]

Marlow. And why not now, my angel? Such beauty fires beyond the power of resistance. Pshaw! the father here! My

old luck; I never nicked seven that I did not throw ames ace [19] three times following. [*Exit* Marlow.

Hardcastle. So, madam! So I find *this* is your *modest* lover. This is your humble admirer, that kept his eyes fixed on the ground, and only adored at humble distance. Kate, Kate, art thou not ashamed to deceive your father so?

Miss Hardcastle. Never trust me, dear papa, but he's still

---

[19] Nicked seven ... throw ames ace—Expressions in dice throwing. The meaning is "I never made a lucky throw that I didn't follow it with three unlucky ones."

the modest man I first took him for; you'll be convinced of it as well as I.

Hardcastle. By the hand of my body, I believe his impudence is infectious! Didn't I see him seize your hand? Didn't I see him haul you about like a milk-maid? And now you talk of his respect and his modesty, forsooth!

Miss Hardcastle. But if I shortly convince you of his modesty, that he has only the faults that will pass off with time, and the virtues that will improve with age, I hope you'll forgive him.

Hardcastle. The girl would actually make one run mad! I tell you I'll not be convinced. I am convinced. He has scarcely been three hours in the house, and he has already encroached on all my prerogatives. You may like his impudence, and call it modesty; but my son-in-law, madam, must have very different qualifications.

Miss Hardcastle. Sir, I ask but this night to convince you.

Hardcastle. You shall not have half the time, for I have thoughts of turning him out this very hour.

Miss Hardcastle. Give me that hour, then, and I hope to satisfy you.

Hardcastle. Well, an hour let it be then. But I'll have no trifling with your father. All fair and open; do you mind me?

Miss Hardcastle. I hope, sir, you have ever found that I considered your commands as my pride; for your kindness is such that my duty as yet has been inclination.[20]   [*Exeunt.*

[20] MY DUTY AS YET HAS BEEN INCLINATION—The things I have so far been required to do have been the things I wanted to do.

ACT IV

Scene 1. *The house.*

Enter Hastings *and* Miss Neville.

Hastings. You surprise me! Sir Charles Marlow expected here this night? Where have you had your information?

Miss Neville. You may depend upon it. I just saw his letter to Mr. Hardcastle, in which he tells him he intends setting out a few hours after his son.

Hastings. Then, my Constance, all must be completed before he arrives. He knows me; and should he find me here, would discover[1] my name, and perhaps my designs, to the rest of the family.

Miss Neville. The jewels, I hope, are safe?

Hastings. Yes, yes. I have sent them to Marlow, who keeps the keys of our baggage. In the meantime, I'll go to prepare matters for our elopement. I have had the Squire's promise of a fresh pair of horses; and, if I should not see him again, will write him further directions. [*Exit.*

Miss Neville. Well, success attend you! In the meantime, I'll go amuse my aunt with the old pretence of a violent passion for my cousin. [*Exit.*

Enter MARLOW, *followed by a* Servant.

Marlow. I wonder what Hastings could mean by sending me so valuable a thing as a casket to keep for him, when he knows the only place I have is the seat of a post-coach[2] at an inn-door. Have you deposited the casket with the landlady, as I ordered you? Have you put it into her own hands?

Servant. Yes, your honor.

Marlow. She said she'd keep it safe, did she?

Servant. Yes; she said she'd keep it safe enough. She asked me how I came by it; and she said she had a great mind to make me give an account of myself. [*Exit* Servant.

Marlow. Ha! ha! ha! They're safe, however. What an unaccountable set of beings have we got amongst! This little barmaid, though, runs in my head most strangely, and drives out the absurdities of all the rest of the family. (She's mine, she must be mine, or I'm greatly mistaken!)

Enter HASTINGS.

Hastings. Bless me! I quite forgot to tell her that I intended to prepare at the bottom of the garden. Marlow here, and in spirits too!

Marlow. Give me joy, George! Crown me, shadow me with laurels! Well, George, after all, we modest fellows don't want for success among the women.

[1] DISCOVER—Reveal.
[2] SEAT OF A POST-COACH—Evidently a post-coach (a coach equipped for rapid travel) is at the door waiting Marlow's departure.

Hastings. Some women, you mean. But what success has your honor's modesty been crowned with now, that it grows so insolent upon us?

Marlow. Didn't you see the tempting, brisk, lovely little thing, that runs about the house with a bunch of keys to its girdle?

Hastings. Well, and what then?

Marlow. Such fire, such motion, such eyes, such lips—but, egad! she would not let me kiss them though.

Hastings. You have taken care, I hope, of the casket I sent you to lock up? It's in safety?

Marlow. Yes, yes; it's safe enough. I have taken care of it. But how could you think the seat of a post-coach at an inn-door a place of safety? Ah! numskull! I have taken better precautions for you than you did for yourself—I have—

Hastings. What?

Marlow. I have sent it to the landlady to keep for you.

Hastings. To the landlady!

Marlow. The landlady.

Hastings. You did?

Marlow. I did. She's to be answerable for its forthcoming, you know.

Hastings. Yes, she'll bring it forth with a witness.

Marlow. Wasn't I right? I believe you'll allow that I acted prudently upon this occasion.

Hastings. [*Aside.*] He must not see my uneasiness.

Marlow. You seem a little disconcerted, though, methinks. Sure nothing has happened?

Hastings. No, nothing. Never was in better spirits in all my life. And so you left it with the landlady, who, no doubt, very readily undertook the charge.

Marlow. Rather too readily; for she not only kept the casket, but, through her great precaution, was going to keep the messenger too. Ha! ha! ha!

Hastings. He! he! he! They're safe, however.

Marlow. As a guinea in a miser's purse.

Hastings. [*Aside.*] So now all hopes of fortune are at an end, and we must set off without it. [*To him.*] Well, Charles, I'll leave you to your meditations on the pretty bar-maid, and he!

he! he! may you be as successful for yourself as you have been for me! [*Exit.*

Marlow. Thank ye, George; I ask no more.—Ha! ha! ha!

Enter HARDCASTLE.

Hardcastle. I no longer know my own house. It's turned all topsy-turvy. His servants have got drunk already. I'll bear it no longer; and yet, from my respect for his father, I'll be calm. [*To him.*] Mr. Marlow, your servant. I'm your very humble servant. [*Bowing low.*]

Marlow. Sir, your humble servant. [*Aside.*] What's to be the wonder now?

Hardcastle. I believe, sir, you must be sensible, sir, that no man alive ought to be more welcome than your father's son, sir. I hope you think so?

Marlow. I do from my soul, sir. I don't want much entreaty. I generally make my father's son welcome wherever he goes.

Hardcastle. I believe you do, from my soul, sir. But though I say nothing to your own conduct, that of your servants is insufferable. Their manner of drinking is setting a very bad example in this house, I assure you.

Marlow. I protest, my very good sir, that is no fault of mine. If they don't drink as they ought, *they* are to blame. I ordered them not to spare the cellar; I did, I assure you. [*To the side-scene.*] Here, let one of my servants come up. [*To him.*] My positive directions were, that as I did not drink myself, they should make up for my deficiencies below.

Hardcastle. Then they had your orders for what they do? I'm satisfied!

Marlow. They had, I assure you. You shall hear from one of themselves.

Enter Servant, *drunk*.

Marlow. You, Jeremy! Come forward, sirrah! What were my orders? Were you not told to drink freely, and call for what you thought fit, for the good of the house?

Hardcastle. [*Aside.*] I begin to lose my patience.

Jeremy. Please your honor, liberty and Fleet-street forever! Though I'm but a servant, I'm as good as another man. I'll drink for no man before supper, sir! Good liquor will sit upon a good supper, but a good supper will not sit upon—hiccup—upon my conscience, sir. [*Exit.*

Marlow. You see, my old friend, the fellow is as drunk as he can possibly be. I don't know what you'd have more, unless you'd have the poor devil soused in a beer barrel.

Hardcastle. Zounds! he'll drive me distracted, if I contain myself any longer. Mr. Marlow, sir! I have submitted to your insolence for more than four hours, and I see no likelihood of its coming to an end. I'm now resolved to be master here, sir, and I desire that you and your drunken pack may leave my house directly.

Marlow. Leave your house!—Sure, you jest, my good friend? What? when I am doing what I can to please you!

Hardcastle. I tell you, sir, you don't please me; so I desire you'll leave my house.

Marlow. Sure you cannot be serious? at this time of night, and such a night? You only mean to banter me.

Hardcastle. I tell you, sir, I'm serious! and now that my passions are roused, I say this house is mine, sir; this house is mine, and I command you to leave it directly.

Marlow. Ha! ha! ha! A puddle in a storm. I shan't stir a step, I assure you. [*In a serious tone.*] This your house, fellow! It's my house. This is my house. Mine, while I choose to stay. What right have you to bid me leave this house, sir? I never met with such impudence, curse me; never in my whole life before.

Hardcastle. Nor I, confound me if ever I did! To come to my house, to call for what he likes, to turn me out of my own chair, to insult the family, to order his servants to get drunk, and then to tell me, "This house is mine, sir!" By all that's impudent, it makes me laugh. Ha! ha! ha! Pray, sir, [*Bantering.*] as you take the house, what think you of taking the rest of the furniture? There's a pair of silver candlesticks, and there's a fire-screen, and here's a pair of brazen-nosed bellows; perhaps you may take a fancy to them?

Marlow. Bring me your bill, sir; bring me your bill, and let's make no more words about it.

Hardcastle. There are a set of prints, too. What think you of the *Rake's Progress*[3] for your own apartment?

Marlow. Bring me your bill, I say, and I'll leave you and your infernal house directly.

Hardcastle. Then there's a mahogany table that you may see your face in.

Marlow. My bill, I say.

Hardcastle. I had forgot the great chair for your own particular slumbers, after a hearty meal.

Marlow. Zounds! bring me my bill, I say, and let's hear no more on 't.

Hardcastle. Young man, young man, from your father's letter to me, I was taught to expect a well-bred, modest man as a visitor here, but now I find him no better than a coxcomb and a bully; but he will be down here presently, and shall hear more of it.
[*Exit.*

Marlow. How's this! Sure I have not mistaken the house? Everything looks like an inn; the servants cry "Coming"; the attendance[4] is awkward; the bar-maid, too, to attend us. But she's here, and will further inform me. Whither so fast, child? A word with you.

Enter MISS HARDCASTLE.

Miss Hardcastle. Let it be short, then. I'm in a hurry. [*Aside.*] I believe he begins to find out his mistake. But it's too soon quite to undeceive him.

Marlow. Pray, child, answer me one question. What are you, and what may your business in this house be?

Miss Hardcastle. A relation of the family, sir.

Marlow. What! a poor relation?

Miss Hardcastle. Yes, sir, a poor relation, appointed to keep the keys, and to see that the guests want nothing in my power to give them.

Marlow. That is, you act as the bar-maid of this inn.

Miss Hardcastle. Inn! O law—what brought that into your head? One of the best families in the county keep an inn!— Ha! ha! ha! old Mr. Hardcastle's house an inn!

---

[3] *Rake's Progress*—A famous set of prints or drawings by a celebrated English artist.
[4] ATTENDANCE—Service.

Marlow. Mr. Hardcastle's house! Is this house Mr. Hardcastle's house, child?

Miss Hardcastle. Ay, sure. Whose else should it be?

Marlow. So, then, all's out, and I have been infernally imposed on. Oh, confound my stupid head, I shall be laughed at over the whole town! I shall be stuck up in caricatura [5] in all the print-shops. The *Dullissimo-Macaroni*.[6] To mistake this house of all others for an inn, and my father's old friend for an innkeeper! What a swaggering puppy must he take me for! What a silly puppy do I find myself! There, again, may I be hanged, my dear, but I mistook you for the bar-maid.

Miss Hardcastle. Dear me! dear me! I'm sure there's nothing in my *behaviour* to put me upon a level with one of that stamp.

Marlow. Nothing, my dear, nothing. But I was in for a list of blunders, and could not help making you a subscriber. My stupidity saw everything the wrong way. I mistook your assiduity for assurance, and your simplicity for allurement. But it's over—this house I no more show *my* face in.

Miss Hardcastle. I hope, sir, I have done nothing to disoblige you. I'm sure I should be sorry to affront any gentleman who has been so polite, and said so many civil things to me. I'm sure I should be sorry [*Pretending to cry.*] if he left the family upon my account. I'm sure I should be sorry people said anything amiss, since I have no fortune but my character.

Marlow. [*Aside.*] By Heaven! she weeps! This is the first mark of tenderness I ever had from a modest woman, and it touches me. [*To her.*] Excuse me, my lovely girl; you are the only part of the family I leave with reluctance. But, to be plain with you, the difference of our birth, fortune, and education, make an honorable connection impossible; and I can never harbor a thought of seducing simplicity that trusted in my honor, or bringing ruin upon one whose only fault was being too lovely.

Miss Hardcastle. [*Aside.*] Generous man! I now begin to admire him. [*To him.*] But I am sure my family is as good as Miss Hardcastle's; and though I'm poor, that's no great mis-

---

[5] CARICATURA—Caricatures.
[6] *Dullissimo-Macaroni*—During this period the term "macaroni" meant a fop or a dandy. *Dullissimo-Macaroni* would therefore mean "the very dullest or most stupid of all dandies."

fortune to a contented mind; and, until this moment, I never thought that it was bad to want [7] fortune.

Marlow. And why now, my pretty simplicity?

Miss Hardcastle. Because it puts me at a distance from one, that, if I had a thousand pound I would give it all to.

Marlow. [*Aside.*] This simplicity bewitches me so, that if I stay I'm undone. I must make one bold effort and leave her. [*To her.*] Your partiality in my favor, my dear, touches me most sensibly; and were I to live for myself alone, I could easily fix my choice. But I owe too much to the opinion of the world, too much to the authority of a father; so that—I can scarcely speak it—it affects me! Farewell. [*Exit.*

Miss Hardcastle. I never knew half his merit till now. He shall not go if I have power or art to detain him. I'll still preserve the character in which I *stooped to conquer,* but will undeceive my papa, who, perhaps, may laugh him out of his resolution. [*Exit.*

Enter Tony *and* Miss Neville.

Tony. Ay, you may steal for yourselves the next time. I have done my duty. She has got the jewels again, that's a sure thing; but she believes it was all a mistake of the servants.

Miss Neville. But, my dear cousin, sure you won't forsake us in this distress? If she in the least suspects that I am going off, I shall certainly be locked up, or sent to my aunt Pedigree's, which is ten times worse.

Tony. To be sure, aunts of all kinds are bad things. But what can I do? I have got you a pair of horses that will fly like Whistle Jacket;[8] and I'm sure you can't say but I have courted you nicely before her face. Here she comes; we must court a bit or two more, for fear she should suspect us.

[*They retire and seem to fondle.*

Enter Mrs. Hardcastle.

Mrs. Hardcastle. Well, I was greatly fluttered, to be sure. But my son tells me it was all a mistake of the servants. I shan't be easy, however, till they are fairly married, and then let her keep her own fortune. But what do I see? Fondling

---

[7] Want—Lack.
[8] Whistle Jacket—A famous race horse.

together, as I'm alive. I never saw Tony so sprightly before. Ah! have I caught you, my pretty doves? What, billing, exchanging stolen glances, and broken murmurs? Ah!

Tony. As for murmurs, mother, we grumble a little now and then, to be sure. But there's no love lost between us.

Mrs. Hardcastle. A mere sprinkling, Tony, upon the flame, only to make it burn brighter.

Miss Neville. Cousin Tony promises to give us more of his company at home. Indeed, he shan't leave us any more. It won't leave us, Cousin Tony, will it?

Tony. Oh, it's a pretty creature! No, I'd sooner leave my horse in a pound, than leave you when you smile upon one so. Your laugh makes you so becoming.

Miss Neville. Agreeable cousin! Who can help admiring that natural humor, that pleasant, broad, red, thoughtless [*Patting his cheek.*],—ah! it's a bold face!

Mrs. Hardcastle. Pretty innocence.

Tony. I'm sure I always loved cousin Con's hazel eyes, and her pretty long fingers, that she twists this way and that over the haspicholls,[9] like a parcel of bobbins.[10]

Mrs. Hardcastle. Ah! he would charm the bird from the tree. I was never so happy before. My boy takes after his father, poor Mr. Lumpkin, exactly. The jewels, my dear Con, shall be yours incontinently.[11] You shall have them. Isn't he a sweet boy, my dear. You shall be married to-morrow, and we'll put off the rest of his education, like Dr. Drowsy's sermons, to a fitter opportunity.

Enter DIGGORY.

Diggory. Where's the Squire? I have got a letter for your worship.
Tony. Give it to my mamma. She reads all my letters first.
Diggory. I had orders to deliver it into your own hands.
Tony. Who does it come from?
Diggory. Your worship mun[12] ask that o' the letter itself.

[*Exit* DIGGORY.

---

[9] HASPICHOLLS—Meant for "harpsichord" which was the forerunner of the modern piano.
[10] BOBBINS—Cylinders or pins used to hold the threads in making lace.
[11] INCONTINENTLY—Immediately; at once.
[12] MUN—Must.

Tony. I could wish to know, though. [*Turning the letter, and gazing on it.*]

Miss Neville. [*Aside.*] Undone, undone! A letter to him from Hastings. I know the hand. If my aunt sees it, we are ruined forever. I'll keep her employed a little if I can. [*To* MRS. HARDCASTLE.] But I have not told you, madam, of my cousin's smart answer just now to Mr. Marlow. We so laughed—you must know, madam—this way a little, for he must not hear us. [*They confer.*]

Tony. [*Still gazing.*] A cramp [13] piece of penmanship as ever I saw in my life. I can read your print-hand very well; but here there are such handles, and shanks, and dashes, that one can scarce tell the head from the tail. "To Anthony Lumpkin, Esquire." It's very odd, I can read the outside of my letters, where my own name is, well enough. But when I come to open it, it's all—buzz. That's hard, very hard; for the inside of the letter is always the cream of the correspondence.

Mrs. Hardcastle. Ha! ha! ha! Very well, very well. And so my son was too hard for the philosopher.

Miss Neville. Yes, madam; but you must hear the rest, madam. A little more this way, or he may hear us. You'll hear how he puzzled him again.

Mrs. Hardcastle. He seems strangely puzzled now himself, methinks.

Tony. [*Still gazing.*] An up-and-down hand, as if it was disguised in liquor. [*Reading.*] "Dear Sir,"—Ay, that's that. Then there's an M, and a T, and an S, but whether the next be an *izzard* [14] or an R, confound me, I cannot tell!

Mrs. Hardcastle. What's that, my dear; can I give you any assistance? [*Taking the letter.*]

Miss Neville. Pray, aunt, let me read it. Nobody reads a cramp hand better than I. [*Twitching the letter from her.*] Do you know who it is from?

Tony. Can't tell, except from Dick Ginger, the feeder.[15]

Miss Neville. Ay, so it is. [*Pretending to read.*] Dear Squire, Hoping that you're in health, as I am at this present. The gentlemen of the Shake-bag [16] club has cut the gentlemen of

---

[13] CRAMP—Hard to decipher.
[14] *Izzard*—The letter Z.
[15] FEEDER—Cock-feeder.
[16] SHAKE-BAG—A large fighting cock.

the Goose-green quite out of feather. The odds—um—odd battle —um—long fighting—um—here, here, it's all about cocks, and fighting; it's of no consequence; here, put it up, put it up. [*Thrusting the crumpled letter upon him.*]

Tony. But I tell you, miss, it's of all the consequence in the world! I would not lose the rest of it for a guinea. Here, mother, do you make it out. Of no consequence! [*Giving* Mrs. Hardcastle *the letter.*]

Mrs. Hardcastle. How's this? [*Reads.*] "Dear Squire, I'm now waiting for Miss Neville with a postchaise and pair, at the bottom of the garden, but I find my horses yet unable to perform the journey. I expect you'll assist us with a pair of fresh horses, as you promised. Despatch is necessary, as the hag — [*ay, the hag*] — your mother, will otherwise suspect us. Yours, Hastings." Grant me patience. I shall run distracted! My rage chokes me!

Miss Neville. I hope, madam, you'll suspend your resentment for a few moments, and not impute to me any impertinence, or sinister design, that belongs to another.

Mrs. Hardcastle. [*Curtseying very low.*] Fine spoken, madam; you are most miraculously polite and engaging, and quite the very pink of courtesy and circumspection, madam. [*Changing her tone.*] And you, you great ill-fashioned oaf, with scarce sense enough to keep your mouth shut,—were you too joined against me? But I'll defeat all your plots in a moment. As for you, madam, since you have got a pair of fresh horses ready, it would be cruel to disappoint them. So, if you please, instead of running away with your spark, prepare, this very moment, to run off with *me*. Your old Aunt Pedigree will keep you secure, I'll warrant me. You, too, sir, may mount your horse, and guard us upon the way. Here, Thomas, Roger, Diggory! I'll show you that I wish you better than you do yourselves. [*Exit.*

Miss Neville. So, now I'm completely ruined.

Tony. Ay, that's a sure thing.

Miss Neville. What better could be expected from being connected with such a stupid fool,—and after all the nods and signs I made him!

Tony. By the laws, miss, it was your own cleverness, and not my stupidity, that did your business. You were so nice and so busy with your Shake-bags and Goose-greens that I thought you could never be making believe.

Enter HASTINGS.

Hastings. So, sir, I find by my servant that you have shown my letter, and betrayed us. Was this well done, young gentleman?

Tony. Here's another. Ask miss, there, who betrayed you. Ecod! it was her doing, not mine.

Enter MARLOW.

Marlow. So, I have been finely used here among you. Rendered contemptible, driven into ill-manners, despised, insulted, laughed at.

Tony. Here's another. We shall have old Bedlam broke loose presently.

Miss Neville. And there, sir, is the gentleman to whom we all owe every obligation.

Marlow. What can I say to him? A mere boy, an idiot, whose ignorance and age are a protection.

Hastings. A poor, contemptible booby, that would but disgrace correction.

Miss Neville. Yet with cunning and malice enough to make himself merry with all our embarrassments.

Hastings. An insensible cub.

Marlow. Replete with tricks and mischief.

Tony. Baw! I'll fight you both, one after the other,—with baskets.[17]

Marlow. As for him, he's below resentment. But your conduct, Mr. Hastings, requires an explanation. You knew of my mistakes, yet would not undeceive me.

---

[17] WITH BASKETS—With basket-hilts. That is, hilts so made as to contain the whole hand and protect it from being wounded.

Hastings. Tortured as I am with my own disappointments, is this a time for explanations? It is not friendly, Mr. Marlow.
Marlow. But, sir—
Miss Neville. Mr. Marlow, we never kept on your mistake, till it was too late to undeceive you. Be pacified.

Enter Servant.

Servant. My mistress desires you'll get ready immediately, madam. The horses are putting to. Your hat and things are in the next room. We are to go thirty miles before morning. [*Exit* Servant.
Miss Neville. Well, well, I'll come presently.
Marlow. [*To* HASTINGS.] Was it well done, sir, to assist in rendering me ridiculous? To hang me out for the scorn of all my acquaintance? Depend upon it, sir, I shall expect an explanation.
Hastings. Was it well done, sir, if you're upon that subject, to deliver what I entrusted to yourself to the care of another, sir?
Miss Neville. Mr. Hastings! Mr. Marlow! Why will you increase my distress by this groundless dispute? I implore, I entreat you—

Enter Servant.

Servant. Your cloak, madam. My mistress is impatient.
Miss Neville. I come. [*Exit* Servant.] Pray, be pacified. If I leave you thus, I shall die with apprehension!

Enter Servant.

Servant. Your fan, muff, and gloves, madam. The horses are waiting. [*Exit* Servant.
Miss Neville. Oh, Mr. Marlow! if you knew what a scene of constraint and ill-nature lies before me, I am sure it would convert your resentment into pity.
Marlow. I'm so distracted with a variety of passions that I don't know what I do. Forgive me, madam. George, forgive me. You know my hasty temper, and should not exasperate it.
Hastings. The torture of my situation is my only excuse.

Miss Neville. Well, my dear Hastings, if you have that esteem for me that I think, that I am sure you have, your constancy for three years will but increase the happiness of our future connection. If—

Mrs. Hardcastle. [*Within.*] Miss Neville! Constance! why, Constance, I say!

Miss Neville. I'm coming! Well, constancy. Remember, constancy is the word. [*Exit.*

Hastings. My heart! how can I support this! To be so near happiness, and such happiness!

Marlow. [*To* Tony.] You see now, young gentleman, the effects of your folly. What might be amusement to you is here disappointment, and even distress.

Tony. [*From a reverie.*] Ecod, I have hit it. It's here! Your hands. Yours, and yours, my poor Sulky.—My boots there, ho!—Meet me, two hours hence, at the bottom of the garden; and if you don't find Tony Lumpkin a more good-natured fellow than you thought for, I'll give you leave to take my best horse, and Bet Bouncer into the bargain! Come along. My boots, ho!

[*Exeunt.*

ACT V

Scene 1. *The house.*

Enter Hastings *and* Servant.

Hastings. You saw the old lady and Miss Neville drive off, you say?

Servant. Yes, your honor. They went off in a post-coach, and the young Squire went on horseback. They're thirty miles off by this time.

Hastings. Then all my hopes are over.

Servant. Yes, sir. Old Sir Charles is arrived. He and the old gentleman of the house have been laughing at Mr. Marlow's mistake this half hour. They are coming this way. [*Exit.*

Hastings. Then I must not be seen. So now to my fruitless appointment at the bottom of the garden. This is about the time. [*Exit.*

Enter SIR CHARLES MARLOW *and* HARDCASTLE.

Hardcastle. Ha! ha! ha! The peremptory tone in which he sent forth his sublime commands!

Sir Charles. And the reserve with which I suppose he treated all your advances.

Hardcastle. And yet he might have seen something in me above a common innkeeper, too.

Sir Charles. Yes, Dick, but he mistook you for an uncommon innkeeper; ha! ha! ha!

Hardcastle. Well, I'm in too good spirits to think of anything but joy. Yes, my dear friend, this union of our families will make our personal friendships hereditary; and though my daughter's fortune is but small—

Sir Charles. Why, Dick, will you talk of fortune to *me?* My son is possessed of more than a competence already, and can want nothing but a good and virtuous girl to share his happiness and increase it. If they like each other, as you say they do—

Hardcastle. If, man! I tell you they *do* like each other. My daughter as good as told me so.

Sir Charles. But girls are apt to flatter themselves, you know.

Hardcastle. I saw him grasp her hand in the warmest manner, myself; and here he comes to put you out of your *ifs,* I warrant him.

Enter MARLOW.

Marlow. I come, sir, once more, to ask pardon for my strange conduct. I can scarce reflect on my insolence without confusion.

Hardcastle. Tut, boy, a trifle. You take it too gravely. An hour or two's laughing with my daughter will set all to rights again. She'll never like you the worse for it.

Marlow. Sir, I shall be always proud of her approbation.

Hardcastle. Approbation is but a cold word, Mr. Marlow; if I am not deceived, you have something more than approbation thereabouts. You take me?

Marlow. Really, sir, I have not that happiness.

Hardcastle. Come, boy, I'm an old fellow, and know what's what as well as you that are younger. I know what has passed between you; but mum.

Marlow. Sure, sir, nothing has passed between us but the most profound respect on my side, and the most distant reserve on hers. You don't think, sir, that my impudence has been passed upon all the rest of the family?

Hardcastle. Impudence! No, I don't say that—not quite impudence—though girls like to be played with, and rumpled a little, too, sometimes. But she has told no tales, I assure you.

Marlow. I never gave her the slightest cause.

Hardcastle. Well, well, I like modesty in its place well enough; but this is over-acting, young gentleman. You *may* be open. Your father and I will like you the better for it.

Marlow. May I die, sir, if I ever—

Hardcastle. I tell you she don't dislike you; and as I am sure you like her—

Marlow. Dear sir,—I protest, sir—

Hardcastle. I see no reason why you should not be joined as fast as the parson can tie you.

Marlow. But hear me, sir—

Hardcastle. Your father approves the match; I admire it; every moment's delay will be doing mischief; so—

Marlow. But why won't you hear me? By all that's just and true, I never gave Miss Hardcastle the slightest mark of my attachment, or even the most distant hint to suspect me of affection. We had but one interview, and that was formal, modest, and uninteresting.

Hardcastle. [*Aside.*] This fellow's formal, modest impudence is beyond bearing.

Sir Charles. And you never grasped her hand, or made any protestations?

Marlow. As heaven is my witness, I came down in obedience to your commands. I saw the lady without emotion, and parted without reluctance. I hope you'll exact no further proofs of my duty, nor prevent me from leaving a house in which I suffer so many mortifications. [*Exit.*

Sir Charles. I'm astonished at the air of sincerity with which he parted.

Hardcastle. And I'm astonished at the deliberate intrepidity of his assurance.

Sir Charles. I dare pledge my life and honor upon his truth.

Hardcastle. Here comes my daughter, and I would stake my happiness upon her veracity.

Enter Miss Hardcastle.

Hardcastle. Kate, come hither, child. Answer us sincerely, and without reserve; has Mr. Marlow made you any professions of love and affection?

Miss Hardcastle. The question is very abrupt, sir. But since you require unreserved sincerity, I think he has.

Hardcastle. [*To* Sir Charles.] You see.

Sir Charles. And pray, madam, have you and my son had more than one interview?

Miss Hardcastle. Yes, sir, several.

Hardcastle. [*To* Sir Charles.] You see.

Sir Charles. But did he profess any attachment?

Miss Hardcastle. A lasting one.

Sir Charles. Did he talk of love?

Miss Hardcastle. Much, sir.

Sir Charles. Amazing! And all this formally?

Miss Hardcastle. Formally.

Hardcastle. Now, my friend, I hope you are satisfied.

Sir Charles. And how did he behave, madam?

Miss Hardcastle. As most professed admirers do; said some civil things of my face; talked much of his want of merit, and the greatness of mine; mentioned his heart, gave a short tragedy speech, and ended with pretended rapture.

Sir Charles. Now I'm perfectly convinced, indeed. I know his conversation among women to be modest and submissive. This forward, canting, ranting manner by no means describes him, and, I am confident, he never sate[1] for the picture.

Miss Hardcastle. Then what, sir, if I should convince you to your face of my sincerity? If you and my papa, in about half an hour, will place yourselves behind that screen, you shall hear him declare his passion to me in person.

Sir Charles. Agreed. And if I find him what you describe, all my happiness in him must have an end. [*Exit.*

Miss Hardcastle. And if you don't find him what I describe —I fear my happiness must never have a beginning. [*Exeunt.*

[1] Sate—Sat.

Then what, sir, if I should convince you to your face of my sincerity?

Scene 2. *The back of the garden.*

Enter Hastings.

Hastings. What an idiot am I to wait here for a fellow who probably takes a delight in mortifying me. He never intended to be punctual, and I'll wait no longer. What do I see? It is he, and perhaps with news of my Constance.

Enter Tony, *booted and spattered.*[2]

Hastings. My honest Squire! I now find you a man of your word. This looks like friendship.

Tony. Ay, I'm your friend, and the best friend you have in the world, if you knew but all. This riding by night, by the bye, is cursedly tiresome. It has shook me worse than the basket of a stage-coach.

Hastings. But how? where did you leave your fellow-travellers? Are they in safety? Are they housed?

Tony. Five and twenty miles in two hours and a half is no such bad driving. The poor beasts have smoked for it: rabbit me! but I'd rather ride forty miles after a fox, than ten with such *varment.*

Hastings. Well, but where have you left the ladies? I die with impatience.

Tony. Left them! Why, where should I leave them but where I found them?

Hastings. This is a riddle.

Tony. Riddle me this, then. What's that goes round the house, and round the house, and never touches the house?

Hastings. I'm still astray.

Tony. Why, that's it, mon. I have led them astray. By jingo, there's not a pond nor slough within five miles of the place but they can tell the taste of.

Hastings. Ha! ha! ha! I understand; you took them in a round,[3] while they supposed themselves going forward. And so you have at last brought them home again.

Tony. You shall hear. I first took them down Feather-bed lane, where we stuck fast in the mud. I then rattled them crack over the stones of Up-and-down Hill. I then introduced them

---

[2] Spattered—Gaitered.
[3] Round—Circle.

to the gibbet on Heavy-tree Heath; and from that, with a circumbendibus,[4] I fairly lodged them in the horse-pond at the bottom of the garden.

Hastings. But no accident, I hope?

Tony. No, no; only mother is confoundedly frightened. She thinks herself forty miles off. She's sick of the journey; and the cattle[5] can scarce crawl. So, if your own horses be ready, you may whip off with Cousin, and I'll be bound that no soul here can budge a foot to follow you.

Hastings. My dear friend, how can I be grateful?

Tony. Ay, now it's "dear friend," "noble Squire." Just now, it was all "idiot," "cub," and run me through the guts. Hang *your* way of fighting, I say. After we take a knock in this part of the country, we kiss and be friends. But if you had run me through the guts, then I should be dead, and you might go kiss the hangman.

Hastings. The rebuke is just. But I must hasten to relieve Miss Neville; if you keep the old lady employed, I promise to take care of the young one.

Tony. Never fear me. Here she comes. Vanish! [*Exit* HASTINGS.] She's got from the pond, and draggled up to the waist like a mermaid.

Enter MRS. HARDCASTLE.

Mrs. Hardcastle. Oh, Tony, I'm killed! Shook! Battered to death! I shall never survive it. That last jolt, that laid us against the quickset[6] hedge, has done my business.

Tony. Alack, mamma, it was all your own fault. You would be for running away by night, without knowing one inch of the way.

Mrs. Hardcastle. I wish we were at home again. I never met so many accidents in so short a journey. Drenched in the mud, overturned in a ditch, stuck fast in a slough, jolted to a jelly, and at last to lose our way! Whereabouts do you think we are, Tony?

Tony. By my guess, we should be upon Crack-skull Common, about forty miles from home.

---

[4] CIRCUMBENDIBUS—What is the meaning here?
[5] CATTLE—Horses.
[6] QUICKSET—Hawthorn.

Mrs. Hardcastle. O lud! O lud! The most notorious spot in all the country. We only want a robbery to make a complete night on 't.

Tony. Don't be afraid, mamma; don't be afraid. Two of the five that kept here are hanged, and the other three may not find us. Don't be afraid. Is that a man that's galloping behind us? No, it's only a tree. Don't be afraid.

Mrs. Hardcastle. The fright will certainly kill me.

Tony. Do you see anything like a black hat moving behind the thicket?

Mrs. Hardcastle. Oh, death!

Tony. No, it's only a cow. Don't be afraid, mamma, don't be afraid.

Mrs. Hardcastle. As I'm alive, Tony, I see a man coming towards us. Ah, I am sure on 't! If he perceives us, we are undone.

Tony. [*Aside.*] Father-in-law, by all that's unlucky, come to take one of his night walks. [*To her.*] Ah, it's a highwayman, with pistols as long as my arm. An ill-looking fellow!

Mrs. Hardcastle. Good Heaven defend us! He approaches.

Tony. Do you hide yourself in that thicket, and leave me to manage him. If there be any danger, I'll cough and cry hem. When I cough, be sure to keep close. [MRS. HARDCASTLE *hides behind a tree in the back scene.*]

Enter HARDCASTLE.

Hardcastle. I'm mistaken, or I heard voices of people in want of help. Oh, Tony, is that you? I did not expect you so soon back. Are your mother and her charge in safety?

Tony. Very safe, sir, at my Aunt Pedigree's. Hem.

Mrs. Hardcastle. [*From behind.*] Ah, death! I find there's danger.

Hardcastle. Forty miles in three hours; sure that's too much, my youngster.

Tony. Stout horses and willing minds make short journeys, as they say. Hem.

Mrs. Hardcastle. [*From behind.*] Sure, he'll do the dear boy no harm.

Hardcastle. But I heard a voice here; I should be glad to know from whence it came.

Tony. It was I, sir, talking to myself, sir. I was saying that forty miles in four hours was very good going. Hem. As to be sure it was. Hem. I have got a sort of cold by being out in the air. We'll go in, if you please. Hem.

Hardcastle. But if you talked to yourself, you did not answer yourself. I'm certain I heard two voices, and resolved [*Raising his voice.*] to find the other out.

Mrs. Hardcastle. [*From behind.*] Oh! he's coming to find me out. Oh!

Tony. What need you go, sir, if I tell you? Hem. I'll lay down my life for the truth—hem—I'll tell you all, sir. [*Detaining him.*]

Hardcastle. I tell you I will not be detained. I insist on seeing. It's in vain to expect I'll believe you.

Mrs. Hardcastle. [*Running forward from behind.*] O lud! he'll murder my poor boy, my darling! Here, good gentleman, whet your rage upon me. Take my money, my life, but spare that young gentleman; spare my child, if you have any mercy.

Hardcastle. My wife, as I'm a Christian! From whence can she come, or what does she mean?

Mrs. Hardcastle. [*Kneeling.*] Take compassion on us, good Mr. Highwayman. Take our money, our watches, all we have, but spare our lives. We will never bring you to justice; indeed we won't, good Mr. Highwayman.

Hardcastle. I believe the woman's out of her senses. What, Dorothy, don't you know *me?*

Mrs. Hardcastle. Mr. Hardcastle, as I'm alive! My fears blinded me. But who, my dear, could have expected to meet you here, in this frightful place, so far from home? What has brought you to follow us?

Hardcastle. Sure, Dorothy, you have not lost your wits? So far from home, when you are within forty yards of your own door! [*To him.*] This is one of your old tricks, you graceless rogue, you! [*To her.*] Don't you know the gate, and the mulberry tree; and don't you remember the horse-pond, my dear?

Mrs. Hardcastle. Yes, I shall remember the horse-pond as long as I live; I have caught my death in it. [*To* Tony.] And is it to you, you graceless varlet, I owe all this? I'll teach you to abuse your mother, I will.

Tony. Ecod, mother, all the parish says you have spoiled me, so you may take the fruits on 't.

Mrs. Hardcastle. I'll spoil you, I will.

[*Follows him off the stage.*

Hardcastle. There's morality, however, in his reply. [*Exit.*

Enter Hastings *and* Miss Neville.

Hastings. My dear Constance, why will you deliberate thus? If we delay a moment, all is lost forever. Pluck up a little resolution, and we shall soon be out of the reach of her malignity.

Miss Neville. I find it impossible. My spirits are so sunk with the agitations I have suffered, that I am unable to face any new danger. Two or three years' patience will at last crown us with happiness.

Hastings. Such a tedious delay is worse than inconstancy. Let us fly, my charmer! Let us date our happiness from this very moment. Perish fortune. Love and content will increase what we possess beyond a monarch's revenue. Let me prevail!

Miss Neville. No, Mr. Hastings, no. Prudence once more comes to my relief, and I will obey its dictates. In the moment of passion, fortune may be despised but it ever produces a lasting repentance. I'm resolved to apply to Mr. Hardcastle's compassion and justice for redress.

Hastings. But though he had the will he has not the power to relieve you.

Miss Neville. But he has influence, and upon that I am resolved to rely.

Hastings. I have no hopes. But, since you persist, I must reluctantly obey you. [*Exeunt.*

Scene 3. *The house.*

Enter Sir Charles Marlow *and* Miss Hardcastle.

Sir Charles. What a situation am I in! If what you say appears, I shall then find a guilty son. If what he says be true, I shall then lose one that, of all others, I most wished for a daughter.

Miss Hardcastle. I am proud of your approbation; and to show I merit it, if you place yourself as I directed, you shall hear his explicit declaration. But he comes.

Sir Charles. I'll to your father, and keep him to the appointment. [*Exit* Sir Charles.

Enter Marlow.

Marlow. Though prepared for setting out, I come once more to take leave; nor did I, till this moment, know the pain I feel in the separation.

Miss Hardcastle. [*In her own natural manner.*] I believe these sufferings cannot be very great, sir, which you can so easily remove. A day or two longer, perhaps, might lessen your uneasiness, by showing the little value of what you now think proper to regret.

Marlow. [*Aside.*] This girl every moment improves upon me. [*To her.*] It must not be, madam; I have already trifled too long with my heart. My very pride begins to submit to my passion. The disparity of education and fortune, the anger of a parent, and the contempt of my equals begin to lose their weight; and nothing can restore me to myself but this painful effort of resolution.

Miss Hardcastle. Then go, sir: I'll urge nothing more to detain you. Though my family be as good as hers you came down to visit, and my education, I hope, not inferior, what are these advantages without equal affluence? I must remain contented with the slight approbation of imputed merit; I must have only the mockery of your addresses, while all your serious aims are fixed on fortune.

Enter Hardcastle *and* Sir Charles Marlow, *from behind.*

Sir Charles. Here, behind this screen.

Hardcastle. Ay, ay; make no noise. I'll engage my Kate covers him with confusion at last.

Marlow. By heavens, madam, fortune was ever my smallest consideration. Your beauty at first caught my eye; for who could see that without emotion? But every moment that I converse with you, steals in some new grace, heightens the picture, and gives it stronger expression. What at first seemed rustic plainness, now appears refined simplicity. What seemed forward assurance, now strikes me as the result of courageous innocence and conscious virtue.

Sir Charles. What can it mean? He amazes me!

Hardcastle. I told you how it would be. Hush!

Marlow. I am now determined to stay, madam, and I have too good an opinion of my father's discernment, when he sees you, to doubt his approbation.

Miss Hardcastle. No, Mr. Marlow, I will not, cannot detain you. Do you think I could suffer a connection in which there is the smallest room for repentance? Do you think I would take the mean advantage of a transient passion to load you with confusion? Do you think I could ever relish that happiness which was acquired by lessening yours?

Marlow. By all that's good, I can have no happiness but what's in your power to grant me! Nor shall I ever feel repentance but in not having seen your merits before. I will stay, even contrary to your wishes; and though you should persist to shun me, I will make my respectful assiduities atone for the levity of my past conduct.

Miss Hardcastle. Sir, I must entreat you'll desist. As our acquaintance began, so let it end, in indifference. I might have given an hour or two to levity; but seriously, Mr. Marlow, do you think I could ever submit to a connection where I must appear mercenary, and you imprudent? Do you think I could ever catch at the confident addresses of a secure admirer?

Marlow. [*Kneeling.*] Does this look like security? Does this look like confidence? No, madam, every moment that shows me your merit, only serves to increase my diffidence and confusion. Here let me continue—

Sir Charles. I can hold it no longer. Charles, Charles, how hast thou deceived me! Is this your indifference, your uninteresting conversation?

Hardcastle. Your cold contempt! your informal interview! What have you to say now?

Marlow. That I'm all amazement! What can it mean?

Hardcastle. It means that you can say and unsay things at pleasure; that you can address a lady in private, and deny it in public; that you have one story for us, and another for my daughter.

Marlow. Daughter!—this lady your daughter?

Hardcastle. Yes, sir, my only daughter—my Kate; whose else should she be?

Marlow. Zounds!

Miss Hardcastle. Yes, sir, that very identical tall, squinting lady you were pleased to take me for [*curtseying*]; she that you addressed as the mild, modest, sentimental man of gravity, and the bold, forward, agreeable Rattle of the Ladies' Club. Ha! ha! ha!

Marlow. Zounds, there's no bearing this; it's worse than death!

Miss Hardcastle. In which of your characters, sir, will you give us leave to address you? As the faltering gentleman, with looks on the ground, that speaks just to be heard, and hates hypocrisy; or the loud, confident creature, that keeps it up with Mrs. Mantrap, and old Miss Biddy Buckskin, till three in the morning? Ha! ha! ha!

Marlow. Oh, curse on my noisy head! I never attempted to be impudent yet that I was not taken down. I must be gone.

Hardcastle. By the hand of my body, but you shall not. I see it was all a mistake, and I am rejoiced to find it. You shall not, sir, I tell you. I know she'll forgive you. Won't you forgive him, Kate? We'll all forgive you. Take courage, man.

[*They retire, she tormenting him, to the back scene.*

Enter Mrs. Hardcastle *and* Tony.

Mrs. Hardcastle. So, so, they're gone off. Let them go, I care not.

Hardcastle. Who gone?

Mrs. Hardcastle. My dutiful niece and her gentleman, Mr. Hastings, from town. He who came down with our modest visitor here.

Sir Charles. Who, my honest George Hastings! As worthy a fellow as lives, and the girl could not have made a more prudent choice.

Hardcastle. Then, by the hand of my body, I'm proud of the connection.

Mrs. Hardcastle. Well, if he has taken away the lady, he has not taken her fortune; that remains in this family to console us for her loss.

Hardcastle. Sure, Dorothy, you would not be so mercenary?

Mrs. Hardcastle. Ay, that's my affair, not yours.

Hardcastle. But you know if your son, when of age, refuses to marry his cousin, her whole fortune is then at her own disposal.

Mrs. Hardcastle. Ay, but he's not of age, and she has not thought proper to wait for his refusal.

Enter HASTINGS *and* MISS NEVILLE.

Mrs. Hardcastle. [*Aside.*] What, returned so soon? I begin not to like it.

Hastings. [*To* HARDCASTLE.] For my late attempt to fly off with your niece, let my present confusion be my punishment. We are now come back, to appeal from your justice to your humanity. By her father's consent I first paid her my addresses, and our passions were first founded in duty.

Miss Neville. Since his death, I have been obliged to stoop to dissimulation to avoid oppression. In an hour of levity, I was ready even to give up my fortune to secure my choice. But I am now recovered from the delusion, and hope from your tenderness what is denied me from a nearer connection.

Mrs. Hardcastle. Pshaw! pshaw; this is all but the whining end of a modern novel.

Hardcastle. Be it what it will, I'm glad they're come back to reclaim their due. Come hither, Tony, boy. Do you refuse this lady's hand, whom I now offer you?

Tony. What signifies my refusing? You know I can't refuse her till I'm of age, father.

Hardcastle. While I thought concealing your age, boy, was likely to conduce to your improvement, I concurred with your mother's desire to keep it secret. But since I find she turns it to a wrong use, I must now declare you have been of age this three months.

Tony. Of age! Am I of age, father?

Hardcastle. Above three months.

Tony. Then you'll see the first use I'll make of my liberty. [*Taking* MISS NEVILLE'S *hand.*] Witness all men, by these presents, that I, Anthony Lumpkin, Esquire, of BLANK place, refuse you, Constantia Neville, spinster, of no place at all, for my true and lawful wife. So Constance Neville may marry whom she pleases, and Tony Lumpkin is his own man again!

Sir Charles. Oh, brave Squire!

Hastings. My worthy friend!

Mrs. Hardcastle. My undutiful offspring.

Marlow. Joy, my dear George, I give you joy sincerely! And could I prevail upon my little tyrant here to be less arbitrary, I should be the happiest man alive, if you would return me the favor.

Hastings. [*To* Miss Hardcastle.] Come, madam, you are now driven to the very last scene of all your contrivances. I know you like him, I'm sure he loves you, and you must and shall have him.

Hardcastle. [*Joining their hands.*] And I say so, too. And, Mr. Marlow, if she makes as good a wife as she has a daughter, I don't believe you'll ever repent your bargain. So now to supper. To-morrow we shall gather all the poor of the parish about us, and the Mistakes of the Night shall be crowned with a merry morning. So, boy, take her; and as you have been mistaken in the mistress, my wish is, that you may never be mistaken in the wife. [*Exeunt Omnes.*

By Way of Appreciation

As was noted at the beginning of the play, the purpose of *She Stoops to Conquer* is entertainment. Its plot, ingenious as it is, is not at all important. The best feature of the play is its skillful characterization. Hardcastle is an excellent picturization of the boresome elderly man who is always attempting to tell long, drawn-out stories. Mrs. Hardcastle is an example of the doting mother always scheming to get what she wants for her pampered son. Young Marlow is the typical "man about town" who suddenly becomes ill at ease in the presence of women of his own class. Tony Lumpkin is so perfect a representation of the practical joker and "Mr. Fixit" that his name has commonly come to be applied to characters of his type in real life. One who has once read or seen the play will know instantly the type of man a chance acquaintance really is if someone remarks, "Well, he's a Tony Lumpkin."

General Suggestions for Reading and Study

Read the play through quickly for the purpose of becoming acquainted with the story or plot. Familiarize yourself with the *Dramatis Personæ*, but do not memorize the names. Try to place each person definitely as to his character and his part in the play. It must be remembered that being a period play the text will have many words and expressions not now common and probably somewhat difficult. Whenever doubt arises, consult the footnotes. After the first reading, reread more carefully, using the suggestions below for intensive study.

THE PLAY BY ACTS AND SCENES

Act I

How would you stage the opening scene? What sort of people do you find the Hardcastles to be? What sort of person do you expect to find in Tony? Why? Does his first appearance bear out your expectations? How does the author contrive to get his characters on and off the stage? Does this seem natural or forced? Be definite in your answer. What in the language of the characters seems to be stilted? Quote examples from the play. What does this teach us about the period?

What details of the plot developed in this scene seem hackneyed here? Were they so at the time of the play? What are we led to expect in young Marlow? How does the author contrive to give us this impression?

Make a sketch of the stage as you would arrange it for Scene 2. What characters would you include for carrying out the direction, "several shabby fellows"? What action would you have as the curtain rises? What is the purpose of this scene? What does it contribute to the plot? Be explicit in your answer.

Act II

Is the opening scene effective? How? If you can get a copy of Molnar's *The Swan*, compare the use of the same idea with Goldsmith's. Which is more effective? Why? Criticize the conversation between Marlow and Hastings. What is its purpose? Is this achieved? What part does Tony play here? What do Tony's friends think of him? Explain your answer. How is the character of young Marlow developed in this scene? Explain the unexpected twist taken by the plot in Act II. What is the part of Hastings in this act? Discuss the ending of the act.

Act III
What is the function of the opening dialogue between Hardcastle and his daughter? What outcome are you led to expect? Can you justify Tony's deceit? His plan? Note the play on words in the scene between Tony and his mother just after her discovery of the robbery. Show how this would amuse an audience. Has it any other purpose than amusement? Is Marlow's failure to recognize Kate in the barmaid believable? Why? What do we learn about Marlow in this scene? How does this affect Kate?

Act IV
What new twist is taken by the plot now? Does this add to suspense? How is it used later in the plot? What is the part played by Jeremy? Is he vital to the success of the play? Explain. Is Marlow's reaction to the revelation of his stupidity natural? Explain.

What new meaning have you learned for the word *macaroni?* Does this explain its use in the American song, *Yankee Doodle?* How would you stage the triangular scene between Miss Neville, Tony, and Mrs. Hardcastle? Is the letter device a good one? Explain. How is suspense aroused at the conclusion of this act?

Act V
Is the scene between Hardcastle and Sir Charles natural? Effective? Why? What is the purpose of Scene 1? Is it achieved?

Trace Tony's cleverness as displayed in Scene 2. What is the effect upon Mrs. Hardcastle? What is the purpose of the dialogue between Hastings and Miss Neville?

Is the use of the screen effective? Why? What is the value of the occasional "asides" given with stage directions? What disposition does the author make of the main characters? Is this effectively done? Are all sufficiently rewarded or punished? Explain. How has young Marlow "improved"? Show definitely how you would stage the closing episode. Would you follow the last stage direction? If not, what would you substitute? Why?

The Play as a Whole
What part does setting play in the development of the plot? How do you account for this? What is the main plot of the play? Outline it briefly. Outline the most important sub-plot. Can these outlines be divided into the five plot divisions, *introduction, rising action, climax, falling action,* and *conclusion?* Whom do you consider to be the chief male character? The chief female character? By definite references to the play, write character sketches of Hardcastle, Mrs. Hardcastle, Tony, and young Marlow. Criticize the ending of the play. Could it have been improved? How? Why is this play classed as a comedy? Contrast this play with a typically modern one; with *Macbeth.*

THE HISTORY OF THE DRAMA IN ENGLAND

The Age of Romanticism (1780–1840)

General Characteristics

Following the dramatic triumphs of Goldsmith and Sheridan, the literature of the latter part of the eighteenth and the beginning of the nineteenth centuries was peculiarly undramatic. This was essentially an age of poetry. The fanciful, the remote, and the whimsical types of ideas seemed to dominate. It has often been said that never in English history were literature and the stage more widely divorced. In spite of this a few dramatists did produce works that were more or less popular. Many of the plays, however, were either produced or found public favor after the close of the Age of Romanticism and toward the end of the nineteenth century.

The Work of Two Poets

Two names famous for the fine literary quality of their poetry also deserve mention for beautiful, though few, contributions to the drama. These names are Walter Savage Landor (1775–1864) and Percy Bysshe Shelley (1792–1822). Landor wrote a noteworthy poetic tragedy, *Count Julian,* and a masterful piece called *Tiberius and Vipsania.* Shelley wrote two outstanding dramatic poems, *The Cenci* and *Prometheus Unbound,* and a poetic drama, *Hellas. Prometheus Unbound* is considered by many critics Shelley's finest work.

Other Dramatists of the Romantic Age

Joanna Baillie is remembered for her *Plays on the Passions* which are particularly effective romantic treatments of various emotions; Sheridan Knowles, an Irish dramatist, and cousin to Richard Brinsley Sheridan, wrote two particularly fine plays, *William Tell* and *The Hunchback;* Tom Taylor was author of two plays still popular with modern audiences, *Our American Cousin* and *The Ticket-of-Leave Man;* and T. W. Robertson wrote a play entitled *David Garrick* which was based on the life of the famous actor.

The Victorian Era (1840–1900)

General Characteristics

Drama remained more or less dull and uninteresting, and dramatists were few and generally mediocre during the early years of the Victorian Era. While conditions in the theater itself improved (more comfortable seats, better stage equipment, etc.), and while the theater-going public in London grew in size and quality, plays presented were revivals and there seemed to be little interest in the production of a new drama. "Strolling players" visited the provinces much as American road and stock companies visit regions of the country outside New York City.

Here again the chief interest lay in revivals of earlier plays. This period has often been called "the age of actors," for British interest centered almost wholly in great acting, to the almost complete exclusion of great plays.

During the latter part of the era a great Norwegian dramatist, Henrik Ibsen, completely revolutionized the drama of the European continent. Very naturally his influence spread to England. His powerful treatment of current social issues stimulated a group of British writers to produce a series of great plays, similar in subject matter and treatment to Ibsen's works, but distinctly British. Simultaneously came a new interest in light opera, found at its best in the often revived favorites by Gilbert and Sullivan, *The Mikado, Trial by Jury,* and *Pirates of Penzance.* Revues, extravaganzas, plays with music, and the like filled London and provincial theaters, but contributed naturally to the slow recovery of true drama.

Pinero, Jones, and Wilde

Three truly noteworthy names in British dramaturgy are those who were in large measure responsible for the modern movement in play writing. Influenced greatly by Ibsen, they began to write social plays of true dramatic power.

Sir Arthur Wing Pinero (1855–   ) is probably best known for his tragedy, *The Second Mrs. Tanqueray.* Others of his best works are *The Magistrate, Trelawney of the Wells, Iris,* and *The Thunderbolt.*

Henry Arthur Jones (1851–1929), a contemporary of Pinero, first won recognition through *The Silver King.* A succession of plays including *The Liars, Mary Goes First,* and *Saints and Sinners,* showed a developing character power, placing him in first rank.

Two plays, *The Importance of Being Earnest,* a skillful comedy, and *Lady Windermere's Fan,* a powerful social drama, also place Oscar Wilde (1856–1900) among the best modern dramatists. He is author of many other plays including *An Ideal Husband* and *Salome.*

Other Victorian Dramatists

Many authorities place the year 1890 as the beginning of the modern era in drama rather than 1900. A number of great dramatists who will be treated in the Twentieth Century Period began their work in the Victorian Era, among whom the two most notable are George Bernard Shaw and Sir James Matthew Barrie.

THE TWENTIETH CENTURY (1900–   )

General Characteristics

The end of the Victorian Era foreshadowed the modern age in drama. Works popular in one age carried over into the next. Playwrights of the 90's still produced new plays after the turn of the century. Others appeared in such rapid succession and such great numbers that an exhaustive list would be almost impossible to construct. The Twentieth Century is an age of internationalism in the theatrical world, and plays produced in one language are sure to be produced in practically all others, if at all successful. Artists are interchanged freely, this being particularly true of the British and American stages.

There is probably no particularly distinguishing characteristic of twentieth century drama. It is frank, daring, socialistic, problem-solving, and almost entirely unlimited as to both subject matter and treatment.

George Bernard Shaw (1856–)

Although Shaw's dramatic career really began about 1890, he more properly belongs to the twentieth century. He is perhaps the most outstanding personality in English drama today. By birth Shaw is an Irishman, born in Dublin in 1856. At the age of twenty he went to London and there during the next ten years went through a variety of experiences, followed a variety of occupations, and became an ardent socialist. During these years his mind was set on a literary career. In 1895 he became a dramatic critic for the *Saturday Review.* Shaw has been a prolific writer and talker; he has written essays and social and literary criticism, and probably none of his contemporaries has given more interviews. He has a habit of prefixing to his plays prefaces, which are oftentimes longer than the play itself, to explain the ideas embodied in the play. In Shaw's hands the play is invariably simply a means for social satire. In the present arrangements of society he finds much which stirs his dissatisfaction. His first play of consequence was *Arms and the Man* produced in 1894. It is a satire upon military glory.

Other outstanding plays are *Candida, Man and Superman, Androcles and the Lion,* and *Saint Joan;* in some respects this last play is his best. There is satire in it but it is subdued and directed against a human weakness of long standing. According to Shaw's interpretation of Joan of Arc, the root of her power was not in the supernatural so much as in her unselfish devotion and sincerity, qualities whose great power Shaw implies the practical man has always been so blind to that he has, as in the case of Joan of Arc, attributed their effect to everything but the true cause. Shaw is versatile, keen, and stimulating.

Sir James Matthew Barrie (1860–1937)

In 1893 there was produced a play *Walker, London,* by the novelist Barrie. This was the beginning of a long dramatic career which placed the author in the first rank. Barrie was not concerned with social problems. First of all he was an able playwright; he wrote plays which would act, and which abounded in charm, whimsical fantasy, and humor. His characters were also well done. Practically all of his plays are well known and many of them have been popularized through amateur production. His chief plays are *The Admirable Crichton, The Little Minister, Peter Pan, A Kiss for Cinderella,* and *Dear Brutus.* He also wrote many superior one-act plays.

Other Great Names of the Twentieth Century

In addition to the works of Shaw and Barrie, fine dramas have been written by John Galsworthy who has used drama especially for the purpose of social criticism in such plays as *The Silver Box, Justice, Strife,* and *Loyalties;* John Masefield, author of *The Tragedy of Man* and *The Tragedy of Pompey the Great;* John Drinkwater, best known probably, for his *Abraham Lincoln;* Arnold Bennett, author of *The Great Adventure;* Granville Barker, a playwright of considerable ability whose best known play is *The Madras House;* and Alfred Sutro, author of *The Two Virtues* and many fine one-act plays.

During the past decade, a number of new playwrights have appeared, among whom are A. A. Milne, Allan Monkhouse, Hubert Davies, Noel Coward, Somerset Maugham, Eden Philpotts, Harold Brighouse, and Clemence Dane.

The Irish Drama

One of the most interesting movements in British drama of the present period has been the attempt to found an Irish National Theater. Rarely do we find careful distinction made among English, Irish, Scottish, and Welsh writers, for all are usually classed as British. Stirred no doubt, by political nationalistic movements, by "little theater group" activities everywhere, several writers of Irish nationality undertook to preserve Irish folklore, traditions and superstitions in dramatic form. Certain outstanding playwrights of this movement, together with some of their better known plays are, John Millington Synge, author of *Riders to the Sea, The Playboy of the Western World,* and *Deidre of the Sorrows;* Lady Augusta Gregory, known for *Spreading the News, The Rising of the Moon,* and *Hyacinth Halvey;* St. John Ervine, author of *Mixed Marriage* and *The First Mrs. Fraser;* Lord Dunsany, author of *The Gods of the Mountain, The Golden Doom,* and *A Night at an Inn;* Sean O'Casey, known for *The Shadow of a Gunman* and *The Plough and the Stars;* and William Butler Yeats, author of *The Land of Heart's Desire, The Hour Class,* and *Cathleen ni Houlihan.*

Twentieth Century Drama

THE LOST SILK HAT *

Lord Dunsany

By Way of Introduction: This play, representative of the work of the Irish group, is merely a whimsical treatment of characterization of several types of Britishers. Its aim is rather to show variations in type characters than to develop any particular plot.

CHARACTERS

The Caller   The Clerk
The Laborer   The Poet
The Policeman

Scene: *A fashionable London street.*

The Caller *stands on a doorstep, "faultlessly dressed," but without a hat. At first he shows despair, then a new thought engrosses him. Enter the* Laborer.

The Caller. Excuse me a moment. Excuse me—but—I'd be greatly obliged to you if—if you could see your way—in fact, you can be of great service to me if——

The Laborer. Glad to do what I can, sir.

Caller. Well, all I really want you to do is just to ring that bell and go up and say—er—say that you've come to see to the drains, or anything like that, you know, and get hold of my hat for me.

Laborer. Get hold of your 'at!

Caller. Yes. You see, I left my hat behind, most unfortunately. It's in the drawing-room [*Points to window.*], that room there, half under the long sofa, the far end from the door. And if you could possibly go and get it, why, I'd be [*The* Laborer's *expression changes.*]—Why, what's the matter?

Laborer. [*Firmly.*] I don't like this job.

---

* From *Five Plays* by Lord Dunsany. Reprinted by permission. Copyright, 1914, by Little, Brown, and Company. All dramatic rights reserved by the author. This play is fully protected by the copyright law, all requirements of which have been complied with. In its present printed form it is dedicated to the reading public only, and no performance of it, either professional or amateur, may be given without the written permission of the owner of the acting rights, who may be addressed in care of the publishers, Little, Brown, and Company.

Caller. Don't like this job! But my dear fellow, don't be silly, what possible harm——?

Laborer. Ah-h. That's what I don't know.

Caller. But what harm can there possibly be in so simple a request? What harm does there seem to be?

Laborer. Oh, it seems all right.

Caller. *Well,* then.

Laborer. All these crack jobs do seem all right.

Caller. But I'm not asking you to rob the house.

Laborer. Don't seem as if you are, certainly, but I don't like the looks of it; what if there's things what I can't 'elp taking when I gets inside?

Caller. I only want my hat— Here, I say, please don't go away—here's a sovereign, it will only take you a minute.

Laborer. *What I want to know*——

Caller. Yes?

Laborer. —Is what's *in* that hat?

Caller. What's *in* the hat?

Laborer. Yes; that's what I want to know.

Caller. What's *in* that hat?

Laborer. Yes, you aren't going to give me a sovereign——?

Caller. I'll give you two sovereigns.

Laborer. You aren't going to give me a sovereign, and rise it to two sovereigns, for an *empty* hat?

Caller. But I must have my hat. I can't be seen in the streets like this. There's nothing *in* the hat. What do you think's in the hat?

Laborer. Ah, I'm not clever enough to say that, but it looks as if the papers was in that hat.

Caller. The papers?

Laborer. Yes, papers proving, if you can get them, that you're the heir to that big house, and some poor innocent will be defrauded.

Caller. Look here, the hat's absolutely empty. I *must* have my hat. If there's anything in it you shall have it yourself as well as the two pounds, only get me my hat.

Laborer. Well, that seems all right.

Caller. That's right, then you'll run up and get it?

Laborer. Seems all right to me and seems all right to you.

But it's the police what you and I have got to think of. Will it seem all right to them?

Caller. Oh, for heaven's sake——

Laborer. Ah!

Caller. What a hopeless fool you are.

Laborer. Ah!

Caller. Look here.

Laborer. Ah, I got you there, mister.

Caller. Look here, for goodness' sake don't go.

Laborer. Ah! [*Exit.*]

[*Enter the* CLERK.]

Caller. Excuse me, sir. Excuse my asking you, but, as you see, I am without a hat. I shall be extraordinarily obliged to you if you would be so very good as to get it for me. Pretend you have come to wind the clocks, you know. I left it in the drawing-room of this house, half under the long sofa, the far end.

Clerk. Oh, er—all right, only——

Caller. Thanks so much, I am immensely indebted to you. Just say you've come to wind the clocks, you know.

Clerk. I—er—don't think I'm very good at winding clocks, you know.

Caller. Oh, that's all right, just stand in front of the clock and fool about with it. That's all they ever do. I must warn you there's a lady in the room.

Clerk. Oh!

Caller. But that's all right, you know. Just walk past up to the clock.

Clerk. But I think, if you don't mind, as there's someone there——

Caller. Oh, but she's quite young and very, very beautiful and——

Clerk. Why don't you get it yourself?

Caller. That is impossible.

Clerk. Impossible?

Caller. Yes, I have sprained my ankle.

Clerk. Oh! Is it bad?

Caller. Yes, very bad indeed.

Clerk. I don't mind trying to carry you up.

Caller. No, that would be worse. My foot has to be kept on the ground.

Clerk. But how will you get home?

Caller. I can walk all right on the flat.

Clerk. I'm afraid I have to be going on. It's rather later than I thought.

Caller. But for goodness' sake don't leave me. You can't leave me here like this without a hat.

Clerk. I'm afraid I must, it's later than I thought. [*Exit.*]

[*Enter the* Poet.]

Caller. Excuse me, sir. Excuse my stopping you. But I should be immensely obliged to you if you would do me a very great favor. I have unfortunately left my hat behind while calling at this house. It is half under the long sofa, at the far end. If you could possibly be so kind as to pretend you have come to tune the piano and fetch my hat for me I should be enormously grateful to you.

Poet. But why cannot you get it for yourself?

Caller. I cannot.

Poet. If you would tell me the reason perhaps I could help you.

Caller. I cannot. I can never enter that house again.

Poet. If you have committed a murder, by all means tell me. I am not sufficiently interested in ethics to wish to have you hanged for it.

Caller. Do I look like a murderer?

Poet. No, of course not. I am only saying that you can safely trust me, for not only does the statute book and its penalties rather tend to bore me, but murder itself has always had a certain fascination for me. I write delicate and fastidious lyrics, yet, strange as it may appear, I read every murder trial, and my sympathies are always with the prisoner.

Caller. But I tell you I am not a murderer.

Poet. Then what have you done?

Caller. I have quarreled with a lady in that house and have sworn to join the Bosnians [1] and die in Africa.

Poet. But this is beautiful.

Caller. Unfortunately I forgot my hat.

---

[1] Bosnians—Natives of Bosnia, a province of Yugoslavia. The Caller simply means any out-of-the-way country.

Poet. You go to die for a hopeless love, and in a far country; it was wont of the troubadours.[2]

Caller. But you will get my hat for me?

Poet. That I will gladly do for you. But we must find an adequate reason for entering the house.

Caller. You pretend to tune the piano.

Poet. That, unfortunately, is impossible. The sound of a piano being unskillfully handled is to me what the continual drop of cold water on the same part of the head is said to be in countries where that interesting torture is practiced. There is——

Caller. But what are we to do?

Poet. There is a house where kind friends of mine have given me that security and comfort that are a poet's necessity. But there was a governess there and a piano. It is years and years since I was able even to see the faces of those friends without an inward shudder.

Caller. Well, we'll have to think of something else.

Poet. You are bringing back to these unhappy days the romance of an age of which the ballads tell.

Caller. Yes, but you know first of all I must get my *hat*.

Poet. But why?

Caller. I cannot possibly be seen in the streets without a hat.

Poet. Why not?

Caller. It can't be done.

Poet. But you confuse externals with essentials.

Caller. I don't know what you call essentials, but being decently dressed in London seems pretty essential to me.

Poet. A hat is not one of the essential things of life.

Caller. I don't want to appear rude, but my hat isn't quite like yours.

Poet. Let us sit down and talk of things that matter, things that will be remembered after a hundred years. [*They sit.*] Regarded in this light one sees at once the triviality of hats. But to die, and die beautifully for a hopeless love, that is a thing one could make a lyric about. That is the test of essential

---

[2] TROUBADOURS—A class of lyric poets who flourished in the twelfth century in southern France. Their poetry was very romantic and usually dealt with love themes.

things—try and imagine them in a lyric. One could not write a lyric about a hat.

Caller. I don't care whether you could write a lyric about my hat or whether you couldn't. All I know is that I am not going to make myself absolutely ridiculous by walking about in London without a hat. Will you get it for me or will you not?

Poet. To take any part in the tuning of a piano is impossible to me.

Caller. Well, pretend you've come to look at the radiator. They have one under the window, and I happen to know it leaks.

Poet. I suppose it has an artistic decoration on it.

Caller. Yes, I think so.

Poet. Then I decline to look at it or to go near it. I know these decorations in cast iron. I once saw a pot-bellied Egyptian god, named Bes, and he was *meant* to be ugly, but he wasn't as ugly as these decorations that the twentieth century can make with machinery. What has a plumber got to do with art that he should dare to attempt decoration?

Caller. Then you won't help me.

Poet. I won't look at ugly things and I won't listen to ugly noises, but if you can think of any reasonable plan I don't mind helping you.

Caller. I can think of nothing else. You don't look like a plumber or a clock-winder. I can think of nothing more. I have had a terrible ordeal and I am not in the condition to think calmly.

Poet. Then you will have to leave your hat to its altered destiny.

Caller. Why can't you think of a plan? If you're a poet, thinking's rather in your line.

Poet. If I could bring my thoughts to contemplate so absurd a thing as a hat for any length of time no doubt I could think of a plan, but the very triviality of the theme seems to scare them away.

Caller. [*Rising.*] Then I must get it myself.

Poet. For Heaven's sake, don't do that! Think what it means!

Caller. I know it will seem absurd, but not so absurd as walking through London without it.

Poet. I don't mean that. But you will make it up. You

will forgive each other, and you will marry her, and then Romance will be dead. No, don't ring that bell. Go and buy a bayonet, or whatever one does buy, and join the Bosnians.

Caller. I tell you I can't without a hat.

Poet. What is a hat! Will you sacrifice for it a beautiful doom? Think of your bones, neglected and forgotten, lying forlornly because of hopeless love on endless golden sands. "Lying forlorn!"[3] as Keats said. What a word! Forlorn in Africa. The careless Bedouins[4] going past by day, at night the lion's roar, the grievous voice of the desert.

Caller. As a matter of fact, I don't think you're right in speaking of it as desert. The Bosnians, I believe, are only taking it because it is supposed to be the most fertile land in the world.

Poet. What of that? You will not be remembered by geography and statistics, but by golden-mouthed Romance. And that is how Romance sees Africa.

Caller. Well, I'm going to get my hat.

Poet. Think! Think! If you enter by that door you will never fall among the foremost Bosnians. You will never die in a far-off, lonely land to lie by immense Sahara. And she will never weep for your beautiful doom and call herself cruel in vain.

Caller. Hark! She is playing the piano. It seems to me that she might be unhappy about it for years. I don't see much good in that.

Poet. No. *I* will comfort her.

Caller. I'm hanged if you do. Look here! I don't mind saying: I'm hanged if you do.

Poet. Calm yourself. Calm yourself. I do not mean in that way.

Caller. Then what on earth do you mean?

Poet. I will make songs about your beautiful death, glad songs and sad songs. They shall be glad because they tell again the noble tradition of the troubadours, and sad because they tell of your sorrowful destiny and of your hopeless love. I shall make legends also about your lonely bones, telling perhaps how some Arabian men, finding them in the desert by

[3] LYING FORLORN—See Keats' *Ode to a Nightingale.*
[4] BEDOUINS—Nomadic Arabs of the Arabian or North African deserts.

some oasis, memorable in war, wonder who loved them. And then as I read them to her, she weeps perhaps a little, and I read instead of the glory of the soldier, how it overtops our transitory——

Caller. Look here, I'm not aware that you've ever been introduced to her.

Poet. A trifle, a trifle.

Caller. It seems to me that you're in rather an undue hurry for me to get a Jubu spear [5] in me; but I'm going to get my hat first.

Poet. I appeal to you. I appeal to you in the name of beautiful battles, high deeds, and lost causes; in the name of love-tales told to cruel maidens and told in vain. In the name of stricken hearts broken like beautiful heart-strings, I appeal to you. I appeal in the ancient holy name of Romance: *do not ring that bell.*

[CALLER *rings the bell.*]

Poet. [*Sits down, abject.*] You will marry. You will sometimes take a ticket with your wife as far as Paris. Perhaps as far as Cannes.[6] You will be like all the rest. No monument will ever be set up to your memory but——

[*Servant answers bell.* CALLER *says something inaudible. Exit through door.*]

Poet. [*Rising, lifting hand.*] But let there be graven in brass upon this house: Romance was born again here out of due time and died young. [*He sits down.*]

[*Enter* LABORER *and* CLERK *with* POLICEMAN. *The music stops.*]

Policeman. Anything wrong here?

Poet. Everything's wrong. They're going to kill Romance.

Policeman. [*To* LABORER.] This gentleman doesn't seem quite right somehow.

Laborer. They're none of them quite right today.

[*Music starts again.*]

Poet. Ye gods! It is a duet.

Policeman. He seems a bit wrong somehow.

Laborer. You should 'a' seen the other one.

CURTAIN

[5] JUBU—The name of a tribe in central Africa.
[6] CANNES—A famous resort in southern France.

Suggestions for Study: The play should first be read in its entirety for the purpose of gaining the general idea of the author and the major incidents of the story. It should then be re-read for more detailed interpretation and criticism.

Since the treatment of the theme is fanciful and whimsical, the reader should approach it in that mood and should strive to enjoy and appreciate the typical strengths and weaknesses of the characters.

Note the simplicity of stage directions. How would you have the stage set for the rising curtain? How should the caller be costumed in order to comply with the direction "faultlessly dressed"? How would you contrast the caller and the laborer? What lines spoken by the very correct English gentleman are characteristic of his type? What lines are truly representative of the laborer as a type? Of the clerk?

Do the various suggestions of the caller as to excuses for entering the house seem too silly? Can you justify them? What do you imagine the laborer and the clerk think of the caller? What shows this?

Read to the class certain lines typical of the poet. Explain your choice. How does the poet rate the caller? Why? Do you believe the poet really reads "every murder trial"? Why? How does the poet treat each suggestion of the caller? Would you call him a student of human nature? Why? Contrast the philosophy of life of the poet and the caller. What is the meaning of the line "But you confuse externals with essentials"? Why does the poet abhor piano tuning and ornaments on radiators?

Do you feel the poet intended influencing the return of the caller? Justify your answer. What one thing makes the caller return? Is this true to life?

Why does the idea of going to Paris or Cannes strike the poet as so undesirable? What is the significance of the line "Romance was born again here out of due time and died young"?

Why is the policeman introduced for only three lines? Does this strengthen or weaken the play? Explain. Criticize the curtain line of the play.

Write character sketches of the caller, the poet, the laborer. Prove your characterizations by definite reference to the play. Which do you like best? Why? Which do you consider the leading character in the drama? Justify your answer.

The Drama in World Literature

General Characteristics

As has already been pointed out, English drama has borrowed from the foreign at all stages of its development. Foreign movements have influenced English native drama, and translations of continental successes are produced almost simultaneously on both England's and America's stages. London and New York plays are produced interchangeably. Truly the condition of drama is international in subject matter, treatment, and form.

On the Reading of Foreign Plays

Every nation has expressed its ideals and its customs in dramatic form. However, a play written by a dramatist of another land for production in his own country may seem strange to us. The stage may look different. The conversation may be different. Expressions may be used that sound strange to our ears. The whole plot may be based upon an incident that would seem absurd to a modern American. Certain ideals may be made important which we consider trivial. But if it is a good play, it will hold us by a sense of reality, a feeling that we are looking at life, and it will be based upon truths that are universal, no matter in what queer language or actions they may be clothed. These things we should remember in reading foreign plays. We should notice expressions, actions, settings, customs, and ideas that are characteristic of the nation. But more than that we should look for the universal theme of the play and discover what changes must be made in the action and plot to make the theme fit our own nation and time.

The Drama Reveals a Nation's Ideals

Every nation and time has its peculiar problems which the dramatist uses for material. So that besides the universal problems which every dramatist uses, we shall find in the dramas of other nations the presentation of social and political questions which are distinctive, and by which one might guess the nationality of the playwright. The theme of *Loyalty* will make quite a different play in Japan from the same theme in England, because social and political ideas are so different. The drama of a nation is an index to its history and ideals.

Suggested Readings in World Drama

Lack of space forbids the inclusion of a world literature play in this book, but the following list is suggestive of some translations of foreign plays that should prove of interest.

Hungarian
Ferenc Molnar
Liliom
The Swan

Belgian
Maurice Maeterlinck
Blue Bird
Pelleas and Melisande

DRAMA IN WORLD LITERATURE

French
Edmond Rostand
  The Romancers
  Cyrano de Bergerac
  D'Aiglon
  Chantecler
Charles Vildrac
  S. S. Tenacity
Alexandre Dumas
  A Marriage of Convenience
Edouard Bourdet
  Captive
Eugene Brieux
  Blanchette
  The Escape
Anatole France
  The Man Who Married a Dumb Wife
  Crinquebille
Romain Rolland
  Liluli
Molière (Jean Baptiste Poquelin)
  Doctor by Compulsion
  The Imaginary Invalid
  The Miser
  The Merchant Gentlemen
Jean Baptiste Racine
  Berenice
  Esther
Victorien Sardou
  The Black Pearl

Spanish
Quinteros (The)
  The Fountain of Youth
  By Their Words Ye Shall Know Them
Jacinto Benavente
  La Malquerida

Italian
Gabrielle D'Annunzio
  Francesca da Rimini
Luigi Pirandello
  As You Desire Me
  Right You Are If You Think You Are

Norwegian
Henrik Ibsen
  Hedda Gabler
  A Doll's House
  Pillars of Society
Björnstjerne Björnson
  The Newly Married Couple
  Between Battles

German
Johann Wolfgang von Goethe
  Faust
  Egmont
  Iphigenia
Johann Schiller
  Don Carlos
  Wilhelm Tell
Gerhart Hauptmann
  Before Sunrise
  The Sunken Bell
  Pippa Dances
Hermann Sudermann
  Joy of Living
  The Homeland
Georg Kaiser
  The Coral
  From Morning to Midnight
Ernst Toller
  Man and the Masses
Hans Chumberg
  Miracle at Verdun
Arthur Schnitzler
  The Green Cockatoo

Swedish
August Strindberg
  Comrades
  The Father
  Pangs of Conscience

Russian
Anton Chekhov
  The Cherry Orchard
  The Seagull
Leonid Andreyev
  He Who Gets Slapped

Indian
Rabindranath Tagore
  Post Office

EXTENSIVE READING PROGRAM—THE DRAMA

The Age of Elizabeth (1550–1625)

William Shakespeare
Hamlet
Julius Caesar
The Merchant of Venice
As You Like It
Midsummer Night's Dream
Twelfth Night
Much Ado about Nothing
King Lear
Romeo and Juliet
Ben Jonson
Every Man in His Humour
The Faery Prince
The Sad Shepherd
Cynthia's Revels
Francis Beaumont
The Maid's Tragedy
Triumph of Love
Triumph of Death

John Fletcher
The Loyal Subject
The Scornful Lady
Thomas Heywood
The English Traveller
The Iron Age
Thomas Dekker
The Shoemaker's Holiday
Old Fortunatus
Thomas Middleton
A Game at Chesse
The Witch
John Webster
The Duchess of Molfy
James Shirley
The Cardinal
The Faithful Servant
Thomas Randolph
The Conceited Pedlar

The Puritan Age and the Restoration (1625–1700)

John Dryden
The Wild Gallant
The Rival Ladies
The Rehearsal
All for Love

William Congreve
Way of the World
Love for Love
Thomas Otway
The Orphan

Classicism and the Age of Johnson (1700–1780)

Colley Cibber
Love's Lost Shaft
The Careless Husband
Mrs. Susanna Centlivre
The Busy Body
The Gamester
Sir Richard Steele
The Tender Husband
Oliver Goldsmith
The Good Natur'd Man
Richard Brinsley Sheridan
The Rivals
The School for Scandal

George Lillo
The London Merchant
Justice Triumphant
Henry Fielding
Tom Thumb
Author's Farce
Samuel Foote
The Nabob
The Capuchin
David Garrick
The Guardian
Miss in Her Teens
The Lying Valet

EXTENSIVE READING PROGRAM

The Age of Romanticism (1780–1840)

Walter Savage Landor
 Count Julian
 Tiberius and Vipsania
Tom Taylor
 Our American Cousin
 The Ticket-of-Leave Man
T. W. Robertson
 David Garrick

Percy Bysshe Shelley
 Prometheus Unbound
 The Cenci
 Hellas
Sheridan Knowles
 Virginius
 William Tell
 The Hunchback

The Victorian Era (1840–1900)

Sir Arthur Wing Pinero
 The Second Mrs. Tanqueray
 Trelawney of the Wells
Henry Arthur Jones
 Michael and His Lost Angel
 The Silver King

Oscar Wilde
 Lady Windermere's Fan
 The Importance of Being Earnest
 A Woman of No Importance
 An Ideal Husband

The Twentieth Century (1900–   )

George Bernard Shaw
 Arms and the Man
 Candida
 Saint Joan
 Fanny's First Play
Sir James Matthew Barrie
 Dear Brutus
 A Kiss for Cinderella
 Peter Pan
 The Little Minister
 Quality Street
 The Admirable Crichton
Arnold Bennett
 The Great Adventure
John Masefield
 Tragedy of Man
 Philip the King
Granville Barker
 The Madras House
 Prunella
John Drinkwater
 Abraham Lincoln
 A Night of the Trojan War
Noel Coward
 The Vortex
 Hay Fever

Allan Monkhouse
 The Conquering Hero
Lady Gregory
 The Rising of the Moon
 The Workhouse Ward
 Hyacinth Halvey
John Galsworthy
 Strife
 Justice
 Loyalties
 The Skin Game
Somerset Maugham
 Our Betters
 The Circle
Clemence Dane
 A Bill of Divorcement
 Granite
A. A. Milne
 Mr. Pim Passes By
 The Romantic Age
 The Ivory Door
St. John Ervine
 Jane Clegg
 John Ferguson
 Mary, Mary, Quite Contrary
 The First Mrs. Fraser

Lord Dunsany
The Gods of the Mountain
A Night at an Inn
John Millington Synge
Riders to the Sea
Playboy of the Western World

Sean O'Casey
The Shadow of a Gunman
The Plough and the Stars
William Butler Yeats
The Hour Glass
The Land of Heart's Desire

Suggested Readings on Shakespeare and His Times

J. Q. Adams
A Life of William Shakespeare
Shakespearean Playhouses
Sir Sidney Lee
A Life of William Shakespeare
Paul Kaufman
Outline Guide to Shakespeare
Oxford University Press
Shakespeare's England
H. T. Stephenson
Shakespeare's London
E. A. G. Lamborn and G. B. Harrison
Shakespeare, The Man and His Stage

George Saintsbury
Shakespeare: Life and Plays
Samuel T. Coleridge
Notes and Lectures on Shakespeare
A. C. Bradley
Shakespearean Tragedy
C. F. Tucker Brooke
Tudor Drama
C. T. Onions
A Shakespeare Glossary
E. A. Abbott
A Shakespearean Grammar
Brander Matthews
A Study of the Drama

Collections of English and World Dramas

Curtis Canfield
Plays of the Irish Renaissance
Bruce Carpenter
A Book of Dramas
Barrett H. Clark
Representative One-Act Plays
Thomas H. Dickinson
Chief Contemporary Dramatists
Esther C. Dunn
Eight Famous Elizabethan Plays
Roland Lewis
Contemporary One-Act Plays
J. W. Marriott
Great Modern British Plays

Brander Matthews and Leider Paul
The Chief British Dramatists
Brander Matthews
The Chief European Dramatists
Montrose J. Moses
Representative British Dramas
Representative Continental Dramas
Representative One-Act Plays by Continental Authors
Frederick Tupper and James Tupper
Representative English Dramas from Dryden to Sheridan

THE NOVEL

THE HISTORY OF THE NOVEL IN ENGLAND

Early Prose Fiction (Beginnings to 1700)

The Beginnings of the Novel

The first English novel did not make its appearance until after the year 1700, but, like the drama, it did not spring into existence fully developed. A novel, properly speaking, is a long fictitious narrative with a more or less well developed plot which has for its purpose the portrayal of life and manners. A number of early writings contributed to this new form.

Sir Thomas Malory in his *Le Morte d'Arthur* (1470) invented a new style of narrative, and although his work does not show anything of the method of the modern novel, it was at least a beginning of prose fiction. In the sixteenth century, interest in Italian novelists was awakened, and an appreciation of Italian stories led to Lyly's *Euphues*, which again, though not strictly a novel, made a distinct addition to fictional writing.

In the seventeenth century came a number of writers, each of whom made some contribution to the modern novel. John Bunyan in *The Pilgrim's Progress* and Jonathan Swift in *Gulliver's Travels* each contributed the gift of writing fictitious narrative so that it had an air of truth. Addison and Steele directed attention to life and manners and also created in Sir Roger de Coverley and his friends a number of well developed fictitious characters. It was Daniel Defoe who, in his immortal narrative of *Robinson Crusoe,* came nearest to writing what we know as the modern novel, but not even yet had this form of literature been fully developed.

Classicism and the Age of Johnson (1700–1780)

General Characteristics

There now came in the Classic Age a number of men who wrote entertaining stories of fictitious characters whose fortunes they pursued over a considerable period, and it is in this age that we find the first English novels.

Samuel Richardson (1689-1761)

The first English novelist was Samuel Richardson, whose *Pamela* was the first real novel. This book was the result, one might say, of accident. Richardson, a printer, had set out to compile a kind of model letter-writer, and in the execution of his plans he conceived the idea of connecting his letters by a story. The book takes its name from its chief character, Pamela Andrews. So entertaining was Richardson's model letter-writer that he followed it up with two other stories told through the medium of a series of letters. These are *Clarissa Harlowe*, and the *History of Sir Charles Grandison*. His stories are somewhat sentimental, a fact which shows him not to have been a classicist, yet they show a classic realism.

Other Novelists of the Classic Age

The greatest, if not the first, of the novelists of the period was Henry Fielding, whose four novels are *Joseph Andrews, Mr. Jonathan Wild the Great, Amelia*, and his masterpiece, *Tom Jones*. Fielding's outstanding characteristics are vigor and energy, humor, and realism. To this period also belongs Tobias Smollett, the author of five novels, the best of which is *Humphrey Clinker;* and Laurence Sterne, author of *Tristram Shandy* and *Sentimental Journey*. Mention should also be made of Horace Walpole whose romantic story, *The Castle of Otranto*, was a forerunner of the medieval romances of the Romantic Age. Oliver Goldsmith, better known as a poet, was author of one of the best novels of the period, *The Vicar of Wakefield*.

THE AGE OF ROMANTICISM (1780-1840)

General Characteristics

During the early years of the Romantic Period the development of the novel continued. Frances Burney, afterward Madame d'Arblay, one of the outstanding women novelists in our literature, continued the type which originated with Richardson in her *Evelina* and her *Cecilia*. The romance now received further impetus in the hands of Mrs. Ann Radcliffe, whose story, *The Mysteries of Udolpho*, is representative of a number of tales of mystery and terror which now began to appear. In *Caleb Williams*, a third writer, William Godwin, made use of the novel to preach social and political reform. It was not until after the turn of the century that the two great novelists of the period, Sir Walter Scott and Jane Austen, made their appearance.

Sir Walter Scott (1771-1832)

One of the delights of Walter Scott's youth had been to wander about on foot or on horseback in his native Scotland. On these wanderings he stored up in his mind romantic scenery and historical events, legends and folklore, ballads and songs, which he was later to incorporate in his own writings. His interest in native Scotch ballads led him to publish his first book, *Minstrelsy of the Scotch Border*. This was so much enjoyed that it was followed by *The Lay of the Last Minstrel, Marmion,* and *The Lady of the Lake*.

But Scott was not to continue writing all his stories in poetry form. One day, when rummaging through a cabinet, in search of some fishing tackle, he found the manuscript of a story which he had begun and laid aside nine years before. He read it eagerly, enjoying it as if it had been some one else's work. In three weeks' time, he had finished the story, and sent it out into the world, without signing his name.

This first novel, *Waverley*, met with instant success. Everyone wanted to know the name of the author, and during the next four years everyone wondered and praised more than ever, for six more books appeared. For seventeen years, Sir Walter wrote about two books a year. At first he wrote entirely about his own land and made Scotland and Scotchmen known and loved throughout the world. Then he wrote about England in *Ivanhoe;* about France in *Quentin Durward;* about Palestine in *The Talisman*. He put such magic in his writing, making the people of the past live and move again, that he was called "The Wizard of the North."

Jane Austen (1775–1817)

Quite different in every respect from the books of Scott were those of Jane Austen. She writes of quiet, uneventful English village life, portraying it in detail with a careful realism and drawing her characters with fidelity and accuracy. Her novels are not at all exciting, but they have never been equaled for their faithful portrayal of the everyday life which she chose to depict. The titles of her books are *Emma, Mansfield Park, Northanger Abbey, Sense and Sensibility,* and *Pride and Prejudice,* which is usually considered her masterpiece.

THE VICTORIAN ERA (1840–1900)

General Characteristics

The English novel reaches its high-water mark in the Victorian Era. Cheap printing and a wide reading public tended to popularize it, and it became the means through which men pictured the life and manners of their own and other times and also a vehicle for criticism of their own age and a means for urging various reforms. There are a number of novelists of the period who deserve special mention.

Charles Dickens (1812–1870)

Born in humble circumstances and brought up in slums and shabby streets, Charles Dickens' story is an illustration of what may be accomplished in the face of handicaps and adverse influences which in every way pointed to discouragement and failure.

He was the second in a family of eight children. His father was a clerk in a navy pay-office and for some time the family lived in comfortable, middle-class circumstances. The father was irresponsible and care-free, however, and finally, when Charles was about ten years old, was arrested and put into a debtors' prison. The lad's dreams of school and college were shattered and "he found himself in a row of ragged boys in a great dreary factory, putting the same kinds of labels on the same kinds of blacking bottles from morning till night." The degradation and misery of these days sank deep into the sensitive boy's soul, and of this particular dark spot in his life he could never speak.

After about two years Charles' father was released from prison and upon the unexpected receipt of a legacy, the financial condition of the family began to improve. Charles was sent to a private school where he remained for three or four years. At the age of seventeen he secured a position as a newspaper reporter, and this work gave him an intimate knowledge of London people in every walk of life. It was while connected with the paper that Dickens began to think of using his leisure hours for writing about the scenes and characters which he daily saw. His first articles, *Sketches by Boz*, appeared in the paper on which he worked, and because of their popularity, he was encouraged to write other character sketches which appeared first in monthly installments and later in book form. These were the *Pickwick Papers*, and within a year 40,000 copies were sold. Dickens' popularity was now assured and the rest of his life was success after success.

The events of his childhood and his youth had impressed his imagination and influenced the whole of his literary career so profoundly that to the very end of his life there was not a single work in which some of the characters, some of the places, were not derived from his early recollections. His own childhood may be read in *David Copperfield*. His father, his mother, his old landlady, his companions in the blacking factory, and the quaint, grotesque figures of the alleys live in the characters of his books. The prison, the lawyer's office, the tavern, warehouses, and shabby streets furnished him with scenes and settings. All that he had learned in his rough initiation into life was poured out into his stories. The bitter memories of his own childhood sufferings gave him great sympathy for children and for the middle and lower classes. He detested cruelty and indifference and oppression and in his stories he attacked many public abuses and aided in many reforms. In *Oliver Twist* he attacked the work-house and in *Little Dorrit*, the debtors' prison. In *Nicholas Nickleby* and *Dombey & Son* he exposed the cruelty practiced in English schools and helped put a stop to the shameful exploitation of children for commercial purposes. He knew well how to produce laughter and horror and tears, and "it is for his deeply human heart that the world will continue to love the memory of Charles Dickens."

William Makepeace Thackeray (1811–1863)

Thackeray was a man of altogether different temperament from Dickens. He was not concerned with social problems, but endeavored to see life whole and see it steadily. He possessed a penetrating insight into human nature, seeing through sham and pretense and viewing life without illusion. His method is that of the realist, who endeavors to picture life faithfully and accurately as it is. The characters in his books come from the higher social levels. His novel, *Henry Esmond,* laid in the days of Queen Anne, is regarded as one of the greatest of English novels. A close second to this is *Vanity Fair,* laid in London in the days of the Napoleonic Wars. *The Newcomes* and *Pendennis* deal with contemporary life. In addition to these he wrote a sequel to *Henry Esmond,* entitled *The Virginians.*

George Eliot (Mary Ann Evans) (1819–1880)

"You may try, but you can never imagine what it is to have a man's force of genius in you, and yet to suffer the slavery of being a girl," wrote George Eliot. From her earliest childhood, Mary Ann Evans was torn between a desire to follow her own intellectual bent and her conviction that a woman's place was in the home doing the duties which naturally fall to the daughter or wife of the house. She was thirty-seven years old before she definitely launched herself on a literary career and then she chose a *nom de plume* because she felt that as a woman she would not gain any recognition in the literary field.

Although she ended her life during the years of scientific discovery and progress of the last quarter of the nineteenth century, it is events of her girlhood before railroads, telegraphs or factories, which appear in most of her writings. Her first novel was *Adam Bede,* followed the next year by *The Mill on the Floss.* The latter is largely a story of her own childhood and her brother Isaac to whom she was deeply devoted. Other well-known novels from her pen are *Silas Marner, Romola,* and *Felix Holt.* As a novelist, she ranks with Dickens and Thackeray.

Other Novelists of the Early Victorian Age

In addition to Dickens, Thackeray, and Eliot, the early years of the period produced a number of novelists of considerable ability. Among these were Bulwer-Lytton who continued the romantic strain of Scott, whose best-known books are *The Last Days of Pompeii, Rienzi, The Last of the Barons,* and *Harold;* Benjamin Disraeli, three times Prime Minister of England, and the author of four novels; Charlotte Brontë, best remembered for her book *Jane Eyre;* Charles Kingsley, author of *Hypatia, Westward Ho!,* and *Herward the Wake;* and Mrs. Elizabeth Gaskell, who produced in *Cranford* a realistic novel of distinction.

ELD

Later Victorian Novelists

The long reign of Victoria covered a period of sixty-four years. The great novelists whose works had appeared in the early days of her reign were all dead by 1880. A new group was appearing, and with the possible exception of Stevenson, these men all exhibit a reaction against the confidence which characterized the early days of the Victorian Era. They are strongly individualistic in their reaction and attitude.

Robert Louis Stevenson (1850-1894)

Stevenson looked upon fiction as a means of escape. He contended that it should be to the grown man what play is to the child. In addition to *Treasure Island,* which is the greatest adventure story in our literature, he wrote a number of romances which have many of the outstanding characteristics of this work. The titles of these are *Kidnapped, The Master of Ballantrae, David Balfour,* and the unfinished romances, *St. Ives* and *Weir of Hermiston.*

George Meredith (1828-1909)

Meredith is entitled to a place among the great English novelists. His recognition by the public was belated and may be said to have been delayed until after his death. Meredith began as a poet. His attitude toward life, or his philosophy, is best illustrated by his masterpiece, *The Egoist.* According to him, it is out of egoism that come all the ills that flesh is heir to. The antidote to this is what he calls the Comic Spirit or the "genius of thoughtful laughter" which, by making folly, vanity and ambition appear ridiculous, destroys them. Meredith's chief novels are *Evan Harrington, The Egoist, The Ordeal of Richard Feberel,* and *Diana of the Crossways.*

Other Victorian Novelists

Among other novelists, the late Victorian years produced Samuel Butler and George Gissing. Butler was a critic of his age which he attacked in two satirical novels, *Erehwon* and *The Way of All Flesh.* Gissing, who saw no romance in life, was an uncompromising realist, whose attention was centered upon poverty and hardship. His masterpiece is *New Grub Street.*

THE TWENTIETH CENTURY (1900-   )

General Characteristics

In the hands of many contemporary English novelists, this form has tended to become an instrument for social criticism. Throughout many novels dissimilar in other respects, the writer is busy with some phase of life or some problem growing out of the new social order which science and the machine age are developing, attempting to interpret this new order or showing it in conflict with the old. Changing standards of public and private morality, new family and social relationships, the effect of new scientific discoveries in biology, medicine, psychology, and sociology upon the individual and upon new relationships, the passing of old conventions—all these find treatment in the contemporary novel. As in other forms, there has been great activity in this field of writing.

Thomas Hardy (1840–1928)

One of the greatest figures in recent English literature is Thomas Hardy. He has the distinction of being both a great poet and a great novelist. Hardy was born in Wessex and began life as an architect. His first novel, *Desperate Remedies,* was published in 1868 and his last, *The Well-Beloved,* in 1897, after which he turned to the writing of poetry. His novels, all of which deal with rustic or provincial life, are all laid in his native Wessex. He is primarily a novelist of character but he is also a master of plot. One of his chief characteristics is his faithful portrayal of life. His philosophy is somewhat fatalistic; he conceives of men and women as the puppets of circumstance in the clutch of great blind forces which they are quite powerless to affect. This idea is also seen in his poetry, as the titles of some of his volumes indicate, such as *Satires of Circumstance* and *Time's Laughing Stocks.* He is no optimist; on the other hand, the term pessimist is hardly applicable to him. He is rather one who hears the still sad music of humanity. His principal novels are *Under the Greenwood Tree, Far from the Madding Crowd, The Return of the Native, The Woodlanders, The Mayor of Casterbridge, Tess of the D'Urbervilles,* and *Jude the Obscure.*

Joseph Conrad (1856–1924)

Conrad was a Pole by birth, born in Ukraine and educated at Cracow. For twenty years he followed the sea, finally becoming a shipmaster in the British merchant marine. Although Conrad could speak no English until he was past twenty and was nearly forty before he did his first novel he is one of the outstanding writers of our generation. Most of his stories have the sea as a background and are distinguished for their rich, poetic descriptions. His principal novels are *Almayer's Folly, The Nigger of the Narcissus, Lord Jim, Nostromo,* and *The Rescue.*

H. G. Wells (1866–   )

Wells has been a prolific writer, having to his credit a great number of stories, essays, novels, and his well known *Outline of History.* He is a popular and stimulating writer with no small fund of humor, and a good story-teller. His novels deal with a number of different phases of the new social order. In one group, of which *The Time Machine* and *The War in the Air* are examples, his imagination goes out to picture for us in a vivid manner the effect of modern science on human affairs. In another group he exploits his views on sociology and religion, as in *New Worlds for Old* and *The Soul of a Bishop;* again his theme is education as in *Joan and Peter* and the sketch of Sanderson of Oundle. Most of his books are probably bound to lose interest to future generations. Some of his best work is to be seen in *Kipps, Tono-Bungay, Veronica,* and *Love and Mr. Lewisham,* in which the interest is not so much in a problem as in character and the life portrayed. His *Mr. Brittling Sees It Through* will probably live as one of the best of the war novels.

Arnold Bennett (1867-)

Like Wells, Bennett has been a prolific writer. The novels for which he is best known show him as a realist. They are *The Old Wives' Tale* and the three novels constituting the Clayhanger trilogy—*Clayhanger, Hilda Lessways,* and *These Twain*. The scene of these novels is the "Five Towns"—Newcastle, Stoke, Burslem, Tunstall, and Longton—in the industrial and mining region of England. Bennett has no doctrine to preach nor any reform program. He is concerned only with picturing the effect of life in the "Five Towns" upon not so much the working man as the lower middle class of which Clayhanger, the owner of a small printing establishment, is a good example. The trilogy follows the development of Clayhanger's youth and his relations with Hilda Lessways whom he marries. Bennett's novels are not stimulating or exciting but they portray life with careful fidelity.

John Galsworthy (1867-1933)

Galsworthy is perhaps the greatest of the twentieth century novelists. He is a realist who has given us a number of novels picturing to us the characters and the background of the English upper middle class, their conventions, philosophy of life, self-satisfaction, complacency, manners, and outlook. Galsworthy goes about his work in an impartial, rather cool manner, keeping himself pretty well out of his novels, picturing for us men and women who, "life flies caught among the impalpable and smoky threads of cobwebs, . . . struggle in the webs of their own natures, giving here a start, there a pitiful small jerking, long sustained, and falling into stillness." Among Galsworthy's principal novels are *The Island Pharisees, The White Monkey, The Dark Flower,* and *The Man of Property*. *The Man of Property* is the first of a series of novels dealing with the Forsyte family to which the name *The Forsyte Saga* is given. Other novels in this series are *In Chancery* and *To Let*.

Other Twentieth Century Novelists

A list of men and women who have produced novels of some consequence would run to great length. In it would appear such names as Maurice Hewlett who has done a number of historical romances; Robert Hichens, author of a number of psychological novels; William De Morgan, who continues the Victorian tradition; Eden Phillpotts, whose best work portrays the Dartmoor country; Hugh Walpole; Rudyard Kipling; Compton McKenzie; William J. Locke; Archibald Marshall; Sheila Kaye-Smith; May Sinclair; D. H. Lawrence; W. Somerset Maugham; Frank Swinnerton; and a host of others.

A TALE OF TWO CITIES

Charles Dickens

Historical Background—The Old Régime in France

The French Revolution was "the terrible reaping of a long sowing of grinding oppression, brutal indifference to human relations, and wanton waste." And, indeed, conditions on the eve of the Revolution were in a deplorable state. The king claimed to rule by divine right and to be responsible to no one but God. He was an absolute monarch. He made the laws, levied taxes, spent them as he saw fit, seized property at will, and imprisoned by mere order, without trial, and for as long a time as he chose. He lived in the most extravagant luxury and wasted millions on his court and on frivolous pleasures. National expenditures were always larger than national income, and taxes were very burdensome. The wealthiest paid the least, however, and the crushing weight of the taxation fell on the peasants.

There were three main classes, or divisions, in French society—the clergy, the nobility, and the so-called third estate. Many of the clergy, especially in the country, were earnest, devout men, but others of the higher clergy drew enormous salaries and neglected their parishes for luxurious pleasure at court. The nobles in earlier times had taken an active part in governing and defending the country but now most of them led frivolous, useless lives at court, and neglected their lands and tenants. The nobles and the clergy were exempted from most of the taxes which therefore fell all the more heavily on the class that remained, known as the third estate. To this estate the mass of the people, of whom the greatest number were peasants, belonged. It had to support not only the king and his court but the clergy and nobles as well. Fully one-half of its annual earnings were exacted by the state in the form of taxes, and in addition there were the tithes to the clergy and the feudal dues to the nobles. The peasant had to pay tolls for the use of roads and bridges, he was compelled to use his lord's wine press, his mill, and his oven, always paying for these privileges. The result was that only about one-fifth of his earnings were left with which to support his family. He lived on the verge of disaster and in a poor year he faced dire want, and even starvation. It happened that the harvest was bad in 1788 and that the following winter was cruelly severe. Hundreds of thousands of men became beggars, driven to frenzy by hunger. It was no wonder that there were abundant recruits for riots and deeds of violence.

Religious liberty was lacking. Protestantism was outlawed and Catholics were required by law to observe the requirements and usages of their religion. There was no liberty of thought. Every book and paper was censored, and no printer might print without permission. There was no political liberty. The people could not hold public meetings nor could they elect any assemblies.

Nor was there any individual liberty. The authorities, without reason and without trial, might arrest any one whom they wished, and the prisons were filled with prisoners there by reason of the *lettres de cachet*. These were orders for arbitrary arrest and one of the most odious and hated features of the Old Régime. "Ministers and their subordinate officials used these letters freely. Nobles easily obtained them, sometimes the place for the name being left blank for them to fill in. Sometimes, even, they were sold. Thus there was abundant opportunity to use them to pay off merely personal grudges."

In view of all these facts it is not strange that "Liberty and Equality" became the battle cry of the Revolution.

Social Conditions in England

While trouble was brewing in France, England was not entirely quiet. George III had come to the throne in 1760 and he was narrow and stubborn to the last degree. The Whig party had held almost uninterrupted possession of the government for nearly half a century and its influence was so supreme that the sovereign had practically become a mere cipher, dependent for his authority on the political support which he received. George III was resolved that this state of things should continue no longer. He was determined to reassert the royal authority, secure a government which should reflect his principles, and have a ministry to whom he could dictate, instead of one that dictated to him. For a long time he struggled in vain, but at last succeeded, and found in Lord North a Prime Minister who bowed to the royal will and endeavored to carry out the royal policy of "governing for, but never by, the people." That obstinate policy finally precipitated the American Revolution, saddled the English taxpayers with a huge debt, and forever separated Great Britain from the richest colonies that she ever possessed.

While the war was in progress in America, the people in England were asserting their independence of many long-established abuses. "The times were brutal. The pillory still stood in the center of London and if the unfortunate offender who was put in it escaped with a shower of mud and other unsavory missiles, instead of clubs and brickbats, he was lucky indeed. Gentlemen of fashion arranged pleasure parties to visit the penitentiaries to see the wretched women whipped. The whole code of criminal law was savagely vindicitive. Capital punishment was inflicted for upwards of two hundred offences, many of which would now be thought to be sufficiently punished by one or two months' imprisonment in the house of correction. Not only men, but women and children even, were hanged for pilfering goods or food worth a few shillings. The jails were crowded with poor wretches whom want had driven to theft, and who were 'worked off' on the gallows every Monday morning in batches of a dozen or twenty, in sight of the jeering, drunken crowds who gathered to witness their death agonies." Through the efforts of influential men a reform was finally effected in this bloody code, laws respecting punishment for debt were changed for the better, and thousands of miserable beings who were without means to satisfy their creditors were set free, instead of being kept in useless life-long imprisonment.

When the French Revolution broke out, the English people at first extended their hearty sympathy to the revolutionists but after the execution of Louis XVI and Marie Antoinette, they became alarmed at the horrible scenes of the Reign of Terror and joined an alliance of the principal European powers for the purpose of restoring the French monarchy. The wars with France lasted more than twenty years and did not end until the defeat of Napoleon at the Battle of Waterloo in 1815.

The French Revolution

At the outbreak of the Revolution Louis XVI was king of France. He was honest and well-meaning, but weak and at the mercy of stronger wills. His queen, Marie Antoinette, beautiful, gracious and of a strong will, was on the other hand wilful, proud, and fond of pleasure, and by her extravagances helped to aggravate the financial situation. The royal couple lived in the most sumptuous and extravagant fashion twelve miles distant from Paris in the palace at Versailles which had been erected at a cost of one hundred million dollars. It is said that in the year 1789 alone, the cost of maintaining the court was over twenty million dollars.

At length the financial situation became so serious that it could no longer be endured and the crisis forced the monarch to make an appeal to the people through the Estates-General. This was an assembly representing the three estates of the people, and although a very old institution, it had not held a meeting in nearly two hundred years. The king called the representatives together and the assembly convened on May 5, 1789. The meeting now became an attempt of the third estate to gain control and for two months a bitter contest was waged. On July 14th, the people of Paris, hungry and poverty-stricken, fearing that the royal troops might break up the assembly, marched on the Bastille, the famous royal prison. Within a few hours the guards were slaughtered and the prison taken, an act which rendered Paris practically independent of royal control. Frenchmen still celebrate July 14th as their national holiday. The storming of the Bastille was followed by similar outbreaks throughout France. Peasants made war upon the châteaux, unpopular tax collectors were assaulted, and lawlessness was triumphant.

Meanwhile the king, with his queen and court, continued to feast at Versailles while Paris was starving. On October 5, 1789, several thousand women, armed with clubs, started to march to Versailles, screaming for bread. They were joined by as many men, forced the gates, and surrounded the palace. Lafayette and his soldiers guarded the royal family through the night, but in the morning the king appeared before the crowd and promised them food. He was persuaded to return to Paris with the mob, and so the procession, with the royal coach in its midst, started back to the city.

Between 1789 and 1792 were swept away all kinds of privileges which had formerly been assumed to be the legal rights of the nobles and the clergy. Brute force had gained its ends, and a democracy was formed in which the common people gained many rights which they had never before possessed. The nobles and the clergy were naturally hostile to all of these reforms and tried desperately to regain property and privilege. As the result of a decree in 1790 which abolished all titles of nobility, they left the country in large numbers, forming a group called the *émigrés*. The king himself made an attempt to escape with his family, but was captured and returned to Paris, almost a prisoner. Many of the *émigrés* intrigued in European courts trying to instigate rulers to invade France, and decrees were passed declaring that unless they returned to France by January 1, 1792, their property would be confiscated, and they would be treated as enemies and exposed to the penalty of death.

All of this time the masses were becoming steadily more excitable and they worshiped Liberty frantically. They displayed the Revolutionary colors and adopted the red cap as a symbol of liberty. Political clubs, the best known of which was the Jacobin Club, were organized, grew steadily more radical, and extended their influence all over France. A crisis was fast approaching.

Just at this time (1792) Austria and Prussia declared war on France, which was hailed with enthusiasm by the French people. They soon began to see, however, that they were in danger of losing all of their privileges which they had secured at such cost. They accordingly revolted against the royalist troops, sacked the royal palace, and seized and imprisoned the king.

The September massacres of that year grew out of the feeling of panic which seized the population of Paris as it heard of the approach of the Prussians and Austrians toward the city. Hundreds of persons, suspected or charged with treason, had been thrown into the prisons, and the more violent members of the Paris mob began to say that before troops were sent to the front, all of the traitors within the city ought to be put out of the way. The result was that day after day from September 2 to September 6, a cold-blooded murder of nearly 1200 persons took place.

On September 20 the Prussians were stopped on their onward march, and on September 21, 1792, France was declared a republic. Louis XVI was brought to trial and was executed on January 21, 1793. And he was not the only one to die by the guillotine. A Revolutionary Tribunal had been instituted for the purpose of trying traitors and conspirators rapidly. No appeal could be taken from its decisions, and under the law of "suspects" practically anyone could be arrested and sent before it. Terror reigned as the Tribunal daily sent its victims to the guillotine, and in October of that year it sentenced Marie Antionette to death.

The bloodshed lasted until July 27, 1794, which date saw the fall of Robespierre who had been a leader of the Jacobin Club and for some time practically dictator in France. With his death France breathed more freely. The storm subsided slowly but surely, and it was not long before there appeared on the horizon the figure of Napoleon who was to dominate the field of history for the next twenty years.

Dickens and the Historical Novel

The historical novel with its emphasis on plot and action, and with its characters secondary, is not characteristic of Dickens' style of writing. As a rule, he cared little for the well-constructed plot, and was run away with by the characters who mostly interested him. His stories seem to be made up of scenes in which new characters are always appearing and playing their disconnected parts and disappearing, with just enough plot to carry the story along. When we think of Dickens' stories we think of the people in them—of Mr. Micawber, Little Nell, Mrs. Nickleby, and Little Dorrit—we almost forget the plot.

A Tale of Two Cities, which puts before us in all their terrible detail the days of the French Revolution, stands out among Dickens' novels as almost unique. It is closely constructed and carefully worked out from beginning to end, and by many critics it is considered to be his best novel. Dickens himself declared that this novel was "the best story I have written." We do know that it is his easiest novel to read, that it is vastly entertaining, and vividly dramatic.

The plot of the story suggested itself to Dickens in 1857 while, as he tells us, he and his children were acting in a play by Wilkie Collins, *The Frozen Deep*. He had been reading Carlyle's book on the French Revolution, and the idea of a dramatic story based upon the events of that period took hold of his imagination. A year later the idea still haunted him and he reports that as it became familiar it gradually shaped itself into its present form. "Throughout its execution," he writes in his preface to the story, "it has had complete possession of me; I have so far verified what is done and suffered in these pages, as that I have certainly done and suffered it all myself. Whenever any reference (however slight) is made here to the condition of the French people before or during the Revolution, it is truly made on the faith of the most trustworthy witnesses. It has been one of my hopes to add something to the popular and picturesque means of understanding that terrible time."

BOOK THE FIRST. RECALLED TO LIFE

I THE PERIOD

It was the best of times, it was the worst of times, it was the age of wisdom, it was the age of foolishness, it was the epoch of belief, it was the epoch of incredulity, it was the season of Light, it was the season of Darkness, it was the spring of hope, it was the winter of despair, we had everything before us, we had nothing before us, we were all going direct to Heaven, we were all going direct the other way.

There were a king with a large jaw and a queen with a plain face,[1] on the throne of England; there were a king with a large jaw and a queen with a fair face,[2] on the throne of France. It was the year of Our Lord one thousand seven hundred and seventy-five.

France was rolling with exceeding smoothness down-hill, making paper money and spending it.[3] Under the guidance of her Christian pastors, she entertained herself, besides, with such

---

[1] KING WITH A LARGE JAW AND A QUEEN WITH A PLAIN FACE—George III, famous for his obstinacy, and Charlotte, fat and homely.

[2] KING WITH A LARGE JAW AND A QUEEN WITH A FAIR FACE—Louis XVI and beautiful Marie Antoinette.

[3] MAKING PAPER MONEY AND SPENDING IT—A reference to the extravagance of the times, and the ruinous financial policy of the government which was one of the immediate causes of the French Revolution.

humane achievements as sentencing a youth to have his hands cut off, his tongue torn out with pincers, and his body burned alive, because he had not kneeled down in the rain to do honour to a religious procession which passed within his view, at a distance of some fifty or sixty yards.[4] It is likely enough that, rooted in the woods of France and Norway, there were growing trees, when that sufferer was put to death, already marked by the Woodman, Fate, to come down and be sawn into boards, to make a certain movable framework [5] with a sack and a knife in it, terrible in history. It is likely enough that in the rough outhouses of some tillers of the heavy lands adjacent to Paris, there were sheltered from the weather that very day, rude carts, bespattered with rustic mire, snuffed about by pigs, and roosted in by poultry, which the Farmer, Death, had already set apart to be his tumbrils [6] of the Revolution.

In England, there was scarcely an amount of order and protection to justify much national boasting. Daring burglaries by armed men, and highway robberies, took place in the capital itself every night; families were publicly cautioned not to go out of town without removing their furniture to upholsterers' warehouses for security; the highwayman in the dark was a city tradesman in the light; the mail was waylaid by seven robbers, and the guard shot three dead, and then got shot dead himself by the other four, "in consequence of the failure of his ammunition": after which the mail was robbed in peace; prisoners in London gaols fought battles with their turnkeys, and the majesty of the law fired blunderbusses in among them, loaded with rounds of shot and ball; thieves snipped off diamond crosses from the necks of noble lords at Court drawing-rooms; musketeers went into St. Giles's,[7] to search for contraband goods, and the mob fired on the musketeers, and the musketeers fired on the mob, and nobody thought any of these occurrences much out of the common way. In the midst of them, the hangman, ever

---

[4] In 1776 such an execution actually did take place, but in order to emphasize his point Dickens does not state that the offender made blasphemous speeches and sang blasphemous songs in the presence of the procession.

[5] A CERTAIN MOVABLE FRAMEWORK—The guillotine, a machine for beheading people, which was used in the French Revolution.

[6] TUMBRILS—Rough carts which were used by the revolutionists to carry the condemned prisoners through the streets to the guillotine.

[7] ST. GILES'S—A section in London inhabited by the lowest classes, and notorious as a resort of criminals.

busy and ever worse than useless, was in constant requisition; now, stringing up long rows of miscellaneous criminals; now, hanging a house-breaker on Saturday who had been taken on Tuesday; now, burning people in the hand at Newgate [8] by the dozen, and now burning pamphlets at the door of Westminster Hall; [9] today, taking the life of an atrocious murderer, and tomorrow of a wretched pilferer who had robbed a farmer's boy of sixpence.

All these things, and a thousand like them, came to pass in and close upon the dear old year one thousand seven hundred and seventy-five. Environed by them, while the Woodman and the Farmer worked unheeded, those two of the large jaws, and those two of the plain and the fair faces, trod with stir enough, and carried their divine rights with a high hand. Thus did the year one thousand seven hundred and seventy-five conduct their Greatnesses, and myriads of small creatures—the creatures of this chronicle among the rest—along the roads that lay before them.

[8] NEWGATE—The most famous prison of London.
[9] WESTMINSTER HALL—Trials for treason were conducted in this hall, and treasonable documents were publicly burned in front of it.

II THE MAIL

IT WAS the Dover road [1] that lay, on a Friday night late in November, before the first of the persons with whom this history has business. The Dover road lay, as to him, beyond the Dover mail, as it lumbered up Shooter's Hill. He walked up-hill in the mire by the side of the mail, as the rest of the passengers did; not because they had the least relish for walking exercise, under the circumstances, but because the hill, and the harness, and the mud, and the mail, were all so heavy, that the horses had three times already come to a stop.

Two other passengers, besides the one, were plodding up the hill by the side of the mail. All three were wrapped to the cheek-bones and over the ears, and wore jack-boots.[2] Not one of the three could have said, from anything he saw, what either of the other two was like; and each was hidden under almost

[1] DOVER ROAD—The main road from London to Dover, a part of the direct route to Paris by way of Dover and Calais on the English Channel.
[2] JACK-BOOTS—Large boots reaching up over the knees.

as many wrappers from the eyes of the mind, as from the eyes of the body, of his two companions. In those days, travellers were very shy of being confidential on a short notice, for anybody on the road might be a robber or in league with robbers.

The Dover mail was in its usual genial position that the guard suspected the passengers, the passengers suspected one another and the guard, they all suspected everybody else, and the coachman was sure of nothing but the horses.

"Wo-ho!" said the coachman. "So, then! One more pull and you're at the top and be damned to you, for I have had trouble enough to get you to it!—Joe!"

"Halloa!" the guard replied.

"What o'clock do you make it, Joe?"

"Ten minutes, good, past eleven."

"My blood! My blood!" ejaculated the vexed coachman, "and not atop of Shooter's yet? Tst! Yah! Get on with you!"

The last burst carried the mail to the summit of the hill. The horses stopped to breathe again, and the guard got down to skid the wheel [3] for the descent, and open the coach door to let the passengers in.

"Tst! Joe!" cried the coachman in a warning voice, looking down from his box.

"What do you say, Tom?"

They both listened.

"I say a horse at a canter coming up, Joe."

"*I* say a horse at a gallop, Tom," returned the guard, leaving his hold of the door, and mounting nimbly to his place. "Gentlemen! In the king's name, all of you!"

With this hurried adjuration, he cocked his blunderbuss, and stood on the offensive.

The passenger booked by this history, was on the coach step, getting in; the two other passengers were close behind him, and about to follow. He remained on the step, half in the coach and half out of it; they remained in the road below him. They all looked from the coachman to the guard, and from the guard to the coachman, and listened. The coachman looked back, and the guard looked back, and even the horses pricked up their ears and looked back.

[3] To SKID THE WHEEL—To place a kind of drag or skid under the wheel to serve as a brake in descending a hill.

The sound of a horse at a gallop came fast and furiously up the hill.

"So-ho!" the guard sang out, as loud as he could roar. "Yo, there! Stand! I shall fire!"

The pace was suddenly checked, and, with much splashing and floundering, a man's voice called from the mist, "Is that the Dover mail?"

"Never you mind what it is!" the guard retorted. "What are you?"

"*Is* that the Dover mail?"

"Why do you want to know?"

"I want a passenger, if it is."

"What passenger?"

"Mr. Jarvis Lorry."

Our booked passenger showed in a moment that it was his name. The guard, the coachman, and the two other passengers eyed him distrustfully.

"Keep where you are," the guard called to the voice in the mist, "because, if I should make a mistake, it could never be set right in your lifetime. Gentleman of the name of Lorry answer straight."

"What is the matter?" asked the passenger, then, with mildly-quavering speech. "Who wants me? Is it Jerry?"

("I don't like Jerry's voice, if it is Jerry," growled the guard to himself. "He's hoarser than suits me, is Jerry.")

"Yes, Mr. Lorry."

"What is the matter?"

"A despatch sent after you from over yonder. T. and Co."

"I know this messenger, guard," said Mr. Lorry, getting down into the road—assisted from behind more swiftly than politely by the other two passengers, who immediately scrambled into the coach, shut the door, and pulled up the window. "He may come close; there's nothing wrong."

"I hope there ain't, but I can't make so 'nation sure of that," said the guard, in gruff soliloquy. "Hallo you!"

"Well! And hallo you!" said Jerry, more hoarsely than before.

"Come on at a footpace; d'ye mind me? And if you've got holsters to that saddle o' yourn, don't let me see your hand go

"So-ho!" the guard sang out, as loud as he could roar. "Yo, there! Stand! I shall fire!"

nigh 'em. For I'm a devil at a quick mistake, and when I make one it takes the form of lead. So now let's look at you."

The figures of a horse and rider came slowly through the eddying mist, and came to the side of the mail, where the passenger stood. The rider stooped, and, casting up his eyes at the guard, handed the passenger a small folded paper. The rider's horse was blown, and both horse and rider were covered with mud, from the hoofs of the horse to the hat of the man.

"Guard!" said the passenger, in a tone of quiet business confidence.

The watchful guard, with his right hand at the stock of his raised blunderbuss, his left at the barrel, and his eyes on the horseman, answered curtly, "Sir."

"There is nothing to apprehend. I belong to Tellson's Bank. You must know Tellson's Bank in London. I am going to Paris on business. A crown to drink. I may read this?"

"If so be as you're quick, sir."

He opened it in the light of the coach-lamp on that side, and read—first to himself and then aloud: "'Wait at Dover for Mam'selle.' It's not long, you see, guard. Jerry, say that my answer was, *Recalled to Life*."

Jerry started in his saddle. "That's a blazing strange answer, too," said he, at his hoarsest.

"Take that message back, and they will know that I received this as well as if I wrote. Make the best of your way. Good night."

With those words the passenger opened the coach-door and got in; not at all assisted by his fellow-passengers, who had expeditiously secreted their watches and purses in their boots, and were now making a general pretense of being asleep, with no more definite purpose than to escape the hazard of originating any other kind of action.

The coach lumbered on again, with heavy wreaths of mist closing round it as it began the descent. The guard soon replaced his blunderbuss in his arm-chest, and looked to the rest of its contents, and to the supplementary pistols that he wore in his belt.

"Tom!" softly over the coach-roof.

"Hallo, Joe."

"Did you hear the message?"

"I did, Joe."
"What did you make of it, Tom?"
"Nothing at all, Joe."
"That's a coincidence, too," the guard mused, "for I made the same of it myself."

Jerry, left alone in the mist and darkness, dismounted meanwhile, not only to ease his spent horse, but to wipe the mud from his face, and to shake the wet out of his hat-brim, which might be capable of holding about half a gallon. After standing with the bridle over his heavily-splashed arm, until the wheels of the mail were no longer within hearing and the night was quite still again, he turned to walk down the hill.

"After that there gallop from Temple-bar,[4] old lady, I won't trust your fore-legs till I get you on the level," said this hoarse messenger, glancing at his mare. *"Recalled to Life.* That's a blazing strange message. Much of that wouldn't do for you, Jerry! I say, Jerry! You'd be in a blazing bad way, if recalling to life was to come into fashion, Jerry!"

[4] TEMPLE-BAR—An old gateway in London where formerly were exposed, as a public warning, the heads of executed traitors.

III   THE NIGHT SHADOWS

THE messenger rode back at an easy trot, stopping pretty often at ale-houses by the way to drink, but evincing a tendency to keep his own counsel, and to keep his hat cocked over his eyes. He had eyes that assorted very well with that decoration, being of a surface black, with no depth in the color or form, and much too near together—as if they were afraid of being found out in something, singly, if they kept too far apart. They had a sinister expression, under an old cocked-hat like a three-cornered spittoon, and over a great muffler for the chin and throat, which descended nearly to the wearer's knees. When he stopped for drink, he moved the muffler with his left hand, only while he poured his liquor in with his right; as soon as that was done, he muffled again.

"No, Jerry, no!" said the messenger, harping on one theme as he rode. "It wouldn't do for you, Jerry. Jerry, you honest tradesman, it wouldn't suit *your* line of business! *Recalled*——! Bust me if I don't think he'd been a drinking!"

His message perplexed his mind to that degree that he was fain, several times, to take off his hat to scratch his head. Except on the crown, which was raggedly bald, he had stiff, black hair, standing jaggedly all over it, and growing down-hill almost to his broad, blunt nose. It was so like smith's work, so much more like the top of a strongly spiked wall than a head of hair, that the best of players at leap-frog might have declined him, as the most dangerous man in the world to go over.

While he trotted back with the message he was to deliver to the nightwatchman in his box at the door of Tellson's Bank, by Temple-bar, who was to deliver it to greater authorities within, the shadows of the night took such shapes to him as arose out of the message, and took such shapes to the mare as arose out of *her* private topics of uneasiness. They seemed to be numerous, for she shied at every shadow on the road.

What time,[1] the mail-coach lumbered, jolted, rattled, and bumped upon its tedious way, with its three fellow-passengers inside. To whom, likewise, the shadows of the night revealed themselves, in the forms their dozing eyes and wandering thoughts suggested.

As the bank passenger nodded in his place with half-shut eyes, the little coach-windows, and the coach-lamp dimly gleaming through them, and the bulky bundle of opposite passenger, became Tellson's Bank, and did a great stroke of business. The rattle of the harness was the chink of money, and more drafts were honoured in five minutes than even Tellson's, with all its foreign and home connection, ever paid in thrice the time. Then the strong-rooms underground, at Tellson's, with such of their valuable stores and secrets as were known to the passenger opened before him, and he went in among them with the great keys and the feebly-burning candles, and found them safe, and strong, and sound, and still, just as he had last seen them.

But, though the bank was almost always with him, and though the coach (in a confused way, like the presence of pain under an opiate) was always with him, there was another current of impression that never ceased to run, all through the night. He was on his way to dig someone out of a grave.

Now, which of the multitude of faces that showed themselves before him was the true face of the buried person, the shadows

---

[1] WHAT TIME—In the meantime.

of the night did not indicate; but they were all the faces of a man of five-and-forty by years, and they differed principally in the passions they expressed, and in the ghastliness of their worn and wasted state. But the face was in the main one face, and every head was prematurely white. A hundred times the dozing passenger inquired of this spectre:

"Buried how long?"

The answer was always the same: "Almost eighteen years."

"You had abandoned all hope of being dug out?"

"Long ago."

"You know that you are recalled to life?"

"They tell me so."

"I hope you care to live?"

"I can't say."

"Shall I show her to you? Will you come and see her?"

The answers to this question were various and contradictory. Sometimes the broken reply was, "Wait! It would kill me if I saw her too soon." Sometimes, it was given in a tender rain of tears, and then it was, "Take me to her." Sometimes, it was staring and bewildered, and then it was, "I don't know her. I don't understand."

After such imaginary discourse, the passenger in his fancy would dig, and dig, dig—now, with a spade, now with a great key, now with his hands—to dig this wretched creature out. Got out at last, with earth hanging about his face and hair, he would suddenly fall away to dust. The passenger would then start to himself, and lower the window, to get the reality of mist and rain on his cheek.

IV THE PREPARATION

When the mail got successfully to Dover, in the course of the forenoon, the head-drawer [1] at the Royal George Hotel opened the coach-door as was his custom. He did it with some flourish of ceremony, for a mail journey from London in winter was an achievement to congratulate an adventurous traveller upon.

By that time, there was only one adventurous traveller left to be congratulated; for the two others had been set down at their respective roadside destinations. The mildewy inside of

[1] Head-drawer—Head waiter. Drawing liquor from the casks was one of his important duties.

the coach, with its damp and dirty straw, its disagreeable smell, and its obscurity, was rather like a larger dog-kennel. Mr. Lorry, the passenger, shaking himself out of it in chains of straw, a tangle of shaggy wrapper, flapping hat, and muddy legs, was rather like a larger sort of dog.

"There will be a packet [2] to Calais tomorrow, drawer?"

"Yes, sir, if the weather holds and the wind sets tolerable fair. The tide will serve pretty nicely at about two in the afternoon, sir. Bed, sir?"

"I shall not go to bed till night; but I want a bedroom, and a barber."

"And then breakfast? Yes, sir. That way, sir, if you please. Show Concord! [3] Gentleman's valise and hot water to Concord. Pull off gentleman's boots in Concord. Fetch barber to Concord. Stir about there, now, for Concord!"

The Concord bed-chamber being always assigned to a passenger by the mail, and passengers by the mail being always heavily wrapped up from head to foot, the room had the odd interest for the establishment of the Royal George that although but one kind of man was seen to go into it, all kinds and varieties of men came out of it. Consequently, another drawer, and two porters, and several maids, and the landlady, were all loitering by accident at various points of the road between the Concord and the coffee-room, when a gentleman of sixty, formally dressed in a brown suit of clothes, pretty well worn, but very well kept, with large square cuffs and large flaps to the pockets, passed along on his way to his breakfast.

The coffee-room had no other occupants, that forenoon, than the gentleman in brown. His breakfast-table was drawn before the fire, and as he sat, with its light shining on him, waiting for the meal, he sat so still, that he might have been sitting for his portrait.

Very orderly and methodical he looked, with a hand on each knee, and a loud watch ticking a sonorous sermon under his flapped waistcoat. He had a good leg, and was a little vain of it, for his brown stockings fitted sleek and close, and were of a fine texture; his shoes and buckles, too, though plain, were trim. He wore an odd little sleek crisp flaxen wig, setting very close

[2] PACKET—A vessel employed in carrying mails, goods, and passengers.
[3] CONCORD—The name of a room.

to his head: which wig, it is to be presumed, was made of hair, but which looked far more as though it were spun from filaments of silk or glass. His linen, though not of a fineness in accordance with his stockings, was as white as the tops of the waves that broke upon the neighboring beach, or the specks of sail that glinted in the sunlight far at sea. A face habitually suppressed and quieted, was still lighted up under the quaint wig by a pair of moist bright eyes that it must have cost their owner, in years gone by, some pains to drill to the composed and reserved expression of Tellson's Bank. He had a healthy colour in his cheeks, and his face, though lined, bore few traces of anxiety. But, perhaps the confidential bachelor clerks in Tellson's Bank were principally occupied with the cares of other people; and perhaps second-hand cares, like second-hand clothes, come easily off and on.

Completing his resemblance to a man who was sitting for his portrait, Mr. Lorry dropped off asleep. The arrival of his breakfast roused him, and he said to the drawer, as he moved his chair to it:

"I wish accommodations prepared for a young lady who may come here at any time today. She may ask for Mr. Jarvis Lorry, or she may only ask for a gentleman from Tellson's Bank. Please to let me know."

When Mr. Lorry had finished his breakfast, he went out for a stroll on the beach. As the day declined into the afternoon, and the air, which had been at intervals clear enough to allow the French coast to be seen, became again charged with mist and vapour, Mr. Lorry's thoughts seemed to cloud too. When it was dark, and he sat before the coffee-room fire, awaiting his dinner as he had awaited his breakfast, his mind was busily digging, digging, digging in the live red coals. Suddenly a rattling of wheels came up the narrow street, and rumbled into the inn-yard. "This is Mam'selle!" said he.

In a very few minutes the waiter came in, to announce that Miss Manette had arrived from London, and would be happy to see the gentleman from Tellson's.

"So soon?"

Miss Manette had taken some refreshment on the road, and required none then, and was extremely anxious to see the gentleman from Tellson's immediately, if it suited his pleasure and convenience.

The gentleman from Tellson's had nothing left for it but to settle his odd little flaxen wig at the ears, and follow the waiter to Miss Manette's apartment. It was a large, dark room, furnished in a funereal manner with black horsehair, and loaded with heavy dark tables. These had been oiled and oiled, until the two tall candles on the table in the middle of the room were gloomily reflected on every leaf; as if *they* were buried, in deep graves of black mahogany, and no light to speak of could be expected from them until they were dug out.

The obscurity was so difficult to penetrate that Mr. Lorry, picking his way over the well-worn Turkey carpet, supposed Miss Manette to be, for the moment, in some adjacent room, until, having got past the two tall candles, he saw standing to receive him by the table between them and the fire, a young lady of not more than seventeen, in a riding-cloak, and still holding her straw travelling-hat by its ribbon in her hand.

As his eyes rested on a short, slight, pretty figure, a quantity of golden hair, a pair of blue eyes that met his own with an inquiring look, and a forehead with a singular capacity of lifting and knitting itself into an expression that was not quite one of perplexity, or wonder, or alarm, or merely of a bright fixed attention, though it included all the four expressions—as his eyes rested on these things, a sudden vivid likeness passed before him, of a child whom he had held in his arms on the passage across that very Channel, one cold time, when the hail drifted heavily and the sea ran high. The likeness passed away, say, like a breath along the surface of the gaunt pier-glass behind her, and he made his formal bow to Miss Manette.

"Pray take a seat, sir." In a very clear and pleasant young voice: a little foreign in its accent, but a very little indeed.

"I kiss your hand, miss," said Mr. Lorry, with the manners of an earlier date, as he made his bow again, and took his seat.

"I received a letter from the Bank, sir, yesterday, informing me that some intelligence—or discovery—respecting the small property of my poor father whom I never saw—so long dead——"

Mr. Lorry moved in his chair, and cast a troubled look towards her.

"—rendered it necessary that I should go to Paris, there to communicate with a gentleman of the Bank, so good as to be despatched to Paris for the purpose."

"Myself."

"As I was prepared to hear, sir."

She curtseyed to him with a pretty desire to convey to him that she felt how much older and wiser he was than she. He made her another bow.

"I replied to the Bank, sir, that as it was considered necessary, by those who know, and who are so kind as to advise me, that I should go to France, and that as I am an orphan and have no friend who could go with me, I should esteem it highly if I might be permitted to place myself during the journey, under that worthy gentleman's protection. The gentleman had left London, but I think a messenger was sent after him to beg the favour of his waiting for me here."

"I was happy," said Mr. Lorry, "to be entrusted with the charge. I shall be more happy to execute it."

"Sir, I thank you indeed. I thank you very gratefully. It was told me by the Bank that the gentleman would explain to me the details of the business, and that I must prepare myself to find them of a surprising nature. I have done my best to prepare myself, and I naturally have a strong and eager interest to know what they are."

"Naturally," said Mr. Lorry. "Yes—I——"

After a pause, he added, again settling the crisp flaxen wig at the ears:

"It is very difficult to begin."

He did not begin, but, in his indecision, met her glance. The young forehead lifted itself into that singular expression—but it was pretty and characteristic, besides being singular—and she raised her hand, as if with an involuntary action she caught at, or stayed, some passing shadow.

"Are you quite a stranger to me, sir?"

"Am I not?" Mr. Lorry opened his hands, and extended them outward with an argumentative smile.

Between the eyebrows and just over the little feminine nose, the line of which was as delicate and fine as it was possible to be, the expression deepened itself as she took her seat thoughtfully in the chair by which she had hitherto remained standing. He watched her as she mused, and the moment she raised her eyes again, went on:

"In your adopted country, I presume, I cannot do better than address you as a young English lady, Miss Manette?"

"If you please, sir."

"Miss Manette, I am a man of business. I have a business charge of which to acquit myself. In your reception of it, don't heed me any more than if I were a speaking machine—truly, I am not much else. I will, with your leave, relate to you, miss, the story of one of our customers."

"Story!"

He seemed wilfully to mistake the word she had repeated, when he added, in a hurry, "Yes, customers; in the banking business we usually call our connections our customers. He was a French gentleman; a scientific gentleman; a man of great acquirements—a Doctor."

"Not of Beauvais?"

"Why, yes, of Beauvais. Like Monsieur Manette, your father, the gentleman was of Beauvais. Like Monsieur Manette, your father, the gentleman was of repute in Paris. I had the honour of knowing him there. Our relations were business relations, but confidential. I was at that time in our French House, and had been—oh! twenty years."

"At that time—I may ask, at what time, sir?"

"I speak, miss, of twenty years ago. He married—an English lady—and I was one of the trustees. His affairs, like the affairs of many other French gentlemen and French families, were entirely in Tellson's hands. In a similar way, I am, or I have been, trustee of one kind or other for scores of our customers. These are mere business relations, miss; there is no friendship in them, no particular interest, nothing like sentiment. I have passed from one to another, in the course of my business life, just as I pass from one of our customers to another in the course of my business day; in short, I have no feelings; I am a mere machine. To go on——"

"But this is my father's story, sir; and I begin to think"—the curiously roughened forehead was very intent upon him—"that when I was left an orphan through my mother's surviving my father only two years, it was you who brought me to England. I am almost sure it was you."

Mr. Lorry took the hesitating little hand that confidingly advanced to take his, and he put it with some ceremony to his lips. He then conducted the young lady straightway to her chair again, and, holding the chair-back with his left hand, and using his right by turns to rub his chin, pull his wig at the ears, or point what he said, stood looking down into her face while she sat looking up into his.

"Miss Manette, it *was* I. And you will see how truly I spoke of myself just now, in saying I had no feelings, and that all the relations I hold with my fellow-creatures are mere business relations, when you reflect that I have never seen you since. No; you have been the ward of Tellson's House since, and I have been busy with the other business of Tellson's House since. Feelings! I have no time for them, no chance of them. I pass my whole life, miss, in turning an immense pecuniary Mangle."[4]

After this odd description of his daily routine of employment, Mr. Lorry flattened his flaxen wig upon his head with both hands, and resumed his former attitude.

"So far, miss (as you have remarked), this is the story of your regretted father. Now comes the difference. If your father had not died when he did—— Don't be frightened! How you start!"

She did, indeed, start. And she caught his wrist with both her hands.

"Pray," said Mr. Lorry, in a soothing tone, bringing his left hand from the back of the chair to lay it on the supplicatory fingers that clasped him in so violent a tremble, "pray control your agitation—a matter of business. As I was saying——"

---

[4] MANGLE—A machine for ironing or smoothing linens. Mr. Lorry is thus illustrating the mechanical, impersonal nature of his business.

Her look so discomposed him that he stopped, wandered, and began anew:

"As I was saying, if Monsieur Manette had not died; if he had suddenly and silently disappeared; if he had been spirited away; if it had not been difficult to guess to what dreadful place, though no art could trace him; if he had an enemy in some compatriot who could exercise a privilege that I in my own time have known the boldest people afraid to speak of in a whisper, across the water there; for instance, the privilege of filling up blank forms [5] for the consignment of anyone to the oblivion of a prison for any length of time; if his wife had implored the king, the queen, the court, the clergy, for any tidings of him, and all quite in vain;—then the history of your father would have been the history of this unfortunate gentleman, the Doctor of Beauvais."

"I entreat you to tell me more, sir."

"I will. I am going to. You can bear it?"

"I can bear anything but the uncertainty you leave me in at this moment."

"You speak collectedly, and you—*are* collected. That's good!" (Though his manner was less satisfied than his words.) "A matter of business. Regard it as a matter of business—business that must be done. Now, if this Doctor's wife, though a lady of great courage and spirit, had suffered so intensely from this cause before her little child was born——"

"The little child was a daughter, sir."

"A daughter. A—a—matter of business—don't be distressed. Miss, if the poor lady had suffered so intensely before her little child was born, that she came to the determination of sparing the poor child the inheritance of any part of the agony she had known the pains of, by rearing her in the belief that her father was dead—— No, don't kneel! In Heaven's name why should you kneel to me!"

"For the truth. O dear, good, compassionate sir, for the truth!"

"A—a matter of business. You confuse me, and how can I transact business if I am confused? Let us be clear-headed. If

---

[5] BLANK FORMS—*Lettres de cachet,* which were blank forms of arrest given by the French kings to their favorites, and bearing the royal signature. These could be filled in with the name of any victim whatsoever.

you could kindly mention now, for instance, what nine times ninepence are, or how many shillings in twenty guineas, it would be so encouraging. I should be so much more at my ease about your state of mind."

Without directly answering to this appeal, she sat so still when he had very gently raised her, and the hands that had not ceased to clasp his wrists were so much more steady than they had been, that she communicated some reassurance to Mr. Jarvis Lorry.

"That's right, that's right. Courage! Business! You have business before you; useful business. Miss Manette, your mother took this course with you. And when she died—I believe broken-hearted—having never slackened her unavailing search for your father, she left you, at two years old, to grow to be blooming, beautiful, and happy, without the dark cloud upon you of living in uncertainty whether your father soon wore his heart out in prison, or wasted there through many lingering years. You know that your parents had no great possession, and that what they had was secured to your mother and to you. There has been no new discovery, of money, or of any other property; but——"

He felt his wrist held closer, and he stopped. The expression in the forehead, which had so particularly attracted his notice, and which was now immovable, had deepened into one of pain and horror.

"But he has been—been found. He is alive. Greatly changed, it is too probable; almost a wreck, it is possible; though we will hope the best. Still, alive. Your father has been taken to the house of an old servant in Paris, and we are going there: I, to identify him, if I can: you, to restore him to life, love, duty, rest, comfort."

A shiver ran through her frame, and from it through his. She said, in a low, distinct, awe-stricken voice, as if she were saying it in a dream,

"I am going to see his Ghost! It will be his Ghost—not him!"

Mr. Lorry quietly chafed the hands that held his arm. "There, there, there! See now, see now! The best and the worst are known to you now. You are well on your way to the poor wronged gentleman, and, with a fair sea voyage, and a fair land journey, you will be soon at his dear side."

She repeated in the same tone, sunk to a whisper, "I have been free, I have been happy, yet his Ghost has never haunted me!"

"Only one thing more," said Mr. Lorry, laying stress upon it as a wholesome means of enforcing her attention: "he has been found under another name; his own, long forgotten or long concealed. It would be worse than useless now to inquire which; worse than useless to seek to know whether he has been for years overlooked, or always designedly held prisoner. It would be worse than useless now to make any inquiries, because it would be dangerous. Better not to mention the subject, anywhere or in any way, and to remove him—for a while at all events—out of France. Even I, safe as an Englishman, and even Tellson's, important as they are to French credit, avoid all naming of the matter. I carry about me not a scrap of writing openly referring to it. This is a secret service altogether. My credentials, entries, and memoranda are all comprehended in one line, *'Recalled to Life'*; which may mean anything. But what is the matter? She doesn't notice a word! Miss Manette!"

Perfectly still and silent, and not even fallen back in her chair, she sat under his hand, utterly insensible; with her eyes open and fixed upon him, and with that last expression looking as if it were carved or branded into her forehead. So close was her hold upon his arm, that he feared to detach himself lest he should hurt her; therefore he called out loudly for assistance without moving.

A wild-looking woman, whom even in his agitation, Mr. Lorry observed to be all of a red color, and to have red hair, and to be dressed in some extraordinary tight-fitting fashion, came running into the room in advance of the inn servants, and soon settled the question of his detachment from the poor young lady, by laying a brawny hand upon his chest, and sending him flying back against the nearest wall.

"Why, look at you all!" bawled this figure, addressing the inn servants. "Why don't you go and fetch things, instead of standing there staring at me? I am not so much to look at, am I? Why don't you go and fetch things? I'll let you know, if you don't bring smelling-salts, cold water, and vinegar, quick!"

There was an immediate dispersal for these restoratives, and she softly laid the patient on a sofa, and tended her with great skill and gentleness: calling her "my precious!" and "my bird!" and spreading her golden hair aside over her shoulders with great pride and care.

"And you in brown!" she said, indignantly turning to Mr. Lorry; "couldn't you tell her what you had to tell her, without frightening her to death? Look at her, with her pretty pale face and her cold hands. Do you call *that* being a Banker?"

Mr. Lorry was so exceedingly disconcerted by a question so hard to answer, that he could only look on, at a distance, with much feebler sympathy and humility, while the strong woman, having banished the inn servants under the mysterious penalty of "letting them know" something not mentioned if they stayed there, staring, recovered her charge by a regular series of gradations, and coaxed her to lay her drooping head upon her shoulder.

"I hope she will do well now," said Mr. Lorry.

"No thanks to you in brown, if she does. My darling pretty!"

"I hope," said Mr. Lorry, after another pause of feeble sympathy and humility, "that you accompany Miss Manette to France?"

"A likely thing, too!" replied the strong woman. "If it was ever intended that I should go across salt water, do you suppose Providence would have cast my lot in an island?"

This being another question hard to answer, Mr. Jarvis Lorry withdrew to consider it.

V THE WINE-SHOP

A LARGE cask of wine had been dropped and broken, in the street. The accident had happened in getting it out of a cart; the cask had tumbled out with a run, the hoops had burst, and it lay on the stones just outside the door of the wine-shop, shattered like a walnut-shell.

All the people within reach had suspended their business, or their idleness, to run to the spot and drink the wine. The rough, irregular stones of the street, pointing every way, and designed, one might have thought, expressly to lame all living creatures that approached them, had dammed it into little pools; these were surrounded, each by its own jostling group or crowd, according to its size. Some men kneeled down, made scoops of their two hands joined, and sipped, or tried to help women, who bent over their shoulders, to sip, before the wine had all run out between their fingers. Others, men and women, dipped in the puddles with little mugs of mutilated earthenware, or even with handkerchiefs from women's heads, which were squeezed dry into infants' mouths; others made small mud-embankments, to stem the wine as it ran; others, directed by lookers-on up at high windows, darted here and there, to cut off little streams

of wine that started away in new directions; others devoted themselves to the sodden pieces of the cask, licking, and even champing the moister wine-rotted fragments with eager relish. There was no drainage to carry off the wine, and not only did it all get taken up, but so much mud got taken up along with it, that there might have been a scavenger[1] in the street, if anybody acquainted with it could have believed in such a miraculous presence.

A shrill sound of laughter and of amused voices—voices of men, women, and children—resounded in the street while this wine-game lasted. There was little roughness in the sport, and much playfulness. There was a special companionship in it, an observable inclination on the part of every one to join some other one, which led, especially among the luckier or light-hearted, to frolicsome embraces, drinking of healths, shaking of

[1] SCAVENGER—Street cleaner.

hands, and even joining of hands and dancing, a dozen together. When the wine was gone, and the places where it had been most abundant were raked into a gridiron-pattern by fingers, these demonstrations ceased, as suddenly as they had broken out. The man who had left his saw sticking in the firewood he was cutting, set it in motion again; the woman who had left on a door-step the little pot of hot-ashes, at which she had been trying to soften the pain in her own starved fingers and toes, or in those of her child, returned to it; men with bare arms, matted locks, and cadaverous faces, who had merged into the winter light from cellars, moved away to descend again; and a gloom gathered on the scene that appeared more natural to it than sunshine.

The wine was red wine, and had stained the ground of the narrow street in the suburb of Saint Antoine,[2] in Paris, where it was spilled. It had stained many hands, too, and many faces, and many naked feet, and many wooden shoes. The hands of the man who sawed the wood, left red marks on the billets;[3] and the forehead of the woman who nursed her baby, was stained with the stain of the old rag she wound about her head again. Those who had been greedy with the staves of the cask, had acquired a tigerish smear about the mouth; and one tall joker so besmirched, his head more out of a long squalid bag of a nightcap than in it, scrawled upon a wall with his finger dipped in muddy wine lees—BLOOD.

The time was to come, when *that* wine too would be spilled on the street-stones, and when the stain of it would be red upon many a citizen there.

The wine-shop was a corner shop, better than most others in its appearance and degree, and the master of the wine-shop had stood outside it, in a yellow waistcoat and green breeches, looking on at the struggle for the lost wine. "It's not my affair," said he, with a final shrug of the shoulders. "The people from the market did it. Let them bring another."

This wine-shop keeper was a bull-necked, martial-looking man of thirty, and he should have been of a hot temperament,

---

[2] SAINT ANTOINE (sän-tŏn-twän')—A section of Paris near the famous prison of the Bastille. At the time of the Revolution, this section was one of the poorest and most dangerous sections of the city. Saint Antoine was called "the patron saint of the Revolution."

[3] BILLETS—Small pieces of wood.

for, although it was a bitter day, he wore no coat, but carried one slung over his shoulder. His shirt-sleeves were rolled up, too, and his brown arms were bare to the elbows. Neither did he wear anything more on his head than his own crisply-curling short dark hair. He was a dark man altogether, with good eyes and a good bold breadth between them. Good-humoured-looking on the whole, but implacable-looking, too; evidently a man of a strong resolution and a set purpose; a man not desirable to be met rushing down a narrow pass with a gulf on either side, for nothing would turn the man.

Madame Defarge, his wife, sat in the shop behind the counter as he came in. Madame Defarge was a stout woman of about his own age, with a watchful eye that seldom seemed to look at anything, a large hand heavily ringed, a steady face, strong features, and great composure of manner. There was a character about Madame Defarge, from which one might have predicted that she did not often make mistakes against herself in any of the reckonings over which she presided. Madame Defarge being sensitive to cold, was wrapped in fur, and had a quantity of bright shawl twined about her head, though not to the concealment of her large ear-rings. Her knitting [4] was before her, but she had laid it down to pick her teeth with a toothpick. Thus engaged, with her right elbow supported by her left hand, Madame Defarge said nothing when her lord came in, but coughed just one grain of cough. This, in combination with the lifting of her darkly defined eye-brows over her toothpick by the breadth of a line, suggested to her husband that he would do well to look round the shop among the customers, for any new customer who had dropped in while he stepped over the way.

The wine-shop keeper accordingly rolled his eyes about, until they rested upon an elderly gentleman and a young lady, who were seated in a corner. Other company were there: two playing cards, two playing dominoes, three standing by the counter lengthening out a short supply of wine. As he passed behind the counter, he took notice that the elderly gentleman said in a look to the young lady, "This is our man."

---

[4] KNITTING—The women played an important part in the Revolution, and appeared in the street always with their knitting. They formed societies and their chief work was to urge on the men to deeds of blood and horror. Madame Defarge is represented as a leader among this class of women.

"What the devil do *you* do in that galley there!" said Monsieur Defarge to himself; "I don't know you."

But he feigned not to notice the two strangers, and fell into discourse with the triumvirate of customers who were drinking at the counter.

"How goes it, Jacques?"[5] said one of these three to Monsieur Defarge. "Is all the spilt wine swallowed?"

"Every drop, Jacques," answered Monsieur Defarge.

When this interchange of Christian names was effected, Madame Defarge, picking her teeth with her toothpick, coughed another grain of cough, and raised her eyebrows by the breadth of another line.

"It is not often," said the second of the three, addressing Monsieur Defarge, "that many of these miserable beasts know the taste of wine, or of anything but black bread and death. Is it not so, Jacques?"

"It is so, Jacques," Monsieur Defarge returned.

At this second interchange of the Christian name, Madame Defarge, still using her toothpick with profound composure, coughed another grain of cough, and raised her eyebrows by the breadth of another line.

The last of the three now said his say, as he put down his empty drinking vessel and smacked his lips.

"Ah! So much the worse! A bitter taste it is that such poor cattle always have in their mouths, and hard lives they live, Jacques. Am I right, Jacques?"

"You are right, Jacques," was the response of Monsieur Defarge.

This third interchange of the Christian name was completed at the moment when Madame Defarge put her toothpick by, kept her eyebrows up, and slightly rustled in her seat.

"Hold then! True!" muttered her husband. "Gentlemen—my wife!"

The three customers pulled off their hats to Madame Defarge, with three flourishes. She acknowledged their homage by bending her head, and giving them a quick look. Then she glanced in a casual manner round the wine-shop, took up her knitting

---

[5] JACQUES (zhäk)—This name was the password of a mysterious secret society which some authorities believe to have organized the Revolution.

with a great apparent calmness and repose of spirit, and became absorbed in it.

"Gentlemen," said her husband, who had kept his bright eye observantly upon her, "good-day. The chamber, furnished bachelor-fashion, that you wished to see, and were inquiring for when I stepped out, is on the fifth floor. The doorway of the staircase gives on [6] the little courtyard close to the left here," pointing with his hand, "near to the window of my establishment. But, now that I remember, one of you has already been there, and can show the way. Gentlemen, adieu!"

They paid for their wine, and left the place. The eyes of Monsieur Defarge were studying his wife at her knitting, when the elderly gentleman advanced from his corner, and begged the favour of a word.

"Willingly, sir," said Monsieur Defarge, and quietly stepped with him to the door.

Their conference was very short, but very decided. Almost at the first word, Monsieur Defarge started and became deeply attentive. It had not lasted a minute, when he nodded and went out. The gentleman then beckoned to the young lady, and they, too, went out. Madame Defarge knitted with nimble fingers and steady eyebrows, and saw nothing.

Mr. Jarvis Lorry and Miss Manette, emerging from the wine-shop thus, joined Monsieur Defarge in the doorway to which he had directed his other company just before. It opened from a stinking little black courtyard, and was the general public entrance to a great pile of houses, inhabited by a great number of people. In the gloomy tile-paved entry to the gloomy tile-paved staircase, Monsieur Defarge bent down on one knee to the child of his old master,[7] and put her hands to his lips. It was a gentle action, but not at all gently done; a very remarkable transformation had come over him in a few seconds. He had no good humour in his face, nor any openness of aspect left, but had become a secret, angry, dangerous man.

"It is very high; it is a little difficult. Better to begin slowly." Thus, Monsieur Defarge, in a stern voice, to Mr. Lorry, as they began ascending the stairs.

---

[6] GIVES ON—Opens upon.

[7] CHILD OF HIS OLD MASTER—In years past Defarge had been the servant of Miss Manette's father.

"Is he alone?" the latter whispered.

"Alone! God help him who should be with him!" said the other, in the same low voice.

"Is he always alone, then?"

"Yes."

"Of his own desire?"

"Of his own necessity. As he was when I first saw him after they found me and demanded to know if I would take him, and, at my peril be discreet—as he was then, so he is now."

"He is greatly changed?"

"Changed!"

The keeper of the wine-shop stopped to strike the wall with his hand, and mutter a tremendous curse. No direct answer could have been half so forcible. Mr. Lorry's spirits grew heavier and heavier, as he and his two companions ascended higher and higher.

At last, the top of the staircase was gained, and they stopped to rest. There was yet an upper staircase, of a steeper inclination and of contracted dimensions, to be ascended, before the garret story was reached. The keeper of the wine-shop, always going a little in advance, and always going on the side which Mr. Lorry took, as though he dreaded to be asked any question by the young lady, turned himself about here, and, carefully feeling in the pockets of the coat he carried over his shoulder, took out a key.

"The door is locked then, my friend?" said Mr. Lorry, surprised.

"Ay. Yes," was the grim reply of Monsieur Defarge.

"You think it necessary to keep the unfortunate gentleman so retired?"

"I think it necessary to turn the key." Monsieur Defarge whispered it closer in his ear, and frowned heavily.

"Why?"

"Why! Because he has lived so long, locked up, that he would be frightened—rave—tear himself to pieces—die—come to I know not what harm—if his door was left open."

"Is it possible!" exclaimed Mr. Lorry.

"Is it possible?" repeated Defarge, bitterly. "Yes. And a beautiful world we live in, when it *is* possible, and when many other such things are possible, and not only possible, but done

—done, see you!—under that sky there, every day. Long live the Devil. Let us go on."

This dialogue had been held in so very low a whisper, that not a word of it had reached the young lady's ears. But, by this time she trembled under such strong emotion, and her face expressed such deep anxiety, and, above all, such dread and terror, that Mr. Lorry felt it incumbent on him to speak a word or two of reassurance.

"Courage, dear miss! Courage! Business! The worst will be over in a moment; it is but passing the room door, and the worst is over. Then, all the good you bring to him, all the relief, all the happiness you bring to him, begin. Let our good friend here assist you on that side. That's well, friend Defarge. Come, now. Business, business!"

They went up slowly and softly. The staircase was short, and they were soon at the top. There, as it had an abrupt turn in it, they came all at once in sight of three men, whose heads were bent down close together at the side of a door, and who were intently looking into the room to which the door belonged, through some chinks or holes in the wall. On hearing footsteps close at hand, these three turned, and rose, and showed themselves to be the three of one name who had been drinking in the wine-shop.

"I forgot them in the surprise of your visit," explained Monsieur Defarge. "Leave us, good boys; we have business here."

The three glided by, and went silently down.

There appearing to be no other door on that floor, and the keeper of the wine-shop going straight to this one when they were left alone, Mr. Lorry asked him in a whisper, with a little anger:

"Do you make a show of Monsieur Manette?"

"I show him, in the way you have seen, to a chosen few."

"Is that well?"

"*I* think it is well."

"Who are the few? How do you choose them?"

"I choose them as real men, of my name—Jacques is my name —to whom the sight is likely to do good. Enough, you are English; that is another thing. Stay there, if you please, a little moment."

With an admonitory gesture to keep them back, he stooped,

and looked in through the crevice in the wall. Soon raising his head again, he struck twice or thrice upon the door—evidently with no other object than to make a noise there. With the same intention, he drew the key across it, three or four times, before he put it clumsily into the lock, and turned it as heavily as he could.

The door slowly opened inward under his hand, and he looked into the room and said something. A faint voice answered something. Little more than a single syllable could have been spoken on either side.

He looked back over his shoulder, and beckoned them to enter. Mr. Lorry got his arm securely round the daughter's waist, and held her; for he felt that she was sinking.

"A—a—a—business, business!" he urged, with a moisture that was not of business shining on his cheek. "Come in, come in!"

"I am afraid of it," she answered, shuddering.

"Of it? What?"

"I mean of him. Of my father."

Rendered in a manner desperate, by her state and by the beckoning of their conductor, he drew over his neck the arm that shook upon his shoulder, lifted her a little, and hurried her into the room. He set her down just within the door, and held her, clinging to him.

Defarge drew out the key, closed the door, locked it on the inside, took out the key again, and held it in his hand. All this he did, methodically, and with as loud and harsh an accompaniment of noise as he could make. Finally, he walked across the room with a measured tread to where the window was. He stopped there, and faced round.

The garret, built to be a depository for firewood and the like, was dim and dark: for, the window of dormer shape, was in truth a door in the roof, with a little crane over it for the hoisting up of stores from the street: unglazed, and closing up the middle in two pieces, like any other door of French construction. To exclude the cold, one half of this door was fast closed, and the other was opened but a very little way. Such a scanty portion of light was admitted through these means, that it was difficult, on first coming in, to see anything; and long habit alone could have slowly formed in anyone the ability to do any work requiring nicety in such obscurity. Yet, work of that kind was being done in the garret; for, with his back towards the door, and his face towards the window where the keeper of the wine-shop stood looking at him, a white-haired man sat on a low bench, stooping forward and very busy, making shoes.

VI   THE SHOEMAKER

"GOOD-DAY!" said Monsieur Defarge, looking down at the white head that bent low over the shoemaking.

It was raised for a moment, and a very faint voice responded to the salutation, as if it were at a distance:

"Good-day!"

"You are still hard at work, I see?"

After a long silence, the head was lifted for another moment, and the voice replied, "Yes—I am working." This time, a pair of haggard eyes had looked at the questioner, before the face had dropped again.

The faintness of the voice was pitiable and dreadful. It was not the faintness of physical weakness, though confinement and hard fare no doubt had their part in it. Its deplorable peculiarity was, that it was the faintness of solitude and disuse. It was like the last feeble echo of a sound made long and long ago. So entirely had it lost the life and resonance of the human voice, that it affected the senses like a once beautiful color, faded away into a poor weak stain.

Some minutes of silent work had passed, and the haggard eyes had looked up again: not with any interest or curiosity, but with a dull mechanical perception, beforehand, that the spot where the only visitor they were aware of had stood, was not yet empty.

"I want," said Defarge, who had not removed his gaze from the shoemaker, "to let in a little more light here."

The opened half-door was opened a little further, and secured at that angle for the time. A broad ray of light fell into the garret, and showed the workman, with an unfinished shoe upon his lap, pausing in his labor. His few common tools and various scraps of leather were at his feet and on his bench. He had a white beard, raggedly cut, but not very long, a hollow face, and exceedingly bright eyes. The hollowness and thinness of his face would have caused them to look large, under his yet dark eyebrows and his confused white hair, though they had been really otherwise; but they were naturally large, and looked unnaturally so. His yellow rags of shirt lay open at the throat, and showed his body to be withered and worn. He, and his old canvas frock, and his loose stockings, and all his poor tatters of clothes, had, in a long seclusion from direct light and air, faded down to such a dull uniformity of parchment-yellow, that it would have been hard to say which was which.

Mr. Lorry came silently forward, leaving the daughter by the door. When he had stood, for a minute or two, by the side of Defarge, the shoemaker looked up. He showed no surprise at seeing another figure, but the unsteady fingers of one of his hands strayed to his lips as he looked at it, and then the hand dropped to his work, and he once more bent over the shoe. The look and the action had occupied but an instant.

"You have a visitor, you see," said Monsieur Defarge.

"What did you say?"

"Here is a visitor."

The shoemaker looked up as before, but without removing a hand from his work.

"Come!" said Defarge. "Here is monsieur, who knows a well-made shoe when he sees one. Show him that shoe you are working at. Take it, monsieur."

Mr. Lorry took it in his hand.

"Tell monsieur what kind of shoe it is, and the maker's name."

There was a longer pause than usual, before the shoemaker replied:

"I forget what it was you asked me. What did you say?"

"I said, couldn't you describe the kind of shoe, for monsieur's information?"

"It is a lady's shoe. It is a young lady's walking-shoe. It is in the present mode. I never saw the mode. I have had a pattern in my hand." He glanced at the shoe, with some little passing touch of pride.

"And the maker's name?" said Defarge.

Now that he had no work to hold, he laid the knuckles of the right hand in the hollow of the left, and then the knuckles of the left hand in the hollow of the right, and then passed a hand across his bearded chin, and so on in regular changes, without a moment's intermission. The task of recalling him from the vacancy into which he always sank when he had spoken, was like recalling some very weak person from a swoon, or endeavouring, in the hope of some disclosure, to stay the spirit of a fast-dying man.

"Did you ask me for my name?"

"Assuredly I did."

"One Hundred and Five, North Tower."

"Is that all?"

"One Hundred and Five, North Tower."

With a weary sound that was not a sigh, nor a groan, he bent to work again, until the silence was again broken.

"You are not a shoemaker by trade?" said Mr. Lorry, looking steadfastly at him.

His haggard eyes turned to Defarge as if he would have transferred the question to him; but as no help came from that quarter, they turned back on the questioner when they had sought the ground.

"I am not a shoemaker by trade? No, I was not a shoemaker by trade. I—I learnt it here. I taught myself. I asked leave to——"

He lapsed away, even for minutes, ringing those measured changes on his hands the whole time. His eyes came slowly back, at last, to the face from which they had wandered; when they rested on it, he started, and resumed, in the manner of a sleeper that moment awake, reverting to a subject of last night.

"I asked leave to teach myself, and I got it with much difficulty after a long while, and I have made shoes ever since."

As he held out his hand for the shoe that had been taken from him, Mr. Lorry said, still looking steadfastly in his face:

"Monsieur Manette, do you remember nothing of me?"

The shoe dropped to the ground, and he sat looking fixedly at the questioner.

"Monsieur Manette;" Mr. Lorry laid his hand upon Defarge's arm; "do you remember nothing of this man? Look at him. Look at me. Is there no old banker, no old business, no old servant, no old time, rising in your mind, Monsieur Manette?"

As the captive of many years sat looking fixedly, by turns at Mr. Lorry and at Defarge, some long obliterated marks of an actively intent intelligence in the middle of the forehead, gradually forced themselves through the black mist that had fallen on him. They were overclouded again, they were fainter, they were gone; but, they had been there. And so exactly was the expression repeated on the fair young face of her who had crept along the wall to a point where she could see him, and where she now stood looking at him, with hands which at first had been only raised in frightened compassion, if not even to keep him off and shut out the sight of him, but which were now extending towards him, trembling with eagerness to lay the spectral face upon her warm young breast, and love it back to life and hope— so exactly was the expression repeated on her fair young face, that it looked as though it had passed, like a moving light, from him to her.

Darkness had fallen on him in its place. He looked at the two, less and less attentively, and his eyes in gloomy abstraction sought the ground and looked about him in the old way. Finally, with a deep long sigh, he took the shoe up, and resumed his work.

"Have you recognized him, monsieur?" asked Defarge, in a whisper.

"Yes; for a moment. At first I thought it quite hopeless, but I have unquestionably seen, for a single moment, the face that I once knew well. Hush! Let us draw further back. Hush!"

She had moved from the wall of the garret, very near to the bench on which he sat. There was something awful in his unconsciousness of the figure that could have put out its hand and touched him as he stooped over his labor.

Not a word was spoken, not a sound was made. She stood, like a spirit, beside him, and he bent over his work.

It happened, at length, that he had occasion to change the instrument in his hand, for his shoemaker's knife. It lay on that side of him which was not the side on which she stood. He had taken it up, and was stooping to work again, when his eyes caught the skirt of her dress. He raised them, and saw her face. The two spectators started forward, but she stayed them with a motion of her hand. She had no fear of his striking at her with the knife, though they had.

He stared at her with a fearful look, and after a while his lips began to form some words, though no sound proceeded from them. By degrees, in the pauses of his quick and labored breathing, he was heard to say:

"What is this! Who are you?"

Not yet trusting the tones of her voice, she sat down on the bench beside him. He recoiled, but she laid her hand upon his arm. A strange thrill struck him when she did so, and visibly passed over his frame; he laid the knife down softly, as he sat staring at her.

Her golden hair, which she wore in long curls, had been hurriedly pushed aside, and fell down over her neck. Advancing his hand by little and little, he took it up, and looked at it. In the midst of the action he went astray, and, with another deep sigh, fell to work at his shoemaking.

But, not for long. Releasing his arm, she laid her hand upon his shoulder. After looking doubtfully at it, two or three times, as if to be sure that it was really there, he laid down his work, put his hand to his neck, and took off a blackened string with a scrap of folded rag attached to it. He opened this, carefully, on his knee, and it contained a very little quantity of hair: not more than one or two long golden hairs, which he had, in some old day, wound off upon his finger.

He took her hair into his hand again, and looked closely at it. "It is the same. How can it be! When was it! How was it!"

As the concentrating expression returned to his forehead, he seemed to become conscious that it was in hers too. He turned her full to the light, and looked at her.

"She had laid her head upon my shoulder, that night when I was summoned out—she had a fear of my going, though I had none—and when I was brought to the North Tower they found these upon my sleeve. 'You will leave me them? They can never help me to escape in the body, though they may in the spirit.' Those were the words I said. I remember them very well."

He formed this speech with his lips many times before he

could utter it. But when he did find spoken words for it, they came to him coherently, though slowly.

"How was this?—*Was it you?*"

Once more, the two spectators started, as he turned upon her with a frightful suddenness. But, she sat perfectly still in his grasp, and only said, in a low voice, "I entreat you, good gentlemen, do not come near us, do not speak, do not move!"

"Hark!" he exclaimed. "Whose voice was that?"

His hands released her as he uttered this cry, and went up to his white hair, which they tore in a frenzy. It died out, as everything but his shoemaking did die out of him, and he refolded his little packet and tried to secure it in his breast; but, he still looked at her, and gloomily shook his head.

"No, no, no; you are too young, too blooming. It can't be. See what the prisoner is. These are not the hands she knew, this is not the face she knew, this is not a voice she ever heard. No, no. She was—and he was—before the slow years of the North Tower—ages ago. What is your name, my gentle angel?"

Hailing his softened tone and manner, his daughter fell upon her knees before him, with her appealing hands upon his breast.

"O, sir, at another time you shall know my name, and who my mother was, and who my father, and how I never knew their hard, hard history. But I cannot tell you at this time, and I cannot tell you here. All that I may tell you, here and now, is, that I pray to you to touch me and to bless me!"

His cold white hand mingled with her radiant hair, which warmed and lighted it as though it were the light of Freedom shining on him.

"If you hear in my voice—I don't know that it is so, but I hope it is—if you hear in my voice any resemblance to a voice that once was sweet music in your ears, weep for it, weep for it! If you touch, in touching my hair, anything that recalls a beloved head that lay on your breast when you were young and free, weep for it, weep for it! If, when I hint to you of a Home that is before us, where I will be true to you with all my duty and with all my faithful service, I bring back the remembrance of a Home long desolate, while your poor heart pined away, weep for it, weep for it!"

She held him closer round the neck, and rocked him on her breast like a child.

Hailing his softened tone and manner, his daughter fell upon her knees before him.

"If, when I tell you, dearest dear, that your agony is over, and that I have come here to take you from it, and that we go to England to be at peace and at rest, I cause you to think of your useful life laid waste, and of our native France so wicked to you, weep for it, weep for it! And if, when I shall tell you of my name, and of my father who is living, and of my mother who is dead, you learn that I have to kneel to my honored father, and implore his pardon for having never for his sake striven all day and lain awake and wept all night, because the love of my poor mother hid his torture from me, weep for it, weep for it! Weep for her, then, and for me! Good gentlemen, thank God! I feel his sacred tears upon my face, and his sobs strike against my heart. O, see! Thank God for us, thank God!"

He had sunk in her arms, with his face dropped on her breast: a sight so touching, yet so terrible in the tremendous wrong and suffering which had gone before it, that the two beholders covered their faces.

When the quiet of the garret had been long undisturbed, and his heaving breast and shaken form had long yielded to the calm that must follow all storms, they came forward to raise the father and daughter from the ground. He had gradually drooped to the floor, and lay there in a lethargy, worn out. She had nestled down with him, that his head might lie upon her arm; and her hair drooping over him curtained him from the light.

"If, without disturbing him," she said, raising her hand to Mr. Lorry as he stooped over them, after repeated blowings of his nose, "all could be arranged for our leaving Paris at once, so that, from the very door, he could be taken away——"

"But, consider. Is he fit for the journey?" asked Mr. Lorry.

"More fit for that, I think, than to remain in this city, so dreadful to him."

"It is true," said Defarge, who was kneeling to look on and hear. "More than that; Monsieur Manette is, for all reasons, best out of France. Say, shall I hire a carriage and post-horses?"[1]

"That's business," said Mr. Lorry, resuming on the shortest notice his methodical manners; "and if business is to be done, I had better do it."

---

[1] Post-horses—Horses for fast traveling.

"Then be so kind," urged Miss Manette, "as to leave us here. You see how composed he has become, and you cannot be afraid to leave him with me now. Why should you be? If you will lock the door to secure us from interruption, I do not doubt that you will find him, when you come back, as quiet as you leave him. In any case, I will take care of him until you return, and then we will remove him straight."

Both Mr. Lorry and Defarge were rather disinclined to this course, and in favor of one of them remaining. But, as there were not only carriage and horses to be seen to, but travelling papers; and as time pressed, for the day was drawing to an end, it came at last to their hastily dividing the business that was necessary to be done, and hurrying away to do it.

Then, as the darkness closed in, the daughter laid her head down on the hard ground close at the father's side, and watched him. The darkness deepened and deepened, and they both lay quiet, until a light gleamed through the chinks in the wall.

Mr. Lorry and Monsieur Defarge had made all ready for the journey, and had brought with them, besides travelling cloaks and wrappers, bread and meat, wine, and hot coffee. Monsieur Defarge put this provender, and the lamp he carried, on the shoemaker's bench, and he and Mr. Lorry roused the captive, and assisted him to his feet.

No human intelligence could have read the mysteries of his mind, in the scared blank wonder of his face. Whether he knew what had happened, whether he recollected what they had said to him, whether he knew that he was free, were questions which no sagacity could have solved. They tried speaking to him; but, he was so confused, and so very slow to answer, that they took fright at his bewilderment, and agreed for the time to tamper with him no more. He had a wild, lost manner of occasionally clasping his head in his hands, that had not been seen in him before; yet, he had some pleasure in the mere sound of his daughter's voice, and invariably turned to it when she spoke.

In the submissive way of one long accustomed to obey under coercion, he ate and drank what they gave him to eat and drink, and put on the cloak and other wrappings that they gave him to wear. He readily responded to his daughter's drawing her arm through his, and took—and kept—her hand in both of his own.

They began to descend; Monsieur Defarge going first with the lamp, Mr. Lorry closing the little procession. They had not traversed many steps of the long main staircase when he stopped, and stared at the roof and round at the walls.

"You remember the place, my father? You remember coming up here?"

"What did you say?"

But, before she could repeat the question, he murmured an answer as if she had repeated it.

"Remember? No, I don't remember. It was so very long ago."

That he had no recollection whatever of his having been brought from his prison to that house, was apparent to them. They heard him mutter, "One Hundred and Five, North Tower"; and when he looked about him, it evidently was for the strong fortress-walls which had long encompassed him. On their reaching the courtyard, he instinctively altered his tread, as being in expectation of a drawbridge; and when there was no drawbridge, and he saw the carriage waiting in the open street, he dropped his daughter's hand and clasped his head again.

No crowd was about the door; no people were discernible at any of the many windows; not even a chance passer-by was in the street. An unnatural silence and desertion reigned there. Only one soul was to be seen, and that was Madame Defarge—who leaned against the door-post, knitting, and saw nothing.

The prisoner had got into the coach, and his daughter had followed him, when Mr. Lorry's feet were arrested on the step by his asking, miserably, for his shoemaking tools and the unfinished shoes. Madame Defarge immediately called to her husband that she would get them, and went, knitting, out of the lamplight, through the courtyard. She quickly brought them down and handed them in;—and immediately afterwards leaned against the door-post, knitting, and saw nothing.

Defarge got upon the box, and gave the word "To the Barrier!"[2] The postilion cracked his whip, and they clattered away under the feeble over-swinging lamps.

Under the over-swinging lamps—swinging ever brighter in the better streets, and ever dimmer in the worse—and by lighted shops, gay crowds, illuminated coffee-houses, and theatre doors,

---

[2] The Barrier—The city gates.

to one of the city gates. Soldiers with lanterns, at the guardhouse there. "Your papers, travellers!" "See here then, Monsieur the Officer," said Defarge, getting down, and taking him gravely apart, "these are the papers of monsieur inside, with the white head. They were consigned to me, with him, at the——" He dropped his voice, there was a flutter among the military lanterns, and one of them being handed into the coach by an arm in uniform, the eyes connected with the arm looked, not an every day or an every night look, at monsieur with the white head. "It is well. Forward!" from the uniform. "Adieu!" from Defarge. And so, under a short grove of feebler and feebler over-swinging lamps, out under the great grove of stars.

The shadows of the night were broad and black. All through the cold and restless interval, until dawn, they once more whispered in the ears of Mr. Jarvis Lorry—sitting opposite the buried man who had been dug out, and wondering what subtle powers were forever lost to him, and what were capable of restoration—the old inquiry:

"I hope you care to be recalled to life?"
And the old answer:
"I can't say."

BOOK THE SECOND. THE GOLDEN THREAD

I FIVE YEARS LATER

TELLSON'S BANK by Temple-bar was an old-fashioned place, even in the year one thousand seven hundred and eighty. It was very small, very dark, very ugly, very incommodious. It was an old-fashioned place, moreover, in the moral attribute that the partners in the House were proud of its smallness, proud of its darkness, proud of its ugliness, proud of its incommodiousness. They were even boastful of its eminence in those particulars, and were fired by an express conviction that, if it were less objectionable, it would be less respectable.

Cramped in all kinds of dim cupboards and hutches at Tellson's, the oldest of men carried on the business gravely. When they took a young man into Tellson's London house, they hid him somewhere till he was old. They kept him in a dark place, like a cheese, until he had the full Tellson flavor and blue-mold upon him. Then only was he permitted to be seen, spectacularly poring over large books, and casting his breeches and gaiters into the general weight of the establishment.

Outside Tellson's—never by any means in it, unless called in—was an odd-job-man, an occasional porter and messenger, who served as the live sign of the house. He was never absent during business hours, unless upon an errand, and then he was represented by his son: a grisly urchin of twelve, who was his express image. People understood that Tellson's, in a stately way, tolerated the odd-job-man. The House had always tolerated some person in that capacity, and time and tide had drifted this person to the post. His surname was Cruncher, and on the youthful occasion of his renouncing by proxy[1] the works of darkness, in the easterly parish church of Houndsditch, he had received the added appellation of Jerry.

The scene was Mr. Cruncher's private lodging in Hanging-sword-alley, Whitefriars;[2] the time, half-past seven of the clock on a windy March morning, Anno Domini seventeen hundred and eighty. (Mr. Cruncher himself always spoke of the year of our Lord as Anna Dominoes: apparently under the impression that the Christian era dated from the invention of a popular game, by a lady who had bestowed her name upon it.)

Mr. Cruncher's apartments were not in a savory neighborhood, and were but two in number, even if a closet with a single pane of glass in it might be counted as one. But, they were very decently kept. Early as it was, on the windy March morning, the room in which he lay a-bed was already scrubbed throughout; and between the cups and saucers arranged for breakfast, and the lumbering deal table, a very clean white cloth was spread.

Mr. Cruncher reposed under a patchwork counterpane, like a Harlequin[3] at home. At first, he slept heavily, but, by degrees, began to roll and surge in bed, until he rose above the surface, with his spiky hair looking as if it must tear the sheets to ribbons. At which juncture, he exclaimed, in a voice of dire exasperation:

"Bust me, if she ain't at it agin!"

---

[1] RENOUNCING BY PROXY—That is, when he was baptized.
[2] WHITEFRIARS—A London district not far from Temple-bar.
[3] HARLEQUIN—A favorite clown character, dressed in a colorful costume.

A woman of orderly and industrious appearance rose from her knees in a corner, with sufficient haste and trepidation to show that she was the person referred to.

"What!" said Mr. Cruncher, looking out of bed for a boot. "You're at it agin, are you?"

After hailing the morn with this second salutation, he threw a boot at the woman as a third. It was a very muddy boot, and may introduce the odd circumstance connected with Mr. Cruncher's domestic economy, that, whereas he often came home after banking hours with clean boots, he often got up next morning to find the same boots covered with clay.

"What," said Mr. Cruncher, varying his apostrophe after missing his mark—"what are you up to, Aggerawayter?" [4]

"I was only saying my prayers."

"Saying your prayers. You're a nice woman! What do you mean by flopping yourself down and praying agin me?"

"I was not praying against you; I was praying for you."

"You weren't. And if you were, I won't be took the liberty with. Here! your mother's a nice woman, Young Jerry, going a-praying agin your father's prosperity. You've got a dutiful mother, you have, my son. You've got a religious mother, you have, my boy: going and flopping herself down, and praying that the bread-and-butter may be snatched out of the mouth of her only child!"

Master Cruncher (who was in his shirt) took this very ill, and, turning to his mother, strongly deprecated any praying away of his personal board.

"And what do you suppose, you conceited female," said Mr. Cruncher, with unconscious inconsistency, "that the worth of *your* prayers may be? Name the price you put *your* prayers at!"

"They only come from the heart, Jerry. They are worth no more than that."

"Worth no more than that," repeated Mr. Cruncher. "They ain't worth much, then. Whether or no, I won't be prayed agin, I tell you. I can't afford it. I'm not going to be made unlucky by *your* sneaking. If you must go flopping yourself down, flop in favor of your husband and child, and not in opposition to 'em. If I had had any but a unnat'ral wife, and this poor boy

---

[4] AGGERAWAYTER—Aggravator.

had had any but a unnat'ral mother, I might have made some money last week, instead of being counterprayed and countermined and religiously circumwented into the worst of luck. Bu-u-ust me!" said Mr. Cruncher, who all this time had been putting on his clothes, "if I ain't, what with piety and one blowed thing and another, been choused[5] this last week into as bad luck as ever a poor devil of a honest tradesman met with! Young Jerry, dress yourself, my boy, and while I clean my boots keep a eye upon your mother now and then, and if you see any signs of more flopping, give me a call."

Mr. Cruncher's temper was not at all improved when he came to his breakfast. He resented Mrs. Cruncher's saying grace with particular animosity.

"Now, Aggerawayter! What are you up to? At it agin?"

His wife explained that she had merely "asked a blessing."

"Don't do it!" said Mr. Cruncher, looking about, as if he rather expected to see the loaf disappear under the efficacy of his wife's petitions. "I ain't a-going to be blest out of house and home. I won't have my wittles[6] blest off my table."

Exceedingly red-eyed and grim, as if he had been up all night at a party which had taken anything but a convivial turn, Jerry Cruncher worried his breakfast rather than ate it, growling over it like any four-footed inmate of a menagerie. Towards nine o'clock he smoothed his ruffled aspect, and, presenting as respectable and business-like an exterior as he could overlay his natural self with, issued forth to the occupation of the day.

It could scarcely be called a trade, in spite of his favorite description of himself as "a honest tradesman." His stock consisted of a wooden stool, made out of a broken-backed chair cut down, which stool Young Jerry, walking at his father's side, carried every morning to beneath the banking-house window that was nearest Temple-bar: where, with the addition of the first handful of straw that could be gleaned from any passing vehicle to keep the cold and wet from the odd-job-man's feet, it formed the encampment for the day. On this post of his, Mr. Cruncher was as well known to Fleet-street and the Temple, as the Bar itself—and was almost as ill-looking.

Encamped at a quarter before nine, in good time to touch his

[5] CHOUSED—Cheated, tricked.
[6] WITTLES—Victuals.

three-cornered hat to the oldest of men as they passed in to Tellson's, Jerry took up his station on this windy March morning, with Young Jerry standing by him, when not engaged in making forays through the Bar, to inflict bodily and mental injuries of an acute description on passing boys who were small enough for his amiable purpose. Father and son, extremely like each other, looking silently on at the morning traffic in Fleet-street, with their two heads as near to one another as the two eyes of each were, bore a considerable resemblance to a pair of monkeys. The resemblance was not lessened by the accidental circumstance, that the mature Jerry bit and spat out straw, while the twinkling eyes of the youthful Jerry were as restlessly watchful of him as of everything else in Fleet-street.

The head of one of the regular in-door messengers attached to Tellson's establishment was put through the door, and the word was given:

"Porter wanted!"

"Hooray, father! Here's an early job to begin with!"

Having thus given his parent God-speed, Young Jerry seated himself on the stool, entered on his reversionary interest in the straw his father had been chewing, and cogitated.

"Al-ways rusty! His fingers is al-ways rusty!" muttered Young Jerry. "Where does my father get all that iron rust from? He don't get no iron rust here!"

II A SIGHT

"You know the Old Bailey [1] well, no doubt?" said one of the oldest of clerks to Jerry the messenger.

"Ye-es, sir," returned Jerry, in something of a dogged manner. "I *do* know the Bailey."

"Just so. And you know Mr. Lorry?"

"I know Mr. Lorry, sir, much better than I know the Bailey. Much better," said Jerry, not unlike a reluctant witness at the establishment in question, "than I, as a honest tradesman, wish to know the Bailey."

"Very well. Find the door where the witnesses go in, and show the doorkeeper this note for Mr. Lorry. He will then let you in."

"Into the court, sir?"

---

[1] OLD BAILEY—The principal English criminal court, near Newgate Prison.

"Into the court."

Mr. Cruncher's eyes seemed to get a little closer to one another, and to interchange the inquiry, "What do you think of this?"

"Am I to wait in the court, sir?" he asked, as the result of that conference.

"I am going to tell you. The doorkeeper will pass the note to Mr. Lorry, and do you make any gesture that will attract Mr. Lorry's attention, and show him where you stand. Then what you have to do, is, to remain there until he wants you."

"Is that all, sir?"

"That's all. He wishes to have a messenger at hand. This is to tell him you are there."

Jerry took the letter, made his bow, informed his son, in passing, of his destination, and went his way.

The Old Bailey was famous as a kind of deadly inn-yard, from which pale travellers set out continually, in carts and coaches, on a violent passage into the other world. It was famous, too, for the pillory, a wise old institution, that inflicted a punishment of which no one could foresee the extent; also, for the whipping-post, another dear old institution, very humanising and softening to behold in action; also, for extensive transactions in blood-money,[2] another fragment of ancestral wisdom, systematically leading to the most frightful mercenary crimes that could be committed under Heaven.

Making his way through the tainted crowd, dispersed up and down this hideous scene of action, with the skill of a man accustomed to make his way quietly, the messenger found out the door he sought, and handed in his letter through a trap in it. After some delay and demur, the door grudgingly turned on its hinges a very little way, and allowed Mr. Jerry Cruncher to squeeze himself into court.

"What's on?" he asked, in a whisper, of the man he found himself next to.

"Nothing yet."

"What's coming on?"

"The Treason case."

"The quartering one, eh?"

---

[2] BLOOD-MONEY—Money paid for false testimony by which a capital conviction is secured.

"Ah!" returned the man, with a relish; "he'll be drawn on a hurdle to be half hanged, and then he'll be taken down and sliced before his own face, and then his inside will be taken out and burnt while he looks on, and then his head will be chopped off, and he'll be cut into quarters. That's the sentence."

"If he's found guilty, you mean to say?" Jerry added, by way of proviso.

"Oh! they'll find him guilty," said the other. "Don't you be afraid of that."

Mr. Cruncher's attention was here diverted to the door-keeper, whom he saw making his way to Mr. Lorry, with the note in his hand. Mr. Lorry sat at a table, among the gentlemen in wigs: not far from a wigged gentleman, the prisoner's counsel, who had a great bundle of papers before him: and nearly opposite another wigged gentleman with his hands in his pockets, whose whole attention, when Mr. Cruncher looked at him then or afterwards, seemed to be concentrated on the ceiling of the court. After some gruff coughing and rubbing of his chin and signing with his hand, Jerry attracted the notice of Mr. Lorry, who had stood up to look for him, and who quietly nodded, and sat down again.

The entrance of the Judge produced a great stir and settling-down in the court, and presently, the dock became the central point of interest. Two gaolers, who had been standing there, went out, and the prisoner was brought in, and put to the bar.

Everybody present, except the one wigged gentleman who looked at the ceiling, stared at him. Eager faces strained round pillars and corners, to get a sight of him; spectators in back rows stood up, not to miss a hair of him; people on the floor of the court, laid their hands on the shoulders of the people before them, to help themselves, at anybody's cost, to a view of him—stood a-tiptoe, got upon ledges, stood upon next to nothing, to see every inch of him.

The object of all this staring was a young man of about five-and-twenty, well-grown and well-looking, with a sunburnt cheek and a dark eye. His condition was that of a young gentleman. He was plainly dressed in black, or very dark grey, and his hair, which was long and dark, was gathered in a ribbon at the back of his neck: more to be out of his way than for ornament. As an emotion of the mind will express itself through any covering of the body, so the paleness which his situation engendered came through the brown upon his cheek, showing the soul to be stronger than the sun. He was otherwise quite self-possessed, bowed to the Judge, and stood quiet.

Silence in the court! Charles Darnay had yesterday pleaded Not Guilty to an indictment denouncing him for that he was a false traitor of our serene, illustrious, excellent, and so forth, prince, our Lord the King, by reason of his having, on divers occasions, and by divers means and ways, assisted Louis, the French King, in his wars against our said serene, illustrious, excellent, and so forth; that was to say, by coming and going between the dominions of our said serene, illustrious, excellent, and so forth, and those of the said French Louis, and wickedly, falsely, traitorously, and otherwise evil-adverbiously, revealing to the said French Louis what forces our said serene, illustrious, excellent, and so forth, had in preparation to send to Canada and North America. This much, Jerry, with his head becoming more and more spiky as the law terms bristled it, made out with huge satisfaction, and so arrived circuitously at the understanding that the aforesaid, and over and over again aforesaid, Charles Darnay, stood there before him upon his trial; that the jury were swearing in; and that Mr. Attorney-General was making ready to speak.

The accused, who was (and who knew he was) being mentally hanged, beheaded, and quartered, by everybody there, neither flinched from the situation, nor assumed any theatrical air in it. He was quiet and attentive; watched the opening proceedings with a grave interest; and stood with his hands resting on the slab of wood before him. As a bar of light struck across his face, he turned to that side of the court which was on his left. About on a level with his eyes, there sat, in that corner of the Judge's bench, two persons upon whom his look immediately rested; so immediately, and so much to the changing of his aspect, that all the eyes that were turned upon him, turned to them.

The spectators saw in the two figures, a young lady of little more than twenty, and a gentleman who was evidently her father; a man of a very remarkable appearance in respect of the absolute whiteness of his hair, and a certain indescribable intensity of face: not of an active kind, but pondering and self-communing. When this expression was upon him, he looked as if he were old; but, when it was stirred and broken up—as it was now, in a moment, on his speaking to his daughter—he became a handsome man, not past the prime of life.

His daughter had one of her hands drawn through his arm, as she sat by him, and the other pressed upon it. She had drawn close to him, in her dread of the scene, and in her pity for the prisoner. Her forehead had been strikingly expressive of an engrossing terror and compassion that saw nothing but the peril of the accused. This had been so very noticeable, so very powerfully and naturally shown, that starers who had had no pity for him were touched by her; and the whisper went about, "Who are they?"

Jerry the messenger, who had made his own observations, in his own manner, and who had been sucking the rust off his fingers in his absorption, stretched his neck to hear who they were. The crowd about him had pressed and passed the inquiry on to the nearest attendant, and from him it had been more slowly pressed and passed back; at last it got to Jerry:

"Witnesses."

"For which side?"

"Against."

"Against what side?"

"The prisoner's."

The Judge, whose eyes had gone in the general direction, recalled them, leaned back in his seat, and looked steadily at the man whose life was in his hand, as Mr. Attorney-General rose to spin the rope, grind the axe, and hammer the nails into the scaffold.

III A DISAPPOINTMENT

MR. ATTORNEY-GENERAL had to inform the jury, that the prisoner before them, though young in years, was old in the treasonable practices which claimed the forfeit of his life. That this correspondence with the public enemy was not a correspondence of today, or of yesterday, or even of last year, or of the year before. That, it was certain the prisoner had, for longer than that, been in the habit of passing and repassing between France and England, on secret business of which he could give no honest account. That, if it were in the nature of traitorous ways to thrive (which happily it never was), the real wickedness and guilt of his business might have remained undiscovered. That Providence, however, had put it into the heart of a person who was beyond fear and beyond reproach, to ferret out the nature of the prisoner's schemes, and, struck with horror, to disclose them to his Majesty's Chief Secretary of State and most honorable Privy Council.[1] That, this patriot would be produced before them. That, his position and attitude were, on the whole, sublime. That, he had been the prisoner's friend, but, at once in an auspicious and an evil hour detecting his infamy, had resolved to immolate the traitor he could no longer cherish in his bosom, on the sacred altar of his country. That, the lofty example of this immaculate and unimpeachable witness for the Crown, to refer to whom however unworthily was an honor, had communicated itself to the prisoner's servant, and had engendered in him a holy determination to examine his master's table-drawers and pockets, and secrete his papers. That, the evidence of these two witnesses, coupled with the documents of their discovering that would be produced, would show the prisoner to have been furnished with lists of his Majesty's forces, and of their disposition and preparation, both by sea and land, and would leave no doubt that he had habitually conveyed such information to a hostile power. That, these lists could not be proved to be in the prisoner's handwriting; but that it was all the same; that, indeed, it was rather the better for the prosecution, as showing the prisoner to be artful in his precautions. That, the proof would go back five years, and would show the prisoner already engaged in these pernicious missions, within a few weeks before the date of the very first action fought between the British troops and the Americans. That, for these reasons, the jury, being a loyal jury (as he knew they were), and being a responsible jury (as *they* knew they were), must

[1] PRIVY COUNCIL—The council of state of the British sovereign.

positively find the prisoner Guilty, and make an end of him, whether they liked it or not.

When the Attorney-General ceased, a buzz arose in the court as if a cloud of great blue-flies were swarming about the prisoner, in anticipation of what he was soon to become. When it toned down again, the unimpeachable patriot appeared in the witness-box.

Mr. Solicitor-General then, following his leader's lead, examined the patriot: John Barsad, gentleman, by name. The story of his pure soul was exactly what Mr. Attorney-General had described it to be—perhaps, if it had a fault, a little too exactly. Having released his noble bosom of its burden, he would have modestly withdrawn himself, but that the wigged gentleman with the papers before him, sitting not far from Mr. Lorry, begged to ask him a few questions. The wigged gentleman sitting opposite, still looking at the ceiling of the court.

Had he ever been a spy himself? No, he scorned the base insinuation. What did he live upon? His property. Where was his property? He didn't precisely remember where it was. What was it? No business of anybody's. Had he inherited it? Yes, he had. From whom? Distant relation. Very distant? Rather. Ever been in prison? Certainly not. Never in a debtor's prison? Didn't see what that had to do with it. Never in a debtor's prison?—Come, once again. Never? Yes. How many times? Two or three times. Not five or six? Perhaps. Of what profession? Gentleman. Ever been kicked? Might have been. Frequently? No. Ever kicked down stairs? Decidedly not; once received a kick on the top of a staircase, and fell down of his own accord. Kicked on that occasion for cheating at dice? Something to that effect was said by the intoxicated liar who committed the assault, but it was not true. Swear it was not true? Positively. Ever live by cheating at play? Never. Ever live by play? Not more than other gentlemen do. Ever borrow money of the prisoner? Yes. Ever pay him? No. Was not this intimacy with the prisoner, in reality a very slight one, forced upon the prisoner in coaches, inns, and packets? No. Sure he saw the prisoner with these lists? Certain. Knew no more about the lists? No. Had not procured them himself, for instance? No. Expect to get anything by this evidence? No. Not in regular government pay and employment, to lay traps?

Oh, dear, no. Or to do anything? Oh, dear, no. Swear that? Over and over again. No motives but motives of sheer patriotism? None whatever.

The virtuous servant, Roger Cly, swore his way through the case at a great rate. He had taken service with the prisoner, in good faith and simplicity, four years ago. He had asked the prisoner, aboard the Calais packet, if he wanted a handy fellow, and the prisoner had engaged him. He had not asked the prisoner to take the handy fellow as an act of charity—never thought of such a thing. He began to have suspicions of the prisoner, and to keep an eye upon him, soon afterwards. In arranging his clothes, while travelling, he had seen similar lists to these in the prisoner's pockets, over and over again. He had taken these lists from the drawer of the prisoner's desk. He had not put them there first. He had seen the prisoner show these identical lists to French gentlemen at Calais, and similar lists to French gentlemen, both at Calais and Boulogne. He loved his country, and couldn't bear it, and had given information. He had known the last witness seven or eight years; that was merely a coincidence. He didn't call it a particularly curious coincidence; most coincidences were curious. Neither did he call it a curious coincidence that true patriotism was *his* only motive too. He was a true Briton, and hoped there were many like him.

The blue-flies buzzed again, and Mr. Attorney-General called Mr. Jarvis Lorry.

"Mr. Jarvis Lorry, are you a clerk in Tellson's Bank?"

"I am."

"On a certain Friday night in November one thousand seven hundred and seventy-five, did business occasion you to travel between London and Dover by the mail?"

"It did."

"Were there any other passengers in the mail?"

"Two."

"Did they alight on the road in the course of the night?"

"They did."

"Mr. Lorry, look upon the prisoner. Was he one of those two passengers?"

"I cannot undertake to say that he was."

"Does he resemble either of those two passengers?"

"Both were so wrapped up, and the night was so dark, and we were all so reserved, that I cannot undertake to say even that."

"Mr. Lorry, look again upon the prisoner. Supposing him wrapped up as those two passengers were, is there anything in his bulk and stature to render it unlikely that he was one of them?"

"No."

"You will not swear, Mr. Lorry, that he was not one of them?"

"No."

"So at least you say he may have been one of them?"

"Yes. Except that I remember them both to have been—like myself—timorous of highwaymen, and the prisoner has not a timorous air."

"Did you ever see a counterfeit of timidity, Mr. Lorry?"

"I certainly have seen that."

"Mr. Lorry, look once more upon the prisoner. Have you seen him, to your certain knowledge, before?"

"I have."

"When?"

"I was returning from France a few days afterwards, and, at Calais, the prisoner came on board the packet-ship in which I returned, and made the voyage with me."

"At what hour did he come on board?"

"At a little after midnight."

"In the dead of the night. Was he the only passenger who came on board at that untimely hour?"

"He happened to be the only one."

"Never mind about 'happening,' Mr. Lorry. He was the only passenger who came on board in the dead of the night?"

"He was."

"Were you travelling alone, Mr. Lorry, or with any companion?"

"With two companions. A gentleman and lady. They are here."

"They are here. Had you any conversation with the prisoner?"

"Hardly any. The weather was stormy, and the passage long and rough, and I lay on a sofa, almost from shore to shore."

"Miss Manette!"

The young lady, to whom all eyes had been turned before, and were now turned again, stood up where she had sat. Her father rose with her, and kept her hand drawn through his arm.

"Miss Manette, look upon the prisoner."

To be confronted with such pity, and such earnest youth and beauty, was far more trying to the accused than to be confronted with all the crowd. Standing, as it were, apart with her on the edge of his grave, not all the staring curiosity that looked on, could, for the moment, nerve him to remain quite still. The buzz of the great flies was loud again.

"Miss Manette, have you seen the prisoner before?"

"Yes, sir."

"Where?"

"On board the packet-ship just now referred to, sir, and on the same occasion."

"You are the young lady just now referred to?"

"O! most unhappily, I am!"

The plaintive tone of her compassion merged into the less musical voice of the Judge, as he said, something fiercely: "Answer the questions put to you, and make no remark upon them."

"Miss Manette, had you any conversation with the prisoner on that passage across the Channel?"

"Yes, sir."

"Recall it."

In the midst of a profound stillness, she faintly began:

"When the gentleman came on board——"

"Do you mean the prisoner?" inquired the Judge, knitting his brows.

"Yes, My Lord."

"Then say the prisoner."

"When the prisoner came on board, he noticed that my father," turning her eyes lovingly to him as he stood beside her, "was much fatigued and in a very weak state of health. My father was so reduced, that I was afraid to take him out of the air, and I had made a bed for him on the deck near the cabin steps, and I sat on the deck at his side to take care of him. There were no other passengers that night, but we four. The prisoner was so good as to beg permission to advise me how I could shelter my father from the wind and weather, better than I had done. I had not known how to do it well, not understanding how the wind would set when we were out of the harbor. He did it for me.

He expressed great gentleness and kindness for my father's state, and I am sure he felt it. That was the manner of our beginning to speak together."

"Let me interrupt you for a moment. Had he come on board alone?"

"No."

"How many were with him?"

"Two French gentlemen."

"Had they conferred together?"

"They had conferred together until the last moment, when it was necessary for the French gentlemen to be landed in their boat."

"Had any papers been handed about among them, similar to these lists?"

"Some papers had been handed about among them, but I don't know what papers."

"Like these in shape and size?"

"Possibly, but indeed I don't know, although they stood whispering very near to me: because they stood at the top of the cabin steps to have the light of the lamp that was hanging there; it was a dull lamp, and they spoke very low, and I did not hear what they said, and saw only that they looked at papers."

"Now, to the prisoner's conversation, Miss Manette."

"The prisoner was as open in his confidence with me—which arose out of my helpless situation—as he was kind, and good, and useful to my father. I hope," bursting into tears, "I may not repay him by doing him harm to-day."

Buzzing from the blue-flies.

"Miss Manette, if the prisoner does not perfectly understand that you give the evidence which it is your duty to give—which you must give—and which you cannot escape from giving—with great unwillingness, he is the only person present in that condition. Please to go on."

"He told me that he was travelling on business of a delicate and difficult nature, which might get people into trouble, and that he was therefore travelling under an assumed name. He said that this business had, within a few days, taken him to France, and might, at intervals, take him backwards and forwards between France and England for a long time to come."

"Did he say anything about America, Miss Manette? Be particular."

"He tried to explain to me how that quarrel had arisen, and he said that, so far as he could judge, it was a wrong and foolish one on England's part. He added, in a jesting way, that perhaps George Washington might gain almost as great a name in history as George the Third. But there was no harm in his way of saying this: it was said laughingly, and to beguile the time."

Mr. Attorney-General now signified to My Lord,[2] that he deemed it necessary, as a matter of precaution and form, to call the young lady's father, Doctor Manette. Who was called accordingly.

"Doctor Manette, look upon the prisoner. Have you ever seen him before?"

"Once. When he called at my lodgings in London. Some three years, or three years and a half ago."

"Can you identify him as your fellow-passenger on board the packet, or speak of his conversation with your daughter?"

"Sir, I can do neither."

"Is there any particular and special reason for your being unable to do either?"

He answered, in a low voice, "There is."

"Has it been your misfortune to undergo a long imprisonment, without trial, or even accusation, in your native country, Doctor Manette?"

He answered, in a tone that went to every heart, "A long imprisonment."

"Were you newly released on the occasion in question?"

"They tell me so."

"Have you no remembrance of the occasion?"

"None. My mind is a blank, from some time—I cannot even say what time—when I employed myself, in my captivity, in making shoes, to the time when I found myself living in London with my dear daughter here. She had become familiar to me, when a gracious God restored my faculties; but, I am quite unable even to say how she had become familiar. I had no remembrance of the process."

Mr. Attorney-General sat down, and the father and daughter sat down together.

[2] My Lord—The judge.

A singular circumstance then arose in the case. The object in hand being to show that the prisoner went down, with some fellow-plotter untracked, in the Dover mail on that Friday night in November five years ago, and got out of the mail in the night, as a blind, at a place where he did not remain, but from which he travelled back some dozen miles or more, to a garrison and dockyard, and there collected information; a witness was called to identify him as having been at the precise time required, in the coffee-room of an hotel in that garrison-and-dockyard town, waiting for another person. The prisoner's counsel was cross-examining this witness with no result, except that he had never seen the prisoner on any other occasion, when the wigged gentleman who had all this time been looking at the ceiling of the court, wrote a word or two on a little piece of paper, screwed it up, and tossed it to him. Opening this piece of paper in the next pause, the counsel looked with great attention and curiosity at the prisoner.

"You say again you are quite sure that it *was* the prisoner?"

The witness was quite sure.

"Did you ever see anybody very like the prisoner?"

Not so like (the witness said), as that he could be mistaken.

"Look well upon that gentleman, my learned friend there," pointing to him who had tossed the paper over, "and then look well upon the prisoner. How say you? Are they very like each other?"

Allowing for my learned friend's appearance being careless and slovenly, if not debauched, they were sufficiently like each other to surprise, not only the witness, but everybody present, when they were thus brought into comparison. My Lord being prayed to bid my learned friend lay aside his wig, and giving no very gracious consent, the likeness became much more remarkable. My Lord inquired of Mr. Stryver (the prisoner's counsel), whether they were next to try Mr. Carton (name of my learned friend) for treason? But, Mr. Stryver replied to My Lord, no; but he would ask the witness to tell him whether what happened once, might happen twice; whether he would have been so confident if he had seen this illustration of his rashness sooner; whether he would be so confident, having seen it; and more. The upshot of which, was, to smash this witness like a crockery vessel, and shiver his part of the case to useless lumber.

Mr. Cruncher had by this time taken quite a lunch of rust off his fingers, in his following of the evidence. He had now to attend while Mr. Stryver fitted the prisoner's case on the jury, like a compact suit of clothes; showing them how the patriot, Barsad, was a hired spy and traitor, an unblushing trafficker in blood, and one of the greatest scoundrels upon earth since accursed Judas—which he certainly did look rather like. How the virtuous servant, Cly, was his friend and partner, and was worthy to be; how the watchful eyes of those forgers and false swearers had rested on the prisoner as a victim, because some family affairs in France, he being of French extraction, did require his making those passages across the Channel —though what those affairs were, a consideration for others who were near and dear to him, forbade him, even for his life, to disclose. How the evidence that had been wrapped and wrested from the young lady, whose  anguish in giving it they had witnessed, came to nothing, involving the mere little innocent gallantries and politenesses likely to pass between any young gentleman and young lady so thrown together:—with the exception of that reference to George Washington, which was altogether too extravagant and impossible, to be regarded in any other light than as a monstrous joke.

Mr. Stryver then called his few witnesses, and Mr. Cruncher had next to attend while Mr. Attorney-General turned the whole suit of clothes Mr. Stryver had fitted on the jury, inside out; showing how Barsad and Cly were even a hundred times better than he had thought them, and the prisoner a hundred times worse. Lastly, came My Lord himself, turning the suit of clothes, now inside out, now outside in, but on the whole decidedly trimming and shaping them into grave-clothes for the prisoner.

And now, the jury turned to consider, and the great flies swarmed again.

Mr. Carton, who had so long sat looking at the ceiling of the court, changed neither his place nor his attitude, even in this excitement. While his learned friend, Mr. Stryver, massing his papers before him, whispered with those who sat near, and from time to time glanced anxiously at the jury; while all the spectators moved more or less, and grouped themselves anew; while even My Lord himself arose from his seat, and slowly paced up and down his platform, not unattended by a suspicion in the minds of the audience that his state was feverish; this one man sat leaning back, with his torn gown half off him, his untidy wig put on just as it had happened to light on his head after its removal, his hands in his pockets, and his eyes on the ceiling as they had been all day. Something especially reckless in his demeanor, not only gave him a disreputable look, but so diminished the strong resemblance he undoubtedly bore to the prisoner (which his momentary earnestness, when they were compared together, had strengthened), that many of the lookers-on, taking note of him now, said to one another they would hardly have thought the two were so alike. Mr. Cruncher made the observation to his next neighbor, and added, "I'd hold half a guinea that *he* don't get no law-work to do. Don't look like the sort of one to get any, do he?"

Yet, this Mr. Carton took in more of the details of the scene than he appeared to take in; for now, when Miss Manette's head dropped upon her father's breast, he was the first to see it, and to say audibly: "Officer! Look to that young lady. Help the gentleman to take her out. Don't you see she will fall!"

There was much commiseration for her as she was removed, and much sympathy with her father. It had evidently been a great distress to him, to have the days of his imprisonment recalled. He had shown strong internal agitation when he was questioned, and that pondering or brooding look which made him old, had been upon him, like a heavy cloud, ever since. As he passed out, the jury, who had turned back and paused a moment, spoke, through their foreman.

They were not agreed, and wished to retire. My Lord (perhaps with George Washington on his mind) showed some surprise that they were not agreed, but signified his pleasure that they should retire under watch and ward, and retired himself. The trial had lasted all day, and the lamps in the court were now being lighted. It began to be rumored that the jury would be out a long while. The spectators dropped off to get refreshment, and the prisoner withdrew to the back of the dock, and sat down.

Mr. Lorry, who had gone out when the young lady and her father went out, now reappeared, and beckoned to Jerry: who, in the slackened interest, could easily get near him.

"Jerry, if you wish to take something to eat, you can. But, keep in the way. You will be sure to hear when the jury come in. Don't be a moment behind them, for I want you to take the verdict back to the bank. You are the quickest messenger I know, and will get to Temple-bar long before I can."

Jerry had just enough forehead to knuckle, and he knuckled it in acknowledgment of this communication and a shilling. Mr. Carton came up at the moment, and touched Mr. Lorry on the arm.

"How is the young lady?"

"She is greatly distressed; but her father is comforting her, and she feels the better for being out of court."

"I'll tell the prisoner so," and Mr. Carton made his way to the outside of the bar. The way out of court lay in that direction, and Jerry followed him, all eyes, ears, and spikes.

"Mr. Darnay!"

The prisoner came forward directly.

"You will naturally be anxious to hear of the witness, Miss Manette. She will do very well. You have seen the worst of her agitation."

"I am deeply sorry to have been the cause of it. Could you tell her so for me, with my fervent acknowledgments?"

"Yes, I could. I will, if you ask it."

Mr. Carton's manner was so careless as to be almost insolent. He stood, half turned from the prisoner, lounging with his elbow against the bar.

"I do ask it. Accept my cordial thanks."

"What," said Carton, still only half turned towards him, "do you expect, Mr. Darnay?"

"The worst."

"It's the wisest thing to expect, and the likeliest. But I think their withdrawing is in your favor."

Loitering on the way out of court not being allowed, Jerry heard no more; but left them—so like each other in feature, so unlike each other in manner—standing side by side.

An hour and a half limped heavily away in the thief-and-rascal-crowded passages below, even though assisted off with mutton pies and ale. The hoarse messenger, uncomfortably seated on a form after taking that refection, had dropped into a doze, when a loud murmur and a rapid tide of people setting up the stairs that led to the court, carried him along with them.

"Jerry! Jerry!" Mr. Lorry was already calling at the door when he got there.

"Here, sir! It's a fight to get back again. Here I am, sir!"

Mr. Lorry handed him a paper through the throng. "Quick! Have you got it?"

"Yes, sir."

Hastily written on the paper was the word *Acquitted*.

"If you had sent the message, *Recalled to Life*, again," muttered Jerry, as he turned, "I should have known what you meant, this time."

He had no opportunity of saying, or so much as thinking, anything else, until he was clear of the Old Bailey; for, the crowd came pouring out with a vehemence that nearly took him off his legs, and a loud buzz swept into the street as if the baffled blue-flies were dispersing in search of other carrion.

IV CONGRATULATORY

From the dimly-lighted passages of the court, the last sediment of the human stew that had been boiling there all day, was straining off, when Doctor Manette, Lucie Manette, his daughter, Mr. Lorry, the solicitor for the defence, and its counsel, Mr. Stryver, stood gathered around Mr. Charles Darnay—just released—congratulating him on his escape from death.

It would have been difficult by a far brighter light, to recognize in Doctor Manette, intellectual of face and upright of bearing, the shoemaker of the garret in Paris. Yet, no one could have looked at him twice, without looking again: even though the opportunity of observation had not extended to the mournful cadence of his low grave voice, and to the abstraction that overclouded him fitfully, without any apparent reason. While one external cause, and that a reference to his long lingering agony, would always—as on the trial—evoke this condition from the depths of his soul, it was also in its nature to arise of itself, and to draw a gloom over him, as incomprehensible to those unacquainted with his story as if they had seen the shadow of the actual Bastille [1] thrown upon him by a summer sun, when the substance was three hundred miles away.

Only his daughter had the power of charming this black brooding from his mind. She was the golden thread that united him to a Past beyond his misery, and to a Present beyond his misery: and the sound of her voice, the light of her face, the touch of her hand, had a strong beneficial influence with him almost always. Not absolutely always, for she could recall some occasions on which her power had failed; but, they were few and slight, and she believed them over.

Mr. Darnay had kissed her hand fervently and gratefully, and had turned to Mr. Stryver, whom he warmly thanked. Mr. Stryver, a man of little more than thirty, but looking twenty years older than he was, stout, loud, red, bluff, and free from any drawback of delicacy, had a pushing way of shouldering himself into companies and conversations, that argued well for his shouldering his way up in life.

He still had his wig and gown on, and he said, squaring himself at his late client to that degree that he squeezed the innocent Mr. Lorry clean out of the group: "I am glad to have brought you off with honor, Mr. Darnay. It was an infamous prosecution, grossly infamous; but not the less likely to succeed, on that account."

"You have laid me under an obligation to you for life—in two senses," said his late client, taking his hand.

"I have done my best for you, Mr. Darnay; and my best is as good as another man's, I believe."

It clearly being incumbent on somebody to say, "Much better," Mr. Lorry said it; perhaps not quite disinterestedly, but with the interested object of squeezing himself back again.

"You think so?" said Mr. Stryver. "Well! you have been present all day, and you ought to know. You are a man of business, too."

"And as such," quoth Mr. Lorry, whom the counsel learned

---

[1] BASTILLE—The most noted and infamous of French state prisons, built in the fourteenth century.

in the law had now shouldered back into the group, just as he had previously shouldered him out of it—"as such, I will appeal to Doctor Manette, to break up this conference and order us all to our homes. Miss Lucie looks ill, Mr. Darnay has had a terrible day, we are worn out."

"Speak for yourself, Mr. Lorry," said Stryver; "I have a night's work to do yet. Speak for yourself."

"I speak for myself," answered Mr. Lorry, "and for Mr. Darnay, and for Miss Lucie, and—Miss Lucie, do you not think I may speak for us all?" He asked her the question pointedly, and with a glance at her father.

His face had become frozen, as it were, in a very curious look at Darnay: an intent look, deepening into a frown of dislike and distrust, not even unmixed with fear. With this strange expression on him his thoughts had wandered away.

"My father," said Lucie, softly laying her hand on his.

He slowly shook the shadow off, and turned to her.

"Shall we go home, my father?"

With a long breath, he answered, "Yes."

The friends of the acquitted prisoner had dispersed, under the impression—which he himself had originated—that he would not be released that night. The lights were nearly all extinguished in the passages, the iron gates were being closed with a jar and a rattle, and the dismal place was deserted until to-morrow morning's interest of gallows, pillory, whipping-post, and branding-iron, should re-people it. Walking between her father and Mr. Darnay, Lucie Manette passed into the open air. A hackney-coach [2] was called, and the father and daughter departed in it.

Mr. Stryver had left them in the passages, to shoulder his way back to the robing-room. Another person who had not joined the group, or interchanged a word with any one of them, but who had been leaning against the wall where its shadow was darkest, had silently strolled out after the rest, and had looked on until the coach drove away. He now stepped up to where Mr. Lorry was taking his leave of Mr. Darnay. "Mr. Darnay, good night, God bless you, sir! I hope you have been this day preserved for a prosperous and happy life.—Chair there!" [3]

---

[2] HACKNEY-COACH—Horse and carriage for hire.
[3] CHAIR THERE!—The call for an inclosed seat supported on poles by two bearers.

Mr. Lorry bustled into the chair, and was carried off to Tellson's, while Carton, who smelt of port wine, and did not appear to be quite sober, turned to Darnay:

"This is a strange chance that throws you and me together. This must be a strange night to you, standing alone here with your counterpart on these street-stones?"

"I hardly seem yet," returned Charles Darnay, "to belong to this world again."

"I don't wonder at it; it's not so long since you were pretty far advanced on your way to another. You speak faintly."

"I begin to think I *am* faint."

"Then why the devil don't you dine? I dined, myself, while those numbskulls were deliberating which world you should belong to—this, or some other. Let me show you the nearest tavern to dine well at."

Drawing his arm through his own, he took him down Ludgate-hill to Fleet-street, and so, up a covered way, into a tavern. Here, they were shown into a little room, where Charles Darnay was soon recruiting his strength with a good plain dinner and good wine: while Carton sat opposite to him at the same table, with his separate bottle of port before him, and his fully half-insolent manner upon him.

"Do you feel, yet, that you belong to this terrestrial scheme again, Mr. Darnay?"

"I am frightfully confused regarding time and place; but I am so far mended as to feel that."

"It must be an immense satisfaction!"

He said it bitterly, and filled up his glass again: which was a large one.

"As to me, the greatest desire I have, is to forget that I belong to it. It has no good in it for me—except wine like this—nor I for it. So we are not much alike in that particular. Indeed, I begin to think we are not much alike in any particular, you and I."

Confused by the emotion of the day, and feeling his being there with this Double of coarse deportment, to be like a dream, Charles Darnay was at a loss how to answer; finally, answered not at all.

"Now your dinner is done," Carton presently said, "why don't you call a health, Mr. Darnay; why don't you give your toast?"

"What health? What toast?"

"Why, it's on the tip of your tongue. It ought to be, it must be, I'll swear it's there."

"Miss Manette, then!"

"Miss Manette, then!"

Looking his companion full in his face while he drank the toast, Carton flung his glass over his shoulder against the wall, where it shivered to pieces; then, rang the bell, and ordered in another.

"That's a fair young lady to hand to a coach in the dark, Mr. Darnay!" he said, filling his new goblet.

A slight frown and a laconic "Yes," were the answer.

"That's a fair young lady to be pitied by and wept for by! How does it feel? Is it worth being tried for one's life, to be the object of such sympathy and compassion, Mr. Darnay?"

Again Darnay answered not a word.

"She was mightily pleased to have your message when I gave it her. Not that she showed she was pleased, but I suppose she was."

The allusion served as a timely reminder to Darnay that this disagreeable companion had, of his own free will, assisted him in the strait of the day. He turned the dialogue to that point, and thanked him for it.

"I neither want any thanks, nor merit any," was the careless rejoinder. "It was nothing to do, in the first place; and I don't know why I did it, in the second. Mr. Darnay, let me ask you a question."

"Willingly, and a small return for your good offices."

"Do you think I particularly like you?"

"Really, Mr. Carton," returned the other, oddly disconcerted, "I have not asked myself the question."

"But ask yourself the question now."

"You have acted as if you do; but I don't think you do."

"*I* don't think I do," said Carton. "I begin to have a very good opinion of your understanding."

"Nevertheless," pursued Darnay, rising to ring the bell, "there is nothing in that, I hope, to prevent my calling the reckoning,[4] and our parting without ill-blood on either side."

[4] CALLING THE RECKONING—Calling for the bill.

Carton rejoining, "Nothing in life!" Darnay rang. "Do you call the whole reckoning?" said Carton. On his answering in the affirmative, "Then bring me another pint of this same wine, drawer, and come and wake me at ten."

The bill being paid, Charles Darnay rose and wished him good night. Without returning the wish, Carton rose too with something of a threat of defiance in his manner, and said, "A last word, Mr. Darnay: you think I am drunk?"

"I think you have been drinking, Mr. Carton."

"Think? You know I have been drinking."

"Since I must say so, I know it."

"Then you shall likewise know why. I am a disappointed drudge, sir. I care for no man on earth, and no man on earth cares for me."

"Much to be regretted. You might have used your talents better."

"Maybe so, Mr. Darnay; maybe not. Don't let your sober face elate you, however; you don't know what it may come to. Good night!"

When he was left alone, this strange being took up a candle, went to a mirror that hung against the wall, and surveyed himself minutely in it.

"Do you particularly like the man?" he muttered, at his own image; "why should you particularly like a man who resembles you? There is nothing in you to like; you know that. Ah, confound you! What a change you have made in yourself! A good reason for taking to a man, that he shows you what you have fallen away from, and what you might have been! Change places with him, and would you have been looked at by those blue eyes as he was, and commiserated by that agitated face as he was? Come on, and have it out in plain words! You hate the fellow."

He resorted to his pint of wine for consolation, drank it all in a few minutes, and fell asleep on his arms, with his hair straggling over the table, and a long winding-sheet in the candle [5] dripping down upon him.

---

[5] WINDING-SHEET IN THE CANDLE—The drapery-like overflow from a guttering candle, sometimes looked upon superstitiously as ominous of death. A winding-sheet is the sheet that wraps a corpse.

V THE JACKAL

Those were drinking days, and most men drank hard. So very great is the improvement Time has brought about in such habits, that a moderate statement of the quantity of wine and punch which one man would swallow in the course of a night, without any detriment to his reputation as a perfect gentleman, would seem, in these days, a ridiculous exaggeration. The learned profession of the Law was certainly not behind any other learned profession in its Bacchanalian propensities;[1] neither was Mr. Stryver, already fast shouldering his way to a large and lucrative practice, behind his compeers in this particular, any more than in the drier parts of the legal race.

A favorite at the Old Bailey, and eke at the Sessions,[2] Mr. Stryver had begun cautiously to hew away the lower staves of the ladder on which he mounted. Sessions and Old Bailey had now to summon their favorite, specially, to their longing arms; and shouldering itself towards the visage of the Lord Chief Justice in the Court of King's Bench,[3] the florid countenance of Mr. Stryver might be daily seen, bursting out of the bed of wigs, like a great sunflower pushing its way at the sun from among a rank garden-full of flaring companions.

It had once been noted at the Bar, that while Mr. Stryver was a glib man, and an unscrupulous, and a ready, and a bold, he had not that faculty of extracting the essence from a heap of statements, which is among the most striking and necessary of the advocate's[4] accomplishments. But, a remarkable improvement came upon him as to this. The more business he got, the greater his power seemed to grow of getting at its pith and marrow; and however late at night he sat carousing with Sydney Carton, he always had his points at his fingers' ends in the morning.

Sydney Carton, idlest and most unpromising of men, was Stryver's great ally. What the two drank together, between Hilary Term and Michaelmas,[5] might have floated a king's ship.

---

[1] Bacchanalian propensities—Tendencies toward intemperate drinking. Bacchanalian is from Bacchus, the god of wine.
[2] Sessions—A lower court, usually criminal.
[3] Court of King's Bench—The highest court.
[4] Advocate—One who pleads in a court of law.
[5] Hilary Term and Michaelmas—January 11 to September 29. The first and last of the four terms during which the courts held sessions.

Stryver never had a case in hand, anywhere, but Carton was there, with his hands in his pockets, staring at the ceiling of the court; they went the same Circuit, and even there they prolonged their usual orgies late into the night, and Carton was rumored to be seen at broad day, going home stealthily and unsteadily to his lodgings, like a dissipated cat. At last, it began to get about, among such as were interested in the matter, that although Sydney Carton would never be a lion, he was an amazingly good jackal,[6] and that he rendered suit and service to Stryver in that humble capacity.

"Ten o'clock, sir," said the man at the tavern, whom he had charged to wake him—"ten o'clock, sir."

"*What's* the matter?"

"Ten o'clock, sir."

"What do you mean? Ten o'clock at night?"

"Yes, sir. Your honor told me to call you."

"Oh! I remember. Very well, very well."

After a few dull efforts to get to sleep again, which the man dexterously combated by stirring the fire continuously for five minutes, he got up, tossed his hat on, and walked out. He turned into the Temple, and, having revived himself by twice pacing the pavements of King's-Bench walk, turned into the Stryver chambers.

The Stryver clerk, who never assisted at these conferences, had gone home, and the Stryver principal opened the door. He had his slippers on, and a loose bedgown, and his throat was bare for his greater ease. He had that rather wild, strained, seared marking about the eyes, which may be observed in all free livers of his class.

"You are a little late, Memory," said Stryver.

"About the usual time; it may be a quarter of an hour later."

They went into a dingy room lined with books and littered with papers, where there was a blazing fire. A kettle steamed upon the hob, and in the midst of the wreck of papers a table shone, with plenty of wine upon it, and brandy, and rum, and sugar, and lemons.

"You have had your bottle, I perceive, Sydney."

[6] LION . . . JACKAL—A jackal is one who does work and furnishes material to serve another's purpose. There is an erroneous supposition that the jackal finds prey for the lion.

"Two to-night, I think. I have been dining with the day's client; or seeing him dine—it's all one!"

"That was a rare point, Sydney, that you brought to bear upon the identification. How did you come by it? When did it strike you?"

"I thought he was rather a handsome fellow, and I thought I should have been much the same sort of fellow, if I had had any luck."

Mr. Stryver laughed, till he shook. "You and your luck, Sydney! Get to work, get to work."

Sullenly enough, the jackal loosened his dress, went into an adjoining room, and came back with a large jug of cold water, a basin, and a towel or two. Steeping the towels in the water, and partially ringing them out, he folded them on his head in a manner hideous to behold, sat down at the table, and said, "Now I am ready!"

"Not much boiling down to be done to-night, Memory," said Mr. Stryver, gaily, as he looked among his papers.

"How much?"

"Only two sets of them."

"Give me the worst first."

"There they are, Sydney. Fire away!"

The lion then composed himself on his back on a sofa on one side of the drinking-table, while the jackal sat at his own paper-bestrewn table proper, on the other side of it, with the bottles and glasses ready to his hand. Both resorted to the drinking-table without stint, but each in a different way; the lion for the most part reclining with his hands in his waistband, looking at the fire, or occasionally flirting with some lighter document; the jackal, with knitted brows and intent face, so deep in his task, that his eyes did not even follow the hand he stretched out for his glass—which often groped about, for a minute or more, before it found the glass for his lips. Two or three times, the matter in hand became so knotty that the jackal found it imperative on him to get up and steep his towels anew.

At length the jackal had got together a compact repast for the lion, and proceeded to offer it to him. The lion took it with care and caution, made his selections from it, and his remarks upon it, and the jackal assisted both. When the repast was fully discussed, the lion put his hand in his waistband again, and lay down to meditate. The jackal then invigorated himself with a bumper for his throttle, and a fresh application to his head, and applied himself to the collection of a second meal; this was administered to the lion in the same manner, and was not disposed of until the clocks struck three in the morning.

"And now we have done, Sydney, fill a bumper of punch," said Mr. Stryver.

The jackal removed the towels from his head, which had been steaming again, shook himself, yawned, shivered, and complied.

"You were very sound, Sydney, in the matter of those crown witnesses [7] to-day. Every question told."

"I always am sound; am I not?"

"I don't gainsay it. What has roughened your temper? Put some punch to it and smooth it again."

With a deprecatory grunt, the jackal again complied.

"The old Sydney Carton of old Shrewsbury School," said Stryver, nodding his head over him as he reviewed him in the present and the past, "the old seesaw Sydney. Up one minute and down the next; now in spirits and now in despondency!"

"Ah!" returned the other, sighing: "yes! The same Sydney, with the same luck. Even then, I did exercises for other boys, and seldom did my own."

"And why not?"

"God knows. It was my way, I suppose."

He sat, with his hands in his pockets and his legs stretched out before him, looking at the fire.

"Carton," said his friend, squaring himself at him with a bullying air, as if the fire-grate had been the furnace in which sustained endeavor was forged, and the one delicate thing to be done for the old Sydney Carton of old Shrewsbury School was to shoulder him into it, "your way is, and always was, a lame way. You summon no energy and purpose. Look at me."

---

[7] CROWN WITNESSES—Witnesses for the crown, or prosecution.

"Oh, botheration!" returned Sydney, with a lighter and more good-humored laugh, "don't *you* be moral!"

"How have I done what I have done?" said Stryver. "How do I do what I do?"

"Partly through paying me to help you, I suppose. But it's not worth your while to apostrophise me, or the air, about it; what you want to do, you do. You were always in the front rank, and I was always behind."

"I had to get into the front rank; I was not born there, was I?"

"I was not present at the ceremony; but my opinion is you were," said Carton. At this, he laughed again, and they both laughed.

"Before Shrewsbury, and at Shrewsbury, and ever since Shrewsbury," pursued Carton, "you have fallen into your rank, and I have fallen into mine. Even when we were fellow-students in the Student-Quarter of Paris, picking up French, and French law, and other French crumbs that we didn't get much good of, you were always somewhere, and I was always—nowhere."

"And whose fault was that?"

"Upon my soul, I am not sure that it was not yours. You were always driving and shouldering and pressing, to that restless degree that I had no chance for my life but in rust and repose. It's a gloomy thing, however, to talk about one's own past, with the day breaking. And now I'll have no more drink; I'll get to bed."

When his host followed him out on the staircase with a candle, to light him down the stairs, the day was coldly looking in through its grimy windows. When he got out of the house, the air was cold and sad, the dull sky overcast, the river dark and dim, the whole scene like a lifeless desert. And wreaths of dust were spinning round and round before the morning blast, as if the desert-sand had risen far away, and the first spray of it in its advance had begun to overwhelm the city.

Waste forces within him, and a desert all around, this man stood still on his way across a silent terrace, and saw for a moment, lying in the wilderness before him, a mirage of honorable ambition, self-denial, and perseverance. In the fair city of this vision, there were airy galleries from which the loves and graces looked upon him, gardens in which the fruits of life hung ripening, waters of Hope that sparkled in his sight. A moment, and it was gone. Climbing to a high chamber in a well of houses, he threw himself down in his clothes on a neglected bed, and its pillow was wet with wasted tears.

Sadly, sadly, the sun rose; it rose upon no sadder sight than the man of good abilities and good emotions, incapable of their directed exercise, incapable of his own help and his own happiness, sensible of the blight on him, and resigning himself to let it eat him away.

VI HUNDREDS OF PEOPLE

The quiet lodgings of Doctor Manette were in a quiet street-corner not far from Soho-square.[1] On the afternoon of a certain fine Sunday when the waves of four months had rolled over the trial for treason, and carried it, as to the public interest and memory, far out to sea, Mr. Jarvis Lorry walked along the sunny streets from Clerkenwell where he lived, on his way to dine with the Doctor. After several relapses into business-absorption, Mr. Lorry had become the Doctor's friend, and the quiet street-corner was the sunny part of his life.

A quainter corner than the corner where the Doctor lived, was not to be found in London. There was no way through it, and the front windows of the Doctor's lodgings commanded a pleasant little vista of street that had a congenial air of retirement on it. There were few buildings then, north of the Oxford-road, and forest-trees flourished, and wild flowers grew, and the hawthorn blossomed, in the now vanished fields. As a consequence, country airs circulated in Soho with vigorous freedom, and there was many a good south wall, not far off, on which the peaches ripened in their season.

The summer light struck into the corner brilliantly in the earlier part of the day; but, when the streets grew hot, the corner was in shadow, though not in shadow so remote but that you could see beyond it into a glare of brightness. It was a cool spot, staid but cheerful, a wonderful place for echoes, and a very harbor from the raging streets.

There ought to have been a tranquil bark in such an anchorage, and there was. The Doctor occupied two floors of a large

[1] Soho-square—The residential district of the foreign element, particularly the French.

still house, and received such patients here as his old reputation, and its revival in the floating whispers of his story, brought him. His scientific knowledge, and his vigilance and skill in conducting ingenious experiments, brought him otherwise into moderate request, and he earned as much as he wanted.

These things were within Mr. Jarvis Lorry's knowledge, thoughts, and notice, when he rang the door-bell of the tranquil house in the corner, on the fine Sunday afternoon.

"Doctor Manette at home?"

Expected home.

"Miss Lucie at home?"

Expected home.

"Miss Pross at home?"

Possibly at home, but of certainty impossible for hand-maid to anticipate intentions of Miss Pross, as to admission or denial of the fact.

"As I am at home myself," said Mr. Lorry, "I'll go upstairs."

Although the Doctor's daughter had known nothing of the country of her birth, she appeared to have innately derived from it that ability to make much of little means, which is one of its most useful and most agreeable characteristics. Simple as the furniture was, it was set off by so many little adornments, of no value but for their taste and fancy, that its effect was delightful. The disposition of everything in the rooms, from the largest object to the least; the arrangement of colors, the elegant variety and contrast obtained by thrift in trifles, by delicate hands, clear eyes, and good sense; were at once so pleasant in themselves, and so expressive of their originator, that, as Mr. Lorry stood looking about him, the very chairs and tables seemed to ask him, with something of that peculiar expression which he knew so well by this time, whether he approved?

There were three rooms on a floor, and, the doors by which they communicated being put open that the air might pass freely through them all, Mr. Lorry, smilingly observant of that fanciful resemblance which he detected all around him, walked from one to another. The first was the best room, and in it were Lucie's birds, and flowers, and books, and desk, and work-table, and box of water-colors; the second was the Doctor's consulting-room, used also as the dining-room; the third, changingly speckled by the rustle of the plane-tree [2] in the yard, was the Doctor's bedroom, and there, in a corner, stood the disused shoemaker's bench and tray of tools, much as it had stood on the fifth floor of the dismal house by the wine-shop, in the suburb of Saint Antoine in Paris.

"I wonder," said Mr. Lorry, pausing in his looking about, "that he keeps that reminder of his sufferings by him!"

"And why wonder at that?" was the abrupt inquiry that made him start.

It proceeded from Miss Pross, the wild red woman, strong of hand, whose acquaintance he had first made at the Royal George Hotel at Dover, and had since improved.

"How do you do?" inquired that lady then—sharply, and yet as if to express that she bore him no malice.

"I am pretty well, I thank you," answered Mr. Lorry, with meekness, "how are you?"

"Nothing to boast of," said Miss Pross.

"Indeed?"

"Ah! indeed!" said Miss Pross. "I am very much put out about my Ladybird."

"May I ask the cause?"

"I don't want dozens of people who are not at all worthy of Ladybird, to come here looking after her," said Miss Pross.

"*Do* dozens come for that purpose?"

"Hundreds," said Miss Pross. "It really is doubly and trebly hard to have crowds and multitudes of people turning up, to take Ladybird's affections away from me."

Mr. Lorry knew Miss Pross to be very jealous, but he also knew her by this time to be, beneath the surface of her eccentricity, one of those unselfish creatures—found only among women—who will, for pure love and admiration, bind themselves willing slaves, to youth when they have lost it, to beauty that they never had, to accomplishments that they were never fortunate enough to gain, to bright hopes that never shone upon their own sombre lives. He knew enough of the world to know that there is nothing in it better than the faithful service of the heart, so rendered and so free as was hers from any mercenary taint.

"There never was, nor will be, but one man worthy of Lady-

---

[2] PLANE-TREE—A sycamore-maple, an ornamental species of maple with very large, dark green leaves.

bird," said Miss Pross; "and that was my brother Solomon, if he hadn't made a mistake in life."

Here again: Mr. Lorry's inquiries into Miss Pross's personal history had established the fact that her brother Solomon was a heartless scoundrel who had stripped her of everything she possessed, as a stake to speculate with, and had abandoned her in her poverty for evermore, with no touch of compunction. Miss Pross's fidelity of belief in Solomon (deducting a mere trifle for this slight mistake) was quite a serious matter with Mr. Lorry, and had its weight in his good opinion of her.

"As we happen to be alone for the moment, and are both people of business," he said, when they had got back to the drawing-room, and had sat down there in friendly relations, "let me ask you—does the Doctor, in talking with Lucie, never refer to the shoemaking time, yet?"

"Never."

"And yet he keeps that bench and those tools beside him?"

"Ah!" returned Miss Pross, shaking her head. "But I don't say he don't refer to it within himself."

"Do you believe that he thinks of it much?"

"I do," said Miss Pross.

"Do you suppose," Mr. Lorry went on, "that Doctor Manette has any theory of his own, preserved through all those years, relative to the cause of his being so oppressed; perhaps, even to the name of his oppressor?"

"I don't suppose anything about it but what Ladybird tells me."

"And that is——?"

"That she thinks he has."

"Now don't be angry at my asking all these questions. Is it not remarkable that Doctor Manette, unquestionably innocent of any crime as we are well assured he is, should never touch upon that question? I will not say with me, though he had business relations with me many years ago and we are now intimate; I will say with the fair daughter to whom he is so devotedly attached, and who is so devotedly attached to him? Believe me, Miss Pross, I don't approach the topic with you, out of curiosity, but out of zealous interest."

"Well! To the best of my understanding," said Miss Pross, "he is afraid of the whole subject."

"Afraid?"

"It's plain enough, I should think, why he may be. It's a dreadful remembrance. Besides that, his loss of himself grew out of it. Not knowing how he lost himself, or how he recovered himself, he may never feel certain of not losing himself again. That alone wouldn't make the subject pleasant, I should think."

It was a profounder remark than Mr. Lorry had looked for. "True," said he, "and fearful to reflect upon. Yet, a doubt lurks in my mind, Miss Pross, whether it is good for Doctor Manette to have that suppression always shut up within him. Indeed, it is this doubt and the uneasiness it sometimes causes me that has led me to our present confidence."

"Can't be helped," said Miss Pross, shaking her head. "Touch that string, and he instantly changes for the worse. Better leave it alone. In short, must leave it alone, like or no like. Sometimes, he gets up in the dead of the night, and will be heard, by us overhead there, walking up and down, walking up and down, in his room. Ladybird has learnt to know then, that his mind is walking up and down, walking up and down, in his old prison. She hurries to him, and they go on together, walking up and down, walking up and down, until he is composed. But he never says a word of the true reason of his restlessness, to her, and she finds it best not to hint at it to him. In silence they go walking up and down together, walking up and down together, till her love and company have brought him to himself."

Notwithstanding Miss Pross's denial of her own imagination, there was a perception of the pain of being monotonously haunted by one sad idea, in her repetition of the phrase, walking up and down, which testified to her possessing such a thing.

The corner has been mentioned as a wonderful corner for echoes; it had begun to echo so resoundingly to the tread of coming feet, that it seemed as though the very mention of that weary pacing to and fro had set it going.

"Here they are!" said Miss Pross, rising to break up the conference; "and now we shall have hundreds of people pretty soon!"

It was such a curious corner in its acoustical properties, such a peculiar ear of a place, that as Mr. Lorry stood at the open window, looking for the father and daughter whose steps he heard, he fancied they would never approach. Not only would the echoes die away, as though the steps had gone; but, echoes of other steps that never came, would be heard in their stead, and would die away for good when they seemed close at hand. However, father and daughter did at last appear, and Miss Pross was ready at the street door to receive them.

Miss Pross was a pleasant sight, albeit wild, and red, and grim, taking off her darling's bonnet when she came upstairs, and touching it up with the ends of her handkerchief, and blowing the dust off it, and folding her mantle ready for laying by, and smoothing her rich hair with as much pride as she could possibly have taken in her own hair if she had been the vainest and handsomest of women. Her darling was a pleasant sight too, embracing her and thanking her, and protesting against her taking so much trouble for her—which last she only dared to do playfully, or Miss Pross, sorely hurt, would have retired to her own chamber and cried. The Doctor was a pleasant sight too, looking on at them, and telling Miss Pross how she spoilt Lucie, in accents and with eyes that had as much spoiling in them as Miss Pross had, and would have had more if it were possible. Mr. Lorry was a pleasant sight too, beaming at all this in his little wig, and thanking his bachelor stars for having lighted him in his declining years to a Home. But, no Hundreds of people came to see the sights, and Mr. Lorry looked in vain for the fulfilment of Miss Pross's prediction.

Dinner-time, and still no Hundreds of people. On Sundays, Miss Pross dined at the Doctor's table, but on other days persisted in taking her meals, at unknown periods, either in the lower regions, or in her own room on the second floor—a blue chamber, to which no one but her Ladybird ever gained admittance. On this occasion Miss Pross, responding to Ladybird's pleasant face and pleasant efforts to please her, unbent exceedingly; so the dinner was very pleasant, too.

It was an oppressive day, and, after dinner, Lucie proposed that the wine should be carried out under the plane-tree, and they should sit there in the air. As everything turned upon her and revolved about her, they went out under the plane-tree, and she carried the wine down for the special benefit of Mr. Lorry. She had installed herself, some time before, as Mr. Lorry's cupbearer; and while they sat under the plane-tree, talking, she kept his glass replenished. Mysterious backs and ends of houses peeped at them as they talked, and the plane-tree whispered to them in its own way above their heads.

Still, the Hundreds of people did not present themselves. Mr. Darnay presented himself while they were sitting under the plane-tree, but he was only One.

Doctor Manette received him kindly, and so did Lucie. But, Miss Pross suddenly became afflicted with a twiching in the head and body, and retired into the house. She was not unfrequently the victim of this disorder, and she called it, in familiar conversation, "a fit of the jerks."

The Doctor was in his best condition, and looked especially young. The resemblance between him and Lucie was very strong at such times, and, as they sat side by side, she leaning on his shoulder, and he resting his arm on the back of her chair, it was very agreeable to trace the likeness.

He had been talking all day, on many subjects and with unusual vivacity. "Pray, Doctor Manette," said Mr. Darnay, as they sat under the plane-tree—and he said it in the natural pursuit of the topic in hand, which happened to be the old buildings of London—"have you seen much of the Tower?"[3]

"Lucie and I have been there; but only casually. We have seen enough of it to know that it teems with interest; little more."

"*I* have been there, as you remember," said Darnay, with a smile, though reddening a little angrily, "in another character, and not in a character that gives facilities for seeing much of it. They told me a curious thing when I was there."

"What was that?" Lucie asked.

"In making some alterations, the workmen came upon an old dungeon, which had been, for many years, built up and forgotten. Every stone of its inner wall was covered with inscriptions which had been carved by prisoners—dates, names, complaints, and prayers. Upon a corner stone in an angle of the wall, one prisoner, who seemed to have gone to execution, had cut, as his last work, three letters. They were done with some very poor instrument, and hurriedly, with an unsteady hand. At first, they were read as D. I. C.; but, on being more carefully examined,

[3] TOWER—The Tower of London, long a prison for political offenders.

the last letter was found to be G. There was no record or legend of any prisoner with those initials, and many fruitless guesses were made what the name could have been. At length, it was suggested that the letters were not initials, but the complete word, Dig. The floor was examined very carefully under the inscription, and, in the earth beneath a stone, or tile, or some fragment of paving, were found the ashes of a paper, mingled with the ashes of a small leathern case or bag. What the unknown prisoner had written will never be read, but he had written something, and hidden it away to keep it from the gaoler."

"My father!" exclaimed Lucie, "you are ill!"

He had suddenly started up, with his hand to his head. His manner and his look quite terrified them all.

"No, my dear, not ill. There are large drops of rain falling, and they made me start. We had better go in."

He recovered himself almost instantly. Rain was really falling in large drops, and he showed the back of his hand with rain-drops on it. But, he said not a single word in reference to the discovery that had been told of, and, as they went into the house, the business eye of Mr. Lorry either detected, or fancied it detected, on his face, as it turned towards Charles Darnay, the same singular look that had been upon it when it turned towards him in the passages of the Court House.

Tea-time, and Miss Pross making tea, with another fit of the jerks upon her, and yet no Hundreds of people. Mr. Carton had lounged in, but he made only Two.

The night was so very sultry, that although they sat with doors and windows open, they were overpowered by heat. When the tea-table was done with, they all moved to one of the windows, and looked out into the heavy twilight. Lucie sat by her father; Darnay sat beside her; Carton leaned against a window. The curtains were long and white, and some of the thunder-gusts that whirled into the corner, caught them up to the ceiling, and waved them like spectral wings.

"The rain-drops are still falling, large, heavy, and few," said Doctor Manette. "It comes slowly."

"It comes surely," said Carton.

They spoke low, as people watching and waiting mostly do;

The floor was examined very carefully under the inscription.

as people in a dark room, watching and waiting for lightning, always do.

There was a great hurry in the streets, of people speeding away to get shelter before the storm broke; the wonderful corner for echoes resounded with the echoes of footsteps coming and going, yet not a footstep was there.

"A multitude of people, and yet a solitude!" said Darnay when they had listened for a while.

"Is it not impressive, Mr. Darnay?" asked Lucie. "Sometimes, I have sat here of an evening, until I have fancied—but even the shade of a foolish fancy makes me shudder to-night, when all is so black and solemn——"

"Let us shudder too. We may know what it is?"

"It will seem nothing to you. Such whims are only impressive as we originate them, I think; they are not to be communicated. I have sometimes sat alone here of an evening, listening, until I have made the echoes out to be the echoes of all the footsteps that are coming by-and-by into our lives."

"There is a great crowd coming one day into our lives, if that be so," Sydney Carton struck in, in his moody way.

The footsteps were incessant, and the hurry of them became more and more rapid. The corner echoed and re-echoed with the tread of feet; some, as it seemed, under the windows; some, as it seemed, in the room; some coming, some going, some breaking off, some stopping altogether; all in the distant streets, and not one within sight.

"Are all these footsteps destined to come to all of us, Miss Manette, or are we to divide them among us?"

"I don't know, Mr. Darnay; I told you it was a foolish fancy, but you asked for it. When I have yielded myself to it, I have been alone, and then I have imagined them the footsteps of the people who are to come into my life, and my father's."

"I take them into mine!" said Carton. "*I* ask no questions and make no stipulations. There is a great crowd bearing down upon us, Miss Manette, and I see them!—by the lightning." He added the last words, after there had been a vivid flash which had shown him lounging in the window.

"And I hear them!" he added again, after a peal of thunder. "Here they come, fast, fierce, and furious!"

It was the rush and roar of rain that he typified, and it

stopped him, for no voice could be heard in it. A memorable storm of thunder and lightning broke with that sweep of water, and there was not a moment's interval in crash, and fire, and rain, until after the moon rose at midnight.

The great bell of Saint Paul's was striking one in the cleared air, when Mr. Lorry, escorted by Jerry, high-booted and bearing a lantern, set forth on his return-passage to Clerkenwell. There were solitary patches of road on the way between Soho and Clerkenwell, and Mr. Lorry, mindful of footpads, always retained Jerry for this service: though it was usually performed a good two hours earlier.

"What a night it has been! Almost a night, Jerry," said Mr. Lorry, "to bring the dead out of their graves."

"I never see the night myself, master—nor yet I don't expect to it—what would do that," answered Jerry.

"Good night, Mr. Carton," said the man of business. "Good night, Mr. Darnay. Shall we ever see such a night again, together!"

Perhaps. Perhaps, see the great crowd of people with its rush and roar, bearing down upon them, too.

VII MONSIEUR THE MARQUIS IN TOWN

A TALL man of about sixty, handsomely dressed, haughty in manner, quietly walked down the stairs of a great mansion in Paris. His face was like a fine mask—a face of a transparent paleness; every feature in it clearly defined; one set expression on it. The nose, beautifully formed otherwise, was very slightly pinched at the top of each nostril. In those two compressions, or dints, the only little change that the face ever showed, resided. They persisted in changing color sometimes, and they would be occasionally dilated and contracted by something like a faint pulsation; then, they gave a look of treachery, and cruelty, to the whole countenance. Examined with attention, its capacity of helping such a look was to be found in the line of the mouth, and the lines of the orbits of the eyes, being much too horizontal and thin; still, in the effect the face made, it was a handsome face, and a remarkable one.

Its owner went down stairs into the courtyard, got into his carriage, and drove away. It appeared rather agreeable to him to see the common people dispersed before his horses, and often barely escaping from being run down. His man drove as if he were charging an enemy, and his furious recklessness brought no check into the face, or to the lips, of the master. The complaint had sometimes made itself audible, even in that deaf city and dumb age, that, in the narrow streets without footways, the fierce patrician custom of hard driving endangered and maimed the mere vulgar in a barbarous manner. But, few cared enough for that to think of it a second time, and, in this matter, as in all others, the common wretches were left to get out of their difficulties as they could.

With a wild rattle and clatter, and an inhuman abandonment of consideration not easy to be understood in these days, the carriage dashed through the streets and swept round corners, with women screaming before it, and men clutching each other and clutching children out of its way. At last, swooping at a street corner by a fountain, one of its wheels came to a sickening little jolt, and there was a loud cry from a number of voices, and the horses reared and plunged.

But for the latter inconvenience, the carriage probably would not have stopped: carriages were often known to drive on, and leave their wounded behind, and why not? But, the frightened valet had got down in a hurry, and there were twenty hands at the horses' bridles.

"What has gone wrong?" said Monsieur, calmly looking out.

A tall man had caught up a bundle from among the feet of the horses, and had laid it on the basement of the fountain, and was down in the mud and wet, howling over it like a wild animal.

"Pardon, Monsieur the Marquis!" said a ragged and submissive man, "it is a child."

"Why does he make that abominable noise? Is it his child?"

"Excuse me, Monsieur the Marquis—it is a pity—yes."

The fountain was a little removed; for the street opened, where it was, into a space some ten or twelve yards square. As the tall man suddenly got up from the ground, and came running at the carriage, Monsieur the Marquis clapped his hand for an instant on his sword-hilt.

"Killed!" shrieked the man, in wild desperation, extending both arms at their length above his head, and staring at him. "Dead!"

The people closed round, and looked at Monsieur the Marquis. There was nothing revealed by the many eyes that looked at him but watchfulness and eagerness; there was no visible menacing or anger. Neither did the people say anything; after the first cry, they had been silent, and they remained so. The voice of the submissive man who had spoken was flat and tame in its extreme submission. Monsieur the Marquis ran his eyes over them all, as if they had been mere rats come out of their holes.

He took out his purse.

"It is extraordinary to me," said he, "that you people cannot take care of yourselves and your children. One or the other of you is forever in the way. How do I know what injury you have done my horses. See! Give him that."

He threw out a gold coin for the valet to pick up, and all the heads craned forward that all the eyes might look down at it as it fell. The tall man called out again with a most unearthly cry, "Dead!"

He was arrested by the quick arrival of another man, for whom the rest made way. On seeing him, the miserable creature fell upon his shoulder, sobbing and crying, and pointing to the fountain, where some women were stooping over the motionless bundle, and moving gently about it. They were as silent, however, as the men.

"I know all, I know all," said the last comer. "Be a brave man, my Gaspard! It is better for the poor little plaything to die so, than to live. It has died in a moment without pain. Could it have lived an hour as happily?"

"You are a philosopher, you there," said the Marquis, smiling. "How do they call you?"

"They call me Defarge."

"Of what trade?"

"Monsieur the Marquis, vendor of wine."

"Pick up that, philosopher and vendor of wine," said the Marquis, throwing him another gold coin, "and spend it as you will. The horses there; are they right?"

Without deigning to look at the assemblage a second time, Monsieur the Marquis leaned back in his seat, and was just being driven away with the air of a gentleman who had accidentally broken some common thing, and had paid for it and could afford to pay for it; when his ease was suddenly disturbed by a coin flying into his carriage, and ringing on its floor.

"Hold!" said Monsieur the Marquis. "Hold the horses! Who threw that?"

He looked to the spot where Defarge the vendor of wine had stood, a moment before; but the wretched father was grovelling on his face on the pavement in that spot, and the figure that stood beside him was the figure of a dark stout woman, knitting.

"You dogs!" said the Marquis, but smoothly, and with an unchanged front, except as to the spots on his nose: "I would ride over any of you very willingly, and exterminate you from the earth. If I knew which rascal threw at the carriage, and if that brigand were sufficiently near it, he should be crushed under the wheels."

So cowed was their condition, and so long and hard their experience of what such a man could do to them, within the law and beyond it, that not a voice, or a hand, or even an eye was raised. Among the men, not one. But the woman who stood knitting looked up steadily, and looked the Marquis in the face. It was not for his dignity to notice it; his contemptuous eyes passed over her, and over all the other rats; and he leaned back in his seat again, and gave the word "Go on!"

VIII MONSIEUR THE MARQUIS IN THE COUNTRY

A BEAUTIFUL landscape, with the corn bright in it but not abundant. Patches of poor rye where corn should have been, patches of poor peas and beans, patches of most coarse vegetable substitutes for wheat. On inanimate nature, as on the men and women who cultivated it, a prevalent tendency towards an appearance of vegetating unwillingly—a dejected disposition to give up, and wither away.

Monsieur[1] the Marquis in his travelling carriage, conducted by four post-horses and two postilions, fagged up a steep hill. A blush on the countenance of Monsieur the Marquis was no impeachment of his high breeding; it was not from within; it was occasioned by an external circumstance beyond his control—the setting sun.

The sunset struck so brilliantly into the travelling carriage

---

[1] MONSIEUR (mo-syû´)—Equivalent to Sir.

when it gained the hill-top, that its occupant was steeped in crimson. "It will die out," said Monsieur the Marquis, glancing at his hands, "directly."

In effect, the sun was so low that it dipped at the moment. When the heavy drag had been adjusted to the wheel, and the carriage slid down-hill, with a cinderous smell, in a cloud of dust, the red glow departed quickly; the sun and the Marquis going down together, there was no glow left when the drag was taken off.

But, there remained a broken country, bold and open, a little village at the bottom of the hill, a broad sweep and rise beyond it, a church-tower, a windmill, a forest for the chase, and a crag with a fortress on it used as a prison. Round upon all these darkening objects as the night drew on, the Marquis looked, with the air of one who was coming near home.

The village had its one poor street, with its poor brewery, poor tannery, poor tavern, poor stable-yard for relays of post-horses, poor fountain, all usual poor appointments. It had its poor people too. All its people were poor, and many of them were sitting at their doors, shredding spare onions and the like for supper, while many were at the fountain, washing leaves, and grasses, and any such small yieldings of the earth that could be eaten. Expressive signs of what made them poor were not wanting; the tax for the state, the tax for the church, the tax for the lord, tax local and tax general, were to be paid here and to be paid there, according to solemn inscription in the little village, until the wonder was that there was any village left unswallowed.

Few children were to be seen, and no dogs. As to the men and women, their choice on earth was stated in the prospect—Life on the lowest terms that could sustain it, down in the little village under the mill; or captivity and Death in the dominant prison on the crag.

Heralded by a courier in advance, and by the cracking of his postilions' whips, which twined snake-like about their heads in the evening air, as if he came attended by the Furies,[2] Monsieur the Marquis drew up in his travelling carriage at the posting-house gate. It was hard by the fountain, and the peasants

---

[2] THE FURIES—In Greek mythology, the daughters of Night and Darkness, supposed to be women with terrible faces and long snaky hair.

suspended their operations to look at him. Monsieur the Marquis cast his eyes over the submissive faces that drooped before him, when a grizzled mender of the roads joined the group.

"Bring me hither that fellow!" said the Marquis to the courier.

The fellow was brought, cap in hand, and the other fellows closed round to look and listen, in the manner of the people at the Paris fountain.

"I passed you on the road?"

"Monseigneur,[3] it is true. I had the honor of being passed on the road."

"Coming up the hill, and at the top of the hill, both?"

"Monseigneur, it is true."

"What did you look at, so fixedly?"

"Monseigneur, I looked at the man."

He stooped a little, and with his tattered blue cap pointed under the carriage. All his fellows stooped to look under the carriage.

"What man, pig? And why look there?"

"Pardon, Monseigneur; he swung by the chain of the shoe—the drag."

"Who?" demanded the traveller.

"Monseigneur, the man."

"May the Devil carry away these idiots! How do you call the man? You know all the men of this part of the country. Who was he?"

"Your clemency, Monseigneur! He was not of this part of the country. Of all the days of my life, I never saw him."

"Swinging by the chain? To be suffocated?"

"With your gracious permission, that was the wonder of it, Monseigneur. His head hanging over—like this!"

He turned himself sideways to the carriage, and leaned back, with his face thrown up to the sky, and his head hanging down; then recovered himself, fumbled with his cap, and made a bow.

"What was he like?"

"Monseigneur, he was whiter than the miller. All covered with dust, white as a spectre, tall as a spectre!"

The picture produced an immense sensation in the little

---

[3] MONSEIGNEUR (mŏn-sĕn-yēr')—A title of honor, equivalent to "My Lord."

crowd; but all eyes, without comparing notes with other eyes, looked at Monsieur the Marquis. Perhaps, to observe whether he had any spectre on his conscience.

"Truly, you did well," said the Marquis, felicitously sensible that such vermin were not to ruffle him, "to see a thief accompanying my carriage, and not open that great mouth of yours. Bah! Put him aside, Monsieur Gabelle!"

Monsieur Gabelle was the postmaster and some other taxing functionary united; he had come out with great obsequiousness to assist at this examination, and had held the examined by the drapery of his arm in an official manner.

"Bah! Go aside!" said Monsieur Gabelle.

"Lay hands on this stranger if he seeks to lodge in your village tonight, and be sure that his business is honest, Gabelle."

"Monseigneur, I am flattered to devote myself to your orders."

"Did he run away, fellow?—where is that accursed?"

The accursed was already under the carriage with some half-dozen particular friends, pointing out the chain with his blue cap. Some half-dozen other particular friends haled him out, and presented him breathless to Monsieur the Marquis.

"Did the man run away, dolt, when we stopped for the drag?"

"Monseigneur, he precipitated himself over the hill-side, head first, as a person plunges into the river."

"See to it, Gabelle. Go on!"

The half-dozen who were peering at the chain were still among the wheels, like sheep; the wheels turned so suddenly that they were lucky to save their skins and bones; they had very little else to save, or they might not have been so fortunate.

The burst with which the carriage started out of the village and up the rise beyond was soon checked by the steepness of the hill and gradually, it subsided to a foot pace. The sweet scents of the summer night rose all around Monsieur the Marquis, and rose, as the rain falls, impartially, on the dusty, ragged, and toil-worn group at the fountain not far away; to whom the mender of roads, with the aid of the blue cap without which he was nothing, still enlarged upon his man like a spectre, as long as they could bear it. By degrees, as they could bear no more, they dropped off one by one, and lights twinkled in little casements; which lights, as the casements darkened, and more stars came out, seemed to have shot up into the sky instead of having been extinguished.

The shadow of a large high-roofed house, and of many overhanging trees, was upon Monsieur the Marquis by that time; and the shadow was exchanged for the light of a flambeau,[4] as his carriage stopped, and the great door of his château was opened to him.

"Monsieur Charles, whom I expect; is he arrived from England?"

"Monseigneur, not yet."

[4] FLAMBEAU—A light made of thick wicks covered with wax.

IX THE GORGON'S HEAD

It was a heavy mass of building, that château of Monsieur the Marquis, with a large stone courtyard before it, and two stone sweeps of staircase meeting in a stone terrace before the principal door. A stony business altogether, with heavy stone balustrades, and stone urns, and stone flowers, and stone faces of men, and stone heads of lions, in all directions. As if the Gorgon's head [1] had surveyed it, when finished, two centuries ago.

Up the broad flight of shallow steps, Monsieur the Marquis, flambeau preceded, went from his carriage, sufficiently disturbing the darkness to elicit loud remonstrance from an owl in the roof of the great pile of stable-building away among the trees. All else was so quiet, that the flambeau carried up the steps, and the other flambeau held at the great door, burnt as if they were in a close room of state, instead of being in the open night-air. Other sound than the owl's voice there was none, save the falling of a fountain into its stone basin; for, it was one of those dark nights that hold their breath by the hour together, and then heave a long low sigh, and hold their breath again.

The great door clanged behind him, and Monsieur the Marquis crossed a hall grim with certain old boar-spears, swords, and knives of the chase; grimmer with certain heavy riding-rods and riding-whips, of which many a peasant, gone to his benefactor Death, had felt the weight when his lord was angry.

[1] GORGON'S HEAD—Medusa, whose hair was changed to serpents so terrible to look upon that they turned the beholder to stone. There are three Gorgons, but the name is usually applied to Medusa only.

Avoiding the larger rooms, which were dark and made fast for the night, Monsieur the Marquis, with his flambeau-bearer going on before, went up the staircase to a door in a corridor. This thrown open, admitted him to his own private apartment of three rooms: his bed-chamber and two others. High vaulted rooms with cool uncarpeted floors, great dogs upon the hearths for the burning of wood in winter time, and all luxuries befitting the state of a marquis in a luxurious age and country.

A supper-table was laid for two, in the third of the rooms, a round room, in one of the château's four extinguisher-topped[2] towers. A small lofty room, with its window wide open, and the wooden jalousie-blinds[3] closed, so that the dark night only showed in slight horizontal lines of black, alternating with their broad lines of stone color.

"My nephew," said the Marquis, glancing at the supper preparation; "they said he was not arrived."

Nor was he; but, he had been expected with Monseigneur.

"Ah! It is not probable he will arrive tonight; nevertheless, leave the table as it is. I shall be ready in a quarter of an hour."

In a quarter of an hour, Monseigneur was ready, and sat down alone to his sumptuous and choice supper. His chair was opposite to the window, and he had taken his soup, and was raising his glass of Bordeaux to his lips, when he put it down.

"What is that?" he calmly asked, looking with attention at the horizontal lines of black and stone color.

"Monseigneur? That?"

"Outside the blinds. Open the blinds."

It was done.

"Well?"

"Monseigneur, it is nothing. The trees and the night are all that are here."

The servant who spoke, had thrown the blinds wide, had looked out into the vacant darkness, and stood, with that blank behind him, looking round for instructions.

"Good," said the imperturbable master. "Close them again."

That was done too, and the Marquis went on with his supper. He was half way through it, when he again stopped with his

---

[2] EXTINGUISHER-TOPPED—Conical shaped, like the old-fashioned extinguisher of a candle.
[3] JALOUSIE-BLINDS—Lattice blinds.

glass in his hand, hearing the sound of wheels. It came on briskly, and came up to the front of the château.

"Ask who is arrived."

It was the nephew of Monseigneur. He had been some few leagues behind Monseigneur, early in the afternoon. He had diminished the distance rapidly, but not so rapidly as to come up with Monseigneur on the road. He had heard of Monseigneur, at the posting-houses, as being before him.

He was to be told (said Monseigneur) that supper awaited him then and there, and that he was prayed to come to it. In a little while, he came. He had been known in England as Charles Darnay.

Monseigneur received him in a courtly manner, but they did not shake hands.

"You left Paris yesterday, sir?" he said to Monseigneur, as he took his seat at table.

"Yesterday. And you?"

"I came direct."

"From London?"

"Yes."

"You have been a long time coming," said the Marquis with a smile.

"On the contrary; I came direct."

"Pardon me! I mean, not a long time on the journey; a long time intending the journey."

"I have been detained by"—the nephew stopped a moment in his answer—"various business."

"Without doubt," said the polished uncle.

So long as a servant was present, no other words passed between them. When coffee had been served and they were alone together, the nephew, looking at the uncle and meeting the eyes of the face that was like a fine mask, opened a conversation.

"I have come back, sir, as you anticipate, pursuing the object that took me away. It carried me into great and unexpected peril; but it is a sacred object, and if it had carried me to death I hope it would have sustained me."

"Not to death," said the uncle; "it is not necessary to say, to death."

"I doubt, sir," returned the nephew, "whether, if it had carried me to the utmost brink of death, you would have cared to stop me there."

The deepened marks in the nose, and the lengthening of the fine straight lines in the cruel face, looked ominous as to that; the uncle made a graceful gesture of protest, which was so clearly a slight form of good breeding that it was not reassuring.

"Indeed, sir," pursued the nephew, "for anything I know, you may have expressly worked to give a more suspicious appearance to the suspicious circumstances that surrounded me."

"No, no, no," said the uncle, pleasantly.

"But, however that may be," resumed the nephew, glancing at him with deep distrust, "I know that your diplomacy would stop me by any means, and would know no scruple as to means."

"My friend, I told you so," said the uncle, with a fine pulsation in the two marks. "Do me the favor to recall that I told you so, long ago."

"I recall it."

"Thank you," said the Marquis—very sweetly indeed.

His tone lingered in the air, almost like the tone of a musical instrument.

"In effect, sir," pursued the nephew, "I believe it to be at once your bad fortune, and my good fortune, that has kept me out of a prison in France here."

"I do not quite understand," returned the uncle, sipping his coffee. "Dare I ask you to explain?"

"I believe that if you were not in disgrace with the court, and had not been overshadowed by that cloud for years past, a *lettre de cachet*[4] would have sent me to some fortress indefinitely."

"It is possible," said the uncle, with great calmness. "For the honor of the family, I could even resolve to incommode you to that extent. A good opportunity for consideration, surrounded by the advantages of solitude, might influence your destiny to far greater advantage than you influence it for yourself. But it is useless to discuss the question. I am, as you say, at a disadvantage. These little instruments of correction, these gentle aids to the power and honor of families, these slight favors that might so incommode you, are only to be obtained now by interest and importunity. They are sought by so many, and they are granted (comparatively) to so few! It used not to be so, but France in all such things is changed for the worse. Our not remote ancestors held the right of life and death over the surrounding vulgar. But we have lost many privileges; a new philosophy has become the mode; and the assertion of our station, in these days, might cause us real inconvenience. All very bad, very bad!"

The Marquis took a gentle little pinch of snuff, and shook his head; as elegantly despondent as he could becomingly be, of a country still containing himself, that great means of regeneration.

"We have so asserted our station, both in the old time and in the modern time also," said the nephew, gloomily, "that I believe our name to be more detested than any name in France."

"Let us hope so," said the uncle. "Detestation of the high is the involuntary homage of the low."

"There is not," pursued the nephew, in his former tone, "a face I can look at, in all this country round about us, which looks at me with any deference on it but the dark deference of fear and slavery."

"A compliment," said the Marquis, "to the grandeur of the family, merited by the manner in which the family has sustained its grandeur. Hah!" And he took another gentle little pinch of snuff, and lightly crossed his legs.

But, when his nephew, leaning an elbow on the table, covered his eyes thoughtfully and dejectedly with his hand, the fine mask looked at him sideways with a stronger concentration of

---

[4] *Lettre de cachet*—The "blank form" to which Mr. Lorry had once referred, the arbitrary order of imprisonment.

keenness, closeness, and dislike, than was comportable with its wearer's assumption of indifference.

"Repression is the only lasting philosophy. The dark deference of fear and slavery, my friend," observed the Marquis, "will keep the dogs obedient to the whip, as long as this roof," looking up to it, "shuts out the sky."

That might not be so long as the Marquis supposed. If a picture of the château as it was to be a very few years hence, and of fifty like it as they too were to be a very few years hence, could have been shown to him that night, he might have been at a loss to claim his own from the ghastly, fire-charred, plunder-wrecked ruins. As for the roof he vaunted, he might have found *that* shutting out the sky in a new way—to wit, for ever, from the eyes of the bodies into which its lead was fired, out of the barrels of a hundred thousand muskets.

"Meanwhile," said the Marquis, "I will preserve the honor and repose of the family, if you will not. But you must be fatigued. Shall we terminate our conference for the night?"

"A moment more."

"An hour, if you like."

"Sir," said the nephew, "we have done wrong, and are reaping the fruits of wrong."

"*We* have done wrong?" repeated the Marquis, with an inquiring smile, and delicately pointing, first to his nephew, then to himself.

"Our family; our honorable family, whose honor is of so much account to both of us, in such different ways. Even in my father's time, we did a world of wrong, injuring every human creature who came between us and our pleasure, whatever it was. Why need I speak of my father's time, when it is equally yours? Can I separate my father's twin-brother, joint inheritor, and next successor, from himself?"

"Death has done that!" said the Marquis.

"And has left me," answered the nephew, "bound to a system that is frightful to me, responsible for it, but powerless in it; seeking to execute the last request of my dear mother's lips, and obey the last look of my dear mother's eyes, which implored me to have mercy and to redress; and tortured by seeking assistance and power in vain."

"Seeking them from me, my nephew," said the Marquis,

touching him on the breast with his forefinger—they were now standing by the hearth—"you will forever seek them in vain, be assured."

Every fine straight line in the clear whiteness of his face was cruelly, craftily, and closely compressed, while he stood looking quietly at his nephew, with his snuff-box in his hand. Once again he touched him on the breast, as though his finger were the fine point of a small sword, with which, in delicate finesse, he ran him through the body, and said,

"My friend, I will die, perpetuating the system under which I have lived."

When he had said it, he took a culminating pinch of snuff, and put his box in his pocket.

"Better to be a rational creature," he added then, after ringing a small bell on the table, "and accept your natural destiny. But you are lost, Monsieur Charles, I see."

"This property and France are lost to me," said the nephew, sadly; "I renounce them."

"Are they both yours to renounce? France may be, but is the property? It is scarcely worth mentioning; but, is it yet?"

"I had no intention, in the words I used, to claim it yet. If it passed to me from you, tomorrow——"

"Which I have the vanity to hope is not probable."

"—or twenty years hence——"

"You do me too much honor," said the Marquis; "still, I prefer that supposition."

"—I would abandon it, and live otherwise and elsewhere. It is little to relinquish. What is it but a wilderness of misery and ruin!"

"Hah!" said the Marquis, glancing round the luxurious room.

"To the eye it is fair enough, here; but seen in its integrity, under the sky, and by the daylight, it is a crumbling tower of waste, mismanagement, extortion, debt, mortgage, oppression, hunger, nakedness; and suffering."

"Hah!" said the Marquis again, in a well-satisfied manner.

"If it ever becomes mine, it shall be put into some hands better qualified to free it slowly (if such a thing is possible) from the weight that drags it down, so that the miserable people who cannot leave it and who have been long wrung to the last point of endurance, may, in another generation, suffer less; but it is not for me. There is a curse on it, and on all this land."

"And you?" said the uncle. "Forgive my curiosity; do you, under your new philosophy, graciously intend to live?"

"I must do, to live, what others of my countrymen, even with nobility at their backs, may have to do some day—work."

"In England, for example?"

"Yes. The family honor, sir, is safe for me in this country. The family name can suffer from me in no other, for I bear it in no other."

The ringing of the bell had caused the adjoining bed-chamber to be lighted. It now shone brightly, through the door of communication. The Marquis looked that way, and listened for the retreating step of his valet.

"England is very attractive to you, seeing how indifferently you have prospered there," he observed then, turning his calm face to his nephew with a smile.

"I have already said, that for my prospering there, I am sensible I may be indebted to you, sir. For the rest, it is my refuge."

"They say, those boastful English, that it is the refuge of many. You know a compatriot who has found a refuge there? A Doctor?"

"Yes."

"With a daughter?"

"Yes."

"Yes," said the Marquis. "You are fatigued. Good night!"

As he bent his head in his most courtly manner, there was a secrecy in his smiling face, and he conveyed an air of mystery to those words, which struck the eyes and ears of his nephew forcibly. At the same time, the thin straight lines of the setting of the eyes, and the thin straight lips, and the markings in the nose, curved with a sarcasm that looked handsomely diabolic.

"Yes," repeated the Marquis. "A Doctor with a daughter. Yes. So commences the new philosophy! You are fatigued. Good night!"

It would have been of as much avail to interrogate any stone face outside the château as to interrogate that face of his. The nephew looked at him, in vain, in passing on to the door.

"Good night!" said the uncle. "I look to the pleasure of seeing you again in the morning. Good repose! Light Monsieur my nephew to his chamber there!—And burn Monsieur my nephew in his bed, if you will," he added to himself, before he rang his little bell again, and summoned his valet to his own bedroom.

The valet come and gone, Monsieur the Marquis walked to and fro in his loose chamber-robe, to prepare himself gently for sleep, that hot still night. Rustling about the room, his softly-slippered feet making no noise on the floor, he moved like a refined tiger:—looked like some enchanted marquis of the impenitently wicked sort, in story, whose periodical change into tiger form was either just going off, or just coming on.

He moved from end to end of his voluptuous bedroom, looking again at the scraps of the day's journey that came unbidden into his mind; the slow toil up the hill at sunset, the setting sun, the descent, the mill, the prison on the crag, the little village in the hollow, the peasants at the fountain, and the mender of roads with his blue cap pointing out the chain under the carriage. That fountain suggested the Paris fountain, the little bundle lying on the step, the women, bending over it, and the tall man with his arms up, crying, "Dead!"

"I am cool now," said Monsieur the Marquis, "and may go to bed."

So, leaving only one light burning on the large hearth, he let the thin gauze curtains of the bed fall around him, and heard the night break its silence with a long sigh as he composed himself to sleep.

For three heavy hours, the stone faces of the château, lion and human, stared blindly at the night. Dead darkness lay on all the landscape, dead darkness added its own hush to the hushing dust on all the roads. The fountain in the village flowed unseen and unheard, and the fountain at the château dropped unseen and unheard—both melting away, like the minutes that were falling from the spring of Time—through three dark hours. Then, the grey water of both began to be ghostly in the light, and the eyes of the stone faces of the château were opened.

Lighter and lighter, until at last the sun touched the tops of the still trees, and poured its radiance over the hill. In the glow, the water of the château fountain seemed to turn to blood, and the stone faces crimsoned. Now, the sun was full up, and movement began in the village. Casement windows opened,

locked doors were unbarred, and people came forth shivering—
chilled, as yet, by the new sweet air. Then began the rarely
lightened toil of the day among the village population. Some,
to the fountain; some, to the fields; men and women here, to
dig and delve; men and women there, to see to the poor live
stock, and lead the bony cows out, to such pasture as could be
found by the roadside.

The château awoke later, as became its quality, but awoke
gradually and surely. First, the lonely boar-spears and knives
of the chase had been reddened as of old; then, had gleamed
trenchant in the morning sunshine; now, doors and windows
were thrown open, horses in their stables looked round over
their shoulders at the light and freshness pouring in at doorways, leaves sparkled and rustled at iron-grated windows, dogs
pulled hard at their chains, and reared impatient to be loosed.

All these trivial incidents belonged to the routine of life, and
the return of morning. Surely, not so the ringing of the great
bell of the château, nor the running up and down the stairs, nor
the hurried figures on the terrace, nor the booting and tramping
here and there and everywhere, nor the quick saddling of horses
and riding away?

What winds conveyed this hurry to the grizzled mender of
roads, already at work on the hill-top beyond the village, with
his day's dinner lying in a bundle that it was worth no crow's
while to peck at, on a heap of stones? Had the birds, carrying
some grains of it to a distance, dropped one over him as they
sow chance seeds? Whether or no, the mender of roads ran, on
the sultry morning, as if for his life, down the hill, knee-high in
dust, and never stopped till he got to the fountain.

All the people of the village were at the fountain, standing
about in their depressed manner, and whispering low, but showing no other emotions than grim curiosity and surprise. Some
of the people of the château, and some of those of the posting-
house, and all the taxing authorities, were armed more or less,
and were crowded on the other side of the little street in a
purposeless way, that was highly fraught with nothing. Already,
the mender of roads had penetrated into the midst of a group of
fifty particular friends, and was smiting himself in the breast
with his blue cap. What did all this portend, and what portended the swift hoisting-up of Monsieur Gabelle behind a serv-

ant on horseback, and the conveying away of the said Gabelle double-laden though the horse was, at a gallop, like a new version of the German ballad of Leonora?[5]

It portended that there was one stone face too many, up at the château.

The Gorgon had surveyed the building again in the night, and had added the one stone face wanting; the stone face for which it had waited through about two hundred years.

It lay back on the pillow of Monsieur the Marquis. It was like a fine mask, suddenly startled, made angry, and petrified. Driven home into the heart of the stone figure attached to it, was a knife. Round its hilt was a frill of paper, on which was scrawled:

"Drive him fast to his tomb. This, from JACQUES."

[5] GERMAN BALLAD OF LEONORA—A ballad popular in England at that time, in which a maiden, mourning for her lover gone on a crusade, is carried off on horseback by her lover, who proves to be a specter carrying her to her grave.

X TWO PROMISES

MORE months, to the number of twelve, had come and gone, and Mr. Charles Darnay was established in England as a higher teacher of the French language who was conversant with French literature. As a tutor, whose attainments made the students' way unusually pleasant and profitable, and as an elegant translator who brought something to his work besides mere dictionary knowledge, young Mr. Darnay soon became known and encouraged. He was well acquainted, moreover, with the circumstances of his country, and those were of ever-growing interest. So, with great perseverance and untiring industry, he prospered.

In London, he had expected neither to walk on pavements of gold, nor to lie on beds of roses; if he had had any such exalted expectation, he would not have prospered. He had expected labor, and he found it, and did it, and made the best of it. In this, his prosperity consisted. A certain portion of his time was passed at Cambridge, where he read with undergraduates. The rest of his time he passed in London.

Now, from the days when it was always summer in Eden, to these days when it is mostly winter in fallen latitudes, the world of a man has invariably gone one way—Charles Darnay's way—the way of the love of a woman.

He had loved Lucie Manette from the hour of his danger. He had never heard a sound so sweet and dear as the sound of her compassionate voice; he had never seen a face so tenderly beautiful, as hers when it was confronted with his own on the edge of the grave that had been dug for him. But, he had not yet spoken to her on the subject; the assassination at the deserted château far away beyond the heaving water and the long, long dusty roads—the solid stone château which had itself become the mere mist of a dream—had been done a year, and he had never yet, by so much as a single spoken word, disclosed to her the state of his heart.

That he had his reasons for this, he knew full well. It was again a summer day when, lately arrived in London from his college occupation, he turned into the quiet corner in Soho, bent on seeking an opportunity of opening his mind to Doctor Manette. It was the close of the summer day, and he knew Lucie to be out with Miss Pross.

He found the Doctor reading in his arm-chair at a window. The energy which had at once supported him under his old sufferings and aggravated their sharpness had been gradually restored to him. He was now a very energetic man indeed, with great firmness of purpose, strength of resolution, and vigor of action. In his recovered energy he was sometimes a little fitful and sudden, as he had at first been in the exercise of his other recovered faculties; but, this had never been frequently observable, and had grown more and more rare.

He studied much, slept little, sustained a great deal of fatigue with ease, and was equably cheerful. To him, now entered Charles Darnay, at sight of whom he laid aside his book and held out his hand.

"Charles Darnay! I rejoice to see you. We have been counting on your return these three or four days past. Mr. Stryver and Sydney Carton were both here yesterday, and both made you out to be more than due."

"I am obliged to them for their interest in the matter," he answered, a little coldly as to them, though very warmly as to the Doctor. "Miss Manette——"

"Is well," said the Doctor, as he stopped short, "and your

return will delight us all. She has gone out on some household matters, but will soon be home."

"Doctor Manette, I knew she was from home. I took the opportunity of her being from home, to beg to speak to you."

There was a blank silence.

"Yes?" said the Doctor, with evident constraint. "Bring your chair here, and speak on."

He complied as to the chair, but appeared to find the speaking on less easy.

"I have had the happiness, Doctor Manette, of being so intimate here," so he at length began, "for some year and a half, that I hope the topic on which I am about to touch may not——"

He was stayed by the Doctor's putting out his hand to stop him. When he had kept it so a little while, he said, drawing it back:

"Is Lucie the topic?"

"She is."

"It is hard for me to speak of her, at any time. It is very hard for me to hear her spoken of in that tone of yours, Charles Darnay."

"It is a tone of fervent admiration, true homage and deep love, Doctor Manette!" he said, deferentially.

There was another blank silence before her father rejoined:

"I believe it. I do you justice; I believe it."

He sat with his face turned away and his eyes bent on the ground. His chin dropped upon his hand, and his white hair overshadowed his face:

"Have you spoken to Lucie?"

"No."

"Nor written?"

"Never."

"It would be ungenerous to affect not to know that your self-denial is to be referred to your consideration for her father. Her father thanks you."

He offered his hand; but, his eyes did not go with it.

"I know," said Darnay, respectfully, "how can I fail to know, Doctor Manette, I who have seen you together from day to day, that between you and your daughter there is an affection so unusual, so touching, so belonging to the circumstances in which it has been nurtured, that it can have few parallels, even in the tenderness between a father and child. I know, Doctor Manette —how can I fail to know—that, mingled with the affection and duty of a daughter who has become a woman, there is, in her heart towards you, all the love and reliance of infancy itself. I know that, as in her childhood she had no parent, so she is now devoted to you with all the constancy and fervor of her present years and character, united to the trustfulness and attachment of the early days in which you were lost to her. I know perfectly well that if you had been restored to her from the world beyond this life, you could hardly be invested, in her sight, with a more sacred character than that in which you are always with her. I have known this, night and day, since I have known you in your home."

Her father sat silent, with his face bent down. His breathing was a little quickened; but he repressed all other signs of agitation.

"Dear Doctor Manette, always knowing this, always seeing her and you with this hallowed light about you, I have forborne, and forborne, as long as it was in the nature of man to do. I have felt, and do even now feel, that to bring my love—even mine—between you, is to touch your history with something not quite so good as itself. But I love her. Heaven is my witness that I love her!"

"I believe it," answered her father, mournfully. "I have thought so, before now. I believe it."

"But, do not believe," said Darnay, upon whose ear the mournful voice struck with a reproachful sound, "that if my fortune were so cast as that, being one day so happy as to make her my wife, I must at any time put any separation between her and you, I could or would breathe a word of what I now say. Besides that I should know it to be hopeless, I should know it to be a baseness. No, dear Doctor Manette. Like you, a voluntary exile from France; like you, driven from it by its distractions, oppressions, and miseries; like you, striving to live away from it by my own exertions, and trusting in a happier future; I look only to sharing your fortunes, sharing your life and home, and being faithful to you to the death. Not to divide with Lucie her privilege as your child, companion, and friend; but to come in aid of it, and bind her closer to you, if such a thing can be."

Her father rested his hands upon the arms of his chair, and looked up for the first time since the beginning of the conference. A struggle was evidently in his face; a struggle with that occasional look which had a tendency in it to dark doubt and dread.

"You speak so feelingly and so manfully, Charles Darnay, that I thank you with all my heart, and will open all my heart —or nearly so. Have you any reason to believe that Lucie loves you?"

"None. As yet, none."

"Is it the immediate object of this confidence, that you may at once ascertain that, with my knowledge?"

"Not even so. I might not have the hopefulness to do it for weeks. I might (mistaken or not mistaken) have that hopefulness tomorrow."

"Do you seek any guidance from me?"

"I ask none, sir. But I have thought it possible that you might have it in your power, if you should deem it right, to give me some."

"Do you seek any promise from me?"

"I do seek that."

"What is it?"

"It is, that if Miss Manette should bring to you at any time, on her own part, such a confidence as I have ventured to lay before you, you will bear testimony to what I have said, and to your belief in it. I hope you may be able to think so well of me, as to urge no influence against me. I say nothing more of my stake in this; this is what I ask. The condition on which

I ask it, and which you have an undoubted right to require, I will observe immediately."

"I give the promise," said the Doctor, "without any condition. I believe your object to be, purely and truthfully, as you have stated it. I believe your intention is to perpetuate, and not to weaken, the ties between me and my other and far dearer self. If she should ever tell me that you are essential to her perfect happiness, I will give her to you. If there were—Charles Darnay, if there were——"

The young man had taken his hand gratefully; their hands were joined as the Doctor spoke:

"—any fancies, any reasons, any apprehensions, anything whatsoever, new or old, against the man she really loved—the direct responsibility thereof not lying on his head—they should all be obliterated for her sake. She is everything to me; more to me than suffering, more to me than wrong, more to me—— Well! This is idle talk."

So strange was the way in which he faded into silence, and so strange his fixed look when he had ceased to speak, that Darnay felt his own hand turn cold in the hand that slowly released and dropped it.

"You said something to me," said Doctor Manette, breaking into a smile. "What was it you said to me?"

He was at a loss how to answer, until he remembered having spoken of a condition. Relieved as his mind reverted to that, he answered:

"Your confidence in me ought to be returned with full confidence on my part. My present name, though but slightly changed from my mother's, is not, as you will remember, my own. I wish to tell you what that is, and why I am in England."

"Stop!" said the Doctor of Beauvais.

"I wish it, that I may the better deserve your confidence, and have no secret from you."

"Stop!"

For an instant, the Doctor even had his two hands at his ears; for another instant, even had his two hands laid on Darnay's lips.

"Tell me when I ask you, not now. If your suit should

prosper, if Lucie should love you, you shall tell me on your marriage morning. Do you promise?"

"Willingly."

"Give me your hand. She will be home directly, and it is better she should not see us together tonight. Go! God bless you!"

It was dark when Charles Darnay left him, and it was an hour later and darker when Lucie came home; she hurried into the room alone—for Miss Pross had gone straight upstairs—and was surprised to find his reading-chair empty.

"My father," she called to him. "Father dear!"

Nothing was said in answer, but she heard a low hammering sound in his bedroom. Passing lightly across the intermediate room, she looked in at his door and came running back frightened, crying to herself, with her blood all chilled, "What shall I do! What shall I do!"

Her uncertainty lasted but a moment; she hurried back, and tapped at his door, and softly called to him. The noise ceased at the sound of her voice, and he presently came out to her, and they walked up and down together for a long time.

She came down from her bed, to look at him in his sleep that night. He slept heavily, and his tray of shoemaking tools, and his old unfinished work, were all as usual.

XI THE FELLOW OF NO DELICACY

IF Sydney Carton ever shone anywhere, he certainly never shone in the house of Doctor Manette. He had been there often, during a whole year, and had always been the same moody and morose lounger there. When he cared to talk, he talked well; but, the cloud of caring for nothing, which overshadowed him with such a fatal darkness, was very rarely pierced by the light within him.

And yet he did care something for the streets that environed that house, and for the senseless stones that made their pavements. Many a night he vaguely and unhappily wandered there, when wine had brought no transitory gladness to him; many a dreary daybreak revealed his solitary figure lingering there, and still lingering there when the first beams of the sun brought into strong relief, removed beauties of architecture in spires of churches and lofty buildings, as perhaps the quiet time brought some sense of better things, else forgotten and unattainable, into his mind. Of late, the neglected bed in the Temple court had known him more scantily than ever; and often when he had thrown himself upon it no longer than a few minutes, he had got up again, and haunted that neighborhood.

On a day in August, when the sight and scent of flowers in the city streets had some waifs of goodness in them for the worst, of health for the sickliest, and of youth for the oldest, Sydney's feet still trod those stones. From being irresolute and purposeless, his feet became animated by an intention, and, in the working out of that intention, they took him to the Doctor's door.

He was shown upstairs, and found Lucie at her work, alone. She had never been quite at her ease with him, and received him with some little embarrassment as he seated himself near her table. But, looking up at his face in the interchange of the first few common-places, she observed a change in it.

"I fear you are not well, Mr. Carton!"

"No. But the life I lead, Miss Manette, is not conducive to health. What is to be expected of, or by, such profligates?"

"Is it not—forgive me; I have begun the question on my lips—a pity to live no better life?"

"God knows it is a shame!"

"Then why not change it?"

Looking gently at him again, she was surprised and saddened to see that there were tears in his eyes. There were tears in his voice too, as he answered:

"It is too late for that. I shall never be better than I am. I shall sink lower, and be worse."

He leaned an elbow on her table, and covered his eyes with his hand. The table trembled in the silence that followed.

She had never seen him softened, and was much distressed. He knew her to be so, without looking at her, and said:

"Pray forgive me, Miss Manette. I break down before the knowledge of what I want to say to you. Will you hear me?"

"If it will do you any good, Mr. Carton, if it would make you happier, it would make me very glad!"

"God bless you for your sweet compassion!"

He unshaded his face after a little while, and spoke steadily.

"Don't be afraid to hear me. Don't shrink from anything I say. I am like one who died young. All my life might have been——"

"No, Mr. Carton. I am sure that the best part of it might still be; I am sure that you might be much, much worthier of yourself."

She was pale and trembling. He came to her relief with a fixed despair of himself which made the interview unlike any other that could have been holden.

"If it had been possible, Miss Manette, that you could have returned the love of the man you see before you—self-flung away, wasted, drunken, poor creature of misuse as you know him to be—he would have been conscious this day and hour, in spite of his happiness, that he would bring you to misery, bring you to sorrow and repentance, blight you, disgrace you, pull you down with him. I know very well that you can have no tenderness for me; I ask for none; I am even thankful that it cannot be."

"Without it, can I not save you, Mr. Carton? Can I not recall you—forgive me again!—to a better course! Can I in no way repay your confidence? I know this is a confidence," she modestly said, after a little hesitation, and in earnest tears; "I know you would say this to no one else. Can I turn it to no good account for yourself, Mr. Carton?"

He shook his head.

"To none. No, Miss Manette, to none. If you will hear me through a very little more, all you can ever do for me is done. I wish you to know that you have been the last dream of my soul. In my degradation, I have not been so degraded but that the sight of you with your father, and of this home made such a home by you, has stirred old shadows that I thought had died out of me. Since I knew you, I have been troubled by a remorse that I thought would never reproach me again, and have heard whispers from old voices impelling me upward, that I thought were silent forever. I have had unformed ideas of striving afresh, beginning anew, shaking off sloth and sensuality, and fighting out the abandoned fight. A dream, all a dream, that ends in nothing, and leaves the sleeper where he lay down, but I wish you to know that you inspired it."

"Will nothing of it remain? O, Mr. Carton, think again! Try again!"

"No, Miss Manette; all through it, I have known myself to be quite undeserving. And yet I have had the weakness, and have still the weakness, to wish you to know with what a sudden mastery you kindled me, heap of ashes that I am, into fire—a fire, however, inseparable in its nature from myself, quickening nothing, lighting nothing, doing no service, idly burning away."

"Since it is my misfortune, Mr. Carton, to have made you more unhappy than you were before you knew me——"

"Don't say that, Miss Manette, for you would have reclaimed me, if anything could. You will not be the cause of my becoming worse."

"Since the state of your mind that you describe is, at all events, attributable to some influence of mine—this is what I mean, if I can make it plain—can I use no influence to serve you? Have I no power for good, with you, at all?"

"The utmost good that I am capable of now, Miss Manette, I have come here to realize. Let me carry through the rest of my misdirected life, the remembrance that I opened my heart to you, last of all the world; and that there was something left in me at this time which you could deplore and pity. Will you let me believe, when I recall this day, that the last confidence of my life was reposed in your pure and innocent breast, and that it lies there alone, and will be shared by no one?"

"If that will be a consolation to you, yes."

"Not even by the dearest one ever to be known to you?"

"Mr. Carton," she answered, after an agitated pause, "the secret is yours, not mine; and I promise to respect it."

"Thank you. And again, God bless you."

He put her hand to his lips, and moved towards the door.

"Be under no apprehension, Miss Manette, of my ever resuming this conversation by so much as a passing word. I will never refer to it again. If I were dead, that could not be surer than it is henceforth. In the hour of my death, I shall hold sacred the one good remembrance—and shall thank and bless you for it—that my last avowal of myself was made to you, and that my name, and faults, and miseries, were gently carried in your heart. May it otherwise be light and happy!"

He was so unlike what he had ever shown himself to be, and

it was so sad to think how much he had thrown away, and how much he every day kept down and perverted, that Lucie Manette wept mournfully for him as he stood looking back at her.

"Be comforted!" he said, "I am not worth such feeling, Miss Manette. An hour or two hence, and the low companions and low habits that I scorn but yield to, will render me less worth such tears as those, than any wretch who creeps along the streets. Be comforted! But, within myself, I shall always be, towards you, what I am now, though outwardly I shall be what you have heretofore seen me. The last supplication but one I make to you, is, that you will believe this of me."

"I will, Mr. Carton."

"My last supplication of all, is this; and with it, I will relieve you of a visitor with whom I well know you have nothing in unison, and between whom and you there is an impassable space. It is useless to say it, I know, but it rises out of my soul. For you, and for any dear to you, I would do anything. If my career were of that better kind that there was any opportunity or capacity of sacrifice in it, I would embrace any sacrifice for you and for those dear to you. Try to hold me in your mind, at some quiet times, as ardent and sincere in this one thing. The time will come, the time will not be long in coming, when new ties will be formed about you—ties that will bind you yet more tenderly and strongly to the home you so adorn—the dearest ties that will ever grace and gladden you. O, Miss Manette, when the little picture of a happy father's face looks up in yours, when you see your own bright beauty springing up anew at your feet, think now and then that there is a man who would give his life, to keep a life you love beside you!"

He said, "Farewell!" said a last "God bless you!" and left her.

XII THE HONEST TRADESMAN

To the eyes of Mr. Jeremiah Cruncher, sitting on his stool in Fleet-street with his grisly urchin beside him, a vast number and variety of objects in movement were every day presented. Who could sit upon anything in Fleet-street during the busy hours of the day, and not be dazed and deafened by two immense processions, one ever tending westward with the sun, the other ever tending eastward from the sun, both ever tending to the plains beyond the range of red and purple where the sun goes down!

It fell out that Mr. Cruncher was thus engaged in a season when crowds were few and when his affairs in general were so unprosperous as to awaken a strong suspicion in his breast that Mrs. Cruncher must have been "flopping" in some pointed manner, when an unusual concourse pouring down Fleet-street westward, attracted his attention. Looking that way, Mr. Cruncher made out that some kind of funeral was coming along, and that there was popular objection to this funeral, which engendered uproar.

"Young Jerry," said Mr. Cruncher, turning to his offspring, "it's a buryin'."

"Hooroar, father!" cried Young Jerry.

The young gentleman uttered this exultant sound with mysterious significance. The elder gentleman took the cry so ill, that he watched his opportunity, and smote the young gentleman on the ear.

"What d'ye mean? What are you hooroaring at? What do you want to conwey to your own father, you young Rip? This boy is getting too many for *me!*" said Mr. Cruncher, surveying him. "Him and his hooroars! Don't let me hear no more of you, or you shall feel some more of me. D'ye hear?"

"I warn't doing no harm," Young Jerry protested, rubbing his cheek.

"Drop it then," said Mr. Cruncher; "I won't have none of *your* no harms. Get a top of that there seat, and look at the crowd."

His son obeyed, and the crowd approached; they were bawling and hissing round a dingy hearse and dingy mourning coach, in which mourning coach there was only one mourner, dressed in the dingy trappings that were considered essential to the dignity of the position. The position appeared by no means to please him, however, with an increasing rabble surrounding the coach, deriding him, making grimaces at him, and incessantly groaning and calling out: "Yah! Spies! Tst! Yaha! Spies!" with many compliments too numerous and forcible to repeat.

Funerals had at all times a remarkable attraction for Mr. Cruncher; he always pricked up his senses, and became excited, when a funeral passed Tellson's. Naturally, therefore, a funeral with this uncommon attendance excited him greatly, and he asked of the first man who ran against him:

"What is it, brother? What's it about?"

"*I* don't know," said the man. "Spies! Yaha! Tst! Spies!" He asked another man. "Who is it?"

"*I* don't know," returned the man: clapping his hands to his mouth nevertheless, and vociferating in a surprising heat and with the greatest ardor, "Spies! Yaha! Tst, tst! Spi-ies!"

At length, a person better informed on the merits of the case, tumbled against him, and from this person he learned that the funeral was the funeral of one Roger Cly.

"Was he a spy?" asked Mr. Cruncher.

"Old Bailey spy," returned his informant. "Yaha! Tst! Yah! Old Bailey Spi-i-ies!"

"Why, to be sure!" exclaimed Jerry, recalling the trial at which he had assisted. "I've seen him. Dead, is he?"

"Dead as mutton," returned the other, "and can't be too dead. Have 'em out, there! Spies! Pull 'em out, there! Spies!"

The idea was so acceptable in the prevalent absence of any idea, that the crowd caught it up with eagerness, and loudly repeating the suggestion to have 'em out, and to pull 'em out, mobbed the two vehicles so closely that they came to a stop. On the crowd's opening the coach doors, the one mourner scuffled out of himself and was in their hands for a moment; but he was so alert, and made such good use of his time, that in another moment he was scouring away up a by-street, after shedding his cloak, hat, long hatband, white pocket-handkerchief, and other symbolical tears.

These, the people tore to pieces, and scattered far and wide with great enjoyment, while the tradesmen hurriedly shut up their shops; for a crowd in those times stopped at nothing, and was a monster much dreaded. They had already got the length of opening the hearse to take the coffin out, when some brighter genius proposed instead, its being escorted to its destination amidst general rejoicing. Practical suggestions being much needed, this suggestion, too, was received with acclamation, and the coach was immediately filled with eight inside and a dozen out, while as many people got on the roof of the hearse as could by any exercise of ingenuity stick upon it. Among the first of these volunteers was Jerry Cruncher himself, who modestly concealed his spiky head from the observation of Tellson's, in the farther corner of the mourning coach.

The officiating undertakers made some protest against these changes in the ceremonies; but, the river being alarmingly near, and several voices remarking on the efficacy of cold immersion in bringing refractory members of the profession to reason, the protest was faint and brief. The remodelled procession started, with a chimney-sweep driving the hearse—advised by the regular driver, who was perched beside him, under close inspection, for the purpose—and with a pieman, also attended by his cabinet minister, driving the mourning coach.

Thus, with beer-drinking, pipe-smoking, song-roaring, and infinite caricaturing of woe, the disorderly procession went its way, recruiting at every step, and all the shops shutting up before it. Its destination was the old church of Saint Pancras, far off in the fields. It got there in course of time; insisted on pouring into the burial-ground; finally, accomplished the interment of the deceased Roger Cly in its own way, and highly to its own satisfaction.

The dead man disposed of, and the crowd being under the necessity of providing some other entertainment for itself, another brighter genius conceived the humor of impeaching casual passers-by, as Old Bailey spies, and wreaking vengeance on them. Chase was given to some scores of inoffensive persons who had never been near the Old Bailey in their lives, in the realization of this fancy, and they were roughly hustled and maltreated. The transition to the sport of window-breaking, and thence to the plundering of public houses, was easy and natural. At last, after several hours, when sundry summer-houses had been pulled down, and some area railings had been torn up, to arm the more belligerent spirits, a rumor got about that the guards were coming. Before this rumor, the crowd gradually melted away, and perhaps the guards came, and perhaps they never came, and this was the usual progress of a mob.

Mr. Cruncher did not assist at the closing sports, but had remained behind in the churchyard, to confer and condole with the undertakers. The place had a soothing influence on him.

He procured a pipe from a neighboring public-house, and smoked it, looking in at the railings and maturely considering the spot.

"Jerry," said Mr. Cruncher, talking to himself in his usual way, "you see that there Cly that day, and you see with your own eyes that he was a young 'un and a straight made 'un."

Having smoked his pipe out, and ruminated a little longer, he turned himself about, that he might appear, before the hour of closing, on his station at Tellson's. Young Jerry relieved his father with dutiful interest, and reported No job in his absence. The bank closed, the ancient clerks came out, the usual watch was set, and Mr. Cruncher and his son went home to tea.

"Now, I tell you where it is!" said Mr. Cruncher to his wife, on entering. "If, as a honest tradesman, my wenturs goes wrong tonight, I shall make sure that you've been praying again me, and I shall work you for it just the same as if I seen you do it."

The dejected Mrs. Cruncher shook her head.

"You are going out tonight?" she asked.

"Yes, I am."

"May I go with you, father?" asked his son, briskly.

"No, you mayn't. I'm a-going—as your mother knows—a fishing. That's where I'm going to. Going a fishing."

"Your fishing-rod gets rayther rusty; don't it, father?"

"Never you mind."

"Shall you bring any fish home, father?"

"If I don't, you'll have short commons tomorrow," returned that gentleman, shaking his head; "that's questions enough for you; I ain't a-going out, till you've been long a-bed."

He devoted himself during the remainder of the evening to keeping a most vigilant watch on Mrs. Cruncher, and sullenly holding her in conversation that she might be prevented from meditating any petitions to his disadvantage.

Thus the evening wore away until Young Jerry was ordered to bed, and his mother, laid under similar injunctions, obeyed them. Mr. Cruncher beguiled the earlier watches of the night with solitary pipes, and did not start upon his excursion until nearly one o'clock. Towards that small and ghostly hour, he rose up from his chair, took a key out of his pocket, opened a locked cupboard, and brought forth a sack, a crowbar of convenient size, a rope and chain, and other *fishing-tackle* of that nature. Disposing these articles about him in skilful manner, he bestowed a parting defiance on Mrs. Cruncher, extinguished the light, and went out.

Young Jerry, who had only made a feint of undressing when he went to bed, was not long after his father. Under cover of the darkness he followed out of the room, followed down the stairs, followed down the court, followed out into the streets. He was in no uneasiness concerning his getting into the house again, for it was full of lodgers, and the door stood ajar all night.

Impelled by a laudable ambition to study the art and mystery of his father's honest calling, Young Jerry, keeping as close to house-fronts, walls, and doorways, as his eyes were close to one another, held his honored parent in view. The honored parent steering northward, had not gone far, when he was joined by another disciple of Izaak Walton,[1] and the two trudged on together.

Within half an hour from the first starting, they were beyond the winking lamps, and the more than winking watchmen, and were out upon a lonely road. Another fisherman was picked up here—and that so silently, that if Young Jerry had been superstitious, he might have supposed the second follower of the gentle craft to have, all of a sudden, split himself into two.

The three went on, and Young Jerry went on, until the three stopped under a bank overhanging the road. Upon the top of the bank was a low brick wall surmounted by an iron railing. In the shadow of bank and wall, the three turned out of the road, and up a blind lane, of which the wall—there, risen to some eight or ten feet high—formed one side. Crouching down in a corner, peeping up the lane, the next object that Young Jerry saw, was the form of his honored parent, pretty well defined against a watery and clouded moon, nimbly scaling an iron gate. He was soon over, and then the second fisherman got over, and then the third. They all dropped softly on the ground within the gate, and lay there a little—listening perhaps. Then, they moved away on their hands and knees.

It was now Young Jerry's turn to approach the gate: which he did, holding his breath. Crouching down again in a corner

---

[1] IZAAK WALTON—The author of *The Compleat Angler,* the most famous book on the art of fishing.

there, and looking in, he made out the three fishermen creeping through some rank grass; and all the gravestones in the churchyard—it was a large churchyard that they were in—looking on like ghosts in white, while the church tower itself looked on like the ghost of a monstrous giant. They did not creep far, before they stopped and stood upright. And then they began to fish.

They fished with a spade, at first. Presently the honored parent appeared to be adjusting some instrument like a great corkscrew. Whatever tools they worked with, they worked hard, until the awful striking of the church clock so terrified Young Jerry, that he made off, with his hair as stiff as his father's.

But, his long-cherished desire to know more about these matters, not only stopped him in his running away, but lured him back again. They were still fishing perseveringly, when he peeped in at the gate for the second time; but now they seemed to have got a bite. There was a screwing and complaining sound down below, and their bent figures were strained, as if by a weight. By slow degrees the weight broke away the earth upon it, and came to the surface. Young Jerry very well knew what it would be; but, when he saw it, and saw his honored parent about to wrench it open, he was so frightened, being new to the sight, that he made off again, and never stopped until he had run a mile or more.

He would not have stopped then, for anything less necessary than breath, it being a spectral sort of race that he ran, and one highly desirable to get to the end of. He had a strong idea that the coffin he had seen was running after him; and, pictured as hopping on behind him, bolt upright upon its narrow end, always on the point of overtaking him and hopping on at his side—perhaps taking his arm—it was a pursuer to shun. It got into shadows on the road, and lay cunningly on its back to trip him up and was incessantly hopping on behind and gaining on him, so that when the boy got to his own door he had reason for being half dead. And even then it would not leave him, but followed him up-stairs with a bump on every stair, scrambled into bed with him, and bumped down, dead and heavy, on his breast when he fell asleep.

From his oppressed slumber, Young Jerry in his closet was awakened after daybreak and before sunrise, by the presence of his father in the family room. Something had gone wrong with him; at least, so Young Jerry inferred, from the circumstance of his holding Mrs. Cruncher by the ears, and knocking the back of her head against the head-board of the bed.

"I told you I would," said Mr. Cruncher, "and I did."

"Jerry, Jerry, Jerry!" his wife implored.

"You oppose yourself to the profit of the business," said Jerry, "and me and my partners suffer. You was to honor and obey; why the devil don't you?"

"I'll try to be a good wife, Jerry," the poor woman protested, with tears.

"Is it being a good wife to oppose your husband's business? Is it honoring your husband to dishonor his business? Is it obeying your husband to disobey him on the wital subject of his business?"

"You hadn't taken to the dreadful business then, Jerry."

"It's enough for you," retorted Mr. Cruncher, "to be the wife of a honest tradesman, and not to occupy your female mind with calculations when he took to his trade or when he didn't. A honoring and obeying wife would let his trade alone altogether. Call yourself a religious woman? If you're a religious woman, give me a irreligious one!"

The altercation was conducted in a low tone of voice, and terminated in the honest tradesman's kicking off his clay-soiled boots, and lying down at his length on the floor. After taking a timid peep at him lying on his back, with his rusty hands under his head for a pillow, his son lay down too, and fell asleep again.

There was no fish for breakfast, and not much of anything else. Mr. Cruncher was out of spirits, and out of temper, and kept an iron pot-lid by him as a projectile for the correction of Mrs. Cruncher, in case he should observe any symptoms of her saying grace. He was brushed and washed at the usual hour, and set off with his son to pursue his ostensible calling.

Young Jerry, walking with the stool under his arm at his father's side along sunny and crowded Fleet-street, was a very different Young Jerry from him of the previous night, running home through darkness and solitude from his grim pursuer. His cunning was fresh with the day, and his qualms were gone with the night—in which particulars it is not improbable that he had compeers in Fleet-street and the City of London, that fine morning.

"Father," said Young Jerry, as they walked along: taking care to keep at arm's length and to have the stool well between them: "what's a Resurrection-Man?"[2]

Mr. Cruncher came to a stop on the pavement before he answered, "How should I know?"

"I thought you knowed everything, father," said the artless boy.

"Hem! Well," returned Mr. Cruncher, going on again, and lifting off his hat to give his spikes free play, "he's a tradesman."

"What's his goods, father?" asked the brisk Young Jerry.

"His goods," said Mr. Cruncher, after turning it over in his mind, "is a branch of scientific goods."

"Persons' bodies, ain't it, father?" asked the lively boy.

"I believe it is something of that sort," said Mr. Cruncher.

"Oh, father, I should so like to be a Resurrection-Man when I'm quite growed up!"

Mr. Cruncher was soothed, but shook his head in a dubious

[2] RESURRECTION-MAN—One who makes a trade of digging up bodies to sell for dissecting, a "body snatcher."

and moral way. "It depends upon how you dewelop your talents. Be careful to dewelop your talents, and never to say no more than you can help to nobody, and there's no telling at the present time what you may not come to be fit for." As Young Jerry, thus encouraged, went on a few yards in advance, to plant the stool in the shadow of the Bar, Mr. Cruncher added to himself: "Jerry, you honest tradesman, there's hopes wot that boy will yet be a blessing to you, and a recompense to you for his mother!"

XIII KNITTING

THIS had been the third morning in succession, on which there had been early drinking at the wine-shop of Monsieur Defarge. It had begun on Monday, and here was Wednesday come. There had been more of early brooding than drinking; for, many men had listened and whispered and slunk about there from the time of the opening of the door, who could not have laid a piece of money on the counter to save their souls. These were to the full as interested in the place, however, as if they could have commanded whole barrels of wine; and they glided from seat to seat, and from corner to corner, swallowing talk in lieu of drink, with greedy looks.

Notwithstanding an unusual flow of company, the master of the wine-shop was not visible. He was not missed; for, nobody who crossed the threshold looked for him, nobody asked for him, nobody wondered to see only Madame Defarge in her seat, presiding over the distribution of wine, with a bowl of battered small coins before her, as much defaced and beaten out of their original impress as the small coinage of humanity from whose ragged pockets they had come.

A suspended interest and a prevalent absence of mind, were perhaps observed by the spies who looked in at the wine-shop, as they looked in at every place, high and low, from the king's palace to the criminal's gaol. Games at cards languished, players at dominoes musingly built towers with them, drinkers drew figures on the tables with spilt drops of wine, Madame Defarge herself picked out the pattern on her sleeve with her toothpick, and saw and heard something inaudible and invisible a long way off.

Thus was Saint Antoine in this vinous feature until midday. It was high noontide, when two dusty men passed through the streets and under the swinging lamps: of whom, one was Monsieur Defarge: the other, a mender of roads in a blue cap. All adust and athirst, the two entered the wine-shop. Their arrival had lighted a kind of fire in the breast of Saint Antoine, fast spreading as they came along, which stirred and flickered in flames of faces at most doors and windows. Yet, no one had followed them, and no man spoke when they entered the wine-shop, though the eyes of every man there were turned upon them.

"Good-day, gentlemen!" said Monsieur Defarge.

It may have been a signal for loosening the general tongue. It elicited an answering chorus of "Good-day!"

"It is bad weather, gentlemen," said Defarge, shaking his head.

Upon which, every man looked at his neighbor, and then all cast down their eyes and sat silent, except one man, who got up and went out.

"My wife," said Defarge aloud, addressing Madame Defarge; "I have travelled certain leagues with this good mender of roads, called Jacques. I met him—by accident—a day and a half's journey out of Paris. He is a good child, this mender of roads, called Jacques. Give him to drink, my wife!"

A second man got up and went out. Madame Defarge set wine before the mender of roads called Jacques, who doffed his blue cap to the company, and drank. In the breast of his blouse, he carried some coarse dark bread; he ate of this between whiles, and sat munching and drinking near Madame Defarge's counter. A third man got up and went out.

Defarge refreshed himself with a draught of wine and stood waiting until the countryman had made his breakfast. He looked at no one present, and no one now looked at him; not even Madame Defarge, who had taken up her knitting, and was at work.

"Have you finished your repast, friend?" he asked, in due season.

"Yes, thank you."

"Come then! You shall see the apartment that I told you you could occupy. It will suit you to a marvel."

Out of the wine-shop into the street, out of the street into a courtyard, out of the courtyard up a steep staircase, out of the staircase into a garret—formerly the garret where a white-haired man sat on a low bench, stooping forward and very busy, making shoes.

No white-haired man was there now; but, the three men were there who had gone out of the wine-shop singly. And between them and the white-haired man afar off, was the one small link, that they had once watched him through the chinks in the wall.

Defarge closed the door carefully and spoke in a subdued voice:

"Jacques One, Jacques Two, Jacques Three! This is the witness encountered by appointment, by me, Jacques Four. He will tell you all. Speak, Jacques Five!"

The mender of roads, blue cap in hand, wiped his swarthy forehead with it, and said, "Where shall I commence, monsieur?"

"Commence," was Monsieur Defarge's not unreasonable reply, "at the commencement."

"I saw him then, messieurs," began the mender of roads, "a year ago this running summer, underneath the carriage of the Marquis, hanging by the chain. Behold the manner of it. I leaving my work on the road, the sun going to bed, the carriage of the Marquis slowly ascending the hill, he hanging by the chain—like this."

Again, the mender of roads went through the old performance; in which he ought to have been perfect by that time, seeing that it had been the infallible resource and indispensable entertainment of his village during a whole year.

Jacques One struck in, and asked if he had ever seen the man before.

"Never," answered the mender of roads, recovering his perpendicular.

Jacques Three demanded how he afterwards recognized him then.

"By his tall figure," said the mender of roads, softly, and with his finger at his nose. "When Monsieur the Marquis demands that evening, 'Say, what is he like?' I make response, 'Tall as a spectre.'"

"You should have said, short as a dwarf," returned Jacques Two.

"But what did I know! The deed was not then accomplished,

neither did he confide in me. Observe! Under those circumstances even, I do not offer my testimony. Monsieur the Marquis indicates me with his finger, standing near our little fountain, and says, 'To me! Bring that rascal!' My faith, messieurs, I offer nothing."

"He is right there, Jacques," murmured Defarge, to him who had interrupted. "Go on!"

"Good!" said the mender of roads, with an air of mystery. "The tall man is lost, and he is sought—how many months? Nine, ten, eleven?"

"No matter, the number," said Defarge. "He is well hidden, but at last he is unluckily found. Go on!"

"I am again at work upon the hill-side, and the sun is again about to go to bed. I am collecting my tools to descend to my cottage down in the village below, where it is already dark, when I raise my eyes, and see coming over the hill, six soldiers. In the midst of them is a tall man with his arms bound—tied to his sides, like this!"

With the aid of his indispensable cap, he represented a man with his elbows bound fast at his hips, with cords that were knotted behind him.

"I stand aside, messieurs, by my heap of stones, to see the soldiers and their prisoner pass, and at first, as they approach, I see no more than that they are six soldiers with a tall man bound, and that they are almost black to my sight—except on the side of the sun going to bed, where they have a red edge, messieurs. Also, I see that their long shadows are on the hollow ridge on the opposite side of the road, and are on the hill above it, and are like the shadows of giants. Also, I see that they are covered with dust, and that the dust moves with them as they come, tramp, tramp! But when they advance quite near to me, I recognize the tall man, and he recognizes me. Ah, but he would be well content to precipitate himself over the hill-side once again, as on the evening when he and I first encountered, close to the same spot!"

He described it as if he were there, and it was evident that he saw it vividly; perhaps he had not seen much in his life.

"I do not show the soldiers that I recognize the tall man; he does not show the soldiers that he recognizes me; we do it, and we know it, with our eyes. 'Come on!' says the chief of that company, pointing to the village, 'bring him fast to his tomb!' and they bring him faster. I follow. His arms are swelled because of being bound so tight, his wooden shoes are large and clumsy, and he is lame. Because he is lame, and consequently slow, they drive him with their guns—like this!"

He imitated the action of a man's being impelled forward by the butt-ends of muskets.

"As they descend the hill like madmen running a race, he falls. They laugh and pick him up again. His face is bleeding and covered with dust, but he cannot touch it; thereupon they laugh again. They bring him into the village; all the village runs to look; they take him past the mill, and up to the prison; all the village sees the prison gate open in the darkness of the night, and swallow him—like this!"

He opened his mouth as wide as he could, and shut it with a sounding snap of his teeth. Observant of his unwillingness to mar the effect by opening it again, Defarge said, "Go on, Jacques."

"All the village," pursued the mender of roads, on tiptoe and in a low voice, "withdraws; all the village whispers by the fountain; all the village sleeps; all the village dreams of that unhappy one, within the locks and bars of the prison on the crag, and never to come out of it, except to perish. In the morning, with my tools upon my shoulder, eating my morsel of black bread as I go, I made a circuit by the prison, on my way to my work. There, I see him, high up, behind the bars of a lofty iron cage, bloody and dusty as last night, looking through. He has no hand free, to wave to me; I dare not call to him; he regards me like a dead man."

Defarge and the three glanced darkly at one another. The looks of all of them were dark, repressed, and revengeful, as they listened to the countryman's story; the manner of all of them, while it was secret, was authoritative too. They had the air of a rough tribunal; Jacques One and Two sitting on the old pallet-bed, each with his chin resting on his hand, and his eyes intent on the road mender; Jacques Three, equally intent, on one knee behind them, with his agitated hand always gliding over the network of fine nerves about his mouth and nose; Defarge standing between them and the narrator, whom he had stationed in the light of the window, by turns looking from him to them and from them to him.

"Go on, Jacques," said Defarge.

"He remains up there in his iron cage some days. The village looks at him by stealth, for it is afraid. But it always looks up, from a distance, at the prison on the crag; and in the evening when the work of the day is achieved and it assembles to gossip at the fountain, all faces are turned towards the prison. Formerly, they were turned towards the posting-house; now, they are turned towards the prison. They whisper at the fountain, that although condemned to death he will not be executed; they say that petitions have been presented in Paris, showing that he was enraged and made mad by the death of his child; they say that a petition has been presented to the King himself. What do I know? It is possible. Perhaps yes, perhaps no."

"Listen then, Jacques," Number One of that name sternly interposed. "Know that a petition was presented to the King and Queen. All here, yourself excepted, saw the King take it, in his carriage in the street, sitting beside the Queen. It is Defarge whom you see here, who, at the hazard of his life, darted out before the horses, with the petition in his hand."

"And once again listen, Jacques!" said the kneeling Number Three: his fingers ever wandering over and over those fine nerves, with a strikingly greedy air, as if he hungered for something—that was neither food nor drink; "the guard, horse and foot, surrounded the petitioner, and struck him blows. You hear?"

"I hear, messieurs."

"Go on then," said Defarge.

"Again; on the other hand, they whisper at the fountain," resumed the countryman, "that he is brought down into our country to be executed on the spot, and that he will very certainly be executed. They even whisper that because he has slain Monseigneur, and because Monseigneur was the father of his tenants —serfs—what you will—he will be executed as a parricide. One old man says at the fountain, that his right hand, armed with the knife, will be burnt off before his face; that, into wounds which will be made in his arms, his breast, and his legs, there will be poured boiling oil, melted lead, hot resin, wax, and sulphur; finally, that he will be torn limb from limb by four strong horses. That old man says, all this was actually done to a prisoner who made an attempt on the life of the last King, Louis XV. But how do I know if he lies? I am not a scholar."

"Listen once again then, Jacques!" said the man with the restless hand and the craving air. "The name of that prisoner was Damiens,[1] and it was all done in open day, in the open streets of this city of Paris; and nothing was more noticed in the vast concourse that saw it done, than the crowd of ladies of quality and fashion, who were full of eager attention to the last —to the last, Jacques, prolonged until nightfall, when he had lost two legs and an arm, and still breathed! And it was done —why, how old are you?"

"Thirty-five," said the mender of roads, who looked sixty.

"It was done when you were more than ten years old; you might have seen it."

"Enough!" said Defarge, with grim impatience. "Long live the Devil! Go on."

"Well! Some whisper this, some whisper that; they speak of nothing else; even the fountain appears to fall to that tune. At length, on Sunday night when all the village is asleep, come soldiers, winding down from the prison, and their guns ring on the stones of the little street. Workmen dig, workmen hammer, soldiers laugh and sing; in the morning, by the fountain, there is raised a gallows forty feet high, poisoning the water."

The mender of roads looked *through* rather than *at* the low ceiling, and pointed as if he saw the gallows somewhere in the sky.

"All work is stopped, all assemble there, nobody leads the cows out, the cows are there with the rest. At mid-day, the roll of drums. Soldiers have marched into the prison in the night, and he is in the midst of many soldiers. He is bound as before, and in his mouth there is a gag—tied so, with a tight string, making him look almost as if he laughed." He suggested it, by creasing his face with his two thumbs, from the corners of his mouth to his ears. "On the top of the gallows is fixed the knife, blade upwards, with its point in the air. He is hanged there forty feet high—and is left hanging, poisoning the water."

They looked at one another, as he used his blue cap to wipe

---

[1] DAMIENS—Robert Damiens attempted to assassinate Louis XV in 1757. He was executed as here described.

his face, on which the perspiration had started afresh while he recalled the spectacle.

"It is frightful, messieurs. How can the women and the children draw water! Who can gossip of an evening, under that shadow! Under it, have I said? When I left the village, Monday evening as the sun was going to bed, and looked back from the hill, the shadow struck across the church, across the mill, across the prison—seemed to strike across the earth, messieurs, to where the sky rests upon it!"

The hungry man gnawed one of his fingers as he looked at the other three, and his finger quivered with the craving that was on him.

"That's all, messieurs. I left at sunset (as I had been warned to do), and I walked on, that night and half next day, until I met (as I was warned I should) this comrade. With him, I came on, now riding and now walking, through the rest of yesterday and through last night. And here you see me!"

After a gloomy silence, the first Jacques said, "Good. You have acted and recounted, faithfully. Will you wait for us a little, outside the door?"

"Very willingly," said the mender of roads, whom Defarge escorted to the top of the stairs, and, leaving seated there, returned.

The three had risen, and their heads were together when he came back to the garret.

"How say you, Jacques?" demanded Number One. "To be registered?"

"To be registered, as doomed to destruction," returned Defarge.

"Magnificent!" croaked the man with the craving.

"The château, and all the race?" inquired the first.

"The château and all the race," returned Defarge. "Extermination."

The hungry man repeated, in a rapturous croak, "Magnificent!" and began gnawing another finger.

"Are you sure," asked Jacques Two, of Defarge, "that no embarrassment can arise from our manner of keeping the register? Without doubt it is safe, for no one beyond ourselves can decipher it; but shall we always be able to decipher it—or, I ought to say, will she?"

*"The château and all the race,"
returned Defarge. "Extermination."*

"Jacques," returned Defarge, drawing himself up, "if madame my wife undertook to keep the register in her memory alone, she would not lose a word of it—not a syllable of it. Knitted, in her own stitches and her own symbols, it will always be as plain to her as the sun. Confide in Madame Defarge. It would be easier for the weakest poltroon that lives, to erase himself from existence, than to erase one letter of his name or crimes from the knitted register of Madame Defarge."

There was a murmur of confidence and approval, and then the man who hungered, asked: "Is this rustic to be sent back soon? I hope so. He is very simple; is he not a little dangerous?"

"He knows nothing," said Defarge; "at least nothing more than would easily elevate himself to a gallows of the same height. I charge myself with him; let him remain with me; I will take care of him, and set him on his road. He wishes to see the fine world—the King, the Queen, and Court; let him see them on Sunday."

"What?" exclaimed the hungry man, staring. "Is it a good sign, that he wishes to see royalty and nobility?"

"Jacques," said Defarge; "judiciously show a cat milk, if you wish her to thirst for it. Judiciously show a dog his natural prey, if you wish him to bring it down one day."

Nothing more was said, and the mender of roads, being found already dozing on the topmost stair, was advised to lay himself down on the pallet-bed and take some rest. He needed no persuasion, and was soon asleep.

Worse quarters than Defarge's wine-shop could easily have been found in Paris for a provincial slave of that degree. Saving for a mysterious dread of madame by which he was constantly haunted, his life was very new and agreeable. But, madame sat all day at her counter, so expressly unconscious of him, and so particularly determined not to perceive that his being there had any connection with anything below the surface, that he shook in his wooden shoes whenever his eye lighted on her. For, he contended with himself that it was impossible to foresee what that lady might pretend next; and he felt assured that if she should take it into her brightly ornamented head to pretend that she had seen him do a murder and afterwards flay the victim, she would infallibly go through with it until the play was played out.

Therefore, when Sunday came, the mender of roads was not enchanted (though he said he was) to find that madame was to accompany monsieur and himself to Versailles. It was additionally disconcerting to have madame knitting all the way there, in a public conveyance; it was additionally disconcerting yet, to have madame in the crowd in the afternoon, still with her knitting in her hands as the crowd waited to see the carriage of the King and Queen.

"You work hard, madame," said a man near her.

"Yes," answered Madame Defarge; "I have much to do."

"What do you make, madame?"

"Many things."

"For instance——"

"For instance," returned Madame Defarge, composedly, "shrouds."

The man moved a little farther away, as soon as he could, and the mender of roads fanned himself with his blue cap: feeling it mightily close and oppressive. If he needed a King and Queen to restore him, he was fortunate in having his remedy at hand; for, soon the large-faced King and the fair-faced Queen[2] came in their golden coach, attended by the shining Bull's Eye[3] of their Court, a glittering multitude of laughing ladies and fine lords; and in jewels and silks and powder and splendor and elegantly spurning figures and handsomely disdainful faces of both sexes, the mender of roads bathed himself, so much to his temporary intoxication, that he cried, "Long live the King, Long live the Queen, Long live everybody and everything!" as if he had never heard of ubiquitous Jacques in his time. During the whole of this scene, which lasted some three hours, he had plenty of shouting and weeping and sentimental company, and throughout Defarge held him by the collar, as if to restrain him from flying at the objects of his brief devotion and tearing them to pieces.

[2] LARGE-FACED KING AND FAIR-FACED QUEEN—Louis XVI and Marie Antoinette.

[3] BULL'S EYE—Meaning here the courtiers in highest favor. The Bull's Eye was a waiting room where the court favorites were permitted to await the King and Queen.

"Bravo!" said Defarge, clapping him on the back when it was over, like a patron; "you are a good boy!"

The mender of roads was now coming to himself, and was mistrustful of having made a mistake in his late demonstrations; but no.

"You are the fellow we want," said Defarge, in his ear; "you make these fools believe that it will last forever. Then, they are the more insolent, and it is the nearer ended."

"Hey!" cried the mender of roads, reflectively; "that's true."

"These fools know nothing. While they despise your breath, and would stop it for ever and ever, in you or in a hundred like you rather than in one of their own horses or dogs, they only know what your breath tells them. Let it deceive them, then, a little longer; it cannot deceive them too much."

Madame Defarge looked superciliously at the client, and nodded in confirmation.

"As to you," said she, "you would shout and shed tears for anything, if it made a show and a noise. Say! Would you not?"

"Truly, madame, I think so. For the moment."

"If you were shown a great heap of dolls, and were set upon them to pluck them to pieces and despoil them for your own advantage, you would pick out the richest and gayest. Say! Would you not?"

"Truly yes, madame."

"Yes. And if you were shown a flock of birds, unable to fly, and were set upon them to strip them of their feathers for your own advantage, you would set upon the birds of the finest feathers; would you not?"

"It is true, madame."

"You have seen both dolls and birds today," said Madame Defarge, with a wave of her hand towards the place where they had last been apparent; "now, go home!"

XIV STILL KNITTING

MADAME DEFARGE and monsieur her husband returned amicably to the bosom of Saint Antoine, while a speck in a blue cap toiled through the darkness, and through the dust, and down the weary miles of avenue by the wayside, slowly tending towards that point of the compass where the château of Monsieur the Marquis, now in his grave, listened to the whispering trees.

The Defarges, husband and wife, came lumbering under the starlight, in their public vehicle, to that gate of Paris whereunto their journey naturally tended. There was the usual stoppage at the barrier guard-house, and the usual lanterns came glancing forth for the usual examination and inquiry. Monsieur Defarge alighted: knowing one or two of the soldiery there, and one of the police. The latter he was intimate with, and affectionately embraced.

When Saint Antoine had again enfolded the Defarges in his dusky wings, and they, having finally alighted near the Saint's boundaries, were picking their way on foot through the black mud of his streets, Madame Defarge spoke to her husband:

"Say then, my friend: what did Jacques of the police tell thee?"

"Very little tonight, but all he knows. There is another spy commissioned for our quarter. There may be many more for all that he can say, but he knows of one."

"Eh, well!" said Madame Defarge, raising her eyebrows with a cool business air. "It is necessary to register him. How do they call that man?"

"He is English."

"So much the better. His name?"

"Barsad," said Defarge, making it French by pronunciation. But, he had been so careful to get it accurately, that he then spelt it with perfect correctness.

"Barsad," repeated madame. "Good. Christian name?"

"John."

"John Barsad," repeated madame, after murmuring it once to herself. "Good. His appearance; is it known?"

"Age, about forty years; height, about five feet nine; black hair; complexion dark; generally, rather handsome visage; eyes dark, face thin, long, and sallow; nose aquiline, but not straight, having a peculiar inclination towards the left cheek; expression, therefore, sinister."

"Eh, my faith. It is a portrait!" said madame, laughing. "He shall be registered tomorrow."

Next noontide saw the admirable woman in her usual place

in the wine-shop, knitting away assiduously. A rose lay beside her, and if she now and then glanced at the flower, it was with no infraction of her usual preoccupied air. There were a few customers, drinking or not drinking, standing or seated, sprinkled about. A figure entering at the door threw a shadow on Madame Defarge which she felt to be a new one. She laid down her knitting, and began to pin her rose in her head-dress, before she looked at the figure.

It was curious. The moment Madame Defarge took up the rose, the customers ceased talking, and began gradually to drop out of the wine-shop.

"Good-day, madame," said the new comer.

"Good-day, monsieur."

She said it aloud, but added to herself, as she resumed her knitting: "Hah! Good day, age about forty, height about five feet nine, black hair, generally rather handsome visage, complexion dark, eyes dark, face thin, long and sallow, aquiline nose but not straight, having a peculiar inclination towards the left cheek which imparts a sinister expression! Good-day, one and all!"

"Have the goodness to give me a little glass of old cognac, and a mouthful of cool, fresh water, madame."

Madame complied with a polite air.

"Marvellous cognac this, madame!"

It was the first time it had ever been so complimented, and Madame Defarge knew enough of its antecedents to know better. She said, however, that the cognac was flattered, and took up her knitting. The visitor watched her fingers for a few moments, and took the opportunity of observing the place in general.

"You knit with great skill, madame."

"I am accustomed to it."

"A pretty pattern too!"

"*You* think so?" said madame, looking at him with a smile.

"Decidedly. May one ask what it is for?"

"Pastime," said madame, looking at him with a smile, while her fingers moved nimbly.

"Not for use?"

"That depends. I may find a use for it, one day. If I do—

well," said madame, drawing a breath and nodding her head with a stern kind of coquetry, "I'll use it!"

It was remarkable; but, the taste of Saint Antoine seemed to be decidedly opposed to a rose on the head-dress of Madame Defarge. Two men had entered separately, and had been about to order drink, when, catching sight of that novelty, they faltered, made a pretence of looking about as if for some friend who was not there, and went away. Nor, of those who had been there when this visitor entered, was there one left. They had all dropped off. The spy had kept his eyes open, but had been able to detect no sign. They had lounged away in a poverty-stricken, purposeless, accidental manner, quite natural and unimpeachable.

"JOHN," thought madame, checking off her work as her fingers knitted, and her eyes looked at the stranger. "Stay long enough, and I shall knit 'BARSAD' before you go."

"You have a husband, madame?"

"I have."

"Children?"

"No children."

"Business seems bad?"

"Business is very bad; the people are so poor."

"Ah, the unfortunate, miserable people! So oppressed too—as you say."

"As *you* say," madame retorted, correcting him, and deftly knitting an extra something into his name that boded him no good.

"Pardon me; certainly it was I who said so, but you naturally think so. Of course."

"*I* think?" returned madame, in a high voice. "I and my husband have enough to do to keep this wine-shop open, without thinking. All we think, here, is, how to live. That is the subject *we* think of, and it gives us, from morning to night, enough to think about, without embarrassing our heads concerning others. *I* think for others? No, no."

The spy, who was there to pick up any crumbs he could find or make, did not allow his baffled state to express itself in his sinister face; but, stood with an air of gossiping gallantry, leaning his elbow on Madame Defarge's little counter, and occasionally sipping his cognac.

"A bad business this, madame, of Gaspard's execution. Ah! the poor Gaspard!" With a sigh of great compassion.

"My faith!" returned madame, coolly and lightly, "if people use knives for such purposes, they have to pay for it. He knew beforehand what the price of his luxury was; he has paid the price."

"I believe," said the spy, dropping his soft voice to a tone that invited confidence, and expressing an injured revolutionary susceptibility in every muscle of his wicked face: "I believe there is much compassion and anger in this neighborhood, touching the poor fellow? Between ourselves."

"Is there?" asked madame, vacantly.

"Is there not?"

"—Here is my husband!" said Madame Defarge.

As the keeper of the wine-shop entered at the door, the spy saluted him by touching his hat, and saying, with an engaging smile, "Good-day, Jacques!" Defarge stopped short, and stared at him.

"Good-day, Jacques!" the spy repeated; with not quite so much confidence, or quite so easy a smile under the stare.

"You deceive yourself, monsieur," returned the keeper of the wine-shop. "You mistake me for another. That is not my name. I am Ernest Defarge."

"It is all the same," said the spy, airily, but discomfited too: "good-day!"

"Good-day!" answered Defarge, dryly.

"I was saying to madame, with whom I had the pleasure of chatting when you entered, that they tell me there is—and no wonder!—much sympathy and anger in Saint Antoine, touching the unhappy fate of poor Gaspard."

"No one has told me so," said Defarge, shaking his head. "I know nothing of it."

Having said it, he passed behind the little counter, and stood with his hand on the back of his wife's chair, looking over that barrier at the person to whom they were both opposed, and whom either of them would have shot with the greatest satisfaction.

The spy, well used to his business, did not change his unconscious attitude, but drained his little glass of cognac, took a sip of fresh water, and asked for another glass of cognac.

Madame Defarge poured it out for him, took to her knitting again, and hummed a little song over it.

"You seem to know this quarter well; that is to say, better than I do?" observed Defarge.

"Not at all, but I hope to know it better. I am so profoundly interested in its miserable inhabitants."

"Hah!" muttered Defarge.

"The pleasure of conversing with you, Monsieur Defarge, recalls to me," pursued the spy, "that I have the honor of cherishing some interesting associations with your name."

"Indeed?" said Defarge, with much indifference.

"Yes, indeed. When Doctor Manette was released, you his old domestic had the charge of him, I know. He was delivered to you. You see I am informed of the circumstances?"

"Such is the fact, certainly," said Defarge. He had had it conveyed to him, in an accidental touch of his wife's elbow as she knitted and warbled, that he would do best to answer, but always with brevity.

"It was to you," said the spy, "that his daughter came; and it was from your care that his daughter took him, accompanied by a neat brown monsieur; how is he called?—in a little wig—Lorry—of the bank of Tellson and Company—over to England."

"Such is the fact," repeated Defarge.

"Very interesting remembrances!" said the spy. "I have known Doctor Manette and his daughter, in England."

"Yes," said Defarge.

"You don't hear much about them now?" said the spy.

"No," said Defarge.

"In effect," madame struck in, looking up from her work and her little song, "we never hear about them. We received the news of their safe arrival, and perhaps another letter or perhaps two; but since then, they have gradually taken their road in life—we, ours—and we have held no correspondence."

"Perfectly so, madame," replied the spy. "She is going to be married."

"Going?" echoed madame. "She was pretty enough to have been married long ago. You English are cold, it seems to me."

"Oh! You know I am English?"

"I perceive your tongue is," returned madame; "and what the tongue is, I suppose the man is."

He did not take the identification as a compliment; but, he made the best of it, and turned it off with a laugh. After sipping his cognac to the end, he added:

"Yes, Miss Manette is going to be married. But not to an Englishman; to one who, like herself, is French by birth. And speaking of Gaspard (ah, poor Gaspard! It was cruel, cruel!), it is a curious thing that she is going to marry the nephew of Monsieur the Marquis, for whom Gaspard was exalted to that height of so many feet; in other words, the present Marquis. But he lives unknown in England, he is no Marquis there; he is Mr. Charles Darnay. D'Aulnais is the name of his mother's family."

Madame Defarge knitted steadily, but the intelligence had a palpable effect upon her husband. Do what he would, behind the little counter, as to the striking of a light and the lighting of his pipe, he was troubled, and his hand was not trustworthy. The spy would have been no spy if he had failed to see it, or to record it in his mind.

Having made, at least, this one hit, whatever it might prove to be worth, and no customers coming in to help him to any other, Mr. Barsad paid for what he had drunk, and took his leave: taking occasion to say, in a genteel manner, before he departed, that he looked forward to the pleasure of seeing Monsieur and Madame Defarge again. For some minutes after he had emerged into the outer presence of Saint Antoine, the husband and wife remained exactly as he had left them, lest he should come back.

"Can it be true," said Defarge, in a low voice, looking down at his wife as he stood smoking with his hand on the back of her chair: "what he has said of Ma'amselle Manette?"

"As he has said it," returned madame, lifting her eyebrows a little, "it is probably false. But it may be true."

"If it is—" Defarge began; and stopped.

"If it is?" repeated his wife.

"—And if it does come, while we live to see it triumph—I hope, for her sake, destiny will keep her husband out of France."

"Her husband's destiny," said Madame Defarge, with her usual composure, "will take him where he is to go, and will lead him to the end that is to end him. That is all I know."

"But it is very strange—now, at least is it not very strange" —said Defarge, rather pleading with his wife to induce her to admit it, "that, after all our sympathy for Monsieur her father and herself, her husband's name should be proscribed under your hand at this moment, by the side of that infernal dog's who has just left us?"

"Stranger things than that will happen when it does come," answered madame. "I have them both here, of a certainty; and they are both here for their merits; that is enough."

She rolled up her knitting when she had said those words, and presently took the rose out of the handkerchief that was wound about her head. Either Saint Antoine had an instinctive sense that the objectionable decoration was gone, or Saint Antoine was on the watch for its disappearance; howbeit, the Saint Antoine inhabitants took courage to lounge in, very shortly afterwards, and the wine-shop recovered its habitual aspect.

XV NINE DAYS

It was Lucie's marriage day. The sun was shining brightly, and they were ready outside the closed door of the Doctor's room, where he was speaking with Charles Darnay. They were ready to go to church; the beautiful bride, Mr. Lorry, and Miss Pross—to whom the event, though a gradual process of reconcilement to the inevitable, would have been one of absolute bliss, but for the yet lingering consideration that her brother Solomon should have been the bridegroom.

"And so," said Mr. Lorry, who could not sufficiently admire the bride, and who had been moving round her to take in every point of her quiet, pretty dress; "and so it was for this, my sweet Lucie, that I brought you across the Channel, such a baby! Lord bless me! How little I thought what I was doing. How lightly I valued the obligation I was conferring on my friend Mr. Charles!"

"You didn't mean it," remarked the matter-of-fact Miss Pross, "and therefore how could you know it? Nonsense!"

"Really? Well; but don't cry," said the gentle Mr. Lorry.

"I am not crying," said Miss Pross; "*you* are."

"I, my Pross?" (By this time, Mr. Lorry dared to be pleasant with her, on occasion.)

"You were just now; I saw you do it, and I don't wonder at it. Such a present of plate as you have made 'em, is enough to bring tears into anybody's eyes. There's not a fork or a spoon in the collection," said Miss Pross, "that I didn't cry over, last night after the box came, till I couldn't see it."

"I am highly gratified," said Mr. Lorry, "though, upon my honor, I had no intention of rendering those trifling articles of remembrance, invisible to any one. Dear me! This is an occasion that makes a man speculate on all he has lost. Dear, dear, dear! To think that there might have been a Mrs. Lorry, any time these fifty years almost! Enough! Now, my dear Lucie," drawing his arm soothingly round her waist, "I hear them moving in the next room, and Miss Pross and I, as two formal folks of business, are anxious not to lose the final opportunity of saying something to you that you wish to hear. You leave your good father, my dear, in hands as earnest and as loving as your own; he shall be taken every conceivable care of; during the next fortnight, while you are in Warwickshire and thereabouts, even Tellson's shall go to the wall before him. And when, at the fortnight's end, he comes to join you and your beloved husband, on your other fortnight's trip in Wales, you shall say that we have sent him to you in the best health and in the happiest frame. Now, I hear Somebody's step coming to the door. Let me kiss my dear girl with

an old-fashioned bachelor blessing, before Somebody comes to claim his own."

For a moment, he held the fair face from him to look at the well-remembered expression on the forehead, and then laid the bright golden hair against his little brown wig, with a genuine tenderness and delicacy, which, if such things be old fashioned, were as old as Adam.

The door of the Doctor's room opened, and he came out with Charles Darnay. He was so deadly pale—which had not been the case when they went in together—that no vestige of color was to be seen in his face. But, in the composure of his manner he was unaltered, except that to the shrewd glance of Mr. Lorry it disclosed some shadowy indication that the old air of avoidance and dread had lately passed over him, like a cold wind.

He gave his arm to his daughter, and took her downstairs to the chariot which Mr. Lorry had hired in honor of the day. The rest followed in another carriage, and soon, in a neighboring church where no strange eyes looked on, Charles Darnay and Lucie Manette were happily married.

Besides the glancing tears that shone among the smiles of the little group when it was done, some diamonds, very bright and sparkling, glanced on the bride's hand, which were newly released from the dark obscurity of one of Mr. Lorry's pockets. They returned home to breakfast, and all went well, and in due course the golden hair that had mingled with the poor shoemaker's white locks in the Paris garret, were mingled with them again in the morning sunlight, on the threshold of the door at parting.

It was a hard parting, though it was not for long. But her father cheered her, and said at last, gently disengaging himself from her enfolding arms, "Take her, Charles! She is yours!" And her agitated hand waved to them from a chaise window, and she was gone.

The corner being out of the way of the idle and curious, and the preparations having been very simple and few, the Doctor, Mr. Lorry, and Miss Pross, were left quite alone. It was when they turned into the welcome shade of the cool old hall, that Mr. Lorry observed a great change to have come over the Doctor; as if he had been struck a poisoned blow.

He had naturally repressed much, and some revulsion might have been expected in him when the occasion for repression was gone. But, it was the old scared lost look that troubled Mr. Lorry; and through his absent manner of clasping his head and drearily wandering away into his own room when they got upstairs, Mr. Lorry was reminded of Defarge the wine-shop keeper, and the starlight ride.

"I think," he whispered to Miss Pross, after anxious consideration, "I think we had best not speak to him just now, or at all disturb him. I must look in at Tellson's; so I will go there at once and come back presently. Then, we will take him a ride into the country, and dine there, and all will be well."

It was easier for Mr. Lorry to look in at Tellson's, than to look out of Tellson's. He was detained two hours. When he came back, he ascended the old staircase alone, having asked no question of the servant; going thus into the Doctor's rooms, he was stopped by a low sound of knocking.

"Good God!" he said, with a start. "What's that?"

Miss Pross, with a terrified face, was at his ear. "O, me, O, me! All is lost!" cried she, wringing her hands. "What is to be told to Ladybird? He doesn't know me, and is making shoes!"

Mr. Lorry said what he could to calm her, and went himself into the Doctor's room. The bench was turned towards the light, as it had been when he had seen the shoemaker at his work before, and his head was bent down, and he was very busy.

"Doctor Manette. My dear friend, Doctor Manette!"

The Doctor looked at him for a moment—half inquiringly, half as if he were angry at being spoken to—and bent over his work again.

He had laid aside his coat and waistcoat; his shirt was open at the throat, as it used to be when he did that work; and even the old haggard faded surface of face had come back to him. He worked hard—impatiently—as if in some sense of having been interrupted.

Mr. Lorry glanced at the work in his hand, and observed that it was a shoe of the old size and shape. He took up another that was lying by him, and asked him what it was?

"A young lady's walking shoe," he muttered, without looking up. "It ought to have been finished long ago. Let it be."

"But, Doctor Manette. Look at me!"

He obeyed, in the old mechanically submissive manner, without pausing in his work.

"You know me, my dear friend? Think again. This is not your proper occupation. Think, dear friend!"

Nothing would induce him to speak more. He looked up, for an instant at a time, when he was requested to do so; but, no persuasion could extract a word from him. He worked, and worked, and worked, in silence, and words fell on him as they would have fallen on an echoless wall, or on the air. The only ray of hope that Mr. Lorry could discover was that he sometimes furtively looked up without being asked. In that, there seemed a faint expression of curiosity or perplexity—as though he were trying to reconcile some doubts in his mind.

Two things at once impressed themselves on Mr. Lorry, as important above all others; the first, that this must be kept secret from Lucie; the second, that it must be kept secret from all who knew him. In conjunction with Miss Pross, he took immediate steps towards the latter precaution, by giving out that the Doctor was not well, and required a few days of complete rest. In aid of the kind deception to be practised on his daughter, Miss Pross was to write, describing his having been called away professionally, and referring to an imaginary letter of two or three hurried lines in his own hand, represented to have been addressed to her by the same post.

These measures, advisable to be taken in any case, Mr. Lorry took in the hope of his coming to himself. If that should happen soon, he kept another course in reserve; which was, to have a certain opinion that he thought the best, on the Doctor's case.

In the hope of his recovery, and of resort to this third course being thereby rendered practicable, Mr. Lorry resolved to watch him attentively, with as little appearance as possible of doing so. He therefore made arrangements to absent himself from Tellson's for the first time in his life, and took his post by the window in the same room.

He was not long in discovering that it was worse than useless to speak to him, since, on being pressed, he became worried. He abandoned that attempt on the first day, and resolved merely to keep himself always before him, as a silent protest against the delusion into which he had fallen, or was falling. He remained, therefore, in his seat near the window, reading and writing, and expressing in as many pleasant and natural ways as he could think of, that it was a free place.

Doctor Manette took what was given him to eat and drink, and worked on, that first day, until it was too dark to see—, worked on half an hour after Mr. Lorry could not have seen, for his life, to read or write. When he put his tools aside as useless, until morning, Mr. Lorry rose and said to him:

"Will you go out?"

He looked down at the floor on either side of him in the old manner, looked up in the old manner and repeated in the old low voice:

"Out?"

"Yes; for a walk with me. Why not?"

He made no effort to say why not, and said not a word more. But, Mr. Lorry thought he saw, as he leaned forward on his bench in the dusk, with his elbows on his knees and his head in his hands, that he was in some misty way asking himself, "Why not?" The sagacity of the man of business perceived an advantage here, and determined to hold it.

Miss Pross and he divided the night into two watches, and observed him at intervals from the adjoining room. He paced up and down for a long time before he lay down; but, when he did finally lay himself down, he fell asleep. In the morning, he was up betimes, and went straight to his bench and to work.

On this second day, Mr. Lorry saluted him cheerfully by his name, and spoke to him on topics that had been of late familiar to them. He returned no reply, but it was evident that he heard what was said, and that he thought about it, however confusedly. This encouraged Mr. Lorry to have Miss Pross in with her work, several times during the day; at those times, they quietly spoke of Lucie, and of her father then present, precisely in their usual manner, and as if there were nothing amiss. This was done without any demonstrative accompaniment, not long enough, or often enough to harass him; and it lightened Mr. Lorry's friendly heart to believe that he looked up oftener, and that he appeared to be stirred by some perception of inconsistencies surrounding him.

When it fell dark again, Mr. Lorry asked him as before:

"Dear Doctor, will you go out?"

As before, he repeated, "Out?"

"Yes; for a walk with me. Why not?"

This time, Mr. Lorry feigned to go out when he could extract no answer from him, and, after remaining absent for an hour, returned. In the meanwhile, the Doctor had removed to the seat in the window, and had sat there looking down at the plane-tree; but, on Mr. Lorry's return, he slipped away to his bench.

The time went very slowly on, and Mr. Lorry's hope darkened, and his heart grew heavier again, and grew yet heavier and heavier every day. The third day came and went, the fourth, the fifth. Five days, six days, seven days, eight days, nine days.

With a hope ever darkening, and with a heart always growing heavier and heavier, Mr. Lorry passed through this anxious time. The secret was well kept, and Lucie was unconscious and happy; but, he could not fail to observe that the shoemaker, whose hand had been a little out at first, was growing dreadfully skilful, and that he had never been so intent on his work, and that his hands had never been so nimble and expert, as in the dusk of the ninth evening.

XVI AN OPINION

Worn out by anxious watching, Mr. Lorry fell asleep at his post. On the tenth morning of his suspense, he was startled by the shining of the sun into the room where a heavy slumber had overtaken him when it was dark night.

He rubbed his eyes and roused himself; but he doubted, when he had done so, whether he was not still asleep. For, going to the door of the Doctor's room and looking in, he perceived that the shoemaker's bench and tools were put aside again, and that the Doctor himself sat reading at the window. He was in his usual morning dress, and his face, though still very pale, was calmly studious and attentive.

Even when he had satisfied himself that he was awake, Mr. Lorry felt giddily uncertain for some few moments whether the late shoemaking might not be a disturbed dream of his own; for, did not his eyes show him his friend before him in his accustomed clothing and aspect, and employed as usual; and was there any sign within their range, that the change of which he had so strong an impression had actually happened?

Within a few minutes, Miss Pross stood whispering at his

side. If he had had any particle of doubt left, her talk would of necessity have resolved it; but he was by that time clear-headed, and had none. He advised that they should let the time go by until the regular breakfast-hour, and should then meet the Doctor as if nothing unusual had occurred. If he appeared to be in his customary state of mind, Mr. Lorry would then cautiously proceed to seek direction and guidance from the opinion he had been, in his anxiety, so anxious to obtain.

Miss Pross, submitting herself to his judgment, the scheme was worked out with care. Having abundance of time for his usual methodical toilette, Mr. Lorry presented himself at the breakfast-hour in his usual white linen and with his usual neat leg. The Doctor was summoned in the usual way, and came to breakfast.

So far as it was possible to comprehend him without overstepping those delicate and gradual approaches which Mr. Lorry felt to be the only safe advance, he at first supposed that his daughter's marriage had taken place yesterday. An incidental allusion, purposely thrown out, to the day of the week, and the day of the month, set him thinking and counting, and evidently made him uneasy. In all other respects, however, he was so composedly himself, that Mr. Lorry determined to have the aid he sought. And that aid was his own.

Therefore, when the breakfast was done and cleared away, and he and the Doctor were left together, Mr. Lorry said, feelingly:

"My dear Manette, I am anxious to have your opinion, in confidence, on a very curious case in which I am deeply interested; that is to say, it is very curious to me; perhaps, to your better information it may be less so."

Glancing at his hands, which were discolored by his late work, the Doctor looked troubled, and listened attentively. He had already glanced at his hands more than once.

"Doctor Manette," said Mr. Lorry, touching him affectionately on the arm, "the case is the case of a particularly dear friend of mine. Pray give your mind to it, and advise me well for his sake—and above all for his daughter's—his daughter's, my dear Manette."

"If I understand," said the Doctor, in a subdued tone, "some mental shock——?"

"Yes!"

"Be explicit," said the Doctor. "Spare no detail."

Mr. Lorry saw that they understood one another, and proceeded.

"My dear Manette, it is the case of an old and a prolonged shock, of great acuteness and severity, to the affections, the feelings, the—the—as you express it—the mind. The mind. It is the case of a shock under which the sufferer was borne down, one cannot say for how long, because I believe he cannot calculate the time himself, and there are no other means of getting at it. It is the case of a shock from which the sufferer recovered, by a process that he cannot trace himself—as I once heard him publicly relate in a striking manner. It is the case of a shock from which he has recovered, so completely, as to be a highly intelligent man, capable of close application of mind, and great exertion of body, and of constantly making fresh additions to his stock of knowledge, which was already very large. But, unfortunately, there has been," he paused and took a deep breath —"a slight relapse."

The Doctor, in a low voice, asked, "Of how long duration?"

"Nine days and nights."

"How did it show itself? I infer," glancing at his hands again, "in the resumption of some old pursuit connected with the shock?"

"That is the fact."

"Now, did you ever see him," asked the Doctor, distinctly and collectedly, though in the same low voice, "engaged in that pursuit originally?"

"Once."

"And when the relapse fell on him, was he in most respects— or in all respects—as he was then?"

"I think, in all respects."

"You spoke of his daughter. Does his daughter know of the relapse?"

"No. It has been kept from her, and I hope will always be kept from her. It is known only to myself, and to one other who may be trusted."

The Doctor grasped his hand, and murmured, "That was very kind. That was very thoughtful!" Mr. Lorry grasped his hand in return, and neither of the two spoke for a little while.

"I think it probable," said the Doctor, breaking silence with an effort, "that the relapse you have described, my dear friend, was not quite unforeseen by its subject."

"Was it dreaded by him?" Mr. Lorry ventured to ask.

"Very much." He said it with an involuntary shudder. "You have no idea how such an apprehension weighs on the sufferer's mind, and how difficult—how almost impossible—it is for him to force himself to utter a word upon the topic that oppresses him."

"Would he," asked Mr. Lorry, "be sensibly relieved if he could prevail upon himself to impart that secret brooding to any one, when it is on him?"

"I think so. But it is, as I have told you, next to impossible. I even believe it—in some cases—to be quite impossible."

"Now," said Mr. Lorry, gently laying his hand on the Doctor's arm again, after a short silence on both sides, "to what would you refer this attack?"

"I believe," returned Doctor Manette, "that there had been a strong and extraordinary revival of the train of thought and remembrance that was the first cause of the malady. Some intense associations of a most distressing nature were vividly recalled, I think. It is probable that there had long been a dread lurking in his mind, that those associations would be recalled—say, under certain circumstances—say, on a particular occasion. He tried to prepare himself, in vain; perhaps the effort to prepare himself, made him less able to bear it."

"Would he remember what took place in the relapse?" asked Mr. Lorry, with natural hesitation.

The Doctor looked desolately round the room, shook his head, and answered, in a low voice, "Not at all."

"Now, as to the future," hinted Mr. Lorry.

"As to the future," said the Doctor, recovering firmness, "I should have great hope. I do not think that anything but the one train of association would renew it. I think, that henceforth, nothing but some extraordinary jarring of that chord could renew it. After what has happened, and after his recovery, I find it difficult to imagine any such violent sounding of that string again. I trust, and I almost believe, that the circumstances likely to renew it are exhausted."

He spoke with the diffidence of a man who knew how slight

a thing would overset the delicate organization of the mind, and yet with the confidence of a man who had slowly won his assurance out of personal endurance and distress.

"The occupation resumed under the influence of this passing affliction so happily recovered from," said Mr. Lorry, clearing his throat, "we will call—blacksmith's work. Blacksmith's work. We will say, to put a case and for the sake of illustration, that he had been used in his bad time, to work at a little forge. We will say that he was unexpectedly found at his forge again. Is it not a pity that he should keep it by him?"

The Doctor shaded his forehead with his hand, and beat his foot nervously on the ground.

"He has always kept it by him," said Mr. Lorry, with an anxious look at his friend. "Now, would it not be better that he should let it go?"

Still, the Doctor, with shaded forehead, beat his foot nervously on the ground.

"You do not find it easy to advise me?" said Mr. Lorry. "I quite understand it to be a nice question. And yet I think——" And there he shook his head, and stopped.

"You see," said Doctor Manette, turning to him after an uneasy pause, "it is very hard to explain, consistently, the innermost working of this poor man's mind. He once yearned so frightfully for that occupation, and it was so welcome when it came; no doubt it relieved his pain so much, by substituting the perplexity of the fingers for the perplexity of the brain, and by substituting, as he became more practised, the ingenuity of the hands for the ingenuity of the mental torture; that he has never been able to bear the thought of putting it quite out of his reach. Even now when, I believe, he is more hopeful of himself than he has ever been, and even speaks of himself with a kind of confidence, the idea that he might need that old employment, and not find it, gives him a sudden sense of terror, like that which one may fancy strikes to the heart of a lost child."

He looked like his illustration, as he raised his eyes to Mr. Lorry's face.

"But may not the retention of the thing involve the retention of the idea? If the thing were gone, my dear Manette, might not the fear go with it? In short, is it not a concession to the misgiving, to keep the forge?"

There was another silence.

"You see, too," said the Doctor, tremulously, "it is such an old companion."

"I would not keep it," said Mr. Lorry, shaking his head; for he gained in firmness as he saw the Doctor disquieted. "I would recommend him to sacrifice it. I only want your authority. I am sure it does no good. Come! Give me your authority, like a dear good man. For his daughter's sake, my dear Manette!"

Very strange to see what a struggle there was within him!

"In her name, then, let it be done; I sanction it. But, I would not take it away while he was present. Let it be removed when he is not there; let him miss his old companion after an absence."

Mr. Lorry readily engaged for that, and the conference was ended. They passed the day in the country, and the Doctor was quite restored. On the three following days, he remained perfectly well, and on the fourteenth day, he went away to join Lucie and her husband. The precaution that had been taken to account for his silence, Mr. Lorry had previously explained to him, and he had written to Lucie in accordance with it, and she had no suspicions.

On the night of the day on which he left the house, Mr. Lorry went into his room with a chopper, saw, chisel, and hammer, attended by Miss Pross carrying a light. There, with closed doors, and in a mysterious and guilty manner, Mr. Lorry hacked the shoemaker's bench to pieces, while Miss Pross held the candle as if she were assisting at a murder—for which, indeed, in her grimness, she was no unsuitable figure. The burning of the body was commenced without delay in the kitchen fire; and the tools, shoes, and leathers were buried in the garden. So wicked do destruction and secrecy appear to honest minds, that Mr. Lorry and Miss Pross, while engaged in the commission of their deed and in the removal of its traces, almost felt, and almost looked, like accomplices in a horrible crime.

XVII A PLEA

When the newly-married couple came home, the first person who appeared, to offer his congratulations, was Sydney Carton. They had not been at home many hours, when he presented himself. He was not improved in habits, or in looks, or in manner; but, there was a certain rugged air of fidelity about him, which was new to the observation of Charles Darnay.

He watched his opportunity of taking Darnay aside into a window, and of speaking to him when no one overheard.

"Mr. Darnay," said Carton, "I wish we might be friends."

"We are already friends, I hope."

"You are good enough to say so, as a fashion of speech; but, I don't mean any fashion of speech. You remember a certain famous occasion when I was more drunk than—than usual? On that occasion I was insufferable about liking you, and not liking you. I wish you would forget it."

"I forgot it long ago."

"Fashion of speech again! But, Mr. Darnay, oblivion is not so easy to me, as you represent it to be to you. I have by no means forgotten it, and a light answer does not help me to forget it."

"If it was a light answer," returned Darnay, "I beg your forgiveness for it. Have I had nothing more important to remember, in the great service you rendered me that day?"

"As to the great service," said Carton, "I am bound to avow to you, when you speak of it in that way, that it was mere professional clap-trap. I don't know that I cared what became of you, when I rendered it.—Mind! I say when I rendered it; I am speaking of the past."

"You make light of the obligation," returned Darnay, "but I will not quarrel with *your* light answer."

"Genuine truth, Mr. Darnay, trust me! I have gone aside from my purpose; I was speaking about our being friends. Now, you know me; you know I am incapable of all the higher and better flights of men. But if you could endure to have such a worthless fellow, and a fellow of such indifferent reputation, coming and going at odd times, I should ask that I might be permitted to come and go as a privileged person here; that I might be regarded as a useless piece of furniture, tolerated for its old service, and taken no notice of. I doubt if I should abuse the permission. It is a hundred to one if I should avail myself of it four times in a year. It would satisfy me, I dare say, to know that I had it."

"Will you try?"

"That is another way of saying that I am placed on the footing I have indicated. I thank you, Darnay. I may use that freedom with your name?"

"I think so, Carton, by this time."

They shook hands upon it, and Sydney turned away. Within a minute afterwards he was, to all outward appearance, as unsubstantial as ever.

When he was gone, and in the course of an evening passed with Miss Pross, the Doctor, and Mr. Lorry, Charles Darnay made some mention of this conversation in general terms, and spoke of Sydney Carton as a problem of carelessness and recklessness. He spoke of him, in short, not bitterly or meaning to bear hard upon him, but as anybody might who saw him as he showed himself.

He had no idea that this could dwell in the thoughts of his fair young wife; but, when he afterwards joined her in their own room, he found her waiting for him with the old pretty lifting of the forehead strongly marked.

"What is it, my Lucie?"

"Will you promise not to press one question on me, if I beg you not to ask it?"

"Will I promise? What will I not promise to my love?"

"I think, Charles, poor Mr. Carton deserves more consideration and respect than you expressed for him tonight."

"Indeed, my own? Why so?"

"That is what you are not to ask me. But I think—I know—he does."

"If you know it, it is enough. What would you have me do, my life?"

"I would ask you, dearest, to be very generous with him always, and very lenient on his faults when he is not by. I would ask you to believe that he has a heart he very, very seldom reveals, and that there are deep wounds in it. My dear, I have seen it bleeding."

"It is a painful reflection to me," said Charles Darnay, quite astounded, "that I should have done him any wrong. I never thought this of him."

"My husband, it is so. I am sure that he is capable of good things, gentle things, even magnanimous things."

He bent over the golden head, and put the rosy lips to his, and folded her in his arms. If one forlorn wanderer then pacing the dark streets, could have heard her innocent disclosure, and could have seen the drops of pity kissed away by her husband from the soft blue eyes so loving of that husband, he might have cried to the night—and the words would not have parted from his lips for the first time—

"God bless her for her sweet compassion!"

XVIII ECHOING FOOTSTEPS

A WONDERFUL corner for echoes, it has been remarked, that corner where the Doctor lived. Ever busily winding the golden thread which bound her husband, and her father, and herself, and her old directress and companion, in a life of quiet bliss, Lucie sat in the still house in the tranquilly resounding corner, listening to the echoing footsteps of years.

At first, there were times, though she was a perfectly happy young wife, when her work would slowly fall from her hand, and her eyes would be dimmed. For there was something coming in the echoes, something light, afar off, and scarcely audible yet, that stirred her heart too much. Fluttering hopes and doubts— hopes, of a love as yet unknown to her; doubts, of her remaining upon earth, to enjoy that new delight—divided her breast. Among the echoes then, there would arise the sound of footsteps at her own early grave; and thoughts of the husband who would be left so desolate, and who would mourn for her so much, swelled to her eyes and broke like waves.

That time passed, and her little Lucie lay on her bosom. Then, among the advancing echoes, there was the tread of her tiny feet and the sound of her prattling words. Let greater echoes resound as they would, the young mother at the cradle side could always hear those coming. They came, and the shady house was sunny with a child's laugh, and the Divine friend of children, to whom in her trouble she had confided hers, seemed to take her child in His arms, as He took the child of old, and made it a sacred joy to her.

Ever busily winding the golden thread that bound them all together, weaving the service of her happy influence through the tissue of all their lives, and making it predominate nowhere, Lucie heard in the echoes of years none but friendly and soothing sounds. Her husband's step was strong and prosperous among them; her father's, firm and equal. Lo, Miss Pross, in harness of string, awakening the echoes, as an unruly charger, whip-corrected, snorting and pawing the earth under the plane-tree in the garden!

The echoes rarely answered to the actual tread of Sydney Carton. Some half-dozen times a year, at most, he claimed his privilege of coming in uninvited, and would sit among them through the evening as he had once done often. He never came there, heated with wine. And one other thing regarding him was whispered in the echoes, which has been whispered by all true echoes for ages and ages.

No man ever really loved a woman, lost her, and knew her with a blameless though an unchanged mind, when she was a wife and a mother, but her children had a strange sympathy with him—an instinctive delicacy of pity for him. What fine hidden sensibilities are touched in such a case, no echoes tell; but it is so, and it was so here, for Carton was the first stranger to whom little Lucie held out her chubby arms and he kept his place with her as she grew.

These were among the echoes to which Lucie, sometimes pensive, sometimes amused and laughing, listened in the echoing corner, until her little daughter was six years old. How near to her heart the echoes of her child's tread came, and those of her own dear father's, always active and self-possessed, and those of her dear husband's, need not be told. Nor, how the lightest echo of their united home, directed by herself with such a wise and elegant thrift that it was more abundant than any waste, was music to her. Nor, how there were echoes all about her, sweet in her ears, of the many times her father had told her that he found her more devoted to him married (if that could be) than single, and of the many times her husband had said to her that no cares and duties seemed to divide her love for him or her help to him, and asked her "What is the magic secret, my darling, of your being everything to all of us, as if there were only one of us, yet never seeming to be hurried, or to have too much to do?"

But, there were other echoes, from a distance, that rumbled menacingly in the corner all through this space of time. And it was now, about little Lucie's sixth birthday, that they began to have an awful sound, as of a great storm in France with a dreadful sea rising.

On a night in mid-July, one thousand seven hundred and eighty-nine, Mr. Lorry came in late, from Tellson's, and sat himself down by Lucie and her husband in the dark window. It was a hot wild night, and they were all three reminded of the old Sunday night when they had looked at the lightning from the same place.

"I began to think," said Mr. Lorry, pushing his brown wig back, "that I should have to pass the night at Tellson's. We have been so full of business all day, that we have not known what to do first, or which way to turn. There is such an uneasiness in Paris, that we have actually a run of confidence upon us! Our customers over there, seem not to be able to confide their property to us fast enough. There is positively a mania among some of them for sending it to England."

"That has a bad look," said Darnay.

"A bad look, you say, my dear Darnay? Yes, but we don't know what reason there is in it. People are so unreasonable! Some of us at Tellson's are getting old, and we really can't be troubled out of the ordinary course without due occasion."

"Still," said Darnay, "you know how gloomy and threatening the sky is."

"I know that, to be sure," assented Mr. Lorry, trying to persuade himself that his sweet temper was soured, and that he grumbled, "but I am determined to be peevish after my long day's botheration. Where is Manette?"

"Here he is!" said the Doctor, entering the dark room at the moment.

"I am quite glad you are at home; for these hurries and forebodings by which I have been surrounded all day long, have made me nervous without reason. You are not going out, I hope?"

"No; I am going to play backgammon with you, if you like," said the Doctor.

"I don't think I do like, if I may speak my mind. I am not fit to be pitted against you tonight. Is the tea-board still there, Lucie? I can't see."

"Of course, it has been kept for you."

"Thank ye, my dear. The precious child is safe in bed?"

"And sleeping soundly."

"That's right; all safe and well! I don't know why anything should be otherwise than safe and well here, thank God; but I have been so put out all day, and I am not as young as I was! My tea, my dear? Thank ye. Now, come and take your place in the circle, and let us sit quiet, and hear the echoes about which you have your theory."

"Not a theory; it was a fancy."

"A fancy, then, my wise pet," said Mr. Lorry, patting her hand. "They are very numerous and very loud, though, are they not? Only hear them!"

Headlong mad and dangerous footsteps to force their way into anybody's life, footsteps not easily made clean again if once stained red, the footsteps raging in Saint Antoine afar off, as the little circle sat in the dark London window.

Saint Antoine had been, that morning, a vast dusky mass of scarecrows heaving to and fro, with frequent gleams of light above the billowy heads, where steel blades and bayonets shone in the sun. A tremendous roar arose from the throat of Saint Antoine, and a forest of naked arms struggled in the air like shrivelled branches of trees in a winter wind: all the fingers convulsively clutching at every weapon or semblance of a weapon that was thrown up from the depths below, no matter how far off.

Who gave them out, whence they last came, where they began, through what agency they crookedly quivered and jerked, scores at a time, over the heads of the crowd, like a kind of lightning, no eye in the throng could have told; but, muskets were being distributed—so were cartridges, powder, and ball, bars of iron and wood, knives, axes, pikes, every weapon that distracted ingenuity could discover or devise. People who could lay hold of nothing else, set themselves with bleeding hands to force stones and bricks out of their places in walls. Every pulse and heart in Saint Antoine was on high-fever strain and at high-fever heat. Every living creature there held life as of no account, and was demented with a passionate readiness to sacrifice it.

As a whirlpool of boiling waters has a center point, so, all this raging circled round Defarge's wine-shop, and every human drop in the caldron had a tendency to be sucked towards the vortex where Defarge himself, already begrimed with gunpowder and sweat, issued orders, issued arms, thrust this man back, dragged this man forward, disarmed one to arm another, labored and strove in the thickest of the uproar.

"Keep near to me, Jacques Three," cried Defarge; "and do you, Jacques One and Two, separate and put yourselves at the head of as many of these patriots as you can. Where is my wife?"

"Eh, well! Here you see me!" said madame, composed as ever, but not knitting today. Madame's resolute right hand was occupied with an axe, in place of the usual softer implements, and in her girdle were a pistol and a cruel knife.

"Where do you go, my wife?"

"I go," said madame, "with you, at present. You shall see me at the head of women, by-and-by."

"Come, then!" cried Defarge, in a resounding voice. "Patriots and friends, we are ready! The Bastille!"[1]

With a roar that sounded as if all the breath in France had been shaped into the detested word, the living sea rose, wave on wave, depth on depth, and overflowed the city to that point. Alarm-bells ringing, drums beating, the sea raging and thundering on its new beach, the attack began.

Deep ditches, double drawbridge, massive stone walls, eight great towers, cannon, muskets, fire and smoke. Through the fire and through the smoke—in the fire and in the smoke, for the sea cast him up against a cannon, and on the instant he became a cannoneer—Defarge of the wine-shop worked like a manful soldier, Two fierce hours.

Deep ditch, single drawbridge, massive stone walls, eight great towers, cannon, muskets, fire and smoke. One drawbridge

---

[1] THE BASTILLE—The Bastille was attacked and captured on July 14, 1789. July 14th is a national holiday in France.

down! "Work, comrades all, work! Work, Jacques One, Jacques Two, Jacques One Thousand, Jacques Two Thousand, Jacques Five-and-Twenty Thousand; in the name of all the Angels or the Devils—which you prefer—work!" Thus Defarge of the wine-shop, still at his gun, which had long grown hot.

"To me, women!" cried madame his wife. "What! We can kill as well as the men when the place is taken!" And to her, with a shrill thirsty cry, trooping women variously armed, but all armed alike in hunger and revenge.

Cannon, muskets, fire and smoke; but, still the deep ditch, the single drawbridge, the massive stone walls, and the eight great towers. Slight displacements of the raging sea, made by the falling wounded. Flashing weapons, blazing torches, smoking wagon-loads of wet straw, hard work at neighboring barricades in all directions, shrieks, volleys, execrations, bravery without stint, boom smash and rattle, and the furious sounding of the living sea; but, still the deep ditch, and the single drawbridge, and the massive stone walls, and the eight great towers, and still Defarge of the wine-shop at his gun, grown doubly hot by the service of Four fierce hours.

A white flag from within the fortress, and a parley—this dimly perceptible through the raging storm, nothing audible in it—suddenly the sea rose immeasurably wider and higher, and swept Defarge of the wine-shop over the lowered drawbridge, past the massive stone outer walls, in among the eight great towers surrendered!

So resistless was the force of the ocean bearing him on, that even to draw his breath or turn his head was as impracticable as if he had been struggling in the surf of the South Sea,[2] until he was landed in the outer courtyard of the Bastille. There, against an angle of a wall, he made a struggle to look about him. Jacques Three was nearly at his side; Madame Defarge still heading some of her women, was visible in the inner distance, and her knife was in her hand. Everywhere was tumult, exultation, deafening and maniacal bewilderment, astounding noise, yet furious dumb-show.

"The prisoners!"
"The records!"

[2] SOUTH SEA—The Pacific Ocean, so-called until the nineteenth century.

"The secret cells!"
"The instruments of torture!"
"The prisoners!"

Of all these cries, and ten thousand incoherencies, "The Prisoners!" was the cry most taken up by the sea that rushed in, as if there were an eternity of people, as well as of time and space. When the foremost billows rolled past, bearing the prison officers with them, and threatening them all with instant death if any secret nook remained undisclosed, Defarge laid his strong hand on the breast of one of these men—a man with a grey head who had a lighted torch in his hand—separated him from the rest, and got him between himself and the wall.

"Show me the North Tower!" said Defarge. "Quick!"

"I will faithfully," replied the man, "if you will come with me. But there is no one there."

"What is the meaning of One Hundred and Five, North Tower?" asked Defarge. "Quick!"

"The meaning, monsieur?"

"Does it mean a captive, or a place of captivity? Or do you mean that I shall strike you dead?"

"Kill him!" croaked Jacques Three, who had come close up.

"Monsieur, it is a cell."

"Show it me!"

"Pass this way, then."

Jacques Three, with his usual craving on him, and evidently disappointed by the dialogue taking a turn that did not seem to promise bloodshed, held by Defarge's arm as he held by the turnkey's. Their three heads had been close together during this brief discourse, and it had been as much as they could do to hear one another, even then: so tremendous was the noise of the living ocean, in its irruption into the Fortress, and its inundation of the courts and passages and staircases. All around outside, too, it beat the walls with a deep, hoarse roar, from which, occasionally, some partial shouts of tumult broke and leaped into the air like spray.

Through gloomy vaults where the light of day had never shone, past hideous doors of dark dens and cages, down cavernous flights of steps, and again up steep rugged ascents of stone and brick, more like dry waterfalls than staircases, Defarge, the turnkey, and Jacques Three, linked hand and arm, went with all the speed they could make. Here and there, especially at first, the inundation started on them and swept by; but when they had done descending, and were winding and climbing up a tower, they were alone. Hemmed in here by the massive thickness of walls and arches, the storm within the fortress and without was only audible to them in a dull, subdued way, as if the noise out of which they had come had almost destroyed their sense of hearing.

The turnkey stopped at a low door, put a key in a clashing lock, swung the door slowly open, and said, as they all bent their heads and passed in:

"One hundred and five, North Tower!"

There was a small heavily-grated unglazed window high in the wall, with a stone screen before it, so that the sky could be only seen by stooping low and looking up. There was a small chimney, heavily barred across, a few feet within. There was a heap of old feathery wood-ashes on the hearth. There were a stool, and table, and a straw bed. There were the four blackened walls, and a rusted iron ring in one of them.

"Pass that torch slowly along these walls, that I may see them," said Defarge to the turnkey.

The man obeyed, and Defarge followed the light closely with his eyes.

"Stop!—Look here, Jacques!"

"A. M.!" croaked Jacques Three, as he read greedily.

"Alexandre Manette," said Defarge in his ear, following the letters with his swart forefinger, deeply engrained with gunpowder. "And here he wrote 'a poor physician.' And it was he, without doubt, who scratched a calendar on this stone. What is that in your hand? A crowbar? Give it me!" And turning on the worm-eaten stool and table, beat them to pieces in a few blows.

"Hold the light higher!" he said, wrathfully, to the turnkey. "Look among those fragments with care, Jacques. And see! Here is my knife," throwing it to him; "rip open that bed, and search the straw. Hold the light higher, you!"

With a menacing look at the turnkey he crawled upon the hearth, and, peering up the chimney, struck and pried at its sides with the crowbar, and worked at the iron grating across it. In a few minutes, some mortar and dust came dropping down, which he averted his face to avoid; and in it, and in the old wood-ashes, and in a crevice in the chimney into which his weapon had slipped or wrought itself, he groped with a cautious touch.

"Nothing in the wood, and nothing in the straw, Jacques?"

"Nothing."

"Let us collect them together, in the middle of the cell. So! Light them, you!"

The turnkey fired the little pile, which blazed high and hot. Stooping again to come out at the low-arched door, they left it burning, and retraced their way to the courtyard: seeming to recover their sense of hearing as they came down, until they were in the raging flood once more.

They found it surging and tossing, in quest of Defarge himself. Saint Antoine was clamorous to have its wine-shop-keeper foremost in the guard upon the governor [3] who had defended the Bastille and shot the people. Otherwise, the governor would not be marched to the Hôtel de Ville [4] for judgment. Otherwise, the governor would escape, and the people's blood (suddenly of some value, after many years of worthlessness) be unavenged.

In the howling universe of passion and contention that seemed to encompass this grim old officer conspicuous in his grey coat and red decoration, there was but one quite steady figure, and that was a woman's. "See, there is my husband!" she cried, pointing him out. "See Defarge!" She stood immovable close to the grim old officer, and remained immovable close to him; remained immovable close to him through the streets, as Defarge and the rest bore him along; remained immovable close to him when he was got near his destination, and began to be struck at from behind; remained immovable close to him when the long-gathering rain of stabs and blows fell heavy; was so close to him when he dropped dead under it, that, suddenly animated, she put her foot upon his neck, and with her cruel knife—long ready—hewed off his head.

The hour was come, when Saint Antoine was to execute the horrible idea of hoisting up men for lamps to show what could

---

[3] GOVERNOR—The commandant of the Bastille was called the governor of the prison. DeLaunay was governor at this time and met his death as here described.

[4] HÔTEL DE VILLE—Most of the trials during the Revolution were held here. It is one of the oldest and most beautiful buildings in Paris.

be done. Saint Antoine's blood was up, and the blood of tyranny and domination by the iron hand was down—down on the steps of the Hôtel de Ville where the governor's body lay—down on the sole of the shoe of Madame Defarge where she had trodden on the body to steady it for mutilation. "Lower the lamp yonder!" cried Saint Antoine, after glaring round for a new means of death; "here is one of his soldiers to be left on guard!" The swinging sentinel was posted, and the sea rushed on.

The sea of black and threatening waters, and of destructive upheaving of wave against wave, whose depths were yet unfathomed and whose forces were yet unknown. The remorseless sea of turbulently swaying shapes, voices of vengeance, and faces hardened in the furnaces of suffering until the touch of pity could make no mark on them,—such, and such-like, the loudly echoing footsteps of Saint Antoine escort through the Paris streets in mid-July, one thousand seven hundred and eighty-nine. Now, Heaven defeat the fancy of Lucie Darnay and keep these feet far out of her life! For, they are headlong, mad, and dangerous; and in the years so long after the breaking of the cask at Defarge's wine-shop door, they are not easily purified when once stained red.

XIX DRAWN TO THE LOADSTONE ROCK

In such rising of the sea—the firm earth shaken by the rushes of an angry ocean which had now no ebb but was always on the flow, higher and higher, to the terror and wonder of the beholders on the shore—three years of tempest were consumed. Three more birthdays of little Lucie had been woven by the golden thread into the peaceful tissue of the life of her home.

Many a night and many a day had its inmates listened to the echoes in the corner with hearts that failed them when they heard the thronging feet. For, the footsteps had become to their minds as the footsteps of a people, tumultuous under a red flag and with their country declared in danger, changed into wild beasts by terrible enchantment long persisted in.

The August of the year one thousand seven hundred and ninety-two was come, and the French nobles were by this time scattered far and wide.

As was natural, the headquarters and great gathering-place

of the nobility, in London, was Tellson's Bank. Moreover, it was the spot to which such French intelligence as was most to be relied upon, came quickest. Again: Tellson's was a munificent house, and extended great liberality to old customers who had fallen from their high estate. Again: those nobles who had seen the coming storm in time, and, anticipating plunder or confiscation, had made provident remittances to Tellson's, were always to be heard of there by their needy brethren. To which it must be added that every newcomer from France reported himself and his tidings at Tellson's, almost as a matter of course. For such variety of reasons, Tellson's was at that time, as to French intelligence, a kind of High Exchange; and this was so well known to the public, and the inquiries made there were in consequence so numerous, that Tellson's sometimes wrote the latest news out in a line or so and posted it in the bank windows, for all who ran through Temple-bar to read.

On a steaming, misty afternoon, Mr. Lorry sat at his desk, and Charles Darnay stood leaning on it, talking with him in a low voice.

"But, although you are the youngest man that ever lived," said Charles Darnay, rather hesitating, "I must still suggest to you——"

"I understand. That I am too old?" said Mr. Lorry.

"Unsettled weather, a long journey, uncertain means of travelling, a disorganized country, a city that may not even be safe for you."

"My dear Charles," said Mr. Lorry, with cheerful confidence, "you touch some of the reasons for my going: not for my staying away. It is safe enough for me; nobody will care to interfere with an old fellow of hard upon four-score when there are so many people there much better worth interfering with."

"I wish I were going myself," said Charles Darnay, somewhat restlessly, and like one thinking aloud.

"Indeed! You are a pretty fellow to object and advise!" exclaimed Mr. Lorry. "You wish you were going yourself? And you a Frenchman born? You are a wise counsellor."

"My dear Mr. Lorry, it is because I am a Frenchman born, that the thought has passed through my mind often. One cannot help thinking, having had some sympathy for the miserable people, and having abandoned something to them," he spoke here in his former thoughtful manner, "that one might be listened to, and might have the power to persuade to some restraint. Only last night, after you had left us, when I was talking to Lucie——"

"When you were talking to Lucie," Mr. Lorry repeated. "Yes. I wonder you are not ashamed to mention the name of Lucie! Wishing you were going to France at this time of day!"

"However, I am not going," said Charles Darnay, with a smile. "It is more to the purpose that you say you are."

"And I am, in plain reality. The truth is, my dear Charles," Mr. Lorry lowered his voice, "you can have no conception of the difficulty with which our business is transacted, and of the peril in which our books and papers over yonder are involved."

"And do you really go tonight?"

"I really go tonight, for the case has become too pressing to admit of delay."

"And do you take no one with you?"

"All sorts of people have been proposed to me, but I will have nothing to say to any of them. I intend to take Jerry. Jerry has been my body-guard on Sunday nights for a long time past, and I am used to him. Nobody will suspect Jerry of being anything but an English bull-dog, or of having any design in his head but to fly at anybody who touches his master."

A clerk approached Mr. Lorry, and laying a soiled and unopened letter before him, asked if he had yet discovered any traces of the person to whom it was addressed? He laid the letter down so close to Darnay that he saw the direction—the more quickly, because it was his own right name. The address, turned into English, ran: "Very pressing. To Monsieur heretofore the Marquis St. Evrémonde, of France, Confided to the cares of Messrs. Tellson and Co., Bankers, London, England."

On the marriage morning, Doctor Manette had made it his one urgent and express request to Charles Darnay, that the secret of his name should be—unless he, the Doctor, dissolved the obligation—kept inviolate between them. Nobody else knew it to be his name; his own wife had no suspicion of the fact; Mr. Lorry could have none.

"No," said Mr. Lorry, in reply to the clerk; "I have referred it, I think, to everybody now here, and no one can tell me where this gentleman is to be found."

Darnay, unable to restrain himself any longer, said, "I know the fellow."

"Will you take charge of the letter?" said Mr. Lorry. "You know where to deliver it?"

"I do."

"Will you undertake to explain that we suppose it to have been addressed here, on the chance of our knowing where to forward it, and that it has been here some time?"

"I will do so. Do you start for Paris from here?"

"From here, at eight."

"I will come back, to see you off."

Very ill at ease with himself, Darnay made the best of his way into the quiet of the Temple, opened the letter, and read it. These were its contents:

"PRISON OF THE ABBAYE,[1] PARIS. June 21, 1792.

"MONSIEUR HERETOFORE THE MARQUIS:

"After having long been in danger of my life at the hands of the village, I have been seized, with great violence and indignity, and brought a long journey on foot to Paris. On the road I have suffered a great deal. Nor is that all; my house has been destroyed—razed to the ground.

"The crime for which I am imprisoned, Monsieur heretofore the Marquis, and for which I shall be summoned before the tribunal, and shall lose my life (without your so generous help), is, they tell me, treason against the majesty of the people, in that I have acted against them for an emigrant. It is in vain I represent that I have acted for them, and not against, according to your commands. It is in vain I represent that, before the sequestration of emigrant property, I had remitted the imposts they had ceased to pay; that I had collected no rent, that I had had recourse to no process. The only response is, that I have acted for an emigrant, and where is that emigrant?

"Ah! most gracious Monsieur heretofore the Marquis, where is that emigrant! I cry in my sleep where is he! I demand of

---

[1] THE ABBAYE—The Abbaye (ä-bā'), La Force, and La Conciergerie (kôn-syerzh-rē') were the three principal prisons after the Bastille.

Heaven, will he not come to deliver me! No answer. Ah, Monsieur heretofore the Marquis, I send my desolate cry across the sea, hoping it may perhaps reach your ears through the great bank of Tellson known at Paris!

"For the love of Heaven, of justice, of generosity, of the honor of your noble name, I supplicate you, Monsieur heretofore the Marquis, to succor and release me. My fault is, that I have been true to you. Oh, Monsieur heretofore the Marquis, I pray you be you true to me!

"From this prison here of horror, whence I every hour tend nearer and nearer to destruction, I send you, Monsieur heretofore the Marquis, the assurance of my dolorous and unhappy service.

"Gabelle."

The latent uneasiness in Darnay's mind was roused to vigorous life by this letter. The peril of an old servant and a good servant, whose only crime was fidelity to himself and his family, stared him so reproachfully in the face, that, as he walked to and fro in the Temple considering what to do, he almost hid his face from the passers-by.

He knew very well, that in his horror of the deed which had culminated the bad deeds and bad reputation of the old family house, in his resentful suspicions of his uncle, and in the aversion with which his conscience regarded the crumbling fabric that he was supposed to uphold, he had acted imperfectly. He knew very well, that in his love for Lucie, his renunciation of his social place, though by no means new to his own mind, had been hurried and incomplete. He knew that he ought to have systematically worked it out and supervised it, and that he had meant to do it, and that it had never been done.

The happiness of his own chosen English home, the necessity of being always actively employed, the swift changes and troubles of the time which had followed on one another so fast, that the events of this week annihilated the immature plans of last week, and the events of the week following made all new again; he knew very well, that to the force of these circumstances he had yielded—not without disquiet, but still without continuous and accumulating resistance. That he had watched the times for a time of action, and that they had shifted and struggled until the time had gone by, and the nobility were trooping from France by every highway and byway, and their property was in course of confiscation and destruction, and their very names were blotting out, was as well known to himself as it could be to any new authority in France that might impeach him for it.

But, he had oppressed no man, he had imprisoned no man; he was so far from having harshly exacted payment of his dues, that he had relinquished them of his own will, thrown himself on a world with no favor in it, won his own private place there, and earned his own bread. Monsieur Gabelle had held the impoverished and involved estate on written instructions to spare the people, to give them what little there was to give—such fuel as the heavy creditors would let them have in the winter, and such produce as could be saved from the same grip in the summer—and no doubt he had put the fact in plea and proof, for his own safety, so that it could not but appear now.

This favored the desperate resolution Charles Darnay had begun to make, that he would go to Paris.

Yes. Like the mariner in the old story, the winds and streams had driven him within the influence of the Loadstone Rock,[2] and it was drawing him to itself. He must sail on, until he struck. He knew of no rock; he saw hardly any danger. The intention with which he had done what he had done, even although he had left it incomplete, presented it before him in an aspect that would be gratefully acknowledged in France on his presenting himself to assert it. Then, that glorious vision of doing good, which is so often the sanguine mirage of so many good minds, arose before him, and he even saw himself in the illusion with some influence to guide this raging Revolution that was running so fearfully wild.

As he walked to and fro with his resolution made, he considered that neither Lucie nor her father must know of it until he was gone. Lucie should be spared the pain of separation; and her father, always reluctant to turn his thoughts towards the dangerous ground of old, should come to the knowledge of the step, as a step taken, and not in the balance of suspense and doubt. How much of the incompleteness of his situation was referable to her father, through the painful anxiety to avoid reviving old associations of France in his mind, he did not dis-

---

[2] LOADSTONE ROCK—A mythical rock that drew ships to itself, fatally, by magnetic attraction of their iron bolts, band, etc.

cuss with himself. But, that circumstance too, had had its influence in his course.

He walked to and fro, with thoughts very busy, until it was time to return to Tellson's, and take leave of Mr. Lorry. As soon as he arrived in Paris he would present himself to this old friend, but he must say nothing of his intention now.

A carriage with post-horses was ready at the bank door, and Jerry was booted and equipped.

"I have delivered that letter," said Charles Darnay to Mr. Lorry. "I would not consent to your being charged with any written answer, but perhaps you will take a verbal one?"

"That I will, and readily," said Mr. Lorry, "if it is not dangerous."

"Not at all. Though it is to a prisoner in the Abbaye."

"What is his name?" said Mr. Lorry, with his open pocket-book in his hand.

"Gabelle."

"Gabelle. And what is the message to the unfortunate Gabelle in prison?"

"Simply, 'that he has received the letter, and will come.'"

"Any time mentioned?"

"He will start upon his journey tomorrow night."

"Any person mentioned?"

"No."

He helped Mr. Lorry to wrap himself in a number of coats and cloaks, and went out with him from the warm atmosphere of the old bank, into the misty air of Fleet-street. "My love to Lucie, and to little Lucie," said Mr. Lorry at parting, "and take precious care of them till I come back." Charles Darnay shook his head and doubtfully smiled, as the carriage rolled away.

That night—it was the fourteenth of August—he sat up late, and wrote two fervent letters; one was to Lucie, explaining the strong obligation he was under to go to Paris, and showing her, at length, the reasons that he had, for feeling confident that he could become involved in no personal danger there; the other was to the Doctor, confiding Lucie and their dear child to his care, and dwelling on the same topics with the strongest assurances. To both, he wrote that he would despatch letters in proof of his safety, immediately after his arrival.

It was a hard day, that day of being among them, with the

first reservation of their joint lives on his mind. It was a hard matter to preserve the innocent deceit of which they were profoundly unsuspicious. But, an affectionate glance at his wife, so happy and busy, made him resolute not to tell her what impended, and the day passed quickly. Early in the evening he embraced her, and her scarcely less dear namesake, pretending that he would return by-and-by (an imaginary engagement took him out, and he had secreted a valise of clothes ready), and so he emerged into the heavy mist of the heavy streets, with a heavier heart.

The unseen force was drawing him fast to itself, now, and all the tides and winds were setting straight and strong towards it. He left his two letters with a trusty porter, to be delivered half an hour before midnight, and no sooner; took horse for Dover; and began his journey. "For the love of Heaven, of justice, of generosity, of the honor of your noble name!" was the poor prisoner's cry with which he strengthened his sinking heart, as he left all that was dear on earth behind him, and floated away for the Loadstone Rock.

BOOK THE THIRD. THE TRACK OF A STORM

I IN SECRET

The traveller fared slowly on his way, who fared towards Paris from England in the autumn of the year one thousand seven hundred and ninety-two. More than enough of bad roads, bad equipages, and bad horses, he would have encountered to delay him, though the fallen and unfortunate King of France had been upon his throne in all his glory; but, the changed times were fraught with other obstacles than these. Every town gate and village taxing-house had its band of citizen-patriots, with their national muskets in a most explosive state of readiness, who stopped all comers and goers, cross-questioned them, inspected their papers, looked for their names in lists of their own, turned them back, or sent them on, or stopped them and laid them in hold, as their capricious judgment or fancy deemed best for the dawning Republic One and Indivisible, of Liberty, Equality, Fraternity,[1] or Death.

[1] Liberty, Equality, Fraternity—The motto of the Revolution.

A very few French leagues of his journey were accomplished, when Charles Darnay began to perceive that for him along these country roads there was no hope of return until he should have been declared a good citizen at Paris. Whatever might befall now, he must on to his journey's end. Not a mean village closed upon him, not a common barrier dropped across the road behind him, but he knew it to be another iron door in the series that was barred between him and England. The universal watchfulness so encompassed him, that if he had been taken in a net, or were being forwarded to his destination in a cage, he could not have felt his freedom more completely gone.

This universal watchfulness not only stopped him on the highway twenty times in a stage, but retarded his progress twenty times in a day, by riding after him and taking him back, riding before him and stopping him by anticipation, riding with him and keeping him in charge. He had been days upon his journey in France alone, when he went to bed tired out, in a little town on the high road, still a long way from Paris.

Nothing but the production of the afflicted Gabelle's letter from his prison of the Abbaye would have got him on so far. His difficulty at the guard-house in this small place had been such, that he felt his journey to have come to a crisis. And he was, therefore, as little surprised as a man could be, to find himself awakened at the small inn to which he had been remitted until morning, in the middle of the night.

Awakened by a timid local functionary and three armed patriots in rough red caps and with pipes in their mouths, who sat down on the bed.

"Emigrant," said the functionary, "I am going to send you on to Paris, under an escort."

"Citizen, I desire nothing more than to get to Paris, though I could dispense with the escort."

"Silence!" growled a red-cap, striking at the coverlet with the butt-end of his musket. "Peace, aristocrat!"

"It is as the good patriot says," observed the timid functionary. "You are an aristocrat, and must have an escort—and must pay for it."

"I have no choice," said Charles Darnay.

"Choice! Listen to him!" cried the same scowling red-cap.

"As if it was not a favor to be protected from the lamp-iron!"

"It is always as the good patriot says," observed the functionary. "Rise and dress yourself, emigrant."

Darnay complied, and was taken back to the guard-house where other patriots in rough red caps were smoking, drinking, and sleeping, by a watch-fire. Here he paid a heavy price for his escort, and hence he started with it on the wet, wet roads at three o'clock in the morning.

The escort were two mounted patriots in red caps and tri-colored cockades, armed with national muskets and sabres, who rode one on either side of him. The escorted governed his own horse, but a loose line was attached to his bridle, the end of which one of the patriots kept girded round his wrist. In this state they set forth, with the sharp rain driving in their faces: clattering at a heavy dragoon trot over the uneven town pavement, and out upon the mire-deep roads. In this state they traversed without change, except of horses and pace, all the mire-deep leagues that lay between them and the capital.

They travelled in the night, halting an hour or two after daybreak, and lying by until the twilight fell. The escort were so wretchedly clothed, that they twisted straw round their bare legs, and thatched their ragged shoulders to keep the wet off. Apart from the personal discomfort of being so attended, and apart from such considerations of present danger as arose from one of the patriots being chronically drunk, carrying his musket very recklessly, Charles Darnay did not allow the restraint that was laid upon him to awaken any serious fears in his breast; for, he reasoned with himself that it could have no reference to the merits of an individual case that was not yet stated, and of representations, confirmable by the prisoner in the Abbaye, that were not yet made.

But when they came to the town of Beauvais—which they did at eventide, when the streets were filled with people—he could not conceal from himself that the aspect of affairs was very alarming. An ominous crowd gathered to see him dismount at the posting-yard, and many voices in it called out loudly, "Down with the emigrant!"

He stopped in the act of swinging himself out of his saddle, and, resuming it as his safest place, said:

"Emigrant, my friends! Do you not see me here, in France, of my own will?"

"You are a cursed emigrant," cried a farrier, making at him in a furious manner through the press, hammer in hand; "and you are a cursed aristocrat!"

The postmaster interposed himself between this man and the rider's bridle and soothingly said, "Let him be; let him be! He will be judged at Paris."

"Judged!" repeated the farrier, swinging his hammer. "Ay! and condemned as a traitor." At this, the crowd roared approval.

Checking the postmaster, who was for turning his horse's head to the yard, Darnay said, as soon as he could make his voice heard:

"Friends, you deceive yourselves, or you are deceived. I am not a traitor."

"He lies!" cried the smith. "He is a traitor since the decree. His life is forfeit to the people. His cursed life is not his own!"

At the instant when Darnay saw a rush in the eyes of the crowd, which another instant would have brought upon him, the postmaster turned his horse into the yard, the escort rode in close upon his horse's flanks, and the postmaster shut and barred the heavy double gates. The farrier struck a blow upon them with his hammer, and the crowd groaned; but, no more was done.

"What is this decree that the smith spoke of?" Darnay asked the postmaster, when he had thanked them, and stood beside him in the yard.

"Truly, a decree for selling the property of emigrants."

"When passed?"

"On the fourteenth."

"The day I left England!"

"Everybody says it is but one of several, and that there will be others—if there are not already—banishing all emigrants, and condemning all to death who return.[2] That is what he meant when he said your life was not your own."

"But there are no such decrees yet?"

[2] There were several decrees as here mentioned. They condemned the emigrants to perpetual banishment, confiscated their property, deprived them of civil rights, and imposed death within twenty-four hours, if found on French soil.

"What do I know!" said the postmaster, shrugging his shoulders; "there may be, or there will be. It is all the same. What would you have?"

They rested on some straw in a lot until the middle of the night, and then rode forward again when all the town was asleep: jingling through the untimely cold and wet, among impoverished fields that had yielded no fruits of the earth that year, diversified by the blackened remains of burnt houses, and by the sudden emergence from ambuscade, and sharp reining up across their way, of patriot patrols on the watch on all the roads.

Daylight at last found them before the wall of Paris. The barrier was closed and strongly guarded when they rode up to it.

"Where are the papers of this prisoner?" demanded a resolute-looking man in authority, who was summoned out by the guard.

Naturally struck by the disagreeable word, Charles Darnay requested the speaker to take notice that he was a free traveller and French citizen, in charge of an escort which the disturbed state of the country had imposed upon him, and which he had paid for.

"Where," repeated the same personage, without taking any heed of him whatever, "are the papers of this prisoner?"

The drunken patriot had them in his cap, and produced them. Casting his eyes over Gabelle's letter, the same personage in authority showed some disorder and surprise, and looked at Darnay with a close attention.

He left both escort and escorted without saying a word, however, and went into the guard-room; meanwhile, they sat upon their horses outside the gate. Looking about him while in this state of suspense, Charles Darnay observed that the gate was held by a mixed guard of soldiers and patriots, the latter far outnumbering the former; and that while ingress into the city for peasants' carts bringing in supplies, and for similar traffic and traffickers, was easy enough, egress, even for the homeliest people, was very difficult. A numerous medley of men and women, not to mention beasts and vehicles of various sorts, was waiting to issue forth; but, the previous identification was so strict that they filtered through the barrier very slowly. Some of these people knew their turn for examination to be so far off, that they lay down on the ground to sleep or smoke, while others talked together, or loitered about. The red cap and tricolor [3] cockade were universal, both among men and women.

When he had sat in his saddle some half-hour, taking note of these things, Darnay found himself confronted by the same man in authority, who directed the guard to open the barrier. Then he delivered to the escort, drunk and sober, a receipt for the escorted, and requested him to dismount. He did so, and the two patriots, leading his tired horse, turned and rode away without entering the city.

He accompanied his conductor into a guard-room, smelling of common wine and tobacco, where certain soldiers and patriots, asleep and awake, drunk and sober, and in various neutral states between sleeping and waking, drunkenness and sobriety, were standing and lying about. The light in the guard-house, half derived from the waning oil-lamps of the night, and half from the overcast day, was in a correspondingly uncertain condition. Some registers were lying open on a desk, and an officer of a coarse dark aspect, presided over these.

"Citizen Defarge," said he to Darnay's conductor, as he took a slip of paper to write on. "Is this the emigrant Evrémonde?"

"This is the man."

"Your age, Evrémonde?"

"Thirty-seven."

"Married, Evrémonde?"

"Yes."

"Where married?"

"In England."

"Without doubt. Where is your wife, Evrémonde?"

"In England."

"Without doubt. You are consigned, Evrémonde, to the prison of La Force."

"Just Heaven!" exclaimed Darnay. "Under what law, and for what offence?"

The officer looked up from his slip of paper for a moment.

"We have new laws, Evrémonde, and new offences, since you were here." He said it with a hard smile, and went on writing.

"I entreat you to observe that I have come here voluntarily, in response to that written appeal of a fellow-countryman which

---

[3] TRICOLOR—Red, white, and blue—the emblem of the Revolution.

"Citizen Defarge," said he, as he took a slip of paper. "Is this the emigrant Evrémonde?"

lies before you. I demand no more than the opportunity to do so without delay. Is not that my right?"

"Emigrants have no rights, Evrémonde," was the stolid reply. The officer wrote until he had finished, read over to himself what he had written, sanded it, and handed it to Defarge, with the words "In secret."

Defarge motioned with the paper to the prisoner that he must accompany him. The prisoner obeyed, and a guard of two armed patriots attended them.

"It is you," said Defarge, in a low voice, as they went down the guard-house steps and turned into Paris, "who married the daughter of Doctor Manette, once a prisoner in the Bastille that is no more."

"Yes," replied Darnay, looking at him with surprise.

"My name is Defarge, and I keep a wine-shop in the Quarter Saint Antoine. Possibly you have heard of me."

"My wife came to your house to reclaim her father? Yes!"

The word "wife" seemed to serve as a gloomy reminder to Defarge, to say with sudden impatience, "In the name of that sharp female newly born and called La Guillotine,[4] why did you come to France?"

"You heard me say why, a minute ago. Do you not believe it is the truth?"

"A bad truth for you," said Defarge, speaking with knitted brows, and looking straight before him.

"Indeed, I am lost here. All here is so unprecedented, so changed, so sudden and unfair, that I am absolutely lost. Will you render me a little help?"

"None." Defarge spoke, always looking straight before him.

"Will you answer me a single question?"

"Perhaps. According to its nature. You can say what it is."

"In this prison that I am going to so unjustly, shall I have some free communication with the world outside?"

"You will see."

"I am not to be buried there, prejudged, and without any means of presenting my case?"

[4] LA GUILLOTINE—The guillotine was the method of execution during the Revolution. It consisted of a heavily weighted knife falling between two grooved posts upon the neck of the condemned who was stretched full length upon a platform. The machine was named from its inventor, Dr. Guillotine.

"You will see. But, what then? Other people have been similarly buried in worse prisons, before now."

"But never by me, Citizen Defarge."

Defarge glanced darkly at him for answer, and walked on in a steady and set silence. The deeper he sank into this silence, the fainter hope there was—or so Darnay thought—of his softening in any slight degree. He, therefore, made haste to say:

"It is of the utmost importance to me that I should be able to communicate to Mr. Lorry of Tellson's Bank, an English gentleman who is now in Paris, the simple fact, without comment, that I have been thrown into the prison of La Force. Will you cause that to be done for me?"

"I will do," Defarge doggedly rejoined, "nothing for you. My duty is to my country and the people. I am the sworn servant of both, against you. I will do nothing for you."

Charles Darnay felt it hopeless to entreat him further, and his pride was touched besides. That he had fallen among far greater dangers than those which had developed themselves when he left England, he of course knew now. That perils had thickened about him fast, and might thicken faster and faster yet, he of course knew now. He could not but admit to himself that he might not have made this journey, if he could have foreseen the events of a few days. And yet his misgivings were not so dark as, imagined by the light of this later time, they would appear. Troubled as the future was, it was the unknown future, and in its obscurity there was ignorant hope. The horrible massacre, days and nights long, which, within a few rounds of the clock, was to set a great mark of blood upon the blessed garnering time of harvest, was as far out of his knowledge as if it had been a hundred thousand years away. The "sharp female newly born and called La Guillotine," was hardly known to him, or to the generality of people, by name. The frightful deeds that were to be soon done, were probably unimagined at that time in the brains of the doers. How could they have a place in the shadowy conceptions of a gentle mind?

Of unjust treatment in detention and hardship, and in cruel separation from his wife and child, he foreshadowed the likelihood, or the certainty; but, beyond this, he dreaded nothing distinctly. With this on his mind, enough to carry into a dreary prison courtyard, he arrived at the prison of La Force.

A man with a bloated face opened the strong wicket, to whom Defarge presented "The Emigrant Evrémonde."

"What the Devil! How many more of them!" exclaimed the man with the bloated face.

Defarge took his receipt without noticing the exclamation, and withdrew, with his two fellow-patriots.

"In secret, too," grumbled the gaoler, looking at the written paper. "As if I was not already full to bursting!"

He stuck the paper on a file, in an ill-humor, and Charles Darnay awaited his further pleasure for half an hour: sometimes, pacing to and fro in the strong arched room: sometimes, resting on a stone seat.

"Come!" said the chief, at length taking up his keys, "come with me, emigrant."

Through the dismal prison twilight, his new charge accompanied him by corridor and staircase, many doors clanging and locking behind them, until they came to a stone staircase, leading upward. When they had ascended forty steps (the prisoner of half an hour already counted them), the gaoler opened a low black door, and they passed into a solitary cell. It struck cold and damp, but was not dark.

"Yours," said the gaoler.

"Why am I confined alone?"

"How do I know!"

"I can buy pen, ink, and paper?"

"Such are not my orders. You will be visited, and can ask then. At present, you may buy your food, and nothing more."

There were in the cell, a chair, a table, and a straw mattress. As the gaoler made a general inspection of these objects, and of the four walls, before going out, a wandering fancy wandered through the mind of the prisoner leaning against the wall opposite to him, that this gaoler was so unwholesomely bloated, both in face and person, as to look like a man who had been drowned and filled with water. When the gaoler was gone, he thought, in the same wandering way, "Now am I left, as if I were dead."

"Five paces by four and a half, five paces by four and a half, five paces by four and a half." The prisoner walked to and fro in his cell, counting its measurement, and the roar of the city arose like muffled drums with a wild swell of voices added to them. "He made shoes, he made shoes, he made shoes." The prisoner counted the measurement again, and paced faster, to draw his mind with him from that latter repetition. "He made shoes, he made shoes, he made shoes. . . . Five paces by four and a half." With such scraps tossing and rolling upward from the depths of his mind, the prisoner walked faster and faster, obstinately counting and counting; and the roar of the city changed to this extent—that it still rolled in like muffled drums, but with the wail of voices that he knew, in the swell that rose above them.

II THE GRINDSTONE

TELLSON'S BANK, established in the Saint Germain[1] Quarter of Paris, was in a wing of a large house, approached by a courtyard and shut off from the street by a high wall and a strong gate. The house belonged to a great nobleman who had lived in it until he made a flight from the troubles, in his own cook's dress, and got across the borders. It had been first sequestrated, and then confiscated, and now upon the third night of the autumn month of September, patriot emissaries of the law were in possession, and had marked it with the tricolor, and were drinking brandy in its state apartments.

What money would be drawn out of Tellson's henceforth, and what would lie there, lost and forgotten; what plate and jewels would tarnish in Tellson's hiding-places, while the depositors rusted in prisons, and when they should have violently perished; how many accounts with Tellson's never to be balanced in this world, must be carried over into the next; no man could have said, that night, any more than Mr. Jarvis Lorry could, though he thought heavily of these questions. He sat by a newly lighted wood fire, and on his honest and courageous face there was a deeper shade than the pendent lamp could throw, or any object in the room distortedly reflect—a shade of horror.

He occupied rooms in the Bank, in his fidelity to the House of which he had grown to be a part, like strong root-ivy. It chanced that they derived a kind of security from the patriotic occupation of the main building, but the true-hearted old gentleman never calculated about that. All such circumstances were

---

[1] SAINT GERMAIN—A fashionable quarter of Paris before the Revolution.

indifferent to him, so that he did his duty. On the opposite side of the courtyard, under a colonnade, was extensive standing for carriages—where, indeed, some carriages yet stood. Against two of the pillars were fastened two great flaring flambeaux, and, in the light of these, standing out in the open air, was a large grindstone: a roughly mounted thing which appeared to have hurriedly been brought there from some neighboring smithy, or other workshop. Rising and looking out of window at these harmless objects, Mr. Lorry shivered, and retired to his seat by the fire. He had opened, not only the glass window, but the lattice blind outside it, and he had closed both again, and he shivered through his frame.

"Thank God," said Mr. Lorry, clasping his hands, "that no one near and dear to me is in this dreadful town tonight. May He have mercy on all who are in danger!"

Soon afterwards, the bell at the great gate sounded, and he thought, "They have come back!" and sat listening. But, there was no loud irruption into the courtyard, as he had expected, and he heard the gate clash again, and all was quiet.

The nervousness and dread that were upon him inspired that vague uneasiness respecting the bank, which a great charge would naturally awaken, with such feelings roused. It was well guarded, and he got up to go among the trusty people who were watching it, when his door suddenly opened, and two figures rushed in, at sight of which he fell back in amazement.

Lucie and her father! Lucie with her arms stretched out to him, and with that old look of earnestness so concentrated and intensified, that it seemed as though it had been stamped upon her face expressly to give force and power to it in this one passage of her life.

"What is this!" cried Mr. Lorry, breathless and confused. "What is the matter? Lucie! Manette! What has happened? What has brought you here? What is it?"

With the look fixed upon him, in her paleness and wildness, she panted out in his arms, imploringly, "O my dear friend! My husband!"

"Your husband, Lucie?"

"Charles."

"What of Charles?"

"Here.'

"Here, in Paris?"

"Has been here, some days—three or four—I don't know how many—I can't collect my thoughts. An errand of generosity brought him here unknown to us; he was stopped at the barrier, and sent to prison."

The old man uttered an irrepressible cry. Almost at the same moment, the bell of the great gate rang again, and a loud noise of feet and voices came pouring into the courtyard.

"What is that noise?" said the Doctor, turning towards the window.

"Don't look!" cried Mr. Lorry. "Don't look out! Manette, for your life, don't touch the blind!"

The Doctor turned, with his hand upon the fastening of the window, and said, with a cool bold smile:

"My dear friend, I have a charmed life in this city. I have been a Bastille prisoner. There is no patriot in Paris—in Paris? in France—who, knowing me to have been a prisoner in the Bastille, would touch me, except to overwhelm me with embraces, or carry me in triumph. My old pain has given me a power that has brought us through the barrier, and gained us news of Charles there, and brought us here. I knew it would be so; I knew I could help Charles out of all danger; I told Lucie so.—What is that noise?" His hand was again upon the window.

"Don't look!" cried Mr. Lorry, absolutely desperate. "No, Lucie, my dear, nor you!" He got his arm round her, and held her. "Don't be so terrified, my love. I solemnly swear to you that I know of no harm having happened to Charles; that I had no suspicion even, of his being in this fatal place. What prison is he in?"

"La Force!"

"La Force! Lucie, my child, if ever you were brave and serviceable in your life—and you were always both—you will compose yourself now, to do exactly as I bid you; for, more depends upon it than you can think, or I can say. There is no help for you in any action on your part tonight; you cannot possibly stir out. I say this, because what I must bid you to do for Charles's sake, is the hardest thing to do of all. You must instantly be obedient, still, and quiet. You must let me put you in a room at the back here. You must leave your father and me alone for two minutes, and as there are Life and Death in the world you must not delay."

"I will be submissive to you. I see in your face that you know I can do nothing else than this. I know you are true."

The old man kissed her, and hurried her into his room, and turned the key; then, came hurrying back to the Doctor, and opened the window and partly opened the blind, and put his hand upon the Doctor's arm, and looked out with him into the courtyard.

Looked out upon a throng of men and women: not enough in number, or near enough, to fill the courtyard: not more than forty or fifty in all. The people in possession of the house had let them in at the gate, and they had rushed in to work at the grindstone; it had evidently been set up there for their purpose, as in a convenient and retired spot.

But, such awful workers, and such awful work!

The grindstone had a double handle, and, turning at it madly were two men, whose faces, as their long hair flapped back when the whirlings of the grindstone brought their faces up, were more horrible and cruel than the visages of the wildest savages in their most barbarous disguise. False eyebrows and false moustaches were stuck upon them, and their hideous countenances were all bloody and sweaty, and all awry with howling, and all staring and glaring with beastly excitement and want of sleep. As these ruffians turned and turned, their matted locks now flung forward over their eyes, now flung backward over their necks, some women held wine to their mouths that they might drink; and what with dropping blood, and what with dropping wine, and what with the stream of sparks struck out of the stone, all their wicked atmosphere seemed gore and fire. The eye could not detect one creature in the group, free from the smear of blood. Hatchets, knives, bayonets, swords, all brought to be sharpened, were all red with it. Some of the hacked swords were tied to the wrists of those who carried them, with strips of linen and fragments of dress: ligatures various in kind, but all deep of the one color. And as the frantic wielders of these weapons snatched them from the stream of sparks and tore away into the streets, the same red hue was red in their frenzied eyes;—eyes which any unbrutalized beholder would have given twenty years of life, to petrify with a well-directed gun.

All this was seen in a moment, as the vision of a drowning man, or of any human creature at any very great pass, could see a world if it were there. They drew back from the window, and the Doctor looked for explanation in his friend's ashy face.

"They are," Mr. Lorry whispered the words, glancing fearfully round at the locked room, "murdering the prisoners. If you are sure of what you say; if you really have the power you think you have—as I believe you have—make yourself known to these devils, and get taken to La Force. It may be too late, I don't know, but let it not be a minute later!"

Doctor Manette pressed his hand, hastened bareheaded out of the room, and was in the courtyard when Mr. Lorry regained the blind.

His streaming white hair, his remarkable face, and the impetuous confidence of his manner, as he put the weapons aside like water, carried him in an instant to the heart of the concourse at the stone. For a few moments there was a pause, and a hurry, and a murmur, and the unintelligible sound of his voice; and then Mr. Lorry saw him, surrounded by all, and in the midst of a line twenty men long, all linked shoulder to shoulder, and hand to shoulder, hurried out with cries of "Live the Bastille prisoner! Help for the Bastille prisoner's kindred in La Force! Room for the Bastille prisoner in front there! Save the prisoner Evrémonde at La Force!" and a thousand answering shouts.

He closed the lattice again with a fluttering heart, closed the window and the curtain, hastened to Lucie, and told her that her father was assisted by the people, and gone in search of her husband. He found her child and Miss Pross with her; but, it never occurred to him to be surprised by their appearance until a long time afterwards, when he sat watching them in such quiet as the night knew.

Lucie had, by that time, fallen into a stupor on the floor at his feet, clinging to his hand. Miss Pross had laid the child down on his own bed, and her head had gradually fallen on the pillow beside her pretty charge. O, the long, long night, with the moans of the poor wife. And O, the long, long night, with no return of her father and no tidings!

Twice more in the darkness the bell at the great gate sounded, and the irruption was repeated, and the grindstone whirled and spluttered. "What is it?" cried Lucie, affrighted. "Hush! The soldier's swords are sharpened there," said Mr. Lorry. "The place is national property now, and used as a kind of armory, my love."

Twice more in all; but, the last spell of work was feeble and fitful. Soon afterwards the day began to dawn, and the great grindstone, Earth, had turned when Mr. Lorry looked out again. The sun was red on the courtyard, but the lesser grindstone stood alone there in the calm morning air, with a red upon it that the sun had never given, and would never take away.

III THE SHADOW

ONE of the first considerations which arose in the business mind of Mr. Lorry when business hours came round, was this:— that he had no right to imperil Tellson's by sheltering the wife of an emigrant prisoner under the bank roof. His own possessions, safety, life, he would have hazarded for Lucie and her child, without a moment's demur; but, the great trust he held was not his own, and as to that business charge he was a strict man of business.

At first, his mind reverted to Defarge, and he thought of finding out the wine-shop again and taking counsel with its master in reference to the safest dwelling-place in the distracted state of the city. But, the same consideration that suggested him, repudiated him; he lived in the most violent Quarter, and doubtless was influential there, and deep in its dangerous workings.

Noon coming, and the Doctor not returning, and every minute's delay tending to compromise Tellson's, Mr. Lorry advised with Lucie. She said that her father had spoken of hiring a lodging for a short term, in that Quarter, near the banking-house. As there was no business objection to this, and as he foresaw that even if it were all well with Charles, and he were to be released, he could not hope to leave the city, Mr. Lorry went out in quest of such a lodging, and found a suitable one, high up in a removed by-street where the closed blinds in all the other windows of a high melancholy square of buildings marked deserted homes.

To this lodging he at once removed Lucie and her child, and Miss Pross: giving them what comfort he could, and much more than he had himself. He left Jerry with them, as a figure to fill a doorway that would bear considerable knocking on the head, and returned to his own occupations. A disturbed and doleful mind he brought to bear upon them, and slowly and heavily the day lagged on with him.

It wore itself out, and wore him out with it, until the bank closed. He was again alone in his room of the previous night, considering what to do next, when he heard a foot upon the stair. In a few moments, a man stood in his presence, who, with a keenly observant look at him, addressed him by his name.

"Your servant," said Mr. Lorry. "Do you know me?"

He was a strongly made man with dark curling hair, from forty-five to fifty years of age. For answer he repeated, without any change of emphasis, the words:

"Do you know me?"

"I have seen you somewhere."

"Perhaps at my wine-shop?"

Much interested and agitated, Mr. Lorry said: "You come from Doctor Manette?"

"Yes. I come from Doctor Manette."

"And what says he? What does he send me?"

Defarge gave into his anxious hand, an open scrap of paper. It bore the words in the Doctor's writing,

> Charles is safe, but I cannot safely leave this place yet. I have obtained the favor that the bearer has a short note from Charles to his wife. Let the bearer see his wife.

It was dated from La Force, within an hour.

"Will you accompany me," said Mr. Lorry, joyfully relieved after reading this note aloud, "to where his wife resides?"

"Yes," returned Defarge.

Scarcely noticing, as yet, in what a curiously reserved and mechanical way Defarge spoke, Mr. Lorry put on his hat and they went down into the courtyard. There, they found two women, one, knitting.

"Madame Defarge, surely!" said Mr. Lorry, who had left her in exactly the same attitude some seventeen years ago.

"It is she," observed her husband.

"Does Madame go with us?" inquired Mr. Lorry, seeing that she moved as they moved.

"Yes. That she may be able to recognize the faces and know the persons. It is for their safety."

Beginning to be struck by Defarge's manner, Mr. Lorry looked dubiously at him, and led the way. Both the women followed; the second woman being a lieutenant who had earned the complimentary name of The Vengeance.

They passed through the intervening streets as quickly as they might, ascended the staircase of the new domicile, were admitted by Jerry, and found Lucie weeping, alone. She was thrown into a transport by the tidings Mr. Lorry gave her of her husband, and clasped the hand that delivered his note—little thinking what it had been doing near him in the night, and might, but for a chance, have done to him.

> DEAREST,—Take courage. I am well, and your father has influence around me. You cannot answer this. Kiss our child for me.

That was all the writing. It was so much, however, to her who received it, that she turned from Defarge to his wife, and kissed one of the hands that knitted. It was a passionate, loving, thankful, womanly action, but the hand made no response—dropped cold and heavy, and took to its knitting again.

There was something in its touch that gave Lucie a check. She stopped in the act of putting the note in her bosom, and with her hands yet at her neck, looked terrified at Madame Defarge. Madame Defarge met the lifted eyebrows and forehead with a cold impassive stare.

"My dear," said Mr. Lorry, striking in to explain; "there are frequent risings in the streets; and, although it is not likely they will ever trouble you, Madame Defarge wishes to see those whom she has the power to protect at such times, to the end that she may know them—that she may identify them. I believe," said Mr. Lorry, rather halting in his reassuring words, as the stony manner of all the three impressed itself upon him more and more, "I state the case, Citizen Defarge?"

Defarge looked gloomily at his wife, and gave no other answer than a gruff sound of acquiescence.

"You had better, Lucie," said Mr. Lorry, doing all he could to propitiate, by tone and manner, "have the dear child here, and our good Pross. Our good Pross, Defarge, is an English lady, and knows no French."

The lady in question, whose rooted conviction that she was more than a match for any foreigner, was not to be shaken by distress and danger, appeared with folded arms, and observed in English to The Vengeance, whom her eyes first encountered, "Well, I am sure, Boldface! I hope *you* are pretty well!" She also bestowed a British cough on Madame Defarge; but, neither of the two took much heed of her.

"Is that his child?" said Madame Defarge, stopping in her work for the first time, and pointing her knitting-needle at little Lucie as if it were the finger of Fate.

"Yes, madame," answered Mr. Lorry; "this is our poor prisoner's darling daughter, and only child."

The shadow attendant on Madame Defarge and her party seemed to fall so threatening and dark on the child, that her mother instinctively kneeled on the ground beside her, and held her to her breast. The shadow attendant on Madame Defarge and her party seemed then to fall, threatening and dark, on both the mother and the child.

"It is enough, my husband," said Madame Defarge. "I have seen them. We may go."

But, the suppressed manner had enough of menace in it—not visible and presented, but indistinct and withheld—to alarm Lucie into saying, as she laid her appealing hand on Madame Defarge's dress:

"You will be good to my poor husband. You will do him no harm. You will help me to see him if you can?"

"Your husband is not my business here," returned Madame Defarge, looking down at her with perfect composure. "It is the daughter of your father who is my business here."

"For my sake, then, be merciful to my husband. For my child's sake! We are more afraid of you than of these others."

Madame Defarge received it as a compliment, and looked at her husband. Defarge, who had been uneasily biting his thumbnail and looking at her, collected his face into a sterner expression.

"What is it that your husband says in that little letter?"

asked Madame Defarge, with a lowering smile. "Influence; he says something touching influence?"

"That my father," said Lucie, hurriedly taking the paper from her breast, but with her alarmed eyes on her questioner and not on it, "has much influence around him."

"Surely it will release him!" said Madame Defarge. "Let it do so."

"As a wife and mother," cried Lucie, most earnestly, "I implore you to have pity on me and not to exercise any power that you possess, against my innocent husband, but to use it in his behalf. O sister-woman, think of me. As a wife and mother!"

Madame Defarge looked, coldly as ever, at the suppliant, and said turning to her friend The Vengeance:

"The wives and mothers we have been used to see, since we were as little as this child, and much less, have not been greatly considered? We have known *their* husbands and fathers laid in prison and kept from them, often enough? All our lives, we have seen our sister-women suffer, in themselves and in their children, poverty, nakedness, hunger, thirst, sickness, misery, oppression and neglect of all kinds."

"We have seen nothing else," returned The Vengeance.

"We have borne this a long time," said Madame Defarge, turning her eyes again upon Lucie. "Judge you! Is it likely that the trouble of one wife and mother would be much to us now?"

She resumed her knitting and went out. The Vengeance followed. Defarge went last, and closed the door.

"Courage, my dear Lucie," said Mr. Lorry, as he raised her. "Courage, courage! So far all goes well with us—much, much better than it has of late gone with many poor souls. Cheer up, and have a thankful heart."

"I am not thankless, I hope, but that dreadful woman seems to throw a shadow on me and on all my hopes."

"Tut, tut!" said Mr. Lorry; "what is this despondency in the brave little breast? A shadow indeed! No substance in it, Lucie."

But the shadow of the manner of these Defarges was dark upon himself, for all that, and in his secret mind it troubled him greatly.

IV CALM IN STORM

DOCTOR MANETTE did not return until the morning of the fourth day of his absence. So much of what had happened in that dreadful time as could be kept from the knowledge of Lucie was so well concealed from her, that not until long afterwards when France and she were wide apart, did she know that eleven hundred defenceless prisoners of both sexes and all ages had been killed by the populace; that four days and nights had been darkened by this deed of horror; and that the air around her had been tainted by the slain.[1] She only knew that there had been an attack upon the prisons, that all political prisoners had been in danger, and that some had been dragged out by the crowd and murdered.

To Mr. Lorry, the Doctor communicated under an injunction of secrecy on which he had no need to dwell, that the crowd had taken him through a scene of carnage to the prison of La Force. That, in the prison he had found a self-appointed tribunal sitting, before which the prisoners were brought singly, and by which they were rapidly ordered to be put forth to be massacred, or to be released, or (in a few cases) to be sent back to their cells. That, presented by his conductors to this tribunal, he had announced himself by name and profession as having been for eighteen years a secret and an unaccused prisoner in

---

[1] THE SLAIN—These eleven hundred were the victims of the September Massacres (September 2–6, 1792). The Revolutionists took possession of the prisons, constituted tribunals, and served as executioners. The prisoners were called, and after a few questions they were put at liberty or led into the courtyard and executed.

the Bastille; that, one of the body so sitting in judgment had risen and identified him, and that this man was Defarge.

That, hereupon he had ascertained, through the registers on the table, that his son-in-law was among the living prisoners, and had pleaded hard to the tribunal—of whom some members were asleep and some awake, some dirty with murder and some clean, some sober and some not—for his life and liberty. That, in the first frantic greetings lavished on himself as a notable sufferer under the overthrown system, it had been accorded to him to have Charles Darnay brought before the lawless court, and examined. That, he seemed on the point of being at once released, when the tide in his favor met with some unexplained check, which led to a few words of secret conference. That, the man sitting as President had then informed Doctor Manette that the prisoner must remain in custody, but should, for his sake, be held inviolate in safe custody. That, immediately, on a signal, the prisoner was removed to the interior of the prison again; but, that he, the Doctor, had then so strongly pleaded for permission to remain and assure himself that his son-in-law was, through no malice or mischance, delivered to the concourse whose murderous yells outside the gate had often drowned the proceedings, that he had obtained the permission, and had remained in that Hall of Blood until the danger was over.

As Mr. Lorry received these confidences, and as he watched the face of his friend now sixty-two years of age, a misgiving arose within him that such dread experiences would revive the old danger. But, he had never seen his friend in his present aspect; he had never at all known him in his present character. For the first time the Doctor felt, now, that his suffering was strength and power. For the first time, he felt that in that sharp fire, he had slowly forged the iron which could break the prison door of his daughter's husband, and deliver him. "It all tended to a good end, my friend; it was not mere waste and ruin. As my beloved child was helpful in restoring me to myself, I will be helpful now in restoring the dearest part of herself to her; by the aid of Heaven I will do it!" Thus, Doctor Manette. And when Jarvis Lorry saw the kindled eyes, the resolute face, the calm strong look and bearing of the man whose life always seemed to him to have been stopped, like a clock, for so many years, and then set going again with an energy which had lain dormant during the cessation of its usefulness, he believed.

Greater things than the Doctor had at that time to contend with, would have yielded before his persevering purpose. While he kept himself in his place as a physician whose business was with all degrees of mankind, bond and free, rich and poor, bad and good, he used his personal influence so wisely, that he was soon the inspecting physician of three prisons, and among them of La Force. He could now assure Lucie that her husband was no longer confined alone, but was mixed with the general body of prisoners; he saw her husband weekly, and brought sweet messages to her, straight from his lips; sometimes her husband himself sent a letter to her (though never by the Doctor's hand), but she was not permitted to write to him; for, among the many wild suspicions of plots in the prisons, the wildest of all pointed at emigrants who were known to have made friends or permanent connections abroad.

But, though the Doctor tried hard, and never ceased trying, to get Charles Darnay set at liberty, or at least to get him brought to trial, the public current of the time set too strong and fast for him. The new Era began;[2] the king was tried, doomed, and beheaded; the Republic of Liberty, Equality, Fraternity, or Death, declared for victory or death against the world in arms; and three hundred thousand men, summoned to rise against the tyrants of the earth, rose from all the varying soils of France. What private solicitude could rear itself against the deluge of the Year One of Liberty—the deluge rising from below, not falling from above, and with the windows of Heaven shut, not opened!

There was no pause, no pity, no peace, no interval of relenting rest, no measurement of time. Though days and nights circled as regularly as when time was young, and the evening and the morning were the first day, other count of time there was none. Hold of it was lost in the raging fever of a nation, as it is in the fever of one patient. Now, breaking the unnatural silence of a whole city, the executioner showed the people the head of the

---

[2] THE NEW ERA BEGAN—France was declared a republic and the King was beheaded as a traitor in January, 1793. The motto of the new Republic was Liberty, Equality, Fraternity. The calendar was revised and France began to reckon from the Year One of the Republic. The description of the times in this story are not exaggerated.

king—and now, it seemed almost in the same breath, the head of his fair wife which had had eight weary months of imprisoned widowhood and misery, to turn it grey.

And yet, observing the strange law of contradiction which obtains in all such cases, the time was long, while it flamed by so fast. A revolutionary tribunal in the capital, and forty or fifty thousand revolutionary committees all over the land; a law of the suspected, which struck away all security for liberty or life, and delivered over any good and innocent person to any bad and guilty one; prisons gorged with people who had committed no offence, and could obtain no hearing; these things became the established order and nature of appointed things, and seemed to be ancient usage before they were many weeks old. Above all, one hideous figure grew as familiar as if it had been before the general gaze from the foundations of the world—the figure of the sharp female called La Guillotine.

It was the popular theme for jests; it was the best cure for headache, it infallibly prevented the hair from turning grey, it imparted a peculiar delicacy to the complexion, it was the national razor which shaved close: who kissed La Guillotine, looked through the little window and sneezed into the sack. It sheared off heads so many, that it, and the ground it most polluted, were a rotten red. It hushed the eloquent, struck down the powerful, abolished the beautiful and good. Twenty-two friends of high public mark, twenty-one living and one dead, it had lopped the heads off, in one morning, in as many minutes.

Among these terrors, and the brood belonging to them, the Doctor walked with a steady head: confident in his power, cautiously persistent in his end, never doubting that he would save Lucie's husband at last. Yet the current of the time swept by, so strong and deep, and carried the time away so fiercely, that Charles had lain in prison one year and three months when the Doctor was thus steady and confident. So much more wicked and distracted had the Revolution grown in that December month, that the rivers of the South were encumbered with the bodies of the violently drowned by night, and prisoners were shot in lines and squares under the southern wintry sun. Still, the Doctor walked among the terrors with a steady head. No man better known than he, in Paris at that day; no man in a stranger situation. Silent, humane, indispensable in hospital and prison, using his art equally among assassins and victims, he was a man apart. In the exercise of his skill, the appearance and the story of the Bastille captive removed him from all other men. He was not suspected or brought in question, any more than if he had indeed been recalled to life some eighteen years before, or were a spirit moving among mortals.

V THE WOOD-SAWYER

ONE year and three months. During all that time Lucie was never sure, from hour to hour, but that the guillotine would strike off her husband's head next day. Every day, through the stony streets, the tumbrils now jolted heavily, filled with condemned. Lovely girls; bright women, brown-haired, black-haired, and grey; youths; stalwart men and old; gentle born and peasant born; all red wine for La Guillotine, all daily brought into light from the dark cellars of the loathsome prisons, and carried to her through the streets to slake her devouring thirst. Liberty, Equality, Fraternity, or Death;—the last, much the easiest to bestow, O Guillotine!

If the suddenness of her calamity, and the whirling wheels of the time, had stunned the Doctor's daughter into awaiting the result in idle despair, it would but have been with her as it was with many. But, from the hour when she had taken the white head to her fresh young bosom in the garret of Saint Antoine, she had been true to her duties. She was truest to them in the season of trial, as all of the quietly loyal and good will always be.

As soon as they were established in their new residence, and her father had entered on the routine of his avocations, she arranged the little household as exactly as if her husband had been there. Everything had its appointed place and appointed time. Little Lucie she taught, as regularly, as if they had all been united in their English home. The slight devices with which she cheated herself into the show of a belief that they would soon be reunited—the little preparations for his speedy return, the setting aside of his chair and his books— these, and the solemn prayer at night for one dear prisoner especially, among the many unhappy souls in prison and the shadow of death—were almost the only outspoken reliefs of her heavy mind.

They had not made the round of their changed life, many weeks, when her father said to her, on coming home one evening:

"My dear, there is an upper window in the prison, to which Charles can sometimes gain access at three in the afternoon. When he can get to it—which depends on many uncertainties and incidents—he might see you in the street, he thinks, if you stood in a certain place that I can show you. But you will not be able to see him, my poor child, and even if you could, it would be unsafe for you to make a sign of recognition."

"O show me the place, my father, and I will go there every day."

From that time, in all weathers, she waited there two hours. As the clock struck two, she was there, and at four she turned resignedly away. When it was not too wet or inclement for her child to be with her, they went together; at other times she was alone; but, she never missed a single day.

It was the dark and dirty corner of a small winding street. The hovel of a cutter of wood into lengths for burning was the only house at that end; all else was well. On the third day of her being there, he noticed her.

"Good-day, citizeness."

"Good-day, citizen."

This mode of address was now prescribed by decree. It had been established voluntarily some time ago, among the more thorough patriots; but, it was now law for everybody.

"Walking here again, citizeness?"

"You see me, citizen!"

The wood-sawyer, who was a little man with a redundancy of gesture (he had once been a mender of roads), cast a glance at the prison, pointed at the prison, and putting his ten fingers before his face to represent bars, peeped through them jocosely.

"But it's not my business," said he. And went on sawing his wood.

Next day, he was looking out for her, and accosted her the moment she appeared.

"What! Walking here again, citizeness?"

"Yes, citizen."

"Ah! A child too! Your mother, is it not, my little citizeness?"

"Do I say yes, mamma?" whispered little Lucie, drawing close to her.

"Yes, dearest."

"Yes, citizen."

"Ah! But it's not my business. My work is my business. See my saw! I call it my Little Guillotine. La, la, la; La, la la! And off his head comes!"

The billet fell as he spoke, and he threw it into a basket.

"I call myself the Sanson[1] of the firewood guillotine. See here again! Loo, loo, loo; Loo, loo, loo! And off *her* head comes! Now, a child. Tickle, tickle! Pickle, pickle! And off *its* head comes. All the family!"

Lucie shuddered as he threw two more billets into his basket, but it was impossible to be there while the wood-sawyer was at work, and not be in his sight. Thenceforth, to secure his good will, she always spoke to him first, and often gave him drink-money, which he readily received.

He was an inquisitive fellow, and sometimes when she had quite forgotten him in gazing at the prison roof and grates, and in lifting her heart up to her husband, she would come to herself to find him looking at her, with his knees on his bench and his saw stopped in its work. "But it's not my business!" he would generally say at those times, and would briskly fall to his sawing again.

In all weathers, in the snow and frost of winter, in the bitter winds of spring, in the hot sunshine of summer, in the rains of autumn, and again in the snow and frost of winter, Lucie passed two hours of every day at this place; and every day, on leaving it, she kissed the prison wall. Her husband saw her (so she

---

[1] SANSON—Sanson was the chief executioner throughout the Reign of Terror. He beheaded both the king and queen.

learned from her father) it might be once in five or six times: it might be twice or thrice running: it might be, not for a week or a fortnight together. It was enough that he could and did see her when the chances served, and on that possibility she would have waited out the day, seven days a week.

These occupations brought her round to the December month, wherein her father walked among the terrors with a steady head. On a lightly-snowing afternoon she arrived at the usual corner. It was a day of some wild rejoicing, and a festival. She had seen the houses, as she came along, decorated with little pikes, and with little red caps stuck upon them; also, with tri-colored ribbons; also, with the standard inscription, Republic One and Indivisible. Liberty, Equality, Fraternity, or Death!

The miserable shop of the wood-sawyer was so small, that its whole surface furnished very indifferent space for this legend. He had got somebody to scrawl it up for him, however, who had squeezed Death in with most inappropriate difficulty. On his house-top, he displayed pike and cap, as a good citizen must, and in a window he had stationed his saw, inscribed as his "Little Sainte Guillotine"—for the great sharp female was by that time popularly canonised. His shop was shut and he was not there, which was a relief to Lucie, and left her quite alone.

But, he was not far off, for presently she heard a troubled movement and a shouting coming along, which filled her with fear. A moment afterwards, and a throng of people came pouring round the corner by the prison wall, in the midst of whom was the wood-sawyer hand in hand with The Vengeance. There could not be fewer than five hundred people, and they were dancing like five thousand demons. There was no other music than their own singing. They danced to the popular Revolution song, keeping a ferocious time that was like a gnashing of teeth in unison. Men and women danced together, women danced together, men danced together, as hazard had brought them together. At first, they were a mere storm of coarse red caps and coarser woollen rags; but, as they filled the place, and stopped to dance about Lucie, some ghastly apparition of a dance-figure gone raving mad arose among them. They advanced, retreated, struck at one another's hands, clutched at one another's heads, spun round alone, caught one another and spun round in pairs, until many of them dropped. While those were down, the rest linked hand in hand, and all spun round together: then the ring broke, and in separate rings of two and four they turned and turned until they all stopped at once, began again, struck, clutched, and tore, and then reversed the spin, and all spun round another way. Suddenly they stopped again, paused, struck out the time afresh, formed into lines the width of the public way, and, with their heads low down and their hands high up, swooped screaming off. No fight could have been half so terrible as this dance. It was so emphatically a fallen sport—a something, once innocent, delivered over to all devilry—a healthy pastime changed into a means of angering the blood, bewildering the senses, and steeling the heart. Such grace as was visible in it, made it the uglier, showing how warped and perverted all things good by nature were become.

This was the Carmagnole.[2] As it passed, leaving Lucie frightened and bewildered in the doorway of the wood-sawyer's house, the feathery snow fell as quietly and lay as white and soft, as if it had never been.

"O my father!" for he stood before her when she lifted up the eyes she had momentarily darkened with her hand, "such a cruel, bad sight."

"I know, my dear, I know. I have seen it many times. Don't be frightened! Not one of them would harm you."

"I am not frightened for myself, my father. But when I think of my husband, and the mercies of these people——"

"We will set him above their mercies, very soon. I left him climbing to the window, and I came to tell you. There is no one here to see. You may kiss your hands toward that highest shelving roof."

"I do so, father, and I send him my soul with it!"

"You cannot see him, my poor dear?"

"No, father," said Lucie, yearning and weeping as she kissed her hand, "no."

A footstep in the snow. Madame Defarge. "I salute you, citizeness," from the Doctor. "I salute you, citizen." This in passing. Nothing more. Madame Defarge gone, like a shadow over the white road.

"Give me your arm, my love. Pass from here with an air

---

[2] THE CARMAGNOLE (kär-mä-nyōl')—A Revolutionary song and dance, the performance of which was usually a wild orgy.

of cheerfulness and courage, for his sake. That was well done"; they had left the spot; "it shall not be in vain. Charles is summoned for tomorrow."

"For tomorrow!"

"There is no time to lose. I am well prepared, but there are precautions to be taken, that could not be taken until he was actually summoned before the tribunal. He has not received the notice yet, but I know that he will presently be summoned for tomorrow, and removed to the Conciergerie;[3] I have timely information. You are not afraid?"

She could scarcely answer, "I trust in you."

"Do so, implicitly. Your suspense is nearly ended, my darling; he shall be restored to you within a few hours; I have encompassed him with every protection. I must see Lorry."

He stopped. There was a heavy lumbering of wheels within hearing. They both knew too well what it meant. One. Two. Three. Three tumbrils faring away with their dread loads over the hushing snow.

"I must see Lorry," the Doctor repeated, turning her another way.

The staunch old gentleman was still in his trust; had never left it. He and his books were in frequent requisition as to property confiscated and made national. What he could save for the owners, he saved. No better man living to hold fast by what Tellson's had in keeping, and to hold his peace.

A murky red and yellow sky, and a rising mist from the Seine, denoted the approach of darkness. It was almost dark when they arrived at the bank. The stately residence was altogether blighted and deserted. Above a heap of dust and ashes in the court, ran the letters: National Property. Republic One and Indivisible. Liberty, Equality, Fraternity, or Death.

Who could that be with Mr. Lorry—the owner of the riding-coat upon the chair—who must not be seen? From whom newly arrived, did he come out, agitated and surprised, to take his favorite in his arms? To whom did he appear to repeat her faltering words, when, raising his voice and turning his head toward the door of the room from which he had issued, he said: "Removed to the Conciergerie, and summoned for tomorrow."

[3] CONCIERGERIE (kôn-syerzh-rē')—A large prison.

VI TRIUMPH

The dread tribunal of five judges, public prosecutor, and determined jury, sat every day. Their lists went forth every evening, and were read out by the gaolers of the various prisons to their prisoners.

"Charles Evrémonde, called Darnay," was at length arraigned.

His judges sat upon the bench in feathered hats; but the rough red cap and tricolored cockade was the head-dress otherwise prevailing. Looking at the jury and the turbulent audience, he might have thought that the usual order of things was reversed, and that the felons were trying the honest men. The lowest, cruellest, and worst populace of a city, never without its quantity of low, cruel, and bad, were the directing spirits of the scene: noisily commenting, applauding, disapproving, anticipating, and precipitating the result, without a check. Of the men, the greater part were armed in various ways; of the women, some wore knives, some daggers, some ate and drank as they looked on, many knitted. Among these last, was one, with a spare piece of knitting under her arm as she worked. She was in a front row, by the side of a man whom he had never seen since his arrival at the barrier, but whom he directly remembered as Defarge. He noticed that she once or twice whispered in his ear, and that she seemed to be his wife; but, what he most noticed in the two figures was, that although they were posted as close to himself as they could be, they never looked towards him. They seemed to be waiting for something with a dogged determination, and they looked at the jury but at nothing else. Under the president sat Doctor Manette, in his usual quiet dress. As well as the prisoner could see, he and Mr. Lorry were the only men there, unconnected with the tribunal, who wore their usual clothes, and had not assumed the coarse garb of the Carmagnole.

Charles Evrémonde, called Darnay, was accused by the public prosecutor as an emigrant, whose life was forfeit to the Republic, under the decree which banished all emigrants on pain of death. It was nothing that the decree bore date since his return to France. There he was, and there was the decree; he had been taken in France, and his head was demanded.

"Take off his head!" cried the audience. "An enemy to the Republic!"

The president rang his bell to silence those cries, and asked the prisoner whether it was not true that he had lived many years in England?

Undoubtedly it was.

Was he not an emigrant then? What did he call himself?

Not an emigrant, he hoped, within the sense and spirit of the law.

Why not? the president desired to know.

Because he had voluntarily relinquished a title that was distasteful to him, and a station that was distasteful to him, and had left his country—he submitted before the word emigrant in the present acceptation by the tribunal was in use—to live by his own industry in England, rather than of the industry of the overladen people of France.

What proof had he of this?

He handed in the names of two witnesses: Théophile Gabelle, and Alexandre Manette.

But he had married in England? the president reminded him.

True, but not an English woman.

A citizeness of France?

Yes. By birth.

Her name and family?

"Lucie Manette, only daughter of Doctor Manette, the good physician who sits there."

This answer had a happy effect upon the audience. Cries in exaltation of the well-known good physician rent the hall. So capriciously were the people moved, that tears immediately rolled down several ferocious countenances which had been glaring at the prisoner a moment before, as if with impatience to pluck him out into the street and kill him.

On these few steps of his dangerous way, Charles Darnay had set his foot according to Doctor Manette's reiterated instructions. The same cautious counsel directed every step that lay before him, and had prepared every inch of his road.

The president asked why had he returned to France when he did, and not sooner?

He had not returned sooner, he replied, simply because he had no means of living in France, save those he had resigned;

whereas, in England, he lived by giving instruction in the French language and literature. He had returned when he did, on the pressing and written entreaty of a French citizen, who represented that his life was endangered by his absence. He had come back, to save a citizen's life, and to bear his testimony, at whatever personal hazard, to the truth. Was that criminal in the eyes of the Republic?

The populace cried enthusiastically, "No!" and the president rang his bell to quiet them. Which it did not, for they continued to cry "No!" until they left off, of their own will.

The president required the name of that citizen? The accused explained that the citizen was his first witness. He also referred with confidence to the citizen's letter, which had been taken from him at the barrier, but which he did not doubt would be found among the papers then before the president.

The Doctor had taken care that it should be there—had assured him that it would be there—and at this stage of the proceedings it was produced and read. Citizen Gabelle was called to confirm it, and did so. Citizen Gabelle hinted, with infinite delicacy and politeness, that in the pressure of business imposed on the tribunal by the multitude of enemies of the Republic with which it had to deal, he had been slightly overlooked in his prison of the Abbaye—in fact, had rather passed out of the tribunal's patriotic remembrance—until three days ago; when he had been summoned before it, and had been set at liberty on the jury's declaring themselves satisfied that the accusation against him was answered, as to himself, by the surrender of the citizen Evrémonde, called Darnay.

Doctor Manette was next questioned. His high personal popularity, and the clearness of his answers, made a great impression; but, as he proceeded, as he showed that the accused was his first friend on his release from his long imprisonment; that, the accused had remained in England, always faithful and devoted to his daughter and himself in their exile; that, so far from being in favor with the aristocrat government there, he had actually been tried for his life by it, as the foe of England and friend of the United States—as he brought these circumstances into view, with the greatest discretion and with the straightforward force of truth and earnestness, the jury and the populace became one. At last, when he appealed by name to

Monsieur Lorry, an English gentleman then and there present, who, like himself, had been a witness on that English trial and could corroborate his account of it, the jury declared that they had heard enough, and that they were ready with their votes if the president were content to receive them.

At every vote (the jurymen voted aloud and individually), the populace set up a shout of applause. All the voices were in the prisoner's favor, and the president declared him free.

Then, began one of those extraordinary scenes with which the populace sometimes gratified their fickleness, or their better impulses towards generosity and mercy, or which they regarded as some set-off against their swollen account of cruel rage. No man can decide now to which of these motives such extraordinary scenes were referable; it is probable, to a blending of all the three, with the second predominating. No sooner was the acquittal pronounced, than tears were shed as freely as blood at another time, and such fraternal embraces were bestowed upon the prisoner by as many of both sexes as could rush at him, that after his long and unwholesome confinement he was in danger of fainting from exhaustion; none the less because he knew very well, that the very same people, carried by another current, would have rushed at him with the very same intensity, to rend him to pieces and strew him over the streets.

His removal, to make way for other accused persons who were to be tried, rescued him from these caresses for the moment. Five were to be tried together, next, as enemies of the Republic, forasmuch as they had not assisted it by word or deed. So quick was the tribunal to compensate itself and the nation for a chance lost, that these five came down to him before he left the place, condemned to die within twenty-four hours. The first of them told him so, with the customary prison signs of death—a raised finger—and they all added in words, "Long live the Republic!"

The five had had, it is true, no audience to lengthen their proceedings, for when he and Doctor Manette emerged from the gate, there was a great crowd about it, in which there seemed to be every face he had seen in court—except two, for which he looked in vain. On his coming out, the concourse made at him anew, weeping, embracing, and shouting, all by turns and all together, until the very tide of the river on the bank of which the mad scene was acted, seemed to run mad, like the people on the shore.

They put him into a great chair they had among them, and which they had taken either out of the court itself, or one of its rooms or passages. Over the chair they had thrown a red flag, and to the back of it they had bound a pike with a red cap on its top. In this car of triumph, not even the Doctor's entreaties could prevent his being carried to his home on men's shoulders, with a confused sea of red caps heaving about him, and casting up to sight from the stormy deep such wrecks of faces, that he more than once misdoubted his mind being in confusion, and that he was in the tumbril on his way to the guillotine.

In wild dreamlike procession, embracing whom they met and pointing him out, they carried him on. Reddening the snowy streets with the prevailing Republican color, in winding and tramping through them, as they had reddened them below the snow with a deeper dye, they carried him thus into the courtyard of the building where he lived. Her father had gone on before, to prepare her, and when her husband stood upon his feet, she dropped insensible in his arms.

As he held her to his heart and turned her beautiful head between his face and the brawling crowd, so that his tears and her lips might come together unseen, a few of the people fell to dancing. Instantly, all the rest fell to dancing, and the courtyard overflowed with the Carmagnole. Then, they elevated into the vacant chair a young woman from the crowd to be carried as the Goddess of Liberty, and then, swelling and overflowing out into the adjacent streets, and along the river's bank, and over the bridge, the Carmagnole absorbed them every one and whirled them away.

After grasping the Doctor's hand, as he stood victorious and proud before him; after grasping the hand of Mr. Lorry, who came panting in breathless from his struggle against the waterspout of the Carmagnole; after kissing little Lucie, who was lifted up to clasp her arms round his neck; and after embracing the ever zealous and faithful Pross who lifted her; he took his wife in his arms and carried her up to their rooms.

"Lucie! My own! I am safe."

"O dearest Charles, let me thank God for this on my knees as I have prayed to Him."

They all reverently bowed their heads and hearts. When she was again in his arms, he said to her:

"And now speak to your father, dearest. No other man in all this France could have done what he has done for me."

She laid her head upon her father's breast as she had laid his poor head on her own breast, long ago. He was happy in the return he had made her, he was recompensed for his suffering, he was proud of his strength. "You must not be weak, my darling," he remonstrated; "don't tremble so. I have saved him."

VII   A KNOCK AT THE DOOR

"I HAVE saved him." It was not another of the dreams in which he had often come back; he was really here. And yet his wife trembled, and a vague but heavy fear was upon her.

All the air around was so thick and dark, the people were so passionately revengeful and fitful, the innocent were so constantly put to death on vague suspicion and black malice, it was so impossible to forget that many as blameless as her husband and as dear to others as he was to her, every day shared the fate from which he had been clutched, that her heart could not be as lightened of its load as she felt it ought to be. The shadows of the wintry afternoon were beginning to fall, and even now the dreadful carts were rolling through the streets. Her mind pursued them, looking for him among the condemned; and then she clung closer to his real presence and trembled more.

Her father, cheering her, showed a compassionate superiority to this woman's weakness, which was wonderful to see. No garret, no shoemaking, no One Hundred and Five, North Tower, now! He had accomplished the task he had set himself, his promise was redeemed, he had saved Charles. Let them all lean upon him.

Their housekeeping was of a very frugal kind: not only because that was the safest way of life, involving the least offence to the people, but because they were not rich, and Charles, throughout his imprisonment, had had to pay heavily for his bad food, and for his guard, and towards the living of the poorer prisoners. Partly on this account, and partly to avoid a domestic spy, they kept no servant; the citizen and citizeness who acted as porters at the courtyard gate, rendered them occasional service; and Jerry (almost wholly transferred to them by Mr. Lorry) had become their daily retainer, and had his bed there every night.

It was an ordinance of the Republic One and Indivisible of Liberty, Equality, Fraternity, or Death, that on the door or doorpost of every house, the name of every inmate must be legibly inscribed in letters of a certain size, at a certain convenient height from the ground. Mr. Jerry Cruncher's name, therefore, duly embellished the doorpost down below; and, as the afternoon shadows deepened, the owner of that name himself appeared, from overlooking a painter whom Doctor Manette had employed to add to the list the name of Charles Evrémonde, called Darnay.

In the universal fear and distrust that darkened the time, all the usual harmless ways of life were changed. In the Doctor's little household, as in very many others, the articles of daily consumption that were wanted, were purchased every evening, in small quantities and at various small shops. To avoid attracting notice, and to give as little occasion as possible for talk and envy, was the general desire.

For some months past, Miss Pross and Mr. Cruncher had discharged the office of purveyors; the former carrying the money; the latter, the basket. Every afternoon at about the time when the public lamps were lighted, they fared forth on this duty, and made and brought home such purchases as were needful. Although Miss Pross, through her long association with a French family, might have known as much of their language as of her own, if she had had a mind, she had no mind in that direction; consequently she knew no more of "that nonsense" than Mr. Cruncher did. So her manner of marketing was to plump a noun-substantive at the head of a shopkeeper without any introduction in the nature of an article, and, if it happened not to be the name of the thing she wanted, to look round for that thing, lay hold of it, and hold on by it until the bargain was concluded. She always made a bargain for it, by holding up, as a statement of its just price, one finger less than the merchant held up, whatever his number might be.

"Now, Mr. Cruncher," said Miss Pross, whose eyes were red with felicity; "if you are ready, I am."

Jerry hoarsely professed himself at Miss Pross's service. He had worn all his rust off long ago, but nothing would file his spiky head down.

"There's all manner of things wanted," said Miss Pross, "and we shall have a precious time of it. Now, Ladybird, never you stir from that fire till I come back. Take care of the dear husband you have recovered, and don't move your pretty head from his shoulder as you have it now, till you see me again! Now, Mr. Cruncher!— Don't you move, Ladybird!"

They went out, leaving Lucie, and her husband, her father, and the child, by a bright fire. Mr. Lorry was expected back presently from the banking house. Miss Pross had lighted the lamp, but had put it aside in a corner, that they might enjoy the firelight undisturbed. Little Lucie sat by her grandfather with her hands clasped through his arm; and he, in a tone not rising much above a whisper, began to tell her a story of a great and powerful fairy who had opened a prison-wall and let out a captive who had once done the fairy a service. All was subdued and quiet, and Lucie was more at ease than she had been.

"What is that!" she cried, all at once.

"My dear!" said her father, stopping in his story, and laying his hand on hers, "command yourself. What a disordered state you are in! The least thing—nothing—startles you. *You*, your father's daughter?"

"I thought, my father," said Lucie, excusing herself, with a pale face and in a faltering voice, "that I heard strange feet upon the stairs."

"My love, the staircase is as still as Death."

As he said the word, a blow was struck upon the door.

"O father, father. What can this be! Hide Charles. Save him!"

"My child," said the Doctor, rising and laying his hand upon her shoulder, "I *have* saved him. What weakness is this, my dear! Let me go to the door."

He took the lamp in his hand, crossed the two intervening outer rooms, and opened it. A rude clattering of feet over the floors, and four rough men in red caps, armed with sabres and pistols, entered the room.

"The Citizen Evrémonde, called Darnay," said the first.

"Who seeks him?" answered Darnay.

"I seek him. We seek him. I know you, Evrémonde, I saw you before the tribunal today. You are again the prisoner of the Republic."

The four surrounded him, where he stood with his wife and child clinging to him.

"Tell me how and why am I again a prisoner?"

"It is enough that you return straight to the Conciergerie, and will know tomorrow. You are summoned for tomorrow."

Dr. Manette, whom this visitation had so turned into stone, that he stood with the lamp in his hand, as if he were a statue made to hold it, moved after these words were spoken, put the lamp down, and confronting the speaker, and taking him, not ungently, by the loose front of his red woolen shirt, said:

"You know him, you have said. Do you know me?"

"Yes, I know you, Citizen Doctor."

"We all know you, Citizen Doctor," said the other three.

He looked abstractedly from one to another, and said, in a lower voice, after a pause:

"Will you answer his question to me then? How does this happen?"

"Citizen Doctor," said the first, reluctantly; "he has been denounced[1] to the Section of Saint Antoine. This citizen," pointing out the second who had entered, "is from Saint Antoine."

The citizen here indicated nodded his head, and added:

"He is accused by Saint Antoine."

"Of what?" asked the Doctor.

"Citizen Doctor," said the first, with his former reluctance, "ask no more. If the Republic demands sacrifices from you, without doubt you as a good patriot will be happy to make them. The Republic goes before all. The People is supreme. Evrémonde, we are pressed."

"One word," the Doctor entreated. "Will you tell me who denounced him?"

"It is against rule," answered the first; "but you can ask him of Saint Antoine here."

---

[1] DENOUNCED—It was the privilege of any citizen to "denounce anyone as a traitor, and the charge would be investigated."

The Doctor turned his eyes upon that man. Who moved uneasily on his feet, rubbed his beard a little, and at length said:

"Well! Truly it is against rule. But he is denounced—and gravely—by the Citizen and Citizeness Defarge. And by one other."

"What other?"

"Do *you* ask, Citizen Doctor?"

"Yes."

"Then," said he of Saint Antoine, with a strange look, "you will be answered tomorrow. Now, I am dumb!"

VIII   A HAND AT CARDS

HAPPILY unconscious of the new calamity at home, Miss Pross threaded her way along the narrow streets, reckoning in her mind the number of indispensable purchases she had to make. Mr. Cruncher, with the basket, walked at her side. They both looked to the right and to the left into most of the shops they passed, had a wary eye for all gregarious assemblages of people, and turned out of their road to avoid any very excited group of talkers.

Having purchased a few small articles of grocery, and a measure of oil for the lamp, Miss Pross bethought herself of some wine they wanted. After peeping into several wine-shops, she stopped at the sign of The Good Republican Brutus[1] of Antiquity, where the aspect of things rather took her fancy. It had a quieter look than any other place of the same description they had passed, and, though red with patriotic caps, was not so red as the rest. Sounding Mr. Cruncher and finding him of her opinion, Miss Pross resorted to the Good Republican Brutus of Antiquity, attended by her cavalier.

Slightly observant of the smoky lights; of the people, pipe in mouth, playing with limp cards and yellow dominoes; of the one bare-breasted, bare-armed, soot-begrimed workman reading a journal aloud, and of the others listening to him; of the weapons worn, or laid aside to be resumed; of the two or three customers fallen forward asleep, who in the popular, high-shouldered shaggy black spencer[2] looked, in that attitude, like slumbering bears or dogs; the two outlandish customers approached the counter, and showed what they wanted.

As their wine was measuring out, a man parted from another man in a corner, and rose to depart. In going, he had to face Miss Pross. No sooner did he face her, than Miss Pross uttered a scream, and clapped her hands.

In a moment, the whole company were on their feet. That somebody was assassinated by somebody vindicating a difference of opinion, was the likeliest occurrence. Everybody looked to see somebody fall, but only saw a man and woman standing staring at each other; the man with all the outward aspect of a Frenchman and a thorough Republican; the woman, evidently English.

What was said in this disappointing anti-climax, by the disciples of the Good Republican Brutus of Antiquity, except that it was something very voluble and loud, would have been as so much Hebrew to Miss Pross and her protector, though they had been all ears. But, they had no ears for anything in their surprise. For, it must be recorded, that not only was Miss Pross lost in amazement and agitation; but, Mr. Cruncher—

---

[1] THE GOOD REPUBLICAN BRUTUS—Brutus and his fellow conspirators believed that Caesar was endangering the republican institutions of Rome. The Revolutionists often adopted names of ancient heroes.

[2] SPENCER—Outer coat.

though it seemed on his own separate and individual account—was in a state of the greatest wonder.

"What is the matter?" said the man who had caused Miss Pross to scream; speaking in a vexed abrupt voice (though in a low tone), and in English.

"Oh, Solomon, dear Solomon!" cried Miss Pross, clapping her hands again. "After not setting eyes upon you or hearing of you for so long a time, do I find you here!"

"Don't call me Solomon. Do you want to be the death of me?" asked the man, in a furtive frightened way.

"Brother, brother!" cried Miss Pross, bursting into tears. "Have I ever been so hard with you that you ask me such a cruel question!"

"Then hold your meddlesome tongue," said Solomon, "and come out, if you want to speak to me. Pay for your wine, and come out. Who's this man?"

Miss Pross, shaking her loving and dejected head at her by no means affectionate brother, said, through her tears, "Mr. Cruncher."

"Let him come out too," said Solomon. "Does he think me a ghost?"

Apparently, Mr. Cruncher did, to judge from his looks. He said not a word, however, and Miss Pross, exploring the depths of her reticule through her tears with great difficulty, paid for the wine. As she did so, Solomon turned to the followers of the Good Republican Brutus of Antiquity, and offered a few words of explanation in the French language, which caused them all to relapse into their former places and pursuits.

"Now," said Solomon, stopping at the dark street corner, "what do you want?"

"How dreadfully unkind in a brother nothing has ever turned my love away from!" cried Miss Pross, "to give me such a greeting, and show me no affection."

"There. Con-found it! There," said Solomon, making a dab at Miss Pross's lips with his own. "Now are you content?"

Miss Pross only shook her head and wept in silence.

"If you expect me to be surprised," said her brother Solomon, "I am not surprised. I knew you were here; I know of most people who are here. If you really don't want to endanger my existence—which I half believe you do—go your ways as soon as possible, and let me go mine. I am busy. I am an official."

"My English brother Solomon," mourned Miss Pross, casting up her tear-fraught eyes, "that had the makings in him of one of the best and greatest of men in his native country, an official among foreigners, and such foreigners! I would almost sooner have seen the dear boy lying in his——"

"I said so!" cried her brother, interrupting. "I knew it! You want to be the death of me. I shall be rendered suspected, by my own sister. Just as I am getting on!"

"The gracious and merciful Heavens forbid!" cried Miss Pross. "Far rather would I never see you again, dear Solomon, though I have ever loved you truly, and ever shall. Say but one affectionate word to me, and tell me there is nothing angry or estranged between us, and I will detain you no longer."

Good Miss Pross! As if the estrangement between them had come of any culpability of hers. As if Mr. Lorry had not known it for a fact, years ago, in the quiet corner in Soho, that this precious brother had spent her money and left her!

He was saying the affectionate word, however, with a far more grudging condescension and patronage than he could have shown if their relative merits and positions had been reversed, when Mr. Cruncher, touching him on the shoulder, hoarsely and unexpectedly interposed with the following singular question:

"I say! Might I ask the favor? As to whether your name is John Solomon, or Solomon John?"

The official turned towards him with sudden distrust. He had not previously uttered a word.

"Come!" said Mr. Cruncher. "Speak out, you know. John Solomon, or Solomon John? She calls you Solomon, and she must know, being your sister. And *I* know you're John, you know. Which of the two goes first? And regarding that name of Pross, likewise. That warn't your name over the water."

"What do you mean?"

"Well, I don't know all I mean, for I can't call to mind what your name was, over the water."

"No?"

"No. But I'll swear it was a name of two syllables."

"Indeed?"

"Yes. T'other one's was one syllable. I know you. You was a spy-witness at the Bailey. What in the name of the

Father of Lies, own father to yourself, was you called at that time?"

"Barsad," said another voice, striking in.

"That's the name for a thousand pound!" cried Jerry.

The speaker who struck in was Sydney Carton. He had his hands behind him under the skirts of his riding-coat, and he stood at Mr. Cruncher's elbow as negligently as he might have stood at the Old Bailey itself.

"Don't be alarmed, my dear Miss Pross. I arrived at Mr. Lorry's, to his surprise, yesterday evening; we agreed that I would not present myself elsewhere until all was well, or unless I could be useful; I present myself here, to beg a little talk with your brother. I wish you had a better employed brother than Mr. Barsad. I wish for your sake Mr. Barsad was not a sheep of the prisons."

Sheep was a cant word of the time for a spy, under the gaolers. The spy, who was pale, turned paler, and asked him how he dared——

"I'll tell you," said Sydney. "I lighted on you, Mr. Barsad, coming out of the prison at the Conciergerie while I was contemplating the walls, an hour or more ago. You have a face to be remembered, and I remember faces well. Made curious by seeing you in that connection, and having a reason, to which you are no stranger, for associating you with the misfortunes of a friend now very unfortunate, I walked in your direction. I walked into the wine-shop here, close after you, and sat near you. I had no difficulty in deducing from your unreserved conversation, and the rumor openly going about among your admirers, the nature of your calling. And gradually, what I had done at random, seemed to shape itself into a purpose, Mr. Barsad."

"What purpose?" the spy asked.

"It would be troublesome, and might be dangerous, to explain in the street. Could you favor me, in confidence, with some minutes of your company—at the office of Tellson's Bank, for instance?"

"Under a threat?"

"Oh! Did I say that!"

"Then why should I go there?"

"Really, Mr. Barsad, I can't say, if you can't."

"Do you mean that you won't say, sir?" the spy irresolutely asked.

"You apprehend me very clearly, Mr. Barsad. I won't."

Carton's negligent recklessness of manner came powerfully in aid of his quickness and skill, in such a business as he had in his secret mind, and with such a man as he had to do with. His practised eye saw it, and made the most of it.

"Now, I told you so," said the spy, casting a reproachful look at his sister; "if any trouble comes of this, it's your doing."

"Come, come, Mr. Barsad!" exclaimed Sydney. "Don't be ungrateful. But for my great respect for your sister, I might not have led up so pleasantly to a little proposal that I wish to make for our mutual satisfaction. Do you go with me to the bank?"

"I'll hear what you have got to say. Yes, I'll go with you."

"I propose that we first conduct your sister safely to the corner of her own street. Let me take your arm, Miss Pross. This is not a good city, at this time, for you to be out in, unprotected; and as your escort knows Mr. Barsad, I will invite him to Mr. Lorry's with us. Are we ready? Come then!"

Miss Pross recalled soon afterwards, and to the end of her life remembered, that as she pressed her hands on Sydney's arm and looked up in his face, imploring him to do no hurt to Solomon, there was a braced purpose in the arm and a kind of inspiration in the eyes, which not only contradicted his light manner, but changed and raised the man. She was too much occupied then, with fears for the brother who so little deserved her affection, and with Sydney's friendly reassurances, adequately to heed what she observed.

They left her at the corner of the street, and Carton led the way to Mr. Lorry's, which was within a few minutes' walk. John Barsad, or Solomon Pross, walked at his side.

Mr. Lorry had just finished his dinner, and was sitting before a cheery little log or two of fire—perhaps looking into their blaze for the picture of that younger elderly gentleman from Tellson's, who had looked into the red coals at the Royal George at Dover, now a good many years ago. He turned his head as they entered, and showed the surprise with which he saw a stranger.

"Miss Pross's brother, sir," said Sydney. "Mr. Barsad."

"Barsad?" repeated the old gentleman, "Barsad? I have an association with the name—and with the face."

"I told you you had a remarkable face, Mr. Barsad," observed Carton, coolly. "Pray sit down."

As he took a chair himself, he supplied the link that Mr. Lorry wanted, by saying to him with a frown, "Witness at that trial." Mr. Lorry immediately remembered, and regarded his new visitor with an undisguised look of abhorrence.

"Mr. Barsad has been recognised by Miss Pross as the affectionate brother you have heard of," said Sydney, "and has acknowledged the relationship. I pass to worse news. Darnay has been arrested again."

Struck with consternation, the old gentleman exclaimed, "What do you tell me! I left him safe and free within these two hours, and am about to return to him!"

"Arrested for all that. When was it done, Mr. Barsad?"

"Just now, if at all."

"Mr. Barsad is the best authority possible, sir," said Sydney, "and I have it from Mr. Barsad's communication to a friend and brother sheep over a bottle of wine, that the arrest has taken place. He left the messengers at the gate, and saw them admitted by the porter. There is no earthly doubt that he is retaken."

Mr. Lorry's business eye read in the speaker's face that it was loss of time to dwell upon the point. Confused, but sensible that something might depend on his presence of mind, he commanded himself, and was silently attentive.

"Now, I trust," said Sydney to him, "that the name and influence of Doctor Manette may stand him in as good stead tomorrow—you said he would be before the tribunal again tomorrow, Mr. Barsad?——"

"Yes; I believe so."

"——In as good stead tomorrow as today. But it may not be so. I own to you, I am shaken, Mr. Lorry, by Doctor Manette's not having had the power to prevent this arrest."

"He may not have known of it beforehand," said Mr. Lorry.

"But that very circumstance would be alarming, when we remember how identified he is with his son-in-law."

"That's true," Mr. Lorry acknowledged, with his troubled hand at his chin, and his troubled eyes on Carton.

"In short," said Sydney, "this is a desperate time, when desperate games are played for desperate stakes. Let the Doctor play the winning game; I will play the losing one. No man's life here is worth purchase. Any one carried home by the people today, may be condemned tomorrow. Now, the stake I have resolved to play for, in case of the worst, is a friend in the Conciergerie. And the friend I purpose to myself to win, is Mr. Barsad."

"You need have good cards, sir," said the spy.

"I'll run them over. I'll see what I hold.—Mr. Lorry, you know what a brute I am; I wish you'd give me a little brandy."

It was put before him, and he drank off a glassful—drank off another glassful—pushed the bottle thoughtfully away.

"Mr. Barsad," he went on, in the tone of one who really was looking over a hand at cards: "Sheep of the prisons, emissary of Republican committees, now turnkey, now prisoner, always spy and secret informer, so much the more valuable here for being English that an Englishman is less open to suspicion of subornation in those characters than a Frenchman, represents himself to his employers under a false name. That's a very good card. Mr. Barsad, now in the employ of the republican French government, was formerly in the employ of the aristocratic English government, the enemy of France and freedom. That's an excellent card. Inference clear as day in this region of suspicion, that Mr. Barsad, still in the pay of the aristocratic English government, is the spy of Pitt,[3] the treacherous foe of the Republic crouching in its bosom, the English traitor and agent of all mischief so much spoken of and so difficult to find. That's a card not to be beaten. Have you followed my hand, Mr. Barsad?"

"Not to understand your play," returned the spy, uneasily.

"I play my ace, denunciation of Mr. Barsad to the nearest section committee. Look over your hand, Mr. Barsad, and see what you have. Don't hurry."

He drew the bottle near, poured out another glassful of brandy, and drank it off. He saw that the spy was fearful of his drinking himself into a fit state for the immediate denunciation of him. Seeing it, he poured out and drank another glassful.

[3] PITT—William Pitt, the Prime Minister of England. At the beginning of the Revolution, public sentiment in England was in favor of the French people, but with the execution of the King, England joined the other nations of Europe in a war against the tyranny of the new Republic.

"Look over your hand carefully, Mr. Barsad. Take time."

It was a poorer hand than he suspected. Mr. Barsad saw losing cards in it that Sydney Carton knew nothing of. Thrown out of his honorable employment in England, through too much unsuccessful hard swearing there—he knew that he had crossed the Channel, and accepted service in France: first, as a tempter and an eavesdropper among his own countrymen there: gradually as a tempter and an eavesdropper among the natives. He knew that under the overthrown government he had been a spy upon Saint Antoine and Defarge's wine-shop; had received from the watchful police such heads of information concerning Doctor Manette's imprisonment, release, and history, as should serve him for an introduction to familiar conversation with the Defarges; and tried them on Madame Defarge, and had broken down with them signally. He always remembered with fear and trembling, that that terrible woman had knitted when he talked with her, and had looked ominously at him as her fingers moved. He had since seen her, in the section of Saint Antoine, over and over again produce her knitted registers, and denounce people whose lives the guillotine then surely swallowed up. He knew, as every one employed as he was, did, that he was never safe; that flight was impossible; that he was tied fast under the shadow of the axe; and that in spite of his utmost tergiversation and treachery in furtherance of the reigning terror, a word might bring it down upon him. Once denounced, and on such grave grounds as had just now been suggested to his mind, he foresaw that the dreadful woman of whose unrelenting character he had seen many proofs, would produce against him that fatal register, and would quash his last chance of life. Besides that all secret men are men soon terrified, here were surely cards enough of one black suit, to justify the holder in growing rather livid as he turned them over.

"You scarcely seem to like your hand," said Sydney, with the greatest composure. "Do you play?"

"I think, sir," said the spy, in the meanest manner, as he turned to Mr. Lorry, "I may appeal to a gentleman of your years and benevolence, to put it to this other gentleman, so much your junior, whether he can under any circumstances reconcile it to his station to play that ace of which he has spoken. I admit that *I* am a spy, and that it is considered a discreditable station—though it must be filled by somebody; but this gentleman is no spy, and why should he so demean himself as to make himself one?"

"I play my ace, Mr. Barsad," said Carton, taking the answer on himself, and looking at his watch, "without any scruple, in a very few minutes."

"I should have hoped, gentlemen both," said the spy, always striving to hook Mr. Lorry into the discussion, "that your respect for my sister——"

"I could not better testify my respect for your sister than by finally relieving her of her brother," said Sydney Carton.

"You think not, sir?"

"I have thoroughly made up my mind about it."

The smooth manner of the spy, curiously in dissonance with his rough dress, and probably with his usual demeanor, received such a check from the inscrutability of Carton,—who was a mystery to wiser and honester men than he,—that it faltered here and failed him. While he was at a loss, Carton said, resuming his former air of contemplating cards:

"And indeed, now I think again, I have a strong impression that I have another good card here, not yet enumerated. That friend and fellow-sheep, who spoke of himself as pasturing in the country prisons; who was he?"

"French. You don't know him," said the spy, quickly.

"French, eh?" repeated Carton, musing, and not appearing to notice him at all, though he echoed his word. "Well he may be."

"Is, I assure you," said the spy; "though it's not important."

"Though it's not important," repeated Carton, in the same mechanical way—"though it's not important—— No, it's not important. No. Yet I know the face."

"I think not. I am sure not. It can't be," said the spy.

"It—can't—be," muttered Sydney Carton, retrospectively, and filling his glass again. "Can't—be. Spoke good French. Yet like a foreigner, I thought?"

"Provincial," said the spy.

"No. Foreign!" cried Carton, striking his open hand on the table, as a light broke clearly on his mind. "Cly! Disguised, but the same man. We had that man before us at the Old Bailey."

"Now, there you are hasty, sir," said Barsad, with a smile that gave his aquiline nose an extra inclination to one side; "there you really give me an advantage over you. Cly, who I will unreservedly admit, at this distance of time, was a partner of mine, has been dead several years. I attended him in his last illness. He was buried in London, at the church of Saint Pancras-in-the-Fields. His unpopularity with the blackguard multitude at the moment, prevented my following his remains, but I helped to lay him in his coffin."

Here, Mr. Lorry became aware, from where he sat, of a most remarkable goblin shadow on the wall. Tracing it to its source, he discovered it to be caused by a sudden extraordinary rising and stiffening of all the risen and stiff hair on Mr. Cruncher's head.

"Let us be reasonable," said the spy, "and let us be fair. To show you how mistaken you are, and what an unfounded assumption yours is, I will lay before you a certificate of Cly's burial, which I happen to have carried in my pocketbook," with a hurried hand he produced and opened it, "ever since. There it is. Oh, look at it, look at it! You may take it in your hand; it's no forgery."

Here, Mr. Lorry perceived the reflexion on the wall to elongate, and Mr. Cruncher rose and stepped forward. His hair could not have been more violently on end, if it had been that moment dressed by the cow with the crumpled horn in the house that Jack built.

Unseen by the spy, Mr. Cruncher stood at his side, and touched him on the shoulder like a ghostly bailiff.

"That there Roger Cly, master," said Mr. Cruncher, with a taciturn and iron-bound visage. "So *you* put him in his coffin?"

"I did."

"Who took him out of it?"

Barsad leaned back in his chair, and stammered, "What do you mean?"

"I mean," said Mr. Cruncher, "that he warn't never in it. No! Not he! I'll have my head took off, if he was ever in it."

The spy looked round at the two gentlemen; they both looked in unspeakable astonishment at Jerry.

"I tell you," said Jerry, "that you buried paving-stones and

Mr. Lorry became aware, from where he sat, of a most remarkable goblin shadow on the wall.

earth in that there coffin. Don't go and tell *me* that you buried Cly. It was a take in. Me and two more knows it."

"How do you know it?"

"What's that to you? Ecod!" growled Mr. Cruncher, "it's you I have got a old grudge again, is it, with your shameful impositions upon tradesmen! I'd catch hold of your throat and choke you for half a guinea."

Sydney Carton, who, with Mr. Lorry, had been lost in amazement at this turn of the business, here requested Mr. Cruncher to moderate and explain himself.

"At another time, sir," he returned, evasively, "the present time is ill-conwenient for explainin'. What I stand to, is, that he knows well wot that there Cly was never in that there coffin. Let him say he was, in so much as a word of one syllable, and I'll either catch hold of his throat and choke him for half a guinea"; Mr. Cruncher dwelt upon this as quite a liberal offer; "or I'll out and announce him."

"Humph! I see one thing," said Carton. "I hold another card, Mr. Barsad. Impossible, here in raging Paris, with suspicion filling the air, for you to outlive denunciation, when you are in communication with another aristocratic spy of the same antecedents as yourself, who, moreover, has the mystery about him of having feigned death and come to life again! A plot in the prisons, of the foreigner against the Republic. A strong card—a certain guillotine card! Do you play?"

"No!" returned the spy. "I throw up. I confess that we were so unpopular with the outrageous mob, that I only got away from England at the risk of being ducked to death, and that Cly was so feretted up and down, that he never would have got away at all but for that sham. Though how this man knows it was a sham, is a wonder of wonders to me."

"Never you trouble your head about this man," retorted the contentious Mr. Cruncher; "you'll have trouble enough with giving your attention to that gentleman. And look here! Once more!"—Mr. Cruncher could not be restrained from making rather an ostentatious parade of his liberality—"I'd catch hold of your throat and choke you for half a guinea."

The sheep of the prisons turned from him to Sydney Carton, and said, with more decision, "It has come to a point. I go on duty soon, and can't overstay my time. You told me you had a proposal; what is it? Now, it is of no use asking too much of me. Ask me to do anything in my office, putting my head in great extra danger, and I had better trust my life to the chances of a refusal than the chances of consent. In short, I should make that choice. You talk of desperation. We are all desperate here. Remember! I may denounce you if I think proper, and I can swear my way through stone walls, and so can others. Now, what do you want with me?"

"Not very much. You are a turnkey at the Conciergerie?"

"I tell you once for all, there is no such thing as an escape possible," said the spy, firmly.

"Why need you tell me what I have not asked? You are a turnkey at the Conciergerie?"

"I am sometimes."

"You can be when you choose?"

"I can pass in and out when I choose."

Sydney Carton filled another glass with brandy, poured it slowly out upon the hearth, and watched it as it dropped. It being all spent, he said, rising:

"So far, we have spoken before these two, because it was as well that the merits of the cards should not rest solely between you and me. Come into the dark room here, and let us have one final word alone."

IX   THE GAME MADE

WHILE Sydney Carton and the sheep of the prisons were in the adjoining dark room, speaking so low that not a sound was heard, Mr. Lorry looked at Jerry in considerable doubt and mistrust. That honest tradesman's manner of receiving the look, did not inspire confidence; he changed the leg on which he rested, as often as if he had fifty of those limbs, and were trying them all; he examined his finger-nails with a very questionable closeness of attention; and whenever Mr. Lorry's eye caught his, he was taken with that peculiar kind of short cough requiring the hollow of a hand before it, which is seldom, if ever, known to be an infirmity attendant on perfect openness of charcater.

"Jerry," said Mr. Lorry. "Come here."

Mr. Cruncher came forward sideways, with one of his shoulders in advance of him.

"What have you been, besides a messenger?"

After some cogitation, accompanied with an intent look at his patron, Mr. Cruncher conceived the luminous idea of replying, "Agricultooral character."

"My mind misgives me much," said Mr. Lorry, angrily shaking a forefinger at him, "that you have used the respectable and great house of Tellson's as a blind, and that you have had an unlawful occupation of an infamous description. If you have, don't expect me to befriend you when you get back to England. If you have, don't expect me to keep your secret. Tellson's shall not be imposed upon."

"I hope, sir," pleaded the abashed Mr. Cruncher, "that a gentleman like yourself wot I've had the honor of odd jobbing till I'm grey at it, would think twice about harming of me, even if it wos so—I don't say it is, but even if it wos. So, wot I would humbly offer to you, sir, would be this. Upon that there stool, at that there Bar, sets that there boy of mine, brought up and growed up to be a man, wot will errand you, message you, general-light-job you, till your heels is where your head is, if such should be your wishes. If it wos so, which I still don't say it is, let that there boy keep his father's place, and take care of his mother; don't blow upon that boy's father—do not do it, sir—and let that father go into the line of the reg'lar diggin', and make amends for what he would have un-dug—if it wos so—by diggin' of 'em in with a will, and with conwictions respectin' the futur' keepin' of 'em safe."

"Say no more now," said Mr. Lorry. "It may be that I shall yet stand your friend, if you deserve it, and repent in action—not in words. I want no more words."

Mr. Cruncher knuckled his forehead, as Sydney Carton and the spy returned from the dark room. "Adieu, Mr. Barsad!" said the former; "our arrangement thus made, you have nothing to fear from me."

He sat down in a chair on the hearth, over against Mr. Lorry. When they were alone, Mr. Lorry asked him what he had done?

"Not much. If it should go ill with the prisoner, I have ensured access to him, once."

Mr. Lorry's countenance fell.

"It is all I could do," said Carton. "To propose too much, would be to put this man's head under the axe, and, as he himself said, nothing worse could happen to him if he were denounced. It was obviously, the weakness of the position. There is no help for it."

"But access to him," said Mr. Lorry, "if it should go ill before the tribunal, will not save him."

"I never said it would."

Mr. Lorry's eyes gradually sought the fire; his sympathy with his darling, and the heavy disappointment of this second arrest, gradually weakened them; he was an old man now, overborne with anxiety of late, and his tears fell.

"You are a good man and a true friend," said Carton, in an altered voice. "Forgive me if I notice that you are affected. I could not see my father weep, and sit by, careless. And I could not respect your sorrow more, if you were my father. You are free from that misfortune, however."

Though he said the last words, with a slip into his usual manner, there was a true feeling and respect both in his tone and in his touch, that Mr. Lorry, who had never seen the better side of him, was wholly unprepared for. He gave him his hand, and Carton gently pressed it.

"To return to poor Darnay," said Carton. "Don't tell Her of this interview, or this arrangement. It would not enable Her to go to see him. She might think it was contrived, in case of the worst, to convey to him the means of anticipating the sentence."

Mr. Lorry had not thought of that, and he looked quickly at Carton to see if it were in his mind. It seemed to be; he returned the look, and evidently understood it.

"She might think a thousand things," Carton said, "and any of them would only add to her trouble. Don't speak of me to her. As I said to you when I first came, I had better not see her. I can put my hand out, to do any little helpful work for her that my hand can find to do, without that. You are going to her, I hope? She must be very desolate tonight."

"I am going now, directly."

"I am glad of that. She has such a strong attachment to you and reliance on you. How does she look?"

"Anxious and unhappy, but very beautiful."

"Ah!"

It was a long, grieving sound, like a sigh—almost like a sob. It attracted Mr. Lorry's eyes to Carton's face, which was turned to the fire. A light, or a shade, the old gentleman could not have said which, passed from it as swiftly as a change will sweep over a hillside on a wild bright day, and he lifted his foot to put back one of the little flaming logs, which was tumbling forward.

"And your duties here have drawn to an end sir?" said Carton, turning to him.

"Yes. I was telling you last night when Lucie came in so unexpectedly, I have at length done all that I can do here. I hoped to have left them in perfect safety, and then to have quitted Paris. I have my leave to pass. I was ready to go."

They were both silent.

"Yours is a long life to look back upon, sir?" said Carton, wistfully.

"I am in my seventy-eighth year."

"You have been useful all your life; steadily and constantly occupied; trusted, respected, and looked-up to?"

"I have been a man of business, ever since I have been a man. Indeed, I may say that I was a man of business when a boy."

"See what a place you fill at seventy-eight. How many people will miss you when you leave it empty!"

"A solitary old bachelor," answered Mr. Lorry, shaking his head. "There is nobody to weep for me."

"How can you say that? Wouldn't She weep for you? Wouldn't her child?"

"Yes, yes, thank God. I didn't quite mean what I said."

"It *is* a thing to thank God for; is it not?"

"Surely, surely."

"If you could say, with truth, to your own solitary heart, tonight, 'I have secured to myself the love and attachment, the gratitude or respect, of no human creature; I have won myself a tender place in no regard; I have done nothing good or serviceable to be remembered by!' your seventy-eight years would be seventy-eight heavy curses; would they not?"

"You say truly, Mr. Carton; I think they would be."

Carton terminated the conversation here, by rising to help him on with his outer coat; "but you," said Mr. Lorry, reverting to the theme, "you are young."

"Yes," said Carton. "I am not old, but my young way was never the way to age. Enough of me."

"And of me, I am sure," said Mr. Lorry. "Are you going out?"

"I'll walk with you to her gate. You know my vagabond and restless habits. If I should prowl about the streets a long time, don't be uneasy; I shall reappear in the morning. You go to the court tomorrow?"

"Yes, unhappily."

"I shall be there, but only as one of the crowd. My spy will find a place for me. Take my arm, sir."

Mr. Lorry did so, and they went down-stairs and out in the streets. A few minutes brought them to Mr. Lorry's destination. Carton left him there; but lingered at a little distance, and turned back to the gate again when it was shut, and touched it. He had heard of her going to the prison every day. "She came out here," he said, looking about him, "turned this way, must have trod on these stones often. Let me follow in her steps."

It was ten o'clock at night when he stood before the prison of La Force, where she had stood hundreds of times. A little wood-sawyer, having closed his shop, was smoking his pipe at his shop-door.

"Good-night, citizen," said Sydney Carton, pausing in going by; for, the man eyed him inquisitively.

"Good-night, citizen."

"How goes the Republic?"

"You mean the guillotine. Not ill. Sixty-three today. We shall mount to a hundred soon. Sanson and his men complain sometimes, of being exhausted. Ha, ha, ha! He is so droll, that Sanson. Such a barber!"

"Do you often go to see him——"

"Shave? Always. Every day. What a barber! You have seen him at work?"

"Never."

"Go and see him when he has a good batch. Figure this to yourself, citizen; he shaved the sixty-three today, in less than two pipes! Less than two pipes. Word of honor!"

As the grinning little man held out the pipe he was smoking, to explain how he timed the executioner, Carton was so sensible of a rising desire to strike the life out of him, that he turned away.

"But you are not English," said the wood-sawyer, "though you wear English dress?"

"Yes," said Carton, pausing again, and answering over his shoulder.

"You speak like a Frenchman."

"I am an old student here."

"Aha, a perfect Frenchman! Good-night, Englishman."

"Good-night, citizen."

"But go and see that droll dog," the little man persisted, calling after him. "And take a pipe with you!"

Sydney had not gone far out of sight, when he stopped in the middle of the street under a glimmering lamp, and wrote with his pencil on a scrap of paper. Then, traversing with the decided step of one who remembered the way well, several dark and dirty streets—much dirtier than usual, for the best public thoroughfares remained uncleaned in those times of terror—he stopped at a chemist's shop, which the owner was closing with his own hands. A small, dim, crooked shop, kept in a tortuous, uphill thoroughfare, by a small, dim, crooked man.

Giving this citizen, too, good-night, as he confronted him at his counter, he laid the scrap of paper before him. "Whew!" the chemist whistled softly, as he read it. "Hi! hi! hi!"

Sydney Carton took no heed, and the chemist said:

"For you, citizen?"

"For me."

"You will be careful to keep them separate, citizen? You know the consequences of mixing them?"

"Perfectly."

Certain small packets were made and given to him. He put them, one by one, in the breast of his inner coat, counted out the money for them, and deliberately left the shop. "There is nothing more to do," said he, glancing upward at the moon, "until tomorrow. I can't sleep."

It was not a reckless manner, the manner in which he said these words aloud under the fast sailing clouds, nor was it more expressive of negligence than defiance. It was the settled manner of a tired man, who had wandered and struggled and got lost, but who at length struck into his road and saw its end.

Long ago, when he had been famous among his earliest competitors as a youth of great promise, he had followed his father to the grave. His mother had died, years before. These solemn words, which had been read at his father's grave, arose in his mind as he went down the dark streets, among the heavy shadows, with the moon and the clouds sailing on high above him. "*I am the Resurrection and the Life, saith the Lord: he that believeth in me, though he were dead, yet shall he live: and whosoever liveth and believeth in me, shall never die.*"

In a city dominated by the axe, alone at night, with natural sorrow rising in him for the sixty-three who had been that day put to death, and for tomorrow's victims then awaiting their doom in the prisons, and still of tomorrow's and tomorrow's, the chain of association that brought the words home, like a rusty old ship's anchor from the deep, might have been easily found. He did not seek it, but repeated them and went on.

With a solemn interest in the lighted windows where the people were going to rest, forgetful through a few calm hours of the horrors surrounding them; in the towers of the churches where no prayers were said; in the distant burial-places, reserved for Eternal Sleep; in the abounding gaols; and in the streets along which the sixties rolled to a death which has become too common and material; with a solemn interest in the whole life and death of the city settling down to its short nightly pause in fury, Sydney Carton crossed the Seine again for the lighter streets.

Few coaches were abroad, for riders in coaches were liable to be suspected, and gentility hid its head in red nightcaps, and put on heavy shoes, and trudged. But, the theatres were all well filled, and the people poured cheerfully out as he passed, and went chatting home. At one of the theatre doors, there was a little girl with her mother, looking for a way across the street through the mud. He carried the child over, and before the timid arm was loosed from his neck asked her for a kiss.

"*I am the Resurrection and the Life, saith the Lord: he that believeth in me, though he were dead, yet shall he live: and whosoever liveth and believeth in me, shall never die.*"

Now that the streets were quiet, and the night wore on, the words were in the echoes of his feet, and were in the air. Perfectly calm and steady, he sometimes repeated them to himself as he walked; but, he heard them always.

The night wore out, and, as he stood upon the bridge listening to the water as it splashed the river walls of the Island of Paris, where the picturesque confusion of houses and cathedral shone bright in the light of the moon, the day came coldly, looking like a dead face out of the sky. Then, the night, with the moon and the stars, turned pale and died, and for a little while it seemed as if Creation were delivered over to Death's dominion.

But, the glorious sun, rising, seemed to strike those words, that burden of the night, straight and warm to his heart in its long bright rays. And looking along them, with reverently shaded eyes, a bridge of light appeared to span the air between him and the sun, while the river sparkled under it.

The strong tide, so swift, so deep, and certain, was like a congenial friend, in the morning stillness. He walked by the stream, far from the houses, and in the light and warmth of the sun fell asleep on the bank. When he awoke and was afoot again, he lingered there yet a little longer, watching an eddy that turned and turned purposeless, until the stream absorbed it, and carried it on to the sea.—"Like me!"

A trading-boat, with a sail of the softened color of a dead leaf, then glided into his view, floated by him, and died away. As its silent track in the water disappeared, the prayer that had broken up out of his heart for a merciful consideration of all his poor blindnesses and errors, ended in the words, "*I am the resurrection and the life.*"

Mr. Lorry was already out when he got back, and it was easy to surmise where the good old man was gone. Sidney Carton drank nothing but a little coffee, ate some bread, and, having washed and changed to refresh himself, went out to the place of trial.

The court was all astir and a-buzz, when the black sheep—whom many fell away from in dread—pressed him into an obscure corner among the crowd. Mr. Lorry was there, and Doctor Manette was there. She was there, sitting beside her father.

When her husband was brought in, she turned a look upon him, so sustaining, so encouraging, so full of admiring love and pitying tenderness, yet so courageous for his sake, that it called the healthy blood into his face, brightened his glance, and animated his heart. If there had been any eyes to notice the influence of her look on Sydney Carton, it would have been seen to be the same influence exactly.

Before that unjust tribunal, there was little or no order of procedure, ensuring to any accused person any reasonable hearing. There could have been no such Revolution, if all laws, and forms, and ceremonies, had not first been so monstrously abused, that the suicidal vengeance of the Revolution was to scatter them all to the winds.

Every eye was turned to the jury. The same determined patriots and good republicans as yesterday and the day before, and tomorrow and the day after. Eager and prominent among them, one man with a craving face, and his fingers perpetually hovering about his lips, whose appearance gave great satisfaction to the spectators. A life-thirsting, cannibal-looking, bloody-minded juryman, the Jacques Three of Saint Antoine. The whole jury, as a jury of dogs empannelled to try the deer.

Every eye then turned to the five judges and the public prosecutor. No favorable leaning in that quarter today. A cruel, uncompromising, murderous business-meaning there. Every eye then sought some other eye in the crowd, and gleamed at it approvingly; and heads nodded at one another, before bending forward with a strained attention.

Charles Evrémonde, called Darnay. Released yesterday. Re-accused and re-taken yesterday. Indictment delivered to him last night. Suspected and denounced enemy of the Republic, aristocrat, one of a family of tyrants, one of a race proscribed, for that they had used their abolished privileges to the infamous oppression of the people. Charles Evrémonde, called Darnay, in right of such proscription, absolutely dead in law.

To this effect, in as few or fewer words, the public prosecutor spoke.

The president asked, was the accused openly denounced or secretly?

"Openly, president."

"By whom?"

"Three voices. Ernest Defarge, wine-vendor of Saint Antoine."

"Good."

"Thérèse Defarge, his wife."

"Good."

"Alexandre Manette, physician."

A great uproar took place in the court, and in the midst of it, Doctor Manette was seen, pale and trembling, standing where he had been seated.

"President, I indignantly protest to you that this is a forgery and a fraud. You know the accused to be the husband of my daughter. My daughter, and those dear to her, are far dearer to me than my life. Who and where is the false conspirator who says that I denounce the husband of my child?"

"Citizen Manette, be tranquil. To fail in submission to the authority of the tribunal would be to put yourself out of law. As to what is dearer to you than life, nothing can be so dear to a good citizen as the Republic."

Loud acclamations hailed this rebuke. The president rang his bell, and with warmth resumed.

"If the Republic should demand of you the sacrifice of your child herself, you would have no duty but to sacrifice her. Listen to what is to follow. In the meanwhile, be silent!"

Frantic acclamations were again raised. Doctor Manette sat down, with his eyes looking around, and his lips trembling; his daughter drew closer to him. The craving man on the jury rubbed his hands together, and restored the usual hand to his mouth.

Defarge was produced, when the court was quiet enough to admit of his being heard, and rapidly expounded the story of the imprisonment, and of his having been a mere boy in the Doctor's service, and of the release, and of the state of the prisoner when released and delivered to him. This short examination followed, for the court was quick with its work.

"You did good service at the taking of the Bastille, citizen?"
"I believe so."
"Inform the Tribunal of what you did that day within the Bastille, citizen."

"I knew," said Defarge, looking down at his wife, who stood at the bottom of the steps on which he was raised, looking steadily up at him; "I knew that this prisoner, of whom I speak, had been confined in cell known as One Hundred and Five, North Tower. I knew it from himself. He knew himself by no other name than One Hundred and Five, North Tower, when he made shoes under my care. As I serve my gun that day, I resolve, when the place shall fall, to examine that cell. It falls. I mount to the cell, with a fellow-citizen who is one of the jury, directed by a gaoler. I examine it, very closely. In a hole in the chimney, where a stone has been worked out and replaced, I find a written paper. This is that written paper. I have made it my business to examine some specimens of the writing of Doctor Manette. This is the writing of Doctor Manette. I confide this paper, in the writing of Doctor Manette, to the hands of the president."

"Let it be read."

In a dead silence and stillness—the prisoner under trial looking lovingly at his wife, his wife only looking from him to look with solicitude at her father, Doctor Manette keeping his eyes fixed on the reader, Madame Defarge never taking hers from the prisoner, Defarge never taking his from his feasting wife, and all the other eyes there intent upon the Doctor, who saw none of them—the paper was read, as follows:

X THE SUBSTANCE OF THE SHADOW

"I, ALEXANDRE MANETTE, unfortunate physician, native of Beauvais and afterwards resident in Paris, write this melancholy paper in my doleful cell in the Bastille, during the last month of year, 1767. I write it at stolen intervals, under every difficulty. I design to secrete it in the wall of the chimney, where I have slowly and laboriously made a place of concealment for it. Some pitying hand may find it there, when I and my sorrows are dust.

"These words are formed by the rusty iron point with which I write with difficulty in scrapings of soot and charcoal from the chimney, mixed with blood, in the last month of the tenth year of my captivity. Hope has quite departed from my breast. I know from terrible warnings I have noted in myself that my reason will not long remain unimpaired, but I solemnly declare that I am at this time in the possession of my right mind—that my memory is exact and circumstantial—and that I write the truth as I shall answer for these my last recorded words, whether they be ever read by men or not, at the Eternal Judgment-seat.

"One cloudy moonlight night, in the third week of December (I think the twenty-second of the month), in the year 1757, I was walking on a retired part of the quay by the Seine for the refreshment of the frosty air, at an hour's distance from my place of residence in the Street of the School of Medicine, when a carriage came along behind me driven very fast. As I stood aside to let that carriage pass, apprehensive that it might otherwise run me down, a head was put out at the window, and a voice called to the driver to stop.

"The carriage stopped as soon as the driver could rein in his horses, and the same voice called to me by my name. I answered. The carriage was then so far in advance of me that two gentlemen had time to open the door and alight before I came up with it. I observed that they were both wrapped in cloaks, and appeared to conceal themselves. As they stood side by side near the carriage door, I also observed that they both looked of about my own age, or rather younger, and that they were greatly alike, in stature, manner, voice, and (as far as I could see) face too.

" 'You are Doctor Manette?' said one.

" 'I am.'

" 'Doctor Manette, formerly of Beauvais,' said the other; 'the young physician, originally an expert surgeon, who, within the last year or two has made a rising reputation in Paris?'

" 'Gentlemen,' I returned, 'I am that Doctor Manette of whom you speak so graciously.'

" 'We have been to your residence,' said the first, 'and not being so fortunate as to find you there, and being informed that you were probably walking in this direction, we followed, in the hope of overtaking you. Will you please to enter the carriage?'

"The manner of both was imperious, and they both moved,

as these words were spoken, so as to place me between themselves and the carriage door. They were armed. I was not.

"'Gentlemen,' said I, 'pardon me; but I usually inquire who does me the honor to seek my assistance, and what is the nature of the case to which I am summoned.'

"The reply to this, was made by him who had spoken second. 'Doctor, your clients are people of condition. As to the nature of the case, our confidence in your skill assures us that you will ascertain it for yourself better than we can describe it. Enough. Will you please to enter the carriage?'

"I could do nothing but comply, and I entered it in silence. They both entered after me—the last springing in, after putting up the steps. The carriage turned about, and drove on at its former speed.

"I repeat this conversation exactly as it occurred. I have no doubt that it is, word for word, the same. I describe everything exactly as it took place, constraining my mind not to wander from the task. Where I make the broken marks that follow here, I leave off for the time, and put my paper in its hiding-place. . . .

"The carriage left the streets behind, passed the North Barrier, and emerged upon the country road. At two-thirds of a league from the Barrier—I did not estimate the distance at that time, but afterwards when I traversed it—it struck out of the main avenue, and presently stopped at a solitary house. We all three alighted, and walked, by a damp soft footpath in a garden where a neglected fountain had overflowed, to the door of the house. It was not opened immediately, in answer to the ringing of the bell, and one of my two conductors struck the man who opened it, with his heavy riding-glove, across the face.

"There was nothing in this action to attract my particular attention, for I had seen common people struck more commonly than dogs. But, the other of the two, being angry likewise, struck the man in like manner with his arm; the look and bearing of the brothers were then so exactly alike, that I then first perceived them to be twin brothers.

"From the time of our alighting at the outer gate (which we found locked, and which one of the brothers had opened to admit us, and had re-locked), I had heard cries proceeding from an upper chamber. I was conducted to this chamber straight, the cries growing louder as we ascended the stairs, and I found a patient in a high fever of the brain, lying on a bed.

"The patient was a woman of great beauty, and young; assuredly not much past twenty. Her hair was torn and ragged, and her arms were bound to her sides with sashes and handkerchiefs. I noticed that these bonds were all portions of a gentleman's dress. On one of them, which was a fringed scarf for a dress of ceremony, I saw the armorial bearing of a Noble, and the letter E.

"I saw this, within the first minute of my contemplation of the patient; for, in her restless strivings she had turned over on her face on the edge of the bed, had drawn the end of the scarf into her mouth, and was in danger of suffocation. My first act was to put out my hand to relieve her breathing; and in moving the scarf aside, the embroidery in the corner caught my sight.

"I turned her gently over, placed my hands upon her breast to calm her and keep her down, and looked into her face. Her eyes were dilated and wild, and she constantly uttered piercing shrieks, and repeated the words, 'My husband, my father, and my brother!' and then counted up to twelve, and said, 'Hush!' For an instant, and no more, she would pause to listen, and then the piercing shrieks would begin again, and she would repeat the cry, 'My husband, my father, and my brother!' and would count up to twelve, and say 'Hush!' There was no variation in the order, or the manner. There was no cessation, but the regular moment's pause, in the utterance of these sounds.

" 'How long,' I asked, 'has this lasted?'

"To distinguish the brothers, I will call them the elder and the younger; by the elder, I mean him who exercised the most authority. It was the elder who replied, 'Since about this hour last night.'

" 'She has a husband, a father, and a brother?'

" 'A brother.'

" 'I do not address her brother?'

"He answered with great contempt, 'No.'

" 'She has some recent association with the number twelve?'

"The younger brother impatiently rejoined, 'With twelve o'clock.'

" 'See, gentlemen,' said I, still keeping my hands upon her breast, 'how useless I am, as you have brought me! If I had known what I was coming to see, I could have come provided. As it is, time must be lost. There are no medicines to be obtained in this lonely place.'

"The elder brother looked to the younger, who said haughtily, 'There is a case of medicines here'; and brought it from a closet, and put it on the table. . . .

"I opened some of the bottles, smelt them, and put the stoppers to my lips. If I had wanted to use anything save narcotic medicines that were poisons in themselves, I would not have administered any of those.

" 'Do you doubt them?' asked the younger brother.

" 'You see, monsieur, I am going to use them,' I replied, and said no more.

"I made the patient swallow, with great difficulty, and after many efforts, the dose that I desired to give. As I intended to repeat it after a while, and as it was necessary to watch its influence, I then sat down by the side of the bed. There was a timid and suppressed woman in attendance (wife of the man down-stairs), who had retreated into a corner. The house was damp and decayed, indifferently furnished—evidently, recently occupied and temporarily used. Some thick old hangings had been nailed up before the windows, to deaden the sound of the shrieks. They continued to be uttered in their regular succession, with the cry, 'My husband, my father, and my brother!' the counting up to twelve, and 'Hush!' The frenzy was so violent, that I had not unfastened the bandages restraining the arms; but, I had looked to them, to see that they were not painful. The only spark of encouragement in the case, was, that my hand upon the sufferer's breast had this much soothing influence, that for minutes at a time it tranquillized the figure. It had no effect upon the cries; no pendulum could be more regular.

"For the reason that my hand had this effect, I had sat by the side of the bed for half an hour, with the two brothers looking on, before the elder said:

" 'There is another patient.'

"I was startled, and asked, 'Is it a pressing case?'

"'You had better see,' he carelessly answered; and took up a light. . . .

"The other patient lay in a back room across a second staircase, which was a species of loft over a stable. There was a low plastered ceiling to a part of it; the rest was open, to the ridge of the tiled roof, and there were beams across. Hay and straw were stored in that portion of the place, fagots for firing, and a heap of apples in sand. I had to pass through that part,

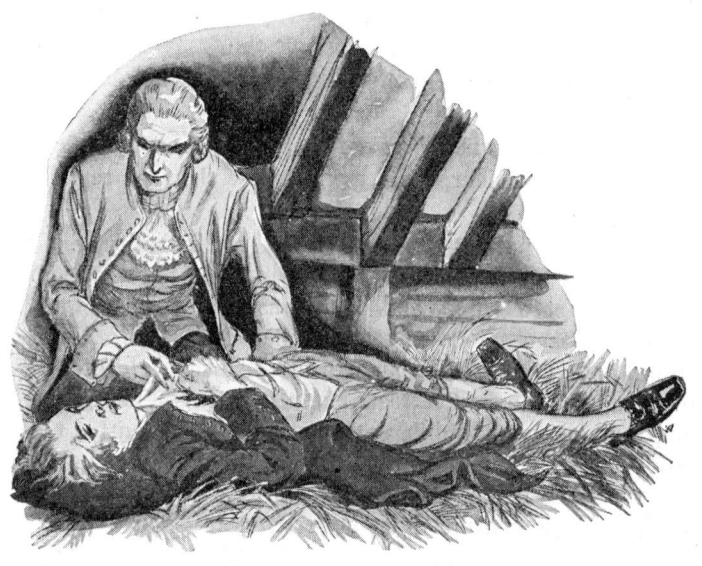

to get at the other. My memory is circumstantial and unshaken. I try it with these details, and I see them all, in this my cell in the Bastille, near the close of the tenth year of my captivity, as I saw them all that night.

"On some hay on the ground, with a cushion thrown under his head, lay a handsome peasant boy—a boy of not more than seventeen at the most. He lay on his back, with his teeth set, his right hand clenched on his breast, and his glaring eyes looking straight upward. I could not see where his wound was, as I kneeled on one knee over him; but, I could see that he was dying of a wound from a sharp point.

"'I am a doctor, my poor fellow,' said I. 'Let me examine it.'

"'I do not want it examined,' he answered; 'let it be.'

"It was under his hand, and I soothed him to let me move his hand away. The wound was a sword-thrust, received from twenty to twenty-four hours before, but no skill could have saved him if it had been looked to without delay. He was then dying fast. As I turned my eyes to the elder brother, I saw him looking down at this handsome boy whose life was ebbing out, as if he were a wounded bird, or hare, or rabbit; not at all as if he were a fellow-creature.

" 'How has this been done, monsieur?' said I.

" 'A crazed young common dog! A serf! Forced my brother to draw upon him, and has fallen by my brother's sword—like a gentleman.'

"There was no touch of pity, sorrow, or kindred humanity, in this answer. The speaker seemed to acknowledge that it was inconvenient to have that different order of creature dying there, and that it would have been better if he had died in the usual obscure routine of his vermin kind. He was quite incapable of any compassionate feeling about the boy, or about his fate.

"The boy's eyes had slowly moved to him as he had spoken, and they now slowly moved to me.

" 'Doctor, they are very proud, these nobles; but we common dogs are proud too, sometimes. They plunder us, outrage us, beat us, kill us; but we have a little pride left, sometimes. She—have you seen her, Doctor?'

"The shrieks and the cries were audible there, though subdued by the distance. He referred to them, as if she were lying in our presence.

"I said, 'I have seen her.'

" 'She is my sister, Doctor. They have had their shameful rights, these Nobles, in the modesty and virtue of our sisters, many years, but we have had good girls among us. I know it, and have heard my father say so. She was a good girl. She was betrothed to a good young man, too; a tenant of his. We were all tenants of his—that man's who stands there. The other is his brother, the worst of a bad race.'

"It was with the greatest difficulty that the boy gathered bodily force to speak; but, his spirit spoke with a dreadful emphasis.

" 'We were so robbed by that man who stands there, as all we common dogs are by those superior beings—taxed by him without mercy, obliged to work for him without pay, obliged to grind our corn at his mill, obliged to feed scores of his tame birds on our wretched crops, and forbidden for our lives to keep a single tame bird of our own, pillaged and plundered to that degree that when we chanced to have a bit of meat, we ate it in fear, with the door barred and the shutters closed, that his people should not see it and take it from us—I say, we were so robbed, and hunted, and were made so poor, that our father told us it was a dreadful thing to bring a child into the world, and that what we should most pray for, was, that our women might be barren and our miserable race die out!'

"I had never before seen the sense of being oppressed, bursting forth like a fire. I had supposed that it must be latent in the people somewhere; but, I had never seen it break out, until I saw it in the dying boy.

" 'Nevertheless, Doctor, my sister married. He was ailing at that time, poor fellow, and she married her lover, that she might tend and comfort him in our cottage—our dug-out, as that man would call it. She had not been married many weeks, when that man's brother saw her and admired her, and asked that man to lend her to him—for what are husbands among us! He was willing enough, but my sister was good and virtuous, and hated his brother with a hatred as strong as mine. What did the two then, to persuade her husband to use his influence with her, to make her willing?'

"The boy's eyes, which had been fixed on mine, slowly turned to the looker-on, and I saw in the two faces that all he said was true. The two opposing kinds of pride confronting one another, I can see, even in this Bastille; the gentleman's, all negligent indifference; the peasant's, all trodden-down sentiment, and passionate revenge.

" 'You know, Doctor, that it is among the rights of these nobles to harness us common dogs to carts, and drive us. They so harnessed him and drove him. You know that it is among their rights to keep us in their grounds all night, quieting the frogs, in order that their noble sleep may not be disturbed. They kept him out in the unwholesome mists at night, and ordered him back into his harness in the day. But he was not persuaded. No! Taken out of harness one day at noon, to feed—if he could find food—he sobbed twelve times, once for every stroke of the bell, and died on her bosom.'

"Nothing human could have held life in the boy but his determination to tell all his wrong. He forced back the gathering shadows of death, as he forced his clenched right hand to remain clenched, and to cover his wound.

"'Then, with that man's permission and even with his aid, his brother took her away; in spite of what I know she must have told his brother—and what that is, will not be long unknown to you, Doctor, if it is now—his brother took her away—for his pleasure and diversion, for a little while. I saw her pass me on the road. When I took the tidings home, our father's heart burst; he never spoke one of the words that filled it. I took my young sister (for I have another) to a place beyond the reach of this man, and where, at least, she will never be *his* vassal. Then, I tracked the brother here, and last night climbed in—a common dog, but sword in hand.—Where is the loft window? It was somewhere here?'

"The room was darkening to his sight; the world was narrowing around him. I glanced about me, and saw that the hay and straw were trampled over the floor, as if there had been a struggle.

"'She heard me, and ran in. I told her not to come near us till he was dead. He came in and first tossed me some pieces of money; then struck at me with a whip. But I, though a common dog, so struck at him as to make him draw. Let him break into as many pieces as he will, the sword that he stained with my common blood; he drew to defend himself—thrust at me with all his skill for his life.'

"My glance had fallen, but a few moments before, on the fragments of a broken sword, lying among the hay. That weapon was a gentleman's. In another place, lay an old sword that seemed to have been a soldier's.

"'Now, lift me up, Doctor; lift me up. Where is he?'

"'He is not here,' I said, supporting the boy, and thinking that he referred to the brother.

"'He! Proud as these nobles are, he is afraid to see me. Where is the man who was here? Turn my face to him.'

"I did so, raising the boy's head against my knee. But, invested for the moment with extraordinary power, he raised himself completely: obliging me to rise too, or I could not have still supported him.

"'Marquis,' said the boy, turned to him with his eyes opened wide and his right hand raised, 'in the days when all these things are to be answered for, I summon you, and yours to the last of your bad race, to answer for them. I mark this cross of blood upon you, as a sign that I do it. In the days when all these things are to be answered for, I summon your brother, the worst of the bad race, to answer for them separately. I mark this cross of blood upon him, as a sign that I do it.'

"Twice, he put his hand to the wound in his breast, and with his forefinger drew a cross in the air. He stood for an instant with the finger yet raised, and, as it dropped, he dropped with it, and I laid him down dead. . . .

"When I returned to the bedside of the young woman, I found her raving in precisely the same order and continuity. I knew that this might last for many hours, and that it would probably end in the silence of the grave.

"I repeated the medicines I had given her, and I sat at the side of the bed until the night was far advanced. She never abated the piercing quality of her shrieks, never stumbled in the distinctness or the order of her words. They were always 'My husband, my father, and my brother! One, two, three, four, five, six, seven, eight, nine, ten, eleven, twelve. Hush!'

"This lasted twenty-six hours from the time when I first saw her. I had come and gone twice, and was again sitting by her, when she began to falter. I did what little could be done to assist that opportunity, and by-and-by she sank into a lethargy, and lay like the dead.

"It was as if the wind and rain had lulled at last, after a long and fearful storm. I released her arms, and called the woman to assist me to compose her figure and the dress she had torn. It was then that I knew her condition to be that of one in whom the first expectations of being a mother have arisen; and it was then that I lost the little hope I had of her.

"'Is she dead?' asked the Marquis, whom I will still describe as the elder brother, coming booted into the room from his horse.

"'Not dead,' said I; 'but like to die.'

" 'What strength there is in these common bodies!' he said, looking down at her with some curiosity.

" 'There is prodigious strength,' I answered him, 'in sorrow and despair.'

"He first laughed at my words, and then frowned at them. He moved a chair with his foot near to mine, ordered the woman away, and said, in a subdued voice,

" 'Doctor, finding my brother in this difficulty with these hinds, I recommended that your aid should be invited. Your reputation is high, and, as a young man with your fortune to make, you are probably mindful of your interest. The things that you see here, are things to be seen, and not spoken of.'

"I listened to the patient's breathing, and avoided answering.

" 'Do you honor me with your attention, Doctor?'

" 'Monsieur,' said I, 'in my profession, the communications of patients are always received in confidence.' I was guarded in my answer, for I was troubled in my mind by what I had heard and seen.

"Her breathing was so difficult to trace, that I carefully tried the pulse and the heart. There was life, and no more. Looking round as I resumed my seat, I found both the brothers intent upon me. . . .

"I write with so much difficulty, the cold is so severe, I am so fearful of being detected and consigned to an underground cell and total darkness, that I must abridge this narrative. There is no confusion or failure in my memory; it can recall, and could detail, every word that was ever spoken between me and those brothers.

"She lingered for a week. Towards the last, I could understand some few syllables that she said to me, by placing my ear close to her lips. She asked me where she was, and I told her; who I was, and I told her. It was in vain that I asked her for her family name. She faintly shook her head upon the pillow, and kept her secret, as the boy had done.

"I had no opportunity of asking her any question, until I had told the brothers she was sinking fast, and could not live another day. Until then, though no one was ever presented to her consciousness save the woman and myself, one or other of them had always jealously sat behind the curtain at the head of the bed when I was there. But when it came to that, they seemed careless what communication I might hold with her; as if—the thought passed through my mind—I were dying too.

"I always observed that their pride bitterly resented the younger brother's having crossed swords with a peasant, and that peasant a boy. The only consideration that appeared really to affect the mind of either of them, was the consideration that this was highly degrading to the family, and was ridiculous. As often as I caught the younger brother's eyes, their expression reminded me that he disliked me deeply, for knowing what I knew from the boy. He was smoother and more polite to me than the elder; but I saw this. I also saw that I was an encumbrance in the mind of the elder too.

"My patient died, two hours before midnight—at a time, by my watch, answering almost to the minute when I had first seen her. I was alone with her, when her forlorn young head drooped gently on one side, and all her earthly wrongs and sorrows ended.

"The brothers were waiting in a room down-stairs, impatient to ride away. I had heard them, alone at the bedside, striking their boots with their riding-whips, and loitering up and down.

" 'At last she is dead?' said the elder, when I went in.

" 'She is dead,' said I.

" 'I congratulate you, my brother,' were his words as he turned round.

"He had before offered me money, which I had postponed taking. He now gave me a rouleau [1] of gold. I took it from his hand, but laid it on the table. I had considered the question, and had resolved to accept nothing.

" 'Pray excuse me,' said I. 'Under the circumstances, no.'

"They exchanged looks, but bent their heads to me as I bent mine to them, and we parted without another word on either side. . . .

"I am weary, weary, weary—worn down by misery. I cannot read what I have written with this gaunt hand.

"Early in the morning, the rouleau of gold was left at my door in a little box, with my name on the outside. From the first, I had anxiously considered what I ought to do. I decided, that day, to write privately to the Minister, stating the nature

---

[1] ROULEAU—A roll of coin made up in paper.

of the two cases to which I had been summoned, and the place to which I had gone: in effect, stating all the circumstances. I knew what court influence was, and what the immunities of the nobles were, and I expected that the matter would never be heard of; but, I wished to relieve my own mind. I had kept the matter a profound secret, even from my wife; and this, too, I resolved to state in my letter. I had no apprehension whatever of my real danger; but, I was conscious that there might be danger for others, if others were compromised by possessing the knowledge that I possessed.

"I was much engaged that day, and could not complete my letter that night. I rose long before my usual time next morning to finish it. It was the last day of the year. The letter was lying before me just completed, when I was told that a lady waited, who wished to see me. . . .

"I am growing more and more unequal to the task I have set myself. It is so cold, so dark, my senses are so benumbed, and the gloom upon me is so dreadful.

"The lady was young, engaging, and handsome, but not marked for long life. She was in great agitation. She presented herself to me, as the wife of the Marquis St. Evrémonde. I connected the title by which the boy had addressed the elder brother, with the initial letter embroidered on the scarf, and, had no difficulty in arriving at the conclusion that I had seen that nobleman very lately.

"My memory is still accurate, but I cannot write the words of our conversation. I suspect that I am watched more closely than I was, and I know not at what times I may be watched. She had in part suspected, and in part discovered, the main facts of the cruel story, of her husband's share in it, and my being resorted to. She did not know that the girl was dead. Her hope had been, she said in great distress, to show her, in secret, a woman's sympathy. Her hope had been to avert the wrath of Heaven from a house that had long been hateful to the suffering many.

"She had reasons for believing that there was a young sister living, and her greatest desire was, to help that sister. I could tell her nothing but that there was such a sister; beyond that, I knew nothing. Her inducement to come to me, relying on my confidence, had been the hope that I could tell her the name and place of abode. Whereas, to this wretched hour I am ignorant of both. . . .

"These scraps of paper fail me. One was taken from me, with a warning, yesterday. I must finish my record today.

"She was a good, compassionate lady, and not happy in her marriage. How could she be! The brother distrusted and disliked her, and his influence was all opposed to her; she stood in dread of him, and in dread of her husband, too. When I handed her down to the door, there was a child, a pretty boy from two to three years old, in her carriage.

"'For his sake, Doctor,' she said, pointing to him in tears, 'I would do all I can to make what poor amends I can. He will never prosper in his inheritance otherwise. I have a presentiment that if no other innocent atonement is made for this, it will one day be required of him. What I have left to call my own—it is little beyond the worth of a few jewels—I will make it the first charge of his life to bestow, with the compassion and lamenting of his dead mother, on this injured family, if the sister can be discovered.'

"She kissed the boy, and said, caressing him, 'It is for thine own dear sake. Thou wilt be faithful, little Charles?' The child answered her bravely, 'Yes!' I kissed her hand, and she took him in her arms, and went away caressing him. I never saw her more.

"As she had mentioned her husband's name in the faith that I knew it, I added no mention of it to my letter. I sealed my letter, and, not trusting it out of my own hands, delivered it myself that day.

"That night, the last night of the year, towards nine o'clock, a man in a black dress rang at my gate, demanded to see me, and softly followed my servant, Ernest Defarge, a youth, upstairs. When my servant came into the room where I sat with my wife—O, my wife, beloved of my heart! My fair young English wife!—we saw the man, who was supposed to be at the gate, standing silent behind him.

"'An urgent case in the Rue St. Honoré, he said. It would not detain me, he had a coach in waiting.

"It brought me here, it brought me to my grave. When I was clear of the house, a black muffler was drawn tightly over my mouth from behind, and my arms were pinioned. The two brothers crossed the road from a dark corner, and identified me with a single gesture. The Marquis took from his pocket the letter I had written, showed it me, burnt it in the light of a lantern that was held, and extinguished the ashes with his foot. Not a word was spoken. I was brought here, I was brought to my living grave.

"If it had pleased God to put it in the hard heart of either of the brothers, in all these frightful years, to grant me any tidings of my dearest wife—so much as to let me know by a word whether alive or dead—I might have thought that He had not quite abandoned them. But, now I believe that the mark of the red cross is fatal to them, and that they have no part in His mercies. And them and their descendants, to the last of their race, I Alexandre Manette, unhappy prisoner, do this last night of the year 1767, in my unbearable agony, denounce to the times when all these things shall be answered for. I denounce them to Heaven and to earth."

A terrible sound arose when the reading of this document was done. A sound of craving and eagerness that had nothing articulate in it but blood. The narrative called up the most revengeful passions of the time, and there was not a head in the nation but must have dropped before it.

Little need, in presence of that tribunal and that auditory, to show how the Defarges had not made the paper public, with the other captured Bastille memorials borne in procession, and had kept it, biding their time. Little need to show that this detested family name had long been anathematised by Saint Antoine, and was wrought into the fatal register. The man never trod ground, whose virtues and services would have sustained him in that place that day, against such denunciation.

And all the worse for the doomed man, that the denouncer was a well-known citizen, his own attached friend, the father of his wife. One of the frenzied aspirations of the populace was, for imitations of the questionable public virtues of antiquity, and for sacrifices and self-immolations on the people's altar. Therefore, when the president said (else had his own head quivered on his shoulders), that the good physician of the Republic would deserve better still of the Republic by rooting out an obnoxious family of aristocrats, and would doubtless feel a sacred glow and joy in making his daughter a widow and her child an orphan, there was wild excitement, patriotic fervor, not a touch of human sympathy.

"Much influence around him, has that Doctor?" murmured Madame Defarge, smiling to The Vengeance. "Save him now, my Doctor, save him!"

At every juryman's vote, there was a roar. Another and another. Roar and roar.

Unanimously voted. At heart and by descent an aristocrat, an enemy of the Republic, a notorious oppressor of the people. Back to the Conciergerie, and Death within four-and-twenty hours!

XI DUSK

THE wretched wife of the innocent man thus doomed to die, fell under the sentence, as if she had been mortally stricken. But, she uttered no sound; and so strong was the voice within her, representing that it was she of all the world who must uphold him in his misery and not augment it, that it quickly raised her, even from that shock.

The judges having to take part in a public demonstration out of doors, the tribunal adjourned. The quick noise and movement of the court's emptying itself by many passages had not ceased, when Lucie stood stretching out her arms towards her husband, with nothing in her face but love and consolation.

"If I might touch him! If I might embrace him once! O, good citizens, if you would have so much compassion for us!"

There was but a gaoler left, along with two of the four men who had taken him last night, and Barsad. The people had all poured out to the show in the streets. Barsad proposed to the rest, "Let her embrace him, then; it is but a moment." It was silently acquiesced in, and they passed her over the seats in the hall to a raised place, where he, by leaning over the dock, could fold her in his arms.

"Farewell, dear darling of my soul. My parting blessing on my love. We shall meet again, where the weary are at rest!"

They were her husband's words, as he held her to his bosom.

"I can bear it, dear Charles. I am supported from above; don't suffer for me. A parting blessing for our child."

"I send it to her by you. I kiss her by you. I say farewell to her by you."

"My husband. No! A moment!" He was tearing himself apart from her. "We shall not be separated long. I feel that this will break my heart by-and-by; but I will do my duty while I can, and when I leave her, God will raise up friends for her, as He did for me."

Her father had followed her, and would have fallen on his knees to both of them, but that Darnay put out a hand and seized him, crying:

"No, no! What have you done, what have you done, that you should kneel to us! We know now, what a struggle you made of old. We know now, what you underwent when you suspected my descent, and when you knew it. We know now, the natural antipathy you strove against, and conquered, for her dear sake. We thank you with all our hearts, and all our love and duty. Heaven be with you!"

Her father's only answer was to draw his hands through his white hair, and wring them with a shriek of anguish.

"It could not be otherwise," said the prisoner. "All things have worked together as they have fallen out. It was the always-vain endeavor to discharge my poor mother's trust, that first brought my fatal presence near you. Good could never come of such evil, a happier end was not in nature to so unhappy a beginning. Be comforted, and forgive me. Heaven bless you!"

As he was drawn away, his wife released him, and stood looking after him with her hands touching one another in the attitude of prayer, and with a radiant look upon her face, in which there was even a comforting smile. As he went out at the prisoners' door, she turned, laid her head lovingly on her father's breast, tried to speak to him, and fell at his feet.

Then, issuing from the obscure corner from which he had never moved, Sydney Carton came and took her up. Only her father and Mr. Lorry were with her. His arm trembled as it raised her, and supported her head. Yet, there was an air about him that was not all of pity—that had a flush of pride in it.

"Shall I take her to a coach? I shall never feel her weight."

He carried her lightly to the door, and laid her tenderly down in a coach. Her father and their old friend got into it, and he took his seat beside the driver.

When they arrived at the gateway where he had paused in the dark not many hours before, to picture to himself on which of the rough stones of the street her feet had trodden, he lifted her again, and carried her up the staircase to their rooms. There, he laid her down on a couch, where her child and Miss Pross wept over her.

"Don't recall her to herself," he said, softly, to the latter, "she is better so; don't revive her to consciousness, while she only faints. Before I go," he paused,—"I may kiss her?"

It was remembered afterwards that when he bent down and touched her face with his lips, he murmured some words. The child, who was nearest to him, told them afterwards, and told her grandchildren when she was a handsome old lady, that she heard him say, "A life you love."

When he had gone out into the next room, he turned suddenly on Mr. Lorry and her father, who were following, and said to the latter:

"You had great influence but yesterday, Doctor Manette; let it, at least, be tried. These judges, and all the men in power, are very friendly to you, and very recognizant of your services; are they not?"

"Nothing connected with Charles was concealed from me. I had the strongest assurances that I should save him; and I did." He returned the answer in great trouble, and very slowly.

"Try them again. The hours between this and tomorrow afternoon are few and short, but try."

"I intend to try. I will not rest a moment."

"That's well. I have known such energy as yours do great things before now—though never," he added, with a smile and a sigh together, "such great things as this. But try! Of little worth as life is when we misuse it, it is worth that effort. It would cost nothing to lay down if it were not."

"I will go," said Doctor Manette, "to the prosecutor and the president straight, and I will go to others whom it is better not to name. I will write too,—But stay! There is a celebration in the streets, and no one will be accessible until dark."

"That's true. Well! It is a forlorn hope at the best, and not much the forlorner for being delayed till dark. I should like to know how you speed; though, mind! I expect nothing! When are you likely to have seen these dread powers, Doctor Manette?"

"Immediately after dark, I should hope. Within an hour or two from this."

"It will be dark soon after four. Let us stretch the hour or two. If I go to Mr. Lorry's at nine, shall I hear what you have done either from our friend or from yourself?"

"Yes."

"May you prosper!"

Mr. Lorry followed Sydney to the outer door, and, touching him on the shoulders as he was going away, caused him to turn.

"I have no hope," said Mr. Lorry, in a low and sorrowful whisper.

"Nor have I."

"If any one of these men, or all of these men, were disposed to spare him—which is a large supposition; for what is his life, or any man's to them!—I doubt if they durst spare him after the demonstration in the court."

"And so do I. I heard the fall of the axe in that sound."

Mr. Lorry leaned his arm upon the door-post, and bowed his face upon it.

"Don't despond," said Carton, very gently; "don't grieve. I encouraged Doctor Manette in this idea, because I felt that it might one day be consolatory to her. Otherwise, she might think 'his life was wantonly thrown away or wasted,' and that might trouble her."

"Yes, yes, yes," returned Mr. Lorry, drying his eyes, "you are right. But he will perish; there is no real hope."

"Yes. He will perish; there is no real hope," echoed Carton. And walked with a settled step, downstairs.

XII DARKNESS

S‌YDNEY C‌ARTON paused in the street, not quite decided where to go. "At Tellson's banking-house at nine," he said, with a musing face. "Shall I do well, in the meantime, to show myself? I think so. It is best that these people should know there is such a man as I here; it is a sound precaution, and may be a necessary preparation. But care, care, care! Let me think it out!"

Checking his steps which had begun to tend towards an object, he took a turn or two in the already darkening street, and traced the thought in his mind to its possible consequences. His first impression was confirmed. "It is best," he said, finally resolved, "that these people should know there is such a man as I here." And he turned his face towards Saint Antoine.

Defarge had described himself, that day, as the keeper of a wine-shop in the Saint Antoine suburb. It was not difficult for one who knew the city well, to find his house without asking any question. Having ascertained its situation, Carton came out of those closer streets again, and dined at a place of refreshment and fell sound asleep after dinner. For the first time in many years, he had no strong drink. Since last night he had taken nothing but a little light thin wine, and last night he had dropped the brandy slowly down on Mr. Lorry's hearth like a man who had done with it.

It was as late as seven o'clock when he awoke refreshed, and went out into the streets again. As he passed along towards Saint Antoine, he stopped at a shop-window where there was a mirror, and slightly altered the disordered arrangement of his loose cravat, and his coat-collar, and his wild hair. This done, he went on direct to Defarge's, and went in.

There happened to be no customer in the shop but Jacques Three, of the restless fingers and the croaking voice. This man whom he had seen upon the jury, stood drinking at the little counter, in conversation with the Defarges, man and wife. The

Vengeance assisted in the conversation, like a regular member of the establishment.

As Carton walked in, took his seat, and asked (in very indifferent French) for a small measure of wine, Madame Defarge cast a careless glance at him, and then keener and keener, and then advanced to him herself, and asked him what it was he had ordered.

He repeated what he had already said.

"English?" asked Madame Defarge, inquisitively raising her dark eyebrows.

After looking at her, as if the sound of even a single French word were slow to express itself to him, he answered, in his former strong foreign accent. "Yes, madame, yes. I am English!"

Madame Defarge returned to her counter to get the wine, and, as he took up a Jacobin journal [1] and feigned to pore over it puzzling out its meaning, he heard her say, "I swear to you, like Evrémonde!"

Defarge brought him the wine, and gave him good-evening.

"How?"

"Good-evening."

"Oh! Good-evening, citizen," filling his glass. "Ah! and good wine. I drink to the Republic."

Defarge went back to the counter, and said, "Certainly, a little like." Madame sternly retorted, "I tell you a good deal like." Jacques Three pacifically remarked, "He is so much in your mind, see you, madame." The amiable Vengeance added, with a laugh, "Yes, my faith! And you are looking forward with so much pleasure to seeing him once more tomorrow!"

Carton followed the lines and words of his paper, with a slow forefinger, and with a studious and absorbed face. They were all leaning their arms on the counter close together, speaking low. After a silence of a few moments, during which they all looked towards him without disturbing his outward attention from the Jacobin editor, they resumed their conversation.

"It is true what madame says," observed Jacques Three. "Why, stop? There is great force in that. Why stop?"

---

[1] JACOBIN JOURNAL—The Jacobins were a party of extreme revolutionists, and were chiefly responsible for the Reign of Terror.

"Well, well," reasoned Defarge, "but one must stop somewhere. After all, the question is still where?"

"At extermination," said madame.

"Magnificent!" croaked Jacques Three. The Vengeance, also, highly approved.

"Extermination is good doctrine, my wife," said Defarge, rather troubled; "in general, I say nothing against it. But this Doctor has suffered much; you have seen him today; you have observed his face when the paper was read."

"I have observed his face!" repeated madame, contemptuously and angrily. "Yes, I have observed his face. I have observed his face to be not the face of a true friend of the Republic. Let him take care of his face!"

"And you have observed, my wife," said Defarge, in a deprecatory manner, "the anguish of his daughter, which must be a dreadful anguish to him!"

"I have observed his daughter," repeated madame; "yes, I have observed his daughter, more times than one. I have observed her today, and I have observed her other days. I have observed her in the court, and I have observed her in the street by the prison. Let me but lift my finger—!" She seemed to raise it (the listener's eyes were always on his paper), and to let it fall with a rattle on the ledge before her, as if the axe had dropped.

"The citizeness is superb!" croaked the juryman.

"She is an angel!" said The Vengeance, and embraced her.

"As to thee," pursued madame, implacably, addressing her husband, "if it depended on thee—which, happily, it does not—thou wouldst rescue this man even now."

"No!" protested Defarge. "Not if to lift this glass would do it! But I would leave the matter there. I say, stop there."

"See you then, Jacques," said Madame Defarge, wrathfully; "and see you, too, my little Vengeance; see you both! Listen! For other crimes as tyrants and oppressors, I have this race a long time on my register, doomed to destruction and extermination. Ask my husband is that so."

"It is so," assented Defarge, without being asked.

"In the beginning of the great days, when the Bastille falls, he finds this paper of today, and he brings it home, and in the middle of the night when this place is clear and shut, we read

"*Magnificent!*" *croaked Jacques.*
The Vengeance, also, approved.

it, here on this spot, by the light of this lamp. Ask him, is that so."

"It is so," assented Defarge.

"That night, I tell him, when the paper is read through, and the lamp is burnt out, and the day is gleaming in above those shutters and between those iron bars, that I have now a secret to communicate. Ask him, is that so."

"It is so," assented Defarge again.

"I communicate to him that secret. I smite this bosom with these two hands as I smite it now, and I tell him, 'Defarge, I was brought up among the fishermen of the seashore, and that peasant-family so injured by the two Evrémonde brothers, as that Bastille paper describes, is my family. Defarge, that sister of the mortally wounded boy upon the ground was my sister, that husband was my sister's husband, that unborn child was their child, that brother was my brother, that father was my father, those dead are my dead, and that summons to answer for those things descends to me!' Ask him, is that so."

"It is so," assented Defarge once more.

"Then tell wind and fire where to stop," returned madame; "but don't tell me."

Both her hearers derived a horrible enjoyment from the deadly nature of her wrath—the listener could feel how white she was, without seeing her—and both highly commended it. Defarge, a weak minority, interposed a few words for the memory of the compassionate wife of the Marquis; but, only elicited from his own wife a repetition of her last reply, "Tell the wind and the fire where to stop; not me!"

Customers entered, and the group was broken up. The English customer paid for what he had had, perplexedly counted his change, and asked, as a stranger, to be directed towards the National Palace. Madame Defarge took him to the door, and put her arm on his, in pointing out the road. The English customer was not without his reflections then, that it might be a good deed to seize that arm, lift it, and strike under it sharp and deep.

But, he went his way, and was soon swallowed up in the shadow of the prison wall. At the appointed hour, he emerged from it to present himself in Mr. Lorry's room again, where he found the old gentleman walking to and fro in restless anxiety.

He said he had been with Lucie until just now, and had only left her for a few minutes, to come and keep his appointment. Her father had not been seen, since he quitted the banking-house towards four o'clock. She had some faint hopes that his mediation might save Charles, but they were very slight. He had been more than five hours gone: where could he be?

Mr. Lorry waited until ten; but, Doctor Manette not returning, and he being unwilling to leave Lucie any longer, it was arranged that he should go back to her, and come to the banking-house again at midnight. In the meanwhile, Carton would wait alone by the fire for the Doctor.

He waited and waited, and the clock struck twelve; but, Doctor Manette did not come back. Mr. Lorry returned, and found no tidings of him, and brought none. Where could he be?

They were discussing this question, and were almost building up some weak structure of hope on his prolonged absence, when they heard him on the stairs. The instant he entered the room, it was plain that all was lost.

Whether he had really been to any one, or whether he had been all that time traversing the streets, was never known. As he stood staring at them, they asked him no question, for his face told them everything.

"I cannot find it," said he, "and I must have it. Where is it?"

His head and throat were bare, and, as he spoke with a helpless look straying all around, he took his coat off, and let it drop on the floor.

"Where is my bench? I have been looking everywhere for my bench, and I can't find it. What have they done with my work? Time presses: I must finish those shoes."

They looked at one another, and their hearts died within them.

"Come, come!" said he, in a whimpering miserable way; "let me get to work. Give me my work."

Receiving no answer, he tore his hair, and beat his feet upon the ground, like a distracted child.

"Don't torture a poor forlorn wretch," he implored them, with a dreadful cry; "but give me my work! What is to become of us, if those shoes are not done tonight?"

Lost, utterly lost!

It was so clearly beyond hope, to reason with him, or try

to restore him, that—as if by agreement—they each put a hand upon his shoulder, and soothed him to sit down before the fire, with a promise that he should have his work presently. He sank into the chair, and brooded over the embers, and shed tears. As if all that had happened since the garret time were a momentary fancy, or a dream, Mr. Lorry saw him shrink into the exact figure that Defarge had had in keeping.

Affected, and impressed with terror as they both were, by this spectacle of ruin, it was not a time to yield to such emotions. His lonely daughter, bereft of her final hope and reliance, appealed to them both, too strongly. Again, as if by agreement, they looked at one another with one meaning in their faces. Carton was the first to speak.

"The last chance is gone: it was not much. Yes; he had better be taken to her. But, before you go, will you, for a moment, steadily attend to me? Don't ask me why I make the stipulations I am going to make, and exact the promise I am going to exact; I have a reason—a good one."

"I do not doubt it," answered Mr. Lorry. "Say on."

The figure in the chair between them, was all the time monotonously rocking itself to and fro, and moaning. They spoke in such a tone as they would have used if they had been watching by a sick-bed in the night.

Carton stooped to pick up the coat, which lay almost entangling his feet. As he did so, a small case in which the Doctor was accustomed to carry the list of his day's duties, fell lightly on the floor. Carton took it up, and there was a folded paper in it. "We should look at this?" he said. Mr. Lorry nodded his consent. He opened it, and exclaimed, "Thank God!"

"What is it?" asked Mr. Lorry, eagerly.

"A moment! Let me speak of it in its place. First," he put his hand in his coat, and took another paper from it, "that is the certificate which enables me to pass out of this city. Look at it. You see—Sydney Carton, an Englishman?"

Mr. Lorry held it open in his hand, gazing in his earnest face.

"Keep it for me until tomorrow. I shall see him tomorrow, you remember, and I had better not take it into the prison."

"Why not?"

"I don't know: I prefer not to do so. Now, take this paper that Doctor Manette has carried about him. It is a similar certificate, enabling him and his daughter and her child, at any time, to pass the barrier and the frontier. You see?"

"Yes!"

"Perhaps he obtained it as his last and utmost precaution against evil, yesterday. When is it dated? But no matter; don't stay to look; put it up carefully with mine and your own. Now, observe! I never doubted until within this hour or two, that he had, or could have, such a paper. It is good, until recalled. But it may be soon recalled, and, I have reason to think, will be."

"They are not in danger?"

"They are in great danger. They are in danger of denunciation by Madame Defarge. I know it from her own lips. I have overheard words of that woman's, tonight, which have presented their danger to me in strong colors. I have lost no time, and since then, I have seen the spy. He confirms me. He knows that a wood-sawyer, living by the prison wall, is under the control of the Defarges, and has been rehearsed by Madame Defarge as to his having seen Her"—he never mentioned Lucie's name—"making signs and signals to prisoners. It is easy to foresee that the pretence will be the common one, a prison plot, and that it will involve her life—and perhaps her child's—and perhaps her father's—for both have been seen with her at that place. Don't look so horrified. You will save them all."

"Heaven grant I may, Carton! But how?"

"I am going to tell you how. It will depend on you, and it could depend on no better man. This new denunciation will certainly not take place until after tomorrow; probably not until two or three days afterwards; more probably a week afterwards. You know it is a capital crime, to mourn for, or sympathize with, a victim of the guillotine. She and her father would unquestionably be guilty of this crime, and this woman would wait to add that strength to her case, and make herself doubly sure. You follow me?"

"So attentively, and with so much confidence in what you say, that for the moment I lose sight," touching the back of the Doctor's chair, "even of this distress."

"You have money, and can buy the means of travelling to the sea-coast as quickly as the journey can be made. Your preparations have been completed for some days, to return to

England. Early tomorrow, have your horses ready, so that they may be in starting trim at two o'clock in the afternoon."

"It shall be done!"

His manner was so fervent and inspiring, that Mr. Lorry caught the flame, and was as quick as youth.

"You are a noble heart. Did I say we could depend upon no better man? Tell her, tonight, what you know of her danger as involving her child and her father. Dwell upon that, for she would lay her own fair head beside her husband's, cheerfully." He faltered for an instant; then went on as before. "For the sake of her child and her father, press upon her the necessity of leaving Paris, with them and you, at that hour. Tell her that it was her husband's last arrangement. Tell her that more depends upon it than she dare believe, or hope. You think that her father, even in this sad state, will submit himself to her; do you not?"

"I am sure of it."

"I thought so. Quietly and steadily, have all these arrangements made in the courtyard here, even to the taking of your own seat in the carriage. The moment I come to you, take me in, and drive away."

"I understand that I wait for you, under all circumstances?"

"You have my certificate in your hand with the rest, you know, and will reserve my place. Wait for nothing but to have my place occupied, and then for England!"

"Why, then," said Mr. Lorry, grasping his eager but so firm and steady hand, "it does not all depend on one old man, but I shall have a young and ardent man at my side."

"By the help of Heaven you shall! Promise me solemnly, that nothing will influence you to alter the course on which we now stand pledged to one another."

"Nothing, Carton."

"Remember these words tomorrow: change the course, or delay in it—for any reason—and no life can possibly be saved, and many lives must inevitably be sacrificed."

"I will remember them. I hope to do my part faithfully."

"And I hope to do mine. Now, good-bye!"

Though he said it with a grave smile of earnestness, and though he even put the old man's hand to his lips, he did not part from him then. He helped him so far to arouse the rocking figure before the dying embers, as to get a cloak and hat upon it, and to tempt it forth to find where the bench and work were hidden that it still moaningly besought to have. He walked on the other side of it and protected it to the courtyard of the house where the afflicted heart—so happy in the memorable time when he had revealed his own desolate heart to it—outwatched the awful night. He entered the courtyard and remained there for a few moments alone, looking up at the light in the window of her room. Before he went away, he breathed a blessing towards it, and a farewell.

XIII FIFTY-TWO

In the black prison of the Conciergerie, the doomed of the day awaited their fate. They were in number as the weeks of the year. Fifty-two were to roll that afternoon on the life-tide of the city to the boundless everlasting sea. Before their cells were quit of them, new occupants were appointed; before their blood ran into the blood spilled yesterday, the blood that was to mingle with theirs tomorrow was already set apart.

Charles Darnay, alone in a cell, had sustained himself with no flattering delusion since he came to it from the tribunal. In every line of the narrative he had heard, he had heard his condemnation. He had fully comprehended that no personal influence could possibly save him, that he was virtually sentenced by the millions, and that units could avail him nothing.

Nevertheless, it was not easy, with the face of his beloved wife fresh before him, to compose his mind to what it must bear. His hold on life was strong, and it was very, very hard to loosen; by gradual efforts and degrees unclosed a little here, it clenched the tighter there; and when he brought his strength to bear on that hand and it yielded, this was closed again. There was a hurry, too, in all his thoughts, a turbulent and heated working of his heart, that contended against resignation. If, for a moment, he did feel resigned, then his wife and child who had to live after him, seemed to protest and to make it a selfish thing.

But, all this was at first. Before long, the consideration that there was no disgrace in the fate he must meet, and that numbers went the same road wrongfully, and trod it firmly, every day, sprang up to stimulate him. Next followed the thought that much of the future peace of mind enjoyable by the dear ones, depended on his quiet fortitude. So, by degrees he calmed into the better state, when he could raise his thoughts much higher, and draw comfort down.

Before it had set in dark on the night of his condemnation, he had travelled thus far on his last way. Being allowed to purchase the means of writing, and a light, he sat down to write until such time as the prison lamps should be extinguished.

He wrote a long letter to Lucie, showing her that he had known nothing of her father's imprisonment until he had heard of it from herself, and that he had been as ignorant as she of his father's and uncle's responsibility for that misery, until the paper had been read. He had already explained to her that his concealment from herself of the name he had relinquished, was the one condition—fully intelligible now—that her father had attached to their betrothal, and was the one promise he had still exacted on the morning of their marriage. He entreated her, for her father's sake, never to seek to know whether her father had become oblivious of the existence of the paper, or had had it recalled to him, by the story of the Tower, on that old Sunday under the dear plane-tree in the garden. If he had preserved any definite remembrance of it, there could be no doubt that he had supposed it destroyed with the Bastille, when he had found no mention of it among the relics of prisoners which the populace had discovered there, and which had been described to all the world. He besought her—though he added that he knew it was needless—to console her father, by impressing him through every tender means she could think of, with the truth that he had done nothing for which he could justly reproach himself, but had uniformly forgotten himself for their joint sakes. Next to her preservation of his own last grateful love and blessing, and her overcoming of her sorrow, to devote herself to their dear child, he adjured her, as they would meet in Heaven, to comfort her father.

To her father himself, he wrote in the same strain; but, he told her father that he expressly confided his wife and child to his care. And he told him this, very strongly, with the hope of rousing him from any despondency or dangerous retrospect towards which he foresaw he might be tending.

To Mr. Lorry, he commended them all, and explained his

worldly affairs. That done, with many added sentences of grateful friendship and warm attachment, all was done. He never thought of Carton. His mind was so full of the others, that he never once thought of him.

He had time to finish these letters before the lights were put out. When he lay down on his straw bed, he thought he had done with this world.

But, it beckoned him back in his sleep, and showed itself in shining forms. Free and happy, back in the old house in Soho, unaccountably released and light of heart, he was with Lucie again, and she told him it was all a dream, and he had never gone away. A pause of forgetfulness, and then he had even suffered, and had come back to her, dead and at peace, and yet there was no difference in him. Another pause of oblivion, and he awoke in the sombre morning, unconscious where he was or what had happened, until it flashed upon his mind, "this is the day of my death!"

Thus, had he come through the hours, to the day when the fifty-two heads were to fall. And now, while he was composed, and hoped that he could meet the end with quiet heroism, a new action began in his waking thoughts, which was very difficult to master.

He had never seen the instrument that was to terminate his life. How high it was from the ground, how many steps it had, where he would be stood, how he would be touched, whether the touching hands would be dyed red, which way his face would be turned, whether he would be the first, or might be the last: these and many similar questions, in no wise directed by his will, obtruded themselves over and over again, countless times. Neither were they connected with fear: he was conscious of no fear. Rather, they originated in a strange besetting desire to know what to do when the time came; a desire gigantically disproportionate to the few swift moments to which it referred; a wondering that was more like the wondering of some other spirit within his, than his own.

The hours went on as he walked to and fro, and the clocks struck the numbers he would never hear again. Nine gone forever, Ten gone forever, Eleven gone forever, Twelve coming on to pass away. After a hard contest with that eccentric action of thought which had last perplexed him, he had got the better of it. He walked up and down, softly repeating their names to himself. The worst of the strife was over. He could walk up and down, free from distracting fancies, praying for himself and for them.

Twelve gone forever.

He had been apprised that the final hour was Three, and he knew he would be summoned some time earlier, inasmuch as the tumbrils jolted heavily and slowly through the streets. Therefore, he resolved to keep Two before his mind, as the hour, and so to strengthen himself in the interval that he might be able, after that time, to strengthen others.

Walking regularly to and fro with his arms folded on his breast, a very different man from the prisoner who had walked to and fro at La Force, he heard One struck away from him, without surprise. The hour had measured like most other hours. Devoutly thankful to Heaven for his recovered self-possession, he thought, "There is but another now," and turned to walk again.

Footsteps in the stone passage outside the door. He stopped.

The key was put in the lock, and turned. Before the door was opened, or as it opened, a man said in a low voice, in English: "He has never seen me here; I have kept out of his way. Go you in alone; I wait near. Lose no time!"

The door was quickly opened and closed, and there stood before him, face to face, quiet, intent upon him, with the light of a smile on his features and a cautionary finger on his lip, Sydney Carton.

There was something so bright and remarkable in his look, that, for the first moment, the prisoner misdoubted him to be an apparition of his own imagining. But, he spoke, and it was his voice; he took the prisoner's hand, and it was his real grasp.

"Of all the people upon earth, you least expected to see me?" he said.

"I could not believe it to be you. I can scarcely believe it now. You are not"—the apprehension came suddenly into his mind—"a prisoner?"

"No. I am accidentally possessed of a power over one of the keepers here, and in virtue of it I stand before you. I come from her—your wife, dear Darnay."

The prisoner wrung his hand.

"I bring you a request from her."

"What is it?"

"A most earnest, pressing, and emphatic entreaty, addressed to you in the most pathetic tones of the voice so dear to you, that you well remember."

The prisoner turned his face partly aside.

"You have no time to ask me why I bring it, or what it means; I have no time to tell you. You must comply with it—take off those boots you wear, and draw on these of mine."

There was a chair against the wall of the cell, behind the prisoner. Carton, pressing forward, had already, with the speed of lightning, got him down into it, and stood over him barefoot.

"Draw on these boots of mine. Put your hands to them; put your will to them. Quick!"

"Carton, there is no escaping from this place; it never can be done. You will only die with me. It is madness."

"It would be madness if I asked you to escape; but do I? When I ask you to pass out at that door, tell me it is madness and remain here. Change that cravat for this of mine, that coat for this of mine. While you do it, let me take this ribbon from your hair, and shake out your hair like this of mine!"

With wonderful quickness, and with a strength both of will and action, that appeared quite supernatural, he forced all these changes upon him. The prisoner was like a young child in his hands.

"Carton! Dear Carton! It is madness. It cannot be accomplished, it never can be done, it has been attempted, and has always failed. I implore you not to add your death to the bitterness of mine."

"Do I ask you, my dear Darnay, to pass the door? When I ask that, refuse. There are pen and ink and paper on this table. Is your hand steady enough to write?"

"It was, when you came in."

"Steady it again, and write what I shall dictate. Quick, friend, quick!"

Pressing his hand to his bewildered head, Darnay sat down at the table. Carton, with his right hand in his breast, stood close beside him.

"Write exactly as I speak."

"To whom do I address it?"

"To no one." Carton still had his hand in his breast.

"Do I date it?"

"No."

The prisoner looked up, at each question. Carton, standing over him with his hand in his breast, looked down.

" 'If you remember,' " said Carton, dictating, " 'the words that passed between us, long ago, you will readily comprehend this when you see it. You do remember them, I know. It is not in your nature to forget them.' "

He was drawing his hand from his breast; the prisoner chancing to look up in his hurried wonder as he wrote, the hand stopped, closing upon something.

"Have you written 'forget them'?" Carton asked.

"I have. Is that a weapon in your hand?"

"No; I am not armed."

"What is it in your hand?"

"You shall know directly. Write on; there are but a few words more." He dictated again. " 'I am thankful that the time has come, when I can prove them. That I do so, is no subject for regret or grief.' " As he said these words with his eyes fixed on the writer, his hand slowly and softly moved down close to the writer's face.

The pen dropped from Darnay's fingers on the table, and he looked about him vacantly.

"What vapor is that?" he asked.

"Vapor?"

"Something that crossed me?"

"I am conscious of nothing; there can be nothing here. Take up the pen and finish. Hurry, hurry!"

As if his memory were impaired, or his faculties disordered, the prisoner made an effort to rally his attention. As he looked at Carton with clouded eyes and with an altered manner of breathing, Carton—his hand again in his breast—looked steadily at him.

"Hurry, hurry!"

The prisoner bent over the paper, once more.

" 'If it had been otherwise;' " Carton's hand was again watchfully and softly stealing down; " 'I never should have used the longer opportunity. If it had been otherwise' ": the hand was at the prisoner's face; " 'I should but have had so much the more to answer for. If it had been otherwise——'" Carton looked at the pen, and saw that it was trailing off into unintelligible signs.

Carton's hand moved back to his breast no more. The prisoner sprang up, with a reproachful look, but Carton's hand was close and firm at his nostrils, and Carton's left arm caught him round the waist. For a few seconds he faintly struggled with the man who had come to lay down his life for him; but, within a minute or so, he was stretched insensible on the ground.

Quickly, but with hands as true to the purpose as his heart was, Carton dressed himself in the clothes the prisoner had laid aside, combed back his hair, and tied it with the ribbon the prisoner had worn. Then, he softly called "Enter there! Come in!" and the Spy presented himself.

"You see?" said Carton, looking up, as he kneeled on one knee beside the insensible figure, putting the paper in the breast: "is your hazard very great?"

"Mr. Carton," the Spy answered, with a timid snap of his fingers, "my hazard is not *that*, in the thick of business here, if you are true to the whole of your bargain."

"Don't fear me. I will be true to the death."

"You must be, Mr. Carton, if the tale of fifty-two is to be right. Being made right by you in that dress, I shall not fear."

"Have no fear! I shall soon be out of the way of harming you, and the rest will soon be far from here, please God! Now, get assistance and take me to the coach."

"You?" said the Spy, nervously.

"Him, man, with whom I have exchanged. You go out at the gate by which you brought me in?"

"Of course."

"I was weak and faint when you brought me in, and I am fainter now you take me out. The parting interview has overpowered me. Such a thing has happened here, often, and too often. Your life is in your own hands. Quick! Call assistance!"

"You swear not to betray me?" said the trembling Spy, as he paused for a last moment.

"Man, man!" returned Carton, stamping his foot; "have I sworn by no solemn vow already, to go through with this, that you waste the precious moments now? Take him yourself to the courtyard you know of, place him yourself in the carriage, show him yourself to Mr. Lorry, tell him yourself to give him no restorative but air, and to remember my words of last night and his promise of last night, and drive away!"

The Spy withdrew, and Carton seated himself at the table, resting his forehead on his hands. The Spy returned immediately, with two men.

"How, then?" said one of them, contemplating the fallen figure. "So afflicted to find that his friend has drawn a prize in the lottery of Saint Guillotine?"

"A good patriot," said the other, "could hardly have been more afflicted if the aristocrat had drawn a blank."

They raised the unconscious figure, placed it on a litter they had brought to the door, and bent to carry it away.

"The time is short, Evrémonde," said the Spy, in a warning voice.

"I know it well," answered Carton. "Be careful of my friend, I entreat you, and leave me."

"Come, then, my men," said Barsad. "Lift him, and come away!"

The door closed, and Carton was left alone. Straining his powers of listening to the utmost, he listened for any sound that might denote suspicion or alarm. There was none. Keys turned, doors clashed, footsteps passed along distant passages: no cry was raised, or hurry made, that seemed unusual. Breathing more freely in a little while, he sat down at the table, and listened again until the clock struck Two.

Sounds that he was not afraid of, for he divined their meaning, then began to be audible. Several doors were opened in succession and finally his own. A gaoler, with a list in his hand, looked in, merely saying, "Follow me, Evrémonde!" and he followed into a large dark room, at a distance. It was a dark winter day, and what with the shadows within, and what with the shadows without, he could but dimly discern the others who were brought there to have their arms bound. Some were standing; some seated. Some were lamenting, and in restless motion; but, these were few. The great majority were silent and still, looking fixedly at the ground.

As he stood by the wall in a dim corner, while some of the fifty-two were brought in after him, one man stopped in passing to embrace him, as having a knowledge of him. It thrilled him with a great dread of discovery; but the man went on. A very few moments after that, a young woman, with a slight girlish form, a sweet spare face in which there was no vestige of color, and large widely opened patient eyes, rose from the seat where he had observed her sitting, and came to speak to him.

"Citizen Evrémonde," she said, touching him with her cold hand, "I am a poor little seamstress, who was with you in La Force."

He murmured for answer: "True. I forget what you were accused of?"

"Plots. Though the just Heaven knows I am innocent of any. Is it likely? Who would think of plotting with a poor little weak creature like me?"

The forlorn smile with which she said it, so touched him that tears started from his eyes.

"I am not afraid to die, Citizen Evrémonde, but I have done nothing. I am not unwilling to die, if the Republic, which is to do so much good to us poor, will profit by my death; but I do not know how that can be, Citizen Evrémonde. Such a poor weak little creature!"

As the last thing on earth that his heart was to warm and soften to, it warmed and softened to this pitiable girl.

"I heard you were released, Citizen Evrémonde. I hoped it was true?"

"It was. But, I was again taken and condemned."

"If I may ride with you, Citizen Evrémonde, will you let me hold your hand? I am not afraid, but I am little and weak, and it will give me more courage."

As the patient eyes were lifted to his face, he saw a sudden doubt in them, and then astonishment. He pressed the work-worn, hunger-worn young fingers, and touched his lips.

"Are you dying for him?" she whispered.

"And his wife and child. Hush! Yes."

"O you will let me hold your brave hand, stranger?"

"Hush! Yes, my poor sister; to the last."

The same shadows that are falling on the prison, are falling, in the same hour of that early afternoon, on the Barrier with the crowd about it, when a coach going out of Paris drives up to be examined.

"Who goes here? Whom have we within? Papers!"

The papers are handed out and read.

"Alexandre Manette. Physician. French. Which is he?"

This is he; this helpless, inarticulately murmuring, wandering old man pointed out.

"Apparently the Citizen Doctor is not in his right mind? The Revolution-fever will have been too much for him?"

Greatly too much for him.

"Hah! Many suffer with it. Lucie. His daughter. French. Which is she?"

This is she.

"Apparently it must be. Lucie, the wife of Evrémonde; is it not?"

It is.

"Hah! Evrémonde has an assignation elsewhere. Lucie, her child. English. This is she?"

She and no other.

"Kiss me, child of Evrémonde. Now, thou hast kissed a good Republican; something new in thy family; remember it! Sydney Carton. Advocate. English. Which is he?"

He lies here, in this corner of the carriage. He, too, is pointed out.

"Apparently the English advocate is in a swoon?"

It is hoped he will recover in the fresher air. It is represented that he is not in strong health, and has separated sadly from a friend who is under the displeasure of the Republic.

"Is that all? It is not a great deal, that! Many are under the displeasure of the Republic, and must look out at the little window. Jarvis Lorry. Banker. English. Which is he?"

"I am he. Necessarily, being the last."

It is Jarvis Lorry who has replied to all the previous questions. It is Jarvis Lorry who has alighted and stands with his hand on the coach door, replying to a group of officials. They leisurely walk round the carriage and leisurely mount the box, to look at what little luggage it carries on the roof; the country people hanging about, press nearer to the coach doors and greedily stare in; a little child, carried by its mother, has its short arm held out for it, that it may touch the wife of an aristocrat who has gone to the guillotine.

"Behold your papers, Jarvis Lorry, countersigned."

"One can depart, citizen?"

"One can depart. Forward, my postilions! A good journey!"

"I salute you, citizens.—And the first danger passed!"

These are again the words of Jarvis Lorry, as he clasps his hands, and looks upward. There is terror in the carriage, there is weeping, there is the heavy breathing of the insensible traveller.

"Are we not going too slowly? Can they not be induced to go faster?" asks Lucie, clinging to the old man.

"It would seem like flight, my darling. I must not urge them too much; it would rouse suspicion."

"Look back, look back, and see if we are pursued!"

"The road is clear, my dearest. So far, we are not pursued."

Houses in twos and threes pass by us, solitary farms, ruinous buildings, dye-works, tanneries and the like, open country, avenues of leafless trees. The hard uneven pavement is under us, the soft deep mud is on either side. Sometimes, we strike into the skirting mud, to avoid the stones that clatter us and shake us; sometimes we stick in ruts and sloughs there. The agony of our impatience is then so great, that in our wild alarm and hurry we are for getting out and running—hiding—doing anything but stopping.

Out of the open country, in again among ruinous buildings, solitary farms, dye-works, tanneries and the like, cottages in twos and threes, avenues of leafless trees. Have these men deceived us, and taken us back by another road? Is not this the same place twice over? Thank Heaven no. A village. Look back, look back, and see if we are pursued! Hush! the posting-house.

Leisurely, our four horses are taken out; leisurely, the coach stands in the little street, bereft of horses, and with no likelihood upon it of ever moving again; leisurely, the new horses come into visible existence, one by one; leisurely, the new postilions follow, sucking and plaiting the lashes of their whips; leisurely, the old postilions count their money, make wrong additions, and arrive at dissatisfied results. All the time, our over-fraught hearts are beating at a rate that would far outstrip the fastest gallop of the fastest horses ever foaled.

At length the new postilions are in their saddles, and the old are left behind. We are through the village, up the hill, and down the hill, and on the low watery grounds. Suddenly, the postilions exchange speech with animated gesticulation, and the horses are pulled up, almost on their haunches. We are pursued!

"Ho! Within the carriage there. Speak then!"
"What is it?" asks Mr. Lorry, looking out at window.
"How many did they say?"
"I do not understand you."

"—At the last post. How many to the guillotine today?"
"Fifty-two."
"I said so! A brave number! My fellow-citizen here, would have it forty-two; ten more heads are worth having. The guillotine goes handsomely. I love it. Hi forward. Whoop!"

The night comes on dark. He moves more; he is beginning to revive, and to speak intelligibly; he thinks they are still together; he asks him, by his name, what he has in his hand. O pity us, kind Heaven, and help us! Look out, look out, and see if we are pursued.

The wind is rushing after us, and the clouds are flying after us, and the moon is plunging after us, and the whole wild night is in pursuit of us; but, so far, we are pursued by nothing else.

XIV THE KNITTING DONE

In that same juncture of time when the fifty-two awaited their fate, Madame Defarge held darkly ominous council with The Vengeance and Jacques Three of the Revolutionary jury. Not in the wine-shop did Madame Defarge confer with these ministers, but in the shed of the wood-sawyer, erst a mender of roads. The sawyer himself did not participate in the conference, but abided at a little distance, like an outer satellite who was not to speak until required, or to offer an opinion until invited.

"But our Defarge," said Jacques Three, "is undoubtedly a good Republican? Eh?"

"There is no better," the voluble Vengeance protested in her shrill notes, "in France."

"Peace, little Vengeance," said Madame Defarge, laying her hand with a slight frown on her lieutenant's lips, "hear me speak. My husband, fellow-citizen, is a good Republican and a bold man; he has deserved well of the Republic, and possesses its confidence. But my husband has his weaknesses, and he is so weak as to relent towards this Doctor."

"It is a great pity," croaked Jacques Three, dubiously shaking his head, with his cruel fingers at his hungry mouth; "it is not quite like a good citizen; it is a thing to regret."

"See you," said madame, "I care nothing for this Doctor. He may wear his head or lose it, for any interest I have in him; it is all one to me. But, the Evrémonde people are to be exterminated, and the wife and child must follow the husband and father."

"She has a fine head for it," croaked Jacques Three. "I have seen blue eyes and golden hair there, and they looked charming when Sanson held them up."

Madame Defarge cast down her eyes, and reflected a little.

"The child also," observed Jacques Three, with a meditative enjoyment of his words, "has golden hair and blue eyes. And we seldom have a child there. It is a pretty sight!"

"In a word," said Madame Defarge, coming out of her short abstraction, "I cannot trust my husband in this matter. Not only do I feel, since last night, that I dare not confide to him the details of my projects; but also I feel that if I delay, there is danger of his giving warning, and then they might escape."

"That must never be," croaked Jacques Three; "no one must escape. We have not half enough as it is. We ought to have six score a day."

"In a word," Madame Defarge went on, "my husband has not my reason for pursuing this family to annihilation, and I have not his reason for regarding this Doctor with any sensibility. I must act for myself, therefore. Come hither, little citizen."

The wood-sawyer, who held her in the respect, and himself in the submission, of mortal fear, advanced with his hand to his red cap.

"Touching those signals, little citizen," said Madame Defarge, sternly, "that she made to the prisoners; you are ready to bear witness to them this very day?"

"Ay, ay, why not!" cried the sawyer. "Every day, in all weathers, from two to four, always signalling, sometimes with the little one, sometimes without. I know what I know. I have seen with my eyes."

He made all manner of gestures while he spoke, as if in incidental imitation of some few of the great diversity of signals that he had never seen.

"Clearly plots," said Jacques Three. "Transparently!"

"There is no doubt of the jury?" inquired Madame Defarge, letting her eyes turn to him with a gloomy smile.

"Rely upon the patriotic jury, dear citizeness. I answer for my fellow-jurymen."

"Now, let me see," said Madame Defarge, pondering again. "Yet once more! Can I spare this Doctor to my husband? I have no feeling either way. Can I spare him?"

"He would count as one head," observed Jacques Three, in a low voice. "We really have not heads enough; it would be a pity, I think."

"He was signalling with her when I saw her," urged Madame Defarge; "I cannot speak of one without the other; and I must not be silent, and trust the case wholly to him, this little citizen here. For, I am not a bad witness."

The Vengeance and Jacques Three vied with each other in their fervent protestations that she was the most admirable and marvellous of witnesses. The little citizen, not to be outdone, declared her to be a celestial witness.

"He must take his chance," said Madame Defarge. "No; I cannot spare him! You are engaged at three o'clock; you are going to see the batch of today executed.—You?"

The question was addressed to the wood-sawyer, who hurriedly replied in the affirmative: seizing the occasion to add that he was the most ardent of Republicans, and that he would be in effect the most desolate of Republicans, if anything prevented him from enjoying the pleasure of smoking his afternoon pipe in the contemplation of the droll national barber. He was so very demonstrative herein, that he might have been suspected of having his small individual fears for his own personal safety, every hour in the day.

"I," said madame, "am equally engaged at the same place. After it is over—say at eight tonight—come you to me, in Saint Antoine, and we will give information against these people at my section."

The wood-sawyer said he would be proud and flattered to attend the citizeness. The citizeness looking at him, he became embarrassed, evaded her glance as a small dog would have done, retreated among his wood, and hid his confusion over the handle of his saw.

Madame Defarge beckoned the juryman and The Vengeance a little nearer to the door, and there expounded her further views to them thus:

"She will now be at home, awaiting the moment of his death. She will be mourning and grieving. She will be in a state of mind to impeach the justice of the Republic. She will be full of sympathy with its enemies. I will go to her."

"What an admirable woman; what an adorable woman!" exclaimed Jacques Three, rapturously. "Ah, my cherished!" cried The Vengeance; and embraced her.

"Take you my knitting," said Madame Defarge, placing it in her lieutenant's hands, "and have it ready for me in my usual seat. Keep me my usual chair. Go you there, straight, for there will probably be a greater concourse than usual, today."

"I willingly obey the orders of my chief," said The Vengeance, with alacrity, and kissing her cheek. "You will not be late?"

"I shall be there before the commencement."

"And before the tumbrils arrive. Be sure you are there, my soul," said The Vengeance, calling after her, for she had already turned into the street, "before the tumbrils arrive!"

Madame Defarge slightly waved her hand, to imply that she heard, and might be relied upon to arrive in good time, and so went through the mud, and round the corner of the prison wall. The Vengeance and the juryman, looking after her as she walked away, were highly appreciative of her fine figure, and her superb moral endowments.

There were many women at that time, upon whom the times laid a dreadfully disfiguring hand; but, there was not one among them more to be dreaded than this ruthless woman, now making her way along the streets.

It was nothing to her, that an innocent man was to die for the sins of his forefathers; she saw, not him, but them. It was nothing to her, that his wife was to be made a widow and his daughter an orphan; that was insufficient punishment, because they were her natural enemies and her prey, and as such had no right to live. To appeal to her, was made hopeless by her having no sense of pity, even for herself. If she had been laid low in the streets, in any of the many encounters in which she had been engaged, she would not have pitied herself; nor, if she had been ordered to the axe tomorrow, would she have gone to it with any softer feeling than a fierce desire to change places with the man who sent her there.

Such a heart Madame Defarge carried under her rough robe. Carelessly worn, it was a becoming robe enough, in a certain weird way, and her dark hair looked rich under her coarse red cap. Lying hidden in her bosom, was a loaded pistol. Lying hidden at her waist, was a sharpened dagger. Thus accoutred, and walking with the confident tread of such a character, and with the supple freedom of a woman who had habitually walked in her girlhood, bare-foot and bare-legged, on the brown sea-sand, Madame Defarge took her way along the streets.

Now, when the journey of the travelling coach, at that very moment waiting for the completion of its load, had been planned out last night, the difficulty of taking Miss Pross in it had much engaged Mr. Lorry's attention. It was not merely desirable to avoid overloading the coach, but it was of the highest importance that the time occupied in examining it and its passengers, should be reduced to the utmost; since their escape might depend on the saving of only a few seconds here and there. Finally, he had proposed, after anxious consideration, that Miss Pross and Jerry, who were at liberty to leave the city, should leave it at three o'clock in the lightest-wheeled conveyance known to that period. Unencumbered with luggage, they would soon overtake the coach, and, passing it and preceding it on the road, would order its horses in advance, and greatly facilitate its progress during the precious hours of the night, when delay was the most to be dreaded.

Seeing in this arrangement the hope of rendering real service in that pressing emergency, Miss Pross hailed it with joy. She and Jerry had beheld the coach start, had known who it was that Solomon brought, had passed some ten minutes in tortures of suspense, and were now concluding their arrangements to follow the coach, even as Madame Defarge, taking her way through the streets, now drew nearer and nearer to the else-deserted lodging in which they held their consultation.

"Now what do you think, Mr. Cruncher," said Miss Pross, whose agitation was so great that she could hardly speak, or stand, or move, or live: "what do you think of our not starting from this courtyard? Another carriage having already gone from here today, it might awaken suspicion."

"My opinion, miss," returned Mr. Cruncher, "is as you're right. Likewise wot I'll stand by you, right or wrong."

"I am so distracted with fear and hope for our precious creatures," said Miss Pross, wildly crying, "that I am incapable of forming any plan. Are *you* capable of forming any plan, my dear good Mr. Cruncher?"

"Respectin' a future spear o' life, miss," returned Mr. Cruncher, "I hope so. Respectin' any present use o' this here blessed old head o' mine, I think not. Would you do me the favor, miss, to take notice o' two promises and wows wot it is my wishes fur to record in this here crisis?"

"Oh, for gracious sake!" cried Miss Pross, still wildly crying, "record them at once, and get them out of the way, like an excellent man."

"First," said Mr. Cruncher, who was all in a tremble, and who spoke with an ashy and solemn visage, "them poor things well out o' this, never no more will I do it, never no more!"

"I am quite sure, Mr. Cruncher," returned Miss Pross, "that you never will do it again, whatever it is, and I beg you not to think it necessary to mention more particularly what it is."

"No, miss," returned Jerry, "it shall not be named to you. Second: them poor things well out o' this, and never no more will I interfere with Mrs. Cruncher's flopping, never no more!"

"Whatever housekeeping arrangement that may be," said Miss Pross, striving to dry her eyes and compose herself, "I have no doubt it is best that Mrs. Cruncher should have it entirely under her own superintendence—O, my poor darling!"

"I go so far as to say, miss, moreover," proceeded Mr.

Cruncher, with a most alarming tendency to hold forth as from a pulpit—"and let my words be took down and took to Mrs. Cruncher through yourself—that wot my opinions respectin' flopping has undergone a change, and that wot I only hope with all my heart as Mrs. Cruncher may be a flopping at the present time."

"There, there, there! I hope she is, my dear man," cried the distracted Miss Pross, "and I hope she finds it answering expectations. If we ever get back to our native land, you may rely upon my telling Mrs. Cruncher as much as I may be able to remember and understand of what you have so impressively said; and at all events you may be sure that I shall bear witness to your being thoroughly in earnest at this dreadful time. Now, pray let us think! My esteemed Mr. Cruncher, let us think!"

Still, Madame Defarge, pursuing her way along the streets, came nearer and nearer.

"If you were to go before," said Miss Pross, "and stop the vehicle and horses from coming here, and were to wait somewhere for me; wouldn't that be best?"

Mr. Cruncher thought it might be best.

"Where could you wait for me?" asked Miss Pross.

Mr. Cruncher was so bewildered that he could think of no locality but Temple-bar. Alas, Temple-bar was hundreds of miles away, and Madame Defarge was drawing very near indeed.

"By the cathedral door," said Miss Pross. "Would it be much out of the way, to take me in, near the great cathedral door between the two towers?"

"No, miss," answered Mr. Cruncher.

"Then, like the best of men," said Miss Pross, "go to the posting-house straight, and make the change."

"I am doubtful," said Mr. Cruncher, hesitating and shaking his head, "about leaving of you, you see. We don't know what may happen."

"Heaven knows we don't," returned Miss Pross, "but have no fear for me. Take me in at the cathedral, at three o'clock or as near it as you can, and I am sure it will be better than our going from here. I feel certain of it. There! Bless you, Mr. Cruncher! Think—not of me, but of the lives that may depend on both of us!"

This exordium, and Miss Pross's two hands in quite agonised

entreaty clasping his, decided Mr. Cruncher. With an encouraging nod or two, he immediately went out to alter the arrangements, and left her by herself to follow as she had proposed.

The having originated a precaution which was already in course of execution, was a great relief to Miss Pross. The necessity of composing her appearance so that it should attract no special notice in the streets, was another relief. She looked at her watch, and it was twenty minutes past two. She had no time to lose, but must get ready at once.

Afraid, in her extreme perturbation, of the loneliness of the deserted rooms, and of half-imagined faces peeping from behind every open door in them, Miss Pross got a basin of cold water and began laving her eyes, which were swollen and red. Haunted by her feverish apprehensions, she could not bear to have her sight obscured for a minute at a time by the dripping water, but constantly paused and looked round to see that there was no one watching her. In one of those pauses she recoiled and cried out, for she saw a figure standing in the room.

The basin fell to the ground broken, and the water flowed to the feet of Madame Defarge. By strange stern ways, and through much staining blood, those feet had come to meet that water.

Madame Defarge looked coldly at her, and said, "The wife of Evrémonde; where is she?"

It flashed upon Miss Pross's mind that the doors were all standing open, and would suggest the flight. Her first act was to shut them. There were four in the room, and she shut them all. She then placed herself before the door of the chamber which Lucie had occupied.

Madame Defarge's dark eyes followed her through this rapid movement, and rested on her when it was finished. Miss Pross had nothing beautiful about her; years had not tamed the wildness, or softened the grimness, of her appearance; but, she too was a determined woman in her different way, and she measured Madame Defarge with her eyes, every inch.

"You might, from your appearance, be the wife of Lucifer," said Miss Pross, in her breathing. "Nevertheless you shall not get the better of me. I am an Englishwoman."

Madame Defarge looked at her scornfully, but still with something of Miss Pross's own perception that they two were at bay.

She saw a tight, hard, wiry woman before her, as Mr. Lorry had seen in the same figure a woman with a strong hand, in the years gone by. She knew full well that Miss Pross was the family's devoted friend; Miss Pross knew full well that Madame Defarge was the family's malevolent enemy.

"On my way yonder," said Madame Defarge, with a slight movement of her hand towards the fatal spot, "where they reserve my chair and my knitting for me, I am come to make my compliments to her in passing. I wish to see her."

"I know that your intentions are evil," said Miss Pross, "and you may depend upon it, I'll hold my own against them."

Each spoke in her own language; neither understood the other's words; both were very watchful, and intent to deduce from look and manner, what the unintelligible words meant.

"It will do her no good to keep herself concealed from me at this moment," said Madame Defarge. "Good patriots will know what that means. Let me see her. Go tell her that I wish to see her. Do you hear?"

"If those eyes of yours were bed-winches," returned Miss Pross, "and I was an English four-poster, they shouldn't loose a splinter of me. No, you wicked foreign woman; I am your match."

Madame Defarge was not likely to follow these idiomatic remarks in detail; but, she so far understood them as to perceive that she was set at naught.

"Woman imbecile and pig-like!" said Madame Defarge, frowning. "I take no answer from you. I demand to see her. Either tell her that I demand to see her, or stand out of the way of the door and let me go to her!" This, with an angry explanatory wave of her right arm.

"I little thought," said Miss Pross, "that I should ever want to understand your nonsensical language; but I would give all I have, except the clothes I wear, to know whether you suspect the truth, or any part of it."

Neither of them for a single moment released the other's eyes. Madame Defarge had not moved from the spot where she stood when Miss Pross first became aware of her; but, she now advanced one step.

"I am a Briton," said Miss Pross, "I am desperate. I don't care an English twopence for myself. I know that the longer

I keep you here, the greater hope there is for my Ladybird. I'll not leave a handful of that dark hair upon your head, if you lay a finger on me!"

Thus Miss Pross, with a shake of her head and a flash of her eyes between every rapid sentence, and every rapid sentence a whole breath! Thus Miss Pross, who had never struck a blow in her life!

But, her courage was of that emotional nature that it brought the irrepressible tears into her eyes. This was a courage that Madame Defarge so little comprehended as to mistake for weakness. "Ha, ha!" she laughed, "you poor wretch! What are you worth! I address myself to that Doctor." Then she raised her voice and called out, "Citizen Doctor! Wife of Evrémonde! Child of Evrémonde! Any person but this miserable fool, answer the Citizeness Defarge!"

Perhaps the following silence, perhaps some latent disclosure in the expression of Miss Pross's face, perhaps a sudden misgiving apart from either suggestion, whispered to Madame Defarge that they were gone. Three of the doors she opened swiftly, and looked in.

"Those rooms are all in disorder, there has been hurried packing, there are odds and ends upon the ground. There is no one in that room behind you! Let me look."

"Never!" said Miss Pross, who understood the request as perfectly as Madame Defarge understood the answer.

"If they are not in that room, they are gone, and can be pursued and brought back," said Madame Defarge to herself.

"As long as you don't know whether they are in that room or not, you are uncertain what to do," said Miss Pross to *her*self; "and you shall not know that, if I can prevent your knowing it; and know that, or not know that, you shall not leave here while I can hold you."

"I have been in the streets from the first, nothing has stopped me, I will tear you to pieces but I will have you from that door," said Madame Defarge.

"We are alone at the top of a high house in a solitary courtyard, we are not likely to be heard, and I pray for bodily strength to keep you here, while every minute you are here is worth a hundred thousand guineas to my darling," said Miss Pross.

Madame Defarge made at the door. Miss Pross, on the instinct of the moment, seized her round the waist in both her arms, and held her tight. It was in vain for Madame Defarge to struggle and to strike; Miss Pross, with the vigorous tenacity of love, always so much stronger than hate, clasped her tight, and even lifted her from the floor in the struggle that they had. The two hands of Madame Defarge buffeted and tore her face; but, Miss Pross, with her head down, held her round the waist, and clung to her with more than the hold of a drowning woman.

Soon, Madame Defarge's hands ceased to strike, and felt at her encircled waist. "It is under my arm," said Miss Pross, in smothered tones, "you shall not draw it. I am stronger than you, I bless Heaven for it. I'll hold you till one or other of us faints or dies!"

Madame Defarge's hands were at her bosom. Miss Pross looked up, saw what it was, struck at it, struck out a flash and a crash, and stood alone—blinded with smoke.

All this was in a second. As the smoke cleared, leaving an awful stillness, it passed out on the air, like the soul of the furious woman whose body lay lifeless on the ground.

In the first fright and horror of her situation, Miss Pross passed the body as far from it as she could, and ran down the stairs to call for fruitless help. Happily, she bethought herself of the consequences of what she did, in time to check herself and go back. It was dreadful to go in at the door again; but, she did go in, and even went near it, to get the bonnet and other things that she must wear. These she put on, out on the staircase, first shutting and locking the door and taking away the key. She then sat down on the stairs a few moments, to breathe and to cry, and then got up and hurried away.

By good fortune she had a veil on her bonnet, or she could hardly have gone along the streets without being stopped. By good fortune, too, she was naturally so peculiar in appearance as not to show disfigurement like any other woman. She needed both advantages, for the marks of gripping fingers were deep in her face, and her hair was torn, and her dress (hastily composed with unsteady hands) was clutched and dragged a hundred ways.

In crossing the bridge, she dropped the door key in the river. Arriving at the cathedral some few minutes before her escort, and waiting there, she thought, what if the key were already taken in a net, what if it were identified, what if the door were opened and the remains discovered, what if she were stopped at the gate, sent to prison, and charged with murder! In the midst of these fluttering thoughts, the escort appeared, took her in, and took her away.

"Is there any noise in the streets?" she asked him.

"The usual noises," Mr. Cruncher replied; and looked surprised by the question and by her aspect.

"I don't hear you," said Miss Pross. "What do you say?"

It was in vain for Mr. Cruncher to repeat what he said; Miss Pross could not hear him. "So I'll nod my head," thought Mr. Cruncher, amazed, "at all events she'll see that." And she did.

"Is there any noise in the streets now?" asked Miss Pross again, presently.

Again Mr. Cruncher nodded his head.

"I don't hear it."

"Gone deaf in a hour?" said Mr. Cruncher, ruminating, with his mind much disturbed; "wot's come to her?"

"I feel," said Miss Pross, "as if there had been a flash and a crash, and that crash was the last thing I should ever hear in this life."

"Blest if she ain't in a queer condition!" said Mr. Cruncher, more and more disturbed. "Wot can she have been a takin', to keep her courage up? Hark! There's the roll of them dreadful carts! You can hear that, miss?"

"I can hear," said Miss Pross, seeing that he spoke to her, "nothing. O, my good man, there was first a great crash, and then a great stillness, and that stillness seems to be fixed and unchangeable, never to be broken any more as long as my life lasts."

"If she don't hear the roll of those dreadful carts, now very nigh their journey's end," said Mr. Cruncher, glancing over his shoulder, "it's my opinion that indeed she never will hear anything else in this world."

And indeed she never did.

XV THE FOOTSTEPS DIE OUT FOREVER

Along the Paris streets, the death-carts rumbled, hollow and harsh. Six tumbrils carry the day's wine to La Guillotine. As the sombre wheels of the six carts go round, they seem to plough up a long crooked furrow among the populace in the streets.

Ridges of faces are thrown to this side and to that, and the ploughs go steadily onward. So used are the regular inhabitants of the houses to the spectacle, that in many windows there are no people, and in some the occupation of the hands is not so much as suspended, while the eyes survey the faces in the tumbrils. Here and there, the inmate has visitors to see the sight; then he points his finger, with something of the complacency of a curator or authorised exponent, to this cart and to this, and seems to tell who sat here yesterday, and who there the day before.

Of the riders in the tumbrils, some observe these things, and all things on their last roadside, with an impassive stare; others, with a lingering interest in the ways of life and men. Some, seated with drooping heads, are sunk in silent despair; again, there are some so heedful of their looks that they cast upon the multitude such glances as they have seen in theatres, and in pictures. Several close their eyes, and think, or try to get their straying thoughts together. Only one, and he a miserable creature of a crazed aspect, is so shattered and made drunk by horror that he sings, and tries to dance. Not one of the whole number appeals, by look or gesture, to the pity of the people.

There is a guard of sundry horsemen riding abreast of the tumbrils, and faces are often turned up to some of them and they are asked some question. It would seem to be always the same question, for, it is always followed by a press of people towards the third cart. The horsemen abreast of that cart, frequently point out one man in it with their swords. The leading curiosity is, to know which is he; he stands at the back of the tumbril with his head bent down, to converse with a mere girl who sits on the side of the cart, and holds his hand. He has no curiosity or care for the scene about him, and always speaks to the girl. Here and there in a long Street of St. Honoré, cries are raised against him. If they move him at all, it is only to a quiet smile, as he shakes his hair a little more loosely about his face. He cannot easily touch his face, his arms being bound.

On the steps of a church, awaiting the coming-up of the tumbrils, stands the Spy and prison-sheep. He looks into the first of them: not there. He looks into the second: not there. He already asks himself, "Has he sacrificed me?" when his face clears, as he looks into the third.

"Which is Evrémonde?" said a man behind him.
"That. At the back there."
"With his hand in the girl's?"
"Yes."

The man cries, "Down, Evrémonde! To the guillotine all aristocrats! Down, Evrémonde!"

"Hush, hush!" the Spy entreats him, timidly.

"And why not, citizen?"

"He is going to pay the forfeit; it will be paid in five minutes more. Let him be at peace."

But, the man continuing to exclaim, "Down, Evrémonde!" the face of Evrémonde is for a moment turned towards him. Evrémonde then sees the Spy, and looks attentively at him, and goes his way.

The clocks are on the stroke of Three and the furrow ploughed among the populace is turning round, to come on into the place of execution, and end. The ridges thrown to this side and to that, now crumble in and close behind the last plough as it passes on, for all are following to the Guillotine. In front of it, seated in chairs as in a garden of public diversion, are a number of women, busily knitting. On one of the foremost chairs, stands The Vengeance, looking about for her friend.

"Thérèse!" she cries, in her shrill tones. "Who has seen her? Thérèse Defarge!"

"She never missed before," says a knitting-woman of the sisterhood.

"No; nor will she miss now," cries The Vengeance, petulantly. "Thérèse."

"Louder," the woman recommends.

Ay! Louder, Vengeance, much louder, and still she will scarcely hear thee. Louder yet, Vengeance, with a little oath or so added, and yet it will hardly bring her. Send other women up and down to seek her, lingering somewhere; and yet, although the messengers have done dread deeds, it is questionable whether of their own wills they will go far enough to find her!

"Bad fortune!" cries The Vengeance, stamping her foot in the chair, "and here are the tumbrils! And Evrémonde will be despatched in a wink, and she not here! See her knitting in my hand, and her empty chair ready for her. I cry with vexation and disappointment!"

As The Vengeance descends from her elevation to do it, the tumbrils begin to discharge their loads. The ministers of Saint Guillotine are robed and ready. Crash!—A head is held up, and the knitting-women who scarcely lifted their eyes to look at it a moment ago when it could think and speak, count One.

The second tumbril empties and moves on; the third comes up. Crash!—And the knitting-women, never faltering or pausing in their work, count Two.

The supposed Evrémonde descends, and the seamstress is lifted out next after him. He has not relinquished her patient hand in getting out, but still holds it as he promised. He gently places her with her back to the crashing engine that constantly whirrs up and falls, and she looks into his face and thanks him.

"But for you, dear stranger, I should not be so composed, for I am naturally a poor little thing, faint of heart; nor should I have been able to raise my thoughts to Him who was put to death, that we might have hope and comfort here today. I think you were sent to me by Heaven."

"Or you to me," says Sydney Carton. "Keep your eyes upon me, dear child, and mind no other object."

"I mind nothing while I hold your hand. I shall mind nothing when I let it go, if they are rapid."

"They will be rapid. Fear not!"

The two stand in the fast-thinning throng of victims, but they speak as if they were alone. Eye to eye, voice to voice, hand to hand, heart to heart, these two children of the Universal Mother, else so wide apart and differing, have come together on the dark highway, to repair home together and to rest in her bosom.

"Brave and generous friend, will you let me ask you one last question? I am very ignorant, and it troubles me—just a little."

"Tell me what it is."

"I have a cousin, an only relative and an orphan, like myself, whom I love very dearly. She is five years younger than I, and she lives in a farmer's house in the south country. Poverty parted us, and she knows nothing of my fate—for I cannot write —and if I could, how should I tell her! It is better as it is."

"Yes, yes: better as it is."

"What I have been thinking as we came along, and what I am still thinking now, as I look into your kind strong face which gives me so much support, is this: If the Republic really does good to the poor, and they come to be less hungry, and in all ways to suffer less, she may live a long time; she may even live to be old."

"What then, my gentle sister?"

"Do you think": the uncomplaining eyes in which there is so much endurance, fill with tears, and the lips part a little more and tremble: "that it will seem long to me, while I wait for her in the better land where I trust both you and I will be mercifully sheltered?"

"It cannot be, my child; there is no time there, and no trouble there."

"You comfort me so much! I am so ignorant. Am I to kiss you now? Is the moment come?"

"Yes."

She kisses his lips; he kisses hers; they solemnly bless each other. The spare hand does not tremble as he releases it; nothing worse than a sweet, bright constancy is in the patient face. She goes next before him—is gone; the knitting-women count Twenty-Two.

"I am the Resurrection and the Life, saith the Lord: he that believeth in me, though he were dead, yet shall he live: and whosoever liveth and believeth in me, shall never die."

The murmuring of many voices, the upturning of many faces, the pressing on of many footsteps in the outskirts of the crowd, so that it swells forward in a mass, like one great heave of water, all flashes away. Twenty-Three.

They said of him, about the city that night, that it was the peacefullest man's face ever beheld there. Many added that he looked sublime and prophetic.

One of the most remarkable sufferers by the same axe—a woman—had asked at the foot of the same scaffold, not long before, to be allowed to write down the thoughts that were inspiring her. If he had given any utterance to his, and they were prophetic, they would have been these:

"I see Barsad, and Cly, Defarge, The Vengeance, the juryman, the judge, long ranks of the new oppressors who have risen on the destruction of the old, perishing by this retributive instrument, before it shall cease out of its present use. I see a beautiful city and a brilliant people rising from this abyss, and, in their struggles to be truly free, in their triumphs and defeats, through long, long years to come, I see the evil of this time and of the previous time of which this is the natural birth, gradually making expiation for itself and wearing out.

"I see the lives for which I lay down my life, peaceful, useful, prosperous and happy, in that England which I shall see no more. I see Her with a child upon her bosom, who bears my name. I see her father, aged and bent, but otherwise restored, and faithful to all men in his healing office, and at peace. I see the good old man, so long their friend, in ten years' time enriching them with all he has, and passing tranquilly to his reward.

"I see that I hold a sanctuary in their hearts, and in the hearts of their descendants, generations hence. I see Her, an old woman, weeping for me on the anniversary of this day. I see Her and her husband, their course done, lying side by side in their last earthly bed, and I know that each was not more honored and held sacred in the other's soul, than I was in the souls of both.

"I see that child who lay upon her bosom and who bore my name, a man, winning his way up in that path of life which once was mine. I see him winning it so well, that my name is made illustrious there by the light of his. I see the blots I threw upon it, faded away. I see him, foremost of just judges and honored men, bringing a boy of my name, with a forehead that I know and golden hair, to this place—then fair to look upon, with not a trace of this day's disfigurement—and I hear him tell the child my story, with a tender and a faltering voice.

"It is a far, far better thing that I do, than I have ever done; it is a far, far better rest that I go to, than I have ever known."

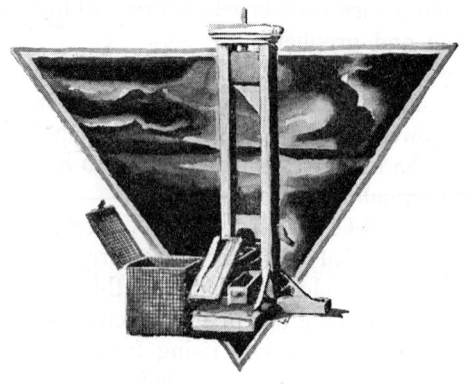

CHARLES DICKENS

BY WAY OF APPRECIATION

The Setting

Reading a novel is very much like watching a play. In your mind's eye you see the setting, watch the people come and go, listen to what they have to say, and hear what others say about them. In *A Tale of Two Cities* you will find that Dickens has set his stage very carefully and that he has arranged his plot with the utmost care. After a rapid sketch, not only of things that are actually happening, but of events that are about to happen, he plunges immediately into the story.

Throughout the opening chapters he aims to produce an atmosphere of mystery and ominous foreboding. Notice how your interest and expectation are aroused by the message brought by Jerry and its startling answer. The feeling of mystery and omen is intensified by the incident of the broken wine cask and the ceaseless knitting of Madame Defarge. Do you not see in the "echoing footsteps" and the thunderstorm ominous foreshadowings of coming events?

The Plot

Keynotes and premonitory hints are frequently given, and it will be interesting for you to notice as you read how many things which happen later in the story are prepared for in the first few chapters. Sometimes entire incidents are prophetic, and sometimes only a few words or a sentence will hint at future happenings. What was the significance of Mr. Lorry's message "Recalled to Life"? Why did Jerry consider it a strange message and admit to himself that he would "be in a blazing bad way if recalling to life was to come into fashion"? See how many other events and prophetic statements you can find which prepare you for things which happen later in the story. This will help you to see how closely each incident is dovetailed into its special place, and how the entire plot is like a beautifully matched puzzle where no part can be detached without harm to the whole.

As a still further study of the plot, it will be interesting for you to trace the parts played by the characters of the story, and to show how they are necessary to the action. Dr. Manette, Sydney Carton, Lucie and Charles Darnay are the major characters and it will not be difficult to trace their parts in the story. You will enjoy following some of the seemingly unimportant and minor characters, too, and see how Dickens has used them in the climax. The spy Barsad apparently plays a minor part in the story, yet explain why he is a necessary character. Jerry Cruncher furnished the only bit of humor in the story, but does he not have a more important part? Is Miss Pross to be remembered only as a faithful and loyal companion to Lucie? Why are Monsieur Gabelle and the road-mender necessary to the action? In most of Dickens' stories characters are many and often seem unrelated to each other. Do you find such a situation in *A Tale of Two Cities*?

The Characters

In a character story our chief concern is with the characters themselves, and with the way in which they grow or change with the passing of the years. In a novel of the type of *A Tale of Two Cities,* however, the reader's interest is more in the action and the story than it is in the people. However, there are a few characters in this book which stand out as worthy of study for themselves, aside from their parts in the development of the plot. Sydney Carton is of course the most important of these. His is the great character for whom the book is famous. Incapable of sustained effort in the direction of his life, nevertheless through the influence of a pure and unselfish love, he rises to the heights of a great sacrifice. As you read the story note his traits of character as they are unfolded by the author. Is your opinion of him at first favorable or unfavorable? When does this opinion begin to change? Why is he the real hero of the story?

While the character of Carton stands out as the only one that shows change and development, there are other characters which are interesting in themselves aside from the parts they play in the story. Miss Pross is an example of unselfish devotion, and Mr. Lorry is a quaint and characteristic figure who hides a world of sentiment behind his insistence on the business aspect of affairs. Madame Defarge is a type character—the type of a powerful nature poisoned by injustice and become the incarnation of implacable and tireless hate. Why is Monsieur the Marquis also a type character?

When you have finished the study of this story, you will agree that what Carlyle writes of Scott's historical novels is also true of *A Tale of Two Cities*—that "historical novels have taught all men this truth . . . that the by-gone ages of the world were actually filled by living men, not protocols, state papers, controversies, and abstractions of men."

EXERCISES AND CREATIVE WORK

A Dramatization of the Novel

A Tale of Two Cities has been said to be more of a drama than a novel. It could hardly have been written by anyone lacking Dickens' keen interest in the stage and in fact, while he was writing the story, he corresponded with a great French actor about a French performance of the dramatization of the story.

Why not try a moving picture scenario of this novel? Such a dramatic story offers wonderful possibilities and it is this type which is most universally used for scenario writing. You will enjoy working out the progression of the plot in a series of scenes, either with or without screen titles. To get the best results you should read the entire story, first in order to get the plot in mind, and to see the way in which it has been worked out. When you can visualize the story as a whole, write a synopsis of it, merely outlining the chief incidents and then group your principal characters which have the closest association with your plot. Begin your story and build up the plot, scene by scene. To get what the scenario writer calls the "punch," keep in mind that every scene is leading up to the climax of the picture. Your scenes may be brief, but should be detailed enough to give the reader an idea of the setting, the characters, and the action.

Oral or Written Reports

There are many historical references in *A Tale of Two Cities* which will furnish interesting material for short reports, either oral or written. Dickens was very skillful in drawing word pictures and in making you see things as they actually happened. By making use of histories and other reference books see if you can describe as vividly some of the following persons and topics:

Louis XVI
Marie Antoinette
George III
The Guillotine
The Jacquerie
The French Aristocracy
The *émigrés*
The Prisons of London
The *lettres de cachet*
The Suburb of St. Antoine
The Storming of the Bastille

The March of the Women to Versailles
The Knitting Women of the Revolution
An English Inn of the Eighteenth Century
The Carmagnole
The Jacobin Club
The Reign of Terror
The September Massacres
Year One of the Republic

SUGGESTIONS FOR STUDY

Book the First

Chapter I—A summarizing picture of the times in both England and France, the scenes of our story, is given in this introductory chapter. The knowledge conveyed by this setting is important to an understanding of the conditions portrayed throughout the novel. The whole narrative evolves about two classes of people in these countries, the nobility and common folk, or peasants. What does the chapter tell of the nobility of England; of France? What does it tell of the commoners in England; of the peasants of France? One other important reference is made in this chapter. What was that "certain movable framework"? Show how smoothly Dickens brought in the significant mention of it. Tell what you know about it from your history readings.

Chapter II—Here the narrative of the story really begins, although in a sense this chapter, too, is introductory. What points make a clear and vivid picture of the stagecoach lumbering up Shooter's Hill? How is the suspense atmosphere of the chapter developed? Tell all you can of "the passenger booked by this history," and your impression of him. It is interesting to note that there were three persons in the stagecoach. Dickens' characters always have a definite purpose for being—is the purpose of the three fulfilled here, or is it possible that we shall see one or more of them again? What would you judge to be the keynote of this chapter? The message seemed to interest the important characters to a great degree. What was Jerry's reaction to it? Note his last sentence—it has an important bearing on the story. Dickens shows genius in novel writing in this chapter, for into its circumstances he has built the substance of his plot and sub-plot, which from this point on he develops with care, holding the reader in suspense until the very end. Watch this work out through the story.

Chapter III—Repeat the description of Jerry in your own words, noting particularly the characteristics of his eyes. You will enjoy knowing Jerry; he will interest and amuse you from time to time. Tell of the disturbed day-dreams of Mr. Jarvis Lorry as he jolted along inside the coach. These musings are most tantalizing at this point, given without explanation. What do you gather from what has been told, thus far? Explain why this chapter is called a "Transition Chapter."

Chapter IV—Describe Mr. Jarvis Lorry. Also describe Miss Manette as she appeared before him. It is important that you have a good picture of each of these characters, as first impressions are usually important in a story. On what occasion had Mr. Lorry seen this girl before? Give the substance of the introductory conversation between the two. Then relate the story Mr. Lorry told Miss Manette. What methods of approach did Mr. Lorry use? Do you learn anything from this of the character of the man? When the chapter climaxes into a serious situation, how does Dickens relieve the tension? Is this a usual device? Give your impression of the red-headed woman. What do you think of her?

Chapter V—The scene changes. Describe the section of St. Antoine. What is the significance of the red wine? Tell what you can of Madame Defarge, giving special attention to the by-play between her and her husband, of her seeing nothing, yet everything, and of her occupation. From your history reading, what do you know about the "Jacques" order in France at that time? Describe the scene in the inn. Tell of the ascent to the garret. What three men were peering into the room? In what manner did Monsieur Defarge enter the garret? What was visible within? What relationship had Monsieur Defarge to the shoemaker in former years?

Chapter VI—Step by step, proceed through the stages of recalling Monsieur Manette to a realization of life and freedom. What significance do you see in the making of a lady's shoe? Can you tell why Miss Manette tried to make her father weep? Tell how the grey-haired man left the garret. What happened at the Barrier? The reverie at the end of the chapter closes this section softly. Is the message delivered on the "Dover Mail" now satisfactorily explained? Where is the climax of Book the First? Sum up your impressions of the important characters thus far—Mr. Lorry, Jerry, Miss Manette, Madame Defarge, and the father—giving predominant traits, occupations, and correlation in the plot, as you now see it.

BOOK THE SECOND

Chapter I—Describe Jerry Cruncher's home life. What did his wife persist in doing that seemed to annoy him greatly? From the attitude Jerry takes against the praying, what do you think about his appellation of "honest tradesman"? Does this have anything to do with the fact that his boots, which are clean when he comes home at night, are often covered with clay in the morning? How did his "honest tradesman's" work turn out last week? How does Young Jerry resemble his father? What suspicions have arisen in Young Jerry's mind?

Chapter II—Why do you think Jerry's eyes "seem to get a little closer together" at the mention of his going to the Bailey? Describe the Old Bailey and tell what a by-stander told Jerry of the punishment that might be meted out to the prisoner. Describe the opening of court. Who was the man standing trial, and for what offense? Who were the witnesses against the accused? Note the gentleman who "concentrated on the ceiling of the court." What does this first impression tell you of the man?

Chapter III—Give a summary of the charges the Attorney General was going to prove against the prisoner. What is your judgment of the worth of the evidence furnished by Barsad? By Cly? Upon what reasons do you base your conclusion? Make close note of these two—they will appear again. What further reference was made to the two men of the Dover Mail? What testimony did Mr. Lorry give? State Miss Manette's testimony. The emotion underlying her one plaintive, heartfelt cry is an important force in this narrative. Repeat this one statement. What did Dr. Manette offer in this case? Was the evidence of father and daughter of help to the Attorney General in his prosecution? How did the case suddenly turn and upon what point? Describe Mr. Carton as he appeared in court. Was it because he saw everything that went on in court that Mr. Carton was the first to notice Miss Manette's faint, or was it because he was unobtrusively and especially watching her? What subject was mentioned between Mr. Carton and Mr. Darnay during their first conversation together? This conversation, and the contrast between the two men as they stood there together is of great significance in the story. It is most interesting, in the development of both plot and character in this novel, to note the clever and significant threads of pure importance which are thrown out in every chapter, and then to watch the author gradually gather them up and weave them together into a completed study of each life and a well-developed history of the times. What was the decision of the jury? What connecting point does Jerry give in his reply to Mr. Lorry? Give Dickens' description of the crowd as it came from the court house.

Chapter IV—Describe the group gathered to congratulate Darnay. Read carefully the paragraph telling what expression came to Dr. Manette as he looked at Darnay. Where was Mr. Carton all this time? Where did Mr. Carton and Mr. Darnay go after the others had departed? Characterize the two men now, as you again see them together. Read the paragraph aloud where Carton soliloquizes to himself before the mirror. Explain it fully, especially his reference to "blue eyes."

Chapter V—Tell the relation of a jackal to a lion. Apply this to Sydney Carton and Mr. Stryver. The purpose of this chapter is the characterization of Sydney Carton. Follow up your first impressions with the best character sketch you can write of him. Of the characters you have met in the book, would you like this man Carton as the hero?

Chapter VI—What is the substance of the conversation between Mr. Lorry and Miss Pross? Here again, note especially the seemingly casual reference to the brother Solomon. He will appear in due time. The important feature of this chapter, however, are the echoes and the footsteps that are heard. In a sense, these echoes cement the relationship between "the two cities," significant of the meaning of the story and its title. They are prophetic—very prophetic! Who was the first caller after dinner? All the people in the group seem very happy and at peace with the world; Dr. Manette appears to us strong and well. What general effect did Darnay's story have on the Doctor? What was the Doctor's specific reaction toward Darnay? Who was the second caller? In the incident of Carton and the family, Dickens has given us another effective summary of the essence of the plot. Explain the situation and its significance, as far as you can visualize. This chapter, which began so peacefully, and ended so tempestuously, is one of the best in the book, and no detail should be overlooked. What is the author's prophecy in the last sentence?

Chapter VII—The picture in this chapter portrays the attitude of the nobility in France toward the peasants, just prior to the French Revolution. Tell the story of the killing of the little girl, giving special attention to the "tall man" and to the Marquis. What connection is given by the appearance of Defarge and of Madame with her knitting?

Chapter VIII—This chapter continues the picture of the misery of the French peasantry, and their treatment at the hands of the nobility. At the beginning of the chapter, why was Monsieur's face red? Do you have any suspicion as to the identity of the man who was under the carriage? Tell further of the treatment of the peasants. Do you connect any previously mentioned name with the one given at the end of this chapter?

Chapter IX—Describe the château. What was the significance of the owl's call? What alarm came to Monsieur the Marquis? Is he the type of man to be jumpy without reason? In what state was the relationship between the Marquis and his nephew? Do you think the Marquis had any part in instigating Darnay's trial in London? Why? What did they discuss? It is interesting to note the reference to "that cloud of years past." How did the nephew say the family name now stood in France? Do you think Darnay was sincere in the philosophy he expressed regarding France, and conditions there? The delineation of the characters in this chapter will bear recalling. Tell what points you gained in knowledge of each of them. How did the peasant begin his day; how waked the noble at the château? What happened at the château during the night? How did the author handle the revelation of this incident? Whom do you suspect of committing the deed?

Chapter X—One year later, how was Charles Darnay occupied in London? What factors contributed to his success? When had he first loved Lucie? Tell the purport of the conference between Dr. Manette and Charles Darnay. What two promises were given? Give the meaning of the paragraph beginning "—any fancies, any reasons, etc." Do you think Dr. Manette is afraid to be told who Darnay really is? What reasons could he have for being afraid? What effect did the conference have on the Doctor?

Chapter XI—This is the most compassionate chapter of the whole book. From it, add to your characterization of Sydney Carton, and check your first impressions. What expression of devotion did Carton give Lucie in the last of this chapter? Do you believe these words to be a sincere pledge, or just fervent emotionalism? Compare Carton to Charles Darnay of the previous chapter.

Chapter XII—Who was at the gateway of Tellson's? How many mourners came down the street, and what happened to the funeral procession? Looking back upon your acquaintance with Cly, whom do you imagine the lone mourner might have been? Did Jerry go to the burying? Why did he remain at the burying ground? Where did he say he was going that night? What remarks were made about it? Explain the work of the "honest tradesman." From his treatment of his wife, what success do you think Jerry had on his "fishing" trip?

Chapter XIII—Describe the activity about the Defarge Wine Shop. Tell the story related by the mender of roads with the blue cap. How was the petition presented to the king? Explain the phrase "hungered for something that was neither food nor drink." What decree was passed at the conclusion of the conference? What was the register, and who kept it? What lesson did Madame Defarge give the mender of roads? Enlarge upon the summary you have written of the conditions of the peasant. Show how the revolutionary spirit was growing.

Chapter XIV—Who was the spy? Where have you seen him before? What was his purpose in visiting Saint Antoine? What information did he convey to the Defarges? How did each accept the information? What was the purpose of the rose in Madame's hair?

Chapter XV—Tell of the day of the wedding, of the preparations and the good-byes. What happened to Dr. Manette? What do you think caused this relapse? What course did Mr. Lorry pursue in attempting to restore the Doctor?

Chapter XVI—This chapter is a psychological study of Dr. Manette's malady. How adroitly did Mr. Lorry get Dr. Manette's opinion on his own case? What, in the Doctor's opinion, was the cause of his malady? What happened to the shoemaker's bench? Again, Mr. Lorry proves himself a true friend.

Chapter XVII—Tell what is again revealed regarding the nature of Sydney Carton. How did Charles react? Lucie? What did she say to her husband? What would you judge to be the purpose of this chapter?

Chapter XVIII—Give the details of the peaceful picture of Lucie's home life. To what stranger did little Lucie first raise her chubby arms? Tell of the footsteps echoing again in Soho Square. The story is suddenly shifted into the midst of what real footsteps? Describe the turmoil in France. Tell of the taking of the Bastille. Did Defarge find anything in cell One Hundred and Five, North Tower? What form of writing does the author use so effectively in this chapter? Notice how closely Dickens is now tying the two situations together. Show the steps in this smooth transition from Soho Square to Saint Antoine.

Chapter XIX—Tell of the importance of Tellson's at this time. When did the first desire come to Darnay to return to France? What was the force that decided him to go? With what arguments did he convince himself that he would be safe, even though he was a nobleman? Were his reasons logical, under the circumstances at home and abroad? What preparations did he make for leaving? What do you think were Darnay's real reasons for wanting to return, unknown, perhaps, to himself? What important developments in plot and character have taken place in this Part II of the story?

BOOK THE THIRD

Chapter I—Tell of Darnay's journey to Paris. Why was Defarge disturbed and surprised when he discovered who the prisoner was? Do you think he was personally in sympathy with Darnay? Tell what happened at the prison of La Force.

Chapter II—How was Mr. Lorry situated in Paris? Why was he thankful, as he looked into the court, that no one dear to him was near? Then what happened? Why did Dr. Manette decide to come to Paris? Describe the courtyard as it now appeared. What effect did the Doctor have on the mob?

Chapter III—Who came to Mr. Lorry with a message? Where did they go, and who accompanied them? What occasioned the sparks between Miss Pross and The Vengeance? Do you see foreboding of evil in this chapter?

Chapter IV—This is Dr. Manette's exclusive chapter. Relate what he was doing and what progress he was making in service.

Chapter V—Where did Lucie go each day between two and four? Who was the wood sawyer? What significance was there in his cutting off the billets of wood? Describe the Carmagnole. Who appeared when Lucie kissed her hand toward the prison? Tell the meaning of the last paragraph. Whom do you suspect this person of the riding coat to be?

Chapter VI—Describe the trial of Darnay. Who was the main figure at the trial? How was Darnay escorted home? Then what did the mob do? Tell of the reunion at home.

Chapter VII—What were the Paris duties of Miss Pross and Jerry? Describe the second arrest. What two denounced Darnay this time? There was yet a third who denounced the prisoner—note the "Do *you* ask, Citizen Doctor" in the last lines.

Chapter VIII—Tell whom Miss Pross and Jerry met while marketing. Relate the different incidents in the book where Barsad has appeared. Who else comes up—the man in the riding coat? When did he arrive in Paris? What did he then propose to Barsad? Give the essence of the beginning conversation when they reached Mr. Lorry's apartment. Explain in detail the paragraph, "In short, etc." What were the cards Sydney Carton held against Barsad? What was Carton's ace trick? What reference was made to Cly, and how did it result? Refer back in your own mind to the incident of the midnight fishing trip. What conclusion do you reach? What duty was among Barsad's service to the Republic? Do you think he will agree to help Carton?

Chapter IX—Why do you think Mr. Lorry was not harsh in judging Jerry, though he now knew of his infamous activity back home? What is the substance of the conversation between Mr. Lorry and Mr. Carton? Trace Mr. Carton's steps after he left Mr. Lorry. Check those you consider most important and significant. Which of the characteristics we know of Mr. Carton have now become most predominant? What did he recall as he walked along the streets alone? Describe Sydney Carton on the bridge, and tell the thoughts that passed through his mind. Describe the court room, and the opening of court.

Chapter X—Relate the story written by Dr. Manette. Who were the twin brothers? By what do you identify them? Who was the little three-year-old boy in the carriage? What kind of woman was Madame St. Evrémonde? How did the jury vote as a result of the story?

Chapter XI—Tell the action of each character in the court room after the trial. What character now looms up with greater strength, forging to the foreground of the narrative? What did Sydney Carton whisper to Lucie as he kissed her? What meaning do you attach to the words and the kiss? Is the chapter title meaningful?

Chapter XII—Where did Sydney Carton go? For what purpose? What did he learn there? Why was Madame Defarge so bitter against the Evrémondes? What happened to Dr. Manette? What specific directions did Sydney Carton give Mr. Lorry?

Chapter XIII—Tell Darnay's thoughts and his preparations for death. Of all his acquaintances, whom did he forget? Who came to visit him? How did he get into the prison? What action did he take with Darnay? What was the purpose of the dictation, and its significance? How was Darnay taken out to the carriage to Mr. Lorry? Tell the conversation between Sydney Carton and the little seamstress. What plea did she make? Relate the incidents of the flight of Mr. Lorry and his party from Paris.

Chapter XIV—Tell the scheme of Madame Defarge, and her plans for carrying it out. Why were Miss Pross and Jerry left behind? What two promises does the situation evoke from Jerry? In what state of mind were Jerry and Miss Pross? What arrangements did they agree upon? Who suddenly appeared at the door before Miss Pross? What happened then? Describe Miss Pross' condition as she went forth to meet Jerry. What effect had the shot on her? How does the last of the chapter lead into the next?

Chapter XV—Give a précis of the first three paragraphs of the chapter. How speaks The Vengeance at La Guillotine? What characteristics does Sydney Carton show during his last moments? How does he care for the little seamstress? Has Sydney Carton found fulfillment of his life and love at last? What two words climax the story?

The concluding prophecy is a most satisfying finale. What is the most beautiful and pleasing element in that inspired reverie?

The Novel as a Whole—Why is this called an historical novel? Did you like the whole story? When did you first become interested in it? Where did you reach the highest point of interest? Where is the semi-climax? Has the author satisfactorily disposed of all the main characters? Have all the mysterious points been explained and correlated to the perfect whole—such as Jerry's rusty fingers; Charles Darnay's real identity; the hidden sister of the murdered peasant boy; the murderer of Monsieur the Marquis; the complete redemption of Sydney Carton? Was Darnay or Carton the hero of the story? Did Barsad redeem himself for testifying falsely against Darnay at his first trial? Comment upon this. What was the author's real purpose of having this first trial in England? What characters might be called humorous? In what chapter in the story do each of the following characters exert their strongest influence—Mr. Lorry, Lucie, Sydney Carton, Charles Darnay, Dr. Manette, Miss Pross, Madame Defarge, Monsieur Defarge, Jerry, and John Barsad?

Write short sketches identifying each of the above-mentioned characters. Of these eleven persons, who made the greatest development through the incidents of the story?

EXTENSIVE READING PROGRAM—THE NOVEL

Classicism and the Age of Johnson (1700–1780)

Samuel Richardson
Pamela
Clarissa Harlowe
Tobias Smollett
Humphrey Clinker
Roderick Random
Oliver Goldsmith
The Vicar of Wakefield

Henry Fielding
Amelia
Tom Jones
Laurence Sterne
Tristram Shandy
Sentimental Journey
Horace Walpole
The Castle of Otranto

The Age of Romanticism (1780–1840)

Frances Burney
Evelina
Cecilia
Sir Walter Scott
Waverley
Ivanhoe
Quentin Durward
The Talisman
Guy Mannering
Kenilworth

Ann Radcliffe
Mysteries of Udolpho
William Godwin
Caleb Williams
Jane Austen
Emma
Mansfield Park
Northanger Abbey
Sense and Sensibility
Pride and Prejudice

The Victorian Era (1840–1900)

Charles Dickens
Pickwick Papers
David Copperfield
Oliver Twist
Nicholas Nickleby
Dombey & Son
Little Dorrit
William Makepeace Thackeray
Henry Esmond
Vanity Fair
The Newcomes
Pendennis
The Virginians
George Eliot (Mary Ann Evans)
Adam Bede
The Mill on the Floss
Silas Marner
Romola
Felix Holt

Edward Bulwer-Lytton
The Last Days of Pompeii
Rienzi
The Last of the Barons
Charlotte Brontë
Jane Eyre
Shirley
Charles Kingsley
Hypatia
Westward Ho!
Herward the Wake
Elizabeth Glaskell
Cranford
Robert Louis Stevenson
Treasure Island
Kidnapped
The Master of Ballantrae
David Balfour
Bottle Imp

THE NOVEL

George Meredith
The Egoist
The Ordeal of Richard Feberel
Diana of the Crossways
Evan Harrington

Samuel Butler
Erehwon
The Way of All Flesh
George Gissing
New Grub Street

The Twentieth Century (1900–)

Thomas Hardy
Under the Greenwood Tree
Far from the Madding Crowd
The Return of the Native
The Woodlanders
Tess of the D'Ubervilles
Jude the Obscure
Joseph Conrad
Almayer's Folly
The Nigger of the Narcissus
Lord Jim
Nostromo
The Rescue
H. G. Wells
The Time Machine
The War in the Air
New Worlds for Old
The Soul of a Bishop
Bealby
Joan and Peter
Tono-Bungay
Mr. Brittling Sees It Through
Arnold Bennett
The Old Wives' Tales
Clayhanger
Buried Alive
Hilda Lessways
These Twain
John Galsworthy
The Forsyte Saga
The Silver Spoon
The Patrician
The Freelands
Maurice Hewlett
Richard Yea and Nay

Compton McKenzie
Carnival
Robert Hichens
The Garden of Allah
Hugh Walpole
The Dark Forest
The Green Mirror
The Cathedral
Fortitude
Duchess of Wrexe
Rudyard Kipling
Captains Courageous
The Jungle Book
Puck of Pook's Hill
Stalky & Co.
Archibald Marshall
The Honor of the Clintons
The Hall and the Grange
Sheila Kaye-Smith
Sussex Gorse
Tamarisk Town
May Sinclair
The Three Sisters
The Divine Fire
D. H. Lawrence
Sons and Lovers
The Plumed Serpent
W. Somerset Maugham
Of Human Bondage
Frank Swinnerton
Nocturne
William De Morgan
Joseph Vance
Alice-for-Short
It Never Can Happen Again

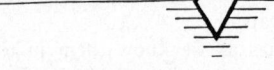

LITERARY PERIODS

A SUMMARY AND REVIEW

A Cross Picture of the Literary Periods

The literature of England has been well represented in this volume of PROSE AND POETRY. Most of the great names and many of the great writings of English literature are to be found in its pages. All types of literature are represented. Each type has been developed historically through each of the literary periods and it now remains to give in brief form a cross picture which will present the various periods, types of literature, and authors in one unified impression of English literature as a whole.

The Anglo-Saxon and Middle English Periods (Page 1)

The Short Story (15)
  Religious Narratives, 15
  Fables, 15
Biography (109)
  Legend and Folklore, 109
Poetry (169)
  Anonymous Poems
    Beowulf, 174
    Sir Gawayne and the Grene Knight, 176
  Cædmon, 175
  Other Religious Writers, 176
  Geoffrey Chaucer, 177

The Essay and Other Prose (447)
  King Alfred, 447
  Religious Writers, 448, 450
  Sir John Mandeville, 448
  Geoffrey Chaucer, 449
The Drama (649)
  Mystery Plays (649)
  Miracle Plays (649)
  Morality Plays (650)
  Interludes, 651
  Other Drama, 651
The Novel (875)
  Beginnings of Biography, 109

Suggestions for Study

Who were the first inhabitants of Britain of whom literature takes an account? Where did they come from? Who were the Angles and the Saxons? Tell of their conquest. What was the nature of the Anglo-Saxon literature? When was Christianity introduced into Britain? What was its effect on literature? Tell of the Danish invasion. Who was King Alfred, and what was his contribution to literature? What were some of the characteristics of the Anglo-Saxon language? Tell of the Norman conquest. Compare the Norman and the Saxon. What was the effect of the Norman conquest on literature? What can you say of the development of literature in the fourteenth and fifteenth centuries? What is meant by the Renaissance?

Were there any short stories as we know them in the early periods of English literature? What were two forms that short narratives took? Was biography known in the early days? How have lives of early heroes come down to us?

What is the greatest Anglo-Saxon poem? Give its story, in brief. Name two other Anglo-Saxon poems. What is the nature of all Anglo-Saxon poetry? Who was Cædmon? Who were other writers of religious poetry? What was the effect of the Norman conquest on poetry? What were the metrical romances? Give the story of Sir Gawayne and the Grene Knight. What early poem expresses an interest in nature? Who was the first great figure in English literature? What was his effect on literature in general? Tell of the development of the ballad. What was the characteristic of Renaissance poetry?

What was the nature of the early prose writing? What was *The Anglo-Saxon Chronicle?* What was the effect of Christianity on prose writing? Who was Sir John Mandeville? Give Chaucer's importance as a prose writer. What were some of the prose writings of the Renaissance?

What were the beginnings of the drama? Give an account of the Mystery and Miracle plays. How did Morality plays differ from the Mystery and Miracle plays? Give a brief outline of *Everyman.* What were the Interludes? What were the contributions of these early forms to the drama? What was the effect of the Renaissance on the drama?

What writings of the Anglo-Saxon and Middle English periods contributed to the form of literature which we know as the novel? Why were most early writings anonymous?

Topics for Discussion and Creative Work

The Celts. The Romans in Britain. The Anglo-Saxon conquest. Anglo-Saxon poetry. Cædmon. The effect of Christianity on literature. Alfred and the West-Saxons. Alfred as a statesman. The Anglo-Saxon language. Anglo-Saxon words in everyday use. The effect of the Danish invasion on the language.

The Norman conquest. The Norman and the Saxon contrasted. The effect of the Norman conquest on the language. Metrical romances. King Arthur, real and legendary. The Round Table. The quest of the Holy Grail. The education of a knight. Medieval warfare. Chivalry. King Arthur and his knights in Malory and in Tennyson.

Chaucer's importance in his own day and in ours. Chaucer as a poet. Chaucer as a prose writer. Chaucer's effect on the language. Pilgrimages. An outline of *The Canterbury Tales.*

Traveling players and plays. A medieval drama in the church. Medieval guilds. A guild play. The ballad—its characteristics and development. Ballads that have lived through the centuries.

SUMMARY AND REVIEW

The Renaissance in Italy. The Renaissance in England. Why Latin is studied in our schools. The Reformation. The effects of the Reformation on literature. The English universities. The Crusades.

The Age of Elizabeth (Page 7)

The Short Story (15)
   Translations from the French and the Italian, 15
   Imitations of the *Novella*, 16
Biography (109)
   Beginnings of Biography, 109
Poetry (183)
   Edmund Spenser, 183
   William Shakespeare, 184
   Ben Jonson, 184
   The Bible, 185
   Sir Walter Raleigh, Christopher Marlowe, Sir Philip Sidney, and John Lyly, 185

The Essay and Other Prose (450)
   Writers of Travel and History, 450
   Other Writers, 451
   Francis Bacon, 452
   Ben Jonson, 454
The Drama (652)
   Christopher Marlowe, 652
   William Shakespeare, 652
   Ben Jonson, 656
   Other Dramatists, 657
The Novel (875)
   Imitations of the Italian and Other Fictitious Narratives, 875

Suggestions for Study

What is meant by the "Elizabethan spirit"? Give an account of internal and external activities in England during this period. What was the effect of the new spirit on the literature? In what types of literature did the new interest in life find best expression? Why?

What attempts were made at short narratives? What is a *novella*? Name two biographies of the period that are deserving of mention as the first forms of biographical writing in English literature.

What was the character of Elizabethan poetry? Who was the first poet of the Elizabethan age? What was his greatest work? Briefly describe its plan. Account for Shakespeare's importance as a poet. Name a third important poet of the Elizabethan age. Why is the Bible important in the study of poetry? Give brief accounts of the work of Sir Walter Raleigh, Christopher Marlowe, Sir Philip Sidney, and John Lyly.

What was the character of Elizabethan prose writing? Who were some of the writers of travel and history? Why did such writings take a prominent place? What was the Authorized Version of 1611? Give an account of the emergence of the essay. Who was the first English essayist? How do his writings reflect his own life and personality? Who was a second Elizabethan essayist?

Of all types of literature, drama was the most important during this period. Why? Who were the University Wits? Give an account of the life of William Shakespeare. Name at least ten of his plays. How do his writings reflect the age in which he lived? Who was the next greatest dramatist after Shakespeare? Name three minor dramatists. Describe the Elizabethan theater, making note of the general plan of the building, the stage, scenery and properties, costumes, music and noise, the audience, and the actors.

What can you say of the novel during this period?

Name three poets who were also dramatists. Uphold by specific examples the statement that the Elizabethan age was one of the most productive in all English literature.

Topics for Discussion and Creative Work

Elizabeth the Queen. Elizabeth as a patron of the arts. Explorations and discoveries of the Elizabethan Age. Sir Walter Raleigh and Sir Philip Sidney—two Elizabethan gallants. Shakespeare as a dramatist. Shakespeare as a poet. A visit to an Elizabethan theater. Some differences between Shakespearean and modern drama. London in Shakespeare's day.

The Puritan Age and the Restoration (Page 8)

The Short Story (16)
   A Decline in the Short Narrative, 16
Poetry (197)
   John Milton, 197
   John Donne, 198
   Robert Herrick, 199
   Other Religious Poets, 199
   The Cavalier Poets, 199
   John Dryden, 200
   Samuel Butler, 200

The Essay and Other Prose (462)
   Puritan Writers, 462
   Cavalier Writers, 463
   Izaak Walton, 463
   John Bunyan, 464
   Samuel Pepys, 465
The Drama (779)
   John Dryden, 779
   Other Dramatists, 779
The Novel (875)
   Fictitious Narratives, 875

Suggestions for Study

What changes were to be observed in literature during the first years of the seventeenth century? Why had these changes come about? Who were the Puritans? the Cavaliers? What was the character of Puritan literature? What was the Restoration? What was the immediate result of the Restoration? What was the effect on literature?

Why was there a decline in narrative writing during the Puritan régime? Give an account of the development of biographical writing. How was the spirit of the age reflected in the biographies?

What is the character of Puritan poetry? Who was the greatest of the Puritan poets? How does his poetry reflect his own life? Who were the religious and metaphysical poets? Who were the Cavalier poets? Compare the poetry of the two groups. Who was the greatest of the Restoration poets?

What kind of prose is to be found in the writings of the Puritans? Why has Izaak Walton's *Compleat Angler* lived through the centuries? How does *The Pilgrim's Progress* reflect John Bunyan's life and also the condition of the times? Who was an important Cavalier writer? Why has his one writing survived the years?

What can you say of the drama during the Puritan régime? during the Restoration? Who was the leading Restoration dramatist? What contributions to the novel were made during the seventeenth century?

SUMMARY AND REVIEW

Topics for Discussion and Creative Work

The Puritan—his effect on politics and on literature. Charles I and his Cavaliers. Puritan versus Cavalier. Oliver Cromwell. Puritan poetry. Puritan prose. Charles II and his court.

Classicism and the Age of Johnson (Page 10)

The Short Story (16)
   English Influence in the Periodical Essay, 16
Biography (110)
   James Boswell, 110, 117
   Other Writers, 110
Poetry (220)
   Alexander Pope, 220
   Other Classic Poets, 221
   Naturalistic Poets, 221
   Thomas Gray, 222
   Oliver Goldsmith, 223
   William Cowper, 223
The Essay and Other Prose (482)
   Jonathan Swift, 482
   Joseph Addison, 483
   Richard Steele, 484

The Essay and Other Prose (Cont'd)
   Samuel Johnson, 485
   Oliver Goldsmith, 486
   Edmund Burke, 486
   Edward Gibbon, 486
The Drama (780)
   Writers of Sentimental Comedy, 780
   Writers of Moralizing Plays, 780
   Samuel Johnson, 780
   Oliver Goldsmith, 781
   Richard Sheridan, 781
   David Garrick, 781
   Other Dramatists, 781
The Novel (875)
   Samuel Richardson, 876
   Other Novelists, 876

Suggestions for Study

What were the general characteristics of the early years of the eighteenth century? What was the effect of the times on literature? What is meant by "classicism"? What are the form, subject, and mood of classic writing? What is meant by "The Age of Johnson"? What indications of changes in literature and life are observable during this age?

Why is this period important in the development of fiction? In what work did biography reach its greatest heights?

What effect did classicism have on poetry? Who was the chief representative of classicism in English poetry? What are the characteristics of his poetry? Who were the forerunners of romantic poetry? How does their poetry resemble classic poetry? How does it differ from classic poetry?

Classicism found its best expression in prose. Why? Who was the first representative of classicism in English prose? How is his life reflected in his writings? Tell of the development of the literary magazine. What was the feature of every issue of the magazines? Name two writers who were leading exponents of the light essay. What was the character of their writings? Account for the importance of Samuel Johnson, both in his own day and in ours. For what writings is he best remembered? What was the Literary Club? What was its influence on literature? For what is Edmund Burke best remembered? Edward Gibbon?

What can you say of the drama of the period? Which two names are most noteworthy in the dramatic literature of the period? Why is David Garrick's name important?

In this period we find the first English novels. How did the first novel come to be written? Name three novelists of the period.

Name one writer who distinguished himself in each of the four fields of poetry, the essay, the drama, and the novel. Name a writer who was important in both essay and drama writing.

Topics for Discussion and Creative Work

Pope and the heroic couplet. London coffee houses. The influence of the literary magazines. Dress and fashions in the early eighteenth century. Education and religion in the Classic Age. A character sketch of Dr. Samuel Johnson. An evening at the Literary Club. What Dr. Johnson would think of present-day fiction. The first novel.

The Age of Romanticism (Page 11)

The Short Story (17)
  Short Story Development, 17
Biography (111)
  Writers of Biography, 111
Poetry (225)
  William Blake, 225
  Robert Burns, 225
  Sir Walter Scott, 257
  Samuel Taylor Coleridge, 258
  Thomas Moore, 259
  George Gordon, Lord Byron, 259
  Percy Bysshe Shelley, 261
  John Keats, 262
  Other Poets, 262

The Essay and Other Prose (518)
  Charles Lamb, 518
  William Hazlitt, 519
  Thomas de Quincey, 520
  Literary Critics, 521
  Other Essayists, 521
The Drama (857)
  Walter Savage Landor, 857
  Percy Bysshe Shelley, 857
  Other Dramatists, 857
The Novel (876)
  Sir Walter Scott, 876
  Jane Austen, 877
  Other Novelists, 876

Suggestions for Study

What influences brought about changes in literature in the latter part of the eighteenth century? What is meant by "romanticism"? Compare it with classicism as to form, subject, and mood. In what type of literature does romanticism find its best expression?

Tell of the development of the short story. Give an account of biographical writing during this period.

Who was the first of the romantic poets? Show how Burns is the best embodiment of all the tendencies exhibited by the romantic movement. What were the characteristics of Wordsworth's poetry? For what is Scott's poetry noted? How is Coleridge's poetry distinguished? Who was a song writer of the period? Byron, Keats, and Shelley are great poets of the period. Give the distinguishing characteristics of the poetry of each. Why is this period considered one of the greatest in English poetry?

What effect did romanticism have on prose writing? Tell of the emergence of the familiar essay. Who were the three leading essayists of the period? Give the character of the writings of each.

SUMMARY AND REVIEW

Why was drama unimportant in this period? What can you say of the development of the novel? Who were the two leading novelists of the period? Which writer distinguished himself in both poetry and prose?

Topics for Discussion and Creative Work

The causes of the French Revolution. Social conditions in England at the outbreak of the Revolution. The effects of the French and American Revolutions in England. The Industrial Revolution. The poetry revival—the nature of romantic poetry. The romantic poets. The effect of romanticism on prose.

The Victorian Era (Page 13)

The Short Story (17)
  Novelists Who Also Wrote Short Stories, 17
  Robert Louis Stevenson, 17
  Other Writers, 18
Biography (111)
  Writers of Critical Biography, 111
  William Makepeace Thackeray, 130
Poetry (350)
  Alfred, Lord Tennyson, 350
  Robert Browning, 351
  Elizabeth Barrett Browning, 352
  Matthew Arnold, 352
  Dante Gabriel Rossetti, 352
  Christina Georgina Rossetti, 353
  Algernon Charles Swinburne, 353
  Oscar Wilde, 354
  William Ernest Henley, 354
  Other Poets, 354
The Essay and Other Prose (554)
  Thomas Carlyle, 554

The Essay (Cont'd)
  Thomas Babington Macaulay, 555
  John Henry Newman, 557
  John Ruskin, 557
  Thomas Henry Huxley, 559
  Robert Louis Stevenson, 559
  Matthew Arnold, 560
  Other Essayists, 560
The Drama (857)
  Arthur Wing Pinero, 858
  Henry Arthur Jones, 858
  Oscar Wilde, 858
  Other Dramatists, 858
The Novel (878)
  Charles Dickens, 877
  William Makepeace Thackeray, 879
  George Eliot, 879
  Robert Louis Stevenson, 880
  George Meredith, 880
  Other Novelists, 879, 880

Suggestions for Study

There were changes in the political and economic conditions of England during the Victorian Era which had direct effect on literature. Discuss these briefly. Was Victorian literature romantic or classic? Why? What types of writing flourished during this period?

During the Victorian Era we find the first English short stories as we know them. Who were some of the novelists who tried their hand at the short story? With whom may the short story be said to have begun? Why did the critical biography become an important type of prose literature? What are some of the best examples of the critical biography?

How were the new tendencies of the times reflected in poetry? Who were the two leading poets of the period? Give the outstanding characteristics which distinguish the writings of each. Name five other Victorian poets. Who were the "Pre-Raphaelites"?

The Victorian Era has been called an age of prose. Why? How does the prose writing of the period reflect the new interests of the times? Who were two important historians of the period? For what historical writing is each remembered? Each of these writers also wrote critical essays. Name one such writing for each. Give the character of the prose writing of John Henry Newman, of John Ruskin, of Thomas Henry Huxley, and of Matthew Arnold. Robert Louis Stevenson was a very versatile writer. What was the character of his prose writing?

Why was there little production in the field of drama? What are the three noteworthy names in the dramatic literature of the period?

The novel reached its high-water mark in the Victorian Era. Why? Name the three leading novelists of the early part of the period, giving the distinguishing characteristics of the writings of each. Name three later Victorian novelists.

Who was perhaps the most versatile writer of the period? In how many fields of literature did he distinguish himself?

Topics for Discussion and Creative Work

Industrial conditions in the early Victorian days. Prison reform. The advance of science and medicine. The expansion of the British Empire. The Pre-Raphaelite society. Tendencies in Victorian poetry. The dramatic monologue. The novel with a purpose.

The Twentieth Century (Page 13)

The Short Story (18)
  Thomas Hardy, 18
  Joseph Conrad, 19
  James Matthew Barrie, 20
  Rudyard Kipling, 21
  John Galsworthy, 22
  Other Writers, 22
Biography (111)
  Lytton Strachey, 140
  Other Writers, 165
Poetry (390)
  Thomas Hardy, 390
  Alfred Edward Housman, 391
  William Butler Yeats, 391
  Rudyard Kipling, 391
  Richard Le Gallienne, 392
  Walter de la Mare, 392
  Gilbert K. Chesterton, 393
  John Masefield, 393
  Alfred Noyes, 394
  Padraic Colum, 394
  Siegfried Sassoon, 394
  James Stephens, 394
  Winifred M. Letts, 395

Poetry (Cont'd)
  Rupert Brooke, 395
  Other Poets, 395
The Essay and Other Prose (596)
  William Henry Hudson, 596
  Arnold Bennett, 597
  John Galsworthy, 598
  Max Beerbohm, 598
  H. M. Tomlinson, 599
  Gilbert K. Chesterton, 599
  Other Essayists, 600
The Drama (858)
  George Bernard Shaw, 859
  James Matthew Barrie, 859
  The Irish Dramatists, 860
  Lord Dunsany, 860
  Other Dramatists, 860
The Novel (880)
  Thomas Hardy, 881
  Joseph Conrad, 881
  H. G. Wells, 881
  Arnold Bennett, 882
  John Galsworthy, 882
  Other Novelists, 882

SUMMARY AND REVIEW

Suggestions for Study

What are some of the characteristics of twentieth century literature? What is meant by "realism"? Can present-day writers be easily classified or grouped with respect to any great movement or tendency of the times? Why?

Name five leading short story writers of the twentieth century. Name at least five minor short story writers. What is meant by the "new biography"? Who was the leader of this movement in England?

Why was there a revolt against Victorian poetry in the early years of the century? What changes in poetry grew out of this revolt? What form does present-day poetry take? What is its subject matter? Who is probably the greatest living English poet? What are the distinguishing characteristics of his poetry? Name at least five other leading present-day English poets.

What is the character of contemporary prose writing? Name six important present-day essayists. Name three of lesser importance.

Who are the two outstanding personalities in English drama today? Compare the dramatic writings of each. Give an account of the Irish drama. Who are some of the playwrights important in this movement?

How does the novel reflect the new tendencies of the day? Name five important present-day novelists. Name five of lesser importance.

Name five novelists who are also short story writers. Name two novelists who are also important in the field of poetry. Name a novelist who is also an important playwright. Which novelists have also distinguished themselves in the field of the essay? Which writer is important in four fields—the short story, the novel, poetry, and the essay?

Topics for Discussion and Creative Work

Realism in twentieth century literature. The effect of the World War on literature. The Irish school of writers. On classifying contemporary writers. My favorite English poet of today. The dramatic revival and the one-act play. The influence of modern magazines. The "new biography." A comparison of contemporary and Victorian poetry. Five outstanding figures in twentieth century English literature.

World Literature

The Short Story (84)
  François Coppée, 84 (French)
  Anton Chekhov, 84 (Russian)
Biography (141)
  André Maurois, 162 (French)
Poetry (435)
  Shi King, 435 (Chinese)
  Su Tung-p'o, 436 (Chinese)
  Moschus, 437 (Greek)
  The Emperor Hadrian, 438 (Latin)

Poetry (Cont'd)
  Giovanni Boccaccio, 439 (Italian)
  Johann Wolfgang von Goethe, 440 (German)
  Henrik Ibsen, 441 (Norwegian)
  Arthur Rimbaud, 442 (French)
The Essay and Other Prose (639)
  Michel de Montaigne, 640
The Drama (870)
  Readings in, 870

Suggestions for Study

It is impossible in a small space to adequately cover the whole subject of world literature. Insofar as possible, however, by means of typical selections and lists of extensive readings, this volume of PROSE AND POETRY has attempted to give a view of the writings of other nations which should stimulate interest in further reading.

Since French and Russian writers have probably developed the short story to a greater degree than the writers of other European nations, typical selections from their writings have been chosen for the short story group. Compare these world literature stories with the English short stories in this volume.

The movement in the "new biography" is world wide. Who is a leader in this movement in Germany? in France? Why is biography a reliable source of information concerning the ideals of individuals and of nations? Why is Maurois' *Disraeli* of particular interest to a student of English literature?

Why is poetry a "universal language"? Because some of the world poetry included in this volume has been translated by great English poets, it is of added interest. Who are some of these translators?

Why is it fitting that Michel de Montaigne be represented in the field of the essay? Is the essay as a type of literature important in countries other than England and America? Why?

How should foreign plays be read? Why is the drama of a nation an index to its history and ideals? Name a leading dramatist from each of the following countries: France, Germany, Norway, Sweden, Russia, Italy, Hungary, Belgium.

INDEX

Addison, Joseph, 496, 501, 506, 509; *biog.*, 483
Against Idleness, Michel de Montaigne, 640
AGE OF ELIZABETH, THE, 7; the short story, 15; biography, 109; poetry, 183, 186; the essay and other prose, 450, 455; the drama, 652, 664; the novel, 875
AGE OF ROMANTICISM, THE, 11; the short story, 17; biography, 111; poetry, 225, 263; the essay and other prose, 518, 522; the drama, 857; the novel, 876
Alfred, King, *biog.*, 779
ANGLO-SAXON AND MIDDLE ENGLISH PERIODS, THE, 1; the short story, 15; biography, 109; poetry, 174, 179; the essay and other prose, 447; the drama, 649; the novel, 875
Anglo-Saxon Chronicle, The, 447
ANGLO-SAXON CONQUEST, THE, 1
Arnold, Matthew, 382; *biog.*, 352, 560
Auld Lang Syne, Robert Burns, 278
Austen, Jane, *biog.*, 877

Bacon, Francis, 455, 458; *biog.*, 452
Bannockburn, Robert Burns, 267
Barrel Organ, The, Alfred Noyes, 420
Barrie, James Matthew, 64; *biog.*, 20, 859
Beerbohm, Max, 618; *biog.*, 598
Bennett, Arnold, 623; *biog.*, 597, 882
Beowulf, 174
Bet, The, Anton Chekhov, 96
Bible, The, 185, 194, 195, 196, 450, 451
BIOGRAPHY: historical development of, 109, 110, 111; biographies of classic age, 112; Victorian era, 119; twentieth century, 131; in world literature, 141; extensive readings in, 164; other writers of, 109, 110, 111, 165

Blake, William, 263; *biog.*, 225
Boccaccio, Giovanni, 439
Book of a Naturalist, The (Selection), William H. Hudson, 601
Boswell, James, 112; *biog.*, 117
Break, Break, Break, Alfred Tennyson, 362
Brooke, Rupert, 431, 432; *biog.*, 395
Browning, Elizabeth Barrett, 381; *biog.*, 352
Browning, Robert, 367, 368, 369, 371, 374, 376; *biog.*, 351
Bunyan, John, 470; *biog.*, 464
Burke, Edmund, *biog.*, 486
Burns, Robert, 264, 265, 267, 268, 270, 271, 278, 280; *biog.*, 225
Butler, Samuel, *biog.*, 200
Byron, Lord, George Gordon, 298, 300, 301, 302; *biog.*, 259

Cædmon, *biog.*, 175
Canterbury Tales, The (Selection), Geoffrey Chaucer, 179
Carlyle, Thomas, 561; *biog.*, 554
Character of the Idler, The, Samuel Johnson, 514
Chaucer, Geoffrey, 179; *biog.*, 177, 449
Chekhov, Anton, 96; *biog.*, 84
Chesterton, Gilbert Keith, 414, 634; *biog.*, 393, 599
Child's Laughter, A, Algernon C. Swinburne, 385
CLASSICISM, *the meaning of,* 10
CLASSICISM AND THE AGE OF JOHNSON, 10; the short story, 16; biography, 110, 112; poetry, 220, 224; the essay and other prose, 482, 487; the drama, 780, 782; the novel, 875
Cloud, The, Percy B. Shelley, 316
Coleridge, Samuel Taylor, 295; *biog.*, 258
Colum, Padraic, 427; *biog.*, 394

INDEX

Compleat Angler, The (Selection), Izaak Walton, 466
Composed upon Westminster Bridge, William Wordsworth, 284
Confessions of an English Opium Eater, Thomas de Quincey, 548
Conrad, Joseph, 47; *biog.*, 19, 881
Consecration, A, John Masefield, 419
Coquette's Heart, The, Joseph Addison and Richard Steele, 509
Coppée, François, *biog.*, 84
Cotter's Saturday Night, The, Robert Burns, 271
Cowper, William, *biog.*, 223
Crossing the Bar, Alfred Tennyson, 366
Cuckoo Song, 177

Daffodils, The, William Wordsworth, 287
Daily Miracle, The, Arnold Bennett, 623
Davies, William Henry, 410; *biog.*, 392
Definition of a Gentleman, The, John H. Newman, 572
"De Gustibus—," Robert Browning, 369
De la Mare, Walter, 411, 412; *biog.*, 392
De Montaigne, Michel, 640; *biog.*, 639
De Quincey, Thomas, 548; *biog.*, 520
Deserted Village, The, Oliver Goldsmith, 236
Destruction of Sennacherib, The, Lord Byron, 298
Diary (Selection), Samuel Pepys, 475
Dickens, Charles, 883; *biog.*, 877
Disraeli (Selection); André Maurois, 141
Disraeli in London, André Maurois, 141
Dissection of a Beau's Head, The, Joseph Addison and Richard Steele, 506
Dissertation upon Roast Pig, A, Charles Lamb, 522
Donkey, The, Gilbert K. Chesterton, 414
Donne, John, *biog.*, 198
Dover Beach, Matthew Arnold, 382
DRAMA, THE: historical development of, 649, 652, 779, 780, 857, 858; dramas of Elizabethan age, 664; classic age, 782; twentieth century, 861; in world literature, 870; extensive readings in, 872; other writers of, 657, 779, 780, 781, 857, 858, 860
Dreamers, Siegfried Sassoon, 429
Dreams, Thomas de Quincey, 548
Dryden, John, *biog.*, 200, 779
Dunsany, Lord, 861; *biog.*, 860

Elegy Written in a Country Churchyard, Thomas Gray, 227
Eliot, George, *see* Evans, Mary Ann
ELIZABETH, THE AGE OF, *see* Age of Elizabeth
ELIZABETHAN THEATER, THE, 657
Eminent Victorians (Selection), Lytton Strachey, 131
English Humorists of the Eighteenth Century, The (Selection), William M. Thackeray, 119
ESSAY AND OTHER PROSE, THE: historical development of, 447, 450, 462, 482, 518, 554, 596; essays and other prose of Elizabethan age, 455; Puritan age, 466; classic age, 487; age of romanticism, 522; Victorian era, 561; twentieth century, 601; in world literature, 639; extensive readings in, 647; other writers of, 448, 449, 450, 451, 462, 521, 560, 600
Essay on Criticism, An (Selection), Alexander Pope, 224
Essays of Elia (Selections), Charles Lamb, 522, 531
Evans, Mary Ann, *biog.*, 879
Eve of St. Agnes, John Keats, 337
Everyman, 650
Example, The, William H. Davies, 410
EXTENSIVE READING PROGRAM: the short story, 107; biography, 164; poetry, 443; the essay and other prose, 647; the drama, 872; the novel, 1179

Faerie Queene, The, Edmund Spenser, 183
Fish in the Forest, A Russian Folk Tale, 104
Florence Nightingale, Lytton Strachey, 131
French Revolution, The (Selection), Thomas Carlyle, 561
From a Diary, Samuel Pepys, 475
Frozen Words, Joseph Addison and Richard Steele, 501
Fuzzy-Wuzzy, Rudyard Kipling, 405

Galsworthy, John, 77, 608; *biog.*, 22, 598, 882

INDEX

Garrick, David, *biog.*, 781
Gibbon, Edward, *biog.*, 486
Goethe, Johann Wolfgang von, 440
Goldsmith, Oliver, 236, 782; *biog.*, 119, 223, 486, 781
Gray, Thomas, 227; *biog.*, 222
Great Lover, The, Rupert Brooke, 432
Green Donkey-Driver, The, Robert L. Stevenson, 587
Greeting, A, William H. Davies, 410
Gulliver's Travels (Selection), Jonathan Swift, 487
Gunga Din, Rudyard Kipling, 402

Hadrian, The Emperor, 438
Hardy, Thomas, 24, 396, 397; *biog.*, 18, 390, 881
Hark, Hark! The Lark, William Shakespeare, 187
Hazlitt, William, 540; *biog.*, 519
Henley, William Ernest, 387, 388; *biog.*, 354
Herrick, Robert, *biog.*, 199
History of England (Selection), Thomas B. Macaulay, 567
Home Thoughts from Abroad, Robert Browning, 368
Housman, Alfred Edward, 398, 399; *biog.*, 391
How Do I Love Thee, Elizabeth B. Browning, 381
How to Live on Twenty-four Hours a Day (Selection), Arnold Bennett, 623
Hudson, William Henry, 601; *biog.*, 596
Huxley, Thomas Henry, 582; *biog.*, 559

Ibsen, Henrik, 441
Idea of a University, The (Selection), John H. Newman, 572
Idler, The, Samuel Johnson, 514
Il Penseroso, John Milton, 211
I Meant to Do My Work Today, Richard Le Gallienne, 409
In Defense of Anglers, Izaak Walton, 466
In Memoriam (Selection), Alfred Tennyson, 361
Inscription for a Portrait of Dante, Giovanni Boccaccio, 439
In Service, Winifred M. Letts, 430
Interludes, 651
In the Orchard, Henrik Ibsen, 441
In the Valley of Humiliation, John Bunyan, 470

Invictus, William E. Henley, 387
IRISH DRAMA, THE, 860
It Is a Beauteous Evening, Calm and Free, William Wordsworth, 285

Jock o' Hazeldean, Sir Walter Scott, 289
John Anderson, My Jo, Robert Burns, 264
JOHNSON, THE AGE OF, *see* Classicism and the Age of Johnson
Johnson as a Conversationalist, James Boswell, 112
Johnson, Samuel, 514; *biog.*, 112, 485, 780
Jones, Henry Arthur, *biog.*, 858
Jonson, Ben, 190, 191; *biog.*, 184, 454, 656

Keats, John, 330, 331, 332, 335, 337; *biog.*, 262
Kipling, Rudyard, 68, 402, 405, 407; *biog.*, 21, 391
Knight, The, Geoffrey Chaucer, 179
Kubla Khan, Samuel T. Coleridge, 295

Lake Isle of Innisfree, The, William B. Yeats, 400
L'Allegro, John Milton, 202
Lamb, Charles, 522, 531; *biog.*, 518
LANGUAGE, THE ENGLISH, 3, 5
Le Gallienne, Richard, 409; *biog.*, 392
Letts, Winifred M., 430; *biog.*, 395
Liberal Education, A, Thomas H. Huxley, 582
Life of Dr. Samuel Johnson, The (Selection), James Boswell, 112
Listeners, The, Walter de la Mare, 412
LITERARY PERIODS, *see* Periods
London, 1802, William Wordsworth, 286
London in 1685, Thomas B. Macaulay, 567
Lost Days, Dante Gabriel Rossetti, 384
Lost Silk Hat, The, Lord Dunsany, 861
Loveliest of Trees, Alfred E. Housman, 398

Macaulay, Thomas Babington, 567; *biog.*, 555
Macbeth, William Shakespeare, 664
Maid of Athens, Ere We Part, Lord Byron, 301
Mandeville, Sir John, *biog.*, 448

Man He Killed, The, Thomas Hardy, 396
Man's a Man for A' That, A, Robert Burns, 265
Margaritae Sorori, William E. Henley, 388
Marlowe, Christopher, *biog.,* 652
Marmion (Selection), Sir Walter Scott, 291
Mary's Little Lamb, William H. Hudson, 601
Masefield, John, 415, 416, 419; *biog.,* 393
Maurois, André, 141; *biog.,* 162
Meredith, George, *biog.,* 880
MIDDLE ENGLISH PERIOD, THE, *see* Anglo-Saxon and Middle English Periods
Milton, John, 201, 202, 211; *biog.,* 197
MIRACLE PLAYS, 649
Moore, Thomas, 297; *biog.,* 259
MORALITY PLAYS, 650
Morning Glory, The, from the *Shi King,* 435
Moschus, 437
Music, When Soft Voices Die, Percy B. Shelley, 329
My Brother Henry, James M. Barrie, 64
My Heart Leaps Up, William Wordsworth, 282
My Heart's in the Highlands, Robert Burns, 270
My Last Duchess, Robert Browning, 371
My Own True Ghost Story, Rudyard Kipling, 68
MYSTERY PLAYS, 649

Newman, John Henry, 572; *biog.,* 557
NORMAN CONQUEST, THE, 4, 176, 448
NOVEL, THE: historical development of, 875, 876, 877, 880; novel of Victorian era, 883; extensive readings in, 1179; other writers of, 876, 879, 880, 882
Noyes, Alfred, 420; *biog.,* 394

Ocean, The, Moschus, 437
Ode on a Grecian Urn, John Keats, 335
Ode to a Nightingale, John Keats, 332
Ode to the West Wind, Percy B. Shelley, 324
Of Books, Of Reading, Of Nations, John Ruskin, 575

Of Studies, Francis Bacon, 455
Of Truth, Francis Bacon, 458
Oft, in the Stilly Night, Thomas Moore, 297
Old China, Charles Lamb, 531
Old Woman of the Roads, An, Padraic Colum, 427
Oliver Goldsmith, William M. Thackeray, 119
On First Looking into Chapman's Homer, John Keats, 330
On Going a Journey, William Hazlitt, 540
On His Blindness, John Milton, 201
On Lying in Bed, Gilbert K. Chesterton, 634
On the Birth of His Son, Su Tung-p'o, 436
OTHER PROSE, *see* The Essay and Other Prose
OTHER WRITERS: of short stories, 17, 18, 22; biography, 109, 110, 111, 165; poetry, 178, 185, 199, 221, 262, 354, 395; the essay and other prose, 448, 449, 450, 451, 462, 521, 560, 600; the drama, 657, 779, 780, 781, 857, 858, 860; the novel, 876, 879, 880, 882
Ozymandias, Percy B. Shelley, 328

Parting of Marmion and Douglas, The, Sir Walter Scott, 291
Pepys, Samuel, 475; *biog.,* 465
PERIODS, LITERARY, 1, 1181; *see also,* Anglo-Saxon and Middle English Periods, The Age of Elizabeth, The Puritan Age and the Restoration, Classicism and the Age of Johnson, The Age of Romanticism, The Victorian Era, The Twentieth Century
Pilgrim's Progress, The (Selection), John Bunyan, 470
Pinero, Arthur Wing, *biog.,* 858
POETRY: poetry forms, 169; versification, 171; historical development of, 174, 183, 197, 220, 225, 350, 390; poetry of the Middle English period, 179; Elizabethan age, 186; Puritan age, 201; classic age, 224; age of romanticism, 263; Victorian era, 355; twentieth century, 396; in world literature, 435; extensive readings in, 443; other writers of, 178, 185, 199, 221, 262, 354, 395
POETRY FORMS, 169
Pope, Alexander, 224; *biog.,* 220
Prisoner of Chillon, The, Lord Byron, 302

INDEX

Prospice, Robert Browning, 374
Psalm 1, The Bible, 194
Psalm 23, The Bible, 195
Psalm 121, The Bible, 196
PURITAN AGE AND THE RESTORATION, THE, 8; the short story, 16; biography, 110; poetry, 197, 201; the essay and other prose, 462, 466; the drama, 779; the novel, 875

Quality, John Galsworthy, 77

Recessional, Rudyard Kipling, 407
RENAISSANCE, THE, 6, 178, 449
Requiescat, Oscar Wilde, 389
RESTORATION, THE, *see* The Puritan Age and the Restoration
Reveille, Alfred E. Housman, 399
Revenge, The, Alfred Tennyson, 355
Richardson, Samuel, *biog.*, 876
Rimbaud, Arthur, 442
Ring Out, Wild Bells, Alfred Tennyson, 361
Road, The, James Stephens, 428
ROMANTICISM, *the meaning of*, 12
ROMANTICISM, THE AGE OF, *see* The Age of Romanticism
Rossetti, Christina Georgina, 384; *biog.*, 353
Rossetti, Dante Gabriel, 384; *biog.*, 352
Rough Wind, That Moanest Loud, Percy B. Shelley, 327
Rounding the Horn, John Masefield, 416
Ruskin, John, 575; *biog.*, 557

Sassoon, Siegfried, 429; *biog.*, 394
Scott, Sir Walter, 289, 291; *biog.*, 257, 876
Sea and the Jungle, The (Selection), Henry M. Tomlinson, 627
Sesame and Lilies (Selection), John Ruskin, 575
Shakespeare, William, 186, 187, 188, 189, 664; *biog.*, 184, 652
Shaw, George Bernard, *biog.*, 859
Shelley, Percy Bysshe, 316, 319, 324, 327, 328, 329; *biog.*, 261
She Stoops to Conquer, Oliver Goldsmith, 782
She Walks in Beauty, Lord Byron, 300
SHORT STORY, THE: historical development of, 15, 16, 17, 18; short stories of the twentieth century, 24; in world literature, 84; extensive readings in, 107; other writers of, 17, 18, 22
Silver, Walter de la Mare, 411
Sir Gawayne and the Grene Knight, 176
Sir Roger at Church, Joseph Addison and Richard Steele, 495
Sleeper of the Valley, The, Arthur Rimbaud, 442
Soldier, The, Rupert Brooke, 431
Solitary Reaper, The, William Wordsworth, 288
Some Platitudes Concerning Drama, John Galsworthy, 608
Song of the Old Mother, The, William Butler Yeats, 401
Sonnet 86—Lost Days, Dante Gabriel Rossetti, 384
Spenser, Edmund, *biog.*, 183
Steele, Sir Richard, 495, 501, 506, 509; *biog.*, 484
Stephens, James, 428; *biog.*, 394
Stevenson, Robert Louis, 587; *biog.*, 17, 559, 880
Storming of the Bastille, The, Thomas Carlyle, 561
Strachey, Lytton, 131; *biog.*, 140
Study in Dejection, A, Max Beerbohm, 618
Substitute, The, François Coppée, 85
Su Tung-p'o, 436
Sweet Afton, Robert Burns, 268
Swift, Jonathan, 487; *biog.*, 482
Swinburne, Algernon Charles, 385; *biog.*, 353

Tale of Two Cities, A, Charles Dickens, 883
Tennyson, Lord, Alfred, 355, 361, 362, 363, 366; *biog.*, 350
Tewkesbury Road, John Masefield, 415
Thackeray, William Makepeace, 119; *biog.*, 130, 879
THEATER, THE ELIZABETHAN, 657
Three Strangers, The, Thomas Hardy, 24
Tiger, The, William Blake, 263
To a Mouse, Robert Burns, 280
To a Skylark, Percy B. Shelley, 319
To Celia, Ben Jonson, 190
Tomlinson, Henry M., 627; *biog.*, 599
To the Memory of My Beloved Master, William Shakespeare, Ben Jonson, 191
Travels with a Donkey (Selection), Robert L. Stevenson, 587

Tremendous Trifles (Selection), Gilbert K. Chesterton, 634
"*Tremolino,*" *The,* Joseph Conrad, 47
TWENTIETH CENTURY, THE, 13; the short story, 18, 24; biography, 111, 131; poetry, 390, 396; the essay and other prose, 596, 601; the drama, 858, 861; the novel, 880

Ulysses, Alfred Tennyson, 363
Under the Greenwood Tree, William Shakespeare, 186
Up at a Villa—Down in the City, Robert Browning, 376
Up-Hill, Christina G. Rossetti, 384

VERSIFICATION, 171
VICTORIAN ERA, THE, 13; the short story, 17; biography, 111, 119; poetry, 350, 355; the essay and other prose, 554, 561; the drama, 857; the novel, 877, 883
Voyage to Brobdingnag, A, Jonathan Swift, 487

Waley, Arthur, 436
Walton, Izaak, 466; *biog.,* 463

Wanderer's Night-Songs, Johann von Goethe, 440
Weathers, Thomas Hardy, 397
Wells, H. G., *biog.,* 881
When I Have Fears That I May Cease to Be, John Keats, 331
When in Disgrace with Fortune and Men's Eyes, William Shakespeare, 189
When to the Sessions of Sweet Silent Thought, William Shakespeare, 188
Wilde, Oscar, 389; *biog.,* 354, 858
Wordsworth, William, 282, 283, 284, 285, 286, 287, 288; *biog.,* 256
World Is Too Much with Us, The, William Wordsworth, 283
WORLD LITERATURE: the short story, 84, 85, 96, 104; biography, 141; poetry, 435, 436, 437, 438, 439, 440, 441, 442; the essay and other prose, 639, 640; the drama, 870

Year's at the Spring, The, Robert Browning, 367
Yeats, William Butler, 400, 401; *biog.,* 391
Yet Again (Selection), Max Beerbohm, 618